LAROUSSE

Dictionary of
WOMEN

LAROUSSE

Dictionary of
WOMEN

Editor
Melanie Parry

LAROUSSE

LAROUSSE
Larousse Kingfisher Chambers Inc.
95 Madison Avenue
New York, New York 10016

First published by Larousse 1996
10 9 8 7 6 5 4 3 2 1

Library of Congress Catalog Card Number: 95–082384
ISBN 07523–0015–6

Cover illustrations: Jackie Kennedy Onassis, Whoopi Goldberg *(Courtesy of Rex Features)*; Mother
Teresa, Elizabeth I *(Courtesy of Camera Press)*

Typeset by Selwood Systems, Midsomer Norton, England
Printed in France

Contents

Acknowledgements

The editor would like to thank Min Lee for her advice and assistance in the early stages of this project; Gail Wood, Director of Libraries and Academic Support Services at SUNY College of Technology at Alfred, New York, for reviewing all the biographies; the reference department at Larousse, Edinburgh, for their invaluable suggestions and support; Ilona Bellos-Morison for her technological expertise; George Davidson for his assistance with the Chinese names; and all the contributors and proofreaders whose work is contained in this volume.

Illustration credits

Copyright The Hulton Getty Picture Collection

Judith Anderson	Annie Oakley
Jean Batten	Frances Perkins
St Birgitta	Phryne
Christian Davis	Beatrix Potter
Amelia Earhart	Dod Procter
Germaine Greer	Janet Reno
Hortense	Gloria Steinem
Angelica Huston	Marie Stopes
Janis Joplin	Junko Tabei
Estée Lauder	Ninette de Valois
Heather McKay	Emma Willard
Aimee Semple McPherson	Rosalyn Yalow
Penny Marshall	Babe Zaharias
Carry Nation	

Copyright Mary Evans

Jane Addams	Ada, Countess Lovelace
Louisa May Alcott	Rosa Luxemburg
Aspasia	Madame de Maintenon
Elizabeth Barry	Margaret of Parma
Isabella Bird	Marie Antoinette
Harriot Stanton Blatch	Queen Mary I
Anne Boleyn	Mata Hari
Charlotte Brontë	Elizabeth Montagu
Caroline of Anspach	Lucretia Mott
Carrie Chapman Catt	La Belle Otero
Colette	Christina Rossetti
Marie Curie	George Sand
Mrs Gaskell	Elizabeth Seton
Emma Goldman	Elizabeth Cady Stanton
Héloïse	Madame de Tencin
Irène Joliot-Curie	Queen Victoria
Bea Lillie	Virginia Woolf

Copyright "PA News"

Diane Abbott	Glenda Jackson
Isabel Allende	Helena Kennedy
Cory Aquino	Eartha Kitt
Joan Armatrading	Winnie Mandela
Jocelyn Bell Burnell	Barbara Mills
Patty Berg	Nancy Mitford
Barbara Taylor Bradford	Jessye Norman
Gro Harlem Brundtland	Sandra Day O'Connor
Kate Bush	Jenny Pitman
Kim Campbell	Joan Plowright
Barbara Castle	Ratushinaskaya
Florence Chadwick	Janet Reger
Hillary Clinton	Joan Ruddock
Tracey Edwards	Cicely Saunders
Queen Elizabeth II	Alison Streeter
Winnie Ewing	Helen Suzman
Dianne Feinstein	Emma Thompson
Celia France	Virginia Wade
Elisabeth Frink	Deborah Warner
Sally Gunnell	Judith Weir
Katharine Hamnett	Oprah Winfrey

Copyright Popperfoto

Lauren Bacall	Deborah Harry
Janet Baker	Rita Hayworth
Sirimavo Bandaranaike	Barbara Hepworth
Simone de Beauvoir	Rosella Hightower
Benazir Bhutto	Billie Holiday
Yelena Bonner	Gypsy Rose Lee
Clara Bow	Vivien Leigh
Helen Gurley Brown	Doris Lessing
Rosalynn Carter	Golda Meir
Cher	Mary Tyler Moore
Kyung-Wha Chung	Toni Morrison
Nadia Comaneci	Dolly Parton
Margaret Smith Court	Sally Ride
Joan Crawford	Anita Roddick
Dorothy Dandridge	Beverley Sills
Takako Doi	Margaret Chase Smith
Faye Dunaway	Susan Sontag
Ella Fitzgerald	Margaret Thatcher
Dawn Fraser	Twiggy
Indira Gandhi	Fatima Whitbread
Shane Gould	

Contributors

Kate Brand
Miranda Britt
Cathy Coll
Gillian Dorricott
Francesca Fearon
Marie Fitzpatrick
Antoinette Galbraith
Liffy Grant
Philip Hillyer
Allan Hunter
Patricia Macdonald
Kenny Mathieson
Brian Morton
Sandy Mullay
Melanie Parry
Jane Stewart
Tilli Tansey
Sophie Warne
Tom and Pamela Wilson
Shane Winser
Gail Wood

Introduction

There is no 'beginning' of feminism in the sense that there is no beginning to defiance in women. Sheila Rowbotham's words in *Women, Resistance and Revolution* are borne out in this work devoted entirely to women's biography which, while making no attempt to analyse female motivation *per se*, documents women's lives and achievements since the dawn of human history. Such a book will inevitably arouse many expectations, varying from the open-minded interest of the general reader to the specific research-oriented requirements of the student of women's studies. Perhaps these expectations reflect the increasing diversification of attitudes to feminism today, which range from the general wish to equalize opportunities in education and occupation within the framework of the traditional family unit, to the radical campaign aimed at overthrowing patriarchal forms of any kind. The *Larousse Dictionary of Women* seeks to satisfy as many as possible of these diverse views, and provides concise biographies of the women commonly perceived to be 'famous' as well as hundreds who seem to have been marginalized until now and deserve to be brought to attention.

Rather than lament the restrictive nature of conventional social roles, the *Larousse Dictionary of Women* seeks to reveal and celebrate a breadth of creativity and courage that testifies to the depth of female influence and intellect. For centuries such qualities were virtually denied, but this is not to say that clever and influential women did not exist, for they did, and some were remarkably powerful. From reading the lives documented here, we may now embrace the beginning of an age where women are seen as capable of holding their own on the world stage in virtually all areas of activity.

As we near the 21st century, these areas grow in variety as their participants do in number. The modern-day woman's opportunities to succeed are multiplying, and can be realised in whichever area she has sufficient ability — be it art or architecture, law or literature, music or mountaineering, science or sport, stage or screen — though in some fields Charlotte Whitton's comment that 'Whatever women do they must do twice as well as men to be thought half as good' is still true.

The *Larousse Dictionary of Women* aims to document many of the women who, in the face of general opposition and prejudice, have been successful in their own right, and whose lives have made a mark on history without reaching the history books. Usually the women here are included for success that is notable regardless of gender, but sometimes they have been included for having broken new ground as a woman in a 'man's' field, often defying society's expectations, or for having achieved something of more interest to women than to men.

As one would expect in such a volume, there is extensive coverage of the leading figures in the women's rights movement, and this is matched with the inclusion of many whose important work — in science and medicine for example — is often ignored. There are also hundreds of creative writers from all over the world whose work has only comparatively recently come to notice, actresses dating from the time that they were disdainfully barred from Christian burial right up to the present day, when they are heralded in high society, and women in international politics, who range from empresses and queens of centuries past to today's country presidents, First Ladies and British Cabinet members.

Although the *Larousse Dictionary of Women* aims to include women from as many parts of the world as possible who have had a significant measure of achievement or influence in every era and in all fields of interest, the coverage is inevitably weighted towards 19th- and 20th-century women in the western world; this is not only due to the development of women in history and the attitudes of different cultures, but also to the more practical concern of accessibility of information.

Of the 3,000 or so articles contained in this volume, about 1,800 have been derived from our extensive database, which includes such previously published books as the *Larousse Biographical Dictionary*, the *Larousse Dictionary of Writers* and the *Larousse Dictionary of Scientists*. These articles have been revised and updated. A further 1,200 entries have been freshly researched and written mainly by specialists in the appropriate field. The selection of women in each area has been carefully made, but in the end there is bound to be an element of subjective choice; the editor regrets any disappointment omissions may cause, and invites readers to suggest or nominate other women who might merit inclusion in a later volume. Constraints of space inevitably cause some degree of frustration, but this is outweighed by the enormous benefit of being able to read about so many exciting and significant lives in a single volume.

Melanie Parry
April 1996

a

Abakanowicz, Magdalena

Born 1930
American–Polish artist, weaver and sculptor who
became a pioneer of abstract woven sculptures

Magdalena Abakanowicz was born in Falenty,
near Warsaw, and her privileged upbringing
was cut short by the Nazi invasion in 1939
and the subsequent Russian 'liberation'. She
was educated at the Warsaw Academy of Fine
Arts (1950–5) during the repressive period of
Socialist Realism, and developed weaving as a
means of escaping conventional art forms. In
1956 she married Jan Kosmowski.

During the 1960s she achieved international
recognition with her monumental abstract
woven fibre installations called *Abakans*.
Later, she abandoned weaving and began
making a series of primitive and disturbing
figurative groups from burlap sacking.

In 1965 she began teaching at the State
College of Arts, Poznan, where she was pro-
fessor from 1979 to 1990. In 1978 she took
part in the pioneering exhibition 'Soft Art' in
Zürich and in 1980 represented Poland at the
Venice Biennale.

Abbott, Berenice

Born 1898 Died 1991
American photographer whose innovative work
included New York cityscapes and illustrations
of the laws of physics

Berenice Abbott was born in Springfield,
Ohio. She studied first at Ohio State University
(1917–18) with the intention of becoming a
journalist, afterwards moving first to New
York in 1918, and subsequently to Europe in
1921, where she studied sculpture. From 1923
to 1925 she worked in Paris as assistant to the
American photographer Man Ray (1890–1976)
and in 1926 opened her own portrait studio
there. Her work was first shown at the Au

Sacre du Printemps gallery, Paris, in 1926,
since when it has been widely exhibited. In
1929 she returned to work in New York, at
first as a practitioner and, from 1934, also as a
teacher of photography. From the early 1930s
she became the companion of art historian
and critic Elizabeth McCausland, and in 1968
settled in Maine.

Abbott is well known for a wide range of
types of work: sensitive portraiture, innovative documentation of town- and cityscape
(especially her project *Changing New York*,
1929–39, also the title of a book, 1939, with
text by McCausland) and pioneering illustrations of the laws and processes of physics.
She is also remembered for her sensitive
curatorship and effective promotion of the
work of the French photographer Eugene
Atget (1856–1927), whom she met and photographed in Paris shortly before his death, and
most of whose work (now in the Museum of
Modern Art, New York) she purchased in
1928. Her other publications include, as editor, *The World of Atget* (1964) and as photographer, *The Attractive Universe* (1969, text by
E G Valens).

Abbott, Diane Julie

Born 1953
English civil rights campaigner and politician,
and the first black woman member of parliament

Diane Abbott was born in Paddington,
London, the daughter of Jamaican parents
who had emigrated to London two years previously. She was an avid reader and a keen
student from childhood, succeeded well at
Harrow City Girls' School despite lack of
encouragement, and went on to Newnham
College, Cambridge.

After two years as a civil service trainee, she
joined the National Council for Civil Liberties

Diane Abbott, 1986

and entered the media world as a television researcher and reporter for five years.

In 1971 she joined the Labour Party, where she made rapid progress; she was appointed Press Officer for the Greater London Council (GLC), then Principal Press Officer for Lambeth Borough Council and served as a member of Westminster City Council from 1982 to 1986. In 1987 she was elected MP for Hackney North and Stoke Newington.

Abbott, Edith

Born 1876   Died 1957
American social worker, educator and author

Edith Abbott was born in Grand Island, Nebraska, and had an illustrious academic career which started at Brownell Hall, in Omaha, and the University of Nebraska, and continued at the University of Chicago, where she graduated PhD in 1905, followed by a period at the London School of Economics.

In 1908 she joined the staff of the Chicago School of Civics and Anthropology in 1908 and lived for 10 years with her sister at Hull House, a famous settlement for the protection of juveniles and for social improvements.

In 1927 she founded the *Social Services Review* which she edited until her retirement; her other works include *Women in Industry* (1910), *The Delinquent Child and the Home* (1912) and *The Tenements of Chicago* (1936).

Abbott, Grace

Born 1878   Died 1939
American social reformer, writer and director of the US Children's Bureau between 1921 and 1934

Grace Abbott was born in Grand Island, Nebraska. She studied at Grand Island College and later at the universities of Nebraska and Chicago. In 1908 she started work at **Jane Addams**'s Hull House, and headed the Immigrants' Protective League (1908–17). In 1917 she joined the staff of the US Children's Bureau, but left two years later to direct the newly founded Illinois State Immigrants' Commission in Chicago. When this commission folded in 1921 she returned to the Children's Bureau as its director (1921–34).

She was responsible for administering the first federal child-labour law and the Maternity and Infancy Act. In addition, she was President of the National Conference of Social Workers (1923–4) and was the unofficial US representative to the League of Nations Advisory Committee on Traffic in Women and Children (1922–34). In 1934 failing health led her to become Professor of Public Welfare at the University of Chicago and editor of *Social Service Review.*

She wrote a series of articles battling for child-labour laws and exposing the exploitation of immigrants, and full-length works calling for social reform, which include *Women in Industry* (1910), *The Immigrant in Massachusetts* (1915), *The Tenements of Chicago* (1936), *The Child and the State* (1938) and *Public Assistance* (1939).

Abdel Rahman, Aisha, *pseud* Bint-al-Shah

Born c.1920
Egyptian writer and professor of literature

Aisha Abdel Rahman was born in Damietta, and educated at Cairo University. After a spell as an assistant lecturer at Cairo University, she worked from 1942 for the Egyptian Ministry of Education as an Inspector for the teaching of Arabic literature. Since 1950 she has taught at Ain Shans University, where she has been Professor of Arabic Literature at the University College for Women.

Her writing includes fiction, but she is best known for her literary criticism with works such as *New Values in Arabic Literature* (1961) and *Contemporary Arab Women Poets* (1963). She has also written extensively about the women members of the prophet Muhammad's family.

Abington, Fanny (Frances), *née* Barton

Born 1737 Died 1815
English actress and milliner whom Reynolds
painted as Miss Prue in Congreve's Love for Love

Fanny Abington was a flower girl, a street singer and milliner in Paris, and a kitchenmaid in London before she made her first appearance on the stage at the Haymarket Theatre in 1755.

She rose to fame in Dublin after 1759, the year she began an unsuccessful marriage to her music teacher, and subsequently returned to Drury Lane under David Garrick. She was extremely versatile, and excelled not only in Shakespearian heroic and romantic roles but also in comedy (Lady Teazle, Polly Peachum, Lucy Lockit). She was succeeded by **Elizabeth Farren**.

Following her milliner's job she had developed a flare for fashion and her 'Abington cap' became popular attire.

Abzug, Bella, *known as* Battling Bella, *née* Savitzky

Born 1920
American lawyer and politician, one of the key
figures of the modern feminist movement

Bella Abzug was born in the Bronx, New York. She was educated at Hunter College, New York, and Columbia University, practised law in New York from 1944 to 1970, and gained a reputation for defending those accused of un-American activities.

She became a prominent peace campaigner, and founded Women Strike for Peace (1961) and the National Women's Political Caucus. She was elected to Congress in 1971, but failed in her attempts to win a Senate seat (1976) and to become Mayor of New York (1977). She returned to her lawyer's practice in 1980, but continued her involvement in political issues.

Inducted into the National Women's Hall of Fame in 1994, she is a vigorous champion of welfare issues and women's rights. Her publications include *Gender Gap: Bella Abzug's Guide to Political Power for American Women* (1984).

Acarie, Madame, *also called* Mary of the Incarnation, *née* Barbe Jeanne Avrillot

Born 1566 Died 1618
French founder of the Carmelites of the Reform
in France

Madame Acarie was prompted by reading a life of **Teresa of Ávila** and receiving visions to promote the establishment of the Paris Carmel in 1603. She also helped found the Paris Ursulines and Bérulle's Oratory.

After the death of her husband Pierre Acarie, Vicomte de Villemore, whom she had married in obedience to her parents' wishes, she entered the Carmel at Amiens in 1613, later moving to Pontoise. Renowned for her charitable works and spiritual advice she was beatified in 1794.

Acheson, Anne Crawford

Born 1882 Died 1962
Northern Irish sculptor whose works include
figures, portraits and architectural subjects

Anne Crawford Acheson was born in Portadown. She studied at Victoria College, Belfast, and at the Royal College of Art, London. She was awarded a CBE in 1919 for her work with the Surgical Requisites Association during World War I.

An annual exhibitor at the Royal Academy, and in Paris, Glasgow and Liverpool, she received the Feodora Gleichen Memorial Award in 1938. Her early work was predominately in wood but she later worked also in metal, stone and concrete.

She was elected a member of Royal Society of British Sculptors and the Society of Artists in Watercolour.

Achurch, Janet

Born 1864   Died 1916
English actress who pioneered many roles in
Ibsen's plays

Janet Achurch was born in Lancashire. She made her London début in 1883, and subsequently toured with the actor-manager Frank Benson, playing various Shakespearian roles.

She is best known for her pioneering association with the works of the Norwegian playwright Henrik Ibsen. She took the role of Nora in *The Doll's House* in 1889, and both produced and starred in *Little Eyolf* in 1896.

After playing the title role in George Bernard Shaw's *Candida* in 1900, she was described by the playwright as a tragic actress of genius. She also toured extensively with her actor-husband Charles Carrington, until she retired from the stage in 1913.

Acosta de Samper, Soledad

Born 1833 Died 1903
Colombian feminist, historian, editor and
novelist, whose works include Los piratas en
Cartegena

Soledad Acosta de Samper was born in Bogotá, Colombia. She was a pioneer feminist, and edited *La Mujer* ('Woman') from 1878 to 1882. She wrote under various pen-names, including Aldebarán, Bertilda and Olga, and her huge output includes 45 novels and historical romances, and several biographies.

Her famous *Los piratas en Cartegena* (1885, 'Pirates in Carthage') is a vivid and psychologically convincing historical novel.

Adam, Juliette, *née* Lamber

Born 1836 Died 1936
French writer who established a salon of
politicians and artists and wrote for the
Republican cause

Juliette Lamber was born in Verberie, Oise. During the time she was married to her second husband, Senator Edmond Adam (1816–77), she established a salon at which she gathered the best collection of wits, artists and advanced politicians. She was a committed Republican, and produced stories and books on social and political questions.

She had begun her writing career in 1858 with a philosophical repudiation of the socialist Joseph Proudhon's anti-feminist stance, entitled *Idées antiproudhoniennes sur l'amour, la femme et le mariage* ('Anti-Proudhonist Ideas on Love, Women and Marriage'), and in 1879 she founded *La Nouvelle Revue*, which became an organ for the Republican cause.

She also wrote novels such as *Paënne* (1883, 'The Pagan Woman') and *Chrétienne* (1913, 'The Christian Woman') and in 1895–1905 published her *Mémoires*.

Adams, Abigail, *née* Smith

Born 1744 Died 1818
American letter writer and the first First Lady
of influence

Abigail Smith was born in Weymouth, Massachusetts, and educated at home. After marrying John Adams in 1764, she managed his farm and maintained a strong interest in politics, often travelling with him.

As the wife of a leader, later Vice-President and second President, in the new republic, she made observations in her letters that were lively and astute. She is considered to have been a strong political influence and her letters, published by her grandson in 1840, paint a vivid picture of the times and outline her strong views on women's rights.

Adams, Hannah

Born 1755 Died 1831
American historian and memoirist often described
as the first professional female author to emerge
in the USA

Hannah Adams was born in Medfield, Massachusetts. She grew up during the independence era and at the age of 29 published her first important book, the *Alphabetical Compendium of the Various Sects* (1784). This was a remarkable survey covering schisms and doctrinal disputes from the Early Fathers to the present day.

Her range of scholarship was also visible in *A Summary History of New England* (1799), one of the best available accounts of the pre- and post-Revolution north-eastern states. Later works were more devotional, except for *The History of the Jews* (1812), which is rather remarkable for its bluntness, and her posthumous autobiography (1832), a vital document in the history of the young republic.

Adams, Maude, *originally* Kiskadden

Born 1872   Died 1953
American actress who is thought to have been the
inspiration for Peter Pan

Maude Kiskadden was born in Salt Lake City. She was a child star before making her New York début in 1888, having taken her actress-mother's maiden name.

After achieving fame as Lady Babbie in J M Barrie's *The Little Minister* (1897), she starred in several more of his plays, and is said to have inspired his most famous character, Peter Pan, a role she took in New York in 1905.

She retired in 1918, but returned to the stage in Shakespearian roles in 1931 and 1934, and taught theatre in Missouri from 1937 to 1950.

Adams, Sarah Flower, *née* Flower

Born 1805 Died 1848
English poet who wrote the hymn 'Nearer, my God,
to Thee' and many others

Sarah Flower was born in Great Harlow, Essex, the daughter of the political writer and publisher Benjamin Flower (1755–1872) and the Sunday-school founder Eliza Gould (1770–1810). She married the engineer-inventor William Bridges Adams (1797–1872) in 1834.

She wrote poems on social and political subjects, and had a brief stage career. But she is best remembered for her hymns written for the Unitarian chapel at South Place, Finsbury, for which her younger sister Eliza (1803–46) frequently composed the music.

Her most famous hymn, 'Nearer, my God, to Thee', is found in the hymnbooks of many denominations.

Adams, Truda (Gertrude), *later known as* Truda Carter, *née* Sharp

Born 1890 Died 1958
English ceramicist who became the leading
decorator for the Poole Pottery

Truda Sharp studied at the Royal Academy Schools, London, and after meeting John Adams, who was on the staff at the Royal College of Art, married him and moved to Durban, South Africa, in 1914. They returned in 1920–1 and were persuaded in 1921 to move to Dorset and help set up the Poole Pottery with Harold Stabler and Cyril Carter.

Truda Adams became resident designer there and provided the majority of the designs that were to be the trademark of the 'Poole' works of the 1920s and 1930s. She was responsible for the first range of brush-stroke floral patterns with the restrained colouring which was popular with the customers of Liberty's and Heals in London, the pottery's main outlets.

The firm of Carter, Stabler and Adams (Poole Pottery) remained popular into the 1930s. Having divorced John Adams, Truda married Cyril Carter in 1931, and continued to design for the company until 1950. Her work was purchased for many Museum Collections, and she exhibited in the Royal Academy's Ceramic Exhibition in 1935, and the International Exhibition in Paris in 1937.

Adamson, Joy Friedericke Victoria, *née* Gessner

Born 1910 Died 1980
Austrian-born British naturalist, writer and
artist remembered for her books about Elsa
the lioness

Joy Gessner was born in Austria. She moved to Kenya in 1937 and began studying and painting the flora and fauna of the country in 1938, the year she married her second husband, a botanist called Peter Bally. In 1943 she married her third husband, British game warden George Adamson, and she accepted a commission by the colonial government to paint the portraits of members of many vanishing tribes (1944–52).

Though Adamson painted over 1,000 pictures, she made her name with a series of books about the lioness Elsa: *Born Free* (1960), *Elsa* (1961), *Forever Free* (1962) and *Elsa and Her Cubs* (1965).

In 1962 she launched the World Wildlife Fund in the USA and continued her career as a leading conservationist. She was murdered at her home in Kenya by tribesmen.

Adcock, (Kareen) Fleur

Born 1934
New Zealand poet who edited the influential
Oxford Book of Contemporary New Zealand
Poetry (1982)

Fleur Adcock was born in Papakura, Auckland, and educated in the UK. She moved to England in 1963 and worked with the Foreign and Commonwealth Office until 1979.

She writes in a lucid, mostly narrative manner, preferring invented situations to autobiographical inscape. Her poems are mostly ironic in tone, often as a means of camouflaging fear or anxiety, and thus very English, though she is most successful when writing about apparently marginal or peripheral locations: New Zealand, Ulster, the English Lakes. This detachment is evident in her (aptly titled) first collection *The Eye of the Hurricane* (1964), but also in the excellent *In Focus* (1977) and among the Wordsworthian echoes of her Lake District sequence *Below Loughrigg* (1977). Her *Selected Poems* appeared in 1983.

She was married to the Maori poet Alistair Te Ariki Campbell and her sister is the novelist **Marilyn Duckworth**.

Addams, Jane

Born 1860 Died 1935
American social reformer and feminist, a tireless
worker for female suffrage who was co-winner of
the Nobel Prize for Peace in 1931

Jane Addams was born in Cedarville, Illinois. She was inspired by a visit to Toynbee Hall in London to found the social settlement in Hull House in Chicago in 1899, which she led for the rest of her life. It comprised several buildings and provided such facilities as training in social work and other courses, a daytime nursery, a community kitchen and a theatre.

Addams worked to promote social justice in housing, factory inspection and the treatment of immigrants and blacks, and her work for women and children resulted in the eighthour working day for women. She became the first woman President of the National Conference of Social Work in 1910, founded the National Federation of Settlements (President, 1911–35) in 1911, and helped found the American Civil Liberties Union in 1920. She was also Vice-President of the National American Woman Suffrage Association (1911–14).

Jane Addams, 1924

She was a committed pacifist and was President of the Women's International League for Peace and Freedom (1919–35). In 1931 she shared the Nobel Prize for Peace with Professor Nicholas Murray Butler. Her many books include *Democracy and Social Ethics* (1902) and *Peace and Bread in time of War* (1922).

Adela

Born c.1062 Died 1137
French mother of King Stephen of England who became an influential regent while her husband fought in the Crusades

Adela was the youngest daughter of William the Conqueror. In 1080 she married Stephen, Count of Meaux and Brie, who later also became Count of Blois and Chartres; the future King Stephen was the third of her nine children and derived his right to the English throne through his mother.

Adela had a flair for administration and was cultured and pious. Her interest in ecclesiastical affairs led her to support the rebuilding of Chartres Cathedral in stone. In 1095 Adela's husband went to join the First Crusade and she became regent. Following his death in the Second Crusade she continued as regent until 1109, when her son Theobald succeeded her.

She retired to a convent but nevertheless retained considerable influence, in 1117 persuading Theobald to side with her brother Henry I of England against the King of France.

Adelaide, Queen

Born 1792 Died 1849
Queen of Great Britain as the wife of William IV (ruled 1830–7) who strove to restore the moral image of the British royal family

Adelaide was the eldest daughter of George, Duke of Saxe-Coburg-Meiningen. In 1818 she married William, Duke of Clarence, with whom she had a happy marriage, although he was twice her age and allegedly the father of several illegitimate children. He succeeded his brother, George IV, to the throne as William IV in 1830.

Adelaide's support of the Tories during the agitation for the Reform Bill in the early 1830s damaged her popularity with the Whig government, and she is thought to have persuaded the King to change from supporting to opposing the Bill and to dismiss Lord Melbourne's government in 1834, though she may be credited with more influence than she really had.

Their two children, both daughters, died in infancy, and William was succeeded by his niece, Queen **Victoria** in 1837. As queen-dowager, Adelaide travelled in Europe, supporting charities as she went. Among the buildings she endowed is the Collegiate Church of St Paul in Valletta, Malta.

Adelaide, St, *German* Adelheid

Born 931 Died 999
Holy Roman Empress who enjoyed a position of influence over three generations of rulers

Adelaide was born in Burgundy, a daughter of Rudolf II of Burgundy. She married Lothair, son of Hugh of Italy, in 947, but he died in 950 and she was imprisoned by his successor, Berengar II. The German king Otto I, 'the Great' of Saxony rescued her and married her as his second wife in 951.

They were crowned emperor and empress in 962. Their son succeeded his father in 973 as Otto II, and as Queen Mother Adelaide exercised considerable influence, although they quarrelled over many things, including her extravagant charities. She became joint regent with her daughter-in-law the empress **Theophano** for her grandson Otto III, and sole regent from 991 to 996.

Thereafter she retired to a convent she had founded at Seltz in Alsace.

Adie, Kate (Kathryn)

Born 1945
English television reporter who has become one of the BBC's top news journalists

Kate Adie was born in Sunderland. She took a degree in Scandinavian studies at Newcastle University, joined BBC radio in 1969 as a technician and then producer, and moved to television in 1977, when she began a two-year spell with BBC TV South.

She has been a reporter on the BBC's network news since 1979, corresponding from trouble spots around the world with a stern, stoical and authoritative delivery. Since 1989 she has held the post of chief news correspondent.

She has twice been the winner of the Monte Carlo International TV News award (1981, 1990) and won the BAFTA Richard Dimbleby award in 1989. She was voted 1992 Reporter of the Year and made an OBE in 1993, and is widely respected by her peers for her unimpeachable integrity.

Adjani, Isabelle Jasmine

Born 1955
French actress who has become a leading lady of stage and screen

Isabelle Adjani was born in Paris to an Algerian father and a German mother. She was an artistic child and ran her own theatre group before making her film début in *Le Petit Bougnat* (1969). She subsequently appeared in a number of film and television roles before being offered a contract with the Comédie–Française in 1972.

Hailed as 'the phenomenon of her generation' by *Le Figaro*, she left the Comédie-Française to pursue a film career, winning acclaim for her performances in *L'Histoire D'Adèle H* (1975, *The Story of Adèle H*), *L'Été Meurtrier* (1983, *One Deadly Summer*) and *Camille Claudel* (1988).

A major star in France, she has also recorded an album of songs and is an active campaigner on human rights issues. She has increasingly limited her screen appearances but after a lengthy absence returned in *Toxic Affair* (1993), *La Reine Margot* (1994) and *Diabolique* (1996).

Adler, Renata

Born 1938
American novelist and journalist whose oblique but precise prose includes her investigative reporting on Watergate

Renata Adler was born in Milan where her German family had gone to escape the Nazis. She was educated at Bryn Mawr and Harvard universities and at the Sorbonne in Paris, and joined the *New Yorker* in 1962. In *A Year in the Dark* (1969), she records her stint as film critic for the *New York Times* (1968–9), *Toward a Radical Middle* (1970) is a collection of other journalism.

These titles perhaps reflect some of the concerns of her two novels to date. *Speedboat* (1976), which won the Ernest Hemingway award, is a series of filmic scenes about loss and abandonment, linked by a compulsive need to tell stories. *Pitch Dark* (1983), in technique, reminds one that to see something clearly at night one looks slightly away, not directly at it. *Reckless Disregard* (1986) is Adler's account of Vietnam commander General Westmoreland's libel litigation against CBS (Columbia Broadcasting System) Inc.

Adler, Stella

Born 1903   Died 1992
American actress and teacher whose technique differed widely from Strasberg's Method acting

Stella Adler was born in New York, the daughter of the great Yiddish actor Jacob Adler. She worked as an actress in both Yiddish theatre and on Broadway, including notable roles in Clifford Odets's *Awake and Sing* and *Paradise Lost* in 1935 for the Group Theatre (founded by her husband, Harold Clurman).

She also directed plays, but is best known for her work as a teacher. She founded the Stella Adler Conservatory of Acting in 1949, where she encouraged students to use imagination and the play itself as their inspiration, in opposition to the self-absorbed Method acting of Lee Strasberg.

Ælflæd, *also known as* Elfleda

Born c.653   Died c.714
English princess and abbess who gave advice to St Cuthbert

Ælflæd was the daughter of Oswiu, King of Northumbria, and Eanflaeda (who was the daughter of Edwin, King of Northumbria, ruled 617–33). Her birth coincided with her father's military success, so she was dedicated to God and brought up by her kinswoman **Hilda**, abbess at Hartlepool and then Whitby.

Her mother joined her at Whitby in 670 and they became co-abbesses in 680 on Hilda's death; on Eanflaeda's death in 704 Ælflæd remained sole abbess. In Church matters mother and daughter favoured Roman rather than Celtic customs.

Ælflæd was a counsellor to Cuthbert, persuading him to accept the bishopric of Lindisfarne. She also brought peace between Theodore of Canterbury and Wilfred of York.

Æthelflæd, *also spelt* Ethelflaed

Born c.870 Died 918
Anglo-Saxon ruler of Mercia who took an active
part in battle against the Danish

Æthelflæd was the daughter of Alfred the Great and sister of Edward the Elder, ruler of Wessex. In about 888 she married Æthelred, ealdorman of Mercia, and fought alongside him against the invading Danes, winning a decisive victory near Tettenhall in 911.

When Æthelred died in the same year, Æthelflæd was recognized as 'Lady of the Mercians', and continued the resistance to the Danes. She built many fortified strongholds throughout Mercia and personally led counter-attacks; in 917, with her brother Edward, she captured Derby, and the following year Leicester. She was preparing to attack Danish-held Northumbria when she died in June 918.

Agassiz, Elizabeth Cabot Cary, *née* Cary

Born 1822 Died 1907
American naturalist and educator who was the
first President of Radcliffe College

Elizabeth Cary was born in Boston. She married the widowed Swiss-American zoologist and geologist Louis Agassiz (1807–73) in 1850 and six years later had established the pioneering Agassiz School for Girls in Boston with him. They also conducted a young ladies' school in Cambridge, Massachusetts. She accompanied her husband on his expeditions to Brazil in 1865–6, which inspired them to write *A Journey in Brazil* (1868), and she also travelled along the Pacific and Atlantic coasts of the Americas (1871–2).

She then served as President of the Society for Collegiate Instruction of Women and was a founder and President (1894–1902) of Radcliffe College for Women, which was founded in 1879 and chartered in 1894. Her other publications include *Seaside Studies in Natural History* (1865).

Agatha, St

Died c.251 AD
Sicilian Christian martyr who remained
committed to God despite severe torture

Agatha was born in Catania or Palermo. Legend has it that as a child she dedicated herself and her virginity to God. When she refused to respond favourably to the amorous advances of the Roman consul Quintinian, he sent her to a brothel, presumably in the hope that the experience would sway her res-olution. She was tortured too, and had both her breasts brutally removed, but it is said that her wounds were healed in prison by a vision of St Peter.

Some versions of her story describe her being martyred by being rolled over burning coals, perhaps the reason for her being invoked against fire (especially eruptians of Mt Etna) and lightning. Others say that Mt Etna erupted as she was about to be burned at the stake and so she was taken down and left to die in prison.

Agatha is the patron saint of Catania and of bell-founders, and is depicted in art carrying a tray bearing her two shorn breasts, which have often been mistaken for bells, or the loaves of bread that are blessed at her feast on 5 February.

Agnes of Poitou

Born c.1024 Died 1077
Wife of Henry III of Germany, Holy Roman
Empress and later regent during the minority of
the future Henry IV

Agnes of Poitou was the daughter of William V of Aquitaine and Poitou; she married the German king Henry III in 1943.

Following her husband Henry's death in 1056, she acted as regent during the minority of her son, the future Henry IV. Discontent at her ineptitude, however, escalated until in 1062 an uprising forced her early retirement and Anno, Archbishop of Cologne, usurped the regency.

Agnes, St

Born c.291 AD Died c.304 AD
Roman Christian and martyr honoured as the
patron saint of virgins and invoked for chastity

Agnes is believed to have been born of a wealthy family, and was martyred in Rome at the age of about 13 during the persecutions of the Christians by Diocletian. Despite her beauty she refused marriage and consecrated her virginity to Christ.

Her name appears in early Christian calendars, and she was praised by early writers, including Ambrose and Jerome. Legends developed around the story of her death, and she was a frequent subject of early Christian art. According to one legend, a man who looked at her with impure thoughts was struck blind, until his sight was restored by her prayers.

Her emblem is a lamb, possibly from the similarity of her name to Latin *agnus*, and her feast day is 21 January.

Agnes of Assisi, St

Born 1197 Died 1253
Italian Christian saint who co-founded the Poor
Clares with her sister

Agnes of Assisi was the daughter of Count
Favorino Scifi and the younger sister of St
Clare. In 1211, despite violent parental oppo-
sition, she joined her sister in a convent, and
they became co-founders of the Order of the
Poor Ladies of San Damiano ('Poor Clares').

One community of the Order was established at Monticelli, and Agnes became abbess
there in 1219.

Agnesi, Maria Gaetana

Born 1718 Died 1799
Italian mathematician and scholar, one of the few
pre-20th-century women mathematicians to gain
a reputation

Maria Agnesi was born in Milan, the eldest
of 21 children of a mathematics professor at
Bologna. She was a child prodigy and was
educated privately, learning to speak six languages by the age of 11.

She published books on philosophy and
mathematics, and her mathematical textbook
Istituzioni analitiche (1784) became famous
throughout Italy. She assimilated the work of
many different authors and developed new
mathematical techniques.

She is best known for her description of a
versed sine curve, which following an early
mistranslation of Italian, became known as the
'witch of Agnesi'.

Agoult, Marie de Flavigny, Comtesse d', *pseud Daniel Stern*

Born 1805 Died 1876
French writer whose salon in Paris was a forum
for revolutionary thinkers

Marie de Flavigny was born in Frankfurt and
educated at a convent in Paris. In 1827 she
married the Comte d'Agoult, who was 20 years
her senior, but in 1834 left him and ran away
with the composer Franz Liszt, by whom she
had three daughters: the eldest married the
French politician Émile Ollivier, while the
youngest, Cosima, married first the German
pianist and conductor Hans von Bülow, and
later the composer Richard Wagner. However
Liszt's career prevented them from settling,
and by 1844 they had separated for good.

In 1839 Madame d'Agoult had returned to
Paris to begin writing. She became a close
friend of **George Sand**, and held a salon in
Paris where the leading thinkers and writers

of the day would discuss their revolutionary
ideals.

She published her first novel, *Nelida*, in
1846, and wrote books on many other subjects, including *Esquisses morales* (1849), *Histoire de la révolution de 1848* (1850), *Dante et
Goethe* (1866) and a play, *Jeanne d'Arc* (1857).

Agreda, María de, *also known as* Mary of Jesus *and* Mary of Agreda

Born 1602 Died 1665
Spanish Franciscan nun and mystical writer

Mary was born in Agreda, one of 11 children.
She took a vow of chastity at the age of eight
and became a Poor Clare at 17, along with her
mother, Catalina de Arana, and one of her
sisters. Her father, Francisco Coronel, became
a Franciscan monk at the same time.

Mary was appointed abbess at 25, a position
she held for most of the rest of her life. Her
sanctity earned her the title Venerable soon
after her death, but the posthumously published account of her mystical experiences,
*The Mystical City of God and the Divine History
of the Virgin Mother of God* (1670), was briefly
placed on the Index of forbidden books in
1681 for giving too high a place to the Virgin
Mary, though scholars later reversed their
judgement.

Agrippina, the Elder

Born c.14BC Died AD33
Roman noblewoman who came to be regarded as
a model of heroic womanhood

Agrippina was the daughter of Marcus Vipsanius Agrippa and granddaughter of the
emperor Augustus. She married the general
Germanicus Julius Caesar, and was the mother
of Gaius Caesar (later the emperor Caligula)
and **Agrippina, the Younger**, who was allegedly born on the banks of the Rhine during a
campaign. She accompanied her husband on
his campaigns, and brought his ashes home
when he was murdered in AD19.

The emperor, Tiberius, was angered by her
popularity and banished her in 30 to the island
of Pandataria. She died of starvation there,
perhaps as a result of hunger strike, but certainly in suspicious circumstances.

Agrippina, the Younger

Born AD15 Died AD59
Roman empress whose successful bid for power
backfired when her presence became too much

Agrippina was the eldest daughter of **Agrippina, the Elder** and Germanicus, and the
sister of Caligula. Her first husband was

Cnaeus Domitius Ahenobarbus, who was the father of her son Domitius (later the emperor Nero, 37–68). Her second husband was Passienus Crispus, whom she allegedly poisoned in AD49, the year she married her third husband, her uncle, Emperor Claudius.

In AD54 Agrippina ruthlessly engineered Domitius's succession to the throne (as Nero) by supplanting the true heir Britannicus, Claudius's son by his fomer wife **Messalina**. She then proceeded to poison all his rivals and enemies and finally (allegedly) the emperor himself (AD54).

Initially she ruled as virtual co-regent with Nero, working with Seneca to improve the nation's economy through trade reorganization and government reform, but Nero tired of her influence and, following an unsuccessful attempt to drown her in a leaking boat, had her murdered.

Ahern, Lizzie (Elizabeth)

Born 1877 Died 1969
Australian socialist and feminist, an ardent
supporter of both movements

Lizzie Ahern was born in Ballarat, Victoria, and became a pupil teacher when she was 14. She later went into domestic service but lost her job because of her political views.

In 1905 she joined the forerunner of the Victorian Socialist Party and became a popular speaker in the Free Speech Campaign, earning 10 days' imprisonment for obstruction. An ardent supporter of women's rights, she co-founded the Domestic Workers' Union and later the Women's Socialist League (1909) and the Women's Anti-Conscription Committee (1916).

In 1908 she married Arthur Wallace, who became a member of parliament in 1919, and together they produced the Victorian Socialist Party's children's newsletter *Dawn*.

Ahlgren, Ernst, *pseud of* Victoria Benedictson

Born 1850 Died 1888
Swedish novelist, considered one of the greatest
talents of her time

Victoria Benedictson was born into a farmer's family in Scania in the south of Sweden. She was disappointed with her father's refusal to allow her to train as an artist, and entered into an ill-matched marriage to an older widower with five children. Her first novel, *Pengar* (1885, 'Money'), is a discussion of marriage and the emancipation of women based on her own experience. *Fru Marianne* (1887, 'Mrs

Marianne'), her other novel, tells of a bookish young woman becoming a model country housewife, representing her own dream of a marriage in which literary interests and traditional women's work are combined.

Benedictson's acquaintance with Georg Brandes, the leading Scandinavian critic of the time, developed into passionate love on her part, but she was met with only chilly flirtation and scornful remarks about her writing and committed suicide in a Copenhagen hotel.

Stora Boken (3 vols, 1978–85, 'The Great Book'), published after her death, contains autobiographical fragments and is a significant document of the period she lived in and of her own struggle for personal liberation.

Ahrweiler, Hélène, *née* Glykatzi

Born 1926
French academic, a specialist in Byzantine social
history who became the first woman President of
the Sorbonne (1976–81)

Hélène Glykatzi was born in Athens where she studied and later taught middle eastern history and archaeology, specializing in Byzantine studies.

In 1950 she moved to France as a researcher for the CNRS (Centre National de la Recherche Scientifique), becoming the first woman head of the history department at the Sorbonne in 1967. As a Vice-President of the Sorbonne in 1970, she was much involved in establishing the schools of humanities and social science as separate entities.

She became the first woman President of the Sorbonne in 1976, and on her retirement became Chancellor of the Universities of Paris (1982–9). Her other prestigious appointments include the presidency of the Centre Nationale d'Art et de Culture Georges Pompidou (1989–91).

Ailian, Dai *see* Dai Ailian

Airy, Anna

Born 1882 Died 1964
English artist and etcher, and author of The Art
of Pastel

Anna Airy was born in Greenwich. She studied at the Slade School of Art (1899–1903) under Henry Tonks and Philip Wilson Steer, winning the Melville–Nettleship prize for three consecutive years. Her subject matter at the beginning of the 20th century was drawn from criminal haunts along the banks of the Thames, where she found cockfighting, gambling and boxing to be of particular interest.

In 1918 she was commissioned by the Imperial War Museum to paint munitions factories. She was Occasional Inspector in Art to the Board of Education, and was elected to many societies, including the Royal Society of Painters and Etchers and the Royal Institute of Oil Painters.

A'ishah, *also spelt* Ayeshah, *in full* A'ishah Bint Abi Bakr

Born c.613   Died 678
Muslim leader known as 'the mother of believers'

A'ishah was the daughter of Abū-Bakr, the first caliph. At the age of nine she married the prophet Muhammad as his third wife. She became his favourite, but had no children.

When Muhammad died in 632 she resisted the claims to the caliphate of Ali, Muhammad's son-in-law (who had accused her of infidelity), in favour of her father, Abū-Bakr. When Ali became the fourth caliph in 656 she led a revolt against him, but was defeated and captured at the Battle of the Camel at Basra, and was exiled to Medina.

Akerman, Chantal

Born 1950
Belgian film director, screenwriter and actress known as a leading feminist filmmaker

Chantal Akerman was born in Brussels. She studied film in Brussels and Paris, and began making short films, inspired by the example of French filmmaker Jean-Luc Godard. Her experimental visual style was sparse and her narratives minimal, but strongly defined. She worked with other experimentalists in New York in 1972, and since then has divided her time between Europe and America.

Her work is demanding and often controversial, and seeks to reverse traditional male perspectives. Her films include *Jeanne Dielman* (1975), *Les Rendez-vous d'Anna* (1978, *Rendezvous with Anna*), and her first English language film, *Histoires d'Amerique* (1989, *American Stories*).

Akhmadulina, Bella (Isabella)

Born 1937
Russian poet and translator, mainly of Georgian poetry

Bella Akhmadulina was born in Moscow into a family of mixed Italian–Russian–Tatar origin, and was married for a time to the poet Yevgeni Yevtushenko. Her writing follows in the intense and candid tradition of **Marina Tsvetayeva**, but does not possess the latter's driven quality, and is not up to the standard established by her, by **Anna Akhmatova** and by **Zinaida Gippius**.

Nonetheless, she is a minor lyric poet of high quality, who has impressed with her fine readings of her poetry, given all over Europe and in New York, and whose first collection, *Struna* (1962, 'String'), attracted much attention. Available in English translation is *Fever* (1969).

Akhmatova, Anna, *pseud of* Anna Andreeyevna Gorenko

Born 1888   Died 1966
Russian poet who became one of Russia's major 20th-century writers despite the repression of the communist regime

Anna Akhmatova was born in Odessa, the daughter of a naval officer, and studied in Kiev before moving to St Petersburg. In 1910 she married the writer Nicholas Gumilev (1886–1921), who at first considerably influenced her style, and with whom she started the neoclassicist Acmeist movement. After her early collections of terse but lyrical poems, including *Vecher* (1912, 'Evening'), *Chokti* (1913, 'The Rosary') and *Belaya Staya* (1917, 'The White Flock'), she developed an impressionist technique. She remained as far as possible neutral to the Revolution. Her husband, from whom she had parted, was shot as a counter-revolutionary in 1921.

After the publication of *Anno Domini MCMXXI* (1922), she was officially silenced until 1940, when she published *Iz checti knig*. Then in 1946 her verse, which had previously been acceptable, was banned as being 'too remote from socialist reconstruction'.

She was 'rehabilitated' in the 1950s, and received official tributes on her death. Her later works include *Poema bez geroya* ('Poem without a Hero') and the banned *Rekviem* (Munich, 1963, 'Requiem'), a moving cycle of poems on the Stalin purges, during which her only son was arrested. *The Complete Poems of Anna Akhmatova* was published in 1993.

Akins, Zoë

Born 1886   Died 1958
American novelist, poet and Pulitzer Prize-winning dramatist

Zoë Akins was born in Humansville, Montana, and moved to New York to train as an actress.

In 1912 she published *Interpretations*, a collection of poetry, but later she concentrated on writing plays. Her most popular were *Déclassée* (1919), a society melodrama; *Daddy's Gone A-Hunting* (1921), a sentimental portrayal of a failing marriage; and *The Greeks had a Word for It* (1930), a comedy about the Ziegfeld showgirls. She won the 1955 Pulitzer Prize for drama for her adaptation of Edith Wharton's novel *The Old Maid*. Her best plays are witty and light, but not without irony or shrewd observation of middle-class women.

Among her other works are a contribution to the screen adaptation of the musical, *Showboat*, and two novels: *Forever Young* (1941) and *Cake upon the Water* (1951).

Akiyoshi, Toshiko

Born 1929
Japanese-born American jazz pianist and composer whose early life in China and Japan influences her music

Toshiko Akiyoshi was born in Dairen, China, of ethnic Japanese parents, and has been resident in the USA since 1956. She studied classical music in her teens, but was exposed to jazz during the American occupation of Japan, where her family had moved after World War II. She already had a substantial reputation as an arranger when the pianist Oscar Peterson encouraged her to move to the USA.

She studied at the Berklee College of Music in Boston and co-led a successful bebop quartet with her first husband, saxophonist Charlie Mariano. Though she has continued to perform as a solo and small-group player in a style influenced by Bud Powell, her interests have increasingly turned to large-scale composition and arrangement, often containing a marked Oriental component. In the early 1970s, she married another saxophone player, Lew Tabackin; their big band was disbanded in 1985, at which point Akiyoshi struck out on her own.

Her career was portrayed in the 1984 documentary film *Jazz is My Native Language*.

Alacoque, St Marguerite Marie

Born 1647 Died 1690
French Visitandine nun who established the feast of the Sacred Heart

Marguerite Marie Alacoque was born in Janots, Burgundy, and suffered a childhood made unhappy largely by the early death of her father. She became a member of the Visitation Order at Paray-le-Monial. She experienced visions of Christ, and managed to convey his message to her contemporaries through the foundation of the devotion to the Sacred Heart, which was later approved by the Pope.

She was canonized in 1920 and her feast day is 17 October.

Albani, Dame Emma, *stage-name of* Marie Louise Emma Cécile Lajeunesse

Born 1852 Died 1930
Canadian operatic soprano who was then one of the few performers to sing in German

Emma Lajeunesse was born in Chambly, Quebec, and was trained in music by her father. She performed for the first time in Albany, New York, at the age of 12 (hence the professional name of 'Albani').

She studied at Paris and Milan, and in 1870 sang in a début performance at Messina with a success that was confirmed in the leading cities of Europe and America. She was noted for her Wagnerian roles of Elsa in *Lohengrin* and Elizabeth in *Tannhäuser*, which she sang in German.

In 1911, the year she retired to teach, she published *Forty Years of Song*. She was appointed DBE in 1925.

Albany, Louisa Maximilienne Caroline, Countess of

Born 1752 Died 1824
British noblewoman whose first husband was Bonnie Prince Charlie

Louisa Maximilienne Caroline was the daughter of Prince Gustav Adolf of Stolberg (d.1757). In 1772 in Florence she married the aging Prince Charles Edward Stuart, Count of Albany (1720–88), who had settled in Italy, long after the failure of the 1745 Jacobite rising.

She left him in 1780 and the marriage was dissolved in 1784, whereupon she took up with the Italian dramatist, Count Vittorio Alfieri. After his death in 1803 she lived with a French painter, François Fabre. Her ashes are buried with those of Alfieri between the tombs of Michelangelo and Machiavelli in the church of Santa Croce, Florence.

Albret, Jeanne d' *see* Jeanne d'Albret

Albright, Madeleine Korbel, *née* Korbel

Born 1937
American diplomat, the first US Ambassador to the UN to have been born outside the USA

Madeleine Korbel was born in Czechoslovakia, educated at Wellesley College and Columbia University in the USA, and was married for a time to Joseph Albright. She is Professor of

Louisa May Alcott

Aleramo, Sibilla, *pseud of* Rina Faccio

Born 1876   Died 1960
Italian novelist, poet and memoirist about whose
work it has been said: 'if men really want to
understand women they must read Aleramo'

Sibilla Aleramo was born in Alessandria. She was married at the age of 16 to a man who had raped her, but left him and her son after about 10 years of misery. She was a woman of great but underrated gifts, whose feminist viewpoint is most poignantly evoked in *Una donna* (1906, Eng trans *A Woman at Bay,* 1908), an early and acute description of the manner in which men, while pretending to celebrate and love women, really treat them as objects.

She was the lover of a number of poets, including the great Dino Campana and Vincenzo Cardarelli, and her other work shows that she understood the poignancy of men who wanted to be exceptional. Always a socialist, she joined the communists after World War II.

Her memoirs were published as *Dal mio diario* (1945, 'From My Diary') and there is a moving collection of the letters between her and Campana entitled *Dino Campana–Sibilla Aleramo: Lettere* (1952). Her *Amo, dunque sono* (1927, 'I Love, Therefore I Am') is yet another of her remarkable books awaiting rediscovery.

International Affairs at Georgetown University and was a staff member of the National Security Council during the administration of President Carter. She has also been a senior adviser to prominent Democrats.

Now head of the Center for National Policy, she has been the USA's permanent representative to the United Nations since 1993, and has been elevated to President Clinton's Cabinet. During this time she has been involved in such events as the crisis in the former Yugoslavia, the retention of US sanctions on Iraq, and the 1995 UN women's conference in China.

Alcott, Louisa May

Born 1832   Died 1888
American author who wrote the children's classic
Little Women

Louisa May Alcott was born in Germantown, Philadelphia, the daughter of the Transcendentalist Amos Bronson Alcott. During the Civil War she was a nurse in a Union hospital, and her letters from this period were published as *Hospital Sketches* in 1864.

In 1868 she achieved enormous success with *Little Women*, which drew on her own home experiences; it was followed by a second volume, *Good Wives* (1869), *An Old Fashioned Girl* (1870), *Little Men* (1871) and *Jo's Boys* (1886).

Alexander, Jane, *originally* Jane Quigley

Born 1939
American actress who has found success on both
stage and screen

Jane Alexander was born in Boston. She was a child actress, and studied in Boston and Edinburgh. She went on to establish a considerable reputation as a character actress in theatre, film and television. Her most famous role was as **Eleanor Roosevelt** in the television film *Eleanor and Franklin* (1977).

She was nominated four times for Academy Awards, for her roles in *The Great White Hope* (1970), *All the President's Men* (1976), *Kramer Vs Kramer* (1979) and *Testament* (1983). She has appeared in many more films and plays, and has always made a powerful impression, even in minor roles. She was appointed chairwoman of the National Endowment for the Arts in 1993.

Alexander, Sadie

Born 1898   Died 1989
American lawyer and civil rights activist

Sadie Alexander was educated at the University of Pennsylvania, graduating in 1918. She was the first African-American woman to practise law in Pennsylvania.

She was secretary of the National Bar Association and became nationally recognized for her work for civil rights and human relations. President Jimmy Carter appointed her to chair the White House Conference on Aging.

Alexandra, Queen

Born 1844 Died 1925
Queen of Great Britain as the dignified,
compassionate and popular wife of Edward VII
(ruled 1901–10)

Alexandra was the eldest daughter of King Kristian IX of Denmark and she was selected by Queen **Victoria** to be engaged to Edward, whom she married in 1863 when he was Prince of Wales. She was a dignified, beautiful and deeply religious lady, and soon gained the affection of the British people. Ladies emulated her style of dress — her wearing of a choker was an innovation — and in the late 19th century a petticoat was named the Alexandra after her.

While supporting Edward through his long wait to ascend the throne, she gave birth to three sons and three daughters and engaged in much charity work, later founding the Queen Alexandra Imperial Military Nursing Service (1902) and instituting the annual Alexandra Rose Day in aid of hospitals (1913) to mark her fiftieth anniversary of coming to Britain.

She began to go deaf at an early age, which perhaps helped her to ignore Edward's extramarital exploits, though her knowledge of these was revealed when she selflessly invited his various mistresses to visit him on his death-bed.

Alexandra, The Hon Mrs Angus Ogilvy, Princess, *in full* Alexandra Helen Elizabeth Olga Christabel of Kent

Born 1936
British princess who is a first cousin of HRH
Queen **Elizabeth II**

Princess Alexandra is the daughter of George, Duke of Kent and Princess Marina of Greece. In 1963 she married the Hon Angus James Bruce Ogilvy (b.1928) and gave birth to a son, James Robert Bruce (b.1964), and a daughter, Marina Victoria Alexandra (b.1966).

She is the patron or president of many charitable organizations, including (since 1966) Princess Mary's RAF Nursing Service.

Alexandra (Alix) Feodorovna

Born 1872 Died 1918
German princess, and empress of Russia as the
wife of Nicholas II (ruled 1894–1917)

Alexandra Feodorovna was the daughter of Grand Duke Louis of Hesse-Darmstadt and **Alice Maud Mary** (Queen **Victoria**'s daughter), and married Nicholas II in 1894.

Though she was deeply pious and superstitious, she came under the evil influence of the fanatical Rasputin, and during World War I, while Nicholas was away at the front, she meddled disastrously in politics.

When the Revolution broke out, she was imprisoned by the Bolsheviks with the rest of the royal family in 1917, and later shot in a cellar at Ekaterinberg.

Aliberty, Soteria

Born 1847 Died 1929
Greek teacher, writer and feminist

Soteria Aliberty was educated in Greece and Italy. She taught in the pioneering Zappeion school for girls in Constantinople (now Istanbul) as later did **Kalliopi Kehajia**. In Romania, where she lived for many years until 1893, she founded a girls' school in the Greek community there.

Back in Athens, she founded the women's association Ergani Athena, and edited the literary journal *Pleiades*. Her writings include her pioneering 'Biographies of Distinguished Greek Women' for the *Women's Newspaper*, published in Athens.

Alice Maud Mary

Born 1843 Died 1878
Princess of Great Britain and Ireland who was a
leading patron of the arts and philanthropist

Princess Alice was the second daughter of Queen **Victoria**. She was an affectionate and light-hearted child, became increasingly accomplished as she grew up, and compassionately nursed her father Albert when he was dying of typhoid (1861). In 1862 she married Prince Frederick William Louis of Hesse-Darmstadt (1837–92), nephew of Louis III, Grand Duke of Hesse-Darmstadt, whom he succeeded (as Louis IV) in 1877.

She became a devoted wife and mother and also a patron of the arts, gathering a circle of German intellectuals around her and learning the art of painting and sculpture herself. All her philanthropic activities were undertaken without ostentation, and after nursing the sick and wounded in the Franco-German War of 1870–1, she founded the Women's Union for

Nursing the Sick and Wounded in War. She also translated some of **Octavia Hill's** essays into German.

Of her four surviving daughters, the eldest became the mother of Louis, Earl Mountbatten, and the youngest, **Alexandra (Alix) Feodorovna**, married Nicholas II of Russia.

Ali-Zadeh, Franghiz

Born 1947
Azeri composer who has emerged triumphantly from the former Soviet Union

Franghiz Ali-Zadeh was born in Baku, Azerbaijan, and trained at the State Conservatory there, where she has subsequently taught. In 1982 she married the influential filmmaker Dzhangir Gasanaga Zeinalov. Her first published work was a piano sonata in memory of Alban Berg, and a tribute to Gustav Mahler followed.

Ali-Zadeh has been as greatly affected by trans-Caucasian folk-music as by Western music, and pieces like her First Symphony (1976) and the cycle *Songs about Motherland* (1978) are typical.

She is widely regarded as one of the most individual composers to emerge from the former Soviet Union.

Allan-Shetter, Liz (Elizabeth), *née* Allan

Born 1947
American water-skier, widely considered the sport's all-time best female competitor

Liz Allan-Shetter has won the overall world championship three times (in 1965, 1969 and 1973), as well as eight individual titles: one tricks, three slalom and four jumps.

Her total of 11 world titles is also a world record, as is her feat of 1969, when she won all four titles for an unique Grand Slam. She has also lifted 42 US national titles, nine Masters Cup for Women titles and the Olympic title when water-skiing was a demonstration sport in 1972.

Allen, Betty

Born 1936
Scottish chef and restaurateur whose expertise has earned the Airds Hotel national fame

Betty Allen was born in Bathgate, West Lothian. Largely self-taught as a chef, she developed her professional skills in her first hotel in Largo (1973–8), which she ran with her husband Eric. In 1978 they moved to Port Appin, Argyll, and opened the Airds Hotel.

Working with their son Graeme (1966–) and employing an imaginative but simple presentation of excellent local produce, she has won wide acclaim there.

National recognition by food writers and restaurant guides was followed by international appreciation. In 1990 she and **Hilary Brown** became the first women in Scotland to receive a Michelin star.

Allen, Dede (Dorothea Carothers)

Born 1924
American film editor who broke new ground with her dynamic work on Bonnie and Clyde

Dede Allen was born in Ohio. She began her career as a messenger in the Columbia studio in 1943, and worked her way up to sound cutter and then assistant editor. Her first important editing assignment came on *Odds Against Tomorrow* (1959).

Her reputation as a leading light in her field was sealed by her imaginative quick-fire cutting on Arthur Penn's *Bonnie and Clyde* (1967). Her other major films have included *The Hustler* (1961), *Little Big Man* (1970), *Serpico* (1974), *Reds* (1981) and *Henry and June* (1990).

Allen, Florence Ellinwood

Born 1884 Died 1966
American judge and feminist, the first woman to sit on a general federal bench and the first on a court of last resort

Florence Allen was born in Salt Lake City, Utah, and educated at Western Reserve University in Cleveland, Ohio (1900–4). She became involved in the New York League for the Protection of Immigrants (1910) and the college Equal Suffrage League.

In 1913 she graduated from New York University Law School, and the next year was admitted to the Ohio Bar. Throughout her career she worked assiduously for women's rights, and won high respect both as a judge and as a feminist.

She retired in 1959, and in 1965 she published the autobiographical *To Do Justly*.

Allen, Gracie (Grace Ethel Rosalie)

Born 1895 Died 1964
American comedy actress who formed an enduring double act with her husband George Burns

Gracie Allen was born into a showbusiness family in San Francisco. She made her stage début as a child and was a regular vaudeville performer from her teenage years onwards. She met her future husband George Burns

(1896–1996) in 1922 and they subsequently formed a double-act under the title 'Sixty-Forty'.

Her persona of a chic, scatter-brained nitwit earned the laughs whilst Burns merely had to register incredulity at his wife's latest non-sensical remark. Their own radio show, *The Adventures of Gracie*, began in 1932 and they eventually transferred to television with the long-running *The Burns and Allen Show* (1950–7). She also appeared in a number of films, often with Burns, including *We're Not Dressing* (1934), *A Damsel in Distress* (1937) and *The Gracie Allen Murder Case* (1939), and they remained a beloved institution of American showbusiness until her retirement through ill health in 1958.

Allen, Paula Gunn

Born 1939
Native American academic and writer mainly concerned with women, women's work and Native American literature

Paula Gunn Allen is of Laguna–Lakota and Lebanese descent. She began her career by writing fiction (*The Woman Who Owned the Shadows*, 1983) and then moved on to literary criticism. She actively encourages the publication of Native American literature, highlighting special themes and structures.

Her works of criticism and her anthologies show a particular interest in the works of women and a concern with women's issues. Among her books are *The Sacred Hoop: Recovering the Feminine in American Indian Traditions* (1986) and *Spider Woman's Grand-daughters: Traditional Tales and Contemporary Writings by Native American Women* (1989).

Allende, Isabel

Born 1942
Chilean novelist best known as the author of The House of the Spirits

Isabel Allende was born in Lima, Peru, the niece and goddaughter of Salvador Allende, the former President of Chile. Several months after the overthrow of Chile's coalition government in 1973 by the forces of a junta headed by General Augusto Pinochet Ugarte, she and her family fled Chile, and Isabel sought sanctuary in Venezuela.

Her first novel, *Casa de los espíritus* (Eng trans *The House of the Spirits*, 1985), arose directly out of her exile and her estrangement from her family, in particular her aged grandfather, who remained in Chile, and achieved huge critical success being hailed as the most exciting talent to emerge from Latin America

Isabel Allende, 1974

since Gabriel García Márquez. *De Amor y de Sombra* ('Of Love and Shadows') followed in 1987, and *El Plan infinito* ('The Infinite Plan') in 1993.

Allgood, Sara

Born 1883 Died 1950
Irish-born American actress whose début coincided with the opening night of the Abbey Theatre

Sara Allgood was born in Dublin. She first appeared in 1904 at the opening night of the Abbey Theatre in Lady **Gregory**'s *Spreading the News*. She also acted in the works of J M Synge, playing Widow Quinn in the *Playboy of the Western World*. She played Isabella in *Measure for Measure* when **Annie Horniman** opened her Manchester company (1908), and toured Australia with *Peg O' My Heart* (1915).

Returning to the Abbey, Allgood created the parts of Juno Boyle and Bessie Burgess in Sean O'Casey's *Juno and the Paycock* and *The Plough and the Stars* (1926) respectively, and her performance of Juno in the Alfred Hitchcock film (1930) gives a glimpse of the dignity and realism she brought to the part.

She settled in Hollywood in 1940, and became a US citizen in 1945. Her roles in over 30 films included haunting appearances in *Jane Eyre* (1943), *The Lodger* (1944) and *Between Two Worlds* (1944), but she was seldom offered parts commensurate with her talent, and died penniless.

Alliluyeva, Svetlana

Born 1926
Russian-born American daughter of Joseph Stalin, who defected to the West and denounced the Soviet authorities

Svetlana Alliluyeva was born in Moscow, the daughter of Joseph Stalin and his second wife, Nadezhola Sergeevna Alliluyeva. The death of her husband, Bradegh Singh, provided her with a reason for leaving Russia to escort his ashes to India, his country of origin, from where she defected to the USA. She became a US citizen in 1966, denouncing the Soviet authorities through extensive interviews and her memoirs, *Twenty Letters to a Friend* (1967).

She married a US architect, William Wesley Peters, in 1970, and gave birth to a daughter, Olga, a year later. The relationship did not last and Alliluyeva relocated, first to England, and then to her homeland in 1984. However the welcome she received upon her return was short-lived, for she soon clashed with the authorities again. She left once more for the USA in 1986, and settled in Wisconsin.

Allingham, Helen, *née* Paterson

Born 1848 Died 1926
English watercolour and graphic artist best known for her rustic landscapes and scenes of idyllic rural England

Helen Paterson was born in Burton-on-Trent. She later moved to Birmingham and trained at Birmingham School of Design for four years before moving to London and studying at the Royal Academy Schools. She began her career as a graphic artist with the *Illustrated London News* and the *Graphic Magazine*.

In 1874 she married the poet William Allingham, and through her husband's literary connections she met John Ruskin, who greatly admired her work. She also executed several portraits of Thomas Carlyle who was a family friend.

She became an Associate Member of the Watercolour Society in 1875 and a full member in 1890. She exhibited in Chicago, where she won the 1893 bronze medal, in Paris, in Brussels, where she took the 1901 silver medal, and had seven exhibitions with the Fine Art Society between 1886 and 1913.

Allingham, Margery Louise

Born 1904 Died 1966
English detective-story writer who created the fictional aristocratic detective Albert Campion

Margery Allingham was born in London. She wrote a string of elegant and witty novels, including *Crime at Black Dudley* (1928), *Police at the Funeral* (1931), *Flowers for the Judge* (1936), *More Work for the Undertaker* (1949), *The Tiger in the Smoke* (1952), *The China Governess* (1963) and *The Mind Readers* (1965).

Allitt, Beverley Gail

Born 1969
English nurse, convicted murderer and alleged sufferer of MSBP

Beverley Allitt was born in Grantham, Lincolnshire. During a period of two months in 1991 while working on the children's ward at Grantham and Kesteven District Hospital she murdered four young children, including one by suffocation and two by lethal injections of insulin, and attacked several others.

In May 1993 she was sent to Rampton top security hospital after being given 13 life sentences for the four murders. She was apparently suffering from Munchausen Syndrome By Proxy (MSPB), a controversial and rare condition which causes carers to create symptoms in the person in their care to attract medical attention.

Allred, Gloria Rachel, *née* Bloom

Born 1941
American lawyer noted for her flamboyant handling of a wide range of cases

Gloria Bloom was born in Philadelphia, Pennsylvania. After studying English at the Universities of Pennsylvania and New York, she taught at an all-black boys' school in Philadelphia, then moved to Los Angeles to teach in the Watts ghetto after the 1965 riots.

Convinced that she could work for social justice if she trained in the law, she graduated from Loyola Law School, Los Angeles, in 1974. She started the law firm Allred, Maroko, Golberg & Ribakoff which specializes in family law.

Known for her flamboyance and dramatic flair, she handled the case that equalized dry-cleaning prices for men and women's clothes, as well as cases involving child custody and support, and sexual abuse.

Almedingen, E M (Martha Edith von)

Born 1898 Died 1971
Russian-born British novelist, biographer, autobiographer and historian

Martha Edith von Almedingen was born in St Petersburg and settled in England, where she became a distinguished academic historian.

She wrote over 60 books, including novels, but is best remembered for her biographies, for both adult and younger readers. These provide a highly readable and atmospheric account of Russia's turbulent history.

A Study of Emperor Paul I of Russia: 1754–1801 (1959) and *Catherine the Great: A Portrait* (1963), drawing upon letters and memoirs, are particularly vivid and politically balanced. Her other works include *Tomorrow Will Come* (1941), *The Almond Tree* (1947) and *Late Arrival* (1952).

Almeida, Brites de

Floreat 1385
Legendary Portuguese heroine who defended her village armed with a baker's shovel

Brites de Almeida was born in Aljubarrota and is thought to have been a baker. About 1385, during the war between John I and the King of Cadiz, she led her townspeople against the Spanish forces who were attacking her village and killed seven of the enemy with her baker's shovel.

The incident was celebrated by the Portuguese poet Luis de Camoens (1524–80) in a poem, and the shovel is believed to have been preserved as a relic in Aljubarrota for several generations.

Aloni, Shulamit

Born 1931
Israeli politician, lawyer and writer

Shulamit Aloni was born in Tel-Aviv. After World War II she became firstly a teacher and then, in 1956, a lawyer. From 1965 to 1969 she was a Labour MP, but left the Labour Party in 1973 to found the Civil Rights Party. For a short time she held a postion as a Minister without Portfolio.

Aloni is a long-term committed campaigner for civil rights, who has written on the rights of both women and children in Israel, and runs a free legal aid service.

Alonso, Alicia, *originally* Alicia de la Caridad del Cobre Martínez Hoyo

Born 1921
Cuban dancer and choreographer who founded the Ballet de Cuba

Alicia Alonso was born in Havana. Her career began in the USA where she studied and performed with the School of American Ballet and the choreographer George Balanchine.

During that time she made several trips back home to make guest appearances with the Cuban company Pro Arte.

In 1948 she returned permanently to form the Alicia Alonso Company. This grew into a national ballet company for Cuba and toured the world to great acclaim. She remained as director when Fidel Castro's régime was established in 1959.

Though best remembered for the development of her company, she was also famed as a dancer, particularly for the title role in *Giselle*. Roles created for her include Antony Tudor's *Undertow* (1945) and *Goya Pastorale* (1940), and Balanchine's *Themes and Variations* (1947); her own works include *La Tinaja* (1943).

Al-Sa'id, Aminah

Born 1914   Died 1995
Egyptian writer, journalist and feminist, a well-known advocate of women's rights

Aminah Al-Sa'id was born in Cairo into an educated family in which women's rights, particularly the right to education, were promoted. (Her eldest sister became the first woman Minister of Education in Egypt in 1965.) Educated at Cairo University, Al-Sa'id became an active advocate of women's rights, most notably as editor of *Hawa*, an influential women's weekly magazine.

She also held important positions as President of Dar al Hilal Publishing House and as a member of the Supreme Board of Journalism. Her books include *Indian Visions, Journey's End, The Great Goal* and *Faces in Shadow*.

Amalia, Anna, *also spelt* Amelia

Born 1739   Died 1807
German Duchess of Saxe-Weimar who became a wise ruler while still only a teenager

Anna Amalia was the daughter of the Duke of Brunswick and niece of Frederick II of Prussia. She married the Duke of Saxe-Weimar at the age of 17 but was widowed in 1758 after only two years of marriage. Though still only a minor herself, she acted as regent for her infant son, Charles Augustus, and ruled her small state with great skill and prudence (1758–75).

During the Seven Years War (1756–63) she had to fight her uncle, but he treated her with respect. Once peace was established, she devoted herself to the education of her sons and to the duchy's public affairs. As a notable patron of German literature, she attracted to the court at Weimar the leading literary figures in Germany — Goethe, Schiller,

Herder, Musaeus and Wieland. She also founded the Weimar Museum and supported the revision of the University of Jena.

When her son came of age in 1775, she withdrew from public life and turned her attention to studying the arts.

Anastasia, *in full* Grand Duchess Anastasia Nikolaievna Romanov

Born 1901   Died 1918
Tsar Nicholas II's youngest daughter who inspired films and books through the mystery of her death

Anastasia was the youngest daughter of Tsar Nicholas II. For 76 years mystery surrounded her death, until in 1994 a Russian government report confirmed that, as previously thought but not confirmed, she had indeed been executed by the Bolsheviks on 19 July 1918 in a cellar in Ekaterinburg, where she had taken refuge with other members of the royal Romanov family in 1917 at the start of the Revolution.

Over the years various people claimed to be Anastasia, such as 'Anna Anderson' from the Black Forest, who in 1968 went to the USA and married a former history lecturer, Dr John Manahan, and died in 1984 in Virginia at the age of 82. She had been rescued from a suicide attempt in a Berlin canal in 1918 and for more than 30 years fought unsuccessfully to establish her identity as Anastasia; most of the surviving members and friends of the Romanov family were sceptical or downright hostile.

Anastasia's story inspired two films (*Anastasia*, 1956, with **Ingrid Bergman**, and *Is Anna Anderson Anastasia?* with Lilli Palmer) and several books.

Anderson, Beth (Barbara Elizabeth)

Born 1950
American composer whose work is varied, innovative and prolific

Beth Anderson was born in Lexington, Kentucky, and educated there and in California, where her teachers included John Cage, Robert Ashley and Terry Riley.

Anderson has worked as a concert pianist and accompanist, was a founder and co-editor of *EAR* magazine (1973–9), and a performing member of the women composers' group Hysteresis (1973–5). Her first opera, *Queen Christina*, was performed in 1973.

Extremely prolific, she turned away from a basically serialist style after 1978 to create a body of work in which hymns, pop tunes and Frank Churchill's Disney songs all play a part; she also pioneered a form of sound-poetry she calls 'text-sound'.

Anderson, Elda Emma

Born 1899   Died 1961
American physicist, an internationally recognized authority on radiation protection and health physics

Elda Anderson was born in Green Lake, Wisconsin. She graduated in physics from the University of Wisconsin in 1924 and taught in local colleges and high schools until 1941, when she gained her PhD.

She then took a break from teaching and worked at Princeton University, where she became a member of the atomic bomb project, and moved to Los Alamos in New Mexico, where she remained until 1947. She briefly returned to teaching, but in 1949 became chief of education at the Health Physics Division of the Oak Ridge National Laboratory in Tennessee.

Anderson, Elizabeth Garrett

Born 1836   Died 1917
English physician who became England's first woman mayor

Elizabeth Garrett Anderson was born in London, the sister of the suffragette **Millicent Fawcett**, and brought up at Aldeburgh in Suffolk. Despite opposition to the admission of women into medical schools, in 1860 she began studying medicine and in 1865 qualified as a medical practitioner by passing the Apothecaries' Hall examination. She was probably only the second woman doctor in England, after **James Barry**.

The following year she established a dispensary for women in London (later renamed the Elizabeth Garrett Anderson Hospital), where she instituted medical courses for women. In 1870 she was appointed a visiting physician to the East London Hospital, and headed the poll for the London School Board, and she was given the degree of MD by the University of Paris.

In 1908 she was elected Mayor of Aldeburgh — the first woman mayor in England.

Anderson, Ethel

Born 1883   Died 1958
English-born Australian writer

Ethel Anderson was born in Leamington, Warwickshire. She was a friend of the Keynes, Darwin, and Vulliamy families and of the poet Frances Cornford. She married an army officer and lived for some time in India.

She wrote two books of verse, *Squatter's Luck* (1942) and *Sunday at Yarralumla* (1947), some essays, and two books of short stories —

Indian Tales (1948) and *The Little Ghosts* (1959) — delicate tales based on her Indian experiences. Her best-known book, *At Parramatta* (1956), turns vignettes of Australian middle-class life in the 1850s into a microcosm of the Seven Deadly Sins.

She also wrote an oratorio, *The Song of Hagar* (1958), set to music by the composer John Antill.

Anderson, Jessica Margaret

Born c.1918
Australian novelist and writer for radio, whose novels have twice won the Miles Franklin award

Jessica Anderson was born in Brisbane. She did not write her first book, *An Ordinary Lunacy* (1963), until she was 40, and her reputation was only established in 1978 with *Tirra Lirra by the River*, which won the Miles Franklin award and recounts Nora Porteous's lifelong search for herself. Anderson won the award a second time for *The Impersonators* (1980).

In *Stories from the Warm Zone and Sydney Stories* (1987), stories of her Brisbane childhood contrast with sophisticated Sydney in the 1980s (where she mainly lives) and demonstrate a command of diverse moods. In her psychological crime story, *The Last Man's Head* (1970), she returns to the detective genre of her first novel. A historical novel, *The Commandant* (1975), based on the true story of an early commander of the Moreton Bay (later Brisbane) penal settlement, had less success.

Anderson, Dame Judith, *originally* Frances Margaret Anderson

Born 1898 Died 1992
Australian actress whose roles included Hamlet on stage and Mrs Danvers in the film Rebecca

Judith Anderson was born of British parentage in Adelaide, South Australia. She made her Sydney stage début in *A Royal Divorce* (1915) and first appeared in New York in 1918. She toured America throughout the 1920s, enjoying successes with *Cobra* (1924) and *Strange Interlude* (1928–9). She first appeared on the big screen in the short *Madame of the Jury* (1930), but she preferred the stage, where her reputation as a distinguished classical and contemporary actress grew following productions like *Mourning Becomes Electra* (1932), *The Old Maid* (1935), *Hamlet* (1936, with John Gielgud) and *Macbeth* (1937) at the Old Vic in London.

Her chilling performance as the sinister Mrs Danvers in *Rebecca* (1940) earned her a cinema

Judith Anderson

career portraying cruel, domineering and often repressed matriarchal figures in films like *Laura* (1944) and *Diary of a Chambermaid* (1946). Her prodigious theatre credits include the title part in the Robinson Jeffers adaptation of *Medea* (1947 and 1982), *The Seagull* (1960) and *Hamlet* (1970–1) in the title role. Her film appearances comprise *Cat on a Hot Tin Roof* (1958), *A Man Called Horse* (1970), *Inn of the Damned* (1974) and *Star Trek III* (1984).

In 1984 a Broadway theatre was named in her honour and, the same year, she joined the cast of the television soap opera *Santa Barbara*. She was created DBE in 1960.

Anderson, Margaret C(aroline)

Born 1886 Died 1973
American author, editor and publisher who co-founded the Little Review

Margaret C Anderson was born in Indianapolis, Indiana. She was a founder in 1914 of the famous literary magazine the *Little Review*, which published pieces by Chicago Renaissance writers Carl Sandburg, Sherwood Anderson, William Carlos Williams, **Amy Lowell** and Wallace Stevens, as well as controversial articles by such writers as W B Yeats, Ernest Hemingway and Ezra Pound. Its extracts of James Joyce's *Ulysses* (published in book form 1922) which appeared between 1917 and 1920 were considered to contain indecent material and several editions of the magazine were burned by the US Post Office, culminating in 1920 with the conviction and fining of Anderson and her colleague Jane Heap for publishing obscene material.

In 1923 she moved to Paris where the *Little Review* appeared from 1924 to 1929.

Anderson, Marian

Born 1902 Died 1993
American contralto who triumphed over racial prejudice and became the first black singer to perform at the Metropolitan Opera

Marian Anderson was born into a poor family in Philadelphia, where her obvious talent as a young gospel singer led to a fund being set up by other church-goers to finance her training. She studied in New York under Boghetti and spent most of her career as a concert singer.

After several trips to Europe between 1925 and 1933, she began to make a name for herself, particularly in New York where she sang at Carnegie Hall in 1929, rising above her earlier problems caused by poverty and racial discrimination. However in 1939 she was prevented from performing at Constitution Hall in Washington DC. There was such a protest that **Eleanor Roosevelt** and others arranged for her to appear in concert at the Lincoln Memorial, and she performed triumphantly to an audience of 75,000.

Renowned for the range and rich tone of her magnificent voice, she became the first black to sing at the White House and at the Metropolitan Opera, as Ulrica in Verdi's *Un ballo in maschera* ('A Masked Ball') in 1955. She published her autobiography, *My Lord, What a Morning*, in 1956 and retired in 1965. President Eisenhower made her a delegate to the United Nations in 1958, and she received many honours and international awards, including the President's Medal for Freedom in 1963.

Anderson, Mary

Born 1859 Died 1940
American actress whose best roles included Rosalind in As You Like It

Mary Anderson was born in Sacramento, California. Her début as Juliet at Louisville in 1875 was successful and she played with growing popularity in America and (after 1883) in England.

By 1890 she had played 18 leading roles and attained the peak of her career, but she retired to marry Antonio de Navarro and settle in England, though she did appear in benefit performances during World War I.

She published two volumes of memoirs, in 1896 and 1930.

Andersson, Bibi (Birgitta)

Born 1935
Swedish actress best known for her roles in Ingmar Bergman films

Bibi Andersson was born in Stockholm. She began her career in 1949 as a film extra. The Ingmar Bergman films in which she has starred include *The Seventh Seal* (1956), *Persona* (1966) and *The Touch* (1971).

As a theatre actress she has been attached to both the Malmö Municipal Theatre and the Royal Dramatic Theatre, Stockholm, and she took many stage roles in the USA during the 1970s. She has been the recipient of many awards, including the British Academy Award for Best Foreign Actress (1971) for her part in *The Touch*.

Andreas-Salomé, Lou

Born 1861 Died 1937
German novelist, biographer, feminist and thinker endowed with beauty and intellect

Lou Andreas-Salomé was born in St Petersburg, Russia, to a German mother and Russian soldier, and became one of Zurich University's first female students. She travelled widely in Europe and befriended many great writers and thinkers of the day. The philosopher Nietzsche loved her and she was a lover of the Austrian poet Rainer Maria Rilke and perhaps of Sigmund Freud, with whom she studied. She too became a practising analyst.

Lou, as she is always called, wrote shrewdly and generously of the efforts of Henrik Ibsen to portray women, gave a piercing account of Nietzsche, and was responsible for releasing much poetry in Rilke, whom she understood better than any other woman in his life.

She was interested in the expression of femininity outside marriage, and her *Die Erotik* (1910) is a key text, although it has been ignored by latter-day feminists. Her psychological and religious novels are now due for revival, as are her work and thought, and her *Rainer Maria Rilke* (1928) remains a seminal work on the poet.

Andrews Sisters, The

LaVerne born 1915; died 1967; Maxene born 1918; died 1995; Patti born 1920
American vocal harmony trio whose record sales remain unsurpassed by another female act

The Andrews Sisters were born and raised in Minneapolis. They began to work on the RKO circuit when in their early teens with the youngest sister Patti singing lead lines, and Maxene and LaVerne singing soprano and contralto harmonies.

Their breakthrough record was 'Bei Mir Bist Du Schön' in 1939, which led to huge wartime success, including 'Pistol Packin' Mama' (1943) with Bing Crosby, 'Boogie Woogie Bugle Boy' and 'Rum and Coca Cola' (1944).

They retired as a group in the late 1950s, but Maxene continued to perform into the 1980s. Andrews Sisters records have continued to outsell every female act in history, accounting for nearly 60 million discs worldwide.

Andrews, Julie, *originally* Julia Elizabeth Wells

Born 1935
English singer and actress whose roles as Mary
Poppins and Maria made her famous

Julie Andrews was born in Walton-on-Thames, Surrey, into a showbusiness family. She trained as a singer, and made her London début in the 1947 revue *Starlight Roof*. Following several successes on radio and stage, she was selected for the New York production of *The Boyfriend* (1954) and several long-running Broadway musicals, notably *My Fair Lady* (1956) and *Camelot* (1960).

She won an Academy Award for her first film, *Mary Poppins* (1964), which was followed by a further nomination for *The Sound of Music* (1965). Her strenuous efforts to move beyond her rather prim image included the portrayal of a breast-baring movie-star in *S.O.B.* (1981) and a transvestite in *Victor/Victoria* (1982). Though she had been active for some time in television, since 1970 she has appeared almost exclusively in films directed by her second husband, Blake Edwards. In 1995 she opened the Broadway version of *Victor/Victoria*.

Angel, Albalucía

Born 1939
Colombian short-story writer and poet, one of the
new wave of feminist writers in Latin America

Albalucía Angel was born in Bogotá. Her fictional works tend to be experimental and, according to some critics, unusually difficult to read because of unexpected narrator changes, manipulations of structure, and verbal fireworks.

Angel is also involved in filmmaking and journalism; she has produced a number of documentaries and written extensively on art.

Her most famous work is *Estaba la pájara pinta sentada en el verde limón* ('The Painted Bird was Sitting on the Green Lemon Tree'), a female *Bildungsroman* dealing with the sexual and political awakening of the protagonist.

Angela Merici, St, *also called* Angela of Brescia

Born 1474 Died 1540
Italian founder of the Ursulines, the oldest
teaching order of women in the Catholic Church

Angela Merici was born in Desenzano, near Lake Garda. After her husband's death she became a Franciscan tertiary, founding girls' schools and caring for the sick.

During a pilgrimage to the Holy Land (1524–5) she became blind for a while. She declined a Papal invitation (1525) to work in Rome, but founded the Ursulines — in her lifetime an uncloistered and informal order dedicated to Christian education in their own homes — in Brescia in 1535, confirming a vision received 29 years earlier.

She was canonized in 1807 and her feast day is 1 June.

Angela of Foligno

Born c.1248 Died 1309
Umbrian Franciscan who is remembered as a
prominent mystic of the 13th century

Angela was from Foligno in Central Italy, the daughter of a wealthy family. She was converted to Christianity around the age of 40 and became a member of the Third Order of St Francis. After the death of her husband and children, she became an anchoress, or recluse.

Her visions are recorded in the *Liber Visionem et Instructionem* ('Book of Visions and Instructions'), which she dictated to her confessor, her cousin Brother Arnaldo. They analyse 20 steps of penitence towards the Vision of God and seven steps into the mystical life. Angela was beatified in 1693.

Angeles, Victoria De Los *see* Los Angeles, Victoria de

Angell, Helen Cordelia, *née* Coleman

Born 1847 Died 1884
English painter of flower subjects who benefited
*from Queen **Victoria**'s support of women artists*

Helen Coleman was the daughter of a doctor. She was trained by her brother William Coleman, and in return assisted him with his decorative work for Minton's Pottery. She married a postmaster for south-west London, and retained her established reputation as a flower painter.

Queen Victoria, herself an amateur artist, was a supporter of women artists and in 1879 appointed Angell 'Flower Painter in Ordinary'. She was elected a member of the Royal Watercolour Society in 1879, but in 1865 joined the Dudley Gallery since it gave women greater freedom in its exhibitions. There her work was considered amongst the best flower painting of the 19th century.

Angelou, Maya

Born 1928
American writer, poet, singer, dancer, performer and black activist best known for I Know Why the Caged Bird Sings

Maya Angelou was born in St Louis, Missouri, and lived with her grandmother in Stamps, Arkansas, after her parents' marriage broke up. She was raped by her mother's boyfriend at the age of eight and for the next five years was mute. As a teenager she moved to California to live with her mother, and at 16 gave birth to her son, Guy.

She has had a variety of occupations in what she describes as a 'roller-coaster life'. In her twenties she toured Europe and Africa in the musical *Porgy and Bess*. She joined the Harlem Writers Guild in New York and continued to earn her living singing in nightclubs and performing in Jean Genet's *The Blacks*. During the 1960s she was involved in black struggles and then spent several years in Ghana as editor of *African Review.*

Her multi-volume autobiography, commencing with *I Know Why the Caged Bird Sings* (1970), was a critical and popular success, imbued with optimism, humour and homespun philosophy. She has published several volumes of verse, including *And Still I Rise* (1987), and in 1981 became the Reynolds Professor of American Studies at Wake Forest University in North Carolina. In 1993 she published a collection of personal reflections, *Wouldn't take nothing for my journey now*. Also that year she read one of her poems at President Clinton's inauguration.

Anglin, Margaret

Born 1876   Died 1958
Canadian actress noted for her portrayal of the darker side of human nature

Margaret Anglin was born in Ottowa, where her father was the Speaker in the Canadian House of Commons. She trained at Charles Frohman's Empire Theatre School in New York, and made her début in Bronson Howard's *Shenandoah* in 1894.

From 1899 to 1905 she was leading lady of the Empire Company, and made her initial reputation in contemporary drama, before turning to the Greek classics and Shakespeare from 1910 to 1914.

She returned to contemporary work for much of her subsequent career, and was particularly valued for her command of the darker, vitriolic emotions. She retired from the stage in 1943.

Anker, Nini Roll

Born 1873   Died 1942
Norwegian novelist and playwright who incorporated her social concerns into her writing

Nini Roll Anker was born in Molde. She became involved in the women's rights movement and in radical politics, and campaigned for working-class people even though she herself lived comfortably.

She explores the conflict between feminine self-realization and the traditional feminine roles set out by the Lutheran Church in *Det svake Kjon* (1915, 'The Weaker Sex'). The 'Stampe' trilogy (1923–7) is an ambitious historical novel, while *Den som henger i en tråd* (1935, 'Hanging by a Thread') highlights the plight of women employed in the textile industry and their joint efforts to improve their situation. *Kvinnen og den svarte fuglen* (completed in 1942, published posthumously in 1945, 'The Woman and the Black Bird') is a powerful feminist-pacifist novel, underlining the need for women to play an active social and political role.

She also wrote books for children under the pseudonym Kaare P.

Anna Carlovna *see* Anna Leopoldovna

Anna Comnena

Born 1083   Died c.1148
Byzantine princess who made two unsuccessful attempts to gain the imperial Crown before withdrawing in shame to a convent

Anna Comnena was the daughter of the emperor Alexius I Comnenus. Helped by her mother, the empress Irene, she tried without success to persuade her father to disinherit his son John II Comnenus in favour of the Bryennium leader Nicephorus Bryennius, whom Anna had married in 1097.

After her father's death in 1118 she tried again to gain the Crown, either by poisoning or overthrowing her brother, but her plot was discovered and she retired from the court disappointed and ashamed.

She found solace in literature and after her husband's death (1137) settled in a convent where she wrote the *Alexiad*, an account in Greek of Byzantine history and society for the period 1069–1118, which includes an account of the First Crusade and a flattering biography of her father.

Anna Ivanovna

Born 1693 Died 1740
Empress of Russia from 1730 whose autocratic rule became a reign of terror

Anna Ivanovna was born in Moscow, the younger daughter of Ivan V and niece of Peter I, the Great. In 1710 she married Frederick William, Duke of Courland, who died the following year. After the early death of Peter II, Anna was elected to the throne by the Supreme Privy Council in 1730, with conditions that severely limited her authority. She went to Moscow where she found much opposition to these conditions, and trumped the Council by abolishing it.

She then ruled as an autocrat with her German lover Ernst Johann Biron, who assumed the title of Duke of Courland and became the real power behind the throne. Together with their group of German advisers, they established a reign of terror, in which 20,000 people are said to have been banished to Siberia.

Anna's extravagant court practices and the high cost of wars such as the War of the Polish Succession (1733–5) and the Russo-Turkish War (1736–9) resulted in unpopularity among the gentry; this was also fuelled by resentment of the Germans and crippling taxes for the peasantry, which were increasing the divide between rich and poor. Just before she died, Anna named her great-nephew, the son of her niece **Anna Leopoldovna**, to succeed her as Ivan VI.

Anna Leopoldovna, *also called* Anna Carlovna, *originally* Elisabeth Katharine Christinem

Born 1718 Died 1746
*Regent of Russia for her infant son Ivan VI who was deposed after a year by **Elizabeth Petrovna***

Anna Leopoldovna was born in Rostock, Mecklenburg, the daughter of Charles Leopold, Duke of Mecklenburg Schwerin, and the niece of Empress **Anna Ivanovna**. In 1739 she married Prince Anton Ulrich, Duke of Brunswick, a nephew of the Holy Roman Emperor Charles VI.

In 1740 their son Ivan was declared Emperor of Russia at the age of eight weeks on the death of Anna Ivanovna. The regent appointed by Anna Ivanovna, her favourite Ernst Johann Biron, was arrested by his German advisers Andrey Osterman and Burkhard Münnich. Instead they appointed Anna regent and assumed important positions in her government, though they were disliked by the Russians and weakened the leadership by their quarrelling.

The following year Ivan was deposed by the Empress Elizabeth Petrovna and his parents were imprisoned soon after. Anna died in exile in Kholmogory.

Anna Pavlovna

Born 1795 Died 1865
Queen of the Netherlands, remembered for bringing international sophistication to the Dutch court

Anna Pavlovna was the sister of Tsar Alexander I. She married William, the Dutch Crown Prince, in 1816, and they ascended the throne on the abdication of William's father, William I, in 1840. She was an indefatigable charity organizer and a stickler for ceremony. William himself died in 1849 and was succeeded by their son, William III.

Anne, Queen

Born 1665 Died 1714
Queen of Great Britain and Ireland and the last Stuart monarch, whose reign saw the union of the parliaments of England and Scotland

Anne was born at St James's Palace in London, the second daughter of James II (then Duke of York) and his first wife, Anne Hyde (daughter of the 1st Earl of Clarendon), who died in 1671. In 1672 her father became a Catholic (he married the Catholic **Mary of Modena** in 1673), but Anne was brought up as a staunch Protestant. In 1683 she married Prince George of Denmark (1653–1708), and over the years bore him 17 children, only one of whom survived infancy — William, Duke of Gloucester, who died in 1700 at the age of 12.

For much of her life Anne was greatly influenced by her close friend and confidante, **Sarah Churchill**, the future Duchess of Marlborough. In the 'Glorious Revolution' of 1688, when her father James II was overthrown, she supported the accession of her sister **Mary II** and her brother-in-law William, and was placed in the succession. However she quarrelled with her sister and was drawn by the Marlboroughs into Jacobite intrigues for the restoration of her father or to secure the succession of his son, James Stewart, the 'Old Pretender'. But in 1701, after the death of her own son, she signed the Act of Settlement designating the Hanoverian descendants of James I as her successors, and in 1702 she succeeded William III on the throne.

As Queen, she was dedicated to national unity under the Crown, and the chief event of her reign was the union of the parliaments of Scotland and England in 1707. The other major event of her reign was the War of the Spanish Succession (1701–13) with Marlborough's victories over the French at Blenheim (1704), Ramillies (1706), Oudenarde (1708) and Malplaquet (1709). Queen Anne finally broke with the Marlboroughs in 1710–11, for Sarah had been supplanted by a new favourite, her cousin Mrs **Abigail Masham**, and the Whigs were replaced by a Tory administration led by Robert Harley (1st Earl of Oxford) and Lord Bolingbroke. Anne was the last Stuart monarch, and on her death in August 1714, she was succeeded by George I.

Anne, Princess, *in full* HRH The Princess Anne Elizabeth Alice Louise

Born 1950
The Princess Royal, daughter of the Queen

Princess Anne is the only daughter of **Elizabeth II** and Prince Philip, Duke of Edinburgh. In 1973 she married Lieutenant (later Captain) Mark Phillips of the Queen's Dragoon Guards, but they separated in 1989 and divorced in 1992; their two children are Peter Mark Andrew (b.1977) and Zara Anne Elizabeth (b.1981). In 1992 she married Commander Timothy Laurence.

She is an accomplished horsewoman and, like Captain Phillips (gold medallist in the 1972 Olympics), she has ridden in the British equestrian team. She is a keen supporter of charities and overseas relief work, and as President of Save the Children Fund has travelled widely promoting its activities.

Her book, *Riding Through My Life*, was published in 1991.

Anne, St

Born 50BC Died AD50
Wife of St Joachim who was freed from her barrenness to give birth to the Virgin **Mary**

Anne is first mentioned in the apocryphal 2nd-century *Protevangelium* of James. She is said to have been born in Nazareth or in Bethlehem and to have lived with Joachim from the age of 20 in Nazareth. Bemoaning her barrenness, and her loneliness, for Joachim had retreated into the wilderness to pray about his apparent sterility, she promised the Lord that any child of theirs would be dedicated to his service. An angel appeared to forecast the birth of Mary, and the couple were reconciled.

The presentation of the three-year-old Mary at the Temple where she was to be brought up became an important feast, and as the cult of the Virgin Mary increased in popularity (especially in the 12th century), so did that of Anne and Joachim.

Later tradition tells of Joachim's death and Anne's remarriages, which led to her being named as the grandmother not only of Jesus Christ, but also of several of the Apostles. She is the patron saint of Brittany and Canada and her feast day is 26 July.

Anne of Austria

Born 1601 Died 1666
Queen of France as the wife of Louis XIII (ruled 1610–43) and Regent of France for her son Louis XIV (ruled 1643–1715)

Anne was the eldest daughter of Philip III of Spain and **Margaret** of Austria. She married the 14-year-old Louis XIII of France in 1615, but the marriage was unhappy and, due to the influence of the king's chief minister Cardinal Richelieu, much of it was spent in virtual separation. Their first son was born in 1638, and he succeeded his father in 1643 as Louis XIV.

Anne was appointed regent for the boy king, and with Richelieu having died in 1642 she wielded power with her own favourite and lover, Cardinal Jules Mazarin, as prime minister. They steered France through the difficult period of the Fronde, and although Louis came of age technically in 1651, they continued to rule the country jointly.

After Mazarin's death in 1661 she retired to the convent of Val de Grâce, and Louis XIV became absolute monarch.

Anne of Bohemia

Born 1366 Died 1394
Queen of England known as 'good Queen Anne', the wife of Richard II (ruled 1377–99)

Anne of Bohemia was the daughter of the emperor Charles IV and Elizabeth of Pomerania. In 1382, shortly after the Peasants' Revolt, a bloody uprising in which many of the poor suffered and perished, she married Richard II of England. The King is said to have become sincerely attached to her, and she managed to persuade him to grant a general pardon, consequently earning the love of the populace and the name 'good Queen Anne'.

She also managed to save the life of the religious reformer John Wycliffe in 1382 when his opinions had been officially condemned and he was facing mortal danger. Her activities and thoughts in many ways anticipated the Reformation, hence her being named in history as the very first of its royal 'nursing mothers'. She died of the plague.

Anne of Brittany

Born 1477 Died 1514
Duchess of Brittany and twice Queen of France
who strove to maintain the autonomy of Brittany

Anne of Brittany was born in Nantes, the daughter of Duke Francis of Brittany. She succeeded to her father's duchy in 1488. Her struggle to preserve her dominion's independence led her in 1490 to form an alliance with Maximilian of Austria, whom she married by proxy. However Charles VIII of France attacked Brittany and in 1491 she was forced to break with Maximilian and marry Charles instead, thus beginning the process of uniting Brittany with the French Crown.

In 1499, a year after Charles's death, she was married to his successor, Louis XII. In addition to her activities as a noted patron of the arts, Anne continued to control the duchy, seeking to preserve its autonomy, but in 1514 her daughter Claude, its inheritor, married the future king of France, Francis I.

Anne of Cleves

Born 1515 Died 1557
Queen of England for six months as the fourth
wife of Henry VIII (ruled 1509–47)

Anne of Cleves was a German princess, the daughter of John, Duke of Cleves, a noted champion of Protestantism in Germany. Her brother William, Duke of Cleves, was a prominent Protestant leader. She was a plain-featured and unattractive girl, and after the death of **Jane Seymour** was selected to marry Henry in 1540 purely for political reasons — part of Thomas Cromwell's plan to develop an alliance with German Protestant rulers because of the apparently imminent alliance of France with the Holy Roman Empire.

The fact that the Catholic powers did not unite after all, coupled with Henry's disappointment with Anne's looks and lack of sophistication, resulted in the marriage being annulled by parliament six months later.

Anne of Denmark

Born 1574 Died 1619
Danish princess, Queen of Scotland and Queen of
England as the wife of James VI and I (ruled
Scotland 1567–1625, England 1603–25)

Anne of Denmark was the daughter of King Frederik II of Denmark and Norway. She married James VI of Scotland in 1589. He became James VI of England in 1603.

She was frivolous by nature (which made her unpopular with the Scottish Presbyterians) as well as extravagant in her tastes, and became a lavish patron of the arts and architecture. She also appeared in dramatic roles in court masques by the dramatists Ben Jonson and Thomas Dekker.

Her second son succeeded James as Charles I of Great Britain.

Anning, Mary

Born 1799 Died 1847
English fossil collector who did much to advance
knowledge through collecting specimens

Mary Anning was born in Lyme Regis, the daughter of a carpenter and vendor of fossil specimens who died in 1810, leaving her to make her own living.

In 1811 she discovered in a local cliff the fossil skeleton of an ichthyosaur, which is now in the Natural History Museum, London. A diligent collector, she also discovered the first pleisiosaur (1821) and the first pterodactyl, *Dimorphodon* (1828).

Anspach, Caroline of *see* Caroline of Anspach

Anthony, Susan B(rownell)

Born 1820 Died 1906
American social reformer and women's suffrage
leader, a key player in the early campaign for
women's rights

Susan B Anthony was born in Adams, Massachusetts. She was active in temperance and anti-slavery movements from her late twenties, and in 1852 founded the Woman's State Temperance Society of New York, because women were not permitted to have important roles in the mainstream temperance movement. Gradually she became a champion of women's rights and a friend of **Elizabeth Cady Stanton** and **Amelia Bloomer**.

During the 1850s she devoted her energies to campaigning against slavery, serving in the American Anti-Slavery Society. In 1869 with Stanton she founded the National American Woman Suffrage Association, of which she later became president of the US branch (1892–1900), and became closely associated also with **Anna Shaw** and **Lucy Stone**. She organized the International Council of Women (1888) and the International Woman Suffrage Alliance in Berlin (1904). With Stanton and **Matilda Joslyn Gage** she compiled the four-volume *History of Women Suffrage* (1881–1906).

Aquino, Cory (Maria Corazon), *née* Cojuango

Born 1933
Filipino politician who was President of the Philippines from 1986 to 1992

Cory Cojuango was the daughter of a wealthy sugar baron in Tarlac province. She gained a degree in mathematics at Mount St Vincent College, New York, before in 1956 marrying a young politician, Benigno S Aquino, who became the chief political opponent and presidential challenger to Ferdinand Marcos. He was imprisoned on charges of murder and subversion (1972–80) and assassinated by a military guard at Manila airport in 1983 on his return from three years of exile for heart surgery in the USA.

Aquino was drafted by the opposition to contest the February 1986 presidential election and claimed victory over Marcos, accusing the government of ballot-rigging.

Cory Aquino, 1990

Marcos refused to step down however, and she proceeded to lead a non-violent 'people's power' campaign which succeeded in overthrowing Marcos. She is a devout Maryist Roman Catholic, and enjoyed strong Church backing in her 1986 campaign. In 1992 she did not run for the presidency again, but instead supported the successful candidacy of General Fidel Ramos.

Arber, Agnes, *née* Robertson

Born 1879 Died 1960
English botanist who specialized in comparative plant anatomy

Agnes Robertson was born in London and educated at University College London and Newnham College, Cambridge. She began her career as research assistant to the plant anatomist Ethel Sargant, from whom she learned the technique of using serial sections to study plant anatomy. She worked, studying gymnosperms, at University College London from 1903 to 1909, when she married Edward Arber, demonstrator in palaeobotany at Cambridge.

At the palaeobotanist Sir Albert Seward's suggestion, she began studying early printed herbals. The outcome was her first and most widely read book, *Herbals, Their Origin and Evolution* (1912), which became the standard work. She was also interested in Johann Wolfgang von Goethe and the philosophy of biology, and published *Goethe's Botany* (1946), *The Natural History of Plant Form* (1950), *The Mind and the Eye* (1954) and *The Manifold and the One* (1957).

Her contributions to comparative plant anatomy included 84 papers published between 1902 and 1957, and three books: *Water Plants: a Study of Aquatic Angiosperms* (1920), *Monocotyledons: A Morphological Study* (1925), where she illuminated the phyllode theory of the origin of the monocotyledonous leaf, and *The Gramineae: A Study of Cereal, Bamboo and Grass* (1934). In 1946 she became the first woman botanist to be elected a fellow of the Royal Society.

Arbus, Diane, *née* Nemerov

Born 1923 Died 1971
American photographer best known for her unconventional portraits of people on the fringes of society

Diane Nemerov was born in New York City. She married fellow photographer Allan Arbus in 1941, but separated in 1960 and divorced in 1969. She rebelled against her wealthy parentage and her work in conventional fashion photography, and in the mid-1950s began, under the influence of her mentor **Lisette Model**, to portray people 'without their masks'.

She achieved fame in the 1960s with her ironic and compelling studies of social poses and the deprived classes, but she became increasingly introverted and depressed over the next few years, and eventually took her own life.

Archer, Robyn

Born 1948
Australian singer and actress often associated
with the German cabaret songs of Kurt Weill,
Hanns Eisler and Paul Dessau

Robyn Archer was born in Adelaide, South Australia, and educated at university there. She worked in Sydney night-clubs before completing her Diploma of Education and teaching English for three years. In 1974 she sang 'Annie I' in Bertolt Brecht and Kurt Weill's *The Seven Deadly Sins*, which led to a contract with New Opera South Australia, and in 1975 she played Jenny in Weill's *Threepenny Opera*.

In 1977 the National Theatre, London, invited her to perform in a Brecht compilation, *To Those Born Later*. She returned to Sydney the following year to write and star in a series of one-woman and political cabaret shows; her one-woman cabaret *A Star is Torn* (1979) ran for two seasons in London's West End in 1982–3, and then became a successful book and record album.

Now concentrating on writing and producing, in 1989 she was commissioned to write a new opera, *Mambo*, for the Nexus Opera, London, but she has also made regular appearances on the BBC television series *Cabaret*.

Archer, Violet Balesteri

Born 1913
Canadian composer whose work-list of over 300
pieces often incorporates native Canadian music

Violet Archer was born in Montreal and educated at McGill University. She also studied for a short time under Béla Bartók in New York City, and Paul Hindemith at Yale. After teaching on various North American campuses, she became professor at the University of Alberta in 1962 (emerita since 1978).

Her work-list consists of more than 300 pieces, largely for voices and chamber forces, written in a broadly traditional but highly personal style. The *Three Sketches for Orchestra* (1961), perhaps her best-known work, shows her use of native Canadian material.

A festival devoted to her work was held in Edmonton in 1985.

Arden, Elizabeth, *originally* Florence Nightingale Graham

Born c.1880 Died 1966
Canadian-born American beautician and
businesswoman whose cosmetics empire gained
worldwide renown

Florence Nightingale Graham was born in Woodbridge, Ontario, and trained as a nurse. She went to New York in 1908 and opened a beauty salon on Fifth Avenue in 1910, adopting the personal and business name of 'Elizabeth Arden'.

She produced and advertised cosmetics on a large scale, developing a worldwide chain of salons which numbered 100 by the time she died.

Arendt, Hannah

Born 1906 Died 1975
German-born American philosopher and political
theorist who could touch political nerves

Hannah Arendt was born in Hanover. She went to the USA in 1940 as a refugee from the Nazis and held academic positions at Princeton, Chicago and in New York as well as becoming chief editor at Shocken Books (1946–8). She also took an active role in various Jewish organizations and wrote about Jewish affairs.

Her study of totalitarianism established her as a major political thinker and she had an effect and a readership far beyond the academic world. Among her books are *Origins of Totalitarianism* (1951), a biography of **Rahel Varnhagen** (1957), *The Human Condition* (1958) and *The Life of the Mind* (published posthumously, 1978).

Arete of Cyrene

5th–4th century BC
Greek philosopher, daughter of Aristippus
of Cyrene

Arete was probably born in Cyrene in Libya. She was educated by her father, the philosopher Aristippus, who is sometimes held to be the founder of Cyreniac or Hedonistic philosophy, though it seems likely that it was Arete's son, also called Aristippus, who formalized this philosophy.

Arete taught philosophy — notably to her son Aristippus (consequently nicknamed 'Mother-taught'). It would seem, therefore, that she was an important link in the evolution and transmission of Hedonistic ideas. Though some authorities credit her with over 40 works, none of these survive, and the authenticity of the single surviving letter from her father to Arete has also been challenged.

Argentina, La, *originally* Antonia Mercé

Born 1890 Died 1936
Spanish dancer who is reportedly the greatest female Spanish dancer in history

La Argentina was born in Buenos Aires. She moved to Spain with her parents, both Spanish dancers, when she was two, and made her début as a classical dancer when she was six.

She became a dancer with Madrid Opera at the age of 11, but gave up classical dance at 14 to study native Spanish dance with her mother. She later became the originator of the Neoclassical style of Spanish dancing and developed outstanding skill on the castanets. Her first foreign tour at the age of 18 was a great success and the blueprint for the rest of her life, during which her international renown earned Spanish dance a new popularity.

Arletty, *originally* Léonie Bathiat

Born 1898 Died 1992
French film and stage actress who rose to stardom in the 1930s

Arletty was born in Courbevoie, the daughter of a miner. She worked in a munitions factory and as a secretary before her radiant beauty brought her modelling assignments and stage work in revues like *Si Que Je Serais Roi* (1922). She made her film début in *La Douceur D'Aimer* in 1930 but continued to star in such stage successes as *L'École Des Veuves* (1936) and *Fric-Frac* (1936) until such roles as a droll Queen of Ethiopia in *Les Perles De La Couronne* (1937, *The Pearls of the Crown*) brought her renown on screen.

She began a fruitful association with director Marcel Carné in *Hotel du Nord* (1938); this went on to include *Le Jour se Lève* (1939, *Daybreak*), a classic of pre-war French fatalism, and the sombre medieval fantasy *Les Visiteurs Du Soir* (1942). Her most famous role was as the enigmatic, mysterious courtesan Garance in his 1944 film *Les Enfants Du Paradis*. A wartime romance with a German officer earned her a time of imprisonment accused of collaboration, but she resumed her career successfully with the thriller *Portrait D'Un Assassin* (1949).

Later films include *Huis Clos* (1955, *No Exit*), *The Longest Day* (1962), her sole appearance in a US production, and *Le Voyage A Biarritz* (1963), her last screen appearance.

Armand, Inessa

Born 1875 Died 1920
Russian politician, one of the most active women Bolsheviks, and a champion of Soviet women's causes

Inessa Armand was born in Paris where her French father lived, and brought up in Russia by a rich family after her parents died. Her intellectual interests and travels brought her into contact with Lenin and she joined his party in 1905.

She was twice exiled, but she returned to Russia in 1917, and in 1919 became the founding head of *zhenotdel*, the women's section of the Communist Party of the Soviet Union. She devoted herself to organizing branches everywhere, but died shortly thereafter of overwork and cholera. *Zhenotdel* continued until it was shut down in 1930.

Armatrading, Joan

Born 1950
West Indian–British singer and songwriter whose song 'Love and Affection' is among her best

Joan Armatrading was born in St Christopher-Nevis in the Caribbean and came to the UK at the age of eight. She gained a reputation as an amateur performer around Birmingham,

Joan Armatrading, 1991

then began writing songs with a friend, Pam Nester, and eventually moved to London in 1971. They made one album, *Whatever's For Us*, before breaking up acrimoniously. Armatrading then signed to A&M and recorded *Back to the Night* (1975), a set of intelligent, patiently crafted songs that caught a new feminist consciousness. The often-reissued 'Love and Affection' (1976) was a big success, but Armatrading was essentially an album artist with only sporadic chart appeal. *Me, Myself, I* (1980) was a personal declaration of independence; shortly afterwards, she was an honoured guest at her native island's independence celebrations.

A later album, *The Key* (1983), included the hit 'Drop the Pilot', but since then she has been less prominent (despite persuading Princess **Margaret** to guest in a video, the first member of the Royal Family to do so).

Armitage, Karole

Born 1954
American dancer and choreographer whose work is described as a 'Molotov cocktail', a controversial blend of wit, high heels and invention

Karole Armitage was born in Madison, Wisconsin, and trained in classical ballet. She moved from the Ballets de Genève, Switzerland (1972–4), to the Merce Cunningham Dance Company in New York (1976–81), where her unique style began to take shape.

Cunningham created several roles for her, including *Squaregame* (1976) and *Channels/Inserts* (1981). During this period she became interested in choreography and with *Drastic Classicism* began a choreographic career which took her to Paris, where she worked with dancers such as Michael Clark and created pieces for Paris Opéra Ballet.

Armour, Mary Nicol Neill, *née* Steel

Born 1902
Scottish painter, one of Scotland's most senior living woman artists in terms of both years and importance

Mary Steel was born in Blantyre. At the age of 11 she won a scholarship to Hamilton Academy where she was taught by Penelope Beaton. She studied at Glasgow School of Art (1920–5) under Maurice Greiffenhagen and Forrester Wilson, and married the artist William Armour in 1927.

She executed a mural commission for the Royal Navy in 1941, the same year she was elected Associate of the RSA (Royal Scottish Academy). During the years that she taught at Glasgow School of Art (1951–62), her work,

which mainly focused on landscape and flower studies, became more free in handling and brighter in colour.

Armour was elected to the RSW (Royal Scottish Water Colour Society) in 1956 and to the RSA in 1958. Though failing eyesight has precluded her from painting since 1988, she lives in the artistic community of Kilbarchan.

Armstrong, Gillian May

Born 1952
Australian film director who had a huge success with My Brilliant Career

Gillian Armstrong was born in Melbourne. She studied theatre design and then film, winning a scholarship to the Film and Television School in Sydney where she directed three short films, including *Gretel* (1974). After her graduation she made documentaries and the drama *The Singer and the Dancer* (1976) which won the Australian Film Institute award for Best Short.

Her first feature film, *My Brilliant Career* (1979), tells the story of a young woman and the sacrifices she makes to assert her individualism in the outback of the 1890s. It was the first Australian feature directed by a woman since the 1930s and won 11 AFI awards, including Best Film and Best Director, and earned her an international reputation of great promise.

She enjoyed a change of pace in the breezy musical comedy *Starstruck* (1982), but has generally continued to focus attention on the difficulties facing independent women in *Mrs. Soffel* (1984), *High Tide* (1987) and *The Last Days of Chez Nous* (1993), an Australian family drama with screenplay by **Helen Garner**.

Armstrong, Lil(ian), *née* Hardin

Born 1898 Died 1971
American jazz musician and composer, one of the great early jazz pianists

Lil Hardin was born in Memphis, Tennessee, and educated at Fisk University before moving to Chicago. She became a brilliant jazz pianist, and played with an aggressive rhythmic style that she had learned from Jelly Roll Morton. Among the Broadway shows, clubs and jazz bands in which she played was King Oliver's Original New Orleans Creole Jazz Band in Chicago, and through it she met the jazz trumpeter Louis Armstrong (1901–71) when he joined them in 1922. Two years later she became his second wife, but they separated in 1931 and divorced in 1938.

She was a member of Oliver's band during the time that many of his masterpieces were recorded, and played in Armstrong's Hot Five and Hot Seven during the later 1920s. Meanwhile she prudently created her own band, which after her divorce had only female musicians.

She died on stage, playing at a memorial concert for Louis.

Arnaud, Yvonne Germaine

Born 1892   Died 1958
French actress noted for her charm, vivacity and inimitably musical accent, who enjoyed a long career on the British stage

Yvonne Arnaud was born in Bordeaux and educated in Paris. She trained as a concert pianist and toured Europe as a child prodigy. With no previous acting experience, she assumed the role of Princess Mathilde in the musical comedy *The Quaker Girl* (1911) and scored an instant success, which she consolidated with *The Girl in the Taxi* (1912).

She appeared in many musicals and farces including *Tons of Money* (1922), *A Cuckoo in the Nest* (1925), *The Improper Duchess* (1931) and *Love for Love* (1943). Her innate kindliness was thought to render her an unsuitable choice for Jean Anouilh's *Colombe* (1951) but she appeared to great effect in *Dear Charles* (1952) and was active until her death.

She made her film début in *Desire* (1920) and appeared in several cinema adaptations of her stage successes as well as films like *On Approval* (1931), *The Ghosts of Berkeley Square* (1947) and *Mon Oncle* (1958). She lived for many years near Guildford, Surrey, where a theatre was opened in her honour in 1965.

Arnauld, (Jeanne-Catherine-) Agnès *see* Arnauld, Angélique

Arnauld, Angélique, *known as* Mère Angélique de Saint Jean

Born 1624   Died 1684
French Jansenist who served for most of her life in the Port-Royal convent in Paris

Angélique Arnauld was the daughter of the lawyer and scholar Robert Arnauld and niece of Mère Angélique (**Marie-Angélique Arnauld**). She entered the convent of Port-Royal in Paris at the age of six and, modelling herself on her virtuous aunts who educated her, became distinguished for her taste and eloquence, serving successively in the positions of subprioress and abbess (1678).

During the persecution of the Port-Royalists (1661–9), she was sustained by her heroic courage and the spirits of the sisterhood and their friends.

Arnauld, (Jacqueline-) Marie-Angélique, *known as* Mère Angélique

Born 1591   Died 1661
French Jansenist religious and monastic reformer who was abbess of the Port-Royal Jansenist centre in Paris

Angélique Arnauld was born in Port-Royal, Paris, one of the six sisters of the Jansenist theologian Antoine ('the Great') Arnauld. Though not truly coverted until 1608, she was made abbess of the Cistercian house of Port-Royal des Champs in 1602 at the age of 11, and ultimately reformed the convent by the severity of her discipline, making it a deeply spiritual place.

She helped with the reform of other convents and was instrumental in transferring the Port-Royal community from near Versailles to Paris in 1625–6. She resigned in 1630, but returned to be prioress under her sister Agnès (1593–1671). From about 1635 she was influenced by Jansenism, which was essentially a reaction against the Catholic dogma of the freedom of the will, but died before the Jansenist persecution (1661–9) reached its peak.

Mère Agnes however was removed in 1664 and detained in a convent at Chaillot where unsuccessful attempts were made to force her to sign an anti-Jansenist document. After the peace organized by Clement IX to stop the persecution in 1669, she was allowed to return to Port-Royal and became a respected writer of spiritual works.

Arnim, Bettina (Elisabeth Katharina Ludovica Magdalena) von, *née* von Brentano

Born 1785   Died 1859
German writer acknowledged as a key personality in the German Romantic movement

Bettina von Brentano was born in Frankfurt-am-Main, the sister of the writer Clemens von Brentano (1778–1842). She married the writer Achim von Arnim (1781–1831) in 1811 and, despite her eccentricities and self-preoccupation, was a loyal wife. She was friendly with Goethe, but he eventually severed connections with her after she quarrelled with his wife Christiane.

Her books, such as one about Goethe and another about her brother, are not novels but somewhat fanciful — yet intelligent — accounts, or else 'documentary' fabrications.

Bettina Arnim is remembered as an outstanding writer of German literature.

Arnim, Mary Annette, Countess von, *pseud* Elizabeth, *née* Beauchamp

Born 1866 Died 1941
New Zealand-born British writer who travelled extensively

Mary Beauchamp, the cousin of **Katherine Mansfield**, was born in New Zealand and travelled to Britain with her family in 1871. She attended Queen's College School in London and won a prize for her organ-playing at the Royal School of Music.

Following her marriage to the Prussian Count von Arnim-Schlagenthin, she went to live on his Pomeranian estate which provided the inspiration for her best-known work, *Elizabeth and her German Garden* (1898), written under her pseudonym Elizabeth. On his death she tried to settle in England, Switzerland and France, and her experiences at this time are described in *All the Dogs of My Life* (1936).

She was courted by the writer H G Wells (1866–1946) but eventually married Francis, 2nd Earl Russell (1865–1931), the elder brother of the philosopher Bertrand Russell, but they separated in 1919.

Arnold, Eve

Born 1913
American photojournalist whose sensitive work covers a wide range of subject matter

Eve Arnold was born in Philadelphia to Russian immigrant parents. She originally studied medicine but changed to photography studies at the New School for Social Research, New York (1947–8). She was the first woman to photograph for Magnum Photos in 1951, becoming a full member of the group in 1957. She moved to London in 1961, and travelled to the Soviet Union five times from 1965, as well as to Afghanistan and Egypt from 1967 to 1971, where she recorded the lives of veiled women, and to China in 1979.

Her photo-essays have appeared in such publications as *Life*, *Look* and the *Sunday Times*. The exhibition 'Eve Arnold in Britain' was shown at the National Portrait Gallery, London, in 1991. She is well known for her sensitive photography of women, childbirth, small-town America, the poor and the elderly as well as celebrities. Among her publications are *The Un-retouched Woman* (1976), *In China* (1980) and *All in a Day's Work* (1989); she also made the film *Behind the Veil* (1973).

Arnold, Roseanne *see* Barr, Roseanne

Arsinoë

Born 316BC Died 270BC
Macedonian princess who became one of the most conspicuous of Hellenistic queens

Arsinoë was the daughter of Ptolemy I and **Berenice I**. Her first husband was the aged King of Thrace, Lysimachus, whom she married about 300BC. She plotted to disgrace her stepson Agathocles, the heir to the throne, in favour of her own eldest son, but this resulted in war between Thrace and the Seleucid Kingdom, whose ruler had responded to a request for help from an ally of Agathocles.

Lysimachus died in battle and Arsinoë went to Cassandrea where she was married (briefly) to Ptolemy Ceraunus. When he executed her two younger sons, she fled to Alexandria, where, about 276BC, she was married for a third time — to her own brother, Ptolemy II Philadelphus.

Her influence in the Egyptian government quickly increased, as she shared in her husband's titles and aided in his victories. She was probably deified during her reign, as was customary in Egypt, and several cities were named after her.

Artemisia

5th century BC
Queen of Halicarnassus who distinguished herself in battle but died of a broken heart

Artemisia was the ruler of Halicarnassus, a city in Caria, and of neighbouring islands including Cos. According to the Greek historian Herodotus, she accompanied the Persian king Xerxes (under whose overlordship she ruled) with five ships on his expedition against Greece in 480–479BC, and distinguished herself at the naval battle of Salamis at which they were defeated.

The Greeks had been infuriated at being challenged by a woman, and had offered 10,000 drachmas as a reward for the capture of Artemisia, but in vain. Xerxes is said to have followed her advice to abandon his invasion. Allegedly distressed by her unrequited love for a younger man, she allegedly committed suicide by jumping off a cliff.

Artemisia

Died c.350BC
Queen of Caria and builder of one of the seven wonders of the world

Artemisia was the wife of her brother, King Mausolus of Caria, and succeeded to his throne when he died in 353 or 352BC. During her reign she erected the magnificent tomb known as the Mausoleum in Halicarnassus (now Bodrum, Turkey) to his memory. It was one of the traditional seven wonders of the ancient world.

Artemisia is remembered also as a botanist, and she gives her name to the plant genus *Artemisia*.

Arthur, Jean, *originally* Gladys Georgianna Greene

Born 1905 Died 1991
American actress, a popular leading lady in the
early talkies

Jean Arthur was born in New York City, the daughter of a photographer, and she left school at 15 to become a model and later an actress. She made her film début in *Cameo Kirby* (1923) and was seen in many unremarkable roles as she survived the transition to sound.

A husky-voiced, vivacious actress, she often played hard-boiled career women with hearts of gold, and was a particularly adept comedienne and co-star for some of Hollywood's most prominent male stars. Her best films include *Mr Deeds Goes to Town* (1936), *Mr Smith Goes to Washington* (1939) and *The More The Merrier* (1943), for which she received a Best Actress Oscar nomination.

She retired from the screen after *Shane* (1953) and later taught drama at Vassar. Her infrequent stage appearances include a highly regarded *Peter Pan* (1950) and *The First Monday in October* (1975) and she was the star of the television series *The Jean Arthur Show*.

Artyukhina, Alexandra Vasilevna

Born 1889 Died 1969
Soviet politician who became an early champion
of Soviet women's rights

Alexandra Artyukhina was a textile worker who was active in the union movement in the pre-revolutionary period and was arrested several times. She held various government jobs after the Russian Revolution (1917), and in 1927 she was appointed head of *zhenotdel*, the women's section of the Communist Party of the Soviet Union.

In this position she did much good work until *zhenotdel* was shut down in 1930. Thereafter, her jobs were more honorific than real.

Arvanitaki, Angélique

Born 1901 Died 1983
French neurobiologist instrumental in developing
the field of cellular neurophysiology

Angélique Arvanitaki was born in Cairo. She obtained her PhD from the University of Lyons in 1938, and worked for most of her career at the Oceanographic Museum of Monaco, sometimes in collaboration with her husband, Dr Nicolas Chalanozitis.

In the new field of cellular neurophysiology, she worked on the giant nerve fibres of the squid, and developed a technique of studying the nerve cells of the sea-slug, *Aplysia*; this provided a major impetus to understanding the cellular mechanisms of neural functioning.

Arzner, Dorothy

Born 1900 Died 1979
American film director who was the only major
woman director in Hollywood in the 1930s

Dorothy Arzner was born in San Francisco. She studied medicine at the University of Southern California and became a volunteer ambulance driver during World War I, then began her film career as a script typist in 1919. Diligently learning the craft of filmmaking, she progressed from script supervisor to editor on such important silent features as *Blood and Sand* (1922).

Encouraged by director James Cruze (1884–1942), she edited several of his westerns including *The Covered Wagon* (1923) and *Old Ironsides* (1926), which she also wrote. She made her directorial début with *Fashions for Women* (1927). She directed Paramount's first sound feature *Wild Party* in 1929 and her best-known films include *Merrily We Go To Hell* (1932), *Christopher Strong* (1933) and *Dance, Girl Dance* (1940).

She worked with many of the top female stars of the era, striving to eschew conventional stereotypes by creating strong, independent women, and earning her unique status in the history of Hollywood as a pioneer and feminist role model.

Ashby, Dame Margery Irene, *née* Corbett

Born 1882 Died 1981
English feminist who was President of the
International Alliance of Women for 23 years

Margery Corbett was the daughter of the Liberal MP for East Grinstead. She was educated at home and studied classics at Newnham College, Cambridge.

She attended the first International Women's Suffrage Congress in Berlin (1904) and subsequently worked with various women's organizations, travelling widely throughout the world and becoming President of the International Alliance of Women (1923–46). She was awarded an honarary LLD by Mount Holyoke College, USA, in recognition of her international work.

Married Arthur Ashby from 1910, she stood as Liberal candidate seven times between 1918 and 1944. She was also co-founder of the Townswomen's Guilds with Eva Hubback.

Ashby, Winifred

Born 1879 Died 1975
English-born American immunologist who carried out vital work on red blood cells

Winifred Ashby graduated from North-western and Washington universities before gaining a PhD at the University of Minnesota in 1921. She then joined the scientific staff of the St Elizabeth's Hospital in Washington (1924–49).

Her pioneering work was first published in 1919 and her observations on patients receiving transfusions during the next few years provided fundamental information about the life-span of red blood cells. She devised the Ashby technique, a method of determining survival rates of red blood cells in the human body.

Her work was little recognized at the time however, and did not achieve widespread usage until World War II.

Ashcroft, Dame Peggy (Edith Margaret Emily)

Born 1907 Died 1991
English actress who was highly successful in films and on the British and US stage

Peggy Ashcroft was born in Croydon. She first appeared on the stage with the Birmingham Repertory Company in 1926, and scored a great London success in *Jew Süss* in 1929. In 1930 she played Desdemona to Paul Robeson's Othello, and acted leading parts at the Old Vic in the season of 1932–3. In 1935 she was a memorable Juliet in John Gielgud's production of *Romeo and Juliet*.

She also worked in films, such as *A Passage to India* (1984), for which she received a Best Actress Oscar. She was created DBE in 1956 and in 1991 received the Olivier award for outstanding service to the theatre.

Ashford, Daisy (Margaret Mary Julia)

Born 1881 Died 1972
English author who is famous for a story she wrote as a child

Daisy Ashford was born in Petersham, Surrey. At the age of nine she wrote *The Young Visiters, or Mr Salteena's Plan*, in which Bernard Clark and Mr Salteena ('not quite a gentleman') vie for the hand of 17-year-old Ethel Monticue. Ashford re-discovered her imperfectly spelt manuscript in 1919, and on its publication it became both a bestseller and a talking point.

The following year *The Young Visiters* became a successful play and in 1968 provided the basis of a musical, albeit with a score which caused one critic to describe it as 'amiably pointless'. Other juvenile Ashford writings appeared in *DA: Her Book* (1920). She wrote nothing as an adult, apparently content to run a market garden with her husband, whom she had married in 1920.

Ashford, Evelyn

Born 1957
African-American track and field athlete, the first woman to run the 100 metres in under 11 seconds in the Olympics

Evelyn Ashford was born in Shreveport, Louisiana. Her talent was first recognized at high school, when she was invited to join the boys' track squad. In 1975 she went to UCLA (University of California at Los Angeles), having accepted the offer of one of its first women's athletic scholarships.

Her continuing success in college athletics gained her All-American honours in 1977 and 1978; also in 1977 she won the AIAW (Association for Intercollegiate Athletics for Women) national championships. In 1979 she set the US record for the 200 metres.

In Olympic competition, she has won one silver medal for the 100 metres in 1988 and three gold medals — for the 100 metres in 1984, and for the 4 × 100-metre relay in both 1984 and 1988. In 1984 she became the first woman to run the 100 metres in under 11 seconds in the Olympics (**Marlies Gohr** was the first to do this outside the Olympics). The Women's Sports Foundation awarded her the **Flo Hyman** Trophy in 1989.

Ashley, Laura, *née* Laura Mountney

Born 1925 Died 1985
Welsh fashion designer who founded the internationally famous chain that bears her name

Laura Mountney was born in Merthyr Tydfil. She married Bernard Ashley in 1949 and they started up in business together four years later, manufacturing furnishing materials and wallpapers with patterns and motifs based upon document sources mainly from the 19th century.

When she gave up work to have a baby she experimented with designing and making clothes; this was to transform the business from one small shop to an international chain of boutiques selling clothes, furnishing fabrics and wallpapers.

Ashley Mountney Ltd became Laura Ashley Ltd in 1968, and her work continued to be characterized by a romantic style and the use of natural fabrics, especially cotton.

Ashton-Warner, Sylvia Constance

Born 1908 Died 1984
New Zealand novelist and schoolteacher whose own life story sparked off her writing career

Sylvia Ashton-Warner was one of eight children of an invalid father and schoolteacher mother who relied on the latter's income to survive. She too became a teacher and taught in several schools that had a large percentage of Maori pupils, where she developed an innovative method of teaching them to read and became interested in educational theory.

She began her writing career with an autobiographical account of her teaching life, *Teacher*, which was at first rejected. She recast it as fiction and it appeared to considerable acclaim as *Spinster* (1958), through the success of which *Teacher* finally appeared in 1963. In *Spinster* the heroine is typical of Ashton-Warner's strong feminine characters who fight against suffocating New Zealand provinciality.

Other novels are *Incense to Idols* (1960), *Bell Call* (1964), *Greenstone* (1966) and *Three* (1971), a closely observed power struggle between mother and daughter-in-law, set in London. Her autobiographical *I Passed This Way* (1979) highlights a sense of alienation from her homeland.

Askew, Anne

Born 1521 Died 1546
English Protestant who was martyred for her Reformed beliefs

Anne Askew was born into a well-to-do family near Grimsby, where she was well educated. She embraced the Reformed doctrines, but was thrown out by her husband after a religious quarrel, and thereupon went up to London to sue for a separation.

Her heretical opinions brought her further trouble while she was employed at the court of **Catherine Parr**, and in 1545 she was arrested. Charged with heresy, she was interrogated, tortured on the rack and burned in Smithfield; her serenity throughout this ordeal earned her a martyr's place in Protestant theology.

Aspasia, *also called* Aspasia of Miletus

5th century BC
Greek mistress of the Athenian statesman Pericles and a larger-than-life figure in Athenian society

Aspasia was born in Miletus and grew up to be a beautiful, intellectual and vivacious woman. Being a foreigner, she was not restricted by Athenian customs and so was free to entertain the philosophers, politicians and artists of the day at her home, which contributed to her own high level of learning. Though she was lampooned in Greek comedy and satire for her private activities and social influence, she was held in high regard by Socrates and his followers.

She became the mistress of the Athenian statesman Pericles after his separation from his Athenian wife in 445BC and was a great inspiration to him. He encouraged the expansion of the arts and architecture, industry and commerce during his rule and also successfully defended her when his political enemies attempted to attack him covertly by charging her with impiety.

After Pericles's death in 429BC she lived with Lysicles, a cattle dealer who had risen to a position of power and influence.

Aspasia

Asquith, Margot (Emma Alice Margaret), née Tennant

Born 1864 Died 1945
Scottish society figure and wit who thrived at the centre of her social and intellectual circles

Margot Tennant was born in Peebleshire, the 11th child of Sir Charles Tennant. She was described as 'unteachable and splendid' and received little formal education, but possessed unusual literary, artistic and musical talents. She 'came out' into society in 1881 and, though far from a beauty ('I have no face, only two profiles clapped together'), was an immense success.

She became a brilliantly witty hostess and led a group of young intellectuals and aesthetes called the 'Souls' who advocated greater freedom for women. Her friends also included Gladstone and **Virginia Woolf**. In 1894 she married H H Asquith (Liberal Prime Minister of Great Britain 1908–16) as his second wife, and had seven children, of whom two survived.

She was highly influential in society, though her devastating wit could be cruel, and was apparently impervious to the opinions of others — she neglected the war effort, continuing her extravagant lifestyle unabashed during World War I. When Asquith was forced to resign in 1916, she wrote two infamously indiscreet autobiographies.

Asquith of Yarnbury, Dame (Helen) Violet Bonham-Carter, Baroness

Born 1887 Died 1969
English Liberal politician and publicist who was prominent in cultural and political movements

Violet Asquith was the daughter of H H Asquith (Liberal Prime Minister of Great Britain, 1908–16) by his first marriage. In 1915 she married Sir Maurice Bonham-Carter (d.1960), a scientist and civil servant. She served as President of the Liberal Party Organization in 1944–5 and as a governor of the BBC (1941–6). She was created a life peeress in 1964, and published *Winston Churchill as I Knew Him* in 1965.

The Scot Baron Jo Grimond (1913–93), who led the Liberal Party from 1956 to 1967, was her son-in-law. Her eldest son Mark Raymond (1922–) stood unsuccessfully as a Liberal in 1945 and 1964 but was Liberal MP for Torrington from 1958 to 1959. He edited his mother's autobiography in 1962.

Astaire, Adele, *professional name of* Adele Austerlitz

Born 1898 Died 1981
American dancer, actress and singer, whose name is largely eclipsed by that of her less-talented sibling, Fred Astaire

Adele Astaire was born in Omaha, as was her younger brother Fred. Her career began in her teens, partnering him in a song-and-dance act that reached Broadway in 1917. Their post-war show *For Goodness Sake* (1922, known in the UK as *Stop Flirting*) was a big success, and they went on to further success in 1924 in George Gershwin shows like *Lady, Be Good* and *Funny Face* — both now inextricably associated with Fred's name. Adele's contribution to Fred Astaire's success was arguably greater than that of any of his other partners, including **Ginger Rogers**, but her activities decreased following her marriage to Lord Charles Cavendish. *Smiles* (1930) was one of her last big successes.

Astell, Mary

Born 1668 Died 1731
English religious writer whose proposal for an Anglican female community was ridiculed

Mary Astell was born in Newcastle, the daughter of a merchant. She lived in Chelsea, and in 1694 her anonymously published *Serious Proposal to the Ladies for the Advancement of their Time and Greatest Interest* proposed an Anglican sisterhood with an academic bias.

Perhaps the first feminist in England, she expanded her pioneering plans for further education for women a few years later but they were strongly criticized by Bishop Gilbert Burnet, ridiculed in journals such as *Tatler*, and did not materialize.

Astley, Thea Beatrice May

Born 1925
Australian novelist and poet who has won the **Miles Franklin** *award three times*

Thea Astley was born in Brisbane. Her first novel, *Girl with a Monkey* (1958), was followed by *A Descant for Gossips* (1960). *The Slow Natives* (1965) became Australian 'Best Novel of the Year' and established her reputation as a satiric and iconoclastic commentator on small-town Australian life.

In *A Kindness Cup* (1974) she denounces Aboriginal treatment in 19th-century Queensland. The narrator of her collection of wrily humorous short stories, *Hunting the Wild Pine-apple* (1979), is a character from *The Slow Natives*, a favourite device of Astley.

Astor of Hever Castle, Nancy Witcher Astor, Viscountess, *née* Langhorne

Born 1879 Died 1964
American-born British politician, the first woman to take a seat in the House of Commons

Nancy Langhorne was born in Danville, Virginia, the daughter of a wealthy tobacco auctioneer. In 1897 she married a Bostonian, but divorced him in 1903 and went to England where in 1906 she married Waldorf Astor, the son of an American millionaire (William Waldorf, 1st Viscount Astor) to whose peerage her husband succeeded in 1919.

Since 1910 Waldorf had been Conservative MP for Plymouth, and following his move to the House of Lords, Lady Astor was elected to the Commons in his place. She abounded in energy and wit, and was known for her interest in social problems, especially temperance, women's rights and education. She was also an influential society hostess at Cliveden, their country home in Buckinghamshire, which was given to the state in 1942.

She retired from parliament in 1945 and from public life after her husband's death in 1952.

Astor, Mary, *originally* Lucille Langhanke

Born 1906 Died 1987
American film actress whose roles ranged from femmes fatales to warm-hearted matriarchs

Mary Astor was born in Quincy, Illinois. To 'make her father's dream come true', she made her film début in *The Beggar Maid* (1921) and was soon established playing beautiful, innocent ingénues in historical dramas like *Beau Brummell* (1924, with John Barrymore) and *Don Juan* (1926, with Douglas Fairbanks). She became an intelligent, prolific actress, carving a special niche as bitchy women of the world, and won an Academy Award for *The Great Lie* (1941, with **Bette Davis**). Her range also included the duplicitous femme fatale of *The Maltese Falcon* (1941), carefree comedy in *The Palm Beach Story* (1942) and tender drama in *Dodsworth* (1936).

In 1936 a court case over custody of her daughter brought press revelations of a scandalous private life and she later suffered from alcoholism. Under contract to MGM, she moved into her 'Mothers for Metro' phase playing warm-hearted matriarchs, most memorably in *Meet Me in St. Louis* (1944), but still making the most of meaty roles in films like *Act of Violence* (1948) and *Return to Peyton Place* (1961).

She retired from film after *Hush...Hush Sweet Charlotte* (1964), as well as from her activities on stage and television, and turned to writing novels and autobiography, including *A Life on Film* (1971).

Astorga, Nora

Born 1949 Died 1988
Nicaraguan revolutionary and diplomat who was involved with the Sandinistas

Nora Astorga was born in Managua and studied sociology at the University of Washington DC, transferring to study law at the *Universidad of Centroamericana* in Managua.

She started working covertly with the Sandinistas as a student. Later, as lawyer and head of personnel for a Nicaraguan construction company, she was involved in luring the National Guard general Perez Varga to her house where he was ambushed and killed by rebels.

Astorga was subsequently named ambassador to the USA. Although this appointment was vetoed by the CIA, she represented Daniel Ortega's regime at the United Nations and was successful in obtaining a World Court Decision which declared US support for the Contra guerillas illegal.

Astrid

Born 1905 Died 1935
Queen of the Belgians as the wife of Leopold III

Astrid was the daughter of Prince Charles of Sweden and Princess Ingeborg of Denmark. On 4 November 1926 she married Leopold, Crown Prince of Belgium, who succeeded to the throne as Leopold III on 23 February 1934, with Astrid as Queen. She had three children, Josephine-Charlotte, Baudouin I (later king) and Albert, and was killed in a car accident near Küssnacht in Switzerland.

Athaliah

Died 837BC
Queen of Judah, the subject of a play by Racine, with incidental music by Mendelssohn

Athaliah was the daughter of King Ahab of Israel (ruled c.869–850BC) and **Jezebel**. She was the wife of Jehoram, King of Judah, and secured the throne of Judah for herself after the death in 843BC of her son Ahaziah at the hands of the usurper Jehu, and by the slaughter of all the royal children save Ahaziah's son Joash.

Her support of Baal-worship led, after six years, to an insurrection headed by the priests; Joash was made king, and Athaliah put to death.

Atherton, Gertrude Franklin, *née* Horn

Born 1857 Died 1948
American novelist who developed the character of the western American heroine

Gertrude Horn was born in San Francisco. After being widowed in 1887, she travelled extensively, living in Europe most of her life, and used the places she visited, which range from ancient Greece to California and the West Indies, as backgrounds for her novels.

She was made Chevalier of the Legion of Honour for her relief work during World War I and in 1934 became President of the American National Academy of Literature. She was a prolific writer whose most popular novels are *The Conqueror* (1902), a fictional biography of Alexander Hamilton, and *Black Oxen* (1923), which is concerned with the possibility of rejuvenation.

Atholl, Katherine Marjory, Duchess of, *née* Ramsay

Born 1874 Died 1960
Scottish Conservative politician who was an early opponent of women's suffrage but fought for other kinds of social justice

Katherine Ramsay was born in Banff, Perthshire, the daughter of historian Sir James Ramsay. She was educated at Wimbledon High School and the Royal College of Music, and became an accomplished pianist and composer. In 1899 she married the future 8th Duke of Atholl, becoming Duchess of Atholl in 1917.

During the Boer War and World War I she organized concerts for the troops abroad and helped in hospital work, and in 1923 became MP for Kinross and Perthshire. From 1924 to 1929 she was the first Conservative woman Minister as Parliamentary Secretary to the Board of Education. She successfully resisted changes in policy which would have adversely affected the education of poorer children, and from 1929 to 1939 she campaigned against the ill-treatment of women and children in the British Empire.

She also translated an unexpurgated edition of *Mein Kampf* to warn of Hitler's intentions, and she published the bestselling *Searchlight on Spain* in 1938. She opposed the Munich agreement, and was dropped as Tory candidate, then resigned her seat in parliament and was defeated in the resultant by-election where she was lampooned as the 'Red Duchess'. From 1939 to 1960 she worked to aid refugees from totalitarianism. Her other publications include *Women and Politics* (1931).

Atkins, Anna, *née* Children

Born 1799 Died 1871
English photographer and illustrator, the first woman photographer and the first person to produce a photographically printed book

Anna Children was born in Tonbridge, England, the daughter of the scientist John George Children who had an early interest in the processes of photography. She became a friend of Sir John Herschel (1792–1871), the originator of the cyanotype (blueprint) process. In 1825 she married John Pelly Atkins, a Jamaican coffee-plantation owner and railway promoter.

Atkins is best known for scientific illustration and particularly for her books of beautifully composed original cyanotype illustrations of plants, the first of which was the privately published and pioneering *British Algae: Cyanotype Impressions* (12 parts, 1843–53). The first part was completed in 1843, making Atkins the first person to produce a photographically illustrated book, and the first to use it as part of an extensive scientific study of the natural world. It pre-dated the *Pencil of Nature* (1844–6) of William Henry Fox Talbot (1800–77).

In addition to their scientific value, Atkins's cyanotypes are also beautiful, and her work is described in N Rosenblum's *A History of Women Photographers* (1994) as 'a testament to the great appeal to women of a pictorial process that called into play both scientific and aesthetic intelligence'.

Atkins, Eileen

Born 1934
English actress whose versatility has brought her an enormous range of roles

Eileen Atkins was born in Birmingham. She made her first London appearance at the Open Air Theatre in 1953, and was a member of the Shakespeare Memorial Theatre in Stratford-upon-Avon from 1957 to 1959.

Having joined the Bristol Old Vic in 1959, she enjoyed a number of substantial successes, notably as Childie in Frank Marcus's controversial *The Killing of Sister George* in 1965.

She is a versatile as well as accomplished

actress, and has played with distinction in Shakespeare, Shaw, Eliot and Bolt, and championed **Marguerite Duras**'s *Suzanna Andler* in London in 1973, for which she was producer as well as leading character.

Atkinson, Ti-Grace

Born 1939
American feminist, a prominent figure in the
American women's liberation movement

Ti-Grace Atkinson strongly advocated non-hierarchal, leaderless groups and was an early member of NOW (National Organization for Women). She became president of the New York Chapter but resigned her presidency in 1968 because the organization followed a traditional and hierarchal structure.

She also co-founded The Feminists, a leaderless group dedicated to the elimination of marriage and patriarchy.

A collection of her essays, *Amazon Odyssey*, was published in 1974.

Attwell, Mabel Lucie

Born 1879 Died 1964
English artist and writer noted for her child
studies and for illustrating children's stories

Mabel Attwell was born in London. She studied at Heatherley's and other art schools, and married cartoonist Harold Earnshaw.

Her child studies were both humorous and serious, and her immensely popular 'cherubic' style was continued in annuals and children's books by her daughter, working under her mother's name.

Atwell, Winifred

Born 1914 Died 1983
Trinidadian pianist and entertainer who had a
string of ragtime hits in the 1950s

Winifred Atwell was born in Trinidad. Though an accomplished musician from early childhood, she originally intended to be a pharmacist but traded in her scientific training and somewhat intermittent classical career for success as a pop cabaret performer.

This led to a lucrative contract with the British Decca record label and a string of 'ragtime' hits featuring a distinctively jangly, public-bar piano sound which had first been heard in the George Botsford tune 'Black and White Rag', recorded on an instrument bought in a Battersea junk shop for little more than 30 shillings.

Her 'Coronation Rag' became *de rigueur* for street parties in 1953 and the medley 'Let's Have a Party' anticipated the jovial Cockney knees-up albums of Chas'n'Dave. Atwell enjoyed success later with classical 'pops' concerts and records, but faded from view in the 1960s and emigrated to Australia, where she spent her final decade.

Atwood, Margaret Eleanor

Born 1939
Canadian novelist, short-story writer, poet and
critic, her country's most important contemporary
writer and a champion of her sex

Margaret Atwood was born in Ottawa and spent her early years in northern Ontario and Quebec bush country. After graduating from the University of Toronto and Radcliffe College, she held a variety of jobs ranging from waitress and summer-camp counsellor to lecturer in English literature and writer-in-residence. Her first published work, a collection of poems entitled *The Circle Game* (1966), won the Governor-General's award.

Since then she has published several volumes of poetry, collections of short stories — *Dancing Girls* (1977) and *Bluebeard's Egg* (1987) — and *Survival* (1972), an acclaimed study of Canadian literature. She is best known, however, as a novelist. *The Edible Woman* (1969) deals with emotional cannibalism and provoked considerable controversy within and beyond the women's movement. It was followed by *Surfacing* (1972), *Lady Oracle* (1976), *Life Before Man* (1979) and *Bodily Harm* (1982), each in some way exploring the place of mythology in an individual's life, and *Alias Grace* (1996), about the Canadian Grace Marks in the 1840s. In 1985 *The Handmaid's Tale* was short-listed for the Booker Prize, as was *Cat's Eye* in 1989. She has been described by one commentator as 'a staunch moralist' who insists 'that modern man must reinvent himself', and she is also a tireless campaigner for social justice.

Auclert, Hubertine

Born 1848 Died 1914
French feminist and writer, an important figure in
the campaign for equality in France

Hubertine Auclert is best remembered as the founder in 1876 of the French women's rights group *Le droit des femmes*, which later became known as *Société de suffrage des femmes*, and of the campaigning newspaper *La Citoyenne* which she edited from 1881 to 1891. She also contributed to *Le radical*, *La libre parole* and *La Fronde*.

In 1888 she married Antonin Levrier and lived with him in Algeria until his death in 1892. Her many publications include *Le Droit politique des femmes* (1878), *L'égalité sociale et politique* (1879), *Les femmes arabes en Algérie* (1900) and her collected writings published posthumously, *Les femmes au gouvernal* (1923).

Auerbach, Charlotte

Born 1899 Died 1994
German-British geneticist who was the first to discover chemical mutagenesis

Charlotte Auerbach was born in Krefeld and educated in Berlin. She attended university courses in Berlin, Würzburg and finally Freiburg (under the zoologist Hans Spemann), graduating in 1925, before taking up schoolteaching. She started her PhD course at the Kaiser Wilhelm Institute under Otto Mangold, but in 1933 all Jewish students were forbidden to enter the university and she moved to Edinburgh, where she completed her thesis at the Institute of Animal Genetics.

In the late 1930s she studied mutation with Hermann Müller. Her discovery of chemical mutagenesis arose from her work on the effects of nitrogen mustard and mustard gas on *Drosophila*. Chemical mutagenesis thereafter became her main research, with particular emphasis on the biological side and the kinds of mutations induced. She was appointed as a lecturer in genetics (1947) and reader (1957) at Edinburgh, and served as professor from 1967 to 1969.

Her many papers and books on how chemical compounds cause mutations and on the comparison between the actions of chemical mutagens and X-rays include *Genetics in the Atomic Age* (1956), *The Science of Genetics* (1961) and *Mutation Research* (1976). She was elected a Fellow of the Royal Society in 1957 and awarded the Royal Society's Darwin Medal in 1976.

Augspurg, Anita Johanna Theodora Sophie, *also spelt* Augsburg

Born 1857 Died 1943
German feminist, pacifist and writer, a prominent campaigner for women's suffrage

Anita Augspurg was born in Verden an der Aller. She trained as a teacher, and worked as an actor and photographer, before her involvement with women's rights led her to study law in Zurich (1893–7).

Back in Berlin she became a leading figure in the *Bund Deutscher Frauenvereine* (Federation of German Women's Associations) alongside **Lida Heymann**, **Minna Cauer** and

Marie Stritt. In 1898 Augspurg left the Bund for the more radical *Verband fortschrittlicher Frauenvereine*.

In 1902, Augspurg, Cauer, Stritt and Heymann founded the *Deutscher Verband für Frauenstimmrecht* to campaign for women's suffrage. Subsequently Augspurg became increasingly identified with the more militant elements in the suffrage movement, forming the *Deutscher Frauenstimmrechtsbund* in 1913. In 1915 she founded the *Internationale Frauenliga für Frieden und Freiheit*. After German women gained the vote in 1919, Augspurg, Heymann and Cauer worked for civil rights, producing the newspaper *Die Frau im Stadt* (1919–33). When Hitler came to power in 1933, Augspurg and Heymann moved to Zurich where they compiled their memoirs, *Erlebtes-Erschautes*.

Aulenti, Gae(tana)

Born 1927
Italian architect whose staggering breadth of work includes the redesigned Musée d'Orsay

Gae Aulenti was born in Aulenti. She trained at Milan Polytechnic Faculty of Architecture and since graduating in 1954 she has maintained her own private practice which is involved with architecture, furniture design, stage design, interiors and product design.

She became a Doctor of Architecture and taught in the Venice (1960–2) and Milan (1964–7) faculties of Architecture. She also spent three years researching with Luca Roncini in Florence. Since 1974 she has been on the board of directors of Lotus International and her name has been associated with the giant business concerns Fiat and Olivetti.

As well as the redesign of the Musée d'Orsay in Paris (1980–6), which was nominated by the International Union of Architects as one of the 10 most important works in the previous three years, her works include the Palazzo Grassi, Venice (1985), Museo de l'Arte Catalana, Barcelona (1985), and the Pirelli Offices, Rome (1986).

Aulnoy, Marie-Catherine Le Jumel de Barneville, Comtesse d'

Born c.1650 Died 1705
French writer famous for her fairy tales, court romances and a 17th-century travel book on Spain

Marie-Catherine Le Jumel de Barneville was born near Honfleur into a well-to-do family. She married in 1666 and became known as

Madame d'Aulnoy. Her five children were not all his, but were probably the reason for her creation of charming fairy-tales or *contes de fées*; these included *La Belle aux cheveux d'or* ('Goldilocks').

She travelled widely in Europe, but after about 1690 lived mainly in Paris. Her works included romances of court life as well as a more authentic account of the Spanish court entitled *Mémoires de la cour d'Espagne* (1690), and a famous document, in letter form, of her travels in Spain: *Relation du voyage en Espagne* (1691, 'Account of Travels in Spain').

Aung San Suu Kyi

Born 1945
Burmese political leader and founder of the National League for Democracy

Aung San Suu Kyi was born in Rangoon, the daughter of Burmese nationalist hero General Aung San (1916–47), who founded the Anti-Fascist People's Freedom League and headed Burma's fight for independence from the UK until his assassination a few months before its realisation. She was educated at Oxford University, married Michael Aris in 1972 and had two sons.

In 1988 Aung San Suu Kyi co-founded the National League for Democracy and became its General Secretary. Between the years 1989 and 1995, however, she was held under house arrest by the ruling military junta for her opposition to its methods of government. Despite the imprisonment of its leader, the National League for Democracy won a tremendous victory in the elections of 1990, although the result was ignored and many newly elected MPs were jailed. Her release did not change her long-standing conviction that the military had no place in politics, but neither did she wish to provoke any violent reactions, hence her constant emphasis on the need for dialogue and reconciliation and her appeal to exiled Burmese opposition groups to practise patience.

Aung San Suu Kyi was awarded the Nobel Peace Prize in 1991. Her publications include *Aung San* (1984) and *Freedom From Fear and Other Writings* (1991).

Auriol, Jacqueline Marie Thérèse Suzanne, *née* Douet

Born 1917
French aviator who broke the women's jet speed record in 1955

Jacqueline Douet was born in Challons. In 1938 she married Paul Auriol, son of the French socialist politician and future President Vincent Auriol.

She took up flying around the age of 30, turned to stunt flying in the late 1940s, then qualified as the first female test pilot in the world and was among the first (who included **Jacqueline Cochran**) to fly faster than sound. In 1955 she broke the women's jet speed record by flying at 715 miles per hour (1150kph) in a French Mystère. She published *I Live To Fly* in 1970.

Austen, Jane

Born 1775 Died 1817
English novelist whose favourite subject was the closely observed and often ironically depicted morals and mores of country life

Jane Austen was born in Steventon, Hampshire, the sixth of seven children of a country rector, an able scholar who also served as her tutor. She spent the first 25 years of her life in Steventon, and the last eight in nearby Chawton, and did almost all her writing in those two places, writing virtually nothing in the intervening years in Bath, which appears to have been an unsettled time in her otherwise ordered and rather uneventful life. She never married, although she had a number of suitors, and wrote percipiently on the subjects of courtship and marriage in her novels.

She began to write at an early age to amuse her family, and by 1790 had completed a burlesque on popular fiction in the manner of Samuel Richardson, entitled *Love and Friendship*, and ridiculed the taste for Gothic fiction in *Northanger Abbey*, which was written at this time, but not published until 1818. Her best-known works in this vein are *Sense and Sensibility* (1811), *Pride and Prejudice* (1813), *Emma* (1816) and the posthumously published *Persuasion* (1817). *Mansfield Park* (1814) is a darker and more serious dissection of her chosen fictional territory, and although never as popular, is arguably her masterpiece.

Her own letters, although carefully filleted by her sister Cassandra after her death, are one of the few revealing documentary sources on her life. Her greatness has been clearer to subsequent generations than to her own, although Sir Walter Scott praised the delicate observation and fine judgement in her work, which she herself characterized as 'the little bit (two inches wide) of Ivory on which I work with so fine a Brush, as produces little effect after much labour'. If she chose a small stage for her labours, however, she worked upon it with exquisite understanding.

Austen, Winifred

Born 1876 Died 1964
English wildlife artist who illustrated bird books
and painted postcards under the signature 'Spink'

Winifred Austen was born in Ramsgate, the daughter of a naval surgeon. She took up painting professionally at an early age and after a tragically brief marriage moved to the village of Orford in Suffolk in 1926. Among the books she illustrated was Patrick Chalmers's *Birds Ashore and Aforeshore* (1935).

Austin, Mary

Born 1868 Died 1934
American novelist and essayist who wrote on
social issues and the culture of Native Americans

Mary Austin was born in Carlinville, Illinois, and educated at Blackburn College. She moved to California in 1888, where she experienced an unsuccessful marriage (1891) and spent some time in a community of artists. The move had a direct influence on her writing, for Native Americans and the land of the Southwest figure prominently in her work. Her first book, *The Land of Little Rain* (1903), won acclaim as a western classic.

Subsequent work addresses women's issues as Austin moved to New York City and became involved in the suffrage movement and other feminist causes; other themes highlighted in her work include mysticism, Christ and 'the individual'. She was a prolific writer, producing 200 articles and 32 books in her lifetime. She is best known for her play *The Arrow Maker* (1911).

Austral, Florence, *stage-name of*
Florence Wilson

Born 1894 Died 1968
Australian soprano who made her name mainly
in Wagnerian roles

Florence Wilson was born in Richmond, Victoria, and educated in Melbourne. She adopted the name of her country as a stage-name prior to her début in 1922 at Covent Garden, London, when she appeared as Brunnhilde with the British National Opera Company.

She toured the USA and Canada in the 1920s, and appeared in the complete cycles of *The Ring* at Covent Garden and at the Berlin State Opera, which she joined as principal in 1930. She also appeared frequently in the concert hall, often with Sir Henry Wood and his BBC Symphony Orchestra, and made many recordings with other leading singers of her day.

After World War II she returned to Australia, where she taught until her retirement in 1959.

Aylward, Gladys

Born 1902 Died 1970
English missionary in China who devoted her life
to spreading the Gospel to the Chinese people and
improving their quality of life

Gladys Aylward was born in Edmonton, London. She left school at 14 and became a parlour-maid, but harboured the ambition to go as a missionary to China. In 1930 she spent her entire savings on a railway ticket to Tianjin (Tientsin) in northern China, and the following year she took Chinese citizenship.

She met up with a Scottish missionary, Jeannie Lawson, in the province of Shanxi (Shansi), and together they founded the Inn of the Sixth Happiness in an outpost at Yangcheng, where they could teach the Gospel to travellers who stopped to rest. Aylward learnt to speak the local dialect and had a job as a local foot inspector, enforcing the new law that forbade the binding of women's feet in infancy. In 1938 she trekked across the mountains, leading over 100 children to safety when the war with Japan brought fighting to the area.

After nine years spent with the Nationalists, fulfilling her mission by caring for the wounded, she returned to England in 1948, preached for five years, then in 1953 settled in Taiwan as head of an orphanage. Her life was the subject of the film *The Inn of the Sixth Happiness* (1958), starring **Ingrid Bergman**.

Ayrton, Hertha (Phoebe Sarah), *née*
Marks

Born 1854 Died 1923
English physicist who worked on the motion of
waves and formation of sand ripples, and studied
the behaviour of the electric arc

Hertha Marks was born in Portsea, near Portsmouth, and educated in mathematics at Girton College, Cambridge. She married William Ayrton in 1885. Her collected papers describing her work on the electric arc were published as *The Electric Arc* in 1902. She did extensive research with her husband on arc lamps, including cinema projector lamps and searchlights, and took out several patents. The improvements that she made to searchlight technology were put into practice in aircraft detection during both world wars.

During World War I she invented the Ayrton fan for dispersing poison gases — this invention was later adapted to various other applications, including the improvement of ventilation in mines. Ayrton was nominated for fellowship of the Royal Society in 1902, but was refused on the grounds that she was a married woman. She received the society's Hughes Medal in 1906.

She was also a suffragette and a friend of **Marie Curie**.

b

Bacall, Lauren, *originally* Betty Joan Perske

Born 1924
American actress whose success was confirmed
when she appeared opposite Humphrey Bogart in
To Have and Have Not

Lauren Bacall was born in New York City and trained at the American Academy of Dramatic Arts. She made her stage début in *Johnny Two-by-Four* (1942) and also worked as a model, in which capacity director Howard Hawks saw her on the cover of *Harper's Bazaar* and signed her to a contract.

Lauren Bacall

He launched her as 'Slinky! Sultry! Sensational!' in the film *To Have and Have Not* (1944), where, with her husky voice and feline grace, she was as tough, shrewd and cynical as her co-star Humphrey Bogart, whom she married in 1945. They appeared together in such hard-boiled thrillers as *The Big Sleep* (1946), *Dark Passage* (1947) and *Key Largo* (1948). She displayed an elegant sense of light comedy in *How To Marry a Millionaire* (1953) and, after Bogart's death in 1957, turned to the stage, enjoying Broadway successes in *Goodbye Charlie* (1959), *The Cactus Flower* (1965–7) and the musical *Applause!* (1970–2), for which she received a Tony award.

Her stylish, witty personality has enhanced such films as *Harper* (1966), *Murder on the Orient Express* (1974) and *Mr. North* (1988) and she received a British Academy award for *The Shootist* (1976). Later stage work includes *Woman of the Year* (1981, Tony award) and *Sweet Bird of Youth* (1986), while her intelligent autobiography, *Lauren Bacall By Myself* (1978), was an international bestseller. She was married to the actor Jason Robards, Jr, from 1961 to 1969.

Bacewicz, Grażyna

Born 1909 Died 1969
Polish composer who made an inspirational
contribution to Polish music

Grażyna Bacewicz was born in Lodz. She studied violin and composition at the Warsaw Conservatory, took a postgraduate course with **Nadia Boulanger** in Paris (1932–4) and returned to teach in her home town until her brief appointment as professor at the State Academy of Music in Warsaw.

Her work suggests the application of Boulanger's neoclassicism to Polish materials, as in the seven violin concerti (1938–65), the seven string quartets (1938–65), the five violin sonatas, the *Polish Overture* (1954) and *Pensieri notturni* (1961).

Bacewicz's premature death robbed Polish music of one of its most inspirational figures.

Bacon, Delia Salter

Born 1811   Died 1859
American writer who tried to prove that
Shakespeare did not write his plays

Delia Salter Bacon was born in Tallmadge, Ohio, a sister of the Congregationalist clergyman Leonard Bacon (1801–81). From 1853 to 1858 she lived in England, where she worked to try and prove her theory that Francis Bacon (no relation), Walter Raleigh, Edmund Spenser and others wrote Shakespeare's plays. She did not originate the idea herself, but was the first to give it currency in her *Philosophy of the Plays of Shakspere Unfolded* (1857), which had a preface by US writer Nathaniel Hawthorne.

Baddeley, Sophia, *née* Snow

Born 1745   Died 1786
English actress and singer who excelled as
Shakespearian heroines

Sophia Snow was the daughter of the trumpeter Valentine Snow. She eloped in 1763 with the actor Robert Baddeley (1732–94), who fought a duel over her with the brother of David Garrick.

While he specialized in low comedy roles, she excelled as Ophelia and other Shakespearian heroines. She was painted by the British artist John Zoffany as Fanny in George Colman and David Garrick's *The Clandestine Marriage*.

Her extravagant lifestyle and drug addiction brought her career to an early end.

Baez, Joan

Born 1941
American folk-singer and prominent civil rights
campaigner who has reached millions of people
through her music

Joan Baez was born in Staten Island, New York. It was at the 1960 Newport Folk Festival that she first gained critical acclaim for her crystalline soprano voice, and her recordings during the 1960s created a mass audience for folk music.

She is a Quaker, and actively opposes racial discrimination, wars and political imprisonment, both on stage and off. In 1966 she escorted some black children to a white Mississippi school but they were refused entry, and the following year she spent 45 days in prison for disturbing the peace by singing anti-war songs outside a selective service centre in California. In 1969 she performed at the Woodstock Music and Art Fair in Bethel, New York, and the following year appeared in the documentary film musical *Woodstock*.

Since then she has widened her repertoire from English ballads and other folk music to include country and western songs and soft rock.

Bagley, Sarah

Born 1806   Died after 1848
American labour leader who played a major role
in the campaign for a 10-hour working day in
Massachusetts

Sarah Bagley was born in Meredith, New Hampshire. In 1836 she was employed as a weaver in the Hamilton Manufacturing Company, where the poor working conditions such as bad lighting, poor ventilation and a 12-hour working day prompted her to voice mill workers' discontent. She became founding President of the Lowell Female Labor Reform Association (LFLRA) in 1845, and after the LFLRA purchased the *Voice of Industry* periodical, she was appointed editor.

Bagley's campaign for a 10-hour working day included collecting 2,000 signatures on petitions, but the Massachusetts state legislature refused to interfere in the operation of textile mills. She resigned her mill position and worked full-time in labour activities, organizing branches of LFLRA in other mill towns and making speeches for the New England Workingman's Association. She founded the Lowell Industrial Reform Lyceum, a forum for speakers such as Horace Greeley (1811–72).

In 1846 she resigned the presidency of LFLRA due to ill health. She then became the first woman telegrapher in the USA on being appointed superintendant of the Lowell Telegraph Office.

Bagnold, Enid

Born 1889   Died 1981
English novelist, playwright and children's writer
who lived on a tightrope between 'society' and the
world of artists and intellectuals

Enid Bagnold began writing poetry as a teenager, and won prizes for it. She had aquired financial independence before the age of 20, and lived in Chelsea, where she became friends with **Vita Sackville-West** and H G Wells. During her life she also met **Virginia Woolf**, who took an instant dislike to her, and

Nancy Mitford, who described her as 'a sort of fearfully nice gym mistress'.

She published *Serena Blandish* (1924, an English upper-class version of **Anita Loos's** *Gentlemen Prefer Blondes*) under the pseudonym 'A Lady of Quality' to spare her father's feelings, and based *The Loved and the Envied* (1951) on an amalgam of her life and that of Lady Diana Cooper. She is best known, however, for *National Velvet* (1935), the skilfully-told story of a girl who wins the Grand National on a piebald horse won in a raffle. The bowdlerized film version of the story provided **Elizabeth Taylor** with her first lead role.

Of Bagnold's plays, only *The Chalk Garden* (1955) was a hit, and solely in New York. Her *Autobiography* (1969) is a lively, impressionistic tumble through a life lived to the full.

Bagryana, Elisaveta, *pseud of* Elisaveta Belcheva

Born 1893 Died 1991
Bulgarian poet and editor, a leading poet and feminist of her day

Elisaveta Bagryana was born in Sliven. She became established as a poet writing for the literary magazine *Zlatorog* ('Golden Horn') from 1922, and her first collection, *Vechnata i suyatata* ('The Eternal and the Saint'), appeared in 1927.

She was an aggressive and Bohemian personality, who urgently advocated the emancipation of women and enjoyed shocking the middle classes of inter-war Bulgaria, announcing that during her many travels she had picked up 'a husband in every country'.

She also wrote novels that are socialist in tone, and 'official verse' under communism, but was clearly uneasy about the latter and was finally able to give it up. Unfortunately none of her vigorous verse, most of the best of it passionate love poetry, has found a translator.

Bailey, Mildred, *originally* Mildred Rinker

Born 1907 Died 1951
American jazz and blues singer, one of the first successful white women in jazz

Mildred Bailey was born in Tekka, Washington, and was married to a xylophonist, 'Red' Norvo, from 1933 to 1945. She became one of the first female band vocalists, and sang with Benny Goodman, Paul Whiteman and others before *pursuing a solo career*. She was also one of the first white singers to earn a reputation as a jazz singer.

Bailey, Pearl Mae

Born 1918 Died 1990
American singer and actress who starred in Hello, Dolly!

Pearl Bailey was born in Newport News. She began her career as a nightclub singer and dancer in Washington DC, and continued to work in jazz throughout her career, notably with arranger Don Redman and drummer Louie Bellson, whom she married in 1952.

Her principal reputation was made on the musical stage, in films, and on television, beginning with *St Louis Woman* on Broadway in 1946. Her greatest success came in the all-black production of *Hello, Dolly!* in 1967. She wrote her autobiography, *The Raw Pearl*, in 1968.

Baillie, Lady Grisell

Born 1822 Died 1921
Scottish philanthropist and first deaconess of the Church of Scotland

Grisell Baillie was the youngest daughter of George Baillie of Mellerstain. She supported the work of the YWCA, the Church of Scotland Woman's Guild, and the temperance movement. She also helped establish the Zenana Mission in 1881 — an early example of ecumenical co-operation among the churches in Scotland.

She was appointed the Church of Scotland's first deaconess in 1888, at Bowden Church, Roxburgh, where she taught in the Sunday school for 50 years.

Baillie, Lady Grizel, *née* Hume

Born 1665 Died 1746
Scottish poet who as a young woman helped the Covenanters and later wrote songs

Grizel Hume was born in Redbraes Castle, Berwickshire. Her father was the Covenanter Sir Patrick Hume, who in 1684 was supplied by her with food during his concealment in the vault beneath Polwarth Church. She also helped shelter the Covenanting scholar Robert Baillie of Jerviswood (1634–84), who was eventually executed, and whose son George she married in 1692.

She is remembered by her songs, particularly 'And werena my heart licht I wad dee'. In 1911 her domestic notebook was published as *The Household Book*, giving a fascinating, detailed insight into the trivia of daily household management.

Baillie, Dame Isobel

Born 1895 Died 1983
Scottish soprano regarded as one of the 20th
century's greatest oratorio singers

Isobel Baillie was born on the estate of the Earl
of Dalkeith in Hawick, the daughter of a baker.
When her family moved to Manchester, the
quality of her voice was recognized and she
had singing lessons from the age of nine. She
worked as an assistant in the piano roll department of a music shop, and then as a clerk in
Manchester Town Hall, and made her début
with the Hallé Orchestra under Hamilton
Harty in 1921.

After studying in Milan, she won immediate success in her opening season in London
in 1923. She regularly sang with such conductors as Thomas Beecham, Arturo Toscanini
and Bruno Walter, and gave over 1,000 performances of Handel's *Messiah*.

Baillie, Joanna

Born 1762 Died 1851
Scottish poet and prolific writer of verse plays

Joanna Baillie was a daughter of the manse of
Boswell in Lanarkshire. She moved to
Hampstead in 1791 and, on being revealed
as the author of the anonymous *Plays on the
Passions* (1798, 1802 and 1812), was welcomed
into London literary society. Sir Walter Scott
especially admired her work and became a
friend.

The plays, such as 'De Montfort' and 'Basil',
were written mainly in verse and published
as scripts before they were staged. They now
seem melodramatic, but were considered to
contain striking treatments of the female
character.

Baillie's *Fugitive Verses* (1790) echo the
rhythms of Scottish folk-song. She was retiring by nature, and in later life took part in
religious and philanthropic projects.

Bainbridge, Beryl Margaret

Born 1934
*English novelist and actress whose novels are
marked by concision, caustic wit and carefully
turned prose*

Beryl Bainbridge was born in Liverpool and
attended ballet school in Tring. She was a repertory actress from 1949 to 1960, then a clerk
for her eventual publisher, Duckworth, from
1961 to 1973. Her first novel was *A Weekend
with Claude* (1967, revised 1981).

Her family (she married at the age of 20 and
has three children) provided raw material for

A Quiet Life (1976), just as her experience
working as a cellar-woman fed into *The Bottle
Factory Outing* (1974), which won the *Guardian* Fiction award. *The Dressmaker* (1973),
Sweet William (1976) and *Injury Time* (1978,
Whitbread award) are typical of her style and
approach. *Young Adolph* (1978) speculates on
Hitler's reputed visit to Liverpool, while *Watson's Apology* (1984) is based on a real Victorian murder. *Mum and Mr Armitage* (1985)
is a short-story collection and *Something Happened Yesterday* (1993) is a collection of essays.
Her novel *An Awfully Big Adventure* (1985)
was adapted for the stage in 1992 and for the
big screen in 1995. She has also written a
number of television plays.

Bajer, Matilde

Born 1840 Died 1934
*Danish feminist and writer, a pioneering advocate
of women's rights in Denmark*

Matilde Bajer was born in Denmark, and much
influenced by John Stuart Mill's *The Subjection
of Women* (1869). With her husband Frederik
Bajer, a member of parliament, she organized
the Danish Women's Association, campaigning for married women's financial independence and opening a trade school for
women workers in Copenhagen in 1872.

Through her work in the 1880s against
state-regulated prostitution, Bajer became
active in the movement for women's suffrage,
founding the Danish Women's Progress Association in 1886.

Baker, Lady Florence Barbara Maria, *née* Finnian von Sass

Born 1841 Died 1916/18
*Hungarian-born explorer of East Africa, one of
the few women to make a major contribution to
the exploration of Africa*

The early life of Florence Finnian von Sass is
unknown. She was purchased by the English
explorer Sir Samuel White Baker (1821–93)
from a Hungarian slave market in 1859, and
became his lifelong companion. He married
her as his second wife in 1860 and together
they searched for the sources of the Nile.

In 1861 they followed the rivers that drain
the Ethiopian highlands and empty into the
Blue Nile. Then they turned their attention to
the White Nile, crossing difficult country to
name both Lake Albert (Albert Nyanza) and
the Murchison Falls, a source of the Nile, in
1864. When her husband was appointed Governor-General of southern Sudan, she was tireless in her attempts to eradicate slavery.

They retired to England, but Florence outlived Sam by some 23 years. Though always happy to live in his shadow, she was an accomplished explorer in her own right.

Baker, Dame Janet Abbott

Born 1933
English mezzo-soprano who has enjoyed an
extensive operatic career

Janet Baker was born in Hatfield, Yorkshire. She sang in various local choirs before going to study music in London in 1953. She made her début in 1956 as Roza in the Czech composer Smetana's *The Secret* at Glyndebourne, and during the 1960s worked as a soloist for Sir John Barbirolli before beginning her operatic career. She excelled particulary in early Italian opera and the works of Benjamin Britten.

Janet Baker, 1966

Also a concert performer, she was a noted interpreter of Mahler and Elgar. In 1982 she retired from the operatic stage and published her autobiography, *Full Circle*. She was created DBE in 1976.

Baker, Josephine, *originally* Freda Josephine McDonald

Born 1906   Died 1975
American-born black French entertainer and
campaigner whose dedication made her a wartime
heroine

Josephine Baker was born in St Louis, Missouri. At the age of 13 she ran away from home and joined a vaudeville company, then in 1925 went to Paris with La Revue Nègre where her natural singing and dancing ability captured the attention of the French as an example of the new hot jazz.

Unable to achieve stardom in the USA, she became a French citizen (1937), and during World War II worked for the Red Cross and the French Resistance. She was awarded the Croix de Guerre, the Rosette de la Resistance and was appointed a Chevalier of the Légion d'Honneur for her efforts to provide entertainment and for her intelligence-gathering work.

After the War, she worked to achieve a Global Village and campaigned for civil rights in the USA, but the expenses surrounding her construction of the World Village impoverished her. She was NAACP (National Association for the Advancement of Colored People) Woman of the Year in 1951.

Baker, Louisa Alice, *née* Dawson

Born 1858   Died 1926
New Zealand romantic novelist who lived in
England but set most of her stories in New
Zealand

Louisa Alice Dawson was born on the South Island. She wrote for some local newspapers, then left for England and marriage in 1894, but continued to contribute articles to publications in New Zealand. Under the pen-name 'Alien', she wrote 16 tales of sacrifice, renunciation, and the sanctity of marriage.

Despite the approbation of the religious press, some contemporary critics believed that Baker dwelt perhaps a little too lovingly on the 'regrettable incidents' in her narratives, some of which included accounts of extramarital affairs as well as of courtship.

Her first book, *A Daughter of the King* (1894), was followed by *The Majesty of Man* (1895). The moral point of *His Neighbour's Landmark* (1907) is heightened by the 1886 eruption of Mt Tarawera. Her other books included *A Double Blindness* (1910).

Baker, Sarah

Born c.1736   Died 1816
English theatre manager who founded theatres in
several towns visited by her touring company

Sarah Baker was born in Kent, where she was active in theatre for over 50 years. Although only semi-literate, she was an energetic and enterprising woman with many eccentric traits, especially regarding money. Widowed in 1769 with three young children, she assumed control of her mother's theatrical company and established a touring circuit around her native county.

After her mother's retirement in 1777, she introduced a more ambitious repertoire, including Shakespeare and Sheridan, and from 1789 set about building permanent theatres in the towns they visited, eventually numbering 10 in all. Edmund Kean (1789–1833) was among the actors who passed through her troupe.

Balabanova, Angelika Isaakovna,
also spelt Balabanov *and* Balabanoff

Born 1878 Died 1965
Russian–Italian socialist who worked for
socialism in several different countries

Angelika Balabanova was born in Chernigov and educated in Belgium, Germany and Italy before studying at the Free University of Brussels.

She became a socialist and moved between Italy and Switzerland where she met and worked with the exiled Benito Mussolini (1883–1945). On her return to Russia in 1917 she became a Bolshevik and was sent to the Soviet Embassy in Switzerland because of her contacts.

By 1920 she was no longer politically active and in 1922 left Russia. Later she worked for Italian socialist organizations in Paris until she left for the USA in 1935. She remained there until after World War II and died in Rome. Her autobiography, *My Life as a Rebel*, was published in 1935.

Balas, Iolanda

Born 1936
Romanian athlete who enjoyed an unparalleled
domination of the high jump

Iolanda Balas was born in Timorsauru. Her achievement was unlike anything seen before in the history of athletics. Hallmarked by consistency, her unbeaten reign stretched from 1956 to 1967.

She was Olympic champion in 1960 and 1964 and European champion in 1958 and 1962, the first Romanian to win an athletics European and Olympic medal. She won the high jump at the world Student Games eight times and the gold at the first European Indoor games in 1966. She set 14 world records at high jump between 1956 and 1961 and by the end of 1963 she had jumped 1.80 metres or higher in 72 competitions. She also won 16 consecutive national titles from the age of 14 onwards.

Balch, Emily Greene

Born 1867 Died 1961
American social reformer and pacifist who was
jointly winner of the 1946 Nobel Prize for Peace

Emily Greene Balch was born in Jamaica Plain, Massachusetts, the daughter of a lawyer and a schoolteacher. She was educated at Bryn Mawr College in the first class to graduate (1886–9), and was described there as having 'extraordinary beauty of moral character'. From 1890 to 1891 she studied political economy at the Sorbonne and in 1893 she published *Public Assistance of the Poor in France*. In 1906 she became a socialist.

She taught economics at Wellesley College from 1896 to 1918 (Professor of Economics and Sociology from 1913), where her innovative courses included coverage of Karl Marx and women's place in the economy. She was an active pacifist, and her open opposition to World War I and the USA's entry into it was viewed by the authorities with increasing suspicion. In 1919 her academic appointment was not renewed.

She helped establish the Women's International League for Peace and Freedom (1919) and subsequently proved an indefatigable administrator, writer and promoter for peace. She shared the 1946 Nobel Prize for Peace with the religious leader and social worker John R Mott. Her works include *Our Slavic Fellow Citizens* (1910) and *Toward Human Unity* (1952).

Balfour, Lady Frances

Born 1858 Died 1931
Scottish suffragist, churchwoman and author who
spoke out against many social issues

Lady Frances Balfour was born in London, and spent her early years at Rosneath Castle and Inverary Castle. Her political ambitions were stifled by the role of women at that time, but she had strong connections with both the Whig and Tory parties, the former through her own family (her father was George, 8th Duke of Argyll) and the latter through her marriage to Eustace Balfour, the brother of Arthur James Balfour (MP from 1874, premier 1902–5).

She was a tireless worker for women's rights, and employed her eloquent and acerbic gift for oratory on behalf of the National Union of Woman's Suffrage Societies. She also spoke out on such issues as Irish Home Rule and free trade. Her crusading, but essentially conservative, spirit — she did not approve of suffragist militants like **Emmeline Pankhurst** — also characterized her work for the

Church of Scotland, and she fought throughout her life for the re-union of 1929, just as her father had opposed the Disruption in 1843.

She wrote a number of memoirs, including those of her sister, Lady Victoria Campbell (1911), and Dr **Elsie Inglis** (1918), and an autobiography, *Ne Obliviscaris* (1930).

Ball, Lucille Desirée

Born 1910 Died 1989
American comedienne who became one of
television's best-loved characters

Lucille Ball was born in Celaron, New York. She was an amateur performer as a child, and became a model and chorus girl before moving to Hollywood, where she spent several years in bit parts and B-pictures before more substantial roles were offered.

An effervescent redhead with a rasping voice and impeccable timing, she began working in television in 1951, starring in such domestic comedies as *I Love Lucy* (1951–5), *The Lucy Show* (1962–8) and *Here's Lucy* (1968–73). She purchased her own studio with her first husband Desi Arnaz and became a successful production executive, occasionally returning to the cinema for popular comedies like *The Facts of Life* (1960) and *Yours, Mine and Ours* (1968).

Balliol, Devorgilla de

Died 1289/90
Scottish philanthropist and patron of Balliol
College, Oxford

Devorgilla was the daughter and co-heiress of Alan, Lord of Galloway, and great-great-granddaughter of David I of Scotland.
She married robber baron John de Balliol of Barnard Castle, who for his misdeeds was given the penance of supporting four Oxford students. Following her husband's death in 1269 she confirmed her support for Balliol College, and in 1282 granted a charter for 16 scholars. In 1273 or 1275 she founded Sweetheart Abbey to the south of Dumfries, where she arranged to be buried with her husband's embalmed heart, which she is said to have carried with her.

Her other civic and religious benefactions were chronicled by the historian Andrew de Wyntoun (1350–1420). Her son John, born at Mons-en-Vimeu, near Abbeville, France, was King of Scotland in 1292–6.

Bambara, Toni Cade, *née* Cade

Born 1939
African-American writer whose depiction of black
experience is imbued with feminist thought

Toni Cade was born in New York City and brought up in a poor area. She was educated at New York's City College and has had jobs ranging from social worker to college professor.

Her writing makes a significant contribution to the development of an African-American literary tradition, and is inspired partly by her experience of African-American urban culture. She writes and lectures on the intersection of Black and feminist consciousness, and has published short stories, essays, novels and screenplays.

She has also edited books on the Black experience in America, including *The Black Woman* (1970), which describes black women's views on the civil rights movement, *Tales and Stories for Black Folks* (1971) and *Southern Black Utterances Today* (1975). Her novels include *The Salt Eaters* (1980) and *If Blessings Come* (1987).

Bancroft, Anne, *originally* Anna Maria Louise Italiano

Born 1931
American actress who has developed a
distinguished career on stage and screen

Anna Italiano was born in New York City. She was a child actress and dancer, and made her television début in 1950 under the name Anne Marno. Her film début, as Anne Bancroft, followed in 1952. She won a Tony for her performance in *Two For a Season* on Broadway in 1958, and another for *The Miracle Worker* in 1959, gaining an Academy Award for the film version in 1962.

Her major films include *The Pumpkin Eaters* (1964), *The Graduate* (1967), *The Turning Point* (1977), *The Elephant Man* (1980), *Agnes of God* (1985) and *84 Charing Cross Road* (1987). She is married to the film director Mel Brooks.

Bandaranaike, Sirimavo Ratwatte Dias, *née* Ratwatte

Born 1916
Sri Lankan politician who became the world's first
woman prime minister

Sirimavo Ratwatte was born in Ratnapura, Sabaragamuwa Province. In 1940 she married Solomon Bandaranaike, who was Prime Minister of Ceylon from 1956 until his assassination in 1959. In 1960 she took over the leadership of his Sri Lanka Freedom Party and headed a left-wing coalition government as the world's first woman prime minister, at the same time holding the Defence and Foreign Affairs portfolios.

Sirimavo Bandaranaike, 1960

She was forced to resign on her electoral defeat in 1965, but after a period in office that was plagued by economic difficulties and communal disturbances, she was premier again between 1970 and 1977. During this time she promoted the new constitution which in 1972 proclaimed a republic, changing the name of the country from Ceylon to Sri Lanka.

From 1980 to 1985 she was banned from active politics for alleged abuse of power while in office; meanwhile the leadership of the SLFP was left to her son Anura. She became Leader of the Opposition again in 1988.

Bankes, Mary, *née* Hawtrey

Died 1661
English Royalist who twice defended Corfe Castle
against Parliamentary attack

Mary Hawtrey married Sir John Bankes (1589–1644) and when Civil War broke out in England in 1642, she and her children retired to Corfe Castle, Dorset, while her husband remained in attendance on Charles I.

In 1643 she and her maidservants and only about five soldiers successfully defended the castle against Oliver Cromwell's Parliamentary forces by throwing down stones and burning coals on the attackers who were trying to scale the walls with ladders. Lady Bankes was given a small garrison of 50 men for protection after this episode, and, not withdrawing from the royal cause even after the death of her husband, successfully defended her home again in late 1645.

In 1646 however she was betrayed by one of her own men who was apparently 'weary of the king's service' and had to surrender the castle to the Roundheads. She and her children were allowed to leave in safety before the castle was sacked and destroyed. The rest of her life was comparatively peaceful.

Bankhead, Tallulah

Born 1903 Died 1968
American actress who developed a larger-than-
life personality despite her conventional
background

Tallulah Bankhead was born in Huntsville, Alabama. She was educated in New York and Washington, and made her stage début in 1918, thereafter appearing in many plays and films.

She won Drama Critics awards for her two most famous stage roles — Regina Giddens in **Lillian Hellman**'s *The Little Foxes* (1939) and Sabina in Thornton Wilder's *The Skin of our Teeth* (1942). Another very popular role was Amanda Prynne in Noël Coward's *Private Lives*.

Her most outstanding film portrayal was in *Lifeboat* (1944), and she also performed on radio and television.

Banks, Lynne Reid

Born 1929
English novelist and playwright whose first novel,
The L-Shaped Room, *was her biggest success*

Lynne Reid Banks was born in London. She began writing plays for television and radio, and was widely acclaimed for *The L-Shaped Room* (1960), the first part of a trilogy completed by *The Backward Shadow* (1970) and *Two Is Lonely* (1974). The first is particularly important, not only because the heroine, a pregnant single woman, defied the social conventions of her class and time by refusing to undergo an abortion, but also because it added a female perspective to other novels being published then, which similarly dealt with young working-class and lower middle-class people coming to terms with sexuality and family life in a grim post-war Britain.

Banks's eight years spent in Israel provided material for the Arab–Israeli background of such novels as *An End to Running* (1962), also focused on the plight of an unfulfilled woman. Although she has continued to write novels, including the 'biographical fiction' *Dark Quartet: The Story of the Brontës* (1976), it is her earlier books which have earned her a place in literary history.

Bannerman, Helen Brodie, *née* Boog Watson

Born 1862 Died 1946
Scottish children's writer and illustrator who
wrote The Story of Little Black Sambo

Helen Boog Watson was born in Edinburgh, the daughter of a Free Church minister. She married a doctor in the Indian Medical Service and spent much of her life in India, where she produced the children's classic, *The Story of Little Black Sambo* (1899).

This is the tale of a black boy and his adventures with the tigers, based on illustrated letters Bannerman had written to her children. It was phenomenally popular when it first appeared, but was judged by some after her death to be racist and demeaning to blacks. She wrote several other illustrated books for children.

Ban Zhao (Pan Chao)

Born AD45 Died AD115
Chinese historian and moralist whose book of
moral admonitions had a lasting influence on
Chinese women

Ban Zhao was born in Anling, Gufang (now Xianyang, Shaanxi (Shensi) province), the sister of the military commander Ban Chao (Pan Ch'ao) and the historian Ban Gu (Pan Ku). She married at the age of 14 but was widowed early and devoted herself to literature.

She helped complete Ban Gu's history of the former Han Dynasty and became a tutor to empresses and court ladies as well as a lady-in-waiting to the empress. She wrote many poems and essays and also compiled *Lessons for Women*, a book of moral admonitions for women, emphasizing the virtues of deference and modesty, which exerted a lasting influence on attitudes towards women in China. A crucial assumption underpinning these moral admonitions was that women should not play any public role.

Bara, Theda, *stage-name of* Theodosia Goodman, *known as* the Vamp

Born 1885 Died 1955
American actress successful as a man-eater before
the Jazz Age changed popular taste

Theodosia Goodman was born in Cincinnati. After making her début on Broadway in 1908 as Theodosia de Coppet she moved to silent films and, beginning with *A Fool There Was* (1915), rapidly became noted for her femme fatale roles. Though she was simply the daughter of a Jewish tailor, mysteries grew up surrounding her background and she was billed by her agent as having been born in the Sahara desert and endowed with mystic powers, so she surrounded herself with symbols of death and popularized the phrase, 'Kiss me, my fool!'.

Her image as a vampire woman who would destroy a man morally, financially and physically (usually through sexual excess) was so popular that audiences would not allow her to break this mould, and by 1919, when her contract with Twentieth Century-Fox ended, she had appeared in around 40 films.

However, changing tastes and the new Jazz Age film style at the beginning of the 1920s left no place for her characterization, and she failed to make a comeback. Her final appearance was in *Madame Mystery* (1926) before she retired to enjoy her happy marriage with film director Charles J Brabin, whom she had married in 1921.

Barat, St Madeleine Sophie

Born 1779 Died 1865
French nun who founded the Society of the
Sacred Heart

Madeleine Sophie Barat was born into a peasant family in Joigny, Burgundy. Her education was managed by her highly religious elder brother Louis. She intended to become a Carmelite nun but instead in 1800 was persuaded by Louis and his superior, Abbé Joseph Varin, to lead a new educational institution, the Society of the Sacred Heart of Jesus, which aimed to promote educational work among all classes.

The following year the first Convent of the Sacred Heart opened at Amiens, with Barat as superior from 1802. It received papal approval in 1826. During her 63-year rule the convent grew in academic excellence and established 100 further foundations in Europe, North Africa and in America under Sister **Rose Philippine Duchesne**, the Society's first missionary.

Barat's work was so highly valued that instead of allowing her to retire at 85, the Order gave her an assistant for her remaining year of life. She was canonized in 1925 and her feast day is 25 May.

Barbara, St

Died c.200AD
Christian virgin martyr of the early church who
was beheaded by her own father

According to legend, which seems to have no foundation in historical fact, Barbara was a Syrian maiden of great beauty whose father immured her in a tower to discourage suitors.

She angered him by refusing the attentions of bachelors he considered eligible and compounded his disgust by becoming a Christian during his absence from home for a time. He had her condemned by the authorities as a Christian and beheaded her himself, but was instantly struck by lightning.

St Barbara is the patron saint of artillerymen and is invoked during thunderstorms. Her emblem in art is a tower, and her feast day, which is now unofficial because her cult was suppressed in 1969 due to the factual uncertainty surrounding her life, is 4 December.

Barbauld, Anna Laetitia, née Aikin

Born 1743 Died 1825
English poet and writer for children who wrote educational material as well as stories

Anna Aikin was born in Kibworth-Harcourt, Leicestershire. Encouraged by the success of her *Poems* in 1773, she and her brother John Aikin jointly published *Miscellaneous Pieces in Prose* later that year. She married a dissenting minister, Rochemont Barbauld, in 1774, and during the next 10 years published her best work, which includes *Early Lessons for Children* (1778) and *Hymns in Prose for Children* (1781).

Also with her brother she began the well-known series *Evenings at Home* in 1792. After her husband's suicide in 1808, she continued writing and editing, and published her long narrative poem *Eighteen Hundred and Eleven* in 1812.

Bardot, Brigitte, originally Camille Javal

Born 1934
French film actress adopted internationally as the symbol of female permissiveness

Brigitte Bardot was born in Paris, the daughter of an industrialist. She trained as a ballet dancer and worked as a model, and her appearance on the cover of *Elle* led to her film début in *Le Trou Normand* (1952). A succession of small roles followed, but it was *Et Dieu Créa La Femme* (1956, 'And God Created Woman') that established her reputation as a sex kitten.

Many of Bardot's roles exploited an image of petulant sexuality that was reinforced by a much publicized off-camera love life. Her many screen credits include *La Verité* (1960, 'The Truth'), *Le Mépris* (1963, 'Contempt') and *Viva Maria* (1965), whilst *Vie Privée* (1962, 'A Very Private Affair') was an autobiographical depiction of a young woman trapped by the demands of her stardom.

She retired from the screen in 1973 and has devoted herself to campaigning for animal rights, forming the Foundation for the Protection of Distressed Animals in 1976.

Barfoot, Joan

Born 1946
Canadian novelist, one of Canada's prominent contemporary writers

Joan Barfoot was born in the province of Ontario, where she became a journalist for the *London Free Press* in London. She published her first novel, *Abra*, in 1978 (reissued as *Gaining Ground* in the UK, 1980), which won the *Books in Canada* First Novel award. It has been followed by *Dancing in the Dark* (1982), which was made into an award-winning film, *Duet for Three* (1985) and *Family News* (1990). Her general theme is that of a woman's search for self-identity in a society which seems to offer no palatable role.

Barfoot's work has attracted comparison with that of her fellow Canadian writer **Margaret Atwood**.

Barlow, Hannah Bolton

Floreat 1870–1913
English ceramic decorator, the first woman artist to work for Henry Doulton, noted for her wildlife decorations

Hannah Barlow was born in Little Hadham, Hertfordshire, the daughter of a bank manager, and showed an early talent for delineating animal life. She studied at Lambeth School of Art and Design from 1868 to 1870, and continued her studies in the evenings after commencing work at Henry Doulton's pottery firm in 1870.

She specialized in 'sgraffito' drawings of animals on raw clay, incising her delicate and articulate drawings onto the damp surface. She kept a small private 'zoo' of 12 to 16 animals to aid her in her studies, including sheep, a pony and a fallow deer.

She exhibited terracotta reliefs and sculptures at the Royal Academy from 1881 to 1890. Along with her sister Florence and Louisa Davis, Hannah did much to secure the success of the Doulton Company. She also exhibited at the Royal Academy, Dudley Gallery, the Society of British Artists and Walker Art Gallery, Liverpool.

Barnard, Marjorie Faith

Born 1897 Died 1987
Australian novelist, critic and writer for children who was also a historian and biographer

Marjorie Barnard was born in Sydney. She wrote many books in conjunction with Flora Eldershaw as 'M Barnard Eldershaw'. Best known are *A House is Built* (1929) and the anti-Utopian novel *Tomorrow and Tomorrow* (1947, eventually published in unexpurgated form as *Tomorrow and Tomorrow and Tomorrow*, 1983).

Her historical writing includes *Macquarie's World* (1941) and the impressive and scholarly one-volume *A History of Australia* (1962). Among her subsequent solo writings are two collections of short stories, biographies of the convict and architect Francis Greenaway and of Governor Lachlan Macquarie, and a critical study of her friend **Miles Franklin**.

She won many prizes, including the 1983 Patrick White Literary award.

Barnes, Djuna

Born 1892 Died 1982
American novelist, poet, dramatist and illustrator whose work and life crossed many conventional boundaries

Djuna Barnes was born in Cornwall-on-Hudson, New York. She began her career as reporter and illustrator for magazines, then became a writer of one-act plays and short stories, published in a variety of magazines and anthologies.

Although little known to the general public, her brilliant literary style has been acclaimed by many critics, including T S Eliot, and she was a prominent figure in the literary society of the 1920s that fostered many Anglo-American modernist writers.

Her works, many of which she has illustrated, range from the outstanding novel *Nightwood* (1936) to her verse play *The Antiphon* (1958), both included in *Selected Works* (1962).

Barnes, Dame (Alice) Josephine (Mary Taylor)

Born 1912
English obstetrician and gynaecologist who has worked her way to the top of her profession

Josephine Barnes was born in Shorlingham, Norfolk. She read physiology at Lady Margaret Hall, Oxford, where she was a member of the Women's Hockey XI (1932–4), before completing her clinical training at University College Hospital, London. She qualified in 1937 and took various junior hospital appointments in obstetrics, gynaecology and surgery in London and Oxford, becoming deputy Academic Head of the Obstetric Unit of University

College Hospital (1947–52), and Surgeon to the **Marie Curie** Hospital (1947–67).

She has served in numerous official medical positions, such as in the Royal Society of Medicine, the British Medical Association (first woman president, 1979–80), the Royal College of Obstetricians and Gynaecologists and the National Association of Family Planning Doctors. She has been awarded several honorary degrees and fellowships, and the many national and international committees to which she has been appointed include the Royal Commission on Medical Education (1965–8), the Committee on the Working of the Abortion Act (1971–3), and the Advertising Standards Authority (1980–93).

She has published extensively on obstetrics, gynaecology and family planning, and was created DBE in 1974.

Barnett, Dame Henrietta Octavia Weston, *née* Rowland

Born 1851 Died 1936
English philanthropist involved with the founding of the first university settlement

Henrietta Rowland was born in Clapham, London. In 1873 she married Samuel Augustus Barnett (1844–1913), curate of St Mary's, Bryanston Square, where she had worked with **Octavia Hill**. They soon moved to the challenging parish of St Jude's Whitechapel, where she supported him in an arduous 33-year ministry that included the founding and running of Toynbee Hall, the first university settlement. Their Christian Socialist beliefs were expounded in *Practicable Socialism* (1885).

Supporting her husband's interests did not prevent Henrietta developing her own. These included the welfare of servants and children, the Children's Country Holiday Fund, the London Pupil Teachers' Association, Whitechapel Art Gallery, the preservation of Hampstead Heath and, from around 1907, the planning of Hampstead Garden Suburb. Barnett was created DBE in 1924.

Barney, Natalie Clifford

Born 1876 Died 1972
American poet, playwright, novelist, essayist, memoirist and epigrammatist, an outspoken lesbian who lived on the Parisian Left Bank

Natalie Barney was born in Bar Harbor, Maine, and inherited vast wealth from her parents. Attracted to Paris by the artistic ambience and the climate of relative moral freedom, she relocated there in 1902 and remained until her death, following her inclination to live her life as a work of art. Being financially independent, she set up and presided over a salon which became one of the most respected and influential of the day, frequented by Ezra Pound and other prominent artistic and literary figures.

She is better known for her active and outspoken lesbianism than for her literary work, which is characteristically inaccessible. She wrote most of her considerable and complex output in French, of which the majority still remains in manuscript. Her infrequent publications were printed by small publishing houses in limited editions, now out of print. She is now receiving more attention from feminist critics, in the light of her continual artistic struggle with the question of female experience.

Among her published works is *The One Who is Legion, or AD's After-Life* (1930), an attempt to explore the western concept of the feminine.

Barns-Graham, Wilhelmina

Born 1912
Scottish painter whose work is in many major
collections throughout the UK

Wilhelmina Barns-Graham was born in St Andrews and trained at Edinburgh College of Art (1931–6). In 1940 she moved to Cornwall where she became involved with Penwith Society of Arts and worked with Ben Nicholson and **Barbara Hepworth**. She subsequently met the younger group of 'St Ives' artists, including Roger Hilton and the writer David Lewis, whom she married in 1949.

Rooted initially in the figurative, her work in the 1960s and 1970s embraced abstraction with the square becoming her predominant motif. In recent years she has returned to direct painting, particularly large watercolours and gouaches in brilliant colour, and in 1973 she returned to live and work in St Andrews.

Barot, Madeleine

Born 1909
French leader in the Resistance movement and
Protestant leader in the ecumenical movement

Madeleine Barot was born in Chateauroux. She joined the French Reformed Church and the French Student Christian Movement, and was a leader at the 1939 First World Conference of Christian Youth.

In 1940 she was appointed general secretary of the refugee relief organization Comité Inter-Mouvement auprès des Evacués (CIMADE), and soon joined the Resistance to assist Jews escaping to Spain and Switzerland. During World War II CIMADE helped internees, deported political activists and persecuted minorities, and after the War it worked for social reconstruction and ecumenical co-operation.

Barot participated in World Council of Churches meetings from 1946 and was appointed director of the Department on the Co-operation of Men and Women in Church and Society (1953–66), later working on development education (teaching on industrial, rural and social affairs in developing countries).

Barr, Roseanne

Born 1952
American comedienne whose television show
brought a new maturity and reality to the
depiction of the American family

Roseanne Barr was born into a Jewish family in Salt Lake City, Utah. She became a teenage mother and a housewife, and later worked as a cocktail waitress, honing her talent for cutting remarks and spontaneous wit on her unsuspecting customers. On turning professional, she built a reputation as a blunt-talking feminist able to articulate the experiences of working-class women.

She moved to Los Angeles in 1985, and became a regular club and television performer before recording her own special, *The Roseanne Barr Show* (1987). She has subsequently starred in the popular television show *Roseanne* (1988–) that conveys the reality of working-class family life. In 1990 she married comedian and former co-star Tom Arnold, but the marriage did not last. Now remarried, she refers to herself simply as Roseanne.

She has also appeared in such films as *She-Devil* (1989), *Even Cowgirls Get the Blues* (1994) and *Smoke* (1995), and has published the books *Roseanne: My Life as a Woman* (1989) and *My Lives* (1994), which describe her personal battles as well as her rise to stardom.

Barraine, Elsa

Born 1910
French composer whose use of instrumentation
was innovative and influential

Elsa Barraine was born in Paris. She studied under Paul Dukas at the Conservatoire National Supérieur de Musique, before working as choirmistress (1936–9) and as head of sound (1944–6) with the Orchestre National de France. She subsequently worked in the recording industry before being appointed

Professor of Musical Analysis at the Conservatoire de Paris (1953–74).

Her first symphony was written when she was 21 and pointed to her very individual use of instrumentation. Her works include effective pieces for organ and saxophone, and for unusual ensembles, such as *Chiens de paille* (1966) for low brasses and ondes Martenot, and *Musique rituelle* (1968) for organ, tam-tam and xylophone.

Though these pieces strongly influenced younger French composers, her music is much less often heard today, even in France.

Barringer, Emily, *née* Dunning

Born 1876　Died 1961
American physician who campaigned for women's access to medical education

Emily Dunning was born in Scarsdale, New York, and was influenced as a teenager by a speech on women's education by **Mary Puttnam Jacobi**. She went to Cornell University and then to the Woman's Medical College of New York, graduating in 1901.

On attempting to get a position at the Mount Sinai Hospital, she was told that, regardless of how well she did in the entrance examination, she would not be appointed. Nearly 40 years later she learned that she had gained higher marks than all the male candidates, some of whom had gone on to receive appointments.

Nevertheless she was able to obtain positions, often with the assistance of Dr Jacobi, although she endured considerable hostility from her male colleagues. From 1903 to 1905 she was a pioneer ambulance surgeon in East Side New York, on call to go out to all emergencies. On leaving this service, she married Benjamin Barringer, a fellow physician.

Barrios De Chamorro, Violeta *see* Chamorro, Violeta Barrios De

Barry, Elizabeth

Born 1658　Died 1713
English actress, the leading tragedienne of her day

As a child Elizabeth Barry was put by her impoverished father in the care of William D'Avenant, manager of Drury Lane Theatre. It is said that she showed little promise at first, but was trained by the Earl of Rochester, whose mistress she became, and rose to be recognized as the first great English actress.

Her earliest known role was in Thomas Otway's *Alcibiades* in 1675, and she earned acclaim for her moving performance of Monimia in *The Orphan* in 1680. Though she

Elizabeth Barry

created a great number of roles in comedy, she was an intense and controlled actress who excelled in tragedy (the comic stage of the day was led by **Anne Bracegirdle**) and many of the parts she played in William Congreve's plays were written specially for her.

She worked with Thomas Betterton at the United Company from the 1680s until 1695, when she and Bracegirdle joined Betterton's group of seceding actors and became co-founders of a company at the Lincoln's Inn Fields Theatre. There she remained until her retirement in 1710.

Barry, James

Born 1795　Died 1865
Scottish surgeon who pretended that she was a man for her entire professional life

James Barry's real name and birthplace are not recorded, although she was said (perhaps romantically) to be the granddaughter of a Scottish earl, and was described by Lord Albemarle in 1819 as having 'an unmistakably Scotch type of countenance', as well as a 'certain effeminacy in his manner'.

She graduated in medicine from Edinburgh University in 1812 and entered the army as a hospital assistant in 1813. She rose to Assistant Surgeon in 1815, Surgeon Major in 1827, Deputy Inspector General of the Army Medical Department in 1851, Inspector General in 1858, and retired on half-pay in 1859.

She fought a duel in Capetown in 1819, and

was reputed to be an excellent surgeon, but quarrelsome and prone to breaches of discipline. Her actions were said, again probably romantically, to have been inspired by her love for an army surgeon. Her pretence that she was male was discovered only on her death.

Barry, (Marie-) Jeanne, Comtesse du, *née* Bécu

Born 1743 Died 1793
French courtesan whose position as Louis XV's favourite mistress brought about her downfall

Jeanne Bécu was born in Vaucouleurs, the illegitimate daughter of a dressmaker. She became a shopgirl (under the name of Jeanne Vaubernier) in Paris and was introduced to society as 'Mademoiselle Lange' by her lover, Jean du Barry. She was presented at court, and in 1768 caught the fancy of the elderly king, who married her off to Jean's brother, a superannuated courtier, the Comte Guillaume du Barry, in order that she could qualify as official court mistress (a position left vacant by the death of Madame de **Pompadour**).

In 1769 she entered the court, where the following year she helped to bring about the downfall of the Finance Minister, the Duke de Choiseul. She wielded considerable influence, but was unpopular with the public and squandered vast sums of money, though she was reputedly a generous patron of the arts. She was banished from court after Louis's death in 1774.

During the French Revolution she was brought before the Revolutionary Tribunal, charged with having wasted the treasure of the state, and guillotined.

Barry, Leonora Kearney, *known as* Mother Lake, *née* Marie Kearney

Born 1849 Died 1923
American labour leader and social reformer

Mary Kearney was born in County Cork, Ireland, and moved to the USA in 1852. She found work in a clothing factory and, as a member of the Women's Knights of Labor, campaigned to improve wages and working conditions for women. She was General Investigator for the women's department of the Knights of Labor from 1886 to 1890 and also lectured at Chautauqua on temperance, labour and women's suffrage.

Barrymore, Ethel

Born 1879 Died 1959
American actress, the leading stage actress of her day

Ethel Barrymore was born in Philadelphia, the daughter of the actor-playwright Maurice Barrymore and the actress Georgina Drew Barrymore, and sister of the actors Lionel and John Barrymore. In 1897–8 she continued the tradition of her family and scored a great success in London with Sir Henry Irving in *The Bells.*

Other noteworthy appearances were in *Trelawney of the Wells* (1911), *The Second Mrs Tanqueray* (1924), *Whiteoaks* (1938) and *The Corn is Green* (1942). She also acted in films, including *Rasputin and the Empress* (1932), the only production in which all three Barrymores appeared together, and *None But the Lonely Heart* (1944, Academy Award), as well as on radio and television.

Barton, Clara (Clarissa Harlowe)

Born 1821 Died 1912
American schoolteacher known as the 'angel of the battlefield' who founded the American Red Cross

Clara Barton was born in Oxford, Massachusetts. From 1836 to 1854 she worked as a teacher in New Jersey in a school that she herself had founded, when she was the federal government's only female employee. She then left to work in the Patent Office in Washington DC (1854–7). During the Civil War (1861–5), she helped to obtain and distribute supplies and comforts for the wounded.

She lived in Europe for the sake of her health from 1869 to 1873, where she worked for the International Red Cross in the Franco-Prussian War (1870–1). When she returned to the USA she established the US branch of the Red Cross in 1881 and became its first president (1881–1904). As a result of her campaigning, the USA signed the Geneva Convention in 1882.

Barton, Elizabeth, *known as the* Holy Maid of Kent *or* Nun of Kent

Born c.1506 Died 1534
English prophet who incited the public to question Henry VIII's matrimonial activities and was executed for her trouble

Elizabeth Barton was a domestic servant at Aldington, and after an illness in 1525, she began to go into trances and make prophetic utterances against the authorities. Archbishop Warham sent two monks to examine her. One of these, Edward Bocking, convinced that she was directly inspired by the Virgin **Mary**, became her confessor at the priory of St Sepulchre at Canterbury. She denounced Henry VIII's divorce and his marriage to **Anne**

Boleyn, and was charged with treason and hanged at Tyburn with Bocking and four others.

Barton, Glenys

Born 1944
English sculptor whose focus since the early 1980s has been on the shape of the human head

Glenys Barton was born in Stoke-on-Trent and trained at the Royal College of Art (1968–71), where she received a travelling scholarship. She began exhibiting in 1973.

From 1976 to 1977 she was artist-in-residence at the Wedgwood factory, where she was able to experiment with clay and the techniques of ceramic figure design. While many of her heads are portraits, her removal of the hair and avoidance of exact facial details gives them a timeless quality. Her work shows a particular interest in the shape of the skull. She uses a great variety of glazes to obtain different effects on the smooth clay surfaces, both in the complete heads and the more recent relief profiles.

Bashkirtseva, Marya Konstantinovna, *also called* Marie Bashkirtseff

Born 1860 Died 1884
Russian diarist and artist whose childhood diary paints a psychological self-portrait

Marya Bashkirtseva was born in Pultowa, south Russia, into a noble family. As a child she travelled in Germany and France with her mother before they settled in Paris.

From the age of 12 she kept a diary in French, selections of which were published posthumously as *Journal de Marie Bashkirtseff, avec un portrait* (1887), which candidly plots the psychological progress of a growing artist's mind.

She studied painting in Paris and became a painter of some promise, exhibiting in the Salon of 1880, but died early of tuberculosis.

Batchelor, Joy

Born 1914 Died 1991
English animated-cartoon producer who made the first British stereoscopic cartoon, The Owl and the Pussycat, *in 1952*

Joy Batchelor was born in Watford. She became a fashion artist for *Harper's Bazaar*, tried her hand at animation with *Robin Hood* (1935), and in 1941 married fellow-producer John Halas, forming the Halas–Batchelor animation unit.

During World War II they made propaganda films for the Ministry of Information, followed by the first British feature-length cartoon, *Handling Ships* (1945), and the *Charley* series (1947).

Later films included George Orwell's *Animal Farm* (1954) and the television series *Tales of Hoffnung* (1965).

Bateman, Kate Josephine

Born 1842 Died 1917
American actress who had a major success in London with Henry Irving in Augustin Daly's Leah the Forsaken

Kate Bateman was born in Baltimore, Maryland, the daughter of the theatrical manager Hezekiah Linthicum Bateman (1812–75). She began acting at the age of four, and after successful tours in America, acted in *Leah the Forsaken* in London in 1863 and in Shakespearian plays (1875–7). She married Dr George Crowe in 1866.

Her sisters Isabel (1854–1934) and Virginia (1853–1940) were both distinguished actresses. The latter married Edward Compton (1854–1918) and was the mother of **Fay Compton** and Sir Compton Mackenzie.

Bates, Daisy May, *née* O'Dwyer

Born 1863 Died 1951
Irish-born Australian anthropologist who devoted much of her life to documenting the life and culture of the Aborigines

Daisy O'Dwyer was born in Tipperary, Ireland. She arrived in Australia in 1884, married Jack Bates the following year, and had a son, Arnold. After a period as a London journalist (1894–9), during which her husband and son remained in Australia, she was commissioned by *The Times* to investigate alleged cruelty to Aborigines, and returned to Australia in 1899 to begin her study of Aboriginal cultures.

In 1902 she accompanied her husband on an overland cattle drive of around 650 miles (1,046km), but this finished off their marriage, and from that time she spent most of her life in the north and west of Australia with remote tribes, by whom she was known as 'Kabbarli' (grandmother). In 1904 she was appointed by the government of Western Australia to research the tribes of that state in 1910–11 she joined Alfred Radcliffe-Brown's anthropological expedition there.

She made detailed notes of Aboriginal life and customs and worked for Aboriginal welfare, setting up camps for the aged and criticizing those who tried to 'westernize' them. When her application in 1912 to become the Northern Territory's Protector of Aborigines was refused on the grounds of her sex, she sold her own cattle station to finance her work. She published an account of her life, *The Passing of the Aborigines*, in 1938. When over 80 she returned to live with a tribe in South Australia, but failing health forced her to retire to Adelaide in 1945. Her life formed the basis of **Margaret Sutherland**'s opera *The Young Kabbarli*.

Bathild, St

Died 680
Anglo-Saxon queen and nun who ruled wisely,
supported the Church and fought against the
slave trade

Bathild was captured by pirates in 641 and sold as a slave to Erchinoald, the mayor of the palace of King Clovis II of the Western Franks. The king was attracted by her beauty and capability and made her his wife in 649. Their three sons all became kings: Clotaire III, Childeric II and Thierry III.

After Clovis died in 657, Bathild acted as regent for the five-year-old Clotaire. She was an intelligent ruler and ably defended the waning Merovingian power against the ascendant Frankish kings. She also supported the Church, endowed monasteries (including Chelles and Corbie), fought against the slave-trade and freed slaves.

A revolution led by nobles in 665 forced Bathild to quit the regency and withdraw to her convent at Chelles, her most famous foundation, where she spent the rest of her life. Her feast day is 26 January.

Bathori, Elizabeth

Died 1614
Hungarian noblewoman who bathed in the blood
of her murder victims

Elizabeth Bathori was the niece of Stephen Bathori, King of Poland, and wife of the Hungarian Count Nádasdy. In 1610 she was discovered to have murdered 650 young girls, so that she could keep her youth by bathing in their warm blood. Her accomplices were burnt, and she was shut up for life in her fortress of Csej.

Bathsheba

Born c.970BC
Biblical character with whom King David
committed adultery

Bathsheba was the daughter of Eliam and the wife of Uriah the Hittite, an army officer. After King David had committed adultery with Bathsheba, Uriah was sent to his death, in order to hide the king's crime, enabling him to take the beautiful Bathsheba for himself. Nathan the prophet forced David to condemn his own action, and prophesied the death of their first child. The second child was Solomon, David's successor.

Jewish tradition holds that the song in praise of a good wife in Proverbs 31 was written by Solomon in memory of his mother.

Batten, Jean, *originally* Jane Gardner Batten

Born 1909 Died 1982
New Zealand pioneer aviator whose record-
breaking solo flights included going from England
to Australia and back

Jean Batten was born in Rotorua. She went to study music in England but abandoned a possible musical career and sold her piano in favour of aviation. At the age of 21 she took her pilot's and ground engineer licences.

In 1934, in a Gypsy Moth, she broke **Amy Johnson**'s record for the flight from England to Australia by nearly five days, completing the journey in 14 days, 23 hours and 25 minutes. She became the first woman to complete the return journey and in 1935 flew over the South Atlantic to Argentina.

Retiring from active flying in the 1940s, she remained an enthusiastic supporter of British aeronautics. Her autobiography *My Life* (1938) was republished as *Alone in the Sky* in 1979.

Jean Batten, 1935

Batten, Mollie (Edith Mary)

Born 1905 Died 1985
English social work pioneer and educationalist
who led a varied and influential life

Mollie Batten was born in London and educated at Southport Girls' High School, Liverpool University and the London School of
Economics. She became warden of Birmingham university settlement, and from 1933
developed training for both youth and social
workers.

During World War II she worked for the
Ministry of Labour, but afterwards declined a
permanent civil service appointment, choosing instead to read theology at St Anne's,
Oxford (1947–9). Her experience and interests
came together at William Temple College,
where she was principal from 1950 to 1966.
The college specialized in short courses,
bringing together people from industry, the
civil service, social work and education.

A supporter of the Labour Party and of the
ordination of women to the priesthood, Batten
was awarded the OBE in 1948.

Baudisch-Wittke, Gudrun, *née* Baudisch

Born 1907 Died 1982
Austrian ceramicist who became an important
member of the Wiener Werkstätte in Vienna

Gudrun Baudisch studied ceramics and sculpture at Graz and, at 19, became the youngest
member in the Kunstlerwerkstätte when she
moved to Grünbach. She quickly established
herself as one of the top designers in the
Wiener Werkstätte, specializing in heads and
figurines. Her heads were smooth and
unadorned, and had elongated faces, painted
with the colours of eyeshadow, lipstick and
mascara.

In 1928 her work was included in the International Exhibition of Ceramic Art at the
Metropolitan Museum in New York. In the
1930s she opened her own studio in Vienna,
but moved to Berlin in 1938 following the
Anschluss with Hitler's Germany. She worked
with the architect Clemens Holzmeister designing architectural faience for churches in
Turkey, Austria and Germany.

In 1946 she settled in Hallstatt in Austria
with her second husband Karl Wittke and
together they set up a pottery, the Keramic
Hallstatt. She retired in 1977, handing over
her pottery to Gruppe H, a group of young
ceramicists that she had organized.

Baum, Vicki (Hedvig)

Born 1888 Died 1960
Austrian-born American novelist who tends to
focus on independent women caught up in the
turmoil of 20th-century society

Vicki Baum was born in Vienna, and married
first a journalist and second the conductor
Richard Lert. After periods as a harp-player,
as a journalist, and as a nurse during World
War I, she began writing novels and short
stories in German in 1920.

She made her name with *Menschen im Hotel*
(1929, Eng trans *Grand Hotel*, 1930), which
became a bestseller and a popular film in 1931
starring **Joan Crawford** and **Greta Garbo**.

She emigrated to the USA in 1931 and
gained citizenship in 1939. Her later novels
include *Falling Star* (1934), *Headless Angel*
(1948) and *The Mustard Seed* (1953).

Baumer, Gertrude

Born 1873 Died 1954
German feminist, leader of the German feminist
movement

Gertrude Baumer was born in Hohenlimburg,
Westphalia, and became involved in feminist
politics while studying at Berlin University.
She wrote many pamphlets to popularize her
views. From 1910 to 1919 she was President of
the League of German Women's Associations,
and in 1917 founded a socialist school for
women. She also edited the newspaper *Die
Frau* from 1893 to 1944.

In 1920 she became a member of the Reichstag, but lost the position in 1933 on the
advent of Nazi power. Motivated by her Christian faith, she continued to express her resistance to the regime and was subjected to
Gestapo interrogation more than once.

After World War II she founded the Christian Social Union party but was soon forced
by ill health to retire from public life.

Bausch, Pina

Born 1940
German choreographer and dancer whose
choreography and unusual stagings mark an
influential turning point in contemporary dance

Pina Bausch was born in Solingen. She trained
first with Kurt Jooss at the Essen Folk-
wangschule and then with José Limón and
Antony Tudor in New York. After a season
with the Metropolitan Opera Ballet Company
and another with American choreographer
Paul Taylor, she returned to Essen where she

staged several operas for the Wuppertal Theatre.

Her success led to an invitation to found her own company. After staging Igor Stravinsky's *Le Sacre du printemps* (1975) and Bertolt Brecht and Kurt Weill's *Seven Deadly Sins*, she began to produce her own work in the late 1970s. Her works have featured stages strewn with dead leaves (*Bluebeard*, 1977), pink and white carnations (15,000 of them in *Carnations*, 1982) and chairs (*Café Muller*, 1978).

Bawden, Nina Mary, *née* Mabey

Born 1925
English novelist whose writing for adults and for young people examines the emotional upheavals experienced at any age

Nina Mabey was born in London. She was educated at Oxford and married Henry Bawden in 1946. Her first adult novel was published in 1953. Much of her work delves into the domestic and emotional turbulence of the middle-classes: their friendships, marriages, divorces and the resulting expanding and contracting families. *Anna Apparent* (1972) is a study of an illegitimate child evacuee, spanning from the London blitz to her life as a wife and mistress, while the middle-aged narrator of *Afternoon of a Good Woman* (1976) reflects on a life of disappointment and emotional betrayal before turning to face her future with renewed resilience. *The Ice House* (1983) casts a discriminating eye on a 30-year female friendship, with all its confidences and conflicts.

The implication in Bawden's adult work that the feelings and thoughts of children are too often overlooked becomes a dominant note in her novels for younger readers. In *Carrie's War* (1973), Carrie's response to being evacuated to Wales during World War II is sharply and sympathetically observed.

Bayes, Nora, *professional name of* Dora Goldberg

Born 1880 Died 1928
American singer and composer whose star rose during World War I

Nora Bayes was born in Joliet, Illinois. Five times married, she enjoyed her greatest success with her second husband Jack Norworth, with whom she wrote and performed 'Shine On, Harvest Moon', the hit song of the *Ziegfeld Follies* of 1908. Her other lasting compositions were 'Has Anyone Here Seen Kelly', included in *The Jolly Bachelors* (1910), and the wartime favourite 'Down at the Old Bull and Bush', which few Londoners realised had originally been called 'Down Where the Wurzburger Flows'.

Between World War I and her death, Bayes made many recordings. Her life story was filmed as *Shine On Harvest Moon* (1944), starring Ann Sheridan (1915–67) as Nora.

Baylis, Lilian Mary

Born 1874 Died 1937
English theatrical manager who established the Old Vic as a centre of Shakespearian production

Lilian Baylis was born in London, the daughter of musicians. She received a musical education and when in 1890 the family emigrated to South Africa, she became a music teacher in Johannesburg. She returned to England in 1898, and helped her aunt **Emma Cons** with the management of the Royal Victoria Hall, which had been turned into a temperance music hall providing cheap family entertainment.

Baylis became manager of the theatre in 1912, and under her it became the Old Vic, a joint home of Shakespeare and opera. By 1923 the entire canon of Shakespeare's first folio plays had been presented.

In 1931 Baylis acquired the Sadler's Wells Theatre for the exclusive presentation of opera and ballet. There she founded the Vic–Wells Ballet, which was to become the Royal Ballet on receiving its Royal Charter in 1956, and the Sadler's Wells Opera, which moved to the Coliseum in 1968 and was renamed English National Opera in 1974.

Bayne, Margaret

Born 1798 Died 1835
Scottish missionary, a pioneer of female missionary work and education in India

Margaret Bayne was born in Greenock. A gifted linguist and able administrator, she married the Bombay missionary John Wilson and from 1829 established schools for girls in India and trained teachers for them.

After her death, her work was continued by her two sisters, Anna and Hay, and supported by the establishment in Edinburgh in 1837 of a society for the advancement of female education in India.

Her life was a clear example of the important role that women could and would come to play on the mission field.

Baynton, Barbara Janet Ainsleigh, née Lawrence

Born 1857 Died 1929
Australian novelist, short-story writer and socialite whose writing evokes the grime and squalor of life in the Australian bush

Barbara Lawrence was born in Scone, New South Wales. Her father was a carpenter of Irish stock, and Baynton afterwards fantasized about her origins. She found work as a governess and married a son of the house, but he later left her for one of her servants. She then married a 70-year-old retired surgeon, Thomas Baynton, and entered a life of leisure and culture.

She began to write stories for the popular periodical *The Bulletin* and became a close friend of its editor, A G Stephens. In search of a publisher for her stories, she visited London in 1902 and was befriended by the English writer and critic Edward Garnett. When her husband died in 1904, leaving Baynton wealthy, she returned to London, made profitable investments on the stock exchange and lived in a series of increasingly grand houses surrounded by choice antiques. She travelled frequently between England and Australia and in 1921 married the fifth Lord Headley, but they soon separated.

She wrote one novel, *Human Toll* (1907), and a number of short stories first collected in *Bush Studies* (1902) and later, with two others, in *Cobbers* (1917). In all her writing the grime and squalor of the real bush, as seen and endured by women and the underprivileged, contrasts hugely with the romanticized male 'mateship' of the Australian writer Henry Lawson and his followers.

Beach, Mrs H H A, *professional name of* Amy Marcy Beach, née Cheney

Born 1867 Died 1944
American concert pianist and composer who became the first US woman to write a symphony

Amy Cheney was born in Henniker, New Hampshire. She made her professional concert début at 16 in Boston where she met and married (in 1885) a local surgeon, Henry Harris Aubrey Beach. She then decided to devote herself to composition, in which she was mostly self-taught.

Her *Mass* of 1892 was an important work, but it was her Symphony in E-minor Op.32 that established her romantic style which was reminiscent of folk. It was written and performed by the Boston Symphony Orchestra in 1896. Like Olivier Messiaen, she also tran-scribed birdsong and made use of it in her work.

After Dr Beach's death in 1910, by which time she had become an established composer, she performed successfully in Europe, returning to the USA on the eve of World War I.

Beale, Dorothea

Born 1831 Died 1906
English pioneer of women's education whose vision bore fruit in some of England's most prestigious female educational establishments

Dorothea Beale was born in London. She attended Queen's college, Harley Street, at the same time as **Frances Buss** and **Adelaide Procter**, and taught there from 1849. In 1857 she was appointed head teacher of Clergy Daughters' School in Westmorland (where the **Brontë** sisters were educated, the model for 'Lowood' in *Jane Eyre*), and from 1858 to 1906 was principal of Cheltenham Ladies' College, the quality and size of which she radically increased.

In 1885 she founded St Hilda's College, Cheltenham, as the first English training college for women teachers, and sponsored St Hilda's Hall in Oxford for women teachers in 1893. She was an ardent suffragette, and was immortalized in verse with Buss ('Miss Buss and Miss Beale, Cupid's darts do not feel').

Beale, Mary, née Cradock

Born 1632 Died 1699
English portrait painter and copyist who worked prolifically in the manner of Lely

Mary Cradock was born in Barrow, Suffolk, the daughter of a clergyman. When in 1651 she married Charles Beale, a landowner and textile manufacturer, she was already a practising portrait painter and a devoted follower of the most celebrated portraitist of her day, Sir Peter Lely (1618–80).

Very little is known of her work before about 1670, but several of her husband's diaries record her painting commissions, including a good number of portraits of clerics. They provide an insight into the artistic circles revolving around Lely's studio. She also executed copies after Lely, whose influence is generally evident in all her work.

Beals, Jessie Tarbox, née Tarbox

Born 1870 Died 1942
American photographer who became one of the first women press photographers

Jessie Tarbox was born in Hamilton, Canada, a daughter of the inventor Nathaniel Tarbox.

She became a teacher in Massachusetts in 1887, and carried out portrait photography in the summers of the 1890s. She married machinist Alfred T Beals in 1897 and taught him photography; in 1900 they became itinerant photographers, with Jessie as photographer and business manager and Alfred as darkroom worker.

She became a journalist in upstate New York in 1902 and then moved to New York City where she established a studio in 1905. In 1910–12 she made documentary photographs of children of the New York slums. Nanette, her daughter with a lover, was born in 1911. Although they continued to work together, she left Alfred in her marital capacity in 1917 and they divorced. Their work was published in the journals *Harper's Bazaar* and *Vogue*, among others. In 1928 she and Nanette went to southern California, where she photographed mainly celebrities and gardens, returning to New York in 1929.

Jessie Tarbox Beals and **Frances Benjamin Johnston** are considered to be among the very first women press photographers.

Beard, Mary Ritter, *née* Ritter

Born 1876   Died 1958
American feminist and historian best remembered for illuminating women's history

Mary Ritter was born in Indianapolis and educated at DePauw University, where she met her future husband, the historian Charles A Beard (1874–1948). They married in 1900 and she immediately became involved in the campaign for women's suffrage, first in England, where her husband was a student at Oxford, then in New York (from 1902), where they both enrolled at Columbia University. Shortly after the birth of a son in 1907, she joined the National Women's Trade Union League, and helped to run strikes and protests.

In 1910 she became a member of the Woman Suffrage movement, and after a period of editing *The Woman Voter* became involved with the more working-class issues of the Wage Earners' League. From 1913 to 1917 she worked assiduously for the Congressional Union (later the National Women's party) under **Alice Paul**'s leadership, but, a polemical, perceptive commentator, gradually became more interested in writing and giving lectures than in practical work.

Her publications included *Woman's Work in Municipalities* (1915), *On Understanding Women* (1931) and, most famously, *Women as a Force in History* (1946). With her husband she wrote several influential works on US history,

such as *History of the United States* (1921) and *The Rise of American Civilization* (1927).

Beat, Janet Eveline

Born 1937
English composer working in Scotland whose speciality is electro-acoustic music

Janet Beat was born in Streetly, Staffordshire, and has been based in Scotland since 1972. After graduating from the University of Manchester, she worked as a freelance horn player (1960–5) and as a teacher. In 1972, shortly after her first compositions were published, she was appointed lecturer at the Royal Scottish Academy of Music and Drama in Glasgow.

Her output includes a large number of electro-acoustic pieces which reflect her scientific and anthropological interests; *A Vision of the Unseen* (1988) and *Mandala* (1990) are both representative. Beat is a founder-member of the Scottish Society of Composers (1980), the Scottish Electro-Acoustic Music Society (1987) and the ensemble Soundstrata (1988).

Beatrix, Queen, *in full* Beatrix Wilhemina Armgard

Born 1938
Queen of the Netherlands who acceded to the throne on her mother's abdication in 1980

Beatrix Wilhemina Armgard is the eldest daughter of Queen **Juliana** and Prince Bernhard Leopold. In 1966 she married the German diplomat Claus-Georg Wilhelm Otto Friedrich Gerd von Amsberg (1926–   ). Their son Prince Willem-Alexander Claus George Ferdinand (b.1967) is the first male heir to the Dutch throne in over a century. The other two sons are Johan Friso Bernhard Christiaan David (b.1968) and Constantijn Christof Frederik Aschwin (b.1969). Beatrix adopts a regal but pragmatic approach to her position and enjoys great popularity with the majority of her subjects.

Beattie, Ann

Born 1947
American novelist and short-story writer who tends to focus on disaffected families or individuals

Ann Beattie was born in Washington DC, and educated at American University and the University of Connecticut. She has worked as a visiting lecturer at the University of Virginia and at Harvard University. She received a Guggenheim Fellowship in 1977 and has several novels and collections of short stories to her name, beginning with the novel *Chilly Scenes of Winter* (1976) and the story collection *Distortions* (1976). Both comic and detached, her work presents the theme of contemporary alienation in a minimalist manner.

Her novel *Picturing Will* (1990), about a young boy brought up by his mother who is preoccupied with her career as a photographer, uses photographic imagery to examine the issues Beattie's earlier novels and short stories explored through language.

Beaufort, Lady Margaret, Countess of Richmond and Derby

Born 1443 Died 1509
English noblewoman whose son became King
Henry VII, and who herself became a generous
patron of education

Margaret Beaufort was the daughter of John Beaufort, 1st Duke of Somerset. In 1455 she married Edmund Tudor, Earl of Richmond. The Lancastrian claim to the English Crown was transferred to her with the extinction of the male line, and it was in the right of his mother's descent as great-granddaughter of John of Gaunt (1340–99, a son of Edward III) that her son ascended the throne as Henry VII after the defeat of Richard III in 1485.

During the Wars of the Roses Margaret had been imprisoned at Pembroke by the Yorkists. In 1464 she married Henry Stafford, son of the Duke of Buckingham, and in 1473 Thomas Stanley, 1st Earl of Derby. She was a generous benefactress of Oxford and Cambridge universities, where she endowed two divinity professorships. She also founded Christ's College, Cambridge, and St John's College, Cambridge, and was a patron of the first English printer, William Caxton (c.1422–91).

Beauharnais, Eugénie-Hortense Cécile *see* Hortense

Beaumont, Agnes

Born 1652 Died 1720
English religious autobiographer and friend of
John Bunyan

Agnes Beaumont was born in Edworth, Bedfordshire, the seventh and youngest child of a widowed yeoman farmer. At 20 she joined one of John Bunyan's congregations at Gamlingay.

Two years later, in 1674, her father forbade her to attend a meeting. When she defied him he locked her out of the house for two days. They were soon reconciled, but the strain of the incident killed him. It took a coroner's jury to clear the accusation that she and Bunyan had conspired to poison him.

The story is related in Beaumont's autobiography, the 'Narrative of the Persecution of Agnes Beaumont', which still survives in manuscript form and was published in 1760 in a collection called *An Abstract of the Gracious Dealings of God with Several Eminent Christians.*

Beauvoir, Simone de

Born 1908 Died 1986
French novelist, feminist, autobiographer and
essayist regarded as one of the 20th century's
major feminist writers

Simone de Beauvoir was born in Paris and educated at the Sorbonne, where she later lectured. There she met the philosopher and writer Jean-Paul Sartre (1905–80) and became his lifelong companion. Together they formulated the philosophy of Existentialism, which influenced her writing.

De Beauvoir will undoubtedly be remembered chiefly for the enormous impact made by her famous book *Le Deuxième Sexe* (1949, Eng trans *The Second Sex*, 1953), which despite its alleged shortcomings as a feminist tract, remains authoritative for its intelligence and the sheer weight of its case. It inspired many women to salutary writings and actions and has caused many of them to refer to its author as 'the mother of us all'.

She was also a notable novelist (in particular in *Les Mandarins*, 1954, Eng trans *The Man-*

Simone de Beauvoir, 1983

darins, 1956) and a supreme autobiographer, as in *Memoires d'une jeune fille rangée* (1954, Eng trans *Memoirs of a Dutiful Daughter*, 1959).

Becher, Hilla, *née* Wobeser

Born 1934
German photographer and conceptual artist best known for her photographs of industrial structures

Hilla Wobeser was born in Potsdam, Germany. She was apprenticed to a commercial photographer from 1951 to 1954 and worked as an aerial photographer in Hamburg in the 1950s before moving to Dusseldorf to study at the Staatliche Kunstacademie Dusseldorf and to work for an advertising agency where her future husband Bernd Becher was an employee.

Both art students, they began to work together in 1959 photographing industrial subjects; they married in 1961 and left the academy to concentrate on their own work, which they carried out during Bernd's travels as a photographer for a cement company. Hilla worked as a freelance designer for industrial fairs and exhibitions. Their son Max was born in 1964.

Hilla and Bernd Becher are well known for their photographs documenting industrial buildings and other structures such as water towers in Germany, Holland, Belgium, Britain and the USA. Their work has been exhibited internationally since 1965. Their publications include *Anonyme Skulpturen: Eine Typologie technische bauten* (1970).

Becker, Lydia Ernestine

Born 1827 Died 1890
English suffragette and a clear speaker who was effective in lobbying parliament for the cause of suffrage

Lydia Becker was born in Manchester, the eldest of 15 children of a prominent manufacturer. Educated at home, she studied botany and corresponded with the naturalist Charles Darwin (1809–82).

When she was 40 she heard **Barbara Bodichon** speak on women's suffrage. She responded with a paper on suffrage published in the *Contemporary Review, and* became secretary and founding member of the Manchester Women's Suffrage Committee in 1867, remaining on the board for 23 years. In 1870 she founded the *Women's Suffrage Journal*.

Beckett, Margaret Mary, *née* Jackson

Born 1943
English Labour politician and a strong influence in the reform of the Labour Party in recent years

Margaret Jackson was born in Ashton-under-Lyne, the daughter of a carpenter and a teacher. She trained as an engineer at Manchester College of Science and Technology and worked as a metallurgist before entering parliament as Labour MP of Lincoln in 1974, remaining until 1979. During this time she held the position, among others, of Parliamentary Under-Secretary of State for the Department of Education and Science (1976–9).

In 1979 she married Lionel Beckett. Also that year she joined Granada Television as chief researcher until 1983, when she was elected MP for Derby South. A fiercely pragmatic politician with steely determination, she continued her rise through the ranks of the Labour Party, serving as Opposition front bench spokesperson on health and social security (1984–9), shadow chief secretary to the Treasury (1989–92), shadow Leader of the House and campaigns co-ordinator (1992–4) and Deputy Leader (1992–4).

After the sudden death of Labour leader John Smith in 1994, she was acting Leader for a few months until Tony Blair took over and she was given the Opposition health portfolio again. In 1995 she was appointed Opposition front bench spokesperson for the Department of Trade and Industry.

Beecher, Catharine Esther

Born 1800 Died 1878
American educationalist and writer who maintained that a woman's proper place was in the home

Catharine Beecher was born in East Hampton, New York, the eldest daughter of the American Presbyterian minister Lyman Beecher, among whose 12 other children were **Harriet Beecher Stowe** and the Congregationalist clergyman Henry Ward Beecher. Catharine Beecher's promotion of the training of women as teachers and the necessity for them to be educated in domestic affairs helped to consolidate, and also to raise, the traditional, conservative view of a woman's role in society, where they could uphold domestic values and thereby improve the development of American society.

Among her activities were the founding of

the Hartford Female Seminary with her sister Mary in 1823, and the organization of the American Women's Educational Association in 1852. Her writings, mainly on female higher education and domestic life, particularly focusing on the duties of women, were widely read and influential. They include *A Treatise on Domestic Economy* (1841), *The Duty of American Women to Their Country* (1845) and *The American Woman's Home* (1869, with Harriet Beecher Stowe).

Beeton, Isabella Mary, *née* Mayson

Born 1836   Died 1865
English writer whose Book of Household Management *made her a household name*

Isabella Mayson was educated in Heidelberg and became an accomplished pianist. In 1856 she married Samuel Orchard Beeton, a publisher. Her *Book of Household Management*, which covers cookery and other branches of domestic science, was first published in parts (1859–60) in a women's magazine founded by her husband. It made Mrs Beeton's name a household word. She died prematurely after the birth of her fourth son.

Behn, Aphra, *née* Johnson

Born 1640   Died 1689
English playwright, poet and adventuress, perhaps the first professional woman author in England

Aphra Johnson was born near Canterbury in Kent, the daughter of an innkeeper, and spent some of her early life in Surinam, where she made the acquaintance of the enslaved negro prince Oroonoko — the subject afterwards of one of her novels, in which she anticipated Rousseau's 'noble savage'.

She returned to England in 1663, and married a merchant called Behn, who died within three years. By then she had entered court circles, and so was available for appointment as a professional spy in government service at Antwerp during the Dutch Wars. She sent back political and naval information (some of her dispatches survive), but received no money and little thanks, and on her return was imprisoned for debt.

She turned to writing poetry and novels (eg *Oroonoko, or the History of the Royal Slave*, 1688), as well as several coarse but popular Restoration plays, including *The Forced Marriage* (1670), *The Rover* (1678) and *The Feigned Courtizans* (1678). She was buried in Westminster Abbey.

Béjart, Madeleine

Born 1618   Died 1672
French actress who was linked with Molière personally and professionally

Madeleine Béjart was the eldest child of a Parisian theatrical family closely associated with the work of Molière (1622–73). When Molière married her youngest sister Armande (1642–1700) in 1662, malicious gossip of the time suggested Armande was really Madeleine's daughter from an affair with Molière that had taken place two decades before.

Madeleine was already an established classical actress when she met Molière. They formed a company, then toured the provinces after its failure, but returned to Paris in 1658, where she shared in his success. She played in a number of his comedies as well as managing the affairs of his company for a time, and is thought to have exerted an importance influence on his achievement.

Bell, Gertrude Margaret Lowthian

Born 1868   Died 1926
English archaeologist and traveller who helped to establish the Hashimite dynasty and to preserve the antiquities of Iraq

Gertrude Bell was born at Washington Hall, Durham. By the age of 16 she was enjoying a brilliant career at Lady Margaret Hall, Oxford, where she became the first woman to obtain a first in modern history. She travelled widely in the Middle East, and learnt to speak Persian and Arabic. In 1913 she began a journey on which she became the second woman (after Lady **Anne Blunt**) to visit Ha'il, but she was not well received. She wrote extensively about many of her travels.

During World War I she was appointed to the Arab Bureau in Cairo and seconded to the Mesopotamia Expeditionary Force in Basra and Baghdad. She later wrote a brilliant report on the administration of Mesopotamia between the armistice of 1918 and the Iraq rebellion in 1920.

She became Oriental Secretary to the British High Commission in Iraq in 1920, and played a part in establishing the Hashimite dynasty by helping to get Faysal I placed on the throne in Baghdad in 1921. She spent three years creating an archaeological museum in Baghdad, and on her death left money to fund the British Institute of Archaeology in Iraq.

Bell, Vanessa, *née* Stephen

Born 1879   Died 1961
English painter and decorative designer, a central figure in the Bloomsbury Group

Vanessa Stephen was born in Kensington, London, a daughter of the scholar and critic Sir Leslie Stephen and elder sister of **Virginia Woolf**. She trained as an artist under Sir Arthur Cope (1896–1900) and studied at the Royal Academy Schools (1901–4). In 1907 she married the critic Clive Bell, but left him in 1916 to live at Firle, Sussex, with Duncan Grant, a fellow-contributor to Roger Fry's Omega Workshops (1913–20).

In 1912 she exhibited four pictures in her decorative style (which was influenced by Matisse) in the second Post-Impressionist exhibition. In 1919 she was elected to the London Group, exhibiting with them regularly from 1920.

Bellamy, George Anne

Born c.1727 Died 1788
English actress who became a leading lady at
Drury Lane under David Garrick

George Anne Bellamy was the illegitimate daughter of a Quaker schoolgirl and Lord Tyrawley. She first appeared in an adult role in Thomas Otway's *The Orphan* at Covent Garden (c.1744).

She was profligate and extravagant and, having squandered her talent and her beauty in a scandalous lifestyle, she spent her last years in poverty. Following her retirement, she published a six-volume autobiographical *Apology* (1785).

Bell Burnell, (Susan) Jocelyn, *née* Bell

Born 1943
English radio astronomer who jointly discovered
the first pulsar

Jocelyn Bell was born in York and educated at the universities of Glasgow and Cambridge, where she received her PhD in 1968, the year she married Martin Burnell.

In 1967 she was a research student at Cambridge, working with Antony Hewish, when they noticed an unusually regular radio signal on the 3.7 metre wavelength radio telescope. This led to the first discovery of a pulsar (PSR 1919 + 21, with a period of 1.337 seconds). Within the first few weeks of discovery the correct conclusions were drawn — the object is stellar as opposed to a member of the solar system, and is a condensed neutron star.

She later joined the staff of the Royal Observatory, Edinburgh, and became the manager of their James Clerk Maxwell Telescope on Hawaii. She was awarded the Herschel Medal of the Royal Astronomical Society

Jocelyn Bell Burnell, 1975

in 1989, and since 1991 has been Professor of Physics at the Open University.

Belmont, Alva Ertskin, *née* Smith

Born 1853 Died 1933
American socialite and reformer who gave
financial support to the suffrage movement in
America

Alva Ertskin Smith was born in Mobile, Alabama, into a well-established Southern family. She developed into a committed socialite, and cleverly worked her way into the New York social élite as the wife of William Henry Vanderbilt (1875, divorced 1895). Her daughter Consuelo married the Duke of Marlborough.

On becoming a wealthy widow after the death of her second husband, Oliver Hazard Parry Belmont, in 1908, she developed an interest in women's rights and became involved with militant feminism. In 1914 she invited **Christabel Pankhurst** to the USA to speak, and she also donated huge sums of money to the cause. From 1921 to 1933 she was President of the National Woman's party. Other good causes that benefited from her generosity included children's hospitals.

Benedict, Ruth, *née* Fulton

Born 1887 Died 1948
American anthropologist who had a profound
influence on cultural anthropology

Ruth Fulton was born in New York City, the

daughter of a surgeon. She studied philosophy and English literature at Vassar before going on to study anthropology under Alexander Goldenweiser and Franz Boas at Columbia University. She married Stanley R Benedict in 1914.

Her most important contribution to the US culture-and-personality movement in the 1930s and 1940s lay in her 'configurational' approach to entire cultures, according to which each culture tends to predispose its individual members to adopt an ideal type of personality. Thus every culture, she believed, could be characterized in terms of its own distinctive ethos.

Her best-known works include *Patterns of Culture* (1934), *Race: Science and Politics* (1940), which is a book against racism, and *The Chrysanthemum and the Sword: Patterns of Japanese Culture* (1946). In 1948, the year of her death, she became professor at Columbia University.

Benesh, Joan, *née* Rothwell

Born 1920
English dance notator whose dance notation system is now used to document all Royal Ballet productions

Joan Rothwell was born in Liverpool. She became a member of the Sadler's Wells Ballet and married a painter, Rudolph Benesh (1916–75), with whom in 1955 she copyrighted a dance notation system called Choreology. This is now used to document all important Royal Ballet productions and has been included in the syllabus of London's Royal Academy of Dancing.

The couple opened their own Institute in 1962 and their influence on a vast number of notators and educators has been incalculable.

Bennett, Jill

Born 1931 Died 1990
English actress who often played in the works of her husband, John Osborne

Jill Bennett was born in London. She made her début at Stratford in 1949, and in London in 1950. She scored her first major success in Jean Anouilh's *Dinner With The Family* in 1957, and went on to establish a considerable reputation as an elegant, sharp-witted actress, both in classical and contemporary drama.

She married the playwright John Osborne (1929–94) in 1968, and played in a number of his works, including *Time Present* (1968), *West of Suez* (1971), *Watch It Come Down* (1976), as well as an acclaimed title role in his version of

Henrik Ibsen's classic drama *Hedda Gabler* in 1972.

Bennett, Louie

Born 1870 Died 1956
Irish trade unionist instrumental in drawing attention to the plight of women workers

Louie Bennett was born in Temple Hill, Dublin, and was educated at Alexandra College, London, before studying singing in Bonn and writing several novels. In 1911 she was involved in the founding of the Irish-women's Suffrage Federation, becoming its secretary in 1913. She was concerned to draw attention to the state of women's wages and their conditions of employment, and jointly founded the Irish Women's Reform League. Through this association she sought to alleviate the conditions of women workers, as well as furthering the cause of women's suffrage.

She campaigned for peace during World War I, representing Ireland on the International Executive of the Women's League for Peace and Freedom. She was also a prominent member of the Women Workers' Union, and in 1932 became the first woman President of the Irish Trades Union Congress. Although a member of the Labour Party Administrative Council, she was an unsuccessful Labour candidate in 1944.

Bennett, Louise Simone, *also known as* Miss Lou

Born 1919
Jamaican poet, one of the leading writers of the oral culture of Jamaica

Louise Bennett was born in Kingston and educated at Excelsior High School. She studied journalism by correspondence course before going to the Royal Academy of Dramatic Art in London in 1945. After graduating she taught drama in Jamaica, performed in theatres in Britain and America and lectured widely on Jamaican folklore and music. In 1954 she married the Jamaican actor and impresario Eric Coverley.

Her numerous books include retellings of Jamaican folk-stories and collections of her own ballads and verse monologues. Her use of Jamaican dialect and speech rhythms, humour and satirical wit for the purposes of social and political comment have made her one of the outstanding performance poets of the 20th century.

Among her publications is the poetry collection *Jamaican Labrish* (1966), of which she was editor.

Benois, Nadia (Nadezhda Leontievna)

Born 1896 Died 1975
Russian painter of landscapes and flowers who
also designed ballet and theatre sets

Nadia Benois was born in St Petersburg, the daughter of a court architect and professor of architecture. She studied first with her uncle and then at a private academy in St Petersburg under Shoukhaer. She married Jonah Ustinov in 1920, and moved with him to England. In 1921 their son Peter Ustinov was born, who became an actor and playwright and wrote the play *House of Regrets* (1942), for which she designed the set.

Benois continued to paint, and her travels in Scotland, France, Wales and Ireland inspired her landscape paintings which were impressionist in style. She exhibited her work in London, Paris, Pittsburgh and in Canada.

From 1932 she began designing sets and costumes for several ballet companies, including the Ballet Rambert. She also worked closely with the French avant-garde theatre company Compagnie Quinze.

Benoit, Joan *see* Samuelson, Joan Benoit

Berberian, Cathy (Catherine)

Born 1925 Died 1983
American soprano and composer whose
remarkable voice inspired many to compose
works for her

Cathy Berberian was born in Attleboro, Massachusetts, of Armenian extraction. She studied music and drama at Columbia University and New York University (1942–3).

She was married to the composer Luciano Berio from 1950 to 1966 and he wrote many works for her, including *Circles* (1960), which she performed on her American début, *Sequenza III* (1963) and *Recital I* (1971). Many other composers, including Stravinsky and Henri Pousseur, wrote pieces for her remarkable voice. She also performed work as diverse as Monteverdi and Lennon/McCartney.

Her own compositions include *Stripsody* (1966), an unaccompanied 'cartoon' for vocalist, and *Morsicat(h)y* (1971) for piano.

Berenice

1st century BC
Princess of the Jewish Idumean dynasty

Berenice was the daughter of Costobarus and Salome, who was a sister of Herod I ('the Great'). She was married to her cousin Aris-

tobulus from c.17BC and their children were Herod of Chalcis, Herod Agrippa I (father of the Jewish **Berenice**), Aristobulus, Herodias and Mariamne.

She allegedly set in motion the plot to murder her husband by her uncle Herod, whose brother-in-law Theudion she later married. Her third husband was Archelaus, whom she married when Theudion was executed for scheming against Herod.

Berenice I

Floreat c.317BC–c.275BC
Macedonian princess who became Queen of Egypt
as the wife of Ptolemy I (ruled 323–283BC)

Berenice was born in Macedonia and came to Egypt as a lady-in-waiting to Eurydice, who became the second wife of Ptolemy I Soter. Ptolemy married Berenice as his third wife in c.317BC and made her Queen of Egypt in 290.

Their son became Ptolemy II Philadelphus when he succeeded his father in 283, and their daughter **Arsinoë** married Ptolemy II as his second wife.

Berenice II

Born c.269BC Died 221BC
Princess of Cyrene who became the wife of
Ptolemy III

Berenice was the daughter of Magas, King of Cyrene. Her mother wanted her to marry a Macedonian prince called Demetrius the Fair, but she arranged for Demetrius to be murdered and married Ptolemy III Euergetes (247BC) instead, thus uniting Cyrene (in modern Libya) with Egypt.

When her husband went to fight in the Third Syrian War to avenge the murder of his sister (**Berenice** Syra), Berenice dedicated a lock of her hair to Aphrodite for his safe return. According to the court astronomer, the hair ended up in heaven and became the constellation Coma Berenices ('Hair of Berenice').

Berenice's son Ptolemy IV Philopater succeeded his father and began his reign by having her poisoned; he married his sister Arsinoë III.

Berenice III

Died c.80BC
Egyptian princess who became queen and ruled
during an unsettled and violent time

Berenice was the daughter of Ptolemy IX and either Cleopatra Selene or Cleopatra IV. Her first husband was her uncle, Ptolemy X, and she became queen after the death in 101BC of the dowager queen Cleopatra III, Ptolemy VIII's widow.

The people of Alexandria, thinking that Ptolemy had murdered Cleopatra, rebelled and expelled him in 87BC, so he raised an army in Syria and returned to Egypt, where he plundered the tomb of Alexander the Great to pay his soldiers. Expelled again, he fled to Asia Minor, taking Berenice with him.

She returned to Egypt after his death in 80BC and became sole ruler of Egypt. With the help of the Roman dictator Cornelius Sulla, Ptolemy Alexander, the son of Ptolemy X, went to Egypt to marry Berenice, but when she refused to marry and surrender her authority, he had her murdered.

Berenice IV

Died 55BC
Egyptian princess who became Queen of Egypt for three years

Berenice was the daughter of Ptolemy XII Auletes and the elder sister of **Cleopatra**. While her father was forced by impending insurrection away from Egypt in 58–55BC, his wife died and Berenice was proclaimed queen.

Towards the end of her reign, Alexandria was attacked by Aulus Gabinius, the Roman proconsul of Syria. Ptolemy XII was recalled in 55BC, whereupon he had his daughter murdered.

Berenice, *known as* Berenice Syra

Born c.280BC Died c.246BC
Queen of Syria as the wife of Antiochus II

Berenice was the daughter of Ptolemy II. In 252BC she married Antiochus II of Syria, which brought about a hiatus in the fighting between the Egyptians and the Seleucids.

When Antiochus died however, Antiochus's divorced wife Laodice (who had been exiled with her children on his marriage to Berenice) plotted the death of the queen and her young son, enabling her own son to succeed as Seleucus II.

Berenice's brother Ptolemy III Euergetes came from Egypt to Syria to avenge his sister's death, an act which resulted in the Third Syrian War.

Berenice, *known as* the Jewish Berenice

Born c.28AD Died after AD79
Princess of the Jewish Idumean dynasty who became the mistress of the Roman emperor Titus but never his wife

Berenice was the daughter of Herod Agrippa I and Cypros. Her first husband died before consummating their marriage, so she was married again, this time to her uncle Herod of Chalcis. After she had given birth to two sons, he died (AD48) and Berenice moved to live at the court of her brother, Agrippa II, with whom she allegedly had an incestuous relationship. To quell such rumours she married a Cilician priest-king, but soon returned to Agrippa, with whom she worked in vain trying to prevent a rebellion by the Jews.

After the recapture of Jerusalem by Rome (AD70), she became the mistress of Flavius Titus (AD39–81), Emperor Vespasian's son, who had noticed her some years earlier during a visit to Judaea. They made no secret of living together in Rome, but Titus was advised, on account of Berenice's race, to send her away. The love affair continued to lack the fulfilment of marriage, even when Berenice returned to Rome around AD79, the year Titus became emperor. She became the model for the tragic heroine of Jean Racine's *Berenice* (1670) and Pierre Corneille's *Tite et Bérénice* (1670).

Berenson, Senda

Born 1868 Died 1954
American physical education instructor and basketball player credited with introducing the game to female players

Senda Berenson was born in Lithuania. She became a physical education teacher at Smith College and introduced the game of basketball to her students in 1893, after reading about the new game in the YMCA publication *Physical Education*. The game had been conceived two years before by Dr James Naismith, a PE instructor at the YMCA Training School in Springfield, Massachusetts.

Berenson established the first official rules for girls in 1899, and chaired the American Association for the Advancement of Physical Education Committee on Basketball for Girls for 12 years. In 1901 she wrote *Line Basket Ball for Women*, the first published rules for women's basketball.

Thirty years after her death, she was inducted into the Naismith Memorial Basketball Hall of Fame and the International Women's Sports Hall of Fame for her contribution to women's basketball.

Beresford-Howe, Constance

Born 1922
Canadian novelist and short-story writer whose later work challenges conventional attitudes to domesticity and sexuality

Constance Beresford-Howe was born in Montreal and educated at McGill and Brown universities. She later taught at the former and at Ryerson Polytechnical Institute in Toronto. With the exception of the historical romance *My Lady Greensleeves* (1955), her novels deal with contemporary women, her first three — *The Unreasoning Heart* (1946), *Of This Day's Journey* (1947) and *The Invisible Gate* (1949)— focusing on young women at critical stages of their worldly development.

Of her later books, *A Population of One* (1977) follows a single woman's plunge into the academic world, while *Night Studies* (1985) records the dismal lives of the students and staff at an urban college of further education. Her most famous novel, however, is *A Book of Eve* (1973), in which the eponymous protagonist, a woman in her mid-sixties, leaves her husband of 40 years to start a new life alone on the other side of Montreal. Like her other novels, it is compassionate, witty and gently effective.

Patty Berg, 1963

Berg, Leila

Born 1917

English children's writer and editor whose work in children's education drew attention to the urban, working-class environment

Leila Berg was born in Salford, Lancashire. Her *Look At Kids* (1972), illustrated with unsentimental black-and-white photographs of urban life, was as influential, in its way, as the Plowden report (see Lady **Plowden**).

While Berg was an editor at Macmillan, she launched the 'Nippers' series of primary-school readers, many of which she wrote herself. These were criticized for the stereotyped portrait they drew of working-class life and have become museum pieces of the 1970s.

As a story-teller her work is longer-lasting. *A Box For Benny* (1958) is still enjoyed.

Berg, Patty (Patricia Jane)

Born 1918

American golfer considered the best woman golfer in the USA by the time she was 20

Patty Berg was born in Minneapolis, Minnesota. She began playing in amateur competition in 1933, and won the Minnesota State championships in 1935, 1936 and 1938. By the age of 20 she was considered the foremost female golfer in the USA.

In 1938 she won the US amateur title in 10 of the 13 tournaments she entered. The Associated Press named her Outstanding Female Athlete of that year, as well as of 1943 and 1955. She co-founded the LPGA (Ladies

Professional Golf Association) which was officially chartered in 1950, serving as its president from 1949 (when discussions began) to 1952. She has earned a place in several Halls of Fame — that of the LPGA (1951), world Golf (1974), PGA (Professional Golfers Association) in 1978, and the International Women's Sports (1980).

Berganza, Teresa

Born 1935

Spanish mezzo-soprano who became noted for her Rossini roles

Teresa Berganza was born in Madrid, where she made her début in 1955. She first sang in England at Glyndebourne (1958). She appeared at Covent Garden in 1960 and subsequently in concert and opera in Vienna, Milan, Edinburgh, in Israel, the USA and elsewhere. She has also given recitals with her pianist husband Felix Lavilla.

Her most noteworthy Rossini roles include Rosina in *Il Barbiere di Siviglia* and Cenerentola (Cinderella) in *La Cenerentola*.

Bergen, Candice

Born 1946

American actress who has found fame on television, especially as Murphy Brown

Candice Bergen was born in Beverly Hills, California, the daughter of ventriloquist Edgar Bergen (1903–78). She attended school in Switzerland and modelled before dropping out of school to pursue an acting career. She made her film début in *The Group* (1966) and emerged as a leading lady in the cinema of the 1970s.

Adept at portraying strong-willed, intelligent women of the world, she has appeared in such films as *Carnal Knowledge* (1971), *The Wind and the Lion* (1975) and *Starting Over* (1979), for which she received an Academy Award nomination. She is also an accomplished photojournalist, and played **Margaret Bourke-White** in *Gandhi* (1982). Her greatest success came with the television series *Murphy Brown* (1988–   ) in which her outspoken character became a barometer of public attitudes to the single mother in modern America.

She was married to French film director Louis Malle (1932–95) from 1980, and published an autobiography, *Knock Wood*, in 1984.

Berggol'ts, Ol'ga Fëdorovna

Born 1910   Died 1975
Russian poet for whom the theme of war pervaded her life and work

Ol'ga Berggol'ts was born in St Petersburg. She married the poet Boris Kornilov, who was murdered by Stalin in the Purges (1937); she herself was imprisoned for two years. Although she had published her first book in 1934, she became well known only when she organized resistance, and made highly effective daily broadcasts in Leningrad (now St Petersburg again) when it was besieged by the Nazis throughout World War II. She survived the blockade, but her second husband died of starvation.

Her autobiographical lyrical prose effusion *Dnevnye zvyozdy* (1959, 'Stars in Daytime' or 'Diurnal Stars') received high praise; her poetry is well constructed and poignant in its sincerity.

Berghmans, Ingrid

Born 1961
Belgian judo player who is to date the most successful female player in the history of the sport

Ingrid Berghmans was born in Hasselt. A tall player, she prefers an upright style of play and is well known for her grace, strength and femininity.

A fourth dan who married fellow player Marc Vallot in 1990, she has won a record six world titles, picking up an additional four silvers and a bronze. She was Olympic champion in 1988, when judo was a demonstration sport, and was European champion three times at the 72kg level and three times at Open level. She has won the British Open numerous times, as well as Japan's Fukuoka title and the Canadian Open title.

Bergman, Ingrid

Born 1915   Died 1982
Swedish film and stage actress, an unaffected and vivacious popular romatic heroine

Ingrid Bergman was born in Stockholm and trained at the Royal Dramatic Theatre. She was offered a contract by Svenskfilmindustri and made her film début in *Munkbrogreven* (1934). She was then signed by producer David O Selznick to appear in an English-language remake of *Intermezzo* (1939), and gained much popularity as a romantic star in such films as *Casablanca* (1942), *Spellbound* (1945) and *Notorious* (1946).

In 1952 she gave birth to the illegitimate child of director Roberto Rossellini — Isabella Rossellini. The ensuing scandal led to her ostracization from the American film industry, but she continued her career in Europe and was welcomed back by Hollywood on her return in 1956. In later years she worked on stage and television.

Her last film was Ingmar Bergman's *Autumn Sonata* (1978), a deeply-felt exploration of a mother–daughter relationship. She received seven Best Actress Academy Award nominations, winning the award for *Gaslight* (1943, Award 1944) and *Anastasia* (1956) and the Best Supporting Actress Award for *Murder on the Orient Express* (1974).

Bergner, Elisabeth

Born 1900   Died 1986
Austrian actress whose major successes were in the works of Wedekind and Shaw

Elisabeth Bergner was born in Vienna. She made her stage début in Zurich, but earned her reputation in Berlin in the 1920s, where she was particularly associated with the Expressionist dramas of Frank Wedekind, and had an international success in the title role of George Bernard Shaw's *St Joan* in 1924.

She moved to London, where her boyish figure and elfin looks so captivated J M Barrie that he wrote *The Boy David* (1936) for her. She fled to Switzerland after its humiliating failure, and spent the war years in America, before returning to Europe in 1951.

She was awarded the Schiller Prize for her contribution to German culture in 1963.

Bernadette of Lourdes, St, *originally* Marie-Bernarde Soubirous

Born 1844 Died 1879
*French visionary who saw the Virgin **Mary** at*
Lourdes, a site now famous for its miracles of
healing

Bernadette was born in Lourdes, Hautes-Pyrénées, the daughter of a miller. She claimed to have received 18 apparitions of the Blessed Virgin during the year 1858, when she was 14, and though she was a sickly child and poorly educated, she managed to convince the authorities of the Church and State of the veracity of her experience.

The visions took place at the Massabielle Rock, which has since become a notable place of pilgrimage as the shrine of Lourdes, renowned for the many miracles of healing that have since occurred there. Bernadette joined the Sisters of Charity at Nevers in 1866, where she was well loved for her kind and holy nature.

She was beatified in 1925 and canonized in 1933. Her feast day is 16 April or sometimes 18 February in France.

Bernard, Jessie Shirley, *née* Ravitch

Born 1903
American sociologist and author of challenging
and popular feminist works

Jessie Ravitch was born in Minneapolis, Minnesota. She studied at the University of Minnesota where she met Luther Lee Bernard, whom she married in 1925. She worked alongside him, and together they produced works which included *Origins of American Sociology* (1943).

In 1947 the couple moved to Pennsylvania State University, where she wrote *American Community Behaviour* (1949), three years before her husband's death and her subsequent extensive trip to Europe. She resigned from Pennsylvania State University in 1964, and pursued a career as an influential and ground-breaking feminist writer. Her pertinent analyses include the following: *The Sex Game* (1968), *Women, Wives and Mothers* (1975) and *The Female World from a Global Perspective* (1987).

Berners, Juliana, *also called* Dame Julyans Barnes *or* Bernes

Born c.1388
English prioress and the author of some of the
earliest published writings in English by a woman

Juliana Berners was either the daughter of Sir James Berners (one of Richard II's favourites who was beheaded soon after his daughter's birth), or the wife of the lord of the manor of Julians Barns near St Albans, which would explain her other name, Dame Julyans Barnes. Some traditions hold that after 1430 she was the prioress of Sopwell nunnery in St Albans, Hertfordshire, but this seems unlikely.

She was a woman of great beauty and learning, and like other fashionable noblewomen of her day, took part in several different fieldsports, which provided material for her writings, such as her *Treatyse perteynynge to Hawkynge, Huntynge, Fysshynge, and Coote Armiris*. This formed part of the multi-authoured *Boke of St Albans*, the last version of which was published in 1486 on the St Albans press which had been established just seven years previously.

Bernhardt, Sarah, *originally* Henriette Rosine Bernard, *known as* the Divine Sarah

Born 1844 Died 1923
French actress, certainly the greatest tragedienne
of her day and possibly the most versatile ever

Sarah Bernhardt was born in Paris. She entered the Paris Conservatoire in 1859, and made her début in 1862 as 'Iphigénie' at the Théâtre Français, but attracted little notice. In 1867 she played minor parts at the Odéon, but won fame as 'Zanetto' in Coppée's *Le Passant* (1869) and as 'Queen of Spain' in *Ruy Blas* (1872), and was recalled to the Théâtre Français.

After 1876 she made frequent appearances in London, America and Europe, becoming renowned for the purity of her diction, among other attributes. In 1882 she married Jacques Daria or Damala (d.1889), a Greek actor, from whom she was divorced shortly afterwards. In 1916 her French nationality was restored. She founded the Théâtre Sarah Bernhardt in 1899.

In 1915 she had a leg amputated, but did not abandon the stage. She was a legendary figure in the theatre world, who also painted and wrote poetry and plays.

Bernstein, Aline, *née* Frankau

Born 1881 Died 1955
American costume and set designer who
contributed to the success of many Broadway
productions

Aline Frankau was born in New York. Her original ambition was to be a portrait painter, but she became involved in theatre as a founder of the Neighbourhood Playhouse in

1915, and went on to great success as a designer for the stage.

She produced sets for the Theatre Guild and **Eva Le Gallienne**'s Civic Repertory Theatre, as well as for Broadway productions, with notable successes in Anton Chekov's *The Cherry Orchard* (1928) and *The Seagull* (1929), and **Lillian Hellman**'s *The Children's Hour* (1934) and *The Little Foxes* (1939).

She also co-founded the Museum of Costume Art in 1937, now part of the Metropolitan Museum of New York.

Bertha of Kent

Born after 561   Died after 601
Early Christian queen who helped to bring about
Augustine's mission to Britain

Bertha was the daughter of the Frankish King Charibert of Paris. She married King Ethelbert of Kent on condition that she was allowed to practise her Christian faith and bring her chaplain, Bishop Liudhard, with her. Ethelbert gave her the old church of St Martin, outside Canterbury, to use as she wished.

Bertha and her chaplain had enough Christian influence in Kent to persuade Pope Gregory to send letters to both her and her husband, commending the coming of Augustine and his band of missionaries. When they arrived they were allowed to use the queen's church until Ethelbert became a Christian and they could preach openly.

Besant, Annie, *née* Wood

Born 1847   Died 1933
English theosophist and social reformer, an early
advocate of birth control and an ardent socialist

Annie Wood was born in London of Irish parentage. After her separation in 1873 from her husband, the Rev Frank Besant, brother of the novelist and reformer Sir Walter Besant, she became in 1874 Vice-President of the National Secular Society. She was closely associated with the social reformer Charles Bradlaugh, and became an ardent proponent of birth control and socialism.

During the 1880s she was influenced by George Bernard Shaw and made her name as a Fabian socialist. In 1889, after meeting Madame **Blavatsky**, she developed an interest in theosophy, and went out to India, where she became involved in politics. She was particulary in favour of Indian independence, and established the Indian Home Rule League in 1916. From 1917 to 1923 she was President of the Indian National Congress.

Her publications include *The Gospel of Atheism* (1877) and *Theosophy and the New Psychology* (1904).

Bessmertnova, Natalya Igorevna

Born 1941
Russian ballerina who has excelled in all the major
roles of the classical repertory

Natalya Bessmertnova was born in Moscow. She trained at the Bolshoi Ballet School (1952–61) and joined the company upon graduation, remaining a soloist there until 1988.

As well as excelling in all the major roles of the classical repertory, she has figured significantly in ballets devised by her husband Yuriy Grigorovich (1927–), particularly *Ivan the Terrible* (1975).

Bethune, Jennie Louise, *née* Blanchard

Born 1856   Died 1913
American architect who in 1888 joined the
American Institute of Architects as the first
woman Fellow

Jennie Blanchard was born in Waterloo, New York, and was educated at home by her parents. She expressed an interest in buildings and prepared to attend Cornell University to study architecture, but instead took an apprenticeship with Richard Waite in an established architectural practice. She soon became his assistant and received what was considered a man's training in a male profession largely through her own self-motivation.

When she was 25 she opened her own office in Buffalo, where she had moved with her family. Louise married a colleague from Waite's office, Robert Bethune, and set up a partnership with him. Her reputation gained her an enthusiastic reception when she was admitted to the Western Association of Architects in 1885, which was followed three years later by admittance to the American Institute of Architects.

Bethune, Mary McLeod, *née* McLeod

Born 1875   Died 1955
American educator and administrator who
advised President Roosevelt on minority groups

Mary McLeod Bethune was born in Mayesville, South Carolina, to parents who had been slaves before the American Civil War. She began her career by teaching in Southern schools, then in 1904 opened the Daytona Normal and Industrial Institute for Girls which merged in 1923 with the Cookman

Institute to become the co-educational Bethune–Cookman College, of which Bethune was president until 1942 and then again in 1946–7. She was also founder-President of the National Council of Negro Women (1935–49).

While serving as adviser to President Franklin D Roosevelt's New Deal administration, she worked to expand awareness of minority issues within government agencies. At a time when 40 per cent of black youths were suffering unemployment, she was director of the division of Negro Affairs within the National Youth Administration, and as such she was quietly insistent that the number of blacks enrolled in the programme be increased despite the reluctance of state administrators. Black college students also benefited from the Special Negro Fund which she administered.

In 1945 she was accredited by the State Department to attend the San Francisco Conference to establish the United Nations.

Bhutto, Benazir

Born 1953
Pakistani politician who as prime minister became the first modern-day woman leader of a Muslim nation

Benazir Bhutto was born in Karachi, the daughter of the former prime minister Zulfikar Ali Bhutto (1928–79, leader 1971–7). She was educated at Oxford University, where she became President of the Union. She returned to Pakistan in 1977 and was placed under frequent house arrest between then and 1984,

Benazir Bhutto, 1994

after the military coup led by General Zia ul-Haq.

Between 1984 and 1986, with her mother Nusrat (1934–), she moved to England and became the joint leader in exile of the opposition Pakistan People's Party (PPP). After the lifting of martial law in December 1985, she returned to Pakistan in April 1986 to launch a nationwide campaign for 'open elections'. She married Asif Ali Zardari, a wealthy landowner, in 1987 and, following the death of General Zia ul-Haq, was elected prime minister in 1988, barely three months after giving birth to her first child.

She led her country back into the Commonwealth in 1989 and became, in 1990, the first head of government to bear a child while in office. That year she was removed from the premiership by presidential decree and defeated in the elections, but she returned to power in the elections of 1993.

Biermann, Aenne, *née* Anna Sibilla Sternefeld

Born 1898 Died 1933
German photographer whose work exemplifies the 'new objectivity' of the time

Anna Sternefeld was born to a prosperous family in Goch am Niederrhein, Germany. She moved to Gera in 1920 on her marriage to a businessman with a strong interest in literature, Herbert Biermann, with whom she had a daughter, Helga (b.1921), and a son, Gershon (b.1923). Her interest in photography began in 1921, with taking pictures of her baby daughter, and continued to grow. Her serious work in photography was initiated by a meeting in 1929 with the geologist Rudolf Hundt, with whom she later collaborated on photographing minerals.

Her best-known work, produced between 1929 and 1932, comprises sensitive studies of childhood and also portraits and photographs of buildings, structures, animals, plants and objects natural and artificial. These are innovative in the manner of the *Neue Sachlichkeit*, or 'new objectivity', in which modernist artists, including practitioners of the 'new photography', adopted strategies which forced the viewer to look at familiar subject matter in an unfamiliar way.

Her photographs were included in important group exhibitions such as 'Film und Foto' (1929, Stuttgart) and 'Die neue Fotographie' (1930, Basle), and a book of her work with text by Franz Roh, *Fototek 2: Aenne Biermann*, was published in 1930.

Bigelow, Kathryn

Born 1952
American film director who has made her mark
in the traditional male preserve of the action
thriller

Kathryn Bigelow began her career as a painter, but switched to filmmaking after enrolling at Columbia University graduate film school in New York. She worked initially as a script supervisor and as an actress before co-directing *The Loveless* (1984).

Her first commercial success arrived with the contemporary horror film *Near Dark* 1987. Her stylish direction earned her attention, and her reputation was enhanced by her best film, the tense police thriller *Blue Steel* (1990), which also offered **Jamie Lee Curtis** a particularly challenging role. Her other films include *Point Break* (1991) and *Strange Days* (1995).

Biggs, Rosemary

Born 1912
English haematologist who is jointly credited with
describing a clotting disorder called 'Christmas
disease'

Rosemary Biggs was born in London. She obtained a PhD in Mycology at the University of Toronto before training in medicine at the London School of Medicine for Women, from which she graduated in 1943.

She worked as an Assistant Pathologist in Oxford from 1944 to 1959, becoming Deputy Director and then Director (1967–77) of the Oxford Haemophilia Centre and an honorary consultant haematologist. She also wrote or co-authored several influential textbooks on blood-clotting mechanisms and disorders.

Bijns, Anna

Born 1493 Died 1575
Dutch poet, a strongly religious woman who
became the first major woman poet writing in
Dutch or Flemish

Anna Bijns was from Antwerp, in what is now Belgium, and worked as a schoolteacher. She took up writing verse at the behest of the Catholic Church. Many of her poems are a response to the spread of Protestantism in the northern Netherlands, others are simply devotional and a few are more earthly love poems.

Her work is still very highly regarded in Holland and Belgium. *Schoon Ende suverlijc*

boecken inhoudende veel — constige refereinen (1987) is a superb facsimile edition of her 1528 original, with the original woodcuts and a modern commentary,

Billington-Greig, Teresa, *née* Billington

Born 1877 Died 1964
English suffragette, socialist and writer, author of
The Militant Suffrage Movement

Teresa Billington was born in Blackburn and educated at a convent school and through Manchester University extension classes. A teacher and a member of the Independent Labour Party, she was secretary of the Manchester Equal Pay League, and first met **Emmeline Pankhurst** when her job was threatened for refusing to teach religious instruction.

A friend of the Pankhursts and **Annie Kenney**, Billington-Greig joined the Women's Social and Political Union in 1903 and became its London organizer in 1907. However in 1907, in dispute with the Pankhursts, she founded the Women's Freedom League with **Charlotte Despard** and **Edith How-Martyn**.

Though an ardent suffragette, twice imprisoned in Holloway for her activities, she became a critic of the more militant suffragists, as she indicates in *The Militant Suffrage Movement* (1911).

Binchy, Maeve

Born 1940
Irish novelist, playwright and short-story writer
who clearly depicts strong female characters
and friendships

Maeve Binchy was born in Dublin and educated at University College, Dublin.

She worked as a teacher and part-time travel writer before joining the *Irish Times* in 1969, later becoming the paper's London correspondent. She has had plays staged in Dublin and won awards in Ireland and Prague for her television play *Deeply Regretted By* (1979).

Her collections of short stories include observations on the lives of Londoners in *Victoria Line, Central Line* (1987) and Dubliners in *Dublin 4* (1982). Her novels include *Light a Penny Candle* (1982), *Firefly Summer* (1987), *The Copper Beech* (1992) and *The Glass Lake* (1994). Binchy excels at exploring the private ambitions, joys and anguish of ordinary individuals and families and at evoking everyday life in small communities.

Bing, Ilse

Born 1899
German photojournalist and advertising photographer whose work was published in various French magazines of the 1930s

Ilse Bing was born in Frankfurt into a rich middle-class family. Trained in music and art, she attended the Universität Frankfurt from 1920. She began a postgraduate degree in history of art in 1924 and began photographing in 1928 to illustrate her dissertation on the German architect Friedrich Gilly.

She abandoned her academic studies in 1929 and the following year went to Paris where her photographic work was widely published in, for example, *Vu* and *Le Monde Illustré*. She visited New York in 1936, where she was offered a staff position on *Life* magazine, which she refused. Her work was included in important exhibitions in the USA, for example the 1937 exhibition at the Museum of Modern Art, New York: 'Photography, 1839–1937'. Also, that year, Bing married pianist and musicologist Konrad Wolff; together they emigrated to New York in 1941.

After 1959 she gave up photography. Her work was 're-discovered' in 1976 when it was included in two major exhibitions in New York at the Museum of Modern Art and the Witkin Gallery. Her publications include *Words as Visions* (1974).

Binh, Nguyen Thi

Born 1927
Vietnamese patriot who played a key role in the Vietnam War

Nguyen Thi Binh was born in South Vietnam into a family of Vietnamese patriots and dedicated herself at an early age to carrying on the work of her father and grandfather. In 1951 she was imprisoned for her political activities until the French rule ended in 1954. Resuming the fight for independence she fought against the Vietnamese dictator Diem and later the USA.

When the provisional government was formed in 1969 she was appointed Foreign Minister and in 1973, as representative of the National Liberation Front, she signed the treaty that ended the war. In 1979 she was appointed Minister of Education in the United Government and 1992 she was appointed Vice-President of Vietnam.

Bird, Bonnie

Born 1914 Died 1995
American dancer and teacher who greatly influenced British dance education and contemporary dance and choreography

Bonnie Bird was born in Portland, Oregon. She was Head of Dance at the Cornish School of Fine Arts between the years 1937 and 1940, where her students included Merce Cunningham and Jane Dudley. She married Ralph Gundlach in 1938. After World War II she founded the dance company the Merry-Go Rounders, chaired the American Dance Guild (1965–7), and was partly responsible for founding the Congress on Research in Dance.

Together with Marion North, Bird reshaped the Laban Centre for Movement and Dance from 1974, introducing professional training for dancers and Britain's first degree course in Dance Studies (1977). Bird also provided the inspiration for the *Dance Theatre Journal*, for which she acted as an editorial adviser from its creation in 1983 until her death. Also in 1983 she formed the Transitions Dance Company, which was designed to provide student dancers with experience in new choreography; a year later she founded the New Choreography Fund, which has both sponsored works and undertaken research.

Isabella Bird (biography on next page)

Bird, Isabella (Lucy), *married name* Bishop

Born 1831   Died 1904
English writer and pioneering traveller of unusual courage

Isabella Bird was born in Boroughbridge, Yorkshire. From 1854 she visited Canada and the USA, the Sandwich Islands, the Rocky Mountains, Yezo, Persia and Kurdistan, Tibet, Korea and Morocco. In 1881 she married another traveller, Dr John Bishop.

Her written work includes *Englishwoman in America* (1856) and many other travel books, such as *The Hawaiian Archipelago* (1874) and *The Yangtze Valley and Beyond* (1899). As well as a being successful writer, she was an active philanthropist and missionary. In 1889 she organized the building of two hospitals in India and in 1894 she set out for China as a missionary and founded three hospitals and an orphanage. In 1892 she became the first woman fellow of the Royal Geographical Society.

Isabella Bird Bishop provides the basis for one of **Caryl Churchill**'s characters in *Top Girls*. (*See illustration on previous page.*)

Birgitta, St, *also called* Bridget

Born 1303   Died 1373
Swedish visionary, one of Sweden's earliest authors whose revelations became popular reading

Birgitta was born in Finsta in Uppland. She had her first revelations of the Virgin **Mary** at the age of seven. At the age of 13 she was married to Ulf Gudmarsson, a young nobleman who became a lawman. They had eight children. She gained considerable political insight through travel and service at the Swedish court and during her life undertook several pilgrimages, to Trondheim (1338), Santiago de Compostela (1341) and Palestine and Cyprus (1372).

She was widowed in 1344, and subsequently moved to Rome where she founded a Swedish hospice and gathered a circle of devoted disciples. Inspired by a series of revelations, she founded the monastery of Vadstena in Sweden; it became the cradle of the new order of Birgittines as a branch of the Augustinian order, which at its peak had more than 80 convents throughout Europe.

Birgitta died in Rome on returning from her Palestinian pilgrimage and was canonized in 1391. Her numerous revelations were recorded and edited by her confessors and

St Birgitta

published in Latin after her death as *Revelationes cælestes* (there is also a 14th-century translation into Swedish). Many were of a political nature and critical of both the throne and the Church in Sweden or of the papal exile in Avignon. Characterized by vivid realistic detail and an abundant imagery, frequently inspired by her experiences as a mother, they were widely circulated and enjoyed a huge international reputation. Birgitta's daughter, St Katarina of Sweden (1335–81), was canonized in 1489.

Biryukova, Alexandra Pavlovna

Born 1929
Soviet politician who achieved a high position of political importance for a woman in the USSR

Alexandra Biryukova was trained as a textile engineer and continued until as late as 1968 with her professional job in a factory. However, she had earlier taken official jobs, and in 1968 she became Secretary of the Trade Union Presidium and in 1985 Deputy Chairman.

In 1986 Mikhail Gorbachev selected her for the Secretariat of the Central Committee of the Communist Party and in 1988 appointed her Deputy Prime Minister responsible for Social Development. She was also made a candidate member of the Politburo, the first woman since **Yekaterina Furtseva** to achieve this distinction.

She was one of the few Soviet women to reach a position of political importance, but in the turmoil of 1990–1, she was pushed aside.

Bishop, Ann

Born 1899   Died 1990
English protozoologist and parasitologist who
investigated the mechanisms of drug resistance

Ann Bishop was born in Manchester. After graduating from Manchester University in 1921, she accepted an unofficial, part-time teaching post in the Department of Zoology at Cambridge, where she and **Sidnie Manton** were the only women. She also became a research fellow at Girton College, which she remained until her retirement in 1967, when she was made a Life Fellow.

In 1929 she was awarded a Beit Fellowship at the Molteno Institute for Parasitology in Cambridge, where she remained for the rest of her career. Her work on understanding the life cycle of parasitic protozoa, especially those causing malaria, provided a valuable resource during World War II, when chemotherapeutic alternatives to quinine were desperately needed. She was elected a Fellow of the Royal Society in 1959.

Bishop, Elizabeth

Born 1911   Died 1979
American poet and short-story writer noted for
the elegance and imaginative power of her verse

Elizabeth Bishop was born in Worcester, Massachusetts, brought up by her grandmother and an aunt in Boston, and educated at Vassar College.

Her witty, precise verse often evokes images of nature. Her first collection, *North and South* (1946), was reprinted with additions as *Poems: North and South — A Cold Spring* (1955) and received the 1956 Pulitzer Prize for poetry. Her short stories were published in the *New Yorker* magazine, among others.

She lived in Brazil from 1952 to 1967, wrote a travel book, *Brazil* (1962), and taught at Harvard from 1970. A *Complete Poems* was published in 1979.

Bishop, Isabella Bird *see* Bird, Isabella

Bjornson, Maria

Born 1949
British stage designer with a painter's eye for
detail and overall effect

Maria Bjornson was born in Paris of Norwegian and Romanian parents.

She has designed sets and costumes for straight drama and opera and is noted for her expressive use of fabrics. She worked extensively in repertory, at the Glasgow Citizens' Theatre and elsewhere.

For the Royal Shakespeare Company she has designed several productions including *A Midsummer Night's Dream* (1981), *The Tempest* (1982), and *Hamlet* and *Camille* (both 1984). She has designed the US director Hal Prince's production of Andrew Lloyd Webber's *The Phantom of the Opera* (1986) and has worked with Trevor Nunn on such productions as Lloyd Webber's *Aspects of Love* (1989), *Cosí Fan Tutti* (1991), **Pam Gems**'s *The Blue Angel* (1991) and Janacek's *Katya Kabanova* (1994).

The opera companies she has worked for include Huston Opera, Netherlands Opera, the Royal Opera House, English National Opera and Welsh National Opera.

Black, Cilla, *originally* Priscilla Maria Veronica White

Born 1943
English singer who rose during three decades to
become UK television's top earner

Cilla Black was born in Liverpool, where she became a friend of the Beatles. She made her vocal début in the legendary Cavern Club and was subsequently signed to a recording contract. She began her television career in *Ready, Steady Go!* (1963) and achieved her first number-one single with 'Anyone Who Had a Heart' (1964) which sold over 900,000 copies. Her first US television appearance was on the *Ed Sullivan Show* in 1965, the year she made the first of many pantomime appearances in *Little Red Riding Hood*.

She appeared in the West End revue *Way Out in Piccadilly* (1966–7) and essayed her only dramatic film role in *Work is a Four Letter Word* (1967). Forever associated with the sounds of the Swinging Sixties, her chart hits include 'Alfie' (1966), 'Step Inside Love' (1968) and 'Surround Yourself with Sorrow' (1969). Throughout the 1970s she concentrated on television, family life and cabaret appearances, but the compilation album *The Very Best of Cilla Black* (1983) returned her to the charts after a decade's absence.

She retained her hold on the public's affections as the gregarious, matchmaking host of such popular light entertainment programmes as *Blind Date* (1985–) and *Surprise, Surprise* (1984–), and on signing a new two-year seven-figure deal with ITV in 1994, became Britain's top earner in television.

Black, Clementina Maria

Born 1853 Died 1922
English suffragist, trade unionist and novelist who
campaigned against sweated industries

Clementina Black, the sister of **Constance Garnett**, was born in Brighton and educated at home. On her mother's death she moved to London where she conducted research for her novels and lectured on 18th-century literature.

After serving as secretary of the Women's Provident and Protective League for a while, she set up the more militant Women's Trade Union Association (1889). This merged with the Women's Industrial Council (1897) and she became its president, playing an important part in collecting data on women's work and campaigning against sweated industries.

Her publications include *Sweated Industry and the Minimum Wage* (1907), *A Case for Trade Boards* (1909), and her best-known book, *Married Women's Work* (1915), as well as a number of novels.

Blackadder, Elizabeth

Born 1931
Scottish artist who has achieved considerable renown and academic distinction

Elizabeth Blackadder was born in Falkirk, Stirlingshire. She studied at Edinburgh University and Edinburgh College of Art, where she later taught. Her early work was mainly landscape painting, but from the 1970s she began to concentrate on still life, for which she is now best known.

In both oil and watercolour she combines recognizable objects with apparently random associations (cats, fans, ribbons, etc) depicted on an abstract empty background. Her interest in calligraphic gesture and the space between motifs shows considerable Japanese influence. By the late 1970s the representational elements increasingly included flowers and plants, which have come to dominate her compositions. She is the first Scottish woman painter to be elected to full membership of both the Royal Academy and the Royal Scottish Academy.

Blackburn, Helen

Born 1842 Died 1903
Irish social reformer, an early leader of the movement for female emancipation in Britain

Helen Blackburn was born in Knightstown, County Kerry, the daughter of a civil engineer and inventor. In 1859 she moved with her family to London. She became a staunch believer in the vote as the key to women's equality, and was secretary of the National Society for Women's Suffrage from 1874 to 1895.

Her many publications include a *Handbook for Women engaged in Social and Political Work* (1881) and *Women's Suffrage: a Record of the Movement in the British Isles* (1902). In 1899, with Jessie Boucherett (owner of *The Englishwoman's Review* which Blackburn edited, 1881–90), she founded the Freedom of Labour Defence League, aimed at maintaining women's freedom and their powers of earning, for she recognized the importance of the role that women played in industry. She also published *Women under the Factory Act* (1903, with Nora Vynne).

Blackburn, Jemima

Born 1823 Died 1909
Scottish painter known for her visual diaries depicting life in the Scottish Highlands

Jemima Blackburn was born in Edinburgh, the youngest child of James Wedderburn, Solicitor General for Scotland. She showed a precocious talent from an early age and by the time she met the English animal painter Sir Edwin Landseer in 1843, he had to admit that in the drawing of animals he had nothing to teach her. The author and art critic John Ruskin claimed that she was the best artist he knew, and while this is an obviously extravagant statement, she was for a period one of the most popular illustrators in Victorian Britain.

She illustrated 27 books, the most important being *Birds from Nature* (1862 and 1868), demonstrating extraordinary skill both with brush and lithographic crayon. Her most enduring works are the albums containing hundreds of watercolours depicting the day-to-day events of late-19th-century family life in the Scottish Highlands.

Blackburn, Jessy (Jessica), née Thompson

Born 1894 Died 1995
British aviation enthusiast who played a crucial role in establishing Blackburn Aircraft (now owned by British Aerospace)

Jessy Thompson was born in Cradley, Worcestershire, and orphaned at an early age. In 1914 she married Robert Blackburn, who a year later (with the help of his wife's inheritance) founded the Blackburn Aircraft Company to supply military biplanes. She undertook her first flight in Roundhay Park, Leeds, becoming one of the first women to fly a British monoplane before World War I. Not only a familiar and popular spectator at all the major flying events in the ensuing years, she also competed twice in the King's Cup Air Races, in 1922 and 1928.

The 1930s were shaped by a series of tragedies for Jessy Blackburn, including the deaths of two close friends and her second son. Her direct involvement with Blackburn Aircraft terminated following her divorce from Robert in 1936. She remarried twice, but neither relationship lasted.

Blackstone, Tessa Ann Vosper Evans, Baroness, *née* Blackstone

Born 1942
English sociologist and Master of Birkbeck College

Tessa Blackstone was born in Bures, Suffolk, and educated at the London School of Economics. She married Thomas Evans (d.1985) in 1963, but later divorced. After lecturing in sociology at Enfield College of Technology (1965–6), she lectured in social administration at LSE for nine years, then became adviser to the Central Policy Review Staff in the Cabinet Office (1975–8).

Following her appointment as Professor of Educational Administration at the University of London Institute of Education (1978–83), she moved to become Director of Education at ILEA, before being appointed Master of London University's Birkbeck College in 1987. Also that year she was awarded a life peerage, and she has served in the House of Lords as Opposition front bench spokesperson on education and science (1988–92) and on foreign affairs (1992–   ).

She is on the board of the Royal Opera House, among others, and has written several books on education and social issues, including *Prisons and Penal Reform* (1990).

Blackwell, Antoinette Louisa Brown, *née* Brown

Born 1825   Died 1921
Early American woman minister of religion and social reformer

Antoinette Brown was born in Henrietta, New York. She completed a theological course at Oberlin College in 1850 but, as a woman, was refused a preaching licence. In 1853 she became pastor of South Butler Congregational Church, New York, but soon resigned following theological controversy. She eventually became a Unitarian.

She turned briefly to social work but following her marriage to Samuel C Blackwell in 1856, she divided her time between raising a family and writing and study, producing books on science, philosophy, and Darwinism. She also supported the causes of temperance, the abolition of slavery, and women's rights.

Blackwell, Elizabeth

Born 1821   Died 1910
English-born American physician, the first woman doctor in the USA

Elizabeth Blackwell was born in Bristol, an elder sister of **Emily Blackwell**. The family emigrated to the USA in 1832 and her father died six years later, leaving a widow and nine children. Elizabeth helped to support the family by teaching, but devoted her leisure time to the study of medical books.

After fruitless applications for admission to various medical schools, she entered that of Geneva, in New York State, and graduated in 1849. She next visited Europe and, after much difficulty, was admitted into La Maternité in Paris, and St Bartholomew's Hospital in London.

In 1851 she returned to New York where she established a successful practice and founded the New York Infirmary, which had only female staff. After 1868 she lived in England, where she founded the London School of Medicine for Women.

Blackwell, Emily

Born 1826   Died 1910
English-born American doctor, the first woman doctor to undertake major surgery on a large scale

Emily Blackwell was born in Bristol, a younger sister of **Elizabeth Blackwell**. The family emigrated to the USA in 1832. She was educated at Cleveland (Western Reserve) University, followed by work in Europe where she was assistant to the obstetrician Sir James Young Simpson.

In 1856 she helped open her sister's dispensary in New York City (The New York Infirmary for Indigent Women and Children). From 1869 to 1910 she ran the dispensary, and from 1869 to 1899 was Dean and Professor of Obstetrics and Diseases of Women at the Women's Medical College which was attached to the infirmary.

Blair, Bonnie

Born 1964
American ice skater, winner of six Olympic medals for speedskating

Bonnie Blair was born in Cornwall, New York. She is the most decorated female Olympian after **Lidya Skoblikova** with six medals (five of them gold), all for speedskating, as well as being the first American speedskater to win in more than one Olympic Games.

The five gold medals were for the 500 metres in 1988, 1992 and 1994, and for the 1,000 metres in 1992 and 1994. In 1994 she became a professional speedskater and motivational speaker, and in 1995 she set the 500 metres world record at Calgary.

Blair, Catherine

Born 1872   Died 1946
Scottish painter and reformer, and a firm advocate
of pottery as a cottage industry

Catherine Blair was born in Bathgate, Midlothian. From her late thirties she was at the forefront of the Women's Suffrage Movement and deeply involved in the Scottish Women's Rural Institute.

A few years later, in 1920, she founded the Mak' Merry Pottery in Macmerry, East Lothian, which specialized in painting pottery blanks to an extremely high standard in a colourful and decorative manner.

Throughout her life she was an outspoken champion of the ordinary Cottar woman and she happily passed on her skills, enabling this cottage industry to develop.

Blais, Marie-Claire

Born 1939
French–Canadian novelist, dramatist and poet

Marie-Claire Blais was born in Quebec city and educated at Laval University, Quebec. At the age of 18 she wrote her first novel, *La Belle Bête* (1959, Eng trans *Mad Shadows*, 1960), a sometimes nightmarish portrayal of a stultified childhood in her native Quebec, though the actual location was, typically, ambiguous. *Tête blanche* followed (1960) and was more conventional, but *Une saison dans la vie d'Emmanuel* (1965) returned to the darkly lyrical strain. She is noted for her fantastical depiction of society's outsiders in their desolation and emptiness

The critic Edmund Wilson gave Blais's career a significant boost with a sensitive appreciation in his pioneering *O Canada* (1967). In the later 1960s, she published a further sequence of novels with an autobiographical theme: *Manuscrits de Pauline Archange* (1968), *Vivre! Vivre!* (1969, published together as *The Manuscripts of Pauline Archange*, 1970) and *Les Apparances* (1970, Eng trans *Dürer's Angel*, 1976).

Later novels have concentrated on the theme of gay and lesbian sexuality, and include the very fine *Les Nuits d'underground*

(1978, Eng trans *Nights in the Underground*, 1979). Her verse was published in *Pays voilés* (1963) and *Existences* (1964, translated and collected as *Veiled Countries/Lives*, 1984). She has been awarded the Prix Médicis of France in 1966, two Governor-General's awards and in 1980 was made a Member of the Order of Canada.

Blankers-Koen, Fanny (Francina)

Born 1918
Dutch athlete who captured the imagination of the
sporting world as the 'flying Dutch housewife'

Fanny Blankers-Koen was born in Amsterdam. She achieved success at the comparatively late age of 30, and dominated women's events in the London Olympics of 1948, winning four gold medals: the 100 metres (11.9 seconds), 200 metres (24.4 seconds), 80 metres hurdles (11.2 seconds) and the 4 × 100 metres relay.

She was unequalled among women as an all-round athlete, and though primarily a sprinter, at various times held world records for both high and long jumps.

Blatch, Harriot (Eaton) Stanton, *née* Stanton

Born 1856   Died 1940
American suffrage leader who participated in
both the British and American suffragette
movements

Harriot Stanton was born in Seneca Falls, New York, the daughter of **Elizabeth Cady**

Harriot Stanton Blatch

Stanton, and educated at Vassar College, where she studied mathematics. In 1882 she moved to Basingstoke, England, on her marriage to William Blatch, an English businessman, and was impressed by the direction and work of the Women's Franchise League.

After her return to the USA in 1902 she set abound reviving the suffrage campaign there and became a staunch activist in support of women's rights, founding the Equality League of Self-Supporting Women in 1907 and the Women's Political Union in 1908. She also organized suffrage parades and directed the Woman's Land Army during World War I.

Her writings include her contribution to the *History of Women Suffrage* (1881–7), which was edited by **Susan B Anthony**, **Matilda Joslyn Gage** and Blatch's mother, and her own *Mobilizing Woman-Power* (1918) and *A Woman's Point of View, Some Roads to Peace* (1920).

Blavatsky, Helena Petrovna, *née* Hahn

Born 1831 Died 1891
Russian-born American spiritualist and author who was a major promoter of theosophy

Helena Hahn was born in Ekaterinoslav. She had a brief marriage in her teens to a Russian officer, later a provincial governor, Nikifor V Blavatsky, but left him and travelled widely in the East, including Tibet, becoming interested in the occult and spiritualism.

She went to the USA in 1873, and in 1875, with Henry Steel Olcott, founded the Theosophical Society in New York to promote Theosophy, a pantheistic religious–philosophical system, later carrying on her work in India. Her psychic powers were widely acclaimed but did not survive investigation by the London Society for Psychical Research; this, however, did not deter her large following, which included **Annie Besant**.

Her writings include *Isis Unveiled* (1877) and *The Voice of Silence* (1889). The former work makes the claim that mystical experience, rather than contemporary religion or science, is the only way to attain spiritual truth.

Blessington, Marguerite, Countess of, *née* Power

Born 1789 Died 1849
Irish journalist, novelist, literary hostess and adventuress who led a brilliant London salon

Marguerite Power was born at Knockbrit near Clonmel, County Tipperary. At the age of 14 she was sold by her dissolute father to her future husband, but abandoned him. When he fell to his death from a window, she married the Earl of Blessington, with whom she had been living for some time.

After his death from apoplexy in 1829, the witty and beautiful Countess became one of Mayfair's most vivacious hostesses, a prolific author (in an attempt to support herself) and dreadful debtor. Her entertaining *Journal of Conversations with Lord Byron* appeared in 1832; two travel books, *The Idler in Italy* and *The Idler in France*, followed in 1839 and 1841. She also produced several intermittently engaging three-volume novels of upper middle-class manners and edited such annual publications as *The Keepsake* and the *Book of Beauty*, volumes containing decorous social advice for young ladies.

Bley, Carla, *née* Borg

Born 1938
American jazz composer, bandleader and pianist who has made inroads into jazz for other women to follow

Carla Bley was born in Oakland, California. She moved to New York as a teenager, and worked as a cigarette girl to supplement her occasional income from music.

She founded the Jazz Composers Orchestra with Michael Mantler in 1964, which she subsequently developed into a distribution network for commercially difficult music. Composition was always her major artistic concern, and she has produced significant works for important jazz musicians like Gary Burton and Charlie Haden, as well as a consistent stream of writing for her own ensembles.

One of the most distinctive figures in contemporary jazz, she has made a major impact in a traditionally male-dominated field; this is now encouraging other women to follow her example.

Bliss, Catherine

Born 1908 Died 1989
English educationist whose primary concern was the role of women in the Church

Catherine Bliss was born in London. She studied theology at Cambridge. Between 1948 (when she chaired the committee on the laity at Amsterdam) and 1968 she took a keen interest in the lay and educational concerns of the World Council of Churches (WCC), especially in the coming together of the WCC and the World Council of Christian Education.

She was on the British Council of Churches

(1942–67), was secretary of the Church of England Board of Education (1957–66), and a lecturer in religious studies at the University of Sussex (1966–73).

Her writings include *The Service and Status of Women in the Churches* (1963) and *The Future of Religion* (1969).

Blixen, Karen, Baroness, *pseud* Isak Dinesen

> Born 1885 Died 1962
> *Danish story-teller and novelist who wrote the story behind the film* Out of Africa

Karen Blixen was born in Rungsted and educated at home and in France, Switzerland and England. She adopted English as her main literary language, translating some of her most important works back into Danish. In 1914 she married her cousin, Baron Bror Blixen Finecke, from whom she contracted syphilis.

Their life on an unproductive coffee plantation in Kenya is recounted in *Den Afrikanske Farm* (1937, Eng trans *Out of Africa*, 1938), which was also the basis of a 1985 Hollywood film starring **Meryl Streep**. After her divorce and the death of her lover Denys Finch-Hatton in a plane crash, she returned to Denmark and began writing the brooding, existential tales for which she is best known.

Like the singer in 'The Wide-Travelling Lioness' (*Seven Gothic Tales*, 1934, Danish translation, 1935), they are usually concerned with identity and personal destiny, and are markedly aristocratic in spirit. This is confirmed in *Winter's Tales* (1942), *Last Tales* (1957) and *Anecdotes of Destiny* (1958). 'Babett's Feast' (1950), also successfully filmed, shows a lighter side to her artistic nature.

Blois, Natalie de

> Born 1921
> *American architect who was senior designer for one of America's largest architecture firms, working on some of its most famous buildings*

Natalie de Blois won a scholarship to Columbia University School of Architecture, where she graduated in 1944. Almost immediately she started working for Skidmore, Owings and Merrill (SOM), a massive architecture firm, which at that stage was known for reliability and competence rather than originality. The corporate structure encouraged anonymity in its staff and De Blois could have gone virtually unnoticed. By 1948 she was working with Louis Skidmore as a design co-ordinator for the Terrace Plaza Hotel, Cincinnati.

In 1952 she went with her family to Paris for a year, then SOM asked her to be senior designer on a series of US consulates in Germany. On returning to the USA she continued as a senior designer, working on some of SOM's most famous buildings, including the General Life Insurance Company Building in Bloomfield, Connecticut (1957), the Pepsi-Cola Building in Park Avenue, New York (1959), and the Union Carbide Building, New York (1960).

In 1968 she was finally made a design associate and worked on the Boots Building in Nottingham, England. In 1974, after 30 years of service, she left SOM, where she had never been fully recognized, to become a senior project designer with Neuhaus and Taylor in Texas.

Bloom, Claire

> Born 1931
> *English actress who has been acclaimed in roles ranging from Cordelia to Blanche du Bois*

Clarie Bloom was born in London. She made her début in Oxford in 1946, and in London in 1947, before joining the Shakespeare Memorial Theatre in Stratford-upon-Avon. She moved to the Old Vic in 1952, and established a reputation as a distinguished Shakespearian actress, her roles including Cordelia opposite John Gielgud in a West End production of *King Lear* in 1955.

An intense, intelligent actress, she has built a distinguished career in films and television as well as on stage, where she has played with distinction in Sartre, Chekov, Ibsen and Bolt. She also had a notable success as Blanche du Bois in Tennessee Williams's *A Streetcar Named Desire* in 1974.

Bloomer, Amelia Jenks, *née* Jenks

> Born 1818 Died 1894
> *American champion of women's rights, temperance and dress reform*

Amelia Jenks was born in Homer, New York. She married a lawyer, Dexter C Bloomer, in 1840, and devoted her time to writing articles and lecturing on such subjects as women's suffrage, unjust marriage laws and education, working closely with **Susan B Anthony** and the Rev Antoinette L Brown (later **Antoinette Brown Blackwell**). She also founded and edited the feminist paper, the *Lily* (1849–55).

Her pursuit of dress equality led her to wear her own version of full trousers for women which came to be called 'bloomers' after her.

Bloor, Ella Reeve, *known as* Mother Bloor, *née* Reeve

Born 1862 Died 1951
American radical and feminist, a founding
member of the American Communist Party

Ella Reeve was born on Staten Island, New York. She married at the age of 19 and was a mother of four by 1892. She became interested in women's rights and the labor movement, but her political interests led to her divorce in 1896. Following a second unsuccessful marriage, she moved into politics as an activist, joining the Socialist Party in 1901.

After adopting the name Ella Bloor in 1906 for a piece of investigative reporting undertaken for the social reformer and novelist Upton Sinclair, she continued to write under this name. She became the party organizer for Connecticut, attracting support for various labor causes, until in 1919 she broke with the Socialists and became one of the founders of the American Communist Party, to which she became utterly committed.

Arrested more than 30 times during her career, she gained a reputation as a distinguished party speaker and became a member of the Party's central committee (1932–48). She wrote *Women of the Soviet Union* (1930) and *We Are Many* (1940).

Blume, Judy

Born 1938
American novelist, perhaps the most controversial
and certainly the most popular contemporary
American writer for teenagers

Judy Blume was born in Elizabeth, New Jersey. She studied early childhood education at New York University. Her first published book was *The One in the Middle is the Green Kangaroo* (1969), but it was her third book, *Are You There, God? It's Me, Margaret* (1970), that brought her acclaim, chiefly for her candid approach to teenage social problems connected with the onset of puberty, such as menstruation and sex, and for her natural, if unsubtle, style.

As with subsequent books, attempts were made to restrict its circulation; her work has allegedly suffered more censorship attempts in US schools and libraries than that of any other author. Her explicitness brought her into conflict with parents, but she has a remarkable rapport with her readers and dares to confront subjects which previously were ignored.

Her other books include *Then Again, Maybe I Won't* (1971), *It's not the End of the World* (1972), *Deenie* (1973), *Blubber* (1974) and *For-*

ever (1975). Her books for adults include *Wifey* (1978) and *Smart Women* (1984), both about women trapped by traditional marriage.

Blundell, Heather *see* McKay, Heather

Bly, Nellie *see* Seaman, Elizabeth Cochrane

Blunt, Lady Anne Isobel, *née* Noel

Born 1837 Died 1917
English traveller, diarist, and letter-writer, the
first English woman to enter the Arabian
peninsula

Lady Anne Noel was the daughter of mathematician Ada, Countess of **Lovelace** and granddaughter of Lord Byron. She was educated at home and in 1858 married the poet Wilfred Scawen Blunt (1840–1922).

On his retiral from the diplomatic service they went to live and travel in the Near and Middle East. Both shared a love of Arab horses and in 1878 they crossed the desert from Aleppo to Bagdad to buy bloodstock for their English estate. They later bought an estate in Egypt (1881), where they also ran a stud.

Lady Anne was the first Englishwoman to travel in the Arabian peninsula, and she describes their travels in her books *The Bedouin Tribes of the Euphrates* (1878) and *A Pilgrimage to Nedj* (1881).

Blyton, Enid Mary

Born 1897 Died 1968
English children's author of over 600 books and
creator of 'Noddy' and the 'Famous Five'

Enid Blyton was born in London. She trained as a Froebel kindergarten teacher, then became a journalist, specializing in educational and children's publications. In 1922 she published her first book, *Child Whispers*, a collection of verse, but it was in the late 1930s that she began writing her many children's stories featuring such characters as Noddy, the Famous Five and the Secret Seven.

Now one of the most translated British authors, she identified closely with children and always considered her stories highly educational and moral in tone; however she has recently been criticized for stereotypical racism, sexism and snobbishness, as well as stylistic inelegance and over-simplicity.

Blyton also edited various magazines, including *Sunny Stories* and *Pictorial Knowledge* for children, and *Modern Teaching*, was part-author of *Two Years in the Infant School*, and wrote school readers and books on nature and religious study.

Bocage, Marie Anne Fiquet du, *née* Le Page

Born 1710 Died 1802
French poet and playwright who was nicknamed
'le Milton français' and 'l'illustre Amazon'

Marie Anne Le Page was born in Rouen to a bourgeois family. She married at the age of 17 and moved to Paris in 1733. In 1749 her play, *Les Amazons*, was performed at the Comédie Française; it was the first work by a woman to be seen there for many years.

Her epic poems *Paradis terrestre* (1748, 'Earthly Paradise'), an imitation of Milton, and *La Colombiade* (1756) gave her an exaggerated fame, perhaps on account of their author's great beauty, and her letters to her sister, written while travelling through England, Holland and Italy, have historical interest. From 1758 she was the hostess of a literary salon, which continued in spite of the Revolution of 1789.

Bodichon, Barbara, *née* Leigh Smith

Born 1827 Died 1891
English feminist and polemicist who was an
active campaigner for women's suffrage and
legal reform

Barbara Leigh Smith was born in London, the daughter of Benjamin Leigh Smith, a radical MP who believed strongly in women's rights. She studied at Bedford College, London, and in 1852 opened a primary school in London. In 1857 she married Dr Eugène Bodichon, a French doctor whom she met on a visit to Algiers.

Following the success of her influential pamphlet *A Brief Summary in Plain Language of the Most Important Laws Concerning Women* (1954), she wrote *Women at Work* (1857) and helped **Bessie Rayner Parkes** and others to found the feminist magazine *The Englishwoman's Journal* (1858). Later, in 1869, she helped **Emily Davies** found the college for women in Hitchin that became Girton College, Cambridge.

She was also a landscape watercolourist and her drawings and paintings were widely exhibited.

Bogan, Louise

Born 1897 Died 1970
American poet and short-story writer who evokes
an erotic celebration of romantic love or else
laments its delusion

Louise Bogan was born in Livermore, Maine. She began writing in high school and published a collection of verse, *Body of this Death*, in 1923. She published comparatively few works, but enough of sufficient quality, powerful and controlled to be considered a 'poet's poet'. She was also a highly respected critic, writing for the *New Yorker* (1931–51) and other publications.

Her two marriages and other relationships with men led her to believe that love almost always ends in acrimony and betrayal. While editions of her collected poetry were published in 1941 and 1954, *The Blue Estuaries* (1968) is the definitive volume, all 105 poems having been selected by the author herself as those by which she wished to be remembered.

Boland, Eavan

Born 1944
Irish poet and critic who is considered one of the
most important poets writing in Ireland today

Eavan Boland was born in Dublin and educated there, in London and in New York. From *New Territory* (1967) onwards she became a poetic commentator on the 'frail compasses and trenchant constellations' that she sees as constituting suburban Irish lives in the style-conscious second half of the 20th century.

Her experience of motherhood lent deep emotion to *Night Feed* (1982) and her subsequent combination of intellectualism and feminism led to the award-winning *Outside History* (1990), a significant step forward for women writing from within a male-dominated Irish culture.

Boleyn, Anne

Born c.1504 Died 1536
Queen of England as the second wife of Henry VIII
(ruled 1509–47)

Anne Boleyn was the daughter of Sir Thomas Boleyn and Elizabeth Howard, daughter of the Duke of Norfolk. She spent some years being educated at the French court, and on her return in 1522 her suitors included Henry Percy, the heir to the Earl of Northumberland, and King Henry himself, who began to shower favours upon her father, having already had an affair with her sister. Anne did not apparently favour him until negotiations for the divorce from **Catherine of Aragon** began in 1527, but, as these dragged on, their association became shameless and they were secretly married in January 1533.

Thomas Cranmer declared her Henry's legal wife in May and she was crowned with great splendour in Westminster Hall on Whit-

Anne Boleyn

sunday; but within three months Henry's passion had cooled. It was not revived by the birth, in September 1533, of a princess, the future Queen **Elizabeth**, still less by that of a stillborn son, in January 1536.

On May Day that year the King rode off abruptly from a tournament held at Greenwich, leaving the Queen behind, and the next day she was arrested and brought to the Tower. A secret commission investigated charges of Anne's adultery with four commoners and incest with her own brother, Lord Rochford. They were tried and convicted of high treason. Her own uncle, Thomas Howard, 3rd Duke of Norfolk, presided over her judges and pronounced the verdict. She was beheaded on Tower Green on 19 May. Eleven days later Henry married **Jane Seymour**.

Bol Poel, Martha, Baroness, *née* De Kerchove de Deuterghem

Born 1877   Died 1956
Belgian patriot and feminist, an effective worker
in the wartime underground

Martha De Kerchove de Deuterghem was born in Ghent and educated at the Kerchove Institute founded by her grandfather. She later attended painting classes in Paris at the Académie Julien and married the industrialist Bol Poel in 1898.

During World War I she was imprisoned for organizing a communications network during the German occupation and was exiled to Switzerland during a period of ill health.

She became a prominent figure in the Belgian women's movement between the wars and was elected President of the International Council of Women from 1935 to 1940. During the German occupation of Belgium in World War II she was banned from public association but nevertheless played her part in underground activities.

Bolt, Carol, *née* Johnson

Born 1941
Canadian playwright whose themes include North
American life

Carol Johnson was born in Winnipeg, Manitoba, and educated at the University of British Columbia, Vancouver. She married David Bolt in 1969. She is a prolific writer whose work is often overtly political, though she also writes for children. Her plays combine an understanding of Canadian life and culture with musical comedy, mythic characters and epic romance. She has written over 20, including three for television, and is noted for her frequent collaborations with other writers.

Her best-known works are *Buffalo Jump* (1972), a play about the riots which occurred during the American Depression, and *Red Emma: Queen of Anarchists* (1973), about **Emma Goldman**.

Bombal, María Luisa

Born 1910   Died 1980
Chilean novelist remembered for writing Chilean
literature's first truly feminist books and for
taking pot-shots at her husband

María Bombal was born in Viña del Mar. She spent much of her youth in Paris, and acquired a degree from the Sorbonne. Back in Chile, she fell in love with the aviator Eugolio Sánchez, but he did not love her, and so, after failing to kill herself, she shot him. Luckily she did not kill him, and under the wing of the poet Pablo Neruda and other friends, she was able to get to Buenos Aires.

There she wrote her first and most famous novel, *La última niebla* (1935, Eng trans *House of Mist*, 1947, taken from a re-working of the original). This, and her second book, *La amortajada* (1938, Eng trans *The Shrouded Woman*, 1948), have been said to have marked a turning point in Latin-American fiction: hallucinated, often unintelligible, they are (or have been taken to be) the first truly feminist books in Chilean literature. Bombal was in the news again in 1940 when she took a pistol shot at her husband — who was alleged to have been intent on killing her — but missed.

She later became involved in the film world, wrote a few more stories (collected in *New Island*, 1982), and on the death of her second husband, a French financier, returned to Chile, where she died in near poverty. Chronic alcoholism prevented her from carrying out many of the projects she had planned. The degree of her achievement has not yet been decided: the charge that she did little more in her novels than render, in words, some notion of the cinematic achievement of Luis Buñuel, is hard to counter; unlike Buñuel, she displayed no sense of humour. However, feminists have pointed to her as a great writer.

Bonaparte, (Marie-Annonciade-) Caroline

Born 1782 Died 1839
Queen of Naples who contributed to the rise and fall of herself and her husband at the hands of her brother Napoleon

Caroline Bonaparte was born in Ajaccio, Corsica, the youngest surviving daughter of Charles and **Letizia Bonaparte**, and sister of Napoleon. In 1800 she was given by her brother in marriage to the French soldier Joachim Murat, who had served with distinction under Napoleon.

They were an ambitious couple, and secured the title of grand duke and duchess of Berg and of Cleves in 1806, before Murat became King of Naples in 1808. As Queen of Naples (until 1815), the ambitious and captivating Caroline brought a brilliant court life to the Neapolitan palaces of Caserta and Portici.

However her husband's loyalty to Napoleon wavered in 1813–15, spoiling her relationship with her brother, and after Murat's execution in 1815 she fled to Austria. She lived there, under surveillance, at Frohsdorf (1815–24), then lived in Trieste (1824–31), where she adopted the title Countess of Lipona, before settling in Florence for the last seven years of her life.

Bonaparte, (Marie-Anne-) Élisa

Born 1777 Died 1820
Sister of Napoleon and Grand Duchess of Tuscany who administered her duchies with competence and intelligence

Élisa Bonaparte was born in Ajaccio, Corsica, the eldest surviving daughter of Charles and **Letizia Bonaparte**, and sister of Napoleon. She married a Corsican noble, Félix Bacciochi, in 1797.

Napoleon made her duchess of the principalities Piombino and Lucca in 1805, and she managed the economy of her small states so profitably that in 1809 he assigned her to Tuscany, where she revived the court glories of the Pitti Palace.

Later however, her relationship with Napoleon grew stale when she supported her brother-in-law Joachim Murat in his disloyal activities. Towards the end of her life she called herself Countess of Compignano, retiring ultimately to Sant'Andrea, near Trieste.

Bonaparte, (Maria) Letizia, *known as* Madame Mère, *née* Ramolino

Born c.1749 Died 1836
Corsican woman and mother of Napoleon

Letizia Ramolino was born in Ajaccio, the daughter of a French army captain. In 1764 she married a Corsican lawyer, Charles Marie Bonaparte. Of her 12 children, five died in infancy; Napoleon (1769–1821) was the fourth child and the second to survive infancy.

She was accorded official status as 'Madame Mère de l'Empereur' in May 1804 but despite acquiring tremendous wealth continued to live a simple and devout life, encouraging her son to seek reconciliation with the Church; her half-brother was Cardinal Fesch (1763–1839), who had become archbishop of Lyons in 1802.

Madame Mère supported the fallen Napoleon on Elba in 1814 but spent most of the last 18 years of her life in dignified, but secluded, retirement in Rome.

Bonaparte, (Marie-) Pauline

Born 1780 Died 1825
Princess Borghese who peppered her life with scandal but showed more loyalty to her brother Napoleon than any other sibling

Pauline Bonaparte was the daughter of Charles and **Letizia Bonaparte** and Napoleon's favourite and most beautiful sister. She married General Leclerc in 1797 and accompanied him on an expedition to Haiti (1802) on which he contracted yellow fever and died.

In 1803 she married Prince Camillo Borghese. Her private life soon shocked the patrician family into which she married, not least because of her willingness to pose as a nude Venus for the sculptor Canova.

Though she had had a disagreement with him over his new empress Marie Louise in 1810, she loyally supported Napoleon in his exile on Elba. Her last years were spent in Florence.

Bond, Mary, *née* McKechnie

Born 1939
Scottish artist deeply rooted in the figurative
tradition who draws inspiration from her travels

Mary Bond was born in Paisley, Renfrewshire, and trained at Glasgow School of Art under David Donaldson and **Mary Armour** from 1955 to 1960. The ancient traditions and folklore from the diverse cultures of India, Mexico, Ireland and Italy provide her with the symbolic and poetic elements in her expressionistic paintings, in which both Eastern and Western artistic traditions are combined. Bond has exhibited widely throughout Britain and has works in many public and private collections at home and abroad. She was Awarded the **Anne Redpath** award in 1984 and elected to the RSW (Royal Scottish Water Colour Society) in 1989.

Bondfield, Margaret Grace

Born 1873 Died 1953
English trade union leader and Labour politician,
the first woman in the British Cabinet

Margaret Bondfield was born in Chard, Somerset, the tenth child in her family. Following a scanty education she started work aged 14 as a draper's assistant, having adopted radical political views from her father and a deep devotion to Christ. Dissatisfied with her working conditions, she became a founding member of the National Union of Shop Assistants and its Assistant Secretary (1898–1908) and was involved in other trade-union initiatives especially concerned with the improvement of working conditions for women, such as the Women's Industrial Council.

She helped **Mary MacArthur** to found the National Federation of Women Workers in 1906, and in 1921 became the chief woman officer of the National Union of General and Municipal Workers. Having been the only woman attending the 1899 Trades Union Congress, she became its first female chairman in 1923, the year she also entered parliament. She was MP for Northampton in 1923–4 and for Wallsend from 1926 to 1931. As Minister of Labour (1929–31) in Ramsay MacDonald's second administration, she was the first woman to be a British Cabinet Minister.

She retired from her work for the trade unions in 1938 and became active instead in various women's welfare groups. She published her autobiography *A Life's Work* in 1949.

Bonheur, Rosa (Marie Rosalie)

Born 1822 Died 1899
French animal painter and sculptor noted for the
exquisite detail of her work

Rosa Bonheur was born in Bordeaux and trained under her father, Raymond Bonheur (d.1853), and in Paris, where from 1841 she exhibited regularly at the Salon.

Known for her detailed depictions of all kinds of animals, particularly horses, she led an unconventional lifestyle, wearing trousers and smoking. It is said that for a time she kept a lioness as a pet and refused to paint domesticated animals. In 1865 she became the first woman to be awarded the Grand Cross of the Légion d'Honneur.

Her paintings include *Ploughing with Oxen* (1849, Luxembourg) and her famous *Horse Fair* (1853, Metropolitan Museum of Art, New York).

Bonner, Yelena, *also* Elena *or* Jelena

Born 1923
Soviet campaigner, an outspoken advocate of civil
rights and leader of the Soviet dissident
movement

Yelena Bonner was born in Moscow. After the arrest of her parents in Stalin's 'great purge' of 1937, and the subsequent execution of her father and imprisonment of her mother, she was brought up in Leningrad (now St Petersburg) by her grandmother. During World War II she served in the army and became a lieutenant, but suffered serious eye

Yelena Bonner, 1990

injuries. After the war she married and worked as a doctor.

On separating from her husband in 1965, she joined the CPSU (Communist Party), but became disillusioned after the Soviet invasion of Czechoslovakia (1968) and drifted into 'dissident' activities. She married the physicist Andrei Sakharov (1921–89) in 1971 and resigned from the CPSU a year later. During the next 14 years they led the Soviet dissident movement.

Following a KGB crackdown, Sakharov was banished to internal exile in Gorky in 1980 and Bonner suffered a similar fate in 1984. After hunger strikes, she was given permission to travel to Italy for specialist eye treatment in 1981 and 1984. The couple were finally released from Gorky and pardoned in 1986, as part of a new 'liberalization' policy by the Gorbachev administration, and remained prominent campaigners for greater democratization.

Bonstelle, Jessie, *originally* Laura Justine Bonesteele

Born 1872 Died 1932
American actress and theatre manager, noted for fostering the talents of rising stars

Jessie Bonstelle was born in New York State. She exhibited an early talent for recitations as a child, and began her professional career as an actress in a touring company under Augustin Daly, later working for the Shubert brothers in Syracuse, New York. She went on to make her reputation in management.

She is most closely associated with Detroit, where she leased and operated the Garrick Theatre from 1910 to 1922, then took on the Playhouse Theatre, turning it into one of America's finest civic theatres. She earned the nickname 'The Maker of Stars', and nurtured the early careers of a number of distinguished players, including **Katharine Cornell** and Melvyn Douglas.

Booth, Catherine, *née* Mumford

Born 1829   Died 1890
English co-founder of the Salvation Army

Catherine Mumford was born in Derbyshire, the daughter of a Wesleyan preacher. She met William Booth at Brixton Wesleyan Church, from which they were both expelled for religious zeal, and they married in 1855.

She became a gifted preacher herself, and shared in her husband's evangelistic work. Following preaching tours round the country, they returned to London in 1864 to start the work that became the Salvation Army. Their eight children all became active in the Salvation Army movement, and she also started the Army's women's work.

Her funeral was attended by 36,000 people. Her belief in woman preachers is outlined in the pamphlet *Female Ministry* (1859).

Booth, Evangeline Cory

Born 1865 Died 1950
English-born American Fourth General of the Salvation Army who gave it her life's work

Evangeline Cory Booth was born in Hackney, East London, the seventh child of the Salvation Army's founders, William and **Catherine Booth**. She attained the rank of sergeant at 15 and captain at 17, and took a leading role in the movement, working as an international trouble-shooter from London and as principal of the International Training Colleges.

She was appointed commander in Canada (1896–1904), and in the USA (1904–34), where she headed the Army's exemplary social work during the World War I and the Depression. She became a US citizen, but after a spell in London as International General (1934–9), retired there. She wrote many songs for the Army and published several books.

Booth, Margaret

Born 1898
American film editor, the first woman to achieve success in her field

Margaret Booth was born in Los Angeles. She began cutting film for D W Griffith, then moved the to Mayer studio in 1921. The studio became MGM in 1924, and she was one of their leading film editors. She was appointed as supervising film editor at MGM in 1939, a prestigious post which she held until 1968.

She returned to more hands-on editing assignments after leaving MGM, working with various independent filmmakers. She received an Academy Award for overall career achievement in 1977. *The Mutiny on the Bounty* (1935) and *The Way We Were* (1973) are among her best-known film credits.

Boothe Luce, Clare *see* Luce, Clare Boothe

Boothroyd, Betty

Born 1929
English Labour politician and the first woman Speaker of the House of Commons

Betty Boothroyd was born in Dewsbury, Yorkshire. She was a Tiller Girl and a political assistant before she became a Hammersmith borough councillor in 1965. Having first stood for parliament in 1957, she was finally elected as MP for West Bromwich in 1973. She has represented West Bromwich West (the constituency boundaries having been redrawn) since 1974.

When she became Deputy Speaker in 1987, she commanded the respect of the House by her magisterial, even-handed performances. She stood successfully for the post of Speaker after the 1992 general election, receiving wide, cross-party support.

Bora, Katherine von

Born 1499 Died 1552
German nun who married Martin Luther and
proved to him the importance of marriage

Katherine von Bora joined the Cistercian convent of Nimptschen, near Grimma, in 1515. She adopted the doctrines of the German religious reformer Martin Luther, and in 1523 she ran away to Wittenberg, the hub of the Reformation.

She married Luther in 1525 and proved to be not only a great help and support to him but also an able businesswoman. So important was Luther's marriage to him that he placed domestic life along with church and political life in his list of the three 'orders of creation' of Christian existence.

Borden, Lizzie Andrew

Born 1860 Died 1927
American alleged murderer whose trial caused a
national sensation

Lizzie Borden was born in Fall River, Massachusetts. In one of the most sensational murder trials in American history, she was accused of murdering her wealthy undertaker father Andrew and hated 14-stone stepmother Abby with an axe, in August 1892. She claimed to have been outside in the barn at the time of the murder, and despite a wealth of circumstantial evidence, she was aquitted.

She lived out her life in Fall River and was buried alongside her father and stepmother. The case is immortalized in a children's nursery rhyme: 'Lizzie Borden took an axe/ And gave her mother forty whacks;/ And when she saw what she had done/ She gave her father forty-one'.

Borgia, Lucrezia

Born 1480 Died 1519
Italian noblewoman and a central character of her
infamous Renaissance family

Lucrezia Borgia was born in Rome, the illegitimate daughter of the Spanish cardinal Rodrigo Borgia (later Pope Alexander VI), and sister of Cesare Borgia, captain-general of the armies of the Church. She was three times married to further her father's political ambitions: first, in 1493, at the age of 12 to Giovanni Sforza, Lord of Pesaro, but this marriage was annulled by her father in 1497 because of his friendship with Naples; second, in 1498, to Alfonso of Aragon, nephew of the king of Naples, but this marriage was ended in 1500 when Alfonso was murdered by her brother Cesare; and third, in 1501, to Alfonso (1486–1534), son of the Duke of Este, who inherited the duchy of Ferrara.

At Ferrara she established a brilliant court of artists and men of letters, including Ariosto and Titian, and devoted herself to the patronage of art and education. In legend she has become notorious, quite unfairly, for wantonness, vice and crime (even including incest with her brother and father).

Boserup, Esther Talke, *née* Börgesen

Born 1910
Danish writer on economic development

Esther Börgesen was born in Frederiksberg and educated at Copenhagen University. As a specialist in economic development, she has worked for the Danish government (1935–47), in Geneva for the UN Economic Committee for Europe (1947–57), and as a freelance consultant in India (1957–9), Senegal (1964–5) and elsewhere since 1957.

She has held several important posts in UN organizations, notably as a member of the UN Expert Committee of Development Planning (1971–80), and of the UN International Research and Training Institute for the Advancement of Women (1979–85).

Boswell, Connee (Connie)

Born 1907 Died 1976
American singer, instrumentalist and arranger,
who as leader of the Boswell Sisters had a
significant impact on pre-war popular music

Connee Boswell was born in New Orleans. She suffered poliomyelitis as a child and, following a later accident, was disabled. Nevertheless, she performed from a wheelchair, compensating for a weakened voice by using a microphone — a pioneer in this regard. As leader of the Boswell Sisters, she prepared much of the group's material and played saxophone, trombone and cello, as well as piano accompaniments for them. Their 'Stormy Weather' was a major success, and a strong influence on **Ella Fitzgerald**'s approach to the blues and jazz (reversing the usual dependence of white artists on black styles). In later years, Connee Boswell adopted a more commercial approach and appeared in several popular films, including *Swing Parade* (1946) and *Senior Prom* (1959).

Bottomley, Virginia Hilda Brunette Maxwell

Born 1948
English Conservative politician who began the
reform of the National Health Service

Virginia Bottomley was born in Dunoon, Scotland, and educated at Putney High School, Essex University and the London School of Economics. She worked as a researcher for a child poverty action group, lecturer in a college of further education and psychiatric social worker before unsuccessfully contesting her first seat, the Isle of Wight, in 1983.

She became MP for Surrey South-West in 1984 and worked as Parliamentary Private Secretary under Chris Patten, then Geoffrey Howe. As junior Minister at the Department of the Environment (1988–9), she tackled such issues as the dumping of toxic waste, lead-free petrol and litter, and in 1989 she became a health Minister under William Waldegrave.

Endowed with admirable presentational skills, she became Secretary of State for Health in 1992, when she began the lengthy reform of the health service, which involved the controversial closure of several hospitals. In July 1995 she became Secretary of State for National Heritage, with responsibilities including the newly launched National Lottery.

Boucicault, Nina

Born 1867   Died 1950
English actress whose career spanned 50 years and
included the creation of the role of Peter Pan

Nina Boucicault was born in London, the daughter of the distinguished Irish playwright and director Dion Boucicault and the Scottish actress Agnes Robertson. Her family pedigree suggested a theatrical career, and she made her acting début in her father's company in the USA in 1885. It was the beginning of a long and largely successful career which ended with her retirement from the stage in 1936.

Although she played many different roles and styles, she is chiefly remembered as the actress who first played Peter Pan in the London première of J M Barrie's immensely popular play in 1904.

Boudicca, *also (incorrectly) called* Boadicea

1st century AD
British warrior-queen who led a great uprising
against the Romans

Boudicca was queen of the native tribe of Iceni (Norfolk, Suffolk and part of Cambridgeshire). Her husband, Prasutagus, an ally of Rome, had shrewdly made the emperor Nero his co-heir, but when he died in AD60 the Romans annexed all the Iceni territory and pillaged it.

According to Tacitus, Boudicca was flogged and her daughters raped. The Iceni rose in fury and, led by Boudicca, destroyed the Roman colony of Camulodunum (Colchester), sacked and burned Londinium (London) and razed Verulamium (St Albans), killing up to 70,000 Romans.

The Roman governor of Britain, Suetonius Paulinus, who had been absent in Mona (Anglesey) in north Wales, gathered two legions and overwhelmed the Iceni in a bloody battle somewhere in the Midlands. Some 80,000 of the tribesmen were slaughtered, against only 400 Roman dead, and Boudicca herself is said to have taken poison rather than surrender.

Bouhired, Djamila, *also spelt* Jamila Bouhaired

Born 1935
Algerian nationalist involved in the revolution

Djamila Bouhired was born in Algeria. As a liaison officer for the nationalist leader Saadi Yacef during the Algerian Revolution, she was captured, accused of terrorism, tortured, tried and sentenced to death in 1957.

Her execution was commuted and in 1958 she was sent to Rheims to be imprisoned there. She was a colleague of Djamila Boupacha, the Algerian nationalist defended by **Gisèle Halimi**. After Algerian independence in 1962, Bouhired returned to Algeria and stood for election to the national assembly.

She came to international attention through the book *Pour Djamila Bouhired* (1957) written by George Arnaud and Jacques Vergès to defend her actions.

Boulanger, Lili

Born 1893   Died 1918
French composer, the first woman winner of the
Grand Prix de Rome

Lili Boulanger was born in Paris. Her elder sister **Nadia Boulanger** encouraged and supervised her, and she studied at the Paris Conservatoire. In 1913 she became the first woman to win the Prix de Rome, with her cantata *Faust et Hélène*.

She returned from Rome to look after the families of musicians fighting in World War I but, having suffered from ill health for most of her life, died young, leaving unfinished an opera based on Maurice Maeterlinck's *La princesse Maleine*.

Among the many pieces she composed are *Pour les funérailles d'un soldat* (1912), *Du fond de l'abîme* (1914–17) and *Vieille prière bouddhique* (1917).

Boulanger, Nadia

Born 1887 Died 1979
French musician, influential teacher of composition and one of the first woman conductors

Nadia Boulanger was born in Paris to a musical family. Her father Ernest Boulanger was a teacher of voice at the Paris Conservatoire, where she studied (1879–1904), under him and under Gabriel Fauré and Charles-Marie Widor. She went on to write many vocal and instrumental works, and won second prize at the Prix de Rome in 1908 for her cantata, *La Sirène*.

After 1918, the year her talented sister **Lili Boulanger** died, she devoted herself to teaching, first at home, and later at the Conservatoire and the École Normale de Musique. In 1921 she moved to the newly founded Conservatoire Américain for US musicians at Fontainbleau, where her first pupil was Aaron Copland. She was also a noted organist and the first woman conductor of several notable US orchestras, pioneering the performance of French Baroque and Renaissance music.

Bourgeois, Louise

Born 1911
French-born American sculptor, one of the most influential of the 20th century

Louise Bourgeois was born in Paris. She studied at the École du Louvre, the Académie des Beaux-Arts and at private art schools before emigrating to the USA in 1938. She began her career as a painter, and had a one-woman show at the Bertha Schaefer Gallery in New York in 1945.

In the late 1940s she turned to woodcarving (eg *The Blind Leading the Blind*, 1947, and *One and Others*, 1955), and in the 1960s to stone and metal, creating fantastical shapes

which suggest figures, or parts of figures, without ever quite becoming 'realistic'.

Other work includes the two-metre long *The Destruction of the Father* (1974) in mixed media, *Nature Study* (1986) in bronze and *Cleavage* (1991) in marble. Bourgeois has been the recipient of numerous awards.

Bourignon, Antoinette

Born 1616 Died 1680
French mystic whose belief that she was the woman clothed with the sun in Revelations led to the foundation of Bourignonism

Antoinette Bourignon was born in Lille. Believing herself called to restore the pure spirit of the Gospel, she fled from home and entered a convent, but her authoritarian approach and innate distrust of human nature meant that she was not suited to convent life, nor to the charge she had of a hospital in Lille.

Around 1667 she gathered followers in Amsterdam, continuing her mission of criticizing all kinds of religious organization and printing enthusiastic works, but was driven out. She later founded a hospital in East Friesland.

Bourignonism spread through the Netherlands and France and prevailed in Scotland to such an extent around 1720 that until 1889 a solemn renunciation was demanded from every entrant into the Presbyterian ministry.

Bourke-White, Margaret, *originally* Margaret White

Born 1906 Died 1971
American photojournalist who pioneered the photo-essay and was the first woman photographer attached to the US armed forces

Margaret Bourke-White was born in New York City, the daughter of a print designer, and trained in photography at Columbia University. In 1927 she started as an industrial and architectural photographer but was engaged by *Fortune* magazine in 1929 and became a staff photographer and associate editor on *Life* magazine when it started publication in 1936. Her 70 photographs for the study by Erskine Caldwell (to whom she was married 1939–42) of rural poverty in the southern USA, *You Have Seen Their Faces* (1937), were highly individual, and contrasted with the more dispassionate records of the US government FSA (Farm Security Administration) workers.

She covered World War II for *Life* and was the first woman photographer to be attached to the US armed forces, producing outstanding reports of the siege of Moscow (1941) and the opening of the concentration camps in 1944. After the War, she recorded the troubles in India, Pakistan and South Africa, and was an official UN war correspondent during the Korean War.

From 1952 she suffered from Parkinson's Disease, but she continued to produce many photo-journalistic essays until her retirement from *Life* in 1969. Her books include *Eyes on Russia* (1931), *Halfway to Freedom* (1946) and an autobiography, *Portrait of Myself* (1963).

Bow, Clara

Born 1905 Died 1965
American film actress and a star of the silent screen who typified the vivacious flapper of the Jazz Age, and spread the concept of 'it'

Clara Bow was born into poverty in Brooklyn, New York. Having won a beauty contest, she went to Hollywood in 1921. Her first part was in *Beyond the Rainbow*, 1922, but even though it was edited out, she went on to become a star.

Elinor Glyn's comment that above all others Bow possessed 'it' (ie sex appeal) led to her role in the film of Glyn's novelette *It* (1927) and Paramount's exploitation of this characterization — an alleged combinaton of **Mary Pickford**'s innocence and **Theda Bara**'s cunning.

Bow's run of successes, such as *The Plastic Age* (1925) and *Dancing Mothers* (1926), in which she often played the working-class woman achieving her own emancipation, was ended early in the 1930s by ill health and scandals concerning her love affairs; she suffered nervous breakdowns for much of her

Clara Bow

life. She eloped with cowboy star Rex Bell, married him in 1931, and settled in Nevada.

Bowen, Elizabeth Dorothea Cole

Born 1899 Died 1973
Irish novelist and short-story writer who set her stories against wartime London

Elizabeth Bowen was born in County Cork, the daughter of a wealthy barrister and landowner, brought up in Dublin, and educated at Downe House School in England. She married in 1923 and in the same year published her first collection of short stories, *Encounters*, followed by *Anne Lee's* (1926).

Her first novel, *The Hotel* (1927), was the first of a string of delicately-written explorations of upper-class relationships, of which *The Death of the Heart* (1938) and *The Heat of the Day* (1949), a war story, are the best known, the latter confirming her reputation as a leading World War II writer.

She moved to London in 1935 and joined the literary circle that included **Virginia Woolf** and **Iris Murdoch**. Her early life provided the material for the autobiographical *Seven Winters* (1942) and *Bowen's Court* (1942), a family history. She was also a perceptive literary critic, and published *English Novelists* (1942) and *Collected Impressions* (1950).

Box, Betty *see* Box, Muriel

Box, (Violette) Muriel, *née* Baker

Born 1905 Died 1991
English screenwriter best known for her writing partnership with her husband Sidney

Muriel Baker was born in Tolworth, Surrey. She began her career as a script girl, and made her writing début with *Alibi Inn* (1935). Her plays often featured all-women casts, anticipating the dominant female roles in her scripts for Gainsborough Films. She married Sydney Box (1907–83) in 1935, and they established a very successful writing partnership that endured until 1958. Their marriage ended in 1969.

They shared an Oscar for *The Seventh Veil* in 1945, and worked together on many films for Sydney Box's production company, Verity Films, before being signed to major studios within the Rank Organization. Sidney's sister, the film producer Betty Box (1920–   ), also became part of the creative team. She took charge of Islington Studios in 1947, and oversaw many films, including *The 39 Steps* (1960) and *Deadlier Than The Male* (1966).

Muriel Box took part in the campaign for women's rights during the 1960s, and founded the feminist press Femina Books in 1966, among other activities. In 1970 she married the Lord Chancellor, Gerald Gardiner, and thereafter turned her attention to political causes.

Boyd, Anne Elizabeth

Born 1946
Australian composer and flautist whose interest in Asian and Australian music influences her work

Anne Boyd was born in Sydney. She studied composition there under Peter Sculthorpe and Richard Meale, and later under Wilfrid Mellers at York University, England. After some years teaching in England and Australia, she became founding head of the department of music at Hong Kong University (1981).

Her interest in ethno-musicology, in Australian Aboriginal music and that of Japan and Java, is reflected in her compositions, many of which have been recorded, such as *As I Crossed the Bridge of Dreams* and her children's opera, *The Little Mermaid*.

Boye, Karin Maria

Born 1900 Died 1941
Swedish poet and novelist who was a leading voice in Swedish modernist poetry

Karin Boye was born in Gothenburg. She studied at Uppsala University and worked for a time as a teacher and journalist. In 1925 she abandoned Christianity in favour of the socialist *Clarté* group, but seems to have been more directly affected by psychoanalytic ideas than by Marxism. She acknowledged herself to be sexually ambivalent, and was profoundly concerned with the relationship between instinct and social convention.

Much of her poetry appeared in the modernist journal *Spektrum*, which she founded and edited from 1931, and in which she also published translations of T S Eliot. Her collections include *Moln* (1922, 'Cloud'), *För trädets skull* (1935, 'For the Tree's Sake') and the posthumous *De sju dödssynderna* (1941, 'The Seven Deadly Sins'), published posthumously. Despite the lyrical simplicity of this last volume, Boye had for some time been profoundly depressed about the rise of totalitarianism; this concern is explored in her novels *Kris* (1934, 'Crisis') and *Kallocain* (1940), a science fiction novel. Her suffering from serious depression continued, and culminated in suicide.

Boyle, Kay

Born 1902 Died 1992
American novelist, short-story writer, poet and essayist, a central figure in the group of expatriates in Paris during the inter-war years

Kay Boyle was born in St Paul, Minnesota, to a wealthy family. She was brought up and educated in the USA, studying music and architecture, then lived in Europe for 30 years, at first within the literary expatriate fraternity of Paris's Left Bank, and latterly as the *New Yorker*'s foreign correspondent (1945–53).

Influenced by the novelist Henry James, she used her experience of expatriation most effectively in *Plagued by the Nightingale* (1931) and *Generation Without Farewell* (1960), but her novels are generally inferior to her stories, which are amassed in several volumes including *The Smoking Mountain* (1951). She won the O Henry award for 'The White Horses of Vienna' in 1935 and 'Defeat' in 1941. Her poems, indebted to William Carlos Williams (1883–1963) and Pádraic Colum (1881–1972), were collected in 1962.

Boyle was professor of English at San Francisco State University from 1963 to 1979, and was imprisoned while in her late sixties for demonstrating against the Vietnam War. She also took an active part in the civil rights movement, campaigning against torture and censorship.

Bracegirdle, Anne

Born c.1663 Died 1748
English actress and one of the earliest women to make a career of the stage

Anne Bracegirdle began her career in 1688 under Thomas Betterton at the United Company in Drury Lane Theatre, then in 1695 moved with him and **Elizabeth Barry** to found a new company at the Lincoln's Inn Fields Theatre. She acted some tragic heroines, but excelled in comedy especially as witty, sophisticated women; she is said to have particularly enjoyed roles that required dressing in breeches.

Bracegirdle was renowned for her beauty and for the characters she created in the plays of William Congreve, such as Angelica in *Love for Love* (1695) and Millamant in *The Way of the World* (1700). She retired in 1707, possibly to make way for the talents of **Anne Oldfield**. Though she maintained a reputation for virtue and chastity, she is also said to have been Congreve's mistress for several years.

Brackeen, JoAnne, *née* Grogan

Born 1938
American jazz pianist and composer who played
in several prominent bands before going solo

JoAnne Brackeen was born in Ventura, California. Though she studied at the Los Angeles Conservatory, she is largely self-taught, replacing an early 'West Coast' influence with a personalized modernist style. She moved to New York City in 1965 with her then husband, black saxophonist Charles Brackeen, their marriage suffering considerable strain due to being interracial.

After playing with Art Blakey's prestigious Jazz Messengers between 1969 and 1972, Brackeen worked with saxophonists Joe Henderson (who has made a practice of employing female musicians) and Stan Getz, before striking out as a solo artist.

She instigated the Concord label's influential *Live at Maybeck Hall* series. Other important recordings include *Special Identity* (1981), which features many of her compositions.

Braddock, Bessie, *née* Bamber

Born 1899 Died 1970
English Labour politician and outspoken
champion of the working classes.

Bessie Bamber was born in Liverpool, the daughter of a successful bookbinder, and grew up with an awareness of the social injustices and inequalities prevalent in her native city. In 1922 she married Jack Braddock.

As a member of the Liverpool City Council between 1930 and 1961, and Alderman from 1955 to 1961, Braddock campaigned for improved housing. In 1945 she was elected to parliament as MP for the Exchange Division of Liverpool.

She was an outspoken parliamentarian with no party allegiance and spoke her mind on issues she cared about, fearless of criticising her party.

Braddon, Mary Elizabeth

Born 1835 Died 1915
English novelist who wrote prolifically and created
the then shocking concept of the beautiful blonde
criminal

Mary Braddon was born in London. She began writing in 1856 to help support first her family — her mother had left her father when she was three — and then the children from a previous marriage of her husband, the publisher John Maxwell, and eventually her own children.

She attained fame with a Victorian thriller, *Lady Audley's Secret* (1862), the melodramatic story of a golden-haired woman murderer. **Margaret Oliphant** credited her with the invention of 'the fair-haired demon of modern fiction'.

Of some 75 popular novels, perhaps the best is *Ishmael* (1884). Her *The Doctor's Wife* (1864) is an adaptation of the theme of Flaubert's *Madame Bovary*. She also edited magazines (eg *The Mistletoe Bough*, 1878–92) and wrote nine plays.

Bradford, Barbara Taylor, *née* Taylor

Born 1933
English novelist known internationally for her
bestselling novels of money, romance and success

Barbara Taylor was born in North Armely, near Leeds. She started writing at the age of seven, had her first book published when she was 12, and at 16 began working as a journalist. In 1963 she married the German-born American Robert Bradford, and soon afterwards left for the USA, where she now lives. She took citizenship in 1993 but still describes herself as English. After settling in New York she continued in journalism, specializing in interior design, and her early publications, books of domestic advice such as *How to Solve Your Decorating Problems* and three volumes of *How to be a Perfect Wife*, appeared during the 1960s and 1970s.

Bradford usually writes about strong, adaptable, sexy women who triumph in a

Barbara Taylor Bradford, 1993

man's world because of their intellect and indomitable spirit, though *The Women in His Life* (1990) ostensibly centres on a man. Her bestsellers include *A Woman of Substance* (1979), a heady, rags-to-riches story taking Emma Harte from obscurity in Yorkshire to a new life as the founder of a retail empire. *Hold the Dream* (1985) and *To Be the Best* (1988) continue the saga.

Her astounding success has resulted in her becoming reportedly the richest English-woman after Queen **Elizabeth II**, with an estimated fortune of well over £600 million.

Bradley, Marion Zimmer, *née* Zimmer

Born 1930
American science fiction and fantasy writer who has become a leader in that genre

Marion Zimmer was born in Albany, New York. Writing under the name of her first husband, she began her prolific career in the 1960s, making her name with exciting, well-plotted adventure novels and stories.

Through her Darkover series and other novels and stories of the 1970s, she became known for her thematic examinations and characterizations. The Sword and Sorceress short-story collections show her interest in the genre as art and in encouraging other writers.

The publication of *The Mists of Avalon* in 1985 established her as a leader in the fantasy genre and highlighted the role of women in fantasy literature.

Bradstreet, Anne Dudley, *née* Dudley

Born 1612   Died 1672
English-born American Puritan poet considered to be the first published English poet in America

Anne Dudley was born probably in Northampton. In 1628 she married a Nonconformist minister, Simon Bradstreet (1603–97), who later became Governor of Massachusetts. In 1630 they emigrated to New England.

Her first volume of poems, *The Tenth Muse lately sprung up in America*, written in the style of English poet Phineas Fletcher (1582–1650), was published by her brother-in-law in London in 1650 without her knowledge. Nevertheless, Bradstreet went on to become the most renowned poet of 17th-century North America.

Bradwell, Myra R, *née* Colby

Born 1831   Died 1894
American lawyer and campaigner for women's rights

Myra Colby was born in Manchester, Vermont, and educated at Portage, and at the Ladies' Seminary, Elgin, near Chicago. She became a school teacher as universities were closed to women.

Following her marriage in 1852 to lawyer James B Bradwell, she studied law to assist him. Despite passing her legal examinations in 1869, she was debarred from practising until 1892 on grounds of gender. She argued her case in both state and national supreme courts, procuring state legislation in 1882 which granted all persons, irrespective of sex, the right to select a profession.

In 1868 she established, managed and edited the *Chicago Legal News* and in 1869 summoned the first Women's Suffrage Convention in Chicago.

Braithwaite, (Florence) Lilian

Born 1873   Died 1948
English actress who played in Arsenic and Old Lace *when she was in her seventies*

Lilian Braithwaite was born in Croydon. She made her professional début in 1897 as a member of a Shakespearian company touring to South Africa, run by her husband Gerald Lawrence. She then joined the celebrated company run by actor-manager Frank Benson in London, where she made an early impression in both Shakespearian roles and in contemporary plays.

She enjoyed a lengthy and successful stage career, reserving some of her most famous performances for its latter stages, which included a three-year run in *Arsenic and Old Lace* from 1942. She was made a DBE in 1943. Her daughter, the actress Joyce Carey, followed her onto the stage.

Bramwell-Booth, Catherine

Born 1883   Died 1987
English Salvation Army leader known for her work among disadvantaged women and children

Catherine Bramwell-Booth was born in London. She was the granddaughter of the Salvation Army's founders William and **Catherine Booth**, and followed her parents Bramwell and Florence into the Army in 1903.

Catherine taught at the SA Training College, was International Secretary for Europe (1917), and did relief work for children after World Wars I and II. During the inter-war years she led women's social work among unmarried mothers and abused children.

She was the author of biographies of her grandmother and father, and had a gift of public speaking that served her well — right up to the celebrations for her hundredth birthday.

Bratenberg, Gerd

Born 1941
Norwegian novelist and radical feminist writer,
one of the few in Scandinavia

Gerd Bratenberg was born in Oslo. She studied at Oslo University and became involved in the new women's movement in the early 1970s. Her first novel was published in 1973 — *Opp alle jordens homofile* (Eng trans *What Comes Naturally*, 1986). It explores the complexities of being lesbian in Oslo in the 1960s, the humorous style tackling conventional prejudices head-on.

Egalias dotre (1977, Eng trans *The Daughters of Egalia*, 1985) is a feminist science-fiction novel that exposes the absurdities of patriarchal society by inverting its norms; it has enjoyed considerable international success. *Favntak* (1983, 'Embraces') depicts lesbian love, while *Sangen om St. Croix* (1979, 'The Song of St Croix'), *Ved fergestedet* (1985, 'At the Ferry Crossing') and *For alle vinder* (1989, 'To the Winds') is a realist trilogy focusing on differences of class and sex.

Braun, Emma Lucy

Born 1889 Died 1971
American botanist, an early champion of the
importance of plant ecology and conservation

Emma Braun was born in Cincinnati and graduated from the University of Cincinnati with a Masters degree in geology in 1912 and a PhD in botany in 1914. She remained in academic positions at the university, becoming Professor of Plant Ecology in 1946, until taking early retirement in 1948.

Her ecological work focused on detailed case studies of the vegetation in a variety of habitats in Ohio and Kentucky, and her analyses of regional variations over a period of time became very important.

She contributed to the growing conservation movement, stressing the importance of preserving natural habitats, and became the first woman to be elected President of the Ecological Society of America.

Braun, Eva

Born 1912 Died 1945
German woman who was the mistress and briefly
the wife of Adolf Hitler

Eva Braun was born in Munich. She met Hitler while employed as secretary to his staff photographer. An athletic person with frivolous interests, she became his mistress in the 1930s, living in a house provided by him until moving to his chalet in Berchtesgaden.

She is thought to have satisfied his need for relaxation and companionship rather than for purely sexual gratification. Though she was never allowed to appear in public with him, she disobeyed his orders and followed him to Berlin in 1945, where he rewarded her loyalty with marriage before they committed suicide together in the air-raid shelter of the Chancellery during the fall of Berlin.

Braun, Lily, *née* von Kretschmann

Born 1865 Died 1916
German socialist writer and feminist prominent
in literary and political circles

Lily von Kretschmann was born in Halberstadt, and first entered literary circles when she published her grandmother's memoirs, *Aus Goethes Freundeskreis* (1892). She married the philosopher Von Gizycki in 1893 and on his death in 1895 she married the socialist politician Heinrich Braun, becoming a member of the Social Democrat Party in 1896.

She is best remembered for her books *Die Frauenfrage* (1901), *Im Schatten der Titanen* (1908) and *Memoiren einer Sozialisten* (1909–11).

Bremer, Fredrika

Born 1801 Died 1865
Swedish novelist and champion of women's rights
credited with contributing the domestic novel to
Swedish literature

Fredrika Bremer was born near Åbo in Finland, and brought up near Stockholm. In her early twenties she travelled with her family in Europe but became unwell and depressed and began to write to occupy herself. Her stories *Teckningar utur hvardagslifvet* (1828, 'Scenes from Everyday Life'), published anonymously, were immediately successful and helped bring about realistic family fiction in Sweden; *Familjen H* (1831, 'The H Family') and *Hemmet* (1839, 'The Home') developed the strain considerably.

Novels like *Hertha* (1856) and *Fader och dotter* (1858, 'Father and Daughter') express her interest in female education and political emancipation, ideas she had absorbed on visits to Britain and the USA. She travelled widely elsewhere in Europe and the Levant and published two volumes of impressions.

Brent-Dyer, Elinor M(ary)

Born 1894 Died 1969
English author of 98 books for schoolgirls famous
especially for her 'Chalet School' stories

Elinor M Brent-Dyer was born in South Shields and educated at Leeds University. She became a schoolmistress and later head-mistress of the Margaret Roper Girls' School in Hereford.

Her first schoolgirl novel, *Gerry Goes to School*, appeared in 1922, inaugurating her 98 titles. Her fourth book, *The School at the Chalet* (1925), established her famous series by showing the 24-year-old Madge Bettany's successful attempt to found an English school in the Austrian Tyrol, to which Austrian as well as English parents were attracted. Centred on Jo Bettany, Madge's younger sister, the series sought to evangelize against English parochialism and xenophobia. Perhaps the best single title was *The Chalet School in Exile* (1940), a horrific if judicious account of the school's flight from Nazi rule.

Later stories were set in the Channel Islands, in Wales, and in the Bernese Oberland; the inevitable decline was offset for many years by the creation of another memorable character, the impetuous and gloriously frank Mary-Lou Trelawney. The final book in the series, *Prefects of the Chalet School*, was published posthumously in 1970.

Breshko-Breshkovskaya, Ekaterina Konstantinova

Born 1844 Died 1934
Russian revolutionary who was nicknamed the
'Grandmother of the Revolution'

Ekaterina Breshko-Breshkovskaya was the colourful and independent-minded daughter of a Polish landowner and a Russian aristocrat. She associated with various liberal and revolutionary groups in the more open society of St Petersburg under Alexander II, before working in the 1870s with the Narodniki revolutionaries (Russian populists who pinned their hopes for political and social change on the peasantry, whom they tried to stir into action). She was arrested and sent to Siberia in 1874, and was not allowed back into European Russia until 1896.

In 1901 she helped to found the Socialist Revolutionary Party but in 1908 she was again exiled to Siberia, from which she was able to return only in 1917. Though she had been dubbed the 'Grandmother of the Revolution', she fell out with the Bolsheviks after their victory in October 1917, and died in Prague a firm anti-communist.

Brice, Fanny, *originally* Fanny Borach

Born 1891 Died 1951
American singer and actress, a star of the lavish
Ziegfeld Follies

Fanny Brice was born in New York. She sang as a child in her parents' saloon, then won a singing contest at 13. She toured in the comedy *College Girls,* and was signed by Florenz Ziegfeld for the *Follies of 1910,* where her vivacious style made her a star.

She played in six further *Follies* for Ziegfeld, and two more for the Shubert family after his death. She performed in many other shows and revues, and was adept at both comic and torch songs. She married a well-known gangster, Nicky Arnstein, and her life provided the basis of the hit musical *Funny Girl* (1964).

Bride, St *see* Brigid, St

Bridget, St *see* Birgitta, St *and* Brigid, St

Bridgman, Laura Dewey

Born 1829 Died 1889
American blind deaf-mute, the first to benefit from
systematic education

Laura Dewey Bridgman was born in Hanover, New Hampshire. At the age of two a violent fever utterly destroyed her sight, hearing, smell and in some degree taste. From 1837 Dr Samuel Howe educated her systematically using a kind of raised alphabet at his Perkins School for the Blind. She was the first person to be so taught, and later became a skilful teacher of blind deaf-mutes. She is referred to in Charles Dickens's *American Notes* (1842).

Brigid, St, *also called* Bride *or* Bridget

Born c.453 Died 523
Irish abbess and great saint of Ireland whose story
comes as much from myth and legend as from
historical fact

Brigid was said to be the daughter of a peasant woman and an Ulster prince, who offered her hand in marriage to the King of Ulster. The King was so impressed by the girl's piety that he refused and released her from the control of her parents. She entered a convent at Meath in her fourteenth year, and founded the first convent in Ireland at Kildare (c.470).

She later founded three other monasteries for women, was regarded as one of the three great saints of Ireland (the others being St Patrick and St Columba) and was held in great reverence in Scotland (as St Bride). Her feast day is 1 February. The many place names and churches throughout Britain that testify to the extent of her cult include St Bride's Bay in Dyfed, Wales, and the church of St Bride's in Fleet Street, London.

Brigman, Anne, *also called* Annie Wardrope, *née* Nott *or* Knott

Born 1868   Died 1950
American pictorialist photographer and poet best known for portraits and for allegorical studies of landscapes

Anne Nott was born in Honolulu, Hawaii, where her mother's family had moved to carry out missionary work. She was educated in Hawaii and moved with her family to Los Gatos, California, c.1886. After about eight years she married sea captain Martin Brigman and went to live in Oakland; they separated in 1910.

Self-taught in photography — her sister, Elizabeth Nott, was also a photographer — she freelanced until the 1930s when, because of failing eyesight, she abandoned photography for writing. She exhibited from 1902 and was elected a fellow of the Photo-Secession group in 1906, and of the Linked Ring pictorialist group in 1909, whose aim was to evoke the meaning beyond the mere appearance of an object. Her allegorical landscapes were characterized by nude or draped figures, and she also painted portraits.

The photographer and gallerist Alfred Stieglitz (1864–1946) became a good friend and promoted her work, which was represented in the first exhibition of the Photo-Secessionists in New York in 1905–6, and first published in Stieglitz's magazine *Camera Work* in 1909. In 1949 a book of her photographs and poetry was published, entitled *Songs of a Pagan*.

Brinsmead, Hesba Fay

Born 1922
Australian author of award-winning fiction for teenagers

Hesba Brinsmead was born in Bilpin, Blue Mountains, New South Wales. Her first work, *Pastures of the Blue Crane* (1964), achieved immediate success, winning two awards and becoming a popular television series in the 1970s. She was one of the first writers of books giving perspectives within an adolescent frame of reference.

Many of her adolescent romances are set in country areas, such as the Tasmania of *Season of the Briar* (1965), but she is aware of the social and racial tensions which affect young people, as in *Beat of the City* (1966). *Longtime Passing* (1971) won the Children's Book of the Year award and was followed by *Longtime Dreaming* in 1982.

Brinvilliers, Marie Madeleine Marguerite d'Aubray, Marquise de

Born c.1630   Died 1676
French murderer who with the help of her lover poisoned nearly all her family

Marie d'Aubray was the daughter of Dreux d'Aubray, lieutenant of Paris. In 1651 she married the Marquis of Brinvilliers, who introduced her to a handsome young officer, Godin de Sainte Croix. He became her lover but in 1663 was sent to the Bastille by her father.

On his release the couple set about poisoning her father and other members of her family. Though Brinvilliers escaped, her father, brothers and sisters died, as eventually did Sainte Croix himself, an accidental victim of his own poison. He left incriminating documents and the marquise fled, but was arrested in Liège, taken to Paris and executed.

Brittain, Vera Mary

Born 1893   Died 1970
English novelist, biographer and poet whose Testament of Youth was an instant bestseller

Vera Brittain was born in Newcastle-under-Lyme and educated at Somerville College, Oxford, despite her parents' objections. She served as a nurse in World War I, and recorded her experiences with war-found idealism in *Testament of Youth* (1933). As well as writing a number of novels, she made several lecture tours in the USA, promoting feminism and pacifism, concerns to which she was to become increasingly committed.

In 1925 she married George Catlin, Professor of Politics at Cornell University. He spent a great deal of time in the USA while Brittain remained in England with her friend **Winifred Holtby**, to whom the next volume of her autobiography, *Testament of Friendship* (1940), was a tribute. The third book in the series was *Testament of Experience* (1957), which is based on the years 1925–50. She also wrote novels and poems. Her daughter is the English politician **Shirley Williams**.

Britton, Alison

Born 1948
English potter who achieved international recognition during the 1970s and is now regarded as a major ceramic artist

Alison Britton was born in Harrow, Middlesex, and trained at Leeds School of Art, the Central School of Art and Design and the Royal College of Art. Her unique handbuilt, high-fired earthenware, often with hand-painted and inlaid patterns, broke new ground in an exciting era when many of the traditional values of wheelmade pottery gave way to a more expressive generation of potters.

Her work can be seen in public collections throughout the world and she has also written many articles. She is a member of the Crafts Council and was awarded the OBE for services to pottery in 1990.

Brodber, Erna

Born 1940
Jamaican novelist whose writing developed from her documentation of Jamaica's social history

Erna Brodber was born in the village of Woodside, St Mary, and educated at the University of West Indies. She is a respected sociologist and social historian and has published extensively in these fields. Her fiction draws on this knowledge and gives a strong sense of the importance of oral history and culture in transmitting traditional wisdom and an appreciation of African ancestry.

Her first novel, *Jane and Louisa Will Soon Come Home* (1980), is a semi-autobiographical prose-poem centring on the character Nellie's search for identity. In both this work and in *Myal* (1989), a lyrical, amusing novel which scrutinizes the educational and religious institutions derived from a colonial past, the acceptance of the varied strands of a multiracial past is shown to be essential for the renewal of individual and society.

Brodber is the sister of the poet, short-story writer and critic, Velma Pollard (1937–   ).

Bronhill, June, *originally* June Gough

Born 1929
Australian operatic soprano who has also had success in musical comedy

June Gough was born in the mining town of Broken Hill, New South Wales, from which she adapted her stage-name. After coming third to **Joan Sutherland** in the Sydney *Sun* Aria competition (1949), and winning it the following year, her home town raised funds to send her to London for further study.

In 1954 she became an immediate success at Sadler's Wells in musicals such as *Robert and Elizabeth* and *The Sound of Music*, and in operetta, particularly as *The Merry Widow*. Later, she took the lead in *Lucia di Lammermoor* at Covent Garden, London (1959).

She continued her career singing mainly for the major opera companies of Australia.

Brontë, *originally* Brunty *or* Prunty

The surname of three sisters, Anne, Charlotte and Emily, who are remarkable figures in English literary history

The Brontë sisters were born in Thornton, Yorkshire. They were the daughters of Patrick Brontë (1777–1861), a clergyman of Irish descent, and his Cornish wife, Maria (1783–1821). They also had two sisters, Maria and Elizabeth, who both died in childhood, and a brother, Branwell (1817–48), who squandered his many talents.

In 1820 the family moved to Haworth, now part of Keighley, when their father became rector there. After the mother's death from cancer, her sister came to look after the children. Their childhood, spent in the sole companionship of one another on the wild Yorkshire moors, was happy enough. They had a harsh schooling at Cowan Bridge, but Roe Head, their second school, proved more amenable. Branwell's debts caused them to leave home and find employment, but they always returned to their beloved Haworth.

Brontë, Anne, *pseud* Acton Bell

Born 1820 Died 1849
The Brontë sister who wrote Agnes Grey and The Tenant of Wildfell Hall

Anne Brontë went as governess to the Inghams at Blake Hall in 1839 and to the Robinsons at Thorpe Green (1841–5), a post she had to leave because of her brother Branwell's love for Mrs Robinson.

She shared in the joint publication, with her sisters **Charlotte** and **Emily**, all under pseudonyms, of their *Poems* (1846), only two volumes of which were sold. Her two novels, *Agnes Grey* (1845) and *The Tenant of Wildfell Hall* (1848), although unsuccessful at the time, show a decided talent, if less vivid than that of her sisters.

Brontë, Charlotte, *pseud* Currer Bell

Born 1816 Died 1855
The Brontë sister whose masterpiece was Jane Eyre

In 1835 Charlotte Brontë returned to her old school, Roe Head, as teacher, but gave up this post and two others, both as governess. Back at Haworth, she and her sisters **Anne** and

Charlotte Brontë

Emily planned to start a school of their own and, to augment their qualifications, Charlotte and Emily attended the Héger Pensionat in Brussels (1842). Their plans foundered, however, and Charlotte returned to Brussels as an English teacher (1843–4) and formed an un-reciprocated attachment to the married M Héger, whom she later scornfully satirized in *Villette* (1852).

Her chance discovery of Emily's remarkable poems in 1845 led to the abortive joint publication, under pseudonyms, of the three sisters' *Poems* (1846). This provoked them all to novel-writing. *The Professor*, which did not achieve publication until Charlotte's death, dwells on the theme of moral madness, possibly inspired by her brother Branwell's degeneration. It was rejected by her publisher, but with sufficient encouragement for her to complete her masterpiece, *Jane Eyre* (1847). This in essence, through the master–pupil love relationship between Rochester and Jane, constituted a magnificent plea for feminine equality with men in the avowal of their passions. It was followed in 1849 by *Shirley*, a novel set in the background of the Luddite riots.

By now her brother and two sisters were dead, and she was left alone at Haworth with her father. *Villette*, founded on her memories of Brussels, was published in 1853. She married her father's curate, Arthur Bell Nich-

olls, in 1854 and died during pregnancy in the following year, leaving the fragment of another novel, *Emma*. Two stories, *The Secret* and *Lily Hart*, were published for the first time in 1978.

Brontë, Emily Jane, *pseud* Ellis Bell

Born 1818 Died 1848
The Brontë sister who wrote Wuthering Heights

Emily Brontë became a governess in Halifax in 1837. She attended the Héger Pensionat in Brussels with Charlotte and in 1845 embarked upon a joint publication of poems after Charlotte's discovery of her *Gondal* verse, including such fine items as *To Imagination, Plead for Me* and *Last Lines*.

Her single novel, *Wuthering Heights* (1847), an intense and powerful tale of love and revenge set in the remote wilds of 18th-century Yorkshire, has much in common with Greek tragedy and has no real counterpart in English literature.

Brooke, Frances, *née* Moore

Born 1723 Died 1789
English novelist and playwright recognized as the author of Canada's first novel

Frances Moore was born in Claypole and educated at home. In the late 1740s she established herself in the literary circles of London, and in 1755 she married the Rev John Brooke, who did not seem to mind her pursuing her literary concerns; these included editing her own periodical, *The Old Maid*, under the name of 'Mary Singleton, spinster'.

Following the publication of the novel *The History of Lady Julia Mandeville* in 1763, she followed her husband to Quebec, as he had become an army chaplain there. She spent five years in Canada, where she wrote the country's first novel, *The History of Emily Montague* (1769). Set in Quebec during the 1760s, the novel explores the differences of a 'woman's place' in England and Canada as well as the complexity of French–English relations, and also details many features of the pioneer settler's life in Canada.

In addition to three novels, she wrote and staged a number of dramatic works, and translated a number of texts from Italian and French. Her work has been reassessed in the light of more recent gender studies.

Brookner, Anita

Born 1928
English novelist and art historian whose main characters are women, self-sufficient in all but love

Anita Brookner was born in London of Polish parentage. She became an authority on 18th-century painting, and was the first woman Slade Professor at Cambridge University (1967–8). From 1977 to 1988 she was a reader at the Courtauld Institute of Art.

She is the author of *Watteau* (1968), *The Genius of the Future* (1971) and *Jacques-Louis David* (1981). As a novelist she was a late starter, but in eight years (1981–8) she published as many novels, elegant, witty and imbued with cosmopolitan melancholy.

By winning the Booker Prize, *Hôtel du Lac* (1984) has become her best-known novel and is regarded by many as her most accomplished. Other titles include *Family and Friends* (1985), *Friends from England* (1987) and *A Private View* (1994).

Brooks, Gwendolyn

Born 1917
American poet and novelist who focuses on the African-American community and was the first black writer to win a Pulitzer Prize

Gwendolyn Brooks was born in Topeka, Kansas, and brought up in the slums of Chicago. She was an active writer from an early age, and had her first poem published at the age of 13. She has taught English in a number of colleges and was Publicity Director of the NAACP (National Association for the Advancement of Colored People) for a time in the 1930s.

Her first collection, *A Street in Bronzeville* (1945), chronicles the cares of city-dwelling black Americans, while *Annie Allen* (1949) traces the growth to maturity of a black woman amid the spiritual and social ills of her race; it earned her a Pulitzer Prize in 1950.

Subsequent works in both poetry and prose have focused on the life and politics of the USA's black community. *Riot* (1969) and *Blacks* (1987) are examples of her increasingly radical tone. *Maud Martha* (1953) is about one woman's growing personal and political maturity, while the autobiography, *Report From Part One* (1972), may be said to account for the same process in Brooks herself.

Brooks, Louise

Born 1906 Died 1985
American actress who displayed a naturalness and ease before the cameras that was rare for the time

Louise Brooks was born in Cherryvale, Kansas. She became a member of the Denishawn Dancers troupe in 1922, then moved to New York and joined the cast of, among others, the

Ziegfeld Follies (1925–6). She made her film début in *Street of Forgotten Men* (1925) and signed a contract with Paramount that led to roles in such comedies as *It's The Old Army Game* (1926) and spirited shenanigans like *Just Another Blonde* (1927), in which she became a luminous embodiment of the flapper age.

She left Paramount and went to Germany for G W Pabst's *Die Büchse von Pandora* (1928, 'Pandora's Box') and her most famous role as Lulu, 'the personification of primitive sexuality'. The purity of her erotic appeal was underlined by Pabst's *Das Tagebüch einer Verlorenen* (1929, 'Diary of a Lost Girl'). Brooks returned to Hollywood but was given only supporting roles and retired after playing opposite John Wayne in the B western *Overland Raiders* (1938).

She later ran a dance studio, worked in radio soap opera, and became a writer on film, publishing an autobiography, *Lulu in Hollywood*, in 1982.

Brophy, Brigid Antonia

Born 1929 Died 1995
English novelist, essayist, playwright, critic and intellectual who fought for the Public Lending Right

Brigid Brophy was born in London and educated at St Paul's Girls' School and at Oxford. Her first novel, *Hackenfeller's Ape*, appeared in 1953, revealing her social, ethical and philosophical concerns, in particular her opposition to vivisection. Other novels, such as *The Finishing Touch* (1963) and *In Transit* (1969), look at lesbianism and transsexuality, while in *Palace Without Chairs* (1978), the lesbian life-force bursts through a bleak Absurdist nightmare. *The Snow Ball* (1964), in which the characters dress up for a ball as characters from *Don Giovanni*, shows Brophy's intense love of Mozart. Her themes often cause her to be linked with **Angela Carter**.

Her critical works among her 25 publications include *Mozart the Dramatist: A New View of Mozart, His Operas and His Age* (1964), the infamous *Fifty Works of English Literature We Could Do Without* (1967), studies of Aubrey Beardsley (1968), on censorship (1972) and a vivacious defence of the work of the novelist Ronald Firbank (1886–1926) entitled *Prancing Novelist* (1973).

In 1972 she began a successful campaign for the Public Lending Right through which authors would be paid a small sum from the government each time one of their books was borrowed from a British library. The campaign was won in 1979. Struck down in the early 1980s with multiple sclerosis, Brophy suffered a long illness but enjoyed the devotion of her husband, Sir Michael Levey, and wrote about her experiences in the collection of essays *Baroque 'n' Roll* (1985).

Brown, Helen Gurley, *née* Gurley

Born 1922
American journalist and commentator on gender affairs, responsible for the success of Cosmopolitan *magazine*

Helen Gurley was born in Green Forest, Arkansas. She studied at Texas State College and Woodbury College, and worked in junior management for three years before embarking upon a career in advertising. In 1959 she married David Brown.

In 1965 she was appointed editor-in-chief of the ailing *Cosmopolitan* magazine which she transformed into an international success, remaining until she retired in 1996 at the age of 73, still convincingly insistent that she was the epitome of the *Cosmo* girl. She is the recipient of many awards, including the Distinguished Achievement Award in Journalism, Stanford University (1977) and the New York Women in Communications Award (1985).

Her first book was the bestseller *Sex and the Single Girl* (1962) which reflected a new mood of female independence. Other works include *Outrageous Opinions* (1966), *Sex and the New Single Girl* (1970) and *Having it All* (1982).

Helen Gurley Brown, 1962

Brown, Hilary

Born 1952
Scottish chef who runs the acclaimed La Potinière with her husband

Hilary Brown was born in Glasgow. She graduated in food and nutrition from Glasgow College of Domestic Science and taught home economics for two years before she and her husband David Brown (1951–   ) decided to start their own restaurant. He attends to the front of house and the celebrated wine list, while she is the chef.

In 1975 they opened La Potinière in Gullane, East Lothian, attending to all branches of the business themselves, an aspect of the operation which they have preserved. The restaurant soon earned acclaim for the excellently chosen and executed no-choice menus and impressive wine list, resulting in tables for Friday and Saturday night dinners being booked up several months ahead.

In 1990 Hilary Brown and **Betty Allen** became the first women in Scotland to receive a Michelin star.

Brown, Olympia

Born 1835 Died 1926
American Universalist minister and woman suffragist, the first American woman to be ordained

Olympia Brown was born in Prairie Ronde, Michigan. She was educated at Antioch College and at St Lawrence University theological school. In 1863 she became the first American woman to be ordained by full denominational authority when she was ordained by the Northern Universalist Association in Malone, New York.

As a supporter of women's rights, she served as President of the Woman Suffrage Association from 1884 to 1912 and was also Vice-President of the National Woman Suffrage Association in 1892.

Brown, Rachel Fuller

Born 1898 Died 1980
American biochemist credited with being an important fungus fighter

Rachel Brown was born in Springfield, Massachusetts and educated at the University of Chicago. She began her career as a chemist at the New York State Department of Health in 1926, where she made important studies of the causes of pneumonia and the bacteria involved.

Shortly after the end of World War II, by which time some methods of controlling bacterial forms of disease had been introduced, Brown, working in collaboration with **Elizabeth Hazen** from 1948, isolated the first antifungal antibiotic, nystatin (1949). It was patented in 1951 and marketed as Mycostatin from 1954.

She was awarded the Pioneer Chemist award of the American Institute of Chemists in 1975.

Brown, Rita Mae

Born 1944
American poet, novelist and essayist, and activist
for homosexual rights

Rita Mae Brown was born in Hanover, Pennsylvania, and grew up an orphan who was adopted by poor people. She attended the University of Florida but was expelled because of her work with the civil rights movement; instead she gained her degree from New York University.

She was an early member of NOW (National Organization for Women) but resigned because of the discrimination she experienced as a lesbian. She formed Radicalesbians and wrote the classic essay, 'The Woman-Identified Woman'. Her books include the novels *Rubyfruit Jungle* (1973), *A Plain Brown Rapper* (1976) and *Southern Discomfort* (1982).

Brown, Tina

Born 1953
English writer and editor of the New Yorker,
called the 'definitive magazine character' of the
mid-1990s

Tina Brown was born in Maidenhead, Berkshire, and educated at Oxford University. She began her career in 1978 as a columnist for *Punch* magazine, won the 1978 Young Journalist of the Year award, and became editor-in-chief of *Tatler* magazine in 1979. She married the English journalist and *Sunday Times* editor Harold Evans (1928–) in 1981.

After leaving *Tatler* in 1983, she moved with Evans to New York, where she became editor-in-chief of Condé–Nast's *Vanity Fair* magazine in 1984. Then in 1992 she was appointed the fourth editor of the élitist weekly the *New Yorker* (founded 1925), a part of the USA's heritage and traditionally the publisher of the best of American writing, however inaccessible. Brown immediately implemented changes that brought censure and praise, enlivening the magazine through the use of more colour and increased focus on current events, and improving its circulation by over 25 per cent.

Her books include the play *Under the Bamboo Tree* (1973), *Loose Talk* (1979) and *Life as A Party* (1983).

Brown, Trisha

Born 1936
American choreographer whose success with her
experimental work led to her own dance company

Trisha Brown was born in Aberdeen, Washington. A meeting in 1959 with the dancer **Yvonne Rainer** at a West Coast summer school, under the direction of the experimental choreographer and dancer Anna Halprin, led her to New York in 1961. There, along with Rainer and others, she founded the experimental Judson Dance Company in 1962.

Throughout the 1960s and 1970s she created a series of daringly original 'equipment pieces' where dancers were rigged in block and tackle harness to allow them to walk on walls or down the trunks of trees. *Walking of the Walls*, *Man Walking Down the Side of a Building* and *Spiral* are from this period, along with *Roof Piece* (1973), which dotted dancers across Manhattan roofs, signalling to one another. She founded the Trisha Brown Dance Co in 1970 and between 1970 and 1976 ran an improvisational group, Grand Union.

In the late 1970s she began to work in traditional theatres, adding design and music to her pieces for the first time. Robert Rauschenberg, the American painter, designed sets for several of her works, including *Glacial Decoy* (1979) and *Set and Reset* (1983). Later work includes *For MG: The Movie* (1991).

Browne, Coral Edith

Born 1913 Died 1991
Australian actress who emerged as a leading
actress on the British stage in the 1940s

Coral Browne was born in Melbourne. She studied painting and costume design, then made her stage début in her native city in 1931. After three years of acting in Australia, she moved to London and worked as an understudy and in experimental theatre until given the opportunity to take the lead in *The Man who Came to Dinner* with Robert Morley in 1941.

Thereafter she was very successsful in a variety of popular plays, including *The Last of Mrs Cheyney* (1944), *Lady Frederick* (1946), W Somerset Maugham's *Canaries Sometimes Sing* (1947) and *Affairs of State* (1952). She moved to Shakespearian roles, including Gertrude in *Hamlet*, a role for which she went with the Stratford Company to Moscow, where she encountered the English spy Guy Burgess.

This meeting was dramatized by Alan Bennett in *An Englishman Abroad* (1983) in which Browne appeared as her younger self and won a BAFTA award for her performance.

In 1950 she married the actor Philip Pearman (d.1964) and in 1974 the US actor Vincent Price (1911–93).

Browner, Carol M

Born 1956
American lawyer and politician who applies her
skills and influence to environmental issues

Carol Browner was born in southern Florida. Her first position concerning government environmental issues was as general counsel for the Florida House of Representatives Government Operations Committee (1979–83). From 1986 to 1989 she worked for Senator Lawton Chiles, helping to negotiate a complex land swap that expanded the Big Cypress National Preserve. She then worked with Senator Al Gore, Jr from 1989 to 1990, drafting amendments to the Clean Air Act.

When Chiles became governor of Florida, she became (1991–3) Secretary of the Department of Environmental Regulation for the State of Florida, the third-largest environmental agency in the USA. In a widely praised agreement, she allowed Walt Disney World to develop its property in exchange for $40 million to reclaim 8,500 acres of endangered land and create a wildlife refuge.

In 1993 she became director of the US Environmental Protection Agency.

Browning, Elizabeth Barrett, *née* Barrett

Born 1806 Died 1861
English poet, the most successful and respected
woman poet of the 19th century

Elizabeth Barrett was born in Coxhoe Hall, Durham. She spent her girlhood mostly on her father's estate, at Hope End in Herefordshire. At the age of 10 she read Homer in the original, and at 14 wrote an epic on *The Battle of Marathon*. During her teens she developed a tubercular complaint that damaged her spine, and was an invalid for a long time. The family ultimately settled in 50 Wimpole Street, London, in 1837. Her *Essay on Mind, and Other Poems* was published in 1826, and in 1833 she issued a translation of Aeschylus's *Prometheus Bound*. This was followed by *The Seraphim, and Other Poems* (1838), a volume containing the fine poem on William Cowper's grave.

During a visit to Torquay, her brother and a party of friends were drowned there in a boating expedition, and the shock confined her to the sickroom for many years, though she continued to write during this time. Her *Poems* appeared in 1844 and the following year she met the poet Robert Browning, six years her junior, who freed her from her sickroom and a possessive father by marrying her in 1846. They settled in Pisa (1846) and then Florence (1847), where their son Robert was born in 1849 and where they became the centre of a brilliant literary circle.

The *Poems* of 1850 contained an entirely new translation of the *Prometheus Bound*. In *Casa Guidi Windows* (1851) Barrett Browning expressed her sympathy with the regeneration of Italy. *Aurora Leigh* (1856) is a long narrative poem into which all the treasures of its writer's mind and heart have been poured. Her so-called *Sonnets from the Portuguese* (published in the *Poems* of 1850) are not translations at all, but express her own love for the country ('my little Portuguese' was Browning's pet name for her). Her *Last Poems* were published the following year.

Bruce, Mary Grant

Born 1878 Died 1958
Australian novelist and prolific writer of
adolescent fiction

Mary Bruce was born in Sale, Victoria. She began writing as a child, but moved to Melbourne in 1898 where she ran the 'Children's Page' of the *Leader* weekly newspaper, in which some of her stories were serialized as *A Little Bush Maid* and later published in book form in 1910. In a long career she published a book nearly every year until 1942, as well as much short fiction and numerous contributions to newspapers and periodicals.

Though she is considered today mainly as a children's writer, her novels in which she created both an idealistic vision of pastoral life in Australia and realistic female characters, were at the time widely read by adults and were so reviewed. Her fame lies mainly in the *Billabong* series of novels of Australian pastoral life and their heroine Norah Linton, perhaps the first Australian female character drawn in an unpatronizing and realistic light.

Brundtland, Gro Harlem, *née* Harlem

Born 1939
Norwegian Labour politician who became
Norway's first woman Prime Minister

Gro Harlem was born in Oslo, the daughter of a doctor who became a Cabinet Minister. She studied medicine at Oslo and Harvard and qualified as a physician, and in 1960 married

Gro Harlem Brundtland, 1993

a leader of the opposition Conservative Party, Arne Olav Brundtland. After working in public medicine services in Oslo, in 1969 she joined the Labour Party and entered politics.

She was appointed Environment Minister (1974–9) and then, as leader of the Labour Party group, became Prime Minister for a short time in 1981. She was Prime Minister again in 1986, with a minority cabinet, and in 1987 chaired the world commission on environment and development which produced the report *Our Common Future*. In 1988 she was awarded the Third World Foundation prize for leadership in environmental issues.

In 1989 she was defeated by a centre-right coalition, but when it collapsed the following year, she became Prime Minister, again with a minority Labour Cabinet, with which she continued in power after the 1993 elections.

Brunhilde

Born c.534 Died 613
Frankish queen whose tyranny made her one of the most influential people of the Merovingian era

Brunhilde was the daughter of the Visigothic king Athanagild. She married King Sigebert I of Austrasia in 567, and after his murder in 575 by her rival **Fredegund**, became regent for her young son Childebert II.

After his death (c.595) she was regent for her two grandsons, Theodebert II, king of Austrasia, and Theodoric II, king of Burgundy, and divided the government of the whole Frankish world with Fredegund, who governed Neustria for the youthful Clotaire II.

On Fredegund's death in 598 she seized Neustria, and for a time united under her rule the whole Merovingian dominions, but was overthrown by the Austrasian nobels under Clotaire II and put to death by being dragged at the heels of a wild horse.

Brunton, Mary, *née* Balfour

Born 1778 Died 1818
Scottish novelist of the 'improver-satirist' school

Mary Balfour was born in Orkney, the daughter of an army officer. In 1798 she married the Rev Alexander Brunton, whom she called 'my companion and instructor', and they settled in the parish of Bolton, East Lothian. Between 1803 and her death she lived in Edinburgh where her husband was minister of the Tron Kirk and Professor of Oriental Languages at Edinburgh University.

She made her name with her first novel *Self Control* (1810), which she dedicated to her close friend **Joanna Baillie**, and which **Jane Austen** called an 'elegantly written work, without anything of nature or probability in it'. Her next novel was *Discipline* (1814). Both were so-called improving works, very popular in their day, and she was included in the school of 'improver-satirists' along with **Susan Ferrier** and Elizabeth Hamilton.

After a visit to England in 1815 she planned a series of domestic sketches on middle-class manners, but only one, *Emmeline* (1819), was completed before her death in childbirth.

Bryant, Sophie, *née* Willock

Born 1850 Died 1922
Irish campaigner for women's education, and the first woman Doctor of Science

Sophie Willock was born in Ireland and educated by her father until she won a scholarship to Bedford College. She married a Dr Bryant at the age of 18 but was widowed at 20.

While studying for a BA in Mental and Moral Science and Mathematics (1881), she taught at North London Collegiate School, where she became headmistress in 1895. She was the first woman DSc (Psychology, Logic and Ethics, 1884), a member of the Board of Studies in Pedagogy for 20 years and served on the Bryce Commission on secondary education. In 1886 she was involved in the campaign for Home Rule for Ireland.

Buchan, Elspeth, *née* Simpson

Born 1738 Died 1791
Scottish founder of the fanatical religious sect
known as the Buchanites

Elspeth Simpson was born near Banff, the daughter of an innkeeper. Around the age of 21 she went to Glasgow, found employment in the manufacture of delft-work, and married a fellow employee, Robert Buchan.

At this time she was an Episcopalian, but she fell in line with the principles held by her husband, a Burgher-Seceder or Antiburgher. Still a regular student of the Bible however, she began to apply peculiar interpretations to the Scriptures, developing her own doctrines, and in 1784 in Irvine she founded a sect called the Buchanites, announcing herself to her followers as the Woman of Revelations 12. She gained the support of a minister, Mr Hugh White, as well as 45 converts, until the people of Irvine attacked White's home and expelled the sect from the town.

The 'Buchanites' settled near Thornhill, Dumfriesshire, and led a holy life like brothers and sisters, for they did not believe in marriage (Robert Buchan seems to have rejected his wife long before); nor did they believe in regular paid employment, believing that God would provide and that Christ would soon return. The sect's numbers were considerably reduced by the time of their founder's death.

Buchanan, Isobel Wilson

Born 1954
Scottish soprano who began her sensational career
in Australia before finding fame nearer home

Isobel Buchanan was born in Glasgow. After studying at the Royal Scottish Academy of Music and Drama, she became a principal singer with Australian Opera (1975–8). In 1978 she made sensational débuts at both Glyndebourne and the Vienna Staatsoper, and the following year appeared at Santa Fé, Chicago, New York and Cologne. She has also sung with Scottish Opera, English National Opera, at Covent Garden and the Paris Opéra. In 1980 she married the actor Jonathan Hyde.

Buck, Pearl S, *née* Sydenstricker

Born 1892 Died 1973
American novelist and Nobel Prize winner noted
for her novels about life in China

Pearl Sydenstricker was born in Hillsboro, West Virginia, the daughter of Presbyterian missionaries. She lived in China from childhood, went to the USA for her education, but returned to China as a missionary and teacher in 1921. She had married another missionary, John Lossing Buck, in 1917, but divorced him in 1934 and in 1935 married her New York publisher, Richard J Walsh, and went back to the USA.

Her earliest novels are coloured by her experiences while living in China, such as *The Good Earth* (1931), a runaway bestseller which won the 1932 Pulitzer Prize. After her return to the USA most of her output was concerned with the contemporary American scene and she was awarded the Nobel Prize for Literature in 1938.

After World War II, in aid of the illegitimate Asian children of US servicemen, she instituted the Pearl S Buck Foundation, to which she gave over $7 million of her earnings in 1967. Her other novels on China include *Sons* (1932), *A House Divided* (1935), *Dragon Seed* (1942) and *Imperial Woman* (1956), and amongst other works are *What America Means to Me* (1944) and *My Several Worlds* (1955).

Budapest, Z, *originally* Zsusanna Mokcsay

Born 1940
American writer and witch who founded a nature-
and woman-based religion

Z Budapest was born in Budapest, Hungary. During the late 1960s and through the 1970s, she worked to found a woman-centred religion — Dianic Wicca.

Based on Budapest's family traditions of spirituality and worship, it is a nature-based, goddess-centred religion. Her books include *Grandmother Moon: Lunar Magic in Our Lives—Spells, Rituals, Goddesses, Legends and Emotions Under the Moon* (1991) and *The Grandmother of Time: A Women's Book of Celebrations, Spells and Sacred Objects for Every Month of the Year*.

Budd, Zola *see* Pieterse, Zola

Bueno, Maria Esther

Born 1939
Brazilian lawn tennis player who won 17 major
championships in 10 years

Maria Bueno was born in Sao Paulo. She began playing tennis around the age of six and won her first tournament at 12, developing a graceful style that incorporated a range of shots and relied on subtlety and placement.

She won Wimbledon in 1959 and 1960 and again in 1964, and was US Open champion on four occasions. Playing in the ladies' doubles competition, she won the Wimbledon doubles title five times and the US doubles four times; her partners included **Althea Gibson**, Darlene Hard, Billie Jean Moffitt (later **Billie Jean King**) and **Margaret Smith Court**.

Ill health brought her retirement from top-class tennis at the relatively early age of 29.

Bülbring, Edith

Born 1903 Died 1990
German-born British pharmacologist known for her work on smooth muscle

Edith Bülbring was born in Bonn. She qualified in medicine in 1928 and after working as a physician she joined the department of pharmacology in Berlin; there she met **Marthe Vogt**, who became a lifelong friend.

Because her Dutch mother was Jewish, she left Germany in 1933 and moved to London, where she worked in the laboratories of the Pharmaceutical Society with J H Burn, moving with him in 1937 to Oxford. She became Reader in 1960 and Professor in 1967, remaining there until her formal retirement in 1971.

Her work on the physiology and pharmacology of smooth muscle — the muscle tissues of visceral organs such as the stomach and intestine — elucidated many of the complex control and regulatory mechanisms of normal functioning, and she was elected a Fellow of the Royal Society in 1958.

Burbidge, (Eleanor) Margaret, *née* Peachey

Born 1923
English astronomer whose work on nucleosynthesis has been of fundamental importance

Margaret Peachey was born in Davenport. She was educated at University College London (1941–7) and in 1948 married the astrophysicist Geoffrey Burbidge. Her lifelong interest in astronomical spectroscopy began in London where she served as Assistant Director of the university observatory (1948–51). In 1951 she moved to the USA and held appointments at Yerkes Observatory, the California Institute of Technology and the University of California at San Diego, where in 1964 she was appointed Professor of Astronomy (Emeritus since 1990).

In 1972 she became Director of the Royal Greenwich Observatory, a post which she relinquished the following year to return to her chair in California. From 1979 to 1988 she was Director of the Center for Astrophysics

and Space Science at San Diego, where since 1990 she has also been Research Physicist.

Together with her husband, and in collaboration with the astronomer Sir Fred Hoyle and the physicist William Fowler, she published the results of theoretical research on nucleosynthesis (the processes whereby the heavy chemical elements are built up in the cores of massive stars), a discovery of fundamental importance to physics. On the observational side, Burbidge's main field of research is in the spectra of galaxies and quasars.

Burdett-Coutts, Angela Georgina Burdett-Coutts, Baroness

Born 1814 Died 1906
English philanthropist who used a fortune inherited from Coutts to help the poor

Angela Burdett was born in London, the daughter of the politician Sir Francis Burdett, and granddaughter of the banker Thomas Coutts. On inheriting her grandfather's fortune in 1837 she took his name and, greatly influenced by Charles Dickens, used the money to mitigate suffering.

She established a shelter for fallen women, built model homes and endowed churches and colonial bishoprics, including those of Capetown, Adelaide and British Columbia. In 1871 she received a peerage, and in 1872 she became the first woman to be given the freedom of the City of London.

When in 1881 she married William Ashmead-Bartlett (1851–1921), who assumed her name, she was obliged to surrender most of her money, and her good works were brought to a halt.

Burgos Seguí, Carmen de, *pseud* Colombine

Born c.1870 Died 1932
Spanish feminist who became a prolific journalist and writer advocating women's rights

Carmen de Burgos Seguí was born sometime between 1867 and 1879 in the remote province of Almeria, the daughter of the Consul of Portugal. She married young and then moved to Madrid after being abandoned by her husband. She became a teacher and was elected to the presidency of the International League of Iberian and Hispanoamerican Women.

She was an outstanding advocate of women's rights, above all through her writing, and published a vast quantity of journalism both in Spain and Latin America (being the first Spanish female war correspondent in

1909) as well as many books on women's issues under the pseudonym 'Colombine'.

Her novels include *Los inadaptados* (1909, 'The Misfits') and *El último contrabandista* (1920, 'The Last Smuggler').

Burnett, Carol

Born 1933
American comedienne and dramatic actress who has found success on stage and screen

Carol Burnett was born in San Antonio, Texas. She majored in theatre arts and English at the University of California in Los Angeles, then moved to New York, secured an agent and found work on children's television. She made her Broadway début in *Once Upon a Mattress* (1959) and became a television regular in *The Garry Moore Show* (1959–62), for which she received her first Emmy Award.

A versatile comedy performer with impeccable timing and a delicious sense of the absurd, she enjoyed enormous success with *The Carol Burnett Show* (1967–78). Her most effective dramatic performances include the television films *Friendly Fire* (1979) and *Life of the Party: The Story of Beatrice* (1982). She has also starred in numerous television specials, but returned to a weekly series format with *Carol and Company* (1990–1).

She was inducted into the Television Hall of Fame in 1985, and published an autobiography, *One More Time*, in 1986.

Burnett, Frances (Eliza) Hodgson, *née* Hodgson

Born 1849 Died 1924
English-born American author of the popular novel Little Lord Fauntleroy *and the children's classic* The Secret Garden

Frances Hodgson was born in Manchester, the daughter of a manufacturer. In 1865 she emigrated with her parents to Knoxville, Tennessee, where she turned to writing to help out with the family finances. She married Dr Swan Moses Burnett in 1873, but divorced in 1898. There is speculation that her second marriage was made under the threat of blackmail; it was an unhappy alliance and did much to cloud her later life.

Her first literary success was *That Lass o' Lowrie's* (1877), about life in a Lancashire coal mining community. Her most popular story was *Little Lord Fauntleroy* (1886) whose boy hero's attire of velvet suit, lace collar and long curls became a firm favourite with mothers, if seldom with their sons.

Later works included plays and *The One I Knew Best of All* (1893, autobiographical), *The*

Little Princess (1905) and *The Secret Garden* (1909), which is still one of the best-loved classics of children's literature. In her lifetime Burnett was rated one of America's foremost writers, and was a friend of Henry James.

Burney, Fanny (Frances), *later* Madame D'Arblay

Born 1752 Died 1840
English novelist and diarist whose Evelina *paved the way for later accounts of social etiquette and faltering heroines*

Fanny Burney was born in King's Lynn, the daughter of the musician Charles Burney.

She educated herself by reading English and French literature and observing the distinguished people who visited her father. By the age of 10 she had begun scribbling down stories, plays and poems, but on her 15th birthday, in a fit of repentance for such waste of time, she burned all her papers. However she could not forget the plot of *Evelina*, which became her first and best novel. Published anonymously in 1778, it describes the entry of a country girl into the gaieties of London life. Her father at once recognized Fanny's talent and confided the secret to Mrs Thrale, who championed the gifted young authoress, as did Dr Johnson.

Cecilia (1782), though more complex, is less natural, and Burney's style gradually declined in *Camilla* (1796) and *The Wanderer* (1814). She was appointed a second Keeper of the Robes to Queen **Charlotte** in 1786, but her health declined; she retired on a pension and married a French émigré, General d'Arblay, in 1793. Her *Letters and Diaries* (1846) show her skill in reporting dramatically. As a portrayer of the domestic scene she was a forerunner of **Jane Austen**, whom she influenced.

Burrows, Eva

Born 1929
Australian with a lifelong involvement in Salvation Army work, appointed world leader of the Salvation Army in 1986

Eva Burrows was born in Newcastle, Australia, and educated at Brisbane High School and at the universities of Queensland, Sydney and London. The daughter of a Salvation Army officer, she committed herself to the Salvation Army while a student.

Subsequently she worked for the Salvation Army in Rhodesia (now Zimbabwe) from 1952 to 1969, England (1970–7), Sri Lanka (1977–9), Scotland (1979–82) and Southern Australia (1982–6), organizing and developing work in such areas as education, battered women's refuges, and youth training schemes.

From 1986 to 1993 she was General of the Salvation Army, only the second woman to hold this office.

Burstyn, Ellen, *née* Edna Rae Gillooly

Born 1932
American actress who established herself as a
leading character actress on stage and screen

Ellen Burstyn was born in Detroit, Michigan. She studied acting in California, and with **Stella Adler** and Lee Strasberg in New York. She made her Broadway début as Ellen McRae in 1957, and has returned regularly since.

Her notable stage successes include *The Three Sisters* (1977) and *84 Charing Cross Road* (1982), as well as both stage (1975) and film (1978) versions of *Same Time, Next Year*. She won an Academy Award for *Alice Doesn't Live Here Any More* in 1974, and was also nominated for *The Last Picture Show* (1971).

Burton, Lady Isabel, *née* Arundell

Born 1831   Died 1896
English explorer and diplomat who accompanied
her husband Sir Richard on his travels

Isabel Arundell was born into a distinguished Roman Catholic family near Marble Arch in London. After a convent education and a debutante season in London, she met and married the notorious British orientalist and explorer Sir Richard Burton (1821–90) in 1861.

Isabel was ambitious for his success and accompanied him on diplomatic postings to Brazil, Damascus and Trieste. She managed his business affairs, playing an active role in the successful publication of his controversial and scholarly translated works of the *Arabian Nights*, and erotica such as the *The Perfumed Garden* and the *Kama Sutra*.

On his death, she burned the papers she considered might tarnish her husband's reputation and wrote his biography. She is buried beside him in Mortlake cemetery in a mausoleum shaped like a Bedouin tent.

Bury, Lady Charlotte Susan Maria

Born 1775   Died 1861
Scottish novelist, the supposed author of a
risqué and controversial account of the court of
George IV

Charlotte Bury was the youngest child of the fifth Duke of Argyll. In 1796 she married Col John Campbell, on whose death in 1809 she became lady-in-waiting to **Caroline of Brunswick**, Princess of Wales. In 1818 she married the Rev Edward John Bury (1790–1832).

A beautiful and accomplished woman, she became the friend of Sir Walter Scott and published at least 14 novels (often anonymously), including *Flirtation* and *Separation*, as well as some poems. Most importantly, she was reputedly the anonymous author of the spicy and controversial two-volume *Diary Illustrative of the Times of George IV* (1838), the material for which she had supposedly gathered during her time as lady-in-waiting.

Bush, Kate (Katherine)

Born 1958
English singer and songwriter whose first hit was
'Wuthering Heights'

Kate Bush was born in Plumstead, South London. Her lyrical skills and uncategorizable voice attracted the attention of Dave Gilmour, guitarist with Pink Floyd, and he subsidized her first recording ventures.

Kate Bush, 1978

'Wuthering Heights' (1978), released on EMI, was an unusual number-one hit, marked by literary words and Bush's yodelling vocal. Her first albums, *The Kick Inside* and *Lionheart* (1978), confirmed her abilities, and live performances made much of her training in mime and drama.

Later records include *The Dreaming* (1982) and *The Hounds of Love* (1986), which touched on every subject from female sexuality to the 'orgone' theories of Wilhelm Reich.

Buss, Frances Mary

Born 1827   Died 1894
English pioneer in women's education and the first
woman to call herself 'headmistress'

Frances Buss was born in London, where she was educated until she began teaching (with her mother) at the age of 14, though she attended evening classes at Queen's College. At the age of 23 she founded the North London Collegiate School for Ladies and was headmistress (the first to be so-described) from 1850 to 1894.

In 1874 she founded the Association of Headmistresses, which she served as president for 20 years, until she was succeeded by her associate **Dorothea Beale** of Cheltenham Ladies' College. She was dedicated to creating and improving teacher-training for women and to emphasizing the need for women's secondary schools and university colleges.

She and Beale were immortalized in verse: 'Miss Buss and Miss Beale/ Cupid's darts do not feel/ How unlike us/ Miss Beale and Miss Buss.'

Butcher, Rosemary

Born 1947
English choreographer, an exponent of New Dance

Rosemary Butcher was born in Bristol. She was the first dance graduate of Dartington College in Devon, and went to New York where she saw the experimental work of **Trisha Brown**, Steve Paxton and **Lucinda Childs**. She began choreographing her own work in 1976 and has made over 30 pieces, often performing them in unusual places — in art galleries and once even on a Scottish mountainside.

She is an influential exponent of New Dance; her work is minimalist and is often made in conjunction with other artists, including film-makers. The fast-moving *Flying Lines* (1985) incorporates music by Michael Nyman and an installation by Peter Noble. The meditative *Touch the Earth* (1986) also has a Nyman score, and sculpture by the artist Dieter Pietsch.

Butcher, Susan

Born 1954
American sled-dog racer who dominated the sport during the 1980s

Susan Butcher was born in Cambridge, Massachusetts. In 1978 she entered the Last Great Race on Earth, the Iditarod Trail Sled Dog Race, an 11-day race from Anchorage to Nome, Alaska. She finished nineteenth, but finished ninth the following year. Entering every year, she won in 1986, 1987, 1988 and 1990. She has finished in the top 10 in 11 out of 14 races, and in 1990 she set the Iditarod speed record. She was named the Women's Sports Founda-

tion's Professional Sportswoman of the Year in 1987 and 1988, and the *Anchorage Times* named her Sled Dog Racer of the Decade in 1989. She was selected Outstanding Female Athlete by the International Academy of Sports in 1989.

Butler, Lady Eleanor

Born 1745 Died 1829
Irish recluse whose resolution to live in seclusion attracted curious onlookers

Lady Eleanor Butler was born in Dublin, the sister of the 17th Earl of Ormonde. In 1779 she and her friend or cousin Sarah Ponsonby (1755–1831) resolved to live in seclusion, and retired to a cottage at Plasnewydd in the vale of Llangollen in Wales, accompanied by a maidservant.

They became famous throughout Europe as the 'Maids of Llangollen' or 'Ladies of the Vale', and attracted visitors from far and wide who must have wanted to witness their eccentricity and devotion to one another for themselves.

Butler, Elizabeth Southerden, *née* Thompson

Born 1846 Died 1933
English painter of patriotic battle scenes which became popular images of the Victorian era

Elizabeth Thompson was born in Lausanne, the daughter of a scholar and concert pianist and sister of **Alice Meynell**. She married the soldier Sir William Butler (1838–1910) in 1877.

She made her reputation with the *Roll Call* (1874) and *Inkermann* (1877) but is perhaps best known for *Scotland for Ever!* (1881), which depicts the charge of the Royal Scots Greys at the Battle of Waterloo.

Though her splendid pictures do seem to glorify war, her focus was on the heroism of the common soldier rather than on the courageous actions of the officers.

Butler, Josephine Elizabeth, *née* Grey

Born 1828 Died 1906
English social reformer whose concerns ranged from promoting education for women to protesting against white slave traffic

Josephine Grey was born in Milfield in the Cheviot Hills, a daughter of John Grey of Dilston, Northumberland. In 1852 she married a Durham University lecturer, George Butler (1819–90), who was later canon of Winchester and author of educational works. She promoted women's education, particularly after meeting **Anne Jemima Clough**, and in 1867 helped to found the North of England Council for the Higher Education of Women, of which she was president until 1873. However her promotion of women's university level examinations was not supported by fellow-reformer **Emily Davies**, who was pressing for women to enter the same examinations as men.

While living in Liverpool, Butler established homes for work-girls and fallen women, for whose cause she later crusaded against the Contagious Diseases Acts (an attempt at state control of prostitution that made women in seaports and military towns liable for compulsory examination for venereal disease). The Act was repealed in 1886.

Butler also campaigned against licensed brothels and white slave traffic, developing a new style of vigorous campaigning, and she travelled on the Continent, urging action especially against under-age prostitution. She wrote *Personal Reminiscences of a Great Crusade* (1896).

Butler-Sloss, Dame (Ann) Elizabeth (Oldfield), *née* Havers

Born 1933
English judge, styled the Rt Hon Lady Justice
Butler-Sloss, the first woman appointed to serve
on the Court of Appeal

Elizabeth Havers was born in Kew Gardens, Richmond, Surrey, the daughter of Sir Cecil Havers QC, a High Court judge. She wanted to study law from an early age, and was educated at Wycombe Abbey School. Called to the Bar in 1955, she practised there for 15 years.

In 1958 she married Joseph Butler-Sloss and in 1959, during her first pregnancy, she contested the Conservative seat at Lambeth, but without success. She was a divorce registrar from 1970, until in 1979 she was appointed to the Family Division of the High Court. Also that year she was appointed DBE.

After chairing the Cleveland Sex Abuse Inquiry in 1987–8, she became the first woman Lord Justice of Appeal.

Butt, Dame Clara Ellen

Born 1872 Died 1936
English contralto singer who was the first to sing
Elgar's Land of Hope and Glory

Clara Butt was born in Southwick, Sussex, educated in Bristol and trained at the Royal College of Music. She made her début in 1892, the year her performances included Ursula in Sir Arthur Sullivan's *The Golden Legend* and Orpheus in Christoph Gluck's opera *Orfeo ed Euridice*.

Earning admiration for her performances of ballads and oratorios, especially those by Handel and Mendelssohn, she also gave recitals with her husband, the baritone Kennerley Rumford.

Sir Edward Elgar composed his *Sea Pictures* (1899) especially for her and acknowledged her as the inspiration for the angel in his *Dream of Gerontius* (1900). She was also the first to sing his *Land of Hope and Glory* (1902) and *Spirit of England* (1916).

Buttrose, Ita Clare

Born 1942
Australian journalist, publisher and broadcaster,
a media personality who is one of the best-known
women in Australia

Ita Buttrose was born in Sydney. She married at 21 and launched into a journalistic career that during the 1970s included the editorships of several women's magazines. She was also a director of the Australian Consolidated Press (1974–81) and publisher of the women's publications by the Australian Consolidated Press (1977–81).

Having been women's editor at the age of 28 for the *Daily Telegraph* and the *Sunday Telegraph*, in 1981 she returned as editor-in-chief, the first woman in Australia to be editor of either a daily or a Sunday paper. In 1983 she entered radio broadcasting and was given her own show by two stations, and in 1985 she became presenter of *Woman's Day* on television. Continuing her radio and television appearances, she also became a newspaper columnist and Chairman of the National Advisory Committee on AIDS (1984–). In 1988 she became Chief Executive of Capricorn Publishing Pty Ltd and editor-in-chief of *The Sun Herald*, launching her own magazine, *Ita*, the following year and editing it until 1994.

Byars, Betsy Cromer

Born 1928
American children's novelist who specialized in
contemporary realism

Betsy Cromer Byars was born in Charlotte, North Carolina. She began to write in the 1960s but had no great impact until *The Summer of the Swans* (1970), the story of a girl and her retarded brother, which was awarded the Newbery Medal.

Specializing in 'kitchen sink' drama (contemporary realism), she produced a number of popular novels, at times perceptive and inventive, at others predictable and reminiscent of soap opera.

Her titles include *The Eighteenth Emergency* (1973), *Goodbye, Chicken Little* (1979), *The Animal, The Vegetable, and John D Jones* (1982) and *Beans on the Roof* (1988).

Byatt, A(ntonia) S(usan), *née* Drabble

Born 1938
English novelist, critic and scholar whose novel
Possession won the Booker Prize

Antonia Drabble was born in Sheffield and educated at Cambridge. She is the elder sister of **Margaret Drabble**. She taught with the Westminster Tutors (1962–5) and at the Central School of Art and Design (1965–9) before joining the extra-mural faculty at University College London (1971); she has subsequently been senior lecturer in English. In 1965 she published *Degrees of Freedom*, the first full-length study of **Iris Murdoch**'s novels, whose philosophical style has influenced her own; in 1976 she added a shorter monograph, *Iris Murdoch*.

Highly respected as a critic, Byatt made her reputation as a novelist with her third novel, *The Virgin in the Garden* (1978). This was followed by *Still Life* (1985), and in 1990 she won the Booker Prize with *Possession* (1990), in which two young academics research the lives of a fictitious mid-Victorian poet, Randolph Henry Ash, and his contemporary, Christabel LaMotte. An excellent example of her style, it is part literary detective story, part romance, part a satirical comedy of English and American academia. She did not write another novel until *Babel Tower* (1996).

Byatt has also written on Ford Madox Ford and on 18th- and 19th-century poetry: *Unruly Times: Wordsworth and Coleridge in their Time* (1970). Her interests extend to art and art history, literary and social history, and philosophy, all of which feature in her novels.

Byron, Annabella (Anne Isabella), *known as* Lady Byron *or* Lady Noel Byron, *née* Milbanke

Born 1792 Died 1860
English philanthropist, wife of Lord Byron,
mother of mathematician Ada, Countess of
***Lovelace**, and grandmother of the traveller*
Anne Blunt

Annabella Milbanke was born at Elmore Hall, Durham, and married the poet Lord Byron in 1815. That year her family inherited the surname Noel through her mother. They separated in 1816 after the birth of their daughter Ada. Lady Byron moved in radical circles — she was a close friend and associate of **Anna Jameson** and **Barbara Bodichon** and is noted particularly for her commitment to schemes for improving education, especially women's education, many of which she funded. In 1854 she purchased the Red Lodge on behalf of the social reformer **Mary Carpenter** who opened it as a home for girl offenders.

Lady Byron was also involved in agricultural and industrial reforms, co-operative movements, the anti-slavery movement (she was a friend of **Harriet Beecher Stowe**) and other radical causes.

C

Caballé, Montserrat

Born 1933
Spanish operatic soprano who became a major
Donizetti and Verdi singer and a notable
performer of Spanish songs

Montserrat Caballé was born in Barcelona,
where she studied at the Conservatorio del
Liceo from the age of nine. She made her
concert début in 1954 and her opera début in
1956 in Basle.

Her first performance at Glyndebourne was
as the First Lady in Mozart's *Die Zauberflöte* in
1965 and at Covent Garden it was as Violetta
in Verdi's *La Traviata* in 1972. Her concert
performance of Gaetano Donizetti's *Lucrezia
Borgia* in New York in 1967 was greatly
admired and made her internationally famous,
leading to her becoming the chief Donizetti
and Verdi singer of her day, acclaimed for her
bel canto style.

She enjoys enormous acclaim in a remarkable variety of stage roles from Rossini to
Puccini, in contemporary opera, in Zarzuela (a
type of Spanish opera) and in the German
tradition (notably Wagner and Strauss). She
has also sung at the Metropolitan Opera, La
Scala and Mexico City, and has made many
recordings.

Caballero, Fernán, *pseud of* Cecilia Francesca de Arrom, *née* Böhl von Faber

Born 1796 Died 1877
Spanish writer who was acclaimed for a time as
Spain's most important novelist

Cecilia Böhl von Faber was born in Morges in
Switzerland, the daughter of Nikolaus Böhl
von Faber (1770–1836), a German merchant in
Spain. She spent most of her childhood in
Germany, but returned to Spain in 1813. She

was married and widowed three times. Her
third husband was Antonio Arrom de Ayala,
who was just 23 when they married in 1837.

She wrote on the history of Spanish literature and introduced in Spain the picturesque
local-colour novel, always celebrating the
country's traditional moral, Catholic and mon-
archist virtues. The first of her 50 romances
was her masterpiece *La Gaviota* (1849, 'The
Seagull'), which is considered a forerunner
to later Spanish realist works; others include
Clemencia (1852), *Un servilón y un liberalito*
(1855, 'A Groveller and a Little Liberal') and *La
Familia de Alvareda* (1856). She also collected
Spanish folk-tales, for example in *Cuentos y
poesías adaluces* (1859, 'Andalusian Tales and
Poetry').

Cable, (Alice) Mildred

Born 1878 Died 1952
English pioneer Christian missionary in China, a
writer and traveller who helped to found one of
the first girls' schools in China

Mildred Cable was born in Guildford. After
training in chemistry and medicine, she went
to China in 1892 under the auspices of the
China Inland Mission and began working with
the sisters Evangeline and Francesca French.

They worked initially in H(w)ochow, Shansi
Province, where they founded one of China's
first girls' schools. In 1923 they toured the
cities of Kansu Province, the first of several
evangelistic journeys in areas until then closed
to both Christianity and single Western women. Around 1928 they moved to Suchow, 'the
City of Criminals', in north-west China.

Their travels are described in several books,
including *Through Jade Gate and Central Asia*
(1927), *A Desert Journal* (1934) and *The Gobi
Desert* (1942).

Cabrini, St Frances Xavier, *known as* Mother Cabrini

Born 1850 Died 1917
Italian-born American nun who helped the
underprivileged and was honoured as America's
first saint

Frances Xavier Cabrini was born named Maria Francesca in Sant 'Angelo, Lodigiano, the thirteenth child of an Italian farmer. She founded the Missionary Sisters of the Sacred Heart (1880), which later became a flourishing order with houses throughout northern Italy.

She travelled to Rome to obtain papal approval for her foundation and also to ask permission to go to China as a missionary. Instead the Pope directed her to serve the Italian immigrants in New York, whose lives were materially miserable and lacking spiritual input.

She emigrated to the USA in 1889 and became renowned as 'Mother Cabrini' for her social and charitable work. She founded 67 houses devoted to nursing, care of orphans and education in the USA, Buenos Aires, Paris and Madrid. She was canonized in 1946, and became the first American saint. Her feast day is 13 November.

Calamity Jane, *real name* Martha Jane Burke, *née* Cannary

Born c.1852 Died 1903
American frontierswoman who became a living
legend for her skill at riding and shooting,
particularly in the Gold Rush days in the
Black Hills of Dakota

Martha Jane Cannary was born in Princeton, Missouri. During the Gold Rush, she teamed up with the renowned US marshal, Wild Bill Hickok (1847–76), at Deadwood, Dakota, shortly before he was murdered. She later alleged that he was her husband and the father of her child born in 1873.

In 1878, disguised as a man, she heroically nursed the victims of a smallpox epidemic in Deadwood, contributing to her legendary status, as did the fact that the Sioux living the area never bothered her. She is said to have threatened 'calamity' for any man who tried to court her, but in 1891 she married Clinton Burke, after living with him for at least six years.

When the marriage failed she toured with Wild West shows, but gained a reputation for drunkenness and offensive behaviour, which resulted in her being fired from the 1901 Pan-American Exposition in Buffalo, New York. Afterwards she retired to Deadwood and died of pneumonia.

Calder, Liz (Elizabeth Nicole), *née* Baber

Born 1938
English publisher, one of the few women at the top
of her profession

Liz Baber was born in London. She grew up in New Zealand and was educated at Canterbury University there. She married Richard Calder in 1958 (divorced 1972) and moved to Brazil, where she worked as a model.

After returning to the UK she managed the publicity department at Victor Gollancz (1971–4), then became editorial director there (1975–8) and at Jonathan Cape (1979–86). In 1986 she was asked by Nigel Newton to help set up Bloomsbury Publishing, and she has been publishing director there ever since.

Among the successful authors whom she has helped to establish during her career are **Anita Brookner**, **Isabel Allende**, **Margaret Atwood** and Salman Rushdie.

Caldwell, Sarah

Born 1924
American opera conductor and impresario who is
considered both eclectic and adventurous

Sarah Caldwell was born in Maryville, Missouri, and educated in Arkansas and at the New England Conservatory. While working as a violist at the Berkshire Music Center, she staged Vaughan Williams's opera *Riders to the Sea* and quickly became an established interpreter of modern repertoire.

In 1958, after heading an opera workshop at Boston University for nearly a decade, she established the forward-looking Opera Company of Boston and specialized in contemporary music, including Schoenberg's unfinished *Moses und Aron* and works by Luigi Nono and Roger Sessions.

In 1976 she was the first female conductor at the Metropolitan Opera in New York City.

Caldwell, Zoë Ada

Born 1934
Australian actress whose career reached a peak
when she played Miss Jean Brodie

Zoë Caldwell was born in Melbourne, where she made her professional début in 1953 as a member of the Union Theatre Repertory Company. She made her British début at Stratford-upon-Avon in 1958, and joined the Royal Court Theatre in 1960. She played Molière and Chekov in her first season on the American stage in Minneapolis in 1963, which was followed by her New York début in John Whiting's *The Devils* in 1965.

Her range of roles is wide, and includes an acclaimed *Medea* in 1982. She had a particularly outstanding success in the title role in *The Prime of Miss Jean Brodie* (1968), and has also directed a number of productions. She was awarded the OBE in 1970.

Callas, Maria, *originally* Cecilia Sophia Anna Mary Kalogeropoulou

Born 1923 Died 1977
American-born Greek singer who was one of the
most distinctive and influential sopranos after
the war

Maria Callas was born in New York of Greek parents. She left the USA in 1937 to study at Athens Conservatory, made her début there as Tosca in 1941, and in 1947 won recognition for her performance at Verona in *La Gioconda*.

She sang with great authority in all the most exacting soprano roles, excelling in the intricate *bel canto* style of pre-Verdian Italian opera and gaining comparison with the great Spanish mezzo-soprano **Maria Malibran**. Her dramatic skill and coloratura range led to the revival of many coloratura roles and infrequently performed operas.

She retired from the stage in 1965, after a legendary Tosca at Covent Garden. She had recorded at least 20 complete operas and performed more than 40 different roles. During the time that she was married to G B Meneghini, she was known as Maria Meneghini Callas.

Callil, Carmen Thérèse

Born 1938
Australian publisher, the co-founder and former
Chairman of Virago Press, and one of the few
women in top positions in UK publishing

Carmen Callil was born to parents of Irish–Lebanese descent in Melbourne, and educated at university there. She went to London in 1960 and worked for Marks and Spencer before beginning her publishing career as editorial assistant at Hutchinson and then at B T Batsford.

She rose swiftly, working in the publicity departments of such companies as Granada Publishing and André Deutsch, and forming her own publicity company. In 1972, with Ursula Owen and Rosie Boycott, she founded the feminist publishing house, Virago Press, with the intention of enabling women to secure a place in the publishing and writing of literature in English. The company earned renown for rediscovering or promoting many successful female authors, including **Maya Angelou**, **Edith Wharton** and **Margaret Atwood**.

When Virago joined the publishing group of Chatto and Windus, Bodley Head and Cape in 1982, Callil remained chairman but took on the additional position of managing director of Chatto and Windus and The Hogarth Press, where she remained for 11 years. In 1993 she was made Publisher-at-Large of the American-owned Random House, the new owners of Chatto and Windus, but left in 1994. She resigned her chairmanship of Virago the following year.

Cam, Helen Maud

Born 1885 Died 1968
English historian who specialized in the
Middle Ages

Helen Cam was born in Oxfordshire and educated at the Royal Holloway College, London, and briefly at Bryn Mawr College in Pennsylvania. After an early teaching career she was appointed Pfeiffer Research Fellow at Girton College, Cambridge, where she lectured and was director of studies until 1948. For the next six years she lectured at Harvard as the first Zenmurray Radcliffe Professor of History.

Cam is best remembered for her detailed research and publications on the legal and constitutional aspects of English medieval history.

Camargo, Maria Anna de

Born 1710 Died 1770
French ballerina whose time at the Paris Opéra
was marked by many innovatory stylistic and
technical changes

Maria Camargo was born in Brussels. She won European fame for her performances at the Paris Opéra, where she made her début in 1726 in Jean Balon's *Les Caractères de la Danse*, and she was one of the first celebrities to lend her name to merchandizing shoes and wigs.

With her remarkable speed and agility she perfected the jumping steps that were previously done only by male dancers, and is said to have established the ballet-dancer's basic leg position as turned-out 90° to the hip. She is also said to have been responsible for the shortening of the traditional ballet skirt to allow more complicated steps to be executed and seen, and she was the first to wear ballet shoes without heels as well as close-fitting drawers underneath her skirt.

Cambridge, Ada

Born 1844 Died 1926
English-born Australian novelist and poet who
wrote books about colonial life

Ada Cambridge was born in Norfolk, the second of 10 children of a gentleman farmer, and educated privately. By the time she met and married George Cross at the age of 26, she had published short stories, poems and a book of hymns. They left almost immediately for Australia where her husband was to be a missionary priest, and settled eventually in Melbourne. In 1873 she began contributing to the *Australian* and published her first novella, *Up the Murray*, in 1875.

She was a woman with a strong sense of class, whose writing called attention to women's social position and encouraged them to think for themselves. She wrote 18 novels, much romantic fiction, and attracted a wide English readership but was modest about her success, regarding herself fortunate to have been the first in the field. **Jane Austen** is the most obvious influence, and her best work is to be found in *A Marked Man* (1890), *The Three Miss Kings* (1891), *Not All In Vain* (1892), *Fidelis* (1895) and *Materfamilias* (1898).

Cameron, Julia Margaret, *née* Pattle

Born 1815 Died 1879
British photographer who became one of the best
portrait photographers of her century

Julia Pattle was born in Calcutta. She married an Indian colonial jurist Charles Hay Cameron (1795–1880) in 1838 and 10 years later moved with him to England. At the age of 48 she was given a camera, so she converted a chicken coop into a studio and a coal bin into a darkroom and went on to become an outstanding amateur photographer in the 1860s.

Her style was influenced by her good friend, the painter George Frederick Watts (1817–1904), and her close-up portraits of such Victorian celebrities as Alfred Lord Tennyson, Charles Darwin and Thomas Carlyle received permanent acclaim, as did her portrayals of the beauty of such women as **Ellen Terry**. Though her technique and accuracy was sometimes criticised, the spiritual depth that she aimed for in her art was undeniable.

In 1875 she and her husband went to Ceylon, where she continued to photograph until her death.

Cameron, Kate (Katharine)

Born 1874 Died 1965
Scottish artist and etcher who was known for her
watercolour flower studies and for her etchings
that often incorporated butterflies or bumble bees

Kate Cameron was born in Hillhead, Glasgow, the sister of the Scottish artist Sir David Young Cameron. She studied at Glasgow School of Art and later with Colarossi in Paris, and married the connoisseur and collector Arthur Kay in 1928.

Her early interior watercolours have a definite arts and crafts flavour in the style of the 'Glasgow 4' (Charles Rennie Mackintosh, **Margaret Mackintosh**, **Frances Mac-Donald** and Herbert MacNair). Although she illustrated many books, including children's fairy tales, she was better known for her watercolour flower studies, in particular her middle- to later- period works which were extremely delicate and highly stylized, and often incorporated butterflies or bumble bees.

Campan, Jeanne Louise Henriette

Born 1752 Died 1822
French educationalist and writer, and companion
*of **Marie Antoinette***

Jeanne Campan was born in Paris. After entering the royal household at the age of 15 as reader to Louis XV's daughters, she became a friend and companion of **Marie Antoinette** (1770–92). Following Robespierre's fall, she opened a boarding-school at St Germain-en-Laye at which the future Queen **Hortense** was a pupil. In 1806 Napoleon appointed her head of the school at Ecouen for the daughters of officers of the Legion of Honour.

She wrote *Vie privée de Marie Antoinette* (1823), *Journal anecdotique* (1824) and *Correspondance avec la Reine Hortense* (2 vols, 1835), and her memoirs were published in 1988 as *Mémoires de Madame de Campan, première femme de chambre de Marie Antoinette, 1774–1792* ('Memoirs of Madame de Campan, Principal Lady-in-Waiting to Marie Antoinette, 1774–1792').

Campbell, Kim (Avril Phaedra)

Born 1947
Canadian politician who became Canada's first
woman Prime Minister in 1993

Kim Campbell was born in British Columbia. She rejected her names Avril Phaedra in favour of 'Kim' at the age of 12. Though a talented musician — she plays piano, cello and guitar — she decided to study political science, first at the University of British Columbia and then at the London School of Economics. After returning to Vancouver she lectured for a while and began the first of her two marriages, both of which have ended in divorce. She failed to secure a teaching post, so trained in law and practised in Vancouver, becoming involved in provincial politics at the same time.

She switched to national politics in the 1988

Kim Campbell, 1993

election, when she was elected to parliament as a member of the Progressive Conservative Party under Brian Mulroney, whose controversial free trade agreement with the USA she openly supported. She was soon admitted into the Cabinet as Justice Minister (1990–3) and then Defence Minister (1993).

Campbell succeeded Mulroney in June 1993, becoming Canada's first woman Prime Minister, but in October that year she and all but two of her Party's candidates lost their parliamentary seats in the national election and the Liberal Party under Jean Chretien took over.

Campbell, Dame (Janet) Mary

Born 1877   Died 1954
British medical reformer and an early state
medical officer

Mary Campbell was the daughter of a banker. She graduated with several qualifications from the London School of Medicine for Women and also trained at the Royal Free Hospital in 1902 and the Belgrave Hospital for Children in 1904. Appointed assistant school medical inspector to London County Council in 1905, she was later the first full-time woman medical officer on the Board of Education. She founded the Medical Woman's Federation in 1917, and from 1919 to 1934 was senior medical officer for maternity and child welfare at the Ministry of Health.

Her writings include *Physical Welfare of Mother and Children* (1917) and *A Comprehensive Report on Maternity Services* (1945). She was created DBE in 1924.

Campbell, Naomi

Born 1970
English model who is among the first to attain
'supermodel' status

Naomi Campbell was born in Streatham to an unmarried teenager and brought up by her grandparents. At first she wanted to be a dancer like her mother and she went to stage school at the age of 11.

Her career as a model began when she was spotted shopping by a modelling agency talent scout. From 1986 she appeared in women's magazines such as *Elle*, became the first black to feature on French *Vogue*, and modelled in fashion shows for top designers including Rifat Ozbek, Gianni Versace and **Vivienne Westwood** (from whose eight-inch platform shoes she had a widely publicized fall).

Seeing modelling as a way into the music business, she released her first album, *Baby Woman*, in 1994, while continuing as a supermodel. Also that year she published *Swan*, a novel about five young models.

Campbell, Mrs Patrick, *née* Beatrice Stella Tanner

Born 1865   Died 1940
English actress who was notoriously volatile in
temperament and famously brilliant in her
portrayal of passionate characters

Beatrice Tanner was born in Kensington of mixed English and Italian parentage. She married Patrick Campbell in 1884, and went on the stage in 1888. Though her mercurial temperament made her the terror of managers, she possessed outstanding charm and talent, and leapt to fame in *The Second Mrs Tanqueray* (1893). Her first husband died in South Africa in 1900; in 1914 she married George Cornwallis-West.

The part of Eliza in George Bernard Shaw's *Pygmalion* (1914) was written specially for her and she formed a long friendship with the author. Among her other notable roles were Mélisande in Maurice Maeterlinck's *Pelléas and Mélisande*, for which the music was composed by Fauré at her request; Mrs Irving in Ibsen's *Ghosts*; the title role in Hermann Sudermann's *Magda*; and Shakespearian roles including Juliet and Lady Macbeth.

Campion, Jane

Born 1954
New Zealand film director who became one of
international cinema's most distinctive new
talents of the 1990s

Jane Campion was born in Wellington and trained at the Australian Film, Television and Radio School in Sydney, Australia. Her début short, *Peel* (1982), won the Cannes Palme D'Or for the best short film.

Following her first feature-length piece, *Two Friends* (1986, for Australian television), she made her feature film début with *Sweetie* (1989), a beautifully composed character study of a roly-poly schizophrenic and the disruptive effect she has on the lives of her nearest and dearest. Next came the cinema release of a three-part television series *An Angel At My Table* (1990), which was a compassionate dramatization of the autobiographies of **Janet Frame**.

Campion won seven separate awards at the Venice Film Festival of 1990, and shared the Cannes Palme D'Or for *The Piano* (1993), the first such award for an Australian production as well as for a woman director.

Campoamor, Clara

Born 1888 Died 1972
Spanish politician and feminist, one of the
principal figures of the 20th century in the struggle
for women's rights in Spain

Clara Campoamor was born into a working-class family. She graduated in law in 1924, and from then onwards agitated widely on behalf of women's issues. She contributed more than anyone else to the inclusion of women's suffrage in Spain's constitution in 1931.

In 1931 she was elected to the Constituent Cortes of the Second Republic as a deputy for the Radical Republican Party, and during the legislature of 1931–3 she was Vice-President of the Labour Commission and participated in the reform of the Civil Code. She also represented Spain at the League of Nations, and founded the Republican Feminine Union; in 1933–4 she was the Director-General of Charity.

Also during the 1930s she wrote extensively on women's rights and aspirations. She chose exile in Buenos Aires in 1938, moving in 1955 to spend the rest of her life in Lausanne.

Cannon, Annie Jump

Born 1863 Died 1941
American astronomer who became a specialist in
the classification of stellar spectra

Annie Jump Cannon was born in Dover, Delaware, the daughter of a wealthy shipbuilder. She was educated at Wellesley College, graduating in 1884. She returned to the college 10 years later as an assistant in the physics department, proceeding to Radcliffe College where she took up the study of astronomy. In 1896 she joined the famous group of women astronomers on the staff of Harvard College Observatory under its director Edward Pickering in a major programme of classification of stellar spectra.

Cannon classified the spectra of no fewer than 225,300 stars brighter than magnitude 8.5, published in the nine volumes of the *Henry Draper Catalogue*. She was already 60 years old when Pickering's successor Harlow Shapley decided to extend the catalogue to fainter stars, upon which she classified another 130,000 stars. She received many honours, among them the Henry Draper Gold Medal of the US National Academy of Sciences and honorary doctorates from the universities of Groningen and Oxford. Her productive career ended only a few weeks before her death. She was inducted into the National Women's Hall of Fame in 1994.

Canth, Minna (Ulrika Vilhelmina), *née* Johnsson

Born 1844 Died 1897
Finnish playwright and feminist, a remarkable
personality who was the first Finnish Realist
writer and an important early Finnish playwright

Minna Johnsson was born in Tampere. She attended the first teachers' college in Finland but without completing her studies married one of her teachers, J F Canth, in 1865. She had seven children and was widowed in 1879, whereupon she travelled to Kuopio to run her parents' shop.

At the same time she undertook an intensive course of self-education in literary and social history. Her reading, and her experience as the single parent of seven children, turned her into a radical. Having only previously written articles for journals, she was inspired by an early visit to the theatre to write for the stage and produced her first play, *Murtovarkens* ('The Burglary'), in 1882.

Canth developed into a powerful exponent of the Realist school, and her work is seen as a catalyst to the modern breakthrough in Finland. Her best-known plays are *Työmiehen vaimo* (1885, 'A Working-Class Wife') and *Kovan onnen lapsia* (1888, 'The Hard Luck Kids') and she also translated the work of the influential Danish critic Georg Brandes (1842–1927). Later she turned to psychological dramas about women, such as *Anna Liisa*

(1895), which recalls Tolstoy and some elements of Ibsen.

Cappello, Bianco, *also spelt* Capello

Born 1548 Died 1587
Italian noblewoman and courtesan whose affairs were the subject of much 16th-century scandal

Bianco Cappello was born in Venice and grew up to be a beautiful and intelligent woman. She eloped with a Florentine man, Pietro Buonaventuri, but secretly became the mistress of Francesco de' Medici, Grand Duke of Tuscany (1541–87, also known as Frances I).

On the murder of her husband in 1569, the affair became public and aroused much animosity in the court, especially from Francesco's brother, Cardinal Ferdinando I de' Medici. She constructed a plot involving an illegitimate child to force Francesco to marry her.

She and Francesco succumbed to an illness within a day of each other, supposedly poisoned by his brother.

Caraway, Hattie (Ophelia) Wyatt, *née* Wyatt

Born 1878 Died 1950
American Democratic politician who became the first woman to be elected to the US Senate

Hattie Wyatt was born near Bakerville, Tennessee. She was married to Senator Thaddeus Horatius Caraway and when he died in 1831 before his term had expired she was appointed by the governor of Arkansas to fill his Senate seat. She ran successfully for the same seat in 1932, becoming the first woman ever elected to the US Senate. She served until 1945, the year she was appointed by President Franklin D Roosevelt to the Federal Employees Compensation Commission.

An independent-minded Democrat, she sponsored an early version of the Equal Rights Amendment in 1943.

Carden, Joan Maralyn

Born 1937
Australian operatic and concert soprano, a principal artist with the Australian Opera since 1971

Joan Carden was born in Melbourne, Victoria. She made her début in 1974 at Covent Garden, London, as Gilda in Verdi's *Rigoletto*, a role she has since made her own. She has appeared at the Glyndebourne Festival, as Donna Anna in Peter Hall's production of *Don Giovanni*, and with the English National Opera, the Scottish Opera and the Metropolitan, New York.

Renowned for her performances of Mozart, Carden's repertoire extends from Mozart and Handel to Richard Strauss and Benjamin Britten, and one of her most celebrated performances is of the four heroines in *The Tales of Hoffmann*.

Carey, Mariah

Born 1969
American singer whose singles and albums have been consistent sellers

Mariah Carey was born in New York City. Her albums of popular rock music include *Mariah Carey* (1990), *Emotions* (1991), *Mariah Carey MTV Unplugged* (1992) and *Music Box* (1993). In 1990 she received two Grammy awards — Best New Artist and Best Pop Vocal-Female.

Carlisle, Lucy Hay, Countess of, *née* Percy

Born 1599 Died 1660
English courtier who became disastrously involved in intrigue and conspiracy

Lucy Percy was the second daughter of Henry Percy, 9th Earl of Northumberland. In 1617 she married James Hay, later Earl of Carlisle (d.1636), and entered wholeheartedly into the life of the court of Charles I. She was witty and beautiful, and became the friend of the King's adviser, the Earl of Strafford, who was impeached by John Pym (a former friend and the leader of the Puritans in parliament) and, at a time when he might have expected backing from the King, was abandoned and executed in 1641.

Perhaps in response to his abandonment, the Countess of Carlisle took to advising the Parliamentary leaders and played an intricate game of intrigue, often informing both Royalists and Parliamentarians of the other side's intentions. Her greatest success was to inform Lord Essex of the King's intention to arrest the five members of parliament (Pym, Hampden, Haselrig, Holles and Strode) so that they could take refuge in London. She openly supported the Presbyterians in 1647 and made a show of great allegiance to the Royalist cause during the second Civil War.

Such meddling landed her in the Tower in 1649 for some months, and following her release she had difficulty resuming her influence in royal circles. The poets Thomas Carew, William Cartwright and Robert Herrick were among several who commemorated her in verse.

Carlson, Carolyn

Born 1943
American dancer and choreographer whose work
influenced dance in Europe, particularly France

Carolyn Carlson was born in California. She studied at San Francisco Ballet School and with Alwin Nikolais, in whose company she danced from 1966 to 1971.

After freelancing in Europe, where her dreamlike, ritualistic dance-spectacles and independent working methods had a great impact on modern and experimental dance, she was invited to create a piece for the Paris Opéra Ballet in 1973. Her solo was so well received that a special post, *Danseuse étoile choreographique*, was invented for her.

From 1980 she directed her own troupe at Venice's Teatro Fenice, but later returned to Paris.

Carlyle, Jane (Baillie) Welsh, *née* Welsh

Born 1801   Died 1866
Scottish literary figure who determined to make a
success of her marriage to the critic and historian
Thomas Carlyle

Jane Welsh was born in Haddington, East Lothian, the only daughter of Dr John Welsh, from whom she received a thorough classical education and inherited a small family estate at Craigenputtock on the moors of Dumfriesshire. She was tutored by the revivalist minister Edward Irving, who in 1821 introduced her to his friend, the critic and historian Thomas Carlyle (1795–1881), whom she married, despite her mother's reservations, in 1826. They became the centre of an intellectual and literary circle.

They lived at Craigenputtock from 1828 to 1834, and thereafter at 5 Cheyne Row, Chelsea (now number 24). Though she was forthright and quick-witted, she declined to become a writer despite Carlyle's promptings. The marriage was a difficult one, and they seem to have had considerable sexual problems; Carlyle was an unhappy, withdrawn, even tormented man, but she supported him loyally through his depressions and chronic ill health.

After her sudden death in 1866, Carlyle was grief-stricken and retired from public life. He wrote an anguished memoir of her in his *Reminiscences* (1881); he also edited her letters and diaries, which are full of vivid insights and writing of high quality, and were eventually published after his death in 1883, revealing her to have been one of the finest letter-writers of her time.

Carmen Sylva, *pseud of* Elisabeth, Queen of Romania

Born 1843   Died 1916
Queen of Romania, poet and prose writer whose
sorrow gave rise to her writing

Elisabeth was the daughter of Prince Hermann of Wied Neuwied. She married King (then Prince) Carol I of Romania in 1869 and her only child, a daughter, died in 1874. The literary activity of 'Carmen Sylva' was born from her sorrow.

Two poems, printed privately at Leipzig in 1880 under the name 'Carmen Sylva', were followed by *Stürme* (1881, 'Storms'), *Leidens Erdengang* (1882, Eng trans *Pilgrim Sorrow*, 1884), *Pensées d'une reine* (1882, 'Thoughts of a Queen'), *The Bard of Dimbovitza* (1891), *Meister Manole* (1892) and other works. In the war of 1877–8 she endeared herself to her people by her devotion to the wounded.

Carmichael, Amy Beatrice

Born 1867   Died 1971
Northern Irish-born missionary to India who
founded the Dohnavur Fellowship

Amy Carmichael was born in Millisle, County Down. After her father's death in 1885 and the loss of a significant amount of money lent to a friend, her family gradually split up. She met Robert Wilson, chairman of the Keswick Convention, at a meeting in Belfast in 1887 and went to live with him as his daughter, since his own wife and daughter had died.

She worked briefly in Japan, then from 1895 onwards worked with the Church of England Zenana Missionary Society in southern India with Thomas Walker of Tinnevelly (Tirunelveli). The Dohnavur Fellowship, which she founded in 1901 for the education of girls rescued from temple prostitution, became an independent interdenominational faith mission in 1926.

Amy Carmichael's work and evangelical spirituality became well known in the West from a series of books, including *Gold Cord* (1932) and *Gold by Moonlight* (1935).

Carner, JoAnne, *née* Gunderson

Born 1939
American golfer, often known as 'Big Momma',
one of the greatest golfers in the world

JoAnne Carner was born in Kirkland, Washington. Her amateur record included an unprecedented win on the US professional tour in 1969 at the Burdine's Invitational competition and five victories in the US amateur championship.

She turned professional in 1970 and finished eleventh on the money list to secure the Rookie of the Year title. In 1971 she won the US Open and so became the first woman to win the US Junior, Amateur and Open titles. She won the title again in 1976.

Caroline of Anspach, *also spelt* Ansbach

Born 1683 Died 1737
Queen of Great Britain and Ireland as the wife of
George II (ruled 1727–60)

Caroline of Anspach was the daughter of the Margrave of Brandenburg-Ansbach. She married George, Electoral Prince of Hanover, in 1705, and went to England with him when his father became King George I in 1714. She became queen when her husband succeeded as George II in 1727.

Caroline of Anspach

As Princess of Wales she established a glittering court of writers and politicians at Leicester House. She was a strong supporter of Sir Robert Walpole, and acted as regent during her husband's absences abroad. They had five children, including Frederick Louis (1707–51), the Prince of Wales and father of George III and William Augustus, Duke of Cumberland (1721–65).

Caroline (Amelia Elizabeth) of Brunswick

Born 1768 Died 1821
Queen of Great Britain and Ireland as the wife of
George IV (ruled 1820–30)

Caroline of Brunswick was the second daughter of Charles William, Duke of Brunswick-Wolfenbüttel, and of George III's sister Augusta. In 1795 she was married to the Prince of Wales, her first cousin. The marriage was disagreeable to him, and although she bore him a daughter, the Princess **Charlotte**, he made her live by herself at Shooters Hill and Blackheath, the object of much sympathy.

Reports to her discredit led the king in 1806 to order an investigation into her conduct, which was found to be imprudent, but not criminal. During George's time as regent for his insane father, she lived mainly in Italy. When George came to the throne in 1820, she was offered an annuity of £50,000 to renounce the title of queen and live abroad; when she refused, and made a triumphal entry into London, the government instituted proceedings against her for adultery.

Much that was very reprehensible was proved, but her husband's treatment of her, and the splendid defence of Lord Brougham, caused such a general feeling in her favour that the ministry gave up the Divorce Bill. She assumed the rank of royalty, but was turned away from Westminster Abbey door at George IV's coronation less than three weeks before she died.

Carpenter, Mary

Born 1807 Died 1877
English educationalist, reformer and
philanthropist

Mary Carpenter was born in Exeter, Devon, the daughter of a Unitarian minister who educated her, and sister of the biologist William Carpenter. She trained as a teacher, opened a girls' school in Bristol with her mother in 1829, and took an active part in the movement for the restoration of neglected children.

In 1846 she founded a ragged school in Bristol, in 1852 a reformatory for boys, in 1854 a reformatory for girls (financed by Lady **Byron**), and in 1859 an industrial school. She visited India on four occasions, and set up a National Indian Association for the purpose of making the needs of India known in England. She also travelled in North America to report on prison conditions there.

She was an advocate of higher education for women, wrote pamphlets about her many concerns, including juvenile delinquency, and influenced changes in the law, particularly concerning poor children's schools. Her books include *Our Convicts* (1864), *The Last Days of Rammohun Roy* (1866) and *Six Months in India* (1868).

Carpenter, Mary Chapin

Born 1959
American singer whose rise to stardom has
encompassed folk, country and pop music

Mary Chapin Carpenter was born in New
Jersey. She settled in Washington DC in the
mid-1970s and began to make her name in folk
clubs, though she has entered the mainstream
through country music.

She and her guitarist John Jennings won
several local awards in the 1980s and went on
to make Carpenter's début album, *Hometown
Girl* (1987). Comprising nine original songs
and Tom Waits's 'Downtown Train', it proved
to be the gateway to stardom.

Her subsequent albums include *State of the
Heart* (1989), *Shooting Straight in the Dark* and
Stones in the Road (1994), all of which confirm
her enduring status in the music world. The
name of her music publishing company is Get-
arealjob Music.

Carpenter-Phinney, Connie

Born 1957
American cyclist who won the USA's first Olympic
cycling medal for 72 years

Connie Carpenter-Phinney was born in Madison, Wisconsin. She began her athletic career as a speed skater, competing on a national level until injury forced her to switch
to cycling.

She won the national championship in road
race and pursuit in 1976, 1977 and 1978, as
well as a silver medal in the 1977 world championship road race. Between 1976 and 1984
she won 12 national championships, four
world championships and three Coors International Classics, a series of wins which culminated in a gold medal at the 1984
Olympics — the first Olympic cycling medal
for the USA since 1912.

Carr, Emily

Born 1871 Died 1945
Canadian artist and writer who has been
described as a 'Canadian cultural icon'

Emily Carr was born in Victoria, British Columbia. She studied painting in San Francisco,
London and Paris, and is best known for her
representations of the West Coast Native
American and British Columbian forest.

Her first book of short stories, *Klee Wyck*
(1941), related her impressions of the Native
Americans of the West Coast, and won a Governor-General's award. It was followed by a
number of further 'autobiographical' writings, including *The Book of Small* (1942), *The*

House of All Sorts (1944) and *Growing Pains*
(1946). Selections from Carr's journals were
published posthumously as *Hundreds and
Thousands* (1966).

Her writings have been used extensively to
compile further biography, but they have been
neglected as literary texts in their own right
and she did not receive acclaim for her paintings until the late 1920s.

Carr, Vikki, *professional name of*
Florencia Bisenta de Casillas Martinez
Cardona

Born 1942
American singer whose fans included two
US presidents

Vikki Carr was born in El Paso, Texas. Her
career began in Pepe Callahan's improbable-
sounding Mexican–Irish Band in Los Angeles,
but she quickly broke through to solo stardom. Her début album was *Color Her Great*
(1963), followed by *Discovery* (1964). 'It Must
Be Him' (1967) was a hit on both sides of the
Atlantic.

She was a favourite with Richard Nixon
(and his successor Gerald Ford), and played
command performances at the White House.
Since being abandoned by Columbia in the
late 1970s, she has devoted much of her time
to charity work for Chicano children.

Carr-Boyd, Ann Kirsten

Born 1938
Australian composer, teacher and music historian
who has become a leading authority on Aboriginal
and early Australian music

Ann Carr-Boyd was born in Sydney and educated at Sydney University. Her many orchestral, chamber and instrumental compositions
include *Symphony in Three Movements* (1964),
Three Songs of Love (1975), *Festival* (1980),
Australian Baroque (1984) and *Suite Veronese*
(1985). Commissions include *Fanfare for Aunty*
(1974), for the opening of the ABC's FM trans-
missions, and *The Bells of Sydney Harbour*
(1979) for the Sydney Organ Society.

Carriera, Rosalba Giovanna

Born 1675 Died 1757
Italian painter and miniaturist famed for her
flattering portraits and for introducing the Rococo
style into Italy and France

Rosalba Carriera was born in Venice and is said
to have trained as a lacemaker before painting
miniatures when the fashion for lace waned.
She was the first artist to paint on ivory rather

than vellum and began by decorating snuff boxes.

Awarded a place at the Roman Academy for her skill, she was also one of the first to use pastels in portraiture, and it was not long before she was employed to paint the portraits of noble visitors to Venice.

In 1720 she went to Paris, where she received numerous commissions, including the infant Louis XV. She later went to Vienna for a time, where she received the patronage of the Holy Roman Emperor Charles VI and taught the empress.

Carson, Rachel Louise

Born 1907 Died 1964
American naturalist and science writer who wrote influentially on the dangers of polluting the sea

Rachel Carson was born in Springdale, Pennsylvania. She studied biology at Johns Hopkins University, taught at the University of Maryland (1931–6) and worked as a marine biologist for the US Fish and Wildlife Service from 1936 to 1949.

Her work in marine ecology established her position in the subject, but her wider reputation came with *The Sea Around Us* (1951), which warned of the increasing danger of large-scale marine pollution, and the hard-hitting *Silent Spring* (1962), which forcefully directed public concern to the problems caused by modern synthetic pesticides and their effect on food chains.

The resulting controls in the USA on the use of pesticides owe much to her work, which also contributed to the increasing ecological and conservationist attitudes which emerged in the 1970s and 1980s.

Carswell, Catherine Roxburgh, *née* Macfarlane

Born 1879 Died 1946
Scottish novelist and critic who was criticised for her controversial views on Lawrence and Burns

Catherine Macfarlane was born in Glasgow, the daughter of a merchant, and educated at the Park School, Glasgow, and in Frankfurt-am-Main. She became a socialist after reading Robert Blatchford at the age of 17, and went on to study English at Glasgow University. Her first marriage was annulled after her husband attempted to kill her, and she married fellow journalist and critic Donald Carswell in 1917.

She made her reputation as a dramatic and literary critic for the *Glasgow Herald* from 1907 to 1915 but lost her job when she wrote a review of D H Lawrence's banned novel *The*

Rainbow. Lawrence encouraged her to complete her autobiographical novel of Glasgow life *Open the Door* (1920), a work depicting a young woman's escape from the confinement of a middle-class, Calvinistic Glasgow family.

Lawrence also encouraged her to emphasize Burns's passionate nature in her *The Life of Burns* (1930). She hoped to bring Robert Burns 'out of the mist they loved to keep about him', but the work was unfavourably received by Burns scholars in Scotland. She also wrote biographies of Lawrence, *The Savage Pilgrim: A Narrative of D.H.Lawrence* (1932), and Boccaccio, *The Tranquil Heart* (1937), but is best remembered as a critic.

Carter, Angela Olive, *née* Stalker

Born 1940 Died 1992
English novelist and essayist whose work is characteristically fantastical and questions conventional attitudes to myth, gender and sexuality

Angela Stalker was born in Eastbourne. She married Paul Carter in 1960 (divorced 1972) and then read English at Bristol University. She taught creative writing in England, the USA and Australia, and lived in Japan for two years, an experience recorded in *Nothing Sacred* (1982).

Her fiction is characterized by imaginative use of fantasy, surrealism, genre pastiche, vibrant humour and psychological symbolism, and her novels include *The Magic Toyshop* (1967), *Heroes and Villains* (1969), *The Passion of New Eve* (1977), *Nights at the Circus* (1985) and *Wise Children* (1991). Her stories are collected in *Fireworks* (1974), *The Bloody Chamber* (1979), *Black Venus* (1985) and *American Ghosts & Old World Wonders* (1993). *The Sadeian Woman* (1979) is a feminist reinterpretation of the Marquis de Sade (1740–1814).

She also wrote poetry, tales for children, radio plays and translated fairy tales, and wrote the screenplay for the film *The Company of Wolves* (1984) with Irish filmmaker Neil Jordan. She died early of cancer, having established herself as one of English fiction's most vivacious talents.

Carter, Betty, *professional name of* Lillie Mae Jones, *also called* Lorraine Carter

Born 1930
American jazz singer who emerged from the late 1940s bop era to launch an enduring solo career

Betty Carter was born in Flint, Michigan, and raised in Detroit. She came of age musically in the bop era, having sung with Charlie Parker. Bandleader Lionel Hampton, who employed her from 1948, nicknamed her 'Betty Bebop'; she resented the belittling comparison with a cartoon character, but adopted the forename.

A brilliant vocal improviser, whose energetic rapport with fans (as on the 1979 record *The Audience with Betty Carter*) has rarely transferred to the studio, she established a solo career in the late 1960s. Her Bet-Car production company has afforded her unprecedented autonomy for a female jazz artist, and she continues to work with gifted young musicians.

Time Waits (1993) marked the culmination of a fruitful association with the Verve label.

Carter, Elizabeth

Born 1717 Died 1806
English scholar, poet and translator who was one of the famous 'bluestocking' circle

Elizabeth Carter was born in Deal, Kent, the daughter of a cleric who taught her Greek, Latin and Hebrew. She persevered in her study of a wide range of academic subjects and became accomplished in domestic skills as well.

She contributed verse to many publications, including *Gentleman's Magazine*, and published her own *Poems upon Particular Occasions* (1738) and *Poems on Several Occasions* (1762). However, being an accomplished linguist, she is best remembered for her translations, particulary that of the Greek philosopher Epictetus (1758).

She belonged to the 'bluestocking' coterie of **Elizabeth Montagu**, and had among her other friends Dr Johnson, Sir Joshua Reynolds, Edmund Burke and Horace Walpole.

Carter, Maybelle, *née* Addington

Born 1909 Died 1978
American country singer and songwriter whose family combined forces to find fame

Maybelle Addington was born in Nickelsville, Virginia. She began singing with her husband's family in 1927 and became known as Mother Maybelle. After the Carter family disbanded as a singing group in 1943, Maybelle began singing with her daughters.

The Carter Sisters were featured on *The Grand Ole Opry*. They sang songs written by her, including 'A Jilted Love', 'Don't Wait' and 'I've Got a Home in Glory'. The Carter Family were elected to the Country Music Hall of Fame in 1970.

Rosalynn Carter, 1979

Carter, Rosalynn Smith, *née* Smith

Born 1927
American humanitarian and First Lady as the wife of President Jimmy Carter

Rosalynn Smith was born in Plains, Georgia, and married James Earl Carter in 1946, when he was serving in the US Navy. When her husband was Governor of Georgia (1971–4), she began to devote herself to developing a national strategy for helping the mentally ill, a work which she continued as First Lady (1977–81).

Dubbed the 'Steel Magnolia' for her mixture of Southern graciousness and relentless ambition, since then she has served on numerous foundations and committees dedicated to helping the mentally ill, and promoting children's health and worldwide peace; these include the board of advisers for Habitat for Humanity, being a sponsor of the National Alliance for Research on Schizophrenia and Depression, and chairing the Carter Center Mental Health Task Force.

She received the Volunteer of the Decade Award from the National Mental Health Association in 1980, the Notre Dame Award for International Humanitarian Service in 1992 and the **Eleanor Roosevelt** Living World award for peace links in 1992. Her books include *First Lady from Plains* (1984), *Everything to Gain: Making the Most of the Rest of Your Life* (with Jimmy Carter, 1987) and *Helping Yourself Help Others: A Book for Caregivers* (1994).

Carter, Truda *see* Adams, Truda

Cartimandua

1st century AD
Queen of the Yorkshire Brigantes whose pro-
Roman bent enabled her to defend her position
and her territory for many years

Cartimandua was the queen of a large tribe in northern Britain. After the Roman conquest (AD43) she made a treaty with Rome, but because there were anti-Roman factions among her subjects, she became dependent on the support of the invading Roman armies to maintain her position. She managed to protect the northern borders of the Roman province of Britain, even surviving an attempted overthrow by her anti-Roman husband and co-ruler Venutius. The couple were reconciled for a time, until she left him for one of his aides and he rebelled again and defeated her. The Brigantes' territory under him was annexed by the Romans in 71.

Cartland, Dame (Mary) Barbara Hamilton

Born 1901
English popular romantic novelist whose
phenomenal output has brought her fame
and wealth

Barbara Cartland was born in Edgbaston, Birmingham. She published her first novel, *Jigsaw*, in 1923, and has since produced well over 400 bestselling books, mostly novels of chaste romantic love designed for women readers, but also including biographies and books on food, health and beauty, and several volumes of autobiography.

She earned a place in the *Guinness Book of Records* for writing 26 books in the year 1983. The step-grandmother of **Diana, Princess of Wales**, she is an ardent advocate of health foods and fitness for the elderly, and has championed causes like the St John's Ambulance Brigade and the provision of campsites for Romany gipsies. She was appointed DBE in 1991.

Casarès, Maria

Born 1922
Spanish-born French actress whose tempestuous
style was innovatory in the French theatre

Maria Casarès was born in Corunna, Spain. She was exiled during the Spanish Civil War, and took up residence in Paris, where she had her intial success in J M Synge's *Deirdre of the Sorrows* in 1942. She became closely associated with the work of the existentialist playwrights Camus and Sartre, and had a success in Racine's *Phèdre* at the Comédie-Française before joining the Théâtre National Populaire in 1955.

She became France's leading tragic actress of her generation, and popularized a more violent and tempestuous style than was traditional in classical French theatre.

Cash, June Carter, *née* Carter

Born 1929
American country singer who was married for a
time to Johnny Cash

June Carter was born in Maces Springs, Virginia, part of The Original Carter Family. She performed at The Grand Ole Opry country music show in Nashville as a member of the Carter Sisters and also sang with her husband, Johnny Cash (1932–).

Her songs include 'Baby It's Cold Outside', 'Love Oh Crazy Love' and 'Leftover Loving'.

Cash, Roseanne

Born 1955
American country singer who followed in her
father's footsteps to success

Roseanne Cash was born in Memphis, Tennessee, the daughter of country singer Johnny Cash (1932–) and his first wife, Vivian Liberto. She began her career as a part-time backup singer to her father. Her first album was recorded for a German label but was never released, even though she married its producer, singer/songwriter Rodney Crowell in 1979.

The difficulties of her family life, her marriage and her cocaine addiction are reflected in her music. After a string of single hits, her 1987 album, *King's Record Shop*, produced four number-one singles and won her a Grammy for Best Album Package in 1988. She is also the recipient of a Special Achievement Award from the Nashville Songwriters Association.

Cáslavská, Vera

Born 1942
Czech gymnast who won 22 Olympic, World and
European titles

Vera Cáslavská was born in Prague. She gave up ice skating in favour of gymnastics as a 15-year-old, and won three Olympic gold medals in 1964 and four in 1968. She donated her medals to each of the four Czech leaders deposed following the Russian invasion (Dubček, Svoboda, Cernik and Smrkorsky).

She was married for a time to Josef Odložil, the Olympic 1,500-metre silver medallist in the Mexico City Olympics. After coaching gymnastics during the 1970s and 1980s, in

Prague (1970–9) and then in Mexico, she became an adviser on social policy to Vaclav Havel, President of the Czech Republic in 1990, and was appointed his assistant in 1991.

Cassatt, Mary

Born 1844 Died 1926
American painter and printmaker who joined the
Impressionists in France

Mary Cassatt was born in Allegheny, Pennsylvania. She studied in Spain, Italy and Holland, but worked mainly in France, where she was a close follower of Degas and joined the Impresssionist movement.

Her *Woman and Child Driving* in the Philadelphia Museum is a typical work, her favourite subjects being women and children. Influenced by Japanese print-making, she was also renowned for her etching and for her drypoint studies of domestic scenes.

She persuaded her fellow-Americans to buy Impressionist art, thus influencing their attitudes and preferences.

Cassidy, Sheila Anne

Born 1937
English physician and religious author who is
particularly involved in palliative care

Sheila Cassidy was born in Lincolnshire, where her father lectured at RAF Cranwell. The family emigrated to Australia in 1949, returning to England in 1957. She studied medicine in Sydney and Oxford, qualifying as a doctor and then as a surgeon.

She went to work in Chile in 1971. In 1975 she was arrested, imprisoned and tortured for two months for treating a wounded guerilla. The experience, related in *Audacity to Believe* (1977), made her a supporter of human rights and re-awakened her Christian faith. After testing her vocation to be a nun in 1978–80, she returned to medicine, becoming medical director at St Luke's Hospice, Plymouth, in 1982 and palliative care physician at Plymouth General Hospital in 1993. She has written several books on prayer and on the care of the suffering and bereaved, including the award-winning *Good Friday People* (1991).

Castellanos, Rosario

Born 1925 Died 1974
Mexican poet, novelist, story writer and
translator, one of the great Latin-American
writers of her century

Rosario Castellanos was born in Mexico City, brought up in Comitán, Chiapas, and educated in Mexico City and in Madrid. Her early work,

described by one influential critic, perhaps not insignificantly, as 'insubstantial and feminine', was in fact full of promise and interest, but she did not develop her full powers until *Poemas 1953–5* (1957), published at the height of her close involvement with the Native Americans of Chiapas, where she had spent her childhood and adolescence.

Her theme, that in such conquered and suffering peoples lies the only residue of hope in a world 'civilized' in the name of barbarism, is movingly expressed. Some of these works are translated in *The Selected Poems of Rosario Castellanos* (1988). Many of her novels and stories have been translated, including *Balúncanán* (1957, Eng trans *The Nine Guardians*, 1958), about the break-up of the old ways under the impact of the reforms of Lázaro Cárdenas.

Castellanos was a professor in Mexico and in the USA, and an ambassador to Israel, during a visit to which she was electrocuted while trying to change a light bulb.

Castle, Irene, *née* Foote

Born 1893 Died 1969
American-born dancer who became a champion
exhibition ballroom dancer partnered by her
husband Vernon

Irene Foote was born in New Rochelle, New York. In 1911 she married an Englishman, Vernon Blythe (1887–1918, later called Vernon Castle), and together they rose to rank among the most popular exhibition ballroom dancers and teachers in history, performing with great style and flair throughout America and Europe.

They devised such famous dances as the one-step and the turkey-trot and popularized the maxixe, the castle walk, the hesitation waltz and the tango, among others. She retired from dancing after his death as an airman in the Royal Flying Corps.

Castle of Blackburn, Barbara Anne Castle, Baroness, *née* Betts

Born 1910
English Labour politician hailed as the 'First Lady
of Socialism'

Barbara Betts was educated at Bradford Girls' Grammar School and St Hugh's College, Oxford. She worked in local government before World War II, and entered parliament in 1945 as MP for Blackburn, having married Edward Cyril Castle (1907–79), a journalist, in 1944. During the 1950s she was a convinced 'Bevanite' and spoke out in defence of radical causes.

Barbara Castle, 1968

She was Chairman of the Labour party from 1958 to 1959, and after Labour came into power in 1964 she attained Cabinet rank as Minister of Overseas Development (1964–5). As Minister of Transport (1965–8), she brought about the controversial introduction of a 70mph speed limit and the 'breathalyzer' test for drunken drivers, in an effort to cut down road accidents. She then took over the newly created post of Secretary of State for Employment and Productivity (1968–70) to deal with the government's difficult prices and incomes policy. In 1974 she became Minister of Health and Social Security, and in 1976 when James Callaghan became the next Labour Prime Minister she returned to the back benches and became Vice-Chairman of the Socialist Group in the European parliament (1979–84).

She published two volumes of her diaries in 1980 and 1984, and was created a life peer in 1990. Her memoirs, *Fighting All the Way*, appeared in 1993.

Castro, Inez de

Born c.1323 Died 1355
Spanish noblewoman famous for her tragic death
at the hands of the King of Portugal

Inez de Castro was the illegitimate daughter of a Spanish nobleman. In 1340 she came to Portugal in the train of her cousin Costança, the bride of the Infante, Dom Pedro (the future Peter I of Portugal). Her beauty captivated him, and, after Costança's death in 1345 he made her his mistress, and in 1354 his wife.

Pedro was greatly influenced by Inez and her brothers and when in 1354 he declared himself pretender to the throne of Castile, his father Afonso IV ordered Inez's assassination by stabbing, an event that has inspired several novels, poems and plays. When Pedro acceded to the throne in 1357 he had her body placed in a magnificent mausoleum.

Castro, Rosalía de

Born 1837 Died 1885
Spanish poet and novelist whose work in both
Galician and Castilian places her among the most
significant poets of the 19th century

Rosalía de Castro was born in Santiago de Compostela and in 1858 married a historian who championed the Galician Renaissance. Her earliest works, such as the poetry collection *La Flor* (1857, 'The Flower'), were written in Spanish, but it is on her later volumes in Galician that her fame rests, such as *Cantares Gallegos* (1863, 'Galician Songs') and *Follas Novas* (1880, 'New Leaves'); her work is a celebration of the Galician people.

Her novels, written in Spanish, brought her to the attention of a wider public; they include *La Hija del Mar* (1859, 'The Daughter of the Sea') and *Ruinas* (1867, 'Ruins').

Despite the currently perilous position of Galician — it receives official support, but the number of mother-tongue speakers is declining — de Castro's reputation as a poet appears secure.

Català, Victor, *pseud of* Caterina Albert i Paradís

Born 1869 Died 1966
Catalan writer who has recently begun to attract
attention as a pioneer of modernist literature

Caterina Albert was born in L'Escala, a fishing village near the Catalan French border. She published her first book, the poetry collection *El Cant del Mesos* ('Song of the Months'), in 1901. She followed this with several volumes of short stories and, in 1905, the psychological novel *Solitud*, a richly atmospheric story of a young bride's experiences and growing self-awareness in an isolated hermitage in the Pyrenees.

Although continuing to write and publish — including a second novel, *Caires Vius*

('Living Aspects'), in 1907 — she largely withdrew from the public eye after the success of her first novel.

Her writing ceased to be published during the Francoist suppression of Catalan writing, and so suffered neglect for many years, but it has recently come to critical attention again and has been translated into many languages.

Catchpole, Margaret

Born 1762 Died 1819
English-born Australian pioneer whose
transportation gave her the opportunity to start
a new life

Margaret Catchpole was born near Ipswich, Suffolk, and became a servant to the Cobbold family of brewers of that town. Twice sentenced to death, for stealing a horse and for subsequently escaping from Ipswich jail, she was transported to New South Wales in 1801, where she was assigned as a servant and nurse.

She managed a farm, ran a store, acted as midwife and led a useful life in the community, dying of an illness brought about by helping a neighbour during the bad winter weather.

Her letters home to her relations and to the Cobbold family, who retained an interest in her welfare, formed the basis of Richard Cobbold's book *Margaret Catchpole* (1845) and give a valuable account of early 19th-century life in the new colony.

Cather, Willa Sibert

Born 1873 Died 1947
American fiction writer, poet and journalist, a
homosexual who wrote about independent women
and frontier life on the plains of America

Willa Cather was born on a farm near Winchester, Virginia. Her formative years were spent in Nebraska, and after university there (1891–5) her career began with a well-written but not significant volume of poetry, *April Twilights* (1903). She moved to New York as Editor of *McClure's* magazine (1906–12).

After her first novel, *Alexander's Bridge* (1912), she wrote three novels dealing with immigrants to the USA: *O Pioneers!* was published in 1913 and *The Song of the Lark* two years later. The third, *My Antonia* (1918), is generally regarded as her best book.

She was a prolific writer, among whose other novels are *Death Comes for the Archbishop* (1927) and *One of Ours* (1922), which won the 1923 Pulitzer Prize.

Catherine I

Born 1684 Died 1727
Empress of Russia who acceded to the throne on
the death of her husband Peter I, the Great

Catherine was of lowly birth, probably of Lithuanian peasant stock, and was baptized a Roman Catholic with the name of Martha Skowronska. She was married as a young girl to a Swedish army officer who deserted her, and subsequently became mistress to a Russian general, Boris Sheremetev, and to the tsar's principal minister, Prince Alexander Menshikov.

In 1705 she became mistress to Tsar Peter (ruled 1682–1725), changing her name to Catherine and converting to Orthodoxy in 1708. The tsar married her (his second wife) in 1712, following her distinguished conduct while on campaign with her husband during the wars against Sweden. In 1722 Peter passed a law allowing the tsar to nominate a successor and in 1724 chose Catherine, having her crowned empress in that year. After his death in 1725, Prince Menshikov ensured her succession to the throne.

Although she continued her husband's reforms, she had neither Peter's strong will nor his sense of purpose. She was, however, concerned to alleviate conditions for the peasantry, lowering taxation and reducing the power of local bureaucracies. She was succeeded by Peter's grandson, Peter II. Later, Russia was ruled by her daughter Elizabeth (from 1741 to 1762) and by her son Peter III (1762).

Catherine II, *known as* Catherine the Great

Born 1729 Died 1796
Empress of Russia whose ambition, ruthlessness,
intelligence and love of her country equate her
forever with a significant epoch in its history

Catherine was born in Stettin, the daughter of the Prince of Anhalt-Zerbst. She married Grand Duke Peter, heir to the Russian throne as Peter III, in 1745, but soon quarrelled with her husband, and became notorious for her love affairs with Gregory Orlov and then with Stanislaw Augustus Poniatowski.

After Peter III's accession in 1762, Catherine was banished to a separate abode, until Peter was dethroned by a conspiracy and forced to abdicate, and Catherine was made empress. A few days afterwards Peter was murdered by Orlov and others. Catherine then made a show of regard for the Greek Church, but her principles were those of the French philosophers. The government was carried on with great energy, and the dominions and power of Russia rapidly increased. When discontent was voiced, the young Prince Ivan, the hope of the disaffected, was murdered in the castle of Schlüsselburg.

From that time internal politics consisted of court intrigues for and against one favourite or another, Grigori Potemkin (1731–91) being the best known. The first partition of Poland in 1772 and the Turkish war (1774) vastly increased the empire; so did a war with Sweden (1790) and another Turkish war (1792), but none without cost to the serfs, on whom the mainly agricultural economy of Russia was based. The second and third partitions of Poland, and the incorporation of Courland into Russia, completed the triumphs of Catherine's reign.

Catherine de' Médicis, *Italian*
Caterina de' Medici

> Born 1519 Died 1589
> Queen of France as the wife of Henri II (ruled 1547–59) who was influential in the Catholic–Huguenot wars and had three sons crowned

Caterina de' Medici was born in Florence, the daughter of Lorenzo de' Medici, Duke of Urbino. In 1533, at the age of 14, she married Henri, Duke of Orléans, the future Henri II of France, second son of Francis I. She became queen on her husband's accession in 1547, but was constantly humiliated by Henry's mistress, **Diane de Poitiers**, who ruled him completely.

When Henri died in 1559, she acted as queen regent during the brief reign of her eldest son, Francis II (1544–60), the first husband of **Mary, Queen of Scots**. She was also queen regent during the minority of her second son, Charles IX (1550–74), who succeeded to the throne in 1560, and whom she dominated throughout his reign. In the religious wars of 1562–9 (the struggle for power between Protestants and Roman Catholics), she at first supported the Protestant Huguenots against the Guise faction, but later supported the Guises and has traditionally been implicated in the fearful St Bartholomew's Day Massacre of 1572.

Her third son, Henri of Anjou, having been elected king of Poland in 1573, succeeded to the French throne in 1574 as Henri III, but her political influence waned throughout his troubled reign.

Catherine of Alexandria, St

> Born c.290AD Died c.310AD
> Legendary saint and virgin who gave her name to the Catherine-wheel

Catherine was born of royal descent in Alexandria. Following her conversion around the age of 18, she publicly denounced the emperor Maxentius for his persecution of the Christians. He attempted to silence her by enforcing a discussion between her and 50 pagan philosophers but, unable to find fault with her argument, they were executed for their trouble.

On discovering that his wife and several soldiers had been converted through Catherine's teaching, Maxentius ordered a spiked wheel (later known as a 'Catherine-wheel') on which she was to be broken. However it was the wheel that broke, and Catherine was beheaded instead.

Her remains were miraculously spirited to Mount Sinai, where her shrine is on display in St Catherine's monastery. Her feast day, which has been removed from the Church calendar, is 25 November.

Catherine of Aragon

> Born 1485 Died 1536
> Queen of England as the first wife of Henry VIII (ruled 1509–47)

Catherine of Aragon was the youngest daughter of Ferdinand and **Isabella I** of Spain. In 1501 she married the 15-year-old Prince Arthur, Prince of Wales, son and heir of Henry VII. Arthur died six months later, and in June 1503 she was betrothed to her brother-in-law, the 11-year-old Prince Henry. They were married in 1509, seven weeks after Henry's accession to the throne, and were happy for a time. Between 1510 and 1514 she bore him four children, who all died in infancy. In 1516 she gave birth to her only surviving child, Princess Mary, later Queen **Mary I** (Mary Tudor).

In the years that followed, Henry's infidelities, and his anxiety for a son and heir, soured the marriage, and in 1527 he began to seek an annulment which would allow him to marry his latest favourite, **Anne Boleyn**. Despite strong opposition from the pope, Henry and Anne were secretly married in 1533, and the annulment of the marriage to Catherine was pronounced by Archbishop Thomas Cranmer a few months later. Catherine, who was well loved by the English people and who had offered a dignified, passive resistance throughout, was sent into retirement at Ampthill in Bedfordshire.

In 1534 the pope pronounced her marriage valid; this provoked Henry's final break with Rome and the onset of the Reformation in England. Catherine steadfastly refused to accept the title of 'princess dowager', or to accept the Act of Succession (1534) which declared Princess Mary illegitimate.

Catherine of Braganza

Born 1638 Died 1705
Queen of England as the wife of Charles II
(ruled 1660–85)

Catherine of Braganza was the daughter of the Duke of Braganza (later King John IV of Portugal) and became a devout Roman Catholic. She married Charles in 1662, and suffered the humiliation of being forced to receive his mistress, **Barbara Villiers**, and their children, at court.

Her own failure to bear children, and her extreme parsimony, alienated her from the people but Charles resisted all pressure for a divorce, though he did force her to live apart from him in retirement. In 1692, seven years after Charles's death, she went home to Portugal. In 1704 she was Regent of Portugal for her brother Pedro II, who was too ill to rule.

Catherine of Genoa, *originally* Caterinetta Fieschi

Born 1447 Died 1510
Italian Christian mystic whose faith led her to care for the sick

Catherine of Genoa was converted to Christianity at the age of 26. Ten years before, through an arranged marriage, she had become the wife of Giuliano Adorno; he too was later converted and became a Franciscan tertiary, helping Catherine care for the sick in Genoa's largest hospital, where she became administrator of the female wards.

From 1475 she took daily Communion, an unusual practice at the time for lay people. Her mystical experiences and teaching, recorded in her *Spiritual Dialogues* and *Treatise on Purgatory*, were evaluated by Friedrich Von Hügel in 1908 in a seminal work in the modern study of Christian mysticism.

Catherine of Siena, St, *originally* Caterina Benincasa

Born 1347 Died 1380
Italian mystic and patron saint of Italy, a prayerful servant of God whose calling led her into the arena of international peacemaking

Caterina Benincasa was the daughter of a dyer in Siena and the youngest of 25 children. She was high-spirited and good looking, but spent much time in penitential prayer and steadfastly refused to marry. She became a Dominican tertiary at the age of 16 and began to experience visions. Gathering a small group of disciples, she took to travelling and preaching.

In 1375, the year in which she is said to have suffered the pain of Christ's stigmata, though not their imprint on her body, she entered the world of public affairs and attempted to arbitrate peace between the rebellious city of Florence and the papal government. Soon afterwards she prevailed upon Pope Gregory XI to move his court back from Avignon to Rome. In 1378, at the start of the reign (in Rome) of Pope Urban VI, whose harshness and insensitivity she had the courage to criticize, Catherine (who had never learnt to write) dictated letters to the European leaders who were showing loyalty to a newly appointed rival in Avignon, Pope Clement VII, begging them to recognize Urban VI instead. In response to Urban's invitation to raise support for him, she moved to Rome and devoted herself to that task, but soon after she suffered a stroke and died.

She wrote devotional pieces, letters and poems, and her *Dialogue*, a work on mysticism, was translated in 1896. She was canonized in 1461, and named patron saint of Italy in 1939. Her feast day is 29 April.

Catherine of Valois

Born 1401 Died 1437
Queen of England as the wife of Henry V
(ruled 1413–22)

Catherine of Valois was the youngest daughter of King Charles VI ('the Foolish') of France. After a stormy courtship, when England and France went to war over Henry's dowry demands, she married Henry at Troyes in 1420.

In 1421 she gave birth to a son, the future Henry VI. After Henry's death in France in 1422, she secretly married Owen Tudor, a Welsh squire, despite parliamentary opposition; their eldest son, Edmund, Earl of Richmond, was the father of Henry VII, the first of the Tudor kings of England.

Catt, Carrie (Clinton) Chapman, *née* Lane

Born 1859 Died 1947
American feminist leader, reformer and pacifist who played a major part in securing female suffrage through the 19th Amendment

Carrie Lane was born in Ripon, Wisconsin. She was educated at Iowa State College, and became a high school principal and one of the first female school superintendants in

Carrie Chapman Catt, 1909

America. She married Leo Chapman in 1884, but he died two years later. Before marrying George W Catt in 1890 she arranged a legal contract with him to allow her to devote herself freely to the suffrage movement for four months each year. His support of her work continued beyond his death in 1905, for he left her financially independent.

She had joined the staff of the National American Woman Suffrage Association in 1890, and later became its president (1900–4 and 1915–47; **Anna Shaw** was president 1904–15), effecting dramatic changes in the organization and helping to bring about the 19th Amendment (1920), thus securing the vote for women. She was also founder-President of the International Woman Suffrage Alliance from 1902 to 1923. She helped establish the two-million-strong League of Women Voters (1919) to continue the movement for legislation reform, and spent the later years of her life campaigning for world peace.

She co-wrote *Woman Suffrage and Politics: The Inner Story of the Suffrage Movement* (1923) and wrote *Why Wars Must Cease* (1935).

Cauer, Minna (Wilhelmine Theodore Marie), *née* Schelle

Born 1841 Died 1922
German feminist and suffragist, also a longtime campaigner for pacifism

Minna Schelle was born in Freyenstein (Ostprignitz) where her father was pastor. After her first husband Latzel's death in 1866,

she qualified as a teacher (1867). After one year's teaching in Paris she and her second husband, whose surname Cauer she adopted, went to Berlin, where he had been appointed as inspector of schools. He died in 1881.

During the 1880s she held leading roles in the *Kaufmannischer Verband für Weibliche Angestellete* and in the *Verein Frauenwohl*. In 1900 she founded with **Anita Augspurg** the important *Verband fortschritter Frauenvereine* (a federation of women's associations) and in 1902 was a founder, with Augspurg and **Lida Heymann**, of a women's suffrage organization, the *Deutscher Verband für Frauenstimmrecht*.

After World War I she was involved with Heymann and Augspurg in publishing the newspaper *Die Frau im Stadt* (1919–33).

Caulkins, Frances Manwaring

Born 1795 Died 1869
American educationalist and historian

Frances Caulkins was born and brought up in Connecticut. When the death of her stepfather impoverished the family, she ran a girls' school in Norwichtown. A convert to Congregationalism, by 1831 she had become involved in evangelical works; her religious tracts published between 1836 and 1842 by the American Tract Society sold millions of copies.

Her two classics of local history, *A History of Norwich* (1845) and *A History of New London* (1852), remain unsurpassed in their field. In 1849 she was the first woman elected to the prestigious Massachusetts Historical Society.

Cavell, Edith Louisa

Born 1865 Died 1915
English nurse and World War I heroine who was executed for helping Allied soldiers escape from German-occupied Belgium

Edith Cavell was born in Swardeston, Norfolk, the daughter of a clergyman. She entered nursing in 1885 and in 1907 became the first matron of the Berkendael Medical Institute in Brussels, which became a Red Cross hospital during World War I.

During the German occupation of Belgium, she joined an underground group helping British, French and Belgian soldiers to escape to neutral Holland; her task was to conceal them at the hospital whilst they were provided with guides and money by the Belgian Philippe Baucq.

In August 1915 she was arrested by the Germans and charged with having helped about 200 Allied soldiers to escape to neutral

Holland. Tried by court-martial, she did not deny the charges and she and Baucq were executed.

Cavendish, Lucy Caroline, Lady Frederick, *née* Lyttleton

Born 1841 Died 1926
British social and educational reformer

Lucy Lyttleton was the daughter of the fourth Lord Lyttleton, and niece of Gladstone. She became Maid of Honour to Queen **Victoria** in 1863, and the following year married Lord Frederick Cavendish, second son of the Duke of Devonshire, with whom she moved in Liberal circles.

After her husband's murder in Phoenix Park in 1882, she used her political connections to devote herself to causes such as religious education, Home Rule for Ireland, unity in South Africa and women's education. She also campaigned for Christians in Turkey. Lucy Cavendish Hall for women graduates at Cambridge was named in her honour in 1965.

Cavendish, Margaret, Duchess of Newcastle

Born 1623 Died 1673
English noblewoman who began writing while in exile during the English Civil War

Margaret Cavendish was born in Colchester, Essex. She was a Maid of Honour at the court of Charles I and **Henrietta Maria**, where she met William, Duke of Newcastle, and became the Duchess of Newcastle on her marriage to him in 1645. She spent the ensuing 15 years of the English Civil War with her exiled husband in Europe, and on her return suffered the ridicule of society for her eccentricities of behaviour and dress.

Her *Poems and Fancies* (1653) contains charming fairy verses, and both her autobiography and the *Life* of her husband show restraint and good sense. Her later poetry is doggerel, her philosophy is pompous and naïve, and Samuel Pepys described one of her plays as 'the most ridiculous thing that was ever wrote'.

Cawley, Evonne Fay, *née* Goolagong

Born 1951
Australian tennis player, the first mother to win Wimbledon and the first aboriginal to be a tennis champion

Evonne Goolagong was born in Barellan, New South Wales, but left for Sydney at the age of 10 to be coached in tennis. She married Roger Cawley, an English metal broker, in 1975. As a teenager she won 37 junior titles and in 1971 she beat **Margaret Smith Court** at Wimbledon, becoming the second-youngest woman to win.

During the subsequent decade before her second Wimbledon win against **Chris Evert** in 1980 (when she became the first mother to do so), she clocked up 92 major tennis tournament wins, including the Australian Open four times, and at the peak of her career was ranked second in the world.

Cecchi d'Amico, Suso, *originally* Giovanna Cecchi

Born 1914
Italian screenwriter whose early career was established in the school of Italian neo-realism that flourished after World War II

Giovanna Cecchi was born in Rome, the daughter of the writer Emilio Cecchi. She studied at Rome and Cambridge, and worked as a journalist and translator before writing the screenplay of the film *Mio Figlio Professore* (1946).

She contributed to the school of Italian neo-realism with her screenplays of *Ladri Di Biciclette* (1948, 'Bicycle Thieves') and *Miracolo A Milano* (1950, 'Miracle in Milan'), but found some of her best opportunities working in collaboration with director Luchino Visconti (1906–76), especially on a number of elegant literary adaptations, including *Il Gattopardo* (1963, 'The Leopard'), *Lo Straniero* (1967, 'The Stranger') and *L'Innocente* (1976, 'The Innocent').

Dedicated to indigenous Italian storytelling, she has provided many of her country's leading filmmakers with expertly crafted and structured screenplays, tailored to the specific sensibility of the director. Among her finest work is *Salvatore Guiliano* (1961), *Jesus of Nazareth* (1977) and *Oci Ciornie* (1987, 'Dark Eyes').

Cecilia, St

Died 230
Christian martyr, and patron saint of music

Cecilia, according to a highly dubious tradition, was a Roman maiden of patrician birth compelled to marry a young pagan, Valerian, despite a vow of celibacy. She succeeded in persuading him to respect her vow, and converted both him and his brother to Christianity, but they were both put to death for their faith. On being caught burying them, she too was sentenced to death by suffocation in her own bathroom, but this was unsuccessful and she was beheaded instead.

Her association with music-making (she is the patron saint of musicians) seems to originate from the legend that during her wedding she 'sang in her heart' to the Lord. Her feast day is 22 November.

Cenci, Beatrice

Born 1577 Died 1599
Italian beauty who has become the tragic central figure in several literary works, including The Cenci *(1819) by Percy Bysshe Shelley*

Beatrice Cenci was the youngest daughter of a wealthy Roman nobleman, Count Francesco Cenci, a vicious man who conceived an incestuous passion for her. He treated her brutally and imprisoned her and her stepmother Lucrezia in a castle.

With the help of the keeper of the castle Calvetti, her brother Giacomo, Lucrezia and others, Beatrice plotted the murder of her father in 1598 by means of two hired assassins.

The Cenci family were arrested and tortured until they confessed. All three were beheaded, despite appeals for clemency, by order of Pope Clement VIII, who also confiscated their property.

Centlivre, Susannah, *née* Freeman

Born c.1667 Died c.1723
English dramatist who became a great woman of the theatre

Susannah Freeman was born probably in Holbeach, Lincolnshire. According to some sources she was taught French by a tutor, and there is a story of her masquerading as a man in order to gain entrance to Cambridge University. There are unsubstantiated stories of her being married at 14, widowed two years later, marrying again and perhaps even being widowed and marrying a third time, all while a relatively young woman.

In 1700 she produced a tragedy, *The Perjured Husband*, and subsequently appeared on the stage in Bath in her own comedy, *Love at a Venture* (1706). She dedicated another play, *The Platonick Lady,* written the same year, to 'all the Generous Encouragers of Female Ingenuity'. Also in 1706 she married Joseph Centlivre, head cook to Queen **Anne** at Windsor.

She wrote 19 plays, of which *The Busie Body* (1709), *A Bold Stroke for a Wife* (1717) and *A Wonder: A Woman Keeps a Secret* (1714) were

farcical comedies of intrigue that became very popular.

Chacel, Rosa

Born 1898
Spanish novelist and poet who since the 1970s has been recognized as an important novelist

Rosa Chacel was born in Valladolid. She spent much time in Italy, and was almost unknown in Spain until 1970, when her novel *La sinrazón* (1960, 'The Wrong'), was reprinted in Barcelona. She has continued to live in Brazil.

Her first novel, *Estación, ida y vuelta* (1930, 'Station, Round Trip'), was more original than it seemed at that time: it was influenced by the Spanish critic and philosopher José Ortega y Gasset (1883–1955), but anticipated the French *nouveau roman* far more clearly than apparently similar contemporaneous works by such novelists as Francisco Ayala. In her work however, Chacel insisted on examining the inner life of her characters at the apparent expense of their outer life, which only gave an impression of the 'dehumanization' then fashionable in Spanish fiction.

Memorias de Leticia Valle (1945, 'Memoirs of Leticia Valle') is a *tour de force* in which a young girl relates the effects upon her of her sexual attractiveness to her male teacher. It is a novel which has annoyed male critics, as it was perhaps intended to do, and, were it translated (a critic has suggested), might become a 'woman's *Lolita*'.

Chadwick, Florence

Born 1918
American long-distance swimmer who seemed to break records almost every time she swam

Florence Chadwick was born in San Diego, California. In 1950 she swam the English Channel from France to England in 13 hours and 20 minutes, breaking **Gertrude Ederle**'s record by over one hour. The following year, when she swam the Channel from England to France, she became the only woman to have swum the Channel in both directions. She later swam the Channel four more times, breaking her France-to-England record twice, in 1953 and 1955.

In 1952 Chadwick swam the 21-mile (34km) Catalina (California) Channel in 13 hours and 47 minutes, the first woman to complete the course, and during a five-week period in 1953, she swam the English Channel, the Straits of Gibraltar and a round-trip across the Bosporus, each in world record times.

(*See photograph on next page.*)

Florence Chadwick, 1957

Chadwick, Helen

Born 1953 Died 1996
English photographer, installation and
performance artist, one of modern art's most
provocative and inspirational figures

Helen Chadwick was born in Croydon, London. She studied at Brighton Polytechnic (1973–6) and Chelsea School of Art (1976–7) and lectured at the latter and at the Royal College.

Her work covered a wide range of disciplines, including sculpture, photography, mixed media installation and performance art, and was often autobiographical in context. Tending to question and challenge stereotypical attitudes in society, many of her works, particularly her series of meat abstracts (eg *Enfleshings 1*, 1989) and her portrayal of the body, which was open to many differing interpretations, courted controversy. Her suggestive *Cacao* (1994) was a fountain of molten chocolate.

In 1987 she had a work shortlisted for the Turner prize, and in 1995 had a solo show at the Museum of Modern Art in New York. Her work is represented in many major public collections in the UK, including the Tate Gallery, the V & A and Birmingham Art Gallery and around the world. She died unexpectedly of heart failure.

Chalker of Wallasey, Lynda
Chalker, Baroness, *née* Bates

Born 1942
English Conservative politician who rose to a high
position in Foreign and Commonwealth Affairs

Lynda Bates was educated at the universities of Heidelberg and London and at the Central London Polytechnic. She married Eric Chalker in 1967 (divorced 1973) and Clive Landa in 1981. After working in market research, she entered parliament as MP for Wallasey in 1974, retaining her seat until 1992.

During the Labour administration she was Opposition spokesperson on social services (1976–9), and once the Conservative government took power, she held two under-secretary positions (DHSS, 1979–82, and Transport, 1982–3) before becoming Minister of State in the Department of Transport (1983–6).

She then moved to the Foreign and Commonwealth Office, and was appointed Minister for Overseas Development in 1989. She has risen to control the world's fifth biggest aid budget and has earned much popularity in the developing world.

Chambefort, Marie

Floreat c.1850
French daguerreotypist photographer who was
active very early in the history of photography

Marie Chambefort was an extremely early female itinerant photographer who worked in the Département de Saône-et-Loire in France during the 1850s. Little is known of her life however, and only a few examples of her work survive, among them a touching portrait entitled *Stephanie Poyet, agée de 7 ans*, in which a solemn little girl is depicted seated, her feet on an embroidered footstool, against which leans, with equal solemnity, a favourite doll.

Chamorro, Violeta Barrios De

Born c.1941
Nicaraguan politician who was elected head of
state 12 years after the murder of her husband

Violeta Chamorro was married to Pedro Joaquin Chamorro from 1950 until his murder in 1978, which sparked off events leading to the Sandinista revolution and the overthrow of the Somozoa regime in 1979. It also marked the beginning of her political career.

She briefly joined the ruling Sandanista junta but, disagreeing with the direction of the revolution, she left in 1980 and, as owner of the influential *La Prensa* newspaper (of which her husband had been editor), used it as an important opposition tool. Her own family of four were split ideologically — one son ran the Sandinista party newspaper *Barricada* while the other joined the contras in exile, and one daughter was a Sandinista diplomat while the other took over the editorship of *La Prensa*.

In 1989 Chamorro stood as the candidate for the National Opposition Union (UNO) which consisted of 14 parties (seven from 1994) with widely differing ideologies. In 1990 she was elected President of Nicaragua after a decisive win over Daniel Ortega. Once in office she focused the policies of her right-wing government on national reconciliation, brought an end to the Contra war and made constitutional changes restricting presidential power. She planned to leave office in 1997 following the elections in October 1996.

Champmeslé, La, *stage name of* Marie Desmares

Born 1642 Died 1698
French actress who became the Comédie-
Française's leading lady and Racine's mistress

Marie Desmares is first mentioned in Rouen, and was probably born there. She took her professional name from her second husband, the actor Charles Chevillet Champmeslé, and by 1668 was in Paris, where she established herself as a leading actress of the day; she is said to have had a particularly moving, semi-sung mode of delivery.

She became the mistress of the playwright Racine, and gave the first performances of his most important works, including *Phèdre* in 1677. She became the leading lady of the newly-formed Comédie-Française in 1680, and

remained on the stage until illness forced her to retire shortly before her death.

Chanel, Coco (Gabrielle)

Born 1883 Died 1971
French couturier and innovative fashion designer
who created the enduring Chanel-style suit that
continues to have worldwide appeal

Coco Chanel was orphaned at an early age. She worked with her sister as a milliner until 1912, when she opened a shop of her own, which she followed by opening a couture house in Deauville (1913). During World War I she served as a nurse. She opened her second couture house in the Rue du Cambon in Paris in 1924, and it was from here that she was to revolutionize women's fashions during the 1920s when, for the first time for a century, women were liberated from the restriction of corsets (an innovation with which Chanel's colleague **Madeleine Vionnet** is credited).

In 1920 Chanel designed her first 'chemise' dress, and in 1925 the collarless cardigan jacket arrived. The combination of simple elegance and comfort in her designs gave them immediate, widespread and lasting appeal, and many of the features she introduced, such as the vogue for costume jewellery, the evening scarf and the 'little black dress', have retained their popularity.

At the height of her career she managed four businesses, including the manufacture of her world-famous perfume, Chanel No.5, and her great wealth and dazzling social life attracted great public interest. She retired in 1938, but made a surprisingly successful comeback in 1954, when, following her original style, she regained her prominence in the fashion world.

Channing, Carol Elaine

Born 1921
American singer and actress, who sang 'Diamonds
Are a Girl's Best Friend' and played the lead in
Hello Dolly!

Carol Channing was born in Seattle, Washington. After an array of small parts, she made her breakthrough as Lorelie Lee in *Gentlemen Prefer Blondes* (1949), singing 'Diamonds Are a Girl's Best Friend', a song now more strongly associated with **Marilyn Monroe**. Channing's big-eyed exuberance was very different from Monroe's more kittenish approach, and it won her the lead in *Hello Dolly!* (1964) and a strong supporting role in the film *Thoroughly Modern Millie* (1967). Her later career has been somewhat hampered by health problems, largely the result of allergies.

Chantal, Jane Francis de *see* Jane Francis de Chantal

Chapone, Hester, *née* Mulso

Born 1727 Died 1801
English poet and writer

Hester Mulso was born in Twywell, Northamptonshire. She was largely self-educated, studying French, Latin, music and drawing. In 1760 she married the lawyer John Chapone, introduced to her by the novelist Samuel Richardson, but he died the next year and thereafter Hester lived with family and friends.

From the 1750s onwards she was a friend of Richardson, Samuel Johnson, **Elizabeth Carter** and **Elizabeth Montagu**, all influential London literary figures. Her most popular work, *Letters on the Improvement of the Mind* (1773), which, among other preoccupations, denounced the current cult of sensibility, was dedicated to Montagu. She also wrote for the periodicals *The Rambler* (in 1750), *The Adventurer* (in 1753) and *The Gentleman's Magazine*.

Charisse, Cyd, *originally* Tula Ellice Finklea

Born 1921
American dancer who was described by Fred Astaire as 'beautiful dynamite'

Cyd Charisse was born in Amarillo, Texas. She trained as a ballet dancer from the age of eight, was signed to the Ballets Russes at 14, and toured in Europe and America. Subsequentely based in Los Angeles, she played small film roles under the name of Lily Norwood before signing a contract with MGM in 1946.

A tall, leggy dancer with a sinuous elegance, she appeared in such classic musicals as *Singin' in the Rain* (1952), *The Band Wagon* (1953), *Brigadoon* (1954) and *Silk Stockings* (1957), partnering both Gene Kelly and Fred Astaire.

Her career faltered with the demise of the original screen musical, although she did work as a dramatic actress and continued to appear on stage, performing in *Charlie Girl* (1986) in London and *Grand Hotel* (1992) on Broadway. She has been married to singer Tony Martin (1912–   ) since 1948.

Charles, Dame (Mary) Eugenia

Born 1919
Dominican politician who spent 27 years in politics and became the first woman Prime Minister in the Caribbean

Eugenia Charles was born in Pointe Michel. After qualifying in London as a barrister she returned to the West Indies to practise in what were the Windward and Leeward Islands. She entered politics in 1968 and two years later became co-founder and first leader of the centrist Dominica Freedom Party (DFP).

She became an MP in 1975. Two years after independence, the DFP won the 1980 general election and she became the Caribbean's first female Prime Minister (also Minister of Foreign Affairs 1980–90). Known as the 'Iron Lady of the Caribbean', she was re-elected Prime Minister in 1985 and 1990, but retired after the DFP was defeated by the United Workers' Party in the general election of June 1995.

Charlotte (Augusta), Princess

Born 1796 Died 1817
Princess of Great Britain and Ireland

Princess Charlotte was the only daughter of King George IV and **Caroline of Brunswick**, who separated immediately after her birth. She was the heir to the British throne, and was brought up in strict seclusion.

She was betrothed to Prince William of Orange in 1813, but broke off the engagement the following year, and in 1816 married Prince Leopold of Saxe-Coburg (the future King Leopold I of the Belgians). She died in childbirth.

Charlotte (Sophia)

Born 1744 Died 1818
Queen of Great Britain and Ireland as the wife of George III (ruled 1760–1820)

Charlotte was the niece of the Duke of Mecklenburg-Strelitz. Her long marriage with George began for political reasons in 1761, shortly after his accession to the throne, and was successful due largely to her strength of character and his need of support. She bore him 15 children, including the future George IV (1762–1830), the eldest son.

Her patronage of the potter Josiah Wedgwood in 1765 led to the name 'Queen's Ware' being given to his simply decorated cream-coloured earthenware, which was marketed successfully worldwide.

Charteris, Catherine Morice Anderson, *née* Anderson

Born 1835 Died 1918
Scottish supporter and promoter of the Church of Scotland's Woman's Guild

Catherine Anderson was the daughter of Sir Alexander Anderson, Lord Provost of Aberdeen. After marrying the churchman Archibald Hamilton Charteris, she found time both to support her husband's many projects and to take the initiative in other areas.

Her activities included promoting the Woman's Guild, which had been set up in 1887 by one of her husband's committees, and serving as its national president until 1906. She also organized slum missions, Bible classes and mothers' meetings, and set up homes for missionaries' children and deaconesses.

Chase, Mary Agnes, *née* Meara

Born 1869 Died 1963
American botanist and suffragist who made
significant contributions to research on grasses,
despite having no formal qualifications

Mary Agnes Chase was born in Iroquois County, Illinois. For many years she worked as a proofreader, developing an amateur interest in botany. Encouraged by a local vicar, she moved towards scientific employment, and in 1903 took a position with the US Department of Agriculture Bureau of Plant Industry and Exploration.

She modernized and extended the national collection of grasses and travelled widely collecting plants. Her work provided important information about cereal and food crops which could be used to develop disease-resistant and nutritionally enhanced strains. Chase was also active in many reform movements, especially female suffrage, and suffered imprisonment and force-feeding during World War I.

Chase, Mary Coyle, *née* Coyle

Born 1907 Died 1981
American playwright whose **Harvey** *was one of*
America's most popular comedies

Mary Coyle was born in Denver, Colorado, where she worked as a journalist before becoming a full-time dramatist. She married Robert L Chase in 1928. Her first play, *Me Third*, was performed in Denver in 1936, and in New York a year later under the title *Now You've Done It*, but it was not a great success.

She is chiefly remembered as the author of the play *Harvey* (1944), a comedy about a drunk whose closest companion is a huge, invisible rabbit. It won her the Pulitzer Prize for drama in 1945, and was made into a highly successful film in 1950. She wrote a number of other plays, including *Mrs McThing* and *Bernardine* (both 1952), which were well received on Broadway, and *Cocktails with Mum* (1974).

She also wrote several books for children,

such as *Loretta Mason Potts* (1958), and should not be confused with **Mary Ellen Chase**.

Chase, Mary Ellen

Born 1887 Died 1973
American novelist, essayist and teacher who
achieved a considerable reputation as a leading
regional writer of her time

Mary Ellen Chase was born in Blue Hill, Maine. From 1926 until her retirement in 1955 she taught English literature in Massachusetts at Smith College, Northampton. She began writing fiction for young people, and her best-known, accomplished novels *Mary Peters* (1934) and *Silas Crockett* (1935) are in the regional, or 'local colour', tradition established by such writers as **Sarah Orne Jewett** and **Mary Wilkins Freeman**.

Silas Crockett is set in the Maine herring industry, and vividly depicts the misery caused by the inhumanely handled introduction of steam-ships. Chase also wrote essays about her summers spent in England, collected in *This England* (1936), and autobiographical books including *A Goodly Fellowship* (1939).

Châtelet-Lomont, Gabrielle Émilie Le Tonnelier de Breteuil, Marquise du

Born 1706 Died 1749
French mathematician, physicist and philosopher
who translated the mathematical and phyisical
theories of Isaac Newton

Gabrielle Émilie Le Tonnelier de Breteuil was born in Paris. She learned Latin and Italian with her father, and after her marriage in 1725 to the Comte du Châtelet-Lomont, she studied mathematics and the physical sciences. He took up a military career, spending little time with his wife, and she took up a lively social life in Paris.

In 1733 she met Voltaire, and became his mistress. Voltaire came to live with her at her husband's estate at Cirey, which became a centre of literary and scientific activity. They set up a laboratory there and studied the nature of fire, heat and light. She connected the causes of heat and light, and believed that both represented types of motion.

She wrote *Institutions de physique* (1740) and *Dissertation sur la nature et la propagation du feu* (1744), but her chief work was her translation into French of Isaac Newton's *Principia Mathematica*, posthumously published in 1759. She died in childbirth.

Chauviré, Yvette

Born 1917
French dancer and teacher, the leading French
ballerina of her generation

Yvette Chauviré was born in Paris. She studied
at the Paris Opéra Ballet School before creating
her first role for the company in 1936. In 1941
she was promoted by her mentor, company
director Serge Lifar, to the rank of *étoile*, a
position she held almost continually until her
retirement from the stage in 1972.

With her lyricism and technical finesse, she
excelled in the classical repertoire and was a
guest star with companies around the world.
In 1970 she became director of the Académie
Internationale de Danse in Paris.

Chen Tiejun (Ch'en T'ieh-chün)

Born 1904 Died 1928
Chinese revolutionary and feminist who was
executed for her Communist activities

Chen Tiejun was the daughter of a merchant.
In 1920 she attended the new Jihua Girls'
School, where she was exposed to radical
ideas. Her family insisted upon a traditional
path for her but she rebelled and entered
teacher training school.

In 1925 she went to university and became
involved in socialism and the women's movement, joining the Communist Party in 1926. In
1927, when Chiang Kai-Shek's (Jiang Jieshi's)
forces became active, she lived with Zhen
Wen-jiang (Chen Wen-chiang), a commander
of the Red Guard, and mobilized a women's
network to supply weapons, but was betrayed
and executed.

Cher, *originally* Cheryl Sarkisian

Born 1946
American pop singer and film actress whose
success spans three decades

Cher was born in El Centro, California, of
partly Cherokee parentage. Bowing to her
childhood desire to be famous, she began her
career in the music industry as a backing
vocalist and soon teamed up with Salvatore
'Sonny' Bono. She married him in 1964. They
had their first major hit single, 'I Got You
Babe', in 1965 and enjoyed great popularity
as part of the 1960s counter-culture.

To revive their celebrity status they appeared on television in *The Sonny And Cher
Show* (1971–4) and after their divorce (1975)
Cher began to gain fame as a solo star. She
stepped off the lucrative pop-music treadmill
to seek work as an actress, eventually being
hired by Robert Altman for a Broadway pro-

Cher, 1980

duction of *Come Back to the Five and Dime,
Jimmy Dean, Jimmy Dean* (1981, film version
1982).

Establishing herself as a film actress, she
won an Oscar nomination as the lesbian friend
of union activist Karen Silkwood in *Silkwood*
(1983), a Cannes Best Actress award in *Mask*
(1985), and a Best Actress Oscar as an Italian
widow in the romantic comedy *Moonstruck*
(1987). Other films include *Mermaids* (1990)
and *The Player* (1992).

Chesler, Phyllis

Born 1940
American educator and writer on psychology

Phyllis Chesler's works on psychology in the
1970s were landmarks in that field, and influenced all future study of women's psychology.
The first, *Women and Madness* (1972), analysed psychology and psychiatry as tools to
oppress women. Later books include *Women,
Money and Power*, written with Emily Jane
Goodman in 1976, and *About Men* (1978).

Chesnut, Mary Boykin Miller, *née*
Miller

Born 1823 Died 1886
American diarist who wrote a valuable and
perceptive personal account of the Civil War

Mary Boykin Miller was born in South Carolina and was educated at private schools in Camden and Charleston. In 1840 she married James Chesnut, who was a US Senator from South Carolina in 1859–60 but resigned to assist in the formation of the Confederacy.

She accompanied him after he joined the Confederate army and kept a diary of her experiences from 1861 to 1865, recording her observations of the military and political leaders of the Confederacy and of life in the American South during the War. Though she apparently intended it for publication, *A Diary from Dixie* did not appear until 1905. It constitutes a highly regarded contribution to the literature and history of the period.

Chiang Ch'ing *see* Jiang Qing

Chicago, Judy, *originally* Judy Cohen

Born 1939
American artist whose work is exhibited in many major collections of the USA

Judy Cohen was born in Chicago, Illinois, and adopted the name of her home town. She co-founded the Feminist Art Program at the California Institute of the Arts to provide women artists with a hospitable place to practise their art, and has been noted for encouraging other women artists. One of her own best-known works is a massive multimedia work called *The Dinner Party,* on which she worked from 1974 to 1979. The work is a banquet table with places set for heroic women, notorious women and goddesses, with each place-setting individually designed to symbolize that woman.

Chicago is represented in the permanent collections of the San Francisco Museum of Modern Art, Oakland Museum of Art, Pennsylvania Academy of Fine Arts and the Los Angeles County Museum. She published her autobiography, *Through the Flower: My Struggle as a Woman Artist*, in 1975.

Chick, Dame Harriette

Born 1875 Died 1977
English nutritionist who discovered how to prevent childhood rickets and carried out pioneering work on vitamins

Harriette Chick was born in London. After attending school in west London, she entered University College London in 1894 and graduated in science two years later, when she began to study for a doctorate. After research visits abroad, she applied for a position at the Lister Institute in 1905, which led some of the staff there to ask the institute's director not to consider appointing a woman. Nevertheless she

won the award, and remained at the Institute for the rest of her long working life, finally retiring aged 95.

After World War I she was sent to Vienna by the British Medical Research Council to study nutritional disorders, and to investigate rickets, then thought to be an infective disease. Chick, and her colleagues Elsie Dalyell and Margaret Hume, established that sunlight and dietary cod-liver oil, rich in vitamin D, could eliminate childhood rickets. She returned to London in 1922 and began extensive studies into the role and standardization of vitamins.

She served as Secretary of the Accessory Food Factors Committee, established by the MRC and the Lister Institute, which co-ordinated, assessed and publicized research and information on nutritional matters. In 1934 Chick was created CBE for her contribution to nutritional science, and in 1949 became a DBE.

Child, Julia

Born 1912
American cookery expert and television personality

Julia Child was born in Pasadena, California. She has hosted the public broadcasting television programme, *The French Chef*, since 1962. In addition to numerous television segments and appearances on cookery programmes, she has written several cookbooks, including *The French Chef Cookbook* (1968), *Mastering the Art of French Cooking* (vol I 1961, vol II 1970, revised 1983) and *The Way to Cook* (1989).

She received a Peabody award in 1964 and an Emmy award in 1966, as well as the French Ordre de Merite Agricole (1967) and the Ordre National de Mérite (1974).

In 1982 she co-founded the American Institute of Food and Wine.

Child, Lydia Maria

Born 1802 Died 1880
American social campaigner, essayist and novelist whose abolitionist writings and campaigns had a major impact

Lydia Maria Child was born in Watertown, Massachusetts. As a committed campaigner for social and political reform, she was editor of the *National Anti-Slavery Standard* and published many essays on political and social issues. Her *The History of the Condition of Women in Various Ages and Nations* (1835) suggested women's equal capacity in the workplace, and *An Appeal in Favor of that Class of Americans Called Africans* (1833) was particularly influential for the abolitionist cause.

She also published several novels, including *Hobomok* (1824), describing the conflict between the Puritans and Native American tribes in the Massachusetts Bay Colony; *The Rebels* (1825), a romance set during the American revolution; *Philothea* (1836), set in Ancient Greece at the time of Pericles; and *A Romance of the Republic* (1867), a 19th-century story which dramatized Child's anti-slavery convictions.

Childs, Lucinda

Born 1940
American dancer and choreographer who
incorporates spoken and filmic elements
in her work

Lucinda Childs was born in New York, where she trained with Merce Cunningham. She was a founder member of the experimental Judson Dance Theatre (1962–4) and was greatly influenced by **Yvonne Rainer**.

She developed a minimalist style of choreography, often incorporating dialogue and, after a five-year gap, made the first of her 'reductionist pattern pieces' in 1973. In 1976 she performed her own solo material in Robert Wilson and Philip Glass's opera *Einstein on the Beach*.

Since the late 1970s she has embraced the work of other artists in her choreography. *Dance 1–5* was set to a 90-minute score by Philip Glass and film by sculptor and painter Sol le Witt. Other works include *Relative Calm* (1981), *Available Light* (1983) and *Premier Orage* in 1984, the year she put her choreography on pointe for the first time.

Chisholm, Caroline, *née* Jones

Born 1808 Died 1877
English-born social worker who undertook
important pioneering philanthropic work
in Australia

Caroline Jones was born near Northampton. She married Archibald Chisholm, an officer in the army of the East India Company, and for a while they were based in Madras. In 1838 they settled in Windsor, New South Wales, but two years later Captain Chisholm returned to duty.

Caroline Chisholm became concerned at the plight of abandoned and impoverished immigrant women in the colony and, with the approval of Governor Gipps, established an office to provide shelter for the new arrivals. She then set about finding them work. In the 1840s she cared for over 11,000 women and children, often enabling them to move to rural areas, and thereby helping to alleviate the overcrowding in Sydney.

She persuaded the British government to grant free passage to families of convicts already transported, and established the Family Colonization Loan Society, to which in 1852 the New South Wales government contributed £10,000. In 1854 she visited the gold-rush settlements of Victoria and publicized the appalling conditions there, but ill health caused her to return to Sydney. In 1866 she left for England where she received a civil pension of £100 a year. Her *Female Immigration Considered in a Brief Account of the Sydney Immigrants' Home* (1842) was the first work by a woman in Australia.

Chisholm, Shirley Anita St Hill, *née* St Hill

Born 1924
American politician who became the first black
woman member of the House of Representatives

Shirley St Hill was born in Brooklyn, New York. She married Conrad Chisholm in 1949 (divorced 1977). After becoming an expert in the education of young children and working as consultant to the New York Bureau of Child Welfare (1959–64), she was elected to the New York State Assembly (1964–8). On her election as a Democrat in 1968, she was the first black woman to become a member of the House of Representatives, and she remained a congresswoman, serving seven terms, until 1983.

She freely voiced her opposition to the war in Vietnam, her criticism of the House seniority system and her support of the urban poor. In the 1972 Democratic Convention she won a 10 per cent vote for the presidential nomination. She has published *Unbought and Unbossed* (1970) and *The Good Fight* (1973).

Chopin, Kate (Katherine) O'Flaherty, *née* O'Flaherty

Born 1851 Died 1904
American novelist, short-story writer and poet
embraced by feminists as a fin de siècle iconoclast
bravely articulating the plight of the 'lost' woman

Kate O'Flaherty was born in St Louis, Missouri, the daughter of an Irish immigrant and a French–Creole mother. She was well educated at the Sacred Heart convent, made her 'début' in society and married Oscar Chopin, a Creole cotton trader from Louisiana. It was a happy marriage, scarred only by business failure.

After her husband died of swamp fever (1882) she returned with their six children to

St Louis where she began to compose sketches of her life in 'Old Natachitoches', such as *Bayou Folk* (1894) and *A Night in Acadie* (1897). This work gives no indication of the furore she aroused with the publication of a realistic novel of sexual passion, *The Awakening* (1899), which was harshly condemned by the public. Thereafter she wrote only a few poems and short stories.

Interest in her work was revived by the critic Edmund Wilson (1895–1972).

Chowdhury, Eulie

Born 1923
Indian architect, the first Indian woman to qualify and be elected to the Royal Institute of British Architects and the Indian Institute of Architects

Eulie Chowdhury was educated at the University of Sydney, Australia, receiving her Bachelor of Architecture in 1947. She worked in the USA before returning to her native India in 1951 to work on Le Corbusier's new Punjab capital, Chandigarh. She worked as senior architect for two periods (1951–63 and 1968–70) and then as chief architect, in charge of the second phase of planning (1971–6).

She was principal of the Delhi school of Architecture from 1963 to 1965, then returned to private practice in 1966, becoming Chief Architect of Harayana State in 1970 and of Punjab State in 1976, a post she held until her retirement in 1981.

She had a remarkable career for a woman in post-independence India.

Christensen, Inger

Born 1935
Danish poet, novelist and essayist, a modernist considered to be Denmark's leading woman writer

Inger Christensen was born in Vejle. She trained as a teacher, and had her first book of poetry published in 1962. Her modernist texts locate the individual within structures that he or she simultaneously creates and is created by; her use of language and form highlight the inclusion of her own works in this process.

The novel *Evighedsmaskinen* (1964, 'The Eternity Machine') is a modern version of the story of Christ, while her second novel, *Azorno* (1967), employs an elaborate series of experiments to explore the borderline between fiction and reality. *Det* (1969, 'It') is a book of poetry which has been characterized as a poetic drama. The magnificent poetic structure of *Alfabet* (1981, 'Alphabet') focuses on creativity and annihilation, adding a prominent ecological dimension.

Christensen was elected a member of the Danish Academy in 1978.

Christie, Dame Agatha Mary Clarissa, *née* Miller

Born 1890 Died 1976
English author whose popular detective novels have become known worldwide

Agatha Miller was born in Torquay into an upper-middle-class family. Under the surname of her first husband (Colonel Christie, divorced 1928), she wrote more than 70 classic detective novels, featuring the Belgian detective Hercule Poirot, or the village spinster Miss Jane Marple, and often painting a nostalgic picture of life before World War I.

In 1930 she married Sir Max Mallowan (1904–78), the noted archaeologist. Between December 1953 and January 1954, she achieved three concurrent West End productions, *The Spider's Web*, *Witness for the Prosecution* and *The Mousetrap*, which continued its record-breaking run into the 1990s.

Her best-known novels are *The Mysterious Affair at Styles* (1920), first featuring the Belgian detective Poirot; *The Murder of Roger Ackroyd* (1926); *Murder at the Vicarage* (1930), introducing Miss Marple; *Murder on the Orient Express* (1934); *Death on the Nile* (1937); *And Then There Were None* (1941) and *Curtain* (1975), in which Poirot meets his end. Christie also wrote under the pen-name 'Mary Westmacott'.

Christie, Julie Frances

Born 1940
English actress who epitomized 'Swinging Sixties' London and continued her fruitful career into the 1990s

Julie Christie was born in Chukua, Assam. She studied at the Central School of Music and Drama and worked in repertory before a television serial, *A is for Andromeda* (1962), led to a small film role in *Crooks Anonymous* (1962). Her portrayal of a free spirit in *Billy Liar* (1963) brought further offers and in 1965 she won an Academy Award for *Darling*.

She consolidated her career with *Dr Zhivago* (1965), *Far From the Madding Crowd* (1967) and *The Go-Between* (1971). Subsequent films have highlighted her involvement with a variety of political issues, although she returned to more mainstream productions with *Heat and Dust* (1982), *Power* (1985), *McCabe and Mrs Miller* (1990) and *The Railway Station Man* (1991).

Christina, *Swedish* Kristina

Born 1626 Died 1689
Queen of Sweden, a very learned woman who was
astute in politics and lavish in her sponsorship
of the arts

Christina was the daughter of King Gustav II
Adolf, whom she succeeded in 1632. She was
educated like a boy during her minority, when
the affairs of the kingdom were ably managed
by her father's chancellor, Count Axel Oxen-
stierna. After she came of age in 1644, she
adopted an independent line in both domestic
and foreign policy and worked to bring an
end to the costly Thirty Years War in which
Sweden was engaged. She patronized the arts
and attracted to her court some of the best
minds in Europe, including Hugo Grotius, Sal-
amatius and Descartes, who died there in 1650.
During her reign the first newspaper in
Sweden was established, the learning of literature and science was promoted, and industry,
especially mining, benefited.

However Christina was strongly averse to
marriage and found child-bearing repugnant.
She refused to marry her cousin (later Charles
X Gustav), but instead had him proclaimed
Crown Prince. Then, having secretly embraced Catholicism (which was prohibited in
Sweden), and impatient of the personal restraints imposed on her as a ruler, she abdicated in 1654, shocking the rest of Europe. She
left Sweden for Italy, was openly received into
the Catholic Church in Innsbruck and entered
Rome on horseback. She made a bid to gain
the throne of Naples and of Poland for herself
but failed and spent the remainder of her life
in her beloved Rome as a pensioner of the
pope and a generous and discerning patron of
the arts, sponsoring the sculptor Bernini and
the composers Corelli and Scarlatti.

Christina of Markyate

Born c.1096 Died after 1155
English recluse and prioress who was renowned
for chastity

Christina was the daughter of an Anglo-Saxon
nobleman, Aute, of Huntingdonshire. Resist-
ing seduction at the hands of Rannulf Flam-
bard, bishop of Durham from 1099, and
refusing to consummate marriage to one of his
friends, she went into hiding as Church court
cases proceeded. Initially at Flamstead, she
moved to a cell at Markyate near St Albans,
under the protection of Roger the Hermit.

From 1130 her fame as a spiritual adviser
spread far and wide, bringing invitations to
lead communities in both England and France,
but she took monastic vows instead. As spiri-

tual adviser to Geoffrey of Gorham, abbot of
St Albans, she took part in Church struggles
against King Stephen (ruled 1135–54). A
priory was built at Markyate in 1145. The last
that is known of Christina of Markyate is that
in 1155 she sent embroidery to the English
Pope Adrian IV.

Christine de Pisan, *also spelt* Pizan

Born c.1364 Died c.1431
French lyric poet and prose writer who may have
been the first professional author and the first
woman to write a book in French praising women

Christine de Pisan was born in Venice, the
daughter of an Italian who became court
astrologer to Charles V in Paris, where she
was brought up. In 1378 she married Étienne
Castel; he became the king's secretary, but died
in 1389, leaving her with three children and no
money. Forced to call upon her literary talents,
she became perhaps the first professional
writer, because she had to write to survive.

Between 1399 and 1415 she produced a
number of brilliant works in both prose and
verse, including a Life of Charles V for Philippe, Duke of Burgundy; *Le livre de la cité
des dames*, a translation from Boccaccio; and
Livres des trois vertus, an educational and
social compendium for women. Her love
poems have grace and charm, but lack depth.
She personally oversaw the copying and
illuminating of her books, which was very
unusual.

Christine is noteworthy for her defence of
the female sex, hitherto a target for satirists.
Saddened by the misfortunes of the Hundred
Years' War she withdrew to a nunnery in
about 1418 but lived to write in celebration of
Joan of Arc's early successes in 1429.

Chudleigh, Elizabeth, Countess of Bristol and Duchess of Kingston

Born 1720 Died 1788
English courtesan and bigamist on whose wilful
and vivacious personality Thackeray based one of
his fictional characters

Elizabeth Chudleigh was beautiful but illiterate. She had several liaisons at court before
secretly marrying a naval lieutenant, Augustus John Hervey, brother of the 2nd Earl of
Bristol, in 1744. Having concealed the birth
and death of a son, she obtained a separation
from her husband; later, when courted by the
2nd Duke of Kingston, she denied the first
marriage on oath and married him in 1769.

On being left heiress to the Duke's estates
in 1773, she was accused of bigamy by his
nephew and found guilty in 1776. In the fol-

lowing year her marriage to Hervey, who had now succeeded his brother as 3rd Duke of Bristol, was declared valid. She was the proto-type of 'Beatrix Esmond' and 'Baroness Bernstein' in Thackeray's *The History of Henry Esmond* (1852) and *The Virginians* (1857–9).

Chudleigh, Mary, *née* Lee

Born 1656 Died 1710
English poet and essayist who wrote The Ladies Defence *to refute claims of male superiority and other misogynist attitudes*

Mary Lee was born in Winslade, Devon. In 1674 she married George Chudleigh, who became baronet in 1691. Though confined to what she called the 'rough and unpolished life' of Devon, she read widely and corresponded with other writers.

The influence of the feminist **Mary Astell** is apparent in her best-known work, *The Ladies Defence* (1701), a spirited verse-debate expos-ing male prejudices and the deficiencies of female education.

She also published *Poems on Several Occasions* (1703) and *Essays upon Several Sub-jects in Verse and Prose* (1710).

Chung, Kyung-Wha

Born 1948
Korean violinist who has made exceptional recordings of concertos by Elgar and Walton in addition to warm and expressive interpretations of many other works

Kyung-Wha Chung, 1971

Kyung-Wha Chung was born in Seoul. She began playing in public at the age of nine, then moved to New York in 1960 and studied at the Juilliard School of Music until 1967, when she made her début with the New York Philharmonic.

Her London début came three years later and she has since performed worldwide with nearly all of the world's best-known orches-tras and conductors, as well as in trio with her sister Myung-Wha (1944–), a distinguished cellist, and her brother Myung-Whung (1953–), a pianist and conductor who was appointed Music Director of the new Opéra de la Bastille, Paris, in 1989.

Churchill, Arabella

Born 1648 Died 1730
English aristocrat and the mistress of James VII of Scotland and II of England (ruled 1685–8)

Arabella Churchill was the elder sister of John Churchill, 1st Duke of Marlborough. Her 'career' began in 1665 when she entered the service of the Duchess of York, wife of the future James VII of Scotland and II of England. She soon became James's mistress and bore him two daughters and two sons — James Fitzjames (Duke of Berwick) and Henry Fitz-james (Duke of Albemarle). Later she was pen-sioned off and married a civil servant.

Churchill, Caryl

Born 1938
English dramatist whose writing is strongly imbued with feminist politics

Caryl Churchill was born in London. She had two of her plays produced whilst an under-graduate at Lady Margaret Hall, Oxford, and became resident dramatist at the Royal Court Theatre in the 1970s, beginning to produce drama that identified with feminist politics, such as *Vinegar Tom* (1976) and *Floorshow* (1977). *Light Shining in Buckinghamshire* (1976) is a historical play about the Levellers, a 17th-century ultra-republican party in the parlia-mentary army.

Churchill's best-known work, *Serious Mo-ney* (1987), was a huge commercial success; it satirizes the world of the young, get-rich-quick City financial brokers. Other plays include *Cloud Nine* (1979), *Top Girls* (1982), *Fen* (1983) and *Softcops* (1984), all of greater dramatic quality than *Serious Money.*

Her involvement with dance began with her collaboration with choreographer Ian Spink on *A Mouthful of Birds* (1986), followed by *Fugue* (1987, for television), *Lives of the Great Poisoners* (1991) and *The Skriker* (1994), a piece that has only three speaking parts but is peopled with characters from folklore and fairy-tale and enlarged with independent sections of music and choreography. She has also made a translation of Seneca's *Thyestes* (1994).

Churchill, Sarah, Duchess of Marlborough, *née* Jennings

Born 1660 Died 1744
English aristocrat who abused Queen **Anne's** favouritism and dominated both her and the government

Sarah Jennings entered the service of the Duke of York (the future James II) in 1673 and became a close friend of his younger daughter Anne Hyde, Princess Anne (the future Queen Anne); in their private correspondence, Anne was called 'Mrs Morley' and Sarah was called 'Mrs Freeman'.

She married John Churchill, 1st Duke of Marlborough, and after the 'Glorious Revolution' of 1688, when William III supplanted James II on the throne, she and her husband tried to draw Anne into Jacobite intrigues for the restoration of her father. After Anne became queen in 1702, Sarah imperiously dominated her household and the Whig ministry.

Queen Anne finally broke with the Marlboroughs in 1711; Sarah had by 1707 been supplanted by a new favourite, her cousin Mrs **Abigail Masham**. She had two daughters: Henrietta, who married Sidney, 1st Earl of Godolphin in 1698; and Anne, who married a son of the 2nd Earl of Sunderland in 1700.

Cibber, Mrs, *née* Susannah Maria Arne

Born 1714 Died 1766
English actress and singer who despite various scandals made a success of her stage career

Susannah Arne was born in London, the sister of the composer Thomas Arne. She had a fine contralto voice, and made her stage début in her brother's *Rosamund* (1733). She became a noted oratorio singer, and Handel wrote parts for her in his *Messiah* and *Samson*. In 1734 she married the disreputable actor Theophilus Cibber (1703–58), son of the actor and dramatist Colley Cibber who gave her some training; from then on she was known as 'Mrs Cibber'.

In an attempt to pay his debts, Theophilus forced her to take a wealthy lover who would pay for her sexual favours. News of this arrangement soon percolated throughout the town and Theophilus was obliged to make a hasty exit for France. The resultant scandal forced her to retire temporarily (some say he attempted to sue her lover) but she devoted herself to drama thereafter and played opposite David Garrick at Drury Lane (1753–66) with enormous success.

Cilento, Lady Phyllis Dorothy, *née* McGlew

Born 1894 Died 1987
Australian medical practitioner, author and broadcaster who stressed the importance of proper nutrition and family planning

Phyllis McGlew was born in Sydney and educated at Adelaide University. She married the medical administrator Raphael West Cilento in 1920. After postgraduate work in Asia, Europe and the USA, she became lecturer in Mothercraft and Obstetrical Physiotherapy at the University of Queensland.

Her life's work, for which she was awarded the AM (membership of the Order of Australia), was devoted to family planning, childbirth education and nutrition, on which subjects she broadcast and wrote many newspaper columns and books, from *Square Meals for the Family* (1934) to *Nutrition of the Elderly* (1980).

She founded the Mothercare Association of Queensland in 1930 and was its president until 1933, and from 1935 to 1948; during this time she also served as President of the Queensland Medical Women's Association (1938–47). Her daughter Diane became an actress and writer.

Çiller, Tansu

Born 1946
Turkish economist and politician who is Turkey's first female Prime Minister

Tansu Çiller was born in Istanbul and educated in the USA. As a teenager she married her husband Ozer, becoming the first woman in Turkey's recent history to make her husband adopt her surname. After working for a time as an academic economist, and the youngest professor in Turkey, she was given ministerial responsibility over government finances when the conservative True Path Party took power in 1991.

In 1993 she was elected head of the Party and Prime Minister of Turkey, breaking ground as the first female leader of that country's 65 million Muslims. In the face of the collapse of the Turkish lira, the crash of the stockmarket, and the rise of inflation and interest rates, her continuation as premier was approved in the municipal elections of 1994. In 1995 however the government resigned and the ensuing general election was won by the

Welfare Party, though it failed to get enough seats to govern alone, and Çiller continued as Prime Minister in the coalition.

Proving herself a glamorous, youthful, but formidably tough leader, Çiller promised pro-European constitutional reforms concerning human rights, a more liberal constitution, ethnic self-expression (though not enough to end the rebellion by the 12-million strong Kurdish population) and democratization, some of which were soon passed in an attempt to convince other European countries that Turkey was serious about reform.

Cixi (Tz'u Hsi), known as the Dragon Empress

Born 1835 Died 1908
Chinese empress, one of the most powerful women in Chinese history

Cixi (whose personal name was Yehenala) was the daughter of a minor Manchu mandarin and was sent at the age of 16 as a concubine to the Xianfeng (Hsien-Feng) emperor (reigned 1851–62). In 1856 she consolidated her position and status within the court by giving birth to his only son, who succeeded at the age of five as the Tongzhi (T'ung-chih) emperor. Her acute grasp of politics soon caused the indecisive Xianfeng to become dependent on her, and she managed to put a stop to the Taiping (T'ai P'ing) rebellion (1850–64) and an invasion of North China by England and France. She gained in influence and power through cruelty, bribery and ingenuity, and rose to become one of the most dominant women in the history of China.

Even after her son came of age in 1873 she kept control, and after his death two years later she flouted the succession laws of the Imperial clan to ensure the succession of Zai Tian (Tsai T'ien), another minor, as the Guangxu (Kuang-hsü) emperor. Again she continued to assert control even when the new emperor reached maturity in 1889, defying a dynastic custom which forbade women to reign.

She was an inveterate intriguer and a conservative force within the Chinese court, and accordingly acquired the nickname 'Old Buddha'. Her support and command of the anti-foreign Boxer movement culminated in the massacre and persecution of hundreds of foreign nationals living in China (1900). On the capture of Tianjin (Tientsin) by international forces, she fled into hiding with Guangxu, to return in 1901 when peace terms were agreed. She proceeded to wipe all reference to the Boxers from the records and thus to exonerate herself from blame.

She died in Beijing (Peking) after a stroke weakened her state of health, having had Guangxu murdered the day before. Only then did it become possible to begin reforms, for she had tried hard to frustrate the country's late-19th-century modernization programme.

Cixous, Hélène

Born 1937
French feminist, dramatist and novelist interested in the links between language by and about women and women themselves

Hélène Cixous was born in Oran, Algeria, into a Jewish family and educated at the Lycée Bugeaud in Algiers. She moved to France in 1955 where she began to teach, at the same time taking further degrees in English. In 1965 she became an assistant lecturer at the Sorbonne and took an active part in the student uprisings of 1968. Later, as Professor of Literature at the University of Paris VIII-Vincennes, she established some experimental literature courses. She also founded the Paris Centre des Recherches en Etudes Féminines in 1974 and became its director.

Her work is mostly concerned with the relationship between psychoanalysis and language, especially in its significance for women, and in exploring the links between the writer and reader. She encourages the expression in language of female sexuality which patriarchal convention has suppressed for so long and, with **Luce Irigaray**, has become associated with a theory called écriture féminine, or 'feminine writing', the aims of which include making the book a means of female liberation and affirmation.

Her publications include Dedans (winner of the 1969 Prix Médicis), Neutre (1972) and Angst (1977), the essays Le Rire de la Méduse (1976, 'The Laugh of the Medusa') and Le Sexe ou la Tête? (1976, 'Castration or Decapitation') and the plays Portrait De Dora (1976, Eng trans Portrait of Dora, 1991) and L'Indiade ou l'Inde de leurs rêves (1987).

Claflin, Tennessee Celeste

Born 1846 Died 1923
American journalist, stockbroker and feminist

Tennessee Claflin was born in Homer, Ohio, like her famous older sister **Victoria Woodhull**, with whom she gave clairvoyance demonstrations in the family's travelling show. She married her first husband, John Bartels, in 1866, but kept her maiden name and later divorced. In 1868 she moved to New York with Victoria, and, through her interest in spiritualism, met the millionaire Cornelius

Vanderbilt who financed the sisters to become stockbrokers. They were extremely successful.

Their success financed *Woodhull and Claflin's Weekly* (1870–6) in which they advocated equal rights, free love, diet reform and the legalization of prostitution. In 1871 it printed *The Communist Manifesto,* its first American publication in English. Both sisters became involved with the women's suffrage movement led by **Susan B Anthony** and **Elizabeth Cady Stanton**.

In 1877 they moved to London where Tennessee became a society hostess, while remaining a colourful advocate of women's rights. She married Francis Cook in 1885, and became Lady Cook when he became a baronet in 1886.

Claiborne, Liz

Born 1929
American fashion designer and founder of one of the world's most successful fashion companies

Liz Claiborne was born in Brussels, Belgium. She studied painting in Belgium and France before moving to the USA and winning a *Harper's Bazaar* design competition. Turning to fashion design, she worked with Omar Kiam in New York and designed for the Youth Guild Inc, before founding her own company with her husband in 1976.

Liz Claiborne's medium-priced ready-to-wear collections, targeted at the 'ordinary' working woman, have made her company one of the largest and most successful womenswear firms in the world. Her trademark practical, wearable separates cross all social barriers and appeal to a mostly young, fashion-conscious public.

The company went public in 1981 and Liz Claiborne retired in 1989, though the company continues.

Clairemont, Claire

Born 1798 Died 1879
English mistress of the poet Lord Byron

Claire Clairemont's mother married the philosopher William Godwin, widower of **Mary Wollstonecraft**, when Claire was three. This union provided Claire with a step-sister, Mary Godwin (see **Mary Shelley**), whom she accompanied when Mary eloped with the poet Percy Bysshe Shelley in 1814.

On their return to London, Claire had a love affair with Lord Byron, which resulted in the birth of their daughter, Allegra, in 1817. However Byron removed Allegra from her mother's care because he disapproved of her methods of raising children. Allegra died in a convent near Ravenna at the age of five and Claire lived abroad for the rest of her life.

Clairon, Mademoiselle, *stage name of* Claire Josèphe Hippolyte Léris de La Tude

Born 1723 Died 1803
French actress who became the leading tragedienne of her day and introduced a new style of acting

Mademoiselle Clairon began life as an illegitimate child born into poverty in Condé-surl'Escaut, and first appeared on stage in 1736 with the Comédie-Italienne. She had a fine singing voice, and joined the Opéra in Paris in 1743, but quickly reverted to her original pursuit of acting, this time with the Comédie-Française.

She became the leading tragic actress of her day, and is credited with developing both a new style of acting which moved beyond the stiff formal gestures and speech of established practice, and a greater concentration on costume which reflected something of the play, rather than simply ostentatious display.

She quit the professional stage in 1765, acting only in private theatres thereafter, and died in poverty in Paris.

Clare, St

Born 1194 Died 1253
Italian Christian saint who founded and led the order of the Poor Clares

Clare was born into a noble family in Assisi, the daughter of Count Favorino Scifi and elder sister of St **Agnes**. At the age of 18 she became a follower of St Francis, and with him and Agnes founded the order of Poor Ladies of San Damiano ('Poor Clares', formerly called 'Minoresses'), of which she became abbess.

The Poor Clares were the first community of women living under the Franciscan rule, and their poverty and austerity were unique among nuns of the day. Clare spent her entire life at the convent in Assisi and, famed for her holiness, contemplation and wisdom, became adviser to many influential church leaders.

She was canonized in 1255, and in 1958 she was designated patron saint of television by Pope Pius XI on the grounds that at Christmas 1252, when she was in her cell at San Damiano, she 'saw and heard' a service being held in the church of St Francis in Assisi. Her feast day is 11 August.

Clark, Petula, *pseud of* Sally Owen

Born 1932
English singer and actress, one of the most
enduring and successful of British popular
entertainers

Sally Owen was born in Epsom, Surrey. A child singer, she entertained troops during World War II, featured in her own radio series *Pet's Parlour* (1943) and made her film début in *Medal for the General* (1944). Her many subsequent film appearances include *Here Come the Huggetts* (1948) and *The Card* (1952).

Sustaining an adult career, she became one of Britain's most successful pop singers, earning 10 gold discs, two Grammy awards and enjoying a string of international hits with such songs as 'Downtown' (1964) and 'My Love' (1966). Her increasingly rare film appearances include the musicals *Finian's Rainbow* (1968) and *Goodbye Mr Chips* (1969), and she has continued to appear on stage in *The Sound of Music* (1981), *Someone Like You* (1987), which she co-wrote, and *Sunset Boulevard* (1995) in London, and on Broadway in *Blood Brothers* (1993–4).

Clarke, Gillian

Born 1937
Welsh poet who since the mid-1980s has been
recognized as a leading female poet

Gillian Clarke was born in Cardiff and educated at the city's University College. She has spent most of her life in South Wales and, while avoiding regional concerns and dealing with such general themes as love, death and relationships, she draws on and incorporates the Welsh experience into her work.

Her earliest collections of poems, *Snow on the Mountain* (1971) and *Sundial* (1978), were followed by the more widely-read *Letter from a Far Country* (1982). *Selected Poems* followed in 1985, then *Letting in the Rumour* (1989). She was editor of *The Anglo-Welsh Review* from 1976 to 1984, and since 1987 has been chair of the Welsh Academy.

Clarke, Martha

Born 1944
American dancer-choreographer who has achieved
worldwide renown

Martha Clarke was born in Maryland. She studied dance as a child and later trained with José Limón, Alvin Ailey, Charles Weidman and **Anna Sokolow** at the American Dance Festival in Connecticut and with **Martha Graham**'s associate Louis Horst at New York's Juilliard School of Music.

She spent a few seasons in Sokolow's company before moving to Europe. On her return to the USA she became in 1972 one of the first female members of Pilobolus, a collectively-run dance-theatre ensemble. As the troupe achieved worldwide popularity, Clarke and dancers Robby Barnett and Felix Blaska formed the trio Crowsnest.

Since the mid-1980s, she has concentrated on unclassifiable dance-theatre productions such as *Garden of Earthly Delights* (1984), *Vienna: Lusthaus* (1986), *The Hunger Artist* (1987) and *Miracolo d'Amore* (1988).

Claudel, Camille

Born 1864 Died 1943
French sculptor who worked alongside Rodin as
mistress and artist before earning renown in her
own right

Camille Claudel was born in La Fère-en-Tardenois, the daughter of a wealthy civil servant, and sister of the poet Paul Claudel. She decided to become a sculptor at an early age and in 1884 was introduced to the sculptor Auguste Rodin (1840–1917). She became his student, model and mistress, producing works which, while close to his, nonetheless show great individuality and mastery. She is also thought to have contributed whole figures to his work, such as to his extensive *Gates of Hell* commission.

Theirs was a fiery relationship, and they eventually parted company in 1898. Claudel continued to sculpt and achieved great renown around 1900. However, the break with Rodin affected her mental stability and from 1913 until her death she was confined to various institutions.

Cleopatra

Born 69BC Died 30BC
Queen of Egypt whose story has become famous in
literature as well as in history

Cleopatra was the last and most famous of the Macedonian dynasty of the Ptolemies. By the will of her father, Ptolemy XII Auletes (d.51BC), she married and shared the throne with her younger brother, Ptolemy XIII Philopater, until in 49BC she was ousted by him and his guardians. She was about to assert her rights, when Julius Caesar arrived in Egypt in pursuit of Pompey (48). Caesar took her side, and after the Alexandrine war placed her back on the throne (47) as the joint ruler and wife of another brother, Ptolemy XIV.

A son born to her the following year, named Ptolemy XV Caesar but known as Caesarion, was claimed by her to be Caesar's (the boy was later put to death by the emperor Augustus). She followed Caesar to Rome in 46, but left after his assassination. After the battle of Philippi (42), Marcus Antonius (Mark Antony) summoned her to Tarsus in Cilicia — their meeting has been made famous in Plutarch's account. She succeeded in charming him as she had done Caesar and they spent the following winter in Alexandria. However, on the death of Antony's wife Fulvia, he married Octavia (40), sister of Octavian (later called Augustus Caesar), and did not see Cleopatra again till 37, by which time he had become estranged from his wife. He acknowledged the paternity of the twins Cleopatra had borne him in 40, and a third child was born in 36. From this time on, their personal and political careers were linked, though how far their aims coincided is not easy to determine.

Cleopatra's ambition was most probably to achieve the restoration of Ptolemaic power to the heights it had once reached under Ptolemy II Philadelphus. But Antony's position in the East and his relations with Cleopatra were ambiguous and susceptible to distortion for propaganda purposes, and at length Octavian was successful in swaying Roman public opinion against his absent rival. War was declared against Cleopatra, who was presented as a threat to the power of Rome, and at the battle of Actium (31) Antony and Cleopatra were defeated and fled to Egypt. When Octavian appeared before Alexandria, Cleopatra opened negotiations with him to try to save her dynasty. Antony, misled by a false report of Cleopatra's death, committed suicide by falling on his sword. Finding that she could not move Octavian, and disdaining to grace his triumph, she killed herself, it is said, by causing an asp to bite her breast.

Cleveland, Duchess of see Villiers, Barbara

Cliff, Clarice

> Born 1899 Died 1972
> English ceramic designer whose richly coloured pottery of the 1930s inspired other artists and brought her lasting fame

Clarice Cliff was born in Tunstall, Staffordshire. She trained at local art schools there and in Burslem, and set up a design studio at Wilkinson's Newport Showroom. There she developed a unique style using bold designs painted with stylized trees and abstract patterns in vivid colours with bold brushwork. By 1929 the Newport Pottery was given over entirely to the decoration of her work which was marketed under the name 'Bizarre'.

Cline, Patsy, stage name of Virginia Petterson Hensley

> Born 1932 Died 1963
> American country singer whose success continued after her sudden death

Patsy Cline was born in Winchester, Virginia. She was spotted on the television show *Talent Scout* (1957) and signed to Decca label. Also in 1957 she married Charlie Dick, having divorced her first husband Gerald Cline.

'Crazy' (1961) is often thought to be her greatest hit, despite never reaching number one; 'She's Got You' (1962) outsold it at the time.

Cline had a forceful delivery that allowed her music to cross over from country to a wider pop audience. Like Buddy Holly, she has been more successful posthumously than in life, which ended suddenly in a plane crash in Tennessee.

Clinton, Hillary Rodham, née Rodham

> Born 1947
> American politician and lawyer, one of the most influential women in America as First Lady, the wife of President Clinton

Hillary Rodham was born in Chicago, Illinois, the daughter of a conservative Republican

Hillary Clinton, 1995

father. She describes herself as a conservative Democrat. She was educated at Wellesley College and received her law degree from Yale University, following which she practised law in private practice, specializing in family issues and children's rights. She is the author of *Handbook on Legal Rights for Arkansas Women*.

She married Bill Clinton in 1975 and has campaigned vigorously for his political offices as Governor of Arkansas (1979–81, 1983–93) and as President of the USA (1993–   ). She was appointed head of his Health Care Task Force, which ran into problems in its plans for health-care reform, and serves as chief presidential adviser.

In 1996 she became the first wife of a president in office to appear before a grand jury, who had to decide whether she should face charges for her dealings in the so-called 'Whitewater affair', an inquiry concerning property deals in Arkansas in the 1980s involving Clinton's former law firm.

Clisby, Harriet Jemima Winifred

Born 1830 Died 1931
English-born Australian journalist, doctor and feminist

Harriet Clisby was born in London. Her family emigrated to Australia when she was eight. In 1845 she became a journalist in Adelaide, moving in 1856 to Melbourne where in 1861 she and **Caroline Dexter** produced the radical political and literary journal *The Interpreter*.

Inspired by **Elizabeth Blackwell**, Harriet decided to become a doctor. Having first worked as a nurse at Guy's Hospital in London, she graduated from the New York Medical College for women in 1865.

She founded the Women's Educational and Industrial Union in Boston, Massachusetts, in 1871, and in retirement in Geneva founded *L'Union des Femmes*.

Clitherow, St Margaret, *née* Middleton

Born 1556 Died 1586
English martyr nicknamed the 'Pearl of York', and one of the 40 martyrs of England and Wales

Margaret Middleton was born in York, the daughter of a candle-maker, and brought up a Protestant. In 1571 she married a wealthy butcher, and three years later converted to Catholicism. Her husband remained a Protestant but their marriage remained intact.

Her increasing outspokenness during these dangerous times following the Reformation

earned her a period in prison, where she learnt to read. She set up a small school at home and also harboured priests there, but the secret room that housed vestments and vessels for Mass was eventually discovered and she was condemned to death by pressing under an 800-pound weight.

She and 39 other martyrs were canonized in 1970; her feast day is 25 October.

Clive, Kitty (Catherine), *née* Raftor

Born 1711 Died 1785
English comic actress and singer who became one of the leading ladies at Drury Lane

Kitty Raftor was born in London, the daughter of William Raftor, a Jacobite lawyer from Kilkenny. She made her début under Colley Cibber at Drury Lane about 1728, where she continued to play till 1769, when she left the stage. Her performance as Nell in Charles Coffey's farce *The Devil to Pay* in 1731 was her first major success. About this time she married George Clive, a barrister, but they soon parted.

She was a founding member of David Garrick's company in 1747, and became one of his leading ladies, performing almost exclusively in comedy roles. She was friendly with Handel, in whose oratorios she sang, and the author Horace Walpole, who gave her a cottage to which she retired. Dr Johnson remarked to Boswell that 'in the sprightliness of humour he never had seen her equalled'.

Close, Glenn

Born 1947
American actress who has established herself as a versatile leading lady of stage and screen

Glenn Close was born in Greenwich, Connecticut. She studied anthropology and acting, and began her career in regional theatre before her Broadway début in *Love for Love* (1974). Her subsequent theatre work includes *The Crucifer of Blood* (1978), *Barnum* (1980–1), *The Singular Life of Albert Nobbs* (1982, for which she received an Obie award), and *The Real Thing* (1984–5) and *Sunset Boulevard* (1994–5), for both of which she received Tony awards.

She made her television début in *Too Far to Go* (1979) and received an Emmy nomination for *Something About Amelia* (1984). Her cinema début in *The World According to Garp* (1982) was followed by several intelligent interpretations of goodness and virtue in such films as *The Big Chill* (1983) and *The Natural* (1984), before a radical change of image as the psychotic mistress in *Fatal Attraction* (1987) brought her international fame that was consolidated with the success of *Dangerous Liaisons* (1988) and continued with such successes as *Reversal of Fortune* and *Hamlet* (both 1990). She was also the executive producer of the documentary *Do You Mean There Are Still Real Cowboys?* (1987).

Clotilda, St

Born 474   Died 545
Queen of the Franks as the wife of King Clovis I

Clotilda was the daughter of a Burgundian king, Childeric. She married Clovis in 493 and eventually persuaded him to convert to Christianity in thanksgiving for a great victory over the Alemmani near Cologne in 496. He was baptised on Christmas day with 2,000 of his soldiers and became a champion of orthodox Christianity against the heretic Arians.

Their four sons were Ingomer and the future kings Clodomir, Childebert I and Chlotar I. After the death of Clovis in 511, Clotilda lived a life of austerity and good works at the abbey of St Martin at Tours, though her sons' behaviour allegedly made her widowhood miserable. Her feast day is 3 June.

Clough, Anne Jemima

Born 1820   Died 1892
English educationalist and feminist, a vigorous and influential proponent of higher education for women

Anne Jemima Clough was born in Liverpool, the daughter of a cotton merchant and sister of the poet Arthur Hugh Clough (1819–61). She began teaching in the late 1830s and in 1852 opened a school in Ambleside.

In her campaign to promote higher education for women, she worked alongside **Emily Davies**, **Frances Buss**, **Josephine Butler** and Henry Sidgwick, and helped to found the North of England Council for the Higher Education of Woman, serving as its secretary (1867–70) and president (1873–4). She also secured the admission of women to Manchester and Newcastle colleges.

In 1871 she became the first principal of the first hall for women students at Cambridge, Newnham Hall, later called Newnham College.

Clough, Prunella

Born 1919
English artist and printmaker whose early figurative style gave way to a more abstract approach

Prunella Clough was born in London and trained at Chelsea School of Art, where her studies were interrupted in 1939 by the outbreak of World War II.

Initially a figurative artist whose subjects included factory workers, lorry drivers and the barbed wire anti-tank spikes of war defence in East Anglia, she also painted and etched workers situated in the industrial landscape of London's dockland. In the 1960s the figurative element in her work gave way to a more abstract geometric approach.

She was friendly with **Ithell Colquhoun** and Robert MacBryde, Keith Vaughan and John Minton, and taught for periods at Chelsea and Wimbledon art schools.

Clyne, Chris

Born 1954
Scottish fashion designer whose exclusive designs are worn by celebrities throughout the western world

Chris Clyne was born in India. She studied at St Martin's School of Art, London, and after working in Paris, she established her own fashion company in London. She moved to Edinburgh in 1980 and forged links with Scottish Borders textile companies.

Concentrating on special occasion and evening wear, she has created exclusive designs and tartans in wool, cashmere and silk, and has a dedicated and growing private clientele in Britain, as well as retail outlets in the USA and Europe.

She also works on special commissions for the theatre and film industry. Her clients include members of the British royal family and celebrities such as **Meryl Streep**, **Glenn Close** and **Diana Rigg**.

Coates, Anne V

Born 1925
English film editor who established herself as a leading practitioner of her craft

Anne Coates was born in Reigate. She began her working life as a nurse, but moved into film editing in the early 1950s. Her early films included *The Pickwick Papers* (1952).

She went on to become a leading film editor, working both in Britain and in Hollywood, and has been responsible for cutting a number of very important films, including the epic *Lawrence of Arabia* (1962), for which she received an Academy Award. She was nominated again for *Becket* (1964), and also cut

Tunes of Glory (1960), *The Eagle Has Landed* (1976) and *Greystoke* (1984).

Cobbe, Frances Power

Born 1822 Died 1904
Irish social worker, feminist, travel writer and essayist who wrote on social and moral issues and was also involved in practical reform

Frances Power Cobbe was born in Newbridge, near Dublin. She became a strong supporter of women's rights, particularly women's suffrage, as well as a prominent anti-vivisectionist, and was associated with **Mary Carpenter** in the founding of ragged schools.

She travelled in Italy and the East, and wrote *Cities of the Past* (1864) and *Italics* (1864). She was also a strong theist, and edited works by the American social reformer and Unitarian clergyman Theodore Parker (1810–60), whose views were too radical to be accepted during his lifetime. She published more than 30 works, mostly on social questions, including *The Duties of Women* (1881) and *The Scientific Spirit of the Age* (1888).

Cochran, Jacqueline

Born 1910 Died 1980
American aviator and businesswoman who led a pioneering, record-breaking career as a pilot

Jacqueline Cochran was born in Pensacola, Florida. She trained as a beautician and in 1932 took a couple of months off work to take flying lessons, soon qualifying for her pilot's licence. In 1934 she started her own cosmetics company and the following year became the first woman to fly in the Bendix transcontinental air race.

In 1938 she secured the transcontinental record at 10 hours and 28 minutes. The International League of Aviators named her the world's outstanding woman pilot from 1937 to 1950 and in 1953, for she had broken the international 1,000km record in 1937 and went on to break the 100km record three times.

She was the first woman to pilot a bomber across the Atlantic in World War II, and became director of Women Auxiliary Service Pilots in the USAF in 1943. In 1953 she became the first woman to fly faster than sound (in an F-86 Sabre fighter). She also made the first landing and take-off by a woman pilot from an aircraft carrier, and in 1964 flew faster than twice the speed of sound.

Colbert, Claudette, *originally* Lily Claudette Chauchoin

Born 1903
French-born American actress, one of the most successful and enduring light actresses in the golden age of Hollywood

Claudette Colbert was born in Paris and educated in New York. She harboured an ambition to be a fashion designer but a bit-part on stage in *The Wild Westcotts* (1923) converted her to acting. Her subsequent theatre work includes *The Marionette Man* (1924), *A Kiss in a Taxi* (1925) and the popular *The Barker* (1927). Her film début in *For the Love of Mike* (1927) led to a long-term contract with Paramount.

A petite, saucer-eyed and apple-cheeked woman, with a deep-throated laugh, she gained attention as historical seductresses in *The Sign of the Cross* (1932) and *Cleopatra* (1934) but sparkled in screwball comedy where her intelligence, wit and glamour enhanced such films as *It Happened One Night* (1934, Best Actress Academy Award), *Midnight* (1939) and *The Palm Beach Story* (1942).

She retired from the cinema in 1961 but has occasionally been seen on stage, as in *The Kingfisher* (1978) and *Aren't We All?* (1984). She also returned to the cameras for the television mini-series *The Two Mrs Grenvilles* (1987).

Cole, Dame Margaret Isabel, *née* Postgate

Born 1893 Died 1980
English writer, historian and political analyst best remembered for her works on Fabian socialism

Margaret Postgate was born in Cambridge, and educated at a private school before winning a scholarship to Roedean School, Brighton. Later, at Girton College, Cambridge, she studied classics and became a socialist and feminist.

She taught for a time at St Paul's School, London, before becoming a researcher for the Fabian Society where she met her husband, G D H Cole. They married in 1918 and together they wrote *An Intelligent Man's Review of Europe Today* (1933), *A Guide to Modern Politics* (1934) and 29 detective stories.

In addition she wrote many distinguished works including *The Makers of the Labour Movement* (1948), and a highly acclaimed biography of **Beatrice Webb** (1945). She was appointed DBE in 1970.

Cole, Natalie

Born 1950
African-American singer who literally sang with
her father's voice

Natalie Cole was born in Los Angeles, California. Her albums include *Everlasting* (1987) and *Thankful, Good to Be Back* (1989). With her 1991 album, *Unforgettable*, she used technology to sing with her deceased father, Nat 'King' Cole (1917–65), for the first time singing standards made famous by him. The album and single garnered her numerous awards, including Grammys.

Coleridge, Sara

Born 1802 Died 1852
English scholar who is best known as the editor of
her father's writings

Sara Coleridge was born at Greta Hall, Keswick, the daughter of the lyric poet and philosopher Samuel Taylor Coleridge (1772–1834). Due to her father's absence from home, she was brought up in the household of another poet, Robert Southey (1774–1843), and well educated.

In 1822 she translated Dobrizhoffer's *Historia de Abiponibus*, and in 1825 the 'Loyal Servitor's' memoirs of the French soldier the Chevalier de Bayard (1476–1524). In 1829 she married her cousin, Henry Nelson Coleridge, and she wrote *Pretty Lessons for Good Children* (1834) and *Phantasmion* (1837), a fairy tale, for their two children. She was a respected figure in the literary circles of London society and enjoyed the friendshp of Thomas and **Jane Carlyle** and other eminent authors.

After her father's death she edited his writings, which she continued to do after her husband's death, despite being plagued by ill health and an addiction to opium. It was a sacrifice to her own literary aspirations that she would later question.

Colet, Louise

Born 1810 Died 1876
French poet who wrote florid, passionate poetry
and had tempestuous affairs with other famous
writers

Louise Colet was born in Aix-en-Provence and lived in Paris following her marriage to Hippolyte Colet, a violin professor at the Conservatoire from whom she later separated.

Her poetry, often on the theme of love's earth-shaking powers, is collected in *Fleurs du Midi* (1836), *Poesies* (1844) and *Ce qui est dans le coeur des femmes* (1852). She won the poetry prize of the Académie Française four times,

though according to some she had more beauty than writing talent.

Infamous for violent, vindictive behaviour and affairs with prominent writers such as Flaubert and Alfred de Musset, she gave the details in *Lui, roman contemporain* (1851, 'Him, A View of Him') which, in the words of critic Marilyn Gaddis Rose, involves 'skilful counterpointing of the personal and professional dilemmas of two women of letters in the 19th century'.

Colette, Sidonie-Gabrielle

Born 1873 Died 1954
French writer of novels, plays, short stories and
screenplays which capture the essence of France,
making her one of the country's greatest writers

Colette was born in Saint-Sauveur-en-Puisaye. Her early novels, the *Claudine* series, were published by her first husband, Henri Gauthier-Villars, under his pen-name of 'Willy'. After their divorce in 1906 she appeared in music-halls in dance and mime, and out of this period came *L'Envers du music-hall* (1913, Eng trans *Music-Hall Sidelights*, 1957).

Her work is characterized by an intense, almost entirely physical preoccupation with immediate sense experiences, and the use of 'Colette' as narrator/character brings into question the relationship between fact and fiction. Her novels include *Chéri* (1920, Eng trans 1929), *La Fin de Chéri* (1926, Eng trans *The Last of Chéri*, 1932), *La Chatte* (1933, Eng trans *The Cat*, 1936) and *Gigi* (1944, Eng trans

Colette

1953). In 1912 she married Henri de Jouvenel, and in 1935, Maurice Goudeket.

Collet, Clara Elizabeth

Born 1860 Died 1948
British feminist and sociologist, an adviser to parliament

Clara Collet was educated at the North London Collegiate School and at University College, London.

She taught at Wyggeston High School, Leicester for seven years, leaving to become assistant commissioner to the Royal Commission on Labour. Following this she was appointed labour correspondent (1893), then senior investigator (1903) to the Board of Trade. Later in life after a spell at the Ministry of Labour, she became Governor of Bedford College.

She presented numerous reports to parliament and her publications include *The Economic Position of Educated Working Women* (1890) and *Women in Industry* (1911). In 1889 she co-authored the *Life and Labour of the People in London* with Charles Booth.

Collins, Jackie

Born 1937
English popular novelist who has had uninterrupted success since the publication of her first book in 1968

Jackie Collins was born in London, the younger sister of the actress **Joan Collins**. Having been expelled from school at 15, she moved to Hollywood in search of fame as a film actress, but instead she has made a career out of writing fiction about the Hollywood set.

Her first novel, *The World is Full of Married Men*, was published in 1968, launching Collins into a consistently successful career. *The Stud* (1969) and *The Bitch* (1972) were both subsequently filmed starring her older sister. *Hollywood Wives* (1983) is perhaps the archetypal Collins novel, being an engaging amalgam of young love, aging lust, sex, shopping, glamour, grime, violence, drugs, rock'n'roll, and more sex.

By the mid-1990s Collins had sold in excess of 170 million copies of her books worldwide and was one of the highest-earning British female authors.

Collins, Joan Henrietta

Born 1933
English actress who has used her sultry appeal and headline-catching private life to build a career as a durable international celebrity

Joan Collins was born in London. She is the older sister of the bestselling novelist **Jackie Collins**. She made her film début in *Lady Godiva Rides Again* (1951) and by the 1970s was appearing in low-budget horror films and softcore pornography. Her fortunes were revitalized with a leading role in the universally popular television soap opera *Dynasty* (1981–9) and she continued acting on stage and screen into the 1990s.

She has been married four times, and has written a tell-all autobiography, *Past Imperfect* (1978); the novels *Prime Time* (1988) and *Too Damn Famous*; *My Secrets* (1994), an illustrated collection of hints on retaining youthful looks; and her memoirs, *Second Act* (1996).

Collins, Judy

Born 1939
American folk-singer whose hits include 'Amazing Grace'

Judy Collins was born in Denver, Colorado. Her recording career began in 1962 with the album *A Maid of Constant Sorrow*. Her later work however, such as *In My Life* (1966), which features string arrangements, is much less conventionally oriented. She had a relationship with songwriter Stephen Stills who wrote 'Suite; Judy Blue Eyes' (performed at Woodstock) in her honour.

In 1970 she reached the peak of her crossover fame with hits 'Both Sides Now' (a **Joni Mitchell** composition) and the traditional 'Amazing Grace', which has re-entered the charts an unprecedented number of times. Though now critically derided, Collins was a leading player in the 'singer-songwriter' boom of the 1960s.

Collot, Marie-Anne

Born 1748 Died 1821
French sculptor who worked with Étienne Falconet on the equestrian statue of Peter the Great

Marie-Anne Collot was born in France, where she became the pupil of Étienne Maurice Falconet (1716–91). She was exceptionally skilled at sculpting portrait busts and accompanied Falconet to Russia in 1766 when he was commissioned to do a monument to Peter the Great in St Petersburg. This was to become one of the 18th century's most famous pieces of sculpture.

They remained in Russia for 16 years, during which period she completed a great number of portrait busts for members of the court of **Catherine II**. Collot married Falconet's son and moved with him to England where he studied with Joshua Reynolds (1723–92).

While in England she sculpted portrait busts, including one of Lady Cathcart, a member of the English Court, but became very unhappy and left to join the elder Falconet in The Hague. When Falconet suffered a paralytic stroke in 1783, she remained with him as his nurse and companion, which meant an abrupt cessation of her work.

Colonna, Vittoria

Born 1490   Died 1547
Italian poet who wrote in a style similar to
Petrarch and was an inspiration and friend to
Michelangelo

Vittoria Colonna was born into a noble Roman family in Marino. She had an arranged marriage to the Marquis of Pescara, but since she saw little of him the marriage turned into one of love-in-absence. He died in battle at Pavi (1525), and she devoted herself to a religious life and good causes, later lamenting his death and that of her father in *Canzoniere* (1544).

Her religious thinking was profound, as were her objections to corruption in her church. She inspired her friend Michelangelo to some of his finest poetry. Her own lyric poetry — Petrarchan in style — is of the first order, and deserves even more extended study than it has already had. Many translations are included in M F Jerrold's *Vittora Colonna* (1906, reprinted 1969).

Colquhoun, Ithell, *originally* Margaret Ithell

Born 1906   Died 1988
English artist and poet whose works drew first
from mythology and later from the occult and
alchemy

Ithell Colquhoun was born in Assam, India. She studied at the Slade School of Art prior to working in various ateliers, or studios, in Paris and Athens. She became associated with the English Surrealists, met André Breton and Salvador Dali in 1933, and exhibited at the International Surrealist Exhibition in 1936. In 1943 she married Tony del Renzio, editor of the Surrealist magazine *Arson*, but the marriage ended after only four years.

Until the 1930s her work dealt with mythological and biblical subjects, then she became involved in portraying dream-like states, and in the 1940s her interest lay in the exploration of fantastic plants using a variety of different mediums. From 1956 she lived in Cornwall where she continued to write and produce

work which incorporated themes from the occult and alchemy. She also contributed articles and poems to the *London Bulletin* and exhibited widely throughout Britain and abroad.

Coltrane, Alice, *also known as* Turiya, Sagittinanda, *née* McLeod

Born 1937
American jazz pianist, organist and harpist, wife
of John Coltrane

Alice McLeod was born in Detroit, Michigan, the sister of bass player Ernie Farrow. She began playing music in church, but soon turned to jazz, working with Kenny Burrell, Johnny Griffin and (as did her brother) Yusef Lateef. While in a band led by Terry Gibbs, she met saxophonist John Coltrane (1926–67). They married in 1965 and Coltrane recruited her to his group, which had an increasingly Oriental sound and philosophy. After Coltrane's death in 1967, Alice continued to play his music and her own for a time, before founding the Vedantic Center in California (1975). Her most distinguished recording is *Transfiguration* (1978), but the past two decades have largely been spent outside music, studying Eastern religion. She has, however, appeared in tribute concerts to John Coltrane, with their sons Ravi and Omar.

Comaneci, Nadia

Born 1961
Romanian gymnast who was the star of the 1976
Olympic Games

Nadia Comaneci was born in Onesti, Moldavia. She entered the 1976 Olympic Games at

Nadia Comaneci, 1978

the age of 14 (coached by Bela Karolyi) and won gold medals for Romania in the beam, vault and floor disciplines. In 1976 she became the first gymnast to obtain a perfect score of 10.00 for her performance on the parallel bars and beam. She retained the beam and floor exercise gold medals in 1980.

She retired in 1984 and became a coach to the Romanian national team, and an international judge. In 1989 she defected to the USA via Hungary, amid much publicity, and became a model. She married US gymnast Bart Conner in 1996.

Compton, Fay (Virginia Lillian Emmeline)

Born 1894 Died 1978
English actress who found fame especially in plays by J M Barrie

Fay Compton was born in London, a daughter of the actor Edward Compton (1854–1918) and sister of the writer Compton Mackenzie (1883–1972). She first appeared on the stage in 1911.

After a successful US visit in 1914, she won acclaim in London as *Peter Pan* in 1918. She subsequently played many famous parts, especially in plays by J M Barrie, W Somerset Maugham and Noël Coward, and latterly in comedies such as **Dodie Smith**'s *Autumn Crocus* (1930) and *Call it a Day* (1935–7).

Compton-Burnett, Dame Ivy

Born 1892 Died 1969
English novelist who examines her upper-class Edwardian characters' relationships by means of their dialogue

Ivy Compton-Burnett was born in Pinner, Middlesex. She graduated in classics from the Royal Holloway College, London University, and published her first novel, *Dolores*, in 1911. She became a prolific writer, producing rather stylized novels that have many features in common: they are often set in upper-class Victorian or Edwardian society, for example, and the characters usually belong to a large family, spanning several generations.

She was noted for her skilful use of dialogue, not because the language is appropriate to character but because it conveys the secret thoughts and understanding of the characters. Her works include *Pastors and Masters* (1925), *Brothers and Sisters* (1929), *Parents and Children* (1941), *Mother and Son* (1955, Tait Black Memorial Prize), *A Father and his Fate* (1957), *The Mighty and their Fall* (1961) and *A God and His Gifts* (1963).

Comstock, Anna, *née* Botsford

Born 1854 Died 1930
American naturalist whose educational programmes received considerable contemporary acclaim

Anna Botsford was born in Otto, New York. She enrolled at Cornell University to study languages, but met and married an entomologist called John Comstock, and became a highly skilled, and recognized, illustrator of her husband's books.

In 1895 she became a member of the Committee for the Promotion of Agriculture in New York State, and she began an extensive programme of lecturing and writing, specifically aimed at encouraging children to appreciate nature study.

Four years later she was elected to a Cornell professorship, although this was withdrawn for political reasons, and she was finally awarded the chair in 1920, from which she continued her educational programmes.

Connolly, Maureen Catherine

Born 1934 Died 1969
American tennis player, nicknamed 'Little Mo', who made an impact on tennis history

Maureen Connolly was born in San Diego, California. She made tennis history by becoming the first woman to win the Grand Slam of the four major titles (British, American, French and Australian) in the same year (1953).

She won the US title in three consecutive years (1951–3) and the Wimbledon singles in three consecutive years (1952–4). Soon after her last Wimbledon triumph she broke her leg in a riding accident and retired from tournament play.

Conran, Shirley Ida, *née* Pearce

Born 1932
English designer, fashion editor and bestselling author of international blockbusters

Shirley Pearce was educated at St Paul's Girls' School and Portsmouth College of Art. From 1955 to 1962 she was married to the first of her three husbands, the English designer and businessman Terence Conran (1931–   ), and she designed fabrics for and was director of Conran Fabrics. Their sons Jasper and Sebastian both became designers. She turned to journalism in 1964 and was woman's editor for the *Observer* colour magazine and then the *Daily Mail*, and then 'life and style' editor for *Over 21* (1972–4).

Her career as a bestselling author began following a debilitating illness when she wrote

Superwoman, a book telling working women and mothers how to cope, for example how to do the minimum amount of housework for the maximum effect. Published in 1975, it went into seven editions in six months, sold 75,000 copies, and was followed by four more superwoman books. In 1979 Conran moved to Monaco, where she still lives, and published her first fiction book, *Lace* (1982), which she describes as being 'about sex from a woman's point of view'. Later novels include *Lace 2* (1985), *Crimson* (1991) and *Tiger Eyes* (1994).

Cons, Emma

Born 1838 Died 1912
English social reformer and artist, the founder of the 'Old Vic' theatre (1880) and its full-time manager from 1894 to 1912

Emma Cons was born in London, studied at Gower Street Art School, and, through the Ladies' Art Guild, became friendly with **Octavia Hill** (whose mother ran the guild) and John Ruskin.

Though she worked as a designer and restorer for Ruskin, she is better known for her work as a social reformer, running crèches, clinics, a girls' hostel, and model housing projects in central London. Her many interests also included women's suffrage, the plight of Armenian refugees and the Women's Horticultural College at Swanley.

She is most famous for buying the Royal Victoria Hall (the 'Old Vic'), established as a prestigious theatre by her niece **Lilian Baylis**. Morley College, founded in 1899, grew out of lectures and classes given at the theatre.

Cook, Beryl

Born 1937
English painter who creates humorous depictions of her family, friends and everyday scenes in her native Plymouth

Beryl Cook was born in Plymouth. She started to paint in the early 1960s, entirely self taught. Her acute character observation, both penetrating and flamboyant, can belie the terms 'naïve' and 'primitive' which are often used to describe her work.

She refuses to admit to any significant artistic influences but has stated that television and in particular 'The Flintstones' cartoon characters have been an influence on her work.

Cook, Eliza

Born 1818 Died 1889
English poet, essayist and feminist whose unaffected, domestic style of verse appealed particularly to ordinary, uncultured people

Eliza Cook was the youngest of a London tradesman's 11 children. She educated herself and in 1835 published her first collection, *Lays of a Wild Harp*, the success of which encouraged her to contribute poems to magazines. She went on to issue volumes of poetry in 1838 and 1864, and her most popular poem, 'The Old Arm Chair', appeared in the *Weekly Dispatch* in 1837.

From 1849 to 1854 she worked on *Eliza Cook's Journal*, a collection of feminist essays on such subjects as marriage, employment and the law; much of this miscellany was republished as *Jottings from my Journal* (1860).

Cookson, Dame Catherine Ann

Born 1906
English popular novelist who is a favourite among habitués of the public library and has published more than 70 books

Catherine Cookson was born in Tyne Dock, County Durham. Her fiction is set in the northeast of England and is replete with tragedy, exploitation and romance. Included in her prolific output are the Mallen trilogy and the Tilly Trotter series, and six written as Catherine Marchant. *Our Kate* (1969) is autobiographical. Cookson was made a DBE in 1993 for her charitable services in the northeast of England.

Coolidge, Martha

Born 1946
American film director who has established herself within the Hollywood system

Martha Coolidge was born in New Haven. She studied at Columbia School of Visual Arts and New York University, and shot documentary films in the late 1960s. She also worked in children's television, including directing episodes of the popular *Sesame Street*.

She came to wider notice with the controversial *Not A Pretty Picture* (1976), which examined the traumas of a rape victim, drawn from her own harrowing experience. Her commercial breakthrough came with the unexpected success of her low-budget feature *Valley Girls* (1983), and she went on to find a niche within the Hollywood system, still a rare achievement for a woman director.

Coolidge, Susan, *pseud of* Sarah Chauncy Woolsey

Born 1835 Died 1905
American poet, literary critic and children's writer who wrote about the escapades of the careless Katy Carr

Susan Coolidge was born in Cleveland, Ohio. She began her writing career as a poet but made her name writing stories for girls, particulary the *Katy* series, which ranged from *What Katy Did* (1872) to *What Katy Did Next* (1886). They are characterized by an easy natural style, free from contemporary sentimentality, and describe the motherless Katy's girlhood adventures, her experience of being bedridden for two years, and her eventual emergence as a competent young lady.

Coolidge also edited the letters of several famous women and wrote *A Short History of Philadelphia* (1887).

Cooper, Anna Julia, *née* Haywood

Born 1858   Died 1964
American teacher and writer, author of A Voice from the South. . .

Anna Haywood was born a slave in Raleigh, North Carolina. She was educated at St Augustine's Episcopalian school in Raleigh and at Oberlin College, Ohio, before returning as a teacher to St Augustine's (1887–1927). In 1901 she became only the second woman to be appointed as a public school principal in Washington DC. She successfully opposed Congress's proposal for a special (academically easier) curriculum for black children.

Cooper gained a doctorate from Columbia University (1917) and from the Sorbonne (1925). In retirement (1929–47) she was President of Freylingham University for Employed Adults (formerly the Freylingham Group of Schools for Employed Colored Persons), Washington DC. Her best-known work is *A Voice from the South by a Black Woman of the South* (1892).

Cooper, Eileen

Born 1933
English artist whose work as a figurative artist explores a wide range of emotions often from a feminist viewpoint

Eileen Cooper was born in Glossop, Derbyshire. She studied at Goldsmiths' College and at the Royal College of Art, London, and became a visiting lecturer at Central St Martins College of Art.

Her works, which focus on the human condition, are executed in a bold linear fashion which can be quite haunting in their simplicity. She has exhibited widely and her work is in the collections of the V & A, Contemporary Art Society and the Arts Council of Great Britain.

Cooper, Dame Gladys Constance

Born 1888   Died 1971
English stage and film actress and theatre manager who was one of the great theatrical personalities and beauties of her day

Gladys Cooper was born in London and became a child model whose features are estimated to have graced over 400 picture postcards. She made her professional stage début in *Bluebell in Fairyland* (1905) and appeared in many musical productions before winning recognition for her dramatic performances in *The Importance of Being Earnest* (1911) and *Milestones* (1912).

She made her film début in *The Eleventh Commandment* (1913) but remained primarily a stage performer, managing the Playhouse Theatre, London (1926–33), and making her first Broadway appearance in *The Shining Hour* (1934). She lived in Hollywood from 1940, and appeared in over 30 films, often cast as aristocratic and embittered older women.

She received Academy Award nominations for her performances in *Now Voyager* (1942), *The Song of Bernadette* (1943) and *My Fair Lady* (1964). A working actress until her death, she starred in the television series *The Rogues* (1964–5) and made her final stage appearance in *The Chalk Garden* (1971). She was appointed DBE in 1967.

Cooper, Jilly

Born 1937
English novelist and author of miscellaneous and humorous non-fiction whose first runaway bestseller was Riders

Jilly Cooper was born in Hornchurch, Essex. Since the appearance of her first book, *How To Stay Married*, in 1969, she has been hugely prolific, specializing initially in cocktail-and-horsey social humour, such as *Jolly Super* (1971) and *Men and Super Men* (1972).

After a series of romantic novels, including *Emily* (1975) and *Prudence* (1978), Cooper published *Riders* (1985), her first huge bestseller, a sensational tale of sex, party-life and horses, dashing young men and highly-charged women. Other similarly raunchy and popular entertainments followed, entitled *Rivals* (1988), *Polo* (1991) and *The Man Who Made Husbands Jealous* (1993).

Cooper, Susie (Susan Vera)

Born 1902   Died 1995
English ceramic designer and factory owner who became the 20th-century British pottery industry's most important and influential woman

Susie Cooper was born in Stoke-on-Trent. She showed a flair for drawing as a child and won a scholarship to the Burslem School of Art where she studied under the Scottish ceramic designer Gordon Forsyth. Though she intended to be a textile designer, she realised that designing pottery could satisfy her artistic potential and joined Gray's Pottery in 1922. By 1924 her work was on show at the British Empire Exhibition at Wembley.

Frustrated with always having to work on ready-made ware, she set up her own firm in 1929, and began by purchasing earthenware locally and decorating it with her individual designs of simple patterns, often in muted shades — coloured bands and polka dots and animals and flowers. She also used lithographic transfers to reduce the inconsistency inherent in handpainting — the printed decoration is indistinguishable from hand painting — and worked closely with the Universal Transfer Company to develop the transfers which have benefited the pottery industry ever since. She received her first major orders in 1935, proving the success of her business slogan: 'Elegance combined with utility'.

She became the first Royal Designer for Industry in 1940 and received many important commissions which show the diversity and originality of her work. In the 1950s she expanded her product to include the manufacture of very fine, almost translucent bone china, while maintaining the established earthenwares. In 1961 the Susie Cooper Pottery merged with R H & S L Plant which became part of the Wedgwood Group in 1966. She was senior designer and director for Josiah Wedgwood & Sons until 1972, following which she continued to be very active, producing new work for her ninetieth birthday 20 years later.

Cooper, Dame Whina (Josephine), née Te Wake

Born 1895 Died 1994
Maori campaigner, one of the most revered leaders of New Zealand's indigenous Maoris

Whina Te Wake was born into poverty in the Hokianga region of Te Karaka in New Zealand. From an early age she showed an interest in debating land ownership and had her education paid for by the then Maori Minister of Native Affairs. She married Richard Gilbert (d.1935) in 1916 and William Cooper (d.1949) in 1941.

Although Maori women were not expected to take part in tribal affairs, at the age of 18 she organized her first protest action and suc-

ceeded in preventing some Maori-owned mudflats being taken over by a European farmer. She went on to devote her life to racial harmony and the Maori cause, working variously as a teacher, shopkeeper, and a cattle and pig breeder. She was founding President of the Women's Welfare League (1951–7) and New Zealand President of the Maori Land Rights from 1975 until the year of her death.

At the age of 80 Cooper led a historic 700-mile march of 5,000 people to Wellington to highlight the fact that all but 2.5 of New Zealand's 66 million acres had been seized by Europeans. Though the more militant Maoris disagreed with her methods, she earned high esteem elsewhere and was appointed DBE in 1981, only the second Maori to be so honoured.

Coppin, Fanny Marion Jackson, née Jackson

Born 1837 Died 1913
American teacher, principal of the Institute for Colored Youth in Philadelphia (1869–1902)

Fanny Jackson was born a slave in the District of Columbia. Her aunt bought her freedom for her when she was a young girl for $125. From 1851 to 1857 she worked for the author George Henry Calvert who encouraged her education, and she went on to study at Oberlin College, Ohio (1860–5).

She became principal of the girls' high school department of the Institute for Colored Youth, Philadelphia (1865), and went on to become its head principal (1869) — the first black woman to hold such a position. During her 37 years at the Institute she extended its curriculum, raising academic qualifications and providing vocational training.

Ill health forced her retirement in 1902. She went with her husband, the Rev Levi Coppin, to Cape Town, where he was Bishop from 1902 to 1912.

Corbin, Margaret, née Cochran

Born 1751 Died 1800
American Revolutionary War heroine, the first woman to receive a military pension from the US government

Margaret Cochran was born in Franklin County, Pennsylvania, and raised by a relative from the age of five when her father had died in a battle with Native Americans and her mother had been taken prisoner. Her husband John Corbin enlisted in the Revolution and she accompanied him to assist in looking after the troops. When he was killed during the fighting at Fort Washington on 16 November

1776, she took over his artillery station and continued firing his cannon until she herself was shot.

Her injuries resulted in the permanent loss of the use of one arm. In 1779 she became the first woman to receive a military pension from Congress and in 1916 a monument at West Point was erected in her honour.

Corday, Charlotte, *in full* Marie Charlotte Corday d'Armont

Born 1768 Died 1793
French Girondist sympathizer and murderer who is remembered for having assassinated the revolutionary Jean Paul Marat in his bath

Charlotte Corday was born in St Saturnin near Sées (Orne). Despite her aristocratic background she initially welcomed the French Revolution. The behaviour of the Jacobins, however, so horrified her that she resolved to kill one of the chief revolutionaries, either Robespierre or Marat.

She went to Paris and, hearing of Marat's demand for 200,000 more victims, gained admittance to his house by pretending to be a messenger. When she arrived Marat was having a bath, and his heartless comment about the fugitive Girondists ('I will have them all guillotined at Paris') incited her to stab him to death. Unrepentant, she was brought before the Revolutionary Tribunal and guillotined.

Corelli, Marie, *pseud of* Mary Mackay

Born 1855 Died 1924
English popular romantic novelist whose melodramas were loved by thousands despite critics' accusations of sentimentality and poor taste

Mary Mackay was born in London, the illegitimate child of Charles Mackay, a journalist, and Ellen Mills, a widow whom he had married as his second wife. She was educated by governesses and trained as a pianist; though accomplished, her métier was writing, to which she devoted herself from 1885.

A Romance of Two Worlds (1886) marked the beginning of an unprecedented career as a bestselling writer. A self-righteous, sentimental moralist, lacking self-criticism or a sense of the absurd, she was the writer that critics loved to hate. Later in a prolific career she refused reviewers access to her latest books, but her aficionados included Liberal Prime Minister William Gladstone and the Irish playwright Oscar Wilde and her readership was immense.

Her novels include *Thelma* (1887), *Barabbas* (1893), *God's Good Man* (1904), *The Devil's*

Motor (1910), *Eyes of the Sea* (1917) and *The Secret Power* (1921).

Cori, Gerty Theresa Radnitz, *née* Radnitz

Born 1896 Died 1957
American biochemist whose work on carbohydrate metabolism earned her the Nobel Prize for Physiology or Medicine in 1947

Gerty Radnitz was born in Prague, Czechoslovakia. She trained in medicine at the German University of Prague and married her fellow student Carl Cori upon graduating. She worked at the Vienna Children's Hospital (1920–2) and then emigrated with her husband to the USA. She was employed at the State Institute for the Study of Malignant Disease, Buffalo, New York (1922–31) and then moved to the Medical School at the Washington University in St Louis (Research Associate in Pharmacology 1931–43; Research Associate Professor of Biochemistry 1943–7; Professor of Biochemistry 1947–57).

With her husband she conducted research into carbohydrate metabolism, and their close collaboration makes it difficult to assess their contributions individually. They elucidated the process whereby glycogen, the stored form of carbohydrate, was enzymatically broken down to glucose, liberating energy in the process. They also discerned how glycogen was synthesized and stored in the body. Their investigations into carbohydrate metabolism were very broad: they studied the effects of many hormones including insulin, adrenaline and pituitary extracts, and examined glycogen and glucose metabolism in biochemically abnormal circumstances, such as in tumours and in inherited metabolic diseases.

The latter work led Gerty Cori to the first demonstration that glycogen storage disease could be caused by abnormalities or deficits in enzymes, a link with her very first position in paediatrics in Vienna. Gerty and Carl shared the Nobel Prize for Physiology or Medicine with the Argentinian Bernardo Houssay in 1947, only the third husband-and-wife team to do so after Pierre and **Marie Curie** in 1903 and Jean and **Irène Joliot-Curie** in 1935.

Corinna

Floreat c.500BC
Greek lyric poet who wrote mainly on mythological themes and was a teacher and rival of Pindar

Corinna came from Tanagra in Boeotia. Her poems, which survive in little beyond substantial fragments of two long pieces, are lyrical narratives derived from Boeotian legends. The titles of others are known and include *The Return of Orion*, *Iolaus* and *Seven against Thebes*.

The two extant poems, written in short, octosyllabic lines and five- or six-line stanzas, describe a singing contest between the mountain gods of Cithaeron and Helicon, and the marriages of the daughters of Asopus. According to tradition, Corinna taught Pindar in his youth and later competed against him in poetic contests.

Cornaro, Caterina

Born 1454 Died 1510
Venetian noblewoman and Queen of Cyprus

Caterina Cornaro was born in Venice. Her marriage in 1472 to James II, King of Cyprus, Jerusalem and Armenia, was organized mainly to give him an alliance with Venice, but he died eight months afterwards and she succeeded him on the throne.

Her reign was troubled due to endless conspiracies to usurp her position, all of which were quelled by the Venetians; eventually in 1489 she was forced to abdicate in favour of a Venetian republic. She was given the castle and town of Asolo, near Bassano, to govern, where she set up a kind of court for poets and scholars.

Her life was celebrated in art (eg by Veronese and Titian), in opera (eg by Fromental Halévy and Gaetano Donizetti) and in her cousin Cardinal Pietro Bembo's Platonic dialogue *Gli Asolani* (1505).

Cornell, Katharine

Born 1893 Died 1974
American actress, producer and manager, 'the first lady of the American theatre', from the 1920s to the 1950s

Katharine Cornell was born in Berlin of American parents. She was educated in New York and made her first stage appearance in 1916. Her first triumph came five years later in **Clemence Dane**'s *A Bill of Divorcement*.

Thereafter she was given many leading roles and appeared in such plays as *Candida*, *The Green Hat*, *The Letter* and *The Age of Innocence* before embarking on a career as producer. Her own productions include a number of Shakespearian and Shavian classics, *The Constant Wife*, *The First-Born* and *Dear Liar*.

After the success of her Elizabeth Moulton-Barrett in *The Barretts of Wimpole Street* in 1931, directed by and co-produced with her husband Guthrie McClintic, she worked closely with him and retired when he died in 1961.

Corrigan-Maguire, Mairéad, *also known as* Mairéad Corrigan

Born 1944
Northern Irish peace activist who co-founded the peace movement in Northern Ireland

Mairéad Corrigan-Maguire was born in Belfast. A Roman Catholic, she worked as a secretary and also became involved with social work in the Catholic areas of Belfast. In 1976 she witnessed the shooting of an IRA (Irish Republican Army) terrorist car driver and the accidental killing of three of her sister's children by the runaway car. From this day onwards, in the face of continuing sectarian violence in Northern Ireland, she devoted herself to organizing programmes working for peace.

The initiative, founded with **Betty Williams**, became a mass movement of Roman Catholic and Protestant women known as the 'Community for Peace People' or the 'Peace People Organization'. They believed that genuine peace could be achieved if Catholics and Protestants were thoroughly integrated — for example in schools, residential areas and leisure clubs.

Corrigan-Maguire was also the first woman in Ulster to denounce the activities of the IRA on television, and she shared with Williams the 1976 Nobel Prize for Peace.

Cossington-Smith, Grace

Born 1892 Died 1984
Australian painter who was one of the first in her country to embrace modernism

Grace Cossington-Smith was born in Neutral Bay, New South Wales. She studied art in Sydney at Dattilo Rubbo's Art School (1909–12, 1914–26), and in England and Germany in 1912–14.

She is credited with introducing post-Impressionism to Australia, and was a pioneer of the modernist movement and co-founded the Contemporary Group in 1926. Her paintings, which are characterized by square brush strokes and bright colours, did not become popular until late in her career. They include *The Sock Knitter* (1915), a key work in the Australian modernist movement, and many still lifes, Sydney landscapes and interiors, such as *The Lacquer Room* (1935).

Cottin, Sophie, *née* Risteau

Born 1770 Died 1807
French writer whom some considered to be the
most accomplished novelist of her time

Sophie Risteau was brought up in Bordeau and at 17 married a Parisian banker, who left her a childless widow at 20. For comfort she turned to writing, and produced verses, a lengthy history and romantic fiction.

She had already written *Claire d'Albe* (1799) and *Mathilde* (1805) when, in 1806, she wrote her most successful work, *Élisabeth, ou les exilés de Sibérie*, ('Elisabeth, or the Siberian Exiles'). The poet Victor Hugo noted 10 years after her death that many regarded her as the most talented of her time.

Court, Margaret Smith, *née* Smith

Born 1942
Australian tennis player who holds more
championship titles than any other player

Margaret Smith was born in Albury, New South Wales. A tall and powerful player, she was the first Australian to win the Wimbledon women's singles title in 1963 (and again in 1965 and 1970). In 1970 she became the second woman, after **Maureen Connolly**, to win the Grand Slam of the four major titles (British, American, French and Australian) in a single year; she also won the Grand Slam in mixed doubles (with Ken Fletcher) in 1963.

In addition she won the Australian singles title 11 times and the US title seven times, making her the holder of more singles, doubles and mixed doubles titles than any other player to date. She has published *The Margaret Smith Story* (1964) and *Court on Court* (1974).

Margaret Smith Court, 1963

Courtneidge, Dame Cicely (Esmerelda)

Born 1893 Died 1980
English actress of light musical comedies who was
acclaimed on her own and in partnership with her
husband

Cicely Courtneidge was born in Sydney, New South Wales. She went on stage at the age of eight, and made her London début at 14 in a musical version of *Tom Jones*, and later became widely known as an actress in musicals, pantomime and revue.

One of her great successes was in *By-the-Way* in 1935, which also starred her husband Jack Hulbert (1892–1978), with whom she had already developed an acclaimed partnership. They appeared together in many shows such as *Clowns in Clover* (1927), *Under Your Hat* (1938) and *Something in the Air* (1943).

She also appeared in several straight comedies, including her final West End stage appearance in Ray Cooney's *Move Over, Mrs Markham* (1971). She published an autobiography, *Cicely*, in 1953.

Courtney, Dame Kathleen D'Olier

Born 1878 Died 1974
English suffragette and world peace activist who
was awarded the UN peace medal in 1972

Kathleen Courtney was born in Gillingham, Kent. She read modern languages at Lady Margaret Hall, Oxford. A woman of independent means, she devoted her life to improving the position of women (promoting, for example, the idea of family allowances) and to world peace. On the outbreak of World War I, like other constitutional suffragettes, she diverted her energies to international Quaker relief work.

A founder of the Women's International League for Peace, she chaired the British section and was on the executive of the British League of Nations Union (1928–39). She took part in the drawing up of the UN Charter, and was Vice-Chairman, then Chairman of the UN Association in Britain (1949–51). She was created DBE in 1952.

Cousins, Margaret, *née* Gillespie

Born 1878 Died 1954
Irish feminist and educationalist remembered
chiefly for her work for women's education
in India

Margaret Gillespie was born in Boyle, County Roscommon, and educated locally in Derry. She studied music at the Royal Irish Academy in Dublin and later taught in an infants' school.

In 1903 she married James Cousins who became a Theosophist in 1908. This led to their removal to India in 1915 where he took up the post of editor of **Annie Besant**'s publication *New India*.

In a continuation of her keen involvement in women's affairs first developed in Ireland, Cousins became the first non-Indian member of the Indian Women's University Association and a founder member of the Indian Women's Association. She was also the first Headmistress of the National Girls' School in Mangalore (1919–20), and the first woman magistrate in India (1920).

Couvreur, Jessie, *née* Huybers

Born 1848 Died 1897
Australian colonial novelist and short-story
writer who often wrote under the pseudonym
'Tasma'

Jessie Huybers was born in Highgate, London, of Dutch–French stock, and in the early 1850s went with her family to Hobart, Tasmania. She married Charles Fraser, a gambler and womanizer, in 1867, but in 1883 instituted divorce proceedings. She returned to Europe where she married Auguste Couvreur, a member of the Belgian parliament (1864–84) and journalist.

On her husband's death (1894), she took over as Belgian correspondent for the London *Times*. Her first and best-known novel, *Uncle Piper of Piper's Hill* (1889), was followed by *In Her Earliest Youth* (1890), *The Penance of Portia James* (1891) and *Not Counting the Cost* (1895). *A Fiery Ordeal* (1897) drew more on her problematic marital experiences.

Unlike many of her Australian contemporaries, such as **Ada Cambridge**, Couvreur wrote not of the land but of the city, families and social divisions. Distinctly English in style, her works give a vivid picture of Australian middle-class life in the latter half of the 19th century.

Couzyn, Jeni

Born 1942
South African-born Canadian poet whose work
often draws on her early experiences of South
Africa

Jeni Couzyn was educated at the University of Natal, taught in Rhodesia and London, and has been a full-time writer since 1968. She took Canadian citizenship in 1975. Her first volume, *Flying* (1970), described her South African background and documented the psychological impact of exile on everyday perceptions and relationships. *Monkeys' Wedding* (1972, revised edition 1978) was much less oblique and by no means as successful. *Christmas in Africa* (1975), *House of Changes* (1978) and *The Happiness Bird* (1978) turn again to South Africa for much of their imagery, but also include poems which develop a consciousness coloured by science fiction and technological fantasy.

With exceptionally balanced irony, Couzyn explores female sexuality as if it were an alien excrescence, but in her most assured collection, *A Time to be Born* (1981), she has come to terms with the world and her own identity within it, a situation reflected in her selection of work for *The Bloodaxe Book of Contemporary Women Poets* (1984). In that same year an expanded edition of her fine selected poems, *Life By Drowning* (originally published 1983), also appeared.

Cowley, Hannah

Born 1743 Died 1809
English playwright and poet, one of the first
exponents of the comedy of manners

Hannah Cowley was the daughter of a Devonshire bookseller. Her first play, *The Runaway* (1776), was written in a fortnight, and produced by David Garrick at Drury Lane. Before retiring to Devon in 1801, she rapidly produced 13 works for the stage, the most successful being *The Belle's Strategem* (1780), which was frequently revived, notably by Henry Irving in 1881, with **Ellen Terry** as Letitia.

She also wrote long narrative verses (1780–94) and, under the pseudonym Anna Matilda, carried on a sentimental, poetic correspondence in the *World*.

Cox, Gertrude Mary

Born 1900 Died 1978
American statistician widely acclaimed for her
design and administration of research projects

Gertrude Cox was born on a farm in rural Iowa. She received her bachelor's degree from the Iowa State College in 1929, and her masters in 1931, specializing in statistics. In 1933 the College opened a statistical laboratory and she assisted in its development until moving in 1941 to the University of North Carolina as Professor of Experimental Statistics, from which she retired in 1965.

As well as for designing and administering research projects, she was widely recognized for incorporating statistical expertise and experimentation design programmess into many other departments of the university. She was awarded several honorary fellowships and degrees, and elected to the National Academy of Sciences in 1975.

Craddock, Charles Egbert, *pseud of* Mary Noailles Murfree

Born 1850 Died 1922
American writer who became a prolific novelist and short-story writer in the local colour genre

Mary Noailles Murfree was born in Murfreesboro, Tennessee. She contributed short stories to the *Atlantic Monthly* from 1878, and the identity behind her pseudonym was only revealed when they were published as *In the Tennessee Mountains* (1884).

As well as her stories of life ignored by the advance of civilisation in the mountain backwoods of Tennessee, she wrote a series of historical novels set in the South, which included *Where the Battle was Fought* (1884). Among her works are *The Despot of Broomsedge Grove* (1889), *The Frontiersman* (1904) and *The Ordeal* (1912).

Craik, Dinah Maria, *née* Mulock

Born 1826 Died 1887
English novelist, short-story writer and poet who encouraged Victorian women to examine their role

Dinah Mulock was born in Stoke-upon-Trent. She settled in London at the age of 20, and published *The Ogilvies* (1849), *Olive* (1850), *The Head of the Family* (1851) and *Agatha's Husband* (1853). Her best-known novel was *John Halifax, Gentleman* (1857).

Her short stories were collected as *Avillion* (1853), and *Collected Poems* appeared in 1881. She also wrote essays, children's stories and fairy tales. In 1865 she married George Lillie Craik, nephew of George Lillie Craik, a partner in the publishing house of Macmillan, and was assigned the benefits of a Civil List pension awarded in 1864 to less well-off authors.

Cranston, Kate (Catherine)

Born 1850 Died 1934
Scottish tea-room proprietress and influential patron of designers from the Glasgow School of Art

Kate Cranston was born in Glasgow, the daughter of a hotelier and dealer in fine teas. Between 1884 and 1904 she opened a chain of highly successful tea rooms in Glasgow, which became known for their distinctive 'artistic' interiors.

In 1896 Charles Rennie Mackintosh was commissioned to redesign the furniture and fittings for the Argyle Street tea rooms, and he later did the interior decorative schemes for the Ingram Street branch (1900) and the Willow tea rooms in Sauchiehall Street (1911). She commissioned George Walton to take charge of the decorative schemes for the Buchanan Street tea rooms, which opened in 1896, though Mackintosh also produced mural designs for these interiors. In 1901 and 1911 she organized and ran the tea rooms for the Glasgow International Exhibitions. After the death of her husband, John Cochrane, she sold the Argyle and Buchanan Street branches (1917) and finally retired in 1919.

Widely known for her eccentric appearance (she wore crinoline dresses long after they had gone out of fashion), Cranston was a highly respected and efficient business woman, who played an important role in drawing attention to the progressive nature of art and design in Glasgow at the turn of the century.

Crawford, Cheryl

Born 1902 Died 1986
American actress, theatre director and producer who had a major influence on the US theatre of the 1930s and 1940s

Cheryl Crawford was born in Akron, Ohio. She began as an actress with the Theatre Guild in New York in 1923, and became its casting manager in 1928. She was centrally involved in some of the most important American theatrical developments of her time, including the Group Theatre (1931, with Harold Clurman and Lee Strasberg, whom she called 'the Old Testament prophets'), the American Repertory Theatre (1946, with **Eva Le Gallienne** and **Margaret Webster**) and the Actors Studio (1947).

She was an important producer in her own right, and mounted productions which ranged from the Alan Jay Lerner and Frederick Loewe musical *Brigadoon* (1947) to Bertolt Brecht's *Mother Courage* (1963), and included four plays by Tennessee Williams.

Crawford, Cindy (Cynthia Ann)

Born 1966
American supermodel, actress and television presenter

Cindy Crawford was born in de Kalb, Illinois. She was an A-grade student with plans to become a chemical engineer before being discovered by photographer Victor Skrebenski in Chicago. In 1986 she moved to New York, where she became established as a top catwalk and photographic model, notching up an unprecedented 300 magazine covers in her career. From 1991 to 1994 she was married to film actor Richard Gere.

Crawford has modelled for *Playboy* magazine and has produced exercise videos and swimsuit calendars. She starred in the film *Fair Game* (1995) with William Baldwin and appears on television as fashion presenter for MTV's *House of Style*. Her advertising contracts include Revlon (due to expire in 1996) and Pepsi.

Crawford, Joan, *originally* Lucille Fay Le Sueur

Born c.1906 Died 1977
American film actress who became the archetypal Hollywood Movie Queen

Joan Crawford was born in San Antonio, Texas. She became a chorus girl and arrived in Hollywood in 1924 to work as an extra at MGM. There she gained some recognition in films like *Our Dancing Daughters* (1928) and *Our Blushing Brides* (1930) before creating a niche for herself as the star of many formula melodramas, usually as a working-class girl with her sights set on wealth and sophistication.

Though declared 'box-office poison' in 1938, she returned as the wickedly witty husband-stealer in *The Women* (1939). Later, she continued to suffer in jewels and ermine as the older woman beset by emotional problems, in *Mildred Pierce* (1945, Academy Award) and *Whatever Happened to Baby Jane?* (1962), a stylish exercise in gothic horror, but she retired after *Trog* (1970).

Joan Crawford

An autobiography, *Portrait of Joan*, appeared in 1962 and her adopted daughter Christina wrote a scathing attack on her domestic tyranny in *Mommie Dearest* (1978).

Crawford, Ruth Porter, *also known for a time as* Ruth Crawford Seeger

Born 1901 Died 1953
American composer and musicologist credited with having a major influence on young American composers

Ruth Crawford was born in Liverpool, Ohio. She studied composition with Charles Seeger, her future husband, and became an avid collector of American folk-songs.

Crawford taught in Jacksonville, Florida, and in Chicago, and her first compositions, daringly unconventional and technically assured, date from this period. Her solitary string quartet (1931), for example, anticipates contemporary styles such as minimalism.

The Seegers' extended family, Peggy, Mike and Pete, all became singers.

Crawford, (Isabella) Valancy

Born 1850 Died 1887
Irish-born Canadian writer remembered as Canada's first important woman poet

Valancy Crawford was born in Dublin, one of 13 children of whom only three survived infancy. Her family emigrated to Canada from Dublin in 1858 and after her father's death her earnings from her writing became the only source of support for her mother and herself.

She produced a range of periodical literature, including many short stories of which a number of selections have been published. However, it is her poetry that has earned her critical recognition, although only one volume, *Old Spookses' Pass, Malcolm's Katie and Other Poems* (1884), was published during her lifetime. In her poems she imbues the Canadian landscape with a mythic significance, imaging the forces of good, evil and love in a symbolic language specific to her Canadian pioneer experience; she was described by Northrop Frye as having 'the most remarkable mythopoeic imagination in Canadian poetry'.

A revival of critical interest in her poetry during the 1970s — principally inspired by the admiration of poet and playwright James Reaney (1926–) for her work — culminated in the important Crawford Symposium of 1977 (collected papers published in Ottawa, 1979).

Cresson, Edith

Born 1934
French politician who was appointed the first
woman Prime Minister of France

Edith Cresson was born in Boulogne-sur-Seine
and educated at the École des Hautes Études
Commerciales. As an active member of the
Socialist Party, she was its youth organizer in
1975, became Mayor of Thuré in 1977, and
was elected a member of the European parliament in 1979.

She earned a reputation as a fiery socialist
equivalent of **Margaret Thatcher**, and for
more than 25 years was a close friend of President François Mitterand. She held various
portfolios during the 1980s (Agriculture
1981–3; Foreign Trade and Tourism 1983–4;
Industrial Redeployment and Foreign Trade
1984–6; European Affairs 1988–90) and was a
member of the national assembly from 1986
until her resignation and return to private
industry in 1990.

In 1991 the moderate premier Michel
Rocard resigned and she was recalled by Mitterand to become France's first woman Prime
Minister, but she too resigned the following
year.

Crispell, Marilyn, *née* Braune

Born 1947
American improvising pianist and composer who
by 1990 had emerged as one of the most
compelling talents of her generation

Marilyn Crispell studied piano at the Peabody
Institute in Baltimore, Maryland, and composition at the New England Conservatory in
Boston, but largely gave up music during her
brief marriage. In the mid-1970s she discovered modern jazz, and in particular the
music of John Coltrane, which inspired her
volcanic improvisational style.

Crispell met composer Anthony Braxton in
the later 1970s and has enjoyed a long association with his work. Her own music, as heard
on such albums as *Spirits Hung in Undrawn
Sky* (1983), *And Your Ivory Voice Sings* (1985)
and *Labyrinths* (1988), drew on Cecil Taylor's
dense, rhythmic piano playing, but within a
few years she had established her own agenda.

Crocker, Hannah Mather, *née* Mather

Born 1752 Died 1829
American advocate of women's education whose
writings were just ahead of their time

Hannah Mather was born into a wealthy Massachusetts family, but had a limited education.
She married and had 10 children. In 1810 she

wrote and published anonymously a series of
fictitious letters in defence of the Freemasons
which suggested women should take an interest in science and literature.

In 1816 she wrote a tract in the hope that
seamen would repent of their licentious habits
if the error of their ways was pointed out to
them by a woman. Two years later her *Observations on the Real Rights of Women* drew on
biblical evidence to demonstrate that women
were equal to men in intelligence and judgement.

Crompton, Richmal, *originally*
Richmal Lamburn

Born 1890 Died 1969
English writer and author of the well-known 'Just
William' *books for children*

Richmal Crompton was born in Bury, Lancashire, and educated in Lancashire and Derby
and at Royal Holloway College, London University, where she graduated in classics (1914).
She taught for some years, but was struck
down with poliomyelitis in 1923.

She published 50 adult titles thereafter but
remains best known for her 38 short-story
collections (and one novel, *Just William's
Luck*) about the perpetual schoolboy, the 11-
year-old William Brown. Children loved the
judicious deliberation with which William's
incursions and imitations are described in
their reduction of ordered adult life to chaos.

Crosby, Fanny (Frances Jane), *later*
Mrs Van Alstyne

Born 1820 Died 1915
American hymnwriter who would not allow
blindness to interfere with her activities

Fanny Crosby was born in Southeast, New
York. She was blind from infancy, and became
a pupil and teacher in New York City's Institute for the Blind.

She composed about 6,000 popular hymns,
including 'Safe in the arms of Jesus' (played
at President Grant's funeral), 'Pass me not,
O gentle Saviour' (reportedly a favourite of
Queen **Victoria**) and 'Rescue the perishing'
(prompted by her mission work on New York's
Lower East Side).

The evangelists Dwight L Moody and Ira D
Sankey acknowledged a great debt to her.

Crossley, Ada Jemima

Born 1871 Died 1929
Australian contralto who sang in seven languages
and was greatly admired for her interpretative
skills

Ada Crossley was born in Tarraville, Victoria. After promising her parents 'never to sing in opera', she left for London in 1894 to study under Sir Charles Santley, and later under Madame Blanche Marchesi, making her début at the Queen's Hall, London, in 1895. After standing in at short notice for the indisposed **Clara Butt**, she was in demand for oratorios and festivals all over Great Britain, and within two years had given five 'command performances' for Queen **Victoria**.

She toured the USA in 1902 and 1903, and recorded for the new Victor Company, later becoming an established international recording artist. Her considerable repertoire included sacred songs and ballads. She returned to Australia for two tours in 1903–4 and 1907–8, with supporting artists including the young pianist Percy Grainger (1882–1961). She later reduced her commitments but performed at many charity concerts during World War I.

Crothers, Rachel

Born 1878 Died 1958
American playwright and feminist whose works examine a woman's quest for freedom in a male-dominated society

Rachel Crothers was born in Bloomington, Illinois. In 1910 she published *A Man's World*, an attack upon moral double standards, the heroine of which proclaims herself 'a natural woman because I am a free one'; at the time this was considered an extremely important work. *Ourselves* (1913) looked at the problem of prostitution.

Crothers succeeded where many playwrights fail, managing to combine polemic with box-office success, although she increasingly veered towards lighter work, as in *As Husbands Go* (1932), which contrasts English and American marriages. While *When Ladies Meet* (1932) recalls her earlier, sharper tone, it is also outwardly a comedy.

Cruft, Catherine Holway

Born 1927
English architectural historian and curator, a leading figure in the field of conservation

Catherine Cruft was born in London and educated at Edinburgh University, where she studied social studies. She subsequently worked with the Scottish National Building Record (SNBR, now the National Monuments Record of Scotland) and the Scots Ancestry Research Society.

After two years producing lists of buildings of special interest for Edinburgh with the architect Ian Lindsay, she became the curator of the SNBR (1958). With another architect, Colin McWilliam, she developed an integrated approach to the Monuments Record, with buildings, photographs, original architectural drawings, survey drawings and biographical material kept in one location.

A leader in the conservation world, she has amassed an extensive knowledge of Scottish architectural history, and her careful representations have saved innumerable archives for the nation.

Cruz, Sor Juana Inés de la

Born 1648 Died 1695
Mexican feminist, poet and playwright, the author of key works in the history of feminism

Sor Juana Inés de la Cruz was born in San Miguel Nepantle, Amecameca, not far from Mexico City. She was a woman of legendary beauty, and has affinities with **Christine de Pisan**, being celebrated for her scholarship at an early age, and invited by the wife of the Viceroy of Mexico to live at the court. At the age of 19 she was led by disgust, probably prompted by the frivolity of court life, to enter the Carmelite Order, but the artificial rigour of that life revolted her too, and she returned to court. A year later she joined the Hieronymite convent (in which she remained) in Mexico City, on account (she declared) of her 'total lack of matrimonial ambition' and of her wish to 'live alone, in order to have no interruption to my freedom and my study'.

When instructed by a bishop, an officer of the Inquisition, to give up learning as 'unbefitting to a woman' she issued the stately *Respuesta* (1691, 'Response'), a key document in the history of feminism. With consummate irony, she pointed out that she wrote secular poetry and drama only because, as a woman, she was incapable of religious devotion — and that merely artistic heresy was not punishable by the Pope. Her own sardonic, parodic, highly erotic and mystical poetry, especially the 'Primero sueño' ('First Dream'), is individualistic and 'modern'. Her poems about male stupidity, in particular 'Rendonillas' ('Verses'), have hardly been forgiven, and have not been translated ('Stupid men, who accuse/women unreasonably/without seeing that you are the cause/of that very thing you blame —').

In one of her plays she demonstrates that her Catholicism was but skin-deep: she explains the Aztec rite of eating the Corn God as a Satanic parody of the Communion. With Christine, **Sappho**, **Laura Riding** and **Emily Dickinson**, she is amongst the greatest and least understood of all writers. She sold all her books, scientific equipment and musical instruments in order to care for the poor, and died of the plague while ministering to them.

Cullberg, Birgit Ragnhild

Born 1908
Swedish dancer, choreographer and ballet director
whose ballets are influenced by modern dance and
characterized by their strong dramatic content

Birgit Cullberg was born in Nyköping. She studied in England with Kurt Jooss (1935–9), and later in New York with **Martha Graham**. In the mid-1940s she toured the Continent with Svenska Dansteatern, a group she co-founded with Ivo Cramér.

The characteristically strong dramatic content of her ballets is often of a psycho-logical nature, and her best-known work is *Miss Julie* (1950). She was resident choreo-grapher of the Royal Swedish Ballet (1952–7), after which she freelanced for companies in-cluding American Ballet Theatre and Royal Danish Ballet.

She formed the Cullberg Ballet at the Swedish National Theatre in 1967, for which her sons Niklas and Mats Ek have danced and choreographed.

Cullis, Winifred Clara

Born 1875 Died 1956
English physiologist, a pioneer in women's
education as well as in her physiological research

Winifred Cullis was born in Gloucester. She won a scholarship to enter Newnham College, Cambridge, and passed both parts of the Natural Sciences tripos in 1899 and 1900; however she was not awarded a degree as women could not then graduate from the uni-versity.

She became a demonstrator in physiology at the London School of Medicine for Women in 1901, a lecturer in 1903, and reader and head of department in 1912, although it was not until 1919 that the University of London granted her the title and status of professor, when she became the first incumbent of the Jex-Blake Chair of Physiology. She earned a doctorate in science in 1908 and was one of the first six women to be elected to the Physio-logical Society in 1915.

She published on a wide array of physio-logical subjects, including urine secretion and the role of the nerves and blood vessels of the heart. Renowned as an inspired teacher of generations of women students, she was a founder of the Federation of University Women, and lectured to audiences as diverse

as the BBC Schools Programmes and British troops, for which she was awarded the OBE in 1929, and the CBE in 1936. She travelled extensively during World War II on behalf of the Ministry of Information and served on numerous public bodies associated with health education and the role of women in professional life.

Cummings, Constance

Born 1910
American-born British actress whose
international reputation spanned many genres

Constance Cummings was born in Seattle, but she spent most of her distinguished career in England after marrying the playwright Benn Wolfe Levy (1900–73) in 1933.

She made her début in San Diego in 1926, and after her first appearance in London in 1934, went on to build a formidable inter-national reputation in both classic and modern drama, including a number of her husband's plays.

Her many roles have included a notable success when she replaced Uta Hagen as Martha in Edward Albee's *Who's Afraid of Virginia Woolf* in London in 1964, and another in Arthur Kopit's *Wings* in New York in 1979.

Cummins, Maria Susanna

Born 1827 Died 1866
American popular novelist whose works were
always women-centred

Maria Cummins was born in Salem, Mas-sachusetts. Her first novel, *The Lamplighter* (1854), was a moralistic fable about a Boston orphan, and became a bestseller in the same way as **Susan Bogert Warner**'s *The Wide, Wide World* had done.

It was followed by the novels *Mabel Vaughn* (1857), *El Fureidis* (1860) and *Haunted Hearts* (1864), all of which focused on a female central character. Cummins also contributed to *Atlan-tic Monthly.*

Cunningham, Imogen

Born 1883 Died 1976
American photographer who earned fame for her
plant photographs

Imogen Cunningham was born in Portland, Oregon. She began taking photographs in 1901, and after working with Edward Curtis (1868–1952), she opened her own portrait studio in Seattle (1910). Her personal style then was Romantic pictorialism, particularly in still-life flower studies, and she earned a national reputation.

In 1915 she married a photographer, Roi Partridge, and moved to San Francisco. She continued with her soft-focus sentimental style until she met Edward Weston (1886–1958) and was converted to his sharply-defined images and use of precise tonal gradation. She joined his association of West Coast 'straight photography' purists, Group f/64, in 1932.

After the break-up of the Group she continued with her portrait gallery for almost another 40 years, and in her nineties was still teaching at the Art Institute in San Francisco.

Curie, Marie (Marya), *née* Skłodowska

Born 1867 Died 1934
Polish-born French radiochemist and twice Nobel Prize winner famous for her work on radioactivity

Marie Skłodowska was born in Warsaw. She was brought up in poor surroundings after her father, who had studied mathematics at the University of St Petersburg, was denied work for political reasons. After brilliant high school studies, she worked as a governess for eight years, during which time she saved enough money to send her sister to Paris to study. In 1891 she too went to Paris where she graduated in physics from the Sorbonne (1893), taking first place; she then received an Alexandrovitch Scholarship from Poland which allowed her to study mathematics.

Marie met Pierre Curie (1859–1906) in 1894 and they married the following year. In 1896, Antoine Henri Becquerel (1852–1908) discovered the radioactive properties of uranium; Marie Curie decided to study this phenomenon for her doctoral thesis topic. She used an apparatus for measuring very small electrical currents, built by her husband, to search for elements that emitted ionizing radiations. In this way she discovered that thorium is also radioactive, and she showed that the radioactivity of uranium was an atomic property, rather than the result of interactions between the element and another substance. In subsequent research she discovered that the radioactivity of the minerals pitchblende and chalcolite was more intense than could be explained by the uranium and thorium content alone, and from this deduced that these minerals must contain new radioactive elements. Pierre left his work on piezoelectricity to help in the laborious process of isolating the new elements by fractional crystallization. No precautions against radioactivity were taken, as the harmful effects were not known at that time.

Marie Curie

In 1898 Pierre and Marie announced the discovery of a new element, which they named polonium in honour of Marie's native country, and later the same year they announced the discovery of radium. In 1903 Marie presented her doctoral thesis (the first advanced scientific research degree to be awarded to a woman in France), and in the same year she was awarded the Nobel Prize for Physics with Pierre and Becquerel for their work on radioactivity. It was around this time that the Curies began to suffer from symptoms later ascribed to radiation sickness. In 1904 Pierre was awarded a new chair in physics at the Sorbonne, but in 1906 he was killed in a street accident; Marie succeeded him as Professor of Physics. She continued her work with radioactivity and in 1911 was awarded the Nobel Prize for Chemistry for her discovery of polonium and radium.

During World War I she developed X-radiography and then became director of the research department at the newly established Radium Institute in Paris (1918–34). She died of leucaemia, probably due to her long exposure to radioactivity. Her daughter **Irène Joliot-Curie** and son-in-law Frédéric Joliot-Curie followed in her footsteps in radiochemistry and also received the Nobel Prize for Chemistry.

Curtis, Jamie Lee, *married name* Lady Haden-Guest

Born 1958
American actress gradually attracting
increasingly substantial roles

Jamie Lee Curtis was born in Los Angeles. She is the daughter of actor Tony Curtis and actress Janet Leigh. In 1984 she married Christopher Haden-Guest, who succeeded to the barony on his father's death in 1996. She appeared on television as a teenager, notably in *Operation Petticoat*. Although not a conventional beauty, her striking looks and athletic physique were exploited in a series of indifferent horror films following her success in John Carpenter's *Halloween* (1978).

She began to find more substantial roles, both in comedies like *Trading Places* (1983) and *A Fish Called Wanda* (1988), and in more serious dramas like *Blue Steel* (1990). Her other films include *Perfect* (1985), *Forever Young* (1992) and *True Lies* (1994).

Cusack, (Ellen) Dymphna

Born 1902 Died 1981
Australian novelist and dramatist whose writings
reflect her commitment to political issues and
women's rights

Dymphna Cusack was born in Wyalong, New South Wales, and educated at Sydney University. She trained as a teacher and wrote 12 novels, the first of which, *Jungfrau*, was published in 1936 and dealt frankly, for its time, with sexual issues. This was followed in 1939 by *Pioneers on Parade*, written jointly with **Miles Franklin**.

Illness forced her to retire from teaching in 1944, but in 1948 she won the Sydney *Daily Telegraph* novel competition with *Come In Spinner*, written in collaboration with **Florence James**; its outspoken handling of adultery and abortion delayed its publication until 1951. An immediate success, it was the story of the intertwined lives of a group of women in wartime Sydney, and the effects of the absence of their menfolk and the presence of American servicemen, but the full text was not published until 1988.

Cusack also wrote eight plays, which illustrate her preoccupation with social and political disadvantage. Her novels and plays have been translated into over 30 languages, and her plays have been broadcast by the BBC and the ABC. She edited and introduced *Caddie, the Story of a Barmaid* (1953, filmed 1976).

Cushman, Charlotte Saunders

Born 1816 Died 1876
American actress and theatre manager acclaimed
as the first native-born star of the American
theatre

Charlotte Cushman was born in Boston. She appeared first in opera in 1834, and as Lady Macbeth in 1835. One of her early successes was as Nancy Sykes in *Oliver Twist* (1839).

She took over the management of the Walnut Street Theatre, Philadelphia, in 1842 and in 1844 accompanied the English actor William Charles Macready on a tour through the northern states. Afterwards she appeared in London, where she was well received in a range of characters that included Meg Merrilies in *Guy Mannering*, Rosalind in *As You Like It*, Lady Macbeth and Romeo, with her sister Susan playing Juliet.

She was best suited to powerfully emotional roles, and, with her tall physique and strong voice, often played male parts, such as Hamlet and Cardinal Wolsey.

Cuthbert, Betty, *known as the* Golden Girl

Born 1938
Australian sprinter whose Olympic wins marked
a comeback for Australian athletics

Betty Cuthbert was born in the Merrylands district of Sydney. As a 15-year-old schoolgirl, encouraged by her headmistress, herself a former Olympic competitor, she won the Australian junior 100 metres title in 11.3 seconds.

Shortly before the 1956 Olympic games, she broke the world record for the 200 metres; she went on to win Olympic gold medals for the 100 metres, 200 metres and 4 x 100 metres relay, setting three Olympic records and the world record for the relay. Over the next nine years she set 16 world records (11 individual and 5 relay), culminating in a fourth gold medal (for the 400 metres) at the Tokyo Olympics in 1964.

The second woman to win four track gold medals (**Fanny Blankers-Koen** was the first), in 1981 she was diagnosed as having multiple sclerosis, and she has since worked to raise public awareness of the disease.

d

Dagover, Lil, *originally* Marie Antonia Sieglinde Marta Liletts

Born 1897   Died 1980
Dutch actress who was an important star in German Expressionist cinema

Lil Dagover was born in Java, where her father was a Dutch forest ranger. She was educated in Germany, and married the actor Fritz Dagover. She broke into German films in Fritz Lang's *Harakiri* (1919), closely followed by Robert Weine's expressionist classic *Das Kabinett das Dr Caligari* (1919, *The Cabinet of Dr Caligari*).

She specialized in playing threatened heroines, and starred in a great many films made in Germany, as well as working in Sweden (1926–7) and France (1928–9). Her only American film was *The Woman from Monte Carlo* (1931). An important star of early cinema, she continued acting until just before her death.

Dai Ailian

Born 1916
Chinese dancer and choreographer who helped to bring the principles and study of western ballet to China

Dai Ailian was born in Trinidad. She trained in Britain during the 1930s with Anton Dolin, Kurt Jooss and Rudolf von Laban, then moved to work in China in 1940.

She performed in dance recitals with various groups before securing leading directorial positions in several companies and institutions, including Central Song and Dance Ensemble (1949–54) and the Beijing (Peking) Dance Academy (1954–64).

In 1959 she co-founded what is now known as the Central Ballet of China, originally an offshoot of the academy's Experimental Ballet Society, and became the company's artistic adviser, and a member of the All-China Dance Association and the International Council of Kinetography/Labanotation. Examples of her works are *Lotus Dance* and the *Women Oil-drillers' Dance*.

Dailey, Janet

Born 1944
American writer of romantic and popular fiction whose works constitute a prolific celebration of Americana

Janet Dailey was born on a farm in Storm Lake, Iowa. Until the age of 30 she worked as her husband William Dailey's secretary. Then she wrote *No Quarter Asked* (1974) and began to produce books at the rate of a dozen a year, claiming that '150 pagers' take her 9 days, and '350 pagers' between 30 and 45 days.

A strict writing schedule, the assignment of research to her husband Bill, and the publication of a fanzine *Janet Dailey Newsletter* have helped to maintain her prodigious output and success.

She has written a novel for every state in the USA (the Americana series) and also found time to compose lyrics for Country and Western songs. At its best, as in the Calder series which began with *This Calder Sky* (1981), Dailey's world is a blockbusting evocation of American grit.

D'Albret, Jeanne *see* Jeanne d'Albret

Dalrymple, Learmouth White

Born 1827   Died 1906
New Zealand teacher, writer and feminist who helped to improve her country's education system

Learmouth Dalrymple was born in Port Chalmers. Throughout her career she was committed to progressive education for girls, corresponding with the British educationalists **Dorothea Beale** and **Frances Buss**.

In the 1860s her campaign for girls' secondary schools led to the opening of the influential Otago Girls' High School in Dunedin in 1871. She also argued for the admission of women students to the new University of New Zealand and, at the other end of the educational spectrum, urged the importance of primary and nursery education. Like many women of her generation, she supported the women's suffrage movement.

Daly, Mary

Born 1928
American feminist and theological writer who has
become influential as a feminist theorist

Mary Daly was born in Schenectady, New York. She studied theology at St Mary's College, Indiana, and Fribourg University, Switzerland, and has taught at Fribourg (1959–66) and Boston College (from 1969). Having analyzed the effects of male bias in *The Church and the Second Sex* (1968), she abandoned her attempts to reform official Roman Catholic attitudes and became a post-Christian radical feminist in *Beyond God the Father* (1973). Her emphasis on pre-Jewish/Christian religion and women's personal experience is developed in *Gyn/Ecology: The Metaethics of Radical Feminism* (1978) and *Pure Lust: Elemental Feminist Philosophy* (1984).

In 1987, with Jane Caputi, she published *Webster's First New Intergalactic Wickedary of the English Language*, containing both serious and factitious reconsiderations of language, or new meanings intended to give women a positive place in society. Daly's outrageous approach reached a peak in 1992 with the publication of her autobiography: *Outercourse: the Be-dazzling Voyage: Containing Recollections from my Logbook as a Feminist Philosopher (be-ing an account of my time/space travels and ideas — then, again, now, and how)*.

d'Andrea, Novella

Born c.1350s Died c.1360s
Italian scholar, renowned for her beauty

Novella d'Andrea was born in Bologna where her father, Giovanni d'Andrea, was Professor of Canon Law at the University of Bologna. He taught her and, despite her youth, she gave lectures for him when he had to be absent from his duties, although she concealed herself behind a curtain to do so, in order that her extreme beauty might not distract the students.

She married John Caldesimus and died young. Little is known of her life and her dates are much disputed, but her story can be found in **Christine de Pisan**'s work *Le livre de la cité des dames* (1405).

Dandridge, Dorothy

Born 1920 Died 1965
American singer and actress who starred in
Carmen Jones

Dorothy Dandridge was born in Cleveland, Ohio. She was a child star in films, but broke through with adult roles in *A Day at the Races* (1937). The most strikingly beautiful African-American actress of her generation, and one of the first ever to be acclaimed a star, Dandridge had her greatest successes in *Carmen Jones* (1954) and *Porgy and Bess* (1959), though in neither case was her rather light voice used, being dubbed in by **Lena Horne** and others.

She died tragically young and an edited memoir, *Everything and Nothing: the Dorothy Dandridge Story*, appeared in 1970.

Dorothy Dandridge, 1956

Dane, Clemence, *pseud of* Winifred Ashton

Born 1888 Died 1965
English novelist, screenwriter and playwright
whose A Bill of Divorcement *achieved a long run*

Winifred Ashton was born in Blackheath, London. She took her pseudonym from the Church of St Clement Danes in The Strand. Having studied art at the Slade School, she went on stage in 1913 under the name 'Diana Cortis', but abandoned her acting career following the success of her first play, *A Bill of Divorcement* (1921), which deals sympathetically with the subject of divorce on the grounds of inherited insanity.

She went on to write two plays on literary subjects: an ingenious reconstruction of the writer's life in *Will Shakespeare* (1921), which was a critical disaster, and *Wild Decembers* (1932), about the **Brontë** sisters. She also wrote a stark tragedy entitled *Granite* (1926), *Call Home the Heart* (1927) and finally *Eighty in the Shade* (1958). Her last play was written especially for the golden wedding anniversay of the actors Lewis Casson and **Sybil Thorndike**, who created the central roles.

Her novels include *Regiment of Women* (1917), *Legend* (1919), *Broome Stages* (1931) and *The Flower Girls* (1954), the last two of which deal with theatrical families.

She was also a literary and social critic of distinction.

Daniels, Bebe (Phyliss)

Born 1901   Died 1971
American actress acclaimed on stage, screen and radio who was honoured for entertaining wartime servicemen

Bebe Daniels was born to a showbusiness family in Dallas, Texas. As a member of her father's theatre company from the age of three, she became known as 'The World's Youngest Shakespearian Actress'. She became a prolific stage performer, and is also reputed to have appeared in over 200 short silent comedies and westerns. Graduating to adult roles, she proved an accomplished comedienne and was often cast in mildly risqué roles as thrill-seeking playgirls. Her films include *Speed Girl* (1921), *Monsieur Beaucaire* (1924) and *She's a Sheik* (1928).

She survived the transition to sound, appearing in musicals like *Rio Rita* (1929) and *42nd Street* (1933), but when her Hollywood career flagged she moved to London with her husband Ben Lyon (1901–79). They remained there throughout the war years, beginning the popular radio show *Hi Gang!* in 1939 and becoming a much-loved showbusiness couple; they enjoyed long-running successes on radio and television, especially with the comedy series *Life With the Lyons* (1955–60).

A dedicated entertainer of American servicemen, she is said to have been the first woman ashore following the D-Day landings in 1944 and was awarded the American Medal of Freedom in 1946 for her war work.

Danilova, Alexandra

Born 1904
Russian dancer and teacher, one of the most popular and versatile ballerinas of her day

Alexandra Danilova was born in Peterhof (Petrodvorets). She trained at the Imperial Ballet School before joining the Maryinsky Theatre (now Kirov Ballet) in 1922. She left the then USSR on a 1924 tour, never to return. That same year she was engaged by Sergei Diaghilev for his Ballet Russe until 1929.

She was a member of Colonel de Basil's Ballet Russe (1933–8) and its splinter group the Ballet Russe de Monte Carlo (until 1952), as well as making guest appearances with many companies. She formed her own group, Great Moments of Ballet (1954–6) before retiring in 1957.

Afterwards she staged ballets for opera companies and in collaboration with George Balanchine, at whose School of American Ballet she has earned a reputation as a superb teacher.

d'Aragona, Tullia

Born 1510   Died 1556
Italian poet and courtesan

Tullia d'Aragona was born in Rome but little is known of her early years. However, in later life she was noted for her succession of lovers and for the salon she conducted in Florence.

Some of her work has survived, including a treatise about love, *Dialogo della infinità di am re* (1547), and *Il meschino d'il guerino* (1560), a narrative poem.

Darbyshire, Jane

Birthdate unavailable
British architect whose first major project set a precedent for many prize-winning designs

Jane Darbyshire graduated from Newcastle University School of Architecture in the early 1970s. She set up her own practice in 1979 and was joined by her then husband, David Darbyshire, in 1980. They won a competition in 1981 to design St Oswald's Hospice, gaining their practice positive publicity and several commissions.

The building, which reflects the sensitive, human nature of Darbyshire's design ethos, was selected RIBA (Royal Institute of British Architects) Building of the Year (1987). In 1987 her marriage and business partnership broke up and she set up a new practice with David Kendall.

She has been the recipient of RIBA or Civic awards for her work virtually every year since

1981 and in 1994 received an OBE for her service to social architecture.

Dare, Zena and Phyllis, originally Dones

Zena born 1887 Phyllis born 1890;
both died 1975
English actress-singer sisters who gained acclaim individually and together

Zena and Phyllis Dare were born in London. Zena made her début in stage musicals, particularly *An English Daisy* (1902) and *The Catch of the Season* (1904), before moving to straight theatre after her marriage in 1910. She later returned to musicals, appearing in *Careless Rapture* (1936), *King's Rhapsody* (1949) and *My Fair Lady* (1958).

Phyllis's début was as an 11-year-old in *Bluebell in Fairyland* (1901), an episode recounted in her memoir *From School to Stage* (1907; sequel *By Herself*, 1921). She joined Zena in *The Catch of the Season* (1904) and *King's Rhapsody* (1949). Her starring roles in *The Girl from Utah* (1913), *Hanky Panky* (1917) and *Lido Lady* (1926) made her a popular pin-up.

The sisters died within weeks of each other in 1975.

Dark, Eleanor, née O'Reilly

Born 1901 Died 1985
Australian writer who became one of her country's bestselling and award-winning novelists

Eleanor O'Reilley was born and educated in Sydney, the daughter of the writer Dowell O'Reilly. Employed briefly as a stenographer, she married a general practitioner, Dr Eric Dark, in 1922 and a year later moved to Katoomba in the Blue Mountains.

Her earliest writings, short stories and verse, were contributed from 1921 to various magazines, mostly under the pseudonym 'Patricia O'Rane' or 'P. O'R'. *Slow Dawning*, her first novel, was completed in 1923 but she had to wait until 1932 to see it published. Her other novels include *Prelude to Christopher* (1934), *Return to Coolami* (1936), *The Little Company* (1945), *Lantana Lane* (1959) and the trilogy, *The Timeless Land* (1941), *Storm of Time* (1948) and *No Barrier* (1953), which charts the early years of European settlement of New South Wales.

A writer of ideas, and a committed socialist and feminist, she was awarded the Australian Literature Society's Gold Medal in 1934 and 1936, and in 1978 received the Australian Society of Women Writers' Alice award.

Darling, Flora, née Adams

Born 1840 Died 1910
American writer who founded the societies Daughters of the Revolution and United States Daughters of 1812

Flora Adams was born in Lancaster, New Hampshire, and married a Southerner whose pro-Southern anti-abolitionist views she shared, but he died during the Civil War. Flora subsequently moved back from Louisiana to Washington DC where she worked as a government clerk and as a writer, expressing views — notably opposing women's suffrage — which can be characterized as reactionary.

She is mostly remembered for her active involvement in the setting up of patriotic women's societies during the 1890s. She was the first Vice-President of the Daughters of the American Revolution (1890) from which she later resigned in acrimony. She went on to found the Daughters of the Revolution (1891) and the United States Daughters of 1812 (1892).

Darling, Grace Horsley

Born 1815 Died 1842
English heroine of a 19th-century sea rescue

Grace Darling was born in Bamburgh, Northumberland. With her father, William Darling (1795–1860), she was a lighthouse keeper on one of the Farne Islands. On 7 September 1838, they rowed out in a storm to rescue the survivors of the shipwrecked *Forfarshire*. She received a medal for her bravery.

Das, Kamala

Born 1934
Indian (Malayalam) poet and novelist generally regarded as one of the best of all Indian poets

Kamala Das was born into a literary family in the southern state of Kerala. She writes her poetry in English and most of her prose in her own language (eg *My Story*, 1976, translated by herself — one of the most important Indian autobiographies ever written).

She is very highly regarded for her poetry, which is sensuous, deeply felt and technically very finely accomplished. Her novel, *Alphabet of Lust* (1977), is also a very remarkable work from an Indian woman who has been much criticized by members of her own sex in her own country for 'departing from traditional norms'.

Dashkova, Ekaterina Romanovna

Born 1743 Died 1810
Russian princess and author who was an
influential patroness of the literary arts in 18th-
century Russia

Ekaterina Romanovna was born in St Petersburg. In 1759 she married Prince Dashkov (d.1762). She was an intimate friend and leading supporter of the Empress **Catherine II** in the conspiracy that deposed her husband, Peter III, in 1762, and placed Catherine on the Russian throne.

She travelled widely in Europe, and was appointed director of the Academy of Arts and Sciences in St Petersburg (1783–96). She wrote several plays, and was the first President of the Russian Academy (1783), the foundation of which she had suggested. Its aim to promote the language and literature of Russia resulted in the publication of a Russian dictionary.

On Catherine's death in 1796 she was ordered by the new emperor, her son Paul I, to retire to her estates at Novgorod.

Daubié, Julie-Victoire

Born 1824 Died 1874
French writer and feminist, the first woman to
obtain the baccalauréat

Julie-Victoire Daubié was born in Eastern France. She had little formal education, but was taught Latin and Greek by her brother and became a governess.

In 1858 she won an essay competition organized by the Académie de Lyon. Encouraged by one of the competition judges, she sat the *baccalauréat* exam in 1861 despite government opposition, and became the first woman to obtain this qualification in 1862. She went on to pass the *licence,* a more advanced exam, in 1871.

Her writings include *La femme pauvre au XIXe siècle* (1866) and *L'émancipation de la femme* (1871).

David, Elizabeth

Born 1913 Died 1992
English cookery writer who could capture the look
of a dish in a few words, and vividly
communicated her passionate views on food

Elizabeth David was born in Sussex. At the age of 16 she was sent to live with a French family and study at the Sorbonne, and she discovered food of a kind that she had never known existed. After living on a Greek island during the 1930s and working in the Ministry of Information office in Cairo during World War II, she returned in 1946 to a Britain in the throes of food rationing.

Her early books — *Mediterranean Food* (1950), *French Country Cooking* (1951), *Italian Food* (1954) and *Summer Cooking* (1955) — did much to remind people of a culinary world not restricted by the lack of butter, cream and imported delicacies. Her work culminated in *French Provincial Cooking* (1960), a book which, together with her columns in *Vogue,* the *Sunday Times* and the *Spectator,* had untold influence on the next generation of cooks, and influenced the eating habits of many Britons. It is a work of reference as well as a collection of recipes, like her authoritative *English Bread and Yeast Cookery* (1977).

David-Neel, Alexandra

Born 1868 Died 1969
French oriental scholar who travelled widely in
Tibet and elsewhere

Alexandra David-Neel was born in Paris. She studied Sanskrit in Sri Lanka and India, and toured internationally as an opera singer. She married an engineer, Phillippe François Neel, who was to be her main sponsor in Tunis in 1904, but she continued to study and travel in Europe until 1911 when she returned to India, visiting the Dalai Lama in exile at Darjeeling and studying Tibetan Buddism.

Invited to Sikkim, she over-wintered in a high mountain cave with a holyman and her life-long servant, Yongden. Having travelled illegally to Tashilhumpo in Tibet, she was expelled from India in 1916 and went to Burma, Japan and Korea with Yongden, arriving in Beijing on 8 October 1917. Together they travelled 2,000 miles to the Kumbum monastery near the Koko Nor and on to Chengdu through northern Tibet, Mongolia and across the Gobi Desert before she donned the disguise of a Tibetan pilgrim, as described in *My journey to Lhasa* (1927).

They returned to Tibet in 1934 to work at Kanting until forced to leave by the Japanese advance of 1944, and retired to Digne in France, where she died aged 100 years.

Davies, Betty

Born 1935
English fashion designer based in Scotland whose
trademark fabrics are tartan, Harris tweed
and silk

Betty Davies was born in Nottingham. She studied at the Guildhall School of Music in London and worked in public relations before founding the Campus group in 1966. In 1987 she launched her award-winning designer label, The Academy Collection, in Glasgow and Paris, and in 1989 the Betty Davies Tartan, winning the Scottish Style award the same year.

She has based her later work on designing Harris tweed as a fashion fabric, specially woven and manufactured for her in the Western Isles. She also works in silk. Hers is now the Betty Davies label, and her clients include **Evelyn Glennie** and **Elizabeth Harwood**. Her projects have included designing new tartans for Japan. She was appointed Governor of the Edinburgh College of Art in 1989.

Davies, Christian, *known as* Mother Ross

Born 1667   Died 1739
Irish woman soldier who served for many years in the army disguised as a man

Christian Davies was born in Dublin, where she inherited an inn. She went to Flanders in search of her husband, Richard Welsh, who had been pressed into Marlborough's army, and enlisted as a private under the name of Christopher Welsh. She fought in the battle of Blenheim (1704) and other battles, and eventually was reunited with her husband in 1706.

Following his death at the battle of Malplaquet (1709), she married a grenadier, Hugh Jones, who was killed the following year. She returned to England to be presented to Queen **Anne**, and then went back to Dublin where she married another soldier, called Davies. She died in Chelsea Pensioners' Hospital for old soldiers.

Davies, (Sarah) Emily

Born 1830   Died 1921
English feminist and champion of educational reform, especially university places for women

Emily Davies, the aunt of **Margaret Llewellyn Davies**, was born in Southampton. She became a vigorous campaigner for higher education for women and joined the feminists **Barbara Bodichon** and **Elizabeth Garrett Anderson**. Later she campaigned with **Dorothea Beale** and **Frances Buss** for women to gain admittance to university examinations (1864–8).

In 1869 she founded a small college for women students at Hitchin, which was transferred to Cambridge as Girton College in 1873. She was mistress of Girton from 1873 to 1875, and honorary secretary from 1882 to 1904. As a member of the London School Board (1870–3), she agitated for London degrees for women, which were granted in 1874.

She wrote *The Higher Education of Women* (1866) and *Thoughts on Some Questions Relating to Women, 1860–1908* (1910).

Davies, Laura

Born 1964
English golfer who won the US Open within two years of turning professional

Laura Davies was born in Coventry. She has never had a year without a win since turning professional in 1985, taking the British Open title at Birkdale in 1986 and winning the US Open the year after when she did not even possess an American player's card. (This is a qualification that has to be earned each year to signify the player's suitability to enter the professional circuit. A player without one is not expected to win.)

She has an impeccable Solheim Cup record, winning all three of her points at the Dalmahoy event to take her total points to five out of six. It was this feat which prompted Trish Johnson to describe her as 'the best golfer in the world'. One of her shots in a long driving contest in 1988 at Stoke Poges was measured at 284 yards (256m).

Christian Davies

Davies, Siobhan, *originally* Susan Davies

Born 1950
English choreographer and dancer who in 1993
won the Laurence Olivier Award for Outstanding
Achievement in Dance

Siobhan Davies was born in London. She was one of the first to study with the London Contemporary Dance Theatre (LCDT) Company in the late 1960s, and began to choreograph early on in her career, becoming resident choreographer with the company in 1971, when she retired as a dancer. She created 17 pieces for LCDT including *New Galileo* (1984) and *Bridge the Distance* (1985). While still at LCDT, she also worked under commission for Ballet Rambert (*Celebration*, 1979), ran the dance company Siobhan Davies and Dancers for a short period during 1981, and became a founding member of Second Stride (a development of Richard Alston's Strider) in 1982, for which she made six pieces.

Working in a style which ranges from personal to abstract, she is also eclectic in her choice of music which includes scores by Benjamin Britten, Michael Nyman and Brian Eno. In 1987 she left LCDT and travelled to the USA on a Fullbright Arts Fellowship with her husband, photographer David Buckland, with whom she also has a working relationship. In 1988 she formed the Siobhan Davies Dance Company, and from 1989 to 1993 was associate choreographer for Ballet Rambert.

Her work often uses living writers and musicians and includes *Wyoming* (1988) and *Arctic Heart* (1991), both to music by John-Marc Gowans, *White Man Sleeps* (1988), *Different Trains* (1990), which combines live and taped music in the score by Steve Reich, and *Winnsboro Cotton Mill Blues* (1992).

Davis, Angela

Born 1944
African-American activist and educator who was
a key campaigner for civil rights in her twenties

Angela Davis was born in Birmingham, Alabama. She was educated at the Sorbonne in France and Brandeis University, and soon began to take part in radical protest and the civil rights movements. In the late 1960s she became involved with the Student Nonviolent Coordinating Committee and the Black Panthers, and in 1968 she joined the Communist Party.

Her activist activities with the Black Panthers led her to support black political prisoners. She was arrested on charges of conspiracy, kidnapping and murder in 1970,

but after a 10-month trial she was acquitted of all charges.

As well as teaching at the University of California, Santa Cruz, she serves on the executive boards of the National Political Caucus of Black Women and the National Black Women's Health Project. Among her many books are *Women, Race and Class* (1981) and *If They Came in the Morning: Voices of Resistance* (1971).

Davis, Bette (Ruth Elizbeth)

Born 1908   Died 1989
American actress and 'first lady of the American
screen' who excelled in her intense portrayals of
strong women

Bette Davis was born in Lowell, Massachusetts. After studying at the John Murray Anderson school, she worked with repertory and summer stock companies before a screen test led to a film contract and her début in *Bad Sister* (1931).

She became highly dedicated, and with her electrifying style she illuminated a vast gallery of characters, bringing an emotional honesty to the most unprepossessing of melodramas. A prime box-office attraction between 1937 and 1946, she was nominated on 10 occasions for the Academy Award, winning for *Dangerous* (1935) and *Jezebel* (1938). Latterly she appeared more often on television, and won an Emmy for *Strangers* (1979).

She was married four times, and wrote several volumes of autobiography: *The Lonely Life* (1962), *Mother Goddam* (1975, with Whitney Stine) and *This 'n' That* (1987, with Michael Herskowitz). In 1977 she became the first woman to receive the American Film Institute's Life Achievement Award.

Davis, Judy

Born 1955
Australian stage and film actress who came to
fame with her role in My Brilliant Career

Judy Davis was born in Perth. She sang in jazz and pop groups, studied at the National Institute of Dramatic Arts in Sydney (1974–7) and made her film début in *High Rolling* (1976). She then worked with the Adelaide State Theatre Company, appearing in such plays as *Visions* (1978).

Her performance as the strong-willed, 19th-century heroine of the film *My Brilliant Career* (1979) earned her international attention. An uncompromising actress, she has portrayed a range of forceful individuals in such films as *Winter of Our Dreams* (1981) and *Heatwave* (1981) whilst continuing a parallel stage career with *Piaf* (1980), *Lulu* (1981) and *Insignificance* (London, 1982).

Her work in *A Passage to India* (1984) brought her an Academy Award nomination but she spurned international offers in order to appear in Australian films like *Kangaroo* (1986) and *High Tide* (1987). Later films include *Barton Fink* (1991), *The Naked Lunch* (1991) and *Husbands and Wives* (1992).

Davis, Katherine Bement

Born 1860 Died 1935
American social worker, prison governor and prison reformer

Katherine Davis was born in Buffalo, New York, and grew up in Rochester, studying at Rochester Free Academy. She taught from 1880 to 1890, then studied at Vassar from 1890 to 1892. Her interest in chemistry led to an interest in providing nutrition on a small income, and so she turned to social work in Philadelphia.

She studied for her doctorate in political economy at Chicago University (1897–1900) and afterwards became superintendent of a new women's reformatory at Bedford Hills, New York (1901–14), where she instituted a modern rehabilitative regime. After chairing the New York City Parole Board from 1915 to 1917, she worked for the Rockefeller Foundation's Bureau of Social Hygiene (1917–28).

Davison, Emily

Born 1872 Died 1913
English suffragette who was trampled by the King's horse

Emily Davison was born in Blackheath and educated at the universities of London and Oxford. In 1906 she became a militant member of the Women's Social and Political Union (WSPU). Her activities included stone-throwing, setting alight letterboxes and attacking a Baptist minister whom she mistook for Lloyd George.

Frequently imprisoned, she often resorted to hunger-striking, and was repeatedly forcefed. Once, while in Holloway prison, she attempted suicide in protest against forcefeeding. In 1913 she went to the Derby and, wearing a WSPU banner, tried to catch the reins of the King's horse, but she was trampled underfoot and died several days later.

Dawes, Sophia, Baronne de (Baroness of) Feuchères

Born 1790 Died 1840
English adventuress who graduated from the workhouse to the French court through being the mistress of the last prince of Condé

Sophia Dawes was born in St Helens on the Isle of Wight, the daughter of a drunken fisherman, and was brought up an inmate in a workhouse. She became an officer's mistress, a servant in a brothel, and then mistress to the Duc de Bourbon, who later became the ninth and last Prince de Condé. Through him she received an excellent education and then she was taken to Paris and in 1818 provided with a military husband, Adrien-Victor de Feuchères, who thinking Condé was her father, was appointed his aide-de-camp and created a baron.

Baronne de Feuchères grew in popularity at the court of Louis XVIII, until her husband discovered the true nature of her relationship with Condé, left her, and informed the King, who banished her from the court. Her status was sufficient however to secure a bequest from Condé of 10 million francs in 1829, which ensured her reception at Charles X's court. The following year Condé planned to leave France, but was found hanging dead in his home. Suspected of murder though not prosecuted, the baroness responded to the Parisiens' dislike of her and retired to London.

Day, Doris, *originally* Doris von Kappelhoff

Born 1924
American singer and vivacious film actress who continued her nationwide popularity into the 1960s

Doris Day was born in Cincinnati. She became a vocalist with several big bands and a radio favourite in the 1940s, and made her film début in *Romance on the High Seas* (1948). Her sunny personality, singing talent and girl-next-door image made her an asset to many standard Warner Brothers musicals of the 1950s. More satisfying material followed with *Calamity Jane* (1953), *Young at Heart* (1954) and *The Pajama Game* (1957).

A top-selling recording artist, she was also able to prove her dramatic worth in *Storm Warning* (1950) and *Love Me or Leave Me* (1955). The popularity of the lightweight sex comedy *Pillow Talk* (1959) earned her an Academy Award nomination and a further career as the perennial virgin in a series of frothy farces in which she was often partnered by Rock Hudson. She retired from the screen after *With Six You Get Egg Roll* (1968), but appeared occasionally on television and also in *The Doris Day Show* (1968–73).

Her autobiography, *Doris Day, Her Own Story* (1976), revealed much of the personal heartache and turmoil beneath her apparently carefree vivacity.

Day, Dorothy

Born 1897 Died 1980
American writer and radical social reformer
whose life was devoted to the practical application
of her political and religious beliefs

Dorothy Day was born in Brooklyn, New York. She became a socialist, and worked in the New York slums as a probationary nurse. Converted to Catholicism in 1927, she co-founded the monthly *Catholic Worker* in 1933, drawing on her earlier experience as a reporter on Marxist publications like *Call* and *The Masses* in lower east side Manhatten.

Under the influence of the French itinerant priest Peter Maurin (1877–1949), she founded the Catholic Worker Movement, which established 'houses of hospitality' and farm communities for people hit by the Depression. This experience is described in her *House of Hospitality* (1939). As a pacifist, and a fervent supporter of farm-worker unionization in the 1960s, she also helped turn her church's attention to peace and justice issues.

Her autobiography, *The Long Loneliness*, was published in 1952. Other works include the autobiographical novel *The Eleventh Virgin* (1924) and *On Pilgrimage: the Sixties* (1972).

Deamer, (Mary Elizabeth Kathleen) Dulcie

Born 1890 Died 1972
New Zealand-born Australian journalist, poet,
playwright and novelist who did much to
encourage literate women of her time

Dulcie Deamer was born in Christchurch. At the age of 17 she won a short-story competition run by the Australian magazine *Lone Hand*. Her winning story is included in the collection *In the Beginning: Six Studies of the Stone Age* (1909, reprinted, with illustrations by Australian artist Norman Lindsay as *As It Was in the Beginning*, 1929). Deamer then joined a theatrical touring company, married the business manager and, when her husband died, sent their six children home to New Zealand to be brought up by her mother.

She toured China, Burma and India with another company and then settled in Sydney in the early 1920s, where she joined Lindsay's artistic and literary circle and became known as the 'Queen of Bohemia'. Her frenetic and heterosexual lifestyle has caused her to be shunned by some modern feminist commentators, despite the fact that she was an encouragement to other literate women.

Her poems and novels deal mainly with mythology and with classical times; an early book of verse, *Messalina* (1932), contained portraits of classical and historic women. Another collection of poems was *The Silver Branch* (1948). Her novels include *The Suttee of Safa: A Hindoo Romance* (1913), *The Street of the Gazelle* (1922) and *The Devil's Saint* (1924). One of her plays, *Easter*, a morality play, was included in *Best Australian One-Act Plays* (1937).

Dean of Thornton-le-Fylde, Brenda Dean, Baroness

Born 1943
English trade union leader who became nationally
known during the SOGAT dispute with the
Murdoch empire

Brenda Dean was born in Manchester. After leaving school in 1959 she became an employee of the printing trade union SOGAT, and slowly rose to prominence. She was secretary of the Manchester branch from 1976 to 1983, when she became president of the renamed and reconstituted SOGAT '82.

From 1985 to 1991 she held the highest post, that of general secretary, and became a national figure during the printers' dispute with Rupert Murdoch's News International. She then became Deputy Chairman of the Graphical Paper and Media Union (1991–2), but resigned on being unsuccessful in the leadership contest. In 1993 she became Chairman of the independent telephone watchdog, the Independent Committee for Supervision of Standards of Telephone Information Services and that same year was awarded a life peerage.

Dean, Laura

Born 1945
American dancer, choreographer and teacher who
makes dances for her own company and for others

Laura Dean was born in Staten Island, New York. She studied at Manhattan's High School of Performing Arts and School of American Ballet, danced in Paul Taylor's company (1965–6) and worked with **Meredith Monk**, Kenneth King and Robert Wilson.

She began choreographing in 1967, developing a style all her own based on an interest in simple, repetitive movement — spinning, stamping, jumping — aligned to rhythmic music. Formed in 1976, Laura Dean Dancers and Musicians mainly features her own scores and those of composer Steve Reich. The other companies for which she has made dances include Joffrey Ballet and New York City Ballet.

Deane, Helen Wendler

Born 1917   Died 1966
American histochemist who worked on the fine
structure of several mammalian tissues

Helen Wendler Deane was born in Massachusetts and educated at Wellesley College. She gained her PhD from Brown University in 1944, married Dr George Markham in 1947, and joined the Department of Anatomy at Harvard.

In 1957 she moved to the Albert Einstein College of Medicine in New York as Professor of Anatomy, although during the McCarthyite era (1954–7) her appointment was allowed to lapse because of her strongly held views on social injustice.

She taught a wide variety of undergraduate and graduate classes in addition to serving on the editorial boards of several books and journals until her early death from cancer.

de Beauvoir, Simone *see* Beauvoir, Simone de

de Blois, Natalie *see* Blois, Natalie de

Deborah

Born 1209BC   Died 1169BC
Biblical character who was respected as a judge
and victorious in battle

Deborah was the wife of Lappidoth, from the tribe of Issachar, and a prophetess and leader of Israel. As a 'judge' she was consulted about inter-tribal disputes and turned to when all Israel was oppressed by the Canaanites.

Deborah accompanied Barak in a military victory that was aided by a tremendous storm disabling the enemy's chariots. The story of the battle and the subsequent murder of Canaanite general Sisera by **Jael** is told in the book of Judges, both in prose and in Deborah's 'song' of victory. The latter is a very early example of Hebrew poetry.

Deffand, Marie de Vichy-Chamrond, Marquise du

Born 1697   Died 1780
French salon hostess who also maintained a lively
correspondence with prominent social and
literary figures of the time

Marie de Vichy-Chamrond was educated in a Paris convent and as a girl she became famous for her wit, audacity and beauty. In 1718 she married the Marquis du Deffand, but they soon separated, and for a number of years she ran a brilliant salon frequented by leading figures in Paris literary society.

She was a correspondent of Voltaire, and of the philosophers Montesquieu and d'Alembert. In 1753 she became blind, and in 1754 invited Mademoiselle de **Lespinasse** to live with her and help her to preside over her salon. Ten years later Mademoiselle de Lespinasse departed after a quarrel, taking away with her d'Alembert and others of the elder lady's former admirers.

From 1766 Madame du Deffand corresponded with Horace Walpole, who offered help when she fell into financial trouble.

DeGaetani, Jan

Born 1933   Died 1989
American mezzo-soprano whose premature death
was a major loss to American music

Jan DeGaetani was born in Massilon, Ohio, and educated at the Juilliard School in New York City. She made her professional début aged 25 and became associated with the avant-garde.

In 1970 she premiered George Crumb's *Ancient Voices of Children* in Washington DC. Three years later, she gave the first performance of Peter Maxwell Davies's *Stone Litany*. She also performed and recorded a wide range of classical songs and lieder, including the works of Schubert, Wolf and Schoenberg. In 1980 she published *The Complete Sightsinger*, based on her master-classes.

de Gouges, Olympe *see* Gouges, Olympe de

de Gournay, Marie le Jars *see* Gournay, Marie le Jars de

De Havilland, Olivia Mary

Born 1916
American actress whose lasting fame began in
films with Errol Flynn in the 1930s

Olivia De Havilland was born in Tokyo, Japan, of British parentage, and raised in California. Her early stage appearances with the Saratoga Community players brought her to the attention of Max Reinhardt (1873–1943), who cast her in both his stage and film versions of *A Midsummer Night's Dream* (1935).

Signed to a long-term contract with Warner Brothers, she first acted with Errol Flynn in the swashbuckler *Captain Blood* (1935). She was to star with him in six more films, her demure charm matching his reckless bravado. Her role as Melanie in *Gone With the Wind*

(1939) established her claim to greater consideration, but it was not until after World War II and her release from Warner Bros (1942) that her career entered its richest phase.

She won Oscars as a self-sacrificing unwed mother in *To Each His Own* (1946) and as an emotionally vulnerable 'ugly-duckling' in *The Heiress* (1949). After her marriage to Paris Match editor Pierre Galante in 1955, her film appearances grew rare, though she appeared in the gothic *Hush. . .Hush, Sweet Charlotte* (1964) at the behest of **Bette Davis** to replace the ailing **Joan Crawford**. Turning to television during the 1970s, she put her increasing resemblance to **Elizabeth**, the Queen Mother, to good use, playing that role in *The Royal Romance of Charles and Diana* (1982), and she also appeared in the story of the romance between Edward VII and Mrs Simpson in *The Woman He Loved* (1988).

Déjazet, (Pauline) Virginie

Born 1798   Died 1875
French actress who became famous for her impish approach to characterization, particulary in breeches roles

Virginie Déjazet was born in Paris. From the age of five she played children's roles with marvellous precocity, and later became famous for her soubrette and 'boy' parts (*déjazets*), which included the young Napoleon in *Bonaparte à Brienne, ou Le Petit Caporal* (1830, 'Bonaparte at Brienne, or the Little Corporal').

She established herself as a leading actress at the Palais-Royal, and later performed at the Variétés and the Gaîté before taking over the management, with her son, of the Folies-Nouvelles (1859–68), renamed the Théâtre Déjazet.

De Keersmaeker, Anne Teresa

Born 1960
Belgian dancer and post-modern choreographer whose dances incorporate features of both American and European styles

Anne De Keersmaeker was born in Mechelen. She studied at the Mudra School in Brussels, and in New York, and created a style which blends the abstract qualities of new American dance with the Expressionist energies of Europeans like **Pina Bausch**.

Her own company, Rosas, premiered in 1983 with *Rosas Danst Rosas*. She has set her pieces to both minimalist and classical music and has used film and speech in her work.

Her recent interests in dance theatre led to a staging of *Verkommenes Ufer Medeamaterial Landschaft mit Argonauten* by German writer Heiner Müller. Other work includes *Elena's Aria* (1984) and *Bartók/Aantekeningen* (1986), a piece about the modern woman which transforms high-heeled restriction into schoolgirl freedom with precision choreography.

Delafield, E M, *pseud of* Edmée Elizabeth Monica Dashwood, *née* de la Pasture

Born 1890   Died 1943
English novelist whose largely autobiographical books about provincial ladies brought her fame

Edmée de la Pasture was born in Llandogo, Monmouthshire. During World War I she worked first as a nurse and then at the Ministry of National Service in Bristol until the end of the war. When she began to write, she anglicized her name to avoid confusion with her mother, also a novelist. Her first novel was published in 1917, but her first real success came with *Messalina of the Suburbs* (1924), based on a famous murder case.

The Diary of a Provincial Lady (1930) brought her to the attention of a wider public, and was the first in a series which included *The Provincial Lady in America* (1934). As the titles suggest, her books examine the intricacies of provincial life; they enjoyed even greater popularity in the USA than in Britain. She also wrote three plays and a study of the **Brontë** sisters.

De La Huntly, Shirley Barbara, *née* Strickland

Born 1925
Australian athlete, the first Australian woman to win an Olympic track and field medal

Shirley De La Huntly was born in Guildford, Western Australia, the daughter of a professional male runner.

Over the course of three Games from 1948 to 1956, she won seven Olympic medals, specializing in the 80 metres hurdles, 200 metres and 100 metres sprint. A re-read of the photo finish at the 1948 Games suggests that she should have taken a bronze in the 200 metres, unofficially taking her medal total to eight.

She also set world record times on successive days in the 80 metres hurdles at the Helsinki Olympics in 1952. Since retiring she has been involved in promoting junior competition.

Delaney, Shelagh

Born 1939
English playwright and screenwriter whose early
work was linked with that of the British social
dramatists

Shelagh Delaney was born in Salford, Lancashire. She left school at 16 and a year later
completed her first and still best-known play,
A Taste of Honey. Produced in London in 1958,
it tells the story of a young white girl's abrasive
home life and her pregnancy following a
casual affair with a black sailor.

It was immediately seen as part of a young,
'angry' movement that dealt realistically with
working-class, provincial life and included the
playwrights John Osborne and Arnold
Wesker.

None of Delaney's more recent writing has
achieved equal critical acclaim or notoriety.
Among her later work is the screenplay for
Dancing with a Stranger (1985), a film depicting
the fraught life of **Ruth Ellis**, who murdered
her lover and became the last woman to be
hanged in England.

Delany, Mary, *née* Granville

Born 1700   Died 1788
English poet who was a prominent member of the
'bluestocking' circle

Mary Granville was born in Coulston, Wiltshire, the niece of Lord Lansdowne. In 1718
she married her first husband, Alexander Pen-
darves (1659–1724), and in 1743 her second,
the Irish divine Rev Patrick Delany (1685–
1768), who was a friend of Jonathan Swift and
the author of a dozen volumes.

After her husband's death she lived chiefly
in London. Her admired 'paper-mosaics', or
flower work, have long since faded, but she is
remembered through her patronage of **Fanny
Burney**, whom she introduced to court, and
by her *Autobiography and Correspondence* (6
vols, 1861–2), which paints a lively picture of
the 18th-century literary and social circles in
which she moved.

De La Roche, Mazo

Born 1885   Died 1961
Canadian novelist remembered for her
'Jalna' books

Mazo De La Roche was born in Newmarket,
Ontario. She wrote *Jalna* (1927), the first of a
series of 16 romantic family history novels
that covered 150 years of the Whiteoak family,
who lived on an estate named 'Jalna'. *Whiteoaks* (1929) was dramatized with considerable success in 1936 and a film, *Jalna*, was

made in 1935. She also wrote children's stories,
history and travel books and an autobiography, *Ringing the Changes* (1957).

Delaunay, Sonia Terk, *née* Stern

Born 1885   Died 1979
Russian-born French painter and textile designer
of international importance

Sonia Stern was born in the Ukraine, the
daughter of a factory owner, and brought up
in St Petersburg. She studied art at Karlsruhe
and in Paris, where she attended the Académie
de la Palette in 1905. In 1909 she made a marriage of convenience with the art critic
Wilhelm Uhde, but that soon ended, and in
1910 she married the French painter Robert
Delaunay.

Together they founded the movement
known as Orphism, and in 1918 they designed
sets and costumes for Sergei Diaghilev's Ballet
Russe. Her textile designs were included in
the important 'Exposition des Arts Décoratifs'
in 1925.

Deledda, Grazia

Born 1875   Died 1936
Italian novelist who received the 1926 Nobel Prize
for Literature for her Sardinian peasant stories

Grazia Deledda moved to Rome after her marriage in 1900, but her work in the next 20
years focused on peasant stories of her native
Sardinia.

She won a considerable reputation for the
lyricism and intensity of novels like *Cenere*
(1904, 'Ashes'), *L'edera* (1908, 'Ivy'), *Marianna
Sirca* (1915) and *La madre* (1920, 'The
Mother'). Her later books left the Sardinian
setting, but were similar in style. The
posthumous *Cosima* (1937) is autobiographical.

Delilah

Biblical character in the Old Testament

Delilah's story in Judges 16 tells how, at the
instigation and bribery of the Philistines, she
enticed Samson, who loved her, to reveal the
secret of his great strength. This was his hair,
which his Nazirite vow, dedicating him to
sacred service for life, forbade him to cut.

Whilst he lay asleep Delilah treacherously
cut his hair to weaken him so that the Philistines could seize and blind him and set him
to work grinding corn in prison. In time,
however, his hair grew back and the Lord
answered his prayer to give him the strength
to pull down the Philistines' temple on them
and himself.

Della Casa, Lisa

Born 1919
Swiss soprano who was noted for her singing of
roles by Mozart and Strauss

Lisa Della Casa was born in Burgdorf near
Berne. She studied in Zürich, and first
appeared at Solothurn-Biel in 1943, subsequently joining the company at the Stadt-
theater, Zürich. Her appearance at the
Salzburg Festival of 1947 led to her engagement with the Vienna State Opera Company.

A noted singer of Mozart, she also specialized in the operas of Richard Strauss, and
shares with **Lotte Lehmann** the distinction of
having sung all three soprano roles in *Der
Rosenkavalier*. She retired in 1974.

Deloria, Ella

Born 1889 Died 1971
American linguist, ethnologist and novelist who
devoted her life's work to preserving the culture
and language of the Dakota people

Ella Deloria was born at White Swan on the
Standing Rock Sioux reservation in South
Dakota, and grew up in a family where traditional Dakota (Sioux) culture merged with
Episcopal Protestantism. After graduating
from Columbia University, she worked for
many years in collaboration with the anthropologist, Franz Boas, gathering material on the
Dakota language and culture she was passionate to preserve.

These researches led to the publication of
Dakota Texts (1932), a bilingual collection of
traditional stories, *Dakota Grammar* (1941)
and *Speaking of Indians* (1944), a description
of Dakota culture written for the popular
market. Her novel, *Waterlily*, written in the
1940s but unpublished until 1988, is set in the
19th century before white impingement on
Dakota culture; more than simply an ethno-
graphic record, it vividly dramatizes the
everyday life of the Dakotas from the often-
overlooked perspective of the women of the
tribe.

Deloria also compiled a Dakota–English dictionary and translated several oral narratives
and autobiographies.

Delorme, Marion

Born 1613 Died 1650
French courtesan and salon hostess who attracted
the leading literary and political figures of
the day

Marion Delorme was born in Paris where at
an early period of her life her beauty and wit
gathered a group of high-born lovers round

her — among them the 1st Duke of Buckingham, Saint-Évremond, the Duc de Brissac
and the Duc de Gramont. Even Richelieu was
not insensible to her charms, and caused her
to be separated from the Marquis de Cinq-
Mars, whose mistress she was until he was
executed for treason in 1642.

During the early days of the Fronde uprising (1648–53), her house was the rallying-
point of its chief rebels, and Mazarin was
about to imprison her when she suddenly
died.

De Los Angeles, Victoria *see* Los Angeles, Victoria de

De Mille, Agnes

Born 1909 Died 1993
American dancer, choreographer and writer who
choreographed several outstandingly successful
musicals

Agnes De Mille was born in New York City, a
niece of the film director Cecil B De Mille.
After graduating from the University of California, she went to London and danced with
Marie Rambert's company in the original
production of Antony Tudor's *Dark Elegies*.
Three Virgins and a Devil (1941) marked her
breakthrough into choreography and, with
Broadway in her sights, she moved into show
business.

Irrepressible, she went on to choreograph
for such hit musicals as *Oklahoma* (1943),
Carousel (1945), *Brigadoon* (1947), *Gentlemen
Prefer Blondes* (1949) and *Paint Your Wagon*
(1951). She was also known for her wit and
eloquent public speaking, and her contribution to television and film.

Her books include *Dance to the Piper* (1952),
The Book of Dance (1963) and *American Dances*
(1980).

De Morgan, Evelyn, *née* Pickering

Born 1855 Died 1919
English painter whose successful career began in
1875 with winning the Slade Scholarship for a life
drawing

Evelyn Oickering was the daughter of a
wealthy lawyer and niece of the artist Roddam
Spencer-Stanhope. After receiving an exceptionally broad education for a girl of the time,
she studied at the Slade School of Art and then
studied further in Rome (1875–7). Her work
at this time reflected an influence of Italian
art, but her later works became more allegorical and Pre-Raphaelite in style and
content.

In 1887 she married the potter William de

Morgan, and from 1893 to 1908 they lived in Florence where William began his career as a writer. Although the sale of Evelyn's paintings had previously provided their income she became increasingly reluctant to exhibit them as the necessity to sell them decreased with her husband's success as a writer. She died within a year of her husband in 1919.

de Méricourt, Théroigne *see*
Méricourt, Théroigne de

Dench, Dame Judi(th Olivia)

Born 1934
English stage, film and television actress and director, one of Britain's most distinguished classical actresses

Judi Dench was born in York and trained at the Central School of Speech Training and Dramatic Art. She made her stage début as Ophelia in *Hamlet* in Liverpool in 1957, joined the Old Vic Company (1957–61) and as her career progressed, appeared with all of the most prestigious theatre companies.

Her distinctive voice, feline features and versatility have brought warmth and emotional veracity to a kaleidoscope of characters from the sensual to the homely. A selection of her numerous stage appearances includes *Macbeth* (1963), *Cabaret* (1968), *The Good Companions* (1974), *Mother Courage* (1984), *Antony and Cleopatra* (1987), *The Plough and the Stars* (1991) and Peter Shaffer's *The Gift of the Gorgon* (1993). Her television credits encompass many individual plays and the popular situation comedy *A Fine Romance* (1981–4) in which she co-starred with Michael Williams (1935–), her husband since 1971. She made her film début in *The Third Secret* (1964) but only became a regular film performer in the 1980s, with incisive character parts in *A Room With a View* (1985), *A Handful of Dust* (1987) and *Henry V* (1989).

She was created DBE in 1988 and made her directorial début in the same year with a production of *Much Ado About Nothing* for Kenneth Branagh's Renaissance Theatre Company. She also directed *Look Back In Anger* for them in 1989. In 1991 in Regent's Park in London she directed *The Boys From Syracuse*, a Rodgers and Hammerstein musical based on *The Comedy of Errors*, and continued to appear in many stage performances.

Deneuve, Cathérine, *originally*
Cathérine Dorléac

Born 1943
French actress who has been a leading screen personality since the 1960s

Cathérine Dorléac was born in Paris into a theatrical family. Assuming her mother's maiden name, she made her film début in *Les Collégiennes* (1956) and was occasionally cast as the sister of her real-life sister, actress Françoise Dorléac (1941–67). Her own career took off with the unexpected popularity of the musical *Les Parapluies de Cherbourg* (1964).

She is a beautiful woman whose remoteness and image of exterior calm concealing passion or intrigue were seen to great effect as the role of a psychopath in *Repulsion* (1965) and a bourgeois housewife turned prostitute in *Belle de Jour* (1967). By then established as a major star, she continued her series of successes with *Tristana* (1970), *Le Sauvage* (1975), *Le Dernier Métro* (1980) and *Indochine* (1992), for which she was nominated for a Best Actress Oscar.

She has also made selective appearances in English language productions like *April Fools* (1969) and *Hustle* (1975). She was married to the photographer David Bailey from 1965 to 1970, and has a child by director Roger Vadim (1963) and another by actor Marcello Mastroianni (1972).

Denman, Lady Gertrude Mary, *née*
Pearson

Born 1884 Died 1954
English founder of the National Federation of Women's Institutes, which remains the largest women's voluntary organization in the UK

Gertrude Pearson was born in London and educated privately. In 1903 she married Thomas, 3rd Baron Denman (1874–1954), and accompanied him when he was appointed Governor General of Australia in 1911, leaving her position on the executive committee of the Women's National Liberal Federation.

Following their return to Britain, she resumed her involvement in various organizations. In 1915 she chaired a sub-committee of the Agricultural Organization Society which that year had founded the Women's Institutes. When the institutes were transferred to the Board of Agriculture in 1917, she insisted they should be self-governing; thus the National Federation of Women's Institutes was formed, with Lady Denman as Chairman until 1946. The institutes' purpose, in her eyes, was to improve the standard of women's lives through increased knowledge and training in 'citizenship'.

She was also involved in the foundation of the National Birth Control (later Family Planning) Association (Chairman from 1930), the Cowdray Club for Nurses and Professional

Women (Chairman, 1932–53), the Ladies' Golf Union (president, 1932–8) and the Women's Land Army. Appointed director of the last-mentioned in 1939, in 1945 she resigned in protest at the government's refusal to give the Land Army the grants and benefits that women in the civil defence and armed services were being given. The Women's Institute residential college in Berkshire was named Denman College in her honour in 1948.

de Noronha, Joana Paula Manso
see Noronha, Joana Paula Manso de

Deraismes, Maria

Born 1828 Died 1894
French writer, journalist and feminist, founder of the first women's rights organization in France

Maria Deraismes was well-educated and wealthy. She moved from writing theatrical criticism to political involvement in Paris, contributing during the 1860s and 1870s to the newspaper *Le Droit des femmes*. With **Paule Mink** and **Louise Michel** she founded the first French women's rights organization, the *Société pour la Revendication des Droits de la Femme*, in 1866, but it was short-lived. She went on to found the *Association pour les Droits des Femmes* in 1870, which became the *Société pour l'Amelioration du sort de la femme et la Revendication de ses Droits* (1881).

With Leon Richier she founded the more conservative *Ligue française pour les Droits des Femmes* (1870), and organized several important national and international conferences on women's rights during the 1870s and 1880s.

Some of her lectures on the position of women were later reprinted in her book *Eve dans l'humanité* (1891). A secularist, she campaigned tirelessly for the separation of Church and State.

Deren, Maya, *originally* Eleanora Derenkowsky

Born 1917 Died 1961
Ukrainian-born American filmmaker who described her work as a 'slow spiral around some central essence'

Maya Deren was born in Kiev and lived in the USA after fleeing with her parents to New York in 1922. Educated at Syracuse University, she was a left-wing activist in the 1930s and regional organizer of the Syracuse Young People's Socialist League. In 1941 she was employed by choreographer **Katherine Dunham** and began a lifelong fascination with dance and movement.

Her interest in the cinema was stimulated by Czech filmmaker Alexander Hammid (1907–) who became her second husband in 1942. They collaborated on *Meshes of the Afternoon* (1943) and *At the Land* (1944), both poetic, trance-like films that used such devices as slow motion to dispense with the conventional narrative requirements of time and space. These were followed by the dance films like *A Study in Choreography for Camera* (1945), *Ritual in Transfigured Time* (1946) and *Mediation on Violence* (1948). She described her final film, *The Very Eye of Night* (1958), to be 'the coolest, the most classicist'.

During the 1940s Deren worked tirelessly on behalf of independent, experimental cinema, establishing a national network of non-theatrical screenings and writing the pamphlet *An Anagram of Ideas on Art, Form and Film* (1946). In 1954 she established the Creative Film Foundation.

Dernesch, Helga

Born 1939
Austrian operatic soprano who has earned renown for her performances in modern German opera

Helga Dernesch was born in Vienna, where she studied at the Conservatory. She made her début in Berne (1961) and at Covent Garden in 1970.

She has sung throughout Europe and the USA, and is specially noted for her portrayals of Wagner, Strauss and the modern German repertory, having created the title role in Wolfgang Fortner's *Elizabeth Tudor* in 1972 and the role of Goneril in Aribert Reimann's *Lear* in 1978.

Since 1979 she has sung mezzo-soprano roles.

Deroin, Jeanne-Françoise

Born 1805 Died 1894
French journalist, teacher, feminist and socialist, the first woman to stand for election to the French National Assembly (1849)

Jeanne-Françoise Deroin was born in Paris. Essentially self-educated, she became a teacher and journalist. She was involved in the Saint-Simonian movement of the 1830s, editing the newspaper *La femme libre*. During the 1840s she was jailed for political activities. She was much involved with the revolutionary societies of 1848. She campaigned for women's emancipation, writing for the newspaper *La Voix des Femmes*, and founding the journal *L'Opinion des femmes* in 1849. She insisted that the complementarity of the sexes necessitated women's participation in political affairs — a participation rejected by the National Assembly (1848).

Her radical beliefs led to imprisonment, and eventually to exile in London, where she continued to publish such works as *Almanack des femmes* (1854). Her refusal to adopt her husband's surname (Desroches) after her marriage in 1832 was a source of continuing comment.

Desai, Anita, *née* Mazumdar

Born 1937
Indian novelist whose impact has extended far beyond her own country

Anita Mazumdar was born in Mussoorie, Uttar Pradesh, the daughter of a Bengali father and a German mother, and educated at Delhi University. She has written novels for adults and children as well as short stories. *Clear Light of Day* (1980) and *In Custody* (1984) were both short-listed for the Booker Prize and *The Village by the Sea* won the Guardian award for children's fiction in 1982.

Her stories often concern urban middle-class women attempting to satisfy their own needs as well as the expectations of traditional Indian society. Her later works include the novel *Baumgartner's Bombay* (1988), the grim story of a German expatriate washed up in India.

Desbordes-Valmore, Marceline

Born 1786 Died 1859
French poet who is considered a significant early exponent of vers libre

Marceline Desbordes-Valmore was born in Douai. From childhood she pursued a theatrical career, appearing in her home town and in Brussels, and eventually at the Opéra-Comique in Paris. She gave up singing around 1803, and began to devote herself seriously to poetry.

She was admired by the poet Paul Verlaine (1844–96), who identified a musicality in her verse akin to his own. Her main themes are domestic, as the titles of her collections show — *Contes et scenes de la vie de famille* ('Tales and Scenes of Family Life') and *Petits Flamands* ('Flemish Children'), for example — with much reference to romantic love and children. She also wrote one short novel, *Domenica*, published in 1885 within a collection of verse entitled *Scènes Intimes* ('Private Scenes'), and based on her experiences of life and art in bohemian circles.

Despard, Charlotte, *née* French

Born 1844 Died 1939
English social reformer and feminist who worked for the poor, for women's rights and for Irish independence

Charlotte French was a younger sister of the soldier John French, 1st Earl of Ypres (1852–1925). Due to their father's early death and mother's mental instability, she was brought up by strict relatives. She suffered an unhappy childhood and developed a rebellious nature. In 1850 she married Maximilien Despard, but was childless; instead she produced novels, such as *Chaste as Ice, Pure as Snow* (1874).

Following her husband's death in 1890 she moved to live among the poor in Nine Elms, Vauxhall, where she later provided subsidized meals and clinics, especially for young mothers. She joined the Independent Labour Party in 1902, which reflected her advocacy of women's rights, particularly suffrage. In 1907 she founded the Women's Freedom League, which, with its inclusion of such causes as women's employment, had wider aims than the **Pankhurst**s' Women's Social and Political Union, namely 'not only the votes for women, but the binding together of all womanhood for human rights'.

After World War I Despard's attention turned to international socialism and Irish self determination. She settled in Dublin (but later had to move to Belfast in 1930 following the condemnation of her visit to Russia) and supported Sinn Féin, becoming a friend of **Maud Gonne**. Her politics seriously embarrassed her brother during his viceroyalty of Ireland (1918–21).

Destivelle, Catherine

Born 1960
French rock-climber who has done much to popularize the sport

Catherine Destivelle was born in Oran, Algeria. She moved to France with her parents in her early teens, and before her seventeenth birthday had made significant climbs at Verdon, Freyr and in the Dolomites.

After her early success she lost interest in rock-climbing and became depressed, but a television contract renewed her interest and she became a professional full-time climber in 1986.

She has since taken part in competitions, advertising and filmmaking, and has acquired superstar status as a rock-climber.

Deutsch, Babette

Born 1895 Died 1982
American poet, novelist and critic whose work is
noted for its perceptive preoccupation with love,
war and desolation

Babette Deutsch was born in New York City. In 1919 she published *Banners*, her first collection of poems, in which the title piece celebrates the initial achievements of the Russian Revolution. Russia became a special interest for her. She translated Alexander Blok's *The Twelve* with a Russian scholar she later married, and continued to translate from both Russian and German.

Showing an interest in the historical place and fate of women, her *Epistle to Prometheus* (1931) is an ambitious, book-length poetic interpretation of human history. Among her novels is *A Brittle Heaven* (1926), an autobiographical tale of a writing mother, while her criticism includes the highly regarded *Poetry in Our Time* (1952). Her collected poems appeared in 1969.

de Valois, Dame Ninette *see* Valois, Dame Ninette de

Devanney, Jean

Born 1894 Died 1962
New Zealand novelist and political activist whose
radical writing addresses political and class
questions and voices a staunchly feminist
approach to the role of women

Jean Devanney was born in Ferntown, South Island, and moved to Australia in 1929. Before leaving New Zealand she had published a book of short stories and four novels, one of which, *The Butcher Shop* (1926), had the distinction of being banned in Australia, New Zealand and Nazi Germany.

Like many with her radical social beliefs, she visited the Soviet Union in the 1930s, but her continual challenging of authority caused her to be expelled from the Communist Party, though she was readmitted in 1944 and resigned in 1950. However, her proletarian sympathies, as in *Sugar Heaven* (1936), the story of industrial action in the Queensland canefields (later translated into Russian), never faltered.

De Varona, Donna

Born 1947
American swimmer, winner of 37 individual
swimming titles and two gold medals

Donna De Varona was born in San Diego, California. As a competitive swimmer, she excelled in the medley — one lap each of backstroke, breaststroke, butterfly and freestyle — for which in 1961 she set a world record time of 5 minutes 34.5 seconds.

At the 1964 Olympics, she won the first gold medal awarded to a woman for the 400-metre individual medley. She also won a gold medal in the 400-metre freestyle relay, setting another world record.

Promoting amateur and women's sports, in 1974 she co-founded the Women's Sports Foundation with **Billie Jean King** and served as its president (1974–84). As special consultant to the US Senate, she lobbied for the Amateur Sports Act and the complete implementation of Title IX of the Education Amendment of 1972, ensuring equal opportunity for women in sports in all levels of education.

She has been inducted into the International Swimming Hall of Fame (1960), the International Women's Sports Hall of Fame (1983) and the US Olympic Hall of Fame (1987).

Devoy, Susan

Born 1964
New Zealand squash player who achieved total
domination of the game in the 1980s

Susan Devoy was born in Rotorua. She came to England in 1982 aged 18 and settled in Marlow, but didn't cause a stir until she won the British championship in 1984.

Improving steadily throughout her career, she won the world championship in 1985 and went on to take the world title another four times and the British Open another seven times, becoming the fourth-top winner of the title of all time, male or female, before she took a complete rest to start a family.

A classically beautiful squash player, who was also noted for her dark good looks, she was the first New Zealand woman to win the world championships.

Dexter, Caroline, *née* Harper

Born 1819 Died 1884
English-born Australian writer and feminist

Caroline Harper was born in Nottingham, and educated in England and in Paris. Having married in 1843, she emigrated to Sydney in Australia in 1855 to join her husband, the artist William Dexter, who had gone there in 1852.

After their art school failed, the Dexters moved to Gippsland. When the marriage broke up, Caroline moved to Melbourne. Here in 1861 she and **Harriet Clisby** founded *The Interpreter*, the first Australian journal produced by women. Also in 1861, her second marriage, to the wealthy William Lynch, enabled her to become a patron of aspiring artists and writers.

Caroline Dexter is also known to have been a friend of **George Sand**.

De Zayas y Sotomayor, Mariá *see* Zayas Y Sotomayor, Mariá de

Diana, Princess of Wales, *née* Lady Diana Frances Spencer

> *Born 1961*
> *English princess of the UK and member of the British royal family by marriage*

Lady Diana Spencer was born in Sandringham, Norfolk, and educated at Riddlesworth Hall, West Heath, and at the Institut Alpen Videmanette in Switzerland. Following her work as a kindergarten teacher in London, she married Charles, Prince of Wales in July 1981. They have two children, Prince William (1982–   ) and Prince Henry (1984–   ), who are heirs to the British throne in succession to their father.

The strain of constant public and media scrutiny, and the pressures of an apparently increasingly unhappy marriage, came to a head at the end of 1992 for various reasons, including the publication of Andrew Morton's *Diana: Her True Story* (1992) which claimed to verify her unhappiness. Buckingham Palace's announcement that the couple would live apart raised constitutional questions and fuelled speculation over a possible divorce.

She continued to carry out her public engagements, apart from a break in late 1993–4, taking a special interest in children and the sick (notably AIDS victims). In 1994 she accepted an advisory role with the International Red Cross.

Diane de France, Duchess of Montmorency *and* Angoulême

> *Born 1538   Died 1619*
> *French noblewoman who enjoyed great influence during the reigns of Henry III and Henry IV of France*

Diane de France was a natural daughter of Henri II of France and a Piedmontese called Filippa Duc (or, according to others, **Diane de Poitiers**). Formally legitimized in 1547, she was married first to a son of the Duke of Parma in 1553, but was widowed that year. In 1559 she married François, the eldest son of the 1st Duke of Montmorency and, during Charles

IX's reign, helped to make her husband the leader of the pacifist Roman Catholic Politiques.

When Henry III succeeded to the throne, she worked to bring about reconciliation between him and Henry of Navarre (later Henry IV). Cultured, beautiful and intelligent, and, as suggested by her letters which have survived, imbued with courage and tolerance, she enjoyed great influence at court under both Henri III (reigned 1574–89) and Henri IV (reigned 1589–1610), superintending the education of the latter's son, the future Louis XIII.

It was Henry III who in 1582 gave her the duchy of Angoulême, following her husband's death in 1579.

Diane de Poitiers, Duchess of Valentinois

> *Born 1499   Died 1566*
> *French mistress of Henri II of France who made her queen in all but name*

Diane de Poitiers was married at 13 and widowed at 32. She was employed at court as lady-in-waiting, and soon after her husband's death she won the affections of the boy dauphin, who was 20 years her junior and already wedded to **Catherine de' Médicis**.

Diane became his mistress (c.1536), enjoyed queen-like influence throughout his reign (1547–59) and was made Duchess of Valentinois. She was also known as a patron and friend of poets and artists. After Henri's death (1559) she retired to her Château d'Anet, which had been built for her by the royal architect Philibert Delorme and enhanced by the works of the Renaissance sculptor Jean Goujon.

Dick, Gladys Rowena, *née* Henry

> *Born 1881   Died 1963*
> *American physician and microbiologist who contributed to the prevention and treatment of scarlet fever*

Gladys Henry was born in Pawnee City, Nebraska. After graduation from the University of Nebraska she overcame parental objections and went on to study at Johns Hopkins School of Medicine, graduating MD in 1907. After junior medical positions she moved to the University of Chicago where she met, married and worked with George Dick.

In 1914 she and her husband became members of the McCormick Memorial Institute for Infectious Diseases, where Gladys remained until retirement in 1953. Their important work on scarlet fever included the development of the 'Dick test', a skin test for scarlet fever susceptibility.

Dickens, Monica Enid

Born 1915 Died 1992
English novelist, author of non-fiction and writer
for children, known for her horse stories

Monica Dickens was born in London, a great-granddaughter of Charles Dickens. After a disrupted education and her presentation at court as a débutante, she produced a series of semi-autobiographical novels. These include *One Pair of Feet* (1942), deriving from her nursing training in the early years of World War II, and *My Turn to Make the Tea* (1951), from her days as a junior reporter on a local newspaper.

She developed in her writing a compassion for human problems such as alcoholism, the subject of *The Heart of London* (1961), and child abuse, which she examined in *Kate and Emma* (1964). For 20 years she was a popular columnist for *Women's Own* magazine. Her children's books are mainly about horses and farming life.

Dickinson, Emily Elizabeth

Born 1830 Died 1886
American poet who published very little during
her lifetime but had a considerable influence on
modern poetry

Emily Dickinson was born in Amherst, Massachusetts, the daughter of an autocratic lawyer who became a Congressman. She was educated at Amherst Academy and Mount Holyoke Female Seminary in South Hadley. She spent her whole life in the family home at Amherst.

A mystic by inclination, she withdrew herself at 23 from all social contacts and lived an intensely secluded life, writing in secret over 1,000 poems. All but one or two of these remained unpublished until after her death, when her sister Lavinia brought out three volumes between 1891 and 1896 which were acclaimed as the work of a poetic genius.

Further collections appeared, as *The Single Hound* (1914) and *Bolts of Melody* (1945). Her lyrics, intensely personal and often spiritual, show great originality both in thought and in form.

Dickson, Barbara

Born 1947
Scottish pop singer and songwriter who had a hit
with 'Another Suitcase, Another Hall' from Evita

Barbara Dickson was born in Dunfermline. While working as a civil servant she started her musical career singing in Scottish folk clubs where her talent was recognized by Bernie Theobald. Her first major break came in 1973 when she starred in Willy Russell's musical *John, Paul, George, Ringo and Bert*.

She had her first chart success with the title track to the album *Answer Me* (1976). Although she did not appear in the West End production of the Tim Rice/Andrew Lloyd Webber musical *Evita*, the show did provide her with the hit single 'Another Suitcase, Another Hall' (1977).

She played the lead role in Willy Russell's *Blood Brothers* (1983) and recorded the album *Tell Me It's Not True*, featuring songs from the show. Other albums have included *You Know It's Me* (1981), *All For A Song* (1982), *The Barbara Dickson Songbook* (1985) and *The Right Moment* (1986).

Dickson, Joan

Born 1921
Scottish cellist who established herself as a sought-
after player and distinguished teacher

Joan Dickson was born in Edinburgh. She studied with Ivor James, Pierre Fournier in Paris and Enrico Mainardi in Rome and Salzburg, and in 1953 gave her début recital in London and became a founder member of the Edinburgh Quartet.

She was soon a leading concerto soloist with all the major UK orchestras, frequently appearing at the London Proms, and in duo performances with her pianist sister Hester Dickson (1924–), with whom she premiered several works specially written for them.

She taught at the Royal Scottish Academy of Music (1954–81) and the Royal College of Music (1967–81). Based in London since 1980, she is a distinguished teacher at various institutions and international masterclasses and chairs the European String Teachers Association.

Didion, Joan

Born 1934
American writer whose work looks at
contemporary society with a sense of cultural
despair

Joan Didion was born in Sacramento, California, and educated at the University of California at Berkeley (1952–6). She married the writer John Gregory Dunne in 1964. From 1956 to 1963 she was associate feature editor of *Vogue* in New York and has worked and written for the *Saturday Evening Post, Esquire* and *National Review*. She has become established as a diarist of late 1990s culture and has documented such subjects as the anti-establishment activities of Patti Hearst (1954–   ) in the 1970s, the Reagan years and the OJ Simpson murder trial in 1995. Her columns have been published as *Slouching Towards Bethlehem* (1968) and *The White Album* (1979).

Her novels portray contemporary social tensions in a laconic style that has aroused much admiration. *Run River* (1963) was her first novel, but she is best known for *A Book of Common Prayer* (1977), set in a banana republic devoid of history, and *Democracy* (1984), about the long and amorous affair between a politician's wife and Jack Lovett, a man who embodies everything her ambitious husband is not.

Didrikson, Babe *see* Zaharias, Babe

Diemer, Emma Lou

Born 1925
American composer, performer and teacher who composed works for several different instruments

Emma Lou Diemer was born in Kansas City, Missouri, and educated at Yale University, where she studied under Paul Hindemith. She completed a doctorate in composition at the Eastman School, Rochester, New York, in 1960, subsequently working as a keyboard performer (piano, organ, synthesizer) and teacher.

She was appointed Professor of Composition at the University of California, Santa Barbara, in 1971, and has been organist at the First Presbyterian Church, Santa Barbara, since 1984.

Her music is expressive and stylistically free, drawing a good deal from jazz, as in the concerti for trumpet (1983) and for marimba (1990).

Dietrich, Marlene, *originally* Maria Magdalena von Losch

Born 1904 Died 1992
German-born American film actress and cabaret performer, one of the most glamorous stars in cinema history

Marlene Dietrich was born in Berlin. She made her film début as a maid in *Der Kleine Napoleon* (1922), but it was her performance in Germany's first sound film *The Blue Angel* (1930) as the temptress Lola that brought her international attention and a contract to film in Hollywood.

Under the direction of Josef von Sternberg

she created an indelible image of enigmatic sexual allure in a succession of exotic and glamorous films like *Morocco* (1930), *Blond Venus* (1932), *The Scarlet Empress* (1934) and *The Devil Is a Woman* (1935). Despite being labelled 'box-office poison' in 1937, she returned in triumph as brawling saloon singer Frenchie in *Destry Rides Again* (1939). Later film work tended to exploit her legendary mystique, although she was effective in *A Foreign Affair* (1948), *Rancho Notorious* (1952) and *Judgement at Nuremberg* (1961).

After extensive tours to entertain troops during World War II she developed a further career as an international chanteuse and cabaret star. Her increasing reclusiveness led her to refuse to be photographed for the 1984 documentary *Marlene*, but she contributed a pugnacious vocal commentary.

Dijkstra, Sjoukje Rosalinde

Born 1942
*Dutch figure skater who like **Sonja Henie** of Norway has won the skating Grand Slam*

Sjoukje Dijkstra was born in Akkrum. From being placed last place at the 1955 world championships when she was just 13 years old, she followed a career of steady progress and had her first major success in 1960, when she won the European title and finished second at both the Olympics and the world championships.

Those victories proved the start of a string of wins which included another four European titles, three world titles (1962–4) and the Olympic title of 1964. She won the Grand Slam in 1964 by lifting the Olympic, European and World titles, as **Sonja Henie** had done twice in her time.

Dilke, Emily (Emilia Frances), *née* Strong

Born 1840 Died 1904
*English writer, art critic, political activist and trade unionist; allegedly, with her first husband the Rev Mark Pattison, the models for Dorothea and Casaubon in **George Eliot**'s Middlemarch*

Emily Strong was born in Ilfracombe, Devon. Her family soon moved to Oxfordshire and, on the advice of John Ruskin who greatly influenced her ideas on art and society, she studied at the South Kensington Art School (1859–61). During her marriage to the Rev Mark Pattison, rector of Lincoln College, Oxford, she became a recognized specialist on French art, and wrote *Claude Lorrain, sa Vie et ses Oeuvres* (1884). She also became involved with the women's suffrage movement, and joined the Women's Protective and Provident League in 1876, the forerunner of the Women's Trade Union League (WTUL). She became President of the WTUL in 1902.

Emily Dilke was committed to trade unionism, arguing for equal pay at TUC meetings and supporting her second husband, the MP Sir Charles Dilke, in his campaigns against sweated labour.

Dillard, Annie

Born 1945
American essayist, fiction writer and prize-winning poet who looks into the ordinary to find the divine

Annie Dillard was born in Pittsburgh, Pennsylvania, and educated at Hollins College. She has worked as a contributing editor at *Harpers* magazine and as an adjunct professor at Wesleyan University, and has contributed to such diverse publications as *Atlantic Monthly* and *Sports Illustrated*.

Her work often concentrates on the search for the spiritual in the natural environment, and in 1974 she won the Pulitzer Prize for general nonfiction for her collection of essays entitled *Pilgrim at Tinker Creek*. She has won a number of other awards, including a Washington Governor's award in 1978 and a Guggenheim Foundation Grant (1984–5).

Dinescu, Violeta, *originally* Violeta Dinescu-Lucaci

Born 1953
Romanian-born German composer who draws on a wide range of contemporary styles

Violeta Dinescu was born in Bucharest and took German citizenship in 1989. She studied at the Ciprian Porumbescu Conservatory in Bucharest, researching Romanian folk music, and later at Heidelberg. She has taught in Romania and Germany, and worked as a correspondent for European and American music journals.

Her substantial work list, which tends to be filtered through Balkan and Transylvanian forms, includes the orchestral piece *Anna Perenna* (1979), a major solo instrumental sequence called *Satya* (1981), and a vocal piece, *Mondnachte* (1986), accompanied by saxophone and percussion.

Ding Ling (Ting Ling), *pseud of* Jiang Bingzhi (Chiang Ping-chih)

Born 1907 Died 1986
Chinese novelist, short-story writer and radical feminist whose outspokenness troubled the authorities of the time but earned her an important place in 20th-century literature

Jiang Bingzhi was born in Linli County, Hunan Province. When she was three her father died and her mother flouted tradition by enrolling in school and becoming a teacher. Jiang was educated at Beijing (Peking) University, where she attended left-wing classes and started publishing stories of rebelliousness against traditional society, such as *The Diary of Miss Sophia* (1928), which dealt candidly with questions of female psychology and sexual desires, *Birth of an Individual* (1929) and *A Woman* (1930).

She joined the League of Left-Wing Writers in 1930 and became editor of its official journal. Two years later she joined the Communist party, and after a spell of imprisonment, escaped to the Communist base at Yenan, where she became a star attraction for Western journalists. Her outspoken comments on male chauvinism and discrimination at Yenan led to her being disciplined by the party leaders, until her novel, *The Sun Shines over the Sanggan River* (1948), about land-reform, restored her to favour. In 1958, however, she was 'purged' and sent to raise chickens in the Heilongjiang reclamation area known as the Great Northern Wilderness (Beidahuang).

She was imprisoned (1970–5) during the Cultural Revolution, but was rehabilitated by the party in 1979, and published a novel based on her experiences in the Great Northern Wilderness, *Comrade Du Wanxiang*.

Dionne, Cécile, Yvonne, Annette, Emilie *and* Marie

Born 1934
Canadian sisters who were the first quintuplets in the world to survive beyond a few days

Cécile, Yvonne, Annette, Emilie and Marie Dionne were successfully delivered to their French–Canadian parents, Oliva and Elzire Dionne, near Callander in Northern Ontario, Canada. They soon became international child celebrities, appearing in advertising and films. Two of the five have since died: Emilie in 1954, and Marie in 1970.

Disraeli, Mary Anne, Viscountess Beaconsfield, *née* Evans

Born 1792 Died 1872
English wife of Benjamin Disraeli who gave him the stability and support he needed

Mary Anne Evans was the daughter of a naval lieutenant, and was neither well educated nor intellectual. She married a member of parliament, Colonel Wyndham Lewis, in 1815, and through him met Benjamin Disraeli, 1st Earl of Beaconsfield (1804–81), who became her 'Parliamentary protegé'.

On Lewis's death she was left a rich widow and, despite the disparity in their ages (she was 12 years older) and her initial suspicions that Disraeli was marrying her for her money, they married and were happy together. She seemed to provide the steadying influence that he needed to make a success of his political career.

She was raised to the peerage as Viscountess Beaconsfield in 1868, the year that Disraeli became Prime Minister for the first time.

D'Istria, Dora *see* Ghica, Helena

Ditlevsen, Tove

Born 1918 Died 1976
Danish poet, novelist and short-story writer whose writing draws on her own painful experiences of marriage, motherhood and psychosis

Tove Ditlevsen grew up in a working-class district of Copenhagen and came to attention with *Pigesind* (1939, 'A Young Girl's Mind'), a sequence of frank and probing lyrics which she continued a decade and a half later with *Kvinesind* (1955, 'A Woman's Mind'). Her autobiographical *Gift* (1971) was a shockingly frank portrayal of the author's sexual and marital problems and her drug addiction; the Danish word *'gift'* for 'married' also means 'toxin' or 'poison'.

The same concerns are also explored in *Vilhelms Vaerelse* (1973, 'Vilhelm's Place'), which exposes a catastrophic marriage to the cold light one associates with Swedish film director Ingmar Bergman (1918–   ). Though often unsettling in their directness, her works retain an essential warmth and humanity, and a great sense of place.

Dix, Dorothea Lynde

Born 1802 Died 1887
American humanitarian and reformer whose shock at the way mentally ill prisoners were held led her to campaign for their proper treatment

Dorothea Dix was born in Hampden, Maine. At the age of 19 she established her own school for girls in Boston (1821–35). She then taught a Sunday School class in a prison in East Cambridge, Massachusetts, where she observed shockingly inhumane treatment of the mentally ill, who were confined in prisons alongside criminals of both sexes and left with neither protection nor treatment.

She compiled a report (1843) on similar shocking conditions that she found across the country and devoted her life to prison reform and the care of the insane in proper state asylums (at least 15 of which were built in the USA and Canada), bringing about change in Europe as well as America. Throughout the Civil War she served as superintendent of women nurses in the army.

Dlugoszewski, Lucia

Born 1925 (other sources 1931 and 1934)
American composer who has pioneered the 'timbre piano' and other innovative percussion instruments

Lucia Dlugoszewski was born in Detroit, Michigan, where she studied piano at the Conservatory (1940–6) and physics and premed courses at Wayne State University (1946–9). She later took piano lessons with Grete Sultan and studied composition under Edgard Varèse, who influenced her interest in unconventional sonics.

Her highly poetic music, which uses a limited range of titles permutated from words such as 'fire', 'flight', 'naked', 'duende' and 'transparent', was first recognized by literary figures John Ashbery and Frank O'Hara. Wider acclaim came with a recording of her trumpet piece *Space is a Diamond* (1970) and of the vocal/orchestral *Fire Fragile Flight* (1973).

Dobson, Rosemary de Brissac

Born 1920 Died 1987
Australian poet who was the recipient of several awards

Rosemary de Brissac Dobson was born in Sydney, the granddaughter of the English poet and essayist Austin Dobson. She worked for some years with the Australian publishing firm Angus & Robertson and married Alec Bolton, then its London editor.

Her poems reflect her love of antiquity and a keen, painterly eye, and her fascination with manuscripts and fine printing, as seen in 'The Missal'. Her first collection was *In a Convex Mirror* (1944); her second, *The Ship of Ice*, won an award in 1948. Later books were *Child with a Cockatoo* (1955) and *Cock Crow* (1965); selections of her verse were published in 1973 and 1980.

She also edited the feminist anthology *Sister Poets* (1979), in which year she received the Robert Frost Prize; in 1984 she won the Patrick White Literary award.

Dod, Lottie (Charlotte)

Born 1871   Died 1960
English sportswoman, the greatest all-rounder
Britain has ever seen

Lottie Dod was born in Cheshire. She was tennis's first child protégé, winning her first Wimbledon title at the age of 15 to become the youngest-ever champion. She went on to win another four singles titles, as well as defeating Wimbledon champion Ernest Renshaw in a handicapped exhibition match in 1885 and six-times winner William Renshaw later the same year.

She then turned her attention to hockey, and represented England in 1899, before taking up golf and going on to win the British Ladies Open Golf championships in 1904 at Troon.

The amazingly versatile Miss Dod completed her career by winning a silver medal in archery at the 1908 London Games.

Dodge, Mary Elizabeth Mapes, *née* Mapes

Born 1831   Died 1905
American writer and editor of books and
magazines for children

Mary Mapes was born in New York City, the daughter of a scientist. She married William Dodge, a lawyer, in 1851, but he died in 1858 and she turned to writing books for children to support her two sons. *Hans Brinker; or, The Silver Skates* (1865) became a children's classic, and she also wrote *A Few Friends and How They Amused Themselves* (1869) and *When Life is Young* (1894).

In 1870 she became *Hearth and Home* magazines' juvenile editor and from 1873 she edited the *St Nicholas* magazine, the USA's most prestigious publication for children. She eschewed the pedantry and didacticism that characterized much previous children's literature and obtained contributions from renowned writers such as Mark Twain and **Louisa May Alcott**.

Takako Doi, 1990

Doi, Takako, *known in Japan as the* Iron Butterfly

Born 1929
Japanese politician and Speaker of the Diet, the
House of Representatives or Lower House of the
Japanese parliament

Takako Doi was born in Kobe and educated at Doshisha University, Kyoto, where she graduated BA (1951) and Master of Laws (1956). In the course of an academic career, she became Professor of Constitutional Law before being elected to the Diet in 1969. From 1983 to 1986 she was the Vice-Chairman of the *Shakaito*, or Japanese Social Party (now the Social Democrat Party of Japan), becoming Chairman in 1986.

She came to national prominence in 1989 when her party almost doubled its seats in the Upper House of Parliament but resigned in 1991 as a result of heavy losses in local elections. Despite this she is respected for her pragmatic approach to politics and was appointed Speaker in 1993.

Dole, Elizabeth Hanford, *née* Hanford

Born 1936
American politician and organizer, and leading
campaigner for her husband

Elizabeth Hanford was born in Salisbury, North Carolina. She trained as a lawyer and in 1975 married Robert J Dole, who became US Senator from Kansas in 1969. She has held numerous posts in the US government, including that of a commissioner on the Federal

Trade Commission and two cabinet level positions — Secretary of Transportation (1983–7) and Secretary of Labor (1989–90).

In 1990 she became the President of the American Red Cross. She has also taken an active role in her husband's campaigns to be elected for the office of Vice-President of the USA in 1976, and supported his bid for the presidency in 1980, 1984, 1990 and 1996.

Dolgorukova, Katharina, Princess Yourieffskaia

Born 1847   Died 1922
Russian noblewoman who was the mistress and then the wife of Alexander II

Katharina Dolgorukova became the mistress of the emperor Alexander II (ruled 1855–81) in about 1864 and had borne him three children by the time he married her in 1880 after the death of his first wife, Wilhelmina (formerly Princess Maria of Hesse-Darmstadt), who had borne him six sons and two daughters.

Though he instituted much reform during his reign, the affair did him considerable harm in the eyes of his family and St Petersburg society. In 1881 he fell victim to a terrorist bomb.

Under the pseudonym of Victor Laferté, Dolgorukova published *Alexandre II, détails inédits sur sa vie intime et sa mort* (1882). Her *Mémoires* (1890) were suppressed by the Russian government.

Dolly Sisters (Rosie *and* Jennie), *professional names of* Roszicka *and* Janszieka Deutsch

Rosie born 1892; died 1970
Jennie born 1902; died 1941
American vaudeville dancers and singers who made a pre-war impact on Broadway

Roszicka and Janszieka Deutsch were born in Hungary and raised in New York City. Both strikingly beautiful, they made an impact on Broadway in *The Echo* (1910) and *Ziegfeld Follies* (1911). After World War I, they brought their revue *The League of Notions* to London. Jennie died tragically during World War II. A film about their early careers was made in 1945 by **Betty Grable** and June Havers.

Donaldson, Margaret Caldwell

Born 1926
Scottish psychologist who has done important work on the development of young minds

Margaret Donaldson was born in Paisley. She graduated in French, and in education, at Edinburgh University, and subsequently completed doctoral studies in psychology at Edinburgh, and studied at Geneva and Harvard.

Following appointments in the Departments of Education and Psychology at Edinburgh, she was appointed Professor of Developmental Psychology in 1980.

Her publications on children's intellectual, linguistic and social skills, *A Study of Children's Thinking* (1963) and *Children's Minds* (1978), have been widely influential in developmental psychology and education.

Doolittle, Hilda, *known as* H. D.

Born 1886   Died 1961
American poet and novelist who was one of the original protagonists of the short-lived but influential imagist movement

Hilda Doolittle was born in Bethlehem, Pennsylvania, the daughter of a professor of astronomy. She was educated at Gordon School and the Friends' Central School in Philadelphia, and Bryn Mawr College (1904–6). She moved to London in 1911, travelled in Europe and joined the literary circle that had gathered around Ezra Pound. In 1913 she married the English poet and novelist Richard Aldington (1892–1962), but after about six years the marriage had foundered and H.D. had found a lifelong lover and companion in Bryher (Winifred Ellerman). After divorcing her husband in 1937, she settled near Lake Geneva.

Her early poems were seen by her literary friends to embody the precision, clarity, restraint and free verse that were associated with the new imagist movement, and her collection *Sea Garden* (1916) was considered a pioneering volume. Other volumes of poetry include *The Walls do not Fall* (1944), *Flowering of the Rod* (1946) and *Helen in Egypt* (1961). She also wrote several novels, notably *Palimpsest* (1926) and *Hedylus* (1928), which were rooted in classical literature, *Tribute to Freud* (1965), an examination of the meaning of the psychoanalysis which she undertook with Sigmund Freud in 1933 and 1934, and *Bid Me to Live* (1960), an autobiographical account of the World War I years.

Dors, Diana, *originally* Diana Fluck

Born 1931   Died 1984
English actress with platinum blonde hair and frank sexuality who became a popular choice as goodtime girls from the 1940s

Diana Fluck was born in Swindon, Wiltshire, and trained at RADA. She made her film début in *The Shop at Sly Corner* (1946) and was signed to a long-term contract with Rank who groomed her for stardom in their 'Charm School'. Promoted as a sex symbol, she was cast in various low-budget comedies, and despite an effective dramatic performance in *Yield to the Night* (1956) and various highly-publicized visits to Hollywood, she was soon seen in blowsy supporting assignments.

Her accomplished stage work in *Three Months Gone* (1970) brought her a selection of good character parts in films like *Deep End* (1970) and *The Amazing Mr. Blunden* (1972). Later roles were undistinguished but her personal popularity never dimmed as she performed in cabaret and on television problem-solving programmes. She returned to the screen in *Steaming* (1984) immediately prior to her death.

Dorval, Marie Thomase Amelie, *née* Delauney

Born 1798   Died 1849
French actress of immense charm whose Romantic style was highly emotive

Marie Delauney was born in Lorient, the daughter of strolling players, and was introduced to the stage at an early age. She married Allan Dorval, a dance-master, in 1813, and appeared in the Parisian theatre from 1818.

She developed a strongly Romantic acting style which audiences of the day found very moving, and was drawn into conflict with the more classically-inclined Mademoiselle **Mars** when they appeared together in 1835.

She worked with considerable success in a number of theatres in Paris, but her health began to fail after her last great triumph in 1845, and she died in poverty.

Douglas, Mary, *née* Tew

Born 1921
English social anthropologist who has written several important and influential studies

Mary Tew was born in Italy. She studied at Oxford, and carried out fieldwork among the Lele of the Belgian Congo (Zaire) in 1949–50 and 1953. She married James Douglas OBE in 1951. From 1970 until 1978 she was Professor of Social Anthropology at University College, London. In 1977 she moved to the USA, where she became Avalon Professor in the Humanities at Northwestern University in 1980, and Professor Emeritus in 1985.

She is especially known for her studies of systems of cultural classification and beliefs about purity and pollution, as in *Purity and Danger* (1966) and *Natural Symbols* (1973). In addition, she has contributed significantly to economic anthropology in *The World of Goods* (1980), and to the study of moral accountability, in *Cultural Bias* (1978) and *Risk and Culture* (1982). Later works include *How Institutions Think* (1986) and *In the Wilderness* (1993).

Dove, Rita Francis

Born 1952
American poet who became the youngest and the first black US poet laureate

Rita Dove was born in Akron, Ohio. Her work characteristically reflects the African-American experience, and her first book was *Ten Poems* (1977). *The Yellow House On The Corner* (1980) contains a sequence of poems told from the point of view of negro slaves, and historical figures have recurred throughout her work.

She was awarded the Pulitzer Prize for poetry in 1987 for *Thomas and Beulah* (1986), in which she re-created the lives of her grandparents from courtship to death. Other collections include *Museum* (1983), *The Other Side of the House* (1988) and *Grace Notes* (1989). *Fifth Sunday* (1985) is a collection of short stories, while *Through the Ivory Gate* (1992) is a novel and *Darker Face of the Earth* (1994) is a verse drama.

In 1989 she was appointed Professor of English at the University of Virginia, Charlottesville, and in 1993 became Commonwealth Professor of English. She was poet laureate of the USA from 1993 to 1995.

Drabble, Margaret

Born 1939
English novelist whose main characters are often young, educated women

Margaret Drabble was born in Sheffield into a bookish family. Her father was a barrister, then a circuit judge, and, in retirement, a novelist; her mother was an English teacher; and her elder sister is the novelist **A S Byatt**. She was educated at the Mount School, York (the Quaker boarding school where her mother taught), and Newnham College, Cambridge. She married the actor Clive Swift, acted briefly, then turned to writing. Divorced from her first husband in 1972 (after having three children), she married the biographer Michael Holroyd in 1982.

Often mirroring her own life, her novels concentrate on the concerns of intelligent, often frustrated middle-class women. *A Summer Bird-Cage* (1963), *The Garrick Year* (1964), *The Millstone* (1965), *Jerusalem the Golden* (1967), *The Needle's Eye* (1972), *The Ice Age* (1977), *The Middle Ground* (1980) and the trilogy comprising *The Radiant Way* (1987), *A Natural Curiosity* (1989) and *The Gates of Ivory* (1991) are among her titles. She was the editor of the fifth edition of the *Oxford Companion to English Literature*, and has written a biography of the English novelist Arnold Bennett (1974).

Draper, Ruth

Born 1889 Died 1956
American diseuse and monologuist famed for her own dramatic monologues

Ruth Draper was born in New York. She made her stage début in 1915, and following successful solo appearances for the American troops in France in 1918, toured extensively, appearing in 1926 before George V at Windsor.

Her repertoire comprised 36 monologues of her own devising, and embraced 57 characters. She was the recipient of many doctorates, including the LLD from Edinburgh University in 1951 when she was also made a CBE.

Drechsler, Heiki, *née* Daute

Born 1964
German athlete who habitually exceeded seven metres in the long jump

Heiki Drechsler was born in Gera. She came to prominence when, competing for East Germany, she won the European youth long jump championship and Heptathlon championship in 1981, setting a world junior record a year later for long jump. In 1983 she won the world championship, becoming the youngest-ever long jump world champion, and in 1985 added wins in the European and World Cup events.

She consistently jumped over seven metres, winning 27 successive competitions at long jump before 1987, when she was injured, and setting three world records before 1988. Although best known for the long jump, she was also a strong sprinter, picking up a variety of Olympic and world medals at 100 and 200 metres and equalling **Marita Koch**'s 200 metres world record. She is a former delegate of the *Volkskammer*, the East German parliament.

Dressler, Marie, *originally* Leila Marie Koerber

Born 1869 Died 1934
Canadian actress who described herself as 'too homely for a prima donna and too ugly for a soubrette'

Marie Dressler was born in Coburg, Ontario, the daughter of a music teacher. She made her official stage début in *Under Two Flags* (1886) and toured extensively with a light opera company before her first Broadway apparance in *Robber on the Rhine* (1892). A popular straight actress, vaudeville headliner and comedienne, she used her substantial girth, jowly face and homely appearance to great advantage.

She made her film début in *Tillie's Punctured Romance* (1914) but her support for an actors' strike in 1917 adversely affected her career and she struggled for a decade before returning to the cinema in small supporting roles. Her effective dramatic performance opposite **Greta Garbo** in *Anna Christie* (1930) revived her fortunes and she was gainfully employed until her death playing drunken dames and wordly wise women with a broad, sympathetic style that stopped short of hamminess.

She received a Best Actress Oscar for *Min and Bill* (1930) and was seen to advantage in *Emma* (1932), *Dinner at Eight* (1933) and *Christopher Bean* (1933). She also published an autobiography, *The Life Story of an Ugly Duckling* (1924).

Drew, Dame Jane Beverley

Born 1911
English architect who was involved in major works in India and Africa as well as in the UK

Jane Drew was born in Thornton Heath, Surrey. She trained at the Architectural Association, London (1929–34), and after graduating worked with J T Alliston (1934–9) and ran her own practice during World War II. She then worked with her husband Maxwell Fry from 1945 until retiring in 1978 after a long and fruitful career of architectural accomplishment. She spent many years in India, where she was a senior architect at Chandigarh, the new capital of Punjab, India (1951–4), supervising work for Le Corbusier and designing the Government College for Women and the High School.

From 1947 to 1965 she often worked in western Africa, responding sensitively to the social, economic and climatic factors affecting poor communities. Her work there includes Wesley Girls' School, Ghana (1946), and the

Olympic Stadium and Swimming Pool in Kaduna, Nigeria (1965).

Deeply influenced by the MARS group who were responsible for the introduction of the Modern Movement into Britain, she persuaded her political friends, including the Prime Minister, of the need for an Open University (Milton Keynes), a project on which she worked from 1969 to 1977. Her other works include the Hospital Building for the Kuwait Oil Company (1949–51) and the Festival of Britain Harbour Restaurant, London (1951). With her husband she wrote *Village Housing in the Tropics* (1945) and *Tropical Architecture in the Humid Zone* (1956). Drew was appointed DBE in 1996.

Drew, Mrs John, *née* Louisa Lane

Born 1820 Died 1897
American actress who managed the Arch Street Theatre Company for nearly 30 years and made the role of Mrs Malaprop her own

Louisa Lane was born in London into a well-established theatrical family. She was a child actress in England, but her father died early in her life, and she went to the USA with her mother in 1827, where her precocious talents were developed with great success.

She was a well-established actress when she married her third husband, John Drew, in 1850, and thereafter adopted his name as her professional name. She was a strong-willed and determined woman, and was equally influential when she turned to theatre management in Philadelphia in 1861, where she ran the Arch Street Theatre Company until 1892.

She made something of a speciality of the role of Mrs Malaprop in Sheridan's *The Rivals* from 1880 until she retired in 1892.

Drexel, Katharine Mary

Born 1858 Died 1955
American nun and educationalist who founded over 60 schools for Native Americans and African Americans

Katharine Drexel was born in Philadelphia into a family of eminent bankers, but she devoted her life and her wealth to follow her religious vocation. She joined the Sisters of Mercy in 1889 and two years later founded the Sisters of the Blessed Sacrament for Indians and Colored People, nuns whose work was focused on Native Americans and blacks. She remained Mother Superior until the year of her death.

Her convents and schools, established in five different states, include St Catherine's School in Santa Fe (1894) and Xavier University in New Orleans (1915). She was beatified in 1988.

Droste-Hülshoff, Annette Elisabeth, Baroness von

Born 1797 Died 1848
German poet who is commonly regarded as Germany's greatest woman writer

Annette von Droste-Hülshoff was born in Westphalia. She led a retired life and from 1818 to 1820 wrote intense devotional verses, eventually published as *Geistliche Jahre* in 1851.

She wrote in a more restrained and classical style than that of most of her contemporaries, especially in her ballads and lyrics, though her long narrative poems, notably *Das Hospiz auf dem Grossen Sankt Bernard* (1838, 'The Hospice on the Great Saint Bernard') and *Die Schlacht im Loener Bruch* ('The Battle in the Loener Marsh'), were influenced by Byron.

She also wrote a novella, *Die Judenbuche* (1841, 'The Jew's Beech-tree'), which was hailed as the most accomplished work of poetic realism in 19th-century German literature.

Drummond, Annabella

Born c.1350 Died 1402
Queen of Scotland as the wife of Robert III (ruled 1390–1406)

Annabella Drummond was born at Stobhill near Perth, the daughter of Sir John Drummond of Stobhill. A beautiful and kindly woman, she married John Stewart in 1367 and was crowned queen when he acceded to the throne as Robert III of Scotland in 1390.

During Henry IV's invasion of England (1399) she assisted her eldest son David, Duke of Rothsay. He later became regent, but shortly after her death from the plague, he was murdered. Her second son became James I.

Drummond, Flora

Born 1869 Died 1949
Scottish suffragette who made up for her small stature with her immense courage and dedication to her cause

Flora Drummond spent most of her childhood in the Scottish Highlands. She trained as a telegraphist, but because she was rotund and very short, she found the position of postmistress denied to her due to her small stature. She had already become involved in social affairs during her teenage years in Glasgow, and went on to become a socialist in Manchester, working in a factory and the Ancoats settlement to gain first-hand experience and joining the Co-operative Movement.

She was later a Women's Social and Political Union organizer, and earned the sobriquet 'General Drummond' for her habit of wearing a uniform and leading a Fife and Drum band on marches. She was a colourful character and an excellent speaker, and once harangued MPs in the House of Commons from a hired launch; she was also imprisoned nine times. Growing more conservative in later years, she was from 1928 the Commander-in-Chief of the Women's Guild of Empire, an organization which opposed strikes and Communism.

Drummond, Margaret

Born c.1472 Died 1502
Scottish noblewoman, one of the many mistresses of James IV of Scotland

Margaret Drummond was the youngest daughter of Lord Drummond. She became James IV's mistress in 1496 and the following year bore him a daughter, who was brought up at the King's expense after Margaret's death.

She and two of her sisters, Eupheme and Sybilla, died suddenly after a suspect breakfast. Suggested culprits include jealous families among the nobility, scheming courtiers wanting to distract James's attention (though he was already engaged to **Mary Tudor**), and the husband of Eupheme.

Du Barry, Jeanne, Comtesse *see* Barry, Jeanne, Comtesse du

Dubravka, *also known as* Dabrowska *or* Dobrawa

Died 977
Polish queen whose influence over her husband Mieszko helped to ensure Christianity was brought to Poland

Dubravka was the Christian daughter of the Czech prince Boleslav I (Boleslav the Cruel, d.967). In 965 she was betrothed to Mieszko I of the Piast Dynasty, and when the wedding took place the following year he and his nobles renounced paganism and were baptised.

Dubravka's influence on her husband, coupled with that of other missionaries, thus led to the conversion of Poland and its becoming part of mainstream Western culture. As for his political reasons, he also wished to avoid further conflict with Germany. Their son Bolesław I (Bolesław the Brave, c.966–1025) ruled Poland from 992, continuing the country's expansion and the organization of the

Church, and was crowned its first king shortly before his death.

Duchesne, St Rose Philippine

Born 1769 Died 1852
French Roman Catholic nun and missionary who was a pioneer of education in the USA

Rose Philippine Duchesne was born in Grenoble, France. She entered the women's community called the Society of the Sacred Heart in 1804, and in 1818 was sent as a missionary and teacher to America.

That year she founded a branch of the society, a convent and school at St Charles, Missouri. With this as her base she went on to establish several convents, orphanages and schools, for example at St Louis, Missouri (1827) and at Grand Cocteau in Louisiana. In the early 1840s she worked to spread the gospel among the Potawatomi in Kansas.

Beatified in 1940, she was canonized in 1988 and her feast day is 17 November.

Duckworth, Marilyn Rose

Born 1935
New Zealand novelist whose themes are predominantly feminist, focusing on the manner in which her heroines cope with challenge

Marilyn Duckworth was born in Otahuhu, Auckland; she is the sister of **Fleur Adcock**. She was an early protégée of Hutchinson's pioneering 'New Authors' imprint with *A Gap in the Spectrum* (1959, 1985). Three others followed: *The Matchbox House* (1960), *A Barbarous Tongue* (1963) and *Over the Fence is Out* (1969).

There was then a 15-year break before *Disorderly Conduct* (1984), with a background of the New Zealand rugby riots of 1981, and four more novels: *Married Alive* (1985), *Rest for the Wicked* (1986), *Pulling Faces* (1987) and *A Message from Harpo* (1989).

Duffy, Maureen Patricia

Born 1933
English novelist, poet and dramatist whose characters are often at the margins of society, hungry for affection

Maureen Duffy was born in Worthing, Sussex. After attending university in London and five years' employment as a schoolteacher, she published her first novel in 1962, *That's How It Was*, which deals with the relationship between a mother and her illegitimate daughter.

One of her most notable novels, *The Microcosm* (1966), looks at lesbian life through the eyes of three women. She has written novels set in the past, the present day and the future, blending realism and fantasy, her subjects ranging from sexual and social themes to animal rights and the moral issues resulting from scientific progress.

Her critical work includes *The Erotic World of Faery* (1972), a Freudian analysis of English literature, and *The Passionate Shepherdess: Aphra Behn 1640–1689* (1977), an excellent study of **Aphra Behn**.

Dugdale, Henrietta

Born 1826 Died 1918
Australian writer and feminist

Henrietta Dugdale was born in London. She emigrated to Australia with her first husband, whose name was Davies. She later adoped the name of her second husband, Dugdale. In 1884 she became president of the first women's suffrage society in Victoria.

Her commitment to women's rights also embraced campaigns on behalf of birth control, dress reform and opposing violence to women, and she argued for greater educational and economic opportunities to be made available to women.

Her pamphlet *A few Hours in a far-off Age* was published in 1883.

Du Maurier, Dame Daphne

Born 1907 Died 1989
English novelist and short-story writer who was often inspired by Cornwall

Daphne du Maurier was born in London, the daughter of the actor-manager Sir Gerald du Maurier. She wrote a number of highly successful period romances and adventure stories, many of which were inspired by Cornwall, where she lived, including *Jamaica Inn* (1936), *Rebecca* (1938), *Frenchman's Creek* (1942) and *My Cousin Rachel* (1951), several of which have been filmed.

Her short story, 'The Birds' (published in *The Apple Tree*, 1952), became a classic Hitchcock movie. Later books included *The Flight of the Falcon* (1965), *The House on the Strand* (1969), *The Winding Stair*, a study of Francis Bacon (1976), *The Rendezvous and other Stories* (1980) and a volume of memoirs, *Vanishing Cornwall* (1967).

Dunaway, (Dorothy) Faye

Born 1941
*American actress whose career of over three decades took off after she played **Bonnie Parker***

Faye Dunaway

Faye Dunaway was born in Bascom, Florida. She trained at the Boston University School of Fine and Applied Arts and made her Broadway début in *A Man for all Seasons* (1962). She was signed to a personal contract with producer-director Otto Preminger (1906–86), appearing in her first film, *The Happening*, in 1966. She quickly acquired star status, winning a Best Actress Oscar nomination for her electrifying performance in the trend-setting *Bonnie and Clyde* (1967), and began to work at a feverish pitch.

After several hits, she made some unwise choices, but managed to rekindle her waning star with *The Three Musketeers* (1973) and *The Towering Inferno* (1974), and went on to win a Best Actress Oscar for her role in *Network* (1976). She also appeared on television, for example as **Aimee Semple McPherson** in *The Disappearance of Aimée* (1976), and in *The Cold Sassy Tree* (1989).

Strongly committed to a career that she hopes will emulate the longevity of such idols as **Bette Davis**, Dunaway remained busy during the 1990s, appearing in *Even Cowgirls Get The Blues* (1993), among other films.

Dunbar, Agnes, Countess of March and Dunbar

Born c.1312 Died 1369
Scottish noblewoman who heroically defended her family castle against marauding Englishmen

Agnes Dunbar was the daughter of the Earl of Moray and grand-niece of Robert Bruce. In 1320 she married Patrick, Earl of March and Dunbar, who was initially a supporter of the English king, Edward II, but became loyal to the nationalist cause from 1334 after changing sides several times.

While Patrick was absent, Dunbar Castle (one of the few important castles remaining in Scottish hands) was besieged by the Earls of Salisbury and Arundel. Agnes, who was known as Black Agnes due to her swarthy complexion, not only organized and sustained the defence, but jeered at the attackers during the 19-week siege. The castle nearly fell twice but the English finally withdrew, defeated by her immense courage.

Duncan, Isadora

Born 1878   Died 1927
American dancer who remains a highly influential and controversial figure

Isadora Duncan was born in San Francisco. She travelled widely in Europe demonstrating her fluid new style of dancing, inspired by classical, particularly Greek, mythology, art and music. She remains one of the most influential and controversial figures in dance, and as well as being a prolific creator, she founded schools in Berlin, Salzburg, Vienna and Moscow.

In 1922 in Moscow she married a young Russian poet, Sergei Yesenin (1895–1925), who later committed suicide. Her private life gave rise to considerable public interest, particularly after her children had been killed in a motor accident. She herself was accidentally strangled when her scarf caught in the wheel of her car. She published her autobiography, *My Life*, in 1926–7.

Duncan, Sara Jeanette (Janet)

Born 1861   Died 1922
Canadian novelist, columnist and travel writer who was the first woman on a Canadian newspaper's editorial team

Sara Jeanette Duncan was born in Brandtford, Ontario. When she joined the *Toronto Globe* in 1886 she became the first woman to work in the editorial department of a Canadian newspaper. Using the pseudonym Garth Grafton she wrote columns for other newspapers.

In 1888 she undertook a round-the-world trip with a friend, Lily Lewis, which resulted in her first full-length book, *Round the World by Ourselves* (1890). After her marriage to Everard Cotes, a museum curator in Calcutta, she spent the next 25 years in India.

Her fiction, whether specifically about India, as in *The Simple Adventures of a Memsahib* (1893), or about generally paternalistic habits of mind, as in *The Imperialist* (1904), a book about small-town life in Ontario, contains acute observation of colonial attitudes.

Dunham, Katherine

Born 1910
American dancer, choreographer and teacher who championed African-American dance

Katherine Dunham was born in Chicago. She studied anthropology at Chicago and researched dance in the West Indies and the Caribbean before her 1938 appointment as dance director of the Federal Theatre Project. Her first New York concert in 1940 launched her career as a leading choreographer of African-American dances.

She subsequently worked on Broadway (most importantly for the 1940 musical *Cabin in the Sky*) and Hollywood (including *Stormy Weather*, 1943), while developing a successful formula for live black performance revues. Her Dunham School of Dance (1945–55) exerted considerable influence on the direction of American black dance with its combination of elements of classical ballet, modern and Afro-Caribbean techniques.

She choreographed for opera, toured extensively with her own company and wrote several books about her field. She published her autobiography, *A Touch of Innocence*, in 1959.

Duniway, Abigail Jane, *née* Scott

Born 1834   Died 1915
American traveller, writer and suffragist, the first woman in Oregon to vote

Abigail Scott was born in Groveland, Illinois. Her education was limited. She kept a journal of her family's 2,400- mile trek from Illinois to Oregon (1852) — an experience recounted in her autobiography *Path Breaking* (1914), and fictionalized in her novels *Captain Gray's Company* (1859) and *From the West to the West* (1905).

Her hard life as a farmer's wife near Lafayette, Oregon, worsened when her husband became disabled. She moved to Portland to found the pro-suffrage newspaper the *New Northwest* (1871–86).

Having organized **Susan B Anthony's** tour in 1871, Duniway became a public speaker for women's suffrage, and in 1873 she helped found the Oregon Equal Suffrage Association. Despite later disagreements with the National Woman Suffrage Association, her long-term commitment was honoured when she was invited to write and sign Oregon's suffrage proclamation in 1912, and to be the first woman in Oregon to vote.

Dunlop, Eliza, *née* Hamilton

Born 1796   Died 1880
Australian poet and Aboriginal sympathizer
inspired by their culture

Eliza Hamilton was born in County Armagh, Ireland, and educated by her grandmother. She married James Law, but he died and she emigrated to Australia in 1838 with her second husband, David Dunlop.

She is best remembered for her poem 'The Aboriginal Mother' which was published in the *Australian* newspaper in 1838 and which was inspired by the notorious Myall Creek massacre earlier that year. She became familiar with Aboriginal customs and languages whilst living in the Hunter Valley, NSW, where her husband was Police Magistrate and Protector of Aborigines, and was the first Australian poet to transliterate Aboriginal songs.

Dunne, Irene, *originally* Irene Marie Dunn

Born 1898   Died 1990
American actress who brought a gracious charm
and ladylike demeanour to a host of roles

Irene Dunne was born in Louisville, Kentucky, and trained at the Chicago Musical College. She made her first Broadway appearance in *The Clinging Vine* (1922) and subsequently established herself as a musical comedy star. She made her Hollywood début in *Leathernecking* (1930) and received the first of five Best Actress Oscar nominations for the Western *Cimarron* (1931).

An intelligent, versatile actress, she took many roles over the next 20 years, proving particularly adept at sophisticated comedies and tear-stained melodramas. Her many successes include *The Awful Truth* (1937), *Love Affair* (1939) and *I Remember Mama* (1948).

She retired from the screen in 1952. In 1957 she served as an alternate delegate to the United Nations 12th General Assembly. Active on behalf of various charitable causes, she was honoured for her lifetime achievement at the Kennedy Arts Centre in 1985.

Dunnett, Dorothy, *née* Halliday

Born 1923
Scottish novelist and painter better known for her
historical novels than for her portraits

Dorothy Halliday was born in Dunfermline and educated at James Gillespie's High School for Girls in Edinburgh. She began her career with the Civil Service as a Press Secretary in Edinburgh, and in 1946 married the journalist Alastair Dunnett.

By 1950 she had become a recognized portrait painter, exhibiting at the Royal Academy, and she joined the Scottish Society of Women Artists.

She has used her maiden name for a series of detective novels, starting with *Dolly and the Singing Bird* (1968), but her best-known works comprise a series of historical novels, including *Game of Kings* (1961) and *Checkmate* (1975). Featuring the fictional Scottish mercenary Francis Crawford of Lymond, these novels continue the Scottish tradition of historical romance. In 1986 she embarked upon a second historical series, this time featuring the house of Charetty and Niccoló.

She became a director of the Edinburgh Book Festival in 1990.

Du Pré, Jacqueline

Born 1945   Died 1987
English cellist whose brilliant playing career was
halted by illness

Jacqueline du Pré was born in Oxford. She studied at the Guildhall School of Music with William Pleeth, with Paul Tortelier in Paris, Pablo Casals in Switzerland and Mstislav Rostropovich in Moscow.

She made her concert début at the Wigmore Hall aged 16, and subsequently toured internationally. In 1967 she married the Israeli pianist Daniel Barenboim. After developing multiple sclerosis in 1972 she pursued a teaching career, including televised master-classes.

Durack, Dame Mary

Born 1913
Australian author of historical and children's
novels and of an operatic libretto

Mary Durack was born into a pioneering Western Australian family in Adelaide, South Australia. *Kings in Grass Castles* (1959) is the saga of the Durack family from 19th-century Ireland to the time of Patsy Durack, one of Australia's greatest landowners, who died in 1898. *Sons in the Saddle* (1983) brings the story up to modern times. Other historical works include *The Rock and the Sand* (1969) and the play *Swan River Saga* (1975).

Durack has also written a number of books for children, some with illustrations by her younger sister, Elizabeth Durack (1916–   ). Her libretto for the opera *Dalgerie*, with music by Australian composer James Penberthy, is based on her own novel *Keep Him My Country* (1955) and was produced at the Sydney Opera House in 1973.

Durand, Marguerite

Born 1864 Died 1936
French feminist and writer, founder of the world's first women's daily paper

Marguerite Durand was born in Paris. She became an actress at the Comédie Française in 1881 but in 1888 abandoned her acting career and married Georges Laguerre, whom she later divorced.

She became a feminist and was for a time Vice-President of *La ligue française pour le droit des femmes*. She established the first women's daily paper in the world — *La Fronde* ('The Insurrectionist') — and campaigned for better working conditions for women and for female suffrage. From 1908 until 1914 she was co-director of the Parisian newspaper *Les Nouvelles*.

In 1922 she organized an exhibition of 19th-century women in Paris and five years before her death endowed a feminist archive, the Bibliothèque Marguerite Durand.

Duras, Marguerite, *pseud of* Marguerite Donnadieu

Born 1914 Died 1996
French novelist and screenwriter regarded as one of the great European writers of the 20th century

Marguerite Donnadieu was born in Gia Dinh, French Indo-China, and went to Paris to study law and political science at the Sorbonne. During World War II she took part in the Resistance at great risk to herself as a Jewess, and in 1945 joined the Communist Party, but was ousted 10 years later for not completely toeing the party line.

A controversial, strong-minded personality, she wrote in a sparse but powerful way on the universal themes of death, memory, love and sexual desire, often deliberately confusing fact and fiction. Among her books are the semi-autobiographical *La Douleur* (1985, Eng trans 1986) and *L'Amant* (1984, Eng trans *The Lover*, 1985, Prix Goncourt), and novels such as *Un Barrage contre le Pacifique* (1950, Eng trans *The Sea Wall*, 1952) and *Détruire, dit-elle* (1969, Eng trans *Destroy, She Said*, 1970)

She transferred *The Square* to the stage in 1955 and entered the group of avant-garde writers of absurdist drama which included Beckett and Ionesco. In 1960 the success of her film script *Hiroshima Mon Amour* ('Hiroshima My Love') confirmed her position in the fashionable world of French film, and she went on to adapt several of her novels, such as *Moderato Cantabile* (1958). She began directing her own highly atmospheric films in 1966.

Durbin, Deanna, *originally* Edna Mae

Born 1921
Canadian actress and singer whose teenage freshness and talent brought her instant stardom

Deanna Durbin was born in Winnipeg, Manitoba. When the family moved to California, her singing voice attracted the attention of talent scouts and she appeared in the short film *Every Sunday* (1936). Already popular on radio, she was signed to a studio contract and became an immediate star with the release of *Three Smart Girls* (1936).

A high-spirited youngster with a lilting soprano and a charmingly fresh personality, she captivated audiences with a succession of lighthearted folderols that included *One Hundred Men and a Girl* (1937), *Mad About Music* (1938) and *Three Smart Girls Grow Up* (1939). Weathering the transition to adulthood, her flair for comedy was evident in *It Started With Eve* (1941) and she gave creditable dramatic performances in *Christmas Holiday* (1944) and *Lady on a Train* (1945).

She lacked strong showbusiness ambitions however, made her last film in 1948 and has enjoyed a long and contented retirement near Paris.

Duse, Eleonora, *known as* The Duse

Born 1859 Died 1924
Italian actress who had George Bernard Shaw among her admirers and ranks among the greatest actresses of all time

Eleonora Duse was born near Venice into a theatrical family whom she accompanied on tour during her childhood. Gradually she achieved recognition, particulary after performing such roles as Emile Zola's Thérèse Raquin in Naples in the late 1870s. After seeing **Sarah Bernhardt** perform she decided to turn to modern French drama and had great success in some of the plays of Dumas fils (1824–95). Following a tour of South America, she established her own company, the Drammatica compagnia dell Città di Roma, and triumphed in cities worldwide, including Vienna, Berlin, New York and London.

The poet Gabriele D'Annunzio, who fell passionately in love with her in the mid-1890s, owed much to her histrionic genius. Convinced of his talent, she supported and encouraged him, acting in and producing several of his plays, including *La Gioconda* (1899) and *Francesca da Rimini* (1902), which he wrote for her. She also excelled in the performance of Henrik Ibsen's dramatic heroines, such as Hedda Gabler and Ellida in *The Lady from the Sea*.

She retired in 1909 due to poor health, but was obliged for financial reasons to return to the stage in 1921.

Dworkin, Andrea

Born 1946
American feminist and critic of contemporary misogynistic society

Andrea Dworkin was born in Camden and educated at Bennington College. She worked as a waitress, a receptionist and a factory employee, before joining the contemporary women's movement.

Her early publications include *Woman Hating* (1974), *Out Blood: Prophecies and Discourses on Sexual Politics* (1976) and *The New Women's Broken Heart* (1980). Her crusade against pornography is detailed in *Take Back the Night: Women on Pornography* (1980) and *Pornography: Men Possessing Women* (1981), where she identifies pornography as a cause rather than a symptom of a sexist culture.

Dworkin portrays contemporary society as one that promotes the hatred of women via debased images of them, and sees this as creating an atmosphere conducive to rape and woman-battering. This stark assessment of a society in which inequality between the sexes is irreversibly promoted, is shared by fellow polemicist **Catherine MacKinnon**, with whom Dworkin battled to have pornography legally condemned as an infringement of equal rights.

Her later works include *Letters from a War-Zone 1976–1987* (1989) and *Mercy* (1990).

Dybwad, Johanne

Born 1867 Died 1950
Norwegian actress and director who dominated Norway's national theatre for four decades

Johanne Dybwad was born in Bergen, where she trained at the National Scene and made her professional début in 1887. She quickly established a reputation as Norway's leading actress with her natural, unaffected style, and became the leading actress of the new National-Theatret when it opened in Oslo in 1899, a position she retained for the next 40 years.

She worked especially well with the great director Bjørn Bjørnson, and was particularly valued for her interpretations of fellow Norwegian Henrik Ibsen's plays. She also directed regularly from 1906, although she was sometimes criticised for a lack of fidelity to the works she undertook.

Dyer, Louise Berta Mosson, *later* Hanson Dyer

Born 1884 Died 1962
Australian music publisher and patron who became a leader in the revival of early music

Louise Dyer was born in Melbourne. She was an accomplished pianist, and studied in Edinburgh and at the Royal College of Music, London. After marrying James Dyer she became the centre of Melbourne's musical life, helping to establish the British Music Society there in 1921.

In 1927 the Dyers left for London and then Paris, where Louise established Editions du Oiseau-Lyre (the Lyre Bird Press), a music publishing business, and in 1933 brought out a complete edition of the works of the French composer François Couperin (1668–1733), followed by works of the English composers Henry Purcell (1659–95) and John Blow (1649–1708). The press set a new standard of music printing and became noted for publishing previously unobtainable older music. In the 1950s it was among the first to issue on LP some of the works of Claudio Monteverdi, Purcell and George Friederic Handel.

She became Mrs Hanson Dyer on remarrying in 1939 after the death of her first husband, and was permanently resident in France and, after World War II, in Monaco, but she maintained her links with Australia and published the works of leading Australian composers **Peggy Glanville-Hicks** and **Margaret Sutherland**. Her considerable Australian estate was left to Melbourne University for music research.

Dyer, Mary

Died 1660
English Quaker who was martyred in the USA

Mary's husband was William Dyer of Somerset, whom she married in London in 1633. They settled in Boston, Massachusetts in 1635, but moved to Portsmouth, Rhode Island, in 1638, following their expulsion from the Church for holding views like those of Mary's friend **Anne Hutchinson**.

Mary became a Quaker on a visit to England in 1650–7, and was persecuted for preaching her beliefs on returning to the USA. She was jailed three times and eventually hanged for repeatedly visiting Quaker prisoners in Boston and refusing to stop.

Dympna

9th century
Legendary Irish princess associated with the
healing of insanity

Dympna is said to have been the daughter of a pagan Celtic chief and a Christian mother. After her mother's death, Dympna was forced to flee with her confessor St Gerebernus, first to Antwerp and then to nearby Gheel, to avoid the incestuous attentions of her father. He managed to trace them through the coins that they had spent and demanded that Dympna return home. On her refusal both she and Gerebernus were murdered on the spot.

The bodies were buried and rediscoverd two centuries later, apparently labelled with an inscription of Dympna's name, giving rise to the above legend. On their translation, miracles of healing of insanity and epilepsy were reported, hence Dympna's patronage of the insane. Her feast day is 15 May.

D'Youville, St Marie Marguerite, *née* Dufrost de Lajemmerais

Born 1701   Died 1771
Canadian founder of the Sisters of Charity

Marie Marguerite Dufrost de Lajemmerais was born in Varennes, Quebec, the eldest of six children. She married François-Madeleine d'Youville in 1722. Widowed in 1730 after an unhappy marriage, she cleared her husband's debts and supported her two surviving sons by running a small shop.

With three companions, and against much initial opposition from both family and local citizens, she founded the Sisters of Charity (Grey Nuns) in Montreal in 1737 to care for the poor. In due course her work was recognized and she was asked to restore the derelict Hôpital Général, which she did in 1749 and again after a fire in 1765.

She was beatified in 1959 and canonized in 1990.

Dyveke, *known as* 'little dove'

Born 1491   Died 1517
Dutch mistress of King Kristian II (ruled
1513–23)

Dyveke was the nickname given to a woman, born in Amsterdam, who became the mistress of King Kristian II of Denmark, Norway and Sweden. She had met him in 1507 in Bergen, Norway, where her mother, Sigbrit Willums, had an inn.

They both went to Denmark with him in 1511, where her mother gained great influence, and the hatred of the nobles. His marriage in 1515 to Elizabeth of Hapsburg, sister of the emperor Charles V, did not extinguish his love for Dyveke.

Dyveke died suddenly, probably by poison.

e

Eames, Ray

Floreat 1940s
American architect who was the first woman to
win the RIBA Gold Medal

Ray Eames was awarded the RIBA (Royal Institute of British Architects) Gold Medal in 1979 with her husband Charles Eames (1907–78). The first time it had been won by a couple, the award was attributed to their record of innovation and excellence in the fields of architecture, furniture design and, more recently, film, graphics and exhibition design.

Their Santa Monica house (1949) was a seminal building in postwar architecture, due to having industrial components in its construction and a contrasting lighthearted feel to it as a whole. Like the house, the Eameses' work contained an abundance of possibility, and was neither precious nor pompous.

Having set up their office in California in 1941, they pushed forward their ideas with inventiveness, displaying a great ability to communicate on all levels and in all mediums. In fact they undertook such a range of different work that their Santa Monica House is almost the only building for which they are known, many people knowing them better for their famous range of furniture designed in 1946.

Eardley, Joan

Born 1921 Died 1963
English painter whose finest work arose from her
love of a tiny Scottish fishing village

Joan Eardley was born in Warnham, Sussex. She began her studies at Goldsmith's College of Art, London (1938), but moved to Glasgow where she enrolled at the School of Art in 1940. After World War II she studied at Hospitalfield, Arbroath, and at Glasgow School of Art, winning various prizes and travelling to France and Italy on a Carnegie bursary.

Greatly influenced by Vincent Van Gogh, both technically and in terms of her choice of subjects, in 1949 she took a studio in Cochrane Street, Glasgow, and began to paint poor children of the nearby tenements. In 1950 she first visited Catterline, the tiny fishing village on the north-east coast of Scotland which inspired her finest landscapes and seascapes. Here she lived and worked until her death.

Earhart, Amelia Mary

Born 1897 Died 1937
American pilot, the first woman ever to fly the
Atlantic

Amelia Earhart was born in Atchison, Kansas. Her early career as a nurse during World War I and a social worker afterwards was eclipsed by the fame she gained for being the first woman to fly the Atlantic — Newfoundland to Burry Point, Wales, on 17 June 1928. She married George Palmer Putnam in 1931 but continued her career under her maiden name.

Feeling that she should earn the fame she had achieved as a passenger in 1928, she successfully crossed the Atlantic alone on 20–21 May 1932. Later notable flights included the first successful journey from Hawaii to California (1935), which covers a greater distance than that between Europe and the USA, and from Mexico City to New York (1935).

During an attempt to fly around the world, her plane was lost over the Pacific in July 1937; her body was never found, and there has been much speculation as to how she died. Her autobiography, *Last Flight* (1938), was edited by her husband.

Amelia Earhart, 1928

Eastman, Crystal

Born 1881   Died 1928
American suffragette and socialist who pioneered
reforms in the workplace as well as in society

Crystal Eastman was born into a family who supported her ambitions. She graduated from New York University with a law degree in 1907 and then spent a year in Pittsburg researching *Work Accidents and the Law*, which illuminated the plight of working families debilitated by industrial accidents.

In 1909 she drafted New York's first worker compensation law, which was later used as a model nationwide, and in 1913 she founded the forerunner of the National Women's Party, which campaigned for the Equal Rights Amendment of 1923. She was also a founder of the Feminist Congress which convened in New York in 1919.

After her second marriage — to Walter Fuller — she moved to England where she

became involved in the women's rights movement there.

Easton, Sheena, *originally* Sheena Orr

Born 1959
Scottish pop singer who came to fame with the hit
single '9 to 5'

Sheena Easton was born in Bellshill, near Glasgow, and trained in drama. Her pop career received a considerable boost when she was the subject of a BBC documentary, *Big Time*, in 1980, which showed how record company EMI went about 'manufacturing' a pop star. The single '9 to 5', released after the programme was aired, gave Easton her first top-10 success.

She had several UK hits, including the theme to the James Bond film *For Your Eyes Only* (1981), before moving to the USA. Since then almost all of her success has been in America, where she has worked with artists ranging from country and western singer Kenny Rogers to Prince. Her television appearances include the *Man of La Mancha* series.

Eaton, Peggy (Margaret), *née* O'Neale

Born 1796   Died 1879
American socialite whose marriage to a prominent
Democrat caused President Jackson's
'Cabinet crisis'

Peggy O'Neill was born in Washington DC, the daughter of an innkeeper. In 1816 she married her first husband, John Timberlake, who died in 1828. In 1829 she married John Henry Eaton, Secretary of State for War under President Jackson.

The wives of the other Cabinet ministers refused to mix with her because of her alleged premarital intimacy with Eaton and because of her humble background. Jackson was enraged and implemented a major Cabinet reshuffle to oust the ringleaders. He also openly supported Martin Van Buren, who was favourably disposed towards Peggy Eaton, in Van Buren's bid to be Vice-President and later President (1836).

Though Eaton had been forced to resign (1831), he later became ambassador to Spain (1836–40) and Peggy enjoyed great social success in Europe. After his death in 1956 she married a fraudulent young Italian dancing instructor who left her for her granddaughter.

Ebba, St, *also called* Ebbe *or* Aebbe

7th century
Northumbrian princess whose name appears in
the place-names Ebchester and St Abb's

Ebba was the daughter of King Ethelfrith of Northumbria. She fled to Scotland on the invasion of Northumbria by Edwin and the death of her father in 616. Later she founded the double monastery of Coldingham in Berwickshire, which she ruled as abbess till her death.

Her niece **Etheldreda** became a nun at Coldingham following her separation from her husband Ecgfrith. Legend relates that when he visisted Etheldreda there, accompanied by his second wife Ermenburga, the wife contracted a strange illness, which was only cured when, on Ebba's advice, Ecgfrith had freed Bishop Wilfrid, whom he had imprisoned, and relics that Ermenburga had stolen had been returned.

Though the pastimes of the nuns at Coldingham allegedly included making beautiful clothes for themselves rather than the discipline of prayer, Ebba's sanctity remained unsullied. She died around the year 670 and her feast day is 25 August.

Eberhardt, Isabelle

Born 1877   Died 1904
Russian writer and traveller, famous for her
travels in the Sahara

Isabelle Eberhardt was born near Geneva, where her mother Nathalie de Moender, a Russian general's wife, had fled with her lover the anarchist Alexander Trophimovsky. She was reared as a boy, and spoke six languages, including Arabic. In 1897 she went to Bone (now Annaba) in Algeria with her mother where they both converted to Islam. Here Isabelle began journeying in the Sahara disguised as an Arab.

Though an enthusiast for all things Arab, she worked for the French government of North Africa. After an assassination attempt on her failed, she was expelled from Algeria, but returned after she married Slimène Ehnni, an Arab. In 1903 she was drowned while reporting for an Algerian newspaper on General Lyautey's campaign in Morocco.

Ebner-Eschenbach, Marie, *née* von Dubsky

Born 1830   Died 1916
Austrian dramatist and writer of novellas which
were among the best of their time

Marie von Dubsky was born to a noble family at Castle Zdislawitz in Moravia and remained in the nobility by marrying her cousin in 1848. Her early writing ventures, which were in the form of drama, failed, but her regional

novellen, starting with her first success, *Ein Spätgwborener* (1874), much influenced by the Russian novelist Ivan Turgenev, were amongst the most skilful and well observed of their time.

The best of her tales include *Das Gemeindekind* (1887, Eng trans *The Child of the Parish*, 1887) and *Unsühnbar* (1890, Eng trans *Beyond Atonement*, 1892). She was an important figure in Viennese society and the first woman to be awarded an honorary doctorate from the University of Vienna.

Eddy, Mary (Morse) Baker, *née* Baker

Born 1821   Died 1910
American founder of the Christian Science Church

Mary Baker was born in Bow, New Hampshire and brought up as a Congregationalist. She was frequently ill as a young woman. After a brief first marriage (to George Glover, 1843–4), she was married a second time, to Daniel Patterson (1853, divorced 1873). In the 1860s she tried all kinds of medication, but turned to faith healing and in 1862 came under the influence of Phineas P Quimby (1802–66).

While recovering from a severe fall in 1866 she turned to the New Testament and was healed; from this time onwards she developed a spiritual and metaphysical system she called Christian Science, explaining her beliefs in *Science and Health with Key to the Scriptures* (1875), which proclaimed the illusory nature of disease.

She married Asa G Eddy in 1877, became known as Mary Baker Eddy and in 1879 founded the Church of Christ, Scientist in Boston. Two years later she founded the Massachusetts Metaphysical College, where she taught until its closure in 1889. She founded various publications, including the *Christian Science Journal* (1883) and the *Christian Science Monitor* (1908).

Edelman, Marian, *née* Wright

Born 1939
American lawyer, an important figure in the civil
rights movement

Marian Edelman was born in Bennettsville, South Carolina. She was educated at the universities of Paris and Geneva, and at Spelman College and Yale University. A significant figure in the Civil Rights movement, she was an executive member of the Student Non-Violent Co-ordinating Committee (1961–3), and has been closely associated with the National Association for the Advancement of

Colored People (NAACP) since the 1960s. She has had a distinguished legal career, and has served on several presidential commissions including the Presidential Commission on Missing in Action (1977).

She has received many honorary degrees and awards, most recently the Gandhi Peace Award (1990).

Ederle, Gertrude Caroline

Born 1906
American swimmer, the first woman to swim the
English Channel

Gertrude Ederle was born in New York City. One of the best-known people in 1920s sport, she swam the crawl using eight kicks for each arm stroke (the eight-beat crawl) and broke several records. She won a gold medal at the 1924 Olympic Games as a member of the US 400-metre relay team, and two bronze medals.

On 6 August 1926 she swam the Channel from Cap Gris Nez to Kingsdown in 14 hours 31 minutes, very nearly two hours faster than the existing men's record. Later she turned professional, becoming a swimming instructor and fashion designer.

Edgeworth, Maria

Born 1767   Died 1849
Irish writer of books on education, novels about
life in Ireland and children's stories

Maria Edgeworth was born in Blackbourton, Oxfordshire, the eldest daughter of the inventor and educationalist Richard Lovell Edgeworth (1744–1817). After being educated in England, in 1872 she returned to Edgeworthstown in County Longford, Ireland, to act as her father's assistant and governess to his many other children. With her father, and to illustrate his educational ideas, she published *Letters to Literary Ladies* (1795), *The Parent's Assistant* (1796) and *Practical Education* (1798).

In 1800 she published her first novel, *Castle Rackrent*, which was an immediate success, followed by *Belinda* in 1801. She received praise from Sir Walter Scott and was lionized on a visit to London and the Continent, where she turned down a proposal of marriage from the Swedish Count Edelcrantz for the sake of her father. The next of her 'social novels' of Irish life was *The Absentee* (1809), followed by *Ormond* (1817).

All her works were written under the influence of her father, which may have inhibited her natural story-telling talent. After her father's death (1817) she did little more writing apart from a late novel, *Helen*

(1834), but devoted herself to looking after the family property, and 'good works'. She is also remembered for children's stories.

Edib (Adivar), Halide

Born 1884   Died 1964
Turkish novelist, dramatist, nationalist politician
and pioneer campaigner for women's rights in
Turkey

Halide Edib was born in Istanbul and educated at the American College for Girls there, becoming the first Muslim to graduate and later the first woman to be a university lecturer (1939) and a member of parliament (1950–4).

In 1919 she became, together with her second husband the politician Professor Adnan Adivar, a leading supporter of Kemal Attatürk — but later they had to go into exile on account of their opposition to his policies. During this period she wrote several books on Turkish affairs in English.

Her novels, the first of which was published in 1909, are competent studies of educated women and their problems and include *Atesten Gömlek* (1922, Eng trans *The Daughter of Smyrna*, 1938) and (in English) *The Clown and his Daughter* (1935).

Edinger, Tilly

Born 1897   Died 1967
German-born American palaeontologist who
established the field of palaeoneurology

Tilly Edinger received her doctorate from Frankfurt University in 1921. She remained in Germany, working on the brain of fossil vertebrates, until 1940 when she emigrated to the USA and joined the staff of the Museum of Comparative Zoology at Harvard.

Her pioneering work in palaeoneurology — the study of the brain and the nervous system — included the promotion of the idea that evolutionary processes are diverse and lateral, rather than linear.

Edmonds, Sarah Emma

Born 1841   Died 1898
Canadian who enlisted in the US Union Army
under the name of Frank Thompson and became
known as the 'Beardless Boy' by her fellow soldiers

Sarah Edmonds was born in Nova Scotia. She was a habitual cross-dresser who claimed to be 'naturally fond of adventure, a little ambitious and a good deal romantic'. These qualities led her not only to pose as a door-to-door Bible salesman among other exploits, but also to enlist as a man in the Union Army's Michigan regiment during the Civil War.

Her talent for subterfuge was well used and she was frequently assigned to serve as a spy, on one occasion infiltrating the Confederate camp as a young black male cook. She also took on the role of nursing the fatally wounded, still in her masculine disguise and proved that she could shoot in cold blood when necessary, by firing a pistol at point-blank range into the face of a Confederate captain.

Her best-selling autobiography, *Nurse and Spy in the Union Army* (1865), is a lively account of her contribution to the history of female impersonation of men as a means of access to masculine work.

Edwards, Amelia Ann Blandford

Born 1831 Died 1892
English Egyptologist and author of novels, short stories and travel writing

Amelia Edwards was born in London. She worked as journalist, then published her first novel, *My Brother's Wife*, in 1855. Historical works such as *The History of France* (1856) and other novels — *Debenham's Vow* (1869) and *Lord Brackenbury* (1880) — followed. She also wrote ghost stories for publication in journals.

She was founder of the Egyptian Exploration Fund, contributed papers on Egyptology to the principal European and American journals and turned her attention to travel-writing in the 1870s; this included *A Thousand Miles up the Nile* (1877), about her own travels through Egypt, and *Pharaohs, Fellahs, and Explorers* (1891).

Edwards, Tracey

Born 1962
English yachtswoman, captain of the first all-female crew in the Whitbread

Tracey Edwards was born in Reading. She learned to sail while serving as a stewardess and then as cook aboard motor and sailing yachts.

In 1985 she decided to compete in the toughest of ocean races, The Whitbread 33,000-mile round-the-world race, and eventually got a spot aboard *Atlantic Privateer*, which won the leg to Auckland, making her the first woman ever to crew a winning yacht in the Whitbread.

Edwards formulated the idea of an all-female crew for the 1989–90 race and started the *Maiden* project, which she financed by selling her house. At the age of 27 she captained and navigated *Maiden* to a win in her

Tracey Edwards on board *Maiden*, 1990

class on the second and third legs of the race, marking the first time a British yacht had won a leg for 12 years. She was voted Yachtsman of the Year by the Yachting Journalists' Association.

Egerton, Sarah, *later* Field, *née* Fyge

Born 1670 Died 1723
English poet and early feminist who wrote spirited verse 'in vindication of her sex'

Sarah Fyge was born in London, the daughter of a well-to-do physician. She left home in disgrace after publishing a lively feminist verse polemic in answer to an attack on women: *The Female Advocate, or an Ansewere to a late Satur against the Pride, Lust and Inconstancy etc., of Women* (1686). She married an attorney who died early, and her second marriage, to the Rev Thomas Egerton, a widower of 50, was unhappy.

She wrote conventional elegies on Dryden (1700), but her more original *Poems on Several Occasions* (1703) contains passionate accounts of her loves, marriages and sufferings, and spirited satire on tyrannical husbands and female prudes.

Ekman, Kerstin

Born 1933
Swedish novelist who is a successful and leading
contemporary writer in her country

Kerstin Ekman was born in Risinge, Öster-götland. She worked as a teacher and in the film industry before emerging as a successful writer of thrillers.

Her tetralogy tracing feminine patterns of civilization within the framework of a Swedish railway town, *Häxringarna* (1974, 'The Witches' Circles'), *Springkällan* (1976, 'The Spring'), *Änglahuset* (1979, 'House of Angels') and *En stad av ljus* (1983, 'City of Light'), established her as one of Sweden's leading contemporary novelists, its carefully researched realist elements mingling with mythical and symbolic dimensions which become particularly prominent in the final volume. *Rövarna i Skuleskogen* (1988, 'The Robbers in the Skule Forest') is a vivid and far-reaching critique of civilization, while *Händelser vid vatten* (1993, 'Events by Water') explores issues of culture and memory in an isolated community in the north of Sweden.

Ekman was elected a member of the Swedish Academy in 1978, but the failure of the Academy to express its support for Salman Rushdie following the death sentence placed on him by Iranian fundamentalists persuaded her to leave it in 1989.

Ekster, Aleksandra Aleksandrovna

Born 1884   Died 1949
Soviet painter and theatre designer who brought
cubist and futurist ideas from France to the USSR

Aleksandra Ekster was born in Georgia. She studied at the School of Art in Kiev and in Paris, where she fell under the influence of Picasso, Braque and Marinetti. She returned to Moscow, bringing cubist and futurist ideas to the radical chamber theatre founded by Tairov, where she worked on highly stylized constructivist sets and costumes within his concept of 'synthetic theatre'.

Her ideas, which were also seen in films, influenced the development of design in the Soviet Union. She moved to Paris in 1924, and enjoyed a successful career as a designer for theatre and ballet.

El Saadawi, Nawal

Born 1931
Egyptian doctor and novelist whose writing voices
her awareness of Arab women's struggles gained
through her medical position

Nawal El Saadawi was born in Kafr Tahla. As a doctor she became aware of women's social and economic problems, and in her first non-fictional work in Arabic, *Women and Sex* (1972), and in her stories in *Two Women in One* (1975, Eng trans 1985), she highlights their plight. *God Dies by the Nile* (1974, Eng trans 1985), considered a 'metaphor for the Sadat regime', further reveals how class and oppression by landlords augments their misery.

As she became increasingly prominent and militant, El Saadawi's outspokenness resulted in her losing her post as Director of Health in Cairo. In her later works, such as *She Has No Place in Paradise* (1987) and *Death of an Ex-Minister* (1987), all published outside Egypt, she further illustrates the impotence of the political and religious system to overcome the influences of imperialism and colonialism.

Elders, M(innie) Joycelyn, *née* Jones

Born 1933
American paediatrician who was US Surgeon
General in 1993

M Jocelyn Elders was born in Skaal, Arkansas, and educated at the Brock Army Medical School and at the University of Arkansas from which she graduated MD in 1960. After post-graduate training and medical posts, she became Professor of Paediatrics at the University of Arkansas in 1974. Her research interests have focused on endocrine mechanisms in growth and development.

In 1987 she was appointed Director of the Arkansas Department of Health, becoming US Surgeon General in 1993 under the Clinton administration, the first woman to hold the position; however she was dismissed at the end of 1994 for expressing controversial views on AIDS and sex education.

Eleanor of Aquitaine

Born c.1122   Died 1204
Queen of France as the wife of Louis VII (ruled
1137–80) and Queen of England as the wife of
Henry II (ruled 1154–89)

Eleanor was the daughter of William X, Duke of Aquitaine, whom she succeeded as Duchess of Aquitaine. In 1137 she married Prince Louis, who became King Louis VII of France a month later. They had two daughters.

She led her own troops on the Second Crusade (1147–9), dressed as an Amazonian warrior, but it was around this time that Louis's adoration of her began to fade. In 1152 the marriage was annulled on the ground of consanguinity, and in the same year Eleanor married Henry Plantaganet, Count of Anjou, who became Henry II of England in 1154. She was soon regarded as the epitome of courtly life and manners and an important supporter of the poetic movements of the time.

As a result of Henry's infidelities she supported two of their five sons, Richard and John (they also had three daughters), in a rebellion against him, and was imprisoned (1174–89) until her son Richard I the Lionheart ascended the throne and released her. She acted as his regent during his crusading campaigns abroad (1189–94) and raised the ransom for his release. In 1200 she led the army that crushed a rebellion in Anjou against her second son, King John. Apparently, rather than succumb to the bitterness engendered by her imprisonment, she enjoyed a wise and benevolent old age and has come to be regarded by some as one of the greatest female rulers.

Eleanor of Castile

Born c.1245   Died 1290
Queen of England as the wife of Edward I (ruled 1272–1307)

Eleanor of Castile was the daughter of Ferdinand III of Castile and Joan of Ponthieu. Her marriage to Edward in 1254 gained England the provinces of Ponthieu and Montreuil (from Eleanor's mother), as well as a claim on Gascony (donated by her half-brother Alfonso X of Castile).

Eleanor accompanied Edward to the Crusades (1270–3), and is said to have saved his life at Acre (now in Israel) by sucking the poison from a wound. She died in Harby, Nottinghamshire, and the 'Eleanor Crosses' at Northampton, Geddington and Waltham Cross are survivors of the nine erected by Edward at the halting places of her cortège. The last stopping place was Charing Cross, where a replica now stands.

Eleanor of Provence

Born 1223   Died 1291
Queen of England as the wife of Henry III (ruled 1216–72)

Eleanor of Provence was the daughter of Raymond Berengar IV, Count of Provence; her mother was the daughter of a Count of Savoy. Married to Henry for political reasons in 1236, Eleanor managed to have her uncles from Savoy and Provence placed in prominent governmental positions, which incurred the hostility of the English nobles, intensifying the problems Henry was already experiencing.

In the Barons' War of 1264 Henry was taken prisoner and Eleanor raised an army of mercenaries in France to support him, but her invasion fleet was wrecked. Nevertheless the insurgents were defeated and Eleanor returned to England. After the death of Henry and the accession in 1272 of her son Edward I, she retired to a convent.

Eleonora of Arborea

Born c.1350   Died 1404
Sardinian ruler regarded as the national heroine of Sardinia

Eleonora was the daughter of a district chieftain (*giudice*). In 1383 she defeated an incursion from Aragon and became Regent of Arborea for her infant son, Frederick. In 1395 she introduced a humanitarian code of laws, *Carta di Logu*, which was far ahead of its time.

She gave special protection to hawks and falcons, and Eleonora's Falcon is named after her. Her statue stands in the Piazza Eleonora in Oristano.

Elgin, Suzette Haden

Born 1936
American linguist and science fiction writer

Suzette Haden Elgin's work as a linguist reflects a concern for women, and her fiction work considers the theme of society's oppression of women.

Her 1984 novel *Native Tongue* combines her interest in language, women, and society's attitudes by depicting a group of women who overcome oppression through developing a language that expresses their experiences and values. As part of this novel, Elgin constructed a language called LAADAN.

Her other works include *The Communipaths* (1970), *The Gentle Art of Verbal Self-Defense* (1987) and *Genderspeak: Men, Women* (1993).

Elion, Gertrude Belle

Born 1918
American biochemist and Nobel Prize winner who developed several drugs useful in medicine today

Gertrude Elion was born in New York City. She was educated at Hunter College and completed a master's degree at New York University before briefly teaching in a high school. World War II opened up laboratory jobs to women, and she joined Burroughs Wellcome in 1944 as a research associate of George Hitchings. She progressed through the company to become Head of Experimental Therapy (1967–83), and since 1983 has been Emeritus Scientist.

With Hitchings she worked extensively on

drug development, and with their 'anti-metabolite' philosophy, they initially synthesized compounds that inhibited DNA synthesis, hoping that these could prevent the rapid growth of cancer cells. Their investigations of the chemistry of purines and pyrimidines, components of DNA, resulted in them jointly holding 18 pharmaceutical patents related to these two compounds, Elion concentrating primarily on pyrimidine chemistry. From their work came drugs active against leucaemia and malaria, drugs used in the treatment of gout and kidney stones, and also drugs that suppressed the normal immune reactions of the body, vital tools in transplant surgery.

In the 1970s they produced an anti-viral compound, acyclovir, active against the herpes virus, which preceeded the successful development by Burroughs Wellcome of AZT, the anti-AIDS compound. In 1988 Elion and Hitchings shared the Nobel Prize for Physiology or Medicine with the Scottish pharmacologist Sir James Black.

Eliot, George, *pseud of* Mary Ann *or* Marian Evans

Born 1819 Died 1880
English novelist who stands among the greatest in British literary history

George Eliot was born on Arbury Farm in Astley, near Nuneaton in Warwickshire. Many of the traits transferred by her to the characters Adam Bede and Caleb Garth were identified in her father Robert Evans, a Warwickshire land agent and a man of strong character. She lost her mother, whom she loved devotedly, in 1836, and soon afterwards took entire charge of the household. Teachers came from Coventry to instruct her in German, Italian and the music of which she was passionately fond throughout her life. She was also an immense reader.

In 1841 her father moved to Coventry, where she met Charles Bray, a writer on the philosophy of necessity from the phrenological standpoint, and his brother-in-law Charles Hennell, who in 1838 had published a rationalistic *Inquiry concerning the Origin of Christianity.* Under their influence she rejected her earlier evangelical Christianity. In 1844 she took on the laborious task of translating Strauss's *Leben Jesu* (published in 1846). After her father's death in 1849 she travelled on the Continent with Mr and Mrs Bray; returning to England in 1850 she began to write for the *Westminster Review.* She became assistant editor in 1851, and the centre of a literary circle, two of whose members were Herbert Spencer and George Henry Lewes. She translated Feuerbach's *Essence of Christianity* (1854), the only book that bore her real name. Gradually her intimacy with Lewes grew, and in 1854 she formed a liaison with him which lasted until his death in 1878.

In 1856 she attempted her first story, 'The Sad Fortunes of the Rev Amos Barton', the beginning of the *Scenes of Clerical Life*. It came out in *Blackwood's Magazine* in 1857, and at once showed that a new author of great power had emerged. 'Mr Gilfil's Love Story' and 'Janet's Repentance' followed quickly. Her first novel, *Adam Bede* (1859), had an enormous success. *The Mill on the Floss* (1860), *Silas Marner* (1861), *Romola* (1863) and *Felix Holt* (1866) appeared next in succession. Her first poem, *The Spanish Gypsy* (1868), was followed the next year by *Agatha, The Legend of Jubal* and *Armgart*; and in 1871–2 appeared *Middlemarch*, generally considered her greatest work. After that came *Daniel Deronda* (1876), her last great novel.

After the death of Lewes, she was coaxed to write *Impressions of Theophrastus Such* (1879), a volume of essays. She fell in love again with a banker 20 years her junior, John Walter Cross (d.1924), a friend of long standing whom she married in May 1880. She died a few months later, and was buried in Highgate Cemetery, in the grave next to that of Lewes. As a novelist, George Eliot will probably always stand among the greatest of the English realist school; her pictures of farmers, tradesmen and the lower middle-class, generally of the Midlands, are hardly surpassed in English literature.

Elizabeth I

Born 1533 Died 1603
Queen of England from 1558

Elizabeth I was the daughter of Henry VIII and his second wife, **Anne Boleyn**. When her father married his third wife, **Jane Seymour**, in 1536, Elizabeth and her elder half-sister Mary Tudor (the future **Mary I**) were declared illegitimate by parliament in favour of Jane Seymour's son, the future Edward VI. Her childhood was precarious but well educated, and unlike her sister she was brought up in the Protestant faith.

In 1549, during the reign of Edward VI, she rejected the advances of Thomas Seymour, Lord High Admiral of England, who was subsequently executed for treason. On Edward's death she sided with her half-sister Mary against Lady **Jane Grey** and the Earl of Warwick (Northumberland), but her identification with Protestantism aroused the suspicions of her Catholic sister, and she was imprisoned in the Tower.

Her accession to the throne in 1558 on Mary I's death was greeted with general approval as an earnest advocate of religious tolerance after the ferocious persecutions of the preceding reigns. Under the able guidance of Sir William Cecil (later Lord Burleigh) as secretary of state, Mary's Catholic legislation was repealed, and the church of England fully established (1559–63). Cecil also gave support to the Reformation in Scotland, where **Mary, Queen of Scots** had returned to Scotland in 1561 to face conflict with the Calvinist reformers led by John Knox. Imprisoned and forced to abdicate in 1567, in 1568 Mary escaped to England, where she was placed in confinement and soon became a focus for Catholic resistance to Elizabeth. The Northern rebellion of 1569 was followed by the Ridolfo plot the following year; and in 1570 the papal bull, *Regnans in Excelsis*, pronounced Elizabeth's excommunication and absolved her Catholic subjects from allegiance to her. Government retribution against English Catholics, at first restrained, became more repressive in the 1580s.

Several plots against the Queen were exposed, and the connivance of Mary in yet another plot in 1586 (known as the Babington conspiracy) led to her execution at Fotheringay Castle in 1587. The harsher policy against Roman Catholics, England's support for the Dutch rebellion against Spain, and the licensed piracy of men like Sir John Hawkins and Sir Francis Drake against Spanish possessions in the New World, all combined to provoke an attempted Spanish invasion in 1588. The Great Armada launched by Philip II of Spain reached the English Channel, only to be dispersed by storms and English harassment, and limped back to Spain after suffering considerable losses.

For the remainder of her reign, Elizabeth continued her policy of strengthening Protestant allies and dividing her enemies. She allowed marriage negotiations with various foreign suitors but with no real intention of getting married, or of settling the line of succession; but with the death of Mary, Queen of Scots, she was content to know that the heir-apparent, James VI of Scotland, was a Protestant. She indulged in romances with court favourites like Robert Dudley, Earl of Leicester, and later with Robert Devereux, Earl of Essex, until his rebelliousness led to his execution in 1601.

Her fiscal policies caused growing resentment, with escalating taxation to meet the costs of foreign military expeditions, and famine in the 1590s brought severe economic depression and social unrest, only partly alleviated by the Poor Law of 1597 which charged parishes with providing for the needy. England's vaunted sea-power stimulated voyages of discovery, with Drake circumnavigating the known world in 1577 and Sir Walter Raleigh mounting a number of expeditions to the North American coast in the 1580s, but England's only real Elizabethan colony was Ireland, where opportunities for English settlers to enrich themselves at the expense of the native Irish were now exploited more ruthlessly than ever before and provoked a serious rebellion under Hugh O'Neill, Earl of Tyrone, in 1597.

At Elizabeth's death in March, 1603, the Tudor dynasty came to an end and the throne passed peacefully to the Stuart James VI of Scotland as James I of England. Her long reign had coincided with the emergence of England as a world power and the flowering of the English Renaissance; and the legend of the 'Virgin Queen', assiduously promoted by the Queen herself and her court poets and playwrights, outlived her to play a crucial part in shaping the English national consciousness.

Elizabeth II

Born 1926
Queen of the United Kingdom and head of the Commonwealth

Elizabeth was born in London as Princess Elizabeth Alexandra Mary, the elder daughter

Queen Elizabeth II, 1995

of George VI and Lady Elizabeth Bowes-Lyon (later Queen **Elizabeth** the Queen Mother). On 20 November 1947 she married Philip Battenburg (created Duke of Edinburgh on the eve of their wedding and styled Prince Philip in 1957).

She was proclaimed Elizabeth II on the death of her father on 6 February 1952 and crowned on 2 June 1953. In December 1952 were announced the styles of the royal title as applicable to the Commonwealth countries, in all of which the Queen is accepted as head of the Commonwealth; she is Queen of the United Kingdom of Great Britain and Northern Ireland, Canada, Australia, New Zealand and of several other more recently independent countries.

Her silver jubilee was celebrated with great enthusiasm in 1977, but her long reign became somewhat troubled in the 1990s by questions about the role of the monarchy in modern Britain. Part of the controversy was fuelled by the breaking up of the marriages of two of her sons, Prince Charles and Prince Andrew and her daughter, Princess **Anne**. Her third and youngest son is Prince Edward.

Elizabeth, *originally* Lady Elizabeth Bowes-Lyon

Born 1900
Queen Mother, and Queen of the United Kingdom as the wife of George VI (ruled 1936–52)

Lady Elizabeth Bowes-Lyon was born at St Paul's Walden Bury, Hertfordshire, and her father became 14th Earl of Strathmore in 1904. Much of her childhood was spent at Glamis Castle in Scotland, where she helped the nursing staff in World War I. In 1920 she met George, the Duke of York, second son of George V; they were married in April 1923. Princess Elizabeth (later **Elizabeth II**) was born in 1926 and Princess **Margaret** in 1930.

The Duchess accompanied her husband on a long tour of Australasia in 1927 and, after he came to the throne as King George VI in 1936, she scored striking personal success in royal visits to Paris (1938) and to Canada and the USA (1939). She was with the king when Buckingham Palace was bombed in 1940, travelling with him to visit heavily damaged towns throughout World War II. In 1947 she became the only Queen of England to tour South Africa.

After George VI's death in 1952, the Queen Mother continued to undertake public duties, flying thousands of miles each year and becoming a widely-loved figure. She never retired and, from 1953 onwards, found a new interest in restoring the Castle of Mey, on the Pentland Firth, as her favourite Scottish home. In 1978 she became Lord Warden of the Cinque Ports, the first woman to hold the office.

Elizabeth

Born 1st century BC Died 1st century AD
Biblical character who was the mother of John the Baptist

Elizabeth was the wife of the priest Zechariah. Though the marriage was childless for many years, her husband received an angelic prophecy concerning the birth and mission of a son who would prepare people for the message of Jesus Christ.

The apparent impossibility of this struck Zechariah dumb until John's birth, while Elizabeth believed and was thankful. When Mary was told by the angel Gabriel about the forthcoming birth of Jesus, she was also informed that her kinswoman Elizabeth was pregnant and went to visit her. When the two women met, Elizabeth prophesied, blessing Mary's faith, and stayed about three months.

Elizabeth de Burgh, *also known as* Lady Elizabeth de Clare

Born 1295 Died 1360
English noblewoman who founded Clare College, Cambridge

Elizabeth de Burgh was the youngest daughter of Gilbert, Earl de Clare, Gloucester and Hereford, and of Joan of Acre, daughter of Edward I. On her brother Gilbert's death at Bannockburn in 1314 she and her sisters inherited the family lands and Elizabeth took the name Lady de Clare. She successively married and outlived John de Burgh (d.1313), Lord Theobald Verdon (d.1316), and Lord Roger Damory (d.1321) by whom she had two daughters.

A close friend of **Marie de St Pol**, Lady de Clare endowed University Hall, Cambridge, in 1346, which soon became known as Clare Hall. She took a close interest in college affairs, giving statutes in 1359, and further endowing the college in her will.

Elizabeth of Bohemia

Born 1596 Died 1662
Queen of Bohemia as the wife of Frederick I (ruled 1619–20)

Elizabeth was the eldest daughter of James VI of Scotland and I of England and **Anne of Denmark**. She married Frederick V, elector Palatine of the Rhine (1610–23), in 1613. She was intelligent and cultured, and enlivened the court at Heidelberg (the capital of the Palatinate) by her presence.

With Frederick's championship of the Protestant cause and his brief, unhappy winter as King Frederick I of Bohemia (1619–20), Elizabeth was known variously as 'the Winter Queen' or 'the Queen of Hearts' and became a potent symbol of the Protestant cause in Europe.

Driven from Prague and deprived of the palatinate by Maximilian of Bavaria, the couple lived in exile in the Hague, continually beset by financial difficulties, with their numerous children, including **Sophia**. Frederick died in 1632, but Elizabeth outlived him by 30 years. Her son, Charles Louis, was restored to the Palatinate in 1648, but she remained in Holland. She died in London in 1662 while on a visit to her nephew, the newly-restored Charles II of England.

Elizabeth of France, *known as* Madame Elizabeth

Born 1764 Died 1794
French princess who was executed for her loyalty
to her brothers

Elizabeth was born in Versailles, a daughter of the dauphin Louis and Maria Josepha of Saxony, and sister of Louis XVI. During the Revolution, out of loyalty to Louis XVI and **Marie Antoinette**, she refused to flee France with her two brothers (the future Louis VXIII and Charles X) and was imprisoned in the Temple after the monarchy was suspended on 10 August 1792.

Her heroic and patient forbearance of her confinement and execution by guillotine gained her much posthumous admiration.

Elizabeth of Hungary, St

Born 1207 Died 1231
Hungarian princess who used her position to
relieve the suffering of the needy

Elizabeth was born in Sáros, Patak, a daughter of Andrew II of Hungary. At the age of four she was betrothed to Louis IV, Landgrave of Thuringia, and educated at his father's court, the Wartburg, near Eisenach. At 14 she was happily married, and she later gave birth to a boy and two girls.

Louis, who admired her for her long prayers and ceaseless alms-giving, died as a crusader at Otranto in 1227, whereupon Elizabeth was deprived of her regency by her husband's brother and evicted from the Wartburg on the grounds that she mismanaged her husband's estates through wasteful charity. After making

provision for her children she enrolled as a Franciscan tertiary at Marburg in Hesse (she had promised Louis she would never marry again) and devoted the rest of her life to the relief of the needy.

She suffered severe privation at the hands of her spiritual adviser, Konrad of Marburg, but nevertheless declined to return to Hungary, seeing her vocation in serving the underprivileged for whom she had built a hostel near her own cottage. It was not long before her physical condition was so weakened, however, that she died at the age of only 24. She was canonized by Pope Gregory IX in 1235 and her feast day is 17 November.

Elizabeth of Portugal, St, *known in Portugal as* Isabel

Born 1271 Died 1336
Portuguese saint and Queen of Portugal as the
wife of King Denis

Elizabeth was the daughter of King Peter III of Aragon and great-niece of **Elizabeth of Hungary**. She was married at the age of 12 to King Denis of Portugal and as queen became known for her piety, social concern and generosity, which she managed to cultivate despite the corrupt life of court. The institutions she founded to meet the needs around her included a hospital, an orphanage and a women's hostel.

She earned the sobriquet of 'peacemaker' because she brought about the reconciliation of Denis and their rebellious son Afonso, who had attempted an armed coup. In 1336 she rode on to the battlefield between the forces of her son (now Afonso IV) and Alfonso of Castile to avert a war between Portugal and Castile.

Though her marriage was an unhappy one, she nursed her unfaithful husband through a long illness before his death. Afterwards she retired to live near a Poor Clare convent which she had founded in Coimbra. She was canonized in 1625 and her feast day is 8 July.

Elizabeth of the Trinity, *also known as* Elizabeth Catez

Born 1880 Died 1906
French Carmelite mystic who believed in the
indwelling of the Trinity in the soul

Elizabeth of the Trinity was born in Bourges. She made a private vow of virginity at 14, but respected her mother's refusal to allow her to become a Carmelite. Her own spiritual experiences were clarified by reading **Teresa of Ávila**'s *Way of Perfection*, the letters of St Paul, and the guidance of a Dominican priest, Iréné Vallée.

She entered the Carmelite house in Dijon in 1901, but before she could take her final vows, she died of an incurable disease. The key to her spirituality, devotion to the indwelling of the Trinity in the soul, is celebrated in a prayer she wrote in 1904. She was beatified in 1984.

Elizabeth of York

Died 1503
English queen as the wife of Henry VII (ruled 1485–1509)

Elizabeth of York was the eldest daughter of Edward IV and **Elizabeth Woodville**, and knew from childhood that she was destined for a political union. She was betrothed first to the Earl of Warwick's heir and then to the French dauphin, son of Louis XII, but on the death of her two brothers in the Tower she became heiress to the House of York and her marriage to the exiled Henry Tudor was arranged.

Following his defeat of Richard III, Henry insisted on delaying the marriage until after he was crowned as Henry VII, because he knew that Elizabeth's claim to the throne was superior to his own. They were married in 1486 and Elizabeth was crowned two years later; despite being arranged, the marriage seems to have been happy.

Elizabeth Petrovna, *also called* Elizabeth of Russia

Born 1709 Died 1762
Empress of Russia from 1741

Elizabeth Petrovna was born in Kolomens-koye, near Moscow, the younger daughter of Peter I, the Great and **Catherine I**. Passed over for the throne on earlier occasions, she came to power in 1741 in a military coup which ousted the infant Ivan VI (1740–64), but left the running of the state largely to her favourites.

An easy-going, intelligent and genial character, she created a brilliant court and superintended a renaissance of Russian arts; she founded the University of Moscow (1755) and the Academy of Fine Arts in St Petersburg (1758) and built the Winter Palace in St Petersburg. She was a patron of the Russian scientist and poet Mikhail Lomonosov (1711–65).

Early in her reign she made war with Sweden (1741–3), which came to a successful conclusion with the Treaty of Abö, and, motivated by a dislike of Frederick II, the Great, plunged Russia into the Seven Years' War (1756–63). She was succeeded by her

nephew Peter III, whom she had designated as her successor in 1742.

Elliot, Cass, *later known as* Mama Cass

Born 1943 Died 1974
American folk and pop singer who was a member of the Mugwumps and the Mamas and the Papas

Cass Elliot was born in Baltimore, Maryland. In the early 1960s, she and first husband John Hendricks formed folk-inclined Cass Elliot and the Big Three, later the Mugwumps. The Mamas and the Papas (formed 1966) were archetypal California hippies, recording 'California Dreamin'' and 'Monday, Monday'.

The band split in 1968, but members continued to work together occasionally, as on Elliot's 'Dream a Little Dream of Me' of that year. She continued to perform in the face of health problems, exacerbated by obesity, and died of a heart attack in London, aged 30.

Elliott, Charlotte

Born 1789 Died 1871
English hymn writer who wrote the famous hymn 'Just as I am, without one plea'

Charlotte Elliott was born and brought up in Clapham, until the family moved to Brighton in 1823. Her maternal grandfather was the Evangelical leader Henry Venn (1725–97). She was converted at the age of 22 and corresponded for 40 years with the Genevan evangelist César Malan.

Left a permanent invalid after a serious illness when she was 32, she wrote some 150 hymns, mostly between 1834 and 1841. Many are included in the 1854 edition of *The Invalid's Hymnbook*. The first line of one of the most enduring, 'Christian, seek not yet repose' well expresses her rejection of idleness. Her hymn of dedication to God, 'Just as I am, without one plea' (1834) prompted more than 1,000 letters to the author in her lifetime.

Elliott, Grace Dalrymple, *née* Dalrymple

Born c.1758 Died 1823
Scottish courtesan whose lovers came from the highest society of the time

Grace Dalrymple was the daughter of an Edinburgh advocate, Hew Dalrymple. In 1771 she married Sir John Elliott, MD (1736–86), who divorced her in 1774.

She was the mistress successively or simultaneously of Lord Valentia, Lord Cholmondley, the Prince of Wales (the future George IV), Charles Windham, George

Selwyn, Philippe Égalité (Duke of Orléans) and many others.

She died at Ville d'Avray near Sèvres, leaving an interesting but untrustworthy *Journal of My Life during the Revolution*, published in 1859 by her granddaughter.

Ellis, Ruth, *née* Neilson

Born 1926 Died 1955
Convicted Welsh murderer and the last person to be hanged in Britain

Ruth Neilson was born in Rhyl, Clwyd. She was a night-club hostess who in a jealous rage repeatedly shot her former lover, David Blakely, a racing-car driver, outside a Hampstead pub on 10 April 1955.

The case achieved notoriety as a 'crime passionnel' — Blakely was trying to extricate himself from their tempestuous, often violent, relationship at the time of his murder.

Ellis was the last woman to receive the death penalty in Britain; she was hanged on 13 July 1955.

Ellis, Sarah, *née* Stickney

Born 1810 Died 1872
English writer, a Victorian forerunner of the women's movement

Sarah Stickney was born into a Quaker family from Yorkshire. She published *Poetry of Life* (1835) and *Pictures of Private Life* (a novel serialized 1833–7) before marrying William Ellis, a missionary, in 1837.

A conservative writer and believer in Christian values who was also involved in teaching and philanthropic work, she wrote a quartet of books which included *The Wives of England* (1843), highlighting the inferiority of educational and career opportunities available to middle-class women.

Elms, Lauris Margaret

Born 1931
Australian operatic and lieder singer

Lauris Elms was born in Melbourne, Victoria. She studied in Paris and made her début in 1957 at Covent Garden in Verdi's *Un Ballo in Maschera*, and became principal resident artist there.

She toured Australia with **Joan Sutherland** in 1965, and appeared at the royal opening of the Sydney Opera House in 1973. She has appeared with all leading Australian companies, and is renowned for her Azucena in Verdi's *Il Trovatore*.

She has broadcast frequently and gives regular lieder recitals with pianist Geoffrey Parsons. Her many acclaimed recordings include *Peter Grimes* under the composer Benjamin Britten.

Elssler, Fanny (Franziska)

Born 1810 Died 1884
Austrian ballet dancer, the first to incorporate theatricalized folk-dance into ballet

Fanny Elssler was born in Vienna, the daughter of a valet and copyist for the composer Franz Joseph Haydn. Her elder sister Therese Elssler (1808–78) was also a dancer, but of the two Fanny was the more fêted, dancing her way through more than 25 years of successful world touring, first in Europe and from 1840 to 1842 in the USA, the only major Romantic ballerina to go there.

She first danced at the Paris Opéra in an adaptation of Shakespeare's *Tempest* (1834), at once challenging the loyalty of the fans of **Maria Taglioni**, her greatest rival, whose lightness and delicacy provided a startling contrast to Elssler's warmth and spontaneity. Elssler is remembered also for having been the first to include theatricalized folk-dance into ballet, for example her performance of the Spanish cachucha in *Le Diable boiteux* (1836) and the Polish cracovienne in *La Gypsy* (1839).

As well as joining her sister on stage as a performer, Therese was one of the few female choreographers of the time. Fanny retired in 1851, and Therese in 1850 married Prince Adalbert of Prussia, nephew of Frederick William III.

Elstob, Elizabeth

Born 1683 Died 1756
English scholar and translator of Anglo-Saxon

Elizabeth Elstob was born in Newcastle-upon-Tyne and orphaned by the time she was eight. Her guardian ceased her education but she obtained permission to learn French and went to live with her brother in Oxford where she learnt eight languages, including Latin. In later life she ran a school and became a governess.

She published a selection of works including a translation of **Madeleine de Scudéry's** *Essay upon Glory* (1708), *An English Anglo-Saxon Homily, On the Birth-Day of St Gregory* (1709) dedicated to Queen **Anne**, and *The Rudiments of Grammar for the Anglo-Saxon Tongue, first given in English with an Apology for the Study of Northern Antiquities* (1715).

Emecheta, (Florence Onye) Buchi

Born 1944
Nigerian-born British sociologist, poet and
novelist who depicts the female condition as a
struggle against the limitations of traditional
society

Buchi Emecheta was born near Lagos and educated at the Methodist Girls' High School there
and at the University of London. She has
worked as a teacher, librarian and social
worker. She moved to England with her
student husband in 1962 and has since lived
in London with her five children.

Speaking of marriage as a battle of the sexes,
her novels are powerful social documents,
graphic in their depiction of man's inhu-
manity to woman (she and her husband
separated). Relevant titles are *In the Ditch*
(1972) and *Second-Class Citizen* (1974), which
were later published together as *Adah's Story*
(1983) and draw on her experiences as an
immigrant. *The Bride Price* (1976), *The Slave
Girl* (1977), *The Joys of Motherhood* (1979),
Double Yoke (1982) and *The Rape of Shavi*
(1983) share the central theme of a woman
adapting to changing circumstances, and
Gwendolen (1989) focuses on the cultural isolation of a young Caribbean immigrant.

Emecheta has also written children's stories
and television plays.

Emerson, Gladys Anderson

Born 1903
American biochemist whose work focused mainly
on nutrition and the role of vitamins

Gladys Emerson was born in Caldwell, Kansas,
and educated at Oklahoma College for
Women. She later received a fellowship to
study nutrition and biochemistry at Berkeley.

Following the identification of vitamin E
by Herbert Evans, Emerson first succeeded
in isolating it in a pure form. At the Merck
Pharmaceutical Company in New Jersey she
studied the role of vitamin B complex
deficiencies in diseases such as arterio-
sclerosis. She also investigated the possible
dietary causes of cancer.

In 1956 she was appointed Professor of
Nutrition at the University of California at Los
Angeles.

Emma (Adelheid Emma Wilhelmina Theresia)

Born 1858 Died 1934
Queen of the Netherlands as the wife of William
III (ruled 1849–90) and Regent during the
minority of her daughter

Emma was the daughter of Prince George
Victor of Waldeck-Pyrmont and Helena of
Nassau-Weilburg. She became the second wife
of the Dutch King William III on 7 January
1879 and the following year her daughter, the
future Queen **Wilhelmina**, was born.

As queen mother, Emma was Regent of the
Netherlands shortly before the death of her
husband in Decemer 1890 until her daughter
came of age in 1898. After William III's
unpopularity, Emma succeeded in restoring
the esteem of the Dutch for their monarchy.

Emma

Died 1052
Queen of England as the wife first of Æthelred II,
'the Unready' and then of Knut Sveinsson (Canute)

Emma was the daughter of Richard, Duke of
Normandy. She married Æthelred in 1002, and
they had a son who was later to be known as
Edward 'the Confessor'. When Svein Haralds-
son, known as 'Fork-Beard', invaded England
in 1013 Emma fled home to Normandy for
safety with Æthelred, and stayed there with
her son Edward when Æthelred returned for
a brief resumption of his reign (1014–16).

In 1017 she was summoned to England to
marry Æthelred's successor, Knut Sveinsson,
by whom she had a son, Hardaknut. On Knut's
death in 1035 she tried to put her son Hardaknut on the throne but was thwarted by her
stepson, Harold Harefoot (Knut's son by his
English mistress Ælgifu) and fled to the court
of Baldwin the Pious, Count of Flanders and
father-in-law of William I, the Conqueror.

She returned to England with Hardaknut
on his election as king in 1040, but after Hardaknut's death in 1042 she found no favour
with his successor, her other son, Edward the
Confessor. In 1043 she had all her lands and
property confiscated by him, apparently for
favouring a rival claimant to the English
throne, Magnus 'the Good' of Norway.

Emmerich, Anna Katharina, *known as the* Nun of Dülmen

Born 1774 Died 1824
German visionary and nun whose visions were
described by Clemens von Brentano

Anna Katharina Emmerich was born near
Coesfeld. She entered the Augustinian order
in 1802, and from 1812 bore the stigmata of
Christ's passion.

Her revelations were recorded by the
German poet Clemens von Brentano (1778–
1842), who had withdrawn to the monastery
of Dülmen to be near her.

Ender, Kornelia

Born 1958
German swimmer who has broken more world
records than any other woman

Kornelia Ender was born in Bitterfeld. Representing East Germany, she won three Olympic silver medals in 1972, aged 13, and between 1973 and 1976 broke 23 world records (the most by a woman under modern conditions). At the 1973 and 1975 World Championships she won 10 medals, including a record eight golds.

In 1976 she became the first woman to win four gold medals at one Olympic Games: the 100m and 200m freestyle, the 100m butterfly and the 4 × 100m medley relay.

Engel, Marian, *née* Passmore

Born 1933 Died 1985
Canadian novelist whose economical style of
writing examines the differences and resentment
between the sexes

Marian Engel was born in Toronto and educated at McMaster University and McGill University. She worked as a teacher in Canada and the USA and lived for a time in London and Cyprus. She married Howard Engel in 1962 but divorced in 1977. Her first novel, *No Clouds of Glory*, was published in 1968.

She chaired the Writers' Union of Canada in 1973–4, and won a Governor-General's award for *Bear* in 1976; her most famous novel, it explores the complex relationship between a woman and a bear, intertwining myth and reality and stirred up much controversy at the time. Her last book, *The Tattooed Woman*, was published posthumously.

Enoki, Miswo

Born 1939
Japanese feminist, a radical campaigner for equal
rights in Japanese society

Miswo Enoki trained as a pharmacist. She is best known as a radical Japanese feminist. She was a leader, during the 1970s, of the Pink Panthers movement which campaigned strongly for abortion rights, greater legal rights for women in marriage and on divorce, and equal pay legislation. She also formed the Japan Woman's Party to contest the general election of 1977.

Ense, Rahel Varnhagen von *see*
Varnhagen von Ense, Rahel

'Ephelia'

Floreat 1679
The unidentified author of Female Poems on
Several Occasions *(1679)*

'Ephelia' was born in London, by her own account, to well-connected parents who died young. Her poems show the frank eroticism typical of Restoration love-songs. Among others published under her name is a political broadside, *Advice to his Grace* (1681), warning the Duke of Monmouth against 'mad ambition'.

Attempts to identify her as the daughter of the poet **Katherine Philips** have not been substantiated, and it remains possible that 'Ephelia' was the pseudonym of a group of male poets.

Ephron, Nora

Born 1941
American screenwriter whose witty,
contemporary romantic comedies have
enjoyed huge success

Nora Ephron was born in New York and educated at Wellesley College. Both her parents were writers. Her début screenplay collaboration *Silkwood* (1983) earned her an Academy Award nomination, and she went on to write two of the most successful romantic comedies of the period: *When Harry Met Sally* (1989) and *Sleepless in Seattle* (1993).

She adapted *Heartburn*, her novel about her failed marriage to Carl Bernstein, one of the *Washington Post* journalists who uncovered the Watergate affair, for the screen in 1985, and added directing to her credits with *This Is My Life* in 1992.

Épinay, Louise Florence Pétronille de La Live, *known as* Madame d'Épinay, *née* Tardieu d'Esclavelles

Born 1726 Died 1783
French writer who spent much of her time with
the famous Encylopaedists

Louise Tardieu was born in Valenciennes. At the age of 19 she married a worthless cousin, Denis-Joseph de La Live D'Épinay. Following their separation she held a brilliant salon at La Chevrette and formed liaisons with the prominent writers and thinkers Baron Friedrich Melchior de Grimm, Jean-Jacques Rousseau and Denis Diderot, the leader of the group who produced the 28-volume *Encyclopédie* (1751–75) — relationships that earned her more fame than her own writing.

She collaborated with Grimm, a long-time friend, on his *Correspondence Littéraire* (1812) and provided Rousseau with the house in which he wrote *Julie, ou la Nouvelle Héloïse* (1761), until they quarrelled and he departed. *Conversations d'Émilie* (1774), a work on education, won her a gold medal from the French Academy.

Eriksen, Gunn

Born 1956
Norwegian-born chef and restaurateur who has made herself a brilliant reputation at the Altnaharrie Inn

Gunn Eriksen was born in Grimstad. A ceramicist and weaver by training, she went to Ullapool to pursue her craft and there met Fred Brown, owner of the Altnaharrie Inn across Loch Broom from Ullapool. She joined him there in 1980 and began to develop the distinctive cooking style which has brought her renown. They married in 1984.

Despite having had no formal culinary training, she combines unusual hedgerow ingredients (nettles, sorrel, hawthorn sprouts) with local seafood and imported ingredients to make memorable meals which reveal her Scandinavian origins.

In 1994 Altnaharrie became the only restaurant in Scotland to have been awarded two Michelin stars, but given the hotel's somewhat isolated location (practical access only by boat), the willingness of visitors to seek out its cooking makes its own point.

Erinna

4th century BC
Greek poet remembered for a few lines of hexameter poetry

Erinna was born on the island of Telos. She is often mistakenly believed in antiquity to have lived in the 7th century. Though she died at the age of only 19, she won fame for her epic, *The Distaff*, on the joys of childhood, which was apparently written in mourning for a friend. Only four lines of this and a handful of epigrams survive of her work.

Ermelova, Mariya Nikolaevna, *also spelt* Maria Yermelova

Born 1853 Died 1928
Russian actress who became the leading tragedienne of the Maly Theatre

Mariya Ermelova was born in Moscow, the daughter of a prompter at the Maly Theatre. She took up an acting career, enjoying early success from 1870, but it was her incendiary role in Lope de Vega's *Fuenteovejuna* that made her name in progressive circles.

She became the leading tragic actress of the Maly Theatre, and played in both classic Western drama and contemporary Russian plays with great success. Her career revived in the early Soviet era, when she played a series of politically approved anti-bourgeois roles. A studio at the Maly Theatre was named after her in 1930.

Erskine, Mary

Born 1629 Died 1707
Scottish pioneer of girls' education in Scotland who gave her name to a famous school in Edinburgh

Mary Erskine was born in Garlet, Clackmannanshire. Relatively little is known about her private life. She was married twice: first in 1661 to an Edinburgh writer called Robert Kennedy (d.1671), then in 1671 to an Edinburgh druggist and apothecary, James Hair. After his death in 1683 she reverted to her maiden name and set up business as a private banker.

In 1694 she contributed to a scheme by the Edinburgh Merchant Company for founding Merchant Maiden Hospital, for the education of the daughters of burgesses. For this purpose she left a benefaction of 10,000 merks Scots. Deacon Brodie is reputed to have been a governor of the school. In 1869 it was transformed into a day school for girls, known as Edinburgh Ladies' College, and in 1944 changed its name to Mary Erskine School.

In 1704 she was instrumental in the establishment of the more vocationally oriented Trades Maiden Hospital which, unlike other similar foundations, did not run its own school but provided boarding and clothing.

Espert Romero, Nuria

Born 1935
Spanish actress and stage director whose company is famous for its productions of both modern and classical works

Nuria Espert Romero began her professional career at the age of 12, played Juliet at 16 and scored a significant success in the role of Medea at 19. At 24 she co-founded the Nuria Espert Theatre Company, which she still leads.

She has played the title role in *Hamlet*, and both Prospero and Ariel in the same production of *The Tempest*. Other productions include Bertolt Brecht's *The Good Person of Setzuan*, Oscar Wilde's *Salome* and a highly acclaimed *Yerma* by Lorca. She has appeared as an actress in productions all over the world.

In 1986 she directed an award-winning revival of Lorca's *The House of Bernarda Alba* with **Glenda Jackson** and **Joan Plowright** in London, and moved into opera with Puccini's *Madame Butterfly* for Scottish Opera.

Espin, Vilma, *married* Castro

Born 1930
Cuban revolutionary and politician, sister-in-law to Fidel Castro

Vilma Espin was born in Santiago de Cuba. While studying to become a chemical engineer at Oriente University, she became politically involved in the resistance to Batista's 1952 coup. She became an important co-ordinator for the resistance network in Santiago de Cuba, after Fidel Castro's attack on the Moncada army barracks (1953).

She undertook postgraduate study at the Massachusetts Institute of Technology, and joined Castro (whose brother Raiul Castro she later married) in Mexico. She was involved in the revolutionary struggle conducted from the Sierra Maestra in Eastern Cuba from 1956, until Batista was overthrown in 1959.

Espin has been President of the Federation of Cuban Women since its founding in 1960, and is a member of the central committee of the Cuban Communist Party.

Estaugh, Elizabeth, *née* Haddon

Born 1680   Died 1762
English-born American Quaker, famous as the founder of the settlement of Haddonfield, New Jersey

Elizabeth Haddon was born in Southwark in London into a Quaker family. She was probably educated in a Quaker school. In 1701 she emigrated to New Jersey to administer the plantation which her father had bought there, intending the whole family to emigrate. She had met the Quaker preacher John Estaugh in London, and felt called to go to America, to work among the Native Americans and establish a base for itinerant preachers.

Although after their marriage (1702) John Estaugh became nominal head of the Haddon plantations, it was Elizabeth who administered the estate. She first lived in the house called Old Haddonfield; in 1713 she established the new house and settlement of New Haddonfield.

Esteve-Coll, Dame Elizabeth Anne Loosemore, *née* Kingdon

Born 1938
English university vice-chancellor who became director of a major London museum

Elizabeth Haddon was educated in Darlington. She married José Esteve-Coll (d.1980) in 1960 and attended London University as a mature student, graduating in 1976. After holding the positions of head of learning resources at Kingston Polytechnic in 1977 and university librarian at Surrey University in 1982, she joined the Victoria and Albert Museum as keeper of the national art library in 1985, being appointed director three years later.

Though accused of weak leadership, Esteve-Coll made the V & A more inviting to the public by improving signposting and encouraging scholarship. She devised the controversially populist slogan 'ace cafe with quite a nice museum attached' to raise awareness of the improvements, but this too was accused of being downmarket in style. In 1995 she resigned to become Vice-Chancellor of the University of East Anglia, and also that year she was created DBE.

Esther

3rd century bc
Biblical queen whose story tells of the origin of the Jewish festival Purim

Esther was a foster-daughter of her cousin, the Jew Mordecai. According to the biblical Book of Esther she was a beautiful woman chosen by the Persian king Ahasuerus (Xerxes I) as his wife in place of the disgraced Queen Vashti, who had been hanged for disobeying her husband's command to show off her beauty to his guests.

By revealing her Jewish identity Esther and Mordecai succeeded in persuading the king not to slaughter the Jews — an event planned for a day which was to be decided by lot (*pur*), which had been organized by the self-important, cruel official Haman, before whom Mordecai had refused to prostrate himself.

Instead the chosen day marked the slaughter of the enemies of the Jews, whose leader was Haman. Tradition holds that this is the origin of Purim, the Jewish feast celebrating the deliverance of the people.

Estrées, Gabrielle d'

Born c.1570   Died 1599
French noblewoman who became the influential mistress of Henry IV of France

Gabrielle d'Estrées was the daughter of the Marquis de Coeuvres. At the court of Henry III she met and became the mistress of Roger de Saint-Lary. He introduced her to Henry IV of France, whose mistress she then became, probably from about 1590. He created her

Marquise de Monceaux and Duchesse de Beaufort.

She had tremendous influence over him and persuaded him to embrace Roman Catholicism, perhaps in the hope that the pope would annul his marriage to Queen Margaret. Henry treated d'Estrées like his queen, and was about to divorce his wife in order to marry her, when she died suddenly in Paris.

From their natural offspring César, Catherine-Henriette and Alexandre, who were legitimized, the house of Vendôme was descended.

Etheldreda, St, *also called* Audrey *or* Aethelthryth

Born c.630　Died 679
Anglo-Saxon founder of a monastery at Ely who is revered as a virgin saint, although twice married

Etheldreda was one of the five daughters of King Anna of East Anglia, all of whom are honoured as saints. She was widowed after three years of her first marriage, which was said never to have been consummated. She then spent five years in solitude on the isle of Ely, which had been her dowry.

In 660, for political reasons, she married the 15-year-old Ecgfrith, future king of Northumbria, who at first agreed that she could preserve her virginity. After 12 years he requested normal conjugal relations, but instead his wife sought the advice of the Bishop of Northumbria, St Wilfrid, and had the marriage dissolved.

She took the veil and withdrew to the double monastery at Coldingham, Berwickshire, founded by her aunt **Ebba**, and in 672 founded a double monastery herself on the isle of Ely, of which she was appointed abbess, and where her sister Sexburga succeeded her following her death from plague. During her illness she had claimed that the tumour on her neck was punishment for her behaviour in her frivolous youth when she had adorned herself with necklaces. Etheldreda is the patron saint of Cambridge University and her feast day is 23 June.

Etheria, *also called* Egeria *or* Aiheria

4th century AD
Pilgrim whose writings are an important source of historical information

Etheria was an abbess or nun, possibly from Spain. She organized a pilgrimage journey to the Holy Land, Egypt, Asia Minor and Constantinople which may have taken place between AD 381 and 384. Information about it is known from an 11th-century manuscript discovered in 1884, which was initially attributed to St Sylvia.

The account is full of geographical observations about religious sites and is an important source of information about early Christian worship, such as the fact that at that time the Nativity was celebrated in Egypt and Jerusalem on 6 January.

Etheridge, Melissa

Born 1962
American singer and songwriter and one of the few openly gay celebrities in the USA

Melissa Etheridge was born in Leavenworth, Kansas. Her 1988 début album *Melissa Etheridge* brought her her first Grammy nomination, and her second album, *Brave and Crazy,* was released the following year.

It was her more experimental album *Never Enough* (1992) that won her a Best Female Rock Perfomance Grammy for the single 'Ain't it Heavy'. After that, her albums and singles sold in the millions and her concert tours (often for AIDS benefits) became sell-outs. In 1993 the album *Yes I Am* had two top-ten single hits. Also that year Etheridge publicly revealed her homosexuality. In 1995 she won her second Grammy for Best Female Rock Performance.

Eudocia, *originally* Athenais

Born AD401　Died AD465
Byzantine princess and wife of Theodosius II (ruled 408–50)

Athenais was the beautiful and accomplished daughter of an Athenian professor of rhetoric. She was chosen by the all-powerful **Pulcheria** to be the wife of her brother, the weak-minded Eastern Roman Emperor, Theodosius II. Before marrying him in 421, Athenais renounced paganism, was baptized a Christian, and changed her name.

After the marriage, she exercised great influence over Theodosius and violent rivalry arose between the sisters-in-law. In 438, the year after her daughter Licinia Eudoxia had married the Western Emperor Valentinian III, Eudocia went on pilgrimage for a year to Jerusalem.

She returned to more quarrels with Pulcheria, often about opposing heresies, and in 443 Eudocia left Constantinople to live the rest of her life in Jerusalem, where she devoted herself to building churches and other works of piety.

She wrote a panegyric about Theodosius's

victories over the Persians in 422, paraphrases of Scripture, hymns and poetry.

Eugénie, Empress, *originally* Eugénia Maria de Montijo de Guzmán

Born 1826 Died 1920
Spanish countess and Empress of France during the Second Empire as the wife of Napoleon III

Eugénie was a Spanish countess, born in Granada. She was educated in Paris and married Napoleon III in 1853 soon after he became Emperor of France.

During the Second Empire (1853–70), the 'Empire Style' exercised considerable influence over European fashion. The couturier Charles Frederick Worth designed Eugénie's dresses, and Paris attained its eminence in the fashion world.

Eugénie's support of the papacy and her anti-democratic beliefs strongly influenced Napoleon. She acted as his regent in 1859, 1865 and 1870. She is credited with promoting Maximilian of Austria's invasion of Mexico (1863) and inciting Napoleon to start the Franco-Prussian war in 1870. After Napoleon's abdication that year Eugénie lived with him in exile at Chislehurst in Kent.

Eustochium, St Julia

Born c.370AD Died AD418 or 419
Disciple of Jerome and first Roman Christian patrician lady to take a vow of virginity

St Julia Eustochium was counselled by Jerome to live an ascetic life in Rome, in response to which she made her vow of perpetual virginity. The circulation of copies of his letter to her — part of a campaign to clean up Church life — prompted a furore which forced Jerome and his friends, including Eustochium, to leave the city.

They travelled to Egypt and settled in Bethlehem, where Eustochium and her mother **Paula** built a monastery and a convent. On Paula's death the convent's direction passed to Eustochium. Jerome praised her asceticism and devotion to scripture which encouraged him to write biblical commentaries. Her feast day is 28 September.

Evangelista, Linda

Born 1965
Canadian model, one of the first to attain 'supermodel' status

Linda Evangelista was born of Italian parentage in St Catherine's Ontario, near Niagara. An early enthusiasm for modelling led her at the age of 16 to enter a Miss Teen Niagara pageant.

Although she did not win, she was spotted by a scout from the model agency Elite. When she was 19 she moved to New York, but only gained recognition when she moved to Paris in 1988 and cropped her hair. Also that year she married Gerald Marie, head of Elite in Paris, but they divorced five years later.

Evangelista is the consummate fashion model, moving with ease between catwalk and photgraphic studio, making a career out of re-inventing her image. She is remembered also for joking to a *Vogue* reporter once: 'We don't wake up for less than $10,000 a day.' She is also a keen amateur photographer, and has had her fashion reportage work published by several magazines.

Evans, Alice

Born 1881 Died 1975
American microbiologist who discovered the common bacterial cause and aetiology of brucellosis

Alice Evans's early education was meagre, but she won a scholarship to study science at Cornell, from which she graduated with a Masters degree in bacteriology in 1910. She accepted a position working in the Dairy Division of the US Department of Agriculture, moving to the US Public Health Service (later the National Institutes of Health) in 1918.

Her investigations into the dangers of non-pasteurized cows' milk, and assertion that cattle brucellosis and human Malta fever had a common origin rather than being two distint diseases, were strongly resisted by veterinarians, dairymen and many physicians. Compelling confirmation during the late 1920s and 1930s led to the recognition of Evans's achievements and she received several honours, including that of being the first woman President of the Society of American Bacteriologists (1928).

Evans, Augusta Jane, *later* Augusta Wilson

Born 1835 Died 1909
American popular novelist whose St Elmo was one of the century's most popular novels

Augusta Evans was born in Columbus, Georgia. From 1868, the date of her marriage, she wrote under her married name of Wilson.

Her novel *St Elmo* (1866) attracted more ridicule than praise, but this story of the prudish Edna Earle's 'taming' of the supposedly Byronic St Elmo, written with much pretentious erudition, became a bestseller and one of the 19th century's most popular novels.

It offers a good example of how 'unwholesome and eminently forgettable trash' can sweep a nation — but only for a short time.

Wilson was less prolific than many of her contemporaries; her other novels include *Vashti* (1869) and *At the Mercy of Tiberius* (1887).

Evans, Dale, *originally* Frances Octavia Smith

Born 1912
American country singer, actress and evangelist who married the 'singing cowboy'

Dale Evans was born in Uvalde, Texas. After business school, she took a job as a secretary. Her boss heard her singing and suggested that she sing on the radio show sponsored by the company. After that she was heard on the radio in Chicago and Dallas.

She went to Hollywood and made her film début in *Swing Your Partner* in 1943, the year she was cast opposite the 'Singing Cowboy' Roy Rogers in *The Cowboy and the Senorita*. They married in 1949 and made nearly 40 films together, mostly westerns with singing numbers. In 1951 her husband formed his own production company and produced a half-hour television western, in which they both starred. Its theme song, 'Happy Trails to You', was one of Evans's many compositions and is regarded as a signature song for the couple.

Evans is known to have a strong evangelical Christian faith and is noted for her charity work. Her 1953 book *Angel Unaware* speaks of her faith and tells of the life and death of her mentally retarded daughter.

Evans, Dame Edith Mary

Born 1888 Died 1976
English actress who earned an enviable reputation for her versatility

Edith Evans was born in London. Throughout her career of over 60 years she appeared in many Shakespeare and Shaw plays, and in others, including William Congreve's *The Way of the World*, Christopher Fry's *The Dark is Light Enough*, which was written for her, James Bridie's *Daphne Laureola* and Oscar Wilde's *The Importance of Being Earnest* (as Lady Bracknell, her most famous role, also on film).

During World War II she entertained the troops at home and abroad and in 1946 was created DBE. In 1948 her successful film career began with her appearance in *The Queen of Spades*, and included *Look Back in Anger*

(1959), *The Chalk Garden* (1964) and *The Whisperers* (1967).

Evans, Janet

Born 1971
American swimmer and winner of four Olympic gold medals

Janet Evans was born in Fullerton, California. She won three gold medals at the 1988 Olympics (400m freestyle, 800m freestyle and 400m medley) and one at the 1992 Olympics (800m freestyle). She holds the world record in the 400m freestyle, the 800m freestyle and the 1,500m freestyle, and was a Sullivan Award winner in 1989.

Evatt, Elizabeth Andreas

Born 1933
Australian lawyer who became Chief Judge of Australia's Family Court

Elizabeth Evatt was born in Sydney, the daughter of a barrister. She trained as the youngest student at Syndey University Law School, where she became the first woman to win the law medal, and at Harvard, before becoming a barrister in New South Wales at the age of 21. In 1958 she was called to the English Bar, and worked in England for several years, focusing on family law with the Law Commission.

Her return to Australia was greeted with senior legal appointments, including the deputy presidency of the Arbitration Commission (1973–89). She chaired the Royal Commission of Human Relationships (1974–7) and the Family Law Council (1976–9) and was chief judge in the Family Court of Australia from 1976 to 1988. She was a member of the UN Committee on the Elimination of Discrimination Against Women from 1984 until 1992, joined the UN Human Rights Committee in 1993. Her other positions include being President of the Law Reform Commission (1988–93), a member of the Australian National Commission for UNESCO (1993–   ), and Chancellor of the University of Newcastle.

Eve

Biblical character, the mother of humankind

According to the Genesis story, Eve was made by God from one of Adam's ribs, as a companion for him. Adam, the first man, named the first woman 'Eve', meaning 'the mother of all living'. They tended the garden of Eden together, until they were expelled for eating the fruit of the tree of knowledge. Although both knew that God had forbidden this, Adam blamed Eve for tempting him. This view has coloured much later interpretation of Eve's character, starting with brief mention in the New Testament of Eve as a weak seducer, and culminating in a negative assessment of women in general.

A few commentators have considered Eve's fellowship with Adam more positively. If Christ can be seen as the Second Adam, reversing the effects of the Fall, then the Virgin **Mary** can be seen as the Second Eve — her 'Yes' to the birth of Jesus being an act of obedience to reverse Eve's disobedience. This interpretation, popular in medieval Catholicism, finds echoes in recent feminist and ecological spirituality that sees women far more in tune with creation than men.

Evert, Chris(tine Marie)

Born 1954
American tennis player who won over 1,000
singles matches

Chris Evert was born in Fort Lauderdale, Florida. Arctic-cool on the courts (hence her nickname, Ice Maiden) she won three times at Wimbledon (1974, 1976, 1981) and took the American title six times; in a long Wightman Cup career which stretched from 1971 to 1982 she never experienced defeat in a singles match. At the Australian Open in 1984 she won her thousandth singles match.

She was married for a time (1979–87) to the English tennis player John Lloyd, during which time she was known as Chris Evert Lloyd and was co-author with him of *Lloyd on Lloyd* (1985). Since retiring from professional tennis playing in 1989 she has become involved in charitable activities.

Ewing, Juliana Horatia, *née* Gatty

Born 1841 Died 1885
English writer for children who was extremely
popular in her time

Juliana Gatty was born in Ecclesfield, Yorkshire, the daughter of Margaret Gatty (1809–73), also a children's writer. She soon began to compose nursery plays, which are said to have suggested to her mother the starting of *Aunt Judy's Magazine* (1866), which she later edited, publishing in it many of her charming (though perhaps now considered too sentimental and moralizing) stories, such as *Jackanapes*.

Her numerous books included *A Flat Iron for a Farthing* (1870), *Lab-lie-by-the-Fire* (1873)

and *Daddy Darwin's Dovecot* (1881). Her *The Brownies and Other Tales* (1870) provided the name by which the junior section of the Girl Guide movement is known.

Ewing, Winnie (Winifred Margaret), *née* Woodburn

Born 1929
Scottish lawyer and Scottish Nationalist
politician, one of the best-known figures in
Scottish politics

Winnie Woodburn was born in Glasgow and educated at Queen's Park School, Glasgow, and Glasgow University. She began practising as a lawyer in 1956, the year of her marriage to Stewart Ewing, and was President of the Glasgow Bar Association in 1970–1. Her victory at the Hamilton by-election of 1967 established the Scottish National Party as a major political force.

Although ousted there in 1970, she won the Moray and Nairn seat in 1974, defeating the Conservative Secretary of State for Scotland. After losing this position in 1979 she was elected to the European parliament in the same year, representing the Highlands and Islands; by 1994 her majority had increased to 55,000.

Her work on behalf of her constituents won her the title 'Madame Ecosse', and her flamboyant electioneering style and combative debating techniques have made her one of the best-known figures in the SNP. She became President of the Party in 1988.

Winnie Ewing, 1967

f

Fabiola, St

Died AD399
Roman Christian matron and patron of Jerome
who founded Europe's first public hospital

Fabiola was a Roman Christian who did public penance in giving away her wealth after the death of her second husband, for her previous divorce, from a notorious debauchee, was not recognized by the Church.

In 390 she founded and worked in a hospital at Ostia, the port of Rome; this was the first public hospital in Europe. In 394–5 she visited the Holy Land, and stayed with **Paula** in Bethlehem, under the direction of Jerome. Her plans to settle there were upset, partly by the scare caused by the Huns invading Palestine. On her return to Rome she set up a harbour-side hospice for the people travelling with Pammachius (c.340–410), Paula's widowed son-in-law.

Fainlight, Ruth Esther

Born 1931
American poet who has been published since
the 1960s

Ruth Fainlight was educated in England and in 1959 married the novelist Alan Sillitoe, with whom she has occasionally collaborated. Most of her work is premised on a refusal to subordinate 'life', with its compromises and hesitations, to 'art'; she refuses to deal in absolutes, calling on fairy tales and popular mythology to demonstrate the merits of adaptation without compromise. This approach lies behind her first completely individual volume, *Cages* (1966), and the aptly titled *To See the Matter Clearly* (1968).

Fainlight seems to have gone through periods of quiet re-assessment and even abnegation at the start of successive decades, but returned to impressive form with *The Region's*

Violence and *Twenty One Poems* (both 1973) and *Climates* and *Fifteen to Infinity* (both 1983). In the latter pair, her perceptiveness is strikingly heightened and a strong-lined metre reinforces her growing philosophical resonance. She has published one collection of short stories, *Daylife and Nightlife* (1971).

Fairbairns, Zoë Ann

Born 1948
English novelist, journalist and pamphleteer
whose concern for the state of contemporary
society is also the central theme of her fiction

Zoë Fairbairns was educated at a convent school in Twickenham and at St Andrews University. She has written on the Campaign for Nuclear Disarmament, women's issues and the consequences of bad housing. *Live as Family* (1968) and *Down: an Exploration* (1969) both deal with the individual's relationships with class and the community.

Her most important novel is perhaps *Stand We at Last* (1983), a family saga spanning the years from the mid-19th century to the present day, and written from a feminist perspective. *Closing* (1987) returns to the modern era to look at the life of women in what the author considers an exploitative society.

Faith, St, *also known as* St Foy

Born c.290AD Died AD303
Gallic Christian virgin and martyr, typical of
medieval devotion, whose shrine was situated on
an important route

Faith, according to legend, suffered with St Caprasius at Agen in Aquitaine, being roasted on a griddle and beheaded. A church was built in their honour in the fifth century.

Her relics were moved around 855 to the abbey of Conques, to which pilgrims were attracted for hundreds of years. These included soldiers on the way to the Crusades and medieval pilgrims going to the shrine of St James at Santiago de Compostela, in Spain.

For a time a magnificent 10th-century gold and jewelled reliquary, which still survives, was displayed behind chains left by former prisoners who attributed their release to St Faith. The many churches dedicated to her in England are probably accounted for by returning pilgrims.

Faithfull, Emily

Born 1835   Died 1895
English publisher and feminist who made a
lifelong contribution to the cause of women's
employment

Emily Faithfull was born in Headley Rectory, Surrey. She took her first step for the sake of women's employment when she became a founder-member of the Society for Promoting the Employment of Women (1859). The following year in London she founded a printing house to provide work for women compositors, employing 19 in the first year.

In 1862 she was appointed Printer and Publisher-in-Ordinary to Queen **Victoria** and in 1863 she started the *Victoria Magazine*, which she edited until 1880, advocating the claims of women to remunerative employment. Among her many activities she also founded a penny weekly, *Women and Work* (1865) and ran the Victorian Discussion Society, providing a forum for women to voice their opinions. In 1868 she published a novel, *Change upon Change*.

Faithfull's *Three Visits to America* (1884) compares the American movement for women's work with that in Britain and gives an account of her lecture tours in the USA (1872–3, 1877, 1882–3).

Faithfull, Marianne

Born 1946
English singer, songwriter and film actress who
first came to notice as Mick Jagger's girlfriend

Marianne Faithfull was born in Hampstead, London. She was 'discovered' by the Rolling Stones' manager and at the age of 18 had a hit with 'As Tears Go By', followed by 'Summer Nights' (1965) and others.

Already known as Mick Jagger's girlfriend, she received headline attention when the Stones were arrested on drugs charges. Her acting career began with *I'll Never Forget Whatshisname* (1967) and the prurient *Girl on a Motorcycle* (1968).

Faithfull's singing career seemed to be over in the 1970s, but the extraordinary *Broken English* (1979) revived her fortunes. Subsequent records include *Dangerous Acquaintances* (1981) and *Strange Weather* (1987). An autobiography, *Faithfull* (1994), set the record straight.

Falconieri, St Juliana

Born 1270   Died 1341
Italian founder of the Third Order of Servites

Juliana Falconieri was born in Florence, the niece of St Alexis Falconieri, one of the seven city councillors who founded the Servite Order (the Order of the Servants of Mary) in 1240. Refusing marriage, at the age of 14 she founded the Servite Third Order, which was devoted to the sick and the poor, and to the education of children. However she waited almost 20 years before undertaking community life after the death of her mother, Ricordata.

The Order received papal recognition in 1424, and Falconieri was canonized in 1737.

Falkender, Marcia Matilda
Falkender, Baroness, *née* Williams

Born 1932
British political worker who was Harold Wilson's
fiercely loyal private and political secretary and
confidante for nearly 40 years

Marcia Williams took a history degree at Queen Mary College, London, then worked at Labour party headquarters before becoming Private and Political Secretary to Harold Wilson (later Baron Wilson of Rievaulx) from 1956 to 1983, working from 10 Downing Street when he was Prime Minister in 1964–70 and 1974–6.

Her background influence during the 1964–70 Labour government is chronicled in her book *Inside No. 10* (1972). She also wrote *Downing Street in Perspective* (1983) and was a political columnist for six years from 1982.

She was awarded a life peerage in 1974.

Faludi, Susan

Born 1960
American journalist and writer, an active voice in
modern feminism

Susan Faludi was born at Yorktown Heights, New York, and educated at Harvard University. She has been a staff member of the *New York Times* and is attached to the San Francisco bureau of the *Wall Street Journal*.

In 1991 she was awarded the Pulitzer prize for her investigative journalism as well as the 1991 National Book Critics Award for Nonfiction for *Backlash* (1991), which argues that despite appearances, women are still controlled and repressed in contemporary society. She is also a contributor to *Ms* and *Mother Jones* magazines.

Farhi, Nicole

Birthdate unavailable
British fashion designer whose name is established worldwide

Nicole Farhi was born in Nice, France, where she worked as a freelance designer before moving to London to work with Stephen Marks on French Connection and the Stephen Marks label. She launched her own company in 1983.

Her comfortable, uncomplicated clothes feature soft structure, subtle colouring and fine quality fabrics in the European style of timeless simplicity rather than fussy detail, and she attributes her phenomenal success simply to 'making clothes that last'.

Farhi has been a nominee in the British Fashion Awards four times, and won the British Classis award in 1989. She recently launched a swimwear collection and has shops in London, Glasgow, Manchester, New York, Oslo and Tokyo, and her collections wholesale to top stores in Europe, America and the Far East.

Farjeon, Eleanor

Born 1881   Died 1965
English novelist and poet, one of the most prolific and highly regarded children's writers of her day

Eleanor Farjeon was born in Hampstead, London, the daughter of a novelist. She was encouraged to write stories and poems as a child and led a richly imaginative fantasy life, which is described in her autobiographical *A Nursery in the Nineties* (1935).

She wrote fantasies and children's stories, beginning with her successful first novel, *Martin Pippin in the Apple Orchard* (1916), and collaborated with her brother Herbert in *Kings and Queens* (1932) and the play *The Glass Slipper* (1944). Her selection of short stories *The Little Bookroom* (1955) won Farjeon the Carnegie Medal and the Hans Christian Andersen International Medal.

The Eleanor Farjeon award was established in 1965 and is given annually by the Children's Book Circle for outstanding service to children's literature.

Farmer, Fannie Merritt

Born 1857   Died 1915
American cookery expert whose Boston Cooking School Cook Book *became one of the best-known in America*

Fannie Farmer was born in Boston. She suffered a stroke at the age of 16 and was unable to attend college, so she turned to cooking at home and then attended the Boston Cooking School. She graduated in 1889 and was a director there from 1891 to 1902, during which time she edited the *Boston Cooking School Cook Book* (1896).

In 1902 she opened Miss Farmer's School of Cookery in Boston, the first to offer courses designed for housewives and nurses rather than servants or teachers. She also wrote for the *Woman's Home Companion* for 10 years. Her insistence on precise measurements in her recipes was innovatory.

Farnese, Isabella, *also called* Elizabeth

Born 1692   Died 1766
Queen of Spain as the second wife of Philip V of Spain (ruled 1700–46).

Isabella Farnese was the daughter of the Duke of Parma. She married Philip in 1714 and warmly supported the aggressive foreign policy of the *de facto* prime minister Giulio Alberoni, which was aimed primarily at removing the Austrians from Italy. She is said to have persuaded him to violate the Treaty of Utrecht by invading Sardinia (1717) and Sicily (1718), which led to confrontation by the Quadruple Alliance of England, France, Austria and Holland, and resulted in the destruction of the Spanish fleet.

She dominated her weak husband and worked to secure the future of her sons: the future Charles III of Spain, who succeeded his half-brother Ferdinand VI and ruled Spain from 1759 to 1788, and Philip, who married Maria Louisa of France and received the duchies of Parma, Piacenza and Guastalla in the Treaty of Aix-la-Chapelle (1748), which resulted from the War of the Austrian Succession.

Farrar, Geraldine

Born 1882   Died 1967
American soprano whose performing career was relatively short, but highly concentrated

Geraldine Farrar was born in Melrose, Maine. She studied in Boston, Paris and Berlin, making her professional début in Germany in *Faust*. Her first role in America came five years later, again in Gounod's work, as Juliet.

Farrar retired from the opera stage in 1922, though continued giving recitals until the early 1930s. Many of her finest roles — including Cio-Cio San and Carmen — were recorded.

She wrote her own life story (rather early, in 1916) as *The Story of an American Singer*, later revised as *Such Sweet Compulsion*; the later title gives a fair impression of her dramatic presence.

Farrell, Suzanne

Born 1945
American ballet dancer who was the principal artist at NYCB for many years

Suzanne Farrell was born in Cincinnati, Ohio, and trained at the School of American Ballet. At the age of 16 she joined the New York City Ballet (NYCB), where she quickly became a major muse of choreographer-artistic director George Balanchine (1904–83), who recognized her exceptional sensitivity to music and emotional depth.

Among the pieces that he created for her were *Movements for Piano and Orchestra* (1963) and the role of Dulcinea in *Don Quixote* (1965). She and her husband, dancer Paul Majia, left the company to join Maurice Béjart's Ballet of the 20th Century (1970–4).

Upon her return to NYCB in 1975, she formed a fruitful onstage partnership with dancer Peter Martins and danced for Balanchine in his *Union Jack* (1976), *Schumann's Davidsbündlertänze* (1980) and *Tizane*, among others. She published her autobiography, *Holding on to the Air*, in 1990.

Farren, Elizabeth

Born c.1759   Died 1829
English actress who saw fame at the Haymarket and at Drury Lane

Elizabeth Farren was the daughter of travelling players. She began her career touring in the Midlands with her family before making her Haymarket Theatre début as Kate Hardcastle in *She Stoops to Conquer* (1777).

She became famous at the Haymarket, particularly for aristocratic roles such as Lady Teazle and Lydia Languish, as well as at Drury Lane, where she succeeded **Fanny Abington**.

She allegedly had a passionate affair with the Earl of Derby for over 10 years before marrying him and retiring from the stage in 1797.

Farrokhzad, Forugh

Born 1935   Died 1967
Iranian poet who is considered as a major writer in her context

Forugh Farrokhzad was born in Tehran. She began writing classical poetry at 14, was unhappily married at 16 and soon lost her

child to the custody of her brutal husband in a travesty of a divorce case. She was killed in a car accident.

Her first two collections (both 1955) were both entitled *Asir* ('The Captive'); the second caused a scandal, since she confessed to sensual feelings for a man, not admitted by women in her country except in private. But the discerning recognized a new and bright talent.

She wrote in a subtle and well-cadenced free verse and is cherished as a major modernist poet.

Farrow, Mia (Maria de Lourdes Villiers)

Born 1945
American actress whose marriages have generated as much interest as her career

Mia Farrow was born in Los Angeles. Her father was the film director John Farrow, and her mother the actress Maureen O'Sullivan. She was a frail child, and put her winsome looks to use as an actress. She made her Broadway début in 1963, but is best known for her screen works since coming to notice in *Peyton Place* on television in the 1960s. Her important films include *Rosemary's Baby* (1968), *The Great Gatsby* (1974), and a number of Woody Allen films, notably *Hannah and Her Sisters* (1986).

She has developed into an authoritative actress, but her high-profile marriages to Frank Sinatra (1966–8) and André Previn (1970–9), and her subsequent relationship with Woody Allen, which ended in court in 1992, have attracted much media attention.

Fatimah, *also spelt* Fatima

Died 633
Arab religious figure and founder of the Fatimid dynasty whose name in Arabic means 'Shining One'

Fatimah was the youngest daughter of the prophet Muhammad, whom she accompanied when he emigrated from Mecca to Medina and nursed during his final illness.

After his death she had a clash over property with Abū-Bakr, Muhammad's successor as leader of the Islamic community, and for a time she and her husband Ali (Muhammad's cousin whom Shiite Muslims believe ought to have inherited the Prophet's property and become the first imam) refused to recognize the new leader's position.

Fatimah is important in the Shiite tradition because from her and Ali were descended the Fatimid dynasty, who ruled over Egypt and

North Africa (969–1171) and later over Syria and Palestine.

Fauset, Jessie Redmon

Born 1882 Died 1961
African-American novelist whose central theme is the problem of race

Jessie Redmon Fauset was born in New Jersey to a poor African-American family and educated at Cornell University. She taught French in Washington DC, earned a Master's degree at the University of Pennsylvania, then moved to New York. There she was associated with the black writer William Dubois and became a co-editor of his magazine *Crisis*.

Her four novels all deal with problems of race; the best is probably *The Chinaberry Tree* (1931), whose oblique theme is the necessity for black women not to try to become white; but its predecessor, *Plum Bun* (1929), which contrasts two sisters, one of whom tries to pass as white in Greenwich Village while the other accepts her heritage in Harlem, runs it a close second.

She has more recently been accused of an illiberal, defeatist attitude, but her work undoubtedly served its cause well. She was the first black woman to become a member of the honorary literary society Phi Beta Kappa.

Faustina, Annia Galeria, *known as* the Elder

Born c.104AD Died AD141
Roman empress whose debauchery did not dampen her husband's ardour

Annia Galeria Faustina the Elder was the daughter of Annius Verus, a prefect of Rome. She became the wife of Emperor Antoninus Pius (ruled 138–61), who apparently so devoted to her, or mesmerized by her beauty and wit, that even when he discovered that she was prone to debauched behaviour he continued to mint coins and medals in her honour.

Their four children included **Annia Galeria Faustina the Younger**. Her husband founded the Puellae Faustinianae, a charitable institution for poor girls, in her memory.

Faustina, Annia Galeria, *known as* the Younger

Died AD175
Roman empress as the wife of the Roman emperor Marcus Aurelius (ruled 161–80)

Annia Galeria Faustina the Younger was the daughter of Emperor Antonius Pius and **Annia Galeria Faustina the Elder**. In AD145 she married her cousin Marcus Aurelius, successor to his adoptive father Antoninus Pius, and bore him at least 12 children.

When he went to fight against the barbarians on the Danube in 170–4, she accompanied him, earning the soubriquet *mater castrorum* ('mother of the camps'). She also accompanied him on other military campaigns.

Like her mother, she was reputed to be promiscuous and faithless, but this was probably baseless. She died on the journey east to confront the governor Avidius Cassius, who had organized a rebellion.

Faverches, Richeldis de

Floreat 1061
English visionary whose response to one of her visions was to build a chapel

According to an anonymous ballad printed around 1460, the widowed Richeldis de Faverches had a vision at Walsingham, Norfolk, in 1061. In it she saw the Nazareth home of the Holy Family and was instructed by the Virgin **Mary** to build a reproduction.

Richeldis and her descendants built and endowed a chapel which remained an important pilgrimage centre until the Reformation. Destroyed in 1538, the shrine was restored in 1938, for the use of both Catholic and Anglican pilgrims.

Fawcett, Dame Millicent, *née* Garrett

Born 1847 Died 1929
English suffragette and educational reformer who led the woman suffrage movement for over five decades

Millicent Garrett was born in Aldeburgh, Suffolk. The seventh of 10 children, one of whom was **Elizabeth Garrett Anderson**, she married the political economist and reformer Henry Fawcett in 1867. She made her first speech on woman suffrage the following year, beginnining her five-decade fight against opposition to female influence in politics and to champion higher education for women.

She opposed the militancy of **Emmeline** and **Christabel Pankhurst**'s techniques and sought to counter the public hostility they engendered. She was a founder of Newnham College, Cambridge (1871), one of the first university colleges for women, and was President of the National Union of Women's Suffrage Societies (1897–1919).

Her works include *Political Economy for Beginners* (1870) and *The Women's Victory — and After* (1920).

Dianne Feinstein, 1985

Feinstein, Dianne, *née* Goldman

Born 1933
American politician who has risen to become US
Senator and the most powerful elected woman
Democrat

Dianne Feinstein was born in San Francisco, California, and educated at Stanford University. She was on the San Francisco Board of Supervisors from 1969 to 1978, serving as board president in 1970–2, 1974–6 and 1978, the year she became Mayor of San Francisco following the assassination of George Mascone. She was elected Mayor in 1979 and re-elected in 1983, remaining in the position until 1988.

She was elected to the US House of Representatives in 1984 and was Senator from California in 1986 and 1992. In 1994 she won on a second term in the US Senate.

Feinstein, Elaine

Born 1930
English poet, translator, novelist and critic who
claims her poetry voices an attempt to 'make sense
of experience'

Elaine Feinstein was born in Bootle, Lancashire, and educated at Cambridge. During the 1960s she was a lecturer in English literature at Essex University. Her first book of poems, *In a Green Eye*, appeared in 1966, placing her in the American tradition of poetry influenced by **Emily Dickinson**, among others.

The Circle (1970), her first novel, deals with a woman's simultaneous craving for emotional

independence and her desire to be insulated by marriage. Subsequent books have also examined the female experience, such as *The Amberstone Exit* (1972), confronting the trauma of birth and motherhood. *The Survivors* (1982), on the other hand, derives partly from the history of her own family and looks at the fate of early 20th-century Jewish refugees from Russia.

Feinstein has also translated several Russian women poets and written an authoritative biography of **Marina Tsvetayeva**, *A Captive Lion* (1987).

Fell, Dame Honor Bridget

Born 1900 Died 1986
British cell biologist who made influential
progress in biochemical study

Honor Fell was educated at the University of Edinburgh where she received her PhD in 1924, and five years later became Director of Strangeways Research Laboratory in Cambridge (1929–70). She was Foulerton Research Fellow of the Royal Society from 1941 to 1967, and Royal Society Research Professor from 1963 to 1967.

Fell greatly advanced biochemical study through her investigations using the organ culture method; she demonstrated that excess vitamin A would destroy intercellular material in the explanted cartilage and bones of foetal mice, with the implication that such organ cultures could be widely used in studies of the physiological effects of vitamins and hormones.

In later life she investigated the pathogenesis of arthritis. Elected a Fellow of the Royal Society in 1952, she was made a DBE in 1963.

Fell, Margaret, *née* Askew

Born 1614 Died 1702
English Quaker who married the founder of the
Quakers and was active in the movement

Margaret Askew was born in Dalton-in-Furness, Lancashire. She was married to Judge Thomas Fell and had nine children. She kept an open house for religious people at Swarthmore Hall, near Ulverston, and was converted by George Fox (1624–91), the founder of the Society of Friends, or 'Quakers'.

Following her husband's death in 1658, she became more involved in Quaker affairs, pleading for prisoners of conscience, including Fox, who was arrested in her house in 1660. They married in 1669. In 1663 and later she was fined and imprisoned for allowing illegal religious meetings to be held in her home and for refusing to take the oath of allegiance (to the Crown) when brought to court.

Her writings include a defence of women speaking in church, and an early protest against a tendency among Quakers to devise and adhere to rigid rules on dress and behaviour.

Fenley, Molissa

Born 1954
American dancer and choreographer of highly energetic solos

Molissa Fenley was born in Las Vegas and raised in Nigeria. She studied dance at Mills College, California, before moving to New York, where she made her choreographic début in 1978.

Although she has created ensemble pieces for her own now-defunct group and other companies, her reputation rests on physically demanding, high-energy solos like *Eureka* (1982) and *State of Darkness* (1988).

Ferard, Elizabeth Catherine

Floreat 1858–73
English deaconess who established the deaconess order in England and became the first deaconess of the Church of England

After the death of her mother, Elizabeth Ferard went in 1858 to stay at the Lutheran Kaiserwerth community in Germany, where the deaconess order or diaconate in the form of an order of nurses had been revived by Theodor Fliedner (1800–64) in 1836, at the same time as the first Protestant hospital was established. Inspired by the work of the order — as was **Florence Nightingale**, who trained there around 1854 — she offered to promote it in London, but under the auspices of the Church of England.

Ferard and two companions undertook a common rule of life in 1861 in a house near Kings Cross, and she was 'set apart' as a deaconess the following year, by A C Tait, Bishop of London. She resigned as leader in 1873, due to ill health, but by that time the idea had spread to other dioceses and the bishops had drawn up guidelines for deaconesses in the Church at large.

Ferber, Edna

Born 1887 Died 1968
American writer who wrote the book behind the 1926 musical Show Boat

Edna Ferber was born in Kalamazoo, Michigan. She was the author of numerous novels and short stories, including *Dawn O'Hara* (1911), *Gigolo* (1922), *So Big* (1924), which won the 1925 Pulitzer Prize, *Cimarron* (1929) and *Saratoga Trunk* (1941).

She is probably best remembered as the writer of *Show Boat* (1926), which inspired the musical play of that name. She also wrote plays with American playwright George S Kaufman (1889–1961), such as *Dinner at Eight* (1932) and *Stage Door* (1936).

Ferguson, Margaret Clay

Born 1863 Died 1951
American plant geneticist and teacher who inspired generations of women at Wellesley College

Margaret Ferguson was born in Orleans, New York. She attended Wellesley College (1888–91), studying chemistry and botany, and in 1893 became an instructor in botany there. She graduated from Cornell University in 1899 and, after obtaining her doctorate in 1901, she returned to Wellesley, becoming head of the department of botany in 1902 and full professor in 1906, remaining there until 1938.

Her research interests focused on plant genetics, especially of *Petunia*, and she analysed the inheritance of features such as petal colour, flower pattern and pollen colour, building up a major database of genetic information.

She received many honours and awards, including election as the first woman President of the Botanical Society of America (1929). Her department became a major centre for botanical education. One of the most distinguished pupils to emerge from Wellesley was the Nobel Prize-winner **Barbara McLintock**.

Ferraro, Geraldine A(nne)

Born 1935
American Democrat politician who was the first woman to be nominated by a major party as vice-presidential candidate

Geraldine Ferraro was born in Newburgh, New York, the daughter of Italian Roman Catholic immigrants. She was educated at Marymount College, Fordham University and New York Law School and, after marrying wealthy businessman John Zaccaro in 1960, established a successful law practice (1961–74).

She served as assistant district attorney for the Queens district of New York between 1974 and 1978 and worked at the Supreme Court from 1978, heading a special bureau for victims of violent crime, before being elected to the House of Representatives in 1981. In Congress, she gained a reputation as an effective, liberal-minded politician and was selected in 1984 by the presidential nominee Walter Mondale to be the first female vice-presidential candidate of a major party, in an effort to add sparkle to the Democrat 'ticket', but the Democrats suffered a convincing defeat. There were unhelpful rumours concerning her husband's business activities at this time and her son's association with drugs, which may also have contributed in 1992 to her narrow defeat in the Democratic senatorial primary election in New York. In 1994 President Clinton appointed her US Ambassador to the United Nations Human Rights Commission.

She has published her memoirs, *Ferraro, My Story* (1985), and *Changing History: Women, Power and Politics* (1993), and was inducted into the National Women's Hall of Fame in 1994.

Ferré, Rosario

Born 1940
Puerto Rican poet and narrator, one of the most expressive authors in Spanish America

Rosario Ferré was born in Ponce. She studied at Wellesley, Manhattanville College, receiving her PhD from the University of Maryland in 1986.

Part of an important emerging group of Puerto Rican authors, she founded and edited the influential literary journal *Zona de Carga y Descarga* (1972–5).

She is also a regular contributor to newspapers, and writes short stories, poetry, essays and translations.

Ferrier, Kathleen

Born 1912 Died 1953
English contralto singer who earned widespread fame and affection

Kathleen Ferrier was born in Higher Walton, Lancashire. An accomplished amateur pianist, she won a prize for singing at a local music festival and was encouraged by this to undertake serious studies in 1940. The range and richness of her voice, together with her remarkable technical control, rapidly won her a great reputation.

In 1946 she sang Lucrezia in Benjamin Britten's *The Rape of Lucrezia* and Orpheus in Christoph Gluck's *Orfeo ed Euridice* at Glyndebourne; from then onwards she was in great demand throughout Europe and America. Her greatest success, perhaps, was in Gustav Mahler's *The Song of the Earth* at the first Edinburgh Festival (1947) and at Salzburg (1949).

Ferrier, Susan Edmonstone

Born 1782 Died 1854
Scottish novelist who painted a satirical picture of 19th-century Scottish high society and became extremely popular

Susan Ferrier was born in Edinburgh, the tenth child of a lawyer who became principal clerk to the Court of Session with Sir Walter Scott. With the death of her mother in 1797, she took over the running of the house and looked after her father until his death in 1829. Through Scott, with whom she enjoyed a close friendship, she became well acquainted with Edinburgh's intellectual society.

Her first work, *Marriage* (1818), a novel of provincial social manners, was followed by *The Inheritance* (1824) and *Destiny* (1831), a Highland romance. For a time it was Scott who was credited by some with the authorship of her books, for they were published anonymously.

Following the publication of these works she was converted to evangelical Christianity and became a member of the Free Church, concentrating on charitable works rather than on writing. Towards the end of her life she lived in relative seclusion, her eyesight failing badly.

Feuchères, Baroness de *see* Dawes, Sophia

Fibiger, Mathilde

Born 1830 Died 1872
Danish novelist whose first book became a seminal text for the women's movement in Denmark

Mathilde Fibiger was born in Copenhagen and found work as a governess. Her fame rests on her first novel, *12 Breve til Clara Raphael* (1851, '12 Letters to Clara Raphael') which, boldly asserting feminine integrity and independence on the basis of Romanticism, liberalism and religious convictions, provoked a major controversy. However it subsequently became a seminal text for the Danish women's movement.

Fibiger's second novel, *En Skizze efter det virkelige Liv* (1852, 'Sketch from Real Life'), was an attempt to appease her readership, but *Minona* (1854), defending the role of feminine eroticism, was attacked as being immoral. Finding it increasingly hard to support herself as a writer, she became Denmark's first woman telegraphist (1863).

Fidler, Kathleen

Born 1899 Died 1980
English author of books for children who gave her name to an award for new children's novel writing

Kathleen Fidler was born in Coalville, Leicestershire. Her first volume, *The Borrowed Garden*, appeared in 1944. Her most popular novels, however, proved to be those about the chirpy Brydon family, whose adventures feature in 17 books, from *The Brydons at Smuggler's Creek* (1946) to *The Brydon's Go Canoeing* (1963). She is also the creator of the Dean family, whose exploits fill nine books, from *The Deans Move In* (1953) to *The Deans' Dutch Adventure* (1982). Her other books include *Stories From Scottish Heritage* (3 vols, 1951) and the *True Tales of* — series, collections of historical stories from various regions of Britain.

In 1982 the annual Kathleen Fidler award was instituted for new novel-writing for children of 8 to 11 years old.

Field, Sally

Born 1946
American film actress who won an Oscar for her role as Norma Rae

Sally Field was born in Pasadena, California, the stepdaughter of Tarzan star Jock Mahoney (1919–89). She gradually gained popularity as the star of the television situation comedy *The Flying Nun* (1966–70) and in various television films. After studying at the Actors Studio she at last had a chance to prove her worth in the television mini-series *Sybil* (1976).

She became romantically and professionally involved with the actor Burt Reynolds, several times his co-star, but was more successful in *Norma Rae* (1979), for which she won a Best Actress Oscar and the respect she had long courted.

Moving from strength to strength, she won a second Oscar for *Places in the Heart* (1984) and formed her own production company in 1988, which was responsible for *Steel Magnolias* (1989), in which she played the mother of the dying Julia Roberts. She has also starred opposite Robin Williams in *Mrs Doubtfire* (1993).

Fielding, Sarah

Born 1710 Died 1768
English translator and writer of one of the earliest novels specifically aimed at children

Sarah Fielding was born in East Stour, Dorset. Her brother was the novelist Henry Fielding (1707–54). Her most popular novel was *The Adventures of David Simple in Search of a Faithful Friend* (1744), a romance dealing with four young people, rejected by their families and society, in which the author's sympathy is clearly with the young women struggling to make an independent and respectable living. A sequel, *Familiar Letters Between the Principal Characters in David Simple*, appeared in 1747, together with a second edition of the first book.

They are ambitious, progressive works and to these two volumes Henry Fielding contributed prefaces. Sarah Fielding was a friend of Samuel Richardson, and wrote the first study of his *Clarissa* in 1749. Also that year she published one of the earliest works for children, *The Governess, or the Little Female Academy*. Other works included a translation of Xenophon's *Memorabilia and Apologia* (1762).

Fields, Dorothy

Born 1904 Died 1974
American lyricist whose hits included 'Big Spender'

Dorothy Fields was born in Allenhurst, New Jersey, the daughter of comedian Lew Fields. She is best known for her successful partnership with Jimmy McHugh, with whom she wrote 'I Can't Give You Anything But Love, Baby' for the Cotton Club revue *Blackbirds of 1928*. Their *International Revue* (1930) included 'On the Sunny Side of the Street'. Fields also wrote numbers for *Annie Get Your Gun* (1946), *A Tree Grows in Brooklyn* (1951) and *Sweet Charity* (1966); her best song in the last of these was 'Big Spender'.

Fields, Dame Gracie, *originally* Grace Stansfield

Born 1898 Died 1979
English comedienne and singer who became a leading music hall entertainer

Gracie Fields was born in Rochdale, Lancashire. A child performer, she progressed, via revues and pantomime, to become one of the country's premier music-hall attractions, affectionately known as 'Our Gracie'. Hers was a chirpy, natural talent, and she was adept at both comic songs and plaintive ballads.

Her long career encompassed radio, recordings, television and films like *Sally in Our Alley* (1931), *Sing As We Go* (1934) and *Holy Matrimony* (1943). In semi-retirement from the

1950s, she won a Silvania TV award for her performance in *The Old Lady Shows Her Medals* (1956) and, in 1960, published her autobiography *Sing As We Go*.

She was a favourite with the royal family, and appeared in 10 command performances between 1928 and 1978, the year she was created a DBE.

Fiennes, Celia

Born 1662 Died 1741
English writer, famous for her writings about her travels throughout Britain during the late 17th and early 18th centuries.

Celia Fiennes was born at Newton Toney near Salisbury into a Puritan, anti-monarchist family.

She travelled extensively throughout England and Scotland, on horseback and by coach, staying at inns or with relatives, and recorded vivid descriptions of her journeys. These journeys, supposedly for her health, were mostly undertaken between 1685 and 1703; during her 'Great Journey' of 1698 she travelled over 1,000 miles. Her travel diaries were first published in 1888 under the title *Through England on a Side Saddle in the time of William and Mary*.

Fiennes admitted that her journeys were inspired by curiosity. She comments on towns, roads, inns, religious practices and particularly on local trade and industry.

Figes, Eva, *née* Unger

Born 1932
German-born British feminist writer

Eva Figes was born in Berlin and escaped from Nazi Germany, coming to England in 1939 and taking British nationality. She was educated at Kingsbury Grammar School, London, and Queen Mary College, London University.

She married George Figes in 1954 and divorced in 1963. Her first novel, *Equinox*, was published in 1966 and in 1967 she became a full-time writer. Her other works include *Patriarchal Attitudes: Women in Society* (1970), a radio play *The True Tale of Margery Kempe* (1985), a highly acclaimed work written in 17th-century prose entitled *The Tree of Knowledge* (1990), and *The Tenancy* (1993).

Figner, Vera

Born 1852 Died 1942
Russian revolutionary activist who suffered over 20 years' internment

Vera Figner was born in Kazan, the daughter of a wealthy nobleman. She was educated at home by governesses and at the Kazan Institute. In 1870 she married and persuaded her husband to study medicine with her at Zurich University. However, she became involved with Russian political activists and abandoned her studies to become a revolutionary agent herself.

In 1879 she became a committee member of *Narodnaia Volia* (The People's Will Party), taking over the leadership in 1881. She was arrested in 1883 and spent 20 years in solitary confinement. Following the 1905 Revolution she was released and travelled the world lecturing on Tsarism. After the 1917 Revolution she became President of the Political Red Cross.

Figuero, Ana

Born 1908 Died 1970
Chilean feminist and political activist, holder of several prestigious UN appointments

Ana Figuero was born in Santiago. She studied at the University of Chile and became a teacher. During World War II she studied at Columbia University and Colorado State College.

On returning to Chile she campaigned for women's suffrage, directed the National School System, and headed the Woman's Bureau in the Ministry of Foreign Affairs. Having in 1951 become Chile's special envoy to the United Nations, she went on to become the first woman head of a UN Committee of the General Assembly, the first woman member of the Security Committee, and the first woman Assistant Director-General of the International Labor Organization.

Fine, Vivian

Born 1913
American composer who at 72 took the solo piano part in Poetic Fires, *perhaps her most important piece of music*

Vivian Fine was born in Chicago, where she studied at the Music College (1919–22) before continuing her studies at the American Conservatory, also in Chicago, under **Ruth Crawford** (1926–8). After moving to New York City in 1931, she took composition classes with Roger Sessions. She married the sculptor Benjamin Karp and taught at New York University and the Juilliard School.

Though her first compositions were professionally performed while she was still in her teens, Fine matured slowly. Her music is dramatically dissonant, being little affected by twelve-tone theory. In 1983 she received a

Pulitzer Prize nomination for the orchestral *Drama*.

Finnbogadóttir, Vigdís

Born 1930
Icelandic politician and President of Iceland, the
first woman in world history to be elected
head of state

Vigdís Finnbogadóttir was born in Reykjavík. She went to France to study French language and literature, specializing in drama at the University of Grenoble and the Sorbonne in Paris (1949–53). She returned to Iceland to work for the National Theatre, while pursuing further studies at the University of Iceland. For 10 years (1962–72) she taught French in senior school in Reykjavík and French drama and theatre history at the university, presented arts programmes on television and worked as a cultural hostess for the Icelandic Tourist Bureau during the summer vacations.

She was the director of the Reykjavík City Theatre from 1972 until 1980, when she was persuaded to stand for the non-political office of President of Iceland. Winning a narrow victory against three male candidates, she became the first woman in world history to be elected head of state.

She was returned unopposed in 1984, re-elected in 1988 and, again returned unopposed, entered her fourth four-year term in 1992. Known as 'President Vigdís', she was married in 1954 and divorced in 1963. She adopted a baby daughter in 1972, one of the first instances in Iceland of a single person adopting a child.

Finnie, Linda

Born 1952
Scottish operatic and concert mezzo-soprano
whose operatic engagements have taken her all
over Europe

Linda Finnie was born in Paisley. She studied at the Royal Scottish Academy of Music and Drama with Winifred Busfield and made her début with Scottish Opera in 1976. After winning the **Kathleen Ferrier** Prize at 's-Hertogenbosch in the Netherlands (1977) she began to sing widely throughout Europe, also with Welsh National and English National Operas (from 1979) and as a guest at Covent Garden.

As a concert singer her touring engagements have included Chicago and San Francisco. Her strong characterizations and firm, warm tone have made her a success in such Wagnerian roles as Brangaene (Cardiff), Wal-

traute (Nice) and Fricka (Bayreuth début, 1988).

Fiorenza, Elisabeth Schuessler

Born 1938
American theologian whose interests include the
role of women in the Church

Elisabeth Schuessler Fiorenza was born in Tschand, Germany. Her written work covers mainly New Testament exegesis and biblical theology. She shows an active interest in women's issues and women's role in the Church, particularly the Roman Catholic Church. Her books include *The Challenge of Liberation Theology* (1981) and *In Memory of Her* (1982).

Firestone, Shulamith

Born 1945
Canadian feminist and women's rights activist

Shulamith Firestone was one of the early organizers of the American women's liberation movement in the 1960s and 1970s. She co-organized the first women's group, Radical Women, in New York City, and also co-founded the radical feminist group, RedStockings, which aimed to combine consciousness-raising theory with action.

Firestone's book, *The Dialectic of Sex* (1970), is a radical analysis of sex and class.

Firsova, Elena Olegovna

Born 1950
Russian composer whose most distinctive, melodic
music is found in her smaller-scale works

Elena Firsova was born in Leningrad (now St Petersburg) and educated in Moscow, where she studied composition at the Conservatory (1970–5) and later worked as a music technician. She married composer Dmitri Smirnov in 1972, the year of her first major orchestral piece, the Cello Concerto.

Her highly unified output is largely for either chamber forces or the voice, and is much influenced by the older Russian, Edison Denisov (1929–   ). She has made many settings of Boris Pasternak, including *Three Romances* (1966–7), and of Osip Mandelstam, such as *The Stone* (1983).

In 1990, Firsova and Smirnov left Russia for the West, settling in the UK.

Fischer, Annie

Born 1914 Died 1995
Hungarian pianist renowned for her performances
of Beethoven, Mozart and Schumann

Annie Fischer was born in Budapest and trained at the Budapest Academy of Music, cunder Ernst von Dohnányi and Arnold Székely. She made her début in 1922 with Beethoven's C Major Concerto, and went on to play throughout Europe between the years 1926 and 1939. She won the first International Liszt Competition in Budapest (1933), and in 1936 married Aldat Toth. The couple spent much of World War II in Sweden, because Fischer was Jewish, and during this period she taught extensively.

On their return to Hungary in 1946, Fischer resumed touring and recording on an international scale. She won the Kossuth Prize in 1949, 1955 and 1965. She was made an Honorary Professor of the Budapest Academy of Music in 1965.

Fisher, Allison

Born 1968
English snooker player, the greatest-ever female competitor in the sport

Allison Fisher was born in Peacehaven, Sussex, and began playing snooker aged eight. She played on her first full-size table at the age of 12 and joined the ladies professional circuit shortly after her fifteenth birthday.

With over 80 titles to her credit, she has won a record seven ladies world titles, five UK titles, four British Opens, three world mixed doubles (with partner Steve Davis) and a world Masters ladies doubles with her chief rival Stacey Hillyard. She boasts a top break of 144 and a competition best break of 133, and was also the first woman to make a televised century.

Fisher, Doris

Birthdate unavailable
American businesswoman and founder of The Gap, one of the world's largest fashion retailers

Doris Fisher founded The Gap Inc in 1969, with her husband Donald, a San Francisco real estate developer, because they had had enough of jeans stores that did not cater for them. The name 'Gap' refers to the generation gap of the time.

Originally selling records and jeans from a small shop on the USA's west coast, Gap now has around 1,370 shops worldwide comprising Gap, Gapkids, babyGap (sic), Banana Republic Brands and Old Navy Clothing Co. Jeans, t-shirts, khaki trousers and checked shirts are the staple stock, continuing the original idea of selling the world the affordable American lifestyle.

Fisher is currently a Gap director as well as the company's merchandizing consultant.

Fisher, M(ary) F(rances) K(ennedy), *née* Kennedy

Born 1908   Died 1992
American cookery writer whose work reflected the universal interest in the eating and enjoyment of food

Mary Frances Kennedy was born in Albion, Michigan, and educated in California and Illinois. Her first husband was an academic called Al Fisher. After six years in France, they settled in California in 1935 (they divorced the following year), where she took a part-time job. She spent much of her spare time in a library containing old cookery books, some dating from Elizabethan times, and began to write about what she had read.

Her first published book, *Serve It Forth*, appeared in 1937, published under her initials to conceal the fact she was a woman (at the time only men wrote about food). After the death of her second husband in 1941, she wrote in earnest, and also translated *The Physiology of Taste* by Brillat-Savarin, whose philosophy she admired.

Sometimes compared to that of **Elizabeth David**, her writing is not so much about cookery itself, but a collection of culinary essays celebrating American regional food and offering reminiscences, anecdotes and reflections. Her books explore her interest in 'the practice and contemplation of adapting the need to eat to the need to be properly nourished'. They include the wartime *How to Cook a Wolf* (1942), *The Art of Eating* (1976) and *With Bold Knife and Fork* (1979). Later in life she became a Hollywood screenwriter and joined the American civil rights movement.

Fiske, Fidelia

Born 1816   Died 1864
American missionary, the first single woman missionary to enter Persia

Fidelia Fiske was born in Shelburne, Massachusetts, a niece of the pioneer missionary to the Near East, Pliny Fisk (1792–1825). She graduated from Mount Holyoke Seminary in 1842 and was appointed by the American Board to the Near East to work in Persia, among women and girls near Lake Urmia, where a central mission station had been opened in 1835.

In 1858 she returned to the USA because of health problems. Always hoping to go back to Persia, she declined the principalship of Mount Holyoke.

Fiske, Minnie Maddern, *née* Maria Augusta Davey

Born 1865   Died 1932
American actress and director who was
instrumental in the development of US theatre
around the turn of the century

Maria Davey was born in New Orleans into a theatrical family. She made her stage début at the age of three under her mother's maiden name of Maddern, graduating to adult roles by the age of 13. She made her New York début in 1882, but retired from the stage after her marriage to the drama critic Harrison Fiske in 1890.

She resumed her career in 1894, and championed realistic theatre and natural acting styles both as a distinguished actress and as an influential director and manager. She campaigned for humanitarian causes outside of theatre, but is remembered chiefly for her important contribution to the development of American drama.

Fitton, Mary

Born c.1578   Died 1647
English courtier whose affair with the poet
William Herbert caused his banishment
from court

Mary Fitton was born probably in Gawsworth, Cheshire. She became maid of honour to **Elizabeth I** in 1595. She was twice married and widowed, and in 1600 became mistress to the poet William Herbert (1580–1630), later 3rd Earl of Pembroke; he was banished from court the following year.

Reputedly of dark complexion, she has been identified by some to have been the 'dark lady' of Shakespeare's Sonnets cxxvii–clvii, although her biography does not indicate that she knew him.

Fitzgerald, Ella, *known as the* First Lady of Song

Born 1918
American jazz singer, one of the most celebrated
and influential performers of the post-war era

Ella Fitzgerald was born in Newport News, Virginia, and raised in New York.

She was 'discovered' at the age of 16 during an amateur night at the Apollo Theatre, Harlem, and began her professional career with the Tiny Bradshaw Band, moving to the Chick Webb Orchestra and taking over the leadership when Webb died in 1939.

Since 1940 Fitzgerald has worked mainly as a featured artiste with her own trio, but there have been notable engagements and record-

Ella Fitzgerald, 1958

ings with Louis Armstrong, Duke Ellington, Count Basie and Jazz at the Philharmonic.

Her vocal range and clarity in her earlier years, and her understanding of jazz interpretation, have made her a consistent influence, and her masterful 'scat' singing has been widely imitated by many different artists.

Fitzgerald, Penelope Mary

Born 1916
English novelist and biographer whose non-fiction
and fiction works show vivid evocation of period,
place and character

Penelope Fitzgerald was born in Lincoln and educated at Oxford. Her biographies include *Edward Burne-Jones* (1975) and *Charlotte Mew and her Friends* (1984). The vivid evocation of period, place and character for which her biographies are noted also distinguishes her elegant, intricately-constructed fiction.

The Bookshop (1978) conjures up the enclosed world of a small Suffolk community, with all its rivalries and in-fighting, while *Offshore* (1979), which won the Booker Prize, deals with a group of people living on barges on the River Thames. This is a novel born of salutory experience: Penelope Fitzgerald had herself, with her family, lived on a Thames barge, which sank. *The Gate of Angels* (1990) is a love story set in Cambridge in 1912.

Fitzgerald, Zelda, *née* Sayre

Born 1900 Died 1948
American novelist and painter whose life as the
wife of F Scott Fitzgerald became more famous
than her work

Zelda Sayre was born in Montgomery, Alabama, the daughter of an Alabama Supreme Court judge. She met the writer F Scott Fitzgerald (1896–1940) while he was stationed in Alabama in 1918 and, after one broken engagement, married him in 1920.

She became a symbol of the liberated flapper and wrote about modern women struggling to establish an identity or career separate from that of their husbands. Ironically, the couple began to emulate the roles of the characters in F Scott Fitzgerald's novels, seeking the American Dream and, aware of their potential fate, they moved to the South of France in 1924.

Zelda suffered mental breakdowns in 1930 and in 1932, the year she published *Save Me the Waltz*, which tells her experiences from her point of view. With her mental instability perhaps exacerbated by her husband's overshadowing success as well as his excesses, she spent much of the rest of her life in sanitariums in Europe and the USA. Other prose fragments by her are of interest, as are many of her paintings.

Fitzherbert, Mrs Maria Anne, *née* Smythe

Born 1756 Died 1837
English widow who was the secret wife of the
future King George IV

Maria Smythe was born probably in Hampshire into an old Roman Catholic family. She was widowed for the second time on the death of her husband Thomas Fitzherbert in 1781, but on finding herself reasonably wealthy was able to enter London high society. The Prince of Wales (later George IV) fell in love with her and they were married in 1785 in secret, for the Act of Settlement (1689) stated that marriage to a Roman Catholic would oblige the prince to forfeit his succession. He moved to live near her home.

However the marriage, contracted without the consent of the king, George III, was declared invalid under the Royal Marriage Act of 1772; the prince later denied that there had been a marriage at all, an act which Mrs Fitzherbert forgave. On his marriage to Princess **Caroline of Brunswick** in 1795 he cruelly broke the connection with Mrs Fitzherbert, but she obtained a formal declaration from the Pope stating that she was the prince's

wife, allowing them to be reunited. Meanwhile George forced his legal wife to live separately from him soon after the birth of their child, Princess **Charlotte**.

The relationship with Mrs Fitzherbert was finally broken off in 1803, as the prince was becoming increasingly dissolute, but it is said that on his death in 1830 he was found to be wearing a locket containing her picture.

Flagstad, Kirsten

Born 1895 Died 1962
Norwegian soprano who was acclaimed the world
over for her Wagnerian roles

Kirsten Flagstad was born in Hamar. She studied in Stockholm and Oslo, where she made her operatic début in 1913. She remained in Scandinavia until 1933.

With her musical intuition and powerful voice she excelled in Wagnerian roles, such as Sieglinde at Bayreuth (1934) and Isolde in New York (1935), and was acclaimed in most of the world's major opera houses.

In 1958–60 she was the first director of the Norwegian State Opera.

Flanner, Janet, *pseud* Genêt

Born 1892 Died 1978
American literary journalist and novelist famed
for her sophisticated cosmopolitan reportage

Janet Flanner was born in Indianapolis and educated privately, in Germany and at the University of Chicago. Following World War I she travelled in Europe and in 1925 became the Paris correspondent of the *New Yorker* under the name Genêt. She remained there with that job for 50 years, apart from during World War II.

She became a leading member of the eventually influential coterie of (mostly) homosexual women (they included **Natalie Barney**, **Djuna Barnes** and Mina Loy) who lived in Paris between the wars. Her 'Letters from Paris' to the *New Yorker* still provide the most articulate guide to all but their sexual affairs. They were edited as *Paris Letters* (1966–71) in two volumes. She also occasionally wrote a 'Letter from London' and translated novels by **Colette**.

Her now neglected feminist novel, *The Cubical City* (1926), about Paris, attacks sexual puritanism and stuffiness.

Flather of Windsor, Shreela Flather, Baroness, *née* Rai

Born 1938
British politician, the first Asian woman to be
awarded a life peerage

Shreela Flather was born in Lahore, Pakistan. She attended University College, London, and was called to the Bar in 1962, as was her husband Gary Flather. After working as a teacher, she entered politics in 1976 as a councillor (until 1991) for the Royal Borough of Windsor and Maidenhead (the first female member of an ethnic minority in Britain to be elected a councillor) and has since served on numerous advisory committees concerned with prison reform, housing, social services and ethnic rights.

She was a member of the Commission for Racial Equality from 1980 to 1986, in which year she was elected Mayor of Windsor and Maidenhead. She served as UK delegate to the European Community's Economic and Social Committee from 1987 until 1990, the year she was awarded a life peerage, making her Britain's first female Asian life peer.

Fleming, Amalia, *née* Coutsouris

Born 1909   Died 1986
Greek-British bacteriologist and politician

Amalia Coutsouris was born in Constantinople (now Istanbul) to Greek parents. She studied medicine at Athens University and married a man named Voureka. During World War II she joined the resistance, was captured, sentenced to death, and rescued by the Allied Advance.

After the War Amalia went to London, where she worked at the Wright–Fleming Institute with Sir Alexander Fleming (1881–1955), whom she married in 1953 as her second husband. After his death, she continued her research as a bacteriologist.

Returning to Greece in 1967, she protested against the military regime which had seized power. Arrested in 1971, she was deported to London. She returned to Greece in 1973, becoming an MP, a European member of parliament, leader of the Greek committee of Amnesty International, and a member of the European Human Rights Commission.

Fleming, May Agnes, *née* Early

Born 1840   Died 1880
Canadian writer whose romantic fiction made her Canada's first bestselling novelist

May Agnes Early was born in Portland, New Brunswick. She began publishing at the age of 15 under a pseudonym, Cousin May Carlton, but after her wedding in 1865 (the result of a whirlwind romance) she used her married name. As Canada's first bestselling

novelist she wrote three novels a year, earning an annual income of $15,000.

Her romantic fantasies about teachers, seamstresses and other poor women achieving prosperity in propitious marriages went against the grain of her own life. She left her alcoholic husband and, when she died at an early age of Bright's disease, he found that she had excluded him from her will.

Fleming, Peggy

Born 1948
American figure skater, winner of the only gold medal won by the USA in the 1968 Olympics

Peggy Fleming was born in San José, California. She became the youngest woman ever to win the women's national senior championships in 1963, a victory that was to be the first of five consecutive wins. Three years later she won the world figure-skating championship, the first American woman to win the competition in more than a decade, and successfully defended her title for the next two years.

After retiring from amateur competition in 1968, she launched a successful commercial career.

Fleming, Williamina Paton, *née* Stevens

Born 1857   Died 1911
Scottish-born American astronomer best known for her pioneering work on the classification of stellar spectra

Williamina Paton Stevens was born in Dundee. She married James Orr Fleming and emigrated to Boston at the age of 20, but the marriage failed and she took up domestic work for the Director of the Harvard College Observatory, Edward Pickering, to support herself and her child.

She joined the research team at the Observatory in 1881 and frequently collaborated with Pickering; some feel the discovery of the duplicity of Beta Lyrae has been wrongly accredited to Pickering rather than to Fleming. Her technique, known as the Pickering–Fleming technique, involved the study of many thousands of celestial photographs. She also discovered new stars and variables, investigated stellar spectra, including 10 of the 24 novae recorded up until 1911, and categorized 10,351 stars in the Draper Catalogue of Stellar Spectra (1890).

In 1906 she became the first American woman to be elected to the Royal Astronomical Society.

Fletcher, Alice Cunningham

Born 1838 Died 1923
American ethnologist and ethnomusicologist

Alice Fletcher was born in Havana, Cuba. Privately educated, she worked for the Peabody Museum at Harvard during the 1870s, joining its staff officially in 1886. She undertook ethnological work among the Native Americans of the Plains, particularly the Omaha, but believing that this policy would best safeguard their land rights, she was a leading proponent during the 1880s of the policy of dividing up the indigenous people's lands into separate farmsteads. For this policy, enshrined in the Dawes Act (1887), she and others have been much criticised.

She held a number of leading posts among American anthropological societies, including Vice-President of the Association of American Anthropological Societies (1895). Her extensive collection and study of traditional Native American melodies have considerable value.

Florence, Mary Sargant, *née* Sargant

Born 1857 Died 1954
English artist, painter of murals in fresco and figure subjects and landscapes in watercolour and tempera

Mary Sargant was born in London and educated privately in Brighton. She studied at the Slade School under Alphonse Legros and later in Paris. In 1888 she married the US musician Henry Smyth Florence and after his death in 1891 returned to the UK and lived in a house which she had designed and decorated.

She exhibited at the Royal Academy and the NEAC (New English Art Club), becoming a member in 1911, and executed a mural, which is still in situ, at Chelsea Old Town Hall, depicting celebrities in science, religion and politics. Her works in Oakham Old School and Bournville School Hall are among her most notable commissions.

She was involved in the suffrage movement, the National Union and the Woman's Freedom League. She also contributed to various publications including articles on colour theory for the *Cambridge Magazine*.

Florentino, Leona (Leonora)

Born 1849 Died 1884
Filipino poet, a cousin of the Filipino patriot and writer José Rizal

Leona Florentino was born into a wealthy family in Vigan, Ilocos Sur, in Northern Luzon. She learnt Spanish, but began writing as a child in her native language of Iloko.

Largely self-educated, she is regarded as the first Filipino woman poet. She wrote love lyrics, celebratory verse and satirical poetry, published in newspapers in Spanish translation.

Although much of her poetry was lost during the 1896 Revolution, her work was exhibited in the Exposition Internationale of 1889 in Paris, through the influence of her son Isabelo de los Reyes. This exposure brought her to European notice, and she was cited in Madame Andzia Wolska's *Bibliothèque Internationale des Oeuvres des Femmes* (1889).

Florey, Lady Margaret Augusta Jennings, *née* Fremantle

Born 1904 Died 1994
English pathologist and scientific collaborator of Nobel Prize-winner Lord Florey

Margaret Fremantle was born in Swanbourne, Buckinghamshire, the second of four daughters of an upper-class family. She went up to Lady Margaret Hall, Oxford, to read English, but was allowed to transfer to physiology to satisfy her desire to study medicine. She married Denys Jennings in 1930, and qualified four years later, after clinical training at the Royal Free Hospital in London.

She joined Florey's department of pathology at Oxford in 1936, and was a member of the team that demonstrated during World War II that penicillin, discovered in the late 1920s by Alexander Fleming, was a potent antibiotic against pathogenic bacteria, but non-toxic to humans.

Howard Florey, Ernst Chain and Alexander Fleming shared the 1954 Nobel Prize for Physiology or Medicine for their work. Margaret Jennings, divorced in 1946, was a Lecturer in Pathology at Oxford from 1945 until 1972, and married Florey in 1967, the year after the death of his first wife.

Flynn, Elizabeth Gurley

Born 1890 Died 1964
American political radical and writer who campaigned for rights for workers and women

Elizabeth Gurley Flynn was born in Concord, New Hampshire. Coming from a socialist background, she embraced socialism at an early age and at 16 delivered her first speech — 'What Socialism will do for Women'. Her marriage in 1908 to John Archibald Jones ended in divorce and a later relationship with a fellow activist, Carlo Tresca, also broke up.

She campaigned for civil rights for immigrants, all categories of workers, and especially for women. In 1951 she was arrested and subsequently imprisoned for subversive activities. Her published works include *Women in the War* (1942), *Women's Place in the Fight for a Better World* (1947) and the autobiographical *I Speak My Piece* (1955).

Fonda, Jane Seymour

Born 1937
American actress whose roles have ranged from sex kitten to aerobics queen

Jane Fonda was born in New York City, a daughter of the actor Henry Fonda, with whom she made her stage début in *The Country Girl* (1955). She studied at the Actor's Studio and modelled part-time before making her film début in *Tall Story* (1960). Work in Europe and marriage to director Roger Vadim labelled her as a 'sex kitten', an image further encouraged by her appearance as comic strip heroine *Barbarella* (1968).

Later she established a new career as a versatile dramatic actress of considerable emotional depth and sensitivity, winning Academy Awards for *Klute* (1971) and *Coming Home* (1978) and an Emmy for *The Dollmaker* (1983). Later films include *Agnes of God* (1985) and *Old Gringo* (1989).

Despite having courted disfavour in the 1970s with her outspoken criticisms of the Vietnam War (she made a controversial trip to North Vietnam), she became a powerful film executive and, during the 1980s, an energetic proselytizer for physical health through bestselling videos. She married the media mogul Ted Turner in her fifties and now spends much of her time in Atlanta, Georgia.

Fonseca, Eleonora Pimentel, Marchesa di (Marchioness of)

Born 1758 Died 1799
Neapolitan noblewoman who was executed for her pro-revolutionary sympathies

Eleonora Pimental was born in Naples. She was educated to a high standard in botany, natural history and anatomy and assisted the biologist and naturalist Lazaro Spallanzani in his investigations; in 1780 he demonstrated the true nature of digestion, and the functions of spermatozoa and ova. She was also lady-in-waiting to Queen **Maria Carolina**, wife of Ferdinand I of the Two Sicilies.

She was an active French partisan, and when in 1799 the royal family was forced to flee Naples, she managed to escape the Lazzaroni who were hostile to supporters of the French interest. The uprising led to the establishment of the Parthenopean Republic (1798–

9), during which she edited a republican journal, the *Neapolitan Monitor*.

On the restoration of the government she was hanged at the queen's instigation, not only for having expressed her pro-revolutionary principles, but also for remarking on her intimacy with Sir John Acton, the queen's English lover who had been appointed Prime Minister.

Fontanne, Lynn, *originally* Lillie Louise Fontanne

Born 1887 Died 1983
English actress who with her husband became a star of the American stage

Lynn Fontanne was born in England. She studied with **Ellen Terry** and made her stage début in 1905. She settled in America in 1916, where she met her husband and stage partner, Alfred Lunt (1892–1977). They went on to become the most successful husband-and-wife team in American theatre, but only after she scored an initial Broadway success in *Dulcy* (1921).

The Lunts first appeared as a partnership in *The Guardsman* (1924). They specialized in high comedy, and developed their trademark style, marked by a then innovative conversational technique and sharp repartee. Their celebrated collaboration lasted until they retired in 1958.

Fonteyn, Dame Margot, *stage-name of* Margaret Hookham

Born 1919 Died 1991
English ballet dancer regarded as one of the finest technicians of this century

Margaret Hookham was born in Reigate. She studied under Nicholai Legat and **Ninette de Valois** among others, then joined the Vic–Wells Ballet, which became the Sadler's Wells Ballet and finally the Royal Ballet, with which she spent her entire career.

She created many roles with De Valois and the choreographer Frederick Ashton, among them *The Haunted Ballroom* (1939), *Symphonic Variations* (1946) and *The Fairy Queen* (1946). She rose in the Royal Ballet to become its queen ballerina, her career extended and enhanced by her acclaimed partnership with Rudolph Nureyev, and performing work by Roland Petit and Kenneth MacMillan.

She also wrote and introduced a six-part television series, *The Magic of Dance* (1979), and her publications include an autobiography (1975) and a study of **Anna Pavlova**. She married Roberto Emilio Arias

(1918–90), Panamanian ambassador to the court of St James, in 1955.

Fontyn, Jacqueline, *professional name of* Jacqueline Schmitt-Fontyn

Born 1930
Belgian composer whose first major work was a choral ballet score

Jacqueline Fontyn was born in Antwerp and educated in Brussels, Paris and Vienna. Shortly after her marriage in 1961 to the organist and composer Camille Schmitt (1908–76), she was appointed Professor of Counterpoint at the Royal Conservatory, Antwerp, leaving in 1970 to take up the same chair in Brussels.

Freely eclectic and communicative in style, she made an impact with the choral ballet score *Piedigrotta* (1958) and with the orchestral *Digressions* (1962) and *Quatre Sites* (1977), the last of these winning her the Prix Arthur Honegger (1977). In 1990 an illuminating study of Fontyn's work was published by Bettina Brandt.

Forbes, (Joan) Rosita

Born 1893   Died 1967
English writer and traveller, particularly in Arabia and North Africa

Rosita Forbes was born in Swinderby, Lincolnshire. Having visited almost every country in the world, she used her experiences as the raw material for exciting travel books, including *The Secret of the Sahara-Kufara* (1922), *From Red Sea to Blue Nile* (1928), *The Prodigious Caribbean* (1940), *Appointment in the Sun* (1949) and *Islands in the Sun* (1950).

Ford, Betty (Elizabeth), *née* Bloomer

Born 1918
American health administrator and First Lady as the wife of President Ford

Betty Bloomer was born in Chicago, Illinois. Her early career was as a dancer, and included a tour with the **Martha Graham** Concert Group.

In 1948 she married Gerald Ford (1913–   ), who later became President of the USA (1974–7). As First Lady, Betty Ford's public battle with breast cancer created awareness of health problems for women.

Her struggle with substance abuse led her to found the Betty Ford Center, of which she is president of the board of directors. She has written two autobiographies, *The Times of My Life* (1979) and *Betty: A Glad Awakening* (1987).

Ford, Isabella

Born 1860   Died 1924
English social reformer who strove to improve working conditions in the garment industry

Isabella Ford was the daughter of a prosperous Quaker. She devoted her life to improving the conditions of working-class women, initially supporting the rights of the seamstresses and the mills girls.

She became a lifelong member of the Leeds Trades and Labour Council, and in 1903 was elected to the executive of the Independent Labour Union, becoming the first woman to speak at the annual conference of the Labour Representation Committee. In 1922 she was a delegate to the International Peace Conference in The Hague.

Forde, Florrie, *professional name of* Florence Flanagan

Born 1876   Died 1940
Australian music-hall singer who encouraged wartime audience participation

Florrie Forde was born in Fitzroy, New South Wales. In Sydney she became known as the Australian **Marie Lloyd**, with a raw, unpolished delivery that encouraged audiences to join in. She was asked to perform at the first ever Royal Command Performance in 1912, but her singalong style had its greatest success during World War I with such songs as 'Pack Up Your Troubles in Your Old Kitbag', 'It's a Long Way to Tipperary' and 'Down at the Old Bull and Bush'.

She formed her own troupe, Flo and Co, and worked regularly through the 1920s and 1930s. Her sudden death on tour in Scotland robbed British entertainment of one of its most enduring stars.

Forgan, Liz (Elizabeth Anne Lucy)

Born 1944
British journalist and broadcaster, the most powerful woman in British broadcasting

Liz Forgan was born in Calcutta, where her Scottish father was posted in the army. She attended Benenden School in England, then Oxford University. Her early jobs in journalism were with an English-language newspaper in Tehran, then the *Hampstead and Highgate Express* in London, and as chief leader-writer on the *Evening Standard* (1974–8). In 1978 she was appointed women's editor at *The Guardian*, where she learnt quickly about women's issues and developed a strong feminist commitment.

In 1981, despite having had no television experience, Forgan was asked to join Channel 4 Television as commissioning editor of factual output. She introduced controversial programmes that allowed a broad range of opinion to be broadcast, such as *Right to Reply*, and by 1988 had become Director of Programmes and the most powerful woman in British television.

In 1993 she left to take up the position of managing director of BBC Network Radio, bringing her creative vitality and determined approach to bear on the BBC's five national radio stations.

Forster, Margaret

Born 1938
English novelist, biographer and critic who examines female family relationships

Margaret Forster was born in Carlisle and educated at Oxford. Her early novels include the topical *Georgy Girl* (1965), depicting the emotional and sexual freedoms and dangers suddenly confronting young women in a liberated decade.

In her later novels, each with a strong sense of character and social context, she has looked at the problems of middle-aged married women (*Marital Rites*, 1981) and adolescent children (*Private Papers*, 1986). Her biographies include a sympathetic *Elizabeth Barrett Browning* (1988), while its companion novel, *Lady's Maid* (1990), speculates intriguingly upon the life of Elizabeth Barrett Browning's maid, Wilson.

Her other non-fiction writing includes *Significant Sisters: the Grassroots of Active Feminism 1839–1939* (1984) and an excellent and authoritative biography, *Daphne du Maurier* (1993).

Fortesque-Brickdale, Mary Eleanor

Born 1872   Died 1945
English painter and illustrator who was also famous as a stained glass designer

Mary Fortesque-Brickdale was born in Surrey and trained at the Crystal Palace School of Art and then at the Royal Academy schools. She began exhibiting at the RA (Royal Academy) in 1896 and in 1897 won a prize for a design for the RA dining room.

She illustrated many books of poetry and prose, and taught for some time at the Byam Shaw School of Art. She also travelled extensively in Italy and the South of France. During World War I she designed posters for the government; after the end of the War her designs for stained glass windows were in great demand. She continued to work into the 1940s. She was the first woman to be elected a member of the Royal Institute of Oil Painters and to be an associated member of the Royal Society of Painters in Water Colour.

Fossey, Dian

Born 1932   Died 1985
American zoologist famed for her work on the social organization of the mountain gorillas of Rwanda and Zaire

Dian Fossey was born in San Francisco. An occupational therapist, in 1963 she went to Africa where she met the anthropologists Louis and **Mary Leakey**, and she first encountered gorillas in the Virunga mountain range of central Africa.

In 1966 she returned to Tanzania, encouraged by the Leakeys, and set up the Karisoke Research Centre in Rwanda in order to study the gorilla population. Her 18-year study is documented in her 1983 book *Gorillas in the Mist* (filmed in 1988, with **Sigourney Weaver** playing Fossey).

Fossey advocated 'active conservation' — rallying international opposition to the threats posed to the gorillas by poaching and by local farming methods. In 1985 she was murdered at the Centre.

Foster, Jodie, *originally* Alicia Christian Foster

Born 1962
American film actress who first found fame in babyhood

Jodie Foster was born in Los Angeles. Starting with her role as the bare-bottom baby in the Coppertone® commercials, Foster's childhood was taken over by acting, both in commercials and films, though she did manage to complete her education with a BA in Literature from Yale. Despite being hailed as one of the most promising young performers of the day, she found surprising difficulty in establishing herself as an adult star.

She made a powerful transition with a harrowing performance as a rape victim in search of justice in *Accused* (1988), which won her a Best Actress Oscar, a feat she repeated with her fiercely intelligent characterization of the fledgling FBI agent in *The Silence of the Lambs* (1991). Also in 1991 she made a thoughtful directorial début with *Little Man Tate*. Her later film appearances include *Nell* (1995).

Fox, Paula

Born 1923
American writer of fiction for children and adults

Paula Fox was born in New York. Her children's books concern characters who remain confused and ill-at-ease for longer than is usual in juvenile fiction. *The Slave Dancer* (1973) is her most powerful narrative story. Set in 1840, it tells the nightmarish tale of a boy being kidnapped into slavery in New Orleans. In similar vein, the earlier *How Many Miles to Babylon* (1967) is the story of a small black boy who is seized by older children.

Fox's adult novels tend to be less dramatic, concerned with suburban domestic themes. *Desperate Characters* (1970) was turned into a movie by Frank D Gilroy.

Frame, Janet Paterson

Born 1924
New Zealand novelist and short-story writer regarded as the greatest fiction writer in her country

Janet Frame was born in Dunedin, a daughter of a railway worker, and trained as a teacher at Otago University Teachers Training College. Her first book was a collection of short stories, *The Lagoon: Stories* (1952), which she followed five years later with a novel, *Owls Do Cry.*

Having spent much time in psychiatric hospitals due to mental breakdowns, Frame writes novels that walk a tightrope between danger and safety, where the looming threat of disorder attracts those it frightens. She was quickly honoured in her homeland but only belatedly received international recognition; her key books are *Scented Gardens for the Blind* (1963), *A State of Siege* (1966), *Intensive Care* (1970) and *Living in the Maniototo* (1979). *The Adaptable Man*, first published in 1965, was reprinted in 1993.

Her short stories were collected in *The Reservoir and Other Stories* (1966) and in *You Are Now Entering the Human Heart* (1983). *The Carpathians* was published in 1988. Some early verse is collected in *The Pocket Mirror* (1967). The background to her work is implicit in three volumes of autobiography, *To the Island* (1983), *An Angel at my Table* (1984) and *The Envoy from Mirror City* (1985), which were collectively made into a film under the title of the second volume.

France, Celia

Born 1921
English ballet dancer and founder of the National Ballet of Canada

Celia France, 1949

Celia France was born in London. She trained under **Marie Rambert**, Antony Tudor and Vera Volkova, and performed with Ballet Rambert from 1937 to 1940, moving to Sadler's Wells Royal Ballet in 1941 where she created roles in Robert Helpmann's *Hamlet* (1942) and *Miracle in the Gorbals* (1944).

Only months after returning to Ballet Rambert in 1950 she was invited by a group of dance patrons in Toronto to set up a new ballet company for Canada. In 1951 the National Ballet of Canada was founded under her directorship, and until her retirement in 1974 she built up a repertoire strong on Russian classics and work from British choreographers like Frederick Ashton and Antony Tudor.

Frances of Rome, St

Born 1384 Died 1440
Italian founder of the Oblate Congregation of Tor de' Specchi for the benefit of the poor and the sick

Frances was born into a wealthy Christian family in Trastevere. From childhood she wanted to be a nun, but instead at 13 was married to Lorenzo Ponziani, whose sister Vanozza joined Frances in her charitable works around Rome, a city beset by plague and war.

During the strife caused by the Great Schism of the Western Church and the capture of Rome by Ladislas of Naples in 1408, the

Ponzianis, known to be strong supporters of the pope, lost their fortune and Lorenzo was forced to flee until 1414. In his absence Frances nevertheless continued to share what she had with the poor and suffering; on his return she nursed him too.

With his approval in 1425 she founded the Oblates of Mary, later known as the Oblate Congregation of Tor de' Specchi, which was associated with the Benedictines of Mount Oliveto. When Lorenzo died in 1436, Frances became superior of the order and spent the rest of her life there. She is said to have experienced many visions, including that of her guardian angel, which may be the reason for her being the patron of motorists. Her feast day is 9 March.

Francesca da Rimini

Died 1285
Italian noblewoman whose story was immortalized in Dante's Inferno

Francesca da Rimini was the daughter of Giovanni da Polenta, Lord of Ravenna.

She was married to Giovanni the Lame, son of Malatesta, lord of Rimini, but she already loved Giovanni's brother Paolo. Giovanni, surprising the lovers together, slew them both.

Francis, Connie, *originally* Concetta Rosa Maria Franconero

Born 1938
American pop singer and film actress whose record sales rivalled those of Frank Sinatra

Connie Francis was born in Newark, New Jersey. She was discovered on a television talent show aged 11, and had her first hit with 'Who's Sorry Now' (1957). In the late 1950s, she rivalled fellow-Newarkian Frank Sinatra for records sold, and capitalized on the new pop boom with songs like 'Lipstick on Your Collar'.

Her first film appearance was in *Where the Boys Are* (1951), and she became known for appearances on military bases and for charity work. Her later career was interrupted by a violent sexual assault in 1974, but her records continue to sell in large numbers.

Franco, Veronica

Born 1546   Died 1591
Italian poet and courtesan celebrated for her beauty and her writing

Veronica Franco was born in Venice. She married a doctor but was widowed early, left with a son. She enjoyed the friendship and correspondence of many of the prominent political and literary figures of the day, and as a woman who had learned much about men, was not uncritical of them. In her thirties she appears to have turned her back on her courtesan's lifestyle and founded a hostel for 'fallen women'.

Her poetry, while ostensibly Petrarchan, is notably erotic, celebrating female sexuality, and abounds in the unusual. Her best-known collection of poetry, written in 1575, *Terza Rima*, was edited in 1912. It is unusual in its rejection of the female chastity and submissiveness advocated by much of the literature of the time. Her *Lettere* ('Letters') of 1580 include one explaining the harshness beneath the glamorous veneer of a courtesan's life.

Frank, Anne

Born 1929   Died 1945
German Jewish concentration camp victim, a symbol of suffering under the Nazis

Anne Frank was born in Frankfurt-am-Main. She fled from the Nazis to Holland in 1933 with her family and after the Nazi occupation of Holland hid with her family and four others in the sealed-off back-room of an office in Amsterdam from 1942 until they were betrayed in August 1944. She died in Belsen concentration camp.

The lively, moving diary she kept during her concealment was published as *Het Achterhuis* (1947, Eng trans *The Diary of Anne Frank*, 1952) and was dramatized in 1958 and filmed in 1959. Her name was given to villages and schools for refugee children throughout western Europe.

Frankenthaler, Helen

Born 1928
American abstract painter of brightly coloured canvases, one of the second generation of Abstract Expressionists

Helen Frankenthaler was born in New York. She studied under the Mexican painter Rufino Tamayo and at Bennington College, Vermont. Influenced by Hans Hofmann, with whom she studied briefly at the Art Students' League in New York in 1950, and Jackson Pollock, she developed a technique of applying very thin paint to unprimed canvas, allowing it to soak in and create atmospheric stains and blots on the surface.

Her best-known picture is *Mountains and Sea* (1952). Married to the artist Robert Motherwell from 1955 to 1971, she has been honoured with several awards (eg first prize for painting at the 1959 Paris Biennale) and has taught at various universities in the USA.

Franklin, Aretha, *known as the* Queen of Soul *and* Lady Soul

Born 1942
American soul singer and pianist whose singles have sold in millions

Aretha Franklin was born in Memphis, Tennessee. The daughter of a well-known Detroit preacher and gospel singer, she had established her name on the gospel circuit with his New Bethel Baptist Church and his gospelling tours before she signed a recording contract with Columbia Records in 1960. Although she spent six years with that label and recorded several successful albums, it was only after moving to Atlantic Records in 1967 that her full potential was realized.

Producer Jerry Wexler capitalized on both her piano-playing skills and her gospel roots, most notably on *I Never Loved A Man The Way I Love You* (1967) and on *Lady Soul* (1968). In 1972 she returned to the church with her album *Amazing Grace*, a two-record set of gospel songs recorded live in Los Angeles. Subsequent albums have included *Everything I Feel in Me* (1974), *Almighty Fire* (1978), *Love All The Hurt Away* (1981), *Get It Right* (1983) and *Aretha* (1986). In 1987 she recorded *One Lord, One Faith, One Baptism* in her father's Detroit church. Her best-known songs include 'Natural Woman' and 'Respect'.

Franklin, Lady Jane, *née* Griffin

Born 1792 Died 1875
English traveller and expedition benefactor who contributed significantly to the search for the North-West Passage

Jane Griffin was born in England and travelled widely with her father before marrying the British naval officer and explorer Sir John Franklin (1786–1847) in 1828. She accompanied him on his tours through Syria, Turkey and Egypt and whilst he was Governor of Van Diemen's Land (Tasmania), she campaigned vociferously for the rights of women prisoners.

When her husband disappeared on a voyage in search of the North-West Passage, she sponsored and raised money for a series of search expeditions, some of them in co-operation with the navy. After 10 years her husband's diaries were recovered, showing he had proved the existence of the North-West Passage.

The expeditions she sponsored made such an important contribution to the exploration of the Canadian Arctic that she was awarded the Royal Geographical Society's Founder's Medal, becoming the first woman to be thus honoured.

Franklin, (Stella Marian Sarah) Miles, *pseud* Brent of Bin Bin

Born 1879 Died 1954
Australian novelist who gave her name to a highly prestigious literary award in Australia

Miles Franklin was born in Talbingo, near Tumut, New South Wales. Known to her family as Stella, she was a fifth-generation Australian, with her great-great-grandfather having been a convict in the First Fleet. She was the eldest of seven children and spent her first 10 years at a farm in the bush country, described in *Childhood at Brindabella* (1963). Later the family moved downmarket to a district fictionalized in *My Brilliant Career* (1901) as Possum Gully. Eventually they settled in a Sydney suburb.

Having flirted with nursing she turned to journalism, became involved in the feminist movement, wrote *My Brilliant Career* and emigrated in 1906 to the USA, where she worked as secretary to the Women's Trade Union League. Moving to England in 1915, despite a deep aversion to war, she helped with the war effort, serving with the Scottish Women's Hospital at Ostrovo, in Macedonia. In 1932 she returned permanently to Australia, where the 'Brent of Bin Bin' series, starting with *Up the Country* (1928), made the pseudonymous author the subject of much speculation.

Her best work appeared under her own name, including the early autobiographical novels *All That Swagger* (1936) and *My Career Goes Bung* (1946), and a collection of essays on Australian literature, *Laughter, Not for a Cage* (1956). The popularity of her novels and the filming of *My Brilliant Career* have tended to obscure the considerable contribution that she made to the social and professional development of Australian women.

Franklin, Rosalind Elsie

Born 1920 Died 1958
English X-ray crystallographer who carried out important work on the structure of DNA

Rosalind Franklin was born in London. She studied physical chemistry at Cambridge and held a research post at the British Coal Utilization Research Association (1942–6), where her work was important in establishing carbon fibre technology. At the Central Government Laboratory for Chemistry in Paris (1947–50), she became experienced in X-ray diffraction techniques.

She returned to London in 1951 to work on DNA at King's College. She produced excellent X-ray diffraction pictures of DNA which were published in the same issue of *Nature* (1953) in which James Watson and Francis Crick proposed their double-helical model of DNA. Finding it difficult to co-operate with Maurice Wilkins, who was also working on DNA at King's College, Franklin left to join John Bernal's laboratory at Birkbeck College, London, to work on tobacco mosaic virus.

She contracted cancer and died in 1958, four years before she could be awarded the 1962 Nobel Prize for Physiology or Medicine jointly with Watson, Crick and Wilkins for the determination of the structure of DNA.

Fraser, Dawn

Born 1937
Australian swimmer, the first woman to win three consecutive Olympic gold medals

Dawn Fraser was born in Balmain, Sydney. Her talent was discovered when as a schoolgirl she used to swim in the harbourside pool in Birchgrove which now bears her name.

In her swimming career she broke 27 world records and won 29 Australian championships. Her outstanding achievement was in winning gold medals at three successive Olympic Games — Melbourne (1956), Rome (1960) and Tokyo (1964) — in each case setting a new Olympic record. At the Rome games she broke three world records within one hour. In 1964 she became the first woman to break the 'magic minute' for the 100 metres with a time of 58.9 seconds, a record which was to stand until **Shane Gould** achieved 58.5 in 1972.

Although her rebellious spirit sometimes brought her into conflict with the swimming authorities, she was awarded the MBE in 1967.

Fraser, Marjory Kennedy *see* Kennedy-Fraser, Marjorie

Fredegund, *also spelt* Frédégonde

Died 598
Queen of the Franks as the murderously cruel wife of Chilperic, King of Neustria

Fredegund was a servant of Chilperic, King of Neustria, but after he had brought about the death of his first wife Galswintha (c.568), she became his mistress and then his wife. She waged a relentless feud with Galswintha's sister **Brunhilde**, wife of Sigbert I, King of Austrasia, a feud that was intensified by the rivalry between the two kingdoms.

Fredegund had Sigbert murdered and organized other assassination attempts, but when Chilperic himself was assassinated (584) she fled to the Paris cathedral with her son Clotaire II, for whom she ruled as regent. When their protector Guntram died, Sigbert's son and heir Childebert II tried in vain to attack Clotaire.

After Childebert's death in 595, Fredegund continued her mercilessly cruel intrigues against Brunhilde, supposedly on Clotaire's behalf, defeating her in war in 596.

Dawn Fraser, 1960

Freeman, Mary (E) Wilkins, née
Wilkins

Born 1852 Died 1930
American novelist and story writer whose regional
stories depict New England life

Mary Wilkins was born in Randolph, Massachusetts. Her schooling was interrupted by poor health. In her youth she acted as secretary to the elder physician and writer Oliver Wendell Holmes (1809–94) and in 1902 she married Dr Charles M Freeman and moved with him to Metuchen, New Jersey.

Her 238 stories about New England life, evoking its colour and frustrations not unlike those of Mrs **Gaskell** in *Cranford*, made an important contribution to American regional, or 'local colour', fiction. Paramount amongst these are her first volume *A Humble Romance and Other Stories* (1887) and the 24 tales in *A New England Nun* (1891).

She was not so happy in the novel form, but in her late collection of tales *Edgewater People* (1918) she recaptured all her old skill and pathos.

French, Annie

Born 1872 Died 1965
Scottish artist and illustrator who developed a
very fine pen-and-ink technique

Annie French was born in Glasgow. She studied at the Glasgow School of Art (1896–1902), where she was a fellow student and later colleague of **Jessie M King**. She first exhibited at the Brussels Salon in 1903 and she married the artist George Woolliscroft Rhead (1854–1920) in 1914.

Her watercolours have a Pre-Raphaelite feel and are 'Romantic' in subject matter, drawing parallels with the work of Sir Edward Burne-Jones and, although less sinister in content, Aubrey Beardsley. She illustrated a number of fairy tales and poems and designed a series of postcards and posters all in a highly decorative manner, emphasizing the unique quality of her fine pen-and-ink linear technique.

French exhibited regularly at the Royal Academy, RGI (Royal Glasgow Institute of Artists) and RSA (Royal Scottish Academy) and settled in Jersey in the late 1950s.

French, Dawn

Born 1957
English comedienne and actress at the forefront of
British comedy

Dawn French was born in Holyhead, Wales, the daughter of an RAF pilot. She was educated at a girls' boarding school in Plymouth,

then trained at the Central School of Speech and Drama, where she made friends with **Jennifer Saunders**. Starting at the Comedy Store in London they created a double act that took them to the forefront of the 'alternative' comedy of the time. In 1980 they joined the new Comic Strip club, which launched the careers of several contemporary comedians. Also during the 1980s French married Jamaican writer and comedian Lenny Henry.

After appearing in all the *Comic Strip Presents* films on television, French and Saunders were given their own outstandingly successful BBC series, which drew its humour from close observation of human foibles, particularly as illustrated by female relationships.

Outside the partnership, French has made many other television appearances, such as in *The Vicar of Dibley* (1994) as a woman priest. She has also had leading roles on stage in **Sharman MacDonald**'s *When I was a Girl I Used to Scream and Shout* and Ben Elton's *Silly Cow*.

French, Marilyn

Born 1929
American novelist and feminist scholar who
examines the limited role of women in a
patriarchal society

Marilyn French was born in New York and educated at Hofstra College and Harvard University. Her first work of fiction was *The Women's Room* (1977), a massive bestseller which, with sympathy and balance, traces its heroine's development from 1950s housewife to 1970s emancipated woman.

Her two subsequent novels, *The Bleeding Heart* (1980) and *Her Mother's Daughter* (1987), have brought a strong feminine philosophy to bear on the social and moral dilemmas of the late 20th century.

She has examined the female role in literature and society in *Shakespeare's Division of Experience* (1981), *Beyond Power: On Women, Men, and Morals* (1985) and *The War Against Women* (1992).

Freud, Anna

Born 1895 Died 1982
Austrian-born British psychoanalyst who
pioneered child psychoanalysis

Anna Freud was born in Vienna, the youngest daughter of the founder of psychoanalysis, Sigmund Freud (1856–1939). She taught at the Cottage Lyceum in Vienna and emigrated with her father to London in 1938, where she organized a residential war nursery for homeless children (1940–5).

In 1947 she founded the Hampstead Child

Therapy Clinic, of which she was director from 1952 to 1982. She made important contributions to child psychology and to elucidating how children learn self-defence through the repression of impulses. Her works include *The Ego and Mechanisms of Defence* (1937), *Normality and Pathology in Childhood* (1968) and *Beyond the Best Interests of the Child* (1973).

Friday, Nancy

Born 1937
American feminist author who explores the collective imagination of women and has thus revolutionized the approach to women and sexuality

Nancy Friday was born in Pittsburgh, Pennsylvania, the daughter of a financier, and was educated at Wellesley College. She worked as a reporter on a newspaper in San Juan, Puerto Rico (1960–1) and as editor of *Islands in the Sun* magazine (1961–3), before turning her efforts to freelance writing.

Her best known work, *My Secret Garden* (1976), a compilation of women's innermost sexual desires, sold over 1.5 million copies worldwide. This work exploded the myth surrounding women's sexual fantasies and exposed 'the woman on the street' as possessing an erotic imagination equal to that of a man. In 1980 she published *Men In Love*, an exploration of men and sexuality and a catalogue of the sexual fantasies men have about women. *Women on Top* (1991) takes another look at the sexual desires of modern women in the context of feminism and renewed sexual freedom, and documents the manner in which women appear to have incorporated male pornography into their sexual fantasies, issues which are dealt with once more in *Forbidden Flowers* (1994).

Frideswide, St

Born c.680 Died c.735
Anglo-Saxon abbess and patron saint of Oxford University and city

St Frideswide was the daughter of Didanus, an alderman. She founded a double monastery in Oxford on the site of what is now Christ Church.

She was canonized in 1481 and has two feast days: 19 October and 12 February.

Friedan, Betty (Elizabeth) Naomi, *née* Goldstein

Born 1921
American feminist, one of the founders of modern feminism

Betty Goldstein was born in Peoria, Illinois, and educated at Smith College. She became a housewife in New York and then began writing for magazines. Finding that her dissatisfaction was shared by others, she wrote a bestseller, *The Feminine Mystique* (1963), a highly influential feminist classic, which analyzed the role of women in American society and articulated their frustrations, particularly in the face of the achievements of the women's rights movement a few decades before.

She was founder and first President of the National Organization for Women (1966) and headed the National Women's Strike for Equality (1970). She warned against the dangers of competing against men by adopting undesirable male qualities and wrote her autobiography *It Changed My Life* (1977) and *The Second Stage* (1981).

Friedlander, Margarete, *married name* Wildenhain

Born 1898
German potter whose work in the 1940s focused on the value of a craftsman's way of life

Margarete Friedlander was born in Lyons, France, to German and English parents. She studied sculpture in Berlin and worked as a designer in a Thuringian porcelain factory, then trained in ceramics under G Marcks at the Bauhaus from 1919, where she produced functional earthenware. In 1925 she began teaching ceramics in Halle-Giebichenstein near Leipzig. She also designed for the Royal Berlin Porcelain Factory.

In 1933 she married F Wildenhain and moved to Holland, where she established a pottery workshop in Putten that produced stoneware for table and kitchen. Seven years later she moved to America and taught in Oakland, California, establishing her own workshops in Gueneville and Pond Farm (California), and working under the name of Margarete Wildenhain. Her work of this time is characterized by urns decorated with human figures and plants.

From the mid-1950s her interest turned increasingly to textured surfaces, created using course sand or grog and incising the decoration.

Friend, Charlotte

Born 1921 Died 1987
American oncologist and medical microbiologist who pioneered research into tumour viruses

Charlotte Friend was born in New York City. She attended Hunter College before serving in the US Navy during World War II. The GI Bill of Rights enabled her to enrol at Yale, from which she graduated PhD in 1950.

She joined the Sloan-Kettering Institute for Cancer Research, and was associate professor of microbiology there until 1966, when she was appointed professor at the Mount Sinai School of Medicine, in which position she remained until her death.

Her discovery that a fatal leucaemia could be induced in experimental animals by a virus, now known as the Friend Leukemia Virus (FLV), was initially received with hostility, but colleagues soon recognized that some viruses could produce cancers. Friend received numerous honours worldwide and was elected to the National Academy of Sciences in 1976.

Frings, Ketti (Catherine), *originally* Hartley

Born c.1910 Died 1981
American novelist, screenwriter and playwright
who won the 1958 Pulitzer Prize for drama

Ketti Frings was born in Columbus, Ohio. She wrote the novels *Hold Back the Dawn* (1942) and *God's Front Porch* (1945) but remains better known as a screenwriter and playwright. In the former capacity she wrote such screenplays as *Come Back Little Sheba* (1952), *Fox Fire* (1955) and *By Love Possessed* (1961).

Her main stage success was the Pulitzer Prize-winning *Look Homeward, Angel* (1957), an adapation of the 1929 novel of the same name by Thomas Wolfe (1900–38). It tells the story of Eugene Grant, who has suffered a dreadful childhood, tyrannized by his domineering mother and frequently drunken father, and an adolescence dominated by unrequited love.

Frink, Dame Elisabeth

Born 1930 Died 1993
English sculptor whose work shows a
preoccupation with figures and the human head

Elisabeth Frink was born in Thurlow, Suffolk. In 1947 she entered Guildford Art School, then trained at Chelsea School of Art (1948–51) under Bernard Meadows, himself influenced by Henry Moore. She later taught there for 10 years and at Central St Martins College of Art and was visiting lecturer at the Royal College. She was appointed a trustee of the British Museum in 1977.

Frink's original, vigorous works display a combination of sensuality, strength and vulnerability, which is seen particularly in her series of horse and rider sculptures. Little concerned with perfect anatomy, they suggest

Elizabeth Frink with her sculpture *Soldier's Head II* (1965), in 1985

movement within the environment and, in many instances, a humanitarian viewpoint.

Her work is in many collections including the Tate Gallery and the MOMA, New York. She undertook many major public commissions and worked in France from 1967 until 1973, when she returned to live and work in Dorset. She was appointed DBE in 1982.

Frith, Mary, *known as* Moll Cutpurse

Born 1584 Died 1659
English highwaywoman, pickpocket and receiver
of stolen goods who ruled the criminal underworld
of London with her audacity and intelligence

Mary Frith was born near the Barbican in London, the daughter of a shoemaker. She quickly frustrated her parent's desire for her to lead a law-abiding life of married domesticity by proving inept and uninterested in all the traditional feminine virtues. She gravitated towards the groups of pickpockets who frequented the crowded markets and fairs of the city, and adopted masculine clothing in order to consolidate her equality among them.

A long period of highway robbery followed this apprenticeship, during which she acquired her nickname from her habit of using a sharp knife to cut the belts on which travellers carried their purses. She became notorious and rich. A declared Royalist, she asserted that she would only rob the king's enemies. She lived well on the proceeds and by the end of her life she was running a brothel.

She left instructions that she was to be buried face down, so that she would remain as preposterous in death as in life.

Fritsch, Elizabeth

Born 1940
English potter, one of the most talented
contemporary potters of her generation

Elizabeth Fritsch was born in Shropshire. She studied harp and piano at the Royal Academy of Music prior to attending the Royal College of Art (1968–71).

Her work is sometimes inspired by music using coiling spires and geometric patterns in coloured slips with a matt texture akin to ivory frescoes.

Her vessels, like those of Hans Coper (1920–81) and **Lucie Rie**, who were both influential in her development, are regarded on equal terms with the important painters and sculptors of today.

Fry, Elizabeth, *née* Gurney

Born 1780   Died 1845
English philanthropist who devoted her life to
prison reform in Europe and improving the
treatment of the hospitalized and the insane

Elizabeth Gurney was born in Norwich, the daughter of a rich Quaker banker, John Gurney, and sister of the banker and reformer Joseph John Gurney. In 1800 she married Joseph Fry, a London Quaker merchant, and in 1810 became a preacher for the Society of Friends.

She visited Newgate Prison for women in 1813 and found 300 women, with their children, in appalling conditions, and thereafter devoted her life to prison and asylum reform at home and abroad.

She also founded hostels for the homeless, as well as charity organizations, despite her husband's bankruptcy in 1828.

Fry, Laura Ann

Born 1857   Died 1943
American wood carver, ceramicist, designer and
sculptor, and a leader in the American decorative
arts movement

Laura Ann Fry was a daughter of the noted wood carver and teacher William Henry Fry. She studied drawing, sculpture, wood carving and china painting at the Cincinnati School of Design (1872–6), continuing her studies in

Trenton, New Jersey, where she learnt the art of throwing, decorating and glazing pottery. She later studied in France and England.

She became the first employee of the Rookwood Pottery in 1881, having been a founder-member of the Cincinnati Art Pottery Club in 1879 with Clara Newton and **Louise McLaughlin**. In 1884 she introduced the use of the atomizer for applying slips to moist pots, and due to her work with underglazing techniques, 'Standard' Rookwood ware became the best-known feature of the firm's Arts and Crafts pottery.

She left Rookwood in 1887 and in 1891 became a Professor of Industrial Art for one year, returning in the 1890s. Between 1891 and 1894 she worked at the Lonhuda Pottery in Steubenville, Ohio.

Fry, (Sara) Margery

Born 1874   Died 1958
English penal reformer

Margery Fry was born in Highgate, London, and was educated at home and at Miss Lawrence's (now Roedean) School, Brighton. She studied mathematics at Somerville College, Oxford, and worked there as librarian until 1904 when she was appointed Warden of the University of Birmingham's women's residence.

During World War I she worked on the War Victims Relief Committee and in 1919 became secretary and subsequently Chairman of the Penal Reform League (later called the Howard League). In 1926 she was appointed Principal of Somerville and on her retirement in 1931 became a governor of the BBC and a member of the Brains Trust.

Her published works include *A Notebook for the Children's Court* (1942), *The Future Treatment of the Adult Offender* (1944) and *Arms of the Law* (1951).

Fuller, Loie (Marie Louise)

Born 1862   Died 1928
American dancer, choreographer and producer, a
pioneer in the field of performance art

Loie Fuller was born in Fullersburg, Illinois. She began her career in vaudeville and as a circus artist (1865–91). In 1891 her exotic solo skirt-dance, using multi-directional coloured lights on the yards of swirling silk she wore, created a sensation, especially in Europe. Her Paris début in 1892 was met with overwhelming acclaim.

In 1900 she appeared at the Paris World Fair. Group pieces also figured among her (more than 100) dances. She founded a school in 1908, and was a model for Toulouse-Lautrec, Auguste Rodin and many other prominent artists.

Fuller, (Sarah) Margaret, Marchioness Ossoli

Born 1810 Died 1850
American feminist and critic who became a
leading transcendentalist and fought to enrich
women's lives through education

Margaret Fuller was born in Cambridgeport, Massachusetts. Rigorously educated by her father before attending the local school at the age of 14, she went on to teach in Boston (1836–7) and Providence (1837–9). There, joining the intellectual élite, she held her celebrated 'conversations', cultural discussions with a circle of Boston ladies, which attracted several prominent reformers and transcendentalists.

From 1840 to 1842 she was editor of *The Dial*, the transcendentalist journal, and in 1844 went to New York where she became literary critic for the *New York Tribune*. When she went to Europe she became the USA's first foreign correspondent. Moving to Italy in 1847, she married Marquis Giovanni Ossoli and with him became involved in the Revolution of 1848.

She was drowned in a shipwreck on her way back to New York, along with her husband and young son. Her publications include *Summer on the Lakes* (1844) and *Woman in the 19th Century* (1845), a feminist statement demanding political equality and overall personal fulfilment for women.

Furtseva, Yekaterina Alexeevna

Born 1910 Died 1974
Soviet politician, the first woman member of the
Soviet Communist Party's Politburo

Yekaterina Furtseva had a technical education, then became a party worker and rose to be district secretary in Moscow in 1942 and a member of the Central Committee in 1956.

A supporter of Nikita Khrushchev, she was brought into the Politburo in 1957 in the aftermath of the Anti-Party Plot (the name given by Khrushchev to the attempt made by senior opponents to oust him from his position as First Secretary of the Communist Party). She was not considered a major political figure however, and was pushed out in 1961.

Nevertheless from 1960 until her death she was Minister of Culture and apparently had no difficulty in insisting on ever greater conformity.

Fyge, Sarah *see* Egerton, Sarah

g

Gabain, Ethel Leontine

Born 1883 Died 1950
English artist and printmaker whose subjects
include portraits and figure studies

Ethel Gabain was born in Le Havre, France, and studied at the Slade School of Art, the Central School of Arts and Crafts, and in Paris. She married the artist John Copley in 1913.

She became known for her many female portraits, such as **Flora Robson** in the role of Lady Audley, which was purchased by Manchester City Art Gallery. She won the De Laszlo Silver Medal in 1933 for that portrait, and in 1940 was appointed an official war artist, initially painting the departing evacuees before turning to the depiction of women in traditionally male occupations.

Gabain was a remarkable draughtsperson who was elected to the membership of both the Royal Society of British Artists and the Royal Institute of Oil Painters.

Gage, Matilda Joslyn, *née* Joslyn

Born 1826 Died 1898
American feminist and early women's rights
activist, a major feminist theoretician and
historian of her day

Matilda Joslyn Gage was born in Cicero, New York. As a young woman, she became a dedicated activist for women's rights, developing a radical feminist perspective and incisive analysis of the nature of patriarchal society, which some thought could alienate the influential men whose support was essential. Nevertheless she worked with the more conservative reformers **Susan B Anthony** and **Elizabeth Cady Stanton** to launch the first wave of the American suffrage movement and with them later compiled the four-volume *History of Woman Suffrage* (1881–1906).

She joined the National Woman Suffrage Association (NWSA) in 1869 and within six years was president of both the national and New York State organizations. She was also editor of the official newspaper of the NWSA, the *National Citizen and Ballot Box* (1878–81), but withdrew from radical suffrage activities in protest at the union between NWSA and the conservative Women's Christian Temperance Union.

Gage believed that a pre-history matriarchy was overthrown by patriarchy and that Church and State colluded to oppress women, and so in 1890 she founded the Women's National Liberal Union, whose central aim was to bring about the separation of Church and State. She expressed her ideas in her *Woman, Church and State: the Original Exposé of Male Collaboration Against the Female Sex* (1893).

Galas, Diamanda, *professional name of* Dimitria Angeliki Elena Galas

Born 1955
American vocalist and composer who was inspired
by AIDS to write Plague Mass

Diamanda Galas was born in San Diego, California. A gifted pianist as a child, she performed the Beethoven Piano Concerto No. 1 with the San Diego Symphony Orchestra while still in her early teens. She then studied biological sciences and music at the University of California, San Diego (1974–9), taking private music lessons. Her work has ranged from improvised performance with Derek Bailey's Company to première interpretations of specially written works by Globokar and Xenakis. Her own compositional output culminates in the huge *Plague Mass* (1990–), a music-theatre work inspired by the AIDS epidemic.

Though she denies the influence of **Cathy Berberian**, their vocal and dramatic style is very similar. Galas's performances are very intense and radical, but she has nevertheless explored blues and gospel in *The Singer* (1990).

Gale, Zona

Born 1874 Died 1938
American novelist, story writer and dramatist
whose depiction of life in the Midwest in Miss
Lulu Bett *made her famous*

Zona Gale was born in Portage, Wisconsin, and educated at the university there. She worked as a journalist before becoming a full-time writer in 1903. Her earliest, regional stories and her first novel, *Romance Island* (1906), were marred by excessive sentimentality, but at the same time so acutely observed that it was evident that she was already a writer of unusual and delicate powers.

She was scorned and disliked for her increasing pacifism and feminism, but, with the novel *Birth* (1918), in which she anticipated the French novelist Georges Duhamel's *Salavin* (1920–32), the iron finally entered her soul; she dramatized this in 1924 as *Mr Pitt*. Meanwhile, with *Miss Lulu Bett* (1920) appearing in the same year as (and artistically superior to) Sinclair Lewis's *Main Street*, she became famous. Her dramatization of it won her a Pulitzer Prize (1921).

Always mystical, she turned to the Armenian mystic and novelist George Gurdjieff and to the English editor and social thinker Alfred Orage, who was teaching the latter's ideas in New York; this strengthened her later work, such as the autobiographical *Portage, Wisconsin* (1928), the story collection *Yellow Gentians and Blue* (1927) and the novel *Papa le Fleur* (1933), now neglected and too hastily written-off, giving it a new psychological accuracy and confidence. She became an avid supporter of Robert La Follette's Progressive Party. The title of her biography by fellow-Wisconsin author August Derleth is singularly appropriate: *Still, Small Voice* (1940).

Galindo, Beatriz, *also known as* La Latina

Born 1465 or 1475 Died 1535
Spanish humanist and scholar, professor at the
University of Salamanca

Beatriz Galindo was probably born in Salamanca, a member of the lower nobility. Some authorities believe she was educated in Italy. She was a famous classical scholar who became tutor to Queen **Isabella I** of Spain and her daughters, and wife of Francisco Ramirez, secretary to Isabella's husband Ferdinand V.

She taught at the University of Salamanca, a rare position for a woman to hold at that time. She also founded schools and hospitals throughout Spain, most significantly the richly-endowed hospital in Madrid where she was buried. A commentary on Aristotle and some Latin poems have been attributed to her.

Gallant, Mavis, *née* de Trafford Young

Born 1922
Canadian novelist and writer of well-crafted short
stories often focusing on the alienation felt by the
foreigner away from home

Mavis de Trafford Young was born in Montreal. Her father was English, her mother German–Russian–Breton, and she spent her childhood going from school to school, 17 in all, which made education 'virtually impossible'. She married John Gallant in 1943, but divorced after three years of marriage. She had various jobs in Montreal before joining the *Montreal Standard* (1944), which she left in 1950 to earn her living entirely by writing, contributing mainly to the *New Yorker*. She travelled in Europe for a time and has lived in Paris since 1960.

Her skilfully observed and crafted short stories, for which she is best known, often evoke personal disquiet attributed to life as a foreigner. They have mostly appeared in the *New Yorker* and have subsequently been collected in such volumes as *The Other Paris: Stories* (1956), *Home Truths: Selected Canadian Stories* (1981) and *In Transit* (1988).

Her novels have been less successful; they include *Green Water, Green Sky* (1959) and *A Fairly Good Time* (1970). Her non-fiction work includes a diary of the 1968 street troubles in Paris.

Galley, Carol

Born 1949/50
British fund manager, one of the few
businesswomen to have reached the top
in UK finance

Carol Galley began her career as a librarian at SG Warburg, the former parent company of Mercury Asset Management (MAM), which she joined in 1970. As one of the world's largest pension fund managers, MAM controls investments worth about £70 billion. In her position as joint Vice-Chairman of MAM, Galley plays a key role in making investment decisions that could, for example, bring about the rise or fall of several multi-national companies. As an illustration of her power, it was her decision that clinched the deal for Granada's takeover bid of Forte in 1996. Reputedly the highest-earning woman in Britain with a salary of around £500,000, she has to deal with sexist hate campaigns that blow up in the male-dominated world of finance, but is widely respected for her pragmatic, head-on approach to her job. She is married to a German banker and has no children.

Galli-Curci, Amelita

Born 1882 Died 1963
Italian soprano who was a self-taught but
outstanding performer of her time

Amelita Galli-Curci was born in Milan. Although a prize-winning piano student at Milan Conservatory, as a singer she was self-taught, first appearing in opera as Gilda in Verdi's *Rigoletto* in 1909. Her brilliance of style was attractive enough to compensate for deficiencies of technique, and in 1916 she joined the Chicago Opera Company.

From 1919 onwards, she worked principally at the Metropolitan Opera, New York, for which her title role in Meyerbeer's *Dinorah* was highly acclaimed. She was first heard in Britain in 1924. After building up her repertory to nearly 30 roles, specializing in high soprano singing, she was forced to retire early, following a throat injury.

Gandhi, Indira

Born 1917 Died 1984
Indian politician whose fourth term as Prime
Minister ended with her assassination

Indira Gandhi was born in Allahabad, a daughter of Jawaharlal Nehru (Prime Minister 1947–64). Her education included a year at Somerville College, Oxford. She was deeply involved in the independence issue and spent a year in prison. She married Feroze Gandhi (d.1960) in 1942 and had two sons, Rajiv (1944–91), who was assassinated, and Sanjay (1946–80), who died in an aircrash.

She became a member of the central committee of Indian Congress (1950), President of Party (1959–60) and Minister of Information (1964), and took over as Prime Minister in 1966 after the death of Lal Bahadur Shastri (1904–66). In June 1975, after her conviction for election malpractices, she declared a 'state of emergency' in India. Civil liberties were curtailed and strict censorship imposed. These restrictions were lifted in 1977 during the campaign for a general election, in which the Congress Party was defeated and Mrs Gandhi lost her seat. Acquitted after her arrest on charges of corruption, in 1978 she resigned

Indira Gandhi

from the Congress Parliamentary party and became leader of the new Indian National Congress (I).

She returned to power as Prime Minister following the 1980 general election, but was assassinated in October 1984 by members of her Sikh bodyguard, resentful of her employment of troops to storm the Golden Temple at Amritsar and dislodge malcontents. This murder provoked a Hindu backlash in Delhi, involving the massacre of 3,000 Sikhs.

Garbo, Greta, *professional name of*
Greta Lovisa Gustafsson

Born 1905 Died 1990
Swedish-born American film actress who was a
glamorous star of 1930s films

Greta Garbo was born in Stockholm. She was a shop-girl who won a bathing beauty competition at 16, then won a scholarship to the Royal Theatre Dramatic School in Stockholm. She was given a starring role in *Gösta Berling's Saga* (1924) by the Swedish director Mauritz Stiller; he also gave his star the name Garbo, chosen before he met her, trained her in acting technique, and insisted that she be given a contract at MGM in Hollywood when he moved there in 1925.

She was an actress of remarkable talent and legendary beauty and her greatest successes, following *Anna Christie* (1930), her first talking picture, were *Queen Christina* (1933), *Anna Karenina* (1935), *Camille* (1936) and *Ninotchka* (1939). She retired from films in 1941, after the failure of *Two-Faced Woman*.

She became an American citizen in 1951 but remained a total recluse for the rest of her life.

García, Pauline Viardot *see* Viardot-García, (Michelle Ferdinande) Pauline

Garden, Mary, *originally* Mary Davidson

Born 1874 Died 1967
Scottish soprano acclaimed for her Mélisande and
her Salome among many other roles, whose career
flourished in America

Mary Garden was born in Aberdeen and taken to America as a child. She studied singing in Chicago and then in Paris, and her career began sensationally when she took over in mid-performance the title role in Charpentier's new *Louise* at the Opéra-Comique in 1900, when the singer was taken ill.

In 1902 she created the role of Mélisande in Debussy's *Pelléas et Mélisande* at the composer's request, and in 1903 she recorded songs with Debussy. Massenet and Erlanger also wrote leading roles for her. She sang at Covent Garden (1902–3), and was a legendary Manon, Thaïs, Violetta, Salomé, Carmen and Juliet (Gounod).

Her American début was as Thaïs in 1907, and in 1910 she began a 20-year association with Chicago Grand Opera, which she also briefly directed (1921–2). She returned to Scotland in 1939.

Gardner, Ava, *originally* Lucy Johnson

Born 1922 Died 1990
American film actress of the 1940s and 1950s who
was voted the world's most beautiful woman

Ava Gardner was born in North Carolina. A green-eyed brunette, she was signed by MGM as a teenager, and emerged from the ranks of decorative starlets with her portrayal of a ravishing femme fatale in *The Killers* (1946).

She remained a leading lady for two decades, portraying an earthy combination of sensuality and cynicism in films like *Mogambo* (1953), for which she was nominated for an Academy Award, *The Barefoot Contessa* (1954) and *Night of the Iguana* (1964). She continued to work as a character actress in films and on television, and was married to the actor Mickey Rooney, the bandleader Artie Shaw and the singer Frank Sinatra.

Gardner, Dame Frances Violet

Born 1913 Died 1989
English physician created DBE in 1975 for
services to medicine and medical education

Frances Gardner was educated in Oxford and then in London, where she qualified in medicine from the Royal Free Hospital School of Medicine in 1940. After medical positions there and in Oxford, and as a research Fellow at Harvard University, she became Consultant Physician at the Royal Free in 1946, remaining there until 1978. She married the surgeon George Qvist in 1958.

She published papers on a wide variety of medical subjects, especially cardiovascular medicine, and served first as Dean of the Royal Free Hospital School of Medicine (1962–75), and then as its president from 1979 until her death. Gardner served on numerous medical committees, including the General Medical Council (1971).

Gardner, Isabella

Born 1915 Died 1981
American poet honoured for her work the year she
*died, whose admirers included **Sylvia Plath***

Isabella Gardner was born in Newton, Massachusetts. She worked in the theatre and published nothing until after her third marriage in 1947. Her husband, whom she divorced 10 years later, encouraged her writing and her first collection, *Birthdays from the Ocean*, appeared in 1955.

Other volumes include *The Looking Glass* (1961), *West of Childhood: Poems 1950–65* (1965) and *That Was Then: New and Selected Poems* (1980). The theme of this last book is death, often in tragic circumstances. Yet although her recurring subjects include the failure of love, an underlying resilience and optimism for life pervade the elegiac fabric of her writing.

She received the first Walt Whitman Citation of Merit in 1981.

Gardner, Kay

Born 1941
American conductor, composer and lecturer whose
interests include music as a means of healing

Kay Gardner was the music director and principal conductor of the New England Women's Symphony in Boston. Her recorded works reflect an interest in the merging of spirituality, healing and music. Among her compositions are *The Cauldron of Cerridwyen* (1978), an opera entitled *Ladies Voices*, and the albums *Mooncircles* and *Rainbow Path*.

In 1990 she published a book (with an album of music) discussing her interests in sound and healing, entitled *Sounding the Inner Landscape: Music as Medicine*.

Garland, Judy, *originally* Frances Gumm

Born 1922 Died 1969
American entertainer who appeared in several of the finest film musicals ever made

Judy Garland was born in Grand Rapids, Minnesota, into a showbusiness family. She partnered two sisters in a vaudeville act that led to a film contract. She was bright and vivacious, with a vibrant singing voice, and appeared in such brilliant film musicals as *The Wizard of Oz* (1939), *Meet Me in St Louis* (1944) and *Easter Parade* (1948).

Personal appearances confirmed the emotional power of her voice, and in *A Star is Born* (1954) she gave an outstanding dramatic performance. Despite emotional and medical difficulties and a reputation for unreliability, she achieved the status of a legendary performer and actress.

She was married five times, and her daughter **Liza Minnelli** from her marriage to film director Vincente Minelli has followed in her showbusiness footsteps, as has her other daughter Lorna Luft. Her premature death was caused by a drug/alcohol overdose.

Garner, Helen

Born 1942
Australian writer whose appeal for teenagers lies in her straightforward approach

Helen Garner was born in Geelong, Victoria. She taught in Melbourne schools until being dismissed for answering frankly her pupils' questions on sex. Her adult fiction appeals strongly to adolescents because it examines contemporary problems in a clear-sighted and non-judgemental manner.

Monkey Grip (1977) deals sympathetically with the subculture of drug addiction; it won the National Book Council award in the same year and was filmed in 1981, springing Garner to near-cult status. Two novellas, *Honour* and *Other People's Children* (both 1980), handle lightly the interplay of adult characters with the legacy of the 'swinging sixties' in Australia. *The Children's Bach* (1984) is a highly regarded treatment of stress in middle-class suburban family life. *Postcards from Surfers* (1985) is a collection of short stories on disparate themes, but with a pervasive Australian atmosphere. *Cosmo Cosmolino* (1993), two short stories and a novella, is a fiction depicting the supernatural within the lives of characters who could easily be the survivors of *Monkey Grip*.

Garner has also written screenplays, such as *The Last Days of Chez Nous* (1993) for **Gillian Armstrong**.

Garnett, Constance Clara, *née* Black

Born 1861 Died 1946
English translator of Russian classic novels

Constance Black, sister of **Clementina Black**, was born in Brighton and educated at home by her brothers and at boarding school in Brighton. She was awarded a scholarship to Newnham College, Cambridge, graduating with a first in classics in 1883.

After teaching privately she married Edward Garnett in 1889 and became librarian at the People's Palace in London. At about this time she joined the Fabian Society and began to learn Russian. In subsequent years she translated a large number of Russian novels into English, making the works of great Russian novelists, such as Chekhov, Tolstoy, Dostoyevsky, Gogol and others, accessible to the Western world. She visited Russia in 1892 and 1904.

Garnett, Eve

Floreat 1930s to 1950s
English children's author and illustrator who pioneered the sympathetic representation of working-class life

Eve Garnett was born in Worcestershire. She studied at the Royal Academy of Art and has combined life as an author with her work as a professional artist, which has included a commission for murals at Children's House, Bow, and an exhibition at the Tate in 1939.

Her name as an author rests upon *The Family from One End Street* (1937, Carnegie Medal), one of the first attempts to present working-class family life sympathetically in children's fiction. This book and its sequel, *Further Adventures of the Family from One End Street* (1956), remain popular.

Garrod, Dorothy Annie Elizabeth

Born 1892 Died 1968
English archaeologist who specialized in the Palaeolithic or Old Stone Age

Dorothy Garrod was the daughter of the physician Sir Archibald Garrod. After studying at Newnham College, Cambridge, she directed expeditions to carry out Paleolithic research in Gibraltar (1925–6) and Kurdistan (1928).

In Palestine (1929–34) a joint British and American team led by Garrod excavated at Mt Carmel and uncovered various remains which were important in the study of human evolution, including a female skeleton estimated to be about 41,000 years old, suggesting there was human life in Palestine in the Paleolithic and Mesolithic (also called Old and Middle Stone Age) eras. She also made studies of Stone Age culture in Bulgaria in 1938 and took part in the excavations in the Lebanon (1958–64).

The first woman to hold a professorial chair at Cambridge, as Professor of Archaeology (1939–52), she published *The Stone Age of Mount Carmel* (2 vols) in 1937–9.

Garson, Greer

Born 1908   Died 1996
Anglo-Irish actress whose red-haired beauty and refined manner made her one of the most popular leading ladies of the 1940s

Greer Garson was born in County Down and educated at the University of London. She worked in an advertising agency and participated in amateur dramatics before making her professional stage début in 1932 with the Birmingham Repertory Company. Two years later, she moved to London's West End and was seen by Hollywood mogul Louis B Mayer (1885–1957) in *Old Music* (1938). He signed her to a contract at MGM, and she made her film début as Mrs Chipping in *Goodbye Mr Chips* (1939).

She won the Best Actress Oscar for her role as the indomitable English matriarch in *Mrs Miniver* (1942) and generally portrayed wholesome, independent women with spirit and wit in such romantic dramas as *Random Harvest* (1942), *Mrs Parkinton* (1944) and *That Forsyte Woman* (1949). She played **Eleanor Roosevelt** in *Sunrise at Campobello* (1960) and made her last film appearance in *The Happiest Millionaire* (1967).

Her later stage work included *Auntie Mame* (1958) on Broadway, and her occasional television appearances include the role of Aunt March in *Little Women* (1978).

Gaskell, Elizabeth Cleghorn, *née* Stevenson

Born 1810   Died 1865
English novelist whose masterful works depict the social problems of the time from a humanitarian viewpoint

Elizabeth Stevenson was born in Cheyne Row, Chelsea, London. Her father was in succession teacher, preacher, farmer, boarding-house keeper, writer and keeper of the records to the Treasury. She was brought up by an aunt in Knutsford — the Cranford of her stories — and grew up well-adjusted and beautiful.

In 1832 she married William Gaskell (1805–

Mrs Gaskell

84), a Unitarian minister in Manchester, where she studied working men and women. She anonymously published *Mary Barton* in 1848, followed by *The Moorland Cottage* (1850), *Cranford* (1853), *Ruth* (1853), *North and South* (1855), *Round the Sofa* (1859), *Right at Last* (1860), *Sylvia's Lovers* (1863), *Cousin Phillis* (1865) and *Wives and Daughters* (1865). Most of her work was published in serial form in Charles Dickens's periodicals *Household Words* and *All the Year Round*. As well as her novels she wrote the first *Life of Charlotte Brontë* (1857). She is usually referred to as Mrs Gaskell.

Gatichon, Françoise, *née* Parturier

Born 1919
French feminist author who campaigned for female equality through writing fiction and newspaper journalism

Françoise Parturier was born into a middle-class family in Paris, where she studied before marrying at the age of 28. Abandoning her literary studies, she launched herself on a career of writing and journalism, contributing regularly to *Figaro* newspaper under the pseudonym 'Nicole'.

In 1959 she began writing under her own name, quickly establishing a reputation as one of France's leading feminists as well as one of the most popular novelists.

Gaudron, Mary Genevieve

Born 1943
Australian lawyer who is the first woman to be
appointed judge in Australia's High Court

Mary Gaudron was born in Moree, New South Wales, and trained at Sydney University, where she won the law medal. She was the youngest person ever to be appointed a federal judge when she became Deputy President of the Arbitration Commission (1975–80), as well as the youngest-ever Solicitor General for New South Wales (1981–7).

In 1987 she became a judge in the High Court of Australia in Canberra, the first woman to reach that position, and was appointed Justice in 1991.

Gaunt, Mary

Born 1861   Died 1942
Australian traveller and writer whose Kirkham's
Find *was one of the earliest novels with a strongly*
feminist theme

Mary Gaunt was born in Chiltern, Victoria, and educated as one of the first two women students at the University of Melbourne. She later lived in England and Italy. She wrote a considerable number of novels, some set in Australia such as her first, *Dave's Sweetheart* (1894).

Kirkham's Find (1897) was an early feminist novel; his find is 'pure gold' — the very independent Phoebe. *The Uncounted Cost* (1910) was banned by London circulating libraries because the fallen heroine did *not* pay the price. Other novels, *As the Whirlwind Passeth* (1923) and *Joan of the Pilchard* (1930), have historical backgrounds.

Her books achieved wide sales and she indulged her love of sailing and travel; her travel books include *Alone in West Africa* (1912) and *A Woman in China* (1914).

Gaynor, Janet, *originally* Laura Gainor

Born 1906   Died 1984
American actress, a leading lady in the late 1920s
who won the first Best Actress Oscar

Janet Gaynor was born in Philadelphia. After attending high school in San Fransisco, she moved to Los Angeles, hoping to break into the film industry, and was a bookkeeper and usherette before securing work as an extra. Small roles in comedies followed, and she made her first notable appearance in *The Johnstown Flood* (1926). Within a couple of years, she had won the first-ever Best Actress Oscar for a trio of performances in *Sunrise* (1927), *Seventh Heaven* (1927) and *Street Angel* (1928).

A waif-like creature with large eyes, she brought a wholesome freshness to the portrayal of vulnerable women, and became a major star in the 1930s. Her many successes include *State Fair* (1933) and *A Star Is Born* (1937). She retired in 1938, making a one-off return to the screen in *Bernadine* (1957). She occasionally performed on television and the stage, and her later theatre work includes *Harold and Maude* (1980) on Broadway.

Geddes, Jenny

Born c.1600   Died c.1660
Scottish vegetable-seller and legendary
stool-thrower

Jenny Geddes is traditionally reputed to have started the riots in St Giles' Cathedral, Edinburgh, when Archbishop Laud's English prayer book was introduced on Sunday, 23 July 1637. According to popular legend she threw her folding stool at Bishop Lindsay, shouting: 'Deil colic the wame of thee (ie may the Devil give you belly-ache); out, false thief! Dost thou say mass at my lug?'.

The ensuing uproar against the attempted anglicization of the Church in Scotland led to the signing of the National Covenant the following year, which abolished the episcopal system.

There is no historical evidence of her exploit. Sydserf in 1661 mentions 'the immortal Jenet Geddes' as having burned 'her leather chair of state' in a Restoration bonfire, and the story appears in full detail in Phillips's continuation of Baker's *Chronicle* (1660).

Gellhorn, Martha Ellis

Born 1908
American journalist, travel and fiction writer who
was inspired by human conflict

Martha Gellhorn was born in St Louis, Missouri, and educated at Bryn Mawr College. She became a foreign correspondent for *Collier's Weekly*, covering the Spanish Civil War, the invasion of Finland, and the European theatre in World War II. She almost certainly saw more violent action than her relentlessly macho first husband, Ernest Hemingway, her marriage to him neatly coinciding (1940–5) with the wider hostilities and proving appropriately stormy.

Her interest in human conflict remained undimmed and she continued to report on wars in Java (1946), Vietnam (1966), the Middle East (1967) and Central America (1983–5). Her earlier reportage was collected in *The Face of War* (1959). Her first novel, *What Mad Pursuit*, had appeared exactly 25 years earlier, followed by others — *A Stricken Field* (1940), *Liano* (1948) and *The Wine of Astonishment* (1948) — which suggested that her instincts were journalistic rather than strictly literary. For that reason, the short stories in *The Trouble I've Seen* (1936), *The Honeyed Peace* (1953), *Two by Two* (1958) and *The Weather in Africa* (1978) are much stronger, marked by acute observation, sympathy for the weak or oppressed and moral straightforwardness.

Gems, Pam (Iris Pamela)

Born 1925
English dramatist and novelist whose courageous feminist drama attracted attention in the 1970s

Pam Gems was born in Bransgore in the New Forest, Hampshire, and educated at Manchester University. Her two short monologues about women living alone, *My Warren* and *After Birthday,* were staged in 1973, but it was her full-length play *Dusa, Fish, Stas and Vi,* a courageous piece of feminist drama dealing with the lives of four women sharing a London flat, that attracted widespread attention when it was staged in London in 1975.

Subsequent plays that have looked at the lives of women in history include *Queen Christina* (1977), an account of the 17th-century intellectual and cross-dressing ruler of Sweden, and *Piaf* (1978), an unsentimental drama based on the life of the French singer **Edith Piaf**, which includes many of Piaf's well-known songs. *Camille* (1984) derives from Dumas's *La dame aux camélias* (1852), but is more critical of bourgeois society than the original. In *The Danton Affair* (1986), she examines the political conflict between Danton and Robespierre.

Gems's more recent work includes a musical stage adaptation of the 1930 film *Blue Angel* (1991), a new play called *Deborah's Daughter* (1994), and several translations, including Henrik Ibsen's *A Doll's House* (1980) and notable versions of Anton Chekhov's *Uncle Vanya* (1979) and *The Seagull* (1994). She has also written two novels: *Mrs Frampton* (1989), the story of a woman who retires to Spain with her husband, and its sequel, *Bon Voyage, Mrs Frampton* (1990).

Geneviève, St

Born c.422 Died c.500
French nun who won the Parisians' respect with her prophecies and became their patron saint

Geneviève was born in Nanterre, near Paris. At the age of seven she met St Germanus of Auxerre and told him of her desire to lead a religious life. With his support, she took the veil at 15 and acquired an extraordinary reputation for sanctity.

Her prophecies concerning danger to Paris contributed to people's misunderstanding and criticism of her until she assured them that during the invasion of Attila and his Huns in 451 Paris would not be harmed, and it would not be necessary to flee the city. Her prediction proved correct, for Attila was defeated at Orléans, and her critics' distrust turned to respect.

She also led an expedition for the relief of the starving city during Childeric's Frankish siege, an act that so impressed Childeric (and Clovis after him) that they released prisoners at her request. In 460 she built a church over the tomb of St Denis, and she persuaded Clovis to build a church to St Peter and St Paul, which was renamed St Geneviève when she was buried there. Her feast day is 3 January.

Genlis, Stéphanie Felicité Ducrest de St Aubin, Comtesse de

Born 1746 Died 1830
French writer, educationalist and mistress of the Duke of Orléans, and one of 19th-century France's most fascinating characters

Stéphanie Ducrest de St Aubin was born in Champcéri, near Autun. At the age of 16 she married the Comte de Genlis, and in 1770 was made lady-in-waiting to the Duchess of Chartres, to whose husband, later Philippe Égalité and Duke of Orléans (1785), she became mistress.

She wrote four volumes of short plays entitled *Théâtre d'education* (1779) for her charges, the royal children, among them the future King Louis-Philippe, and nearly 100 volumes of historical romances and 'improving' works. Both her husband and her lover perished at the guillotine in the 1790s, while she travelled throughout Europe. Her *Précis de la conduite de Mme de Genlis depuis la Révolution* (1796, 'Summary of the Conduct of Madame de Genlis Since the Revolution') was written to appease the Republican regime, who were highly suspicious of her, and to make it possible for her to return to France in safety.

Napoleon admired her work so much, particularly the novella *Mademoiselle de Clermont* (1802) that he gave her a pension. She went on to write in praise of the *ancien regime*, reviving the historical novel genre, and completed 10 volumes of *Mémoires* (1825), which contain interesting social comments on the period.

Gentileschi, Artemisia

Born c.1597   Died c.1652
Italian painter who derived special inspiration
from the idea of a woman decapitating a man

Artemisia Gentileschi was born in Rome, the vivacious daughter of the painter Orazio Gentileschi and a major disciple of Caravaggio (1571–1610). Following a period in Florence she settled in Naples (c.1630) and developed a powerful type of painting in the Caravaggesque style. She visited her father in England (1638–9) and left a self-portrait at Hampton Court.

One of her favourite themes, painted in clear, bright colours, is that of the decapitation of a man by a woman (as in the legend of Judith and Holophernes), which has since been attributed on feminist psychological grounds to her alleged rape 'many times' by the landscape painter Agostino Tassi.

Her chief work is the bloodthirsty *Judith and Holophernes* exhibited in the Uffizi, Florence.

Geoffrin, Marie Thérèse de, *née* Rodet

Born 1699   Died 1777
French patron of literature and salon hostess

Marie-Thérèse Rodet was born in Paris and orphaned at a young age. Educated by her grandmother, she was married at the age of 15 to the much older and wealthier François Geoffrin, who died in 1749, leaving her an immense fortune. She had a genuine love of learning and art, and from about 1750 her Parisian salon in the Hôtel de Rambouillet, which she had taken over on the death of Madame de **Tencin**, became a respectable international rendezvous of the important artists and men of letters of the time.

These included the *Encyclopédistes* of Paris, whose *Encyclopédie* (1751–65) she supported financially. She ruled her salon with generosity and discretion, but forbade the discussion of either religion or politics. She also distributed her wealth in charitable and philanthropic ways.

George, Mademoiselle, *stage-name* of Marguerite Joséphine Weimar

Born 1787   Died 1867
French actress who earned fame for her early
tragic roles

Mademoiselle George was born in Bayeux, the daughter of travelling players. She made her début at the Comédie Française in 1802 and became known for her playing in both classical tragedy and, from the late 1820s, the early romantic dramas. She also achieved great popularity in Russia (1808–13).

Among her great roles were Marguerite de Bourgogne in *La Tour de Nesle* (1832) and **Lucrezia Borgia** and **Marie Tudor** (1833) in the plays of Victor Hugo (1802–85). However by the mid-1840s her voice was losing its former splendour, she had become terribly overweight, and her majestic style of acting was going out of fashion. She gave two farewell performances — in 1849 and 1853.

In her *Mémoirs* she left an account of her celebrated liaison with Napoleon.

Gerard, Marguerite

Born 1761   Died 1837
French artist, one of the first French women
painters to achieve professional success

Marguerite Gerard was born in Grasse and moved to Paris to live with the Fragonard family in the 1780s. She was the sister-in-law of the celebrated Rococo painter Jean-Honoré Fragonard (1732–1806) and became his informal apprentice.

She achieved success painting genre scenes of Enlightenment women in domestic surroundings, developing a particular glaze medium, painstakingly applying layers of translucent colour to create a luminosity in her painting of gowns and fabrics.

When the Salon opened to women artists in the 1790s, Gerard exhibited regularly until 1824, when she retired from painting professionally. Some of her works were bought by Napoleon and Louis XVIII.

Gérin-Lajoie, Marie, *née* Lacoste

Born 1867   Died 1945
French–Canadian writer and feminist

Marie Gérin-Lajoie was born in Montreal, into an intellectual family. A lecturer at Montreal University, she campaigned for women's suffrage and women's rights, writing two important works: *Traité de droit usuel* (1902) and *La femme et le code civil* (1929).

She gave up her position as head of the French-speaking (francophone) wing of Quebec's Provincial Franchise Committee because the Bishop of Montreal expressed disapproval of women's suffrage. However, she continued to work for women's rights.

She founded and directed the French–

Canadian women's charitable organization, the *Fédération nationale St-Jean-Baptiste* (1907).

Germain, Sophie

Born 1776   Died 1831
French mathematician who began her career
disguised as a man and made major contributions
in the study of numbers, acoustics and elasticity

Sophie Germain was born in Paris. Self-educated until the age of 18, she studied lecture notes procured from the newly established École Polytechnique, to which women were not admitted. In the guise of a male student named Le Blanc, she submitted a paper on analysis which so impressed the eminent mathematician Joseph-Louis Lagrange (1736–1813) that he became her personal tutor.

During a career in which she corresponded with the French mathematician Adrien-Marie Legendre (1752–1833) and the German Carl Friedrich Gauss (1777–1855), she gave a more generalized proof of the 'last theorem' (the most famous unsolved problem in mathematics) of Pierre de Fermat (1601–65) than had previously been available, and developed a mathematical explanation of the 'Chladni figures' (the patterns that Ernst Chladni (1756–1827) had found to appear in sand sprinkled on vibrating plate) in response to a challenge from the French Academy of Sciences.

She went on to derive a general mathematical description of the vibrations of curved as well as plane elastic surfaces. Her *Recherches sur la théorie des surfaces élastiques* was published in 1821; she also wrote philosophical works such as *Pensées diverses*, published posthumously.

Gertrude of Helfta, St, *also known as* Gertrude the Great

Born 1256   Died c.1302
German Benedictine nun and medieval mystic,
regarded as the patron saint of the West Indies

Gertrude lived from the age of five and studied in the convent of Helfta near Eisleben in Saxony, cared for by Benedictine nuns. She experienced a deep conversion at the age of 25 and was blessed with visions of Christ and other supernatural revelations.

She recorded her mystical experiences and her contemplations in Latin in several books which later had a wide influence. She focused particularly on the humanity of Christ, prefiguring the development of the devotion to the Sacred Heart.

Gertrude was never formally canonized but she has a feast day, 16 November.

Gertrude of Nivelles, St

Born 626   Died 659
Frankish nun regarded as the patron saint of
travellers in life and beyond

Gertrude was the daughter of Pepin the Elder and his wife Itta. After Pepin's death, Itta established a double monastery at Nivelles, Brabant, where Gertrude later became abbess, after refusing to marry the Merovingian king Dagobert I. As abbess she was renowned for her hospitality, particulary to pilgrims and monks, hence her patronage of travellers.

She resigned in 656 in order to devote herself to prayer without the distraction of administration, but the years of austerity had taken their toll and she suffered poor health thereafter.

She is also the patron saint of the recently dead (travelling from earth to heaven) and of gardeners, perhaps because her feast day (17 March) heralds the beginning of spring.

Ghica, Helena, *also spelt* Gjika, *pseud* Dora d'Istria

Born 1829   Died 1888
Romanian author and traveller who supported the
education of women and of the poor

Helena Ghica was born in Bucharest to aristocratic parents of Albanian origin; her father was Prince Michael Ghica. She married Prince Koltzoff-Massalsky of St Petersburg, in 1849, but separated in 1855. After travelling in Switzerland and Greece, she lived mainly in Florence.

She was concerned for the education of poor people as well as the rich, equal rights for women, and the better treatment of minority groups in the Austro-Hungarian empire. Her works include *La Vie monastique dans l'Église orientale* (1855), *La Suisse allemande* (1856), *Les Femmes en orient* (1860) and a family history.

Gibbons, Stella Dorothea

Born 1902   Died 1989
English novelist, poet and journalist who wrote
the satirical classic Cold Comfort Farm

Stella Gibbons was born in London. She worked as a journalist and later began a series of successful novels. Her *Cold Comfort Farm* (1932), a light-hearted satire on the melodramatic rural novels such as those written by **Mary Webb**, won the Femina Vie Heureuse prize in 1933 and established itself as a classic of parody. Her other novels included such comedies of manners as *A Pink Front Door* (1959) and *The Snow-Woman* (1969).

She also wrote poetry, collections of which include her first publication *The Mountain Beast* (1930), and short stories such as *Conferences at Cold Comfort Farm* (1949).

Gibson, Althea

Born 1927
American tennis player, the first black competitor to achieve success at the highest levels of the game

Althea Gibson was born in Silver City, South Carolina. Tall and elegant, she was the first black player at Forest Hills and Wimbledon in 1950 and 1951 respectively. She dominated women's tennis during the 1950s, winning the French and Italian singles championships in 1956 and the British and American titles in both 1957 and 1958.

She turned professional in 1959 and won the professional singles title in 1960. Later she appeared in some films and played professional golf.

Her autobiography is *I Always Wanted to be Somebody* (1958) and she was named to the National Lawn Tennis Hall of Fame in 1971.

Gielgud, Maina

Born 1945
English dancer, artistic director and teacher who has done much to rehabilitate ballet in Australia

Maina Gielgud was born in London, the niece of the actor Sir John Gielgud (1904–   ). She studied with many distinguished teachers and made her début in 1961 with Roland Petit's company.

She performed with such companies as Ballet of the 20th Century (1967–71), London Festival Ballet (1972–5) and the Royal Ballet (1977–8), before working freelance from 1978.

In 1983 she was appointed artistic director of the Australian Ballet, for which her productions include *Giselle* (1992).

Gilbreth, Lillian Evelyn, *née* Moller

Born 1878   Died 1972
American psychologist who was a pioneer of scientific management

Lillian Moller was born in Oakland, California. She graduated in English literature from Berkeley, and after marrying Frank Gilbreth, acquired a PhD from Brown University.

As Professor of Management at Purdue University from 1935, she established the Time and Motion Study Laboratory there. Her large family of 12 and their active life were represented in a book and film, *Cheaper by the Dozen* (1950).

Gildersleeve, Virginia

Born 1877   Died 1965
American Dean of Barnard College, and spokeswoman on international affairs

Virginia Gildersleeve was born and educated in New York City, obtaining her PhD from Columbia in 1908. In 1911, after an early teaching career at Barnard and Columbia and having published several books on education, she was appointed Dean of Barnard, where she remained for 36 years. Under her influence the college retained its high academic standards and broadened its curriculum.

Gildersleeve was also a leader in international affairs, and she was the only US woman delegate at the United Nations founding conference in San Francisco in 1945.

Gilks, Gillian, *née* Perrin

Born 1959
English badminton player, a talented all-round player

Gillian Perrin was born in Surrey. She won 27 national titles — nine singles, seven ladies doubles and 11 mixed doubles — and was also a treble champion at the 1974 Commonwealth Games. She earned a record number of caps for England and won 11 All-England championship titles. Also the holder of 12 European championship titles, in 1984 she won 16 world class events and a silver medal at the Uber Cup.

Gilks became well known for her struggles with the Badminton Association of England, who tried to decide where she would play and with whom, an imposition on her freedom which she strongly disliked.

Gilliatt, Penelope

Born 1932   Died 1993
English film and theatre critic, novelist and screenwriter

Penelope Gilliatt was born in London. She wrote a handful of novels, including *The Cutting Edge* (1978), which describes the relationship between two brothers, and six collections of short stories, including *Splendid Lives* (1977), a sympathetic study of a fleet of eccentrics.

She was nominated for an Oscar for her screenplay for *Sunday Bloody Sunday* (1971), a highly topical piece dealing with the triangular relationship between a middle-aged man and woman and their shared, younger male lover.

Her profiles of filmmakers, several of which

appeared in the *New Yorker*, are considered among the best of their kind.

Gilligan, Carol

Born 1936
American psychologist who specializes in female behaviour

Carol Gilligan was born in New York City. Her studies in gender differences in moral development, published in *A Different Voice* (1982), point out the biases in studies that establish male behaviour as normal and female behaviour as different or abnormal.

In 1984 she was recognized by *MS Magazine* (founded by **Gloria Steinem**) as Woman of the Year, and in 1987 she founded the Harvard Project on Women's Psychology and the Development of Girls.

Her other books include *Mapping the Moral Domain: A Contribution of Women's Thinking to Psychological Theory and Education* (1988) and *Meeting at the Crossroads: Women's Psychology and Girls' Development* (with Lynn Mikel Brown, 1992).

Gilman, Charlotte (Anna) Perkins, *née* Perkins

Born 1860 Died 1935
American feminist and writer whose utopic novel Herland, *about an all-woman society, has brought her to the forefront of women's studies*

Charlotte Perkins was born in Hartford, Connecticut, and brought up by her mother. She was educated at Rhode Island School of Design and married a painter, Charles Stetson, in 1884, but separated in 1888, divorcing in 1894. Moving to California, she published her first stories, most memorably 'The Yellow Wall-Paper' (1892) and a collection of poetry, *In This Our World* (1893).

She lectured on women's issues, as well as wider social concerns, and in 1898 wrote *Women and Economics*, now recognized as a feminist landmark. In 1902 she married her cousin George Gilman, a New York lawyer. She founded, edited and wrote for the journal *Forerunner* (1909–16). Her later works include *The Man-made World* (1911) and *His Religion and Hers* (1923).

A famous figure in her own time — for her private life as well as her books and lecture tours — she commited suicide on being told that she was suffering from incurable cancer. She was inducted into the National Women's Hall of Fame in 1994.

Gilmore, Dame Mary Jean, *née* Cameron

Born 1865 Died 1962
Australian poet and journalist who came to be regarded as the 'grand old lady' of Australian letters

Mary Cameron was born in Cotta Walla, near Goulburn, New South Wales. Her early teaching career in the mining town of Broken Hill gave her an abiding interest in the labour movement. She became the first woman member of the Australian Workers' Union and in 1896 joined William Lane's Utopian 'New Australia' settlement in Paraguay, South America. There she met and married a shearer, William Gilmore, and they returned to Australia in 1902, settling in Sydney in 1912.

Her socialist sympathies were now harnessed to campaigning for the betterment of the sick and the helpless, through the women's column which she edited for over 20 years in the Sydney *Worker* newspaper, but also in her six volumes of poetry. *Marri'd and Other Verses* (1910) was followed by *The Passionate Heart* (1918), *The Wild Swans* (1930) and the radical *Battlefields* (1939). Selected verse was published in 1948 (revised edition 1969) and in her 89th year she published her last collection, the more tranquil *Fourteen Men* (1954). A further *Selected Poems* came out in 1963.

Her reminiscences *Old Days: Old Ways* (1934) and *More Recollections* (1935) illustrate her lifelong efforts to preserve early Australian traditions and folklore. She was created DBE in 1937, and William Dobell's controversial portrait of her was unveiled on her ninety-second birthday in 1957. A collection of tributes to her was published in 1965, and an edition of her letters in 1980.

Gilpin, Laura

Born 1891 Died 1979
American photographer, best known for luminous platinum-printed landscapes and for intimate portraits, particularly of the Navaho people

Laura Gilpin was born in Colorado, a cousin of the photographer and peace officer Henry Gilpin (1922–   ). She was given a Kodak 'Brownie' camera in 1903, and she made autochromes (the first true colour photographic process to be widely and commercially available) in Colorado Springs from 1908. In 1916 she photographed in the Grand Canyon. Also that year, on the advice of **Gertrude Käsebier**, she began a year's study at the Clarence H White School of Photography in New York.

She opened a portrait studio in 1918,

worked on commercial commissions from the 1920s, and held solo exhibitions from 1924, the year she travelled in southern California and New Mexico photographing ruins. From 1942 to 1945 she undertook public relations photography for the Boeing Aircraft Company in Wichita, Kansas. Beginning in 1945, the year she moved to Santa Fe, she photographed the Rio Grande from source to mouth, and documented the lifestyle of the Navaho people, noting their special relationship with the land.

An important solo exhibition of her work was held at the Witkin Gallery in New York in 1973–4, and a retrospective at the Museum of New Mexico, Santa Fe, in 1974–5. Her publications include *The Rio Grande: River of Destiny* (1949) and *The Enduring Navaho* (1968).

Ginsburg, Ruth Bader, *née* Bader

Born 1933
American federal judge, the second woman to be appointed an associate justice of the US Supreme Court

Ruth Bader was born in Brooklyn, New York, and educated at Cornell and at Harvard and Columbia law schools. She married Martin Ginsburg in 1954 and taught law at Rutgers in the 1960s before becoming professor at the Columbia University School of Law (1972–80).

She was US Circuit Court Judge with the US Court of Appeals from 1980 to 1993, when she was nominated by President Clinton to the Supreme Court of the USA, the highest court in the country. As well as being the second woman Supreme Court Justice (**Sandra Day O'Connor** was the first), she was also the second Jewish justice.

Ginzburg, Natalia

Born 1916   Died 1991
Italian novelist, short-story writer and dramatist who remains among Italy's most highly respected modern writers

Natalia Ginzburg was born in Palermo into a liberal Jewish family who resisted the rise of fascism in the 1930s. Her first husband died in a Nazi prison and she was forced to leave her home in Turin and live in a small town in the Abruzzi. This is where her first work *La strada che va in città e altri raconti* (1942, Eng trans *Road to the City and Other Stories*, 1952) was written, evoking a striking sense of an enclosing environment.

Her spare, deceptively simple prose communicates the inarticulacy and emotional deprivation of her female protagonists. Do-

mestic life remained her subject in her more lighthearted family memoir *Lessico famigliare* (1963, 'Family Sayings'), which won the Strega Prize, and in her later novels and plays which reveal how the break-up of the restrictive family unit has had little beneficial effect on the female condition.

Giovanni, Nikki, *née* Yolande Cornelia Giovanni, Jr

Born 1943
American poet, a prominent figure in the development of Black literature

Yolande Giovanni was educated at Fisk University, an important location in the development of Black consciousness. Though her earlier work, *Black Judgement* (1968), *Black Feeling, Black Talk* (1968) and *Poem of Angela Yvonne Davis* (1970), was closely associated with the radical and quasi-separatist mood of the 1960s, her later verse became more introspective and personal, more akin to the work of **June Jordan** and **Alice Walker**, with whom she conducted a significant debate, published as *A Poetic Equation* (1974).

An encounter the year before with another American black writer, James Baldwin, described in *A Dialogue* (1973), was even more influential. Giovanni's more recent collections include the lyrical *Cotton Candy on a Rainy Day* (1978) and *Those Who Ride the Night Winds* (1983). Like Jordan, she has also written successfully for children. Her other works include *Gemini: An Extended Autobiographical Statement of My First Twenty-Five Years of Being a Black Poet* (1971).

Gippius, Zinaida Nikolayevna, *also called* Hippius

Born 1869   Died 1945
Russian poet, novelist and critic (under the names of 'Anton the Extreme' and 'Comrade Herman')

Zinaida Gippius was born in Belev, Tula. After she went into exile (1919) she spelled her name 'Hippius', and she is sometimes known under it. She was married to the Russian writer Dmitri Merezhkovski, who was more popular in his time, but who was infinitely less gifted.

It took some time for Gippius's poetic merits to become widely acknowledged; as a critic she poured deserved scorn on several now forgotten writers. In fact, Gippius not only played a paramount part in freeing Russian poetry from a prosody it had outworn, but also was one of the best woman poets of the 20th century. With her husband, she founded a new mystical faith.

She had welcomed the February Revolution

of 1917, but rejected the Bolsheviks on account of their godlessness. Her memoirs *Zhivye litsa* (1925, 'Living Faces') are sober prophecies of the fall of Stalinism. Even more wisdom may be gleaned from the English translation of selections from her diaries, *Between Paris and St Petersburg* (1975), but paramount are her love lyrics and religious poetry. *Moy lunny drug* (1925, 'My Moonlight Friend') is an evocative portrait of the Russian poet Alexander Blok. There are English translations of her work in *Selected Works of Zinaida Gippius* (1972) and *Intellect and Ideas in Action: Selected Correspondence* (1972).

Girardin, Delphine de, *née* Gay

Born 1804 Died 1855
French writer whose elegiac poetic essays typified early French Romantic writing

Delphine Gay was born in Aix-la-Chapelle, a daughter of the novelist Sophie Gay (1776–1852). A fashionable figure, graced by beauty, charm and wit, she became the first wife of Émile de Girardin and was acclaimed by the outstanding literary men of the period.

Her elegiac *Essais Poétiques* (Poetic Essays) appeared in 1824 and she contributed *feuilletons* or *lettres parisiennes*, elegant sketches of society life, to her husband's newspaper under the pseudonym of the Vicomte Charles de Launay. She also wrote some poetry, plays and novels, of which *Le Lorgnon* (1831, 'The Eyeglasses') is the best.

Giroud, Françoise, *originally* Françoise Gourdji

Born 1916
French journalist, feminist, broadcaster and politican

Françoise Giroudji was born in Geneva and educated at the Lycée Molière, Paris, and the Collège de Groslay. Rejected by her Turkish father, she selected a new name.

She began her career as a typist but was soon writing screenplays. In 1953 she co-founded the news magazine *l'Express* which she also edited. She has been prominent in post-war feminism and in 1974 accepted the post, which she held for two years, of Minister for the Status of Women in Giscard d'Estaing's government.

Much of her writing has been translated into English, including *Ce que je crois* (1975), *La Comédie du pouvoir* (1977) and the bestseller *Les hommes et les femmes* (1993).

Gish, Lillian Diana, *originally* Lillian de Guiche

Born 1893 Died 1993
American actress remembered for her portrayal of vulnerable heroines in silent era classics

Lillian de Guiche was born in Springfield, Ohio. After making her stage début at the age of five, she acted in touring theatre companies with her sister Dorothy (1898–1968), with whom she made a joint film début in *An Unseen Enemy* (1912). A long association with film director D W Griffith brought her leading roles in *Birth of a Nation* (1915), *Intolerance* (1916) and *Broken Blossoms* (1919) and created a gallery of waif-like heroines with indomitable spirits.

Ill-served by talking pictures, she returned to the stage in 1930 where her many credits include *The Trip to Bountiful* (1953), *Romeo and Juliet* (1965) and *Uncle Vanya* (1973). She continued to play supporting roles in television and on film, including *Duel in the Sun* (1946) and *The Night of the Hunter* (1955), and returned to a major screen role in *The Whales of August* (1987).

She directed one film, *Remodelling Her Husband* (1920), and wrote several volumes of autobiography. She received an honorary Academy Award in 1971.

Glantz, Margo

Born 1930
Mexican novelist and journalist who is one of the most active women writers in Latin America

Margo Glantz was born in Mexico City. She earned her doctorate in literature at the Sorbonne in Paris and has written widely, taught literature, founded a literary journal (*Punto de partida*) and served as President of the Interamerican Congress of Women Writers. She regularly contributes to Mexican newspapers and teaches at the University of Mexico.

Her interest lies in language and repression, and the role of women in subversion of patriarchy and of language itself. Her most famous work is *Las mil y una calorias* ('The Thousand and One Calories'), which is subtitled 'a dietetic novel'.

Glanville-Hicks, Peggy

Born 1912 Died 1990
Australian-born American composer of opera, ballet, and orchestral and chamber music

Peggy Glanville-Hicks was born in Melbourne, Victoria. She studied at the Conservatorium of Music, Melbourne, at the Royal College of Music, London, and with Ralph

Vaughan Williams, **Nadia Boulanger**, Arthur Benjamin and Egon Wellesz.

In 1942 she went to New York where she organized concerts of modern music and between 1948 and 1958 was music critic of the *New York Herald Tribune*. In 1959 she moved to Greece where her opera *Nausicaa* (to a text by Robert Graves) was produced for the 1961 Athens Festival.

Much of her output was for theatre and ballet. Other major works include the operas *The Transposed Heads* (story by Thomas Mann) and *Sappho* (by Lawrence Durrell), an *Etruscan Concerto, Letters from Morocco* and *Concerto Romantico*. From 1975 she was director of Asian studies at the Australian Music Centre, Sydney.

Glasgow, Ellen Anderson Gholson

Born 1874 Died 1945
American novelist best known for her radical stories of the South

Ellen Glasgow was born into an old colonial family in Richmond, Virginia, where she spent all her life. Reacting against the romantic image of Southern life, with its outdated social code of male superiority, she determined to become a high-calibre novelist and began writing an account of social change in Virginia since 1850.

This project spanned to five books, starting with *The Voice of the People* (1900) and including *Virginia* (1913). Among her other works are *The Descendant* (1897), *Barren Ground* (1925), which is a more optimistic and progressivist narrative, *The Sheltered Life* (1932) and *In This Our Life* (1941), which won the 1942 Pulitzer Prize.

Glaspell, Susan Keating

Born 1882 Died 1948
American novelist and playwright who co-founded the Provincetown Players

Susan Glaspell was born in Davenport, Iowa, and educated at Drake University. She began her career as a news reporter before writing short stories (collected in *Lifted Masks*, 1912) and her first novel *The Glory of the Conquered* (1909).

With her husband George Cook, whom she married in 1913, and playwright Eugene O'Neill (1888–1953) she founded the Provincetown Players, which marked the beginning of the New York little theatre movement.

Her other novels include *Fidelity* (1915), *Brook Evans* (1928) and *The Fugitive's Return* (1929), and her plays include *Trifles* (1917) and *Alison's House* (1930), based on the life of

Emily Dickinson, which won the 1931 Pulitzer Prize for drama.

Glass, Ruth, *née* Lazarus

Born 1912 Died 1990
German-born sociologist who became a leading pioneer in urban sociology in Britain

Ruth Lazarus was born of Jewish parentage in Berlin, where she began her career as a journalist. With the advent of Nazi rule, she escaped to London and studied at the London School of Economics.

Driven by a burning passion for justice, she was known for her research in various fields, including new housing developments and planning and, in particular, the status of ethnic minorities in the community.

She was director of the Centre for Urban Studies at University College, London (1958–90), and instrumental in establishing sociology as an academic subject. A collection of her essays, *Clichées of Urban Doom*, was published in 1988.

Glen, (Alice) Esther

Born 1881 Died 1940
New Zealand journalist and influential writer for children

Esther Glen grew up in New Zealand. She became a journalist and, aware of the lack of journalistic writing for children, she started writing a children's supplement for the family newspaper, the Christchurch *Sun*, and later for the *Press*. Her first novel for younger readers was *Six Little New Zealanders* (1917), followed by its sequel *Uncles Three at Kamahi* (1926).

Although she only wrote four books — the others were *Twinkles on the Mountain* (1920) and *Robin of Maoriland* (1929) — her influence on New Zealand children's writing was considerable, and in 1945 the New Zealand Library Association established the annual Esther Glen award for distinguished contributions to the genre.

Glennie, Evelyn

Born 1965
Scottish percussion player who is the only full-time professional percussionist in the world

Evelyn Glennie was born in Aberdeen. She studied timpani and percussion from the age of 12, and from 1982 at the Royal Academy of Music, gaining an honours degree. She also studied marimba with Keiko Abe in Japan. Judged by the highest critical international standards to be a percussionist of outstanding abilities, her achievement is additionally remarkable as she experienced a gradual but total loss of hearing in her early teens.

She has received innumerable prizes and awards, is a Fellow of the Royal College of Music and an honorary Doctor of Music (Aberdeen, 1991), and many leading composers have written specially for her. She has recorded and appeared widely throughout Europe, the USA, Australia and the Far East, and has been the subject of many television and radio documentaries.

She published an autobiography, *Good Vibrations*, in 1990.

Glenorchy, Willielma Campbell, Viscountess

Born 1741   Died 1786
Aristocratic Scottish patroness of evangelical
religious causes

Viscountess Glenorchy was born in Galloway. Widowed in 1771 after 10 years of marriage to the wealthy landowner John, Viscount Glenorchy, she decided to devote her life and fortune to religion.

She held services in her home, employed chaplains and established chapels, including two in Edinburgh: one in 1770 was intended to attract preachers from different denominations, and a second in 1774 was connected with the Church of Scotland. She later founded several chapels in England. In her will she made bequests for her chapels, for schools and for ministerial training.

Gloag, Ann Heron, *née* Souter

Born 1942
Scottish businesswoman who is managing director
of the UK's biggest bus company

Ann Souter was born in Perth, the daughter of a bus conductor. She attended Perth High School, then trained as a nurse, and married her first husband Robin Gloag in 1965. She worked as a nurse for over 17 years before becoming a founding partner with her brother Brian Souter of a bus and coach company called Gloagtrotter in 1980.

The Perth-based company began with a Dundee–London service and operations in and around small Scottish towns, beginning to move into larger metropolitan areas such as London in 1994. Renamed Stagecoach Holdings plc on being floated on the stockmarket in 1993, it became increasingly acquisitive and by the mid-1990s owned a fleet of 7,300 vehicles, employed 20,000 people and had won the franchise to run British Rail's South West Trains. It also owns businesses in Africa, New Zealand and Hong Kong.

Gloag has been managing director of the company since 1986, with Brian Souter as executive chairman, and it is said that they are among the wealthiest business people in the UK. Since 1995 she has lived at Beaufort Castle, former home of the Frasers of Lovat.

Glover, Jane Alison

Born 1949
English conductor and musicologist who has risen
to become the leading woman conductor in the UK

Jane Glover was born in Helmsley, Yorkshire, and educated at St Hugh's College, Oxford, where she became a lecturer in music in 1976 and carried out research on the Italian composer Francesco Cavalli. She joined the Open University faculty of music in 1979, and also became known as a television presenter of such BBC programmes as *Orchestra* (1983) and *Mozart* (1985).

She made her début as a professional conductor at the Wexford Festival in 1975, and since then has conducted nearly all the top orchestras in the world's most famous opera houses. After joining the Glyndebourne Opera in 1979, she worked as chorus director (1980–4) and as musical director of the touring opera (1982–5). She made her first appearance at the Royal Opera House, Covent Garden, in 1988, and was artistic director of the London Mozart Players from 1984 to 1991.

Glover, Julia, *née* Betterton

Born 1779   Died 1850
Irish comic actress who became a leading lady of
the London stage

Julia Betterton was born in Newry. She toured with her father from 1789 until he 'sold' her in 1798 to be married to Samuel Glover. It is said that no money passed hands, but the marriage nevertheless took place in 1800. In 1802 she appeared at Drury Lane, London.

She was the original Alhadra in S T Coleridge's *Remorse* (1813) and excelled in such comic roles as Lydia Languish and Mrs Malaprop in R B Sheridan's *The Rivals* (1775). In her youth, with her hearty humour and plump figure, she was a perfect Mrs Malaprop, but when she played it at her farewell performance in 1850, she was almost too ill to speak.

Her second son, William Howard (1819–75), became a composer and conductor.

Glück, Louise Elisabeth

Born 1943
American poet who examines the anxieties of
young women using myth and symbolism

Louise Glück was born on Long Island, New York, and educated at Sarah Lawrence College and Columbia University. Though her first verses were obviously influenced by Robert Lowell and other male poets, she has developed a distinctively female perspective, most noticeably in her reworking of the story of King David's concubine Abishag the Shunamite in *The House on the Marshland* (1975).

In the 1970s she gradually modulated the staccato contractions of her début collection *Firstborn* (1968) in favour of more varied and expressive rhythms that sometimes recall the Austrian lyric poet Rainer Maria Rilke and even the 19th-century German poet Heinrich Heine.

Later collections include *Descending Figure* (1980), *The Triumph of Achilles* (1985), *Ararat* (1990) and *The Wild Iris* (1992), which won the 1993 Pulitzer Prize for poetry. She has also published *Proofs and Theories: Essays on Poetry* (1994).

Glyn, Elinor, *née* Sutherland

Born 1864 Died 1943
British popular novelist who tantalized her audience with tales of 'it'

Elinor Sutherland was born in Jersey, Channel Islands, and married in 1892. She began her writing with *The Visits of Elizabeth* (1900), but found fame with *Three Weeks* (1907), a book which gained a reputation for being risqué.

She kept her public enthralled with such books as *Man and Maid* (1922), *Did She?* (1934) and *The Third Eye* (1940). Nonsensical, faulty in construction and ungrammatical, her novels were nevertheless avidly read.

She went to Hollywood (1922–7), where 'it' (her version of sex appeal) was glamorized on the screen by **Clara Bow**.

Goddard, Mary Katherine

Born 1738 Died 1816
American printer and publisher, whose newspaper published the first printed copy of the Declaration of Independence

Mary Goddard was born in Connecticut either at Groton, or at New London where she grew up and was educated at home. In 1762, after her father's death, she joined her brother William in Providence, Rhode Island, where he printed the *Providence Gazette* (1765–8). Subsequently she joined him in Philadelphia where they published the *Pennsylvania Chronicle*, and in Baltimore where they began publishing the *Maryland Journal* (1773).

From 1775 the *Maryland Journal* was officially published by Mary Goddard, and in that year it printed the first copy of the Declaration of Independence. In 1784 William and Mary quarrelled, ending her career as a printer, though she continued to run her book shop until about 1810. She was also postmaster of Baltimore from 1775 until forced to retire in 1789.

Godden, (Margaret) Rumer

Born 1907
English novelist, poet and children's author highly regarded for the atmospheric lucidity of her prose

Rumer Godden was born in Eastbourne, Sussex. She lived for many years in India, a country and culture which provide the backdrop to much of her fiction, and has now settled in Scotland. Twice widowed, she writes under her maiden name. Her third novel and first major success, *Black Narcissus* (1939), describes the struggles of nuns attempting to found a mission in the Himalaya region.

Her first book for children was *The Dolls' House* (1947). She frequently writes from the point of view of a young person, most notably in *The Greengage Summer* (1958), a delicate story of love and deception set in the Champagne area of the Marne.

Godden's most recent books include *Coromandel Sea Change* (1991), a love story set in southern India. Her two volumes of autobiography are *A Time to Dance, No Time to Weep* (1987) and *A House with Four Rooms* (1989). She was appointed an OBE in 1993.

Godfree, Kitty (Kathleen), *née* McKane

Born 1896 Died 1992
English tennis player who was twice champion of Wimbledon

Kitty McKane was born in London. Her father encouraged the whole family to participate in sports; they played tennis on the lawn of their home near Henley and cycled to Berlin in 1906.

As Kitty McKane, she lost to **Suzanne Lenglen** in the 1923 Wimbledon final but defeated the young US player **Helen Wills** the next year. In 1926, as Kitty Godfree, she defeated Lili de Alvarez to win the title again.

In 1986 she presented a silver salver to **Martina Navratilova**, when the younger woman won her seventh title.

Godiva, Lady, *Old English* Godgifu

Died 1080
English noblewoman and religious benefactor who
entered legend for her naked ride through
Coventry

Lady Godiva was the wife of Leofric, Earl of
Mercia (d.1057). According to the 13th-
century chronicler Roger of Wendover, in
1040 she rode naked through the market-place
of Coventry, with most of her body covered
by her hair, in order to persuade her husband
to reduce the taxes he had imposed.

A later embellishment of the legend suggests that she requested the townspeople to
remain indoors, which they all did except for
a tailor, 'Peeping Tom', who was struck blind.
Godiva built and endowed monasteries at
Coventry and Stow.

Godwin, Fay Simmonds

Born 1931
English photographer who is known for her
environmentally aware landscapes

Fay Godwin was born in Berlin, the daughter
of a diplomat, and educated in numerous
schools worldwide. She began her career by
taking photographs of her two young sons but
has become best known for her landscapes,
including Welsh and Scottish scenes; they
now often make a sociological or ecological
statement by incorporating pollution, in order
to alert people to the potential for environmental disaster.

Since 1970 she has worked as a freelance
photographer, based in London. Her many
publications include *The Oldest Road: The
Ridgeway* (1975, co-authored with J R L
Anderson).

Godwin, Gail

Born 1937
American writer who examines the trauma faced
by women rejecting conventional female roles

Gail Godwin was born in Birmingham, Alabama, and was raised in North Carolina. Her
first novel was *The Perfectionists* (1970), but
her most famous and highly regarded has been
The Odd Woman (1974), a well-made and sus-
penseful study of an introspective college
instructor who, although intelligent and
aware, cannot prevent herself from over-ideal-
ism in her affair with an over-cautious academic. Her other work includes a collection
of stories entitled *Dream Children* (1976), *A
Mother and Two Daughters* (1982) and *The Finishing School* (1985).

Goegg, Marie, *née* Pouchoulin

Born 1826 Died 1899
Swiss writer, feminist, founder member of the
International League of Peace and Freedom

Marie Pouchoulin was born in Geneva into
a clockmaker's family. She had little formal
education, but her second marriage to the
German revolutionary Armand Goegg (who
had fled to Switzerland in 1849) was crucial in
developing her political activities and beliefs.

With her husband she was involved with
the International League of Peace and Freedom, founded in Geneva in 1867. She was,
however, committed to her belief that in order
to ensure equality for women within revolutionary and progressive movements, they
must also be allowed to organize separately.
To this end she founded the *Association International des Femmes* (later renamed *Solidarité*)
in 1868. She also campaigned for women to
be admitted as students to the University of
Geneva.

Goeppert-Mayer, Maria, *née* Goeppert

Born 1906 Died 1972
German-born American physicist who carried out
important work on the nucleus

Maria Goeppert was born in Kattowitz (now
Katowice in Poland). She graduated at Göttingen in 1930, emigrated to the USA and
taught at Johns Hopkins University, where
her husband, Joseph Mayer, was Professor of
Chemical Physics. From 1960 she held a chair
at the University of California.

She developed the shell model of the
nucleus based on the fact that certain nuclei
are very stable, having 'magic numbers' of
protons and neutrons, and drawing an analogy
with atomic physics in which a closed shell of
electrons leads to stable atoms, eg the noble
gases.

Some initial problems with the theory were
resolved by discussions with the Italian–
American physicist Enrico Fermi who pointed
out that spin-orbit coupling should be taken
into account. A similar model was developed
in Germany by Hans Jensen. Goeppert-Mayer
shared the 1963 Nobel Prize for Physics with
Eugene Wigner and Jensen.

Gohr, Marlies, *née* Oelsner

Born 1958
German track and field athlete, the first woman to
run the 100 metres in under 11 seconds

Marlies Gohr was born in Gera. She battled
with **Evelyn Ashford** for over a decade to see

who would be the fastest woman in the world.

Running for East Germany, she won a record number of European Cup titles, winning the 100 metres in six successive European Cup finals, and was European outdoor champion three times at 100 metres. She was also world champion at 100 metres in 1983 and held nine successive East German national 100 metres titles between 1977 and 1985 as well as another 100 metres title in 1988.

Gohr was consistently ranked in the world's top two for 100 metres and set three world records for this distance.

Goldberg, Leah

Born 1911   Died 1970
Lithuanian poet, critic and university teacher who wrote in Hebrew

Leah Goldberg settled in Palestine from 1935 and became well known as the translator of classics such as Leo Tolstoy's *War and Peace* into Hebrew. She wrote in Hebrew and was one of the most prized of the lyrical poets of Israel, but despite her acclaimed position little of her work has been translated.

Goldberg, Whoopi

Born 1949
American actress whose roles range from stand-up comic to singing nun

Whoopi Goldberg was born in New York City. Appearing on stage from the age of eight, she gradually developed her talent as a mimic and comedienne and built up a stand-up act of pointed humour and humanitarian concerns, which culminated in her Broadway triumph *Whoopi Goldberg* (1984–5).

She made her major film début in *The Color Purple* (1985) with a remarkable performance as a black woman on a voyage of self-discovery that won her a Best Actress Oscar nomination. Determined not to be restricted by her colour, sex or perceived image as a comic, she made the best of the choices offered to her but was rarely faced with first-rate material. Unsurprisingly, she turned to television, finding a recurring role as Guinan in the series *Star Trek: The Next Generation* and in the short-lived situation comedy *Bagdad Café*. Along with comedians Billy Crystal and Robin Williams she has for several years organized a cable-television show, *Comic Relief*, to raise money for the homeless in the USA.

However she returned to the limelight in 1990 with her performance as a Madame Arcati-like phony medium in *Ghost*, which earned her a Best Supporting Actress Oscar, and in the comedy *Sister Act* (1992), playing a Reno singer who takes refuge from her gangster lover in a convent. *Sister Act 2* appeared the following year, further consolidating Goldberg's star status.

Golden, Diana

Born 1963
American Alpine skier whose disability has not prevented her becoming a champion

Diana Golden was born in Cambridge, Massachusetts. She contracted cancer as a child and lost her right leg at the age of 12, but nevertheless joined the high school ski team and became one of the best skiers on the squad. She became involved in competitive disabled racing, joining the national US Disabled Ski Team at the age of 17. In 1982 she came second in the giant slalom at the world handicapped championships.

Golden began to campaign for disabled skiers to be allowed to compete with non-disabled skiers, and in 1985 the 'Golden Rule' of the United States Ski Association (USSA) stated that places were to be reserved at the end of the top seed for top disabled skiers. Two years later Golden finished tenth in a USSA race where all the other competitors were non-disabled. In 1986 she had won the USSA's Beck Award, given to the best American racer in international skiing. In 1987 she was ranked tenth best three-track skier in the world.

Ski Racing magazine named Golden the 1988 US Female Alpine Skier of the Year and also in 1988 she was named Female Skier of the Year by the US Olympic Committee. She retired from competitive ski racing in 1990, and was awarded the **Flo Hyman** Trophy in 1991.

Goldman, Emma, *known as* Red Emma

Born 1869   Died 1940
Lithuanian-born American anarchist who travelled widely, lecturing and inciting anarchic activities

Emma Goldman was born in Kaunas of Jewish parents. She was brought up in East Prussia, but moved in 1882 to St Petersburg, where she worked in a glove factory and absorbed prevailing nihilist ideas. She emigrated to the USA in 1885, where she worked in the garment industry and joined the anarchists in New York who were protesting against the unjust executions of four of their number for the Haymarket bomb-throwing on 4 May 1886 in Chicago.

Emma Goldman, 1901

Vida Goldstein was born in Portland, Victoria, and educated in Melbourne at the Presbyterian Ladies' College and at Melbourne University. She ran a school with her sister and became involved with the campaign for women's suffrage

She was a member of the first Australian suffrage group, the Woman's Suffrage Society, and later formed the Woman's Federal Political Association. She also founded the feminist publication *Australian Woman's Sphere* and stood as an independent candidate in Victoria five times between 1903 and 1917. Full suffrage and eligibility to stand in national elections was granted to women in Australia in 1902, just after federation, and Goldstein was the first woman in the British Empire to stand in national parliamentary elections.

Gomez de Avellaneda y Arteaga, Gertrudis

Born 1814 Died 1873
Cuban poet, playwright and novelist, one of the
most prominent Romantic writers of her century

Gertrudis Gomez de Avellaneda was born in Puerto Príncipe and educated by her parents. She travelled to Europe in the 1830s and lived in Spain for most of her life. There she was widely praised for her work and took part in some of the most important literary *tertulias* (organized literary conversations) of her day. She was important for her anti-slavery stance, for her erotic poetry, her prolific theatrical production and for her early feminism.

Her first poems were published under the pseudonym 'La Peregrina' ('The Pilgrim') and are considered among the most poignant in all of Spain's literature. Her plays were based on the lives of historical models and included the Biblical drama *Saúl* (1849), and her novels treated such themes as abolitionism, but are now largely forgotten.

Gomez was nominated to enter the Spanish Royal Academy but was rejected because of her gender.

Goncharova, Natalia Sergeyevna

Born 1881 Died 1962
Russian-born French painter who was inspired by
Russian folk art and became a Ballets Russes
designer

Natalia Goncharova was born in Ladyzhino, Tula province, south of Moscow. She began as a science student but turned to sculpture around 1898 and studied at the Moscow Academy of Art.

She began painting in 1904 and, like the painters Mikhail Larionov (whom she lived

She was active in anarchist agitation against tyrannical employers and was jailed in 1893 for incitement to riot in New York. She founded and edited the anarchist monthly *Mother Earth* (1906–17) in partnership with Alexander Berkman, who had in 1892 attempted to assassinate the industrialist Henry Clay Frick. Winning international celebrity through her stirring speeches and her visits to anarchist congresses in Paris (1899) and Amsterdam (1907), she worked extensively in American urban slums, but in 1917 was fined $10,000 and sentenced to two years' imprisonment for opposing registration of military recruits. In 1919 she was deported to the USSR (to which she was ideologically opposed).

She returned to the USA in 1924, supported the anarchists in the Spanish Civil War and published an autobiography *Living My Life* (1931) and several other works, including *Anarchism and Other Essays* (1910) and *My Disillusionment in Russia* (1923).

Goldstein, Vida

Born 1869 Died 1949
Australian feminist, an important player in the
Australian campaign for suffrage

with and eventually married on her 74th birthday) and Kasimir Malevich, was attracted to the flat colours and primitive forms of Russian folk art, combining these with the new influences of Cubism and Fauvism and an original flair. She took part in a post-Impressionist exhibition in London in 1912, as well as the second exhibition of Der Blaue Reiter (The Blue Rider) in Munich.

She moved to Geneva in 1915 with Larionov to design for Sergei Diaghilev's Ballets Russes and went to Paris in 1921. She became a French citizen in 1938.

Gonne, Maud, *married name* Maud MacBride

Born 1865 Died 1953
English-born Irish nationalist, feminist and
actress who helped to found Sinn Féin

Maud Gonne was born in Aldershot, Surrey, the daughter of an army officer of Irish descent and an English mother. She became an agitator for the cause of Irish independence, by speaking for the Land League, founding the nationalist Daughters of Ireland and editing a nationalist newspaper, *L'Irlande libre*, in Paris. She also became an actress much admired on the Irish stage, particulary by W B Yeats, who fell in love with her. She played the heroine in his first play *Cathleen ni Houlihan* (1892) and joined his theatre movement, but refused his marriage proposals, marrying instead (1903) Major John MacBride, who fought against the British in the Boer War.

Gonne remained active in campaigns to release Irish political prisoners and took part in the Easter Rising of 1916, following which her husband was executed as a rebel and she was imprisoned. After his death she was an active founder-member of Sinn Féin in Ireland and on the creation of the Irish Free State in late 1921, she was appointed its first French diplomat.

Her son Sean MacBride (1904–88) was Foreign Minister of the Irish Republic from 1948 to 1951 and was awarded the 1974 Nobel Prize for Peace.

Gonzalès, Eva

Born 1849 Died 1883
French painter, a pupil and model of Edouard
Manet also known for her own Impressionistic
paintings

Eva Gonzalès was born in Paris to members of the 'haute bourgeoisie' and was noted for her great beauty at an early age. She studied first with Charles Chaplin, an academic who was also the teacher of **Mary Cassatt**. When she was 20 Edouard Manet requested her family's permission to paint her portrait. She became not only his model, but also his pupil, and was the only artist permitted by him to sign 'pupil of Manet' on Salon entries. Her first entry to the Salon in 1870 was *L'Enfant de Troupe* which was purchased by the government.

Her entries to the Salon in 1872 were well received by Zola and others and in 1874 *La Nichée* was praised by Leroy who said, 'The canvas is nearly as pretty as its author, which is not saying little'.

In 1876 she married the engraver Henri Guérard, a member of the Impressionist table at the Café Guerbois. She gave birth to her first child in 1883 and died of an embolism five days later, one day after Edouard Manet.

Goodall, Jane

Born 1934
English primatologist and conservationist whose
research has been fundamental in the
understanding of chimpanzee behaviour

Jane Goodall was born in London. She worked in Kenya with the anthropologist Louis Leakey who in 1960 raised funds for her to study chimpanzee behaviour at Gombe in Tanzania. She obtained her PhD from Cambridge in 1965 and subsequently set up the Gombe Stream Research Centre. She was visiting professor at the Department of Psychiatry and Program of Human Biology at Stanford University (1971–5) and became visiting professor of zoology at Dar es Salaam in 1973. Since 1967 she has been Scientific Director of the Gombe Wildlife Research Institute.

With her co-workers at Gombe, she has carried out a study of the behaviour and ecology of chimpanzees which at over 30 years is the longest unbroken field study of a group of animals in their natural habitat. This research has transformed the understanding of primate behaviour by demonstrating its complexity and the sophistication of inter-individual relationships. Among Goodall's major discoveries was the ability of chimpanzees to modify a variety of natural objects such as the stems of plants to use as tools to collect termites, and sticks and rocks as missiles for defence against possible predators. She also showed that they hunt animals for meat and that the adults share the proceeds of such kills. She has been active in chimpanzee conservation in Africa and their welfare in those countries where they are extensively used in medical research.

Her books include *In the Shadow of Man* (1971) and *The Chimpanzees of Gombe: Pat-*

terns of Behavior (1986). She has received many awards for conservation and for her scientific research including the Albert Schweitzer award (1987), the Encyclopaedia Britannica award (1989) and the Kyoto Prize for Science (1990).

Goodrich, Frances

Born 1891 Died 1984
American playwright who won a Pulitzer Prize
for her joint adaptation of Anne Frank's diary

Frances Goodrich was born in Belleville, New Jersey. She worked in collaboration with her husband Albert Hackett (1900–95), a New York-born writer and actor. They are best remembered for their highly successful stage adaptation of *The Diary of Anne Frank* in 1955, which won them a Pulitzer Prize in 1956. Their other stage works include *Western Union, Please* (1939) and *The Great Big Doorstep* (1942).

They were also very successful screenwriters, and their many credits include such Hollywood favourites as *The Thin Man* (1934), *Easter Parade* (1948) and *Seven Brides for Seven Brothers* (1954).

Goolagong, Evonne see Cawley, Evonne

Gorbachev, Raisa Maksimova, *née* Titorenko

Born 1934
Russian educationalist, organization official and
former 'first lady' as the wife of Mikhail
Gorbachev (Soviet head of state 1988–91)

Raisa Titorenko was born of a railway family in the Altai region. She graduated from Moscow University and pursued a career in sociological research and lecturing, which included positions as sociologist at Stavropol Teacher Training Institute (1957–61) and as lecturer at Moscow University (1977–85).

A woman of considerable intelligence and obvious charm, she had gained standing in her own right before 1985 when, as the wife of the General Secretary of the Communist Party of the Soviet Union (Gorbachev held this post from 1985 to 1991), she began to appear with him on important occasions, including overseas tours. Being the first wife of a Soviet leader ever to play a public role, in an unsettled society she attracted criticism, but abroad she added to her husband's political and popular prestige and did a great deal to make a success of East–West arms talks.

Since the end of his presidency she has con-tinued as a member of the board of the Cultural Heritage Commission (1987–   ), and she published her autobiography, *I Hope: Reflections and Reminiscences*, in 1991.

Gorbanevskaya, Natalya Evgen'evna

Born 1936
Russian poet who became known for her political
activism

Natalya Gorbanevskaya was born in Moscow and educated at Leningrad (now St Petersburg), having been expelled from Moscow University. A period of hospitalization which resulted from acute vertigo attacks prefigured a more sinister committal in a state psychiatric hospital a decade later (1970–2), before which she had engaged in anti-Soviet activities, including the founding of a *samizdat* journal and protesting against the invasion of Czechoslovakia; the latter event was documented in her book *Polden'* (1970, published in the UK as *Red Square at Noon*, 1972). Shortly after her release she emigrated to France.

Gorbanevskaya's work is known in the West through Daniel Weissbort's 1972 translation, which probably contained more of her poems than had been officially published in the Soviet Union up to that time. Her verse is highly musical and lexically playful, to a degree that renders 'translation' problematic. She also uses a rather personal and highly flexible symbolic system in which external states — cold, snow and ice — take on and shed significance with bewildering speed. Since moving to France, she has edited a new journal, *Kontinent*.

Gordimer, Nadine

Born 1923
South African novelist and a winner of the Nobel
Prize for Literature

Nadine Gordimer was born in Springs, Transvaal, and educated at a convent school and at the University of the Witwatersrand, Johannesburg. Her work is rooted in South Africa, where she has continued to live. Her first book was a collecton of short stories, *Face to Face* (1949), followed by another collection, *The Soft Voice of the Serpent* (1952). In 1954 she married her second husband, Reinhold Cassirer, a Jewish refugee from Nazi Germany.

In 1953 she had published her first novel, *The Lying Days*, in which a white girl triumphs over the provincial narrowness and racial bigotry of her parents' mining village existence, though she too has to come to terms with the limitations of her social background. This recurrent theme dominated Gordimer's early books, such as *Occasion for Loving* (1963) and *The Late Bourgeois World* (1966). Apartheid, and her characters' reaction to it, is ever present in her fiction, most powerfully in *The Conservationist* (1974), joint winner of the Booker Prize with Stanley Middleton's *Holiday*. Other important titles are *A Guest of Honour* (1970), *Burger's Daughter* (1979), *July's People* (1981), *A Sport of Nature* (1987), in which a self-possessed white girl is transformed into a political activist intent on returning Africa to the rule of the Africans, and *None to Accompany Me* (1994), a novel that reads like poltical journalism chronicling the lives of liberal whites in South Africa between the time of Mandela's release and the first multi-racial elections.

Much fêted, Gordimer has received many awards, including the Malaparte Prize from Italy, the **Nelly Sachs** Prize from Germany, the Scottish Arts Council's Neil Gunn Fellowship and the French international award, the Grand Aigle d'Or. She was awarded the 1991 Nobel Prize for Literature.

Gordon, Hannah Cambell Grant

Born 1941
Scottish actress who portrays the humorous and serious aspects of middle-class life

Hannah Gordon was born in Edinburgh. She won the James Bridie Gold Medal at the Royal College of Dramatic Art in Glasgow in 1962, then worked at the Dundee Repertory Theatre and the Glasgow Citizens' Theatre, and made her television début in *Johnson Over Jordan* (1965). Her vast array of television credits includes the situation comedies *My Wife Next Door* (1972) and *Joint Account* (1989–   ), as well as such popular drama series as *Upstairs, Downstairs* (1974) and *Telford's Change* (1979).

Her rare film appearances include *Spring and Port Wine* (1969), *Alfie Darling* (1974) and *The Elephant Man* (1980). Theatre work has provided more opportunities to display her versatility, and her credits include *Can You Hear Me At The Back?* (1979), *The Jeweller's Shop* (1982), *The Country Girl* (1983) and *Shirley Valentine* (1989). She has also worked extensively in radio drama.

Gordon, Ishbel, Marchioness of Aberdeen

Born 1857 Died 1939
Scottish champion of women's interests in Church and society

Ishbel Gordon was married to John Cambell Gordon, seventh Earl and first Marquis of Aberdeen, and wherever public duties took her husband, she made her own distinctive contribution. In particular she was instrumental in promoting the ordination of women to the ministry of the Church of Scotland in 1931.

While he was Lord-Lieutenant of Ireland, she founded an association to combat tuberculosis; while he was Governor-General of Canada she founded a nursing order. She also worked with the Red Cross, served as the elected President of the International Council of Women for 36 years, and was an unremitting advocate of world peace.

Gordon, Mary Catherine

Born 1949
American novelist whose work is strongly influenced by both her feminism and her Catholicism

Mary Gordon was born in Long Island, New York, and educated at Barnard College and Syracuse University. She has worked as a teacher in a community college and as a lecturer at Amherst College.

Her first novel, *Final Payments* (1978), presents a protagonist who accepts the role of caring for her bedridden father and finds herself both liberated and frightened by his death. Subsequent works include *The Company of Women* (1980), *Men and Angels* (1985), *The Other Side* (1990), and the short-story collection *Temporary Shelter* (1987). She has twice received the Janet Kafka Prize (1979 and 1982).

Gordon, Noele

Born 1922 Died 1985
English actress who was also an early specialist in colour television technique

Noele Gordon was born in East Ham, London. She made her first stage appearance at the age of two in a concert staged by the Maud Wells Dancing Academy. After studying at RADA she worked in repertory and pantomime before such London successes as *Diamond Lil* (1948) and *Brigadoon* (1949–51).

She assisted John Logie Baird with his early experiments in colour television and first appeared on that medium in *Ah, Wilderness* (1938). She later studied television techniques in the USA and returned to Britain as an adviser to ATV and host of such series as *Lunch Box* (1955) and *Fancy That* (1956).

She became a household name in the UK as the owner of the motel in the television soap-opera *Crossroads* (1964–81). Unceremoniously dismissed from the series, she returned to the stage in barnstorming musicals like *Gypsy* (1981), *Call Me Madam*, (1982–3) and *No, No Nanette* (1983).

Gordon, Ruth, *née* Jones

Born 1896 Died 1985
American actress, one of the leading women of the American stage

Ruth Jones was born in Wollaston, Massachusetts. She studied at the American Academy of Dramatic Arts, and made her stage début as Nibs in *Peter Pan* in 1915. She finally established herself as a leading actress in Wycherly's *The Country Wife* at the Old Vic in London and Owen Davis's *Ethan Frome* on Broadway, both in 1936.

Her other major roles included Ibsen's *A Doll's House* (1937), Chekhov's *The Three Sisters* (1942) and Thornton Wilder's *The Matchmaker* (1954). She also acted in films and wrote both plays and screenplays, the latter in collaboration with her second husband, Garson Kanin.

Gordon Cumming, Eka (Constance Fredereka)

Born 1837 Died 1924
Scottish traveller who wrote popular books about her extensive journeys

Eka Gordon Cumming was the twelfth child of Sir William Gordon-Cumming, Baronet of Altyre and Gordonstown. She began her travels in 1867 with a visit to her married sister in India.

Over the next 12 years she journeyed through the Pacific to Fiji and Hawaii, California and the Sierrra Nevada, Egypt, China and Ceylon (Sri Lanka), and wrote eight widely popular books, which she illustrated with her own paintings.

Gore, Catherine Grace Frances, *née* Moody

Born 1799 Died 1861
English novelist whose prolific ouput belongs to the 'silver-fork' school of fiction

Catherine Moody was born in East Retford, Nottinghamshire, and married Captain Charles Gore in 1823. She was a prolific and immensely popular writer of over 70 books, mainly novels of fashionable life in the manner of the 'silver fork' school. These show a concern with upper-class mores, correct dress and propitious marriage, and an antipathy to feminist thought.

They include *Mothers and Daughters* (1831), *Mrs Armytage* (1836) and *The Banker's Wife*

(1843). Gore also wrote three plays and some short stories.

Gore-Booth, Eva

Born 1870 Died 1926
Irish poet and suffragette

Eva Gore-Booth was the daughter of a wealthy Irish landowner and the younger sister of Constance Gore-Booth, later Countess **Markievicz**. She met Esther Roper in Italy and decided to spend her life working with her among the Lancashire textile workers.

She ran the North of England Society for Woman's Suffrage, founded the Manchester and Salford Women's Trade Union Council and edited the *Woman's Labour News*. She also supported the Women's Right to Work campaign and was a pacifist during World War I.

Gosse, (Laura) Sylvia

Born 1881 Died 1968
English artist and printmaker who co-founded the London Group

Sylvia Gosse was born in London, a daughter of the writer Sir Edmund Gosse. She studied at St John's Wood School of Art before attending the Royal Academy Schools (1903–6). In 1908 she met Walter Sickert who encouraged her and she became co-principal at his school of painting and etching at Rowland House.

In 1913 she had the first of many solo shows and the following year became a founder-member of the London Group. Her subject matter owes much to Sickert and Spencer Gore, encompassing genre subjects, everyday interiors, often with a single figure, as well as urban, town and Continental scenes. Gosse was also an accomplished etcher and her work can be seen in a number of public collections throughout the UK.

Gouges, Olympe de, *originally* Marie Gouze

Born 1748 Died 1793
French patriot, playwright and pamphleteer guillotined for her anti-revolutionary stance

Olympe de Gouges was born in Languedoc and first came to prominence when she had one of her plays, an attack on slavery entitled *L'Esclavage des noirs*, staged at the Théâtre Française during the 1780s.

With the coming of the revolution her writing became more political. She pleaded publicly for the king's life to be spared in a letter to the National Assembly in 1792, and further aroused public ire by criticising the revolutionary heroes Marat and Robespierre.

She was finally accused of undermining the Republic when her broadsheet *Les Trois urnes*, advocating a plebiscite to let the people decide between a Republican government, a federal government and the monarchy, appeared on bills around Paris. She was tried and sent to the guillotine.

Gould, Shane Elizabeth

Born 1956
Australian swimmer who broke or equalled 11
world records, all as a teenager

Shane Gould was born in Brisbane, Queensland, the day after the opening ceremony of the 1956 Melbourne Olympics. Between 1971 and 1972 she set world records at every freestyle distance from 100 metres to 1,500 metres. Her time of 58.5 seconds for the 100m freestyle broke the record set by **Dawn Fraser** in 1964. Gould became the first woman to win three individual swimming golds in world record times at the 1972 Olympics — in the 200 metres individual medley and 200 metres and 400 metres freestyle — and also won a silver and a bronze medal.

As well as breaking or equalling 11 world records throughout her short career, she won

Shane Gould, 1972

numerous Australian individual championships, all before retiring at the age of 17 to marry and become a social welfare worker.

Gourd, Emilie

Born 1879   Died 1946
Swiss feminist and writer, founder of the
newspaper Le mouvement féministe

Emilie Gourd founded and edited the newspaper *Le mouvement féministe*. She campaigned on behalf of women's rights, particularly taking up the cause of women's suffrage on which she continually lobbied the Swiss authorities at both regional and national level.

She was President of the Swiss Women's Association from 1914 to 1928, and secretary of the International Alliance of Women. Her writings include a biography of the American suffragist **Susan B Anthony**.

Gournay, Marie le Jars de

Born 1565   Died 1645
French writer and feminist who was adopted by
Montaigne and edited his essays

Marie le Jars de Gournay was born in Paris and on her father's death her family moved to the family estate in Picardy. Despite her mother's opposition to a formal education for girls, Marie read widely and also learned Latin.

At the age of 18 she read Montaigne's *Essais* and when she went to Paris in 1588 to be presented at court, she arranged to meet him. He adopted her and subsequently spent some time at her family estate. She published *Le Proumenoir de M de Montaigne* (1594) after his death in 1592 and a posthumous edition of his *Essais* (1595). She is also remembered for her translations of Virgil, Ovid and Tacitus and for her controversial feminist work *Égalité des hommes et des femmes* (1622).

Grable, Betty (Elizabeth Ruth)

Born 1916   Died 1973
American actress whose legs were insured with
Lloyds of London for $1 million

Betty Grable was born in St Louis, Missouri. From 1928 she lived in Los Angeles, studying dancing and subsequently making her film début as a chorus girl in *Let's Go Places* (1930). Under contract to several major studios, she appeared in numerous small roles throughout the next decade but began to build a strong following at Twentieth Century-Fox when she appeared in such popular fare as *Down Argentine Way* (1940) *and Moon Over Miami* (1941).

A pleasing singer, capable dancer and competent actress, her girl-next-door good looks and shapely legs made her a favourite pin-up girl of wartime troops. Her most successful films, usually colourful, escapist musicals, include *The Dolly Sisters* (1945), *Mother More Tights* (1947) and *How To Marry A Millionaire* (1953).

She made her last film appearance in *How To Be Very Very Popular* (1955), but continued to work in cabaret and on stage in such productions *as Hello, Dolly!* (1965–7) and *Belle Starr* (1969).

Grace, Patricia, *also known as* Ngati Toa, Ngati Raukawa *and* Te Ati Awa

Born 1937
New Zealand writer for adults and children, the first Maori writer to publish a story in English and the first Maori novelist

Patricia Grace was born in Wellington. She specialized in English as her second language and began writing while her seven children were still young. Her first publication was a collection of short stories, *Waiariki* (1975), which was followed by her novel *Mutuwhenua: The Moon Sleeps* (1978) on cultural conflicts in a mixed marriage. Next came *The Dream Sleepers and Other Stories* (1980), a further novel, *Potiki* (1986), with its emphatic Maori viewpoint of Paheka (white settler) standards, and *Electric City and Other Stories* (1987).

She treats the Maori culture and community in realistic narrative and deals much with the significance of their extended family relationships. Her later books also examine the treatment of the Maoris within New Zealand culture and consequently are more political in tone.

Graf, Steffi

Born 1969
*German lawn tennis player, six times winner at Wimbledon, and joint world No. 1 with **Monica Seles***

Steffi Graf was born in Bruehl. In 1982 she became the youngest person to receive a World Tennis Association ranking, aged 13, and she first came to prominence in 1984 when she won the Olympic demonstration event and reached the last 16 at Wimbledon.

In 1985 she reached the semi-final of the US Open, though she won it 10 years later, and in 1988 she won the Grand Slam of the four major singles titles (American, British, French and Australian) as well as the gold medal at the Seoul Olympics. Surprisingly, she was de-feated in the 1989 French final, by Arantxa Sanchez, but retained her Wimbledon title that year and won again in 1991–3 and 1995. She has also won various doubles titles.

Graham, Katherine Meyer, *née* Meyer

Born 1917
American newspaper owner and publisher hailed as the 'most powerful woman in America' in the mid-1970s

Katherine Meyer was born in New York City, the daughter of the financier and publisher Eugene Meyer. She was educated at Vassar College and the University of Chicago before beginning her career at the San Francisco *News*. In 1939 she joined the editorial team of the her father's newspaper, the Washington *Post*. The following year she married Philip Graham, who also joined the *Post* as associate publisher in 1946.

Meyer sold the paper to his daughter and her husband in 1948 for a token amount of money, and their newly formed Washington Post Company, with Philip as its president, bought *Newsweek* magazine in 1961 and began to enlarge in circulation and influence. However Philip suffered a mental illness and committed suicide in 1963. Though nearly overcome by grief, Katherine Graham stepped into the presidency (1963–73) and emerged as a tough media tycoon, also taking charge of several television and radio stations.

In 1971 the *Post* won a legal battle over press freedom and was supported in the publication of the 'Pentagon Papers', an exposé of high-echelon military activities. The following year it came to international attention when its editors, who benefited from a policy of editorial freedom, investigated the Watergate scandal, which led to the resignation of President Nixon in 1974. In 1979 Graham was succeeded as publisher of the Washington *Post* by her son Donald Graham, who became the company's president and chief executive in 1991.

Graham, Martha

Born 1894 Died 1991
American dancer, teacher and choreographer acclaimed as a pioneer of modern dance

Martha Graham was born in Pittsburgh. She trained in Los Angeles with the Denishawn School and appeared on stage first in vaudeville and revue. In 1926, after a period performing with the Ruth St Denis and Ted

Shawn companies, she made her independent début in Manhattan.

Influenced greatly by the composer Louis Horst, her early work constitutes a remarkable contribution to the American Constructivist movement and to the development of modern dance. *Lamentation* (1930) and *Frontier* (1935) are among her better-known early works. In 1930 she founded the Dance Repertory Theatre, in which she trained the company in her own method, which was to use every aspect of the body and the mind to dramatic purpose — movement, breathing and muscular control.

Her ballets are based on the same idea of unity in décor, choreography and music and, frequently, spoken dialogue. One of her best-known ballets, *Appalachian Spring* (1958), was a product of her great interest in Native American life and mythology and the early American pioneer spirit, and much of her work was based on the reinterpretation of ancient myths and historical characters. She was director and teacher of dancing at the Martha Graham School of Contemporary Dance in New York from 1927, and her method of dance training has been widely adopted in schools and colleges around the world.

Grahn, Lucile

Born 1819 Died 1907
Danish ballet dancer who was acclaimed as one of the most accomplished of her time

Lucile Grahn was born in Copenhagen. She made her official début at the age of seven, and subsequently studied and worked in the Royal Danish Ballet with choreographer Auguste Bournonville, creating Astrid in his *Valdemar* (1835) and then becoming his first *La Sylphide* in 1836.

To escape his influence she based herself in Paris, also dancing in Hamburg, St Petersburg and London. Nicknamed the 'Taglioni of the North', her lightness was outstanding and her ability to pirouette legendary. She retired from the stage in 1856, and became ballet mistress at the Leipzig State Theatre (1858–61) and then with the Munich Court Opera (1869–75), where she assisted Richard Wagner in the production of *Das Rheingold* and *Die Meistersinger von Nürnberg*.

There is a street in Munich named the Lucile Grahn Strasse after her.

Grand, Sarah, *pseud of* Frances Elizabeth Bellenden McFall, *née* Clarke

Born 1854 Died 1943
British novelist who is credited with coining the phrase 'new woman'

Frances Clarke was born of English parentage in Donaghadee, Ireland. At the age of 16 she married an army doctor, D C McFall (d.1898), but left him after about 23 years and adopted a pseudonym under which she published her first few volumes.

Her reputation rests on *The Heavenly Twins* (1893) and *The Beth Book* (1898). In the former she skilfully handles sex problems, such as syphilis, and denounces the immorality of the Contagious Diseases Act. The latter book is partly autobiographical, covering the heroines' girlhood, disillusionment in marriage and goal of independence.

Grand reportedly coined the phrase 'new woman' in 1894 to describe herself and a new generation of women who were in favour of women's rights, female suffrage, higher education for women and dress equality. Her later works, including *The Winged Victory* (1916), are advocacies of feminine emancipation.

Grange, Lady Rachel, *née* Chiesley

Died 1745
Scottish noblewoman whose husband silenced her with imprisonment in the Hebrides

Lady Grange was the wife of the Lord Justice Clerk of Scotland, James Erskine, Lord Grange (1679–1754). She was a bad-tempered woman, and was opposed to her husband's Jacobite views (he was the brother of the leader of the 1715 Jacobite rising, the 6th Earl of Mar, 1675–1732). On threatening to expose her husband's conspiratorial views one night in 1731, she was spirited away to the Hebrides, while her death was announced in Edinburgh and a mock funeral held.

After three years of captivity on a lonely island off North Uist, she was sent to the remote island group of St Kilda, where she was held incommunicado on the island of Hirta for eight years (1734–42). She was then taken back to the Western Isles, where she managed to smuggle a letter to her cousin, the Lord Advocate, who sent a gunboat to look for her, but failed to trace her whereabouts. She died on the Vaternish peninsula.

Grant of Rothiemurcus, Elizabeth

Born 1797 Died 1885
Scottish diarist of social history known for her posthumous work Memoirs of a Highland Lady *(1898)*

Elizabeth Grant was born in Edinburgh, the daughter of Sir John Peter Grant, a lawyer, Whig MP and Highland landowner, who moved his family from Edinburgh to London and back in search of a profitable legal practice. His final Edinburgh venture failed and the family moved under the shadow of debt to the family house at The Doune, near Aviemore.

Elizabeth and her sisters were obliged to write stories and articles to raise money. Her brother was imprisoned by his creditors in 1826 and the next year her father fled to India to escape a similar fate. There he became Judge of Bombay and Chief Justice of Calcutta, and Elizabeth married Colonel Henry Smith of Baltiboys, County Wicklow, Ireland (1829), who had 10 days previously inherited the 1,200-acre estate from his brother. She raised a family, Smith dying in 1867, managed the estate with an awe-inspiring maternalism through the Irish great famine and beyond, and wrote memoirs and diaries for the amusement of her children.

These memoirs, written under her maiden name, are famous for their account of Edinburgh society and customs. Her diaries were published in part as *The Irish Journals of Elizabeth Smith 1840–1850* (1980), and in part as *The Highland Lady in Ireland* (1991). A strikingly forceful, if self-righteous witness, she makes the reader a confidant while describing her difficult life in an interesting period of personal and national change.

Grasso, Ella Tambussi

Born 1919 Died 1981
American politician, the first woman elected to the post of governor on her own merit and stature, rather than that of her husband

Ella Tambussi Grasso was born in Windsor Locks, Connecticut. After serving in numerous political and state posts, she became Secretary of State in the Connecticut legislature in 1958.

A Democrat, she was elected to the US House of Representatives in 1970 and began her first term as governor in 1974 with her state of Connecticut in financial trouble. By developing an austerity budget (ie spending only on programs mandated by law and necessities such as hospitals) and making harsh cuts, she was able to balance the state budget and create a surplus in revenues.

Midway through her second term as governor, she was diagnosed with ovarian cancer and resigned in 1980.

Grau, Shirley Ann

Born 1929
American novelist and short-story writer whose writing examines the difficulty of coping with racism

Shirley Ann Grau was born in New Orleans, Louisiana, and educated at Tulane University. Her short stories began appearing in magazines such as the *New Yorker* and *The Saturday Evening Post* as early as 1954.

Her first book, *The Black Prince and Other Stories* (1955), was highly acclaimed. In 1965 she won a Pulitzer Prize for her novel *The Keepers of the House* (1964), which tells the story of a mixed race family whose members are related to the Klan. Her other works include *The Condor Passes* (1971) and *Nine Women* (1985).

She has been termed a 'regional writer' because of her concerns with the South and race relations. She taught creative writing at the University of New Orleans in 1966–7.

Gray, Eileen

Born 1878 Died 1976
Irish architect and designer famous for her lacquer screens and furniture

Eileen Gray was born in Enniscorthy, County Wexford. She entered the Slade School of Art in 1898 and developed an interest in Japanese lacquer, then moved to Paris in 1902 and studied at both the Académie Colarossi and Académie Julian. She also worked with Japanese craftsman Sugawara.

Having mastered the art of laquering, she began to design furniture and started making carpets, lamps and wall hangings. In 1922 she opened her widely admired Galerie Jean Désert in the Rue du Faubourg Saint-Honoré, where she showed her famous lacquer screens. Among her patrons were Jacques Doucet and Suzanne Talbot, for whom she designed a spectacular apartment in the Rue de Lota. Self-taught as an architect, at a time when women architects were very rare, in 1929 she worked in the modern movement with Jean Badovici, designing the first of her two houses (called E1027) in the South of France. She later exhibited at the Paris 1937 Exhibition with Le Corbusier.

Though Gray was an extremely influential and prolific designer of the 1920s and 1930s, in her later years she lived a lonely, reclusive life. However in the 1960s her work was 'rediscovered' and she witnessed the revival of her art while in her nineties. Her furniture designs were reproduced in Italy, France and the UK.

Gray, Hanna Holborn, *née* Holborn

Born 1930
German-born American historian who became the first woman to head a major university in the USA

Hanna Holborn was born in Heidelberg, Germany, the daughter of the historian Hajo Holborn who fled the Nazis with his family in 1934 and settled in the USA. She married Charles Montgomery Gray in 1954 and, as a Renaissance and Reformation scholar, worked in various universities during the 1950s and 1960s.

In 1974 she was appointed Professor of History and provost of Yale, becoming acting President in 1977–8. Her appointment as President of the University of Chicago (1978–93) made her the first woman to head a major US university.

Gréco, Juliete

> Born 1927
> French singer and actress who sang 'Je suis bien'

Juliete Gréco was born in Montpelier, and she began her career in Left Bank clubs at the end of World War II. In 1949, at the height of Existentialism, she made her first cabaret appearance at Le Boeuf sur le Toit, establishing herself as the archetypal interpreter of world-weary lyrics, delivered in a half-sung, half-spoken style.

As 'diseuse', she recorded many songs by Jacques Prévert and Josef Kosma (notably 'Les feuilles mortes'), Charles Aznavour ('Je hais les dimanches') and above all Jacques Brel ('Je suis bien'). Gréco had a much-publicized relationship with another contemporary icon, the jazz trumpeter Miles Davis (1926–91).

Her film appearances include Au royaume des cieux (1949), The Sun Also Rises (1957) and Crack in the Mirror (1957).

Green, Anna Katherine

> Born 1846 Died 1935
> American detective-story writer, the first female author of crime fiction

Anna Green was born in Brooklyn. She began her writing career with well-turned and well received verse, no longer read today.

Her father was a trial lawyer, and The Leavenworth Case (1878) was the first crime fiction to be written by a woman. The style of this well-plotted and exciting novel — it was successfully dramatized, and she married one of the actors — now seems awkward, but it was successfully reprinted in 1934.

Green wrote more of the same, including The Doctor, His Wife, and the Clock (1895).

Green, Lucinda Jane, née Prior-Palmer

> Born 1953
> English equestrian event rider who has won the Badminton Horse Trials six times

Lucinda Prior-Palmer was born in London. She became an outstanding three-day eventer, winning the Badminton Horse Trials a record six times (1973, 1976–7, 1979, 1983–4) and the Badminton and Burghley Horse Trials in the same year, on 'George' in 1977. She was individual European champion in 1975 and 1977, and the 1982 world champion on 'Regal Realm', when she also won a team gold medal.

She later turned to commentating — she was the BBC television commentator for Badminton (1987–92) and for the 1988 Olympics, and commentator on Australian television for the 1992 Olympics — and was an editorial consultant for the magazine Eventing (1989–92). She married Australian eventer David Green in 1981.

Green, Mary Anne Everett, née Wood

> Born 1818 Died 1895
> English historian who indexed the state papers of the reigns of James I, Charles II and Elizabeth I

Mary Wood was born in Sheffield, the daughter of a Methodist minister. Following a home education, she continued her studies in the British Museum reading room. Her early publications included Letters of Royal Ladies of Great Britain and Lives of the Princesses of Great Britain (1849); the latter had to be delayed for six years because of a rival publication on the queens of England by Agnes Strickland.

In 1846 she married the painter George Pycock Green and travelled with him in Europe for a couple of years. Later he was to become disabled, and she learnt the technique of painting in order to help him.

In 1853 she was appointed to calendar the state papers of the reigns of James I (1857–8) and Charles II (1860–8), and later of Queen Elizabeth I, with addenda (1869–74). She also later edited the Commonwealth papers (1875–88). Inspired by her own children's studies, she also wrote on education.

Greenaway, Kate (Catherine)

> Born 1846 Died 1901
> English writer, artist and illustrator of children's books

Kate Greenaway was the daughter of a London wood-engraver. She started publishing her immensely popular portrayals of child life in magazines, then made them into books, beginning in 1879 with a collection of her children's verse entitled *Under the Window*, followed by *Kate Greenaway's Birthday Book* (1880), *Mother Goose* (1881), *Little Ann* (1883) and *Marigold Garden* (1885). Though she preferred to write her own text, she illustrated Robert Browning's *Pied Piper of Hamelin* (1889).

Her charming drawings evoking an idyllic world of happily playing children and flower-filled gardens were praised by art critics worldwide and influenced both the literary area of book illustration and the social area of children's dress. During the late 1890s she exhibited her watercolour drawings at the Fine Art Society gallery. The Greenaway medal is awarded annually for the best British children's book artist.

Greenhow, Rose O'Neal

Born 1817   Died 1864
American Confederate spy in the American
Civil War

Rose O'Neal Greenhow, who was born in Port Tobacco, Maryland, was the wife of the doctor and historian, Robert Greenhow, and lived in Washington DC during the Civil War. As a society hostess she overheard information regarding Union troop movements which she is reputed to have passed to the Confederate government.

She was placed under house arrest in 1861 and later exiled to the Confederacy in 1862. She ran the blockade and travelled to England and France representing the Confederate states, but her ship foundered on her return and she drowned off the North Carolina coast. She published an account of her exploits in 1863, *My Imprisonment and the First Year of Abolition Rule at Washington*.

Greenwood, Joan

Born 1921   Died 1987
English actress who was a leading lady of the
1940s

Joan Greenwood was born in Chelsea. She studied at RADA before making her stage début in *Le Malade Imaginaire* (1938). Her film début came in *John Smith Wakes Up* (1940) and her early theatre work included *The Women* (1939) and *Peter Pan* (1941–2).

A woman of distinctive style, her husky tones and feline grace allowed her to be witty and sensual in the portrayal of classical roles and contemporary *femmes fatales*. She toured

with ENSA during the war and appeared with Donald Wolfit's company thereafter.

Her film credits include the influential and enduring Ealing comedies *Whisky Galore* (1948), *Kind Hearts and Coronets* (1949) and *The Man in the White Suit* (1951), and later, *Tom Jones* (1963) and *Little Dorrit* (1987). Later stage successes numbered *Lysistrata* (1957), *Hedda Gabler* (1960) and *Oblomov* (1964). She married actor André Morell in 1960.

Greer, Germaine

Born 1939
Australian feminist, author and lecturer who has
become established as a significant feminist voice

Germaine Greer was born in Australia. She attended the universities of Melbourne, Sydney and Cambridge before becoming a lecturer in English at Warwick University (1968–73). Her controversial and highly successful book *The Female Eunuch* (1970) portrayed marriage as a legalized form of slavery for women and attacked the systematic denial and misrepresentation of female sexuality by male-dominated society.

She is a regular contributor to newspapers and periodicals, and a frequent television panellist, and in 1979 became director of the Tulsa Centre for the Study of Women's Literature.

Her later works include *Sex and Destiny: the Politics of Human Fertility* (1984) and *The Change* (1991), the latter documenting her discoveries and conclusions concerning the menopausal transformation in women.

Germaine Greer, 1975

Gregory, (Isabella) Augusta, *née* Persse

Born 1852 Died 1932
Irish playwright and a leading figure in the Irish
literary revival whose home at Coole Park became
a focus for the movement

Augusta Persse was born into a wealthy family at Roxborough House near Coole, County Galway. The Gregory family were nearby landowners, and in 1880 Augusta Persse married Sir William Henry Gregory (1817–92), who was Governor of Ceylon (1872–7).

After her husband's death, Lady Augusta plunged deeper into her study of Irish mythology and folklore, an interest which led in 1896 to her meeting W B Yeats (1865–1939). She shared his vision of a reinvigorated Irish drama, and with Yeats and the writer Edward Martyn (1859–1923), co-founded the Abbey Theatre, Dublin, which opened in December 1904.

Lady Gregory wrote or translated about 40 short plays about the Irish rural peasantry, including the comedy, *Spreading the News* (1904), the patriotic *Cathleen ni Houlihan* (1902, with Yeats) and *The Rising of the Moon* (1906). *The Gaol Gate* (1906) is a tragedy, while *The White Cockade* (1905) and *The Deliverer* (1911) are history plays. She also translated Molière and wrote versions of the Irish legends in dialect.

Grenfell, Joyce

Born 1910 Died 1979
English entertainer whose comic monologues were
fuelled by the foibles of middle-class spinsters

Joyce Grenfell was born in London. She made her début in *The Little Revue* in 1939 and, after touring hospitals with concert parties during World War II, appeared in revue until the early 1950s, delivering comic monologues.

She later appeared in her own one-woman shows, such as *Joyce Grenfell Requests The Pleasure*. Her monologues exploited the foibles and manners of middle-class, home counties schoolmistresses and ageing spinster daughters.

Her autobiography is *Joyce Grenfell Requests the Pleasure* (1976), and she also wrote *George, Don't Do That* (1977).

Gréville, Henry, *pseud* of Alice Marie Céleste Fleury Durand-Gréville, *née* Fleury

Born 1842 Died 1902
French writer who wrote over 70 volumes of novels
and short stories about Russian society

Alice Fleury was born in Paris. She was highly educated and accompanied her journalist father to St Petersburg in 1857 when he became Professor of French at the university there. She learnt the Russian language and began writing articles about Russian culture under the pseudonym Henry Gréville. She married Emile-Alex Durand (1838–1914), also a Professor of French, and they returned to France in 1872.

Her Russian society novels are no longer read, but were very popular in their day. They include *Les Epreuves de Raïssa* (1877, 'The Trials of Raïssa') and *Louk Loukitch* (1890). Her *Instruction morale et civique des jeunes filles* (1881, 'Moral and Civil Education for Girls') was put on the *Index Librorum Prohibitorum*, a list of books which members of the Roman Catholic Church were forbidden to read, even though it voiced the conventional opinion that a woman's place is at home serving her family and/or husband.

Grey, Dame Beryl Elizabeth, *stage-name of* Mrs Beryl Svenson, *née* Groom

Born 1927
English ballet dancer who performed the role of
Giselle at the age of 16

Beryl Groom was born in London. She won a scholarship to Sadler's Wells Ballet School at the age of nine, and her first solo appearance at Sadler's Wells Theatre was in the part of Sabrina, in *Comus*, in 1941. She married Dr Sven Gustav Svenson in 1950.

The youngest Giselle ever at the age of 16, she was prima ballerina of the Sadler's Wells Ballet (1942–57), and has also appeared with the Bolshoi Ballet in Russia (1957–8) (the first English ballerina to do so) and the Chinese Ballet in Peking and Shanghai (1964, the first Western ballerina to do so).

She was artistic director (1968–79) of the London Festival Ballet, which became the English National Ballet in 1988, and now serves on various committees connected with her art.

Grey, Lady Jane

Born 1537 Died 1554
Queen of England for only nine days who was
executed for the privilege

Jane Grey was born in Bradgate, Leicestershire, the eldest daughter of Henry Grey, Marquess of Dorset, and Frances Brandon, daughter of the Duke of Suffolk. A beautiful and intelligent girl, she was well educated under the tutorship of John Aylmer (later

Bishop of London), proving to be especially proficient at languages.

During the final illness of Edward VI, she was married against her will on 21 May 1553 to Lord Guildford Dudley, fourth son of the lord protector, John Dudley, the Earl of Warwick, as part of the latter's schemes to ensure a Protestant succession.

Declared queen on 10 July, four days after Edward's death, she was rapidly superseded on 19 July by the rightful heir, Edward's Catholic sister **Mary I**, and made prisoner in the Tower. Following a rebellion in her favour under Sir Thomas Wyatt, in which her father (from 1551 Duke of Suffolk) also took part, she was beheaded with her husband on 12 February 1554.

Grey, Maria Georgina, née Shirreff

Born 1816   Died 1906
English writer and pioneer of women's education
who worked to set new standards for girls'
education

Maria Shirreff was the sister of **Emily Shirreff**, and she married her cousin William Thomas Grey in 1841. With her sister she helped to found the National Union for Promoting the Higher Education of Women (1871), which created the Girls' Public Day School Company (later Trust) in 1872 to establish 'good and cheap Day Schools for Girls of all classes above those attending the Public Elementary Schools'.

Eventually it had some 38 schools, of which one of the first, Croydon, had a kindergarten. Also with her sister, Maria Grey revived interest in the work of the German educationalist Friedrich Froebel and promoted the Froebel Society. The Women's Educational Union opened what was later called Maria Grey College in 1878 as a training college for teachers in higher grade girls' schools.

Her writings include *Passion and Principle* (1853) and *Love Sacrifice* (1868), both written with her sister, and works on women's enfranchisement and education.

Grey, Tanni

Born 1969
Welsh wheelchair track sprinter who became a
champion in the 1992 Paralympics

Tanni Grey is a political science graduate, and well known as an articulate and intelligent representative of her sport.

She won four gold medals at the 1992 Barcelona Paralympics — in the 100 metres, 200 metres, 400 metres and 800 metres, setting world records at 100 and 400 metres and Par-

alympic records in the other two events. Two years later she won another four golds at the world championships in Berlin, as well as a bronze in the 10,000 metres. She was also victorious in the wheelchair event at the London marathon.

Griffith, Melanie

Born 1957
American film actress who has overcome drug
dependency to win favourable comparison with
Marilyn Monroe

Melanie Griffith was born in New York City, the daughter of actress Tippi Hedren (1935–   ). She was a child model and actress who is said to have made her first television commercial at the age of nine months. She was briefly seen in the film *Smith!* (1969) but made her first impact as an actress with roles as promiscuous teenagers in *Night Moves* (1975) and *The Drowning Pool* (1975). This early promise was not fulfilled as she developed a drink and drug dependency that left her with an unreliable reputation in Hollywood.

After studying acting in New York she began to make a breakthrough in the 1980s, such as a pornographic film star in *Body Double* (1984) and in *Something Wild* (1986). A curvacious blonde, with a breathy, little-girl voice, she has managed to combine sensuality and vulnerability, winning generally favourable comparisons to the comic talents of Marilyn Monroe. She was nominated for a Best Actress Oscar for her role as an ambitious secretary in *Working Girl* (1988), and has proved herself a tough and resourceful heroine in thrillers such as *Pacific Heights* (1990) and *A Stranger Among Us* (1992).

She was married to the actor Don Johnson from 1989 to 1995, and appeared with him in *Paradise* (1991).

Griffith-Joyner, Florence, known as Flo-Jo

Born 1959
African-American track and field sprinter who
has been labelled the world's fastest woman

Florence Griffith-Joyner was born in Los Angeles, California. After excelling in high school and college, she won the National Collegiate Athletic Association 200-metre title in 1982. Two years later she won an Olympic silver medal in the 200 metres, and in 1987 she competed in the world track and field championships.

At the 1988 Olympics she won three gold medals — for the 100 metres and 200 metres, setting world records of 10.54 seconds for the former and 21.34 seconds for the latter — and for the 4 × 400-metre relay. That year she was given three major awards: the Jesse Owens Award as the year's outstanding athlete, the 1988 Sullivan Award as the top amateur athlete in the USA, and the 1988 Associated Press Female Athlete of the Year Award.

Griffiths, Ann, *née* Thomas

Born 1776   Died 1805
Welsh hymnwriter whose works were recorded by her maid's husband

Ann Thomas was born in Dolwar-Fechan, Montgomeryshire, the eldest daughter of a farmer. Following her conversion to Christianity through evangelical preaching, she joined the Methodist society at Pont Robert in 1797, entering into correspondence with the Methodist minister and preacher John Hughes.

Ann composed hymns in Welsh and recited them to her maid Ruth Evans, who later married Hughes, who wrote the hymns down for his wife. They were published after Ann had died in childbirth, just a year after her marriage in 1804 to the farmer Thomas Griffiths of Meifod.

Though difficult to set to music, the hymns, written in Welsh, are renowned for their depth of feeling and bold metaphors.

Grigson, (Heather Mabel) Jane

Born 1928   Died 1990
English cookery writer whose books have become cookery classics

Jane Grigson was educated at Newnham College, Cambridge, and after graduating she worked as an editorial assistant (1953–5) before becoming a translator from Italian (1956–67). Her first book *Charcuterie and French Pork Cookery* (1967) acknowledged the influence of **Elizabeth David** on her work, but she developed her own style of elegant and appetite-awakening description.

As cookery correspondent for the *Observer* magazine, she continued to write books, three of which are acknowledged to be classics in their field: *English Food* (1974), *Jane Grigson's Vegetable Book* (1978) and *Jane Grigson's Fruit Book* (1982).

She was married to the poet Geoffrey Grigson (1905–85) and lived with him in Wiltshire, with frequent visits to Trôo in France; her country lifestyle much influenced her cookery interests.

Grimké, Sarah Moore *and* Angelina Emily

Sarah born 1792; died 1873
Angelina born 1805; died 1879
American feminists and social reformers who led a combined campaign for the emancipation of both slaves and women

Sarah and Angelina Grimké were born in Charleston, South Carolina, the daughters of a slave-owning judge. Revolted by the practice of slavery, Sarah moved to Philadelphia in 1821, becoming a Quaker, and was joined in 1829 by her sister. Together they set out to eradicate slavery.

Angelina vigorously appealed to the women of America to support their fight against slavery in *Appeal to the Christian Women of the South* (1836) and *Appeal to Women of the Nominally Free States* (1837). Sarah wrote *Epistle to the Clergy of the Southern States* (1836), but in response to these works the two were threatened with imprisonment should they return to South Carolina. Nevertheless they freed the slaves whom they had inherited as part of their father's estate.

The sisters moved to New York in 1836, where they lectured for the American Anti-Slavery Society (the first women to do so), and broadened their concern to include women's emancipation; the Grimkés were largely responsible for linking the anti-slavery and women's rights movements. In 1838 Angelina married the abolitionist Theodore Dwight Weld and Sarah joined them. The sisters both lectured and taught until their joint retirement in 1867. Sarah's other works include *The Condition of Women* (1838) and their most significant joint work is *American Slavery as it is: Testimony of a Thousand Witnesses* (1838).

Gripe, Maria

Born 1923
Swedish writer of novels for children and young adults who has seen her books translated into more than 20 languages

Maria Gripe was brought up in Örebro and educated at Stockholm University. Her first real success was her ninth novel, *Josefin* (1961), about a lonely young girl, struggling to cope with the puzzling and frightening world of the grown-ups around her; as in her five later novels about the young boy Elvis Karlsson (1972–9), events are told strictly from the child's point of view.

These novels remained within the confines of realism, but in later books Gripe incorporates supernatural elements within a realistic frame, such as in the fairy-tale *Glas-*

blåsarnas barn (1964, 'The Glass-blower's Children'), and in *Tordyveln flyger i skymningen* (1978, 'The Chafer Flies at Dusk'), in which past and present, natural and supernatural are skilfully interwoven. In *Skuggan över stenbänken* (1982, 'The Shadow across the Stone Bench'), the first of a series of 'shadow' novels set at the turn of the century, she further develops this style, blending the realistic with elements of a classical horror story.

Maria Gripe is the recipient of numerous national and international awards, among them the Hans Christian Andersen International Medal in 1974. She works in close conjunction with her illustrator husband, Harald Gripe.

Grisi, Carlotta, *originally* Caronne Adele Josephine Marie Grisi

Born 1819   Died 1899
Italian ballet dancer who created the title role in Giselle

Caronne Grisi was born in Visinada, Istria, the cousin of the Italian sopranos **Giuditta** and **Giulia Grisi**. She was trained in Milan at the ballet school of La Scala and made her début before the age of 10. She danced with and studied under Jules Perrot, who became her husband.

Following enormous successes in London and Venice, she went to the Paris Opéra, where she was highly acclaimed and became the first to dance the title role of the Romantic ballet *Giselle* in 1841. Other ballets in which Grisi danced original roles include *Esmerelda* (1844) and *Paquita* (1846).

After dancing in the 1854 season in Warsaw, she retired to spend the rest of her life near Geneva, Switzerland.

Grisi, Giuditta

Born 1805   Died 1840
Italian mezzo-soprano who created the role of Romeo in I Capuleti ed i Montecchi

Giuditta Grisi was born in Milan, the older sister of **Giulia Grisi**. She was trained at the Milan Conservatory, and in 1826 she made her début in Vienna in Gioacchino Rossini's *Bianco e Faliero*.

She was the original Romeo in Vincenzo Bellini's *I Capuleti ed i Montecchi* in 1830, and also sang in his *Il pirata* and *La straniera*. Her career took her to London, Paris and Madrid.

She married Count Barni, and retired in 1838.

Grisi, Giulia

Born 1811   Died 1869
Italian soprano who was one of the great singers of her day

Giulia Grisi was born in Milan, the younger sister of **Giuditta Grisi**, who taught her. During her magnificent career of 30 years, she was renowned for her performances in the operas of Vincenzo Bellini. The roles he created for her included Giulietta in *I Capuleti ed i Montecchi* (1830), in which Grisi played opposite her sister's Romeo, and Adalgisa in *Norma* (1831). In 1835 he wrote *I Puritani* for a famous quartet which included her.

She also performed in the operas of Gioacchino Rossini, such as the title role of *Semiramide* (Paris, 1832) and Ninetta in *La gazza ladra* (London, 1834). From 1839 she enjoyed a successful professional partnership with the Italian tenor Giovanni Mario, and, though they never married, their personal relationship continued until she died.

Grotell, Maija

Born 1899   Died 1973
Finnish potter who won prizes for her early Art Deco style work

Maija Grotell was born in Finland. She studied painting, sculpture and design at the school of industrial arts, and was a post-graduate student of A W Finch. In 1927 she moved to the USA, where she worked for a ceramics studio in New York and then taught at Rutgers University in New Jersey (1936–8). She won prizes in Barcelona and Paris for her early work in Art Deco style, decorated with harbour scenes.

She became head of the ceramics department of the Cranbrook Academy of Art, Michigan, in 1938, where she continued to teach and inspire her students until her retirement in 1966. She also continued to experiment with her own work, throwing earthenware and stoneware bowls and vases, and became noted for rough-textured glazes, including a cratered glaze achieved by using a stoneware glaze over Albany Slip.

Her work is in many private and public collections in the USA.

Groza, Maria

Born 1918
Romanian economist and politician

Maria Groza was born in Deva and educated at the Bucharest Academy of Economics. She worked for the Ministry of Foreign Affairs (1948–55) while continuing to teach for the

Academy of Economics; she became a full-time teacher at the Academy in 1955.

A long-time influential figure in the Romanian National Council of Women (she was its Vice-President from 1965 to 1975, having previously been its secretary), Groza has also held important positions within the Romanian government administration. She has been an official delegate to various international women's conferences, UNESCO and UN congresses and has chaired various UN committees.

Grumbach, Argula von, *née* von Stauffer

Born 1492   Died after 1563
German Protestant who is remembered as an early
theological debater

Argula von Stauffer was brought up as maid to Kunigunde, mother of Duke William of Bavaria who declared himself her protector on the death of her parents, soon after she arrived at court at the age of 10. She was married to Friedrich von Grumbach in 1516.

In 1523 Argula publicly protested to the University of Ingolstadt for forcing a young lecturer, Arsacius Seehofer, to retract Protestant views. Her letter to the university, and a copy to the Duke — along with a further protest about clerical abuses — went unanswered, although her husband lost his job and maltreated her, and her family opposed her.

Argula corresponded with Luther, whom she met in 1530, shortly before her husband's death. After a brief second marriage, she devoted her energies to her estates and family, although she was imprisoned for a time in 1563 for religious activities forbidden to women.

Gubaidulina, Sofia Asgatovna

Born 1931
Russian composer who made her name in the late
1960s using avant-garde techniques

Sofia Gubaidulina was born in Chistopol in the Tatar SSR and has been resident in Germany since 1991. She was educated at Kazan (1949–54) and Moscow (1954–63) conservatories and for the next decade worked in the Soviet theatre and film industry, as accompanist and composer, with a special interest in electronic music.

In 1975, the year her choral/orchestral *Steps* won an International Composers' Competition in Rome, she co-founded the improvising ensemble Astreja, of which she remains a member.

Her work is devotional, drawing on her complex cultural background; major pieces include the violin concerto *Offertorium* (1980–6), the remarkable *Seven Words* (1982), which was initially suppressed, and the symphony *Stimmen . . . Verstummen* (1986).

Guggenheim, Peggy (Marguerite)

Born 1898   Died 1979
American art collector who made one of the best
collections of post-1910 modern art in Europe

Peggy Guggenheim was born in New York City. She married in 1922 but divorced after eight years and decided to flee her bourgeois and conventional upbringing and lifestyle. From 1930 to 1941 she lived in Paris, socializing with all the prominent figures in the art world there, and purchasing many paintings by new (now famous) artists.

During World War II she returned to the USA with the artist Max Ernst, to whom she was married (1941–5), and opened a gallery called 'Art of This Century' in New York. There the works of the European artists whom she supported, including Jackson Pollock, Mark Rothko and Hans Hofmann, were exhibited, changing the course of American art.

After the War Guggenheim moved to Venice, where she lived on the Grand Canal in the Palazzo Venier dei Leoni, which now houses the famous Guggenheim Collection.

Guilbert, Yvette, *originally* Emma Laure Esther Guilbert

Born 1865   Died 1944
French comedienne who rose to stardom with her
apparently innocent delivery of highly risqué
songs

Emma Guilbert was born in Paris. She was a penniless seamstress before she turned to acting and won fame for her songs and sketches of all facets of Parisian life. After 1890 she became known for her revivals of old French ballads and also sang songs written for her by Aristide Bruant.

Of very thin stature and usually heavily made-up, she often wore a yellow dress and long black gloves, and is depicted in this attire in portraits by Henri Toulouse Lautrec. She visited America and founded a school of acting in New York in 1920.

In 1918 she published *L'Arte de chanter une chanson* (How to Sing a Song), the first textbook on the subject. The novels *La Vedette* and *Les Demi-Vieilles* followed in 1920, and her autobiography, *La Chanson de ma vie* (Song of My Life; My Memories), appeared in 1929.

Sally Gunnell, 1994

Gunnell, Sally Jane Janet

Born 1966
English athlete who won the 'Grand Slam' of
hurdling titles in 1994

Sally Gunnell was born in Chigwell, Essex, the daughter of a farmer, and was brought up in Sussex. Her first national title, at the WAAA (Women's Amateur Athletic Association) junior championships in 1980, was in the long jump. She combined that event with the 100 metres hurdles, but, although she won a Commonwealth gold at that distance in 1986, it slowly became clear that her most successful event would be the 400 metres hurdles.

She made her début in the longer race in 1987, and the following year came fifth in the Seoul Olympics. She took the Commonwealth Games title in 1990 (coming second in the 100m), and then capped a remarkable rise at the Barcelona Olympic Games of 1992, winning the 400m hurdles in a race she dominated from gun to tape. In 1993 at Stuttgart she set her world record time of 52.74 seconds (broken in 1995 by Kim Batten), and the following year at Helsinki she won the European title, achieving her ambition of winning the Grand Slam of Commonwealth, Olympic, World and European titles.

In 1994 she launched a Step and Slide fitness video and planned a range of vitamins with her husband Jonathan Bigg, the former junior England representative in the 800 metres race. The surgical removal of a bone spur in Gunnell's right heel in August 1995 meant a lengthy and painful hiatus in her starstruck career, but by the end of the year she was back in training for the 1996 Olympic Games.

Gunning, Elizabeth

Born 1734 Died 1790
Irish socialite who progressed through the ranks
of society to become a baroness

Elizabeth Gunning was born near St Ives, Cambridgeshire, the younger sister of **Maria Gunning**. With her sister, she became famous for her beauty and good figure when they entered London society in 1751. She married the Duke of Hamilton in 1752 and, on his death in 1759, the future Duke of Argyll.

When her sister was suffering from consumption, she too became ill, but after a trip to Italy and France she recovered and was commissioned to accompany Princess **Charlotte** from Germany to England on the occasion of her marriage to George III in 1761. She then became a lady-of-the-bedchamber to the Queen.

In 1770 her husband acceded to his dukedom and in 1776 she was created Baroness Hamilton of Hambledon in Leicestershire.

Gunning, Maria

Born 1733 Died 1760
Irish socialite who was so popular that she needed
a bodyguard

Maria Gunning was born near St Ives, Cambridgeshire, the sister of **Elizabeth Gunning**. Her family were so poor that she is said to have had to borrow clothes from the actress **Mrs Woffington** before she could be presented to the Lord-Lieutenant of Ireland. Both she and her sister were extremely good-looking and when they went to London in 1751 they became known as 'the beauties'.

Maria married the Earl of Coventry in 1752 and, though naïve and unintellectual, was so popular that she was mobbed in Hyde Park in 1759 and thereafter had to be accompanied by a guard. She went to Paris for a time with her husband but her lack of sophistication prevented her from enjoying the same kind of reception there.

She died after a long bout of pulmonary tuberculosis, possibly exacerbated by an addiction to white lead, a white pigment popular with the ladies of the time.

Guthrie, Janet

Born 1938
American motor-racing driver, the first woman to
complete the Indianapolis 500

Janet Guthrie was born in Iowa City, Iowa, and began building and racing cars in 1962. In 1976 she became the first woman to race in a NASCAR Winston Cup event, and also that year qualified for the Indianapolis 500, but was unable to compete because of equipment failure. The following year she became the first woman to compete in the Indianapolis 500, though she did not finish, and in 1978 she competed and finished ninth, establishing herself as the first woman to complete the race.

Her 1978 Indianapolis 500 driver's suit and helmet are in the Smithsonian Institution in Washington DC, and she is a member of the International Women's Sports Hall of Fame.

Guyard, Marie, *also called* Venerable Marie de l'Incarnation

Born 1599   Died 1672
French Catholic missionary to Quebec

Marie Guyard was born in Tours. Widowed after a three-year marriage undertaken to please her parents, she entered the Ursulines in Tours in 1632. She was sent in 1639 with three companions to the Jesuit mission in Quebec to found another religious community there, of which she became the first superior.

Their primarily educational work among the French and the Indians was carried out despite hardship and opposition. Her mystical experiences, which began soon after her husband's death, were recorded in her *Relations* of 1633 and 1654. Her letters, published posthumously, are important sources of early Canadian history.

Guyon, Jeanne Marie de la Motte, *known as* Madame Guyon, *née* Bouvier

Born 1648   Died 1717
French writer, mystic and advocate of Quietism, who became a prominent theological figure

Jeanne Bouvier was born in Montargis. She had intended to become a nun but was married at 16 to the wealthy and elderly Jacques de la Motte Guyon, Lord du Chesnay. On becoming a widow at the age of 28, she determined to devote her life to the poor and needy, and to the cultivation of spiritual perfection. The former part of her plan she began to carry out in 1681 in Geneva, but three years later she was forced to leave on the grounds that her Quietist doctrines (maintaining that religious perfection on earth could be found in passive contemplation of the Deity) were heretical.

In Turin, Grenoble, Nice, Genoa, Vercelli and Paris, where she finally settled in 1686, she became the centre of a movement for the promotion of 'holy living'. In January 1688 she was arrested for heretical opinions and for having been in correspondence with Miguel de Molinos, the leader of Quietism in Spain. Released by the intervention of Madame de **Maintenon**, she entered the royal circle and found an ardent disciple in Abbé de Fénelon, who in 1694 tried to defend her teachings. However the Roman Catholic Church condemned Quietism and Madame Guyon was again imprisoned in 1695. Not released from the Bastille until 1702, she went to Blois to spend the rest of her life writing.

Her works include *Moyen court de faire oraison* (The Short and Very Easy Method of Prayer', 1685); *Le Cantique des Cantiques* (1688), a mystical interpretation of the Song of Solomon; an autobiography; letters; and some spiritual poetry.

Gwyn, Nell (Eleanor)

Born c.1650   Died 1687
English actress who became the vivacious mistress of Charles II

Nell Gwyn was born presumably in Hereford, of humble parentage. She lived precariously as an orange girl before going on the boards at Drury Lane, where she quickly established herself as a comedienne, especially in 'breeches parts'.

Lord Buckhurst was the first protector of 'pretty, witty Nellie's', but the transfer of her affections to Charles II in 1669 was genuine. She had at least one son by the King — Charles Beauclerk, Duke of St Albans — and James Beauclerk is often held to have been a second. She is also said to have urged Charles to found Chelsea Hospital.

She was Charles's only mistress to earn the affection of the people, who enjoyed her presence as the living example of everything that Puritanism denied.

Gwynne-Vaughan, Dame Helen Charlotte Isabella, *née* Fraser

Born 1879   Died 1967
English botanist and servicewoman, honoured for her work during World War I

Helen Fraser was educated at Cheltenham Ladies' College and King's College, London, and in 1911, married Professor Gwynne-Vaughan (d.1915). She was departmental head and later Professor of Botany at Birkbeck College, London (1909–17, 1921–39, 1941–44), and became an authority on fungi.

Her career was interrupted by both World War I and World War II. In the former she was organizer (1917) and later controller of the

Women's Army Auxiliary Air Force in France, and commandant of the Women's Royal Auxiliary Air Force (1918–19), following which she was created DBE. In the latter she was chief controller of the Women's Auxiliary Territorial Service (1939–41). She retired from Birkbeck College in 1944.

Gyp, *pseud of* Gabrielle de Mirabeau, Comtesse de Martel de Janville

Born 1849   Died 1932
French novelist who is remembered both as a prolific author of high-society novels and as an influential anti-Semitic writer

Gabrielle de Mirabeau was born in the château of Koëtsal in Brittany, a descendant of the revolutionary politician Mirabeau. She wrote a series of more than 100 humorous novels, describing fashionable society, of which the best known are *Petit Bob* (1868, 'Little Bob') and *Mariage de Chiffon* (1894, 'Chiffon Marriage').

An ardent nationalist, she was considered influential in her blatant anti-Semitism, and became involved in the scandal concerning Alfred Dreyfus, a Jewish army officer whose tranportation on a false charge caused much division in the French political and literary world.

h

Hadewijch, *also spelt* Hadewych

Born 1230 Died 1297
Dutch poet who was one of the key mystics
of her time

Hadewijch was from the south of The Netherlands. Very little is known of her life, though she is thought to have been involved with a group of women similarly devoted to God.
She wrote devotional prose in the tradition of St Bernard, and established a new genre of mystic love poetry. Some of her letters are translated in *Medieval Netherlands Religious Literature* (1965), by E Colledge.

Hadid, Zaha

Born 1950
Iraqi architect, one of the 'new breed' of
modernists

Zaha Hadid was born in Baghdad and educated at the Architectural Association, London (1972–7). She left college to start her own architectural practice and has already worked in places as far afield as Tokyo, Berlin and Hong Kong.
   Her work is of a conceptual and spatial nature, characterized by zig-zag lines and geometric shapes. It shows the influence of the Russian Constructivists earlier in the 20th century and includes the 'What a Wonderful World' Project (a centre for music, video and architecture) and one of the Pavilions at the Groningen Museum.
   Her design for the Vitra Fire Station was nominated for the 1994 BBC design awards. Also in 1994 she won the competition to design the Cardiff Bay Opera House, which sparked off a lively debate among the local population over the value of modernist architecture.

Hagar

19th century BC
Egyptian servant who features in the Old
Testament narratives about Abraham and his
wife Sarah

Hagar was an Egyptian servant. Since Abraham's wife **Sarah** was apparently barren, tradition held that Abraham should have an heir by Hagar, but when she conceived she 'despised' her mistress, who ill-treated her until she ran away.
   Once in the wilderness, Hagar encountered a messenger from God who persuaded her to return and submit to Sarah, promising her that her descendants would be many. Hagar obeyed and gave birth to a son, Ishmael (Genesis 16). About 14 years later Sarah at last produced a son of her own, Isaac, and at the request of Sarah — who did not want Isaac, who would be considered the firstborn, to have to share his inheritance — Abraham reluctantly expelled Hagar and Ishmael into the wilderness (Genesis 21).
   A divine messenger again came to Hagar's aid, when they had run out of water, and again assured her that Ishmael would become a great nation.

Hainisch, Marianne

Born 1839 Died 1936
Austrian writer and feminist, mother of the
Austrian President Michael Hainisch

Marianne Hainisch was born in Vienna. She campaigned for better educational and employment opportunities for women, including university education and entry to the professions. She also supported the campaign for women's suffrage, and, as founder and President of the *Allgemeiner Osterreichischer Frauenverein*, argued for the reform of the marriage laws and the abolition of legalized prostitution.

Her works include *Die Brötfrage der Frau* (1875), *Frauenarbeit* (1911) and *Die Mutter* (1913). As a pacifist she opposed World War I, and later worked for the Austrian Red Cross, becoming its vice-president.

Haldane, Elizabeth Sanderson

Born 1862 Died 1937
Scottish author and welfare worker, a firm advocate of opportunities for women and improved conditions for the poor

Elizabeth Sanderson Haldane was born in Edinburgh, a sister of the physiologist John Scott Haldane and the statesman Richard Burdon Haldane. She studied nursing and for a while managed the Royal Infirmary, Edinburgh. Influenced by the English reformer **Octavia Hill**, in 1884 she set up a housing organization in Edinburgh to deal with the reconstruction of slums.

After moving to London she was instrumental in saving the Sadler's Wells Theatre and Ballet from bankruptcy. Though not a militant campaigner in the women's rights movement, she was a firm, longstanding supporter, particulary concerning further education for women and entry into the professions. She herself became the first woman justice of the peace in Scotland (1920).

Among her publications are translations of the philosophical works of Descartes and Hegel, a Life of Descartes (1905), commentaries on **George Eliot** (1927) and Mrs **Gaskell** (1930) and other books including *The British Nurse in Peace and War* (1923) and her reminiscences, *From One Century to Another* (1937).

Hale, Sarah Josepha, *née* Buell

Born 1788 Died 1879
American writer who was the first female editor of a magazine and chronicler of her sex

Sarah Josepha Buell was born in Newport, New Hampshire. She was widowed in 1822 with five young children to support and turned to writing, beginning with the two-volume novel *Northwood* (1827). In 1828 she became the first female editor of a magazine — the *Ladies' Magazine*, Boston — and as such was able to influence and shape the thinking of its readership. In 1837 the magazine was bought and for the next 40 years she was employed by its new owner as editor of the *Lady's Book* (later called *Godey's Magazine and Lady's Book*).

Also partly due to her work is the estab-

lishment of the national Thanksgiving celebration. She wrote a book of *Poems for Our Children* (1830) containing 'Mary had a Little Lamb', a collection of poetry by English and American women *The Ladies' Wreath* (1837) and a 2,500-entry biographical book of women entitled *Woman's Record: Or, Sketches of All Distinguished Women from 'the Beginning' till A.D. 1850* (1853).

Halide Edib, (Adivar) *née* Edib

(Adivar), Halide

Halimi, Gisèle Zeïza Elise, *née* Taïeb

Born 1927
French lawyer, writer and feminist, the founder of Choisir

Gisèle Taïeb was born in La Goulette, Tunisia, and educated in Tunis, and at the law faculty and the Institute of Political Studies in Paris. She has married twice; her first husband was Paul Halimi and her second Claude Faux.

She became an advocate in 1948 and practised as a lawyer in Tunisia (1949–56) before being called to the Bar in Paris and practising there, becoming known for her high-profile cases and clients, such as Jean-Paul Sartre and **Simone de Beauvoir**. She also acted as defence lawyer for the Algerian National Liberation Front (FLN) during the Franco-Algerian war, and for the defendants in the notorious Bobigny test-case abortion trial (1972). In 1966 she chaired the Commission of Inquiry into War Crimes in Vietnam.

Halimi's involvement with women's studies includes her co-founding in 1971 of *Choisir*, an organization formed to challenge abortion law in 1972 by defending the women who signed *Manifeste des 343* (thereby admitting that they had had abortions at a time when to do so was illegal in France). *Choisir* also led campaigns on contraception and abortion, contributing to the new laws passed in 1974.

Her publications include two co-authored works, *La Cause des femmes* (1973) and *Le programme commun des femmes* (1978), as well as *Le Lait de l'oranger* (1988). She was elected to the French National Assembly in 1981.

Hall, Jerry Faye

Born 1956
American model whose career has incorporated a successful transition to stage and screen acting

Jerry Hall was born into a Texan farming community and has four sisters and a twin. At first she wanted to be an astronaut or a biologist, but during a trip to Paris in 1973 she was spotted by agents and began modelling for French *Vogue* and designers St Laurent and Thierry Mugler, for whom she still models. Her successful career includes fashion shows, advertising, pop and exercise videos and numerous television appearances.

As an actress she has appeared in US and UK television series, films such as *Batman* (1989) and *Princess Carrabou* (1994), and she starred in the play *Bus Stop* in New Jersey (1987) and London (1989). Her book *Tall Tales* was published in 1984.

With farming still in her blood, she has invested in a Texas horse-breeding ranch. She has lived with Mick Jagger since 1977, marrying him in 1989. They have three children.

Hall, (Marguerite) Radclyffe

Born 1880 Died 1943
English poet and novelist whose treatment of lesbianism in The Well of Loneliness *caused the book to be banned until after her death*

Radclyffe Hall was born in Bournemouth, Hampshire, and educated at King's College, London, and then in Germany. She began as a lyric poet with several volumes of verse, some of which (eg 'The Blind Ploughman') have become songs, but then turned to novel writing with *The Unlit Lamp* (1924) and *The Forge* (1924), the former being the first to include lesbian themes (Radclyffe Hall was a lifelong lesbian).

Her *Adam's Breed* (1926) won the Femina Vie Heureuse and the James Tait Black Memorial prizes, but *The Well of Loneliness* (1928), a largely autobiographical work embodying a sympathetic approach to female homosexuality, caused a prolonged furore and was banned in Britain for many years, though the American court involved disagreed that it was obscene. Her later novels were not controversial.

Hambling, Maggi (Margaret)

Born 1945
English artist who is best known for her portraits of the actor Max Wall

Maggi Hambling was born in Sudbury, Suffolk. She attended Ipswich and Camberwell School of Art prior to studying at the Slade (1967–9), where she won a travelling scholarship to New York.

Whilst she was artist in residence at the National Gallery in London, she met Max Wall (1908–90), and though she has experimented with a variety of subject matter, she is best known for her powerful and expressive portraits of him.

She handles paint in a free manner, occasionally leaving a white ground between areas of colour to highlight atmospheric content. She has exhibited regularly since 1967.

Hamer, Fannie Lou, *née* Townsend

Born 1918 Died 1977
American civil rights leader inspired by her own experiences to fight for justice

Fannie Lou Townsend was born in Montgomery County, Mississippi, and married Perry Hamer in 1942. The grand-daughter of a slave, her life as a plantation worker changed in 1962 when she started to work for the Student Non-Violent Co-ordinating Committee. Her growing commitment to the civil rights movement was affected by her own experiences: in 1961 she was sterilised without her consent, and sacked for attempting to register as a voter.

Throughout the 1960s and 1970s Hamer campaigned for black people's civil rights, promoting voter registration and desegregation of schooling in Mississippi and other states. In 1964, with her co-workers, she founded the Mississippi Freedom Democratic Party. She was elected to the Central Committee of the National Women's Political Caucus at its founding in 1971.

Hamill, Dorothy

Born 1956
American ice-skater who invented the Hamill Camel move

Dorothy Hamill was born in Riverside, Connecticut, and began competing at a young age. In the course of her amateur figure-skating career, she won one world title and three national titles, culminating in a gold medal in the 1976 Olympics.

She is the inventor of the figure-skating move named the Hamill Camel, a spiral spin to a sit spin. After retiring from amateur competition in 1976, she began a successful commercial and media career. She became a member of the US Olympic Hall of Fame in 1991.

Hamilton, Alice

Born 1869 Died 1970
American physician and social reformer who pioneered the study of industrial toxicology

Alice Hamilton was born in New York City. After being educated at home she studied medicine at the University of Michigan, graduating in 1893. She undertook further training in pathology and bacteriology in Europe and was appointed Professor of Pathology at the Woman's Medical College of North Western University in 1897.

Throughout her working life she combined professional medical practice with social concerns, particularly the links between environment and disease, and served on state and national advisory committees on occupational disease. In 1919 she became the first woman professor at Harvard, almost 30 years before Harvard accepted women medical students, and retired in 1935.

Considered the leading authority on lead poisoning in particular and industrial diseases in general, she published extensively, her works including a classic textbook, *Industrial Toxicology*, in 1934.

Hamilton, Edith

Born 1867 Died 1963
American classical scholar and educationalist

Edith Hamilton was born in Dresden and raised in Fort Wayne, Indiana. Educated at home and at Miss Porter's School Farmington, Connecticut, she went on to become Bryn Mawr Fellow in Latin (1894–5), and held the Bryn Mawr European Fellowship in 1895 when she attended Munich and Leipzig Universities. She was headmistress of Bryn Mawr preparatory school in Baltimore from 1896 until 1922.

She was devoted to classical studies; her publications include *The Greek Way* (1930), *The Roman Way* (1932), *The Great Age of Greek Literature* (1943), and her translation of ancient myths, *Mythology* (1942). She was made an honorary citizen of Athens at the age of 90.

Hamilton, Lady Emma, *née* Amy Lyon

Born c.1765 Died 1815
English woman who became the mistress of the naval hero Lord Nelson

Amy Lyon was born in Great Neston, Cheshire, a daughter of a blacksmith. Her girlhood was passed at Hawarden. By 1782 she had had three residences in London, had borne two children to a navy captain and a baronet and had posed as Hygieia in the 'Temple of Health' of James Graham the famous quack; that year she accepted the protection of the Hon Charles Greville (1749–1809) and moved to his home.

Four years later Greville sent her to his uncle, Sir William Hamilton (1730–1803), on the condition that Hamilton would pay his

debts. She became Hamilton's mistress and after five years at Naples, where her beauty captivated Neapolitan society, she married him in 1791.

Already an intimate companion of Queen Maria Caroline, wife of Ferdinand I, she met Admiral (later Viscount) Horatio Nelson in 1793, and on his triumphal return from the Battle of the Nile in 1798, they became lovers. In 1801 she gave birth to a daughter, Horatia (d.1881), later acknowledged by Nelson as his child. After Nelson's death (1805) she squandered her inheritance from her husband and in 1813 was arrested for debt. She died exiled and impoverished.

Hamilton, Mary

Born 1884 Died 1962
English Labour politician, journalist and public servant

Mary Hamilton was the daughter of a professor at Glasgow University. She graduated from Newnham College, Cambridge, with an interest in politics and a first class degree in economics. She became a well known journalist and public speaker and published several novels, including *Dead Yesterday* (1916)

Having joined the Labour Party as a young woman, after two abortive attempts she was elected to parliament in 1929 for Blackburn and became Parliamentary Private Secretary to the Postmaster-General Clement Attlee.

Hammond, Dame Joan Hood

Born 1912
New Zealand-born Australian operatic soprano

Joan Hammond was born in Christchurch. She studied at the Sydney Conservatorium of Music, originally as a violinist. She was an active sportswoman, and won a number of golf and swimming championships up to 1935. When an arm injury forced her to give up the violin, she turned to singing, performing Handel's *Messiah* in London in 1938 and making her operatic début the following year in Vienna.

From 1945 she sang leading roles in some 30 operas and made many recordings; her *O mio babbino caro* from Puccini's *Gianni Schicchi* was the first classical record to win a gold disc for sales of over one million. She retired from singing in 1965 and later became artistic director of the Victoria Opera, and was head of vocal studies at the Victorian College of the Arts (until 1992).

In 1970 she received the Sir Charles Santley award (for musician of the year) from the

Worshipful Company of Musicians in London, and in 1974 she was appointed DBE.

Hamnett, Katharine

Born 1952
English fashion designer who draws inspiration
from the workplace and the environment

Katharine Hamnett was born in Gravesend, Kent, the daughter of a diplomat. She was educated at Cheltenham Ladies College, studied fashion at St Martin's School of Art in London, then worked as a freelance designer, setting up a company (1969–74) and then her own business in 1979, which has been very successful, particularly in selling to other countries such as Japan.

Outspoken and environmentally concerned, she prefers to use natural fibres and draws inspiration for designs from workwear, and from movements such as the peace movement, which she supports.

She made her début in theatrical design for a production of Japanese writer Yukio Mishima's *Madame de Sade* in 1991.

Katharine Hamnett, 1995

Han Suyin, *née* Elizabeth Chow

Born 1917
Chinese-born British novelist and medical
practicioner best known for A Many
Splendoured Thing

Elizabeth Chow was born in Beijing (Peking), the daughter of a Belgian mother and a Chinese railway engineer. She studied medicine at Beijing, Brussels and London, where after the death in 1947 of her husband, General Tang, in the civil war, she completed her studies. She then practised in Hong Kong which, with its undercurrents of pro-Western and anti-Western loyalties, Old China versus the New, White versus Yellow, provided the background for her first partly-autobiographical novel *A Many Splendoured Thing* (1952). This, through the love affair of an emancipated Chinese girl and an English journalist, symbolizes the political and ideological climate of the British colony. It was made into a film in 1955.

In 1952 she married an English police officer in Singapore, where she practised in an anti-tuberculosis clinic and in a private medical practice before becoming a lecturer in contemporary Asian Literature at Nanyang University (1958–60). Her other novels include *Destination Chungking* (1953), ...*And the Rain my Drink* (1954), *The Mountain is Young* (1958) and *Four Faces* (1963). She also wrote a semi-autobiographical and historical trilogy comprising *The Crippled Tree* (1965), *A Mortal Flower* (1966) and *Birdless Summer* (1968) and two volumes of contemporary Chinese history: *The Morning Deluge* and *The Wind in the Tower* (1972).

Hani, Motoko, *originally* Matsuoka Moto

Born 1873   Died 1957
Japanese journalist and educationalist, the first
Japanese woman newspaper reporter

Motoko Hani was born in Hachinohe, Aomori Prefecture and educated at the Meiji Girls' School, Tokyo, where she was influenced by the educationalist Iwamoto Yoshiharu. Having taught briefly in Aomori, she returned to Tokyo where she joined the newspaper *Hochi Shimbun*. In 1897 she became its first full-time woman reporter.

After her marriage to fellow reporter Yoshikazu Hani in 1901, she and her husband joined the magazine *Katei no tomo* in 1903, which eventually, under their ownership, became the highly influential woman's magazine *Fujin no Tomo*.

In 1921 the Hanis founded the progressive school Jiyu Gakuen, which combines Christian and Confucian ethics.

Hannah

Born c.1105 BC
Biblical character, mother of Samuel the prophet

Hannah was the favourite wife of Elkanah the Ephraimite. Elkanah's other wife Peninnah taunted Hannah cruelly because she was childless, but Hannah's prayers for a son were answered. She later had five other children.

As she had promised, Hannah dedicated her son Samuel to God's service as a Nazirite. Her song of thanksgiving, which suggests she was a prophetess, found echoes many generations later in the *Magnificat*, **Mary**'s song at the birth of Jesus Christ.

Hansberry, Lorraine Vivian

Born 1930 Died 1965
American playwright who became the first black
woman author of a play produced on Broadway

Lorraine Hansberry was born in Chicago to middle-class African-American parents. She was educated at the University of Wisconsin, Roosevelt College and the School of Art Institute in Chicago, and in 1959 became the first black woman to have a play produced on Broadway — *A Raisin in the Sun* (1959), a semi-autobiographical account of the emotional and racial problems encountered by a black family attempting to move into a neighbourhood traditionally dominated by whites. It was enormously successful, won the New York Drama Critics Circle Award, and became the basis for *Raisin*, a musical, in 1973. Other plays include *The Sign in Sidney Brustein's Window* (1964), about a community of mixed racial and religious background in Greenwich Village, New York.

Following Hansberry's death from cancer, her husband assembled *To Be Young, Gifted and Black: Lorraine Hansberry in Her Own Words* (1969) from her miscellaneous writings, and completed the unfinished *Les Blancs*, about the post-colonial African experience, in 1972.

Hansford-Johnson, Pamela *see* Johnson, Pamela Hansford

Hanson, (Emmeline) Jean

Born 1919 Died 1973
English physiologist whose studies of the
mechanisms of muscular contraction were widely
recognized

Jean Hanson was born in Newhall, Derbyshire, and graduated from Bedford College, London, in 1941. She undertook wartime research on wound healing, and completed a PhD in 1951.

By this time she was working in the Medical Research Council's Biophysics Research Unit at King's College, London, and had started studies on the ultrastructure of skeletal muscle. This she continued for the rest of her life, utilising the power of the electron microscope then coming into routine use.

She became Professor of Biology at the University of London in 1966, a Fellow of the Royal Society the following year, and director of a specialized Muscle Biophysics Research Unit in 1970.

Hardie, Gwen

Born 1962
Scottish painter and sculptor who takes an
original and feminist approach to the female form

Gwen Hardie was born in Newport, Fife. After studying at Edinburgh College of Art (1979–84), she moved to West Berlin where she studied under Georg Baselitz. She first received critical notice in her postgraduate diploma show at Edinburgh, in which she exhibited a number of paintings of close-ups of female heads and torsos on a monumental scale.

She has continued to explore the theme of the female form from a feminist viewpoint, sometimes schematizing the figure by opening it up to reveal internal organs. The importance of these works lies particularly in the intention to re-invent the female form in pictorial art.

Hardin, Lil *see* Armstrong, Lil

Hardwick, Elizabeth

Born 1916
American essayist, critic and novelist whose
works examine prejudice and the value of truth

Elizabeth Hardwick was born in Lexington, Kentucky. She established her literary reputation by writing essays for the *Partisan Review*. Her first novel, *The Ghostly Lover* (1945), describes the relationship between a white woman and her black servant during the era of racial segregation, while the second, *The Simple Truth* (1955), again scrutinizes prejudice and versions of the truth, this time within the legal system and the judiciary.

Equally as important as her novels are her collections of essays, ranging across a wide variety of cultural and political issues, but with a keen sensitivity to moral values and human worth. They are collected in *A View of My Own* (1962), *Seduction and Betrayal: Women and Literature* (1974) and *Bartleby in Manhattan* (1983).

Hardwick was also, in 1963, a founding editor of the *New York Review of Books*, and for some time (1949–72) she was married to the American poet Robert Lowell (1917–77).

Hargreaves, Alison, *married name* Ballard

Born 1962 Died 1995
English mountaineer, the first woman to climb Everest solo without supplementary oxygen

Alison Hargreaves was born in Belper, Derbyshire, and she learned to climb whilst at Belper High School. She decided not to go to university, preferring instead to join her boyfriend Jim Ballard (whom she later married) in his outdoor climbing business.

In 1988, six months pregnant with her first child, she became the first British woman to climb the north wall of the Eiger. Her second child, Kate, was born two years later. In 1993 the family went on a summer expedition, and Hargreaves scaled the six main Alpine north faces solo in a single season — the Eiger, Matterhorn, Grandes Jorasses, Dru, Badille and Cima Grande. She then turned her attention to Mount Everest, which she climbed, on her second attempt, alone and without supplementary oxygen in May 1995.

After a short visit back to Scotland, where they had moved the previous year to be within easy reach of the ice-climbing in the Highlands, Hargreaves went on to climb the world's second biggest mountain, K2, but died in a blizzard on the descent on 13 August 1995.

Harjo, Joy

Born 1951
American poet who draws on Native American history, mythology and contemporary culture

Joy Harjo was born in Tulsa, Oklahoma, of mixed Creek, Cherokee and French descent. She was educated at the University of New Mexico and the Iowa Writers' Workshop and became a university teacher at Colorado and Arizona.

She has published five collections of poetry, which contain a blend of social and spiritual themes: *The Last Song* (1975), *What Moon Drove Me to This?* (1980), *She Had Some Horses* (1983), *Secrets from the Center of the World*, (1989, with Steven Strom) and *In Mad Love and War* (1990).

Harjo also plays the saxophone, and often incorporates music in public readings of her poems.

Harkness, Georgia Elma

Born 1891 Died 1974
American Methodist scholar and writer of many books about religious and academic life

Georgia Elma Harkness was born in Harkness, New York. She studied at Cornell, Boston, Harvard, Yale, and Union Theological Seminary, New York. A lifetime of teaching at Elmira College, Mount Holyoke College and Garrett Biblical Institute, and appointment as Professor of Applied Theology at the Pacific School of Religion (1950–61) is reflected in her many books. These include studies of ethics, of prayer, and of the position of laypeople, especially women, in the Church. She herself accepted ordination as a Methodist deacon and elder, but not as a minister.

The development of her ideas, including her commitment to Christian pacifism and Christian unity, is related in the autobiographical *The Dark Night of the Soul* (1945), *A Special Way to Victory* (1964) and *Grace Abounding* (1969).

Harlow, Jean, *originally* Harlean Carpentier

Born 1911 Died 1937
American actress whose screen image matched the glamour but not the unhappiness of her private life

Harlean Carpentier was born in Kansas City, Missouri. After attending the Hollywood School for Girls in Los Angeles, she eloped with a local business tycoon at the age of 16 and moved to Los Angeles, where she made her film début in *Moran of the Marines* (1928) and appeared as an extra before being signed to a contract by film director Howard Hughes. She divorced in 1929, changed her name to her mother's maiden name, and appeared in *Hell's Angels* in 1930.

Roles in *Platinum Blonde* (1931), *Red-Headed Woman* (1932) and *Red Dust* (1932) established her screen image as a fast-talking, wisecracking platinum blonde who gave as good as she got and brazenly flaunted her sexuality. Under contract to MGM from 1932 she proved a memorable sparring partner for the studio's top male stars and developed into a deft comedienne in films like *Dinner at Eight* (1933), *Bombshell* (1933) and *Libelled Lady* (1936).

Her death at the age of 26 from cerebral oedema followed a life blighted by ill health and personal problems, including three failed marriages.

Harman, Harriet

Born 1950
English politician, an increasingly prominent spokesperson for the Labour Party

Harriet Harman was born in London. She

trained as a lawyer and became an outstanding legal officer for the National Council of Civil Liberties (1978–82), before entering parliament as MP for Peckham in 1982. Also in that year she married Jack Dromey, a TGWU official.

She was the first Labour frontbencher to take maternity leave and now has three children. Early in 1996 she weathered much criticism for her apparent contradiction of Labour education policy by deciding to send her son to St Olave's grammar school in Kent rather than to a non-elective school.

She became opposition front bench spokesperson on health in 1987, shadow chief secretary to the Treasury in 1992, a member of the Labour Party's National Executive Committee in 1993, opposition front bench spokesperson on employment in 1994 and again on health in 1995. Her publications include *The Century Gap* (1993).

Harper, Frances E(llen) W(atkins)

Born 1825 Died 1911
African-American poet, novelist and activist, the first known writer in the Black tradition

Frances E W Harper was born in Maryland of free parents and educated in her uncle's school. She became an activist in the abolitionist, temperance and women's rights movements, as well as a popular poet of her day and the first known African-American novelist.

The themes in Harper's writings mainly reflect the causes she supported, such as anti-slavery, black women and education. She collected her poems as *Forest Leaves* (1854), *Poems on Miscellaneous Subjects* (1854) and *The Martyr of Alabama and other Poems* (1894). She also wrote two novels: *Iola Leroy; of Shadows Lifted* (1892) and *Sketches of Southern Life* (1872).

Harper, Ida A, *née* Husted

Born 1851 Died 1931
American suffragist, journalist and writer, companion and biographer of Susan B Anthony

Ida Husted was born in Fairfield, Indiana. She briefly attended Indiana University, leaving it to become a school principal in 1869. In 1871 she married and moved to Terre Haute where, despite her husband's disapproval, she started writing for local newspapers. After their divorce in 1890, she joined the Indianapolis *News*. Later, living in New York, she wrote for a number of prestigious magazines including *Harper's Bazaar*.

Harper is most famous for her association with the suffragist Susan B Anthony, with whom she lived from 1897, and with whom she worked closely, editing Anthony's papers, and writing her biography. She worked on the fourth volume of the *History of Women's Suffrage* (1902) with Anthony, and went on to write the final two volumes (vols 5 and 6, published in 1922).

Harris, Barbara Clementine

Born 1930
American cleric in the US Episcopal Church, the first female Anglican bishop

Barbara Harris was born in Philadelphia, the daughter of a steelworker and a church organist. She worked as a public relations and community relations executive, a social activist in the 1960s and a supporter of the ordination of women and of homosexuals in the 1970s.

Harris attended Villanova University in the late 1970s, doing some of her theological training by part-time and correspondence courses. She was ordained priest in 1980, and after parish and prison chaplaincy work was appointed director of the Episcopal Church Publishing Co in 1984. She was consecrated suffragan (assistant) bishop of Massachusetts in 1989. Though not a diocesan bishop, she was the first female bishop in the Anglican Communion.

Her consecration marked a new departure for the worldwide Anglican Communion which was ratified in 1990 when Penelope Jamieson (1942–   ) was consecrated the first female Anglican diocesan bishop, in Dunedin, New Zealand.

Harris, Emmylou

Born 1947
American singer known for her country and country/rock music

Emmylou Harris was born in Birmingham, Alabama. She began her career as a folk singer and in 1970 produced her first album, *Gliding Bird*, which included some Bob Dylan songs and the title song written by her first husband, Tom Slocum. After the failure of her marriage she moved to Washington DC and teamed up with singer Gram Parsons (d.1973), who is credited with inventing the country/rock genre.

Gaining in popularity during the 1970s, Harris won Grammy awards for *Pieces of the Sky* (1975) and *Elite Hotel* (1976) and in 1981 for singing 'That Lovin' You Feelin Again' with Roy Orbison. She married Brian Ahern, the producer of three of her hit albums, in 1977, but the marriage did not last beyond the mid-1980s. Her later recordings include the bluegrass album *Roses in the Snow* (1980), the cross-over *Evangeline* (1981), comprising a collection of bluegrass, country, rock and pop tunes, *Trio* (1987), with **Dolly Parton** and Linda Ronstadt, and *Wrecking Ball* (1995).

Harris, Julie (Julia) Ann

Born 1925
American stage and film actress who rose to fame with her sensitive approach to complex emotional roles

Julie Harris was born in Michigan. She made her New York stage début in 1945 as a student at Yale School of Drama, and in 1946 won critical acclaim as a member of the Old Vic New York company for her roles in *Henry IV Part Two* and Sophocles' *Oedipus*. She established her reputation as a leading actress with her performance as Frankie Adams in **Carson McCullers**'s *The Member of the Wedding* in 1950, following this with an appearance as Sally Bowles in *I am a Camera* in 1951.

She played Juliet at Stratford, Ontario in 1960 and Ophelia in Joseph Papp's production of *Hamlet* in New York in 1964 and is renowned for her solo performance as **Emily Dickinson** in *The Belle of Amherst* in 1976.

Her film début in *The Member of the Wedding* (1952) gained her an Academy Award nomination, and she has since appeared in films such as *The Hiding Place* (1975) and *Gorillas in the Mist* (1988), and on television in such series as the popular *Knots Landing* (1979–) from 1981 to 1987.

Harris, Patricia, *née* Roberts

Born 1924 Died 1985
African-American lawyer and politician, the first black woman to hold a US Cabinet post

Patricia Roberts was born in Mattoon, Illinois. She studied at Howard University (1945), University of Chicago (1947), American University (1950) and George Washington University (1960), and was appointed Dean of Howard University Law School in 1969. She became a director of IBM in 1971, and was appointed ambassador to Luxembourg under President Lyndon B Johnson.

She became the first African-American woman to hold a US cabinet post on being appointed Secretary of Housing and Urban Development (1977–9) by President Jimmy Carter. She then served as Secretary of Health, Education and Welfare (in 1980 redesignated Health and Human Services) from 1979 to 1981.

Harris, Rosemary Jeanne

Born 1930
English actress who has played leading character parts in British and American classics

Rosemary Harris made her début on the New York stage in 1952, and in London a year later, in *The Seven Year Itch*. She appeared with the Bristol Old Vic and the Old Vic in London, before visiting New York again in 1956, this time with the Old Vic Company, as Cressida in Tyrone Guthrie's modern dress version of *Troilus and Cressida*.

She appeared in many plays in the USA before returning to Britain and joining the Chichester Festival Theatre for its inaugural 1962 season. She won huge acclaim in London in 1969, playing three characters in Neil Simon's *Plaza Suite*.

More recently, in 1991 she appeared as the old aunt in *Arsenic and Old Lace* and in Pinero's *Preserving Mr Panmure*, and her performance as Vivienne's mother in the film based on the life of T S Eliot, *Tom and Viv* (1994), was highly acclaimed.

Harrison, Jane Ellen

Born 1850 Died 1928
English classical scholar who pioneered the use of information from other fields of study to support her own

Jane Harrison was born in Cottingham, Yorkshire. She won a scholarship to Newnham College, Cambridge, where she attained the best marks achieved by a woman in Classics. She studied archaeology in London and lectured on Greek art before returning to Newnham as lecturer in classical archaeology (1898–1922). From 1900 to 1903 she was the college's first Research Fellow.

Harrison was among the first to support the movement in classical studies that accepted supporting information from the areas of anthropology, archaeology and philosophy. She wrote *Myths of the Odyssey in Art and Literature* (1882) and *Introductory Studies in Greek Art* (1885) before her interest in religion inspired her most important works — *Prolegomena to the Study of Greek Religion* (1903), *Themis, a Study of the Social Origins of Greek Religion* (1912) and *Ancient Art and Ritual* (new ed 1948).

She was also one of the first magistrates in Cambridge, and though she did not take an active interest in politics, she was a keen supporter of female suffrage.

Deborah Harry, 1983

Harry, Deborah, *also known as* Debbie

Born 1945
American singer and actress who made her name
with Blondie before going solo

Deborah Harry was born in Miami, Florida.
She worked as a beautician, waitress and
Playboy Bunny before recording with the
short-lived Wind in the Willows. In 1973,
with her lover Chris Stein, she formed the
Stilettoes, which later became Blondie. People
tended to believe that the name referred to
her alone, and after a string of new wave
hits — 'Heart of Glass', 'Presence Dear',
'Denise' — and albums *Parallel Lines* and *Eat
to the Beat*, Harry went solo under her own
name, a decision compounded by Stein's long
illness.

Her first solo record was *Koo-Koo*, followed
by the unfortunately titled *Rockbird*. Harry
(who had reverted to 'Deborah' rather than be
considered a mere rock-bird) also turned to
acting, with parts in *Atlantic City* (1980) and
Videodrome geared to her almost Monroe-like
appearance.

Hart of South Lanark, Dame Judith Constance Mary Hart, Baroness

Born 1924 Died 1991
English Labour politician who made efforts to
improve the status of women in every sphere

Judith Hart was born in Burnley, Lancashire,
and educated at the London School of Economics. A lifetime Labour Party member, she
entered the House of Commons, representing
Lanark, in 1959, and joined Harold Wilson's
government in 1964, reaching Cabinet rank as
Paymaster-General in 1968.

She had three successful terms as Minister
of Overseas Development (1969–70, 1974–5
and 1977–9), and was front bench spokesperson on Overseas Aid (1979–80). She was
a popular and influential left-winger, with a
strong concern for the needs of Third World
countries; with her family she was also involved with CND and the abolition of apartheid.

She was appointed DBE in 1979, retired
from parliament in 1987, and was made a life
peer in 1988.

Hart, Nancy, *née* Morgan

Born 1735 Died 1830
American woman who though illiterate and 'rude
of speech' became a legendary heroine of the
American Revolution

Nancy Morgan was born into a frontier family
who moved to Georgia about 1771 and who
during the 'War of Extermination' chose to
stay and fight the Tories.

None of her exploits have been formally
documented, though they are well known in
folklore. The most famous incident occurred
when five Tories appeared at the family cabin
demanding food. Nancy plied them with
whiskey, seized one of their rifles, killed a
soldier and held the rest to hostage until her
young daughter succeeded in signalling for
help.

Harvey, Ethel, *née* Browne

Born 1885 Died 1965
American embryologist and cell biologist
renowned for her discoveries of the mechanisms
of cell division

Ethel Browne was born in Baltimore, Maryland. She was educated at Bryn Mawr School
and the Women's College of Baltimore, then
attended Columbia University, graduating in
1907 and gaining her PhD in 1913. In 1916
she married Edmund Harvey, a professor of
biology at Princeton, and worked part-time or
as an independent research worker for most
of her career.

Her work in cytology (the study of cells), in
which she used sea urchin eggs as her experimental model, was internationally recognized
and she was awarded many honours, including fellowships of the American Association
for the Advancement of Science and the New
York Academy of Sciences.

Harvie Anderson, Betty

Born 1914 Died 1979
Scottish Conservative politician and first woman
Deputy Speaker

Betty Harvie Anderson was born into a political family. Elected MP for Renfrewshire (East) in 1959, she refused to pay special attention to women's problems, but gained a reputation as a good, hardworking constituency MP and became a member of the 1922 Committee of Backbench MPs.

In 1970 she became the first woman to take the Speaker's Chair, proving that a woman could keep order during turbulent times — the passage of the Industrial Relations Act (1970–1) and the Common Market debates. She was appointed a Privy Councillor in 1974.

Harwood, Elizabeth

Born 1938 Died 1990
English concert soprano best remembered for her fine interpretation of the music of Mozart and Strauss

Elizabeth Harwood was born in Barton Seagrave, near Kettering. She grew up in Yorkshire and studied at the Royal Northern College of Music, Manchester, making her début at Glyndebourne in 1960.

She joined Sadler's Wells Opera in 1961 and moved to Covent Garden in 1967, where she made her début in *Arabella*. From 1970 she appeared regularly for the Austrian conductor Herbert von Karajan (1908–89) at the Salzburg Festival.

Harwood, Gwen(doline Nessie)

Born 1920
Australian poet and librettist, recognized as one of Australia's finest living poets

Gwen Harwood was born in Taringa, Brisbane. After studying music she became a teacher of music, and did not publish her first book of verse, *Poems*, until 1963. *Poems, Volume Two* followed in 1968, and then *Selected Poems* (1975) and *The Lion's Bride* (1981). Much of her poetic work, appearing originally under a number of pseudonyms, is suffused with physical or emotional pain.

During that period she wrote librettos for leading Australian composers: Larry Sitsky's operas *The Fall of the House of Usher* (1965), *Lenz* (1972) and *The Golem* (1979), as well as James Penberthy's *Choral Symphony* and Ian Cugley's *Sea Changes*.

Harwood has received the Robert Frost award (1977) and the Patrick White Literary award (1978). *Blessed City* was the Melbourne *Age* Book of the Year for 1990.

Hasegawa, Itsuko

Born 1941
Japanese architect who strives to reach agreement with the local community before implementing her designs

Itsuko Hasegawa was born in Yaizu City and trained at Kanto Gakuin University, where she graduated in 1964. She worked in Japan until 1969, when she undertook two years of research at the Institute of Technology in Tokyo. In 1976 she set up Itsuko Hasegawa Architectural Design Studio in Tokyo.

In 1987 the practice won first prize in a competition for Shonandai Cultural and Community Centre, Fujisawa. The design was not initially popular with local residents, but Hasegawa held lengthy discussions with community groups. The centre is partially sunken with a public park at ground level to extend the building into the community.

Her careful attitude to design was later shown during a three-year discussion period for a stress care centre in Shiranui Hospital, Omuta (1989), and she applied the same thoroughness to the Nagoya Design Exhibition Pavilion (1989) although it was only a temporary structure.

Hashman, Judy (Judith), *née* Devlin

Born 1935
American badminton player who had an outstanding number of wins during her career

Judy Devlin was born in Winnipeg, Canada, the daughter of the Irish-born Frank Devlin (1899–1988), winner of 18 All-England titles.

She won the singles title at the All-England Championships a record 10 times (in 1954, 1957–8, 1960–4 and 1966–7), and also won seven doubles titles (six with her younger sister, Susan Peard, 1940–).

She was a member of the United States Uber Cup winning teams in 1957, 1960 and 1963.

Hassal, Joan

Born 1906 Died 1988
English artist who produced an enormous body of work mainly in the form of book illustration

Joan Hassal was born in Notting Hill, London. She studied at the Royal Academy schools prior to moving to the LCC (London Central College) School of Photo Engraving and Lithography where she studied wood engraving under Ralph Beedham.

She was a prolific artist with subject matter ranging from natural history to illustrating editions of the classics of English literature. Her perfectionist, sensitive approach, similar in style to Thomas Bewick, found many admirers; she became the first woman master member of the Art Workers Guild and was awarded the OBE in 1987.

Hatshepsut

Born c.1540BC   Died c.1418BC
Queen of Egypt of the 18th dynasty who achieved the status of a pharaoh during her reign

Hatshepsut was the daughter of Tuthmosis I. He associated her with him on the throne (or was forced to do so), since she was the only one of the family of royal birth, and married her to Tuthmosis II, his son by another wife. On Tuthmosis II's accession in 1516, she became the real ruler and, on his death in 1503, she acted as regent for her nephew, Tuthmosis III. However after a few years she had herself crowned as pharaoh and assumed full pharaonic power and status, signified by her wearing of the kingly false beard.

Pursuing a peaceful policy, thereby perhaps endangering Egypt's Asian possessions, she built up the economy of the country. She opened the turquoise mines at the Wadi Maghareh, built the great mortuary temple at Deir-el-Bahri, sent a marine expedition to Punt (the southern coast of the Red Sea, now coastal Ethiopia and Djibouti) and erected two obelisks at Karnak (1485).

Hatz, Elizabeth

Born 1953
Swedish architect whose designs incorporate careful maximization of daylight due to the lack of natural light during the Scandanavian winter

Elizabeth Hatz was born in Lund and educated in the Architectural Association (1972–7). After graduating she worked in Paris for two years before returning to Sweden to join Berg Arkitektkontor, a large Swedish practice based in Stockholm, initially working on the headquarters of Kodak in Gothenburg (1979–82).

The projects undertaken by her in the office grew in size and prestige: she was a leading member of the design team for the largest spherical building in the world, a sports centre called the Globe (1986–9), which contains a sports arena with seating for 16,000, training areas, offices and a hotel.

Hatz has taught in the School of Architecture, Stockholm (1983–6) and is a member of the board of ATHENA, the Swedish Women Architects Association.

Haven, Emily Bradley Neal, *née* Bradley

Born 1827   Died 1863
American author and magazine editor whose works were praised for their moral character and lack of sensation

Emily Bradley was born in Hudson, New York. Under the name 'Aunt Alice' she wrote stories for Neal's *Saturday Gazette and Lady's Literary Museum* and in 1846 she married the *Gazette's* editor, Joseph Neal. A year later she was widowed and became editor of the *Gazette*. She was editor for six years and showed a special interest in the juvenile department.

Havergal, Frances Ridley

Born 1836   Died 1879
English poet who wrote the hymn 'Take my life and let it be'

Frances Ridley Havergal was born in Astley, Worcestershire, the daughter of William Henry Havergal (1793–1870), a rector and composer. Her mother Jane died when Frances was 12, and her father soon remarried.

Frances wrote poetry from the age of seven, and became an accomplished classical scholar. She visited Germany with her father's second wife, Caroline, in 1852, and stayed for more than a year, at a school in Düsseldorf and in a pastor's family. She revisited Germany in 1865–6.

She became a Christian at the age of 15, and from 1870 onwards composed several volumes of poetry, such as *Kept for the Master's Use*. She also wrote many hymns, of which the best known is one of consecration and discipleship: 'Take my life and let it be'.

Hawkes, Jacquetta, *née* Hopkins

Born 1910   Died 1996
English archaeologist and writer, wife of J B Priestley

Jacquetta Hopkins was born in Cambridge and educated at the Perse School and Newnham College, Cambridge, where she was the first woman to study archaeology and anthropology to degree level. Her first serious excavation was directed by Christopher Hawkes, whom she married in 1933 and with whom she later published *Prehistoric Britain* (1944).

Her first publication was *The Archaelogy of Jersey* (1939), and her books on British archaeological sites, such as *Early Britain* (1945), and general works on prehistory helped to popularize archaeology. She also wrote on Egyptian topics, produced a biography of the pioneering archaeologist Sir Mortimer Wheeler, and wrote a book of poetry, *Symbols and Speculations* (1948). With her second husband, novelist and playright J B Priestley (1894–1984), whom she married in 1953, she wrote *Journey Down the Rainbow* (1955), a jovial indictment of American life in letter form, and other fictional works.

From the 1940s she was involved with UNESCO (as well as with many other cultural bodies at home and abroad), serving on the Central Committee of UNESCO from 1966 to 1979, and in 1957 she was a co-founder of the Campaign for Nuclear Disarmament.

Hawley, Christine

Born 1949
English architect whose London firm has won five international awards for its work

Christine Hawley was born in Shrewsbury and trained at the Architectural Association, London (1969–75), registering as an architect in 1978. She and her business partner Peter Cook were both members of Archigram, an influential group of teachers at the Architectural Association in the 1960s and 1970s, motivated by the possibilities of 'high technology' and 'dense urban design', philosophies which their firm Cook and Hawley turned into buildable ideas.

Their work includes the unbuilt Stained Glass Museum, Hesse (1989), exhibition pavilions in Nagoya, Japan (1989) and Osaka, Japan (1990), and apartments and shops for the Internationale Bau Ausstellung, Berlin (1984–90), a prestigious site alongside work by Mario Botta. In 1988 Hawley was appointed head of the Department of Architecture at the Polytechnic of East London.

Hawn, Goldie Jeanne

Born 1945
American film actress whose dedication to her family has not thwarted her popularity

Goldie Hawn was born in Washington DC, the daughter of a professional musician. She trained in ballet and tap and dropped out of college to form her own dancing school, soon becoming a television favourite as one of the ensemble troupe in *Rowan and Martin's Laugh-In* (1968–70), where her bikini-clad, perennially giggling, blonde scatterbrain persona proved irresistible.

She won a Best Supporting Actress Oscar in *Cactus Flower* (1969) and went on to gain much popularity, particularly in comedy roles, throughout the 1970s. In 1980 she was the executive producer for *Private Benjamin*, in which she also acted, and took considerable, shrewd control over her subsequent career.

Occasionally absent from the screen for years at a time, devoting herself to husband Kurt Russell and their family, she always seems to find her popularity intact on her return, such as when she played a dizzy lawyer in the immensely successful *Bird on a Wire* (1990). Later films include the comedies *Housesitter* (1992) and *Death Becomes Her* (1992).

Hayashi, Fumiko

Born 1903 Died 1951
Japanese writer whose stories provide a realistic depiction of working-class life and the harshness of post-war Japan

Fumiko Hayashi was born into a family of itinerant gypsy-like pedlars. Her childhood was deeply unstable and left her with an overwhelming desire for security, which turned her into a workaholic and fostered a hedonism which led her into the Tokyo bohemian set of the 1930s.

Her first book, *Horoki*, was closely drawn from her childhood experiences and those of Tokyo and was hugely successful. It was the first of an enormous number of works (well over 200). Her best, and bleakest, is *Ukigumo* ('Drifting Cloud'), which was written in the aftermath of collapse and defeat in 1945 (she had been a war correspondent in China and South-East Asia for *Mainichi Shimbun* from 1937 to the end of the war). It is an extremely powerful tale of doomed love amid the superbly evoked ruins of a nation utterly destroyed.

Haydée, Marcia

Born 1939
Brazilian dancer and director who became one of the greatest dramatic ballerinas of her time

Marcia Haydée was born in Niteroi, near Rio de Janeiro. After studying with Vaslav Veltchek she made an early début with the Rio de Janeiro Teatro Municipal. Further study with the Sadler's Wells Ballet School led to her joining the Grand Ballet of Marquis de Cuevas in 1957 and then Stuttgart Ballet in 1961, where she became leading ballerina.

Her talents blossomed under the direction of the Stuttgart's founder, choreographer John Cranko, for whom she created roles in *Romeo and Juliet* (1962), *Onegin* (1965), *Carmen* (1971) and *Initials R.B.M.E.* (1972). She guested frequently around the world and worked for major choreographers like Kenneth MacMillan and Glen Tetley.

In 1976 she was appointed artistic director of Stuttgart Ballet.

Hayes, Helen

Born 1900   Died 1993
American star of stage, film and television

Helen Hayes was born in Washington. She first went on stage at the age of five and went on to win fame in a wide variety of stage productions, such as *Pollyanna* (1917–18) and *Dear Brutus* (1919). In 1928 she married the playwright and journalist Charles MacArthur (d.1956), a union that because of his drunkenness and womanizing was not without public interest. Her leading roles in Maxwell Anderson's *Mary of Scotland* and Laurence Housman's *Victoria Regina* occupied her for most of the 1930s and consolidated her status as a star.

Though she continued to appear on stage throughout her career, she also appeared in several films, including MacArthur's *The Sin of Madelon Claudet* (1931), for which she won a Best Actress Academy Award in 1932. She was successful too in *Arrowsmith* (1931) and *A Farewell to Arms* (1932). In 1935 she left the cinema, but returned in 1952 in *My Son John* and gave a highly acclaimed performance as the Romanov Grand Duchess in the title role of *Anastasia* (1956). Around this time she began appearing regularly on television, such as in *Arsenic and Old Lace* (1956).

She returned to the big screen again in 1970 to play in *Airport*, earning herself Best Actress and Best Supporting Actress Oscars, the first player to win both awards. By then she had been typed as a cute but steely 'little old lady' and became a memorable Miss Marple in several television murder dramas.

Hays, Mary

Born 1760   Died 1843
*English writer and feminist, close friend of **Mary Wollstonecraft***

Mary Hays was born in Southwark, London, into a dissenting family. She was largely self-educated. Through attending the Dissenting Academy in Hackney in the late 1780s, and through her pamphlet *Cursory Remarks* (1791) defending dissenters, she encountered the publisher Joseph Johnson's radical circle which included William Godwin and **Mary Wollstonecraft**.

Among her many radical works the best-known is her *Appeal to the Men of Great Britain in behalf of the Women*, published anonymously in 1798, in which she deplores the 'perpetual babyism' of women's state,

urging their educational, legal and financial independence. Also important is her *Letters and Essays, Moral and Miscellaneous* (1793) which shows the influence of Wollstonecraft's *A Vindication of the Rights of Women* (1792).

After Wollstonecraft's death (1797), Hays moved away from Godwin's circle. She wrote a number of novels, including the notorious *Memoirs of Emma Courtney* (1796). She also wrote a history of famous women, *Female Biography* (1803).

Hayward, Susan, *originally* Edythe Marrenner

Born 1917   Died 1975
American film actress whose roles were as fiery as her flame-red hair

Susan Hayward was born in Brooklyn, New York. In 1936 she left her job as a cloth designer in a Manhattan handkerchief factory and used her modest savings to enrol at the Feagin School of Dramatic Arts. Subsequently, she pursued a modelling career and was offered a screen test for the part of Scarlett O'Hara in *Gone With The Wind*. Though unsuccessful, she remained in Hollywood, changing her name and taking elocution lessons to deepen her voice and remove her Brooklyn accent.

She excelled in material that exploited her abrasive personality and hankered after larger-than-life emotional torments, and received her first Best Actress Oscar nomination for her performance as an alcoholic in *Smash-Up: The Story of a Woman* (1947, UK: *A Woman Destroyed*). Most popular playing ruthlessly ambitious or crisis-ridden women, Hayward received her fifth Best Actress Oscar nomination and the award itself for portraying the first woman in California to be sent to the gas chamber in *I Want to Live!* (1958).

She continued to act until the early 1970s and spent her last years battling with brain tumours, making a final, typically defiant, public appearance as a presenter at the 1974 Oscar ceremony.

Haywood, Eliza, *née* Fowler

Born c.1693   Died 1756
English novelist whose libellous work elicited a denunciation by Alexander Pope

Eliza Fowler was born in London. She married, but was deserted by her husband. She became an actress and wrote a number of scandalous society novels in which the characters resembled living persons so closely, the names being thinly concealed by the use of asterisks, as to be libellous. Pope denounced her in the *Dunciad*.

She issued the periodical *The Female Spectator* (1744–6) and *The Parrot* (1747). Her works include *Memoirs of a Certain Island Adjacent to Utopia* (1725), and two 'straight' novels, *The History of Betsy Thoughtless* (1751) and *The History of Jemmy and Jenny Hessamy* (1753).

Hayworth, Rita, *originally* Margarita Carmen Cansino

> *Born 1918   Died 1987*
> *American film actress and dancer who rose to become the epitome of glamour and beauty in the 1940s and 1950s*

Rita Hayworth was born into a showbusiness family in New York, a cousin of **Ginger Rogers**. Her nightclub appearances, beginning at the age of 12 in her father's nightclub, led to a succession of small roles in B-pictures.

Blossoming into an international beauty, she was both an enigmatic temptress, as in *Blood and Sand* (1941) and *Gilda* (1946), and a vivacious leading lady in musicals such as *Cover Girl* (1944). Her allure dimmed in middle-age and later roles were lacklustre, although she was effective as the faded beauty in *Separate Tables* (1958).

Her five husbands included film director Orson Welles and Prince Aly Khan. She suffered from Alzheimer's disease for many years prior to her death.

Rita Hayworth in *Blood and Sand*, 1941

Hazen, Elizabeth

> *Born 1885   Died 1975*
> *American chemist and bacteriologist credited with the joint discovery of an antifungal antibiotic*

Elizabeth Hazen was born in Rich, Mississippi. She studied science in Mississippi before graduating from Columbia University with a PhD in 1927.

Her work at the Mycology Laboratory, in collaboration with **Rachel Brown** from 1948, there led to the discovery in 1949 of nystatin, a wide-range antibiotic, which has also been used extensively to treat books and art-works damaged by fungus and mould. It was patented in 1951 and marketed as Mycostatin from 1954.

Hazen and Brown directed royalties from the drug to promoting mycology research for many years, and the two women received many awards and honours for their work.

Hazzard, Shirley

> *Born 1931*
> *Australian-born American novelist who was heralded as a major contemporary writer in 1980*

Shirley Hazzard was born and educated in Sydney. Her first book, *The Evening of the Holiday*, was published in 1966. Between 1952 and 1962 she worked in New York at the United Nations, an organization she was to satirize in her second novel, *People in Glass Houses* (1967). She later published a factual exposé of the UN in *Defeat of an Ideal* (1973).

Other novels are *The Bay of Noon* (1970) and *The Transit of Venus* (1980), which charts the turbulent emotional involvements of an Australian woman in sophisticated America; this book established her as a major contemporary writer. Many of her short stories have appeared in the *New Yorker* magazine; some are collected in *Cliffs of Fall* (1963).

Head, Bessie

> *Born 1937   Died 1986*
> *South African-born Botswanian novelist for whom the escape from apartheid is a prominent theme*

Bessie Head was born in Pietermaritzburg and became a citizen of Botswana after working as an agricultural labourer there. The central character of her first novel, *When Rain Clouds Gather* (1968), repeats her escape from apartheid to the relative, but still compromised, freedom of Botswana.

Later books — *Maru* (1971), *A Question of Power* (1974) and *A Bewitched Crossroad* (1984) — document different aspects of the same basic situation, always concentrating on the fine line between heroism and self-reliance on the one hand, and abject cultural surrender on the other.

The Collector of Treasures (1977) was a transcription of native folk-tales.

Head, Edith

Born 1907   Died 1981
American costume designer who worked on many
famous films

Edith Head was educated at UCLA and Stanford. She taught art and languages for a time before joining Paramount in the late 1930s. She became one of the leading Hollywood costume designers, along with **Irene Sharaff** and MGM's Irene Lentz (1901–62). She later moved to Universal in 1967.

She designed opulent dresses for many of the major stars of the era, including **Barbara Stanwyck, Elizabeth Taylor, Audrey Hepburn** and **Bette Davis**, as well as the stylish suits worn by Robert Redford and Paul Newman in *The Sting* (1973), one of eight films for which she received the Academy Award for costume design.

Hearst, Phoebe, *née* Apperson

Born 1842   Died 1919
American philanthropist who endowed part of the
University of California campus at Berkeley

Phoebe Hearst was born in Missouri, the daughter of a farmer. In 1862 she married the mining magnate George Hearst (1820–91), US Senator from California from 1886, who allowed his wife to use his money to indulge the people of California by endowing schools, kindergartens, libraries and hospitals and by sponsoring archaeological expeditions. She encouraged women to pursue careers in all the fields of activity that she patronised.

The Hearsts had a son, William Randolph Hearst (1863–1951), who in 1887 took over the *San Francisco Examiner* from his father. He also received $7.5 million from his mother and went on to build up the largest newspaper chain in the USA.

One of Phoebe Hearst's most enduring philanthropies was the endowment of some of the buildings of the main campus of the University of California at Berkeley in 1873, for which she was honoured with the position of first woman regent of the university.

Hébert, Anne

Born 1916
Francophone Canadian poet, novelist, playwright
and story writer, hailed as 'one of the greatest
contemporary poets' in her language

Anne Hébert was born in Sainte-Catherine-de-Fossambault, near Québec. She is cousin to the poet Hector de Saint-Denys Garneau (1912–43), who personally influenced her

early poems. The harsh, bright, dry 'nun-like' poems of her first collection, *Les Songes en équilibre* (1942, 'Dreams in Equilibrium'), immediately attracted attention, and won a prize.

The extreme hardness of her approach produced in critic Edmund Wilson 'a mortal chill'. She is especially highly praised in France. Her play *Le Temps sauvage* (1963, 'The Savage Time'), about an over-possessive mother, was successful, as was her rather more conventional novel *Kamouraska* (1970, Eng trans 1973), based on a real-life case of murder.

Heck, Barbara Ruckle, *née* Ruckle

Born 1734   Died 1804
Irish American immigrant who became known as
the 'Mother' of US Methodism

Barbara Ruckle was born in Ballingrane, of a German Palatinate refugee family. Converted to Methodism at 18, she married Paul Heck and migrated with a group of people to New York in 1760.

Upset by the way a change of scene seemed to have dampened her companions' spiritual zeal, she encouraged her cousin Philip Embury (1728–73), a carpenter, to hold the first Methodist meeting in the USA in his own home in 1766, and prompted him to build the first chapel, in 1768.

Her family was forced by the Revolutionary War to move to Canada, first to Sorel near Montreal, then to Augusta township, Lake Ontario.

Heilbron, Dame Rose

Born 1914
English judge, the second woman to be appointed
to serve on the High Court

Rose Heilbron was educated at Liverpool University and won a scholarship to Gray's Inn in 1936. In 1945 she married Dr Nathaniel Burstein. Their daughter Hilary (1949–   ) is also a barrister.

Called to the Bar in 1939, Heilbron progressed quickly to become a QC in 1949 and Recorder of Burnley — the UK's first woman recorder — from 1956 until 1974, when she was appointed a judge of the High Court in the Family Division. She also chaired the Home Secretary's Advisory Group on Rape in 1975 and was presiding judge of the Northern Circuit (1979–82). She retired from the High Court in 1988.

Heiss, Carol, *married name* Carol Heiss-Jenkins

Born 1940
American ice-skater who has been world
champion several times

Carol Heiss was born in New York City. She took up figure-skating and in 1956 became the youngest woman to skate for the USA, winning a silver medal at the Olympics. Her first world title was won at the 1957 world championships. Between then and 1960 she won four straight US national ladies singles titles, two North American crowns and four consecutive world titles.

She won a gold medal at the 1960 Olympics and retired from amateur competition that year, when she turned to sports teaching and coaching and working in the media.

Held, Anna

Born 1873 Died 1918
Polish-born actress and singer, and originator of
the Ziegfeld Follies *idea*

Anna Held was raised in Paris. After being orphaned in Warsaw she joined a travelling troupe and toured Europe, establishing herself as a teenage star of musical comedy in Paris. Her almost caricatured version of French 'naughtiness' made her a huge star in London, and in New York, where she was taken in by her future husband Florenz Ziegfeld (1869–1932) in 1896.

The marriage lasted from 1897 to the eve of World War I, and it was at Anna's suggestion that the *Ziegfeld Follies* were established.

Helena, St

Born c.255AD Died AD330
Roman Empress who is credited with re-
discovering the tomb of Jesus Christ

Helena traditionally came from Bithynia, the daughter of an innkeeper. She became the wife of the emperor Constantius Chlorus and mother of Constantine I, the Great. For political reasons Constantius divorced her in 292, but when he was declared emperor by his army in York in 306, he made her Empress Dowager.

In 312, when toleration was extended to Christianity, she was baptized. In 326, according to tradition, she discovered the Holy Cross and the Holy Sepulchre (tomb of Jesus Christ) in Jerusalem, and founded the basilicas on the Mount of Olives and at Bethlehem. Her feast day is 18 August.

Hellman, Lillian Florence

Born 1907 Died 1984
American playwright who was also a famously
temperamental actress

Lillian Hellman was born into a Jewish family in New Orleans and educated at New York University and Columbia University. She worked for the New York *Herald Tribune* as a reviewer (1925–8) and for MGM in Hollywood as reader of plays (1927–32). She was married for a time to the dramatist Arthur Kober, but lived for many years with the detective writer Dashiell Hammett, who encouraged her writing.

She had her first stage success with *The Children's Hour* (1934), which ran on Broadway for 86 weeks but was prohibited on account of its allusions to lesbianism from playing in several other cities. It was followed by *Days to Come* (1936) and *The Little Foxes* (1939), which was later adapted into a film starring **Bette Davis**. During World War II she also wrote the bravely anti-fascist plays *Watch on the Rhine* (1941, winner of the Critics Circle award) and *The Searching Wind* (1944). When she came before the Un-American Activities committee in 1952 during the Joseph McCarthy era she coined the famous phrase 'I can't cut my conscience to fit this year's fashions'. This period was described in her *Scoundrel Time* (1976). Her other plays included *The Autumn Garden* (1951) and *Toys in the Attic* (1960). Hellman also translated plays, made stage adaptations, and contributed to the libretto of Leonard Bernstein's operetta *Candide* (1956). Her four volumes of memoirs include *An Unfinished Woman* (1969) and *Pentimento* (1973).

She was a left-wing activist, sensitive to social injustice and personal suffering, and her voice was one of the most persuasive in the modern American theatre. Mercurial, she nurtured her animosities, and sued for libel when **Mary McCarthy** said of her that 'every word she writes is a lie, including "and" and "the"', a reference to the misrepresentations in her memoir *Scoundrel Time*. But Hellman died before the case came to court.

Héloïse

Born c.1098 Died 1164
French abbess whose love affair with Peter
Abelard is one of the best known in history

Héloïse

Héloïse was the brilliant niece of canon Fulbert of Notre Dame, who arranged for her education to take place at his own home under the care of the theologian and philosopher Peter Abelard (1079–1142). Héloïse and Abelard fell passionately in love but had to flee to Brittany when Fulbert discovered their affair. They had a son, Astralabe, and were secretly married, but Héloïse's family were angered when the secret was disclosed.

She entered the convent at Argenteuil for safety but Abelard was attacked one night and castrated. Filled with shame, he became a monk at St Denis and persuaded his wife to take the veil at Argenteuil. Later he gave her the Benedictine convent, the Paraclete, that he had founded and she became abbess there, despite her self-confessed devotion to Abelard rather than God.

Their famous correspondence, which allegedly began when a copy of Abelard's account of their tragic story, *Letters to a Friend*, came into her possession, speaks of their passionate love for one another and forms the basis for a plethora of literature on the subject.

Hemans, Felicia Dorothea, *née* Browne

Born 1793 Died 1835
English poet who wrote 'The boy stood on the burning deck'

Felicia Browne was born in Liverpool, the daughter of a merchant. Between 1808 and 1812 she published three volumes of poems, and in 1812 married an Irishman, Captain Alfred Hemans. He deserted her in 1818, and she turned to writing for a living to support her five sons.

She produced a large number of books of verse of all kinds — love lyrics, classical, mythological and sentimental — including *The Siege of Valencia* (1823) and *Records of Women* (1828). She was regarded as an epitome of feminine charm in her time, but is perhaps best remembered for the poem *Casabianca* — better known as 'The boy stood on the burning deck' — and 'The stately homes of England'.

Hemessen, Catharina van

Born c.1528 Died c.1587
Flemish painter best known for her portraits of well-known contemporary figures

Catharina van Hemessen was born in Antwerp, Flanders, the daughter of a well-known artist, Jan Sanders van Hemessen. She studied in her father's studio and collaborated with him on some of his best-known works. In 1554 she married Chrétien de Morien, the organist of Antwerp Cathedral.

She painted many portraits of well-to-do men and women, examples of which now hang in the Rijksmuseum, Amsterdam, and the National Gallery, London. Her famous self portrait *I, Caterina de Hemessen, painted myself in 1548*, now hangs in Basle Museum.

Catharina enjoyed the patronage of Queen **Mary of Hungary**, Regent of the Low Countries, and when Mary resigned her regency in 1556, Catharina was invited to accompany her to Spain; on the death of their patron however, she and her husband returned to their beloved Antwerp.

Henie, Sonja

Born 1912 Died 1969
Norwegian-born American ice-skater who transformed the style of competitive ice-skating

Sonja Henie was born in Oslo. She trained as a ballet dancer and incorporated balletic movements into ice-skating, transforming its style of competitive exhibition. She won the world amateur championship for women in

10 consecutive years (1927–36) and the gold medal in figure-skating at the Winter Olympics of 1928, 1932 and 1936 (her record for the most wins in each competition still holds).

In 1932 and 1936 she took the 'Grand Slam' — the Olympic, World and European titles — then turned professional and starred in touring ice-shows in Europe and the Americas, some of which she produced herslf. She later went to Hollywood where she made 10 films (1937–45) and proved herself to be a highly capable businesswoman and a major box-office attraction.

Married twice to Americans (she took citizenship in 1941), with her third husband the Norwegian shipowner Niels Onstad, she made her name as a modern art collector and patron. In 1968 they founded a modern art centre near Oslo: the Sonja Henies and Niels Onstads Foundation.

Henley, Beth (Elizabeth)

Born 1952
American actress, dramatist and screenwriter
who writes about the American deep South

Beth Henley was born in Jackson, Mississippi. Her first major success was *Crimes of the Heart* (1978), describing a poignant, often comic reunion of three sisters, whose self-reliance and combined emotional strength enables them to overcome the effects of violence and despondency. Staged by the Actors' Theatre of Louisville in 1979, it transferred to Broadway two years later and received the 1981 Pulitzer Prize for drama. It has also been made into a successful film.

Several plays have followed, of which the most familiar is *The Miss Firecracker Contest* (1980), which incorporates Henley's recurring theme — family relationships in the American deep south.

Henningsen, Agnes

Born 1868 Died 1962
Danish novelist and playwright who has earned
most renown for her memoirs

Agnes Henningsen was born on the island of Funen. She married twice, gave birth to four children and lived out the life of sexual, cultural and political freedom that she was known to advocate.

Her work, depicting women in a notable range of roles, focuses on their relations to men and to eroticism. While her novel *De spedalske* (1903, 'The Lepers') defines sexuality as fundamental to all human relations, her play *Elskerinden* (1906, 'The Mistress') exposes the implications of the conventional feminine role. *Kærlighedens Aarstider* (3 vols, 1927–30, 'Love's Seasons'), in which naturalism is fused with psychological realism, asserts the significance of women's eroticism, challenges the centrality of motherhood to women's lives and underlines the impact of self-realization through work. Her eight volumes of *Erindringer* (1941–55, 'Memoirs') have won considerable acclaim.

Her avant-garde subject-matter links her in literary history with **Thit Jensen** and **Karin Michaëlis**.

Henri, Florence

Born 1893 Died 1982
American pianist-turned-artist and
photographer

Florence Henri was born in New York to a French father and a mother from Silesia (now Poland). After her mother's death in 1895, she travelled widely with her father, beginning music studies in Paris in 1902, which she continued in Italy and Berlin until 1914. Until 1918 she was a pianist, but she had studied painting in Berlin in 1914 and returned to these studies in 1922–3. In 1924 she married a Swiss man, Karl Anton Koster (divorced 1954) to facilitate her entry into France, and went on to study painting at the Académie Moderne in Paris (1925–6). In 1927 she attended a session at the Bauhaus, Dessau and there developed an interest in photography.

She opened a photographic studio in Paris in 1929, also teaching and publishing in journals such as *Vogue* and *Art et métiers graphiques*, and her work, which included still lifes and industrial photography, was represented in influential exhibitions such as 'Film und Foto' (1929, Stuttgart). After 1945 she turned again to painting. A major retrospective of her work was shown at the San Francisco Museum of Modern Art in 1990–1.

Florence Henri is best known for her late 1920s and 1930s explorations of abstract, Cubist and purist ideas.

Henrietta Anne, Duchess of Orléans

Born 1644 Died 1670
English princess who spent much of her time at
the court of Louis XIV of France

Henrietta Anne was the youngest daughter of Charles I of Great Britain and **Henrietta Maria**. She was born in Exeter while the English civil wars were still at their height and brought up by her mother in France. Her brother Charles II was restored to the English throne in 1660 and in 1661 she married Louis

XIV's homosexual brother Philippe of France, Duke of Orléans. She was also rumoured to have been for a time the mistress of the French king himself.

Known as 'Minette', she was Charles II's favourite sister and played an important part in the negotiations of the Secret Treaty of Dover (1670) between Charles and Louis, which made England and France allies against the Dutch. There were strong rumours that her subsequent death was caused by poison, although it was more probably a case of a ruptured appendix. She was the mother of Marie-Louise, who married Charles II of Spain, and Anne-Marie, who became Queen of Sardinia.

Henrietta Maria

Born 1609 Died 1669
Queen of Britain as the wife of Charles I (ruled 1625–49)

Henrietta Maria was born in the Louvre, Paris, the youngest child of Henri IV of France. Her father's assassination six months afterwards left her to the upbringing of her mother, **Marie de' Médicis**. She was married in 1625 to Charles I. Her French attendants and Roman Catholic beliefs made her extremely unpopular, but after the assassination of one of her main adversaries, George Villiers, 1st Duke of Buckingham, the couple fell in love and lived reasonably happily.

In February 1642, under the threat of impeachment, she fled to Holland and raised funds for the Royalist cause. A year later she landed at Bridlington, and met Charles near Edgehill, and again tried to bolster the Royalist position. On 3 April 1644 however, they separated at Abingdon for the last time. At Exeter, on 16 June, she gave birth to **Henrietta Anne** and a fortnight later she was compelled to flee to France.

The war of the Fronde (1648) reduced her temporarily to destitution, despite the liberal allowance assigned to her. She paid two visits to England after the Restoration (1660–1 and 1662–5) before settling in Paris. She was the mother of Charles II and James II.

Henry, Alice

Born 1857 Died 1943
Australian writer and journalist, trade unionist and feminist

Alice Henry was born in Richmond, Victoria. She was educated at Melbourne's Educational Institute for Ladies, and became a teacher and then a journalist. Between 1884 and 1904 she wrote for various Melbourne newspapers, and

campaigned for women's suffrage and trade union rights. In 1905 she left to visit England and the USA and remained in Chicago as secretary of the Chicago branch of the National Women's Trade Union League. With **Miles Franklin** she edited the League's official journal (1910–19).

Her works include *The Trade Union Woman* (1915) and *Women and the Labour Market* (1923). After returning to Australia in 1933 she compiled a pioneering bibliography of Australian women writers (1937).

Henshall, Audrey Shore

Born 1927
English archaeologist whose specialities include chambered tombs

Audrey Henshall was born in Oldham, Lancashire, and educated at Edinburgh University. She was Assistant Keeper of Archaeology in the National Museum of Antiquities of Scotland and latterly Assistant Secretary to the Society of Antiquaries of Scotland, as well as being a founder member of the Scottish Archaeological Forum.

She has become a leading authority on early textiles, prehistoric pottery and neolithic chambered tombs, and her corpus *The Chambered Tombs of Scotland* (2 vols, 1963, 1972), currently being updated, has been the essential database for all subsequent work on chambered tombs.

Hepburn, Audrey, *originally* Edda Van Heemstra Hepburn-Ruston

Born 1929 Died 1993
Belgian actress whose starring roles of the 1950s and 1960s included Eliza Doolittle

Audrey Hepburn was born in Brussels. She trained in ballet in Amsterdam and London and made her film début in Nederland in *7 Lessen* (1948). She was given the lead in the Broadway production of *Gigi* and won a Best Actress Oscar for her beguiling performance as a princess wooed by journalist Gregory Peck in *Roman Holiday* (1953).

One of the major stars of the 1950s and 1960s, her greatest successes include *The Nun's Story* (1959) and *Breakfast At Tiffany's* (1961). She also played the lead in *My Fair Lady* (1964), but some felt that **Julie Andrews**, the stage Eliza Doolittle, merited the role.

Being a star, she had an influence on fashion, particularly the wearing of a shirt over a sweater. She is also credited for popularizing Capri pants and flat pumps. Due to family commitments, Hepburn appeared increasingly infrequently and in the 1990s took up extensive travelling as a goodwill ambassador for UNICEF.

Hepburn, Katharine Houghton

Born 1909
American film and stage actress, a versatile and strong-charactered leading lady

Katharine Hepburn was born in Hartford, Connecticut, and educated at Bryn Mawr College. She made her professional stage début in *The Czarina* (1928) in Baltimore, but attained international fame as a film actress where her distinctive New England diction and fine bone structure complemented a versatile talent capable of all shades of drama and farce.

She won Academy Awards for *Morning Glory* (1933), *Guess Who's Coming to Dinner* (1967), *The Lion in Winter* (1968) and *On Golden Pond* (1981). On stage she continued to tackle the classics and enjoyed enormous success in the musical *Coco* (1970). Among many of her outstanding films were *Bringing Up Baby* (1938), *The Philadelphia Story* (1940), *Woman of the Year* (1942), which saw the beginning of a 25-year professional and personal relationship with co-star Spencer Tracy, *The African Queen* (1951) and *Long Day's Journey Into Night* (1962).

She continued to act into her mid-eighties despite suffering from Parkinson's Disease, and her last cinema appearance was a cameo role in *A Love Affair* (1994). Television work includes *The Glass Menagerie* (1973), *Love Among the Ruins* (1975), *Mrs Delafield Wants to Marry* (1986) and *The Man Upstairs* (1992); her last appearance was in cable television's *One Christmas* (1994).

Hepworth, Dame (Jocelyn) Barbara

Born 1903   Died 1975
English sculptor who was one of the foremost nonfigurative sculptors of her time

Barbara Hepworth was born in Wakefield. She studied at the Leeds School of Art (with Henry Moore (1898–1986), who later commented that women sculpture students in those days were not taken seriously), the Royal College of Art, and in Italy. She married, first, the sculptor John Skeaping (1901–80) and then the painter Ben Nicholson (1894–1982), by whom she had triplets.

A leading nonfigurative sculptor, she was notable for the strength and formal discipline of her carving (eg the *Contrapuntal Forms* exhibited at the Festival of Britain, 1951). Until the early 1960s her works were mainly

Barbara Hepworth

in wood, including *Forms in Echelon* (1938) and *Group II (People Waiting)* (1952). She then worked in stone, producing *Two Forms with White (Greek)* (wood and stone, 1963) and *Three Monoliths* (marble, 1964), and in metal — *Four Square (Walk Through)* (bronze, 1966). Her representational paintings and drawings are of equal power.

She suffered from throat cancer, and died in a fire in her studio in Cornwall.

Herbert, Mary, Countess of Pembroke, *née* Sidney

Born 1561   Died 1621
English writer and patron, and sister of Sir Philip Sidney who edited his Arcadia *after his death*

Mary Sidney was probably born in Penshurst, Kent. She grew up in Ludlow Castle, and was well educated, learning Latin, Greek, Hebrew and French. She entered **Elizabeth I**'s household in 1575, and married Henry Herbert, Earl of Pembroke in 1577. Thereafter she lived at Wilton.

She was close to her older brother, the poet Sir Philip Sidney (1554–86) who dedicated *The Countess of Pembroke's Arcadia* (written 1577–83) to her. After Sidney's death in 1586, she completed the verse translation of the psalms on which they had been collaborating (43 by

Sidney; 107 by Mary). She also published revised versions of *Arcadia* (in 1593 and in 1598), which had first been published in 1590. She was a patron to the poets Edmund Spenser and Samuel Daniel.

Hermes, Gertrude

Born 1901 Died 1983
English printmaker and sculptor, a highly skilled and technical engraver whose work often has a post-cubist approach in plane and form

Gertrude Hermes was born in Bromley, Kent. She studied at the Beckenham School of Art before attending Leon Underwood's School in London (1922–5) alongside Henry Moore and her future husband Blair Hughes-Stanton, whom she married in 1926. The couple moved to Gregynog in 1930 and divorced in 1933.

Hermes continued to work in collaboration with Hughes-Stanton at the Gregynog press, bringing up her two children on the income from her sculpture and printmaking work.

She exhibited at the Paris and New York World Fairs and was chosen to represent Britain at the Venice Biennale in 1939. She was elected a Royal Academician in 1971 and awarded the OBE in 1982.

Hermodsson, Elisabet Hermine

Born 1927
Swedish writer, composer and artist whose work combines different art forms

Elisabet Hermodsson was born in Göteborg and educated at the University of Stockholm and at art school. Her work encompasses a range of media and genres, such as in the volume *Dikt-ting* (1966, 'Poems Objects') which conflates poetry and pictures.

On the basis of humanist, Christian and subsequently feminist convictions she has formulated a far-reaching cultural critique to which environmental concerns are central, for example in the poems in *Mänskligt landskap, orättvist fördelat* (1968, 'Human Province, Unfairly Distributed'), in the essays in *Synvända* (1975, 'Sight Distortion'), and in the 'ecological oratorio' *Skapelse utlämnad* (1986, 'Creation Abandoned').

Her feminism first found expression in the 1970s, notably in *Disa Nilssons visor* (1974, 'Disa Nilsson's Songs'), a volume of poems set to music and illustrated by the author, and designed to offer an antithesis to the conventional image of woman presented in the poet Birger Sjöberg's popular *Fridas visor* of 1922.

Herrad of Hohenbourg, *also called* Herrad of Landsburg

Born 1130 Died 1195
Alsatian abbess who became the first woman to organize the compilation of an encyclopedia

Herrad held the position of abbess at Hohenbourg, Alsace, from 1167. An energetic foundress, she was responsible for a priory, church, farm, hospital and hospice.

She had a similar concern for her nuns' education and supervised their production of the *Hortus Deliciarum*, a major religious and scientific illustrated encyclopedia compiled between 1160 and 1170. The original of this summary of 12th-century knowledge was destroyed in the siege of Strasbourg in 1870, but earlier tracings of many of the miniatures survive.

Herschel, Caroline Lucretia

Born 1750 Died 1848
German-born British astronomer who discovered eight comets

Caroline Herschel was born in Hanover. Her brother William Herschel (1738–1822) brought her to England in 1772 as assistant with his musical activities, and she became his devoted collaborator when he abandoned his first career for astronomy (1782).

Between 1786 and 1797 she discovered eight comets, and among her other discoveries was the companion of the Andromeda nebula (1783). In 1787 she was granted a salary of £50 a year from the king as her brother's assistant at Slough. Her part in William's observational work made her thoroughly familiar with the heavens: her *Index to Flamsteed's Observations of the Fixed Stars* and a list of errata were published by the Royal Society (1798).

Following her brother's death she returned at the age of 72 to Hanover where she worked on the reorganization of his catalogue of nebulae. For this *Reduction and Arrangement in the Form of a Catalogue in Zones of all the Star Clusters and Nebulae Observed by Sir William Herschel*, though unpublished, she was awarded the Gold Medal of the Royal Astronomical Society (1828). She was elected (with **Mary Somerville**) an honorary member of the Royal Astronomical Society (1835) and a member of the Royal Irish Academy (1838). On her 96th birthday she received a gold medal from the King of Prussia.

Herz, Henriette, *née* de Lemos

Born 1764 Died 1847
German-Jewish socialite famed for her salon in Berlin

Henriette de Lemos married the doctor and philosopher Markus Herz (1747–1803). She was a woman of outstanding beauty and culture, and presided over a brilliant salon for the greatest intellectual figures of the day, including the statesman and philologist Karl von Humboldt, the philosopher Johann Fichte and the philosopher and theologian Friedrich Schleiermacher. She became a Christian in 1817.

Hess, Dame Myra

Born 1890 Died 1965
English pianist famed for her arrangement of Bach's 'Jesu, joy of man's desiring'

Myra Hess was born in London. She studied under Tobias Matthay at the Royal Academy of Music and was an immediate success on her first public appearance in 1907. She worked as a chamber musician, recitalist and virtuoso, achieving fame in North America as well as Britain.

Her interpretation of the music of Mozart, Robert Schumann, Beethoven and Bach was especially famed, and she successfully transcribed the chorale from Bach's church cantata No.147 under the title 'Jesu, joy of man's desiring'.

During World War II she organized the lunchtime concerts in the National Gallery, for which she was awarded the DBE in 1941.

Hesse, Eva

Born 1936 Died 1970
German-born American sculptor whose imaginative work exerted a strong influence on later sculptors

Eva Hess was born in Hamburg into a Jewish family who emigrated to the USA in 1939 and settled in New York, where she remained until her death. She attended the Pratt Institute, New York (1952–3), and Cooper Union (1954–7).

From 1965 she worked in a variety of unusual materials, including rubber, plastic, string and polythene. Using unconventional techniques, these were made into hauntingly bizarre objects designed to rest on the floor or against a wall or even be suspended from the ceiling.

Hewett, Dorothy Coade

Born 1923
Australian dramatist, novelist and poet, who is perhaps best known for her plays

Dorothy Hewett was born in Wickepin, Western Australia, and educated at the University of Western Australia. She joined the Communist Party at the age of 19 and worked in a factory. Her poetry is collected in *What about the People?* (1961, a collaboration with her third husband Merv Lilley) and four other volumes including *Journeys* (1982).

Little of her prolific output of plays has been published, but *This Old Man Comes Rolling Home* (1976) and *The Man from Mukinupin* (1979) deserve notice. Her first novel, *Bobbin Up* (1959), received acclaim; its story of the political and sexual awakening of a group of factory girls stands in direct line of descent from feminist writings of the 1920s and 1930s. *The Toucher* (1993) tells of an elderly novelist and her relationship with a much younger man.

Hewett has been awarded several literary prizes as well as the Order of Australia.

He Xiangning (Ho Hsiang-ning)

Born 1880 Died 1972
Chinese revolutionary and feminist and one of the first Chinese women to cut her hair short

He Xiangning was born in China and educated in Hong Kong and Japan. She married fellow revolutionary Liao Zhongkai (Liao Chung-k'ai) in 1905 and was an active advocate of links with the communists and Russia.

Her husband was assassinated in 1925, and when two years later the Chinese military leader Chiang Kai-shek (Jiang Jieshi) broke with the communists, she returned to Hong Kong. Here she was an outspoken critic of his leadership and one of the first women to publicly advocate nationlism, revolution and female emancipation. She returned to Beijing (Peking) in 1949 as head of the overseas commission.

Heyer, Georgette

Born 1902 Died 1974
English historical and detective novelist of over 60 books who helped to develop the detective genre

Georgette Heyer was born in London of partly South Slav descent. She studied at Westminster College, London, and after marriage in 1925 travelled in East Africa and Yugoslavia until 1929. By that time she had produced several well-researched historical novels from various periods, including *The Black Moth* (1921) and *Beauvallet* (1929).

She risked fictional studies of real figures in crisis with books on William the Conqueror, Charles II and the battle of Waterloo. It was not until *Regency Buck* (1935) and later novels that she really came into her own with the Regency period (1811–20), on which she made herself an outstanding authority. *My Lord John* (1976), on Henry V's brother, was unfinished at her death.

She also wrote modern comedy detective novels with dexterity, such as *Death in the Stocks* (1935) and *Behold, Here's Poison* (1936), and used detective and thriller plots with pace and irony in historical fiction such as *The Talisman Ring* (1936), *The Reluctant Widow* (1946) and *The Quiet Gentleman* (1951).

Heymann, Lida Gustava

Born 1867 Died 1943
German feminist and political activist, a prominent campaigner for women's suffrage

Lida Heymann was born in Hamburg. She was rich and independent, and during the 1890s she organized a number of projects for women, including a day nursery, a women's home and training for apprentices. In 1898, with **Minna Cauer**, she campaigned against legalized prostitution. She was a founder-member of the women's suffrage society *Deutscher Verband für Frauenstimmrecht* (1902) alongside Cauer and **Anita Augspurg**. In 1907 Heymann, Cauer and Augspurg moved to Munich where they carried on a militant suffrage campaign, joining the more radical *Deutscher Frauenstimmrechtsbund* in 1913.

Heymann's pacifism, shared by Cauer and Augspurg, cost them support within the suffrage movement during World War I. Afterwards, the three colleagues started the newspaper *Die Frau im Staat* (1918–33). When Hitler gained power in 1933 Heymann and Augspurg fled to Zurich, continued to work for women's rights and wrote their memoirs, *Erlebtes-Erschautes*.

Hicks, Amie (Amelia Jane)

Born 1839/40 Died 1917
English trade unionist, one of the founders of the Women's Trade Union Association

Amie Hicks's early life is unknown except that her father was a Chartist. She married William Hicks, emigrated to New Zealand, and worked as a rope-maker. On the family's return to England in the early 1880s, she, her husband and eldest children became active in the Social Democratic Federation.

A midwife and member of the Ladies' Medical College, during the 1880s she became involved in the campaign against the Contagious Diseases Act. She was a founder of the Women's Trade Union Association (1889), the Women's Industrial Council, and other organizations concerned with the education and working conditions of female employees. She was particularly involved with working girls' clubs, and became their vice-president.

Higgins, Rosalyn, *née* Inberg

Born 1937
English lawyer, the first female judge to be appointed to the International Court of Justice in the Hague

Rosalyn Inberg was educated at Cambridge and Yale universities, where she developed an interest in United Nations law. In 1961 she married Terence Higgins, an economist who became Conservative MP for Worthing in 1964. Among other positions, she was staff specialist in international law at the Royal Institute of International Affairs (1963–74).

She was appointed Professor of International Law at the University of Kent at Canterbury in 1978, then moved to the chair at the London School of Economics (1981–95). She became the UK representative on the United Nations Committee on Human Rights in 1985 and was appointed QC the following year, until in 1995 she left these positions to become a judge in the International Court of Justice, an appointment widely welcomed by those who have experienced her strong character, legal expertise, idealism and common sense. Her publications include *Problems and Process: International Law and How We Use It* (1995).

Highsmith, Patricia

Born 1921 Died 1995
American writer of crime fiction whose first thriller became a successful Hitchcock film

Patricia Highsmith was born in Fort Worth, Texas, and educated at Columbia University. She created a world which the novelist Graham Greene characterized as claustrophobic and irrational, one 'we enter each time with a sense of personal danger'.

Her first novel, *Strangers on a Train* (1950), was filmed by Alfred Hitchcock. Her third, *The Talented Mr Ripley* (1955), was awarded the Edgar Allan Poe Scroll by the Mystery Writers of America, and began the adventures of the detective Tom Ripley for which Highsmith is best known. Later novels featuring Ripley include *Ripley Under Ground* (1971), *Ripley's Game* (1974) and *Ripley Under Water* (1991). She also published several volumes of short stories.

Hightower, Rosella

Born 1920
American ballerina, brilliant technician and leading director of dance companies

Rosella Hightower

Paddy Frew was born in Belfast. She began her career in radio and television as a production secretary and assisted her first husband, editor and director Patrick Higson (1931–83), in his documentary and promotional productions as well as the cinéma vérité documentary *Big Banana Feet* (1975), an account of comedian Billy Connolly on tour. Gaining experience, she was associate producer of the Bill Forsyth films *That Sinking Feeling* (1979), *Gregory's Girl* (1980) and *Comfort and Joy* (1984).

Following her husband's death, she became a full-time producer and the doyenne of the Scottish film industry, instrumental in instigating the careers of many first-time directors. Her films include *The Girl in the Picture* (1986) and the award-winning *Silent Scream* (1990). In 1985 she purchased Black Cat Studios in Glasgow to provide facilities for the burgeoning Scottish independent production scene, but was forced into liquidation (1990).

She later worked in the drama department of BBC Scotland, and subsequently returned to independent production with her revived company Antonine Films.

Hilda, St

Born 614   Died 680
Anglo-Saxon abbess whose monastery became an important centre of learning

Hilda was the daughter of a nephew of King Edwin of Northumbria, with whom she was baptized at the age of 13 by Paulinus, the first archbishop of York. In 649 she became abbess of Hartlepool Abbey, a double monastery of monks and nuns.

In 657, on land donated by Edwin's successor King Oswiu, she founded a double monastery at Streaneshalch (now Whitby), over which she ruled wisely for 22 years. It became an important centre of learning and hosted the Synod of Whitby in 663–4, which was called by King Oswiu to resolve the argument over the date for Easter.

Hilda's feast day is 17 November.

Rosella Hightower was born in Ardmore, Oklahoma, of Native American extraction. She studied in Kansas City, Missouri, before beginning her long career as a leading ballerina with Ballet Russe de Monte Carlo (1938–41), American Ballet Theatre (1941–5), Léonide Massine's Ballet Russe Highlights and the Original Ballet Russe (both 1945–6).

She joined Nouveau Ballet de Monte Carlo in 1947 and, later, the Grand Ballet du Marquis de Cuevas (until 1961), touring the world and making guest appearances with various companies.

She became founding director of the Centre de Danse Classique in Cannes in 1962, and was ballet director of the Marseille Opéra Ballet (1969–71), Ballet de Nancy (1973–4) and Paris Opéra Ballet from 1980.

Higson, Paddy, *née* Frew

Born 1941
Northern Irish film producer who became a driving force in the Scottish film industry

Hildegard von Bingen

Born 1098   Died 1179
German Benedictine abbess, mystical philosopher, healer and musician

Hildegard was born to a noble family in Böckelheim and from the age of eight was brought up by a recluse named Jutta. At the age of 15 she entered the convent at Diessenberg, where she succeeded Jutta as abbess in 1136. Sometime between 1147 and 1152, the community moved to a larger house at Rubertsberg, near Bingen.

From an early age Hildegard experienced apocalyptic visions, 26 of which were collected in the *Scivias* (1141–52). Her *Liber vitae meritorum* (1158–63) and *Liber divinorum operum* (1163–74) were also prompted by visions. Her other writings include saints' lives and studies in medicine and natural history. The body of religious music that she wrote has become widely known only in the 1980s.

Her spiritual advice — given during travels in France and Germany and in many surviving letters — was sought by people of all classes, and in parts of Germany she is treated as a saint. Sabina Flanagan's *Hildegard of Bingen: A Visionary Life* (1989) is the major critical study.

Hill, Anita Faye

Born 1956
African-American lawyer and teacher who has become a symbol of race relations and sexual harassment

Anita Hill was born in Morris, Oklahoma. After receiving her law degree from Yale University in 1977, she practised law in Washington DC in a private practice as well as for American government agencies including the US Department of Education and the Equal Employment Opportunity Commission (EEOC).

In 1983 she began teaching law at Oral Roberts University and then moved to become professor at the University of Oklahoma College of Law.

When she was employed by the EEOC, she was special assistant to Clarence Thomas. During the televised hearings of his nomination to join the US Supreme Court in October 1991, she riveted the nation with her testimony of sexual harassment, which he denied. Although Thomas was endorsed and is now serving as an associate US Supreme Court Justice, Hill had paved the way for future charges to be brought against men in high positions.

Hill, Octavia

Born 1838   Died 1912
English social reformer who worked to improve slum conditions and became a founder of the National Trust

Octavia Hill was born in London, the granddaughter of the physician and sanitary reformer Thomas Southwood Smith (1788–1861). She was influenced by the Christian socialism of theologian Frederick Denison Maurice (1805–72) and tutored in art by art critic and author John Ruskin (1819–1900).

She became an active promoter of improved housing conditions for the poor in London and from 1864, with Ruskin's financial help, she bought slum houses for improvement projects. With Maurice she founded the Charity Organization Society (1869).

Her books included *Homes of the London Poor* (1875) and *Our Common Land* (1878). She was also a leader of the open-space movement, and in 1895 became a co-founder (with Canon Hardwicke Rawnsley and Sir Robert Hunter) of the National Trust for Places of Historic Interest or Natural Beauty.

Hill, Susan Elizabeth

Born 1942
English novelist and radio dramatist whose characteristic themes are isolation and despair

Susan Hill was born in Scarborough. She published her first novel, *The Enclosure* (1961), while a student at London University. Her novels are strong in terms of character and atmosphere, particularly climate. A recurring theme, and one which permeates *The Albatross and other Stories* (1971) and *The Bird of Night* (1972), is a sense of malevolence, violence and despair, while *In the Springtime of the Year* (1974) vividly evokes the aftermath of bereavement, and the pain of memory and loneliness.

After a long silence, Hill published *Air and Angels* in 1991, a love story set in India and Cambridge. *Mrs de Winter* (1993), a sequel to **Daphne du Maurier**'s *Rebecca*, is the most successful of a vogue for sequels, because, as **Anita Brookner** observed, the author 'gives us a Susan Hill novel'.

Her stage adaptation of *The Woman in Black* (1983), a musical chiller in which a ghost takes revenge for her child's death by murdering other children, has been a long-running success in London.

Hiller, Dame Wendy

Born 1912
English actress whose clarity of diction and spirited personality made her one of Britain's leading stage performers

Wendy Hiller was born in Bramhall, Cheshire. She became interested in dramatics as a child, and joined the Manchester Repertory Theatre straight from school in 1930. She made her London début in *Love on the Dole* (1935) and her film début in *Lancashire Luck* (1937).

At the 1936 Malvern Festival she played

Saint Joan and Eliza Doolittle, a role she re-created at the behest of playwright George Bernard Shaw in the 1938 film of *Pygmalion*. She gave a moving performance as Tess in Thomas Hardy's *Tess of the D'Urbervilles* in 1946, adapted by the dramatist Ronald Gow (1897–1993), whom she had married in 1937.

Her sporadic film career includes performances of distinction in *Major Barbara* (1940), *I Know Where I'm Going* (1945), *Sons and Lovers* (1960), *A Man for All Seasons* (1966) and *Separate Tables* (1958), for which she received an Academy Award. She continued to work on television and radio into the 1990s.

She was appointed DBE in 1975.

Himiko

Died AD 247
Queen of Japan who was Japan's first known ruler

Himiko is traditionally thought to be the daughter of the emperor Suinin. Originally the ruler of a Japanese tribe known as the Yamato, she extended her control over other tribal groups in the area around Nara (Kyushu) at the eastern end of the Inland Sea and became Japan's first known ruler. Chinese chronicles of the 3rd century describe her as a shamaness-ruler whose younger brother served as the non-spiritual ruler.

She may have been killed by chieftains disillusioned with her waning religious powers in war, or else in battle. Her death sparked off civil war when her brother ignored the female right of inheritance and usurped the throne. Evidence of female rule at this time and the claim of Yamato rulers that they were descended from the Sun Goddess (Amaterasu) have led some historians to suggest that early Japan may originally have been a matriarchal society that was only gradually transformed into the strongly male-dominated family system of later times.

Hindley, Myra

Born 1942
Convicted English criminal who is known as one of the infamous 'Moors Murderers'

Myra Hindley was born in Gorton, near Manchester. While working as a typist she met Ian Brady. They became lovers and soon embarked on a series of murders which were to horrify the public. The couple lured children back to their house in Manchester and tortured them before killing them.

David Smith, Hindley's brother-in-law, contacted the police on 7 October 1965 about the murders. Hindley and Brady were arrested, the body of 17-year-old Edward Evans was found at their house, and a huge search for other victims' bodies began on the Pennine moors. The graves and remains of 10-year-old Lesley Ann Downey and 12-year-old John Kilbride were found on Saddleworth Moor, which is why the couple were called the 'Moors Murderers'. Hindley was convicted on two counts of murder and was sentenced to life imprisonment.

Her claims in recent years that she has reformed have not led to her release. She made a private confession to two other murders in 1986 and the body of Pauline Reade was found in August 1987, 24 years after her disappearance. The body of 12-year-old Keith Bennett has never been found.

Hiratsuka Raicho, *pseud of* Hiratsuka Haru

Born 1886   Died 1971
Japanese feminist whose concerns ranged from consumer affairs to banning the bomb

Hiratsuka Haru was born in Tokyo and educated at Ochanomizu Girls' School. She graduated in home economics from the Japanese Women's University in 1906.

In 1911 she founded the literary magazine *Seito* ('Bluestockings') which focused on 'the new woman' and suffered from personal attacks for the views it proposed. Despite this she lived with Okumara Hiroshi for four years before marrying him in 1918.

In 1920 she formed a women's consumers' union *Wareranole* of which she was also director. In 1953 she became President of the Federation of Japanese Women's Organizations and in 1954 called upon the women of the world to ban the H–bomb, a call which led to the World Mothers' Convention.

Hite, Shere, *originally* Shirley Diana Gregory

Born 1943
American feminist writer and self-appointed sex expert

Shere Hite was born in St Joseph, Missouri, and brought up by her grandparents in Missouri. She studied history at the universities of Florida and Columbia and worked as a model before entering the feminist arena. She directed the feminist sexuality project National Organization for Women in New York (1972–8), and lectured at the universities of Harvard, McGill and Columbia, as well as for numerous women's groups.

In 1976 she published *The Hite Report: A Nationwide Study of Female Sexuality*, the result of five years' research; it sold two million copies amidst great uproar. It was followed in 1981 with *The Hite Report on Male Sexuality*, and in 1987 with *The Hite Report of Women*. Through recording the testimonies of real people, she has exploded traditional attitudes to sex. Her method of research, based on questionnaires, has been criticised for allegedly not using random samples and not taking into account the age, race, economic status and class of respondents, as well as basing statistics on a low level of return of questionnaires.

Irrespective of whether such criticisms invalidate her findings, the interest her work has generated cannot be questioned.

Ho, Xuan Hu'o'ng, *also spelt* Huo

Floreat c.1780–1820
Vietnamese poet whose work constitutes some of Asia's finest 19th-century poetry

Xuan Hu'o'ng Ho's precise identity is unknown, although we know from her work that Ho is her real family name, and Xuan Hu'o'ng is a pseudonym. She was an educated, cultured woman, and produced some of the most sensuous, witty and readable verse to come out of Asia in the 19th century.

Typically, a poem by Ho pretends to be about a harmless domestic activity (weaving or making rice cakes), making it seem innocent, but there is a second level of meaning, usually sexual.

She has been hailed as a proto-feminist, as she argues in her verse that the sexes should be more equal, and often comes out against marriage, saying that love between men and women should be freely given.

Hodgkin, Dorothy Mary, *née* Crowfoot

Born 1910 Died 1994
British crystallographer who became the only British woman to win a Nobel science prize

Dorothy Crowfoot was born in Cairo, Egypt. She studied chemistry at Somerville College, Oxford, moved to Cambridge to study for her PhD and became a Fellow and Tutor at Somerville in 1934. After various appointments within the university, she became the first Royal Society Wolfson Research Professor at Oxford (1960).

In X-ray crystallography studies at Cambridge, Irish crystallographer John Bernal (1901–71) introduced her to the study of biologically interesting molecules, which was extremely difficult and tedious in the 1930s.

With him she began work on sterols, which she continued after her return to Oxford. Her detailed X-ray analysis of cholesterol was a milestone in crystallography, but an even greater achievement was the determination of the structure of penicillin (1942–5). After World War II computational facilities increased; even so, the determination of the structure of vitamin B_{12} (used to fight pernicious anaemia), which was her real triumph, occupied eight years (1948–56). For her later work on insulin, an even more complicated molecule, sophisticated computers were used.

She received the Nobel Prize for Chemistry in 1964, only the third woman to do so (the first two were **Marie Curie** and **Irène Joliot-Curie**), and in 1965 was admitted to the Order of Merit, the first woman to be so honoured since **Florence Nightingale**. She had been elected FRS in 1947 and throughout her career received several other honours.

Hodgkins, Frances Mary

Born 1869 Died 1947
New Zealand artist who was ranked as a leader of contemporary romanticism

Frances Mary Hodgkins was born in Dunedin, the second daughter of the Liverpool-born painter William Matthew Hodgkins (1833–98). She trained at the Dunedin School of Art and began to establish herself as an artist there before travelling extensively in Europe with long sojourns in Paris, where she taught at the Académie Colarossi, and in England, where she spent World War I.

Her paintings, examples of which are in the Tate Gallery and the Victoria and Albert museum, are characterized by a harmonious use of flat colour somewhat reminiscent of French Impressionist painter Henri Matisse (1869–1954). Although she was older than most of her circle, she was regarded as a leader of contemporary Romanticism.

Hoffman, Alice

Born 1952
American novelist regarded by many as one of the leading writers of her generation

Alice Hoffman was born in New York City and educated at Adelphi University, New York, and Stanford University. Her first novel, *Property Of* (1977), concerns a 17-year-old entranced by the leader of a street gang involved with violence and drugs.

In much of Hoffman's subsequent fiction, which also considers the search for identity in a turbulent world, realism is fused with fantasy so that the everyday events about which she writes attain an almost mythical importance. *White Horses* (1982) examines a young girl's obsession with an older brother, while the austere and haunting *At Risk* (1988) deals with the effect upon her family of a young woman suffering from AIDS.

Hoffman, Malvina

Born 1887 Died 1966
American sculptor famed for her figures of
ethnic types

Malvina Hoffman was born in New York City and trained under the French sculptor Auguste Rodin (1840–1917) in Paris, who sent her to study anatomy at the local medical school. She created busts and full figures, taking her early subjects from her social circle of artistic and literary people, such as **Anna Pavlova**. In 1929 she received a commission from the Field Museum of Natural History in Chicago to sculpt figures of ethnic types observed all over the world, and it is for her series of over 100 bronze figures for this commission (1930–3) that she remains best known.

She published the books *Heads and Tales* (1936), about her travels researching the ethnic types, and *Sculpture Inside and Out* (1937), on the techniques of sculpture.

Hogan, Linda

Born 1947
American writer whose main concerns are the
Native American culture and environmental
issues

Linda Hogan was born in Denver, Colorado, of Chickasaw descent. She has published six volumes of poetry — *Calling Myself Home* (1979), *Daughters, I Love You* (1981), *Eclipse* (1983), *Seeing Through the Sun* (1985), *Savings* (1988) and *The Book of Medicines* (1993) — and the short-story collections *That Horse* (1985), *The Big Woman* (1987) and *Red Clay* (1991). She is also the co-editor of the anthology of women's short fiction, *The Stories We Hold Secret* (1986).

Her first novel, *Mean Spirit* (1990), is set in Oklahoma during the time of the Osage oil boom in the 1920s, and describes a series of brutal murders against a background of judicial corruption, aimed at disinheriting the Osages of their land and mineral rights.

Hogg, Pam

Born 1958
Scottish fashion designer who is regarded as one
of Britain's most innovative contemporary
independent designers

Pam Hogg was born in Paisley and brought up in Glasgow. She studied Fine Art and Printed Textiles at Glasgow School of Art, winning the Newbery Medal of Distinction, the Frank Warner Memorial Medal, the Leverhulme Scholarship and the Royal Society of Arts bursary, before pursuing Printed Textiles at the Royal College of Art in London.

She launched her first collection in 1984, and her use of psychedelic colours on figure-hugging bodysuits has since become her trademark. She is based at Harrods in London and has outlets in Glasgow, Manchester, Belfast, New York and Los Angeles, as well as her own shop.

Three of her outfits are now part of the permanent collection of Kelvingrove Art Gallery in Glasgow.

Hogg, Dame Sarah Elizabeth Mary, *née* Boyd-Carpenter

Born 1946
English economist, journalist and former head of
the British Prime Minister's policy unit

Sarah Boyd-Carpenter graduated from Oxford University with a first class degree in philosophy, politics and economics and began her journalistic career at the *Economist* in 1967. The following year she married the lawyer and politician Douglas Hogg (1945–).

Through her writing for the *Economist*, the *Sunday Times*, the *Independent*, the *Telegraph* and *Sunday Telegraph* and as presenter on *Channel 4 News*, she came to be regarded as a top-ranking journalist, and from 1985 to 1992 she also served as governor of the Centre for Economic Policy Research.

In 1990 she was put in charge of the political advisers in Prime Minister John Major's policy unit, which is responsible for long-term strategic thinking and short-term problem solving. She remained through two general elections that brought success to the Conservative Party and though she received some of the blame for the failure of Major's 1993 'back to basics' campaign, she was praised by the Prime Minister for her staunchness and wise advice. She resigned in 1994 and was appointed DBE in 1995.

Holiday, Billie (Eleanora), *known as* Lady Day

Born 1915 Died 1959
American jazz singer who is one of the most
influential but tragic singers in jazz histroy

Billie Holiday was born in Baltimore, Maryland. She had an insecure childhood and was

Billie Holiday, 1954

Provincial Actors tied for the International Critics Prize at Cannes in 1980. She left Poland for Paris in 1981 to escape political repression, but returned after the political changes of 1989. Her work is marked by a strong sense of political and historical engagement.

Holliday, Judy, *originally* Judith Tuvim

Born 1922 Died 1965
American comic actress whose first Broadway
triumph came when she understudied the lead role

Judy Holliday was born in New York. She became a telephonist for Orson Welles's Mercury theatre, and performed as part of the Revuers cabaret group from 1939 to 1944. An engagement in Los Angeles earned her a contract with Twentieth Century-Fox and some minor film roles.

Hired as an understudy for *Born Yesterday* in 1946, she replaced the original star and enjoyed a long-running Broadway triumph in the role of Billie Dawn, a dumb blonde with a heart of gold. The film version in 1950 earned her the Best Actress Oscar.

Investing her roles with a touching naïvety and a deft sense of timing, she made a scene-stealing appearance in *Adam's Rib* (1949) and starred in such comedy classics as *It Should Happen To You* (1954) and *The Solid Gold Cadillac* (1956). A further Broadway success in *Bells Are Ringing* in 1956 became her final film role in 1960.

jailed for prostitution while a teenager. In the early 1930s she worked as a singer in New York clubs and her wistful voice and remarkable jazz interpretation of popular songs resulted in work with clarinettist Benny Goodman and recording sessions with such leading soloists as Teddy Wilson and saxophonist Lester Young.

Later in the 1930s she worked with the big bands of Count Basie and Artie Shaw. During the 1940s she appeared in several films (including *New Orleans*, with trumpeter and singer Louis Armstrong) but by the end of that decade she was falling victim to drug addiction.

Despite the deterioration of her voice from that period, the melodic and rhythmic subtlety of her singing has inspired many followers.

Holland, Agnieszka

Born 1948
Polish film director who was a leading figure in
the influential Polish New Wave

Agnieszka Holland graduated from the Polish Film School in 1971, and worked as assistant director on Zanussi's *Illuminations* in 1973. She made her directing début the following year with *Evening At Abdan's*. She also worked as a screenwriter for the leading Polish director, Andrzej Wadja.

She became a leading figure in the Polish New Wave during the 1970s, and her film

Hollingworth, Leta, *née* Stetter

Born 1886 Died 1939
American educational psychologist working in
medical, legal and educational insitutions

Leta Stetter was born in Chadron, Nebraska, and was educated locally before attending high school at Valentine, Nebraska. She graduated BA from the University of Nebraska (1906) and was also awarded a state teacher's certificate. In 1908 she married Harry Hollingworth and from 1913 she was a graduate student at Columbia University (PhD 1916).

She became psychologist to the city of New York civil service with responsibility for hospitals, schools and law courts. In 1919 she became a member of staff at Teachers College, and was appointed Professor of Education in 1929.

Her publications include *The Psychology of Subnormal Children* (1920), *Special Talents and Defects* (1923), and *The Psychology of the Adolescent* (1928).

Holm, Hanya, *originally* Johanna Eckert

Born 1893 Died 1992
German-born American dancer, choreographer
and teacher, a key figure in modern dance

Hanya Holm was born in Worms. She studied under the Swiss composer Émile Jaques-Dalcroze, and in 1921 started working as both teacher and dancer with **Mary Wigman**, who sent her to New York in 1931 to establish the American branch of her school.

In 1936 Holm founded her own studio, developing a technique that fused the disciplines of Wigman's approach to movement with a more American emphasis on speed and rhythm.

An important figure in modern dance, she divided her time between concert work and the staging of dances for such Broadway musicals as *Kiss Me Kate* (1948), *My Fair Lady* (1956) and *Camelot* (1960).

Holt, Victoria, *pseud of* Eleanor Alice Burford Hibbert

Born 1906 Died 1993
English writer of popular historical novels, Gothic
romances and family sagas

Eleanor Hibbert was born in London. She is also published as Eleanor Burford, Philippa Carr, Kathleen Kellow and (by far her best known) Jean Plaidy. Privately educated, she published her first novel under her own name in 1941, introducing 'Jean Plaidy' shortly afterwards with *Together They Ride* (1943) and 'Victoria Holt' in 1960 with *Mistress of Mellyn*.

The pattern of the novels always remains unchanged, consisting of insubstantial love stories and power struggles erected on a modestly researched background of historical fact. Perhaps the best known of the early Plaidy books is *The Royal Road to Fotheringay* (1955), which dramatized the life of **Mary, Queen of Scots**.

In the 1960s (as Plaidy again), she embarked on a series of dynastic romances or 'sagas' which confirmed the general suspicion that, whatever the ostensible period of the stories, she essentially wrote about the English upper middle class that was beginning to lose its role as she grew up in the aftermath of World War I.

Holtby, Winifred

Born 1898 Died 1935
English novelist and feminist

Winifred Holtby was born in Rudston, Yorkshire. She was educated at Oxford but her degree was interrupted by World War II, when she served in France with the Women's Auxiliary Army Corps. On her return to Oxford, she became friends with **Vera Brittain**, who later wrote *Testament of Friendship* (1940) as a tribute to her.

Holtby was a prolific journalist and was a director from 1926 of *Time and Tide*. She wrote a number of novels, including *The Crowded Street* (1924) and *The Land of Green Ginger* (1927), but is chiefly remembered for her last and most successful, *South Riding* (1935), which won the James Tait Black Memorial Prize.

Hoodless, Adelaide, *née* Hunter

Born 1857 Died 1910
Canadian campaigner for home economics
teaching in schools, and founder of the Women's
Institutes organization

Adelaide Hunter was born in St George, Canada. She married a rich businessman and had a baby son, but he died in 1889 through drinking contaminated milk; this sparked off her lifelong campaign for home economics classes in schools. She ran domestic science classes at Hamilton YWCA in 1889 and, as President of the national YWCA, opened a school for home economics in 1892. In 1897 she founded the first Women's Institute at Stoney Creek, Ontario; within years it had become an international movement.

Hoodless was focused on the belief that women are destined for home-making and parenthood—a potentially controversial position. However, she did promote the status of housework and child rearing, and challenged the education authorities through her insistence that such skills were not instinctive but needed careful teaching.

Hope, Emma

Born 1964
English shoe designer who creates stylish and
practical 'regalia for feet'

Emma Hope was born in London. She graduated from Cordwainers College, East London, in 1984 and launched her first collection in 1985, selling to Whistles, Jones and Joseph.

Her handfinished women's, men's and bridal collections, featuring period detail and sumptuous fabrics such as brocade, velvet, satin, dupion silk and fine leather, have won her numerous awards for their practicality and style.

She has worked with British fashion designers **Betty Jackson** and **Jean Muir** and currently designs for **Nicole Farhi**. Her shoes, which she calls 'regalia for feet', are now sold in the USA, Germany and Japan.

Hopkins, Patty, *née* Wainwright

Born c.1942
English architect who with her husband became in 1994 the first British couple to win the RIBA Gold Medal

Patty Wainwright was born in Staffordshire and trained at the Architectural Association, London, where she met her future husband and partner Michael Hopkins (1935–   ). Since they set up their practice in 1976, she has worked on all its major projects, including the Mound Stand at Lords Cricket Ground and the extension to Glyndbourne Opera House (1987–   ).

Their designs characteristically combine high-tech design with traditional materials, and that of their steel and glass house in Hampstead, London (1975), owes much to the work of the American architects Charles and **Ray Eames**, earlier RIBA (Royal Institute of British Architects) winners.

Hopper, Grace Murray

Born 1906 Died 1992
American computer programmer and naval officer who made a major impact on the history of computing

Grace Hopper was born in New York City. She was educated at Vassar College, where she later taught in the mathematics department (1931–44). She joined the WAVES (Women Accepted for Voluntary Emergency Service) during World War II and stayed in the Naval Reserve for the rest of her career.

Hopper was drafted by the navy to join Howard Aiken's team at Harvard as a coder for the Mark I with no guidance except the coding book. She gradually developed a set of built-in routines and was eventually able to use the machine to solve complex partial differential equations using only the 72 words of storage at her disposal.

In 1949 she joined the Eckert & Mauchly Corporation as a senior mathematician and in 1951 she conceived of a new type of internal computer program that could perform floating-point operations and other tasks automatically. The program was called a compiler; it was designed to scan a programmer's instructions and produce (compile) a roster of binary instructions that carried out the programmer's commands.

Though the compiler and high-level language were not immediately successful, Hopper's ideas spread and were influential in setting standards for software developments, such as for COBOL. She retired from the navy as a Rear Admiral at the age of 80 when she joined the Digital Equipment Corporation as a senior consultant. She was inducted into the National Women's Hall of Fame in 1994.

Hopper, Hedda, *originally* Elda Furry

Born 1885 Died 1966
American actress who later became an influential gossip columnist

Hedda Hopper was born in Hollidaysburg, Pasadena, the daughter of a butcher. She studied piano and voice in Pittsburgh before making her stage début in 1907 with the Aborn Light Opera Company. She went on the New York stage before moving to Hollywood where she established a successful career in silent films, appearing in as many as 50 productions a year. As that career waned, she began a second one as a gossip columnist in 1938 and was built up as a rival to **Louella Parsons**.

Informed by a wide-ranging network of contacts, her column of Hollywood chit-chat and scandal was syndicated to an estimated 3,000 daily newspapers and 2,000 weeklies. Her luxurious Beverly Hills mansion was called 'The House That Fear Built'.

She was a vocal supporter of many right-wing causes, appeared frequently on radio and published two bestselling books: *From Under My Hat* (1952) and *The Whole Truth and Nothing But* (1963).

Horan, Alice

Born 1895 Died 1971
English trade union organizer who spent 20 influential years with a union in Lancashire

Alice Horan was born in London. She began work at the age of 14, and during World War I she was employed in a factory making service equipment. A strike there aroused her interest in trade unionism; she became a shop steward, then won a scholarship to Ruskin College, Oxford and obtained a diploma in political science.

She became a full-time union official in 1926, as Women's District Organizer for the National Union of General and Municipal Workers in Lancashire, a position which she held for 20 years, during which time the membership increased sevenfold. In 1946 she was appointed National Women's Officer.

Horne, Lena Calhoun

Born 1917
American singer and actress who in 1942 became
the first black singer to win a contract from a
major Hollywood company

Lena Horne was born in Brooklyn, New York. She made her début at the legendary Cotton Club, aged 16, but gradually switched from dancing to band singing.

After winning the contract from MGM she appeared in *Cabin in the Sky* (1943, with **Ethel Waters**) and *Stormy Weather* (1943). The latter became her signature song, and the perfect vehicle for her deep, sensuous voice, with its bluesy edge.

Horne has courageously confronted racism throughout her career. She describes its impact in her two memoirs, *In Person* (1950) and *Lena* (1965).

Horne, Marilyn Bernice

Born 1934
American operatic mezzo-soprano famed for the
range of her voice and for championing lesser-
known operas

Marilyn Horne was born in Bradford, Pennsylvania. She made her début as Háta in *The Bartered Bride*, Los Angeles (1954), at Covent Garden as Marie in *Wozzeck* (1964) and at the New York Metropolitan as Adalgisa in *Norma* (1970).

She had a long association with **Joan Sutherland** and has helped in the revival of operas by Rossini, Bellini and Donizetti. She is also a noted recitalist and dubbed the voice of **Dorothy Dandridge** in the film of *Carmen Jones* (1954).

Horney, Karen, *née* Danielssen

Born 1885 Died 1952
German-born American psychiatrist who refuted
some of Freud's basic theories and began a new
approach to psychoanalytic treatment

Karen Danielssen was born in Hamburg. She completed her medical training in Berlin with a thesis on traumatic psychosis, married Oscar Horney, a fellow student, in 1909, and after several years of working and teaching in Berlin moved to the USA in 1932, where she held posts at Chicago and New York City.

It was at the New School of Social Research there that she wrote her seminal texts, an attack on Freudian anti-feminism entitled *The Neurotic Personality of Our Time* (1937) and *New Ways in Psychoanalysis* (1939), which contradicted several of Freud's tenets and claimed that people were more commonly dis-turbed by social and cultural problems than by their biological make-up. Her reassessment of the accepted theory of personality and her research into the causes of mental breakdown in people were very influential.

She was expelled from the New York Psychoanalytic Institute in 1941 for her refusal to accept Freudian theory and instead formed the Association for the Advancement of Psychoanalysis. Her other publications include *Neurosis and Human Growth* (1950).

Horniman, Annie Elizabeth Fredericka

Born 1860 Died 1937
English theatre manager and patron,
instrumental in establishing Irish national
theatre and the British Repertory Theatre
Movement

Annie Horniman was born in Forest Hall, London, the daughter of a wealthy Quaker tea-merchant. She developed a secret passion for the theatre in her teens, studied at the Slade School of Art and travelled widely, especially in Germany. She failed with a play on the London stage in 1894 and went to Ireland in 1903.

She later financed the first staging of W B Yeats's *The Land of Heart's Desire* and George Bernard Shaw's *Arms and the Man*. She even acted a little, for example as the Gipsy Woman in Shaw's *The Gadfly* (a curtain-raiser) in 1898. In 1904 she sponsored the building of the Abbey Theatre in Dublin. She later quarrelled with Yeats, but Shaw never failed to pay her tribute.

In 1908 she purchased the Gaiety Theatre in Manchester, which she called 'the first theatre with a catholic repertoire in England'. Until the company disbanded in 1917 for want of financial success, she put on over 100 new plays by the so-called 'Manchester School', mostly directed by Lewis Casson who married a member of the company, **Sybil Thorndike**. In Britain, the Repertory Theatre Movement and many reputations among playwrights and actors are her legacy; in Ireland, perhaps Irish national theatre itself.

Hortense, *originally* Eugénie-Hortense Cécile de Beauharnais

Born 1783 Died 1837
Queen of the Kingdom of Holland as the wife of
Louis Napoleon

Eugénie-Hortense Cécile de Beauharnais was born in Paris, the daughter of Alexandre, Vicomte de Beauharnais and the future French Empress **Joséphine**. As a child she was a great

Hortense

favourite of her stepfather, Napoleon I, and she married his brother Louis Napoleon in 1802; hence she became Queen of Holland (present-day Netherlands) when her husband became king in 1806.

She took many lovers and had several children of uncertain fatherhood, including the future Emperor Napoleon III, who was said to be the child of a Dutch admiral. In 1810 she separated from her husband and went to Paris, where in 1811 she gave birth to a son (later Duc de Morny) by her lover, Count Charles de Flahaut. In May 1814 she was created Duchess of St Leu by Louis XVIII at Tsar Alexander I's request.

She became involved in Bonapartist intrigue when Napoleon was exiled that year and was banished from France in 1815 for supporting him during the Hundred Days. She retired to Switzerland and turned to writing, publishing her memoirs in 1831–5. She was a gifted artist and a composer, whose marching song, 'Partant pour la Syrie', became the national anthem of France's Second Empire.

Houselander, (Frances) Caryll

Born 1901   Died 1954
English Catholic mystic, artist and poet

Caryll Houselander was born in Bath and became a Catholic at the age of six. After a varied education in a Jewish kindergarten, French and English convents, and state and private schools, she studied at St John's Wood and Central St Martins art colleges in London.

She later worked in an advertising agency, as an ecclesiastical carver, in house decoration, and in book and magazine illustration. Her writings include the autobiographical *A Rocking-Horse Catholic* (1935), many books on the suffering Christ in humankind, and three collections of children's stories published posthumously. From 1942 onwards, doctors sent children and adults to her for therapy.

Houston, Renée, *originally* Katerina Gribbin

Born 1902   Died 1980
Scottish comedienne and character actress

Renée Houston was born in Johnstone, Renfrewshire. She made her stage début as a double-act with her sister Billie in 1920, in which they dressed as a precocious girl and boy. A booking in Tommy Lorne's revue *Froth* (1924) at the Glasgow Pavilion led to their London début in 1925.

Their swift rise to popularity is shown by their appearance in the Royal Variety Performance (1926). For a while the act was a threesome, including their younger sister Shirley, but when Billie retired in 1936, Renée formed a new type of double-act with her husband, Donald Stewart. This too led to a Royal Variety Performance (1938).

In her later years she became a notable character actress, appearing in over 40 films, and was a popular, if opinionated, panellist on the radio series *Petticoat Line*.

Houston, Whitney

Born 1963
American pop and soul singer who began her career singing gospel music with her mother

Whitney Houston was born in Newark, New Jersey, the daughter of singer Cissy Houston, and cousin of **Dionne Warwick**. She started out as a gospel singer and as her mother's partner, supplementing her income with modelling.

Her début album on Arista, *Whitney Houston* (1985), was a huge seller and helped her cross over to a pop market. In 1988 she had her seventh American number one with 'Where Do Broken Hearts Go', thus breaking the Beatles' record.

'I Will Always Love You' (1990), written by

Dolly Parton, is her biggest success to date, boosted by her role in *The Bodyguard*, the film featuring the song.

Howard, Catherine

Born c.1520 Died 1542
Queen of England as the fifth wife of Henry VIII
(ruled 1509–47)

Catherine Howard was the granddaughter of Thomas Howard, 2nd Duke of Norfolk, and niece of Thomas Howard, 3rd Duke of Norfolk. She married Henry VIII in 1540, immediately after his divorce from **Anne of Cleves**.

In November 1541, after clandestine meetings with a musician (Henry Mannock) and a kinsman (Thomas Culpepper), whom she had known before her marriage, she was charged by Archbishop Thomas Cranmer with sexual intercourse before her marriage.

On her confession, both men were executed and Catherine was attainted for treason by parliament and beheaded in February 1542.

Howatch, Susan

Born 1940
English novelist whose popularity increased with the televisation of her romantic sagas

Susan Howatch was born in Leatherhead, Surrey. She had published six novels before achieving success in 1971 with *Penmarric*, a romantic saga about three generations of a Cornish family, owners of a tin mine and dwellers in a grand house which stands atop a cliff.

Such novels as *The Rich are Different* (1977) maintained her popularity with the same formula of glamour, romance and riches until, in 1979, a BBC television adaptation of *Penmarric* introduced her to a new readership and gave her career a second wind. Her later works include a series of novels, among them *Ultimate Prizes* (1989), about the present-day Church of England.

Howe, Julia Ward, *née* Ward

Born 1819 Died 1910
American feminist, reformer and writer who wrote the 'Battle Hymn of the Republic'

Julia Ward was born in New York, a wealthy banker's daughter. In 1843 she married the reformer and educator of the blind, Samuel Gridley Howe. Painfully conscious of the difficulties encountered by Civil War widows, she became a prominent suffragette and abolitionist, and founded the New England Woman Suffrage Association (1868) and the New England Women's Club (1868).

She published several volumes of poetry, including *Passion Flowers* (1854) and *Words for the Hour* (1857), as well as travel books and a play. She also wrote the 'Battle Hymn of the Republic' (published in *Atlantic Monthly*, 1862) and edited *Woman's Journal* (1870–90).

In 1908 she became the first woman to be elected to the American Academy of Arts and Letters.

How-Martyn, Edith, *née* How

Born c.1875 Died 1954
English suffragette and promoter of the birth control movement

Edith How was born in Cheltenham and educated at the North London Collegiate School for Girls, at University College, Aberystwyth, and at London University. She married Herbert Martyn in 1899.

In 1906–7 she was the secretary of the Women's Social and Political Union but left to co-found the Women's Freedom League with **Charlotte Despard** and **Teresa Billington-Greig**. When the franchise was extended to include property-owning women over the age of 30, she stood unsuccessfully for parliament as an independent candidate representing feminist issues (1918). In 1919 she was elected as the first woman member of Middlesex Council.

As founder of the Birth Control International Information Centre (1929) she travelled widely lecturing on women's issues, and published *The Birth Control Movement in England* (1931).

Hrostwitha, *also* Roswita *or* Hroswita *or* Hroswitha

Born c.932 Died c.1002
German Benedictine nun who was also the first known female poet and playwright

Hrostwitha was from Gandersheim, near Göttingen, where she spent most of her life in a convent. She chronicled the life of Otto II (955–83) and wrote six comedies in Latin (*Gallicanus, Dulcitus, Callimachus, Abraham, Pafnutius* and *Sapientia*) which are closely modelled on the work of the Roman comedy writer Terence (c.190–159BC), but instead of echoing the pagan themes of Classical literature, they are specifically Christian in theme and seem to have been intended for the spiritual education of her fellow nuns rather than for performance.

As the first known plays by a woman, they are of great historical importance. Furthermore, the verse in which they are written is lively and witty; her works are now ripe for revival.

Huch, Ricarda

Born 1864 Died 1947
German novelist, historian and feminist who revived interest in the important women in Germany's culture

Ricarda Huch was born in Brunswick into a wealthy Protestant merchant family. She studied history at Zürich, taught at a girls' school there, travelled extensively in Italy, married twice (unhappily) and finally settled in Munich in 1910.

A neo-romantic, she rejected naturalism and wrote novels including the semi-autobiographical *Erinnerungen von Ludolf Ursleu dem Jüngeren* (1893, 'Memoirs of Ludolf Ursleu the Younger'), *Aus der Triumphgasse* (1902, 'Out of Triumph Lane') and *Der letzte Sommer* (1910, 'The Last Summer'), criticism including *Die Blütezeit, Ausbreitung und Verfall der Romantik* (1899–1902, 'The Blossoming, Spread and Decline of Romanticism') and social and political works including *Der Grosse Krieg in Deutschland* (1912–14, 'The Great War in Germany'). She also wrote on religious themes, in *Luthers Glaube* (1915, 'Beliefs of Luther') and *Das Zeitalter der Glaubenspaltung* (1937, 'The Age of Schism'), and on such infuential literary women as **Annette von Droste-Hülshoff**.

She was the first woman to be admitted to the Prussian Academy of Literature in 1931, but resigned in 1933 over the expulsion of Jewish writers. She lived in Jena during World War II.

Huerta, Dolores

Born 1930
American union organizer whose registration of Chicano voters influenced the reform of farm labour

Dolores Huerta was recruited in the 1950s to work with a grassroots advocacy group in Stockton, California, called the Community Service Organization (CSO). Working with its founder Fred Ross, and with Cesar Chavez, she registered Chicano voters (typically farm labourers who did not vote) in order that they could vote for policies and politicians to influence such things as farm labour reform and immigration.

In 1962 she joined the United Farmworkers Union (UFW), as whose vice-president and chief negotiator she now serves.

Hulanicki, Barbara

Born 1936
Fashion designer whose designs had a major influence on 1960s fashions

Barbara Hulanicki was born in Palestine of Polish parents. She moved to Britain in 1948 and attended Brighton Art College. She won a design competition in the London *Evening Standard* in 1955 and became a fashion illustrator. In 1963 she launched Biba's Postal Boutique with a skirt offer in the *Daily Express* and a pink gingham mini dress in the *Daily Mirror*. Success led to the opening of three Biba stores in London (Biba is her sister's name) which became the fashion Mecca of the 1960s.

Her clothes were targeted at the young: smocks, mini-dresses and trouser suits in muted colours, worn with hats and feather boas, were all designed to look different from the 'adult' fashions of the l950s. 'Dolly birds' **Cilla Black**, Cathy McGowan, **Twiggy** and **Brigitte Bardot** were customers.

The mail-order catalogue was launched in 1968 and make-up range in 1970. Biba closed in 1973 and Hulanicki and her family moved to Brazil in 1976. Her autobiography, *From A to Biba*, was published in 1983.

Hull, Hannah Hallowell Clothier, *née* Clothier

Born 1872 Died 1958
American pacifist and suffragist whose life was devoted to world peace

Hannah Hull was born in Sharon Hill, Pennsylvania, and raised with the Quaker principle of peacemaking. She attended the Second Hague Conference for International Peace in 1907 and remained committed to world peace throughout World War I, despite pressure to support the war effort, becoming chair of the Pennsylvania branch of the Women's Peace Party (1917–20).

She also worked with the American Friends Service Committee (AFSC) and was vice-chair of the AFSC board (1928–47), as well as being active in the Women's International League for Peace and Freedom (WILPF). There she met **Jane Addams**, with whom she worked closely for many years, succeeding her as the national chair of the American section of WILPF in 1924.

She continued to hold that office and a variety of other WILPF offices until the death of her husband in 1939, following which she held a variety of local offices in Quaker and peace organizations until her own death.

Hulme, Keri Ann Ruhi

Born 1947
New Zealand writer who won the Booker Prize
with her first novel

Keri Hulme was born in Otautahi, Christchurch, of mixed Maori, Orkney and English descent. She came to notice when she won the Booker Prize in 1985 with her first novel, *The Bone People* (1984), a spell-binding mixing of Maori myth and Christian symbolism.

After another novel, *Lost Possessions* (1985), she published a collection of short stories, *Te Kaihau: The Windeater* (1986). Some of her verse in Maori and English is collected in *The Silences Between* (1982). The themes of gender, race, culture, religion and the environment reappear throughout her work, and she is now one of the country's best-known writers.

Humphrey, Doris

Born 1895 Died 1958
American dancer, choreographer and teacher who
was an innovative founder of modern dance

Doris Humphrey was born in Oak Park, Illinois. She started dancing at the age of eight, and in 1913 began a career as a teacher of ballroom dancing in Chicago. From 1917 to 1927 she was with the Denishawn Company as a dancer, beginning to choreograph in 1920 with *Tragica*.

With her partner Charles Weidman (1901–75), also ex-Denishawn, she founded the Humphrey–Weidman school and company in 1928, which thrived in New York City until the early 1940s. She originated the Juilliard Dance Theatre (1935), and ran the Bennington College Summer School of Dance (1934–42). She choreographed highly original work including *The Shakers* (1931), the trilogy *New Dance* (1935), *Theatre Piece* (1935), and *With My Red Fires* (1936), building the foundations for the future vocabulary and philosophy of modern dance. Her style made extensive use of gravity, and the dancer's need to balance a near-fall with a recovery of equal energy, and of her theory that meaning can be generated by movement alone, even without music.

Disabled by arthritis, she gave up dancing in 1944 but choreographed for the company set up by one of her most talented students, José Limón (1908–72). She was artistic director of the Limón company from 1946 to 1958. She left a legacy rivalled only by her contemporary **Martha Graham** in its influence on modern dance. She wrote *The Art of Making Dances* (1959).

Hunt, (Isobel) Violet

Born 1866 Died 1942
English novelist and biographer who was an early
writer on sexual repression

Violet Hunt was born in Durham, the daughter of a painter, Alfred William Hunt. Having trained as a painter, she turned to writing, and her first novel, *The Maiden's Progress: A Novel in Disguise*, appeared in 1894. She was an outspoken supporter of women's suffrage and most of her 17 books, such as *Unkist, Unkind!* (1897) and *Tales of the Uneasy* (1911), deal frankly, for the time, with the psychological effects on women of sexual repression.

White Rose of Weary Leaf (1908), in which human relationships are restricted by social conventions, is often judged to be her finest novel. Her memoirs include a rather unreliable book about the Pre-Raphaelite painters, *Those Flurried Years* (1926).

Although she never married, Violet Hunt had some turbulent and well-publicized affairs, and later withdrew into virtual seclusion.

Hunter, Holly

Born 1958
American actress who was highly acclaimed for
her role as the mute pianist in The Piano

Holly Hunter was born in Conyers, Georgia, the youngest of seven children. She studied at Carnegie Mellon University in Pittsburgh, and made her film début in *The Burning* (1981). Thereafter mainly a stage actress, her role in *Places of The Heart* (1982) began a continuing association with the plays of **Beth Henley**. She established herself in the cinema with the comedy *Raising Arizona* (1987) and *Broadcast News* (1987).

A diminuitive figure, whose versatility ranges from touching vulnerability to brash dynamism, she won Best Actress Emmy awards for her roles as an unwed mother in *Roe Vs Wade* (1989) and an obsessive Houston housewife in *The Positively True Adventures Of The Alleged Texas Cheerleader-Murdering Mom* (1993), and received a Best Actress Oscar for playing the mute 19th-century Scots woman at the heart of *The Piano* (1993). In 1996 she appeared with **Sigourney Weaver** in *Copycat*.

Hunter, Mollie

Born 1922
Scottish author of historical novels and children's
books, often rooted in Scottish folklore

Mollie Hunter was born in Longniddry, East Lothian. Until 1960 she worked as a freelance journalist, but she is best known for her work in children's fiction, and has published 25 books of various types in this field, including fantasy and historical fiction.

She has been Writer-in-Residence at Dalhousie University in Halifax, Canada, and has lectured and written on writing for children. Her works include *Hi Johnny* (1963), *Haunted Mountain* (1972) and *A Stranger Came Ashore* (1975) and she has been the recipient of many major awards, including the Scottish Arts Council Literary award (1972), the Carnegie Medal (1975, for *The Stronghold*), and the Arbuthnot Lectureship (1975).

Huntingdon, Selina Hastings, Countess of, *née* Shirley

Born 1707 Died 1791
English Methodist leader who played a major part in the 18th-century evangelical revival

Selina Shirley was the daughter of the 2nd Earl Ferrers. In 1728 she married Theophilus Hastings, 9th Earl of Huntingdon (d.1746). Influenced by her sister-in-law, she joined the Methodists in 1739, and in 1748 used her right as a peeress to make George Whitefield, one of the founders of Methodism (whose work in America she also supported), her chaplain. She assumed a leadership among his followers, a Calvinist Methodist sect who became known as 'The Countess of Huntingdon's Connection'.

On learning that some theological students had been sent down from Oxford suspected of Methodism, in 1768 she established a college at Trevecca in Brecknockshire (removed in 1792 to Cheshunt, Hertfordshire, and in 1904 to Cambridge) for the education of evangelical clergymen, and she also built or bought numerous chapels, especially in fashionable places such as Bath where the aristocracy might be introduced to Methodism.

Opposition to her method of supporting Methodism, as well as the development of two different factions within the society, resulted in the necessity to register her chapels under the Toleration Act of 1689 as dissenting houses of worship in order to save them, though this meant that all her Anglican chaplains resigned. She died in London, bequeathing to four persons her 64 chapels, most of which became identical with the Congregational churches.

Huppert, Isabelle

Born 1955
French film actress whose innocent looks enforce the ambiguity of the characters she portrays

Isabelle Huppert was born in Paris. She studied acting at the Conservatoire National D'Art Dramatique and made her film début in *Faustine Et Le Bel Été* (1971, UK: *Faustine*). She won international acclaim for her performance in *La Dentellière* (1977, UK: *The Lacemaker*), which she followed by winning the Best Actress Prize at the Cannes Film Festival for *Violette Nozière* (1978), the story of a teenager leading a double life of wild promiscuity and domestic demureness.

Adept at capturing the mix of good and evil in one person, her freckled features aid her in the depiction of ambiguous characters with surface innocence. She continues to work prolifically, having won acclaim in her best performances of the 1980s — *Coup De Foudre* (1983, UK: *At First Sight*) and *Une Affaire De Femmes* (1988).

Hurst, Margery

Born 1913 Died 1989
English businesswoman who founded the Brook Street temping agency

Margery Hurst was educated at Kilburn High School and RADA. Invalided out of the Auxiliary Territorial Service in 1943, and left by her husband with a new baby, she set up a secretarial company in her parents' home in Portsmouth, with herself as the sole employee. She moved to a one-room office in Brook Street, Mayfair, in 1946 and within 10 years had opened 20 offices providing 'temps' in London and the south-east.

Expansion continued, with offices being opened all over the UK, in the USA, and in Australia. In 1970 she was one of the first women to be elected to the membership of Lloyds, and was also the first woman to be elected to the New York Chamber of Commerce.

The Brook Street Bureau was sold to Blue Arrow for nearly £20 million in 1985 but Mrs Hurst continued as chairman until ill health forced her to resign in 1988.

Hurston, Zora Neale

Born 1901 Died 1960
African-American novelist recognized in the Harlem Renaissance and in the establishment of black literature as a genre

Zora Neale Hurston was born in Eatonville, Florida. The nine secure years she spent there, described in *Dust Tracks on a Road* (1942), ended when her mother died and her father, a Baptist preacher and thrice mayor of the town, remarried. Her life from then on was 'a series of wanderings' — occasional work, interrupted education, working as a wardrobe assistant with a theatre troupe — until she enrolled as a full-time student at Baltimore's Morgan Academy. She moved to Washington DC, enrolled as a part-time student at Howard University and began to write.

Influenced by her studies in cultural anthropology at Barnard College and Columbia University, she became a prominent figure in the Harlem Renaissance. She is a precursor of black women writers like **Alice Walker** and **Toni Morrison**, and her novels include *Jonah's Gourd Vine* (1934), *Their Eyes Were Watching God* (1937), *Moses, Man of the Mountain* (1939), and *Seraph on the Suwanee* (1948).

In the 1950s she withdrew from public life, and was distanced from many contemporaries by her controversial attack on the Supreme Court's ruling on school desegregation. She argued that pressure for integration denied the value of existing black institutions. Her last years were plagued by ill health and she died in poverty. She was inducted into the National Women's Hall of Fame in 1994.

Angelica Huston, 1971

Carolina from a novel by Dorothy Allison and then *Terrible Beauty*, based on the life of **Maud Gonne**.

Huston, Angelica

Born 1951
American film actress who has become
increasingly accomplished since the mid-1980s

Angelica Huston was born in Los Angeles, California. The daughter of director John Huston (1906–87) and granddaughter of character actor Walter Huston (1884–1950), she enjoyed an idyllic childhood on her father's estate in County Galway and at school in London.

She made her film début in her father's *A Walk With Love And Death* (1969) but had her aspirations crushed by the critics and instead became a successful model and the off-screen companion of actor Jack Nicholson. Resurrecting her career in the 1980s, she won a Best Supporting Actress Oscar for her part in *Prizzi's Honor* (1985).

Suitably encouraged, she developed to become one of the most accomplished character actresses of her generation, appearing as a hysterical, lovelorn mistress in *Crimes and Misdemeanours* (1989), a tough-as-nails con-artist in *The Grifters* (1990), and a stylishly seductive Mortitia in *The Addams Family* (1991), among others. In 1996 she moved behind the camera to direct *Bastard Out of*

Hutchinson, Anne, *née* Marbury

Born 1591   Died 1643
English religious leader and pioneer in America
who was an early settler of Rhode Island

Anne Marbury was the daughter of a Lincolnshire clergyman. In 1634 she emigrated with her merchant husband William Hutchinson to Boston, Massachusetts, where she organized regular meetings to discuss sermons and to present her own unorthodox religious views.

She denounced the Massachusetts clergy as being 'under the covenant of works, not of grace' because she regarded them as enslaved by religious doctrine and legalism, rather than liberated through Christ, but was accused of antinomiansim (the doctrine that Christians are emancipated by the Gospel from the obligation to keep the moral law). Tried for heresy and sedition and excommunicated, she, with some friends, acquired territory on the island of Aquidneck from the Narragansetts of Rhode Island, and set up a democracy (1638).

After her husband's death (1642), she removed to a new settlement in what is now Pelham Bay in New York state, where she and all but one of her family of 15 were murdered by Native Americans. She was inducted into the National Women's Hall of Fame in 1994.

Huxley, Elspeth Josceline, *née* Grant

Born 1907
British novelist and travel writer who has written
extensively on Kenya, its history and problems

Elspeth Grant was born in Kenya and brought up on a coffee farm. In 1931 she married Gervas Huxley (1894–1971), grandson of the English biologist Thomas Henry Huxley (1825–95). Her writing is coloured with her experience of colonialism and observation of inter-cultural difficulties.

Her best-known novel is *The Flame Trees of Thika* (1959), which deals with her childhood, as do *The Mottled Lizard* (1962) and *Death of an Aryan* (1986, also known as *The African Poison Murders*). *Murder on Safari* (1938) and *Livingstone and his African Journeys* (1974) are examples of her crime fiction and travel writing respectively.

Huxtable, Ada Louise, *née* Landman

Born 1921
American critic of architecture whose writings
have had a strong influence on public attitude

Ada Huxtable was born in New York. With a background in architectural history, she started work for the *New York Times* in 1963 as an architectural critic, the first to be appointed by a newspaper.

Huxtable stimulated an interest in preserving the US heritage and had a powerful influence on decisions concerning zoning laws and historic building preservation. Her views have always been broad and flexible, addressing architectural issues from sometimes surprising standpoints, even criticising the Modern Movement, which was accepted without question by the majority of the architectural community.

She has published a book, *Pier Luigi Nervi* (1960), and she received the first Pulitzer Prize for distinguished criticism in 1970. In 1982 she left the *Times*, having been on its editorial board since 1973, and became an independent architectural consultant and critic.

Hyde, Ida Henrietta

Born 1857   Died 1945
American physiologist

Ida Hyde was born in Ohio. She graduated from Cornell University in 1891, before moving to Strasbourg in 1893, and then to Heidelberg, where in 1896 she became the first woman to be awarded a doctorate there. In 1898 she joined the University of Kansas, and became a full professor in 1905, retiring in 1920. During World War I she chaired the national Women's Commission on Health and Sanitation.

Her work centred on systems physiology in both vertebrates and invertebrates and she pioneered the use of micro-electrode techniques in single cells. She later endowed science scholarships for women at both Cornell and Kansas Universities and established the Ida H Hyde Woman's International Fellowship of the American Association of University Women. She became the first woman to be elected to the American Physiological Society in 1902.

Hyde, Robin, *pseud of* Iris Guiver Wilkinson

Born 1906   Died 1939
New Zealand journalist, poet and novelist recently
acknowledged as one of New Zealand's major
women writers

Robin Hyde was born in Cape Town, South Africa, of an Anglo-Indian father and Australian mother who settled in Wellington, New Zealand, when she was a baby. She trained as a journalist and through her writing challenged gender-related sterotypes, assumptions and inequality, features which have brought her to the attention of modern feminists.

Her newspaper background is evident in her novels, which often blend fact and fiction as in *Passport to Hell* (1936) and *Nor the Years Condemn* (1938). In *Check to Your King* (1936), a novelized account of Baron Charles de Thierry (the French adventurer and eccentric who sought to establish himself as Sovereign Chief of New Zealand in the 1830s), Hyde shows her empathy with the outcast and under-dog.

She wrote three collections of verse, *The Desolate Star* (1929), *The Conquerors* (1935) and *Persephone in Winter* (1937), and in the autobiographical *A Home in this World* (1937) she describes the social pressures which drove her to drugs and eventual suicide. She visited China in 1938, a time when she produced her best work in *Houses by the Sea*, and *Later Poems* (1952), which also includes backward glances at the innocence of her childhood.

Hyman, Flo

Born 1954   Died 1986
African-American volleyball player who gave her
name to a women's athletics award

Flo Hyman was born in Inglewood, California. She became a top-ranked player in high school and joined the US national team in 1974.

Despite their inexperience, the team won the 1978 and 1982 world championships.

In 1979 Hyman was named most valuable player at the North/Central and Caribbean American (NORCECA) championship; two years later she was chosen as one of six for the All-World Cup team. The US women's volleyball team won the silver medal in 1984.

After retiring from amateur competition, Hyman played on the Japanese professional circuit until her death. In 1987 the Women's Sports Foundation created the Flo Hyman Award for women athletes who capture 'Flo's dignity, spirit and commitment to excellence'.

Hyman, Libbie Henrietta

Born 1888 Died 1969
American zoologist whose texts on vertebrate and invertebrate zoology became widely used

Libbie Hyman was born in Des Moines, Iowa. She studied zoology at the University of Chicago (1906–10) and remained there as research assistant until 1931. Dissatisfied with the practical texts then available, she wrote *A Laboratory Manual for Elementary Zoology* (1919) and *A Laboratory Manual for Comparative Vertebrate Anatomy* (1929). Both these texts, in the form of later editions, are still in use and their great success made Hyman financially independent.

She resigned her position at Chicago, and after a period of travel in Europe, took up residence near the American Museum of Natural History in New York. She carried out research on many aspects of the biology of the lower invertebrates and became a research associate at the museum in 1937.

Until her death she worked on her *magnum opus*, a series of comprehensive volumes on the invertebrates (*The Invertebrates*, 6 vols, 1940–68). These dealt with the protozoa, coelenterates, flatworms, nematodes, echinoderma, and molluscs. Such single-author works, while common in the 18th and 19th centuries, are now almost impossible due to specialization and the growth of knowledge, and Hyman's books may well represent one of the last examples of this type of scholarship.

Hypatia

Born c.370 AD Died AD415
Greek philosopher credited with being the first notable female astronomer and mathematician

Hypatia was the daughter of Theon, a writer and commentator on mathematics. She studied under Plutarch the Younger, taught in Alexandria, and became head of the neoplatonist school there. She collaborated on her father's writings, and was herself the author of commentaries on mathematics and astronomy, though none of these survives.

Renowned for her beauty, eloquence, and learning, Hypatia drew pupils from all parts of the Greek world, Christian as well as pagan, but Cyril, archbishop of Alexandria, came to resent her influence and she was brutally murdered by a Christian mob he may have incited to riot.

i

Ibarbourou, Juana de, *née* Juana Fernandéz Morales

Born 1895 Died 1979
Uruguayan poet who wrote the most 'erotic' poetry that Spanish literature had ever seen

Juana Fernandéz Morales was born in Melo, on the border with Brazil. She was one of the most distinguished 'wife and mother' poets of the 20th century, not unlike **Judith Wright**, but with more Latinate opportunity to express her passions (for the military man whom she married in 1914). Her poems became famous throughout Argentina and, indeed, Spanish America.

Feeling misunderstood, she declared: 'the adjective erotic attached itself to those poems like a fly on a pile of butcher's refuse'. But it was widely understood that no one had before published such erotic poetry in Spanish in modern times. She was named 'Juana of America' at a grand ceremony in Montevideo (1929), at which men, including poets such as Alfonso Reyes, broke down and wept with joy.

However, when she published more verse, in 1930, it went almost unnoticed, and by the end of her life she had become prone to depression and religious devotion. She was perhaps more of a phenomenon than a writer, but her early verse does have the spontaneity of complete subjectivity within a patriotic and conventional context.

Ibarruri (Gómez), (Isidora) Dolores, *known as* La Pasionaria

Born 1895 Died 1989
Spanish writer, Communist politician and revolutionary who became a prominent national figure

Dolores Ibarruri was born in Gallarta, in Vizcaya province, the daughter of a Basque miner. She worked as a maidservant, then joined the Socialist party in 1917 and worked as a journalist for the workers' press, using the pseudonym 'La Pasionaria' ('the passion flower').

She helped to found the Spanish Communist party in 1920, edited several communist newspapers, founded the Anti-Fascist Womens' League in 1934 and was elected to parliament in 1936. During the Civil War (1936–9) she became legendary for her passionate exhortations to the Spanish people to fight against the Fascist forces, declaring 'It is better to die on your feet than to live on your knees'.

When General Franco came to power in 1939 she left for the Soviet Union, returning to Spain in 1977, when, at the age of 81, she was re-elected to the National Assembly.

Ichikawa, Fusaye

Born 1893 Died 1981
Japanese feminist and politician who campaigned successfully for several areas of women's rights

Fusaye Ichikawa started her working life as a teacher, moved to Tokyo as a young woman and became involved in politics and feminism, helping to found the New Women's Association (c.1920) which successfully fought for women's right to attend political meetings.

During her time in the USA (1921–4) she was impressed by the US suffrage movement, and in 1924 formed the Women's Suffrage League in Japan. Following World War II she became head of the New Japan Women's League, which secured the vote for women in 1945, and went on to fight for their wider rights.

She campaigned against legalized prostitution and from 1952 to 1971 served in the Japanese Diet, where she continued to press for an end to bureaucratic corruption. After defeat in 1971 she was triumphantly returned to parliament in 1975 and 1980.

Inchbald, Elizabeth, *née* Simpson

Born 1753 Died 1821
English novelist, playwright and actress who wrote sentimental comedies and early romantic novels

Elizabeth Simpson was born in Bury St Edmunds, the daughter of a farmer. She ran away to go on the stage and in 1772 married John Inchbald, an actor in London. She made her début at Bristol as Cordelia.

After the death of her husband in 1779 she appeared at Covent Garden, but from 1789 made her name as a playwright and author of 19 sentimental comedies, including *The Wedding Day* (1794) and *Lover's Vows* (1798), the play which the Bertram children are acting in a famous scene in **Jane Austen's** *Mansfield Park*.

She also wrote the highly successful novels *A Simple Story* (1791) and *Nature and Art* (1796), and was editor of the 24-volume *The British Theatre* (1806–9).

Inglis, Elsie Maud

Born 1864 Died 1917
Scottish surgeon and reformer who had practical solutions to the prejudice towards women in medicine

Elsie Inglis was born in Naini Tal, India. She was one of the first women medical students at Edinburgh and Glasgow, and inaugurated the second medical school for women at Edinburgh (1892).

In 1901, appalled at the lack of maternity facilities and the prejudice held against women doctors by their male colleagues, she founded a maternity hospital in Edinburgh, completely staffed by women. In 1906 she founded the Scottish Women's Suffragette Federation, which sent two women ambulance units to France and Serbia in 1915.

She set up three military hospitals in Serbia (1916), fell into Austrian hands, was repatriated, but in 1917 returned to Russia with a voluntary corps, which was withdrawn after the revolution. Her biography was written by Lady **Frances Balfour** (1918).

Irene

Born 752 Died 803
Byzantine empress and saint of the Greek Orthodox Church

Irene was a poor orphan in Athens but her beauty and talents led the Emperor Leo IV to marry her in 769. After his death in 780 she ruled as regent for her 10-year-old son, Constantine VI, during which time she sought to restore the veneration of icons, which had been officially prohibited since 730. Despite much opposition from the Iconoclasts, she summoned the Seventh Ecumenical Council to meet in Nicaea in 787 and the cult of images was restored, for which, as well as for her support of the monasteries, she was recognized as a saint by the Greek church.

As Constantine approached adulthood his mother's control over the Empire irked him. He attempted to seize power but failed, an event that led to her demand to be recognized as senior ruler and her banishment from court in 790. On her return in 792 she began to conspire against her son, having him imprisoned and blinded together with her husband's five brothers. She ruled in her own right as empress of the Eastern Roman Empire from 797, but in 802 she was deposed and banished to Lesbos.

Her feast day is 9 August.

Irigaray, Luce

Born 1939
French psychoanalyst whose interest lies in the relationship of women to the language they use

Luce Irigaray's works on femininity and language are a response to the works of the French psychoanalyst Jacques Lacan (1901–81) and a study of the connection between sexuality and writing.

Her theory is that women have their own language related to their sexuality and bodies which has been repressed and denied by the traditionally androcentric language and by patriarchy. Her works include *Les Language des dements* (1973), *Speculum de l'autre femme* (1974) and *Ce sexe qui n'en est pas un* (1977, 'This Sex Which Is Not One').

Isaacs, Susan Brierley, *née* Fairhurst

Born 1885 Died 1948
English psychologist and influential specialist in the education of young children

Susan Fairhurst was born in Bromley Cross, Lancashire. She studied philosophy and psychology at Manchester and Cambridge, and lectured in Manchester and London. A disciple of the founder of psychoanalysis, Sigmund Freud, and believer in the enduring effects of early childhood experiences, she ran an experimental progressive school, Malting House, in Cambridge (1924–7), which aimed at letting children find out for themselves rather than by direct instruction, and at allowing them emotional expression rather than imposing a restrictive discipline.

She was the influential head of the Department of Child Development at the Institute of Education, London (1933–43). She published *Intellectual Growth in Young Children* (1930) and *Social Development of Young Children* (1933). Some of her conclusions challenged the theories of the Swiss pioneer Jean Piaget (1896–1980) concerning the stages of children's intellectual development, before it was acceptable to question Piaget's work.

Isabella

Born 1292 Died 1358
Queen of England as the wife of Edward II (ruled 1307–27)

Isabella was a daughter of Philip IV of France. After her marriage at Boulogne in 1308, she was treated with little consideration, and returned to France in 1325 when her brother, Charles IV, seized Edward's territories in France.

She fell in love with one of Edward's disaffected nobles, Roger de Mortimer (later Earl of March), invaded England in 1326 and routed Edward's troops, forcing him to abdicate in favour of her young son, Edward III, with herself and Mortimer as regents. In September 1327, they brought about the murder of Edward in Berkeley Castle.

Three years later Edward III asserted his authority, and Isabella and Mortimer were arrested. Mortimer was hanged, drawn and quartered, while Isabella withdrew to Castle Rising, near King's Lynn, for the rest of her life.

Isabella I, *also called* Isabella of Castile *and* Isabella the Catholic

Born 1451 Died 1504
Queen of Castile whose union with Ferdinand V of Aragon formed the basis of modern Spain

Isabella was born in Castile, the daughter of King John II of Castile and Leon. She succeeded her half-brother, Henry IV, to the throne in 1474. For political reasons she had many suitors, but in 1469, without the king's consent, she married Ferdinand 'the Catholic' of Aragon. Immediately an anti-Aragonese faction grew up and an alternative heiress, Henry's daughter Joan, supported by Alfonso V of Portugal, was put forward.

When Isabella succeeded in 1474, the inevitable war of succession flared up, but in 1479 the Castilian faction with the Portuguese were defeated. That year Ferdinand succeeded to the rule of Aragon, his title being Ferdinand V of Aragon and Castile, and Isabella became joint sovereign with him.

Isabella is remembered also for having approved and supported Columbus's voyage in 1492 on which he discovered the New World, which was consequently annexed to the Crown of Castile. She was a wise and intensely religious woman, and during her reign gathered good spiritual advisers around her and organized the reform of both the Spanish churches and the Poor Clares.

Isabella II

Born 1830 Died 1904
Queen of Spain whose rule was hampered by rival political factions

Isabella was born in Madrid. On the death of her father, Ferdinand VII (1833), she succeeded to the throne with her mother, Queen **Maria Christina**, as regent. She attained her majority in 1843, and in 1846 married her cousin, Francisco de Assisi.

Although popular with the Spanish people, her scandalous private life made her the tool of rival factions and in 1868 she was deposed and exiled to France, where in 1870 she abdicated in favour of her son, Alfonso XII.

Isabella of Angoulême

Died 1246
Queen of England as the wife of King John (ruled 1199–1216)

Isabella was the daughter of Aymer, Count of Angoulême. Although she was engaged to Hugh IX de Lusignan, Comte de la Marche, she was married in 1200 to John, his overlord. Hugh was outraged; he turned to King Philip II Augustus of France and formed an alliance that through the Barons' War led to John's loss of his Continental lands, including Normandy.

After John's death in 1216 she returned to France, where in 1220 she married Hugh X, the Comte de la Marche, the son of her former fiancé. The marriage caused problems in both England and France, for Isabella was ambitious and liked to push her husband into political activity.

Isabella was the mother of Henry III of England (ruled 1216–72), and her daughter Isabella (1214–41) married the Emperor Frederick II as his third wife in 1235.

j

Jackson, Betty

Born 1949
English fashion designer who was 1985 British
Designer of the Year

Betty Jackson was born in Bacup, Lancashire. Following a three-year fashion course at Birmingham College of Art, she became a freelance illustrator in London before joining Wendy Dagworthy in 1973 as assistant designer and Quorum as designer from 1975 to 1981. With her husband David Cohen she launched her own label in October 1981 and quickly gained a reputation for flattering designs in bold patterned fabrics.

Jackson has won numerous awards, including British Designer of the Year in 1985, the year in which she launched her menswear collection. In 1987 she signed an agreement with Vogue Patterns/Butterick Co to produce Betty Jackson patterns for home dressmakers, and also that year received an MBE for services to British industry and exports. She has since launched Betty Jackson Accessories, BJ Beachwear and BJ Knits.

Jackson, Glenda

Born 1936
English actress and politician who has followed
an award-winning career in the arts with a
successful one in politics

Glenda Jackson was born in Birkenhead, Cheshire. She studied at RADA and made her theatrical début in *Separate Tables* (1957) at Worthing and her London début in the same year in *All Kinds of Men*. She made her film début in *This Sporting Life* (1963) but remained primarily a stage actress in such productions as *Alfie* (1963), *Hamlet* (1965) and *Marat/Sade* (1965).

Her performance in the film *Women in Love* (1969) earned her international recognition and the 1970 Best Actress Academy Award. She won a second Academy Award for *A Touch of Class* (1973). Her film appearances include *Sunday, Bloody Sunday* (1971), *Hedda* (1975), *Stevie* (1978), and *Business as Usual* (1987), and her stage career has encompassed *Hedda Gabler* (1975), *Rose* (1980), *Strange Interlude* (1984), *The House of Bernarda Alba* (1986), *Macbeth* (1988), and *Mother Courage* (1990). Her television work includes the series *Elizabeth R* (1971) and the film *The Patricia Neal Story* (1981).

She later turned to a career in politics, and

Glenda Jackson, 1994

in 1992 successfully overturned a Conservative majority to be elected as Labour MP for Hampstead and Highgate. In 1994 she contributed to a book of writings by single parents, *Soul Providers*.

Jackson, Helen Maria Hunt, *née* Fiske

Born 1830 Died 1885
American writer known for her novel Ramona and her acquaintance with Emily Dickinson

Helen Fiske was born in Amherst, Massachusetts, where she went to school with Emily Dickinson. She married an army captain, Edward Hunt, but by 1863 he and her two sons had died and she had turned to writing. In 1875 she married William Jackson.

Ralph Waldo Emerson acclaimed Helen Hunt Jackson as 'America's greatest woman poet', but this opinion is usually now considered over-valued. In fact it is her two prose works championing the Native American cause which have survived best: the polemical *A Century of Dishonor* (1881) and the sentimental but highly popular novel *Ramona* (1884).

Even so, it is the connection with Emily Dickinson which has done most to keep Jackson's name alive. The novel *Mercy Philbrick's Choice* (1876) is generally considered to contain a fictional portrait of her Amherst schoolfriend.

Jackson, Mahalia

Born 1911 Died 1962
American gospel singer who achieved chart success despite refusing most secular engagements

Mahalia Jackson was born in New Orleans, Louisiana. She grew up in a strict Baptist environment, but was attracted to the blues of **Bessie Smith** and to the evangelical fervour of the Holiness Church.

Like many African-Americans of her generation, she moved north and began singing in the choir of the Great Salem Baptist Church in Chicago (1927) and, from 1932, with the Johnson Gospel Singers. She subsequently worked with the hymn writer Thomas A Dorsey and scored chart successes with 'Move On Up a Little Higher' and other blues-inflected gospel themes.

Despite commercial success, she refused all secular engagements, particularly nightclubs. She did, however, sing at John F Kennedy's inauguration, and her emotional contralto and fervid delivery did much to underline the social imperatives of the New Frontier, Kennedy's ground-breaking proposals in social legislation.

Jackson, Marjorie

Born 1931
Australian sprinter who was the first Australian woman athlete of undoubted world class

Marjorie Jackson was born in Coffs Harbour, New South Wales. She came to prominence by twice defeating the hitherto invincible **Fanny Blankers-Koen** in 1948, after she had swept the boards at the London Olympics.

Her career blossomed and she won both sprints and was in the winning sprint relay team at the Commonwealth Games of 1950. The peak of her achievement came at Helsinki in 1952 when she won both Olympic sprints, crowning a two-year period in which she had set 13 world sprinting records.

Jackson of Lodsworth, Dame Barbara Mary Ward, Baroness

Born 1914 Died 1981
English economist, journalist and conservationist who wrote prolifically on her subjects

Barbara Ward was born in Sussex and educated in Paris, Germany, and Somerville College, Oxford. She became foreign editor of the *Economist* in 1939. After World War II she lectured in the USA, including Harvard (1957–68) and Columbia (1968–73) and from 1973 to 1980 she was President of the International Institute for Environment and Development.

She was married to a UN official, Robert Jackson, and was awarded a life peerage in 1976. Also a prolific and popular writer on politics, economics, and ecology, she wrote such books as *The International Share Out* (1936), *The Rich Nations and the Poor Nations* (1962), *Spaceship Earth* (1966), and *Only One Earth — the Care and Maintenance of a Small Planet* (1972).

Jacob, Mary Phelps, *also known as* Caresse Crosby

Floreat 1913–14
American society lady who is credited with inventing the modern-day bra

Mary Phelps Jacob has entered fashion legend as a social lady who, one evening in 1913 while dressing for a ball, became so frustrated with the tightly-boned, bust-enhancing corset of her era that she dispensed with hers altogether. With the help of a maid, she skilfully tied two silk handkerchiefs together to create the very first 'backless brassière' which gave support yet natural definition to the breasts.

The following year, allegedly haven fallen on hard times, she reputedly sold the patent to Warner's for $1,500. They developed the concept of the bra as an item of underwear separate from the body-shaping all-in-one corset, and marketed it in 1915 as the step-sister of the corset, which reduced in length as well as in popularity.

Jacobi, (J) Lotte

Born 1896   Died 1990
German-born American photographer, best known for her striking modernist portraits

Lotte Jacobi was born in Thorn, Germany (now Torun, Poland), and became the fourth-generation member of her father's family to practise as a commercial photographer; her great grandfather Samuel Jacobi was a pupil of Jacques-Louis-Mande Daguerre (1787–1851). She studied art history in Posen (1912–16) and Munich (1925–7) and photography and film at the Staatliche Höhere Fach Schule für Phototechnik. She was twice married: to timber merchant Fritz Honig from 1916 until they divorced in 1924, with whom she had a son, John Frank (b.1917), and subsequently to publisher Erich Reiss from 1940 until his death in 1951.

In 1927 she took over her father Sigismund Jacobi's Berlin photography studio and ran it until the political situation in Germany made her move to the USA in 1935. She operated a studio in New York until 1955, when she went to Deering, New Hampshire, and practised there. She is known for her portraits of artists, photographers, scientists, politicians and writers, for dance photographs and for photogenic drawings.

Jacobi, Mary Corrinna Puttnam,
née Puttnam

Born 1842   Died 1906
American physician who was considered the leading woman physician in America

Mary Puttnam was born in London, England. She was educated at home in Yonkers, New York, and at private school, and graduated from the New York College of Pharmacy in 1863.

She qualified MD from the Female Medical College of Pennsylvania the following year and worked in **Marie Zakrzewska**'s clinic in Boston for a few months before moving to Paris to study further. She was the first woman to enter the École Médecine, graduating from there in 1871.

Later in 1871 she returned to New York and combined private practice with hospital, educational and professional activities, building fast on her reputation. She was active in social causes and women's suffrage, and married Dr Abraham Jacobi, a paediatrician, in 1873.

Jacobs, Aletta

Born 1851   Died 1929
Dutch doctor and birth control pioneer, the first woman physician in Holland

Aletta Jacobs, a doctor's daughter, was one of 11 children and was educated at home and at her local school. She wanted to become a doctor but medical school was closed to women. After training as a dispenser, she petitioned the Prime Minister of the Netherlands for the right to study medicine and was granted a place at the University of Groningen, later becoming the first female medical doctor in Holland.

Working with her father, she set up free clinics for the poor. In 1882 she established the world's first birth control clinic for women in Amsterdam and campaigned for improvements in health education, for changes in marriage and prostitution laws, and for female suffrage.

In 1892 she married Carel Victor Gerritsen.

Jacqueline of Holland, *also called*
Jacoba of Bavaria

Born 1401   Died 1436
Dutch noblewoman who made a series of controversial marriages

Jacqueline was the daughter of William, Count of Zeeland, Holland and Bavaria. She married, first (1415), Prince John, dauphin of France, who died in 1417. She waged war against John of Bavaria for the right to succeed to her father's title there, then in 1418 married her weak cousin, the Duke of Brabant, who mortgaged Holland and Zeeland to John of Bavaria.

Repudiating the marriage, she went to England, where she married (illegally) Humphrey, Duke of Gloucester, in 1422. Deserted by him during an invasion to regain her lands in Hainault, which destroyed the alliance between England and Burgundy, she was captured by Philip the Good of Burgundy, and relinquished to him her claims to sovereignty through the Treaty of Delft. This act brought together the lands under Burgundian rule in the Netherlands.

In 1433 she married (again illegally), Frans van Borsselen, a Zeeland noble, but Philip suspected action against him; he imprisoned Frans and forced Isabella to give up her title of countess of Holland, Zeeland and Hainaut, which she had been allowed to retain. She was released the following year.

Jadwiga

Born 1374   Died 1399
Queen of Poland, who with her husband brought
Christianity to Lithuania

Jadwiga was the daughter of Louis d'Anjou, King of Hungary and Poland. At the age of four she was betrothed to Duke William of Hapsburg, but two years after succeeding to the Polish throne in 1384, she married Jagiello (1351–1434), the Grand Duke of Lithuania, who later ruled as Wladyslaw (Ladislaus) II Jagiello.

Their joint rule united the two realms, brought Christianity to Lithuania, and heralded the prosperity of the Jagiellon dynasty. Jadwiga devoted her short life and her fortune to the poor, for she died in childbirth, leaving her wealth to re-establish the University of Krakow. A cloak she used to cover a coppersmith who had drowned in the river became the banner of the coppersmiths' guild.

Jael

12th century BC
Biblical character who murdered the Canaanite
general Sisera

Jael was the wife of Heber the Kenite. After the Israelites, under **Deborah** and Barak, had defeated their arch-enemies the Canaanites, the Canaanite commander Sisera fled. Jael — whose family was at peace with the Canaanites — offered the general food and shelter, but while he slept she killed him by driving a tent peg through his temple with a mallet.

The story of the battle and Sisera's murder, which resulted in a 40-year peace for Israel, is told in prose and verse in the book of Judges.

Jakobsdóttir, Svava

Born 1930
Icelandic short-story writer, novelist and
playwright who is the best-known modern woman
writer of her country

Svava Jakobsdóttir was born in Neskaupstadur. She worked as a journalist and also studied in the USA and England. In 1970 she was active in the Icelandic women's movement, and from 1971 to 1979 she represented the Socialist Party in the Icelandic parliament.

Her first collection of short stories, *12 konur* ('12 Women'), appeared in 1965, followed in 1967 by *Veizla undir grjótvegg* ('Party beneath a Stone Wall'). Her texts, highlighting the problems of alienation in modern society and, especially, the position of women in a patriarchal system, tend to open in an atmosphere of everyday realism which alarmingly assumes Surrealist and absurd proportions.

The novel *Leigjandinn* (1969, 'The Lodger') is an allegory about oppression, the central female character representing a curtailment of freedom that is not only sexual but also political and military. *Gunnladar saga* (1987, 'The Story of Gunnlod') is a novel making extensive use of myth as a means of illuminating the present.

James, Florence

Born 1902   Died 1993
New Zealand writer who has collaborated with
and encouraged other Anitopodean writers

Florence James was born in Gisborne. She went to Australia as a child, began a career in music but later moved to art, and then read philosophy. At Sydney University she met **Dymphna Cusack** with whom she wrote *Come In Spinner*. In 1848 this long novel won first prize in a competition in the Sydney *Daily Telegraph* which promised publication, but the strict indecency laws of Australia at that time meant that it was only issued after much debate in a bowdlerized version, edited by James, in 1951.

She was a strong Quaker, and spent time in London's Holloway Women's Prison in the 1960s for her activities with the Campaign for Nuclear Disarmament. A close friend and supporter of **Christina Stead**, she worked in London for the publishing firm of Constable and helped publish younger Australian writers such as **Kylie Tennant**. With Cusack she also wrote a children's book, *Four Winds and a Family* (1947).

James, P(hyliss) D(orothy)

Born 1920
English thriller writer who is hailed as one of the
new 'queens of crime'

P D James was born in Oxford, the eldest child of an official in the Inland Revenue, and educated at Cambridge Girls' High School. Before World War II she worked in the theatre, and during the War she was a Red Cross nurse, and also worked in the Ministry of Food. Later she was employed in hospital administration before working in the home office, first in the police department, where she was involved with the forensic science service, thereafter in the criminal law department. She has devoted herself to writing since 1979.

Cover Her Face, published in 1962, was her first novel, a well-crafted, but slight detective story. She has written steadily since, many of her works featuring the superior detective who is also a minor poet, Commander Adam Dalgleish; these include *A Mind to Murder* (1963), *The Black Tower* (1975), and *Death of an Expert Witness* (1977). *A Taste for Death* (1986), a macabre, elegant, and substantial story, enjoyed an international vogue and was followed by *Devices and Desires* (1989). *The Skull Beneath the Skin* (1982) featured a female private detective, Cordelia Gray. *The Children of Men* (1992), a departure from detective writing, is set in the year 2021 and posits a world where all men have been infertile since 1995. *Original Sin* (1994) is set against the background of a distinguished British publishing house.

James was awarded the Crime Writers Association Diamond Dagger in 1987. She was made a life peer in 1991, becoming Baroness James of Holland Park.

Jameson, Anna Brownell, *née* Murphy

Born 1794 Died 1860
Irish author and art critic who also gave practical support to feminist reform

Anna Brownell Murphy was born in Dublin, the eldest of five daughters. When she was a young child her family moved to London and she received a moderate education. She was governess to the Marquis of Winchester and had a position as a governess in Italy before beginning in 1825 her unsuccessful marriage to Robert Jameson, who was often posted abroad and from whom she separated in 1836.

Her writing career, which later had to support several of the female members of her family, began with *Diary of an Ennuyée* in 1826 and includes *Characteristics of Shakespeare's Women* (1832), *Beauties of the Court of Charles II* (1833), *Winter Studies and Summer Rambles in Canada* (1838), which became the best-known Canadian travel book of its time, and *Sacred and Legendary Art* (4 vols, 1848–60).

Her wide group of well-established literary friends included **George Eliot** and Mrs **Gaskell**. During the mid-1850s she turned to lecturing on the role of women as reformers and she gave financial support to such feminist reformers as **Barbara Bodichon** and **Adelaide Procter**.

Jameson, (Margaret) Storm

Born 1891 Died 1986
English novelist whose works often examine the practical and emotional effects of war

Storm Jameson was born in Whitby. Her first success was *The Lovely Ship* (1927), which was followed by more than 30 books that maintained her reputation as storyteller and stylist. These include *The Voyage Home* (1930), *The Delicate Monster* (1937), *Cloudless May* (1943), *The Black Laurel* (1948), *The Hidden River* (1955), *A Cup of Tea for Mr Thorgill* (1957), *Last Score* (1961), *The Aristide Case* (1964), and *The White Crow* (1968).

Many of her early works focused on the effect that World War I had on male–female relationships. She also wrote poems, essays, criticism, and biography, and several volumes of autobiography, including *No Time Like the Present* (1933) and *Journey from the North* (1969).

Jamet, Marie, *known as* Marie Augustine de la Compassion

Born 1820 Died 1893
French nun who founded the Little Sisters of the Poor

Marie Jamet was a St Servan seamstress. In 1840 she was a founder of the order of the Little Sisters of the Poor, of which she was appointed superior in 1843.

Jamison, Judith

Born 1943
American black dancer who has been a top soloist since the 1960s

Judith Jamison was born in Philadelphia. She studied piano and violin in her home town at the Judimar School before making her New York début as a guest dancer with American Ballet Theatre in 1964. She joined Alvin Ailey's American Dance Theatre the following year, becoming one of his top soloists. He choreographed the solo *Cry* for her in 1971, a showcase for her statuesque physique, musical sensitivity, and dramatic stage presence.

She toured the USA and Europe in 1980 and then starred in the Broadway musical *Sophisticated Ladies* (1981). She later choreographed *Divining Hymn* for the American Dance Theatre as well as works for various other companies. She was with the Maurice Hines Dance School in New York City for a time before rejoining Alvin Ailey's American Dance Theatre as artisitic director in 1990. She is married to the Puerto Rican dancer, Miguel Godreau.

Jane Francis de Chantal, St, *née* Jeanne-Françoise Frémiot

Born 1572   Died 1641
French founder of the Congregation of the
Visitation of Our Lady

Jeanne-Françoise Frémiot was born in Dijon. She was widowed in 1601 after her husband, Baron de Chantal, was killed in a hunting accident. She took Frances de Sales as her spiritual director in 1604 and they became close friends.

Having seen that her son and eldest daughter were provided for, she went with the two youngest daughters to Annecy, in Savoy, where in 1610 she founded the Visitation Order. These Visitandines, or Salesian Sisters, were originally devoted to nursing, but soon became an enclosed contemplative Order.

By the time of Jane Francis de Chantal's death, 86 religious houses of the Order had been established. Her sanctity was recognized by her contemporary, St Vincent de Paul. She was canonized in 1767.

Jansson, Tove

Born 1914
Finno-Swedish author and artist known for her
Moomintroll books for children

Tove Jansson was born in Helsinki, the daughter of artists. She studied art in Helsinki, Stockholm and Paris and began exhibiting her work in 1943. She started the Moomintroll books with *Trollkarlens hatt* (1949, Eng trans *The Magician's Hat*), illustrating them herself. They are as much appreciated by adults and are sometimes made into cartoons or films. Set in the fantastic yet real world of the Moomins, they emphasize the security of family life.

In later years Jansson wrote a number of books for adults, including *Sommarboken* (1972, 'The Summer Book') and a psychological thriller *Den ärliga bedragaren* (1982, 'The Honest Deceiver'). She has been the recipient of many literary prizes.

Jaricot, Pauline

Born 1799   Died 1862
French pioneer fundraiser for Catholic missions

Pauline Jaricot was born in Lyons. At the age of 17 she made a private vow of perpetual virginity and founded a prayer union for servant girls, for whom she later set up the Loretta home, a hostel for young women.

In 1820 she founded an association for the missions, in which she was joined in 1822 by a like-minded group of 12 laymen raising funds for work in New Orleans. This Missionary Society of Lyons or St Francis Xavier Society became the Society for the Propagation of the Faith. In its first year it raised over $4,000 from one-cent contributions.

Jeanne d'Albret

Born 1528   Died 1572
Queen of Navarre and mother of Henry IV of
France (known as Henry of Navarre)

Jeanne d'Albret was the only daughter and heiress of Henry d'Albret (Henry II) of Navarre and **Margaret of Angoulême**, by whom she was taught until the age of 10. She married Antoine de Bourbon, Duc de Vendôme, in 1548, gave birth to Henry in 1553, and succeeded in 1562.

For nearly all of her reign she retained a neutral stance, trying to improve her small Kingdom's administration, among other tasks, and drawing together a group of aristocratic women who were later to wield much influence. However in 1572 she took sides in the Third Civil War as a leader of the Protestant Huguenots and Calvinists, establishing their stronghold at La Rochelle. With grave reservations, due to the inordinate power wielded by **Catherine de' Médicis**, the mother and former regent of Charles IX of France, she agreed to the marriage in March 1572 of her son to **Margaret of Valois**, Charles IX's sister, to mark a truce between the two sides.

Soon after Jeanne d'Albret's death, the horrific St Bartholomew's Day Massacre of Protestants, in which Catherine de' Médicis is traditionally implicated, took place. Henry saved himself only by a pretended conversion to Catholicism.

Jebb, Eglantyne

Born 1876   Died 1928
English philanthropist who founded Save the
Children

Eglantyne Jebb was born in Ellesmere, Shropshire. She graduated from St Margaret Hall, Oxford, in 1898 and taught for a year at an elementary school in Marlborough, but was forced by ill health to leave the profession. After doing social work in Cambridge, she went to Macedonia to administer the relief fund for the victims of the Balkan wars.

At the end of World War I the plight of the 4–5 million children starving in Europe prompted her to set up the Save the Children Fund (1919), for which she managed to raise large sums of money. The Save the Children International Union was established in

Geneva, where she remained and worked until her early death.

Jekyll, Gertrude

Born 1843 Died 1932
English horticulturalist and garden designer who championed the ordered disorder of the natural cottage garden

Gertrude Jekyll was born in London. She trained as an artist but was forced by failing eyesight to abandon painting and took up landscape design at her garden at Munstead Wood, Surrey.

She worked for a time with the Irish gardener and horticultural writer William Robinson (1838–1935), but remains best known for her association with the young architect Edwin Lutyens (1869–1944) — she designed more than 300 gardens for his buildings that had a great influence on promoting colour design in garden planning.

Her books include *Wood and Garden* (1899), *Home and Garden* (1900), *Wall and Water Gardens* (1901), *Colour in the Flower Garden* (1918) and *Garden Ornament* (1918).

Jensen, Thit

Born 1876 Died 1957
Danish novelist and lecturer who held controversial views on equality, marriage, motherhood and contraception

Thit Jensen was born in Farso on Jutland, one of 10 sisters and brothers, one of whom was the Nobel Prize-winning novelist Johannes Jensen (1873–1950). She published her first novel in 1903.

Early works, for example *Martyrium* (1905, 'Martyrdom') and *Orkenvandring* (1907, 'Through the Desert') are pleas for women's equality in marriage. However, her later work deals with the conflict between the demand for equality and motherhood. While the central character in *Gerd* (1918) rejects conventional feminine roles in favour of a career, the renowned MP in the sequel *Aphrodite fra Fuur* (1925, 'Aphrodite from Fuur') experiences a sense of fragmentation that forces her back into a more traditional existence.

The theme of motherhood was subsequently explored by Jensen in a number of historical novels. Her public lectures, most famously in favour of contraception, made her a highly controversial figure.

Jesenská, Miléna

Born 1890 Died 1944
Czech journalist and lover and correspondent of the writer Franz Kafka

Miléna Jesenská was born in Prague into an intellectual family and educated at the Minerva Gymnasium for Girls. She married the Jewish writer Ernst Polak and moved with him to Vienna, despite her father's anti-semitic opposition (he had her placed in a mental asylum to separate them). In Vienna she became a well-known journalist.

Through her work she came in contact with the novelist Franz Kafka around 1920. They corresponded (1920–3) and fell in love, but Miléna refused to leave her husband. Kafka's letters to her (*Briefe an Miléna*) were published in 1952.

An opponent of Nazism, she died in Ravensbrück in 1944.

Jesse, F(riniwyd) Tennyson, *known as* Fryn

Born 1889 Died 1958
English novelist, dramatist, journalist and editor whose interest in criminology pervades her writing

Fryn Jesse was born in Chislehurst, Kent, a great-niece of Alfred, Lord Tennyson (1809–92). She studied painting, but during World War I took up journalism as one of the few female war correspondents. Afterwards she served on the future US President Herbert Hoover's Relief Commission for Europe.

In 1918 she married the dramatist H M Harwood, and with him collaborated in a number of light plays and a series of war-time letters, *London Front* (1940) and *While London Burns* (1942). Jesse herself is best known for her novels set in Cornwall, such as *The White Riband* (1921), *Tom Fool* (1926), and *Moonraker* (1927), as well as *The Lacquer Lady* (1929), set in Burma and regarded by many as her best novel, and *A Pin to See a Peepshow* (1934), based on the Thompson-Bywaters murder case.

She also published collected poems, *The Happy Bride* (1920), and edited several volumes of the *Notable British Trials* series, including remarkable accounts of the trials of **Madeleine Smith** (1927), and of the murderers Timothy Evans and John Christie (1958).

Jett, Joan

Born 1960
American singer and guitarist

Joan Jett was born in Philadelphia, Pennsylvania. After some difficult and rocky beginnings, her rock stage shows became known for their intensity and vitality.

In the 1980s, she formed the group The

Blackhearts; among their albums are *Glorious Results of a Misspent Youth* (1984) and *Up Your Alley*. Her well-known songs include 'I Love Rock 'n' Roll'.

Jewett, (Theodora) Sarah Orne

Born 1849 Died 1909
American novelist, regional realist writer and first President of Vasser College

Sarah Orne Jewett was born in South Berwick, Maine. She wrote a series of sketches, *Deephaven* (1877), and a more structured fiction, *The Country of the Pointed Firs* (1896), which developed her interest in the psychology of small, out of the way places and their inhabitants, particularly women.

She also wrote romantic novels and stories based on the provincial life of her state, such as *A Country Doctor* (1884) and *A White Heron* (1886), and a historical romance, *The Tory Lover* (1901).

She was the first President of Vassar College (1862–4), and regarded as an inspiration and mentor to **Willa Cather**.

Jewsbury, Geraldine (Endsor)

Born 1812 Died 1880
English novelist, wit and conversationalist

Geraldine Jewsbury was born in Measham, Derbyshire, the daughter of a businessman. From 1854 she lived in Chelsea, to be near her friend Jane Welsh Carlyle.

She contributed articles and reviews to various journals, and wrote six novels, including *Zoë* (1845), *The Half Sisters* (1848), *Marion Withers* (1851) and *Right or Wrong* (1859). *A Selection from the Letters of Geraldine Jewsbury to Jane Carlyle* (1892) aroused controversy over the emotional nature of their relationship.

Jex-Blake, Sophia Louisa

Born 1840 Died 1912
English physician and pioneer of medical education for women

Sophia Jex-Blake was born in Hastings. She was the sister of Thomas William Jex-Blake (1832–1915), headmaster of Rugby and Dean of Wells. She studied at Queen's College for Women, London, and became a tutor in mathematics there (1859–61).

From 1865 she studied medicine in New York under **Elizabeth Blackwell**, but since English medical schools were closed to women she could not continue her studies on her return. She fought her way into Edinburgh University, however, where with five other women she was allowed to matriculate in 1869, but the university authorities reversed their decision in 1873.

She waged a public campaign in London, opened the London School of Medicine for Women in 1874 and in 1876 won her campaign when medical examiners were permitted by law to examine women students. In 1886 she founded a medical school in Edinburgh, where from 1894 women were finally allowed to graduate in medicine.

Jezebel

Died 842BC
Phoenician princess in the Old Testament who is considered the archetypal wicked woman

Jezebel was the daughter of Ethbaal, king of Tyre and Sidon, and wife of King Ahab of Israel (869–850BC). She introduced Phoenician habits and the worship of Baal and Asherah to the capital, Samaria, thus provoking the wrath of God against Ahab and earning the undying anger of the prophet Elijah and his successors.

One of her many malicious schemes was to procure Naboth's vineyard for her husband by having Naboth accused of blasphemy and stoned to death. Ahab was subsequently confronted by Elijah and told that not only would his heirs be destroyed, but Jezebel's corpse would be eaten by dogs.

After Ahab's death, Jezebel was the power behind the throne of her sons until the usurper Jehu seized power in an army coup; he had Jezebel thrown from a window, and trampled her to death under his chariot. When the time came to bury her, dogs were found to have eaten most of the body.

Jhabvala, Ruth Prawer, *née* Prawer

Born 1927
British writer of novels and short-stories and such acclaimed screenplays as A Room with a View

Ruth Prawer was born in Cologne, Germany, of Polish parents who emigrated to Britain in 1939. She graduated from Queen Mary College, London University, married a visiting Indian architect, and lived in Delhi (1951–75).

Most of her fiction relates to India, taking the viewpoint of an outsider looking in. Significant novels include *To Whom She Will Marry* (1955), *Esmond in India* (1958), *The Householder* (1960), *A Backward Place* (1963) and *Heat and Dust* (1975), which won the Booker Prize. Her short stories have been collected in several volumes.

In association with the film makers James Ivory and Ismail Merchant, she has written several accomplished screenplays, among them *Shakespeare Wallah* (1965), and the Academy Award (Best Adapted Screenplay) winning *A Room with a View* (1986) and *Howard's End* (1992).

Jiang Qing (Chiang Ch'ing)

Born 1914 Died 1991
Chinese politician, a leader of the suppressive Cultural Revolution and third wife of Mao Zedung

Jiang Qing was born in Zhucheng, Shandong (Shantung) Province, the daughter of a carpenter. She trained in drama before studying literature at Qingdao University, and became a stage and film actress in Shanghai. In 1936 she went to the Chinese Communist Party headquarters at Yenan to study Marxist-Leninist theory, and met the Communist leader, Mao Zedong (Mao Tse-tung, 1893–1976); she became his third wife in 1939.

She was attached to the ministry of culture in 1950–4, but it was in the 1960s that she began her attacks on bourgeois influences in the arts and literature, and she became one of the leaders of the 1965–9 'Cultural Revolution'. In 1969 she was elected to the Politburo, but after Mao's death in 1976 she was arrested with the three other members of the reviled 'Gang of Four' for attempting to seize power.

She was imprisoned, expelled from the Communist party, and tried in 1980 with subverting the government and wrongly arresting, detaining, and torturing numbers of innocent people. Although she was sentenced to death, this was later commuted.

Jinnah, Fatima, *known as* Madar-i-Millat ('Mother of the Country')

Born 1893 Died 1967
Pakistani politician, sister and companion of the first Governor-General of Pakistan, Mohammed Ali Jinnah

Fatima Jinnah was born in Karachi and moved to Bombay in 1901 to live with her brother Mohammed Ali Jinnah. She was educated at a mission school, and studied dentistry. Living with her brother in London (1929–34) affected her attitude to women's status. On returning to India in 1934 she joined the Muslim League, arguing against traditional conservative attitudes towards women. She was the first leader of the All-India Muslim Women's Committee (founded 1938), and toured India campaigning on behalf of women's welfare, education and training. She founded the Fatima Jinnah Women's Medical College in Lahore.

Her brother Ali Jinnah became the first Governor-General of Pakistan in 1947, and she retired from politics after his death. However, during the 1950s she resumed work for the Muslim League, and emerged during the 1960s as a significant opponent of the East Pakistan government.

Jiricna, Eva

Born 1939
Czechoslovakian architect whose engineering training shows clearly in many of her designs

Eva Jiricna was trained at the Prague School of Architecture, graduating in 1962. She moved to London in 1968 and registered as an architect with the RIBA (Royal Institute of British Architects) in 1973. Eva Jiricna Architects opened in London in 1987 and has become known for its sophisticated shop interiors.

The initial shop interiors for Joseph brought commissions from all over the world, including the Lloyds headquarters, London (1985), in collaboration with English architect Richard Rogers. The international furniture company Vitra gave Jiricna her first major building commission for a new headquarters building. Unfortunately the project was never realised, but Vitra also commissioned an entrance bridge to their headquarters shop in Basle (1989), which embodies the delicacy of Jiricna's work.

Joan

No date
A fictitious personage long believed to have been pope, as John VIII (855–8)

Joan was, according to one legend, born in Mainz in Germany, the daughter of English parents. She was so well educated by her lover, a monk, that she in due time became cardinal and pope.

Her reign was said to have ended abruptly when she gave birth to a child during a papal procession between St Peter's and the Lateran, a route since avoided on such occasions, and was taken out of the city and stoned. Other accounts claim that she died in childbirth, and that she was known as Agnes or Gilberta until the name Joan was standardized in the 14th century.

However the story of Pope Joan is apocryphal as there was a break of only a few weeks between the pontificates of Leo IV and Benedict III, between whom she is said to have reigned.

Joan of Arc, St, *French* Jeanne d'Arc, *known as the* Maid of Orléans

Born c.1412 Died 1431
French patriot, martyr and national heroine

Joan of Arc was born in Domrémy, on the border of Lorraine and Champagne, the daughter of well-off peasants. The English over-ran the area in 1421 and in 1424 withdrew. Joan received no formal education but had an argumentative nature and shrewd common sense. At the age of 13 she thought she heard the voices of St Michael, St **Catherine** and St **Margaret** bidding her to rescue the Paris region from English domination. She persuaded the local commander, Robert de Baudricourt, after he had had her exorcised, to take her in 1429 across English-occupied territory to the dauphin (the future Charles VII) at Chinon. According to legend, she was called into a gathering of courtiers, among them the dauphin in disguise, and her success in identifying him at once was interpreted as divine confirmation of his previously doubted legitimacy and claims to the throne. She was equally successful in an ecclesiastical examination to which she was subjected in Poitiers and was consequently allowed to join the army assembled at Blois for the relief of Orléans.

Clad in a suit of white armour and flying her own standard, she entered Orléans with an advance guard on 29 April and by 8 May had forced the English to raise the siege and retire in June from the principal strongholds on the Loire. To put further heart into the French resistance, she took the dauphin with an army of 12,000 through English-held territory to be crowned Charles VII in Reims Cathedral. She then found it extremely difficult to persuade him to undertake further military exploits, especially the relief of Paris.

At last she set out on her own to relieve Compiègne from the Burgundians, was captured in a sortie (1430) and sold to the English by John of Luxembourg for 10,000 crowns. She was put on trial (1431) for heresy and sorcery by an ecclesiastical court of the Inquisition, presided over by Pierre Cauchon, Bishop of Beauvais. Most of the available facts concerning Joan's life are those preserved in the records of the trial. She was found guilty, taken out to the churchyard of St Ouen on 24 May to be burnt, but at the last moment broke down and made a wild recantation. This she later abjured and suffered her martyrdom at the stake in the market place of Rouen on 30 May, faithful to her 'voices'. In 1456, in order to strengthen the validity of Charles VII's coronation, the trial was declared irregular.

It was her belief in her divine mission that made her flout military advice — in the end disastrously — but she rallied her countrymen, halted the English ascendancy in France for ever and was one of the first in history to die for a Christian-inspired concept of nationalism. In 1904 she was designated Venerable, declared Blessed in 1908 and finally canonized in 1920. Her feast day is 30 May.

Joan of Navarre, *also called* Joanna, *French* Jeanne de Navarre

Born c.1370 Died 1437
Queen of England as the wife of Henry IV (ruled 1399–1413)

Joan of Navarre was born in Havering atte Bowe in Essex, the daughter of Charles the Bad, King of Navarre. She married first John V, Duke of Brittany (1386), by whom she had eight children. When he died in 1399, she became Regent of Brittany for her son John VI until 1401, then married Henry IV of England in 1402.

Since there was hostility between Brittany and England, she was not a popular choice as consort, and after Henry's death in 1413, though she remained on good terms with her stepson Henry V, difficulties arose because she was the mother of Brittany's ruler (John VI).

She was imprisoned for three years (1419–22) on specious allegations of witchcraft, but was well treated, leading many to conclude that it was her son's way of having access to her wealth.

Joanna, *also called* Joan *or* Juana, *known as* Joanna the Mad ('la loca')

Born 1479 Died 1555
Queen of Castile (1504–55) and Aragon (1516–55)

Joanna was the daughter of Ferdinand II and **Isabella** of Spain. She became the wife of Philip 'the Handsome' of Burgundy in 1495. The couple settled in Ghent and had several children, of whom the eldest was the future Holy Roman Emperor, Charles V.

On her mother's death in 1505, Joanna became Queen of Castile and she and Philip moved to Spain in 1506. Philip died the same year and Joanna, who suffered from severe melancholia, was declared unfit to govern and was shut away under close watch in a castle at Tordesillas while her father assumed the regency of Castile.

Although Ferdinand died in 1516, her son Charles, now King of Spain, did not release her and Joanna remained in Tordesillas, along with her youngest daughter Catalina, until her death. Revolts against Charles were sometimes led under the pretext that Joanna was not insane at all.

John, Gwen

Born 1876 Died 1939
Welsh painter and mistress of Auguste Rodin

Gwen John was born in Haverfordwest, Pembrokeshire, the elder sister of the painter Augustus John (1878–1961). She lived in Tenby, Pembrokeshire, before studying at the Slade School (1895–8).

In 1904 she moved to Paris, where she worked as an artist's model and after about two years became the mistress of the sculptor Auguste Rodin (1840–1917). After converting to Roman Catholicism in 1913 she lived at Meudon, where she became increasingly religious and reclusive. She was very different in character and style to her exuberant brother, and painted many individual portraits of girls and nuns in muted, greyish tones.

She exhibited with the New English Art Club (1900–11), and her work was included in the Armory Show of 1913. Her only one-woman show during her lifetime was in London in 1926.

Johnson, Amy

Born 1903 Died 1941
English pioneering aviator who flew solo from England to Australia

Amy Johnson was born in Hull, the daughter of a fish merchant. She studied economics at Sheffield University, then worked as a typist, joined the London Aeroplane Club and gained her certificate as a ground engineer (the first woman to do so) and pilot in 1929.

In 1930 she became the first woman to fly solo from England to Australia; this she achieved in her aircraft *Jason*, winning £10,000 from the London *Daily Mail*. In 1931 she flew to Japan via Moscow and back, and in 1932 made a record solo flight to Cape Town and back.

She married the Scottish airman James Mollison in 1932, and with him crossed the Atlantic in a de Havilland biplane in 39 hours (1933) and flew to India in 22 hours (1934). In 1936 she set a new record for a solo flight from London to Cape Town. She divorced in 1938, joined the Air Transport Auxiliary as a pilot in World War II, and was lost after baling out over the Thames estuary.

Johnson, Anna Maria, *also known as* Anna Mackenzie, *née* Wight

Floreat 1783–1811
English novelist who wrote some of the earliest historical romances

Anna Wight was born in Essex, the daughter of a coal merchant, and was educated at a girls' school. Abandoned by her husband (whose surname was Cox), with children to support, she turned to teaching and writing. Though she wrote for magazines, she is best known as a novelist.

Often writing for William Lane's Circulating Libraries, she produced popular romances, and also wrote in the new genre of historical romance (*Monmouth*, 1790) and opposed slavery in her novel *Slavery* (1793). She wrote at least 16 known works (she herself claimed, in 1800, to have written 28 volumes), and it is suspected that she published several novels anonymously; others give her surname variously as 'Johnson' (1789) and 'Mackenzie' (1795).

Johnson, Dame Celia

Born 1908 Died 1982
English actress whose career ranged from exquisitely modulated portraits of quiet despair to sophisticated high comedy

Celia Johnson was born in Richmond, Surrey. She studied at RADA, and made her stage début in *Major Barbara* (1928) at Huddersfield and her London bow in *A Hundred Years Old* (1929). Soon cast as a leading lady, often in well-bred roles, she made her first New York appearance as Ophelia in *Hamlet* (1931) and enjoyed a long run in *The Wind and the Rain* (1933–5) in London.

Dirty Work (1934) marked the first of her rare screen appearances, although she created an unforgettable impression as the sad-eyed suburban housewife in *Brief Encounter* (1945) and won a British Film award for *The Prime of Miss Jean Brodie* (1969).

Her many theatrical successes included *The Three Sisters* (1951), *The Reluctant Debutante* (1955), *The Grass is Greener* (1958), *Hay Fever* (1965) and *The Kingfisher* (1977). She was married to the writer Peter Fleming from 1935 until his death in 1971.

Johnson, Josephine Winslow

Born 1910
American novelist and poet whose first novel won a Pulitzer Prize

Josephine Winslow Johnson was born in Missouri and brought up on a farm. She wrote short stories for a few years and then won a Pulitzer Prize with her first novel *Now in November* (1934), a celebration of unmechanized farming life, a subject she knew well. (Johnson's husband eventually became editor of *Farm Quarterly*.)

Other novels, written in a distinctively quiet but stylish manner, have sombre themes. *Wildwood* (1946) is about a frustrated and lonely young girl growing up in the oppressive home of relatives, and the main character of *The Dark Traveller* (1963) is a schizophrenic.

Johnson, Pamela Hansford, Lady Snow

Born 1912 Died 1981
English novelist, playwright and critic best known for her 'quintessentially British' writing

Pamela Hansford-Johnson was born in London to theatrical parents. Her background provided what **Margaret Drabble** has called 'a peculiar vantage point for an unprejudiced insight into a wide range of behaviour'. She left school at 18, and worked in a bank and as a book reviewer. For a short time in the early 1930s she was engaged to be married to the Welsh poet Dylan Thomas (1914–53).

Her first novel, *This Bed Thy Centre* (1935), was set in working-class south London, and her many subsequent novels are observant both of the world of her youth, and of society in the 1960s and 1970s, and range from the comic to the morally insightful. They include *An Avenue of Stone* (1947) and its sequel *A Summer to Decide* (1948); the tragi-comical *The Unspeakable Skipton* (1958), the first in a trilogy featuring her comic creation Dorothy Merlin; *An Error of Judgement* (1962); *The Honours Board* (1970); and *The Good Husband* (1978). Her critical works include a study of **Ivy Compton-Burnett** (1953) and writing on Thomas Wolfe, and her plays include *Corinth House* (1948, published 1954) and *Six Proust Reconstructions* (1958), for radio broadcast.

In 1950 she married the novelist C P Snow (1905–80), becoming Lady Snow, and collaborated with him on many literary projects.

Johnson, (Emily) Pauline

Born 1861 Died 1913
Canadian poet, the most famous Native Canadian writer of her time

Pauline Johnson was born on the Six Nations Reservation near Ontario. Her father was a Mohawk, while her English mother was related to William Dean Howells. Her earliest poems were published in magazine form in 1884, and her work was collected in several volumes, including *Canadian Born* (1903) and *Flint and Feather* (1912). From 1892 to 1909 she gave extensive public readings of her work, often dressed in Native Canadian costume and using the name Tekahionwake. She also wrote short prose works, collected in *Legends of Vancouver* (1911) and other volumes.

Johnson, Sonia

Born 1936
American feminist and writer who was excommunicated from the Mormon faith for her belief in equal rights for women

Sonia Johnson was born in Malad City, Idaho. She was a Mormon and in 1978 founded Mormons for ERA (the Equal Rights Amendment), which lobbied extensively for a constitutional amendment stating equal rights for women. The following year she was excommunicated from the Mormon faith, as the Church of the Latter-Day Saints, which stresses women's obedience and submission, saw her work for the ERA as disbedient to her faith.

In 1981 she wrote *From Housewife to Heretic*. In 1984 she was the presidential candidate of the Citizen's Party. Her other books include *Wildfire: Igniting the She-Volution* (1989) and *The Ship that Sailed into the Living Room: Sex and Intimacy Reconsidered* (1991).

Johnson, Virginia E(shelman)

Born 1925
American psychologist and sexologist best known for her pioneering research with her husband, William Masters

Virginia Johnson was born in Springfield, Missouri, and educated at Missouri University. She joined the research group of the gynaecologist and sexologist William Masters (1915–) in 1957. They achieved fame through their pioneering investigations of the physiology of sexual intercourse, using volunteer subjects under laboratory conditions at their Reproductive Biology Research Foundation in St Louis, which they established in 1970.

Johnson and Masters (who were married from 1971 to 1993) co-authored *Human Sexual Response* in 1966. They also wrote *Human Sexual Inadequacy* (1970), *Homosexuality in Perspective* (1979) and *On Sex and Human Loving* (1986).

Johnston, Frances Benjamin

Born 1864 Died 1952
American photographer who became one of the first women press photographers

Frances Benjamin Johnston was born in Grafton, West Virginia. She studied painting and drawing at the Académie Julian in Paris (1883–5), and then at the Art Students League in Washington DC (1885). Shortly afterwards, she studied photography with Thomas William Smillie of the Smithsonian Institution, and opened a professional studio in Washington DC in 1890.

She and **Jessie Tarbox Beals** were two of the first women press photographers. Johnston worked first as a magazine correspondent (c.1889) and later operated a studio in New York with a partner, Mattie Edwards Hewitt, specializing in architectural photography (1913–17). After 1917 she photographed mainly gardens, architecture and estates.

She is best known for careful social documentary work, particularly of industrial workers, for portraits and for architectural photography, using medium- to large-format gelatin dry-plate negatives and printing in platinum and silver. She became known as a champion of women as photographers and organized an important exhibition of prints by 28 American women practitioners to coincide with the Exposition Universelle in Paris in 1900.

Johnston, Jennifer Prudence

Born 1930
Irish novelist

Jennifer Johnston was born in Dublin into a Protestant family and educated at Trinity College, Dublin. Her mother, Shelagh Richards, was an actress and director at the Abbey Theatre, and her father was the playwright Denis Johnston (1901–84).

In such works as *The Gates* (1973), Johnston monitors the class and religious divisions in contemporary Ireland, and the slow erosion of the Irish Protestant gentry. *How Many Miles to Babylon?* (1974), in which two childhood friends from either end of the social scale are plunged into World War I, is particularly notable for its atmospheric portrayal of life in the trenches.

In *Shadows on Our Skin* (1977), Joe Logan, a Londonderry Catholic youth, dreams of becoming a poet, his schoolteacher becomes engaged to a British soldier, and Joe's brother returns from England to join the Provisional IRA. Subsequent novels, including *Fool's Sanctuary* (1987), deploy similar themes focusing on the cultural and political tensions in Irish history.

Johnstone, Dorothy

Born 1892 Died 1980
Scottish artist known for her portraits and figure studies

Dorothy Johnstone was born in Edinburgh on Christmas day, the daughter of the artist George Whitton Johnstone RSA. She studied at Edinburgh College of Art and won a travelling scholarship to Italy in 1910.

She first exhibited at the RSA in 1912 and spent some time painting in Kirkcudbright with her friends **Cecile Walton**, **Jessie M King** and E A Taylor. She taught at the Edinburgh College of Art from around 1918 but gave up teaching when she married the artist D M Sutherland in 1924.

She was elected ARSA (Associate of the Royal Scottish Academy) in 1962 and Aberdeen Art Gallery and the Fine Art Society honoured her in 1983 with a major memorial exhibition.

Johnstone, (Christian) Isobel

Born 1781 Died 1857
Scottish cookery writer, novelist and journalist

Isobel Johnstone was born in Fife. She married her second husband, John Johnstone, in 1812, and wrote for the *Inverness Courier* when he was its owner and editor. Whilst in Inverness she wrote *Clan Albyn, A National Tale* (1815) and followed this with *Elizabeth de Bruce* (1827), both historical novels which enjoyed considerable popularity.

She made her name, however, with *The Cook and Housewife's Manual* (1826), popularly known as *Meg Dod's Cookery*. A source of advice on kitchen practice, with recipes for national specialities and a lively commentary on food, using characters from Sir Walter Scott's St Ronan's Well, it was purportedly written by a Margaret Dods of the Cleikum Inn, St Ronan's. It remains an invaluable source-book for modern cooks.

Isobel Johnstone also maintained a successful career as a literary journalist, writing for the *Schoolmaster, Johnstone's Magazine* and *Tait's Magazine*.

Jolas, Betsy (Elizabeth)

Born 1926
Franco-American composer whose works are characterized by an interest in unusual sonorities and in music/text relationships

Betsy Jolas was born in Paris to American parents, the daughter of translator Maria MacDonald and Eugène Jolas, who published James Joyce's *Ulysses*. She was educated in France and, during World War II, in the USA, returning in 1946 to study under Olivier Messiaen and Darius Milhaud at the Conservatoire National Supérieur de Musique, where she became Professor of Analysis in 1975. She married Gabriel Illouz in 1949.

Among her works are orchestral pieces, such as *Tales of a Summer Sea* (1977), a wide range of instrumental pieces, including a cycle of solo *Episodes* (1964–84), and three operas, the latest being *Schliemann* (1987).

Joliot-Curie, Irène, *née* Curie

Born 1897 Died 1956
French physicist who was jointly awarded the
Nobel Prize with her husband

Irène Curie was born in Paris, the daughter of Pierre and **Marie Curie**. She was educated at home by her mother, and during World War I served as a radiographer in military hospitals. In 1918 she joined her mother at the Radium Institute in Paris and began her scientific research in 1921. In 1926 she married Frédéric Joliot, and they collaborated in studies of radioactivity from 1931.

In work on the emissions of polonium, they studied the highly penetrating radiation observed by the German physicist Walther Bothe and demonstrated its ability to eject

Irène Joliot-Curie

protons from paraffin-wax; the radiation emitted was in fact neutrons, but they misinterpreted their results and attributed it to a consequence of the Compton effect. The English physicist James Chadwick read their paper and built on this work in his discovery of the neutron. In 1933–4 the Joliot-Curies made the first artificial radioisotope by bombarding aluminium with alpha particles to produce a radioactive isotope of phosphorus. It was for this work that they were jointly awarded the Nobel Prize for Chemistry in 1935. Similar methods led them to make a range of radioisotopes, some of which have proved indispensable in medicine, scientific research and industry.

During World War II Irène Joliot-Curie escaped to Switzerland. Back in Paris after the War, she became director of the Radium Institute in 1946 and a director of the French Atomic Energy Commission. She died from leucaemia due to long periods of exposure to radioactivity.

Jolley, (Monica) Elizabeth

Born 1923
English-born Australian author of novels, short
stories and plays who uses lesbianism as a major
theme

Elizabeth Jolley was born in Birmingham. She settled in Western Australia in 1959 and in *Five Acre Virgin* (1976) collected some of her writing produced since then. It received immediate critical praise and was followed by *The Travelling Entertainer* (1979), longer pieces from the same period.

Her first novel was *Palomino* (1980), *The Newspaper of Claremont Street* (1981) is the story of a small-town gossip, and *Mr Scobie's Riddle* won the Melbourne *Age* Book of the Year award in 1982. In her later books *My Father's Moon* (1989) and *Cabin Fever* (1990) she returns to her earlier years in post-war England. This partly autobiographical trilogy was completed with the elegiac *The Georges' Wife* (1993). She has also written a number of plays, mostly for radio.

With her translator Françoise Cartano she won the inaugural 1993 France-Australia Award for Literary Translation for her novel *The Sugar Mother* (1988, as *Tombe du Ciel*).

Jones, Ann (Adrianne Shirley), *née* Haydon

Born c.1940
English tennis player, table tennis player, and
broadcaster

Ann Haydon was educated at King's Norton Grammar School, Birmingham. She reached the finals in the World Table Tennis championships in 1954 and 1959, and won her first tennis title at the French Open in 1961. The following year she married Philip Jones (d.1993).

At Wimbledon she was nine times a semi-finalist in the ladies singles, a finalist in 1967, and winner of the title in 1969. Since 1970 she has been a tennis commentator for the BBC, and in 1990 she became director of Women's Tennis, Lawn Tennis Association.

Jones, Grace

Born 1953
West Indian model, singer and film actress, a
transatlantic success

Grace Jones was born in Jamaica. She began modelling in Europe in the 1970s and became an international star with cover photographs appearing on *Elle*, *Vogue* and *Der Stern* magazines.

As a disco artist and concert performer, she was so successful in Europe that she developed a successful American recording career; this included a remake of **Edith Piaf**'s 'La Vie en Rose'. In the 1980s she turned to film and appeared in such American features as *Conan the Barbarian* (1981) and *A View to A Kill* (1985).

Jones, Dame Gwyneth

Born 1936
Welsh dramatic soprano

Gwyneth Jones was born in Pontnewynydd. Her studies included a period at the Royal College of Music. She has been a principal soprano since her débuts at the Royal Opera House, Covent Garden (1963), at the Vienna State Opera (1966), and at the Bavarian State Opera (1967). She has also performed at Bayreuth, Munich, La Scala Milan, and other great houses of the world and is renowned as an interpreter of the heroines of Wagner and Strauss operas.

Jones, Lois Mailou

Born 1905
American painter who is recognized as the first
black female painter of importance

Lois Mailou Jones was born in Boston and won a scholarship to the School of the Museum of Fine Arts in 1923. After graduating she worked as a textile designer and took

advanced courses at Harvard University and then at Howard and Columbia universities. In 1937 she travelled to Paris to study at the Académie Julian and said that for the first time she felt free to paint, free of the prejudice she had experienced in the USA. Returning home in 1938, she had an exhibit in the Vose Gallery in Boston.

She began to paint works like *Mob Victim* in 1944, dealing explicitly with her own background as a black American. She married Vergiaud Pierre-Noel in 1953. A sabbatical in Haiti influenced her work towards a more angular, abstract style, and her more recent work has been inspired by several trips to Africa. Paintings such as *Moon Masque* and *Magic of Nigeria* combine the stylized forms of African art with her powerful flat design shapes.

Lois Mailou Jones was Professor of Art at Howard University in Washington DC for 45 years and is a fellow of the Royal Society of the Arts in London.

Jones, Marion Patrick

Born 1934
Trinidadian novelist and campaigner against
racial discrimination

Marion Patrick Jones was educated at St Joseph's convent, Port of Spain, and then obtained a scholarship to the Imperial College of Agriculture. She moved to the USA in the 1950s and worked in a Brooklyn ceramics factory for a year before returning to Trinidad to qualify as a librarian. In 1959 she undertook postgraduate work in London, where she founded the Campaign Against Racial Discrimination.

Her first novel, Pan Beat (1973), deals impressively with several middle-class marriages in Port of Spain. *J'Ouvert Morning* (1976) is about a Port of Spain family, the Grants; it has been described as 'soap-opera-ish' but also as a 'riveting document of a troubled society in a state of transition'.

Jones, Mary Harris, *known as* Mother Jones, *née* Harris

Born 1830 Died 1930
American labour agitator who was a prominent
figure in the labour movement

Mary Harris was born in Co Cork, Ireland. She migrated to the USA via Canada, lost her family, including her iron-moulder husband, to an epidemic in 1867, and her home to the

Chicago fire of 1871, and thereafter devoted herself to the cause of labour, becoming a courageous campaigner especially on behalf of coalminers and against child labour.

Homeless after 1880, she travelled to areas of labour strife, especially in the coal industry. She was ordered out of Colorado for her dealings with striking miners in 1904, and was imprisoned in West Virginia on a charge of conspiracy to murder in 1912, at the age of 82.

After being freed by a new governor she returned to labour agitation, which she continued almost until her death. She wrote *The Autobiography of Mother Jones* in 1925.

Jones, Rickie Lee

Born 1954
American singer and songwriter whose early
successes included 'Chuck E's in Love'

Rickie Lee Jones was born in Chicago, Illinois. Strongly influenced by jazz and American composers like Gershwin and Cole Porter, she had an unexpected hit with the quirky 'Chuck E's in Love' (1979), from her eponymous début album.

Her subsequent career has been patchy in both critical and commercial terms. Her later recordings include the 10-inch *Girl at her Volcano* (1983), which dug into her musical ancestry, and *The Magazine* (1985), which was more ambitious but failed to recapture her early successes.

Jong, Erica, *née* Mann

Born 1942
American novelist and poet whose books have a
serious core inside their mass-market appeal

Erica Mann was born and educated in New York City, where she taught in a college for several years. She has been thrice married and divorced, and retains the name of her second husband.

Approaching Jong's fiction by way of her verse helps confirm that her novels are more serious and sombre than their eroticism and mass-market appeal initially suggest. The wry and sardonic poems in *Fruits and Vegetables* (1971) and *Half-Lives* (1973) are superficially reminiscent of **Sylvia Plath** and they clearly establish Jong's Jewish background as an essential aspect of her literary personality. In 1973 she published the massively bestselling *Fear of Flying*, which was hailed as a sort of female *Portnoy's Complaint*. The novel introduced the angst-haunted Isadora Wing, and documents her search for a degree of self-determination in her sexuality. Isadora returns

in *How to Save Your Own Life* (1977) and in *Parachutes and Kisses* (1984), in which her eternal quest is renewed.

In between, Jong wrote *Fanny, Being the True History of the Adventures of Fanny Hackabout-Jones* (1980), a clever, feminist send-up of 18th-century erotic novelists like John Cleland (1709–89). Isadora also narrates *Any Woman's Blues* (1990).

Joplin, Janis

Born 1943 Died 1970
American rhythm and blues singer, perhaps the
finest white female blues singer of all time

Janis Joplin was born in Port Arthur, Texas. She was a rebellious teenager, but unquestionably talented. In the mid-1960s, she sang in clubs in Houston, before joining Big Brother and the Holding Company, with whom she recorded two albums (1967–8).

She broke up a successful group to form the critically slated Kozmic Blues Band (1969), and then the Full Tilt Boogie Band, with whom she recorded the unfinished *Pearl* (released 1971). On this album she included 'Me and Bobby McGee', which, alongside the earlier 'Ball and Chain' and 'Piece of My Heart', represents her status as the finest white female blues singer of all time.

Joplin died of an apparently accidental drugs overdose.

Janis Joplin

Jordan, Barbara Charline

Born 1936   Died 1996
African-American politician, lawyer, educator
and former congresswoman

Barbara Jordan was born in Houston, Texas, and educated at Texas Southern and Boston Universities; she was the first black student at Boston University Law School (1956–9). She was admitted to the Bars of Massachusetts and of Texas in 1959, and later served in the Texas Senate (1966–72) as the only woman and the only black, and in the US Congress (1973–8). During the Watergate impeachment hearings concerning President Nixon in 1974, she impressed the nation with her eloquence and firm faith in the US Constitution.

At the University of Texas, she was a Lyndon B Johnson public services professor from 1979 to 1982, when she was appointed Lyndon Johnson Centennial Chair in National Policy. She later became a member of the House Judiciary Committee and in 1991 was appointed special counsel on ethics by the governor of Texas.

She received numerous awards and honours, including induction into the National Women's Hall of Fame (1990), the Texas Women's Hall of Fame (1984) and the African-American Hall of Fame (1993). Her autobiography, *Barbara Jordan: A Self-Portrait*, appeared in 1979.

Jordan, Dorothy, *also called* Dorothea, *née* Bland

Born 1761   Died 1816
Irish actress popular for her lively breeches parts,
and the procreant mistress of William IV

Dorothy Bland was born near Waterford, the illegitimate daughter of an actor. After making her début in Dublin in 1777 as 'Miss Francis' she soon became popular, obtaining in 1782 an engagement from Tate Wilkinson (1739–1803) at Leeds, where she was advised due to her pregnancy to change her name to 'Mrs Jordan'. She appeared with phenomenal success at Drury Lane as Peggy in *The Country Girl* in October 1785.

She had had five illegitimate children by 1790, when she began a liaison with the Duke of Clarence, later William IV, bearing him 10 children surnamed FitzClarence. The affair was one of affection and fidelity on her part, and lasted until they parted forever in 1811. In 1831 King William made their eldest son Earl of Munster.

After playing in London and in the provinces until 1814, Mrs Jordan is said to have been compelled to retire to France, where she died in poverty.

Jordan, June

Born 1936
American political activist and writer concerned
with the African-American experience

June Jordan was born in New York City to Jamaican immigrant parents and educated at Barnard College and the University of Chicago. After working as assistant movie producer, she became a college teacher in Connecticut and New York; she was Professor of English at the State University of New York, Stony Brook, and is now Professor of African American Studies and Women's Studies at the University of California, Berkeley.

Jordan's main literary model is George Orwell. In 1973 she published *Poem: On Moral Leadership as a Political Dilemma*, voicing her response to Watergate. *Things That I Do in the Dark* (1977) was a selection that for the first time made clear the extent to which her militancy was not so literal and dogmatic as to leave no room for a more oblique, metaphoric vision and a chancy, experimental prosody.

In 1993 she published a volume of love poetry, *Haruko*, which touched on bisexuality and feelings of loss and was remarkable for its stoically maintained pessimism. Among Jordan's works for young people are *His Own Where—* (1971) and *Kimako's Story* (1981).

Jordan, Sheila Jeanette, *née* Dawson

Born 1928
American jazz singer who began making her name
as a solo artist with her 1960s version of 'You
Are My Sunshine'

Sheila Dawson was born in Detroit, Michigan, and raised in a poor, coal-mining district of Pennsylvania. She was attracted to bebop as a teenager and became increasingly involved in it after moving to New York City in 1951. The following year she married black pianist Duke Jordan, but she was more obviously influenced by Lennie Tristano, with whom she studied for a time.

The interracial nature of the marriage apparently contributed to its breakdown and in 1962 she and Jordan were divorced. Also that year she recorded a famous version of 'You Are My Sunshine', arranged for her by George Russell on his album *The Outer View*. Increasingly, she worked as a solo artist, often with just a bass player (Harvie Swartz in particular) as accompanist. Her 1990 record *Lost and Found* was a major critical success.

Joséphine de Beauharnais, *née* Marie Joséphine Rose Tascher de la Pagerie

Born 1763 Died 1814
French empress, as wife of Napoleon

Joséphine Tascher de la Pagerie was born in Martinique, where in 1779 she married the Vicomte de Beauharnais. She bore him two children, Hortense (who married Napoleon's brother Louis) and Eugène (who married the daughter of the Duke of Bavaria), but he was embarrassed by her lack of sophistication and in 1785 they separated. Over the next few years, two of which she spent in Martinique until forced back to France by a slave uprising, she gradually carved a niche for herself in Parisian high society.

In 1794 her husband, who served in the Revolutionary army but fell out with the Jacobins, was executed; two years later she married Napoleon. She accompanied him in his Italian campaign, but soon returned to Paris. At Malmaison, and afterwards at the Luxembourg and the Tuileries, she attracted round her the most brilliant society of France, and contributed considerably to the establishment of her husband's power. But the marriage, being childless, was dissolved by Napoleon in 1809.

Joséphine retained the title of empress, and continues to lie at Malmaison where she died while Napoleon was sovereign of Elba.

Joyce, Eileen Alannah

Born 1912 Died 1991
Australian concert pianist who toured every continent and played with many major orchestras

Eileen Joyce was born in Zeehan, Tasmania. Her talent was discovered by the pianist Percy Grainger (1882–1961) when she was a child, and she was sent at the age of 15 to study at Leipzig conservatorium under the Austrian composer and pianist Artur Schnabel. In 1930 she was introduced to the English conductor Henry Wood (1869–1944), who immediately arranged her début at one of the famous promenade concerts under his baton.

She became a prolific broadcaster and during World War II frequently visited the blitzed towns of Britain with conductor Malcolm Sargent (1895–1967) and the London Philharmonic, developing a repertoire of over 50 piano concertos and numerous recital programmes.

She was particularly known for her work on film soundtracks, especially of *Brief Encounter* and *The Seventh Veil* (both 1945) and the film of her childhood, *Wherever She Goes*. She retired prematurely in 1960 but returned to the concert platform in 1967.

Joyce, Joan

Born 1940
American softball player who played the position of pitcher for 22 seasons in amateur softball

Joan Joyce was born in Waterbury, Connecticut. Dubbed the '116 mile-an-hour pitcher', she compiled 509 wins and 33 losses, and holds many records including the most total strikeouts in a national championship and the most innings pitched in one tournament. She is also credited with pitching 130 no-hitters.

In 1975, with the help of tennis player **Billie Jean King** and Dennis Murphy, she founded the International Women's Professional Softball Association (IWPSA). She led the Connecticut Falcons to the World Series for four years before IWPSA folded.

She was inducted into the National Softball Hall of Fame in 1983.

Joyner-Kersee, Jackie (Jacqueline)

Born 1962
American athlete who has won consecutive Olympic gold medals in the heptathlon

Jackie Joyner-Kersee was born in East St Louis, Illinois. At the Los Angeles Olympics of 1984, she won the silver medal in the heptathlon (a seven-event contest consisting of 100 hurdles, shot-put, javelin, high jump, longjump, 200m sprint and 800m race). Four years later, at Seoul, she won gold in both heptathlon and long jump, setting the gold-medal record in the former, and at Barcelona in 1992 she won gold in the heptathlon.

She is the sister of triple jumper Al Joyner, and sister-in-law of the sprinter **Florence Griffith-Joyner**.

Judith

Jewish heroine in the apocryphal Old Testament Book of Judith

Judith was a wealthy, beautiful, and saintly widow. Strengthened by her faith in the God of Israel, she made her way into the tent of Nebuchadrezzar's Asian general Holofernes and cut off his head, thus saving her native town of Bethulia.

Jugan, Jeanne, *also known as* Sister Mary of the Cross

Born 1792   Died 1879
French founder of the Little Sisters of the Poor
whose lifetime saw the care of some 20,000 elderly
poor in over 170 homes

Jeanne Jugan was born in Petites-Croix, Brittany. Following domestic service and hospital work she founded the Little Sisters of the Poor, a pioneer mission for the care of the elderly. Every day she begged for alms, along with two colleagues, Virginie Marie and Tredaniel Jamet.

Although sponsored by townspeople for a French Academy award for virtue in 1845, Jeanne Jugan received little church recognition. Her re-appointment as Superior in 1843 of the original group of three was overturned, and from 1852 onwards she was allowed no part in the Order's development. She was beatified in 1982.

Juhacz, Marie

Born 1880   Died 1956
German feminist and politician

Marie Juhacz was born near Brandenburg. She began work in a factory in 1894, then worked as a seamstress in Berlin where she became active in the struggle for women's suffrage.

Committed to socialist politics, she joined the Social Democratic Party and became a member of the National Assembly in 1919. She went on to become a member of the Reichstag from 1923 until Hitler came to power in 1933.

She then went abroad, spending World War II in France, Martinique and America. She returned to Germany in 1949.

Julia

Born 36BC   Died AD14
Roman noblewoman who was exiled by her father
for her promiscuous behaviour

Julia was the daughter of Octavian (later the emperor Augustus) and Scribonia. She was married at the age of 14 to her cousin Marcellus, a nephew of Augustus, and after his death in 23BC she married in 21BC Marcus Vipsanius Agrippa, to whom she bore three sons and two daughters.

He died in 12BC, whereupon Julia was married to Tiberius (11BC). The marriage was unhappy and her conduct was far from irreproachable, though she was popular with the people. In 2BC her father Augustus learned of her adulteries and banished her to the isle of Pandataria, and from there to Reggio, where she died voluntarily of starvation. Her mother shared her exile.

Julian of Norwich, *also called* Juliana

Born c.1342   Died c.1416
English mystic and writer whose remarkable
religious experience is read about to this day

Julian was born probably in Norwich, where later in life she lived as an anchoress or recluse at St Julian's Church. She was a modest and self-critical woman who illuminated her visions of the Passion of Christ with a clarity and depth that has made her seem highly convincing even to sceptics of her mystical experience.

On 8 May 1373, following an illness, she received a series of visions. The account she wrote of them shortly afterwards, and her meditations on their significance made 20 years later (almost the only information we have about her), have survived in mid-15th- and mid-16th-century manuscript copies, published in modern versions as *A Shewing of God's Love* (Eng trans 1958) and *Revelations of Divine Love* (of which the most accessible edition is that of 1966).

Her prayers, her assurance that everything is held in being by the love of God so 'all will be well', and her characterization of the Trinity as Father, Mother, and Lord, speak to many in search of a contemporary spirituality.

Juliana of Cornillon, *also known as* Juliana of Liège

Born 1192   Died 1258
French prioresss at Mont Cornillon who promoted
the feast of Corpus Christi

Juliana was born at Rétinnes, near Liège, but was orphaned early and brought up by the Canonesses Regular at Mont Cornillon.

She became prioress there in 1222, but was condemned as a visionary and embezzler, and expelled from the monastery for promoting the feast of Corpus Christi — the celebration of the institution of the Eucharist. She was restored by the Bishop of Liège but expelled again on his death, whereupon she went to the Béguines at Salzinnes, Namur, and later to Saint-Feuillon, Fosses.

Six years after death, Juliana's chief supporter, now Pope Urban IV, affirmed the feast; the services and hymns were written by Thomas Aquinas.

Juliana, Queen, *in full* Juliana Louise Emma Marie Wilhelmina

Born 1909
Queen of the Netherlands (1948–80)

Juliana was born in The Hague, the only child of Queen **Wilhelmina** and Prince Henry of Mecklenburg-Schwerin, and educated in law at Leiden University. In 1937 she married Prince Bernhard zur Lippe-Biesterfeld, and they have four daughters: Queen **Beatrix**; Princess Irene Emma Elizabeth (1939–), who in 1964 married Prince Hugo of Bourbon-Parma (1939–), son of Prince Xavier, the Carlist pretender to the Spanish throne (against her parents' wishes, and forfeiting her right of succession); Princess Margriet Fran-cisca (1943–), who married Pieter van Vollenhoven in 1967; and Princess Maria Christina (1947–), who married Jorge Giullermo in 1975.

On the German invasion of Holland in 1940 Juliana escaped to Britain and later resided in Canada. She returned to Holland in 1945, and in 1948, on the abdication of her mother Queen **Wilhelmina**, became queen. She herself abdicated in favour of her eldest daughter, Beatrix, in 1980.

k

Kael, Pauline

Born 1919
American film critic associated with the New
Yorker

Pauline Kael was born in Petaluma, California.
Educated at the University of California at
Berkeley, she became a waspish, insightful
reviewer, and was movie critic of the *New
Yorker* from 1968 to 1991.

She has published several anthologies of her
articles: *Kiss Kiss Bang Bang* (1968), *When the
Lights Go Down* (1980), *5001 Nights at the
Movies* (1982), *State of the Art* (1985), and
Movie Love (1991).

Kaffka, Margit

Born 1880   Died 1918
Hungarian poet, novelist and short-story writer,
and Hungary's first major feminist woman writer

Margit Kaffka was brought up in eastern
Hungary, the daughter of an established but
poor Catholic family. She worked as a teacher
and began writing poetry, influenced by her
friend the leading Hungarian poet Endre Ady
(1877–1919). She also wrote short fiction, such
as *Nyár* (1909, 'Summer'), before coming to
notice with such novels as *Szinék és évek* (1912
'Colours and Years') and *Allomások* (1917,
'Stations').

Her life and achievement were, like those of
the French poet Guillaume Apollinaire (1880–
1918), cut short by the influenza epidemic
which swept over Europe after World War
I. She has become significant to Hungarian
writers in recent years, but her stories — her
best work — have yet to be translated.

Kahlo, Frida

Born 1907   Died 1954
Mexican surrealist artist whose work is imbued
with power and emotion

Frida Kahlo was born in Coyoacán, Mexico
City, the daughter of a Jewish German immigrant photographer and a Catholic Mexican
mother. At the age of 15 she suffered a serious
road accident, which destroyed her ambition
to become a doctor. She started painting
during her convalescence, and sent her work
to the painter Diego Rivera, whom she married
in 1928. It was a colourful but tortured marriage; they divorced, but ultimately remarried.

Kahlo's pictures, which are surrealistic and
often shocking, are characterized by vibrant
imagery, and the themes of pain, which
dogged her all her life, and the suffering of
women. Many of them are striking self-por-
traits.

Kahlo and Rivera mixed in a well-known
circle of artists, photographers and politically
controversial figures such as Trotsky. The surrealist poet and essayist André Breton likened
her paintings to 'a ribbon around a bomb'
(1938). In 1940 she participated in the International Exhibition of Surrealism in Mexico
City, and in 1946 won a prize at the Annual
National Exhibition at the Palace of Fine Arts.
The Frida Kahlo Museum was opened in her
house in Coyoacán in 1958.

Kain, Karen

Born 1951
Canadian ballet dancer who is hailed as the
country's most popular ballerina

Karen Kain was born in Hamilton, Ontario.
After training with the Canadian National
Ballet School she joined the company in 1969,
becoming principal dancer in 1970.

She has danced almost all the major classical
leads as well as interpreting roles in works by
contemporary   choreographers,   such   as
Daphnis and Chlöe (1988) by Glen Tetley
(1926–).

She partnered Rudolf Nureyev (1938–93) in New York, and as guest artist at the Ballet de Marseille she created a leading role in Roland Petit's *Les Intermittences du Coeur* (1974). She has also appeared in televised productions of ballets on Canadian television.

Kairi, Evanthia

Born 1799 Died 1866
Greek teacher who was active at the start of the Greek uprising against the Turks

Evanthia Kairi was born on the Greek island of Andros, where she studied philosophy and ancient Greek with her brother, the philosopher Theophilos Kairis. She taught Latin and Greek literature and history at the girls' school in Kydonies (now in Turkey) where she became principal, and concerned herself with progressive ideas in women's education.

In 1821 she appealed to women's organizations throughout Europe for help in the Greek uprising against Turkish rule. Her appeal was important in fostering the international pro-Greek/anti-Turkish movement throughout Europe and America. In 1826, when Missolonghi fell to the Turks, she wrote her play *Nikiratos*. After Greek independence was achieved she returned to Andros where she founded a school for war orphans.

Kang Keqing (K'ang K'o-ching)

Born 1911
Chinese political leader, long-time influential leader of the national women's organization

Kang Keqing was born in Wan'an, Jiangxi (Kiangsi) province, and adopted by a poor peasant family. She studied at Jinggangshan Red Army College, and the Anti-Japan Military and Political Academy. She joined the Chinese Youth League in 1927, and organized Red Army guerrilla units. After her marriage in 1929 to General Zhu De (Chu Te) she rose to become Commander of the Red Army's Women's Department, and was one of the few women on the Long March (1934–5). After studying she held important posts in the Red Army's political department.

In 1957 she was elected to the committee of the Chinese Democratic Women's Federation, becoming its president in 1978, and an honorary president from 1988. Since her election in 1977 to the 11th Central Committee, she has gone on to hold influential political posts, including membership of the Praesidium of the National Peoples' Congress since 1980.

Kania, Karin, *née* Enke

Born 1961
German figure and speed skater

Karin Kania began her career as a figure skater and, competing for East Germany, finished ninth in the European championships of 1977. Believing that she would be unable to better that performance, she took up speed skating and quickly showed a high level of aptitude.

After only weeks of training, she produced an excellent 1,500 metres time and went on to win her first East German national title in 1980, the same year she won the world sprint championship and the Olympic 500 metres gold. She won another 14 national titles, another five world sprint championship titles and the overall world championship title a record five times. She also won another two Olympic golds, as well as a further four silvers and a bronze.

Karan, Donna

Born 1948
American designer, possibly the most famous woman designer in America today

Donna Karan was born in Donna Faske, New York, the daughter of a haberdasher and a model. She dropped out of Parson's School of Design to work for **Anne Klein**, becoming her successor in 1974.

In 1984 she launched her own company with luxurious, user-friendly clothes that appeal to successful working women — advertising campaigns feature extremely stylish working mothers. Her sassy head-to-toe collections in cashmere, stretch and wraparound fabrics, bodysuits and unitards include own-label jewellery, shoes, accessories, lingerie, hosiery and eyewear.

In 1988 she launched the cheaper DKNY label, followed by DKNY Jeans in 1990, Menswear in 1991, the Beauty Company and DKNY Menswear in 1992, the Shoe company in 1992, and DKNY Kids in 1993. She won the Coty award in 1977, 1981 and 1984 and now employs around 1,000 people worldwide.

Karle, Isabella Helen, *née* Lugoski

Born 1921
American chemist and crystallographer who developed techniques to study electron diffraction

Isabella Lugoski was born in Detroit, Michigan, to a Polish immigrant family. She was educated at the University of Michigan, where in 1942 she married her fellow student Jerome Karle, co-winner of the Nobel Prize for Chemistry in 1985.

Since she and her husband were prevented from holding positions at the same university, they accepted positions at the Naval Research Laboratory in Washington. Their new techniques of studying electron diffraction led Isabella Karle to study living structures by X-ray diffraction.

Among the many important chemical structures she has discovered is that of enkephalin, a naturally occurring analgesic found in the brain, which is a class of chemicals co-discovered by **Candace Pert**. Karle has been honoured by scientific academies around the world.

Karsavina, Tamara Platonovna

Born 1885 Died 1978
Russian-born British dancer who enjoyed a long association with the work of Sergei Diaghilev

Tamara Karsavina was born in St Petersburg. She trained at the Imperial Ballet School at the time the Italian dancer and choreographer Enrico Cecchetti was teaching, and joined the Maryinsky Theatre in 1902. In 1909 she also became one of the original members of Sergei Diaghilev's company for which she created roles in ballets by Michel Fokine and Vaslav Nijinsky.

She moved to London in 1918 with her husband, an English diplomat, though always remained associated with the Russian ballet, guesting with Diaghilev's Ballets Russes and later advising on recreating Diaghilev productions.

She was Vice-President of the Royal Academy of Dancing until 1955 and wrote several books, including the autobiographical *Theatre Street* (1930), *Ballet Technique* (1956), and *Classical Ballet* (1962).

Kartini, Raden Adjeng

Born 1879 Died 1904
Javanese noblewoman who was one of the first to advocate equal opportunities for Indonesian women

Raden Kartini was born into an aristocratic family in Majong on the island of Java, in the Dutch East Indies (now Indonesia). Since her father was employed by the Dutch colonial administration, she attended a Dutch school and learned to speak the language. Thus exposed to Western ideas, she became aware of the inequality experienced by Indonesian women as well as the bad conditions suffered by the Indonesians under colonial rule, and resolved to improve both.

She set up a school in her house in 1903, with the blessing of the country's education minister, and later started another school with her husband, the Regent of Rembang. However she died soon after giving birth to her first child. Her ideas and aspirations, as expressed in letters to a Dutch pen-friend, were published as *Door duisternis tot licht* (1911), the popularity of which led to the Kartini Foundation's establishment of the first girl's school in Java. Despite the fact that she never realised her aims, Kartini became a popular symbol of Indonesian nationalism.

Käsebier, Gertrude, *née* Stanton

Born 1852 Died 1934
American photographer best known for her pictorialist photographs and portraits

Gertrude Stanton was born in Fort Des Moines (now Des Moines), Iowa. As a child she lived in Golden, Colorado Territory, then in Brooklyn. She married a prosperous German immigrant importer, Eduard Käsebier, in 1874 and went to live in New Jersey, where they had three children.

Having begun photographing her family in the late 1880s, she studied painting at the Pratt Institute, Brooklyn (1889–96), worked with a chemist in Germany to learn the technical aspects of photography (1893), and found work in 1896 with a Brooklyn portrait photographer to learn studio management. She opened her own first portrait studio in Manhattan in 1897–8 and built up a successful business. Her portraits were considered radical at the time, rejecting as they did the flat lighting and artificial settings of the portrait studio.

Her photographs were first exhibited in New York in 1897 at the Pratt Institute. She went on to become one of the first women members of the Linked Ring group in 1900 and a founder-member of Photo-Secession in 1902. She was represented in **Frances Benjamin Johnston**'s exhibition of US women photographers (1900–1), and photographer and gallerist Alfred Stieglitz (1864–1946) devoted the first issue of his influential magazine *Camera Work* to her in 1903. She resigned from Photo-Secession in 1912, but continued to produce significant work, and in 1916 became co-founder with Alvin Langdon Coburn (1882–1966) and Clarence White (1871–1925) of the Pictorial Photographers of America.

Kassenbaum, Nancy Landon

Born 1939
American politician who has held several influential positions

Nancy Landon Kassenbaum was born in Topeka, Kansas, and educated at the universities of Kansas and Michigan.

A Republican, she has been a member of the US Senate as Senator from Kansas since 1979, serving on the powerful Foreign Relations Committee, Labor and Human Resources Committee and the Select Committee on Indian Affairs.

She announced in 1995 that she would not seek re-election.

Kassiane, *also known as* Eikasia Kassia

Born c.800/810   Died c.843/867
Byzantine abbess who also compiled many hymns
in the Orthodox liturgy

Kassiane was born in Constantinople. According to legend, she took part in the bride show of 830 when a wife was chosen for the emperor Theophilus, but lost to Theodora (c.810–62). Kassiane was praised for her learning and piety by St Theodore of Studios (759–826), doubtless because she supported him on the veneration of icons.

She founded the Icassion convent at Constantinople and became its abbess. More than 20 of the hymns of the Orthodox liturgy are ascribed to her, but some may date back to Kosmas the Hymnographer (675–752).

Kauffmann, Angelica

Born 1741   Died 1807
Swiss decorative painter whose wall- and
ceiling-paintings adorned houses designed by
Robert Adam

Angelica Kauffmann was born in Chur in the Grisons. At the age of 11 she was painting portraits of notables in Italy, and by 1766 had settled in London, where she became friends with the portrait painter Sir Joshua Reynolds, whose style she imitated. She soon became famous as a painter of classical and mythological pictures, and as a portrait-painter, and was nominated one of the first Royal Academicians (1769).

In the 1770s she executed decorative wall-paintings for houses built by the Adam brothers, and it is for this that she is best known. After an unhappy first marriage in 1781 she married the Venetian painter, Antonio Zucchi, and returned to Italy. Some of her works, which had Neoclassical elements but retained a Rococo prettiness, are well known from engravings by Bartolozzi.

Kautsky, Luise, *née* Ronsperger

Born 1864   Died 1944
Austrian publisher and translator, socialist and
feminist, wife of the Marxist theorist Karl Kautsky

Luise Ronsperger was born in Vienna. Her family had a confectioner's shop. She married the Marxist theorist Karl Kautsky in 1890 and went with him to Stuttgart where she worked with him on his newspaper *Die Neue Zeit*. She translated English, French and Russian socialist writings into German. An active socialist and feminist, she was a close friend of **Rosa Luxemburg**, whose letters she saved for posterity. In Berlin she was, briefly, a delegate for the USPD, the socialist party which her husband helped to found.

The Kautskys returned to Vienna in 1924. After the *Anschluss* Luise joined her husband in Prague (where he had fled after Chancellor Dollfuss suspended parliament and dismissed its socialist members in 1933). They escaped, ahead of the Nazi invasion of Czechoslovakia, to Amsterdam where Karl died in 1938. She was arrested by the Nazis in 1944, and died in Auschwitz–Birkenau.

Kawakubo, Rei

Born 1942
Japanese fashion designer and founder of Comme
des Garçons

Rei Kawakubo was born in Tokyo and graduated in Fine Art from Keio University in 1964. She became a fashion stylist and designed her own clothes, founding her own company in 1969. The label means 'like boys', underscoring her conviction that her clothes are made for modern working women 'who do not need to assure their happiness by looking sexy to man, by emphasizing their figures'.

Her early 1980s collections shocked European critics with their lack of colour and androgenous shapes. They were described as 'funereal' and 'atomic'. However, her controversial 1980s 'ripped' sweater is now in the clothing collection at the Victoria and Albert Museum, recognized as important a development in 20th-century style as Dior's 1950s New Look.

Regarded as the quintessential modernist-designer, Kawakubo now has around 450 employees, 254 CDG stores in Japan, eight stores and 87 outlets worldwide, and also designs her own store interiors and furniture.

Kaye, M(ary) M(argaret)

Born 1909
English novelist who is best known for her
romantic saga, The Far Pavilions

M M Kaye was born in Simla, India, a daughter of the Raj. She married into the army and subsequently travelled extensively with her husband. She is the author of several detective novels with exotic settings, written with a lively mixture of mystery and romance; *Death in Kenya* (1983) is a representative example.

She is best known for her bestselling historical romantic epics. *Trade Wind* (1963), set in 19th-century Zanzibar, is a story of the slave trade, while her two most famous books, *Shadow of the Moon* (1957) and *The Far Pavilions* (1978), are both set in 19th-century India.

She published a volume of autobiography, *The Sun in the Morning*, in 1990.

Kaye, Nora, *originally* Nora Koreff

Born 1920   Died 1987
American dancer who became the leading
dramatic ballerina of her generation

Nora Koreff was born in New York. She studied at the School of American Ballet and the New York Metropolitan Opera Ballet School, dancing as a child with the latter company and also at Radio City Music Hall.

She joined American Ballet Theatre at its inception in 1939 and soon became the leading ballerina, creating the role of Hagar in Antony Tudor's *Pillar of Fire* (1942), and appearing in other modern ballets as well as the classics. She was a member of New York City Ballet (1951–4), and then returned to ABT until her retirement in 1961.

She co-founded Ballet of Two Worlds with her choreographer-husband Herbert Ross, and assisted him in his stage and film work, including *The Turning Point* (1977), until her death.

Kazankina, Tatyana Vasilyevna

Born 1951
Soviet athlete, the only woman to achieve an
Olympic double at 800 metres and 1,500 metres
in the same year

Tatyana Kazankina was born in Petrovsk. In 1976 she won an Olympic double at 800 metres and 1,500 metres, the only woman to have done so to date. Also that year she became the first woman to run the 1,500 metres in under four minutes; this was one of a total of three world records at that distance that she set during her career. She also set world records at 2,000 metres and 3,000 metres.

She was suspended from competition in 1984 for failing to take a drugs test after running a personal best time for the 5,000 metres in Paris, but returned to competition in 1986.

Keane, Molly (Mary Nesta), *née* Skrine

Born 1904   Died 1996
Irish novelist and playwright whose works focus
on the foibles of the upper classes

Molly Keane was born in County Kildare into 'a rather serious Hunting and Fishing and Church-going family' and her mother was a poet. She married Robert Keane in 1938. When young she wrote only to finance her hunting and supplement her dress allowance, adopting the pseudonym M J Farrell. *The Knight of the Cheerful Countenance*, her first book, was written when she was 17. Between 1928 and 1952 she wrote 10 novels, including *Devoted Ladies* (1934), *The Rising Tide* (1937), *Two Days in Aragon* (1941) and *Loving Without Tears* (1951), drawing her material from the foibles of her own class.

A spirited, impish writer, she was also a good playwright; her successes included *Spring Meeting* (1938), *Ducks and Drakes* (1942), *Treasure Hunt* (1949), and *Dazzling Prospect* (1961). When in 1946 her husband died at 37, she stopped writing for many years, but *Good Behaviour* (1981), short-listed for the Booker Prize, led to the reprinting of many of her books and a revival of critical appreciation. *Loving and Giving* (1988) is a bleak comedy seen through the eyes of an eight-year-old girl who is a witness to the break-up of her parents' marriage and the desuetude of the family mansion.

Keaton, Diane, *originally* Diane Hall

Born 1946
American actress closely associated with Woody
Allen both professionally and privately

Diane Keaton was born in Los Angeles, California. She won a scholarship to study at The Neighbourhood Playhouse in Manhattan and began her association with Woody Allen with her Broadway appearance in *Play It Again, Sam* (1969–70).

Though she appeared in several films during the 1970s, the true force of her personality and range as an actress were not fully revealed until her performances as the flustered, eccentrically chic object of affection in Allen's *Annie Hall* (1977), which won her a Best Actress Oscar, and in *Looking For Mr Goodbar* (1977) as a teacher of deaf children whose extra-curricular promiscuity results in death.

She continued to work for Allen — *Interiors* (1978), *Manhattan* (1979) — and though she excels in the portrayal of women struggling to ascertain their independence and assert their sexuality, the public seem to prefer her as a dizzy comedienne in such films as *Father of the Bride* (1991). Keaton is a noted photographer too, and has directed television programmes and pop videos.

Keeler, Christine

Born 1942
English model and show girl whose affair with John Profumo developed into a major scandal

Christine Keeler had an unhappy childhood spent mainly at Wraysbury, in the Thames Valley. She left home at 16 and migrated to London, where she obtained work at Murray's Cabaret Club. Here she met **Mandy Rice-Davies**, a girl who had arrived in similar circumstances, and was to become a close friend.

Stephen Ward, an osteopath, was a frequent visitor to the club and he and Keeler formed a relationship whereby she eventually lived with him, although there were frequent rifts between them. Ward introduced her and Rice-Davies into his circle of influential friends, which included the Conservative Cabinet Minister, John Profumo, with whom she had an affair. She also had an affair with the Soviet naval attaché Yevgeny Ivanov. Consequently Profumo had to resign from politics, Ward, who eventually committed suicide, was prosecuted for living on immoral earnings, and Keeler herself served a prison sentence for related offences.

In the late 1980s, her autobiography, studies of the Ward trial and its aftermath, and the film *Scandal*, in which she collaborated, revived interest in the events and raised doubts about the validity of the charges made against her and Ward.

Keene, Laura

Born 1830 or 1836   Died 1873
English-born actress who became America's first woman theatre manager

Laura Keene was born in England and moved to New York in 1855. Little is known of her early life (hence the uncertainty over her date of birth), but she is thought to have made her London début as an actress in 1851. She joined an American company in 1852, and opened her own theatre in New York in 1856, where she ran a successful repertory company, and developed opportunities for local actors.

During the Civil War her theatre operated as an outlet for variety rather than serious drama; it closed in 1863. Keene resumed touring, and was on stage in Tom Taylor's *Our American Cousin* at Ford's Theatre in Washington DC on the night that Abraham Lincoln was assassinated in 1865.

Kehajia, Kalliopi

Born 1839   Died 1905
Greek teacher and educationalist

Kalliopi Kehajia trained in London as a teacher, before becoming principal of the Hill School for Girls in Athens. In Athens she established a reputation as an innovative and progressive teacher, and showed her commitment to extending women's access to education through her series of open lectures, and through forming The Society for Promoting Women's Education (1872). From 1875 to 1890 she was principal of the Zappeion School for Girls in Constantinople (now Istanbul).

Comparing Greek education unfavourably with what she had observed in France (1874) and in the USA (1888), Kehajia pioneered a reform of educational practices in Greece.

Kehew, Mary Morton, *née* Kimball

Born 1859   Died 1918
American trade unionist and social reformer, one of the founders of the Union for Industrial Progress

Mary Kimball was born in Boston into a wealthy, well-established family, educated privately, and in 1880 married a Boston merchant. Concerned by the growing numbers of young women moving into Boston in search of work, she joined the Women's Educational and Industrial Union in 1886, and rose to become its president (1892–1913; 1914–18). She was active in improving training and education for women employees. Significantly she also promoted research and legislation to improve women's situation, shifting the Union from its original essentially philanthropic focus to become a central agent for social research and reform.

With Mary Kenney O'Sullivan she founded the Union for Industrial Progress which between 1886 and 1901 brought together women working in various poorly-paid trades including the tobacco, laundry and garment industries. In 1903 she became the first President of the National Women's Trade Union League.

Keller, Helen Adams

Born 1880   Died 1968
American writer whose achievement was all the more remarkable because she was deaf and blind

Helen Keller was born in Tuscumbia, Alabama. She became both deaf and blind at 19 months, but, educated by Anne Mansfield Sullivan (later **Anne Sullivan Macy**), she learned to speak by feeling and imitating the tongue and lip movements of other people.

She graduated from Radcliffe College in 1904 and began writing about blindness, which was a taboo subject at the time because of its association with venereal disease. Her book, *The Story of My Life*, appeared in 1902.

She began lecturing in 1913 to raise money for the American Foundation for the Blind, and, becoming a respected lecturer and scholar, devoted her life to working for the blind and deaf.

Kelley, Florence

Born 1859 Died 1932
American feminist and social reformer whose work contributed to changes in the legislation governing working hours, child labour and minimum wages

Florence Kelley was born into a middle-class family in Philadelphia and educated at Cornell University and at Zürich, where she became a socialist. From 1891 to 1899 she worked at **Jane Addams's** Hull House Settlement and subsequently became the first woman factory inspector in Illinois, successfully fighting to reduce working hours and improve methods and conditions of production.

She graduated in law from Northwestern University in 1895 and moved to New York in 1899, becoming general secretary of the National Consumers' League. In 1910 she was one of the founders of the National Association for the Advancement of Colored People and in 1919 she helped establish the Women's International League for Peace and Freedom.

Her works include *Some Ethical Gains Through Legislation* (1905) and a translation of the German socialist Friedrich Engels's *Condition of the Working Class in England in 1844* (1887).

Kelly, Grace Patricia

Born 1929 Died 1982
American film actress who had a short but highly successful film career as a coolly elegant beauty

Grace Kelly was born in Philadelphia, the daughter of a wealthy self-made Irish businessman. After studying at the American Academy of Dramatic Art she acted in television and on Broadway, and made her film début in *Fourteen Hours* (1951).

Her short career included such classics as the Western *High Noon* (1952, with Gary Cooper), *Rear Window* (1954), *The Country Girl* (1954, Academy Award), *To Catch a Thief* (1955, with Cary Grant), and *High Society* (1956).

In 1956 she married Prince Rainier III of Monaco, and retired from the screen. She was killed in a car accident.

Kelly, Jo Ann

Born 1944 Died 1990
English blues and jazz singer and guitarist

Jo Ann Kelly's abilities were nurtured by the skiffle movement and encouraged at the Swing Shop record store in Streatham Hill, London. She favoured the country blues at the beginning of her career, and signed to a contract with CBS records in the 1960s. However, she preferred to work small venues rather than superstar stadiums, and her connection with CBS did not last.

She interpreted the lyrics of American blues composer, guitarist and singer Robert Johnson (c.1911–1938) more successfully than any other singer, and was the only British singer to be invited to the centenary blues festival in Memphis, Tennessee, in 1969.

In later years she was developing as a jazz singer, in the footsteps of **Billie Holiday**.

Kelly, Petra, *originally* Petra Karin Lehmann

Born 1947 Died 1992
German politician, campaigner on ecological issues, and founder of the Green Party (Die Grünen) in Germany

Petra Lehmann was born in Günzburg, Bavaria but moved to the USA at the age of 13 following her parents' divorce and her mother's remarriage to a US army officer. After studying for a degree in political science and international relations at the American University, Washington, she worked for the EEC in Brussels.

In 1979 she co-founded *Die Grünen* and in 1983 they entered the Bundestag with 28 seats. However, in the 'unification election' of 1990 they lost all their parliamentary seats and were dogged by internal divisions.

She died in an apparent suicide pact along with her partner, Gert Bastian, but subsequent reports have cast a shadow on this finding, by linking his name with the Stasi, the secret police of the former East Germany. Kelly's biography, written by **Sara Lamb Parkin**, appeared in 1994.

Kemble, Fanny (Frances Anne)

Born 1809 Died 1893
English playwright and poet who turned to the stage and was successful in both comic and tragic roles

Fanny Kemble was born in London, the daughter of the actor and theatre manager Charles Kemble (1775–1854). She had little inclination to go on the stage, but her father, who was then manager of Covent Garden, was in financial trouble and needed her help. She made her début there in October 1829, when her Juliet (to her father's Mercutio and her mother's Lady Capulet) created a great sensation.

For three years she played leading parts in London. then in 1832 published her first play, *Francis I*, which was performed but quickly withdrawn. She went on tour with her father to America, where in 1834 she married Pierce Butler, a Southern planter. The marriage was not a success, partly because her husband objected to her writing, and partly because she apparently did not realize that he was a slave owner; although they had two children, Fanny sailed back to London alone in 1845 and she and Butler divorced three years later.

Resuming her maiden name, she published poetry and travel writing, eight volumes of autobiography, and a powerful, abolitionist polemic, *Journal of a Residence on a Georgian Plantation in 1838–9* (1863). Between 1848 and 1868 she toured, giving Shakespearian readings, living mostly in Massachusetts, and then Philadelphia, near her daughters. She afterwards settled in London. Her plays, *The Star of Seville* (1837) and *The Adventures of John Timothy Homespun in Switzerland*, a short farce published when she was 80, do not appear to have been performed.

Kempe, Margery, *née* Brunham

Born c.1373   Died c.1440
English mystic who was one of the first English writers to write an autobiography

Margery Brunham was the daughter of a mayor of Lynn. She married a burgess in Lynn and had 14 children. After a period of insanity she experienced a conversion and undertook numerous pilgrimages.

Between 1432 and 1436 she dictated her spiritual autobiography, *The Book of Margery Kempe*, which recounts her persecution by devils and men, repeated accusations of Lollardism (following the teachings of the 14th-century reformer John Wycliffe), her copious weepings, and her journeys to Jerusalem and to Germany.

It is one of the earliest autobiographies in English literature (published in modern English in 1936 and in Middle English in 1940), and has been hailed as a classic.

Kendal, Duchess of *see* Schulenburg, Gräfin von der

Kendal, Felicity Anne

Born 1946
English actress who appears in leading roles on stage and television

Felicity Kendal was born in India into a theatrical family. She made her London début in 1967 in *Minor Murder* at the Savoy and though often popularly associated with mischievous or winsome roles, epitomized by her appearance as Barbara in the television series *The Good Life* (1975–7), she is now recognized as a stage actress of depth and considerable sensitivity.

She has played the title role in *The Second Mrs Tanqueray* (1981), Louise in *Hidden Laughter* (1990) and Ariadne Utterwood in *Heartbreak House* (1992). Also particularly noted for her work with playwright Tom Stoppard (1937–   ), she has played leading roles in his plays *The Real Thing* (1982), *Jumpers* (1985), *Hapgood* (1988), *Arcadia* (1993) and *Indian Ink* (1995).

In 1994 she starred in a new television comedy series, *Honey For Tea*.

Kendal, Dame Madge, *stage-name of* Margaret Brunton Grimston, *née* Margaret Shafto Robertson

Born 1849   Died 1935
English actress who formed a successful acting and managing partnership with her husband

Margaret Robertson was born in Cleethorpes, a sister of the dramatist T W Robertson (1829–71). She first appeared on stage with her parents, and made her London début as Ophelia in *Hamlet*. She continued to be acclaimed in Shakespearian roles and by the 1870s was leading lady at the Haymarket Theatre.

In 1869 she married the actor William Hunter Kendal, properly Grimston (1843–1917), with whom she appeared in many, particularly Shakespearian, productions. They began touring the provincial theatres in 1874 and continued to do so annually until they retired in 1908. Together with Sir John Hare they managed the St James's Theatre in London from 1879 to 1888, which was successful and prosperous because she was a brilliant actress and he had an astute business mind and an eye for a good play.

The Kendals are credited with bringing a new respectability to the acting profession. She was created a DBE in 1926.

Kendall, Kay, *originally* Justine Kendall McCarthy

Born 1926 Died 1959
English actress whose flair for comedy brought her brief fame before her early death

Justine McCarthy was born in Withersnea, near Hull. She came from a long-established showbusiness lineage, and at the age of 12 appeared in the chorus line at the London Palladium and toured extensively in revue and music hall before making a youthful film début in *Fiddlers Three* (1944).

She honed her craft in provincial theatre and further unworthy film assignments before *Genevieve* (1953) revealed her flair for comedy and earned her international recognition. Developing into a polished and elegant comedienne, she appeared in such US films as *Les Girls* (1957) and *The Reluctant Debutante* (1958) with her husband, actor Rex Harrison (1908–90), and seemed on the brink of major stardom at the time of her death from leucaemia.

Kennedy, Helena Ann

Born 1950
Scottish barrister, broadcaster and writer who is overtly left-wing and feminist

Helena Kennedy was born in Glasgow into a working-class, Labour-voting family. Hearing of the unfairness of personal injury claims at her father's place of work, she became interested in law and its use, particularly in relation to working-class people. She went to London

Helena Kennedy, 1979

to study law in 1968 and set up practice with several like-minded colleagues, taking on a variety of radical cases.

She is renowned for her persuasive charm in court, and has hastened changes in attitudes within the English legal system. Her clients have been as diverse as anarchists, a member of the Guildford Four, and **Myra Hindley**. She achieved public recognition with her appearance on the BBC documentary series *The Heart of the Matter* (1987) and with *Blind Justice* (1988), a television drama loosely based on her own legal experiences.

In 1991 she was made a QC and was appointed to the Bar Council, and in 1994 she became Chancellor of Oxford Brookes University.

Kennedy, Louise St John

Born 1950
Australian architect, the first woman to be appointed to the Architects Board of Western Australia

Louise St John Kennedy was educated at the University of Western Australia and the University of Melbourne. She is principal in her own practice in Cottlesloe, Australia, a practice that began designing mostly smaller-scale buildings, and won an award for the most outstanding piece of domestic architecture in Australia.

Clients flooded in, resulting in Kennedy designing 24 houses in an eight-year period. In 1986 her design for tearooms jutting out over Mosman Bay caused an uproar among the wealthy residents of this exclusive area, but after much wrangling they were built and gained acclaim from the public, the architectural press and even the residents themselves.

Kennedy-Fraser, Marjorie, *née* Kennedy

Born 1857 Died 1930
Scottish singer remembered for her knowledge and collection of Hebridean folk-songs

Marjory Kennedy was born in Perth into a large musical family, a daughter of the singer David Kennedy. She trained with him and in Paris as a concert singer and married a man named A J Fraser. In 1882 she started studying Gaelic music, took lessons in Gaelic and started collecting Hebridean folk-songs, to which she gave modern harmonic settings.

She travelled widely, giving lectures and recitals on different types of singing, and in 1909 published the first of her three volumes of *Songs of the Hebrides*. She also wrote the libretto of Granville Bantock's opera *The Seal Woman* (1924), which incorporates Hebridean melodies.

Kenney, Annie

Born 1879 Died 1953
English suffragette who was a tenacious campaigner alongside **Christabel Pankhurst**

Annie Kenney was born in Springhead, near Oldham. She began working part-time in the Woodend Mill when she was 10, and full-time from the age of 13. She started a union, then began a correspondence course at Ruskin College, Oxford. When she met Christabel Pankhurst, she became involved in the struggle for women's suffrage, the only working-class woman in the leadership.

In 1905 she was arrested with Pankhurst for interrupting a meeting in Manchester, and again the next year for interrupting a speech by the Prime Minister, Sir Henry Campbell-Bannerman. She took over the leadership during Pankhurst's exile in Paris, crossing the Channel every week to receive instructions. When World War I started she campaigned for women to be allowed to work in the munitions factories.

She published her autobiography *Memories of a Millhand* in 1924; after her marriage to James Taylor in 1926 she withdrew from public life.

Kenny, Elizabeth

Born 1886 Died 1952
Australian nurse known as 'Sister Kenny' who found a new way of treating polio sufferers

Elizabeth Kenny began practising as a nurse in the bush country in Australia (1912), and then joined the Australian army nursing corps (1915–19). She developed a new technique for treating poliomyelitis by muscle therapy rather than immobilization with casts and splints.

She established clinics in Australia (1933), Britain (1937) and America (Minneapolis, 1940), and travelled widely to demonstrate her methods. She published her autobiography, *And They Shall Walk*, in 1943.

Kenyon, Dame Kathleen Mary

Born 1906 Died 1978
English archaeologist who made important discoveries about the history of ancient biblical sites

Kathleen Kenyon was born in London, the daughter of the director of the British Museum. She was educated at St Paul's Girls' School and Somerville College, Oxford, and went on her first dig in 1929, investigating King Solomon's mines in Rhodesia (now Zimbabwe). Later she became a lecturer in Palestinian archaeology at London University (1948–62) and principal of St Hugh's College, Oxford (1962–73).

During her time as director of the British School of Archaeology in Jerusalem (1951–66), she undertook research in Jordan (Old Testament Jericho) and discovered not only when it was first settled (8th millenium BC) and when the Israelites had destroyed it (c.1425 BC), though she believed the walls to have fallen due to an earthquake, but also that it is the oldest human settlement to have been continually occupied and that agriculture began there around 7000 BC. She turned her attention to Jerusalem between 1961 and 1967, and established that both Jericho and Jerusalem were permanent and not nomadic settlements.

Her most notable books are *Digging up Jericho* (1957), *Archaeology in the Holy Land* (1965) and *Digging up Jerusalem* (1974).

Kerin, Dorothy

Born 1889 Died 1963
English mystic whose ministry encouraged mainstream Anglicanism to take divine healing seriously

Dorothy Kerin was born in London of Irish extraction. After suffering five years as a chronic and 'incurable' invalid, in 1912 she was suddenly healed and entrusted with a mission of healing. Other visions and the stigmata followed.

After some years of prayer and quiet preparation, her public ministry began in 1930 in Ealing, under the guidance of Bishop Philip Lloyd. The work grew and in 1948 she moved to Burrswood in Groombridge, Kent. From 1959 Dorothy held healing missions in Sweden, Geneva, Paris, and the USA.

Her vocation — recounted in successive editions of *The Living Touch* and *Fulfilling* — was firmly integrated with Anglican life and did much to bring healing back to the Church's normal ministry.

Kerr, Deborah, *originally* Deborah Jane Kerr-Trimmer

Born 1921
Scottish actress usually cast in well-bred roles who received six Academy Award nominations

Deborah Kerr-Trimmer was born in Helensburgh. She trained as a dancer, and made her stage début in the corps de ballet of a Sadler's Wells production of *Prometheus* (1938). Choosing instead to act, she appeared in repertory in Oxford before making her film début in *Major Barbara* (1940), which was followed by British successes in *The Life and Death of Colonel Blimp* (1943) and *Black Narcissus* (1947) that brought her a Hollywood contract.

Invariably cast in well-bred, ladylike roles, she played numerous governesses and nuns but strayed sensationally from her established image to play a nymphomaniac in *From Here to Eternity* (1953). In 1969 she retired from the screen and returned to the theatre in works such as *Seascape* (1975), *Long Day's Journey Into Night* (1977) and *Overheard* (1981), and after sustained activity on stage and television, she returned to the cinema in *The Assam Garden* (1985).

She was awarded the BAFTA special award in 1991.

Kesson, Jessie, *originally* Jessie Grant McDonald

Born 1915 Died 1994
Scottish novelist, short-story writer, and playwright

Jessie McDonald was born in Inverness. She did not know who her father was, and soon moved with her mother to Elgin. There, estranged from many of the family, mother and daughter lived meagrely on their own resources, becoming adept at evading the Cruelty Inspector and the rent man. In her teens, however, Jessie was sent to an orphanage in Skene, Aberdeenshire.

Later she entered service, and settled in 1934 on a farm with her husband Johnnie, a cottar. Although she managed eventually to devote herself to writing, she worked for many years as a cinema cleaner, artists' model, and a social worker in London and Glasgow.

The White Bird Passes (1958), *Glitter of Mica* (1963), *Another Time, Another Place* (1983) and *Where the Apple Ripens* (1985) recreate faithfully, and without sentimentality, her hard early years in a farming community.

Key, Ellen Karolina Sophia

Born 1849 Died 1926
Swedish reformer, educationalist and writer with a radical view of the role of women

Ellen Key was born in Sundsholm, Småland, the daughter of a politician and landowner. She became a teacher in Stockholm (1880–99) when her father lost his fortune.

Earning the soubriquet 'Pallas of Sweden', she made her name as a writer on the feminist movement, child welfare, sex, love and marriage, in *Barnets århundrade* (1900, Eng trans *The Century of the Child*, 1909) and *Lifslinjer I–III* (1903–6, 'Life-Lines'). Her philosophy focused on the role of women in society, placing mothers in the home and women without children in the political arena, campaigning for peace. She also developed a pioneering method of teaching that was anti-authoritarian in style and highly influential.

Though her radical and liberal views were controversial, her writings were translated into several languages and she lectured abroad, influencing many writers.

Khan, Ra'ana Liaquat Ali, *née* Ra'ana Pant

Born 1905 Died 1990
Pakistani politician who received the 1979
Human Rights Award

Ra'ana Pant was born in Almora, North India, and graduated in economics from Lucknow University. She became lecturer in economics at Indraprastha College for Women in New Delhi where she worked until she married politician Zada Liaquat Ali Khan in 1933.

On partition (1947) he became Prime Minister and Begum Ra'ana was one of the first to organize assistance for refugees during the mass transit. Following her husband's assassination at Rawalpindi in 1951, she devoted herself to social work, but remained politically active. She was appointed UN delegate in 1952, and from 1954 to 1966 represented her country as the first woman ambassador to Holland, Italy and Tunisia. In 1973 she became the first woman governor of Sind.

Kidd, Carol

Born 1944
Scottish jazz singer who is hailed as one of the finest in Britain

Carol Kidd was born in Glasgow. While still at school she began to sing with traditional jazz bands, later joining the Glasgow-based band of Jimmy Feighan, whose style allowed her to develop her talent for interpreting ballads. She married pianist George Kidd at the age of 17 and began to work with her own permanent trio, developing a loyal following in Scotland but little known outside until, in the late 1970s, she was featured in London at Ronnie Scott's club and the Pizza Express jazz clubs.

Then followed occasional work in Scotland on radio and television, as a singer and presenter, and the start of her recording career. During the late 1980s she began to give performances with specially assembled larger orchestras, including string sections, notably at the Glasgow and Edinburgh jazz festivals, winning various awards which gave her overdue recognition as one of Britain's finest jazz singers.

By 1990 she had moved to England to develop her career, working and recording with a regular trio of London-based musicians, and was chosen to support Frank Sinatra at his Ibrox Stadium concert (1990).

Kidd, Dame Margaret Henderson

Born 1900 Died 1988
Scottish pioneering lawyer whose determination
to reach the top paved the way for other women
making their careers in law

Margaret Henderson was the daughter of a Linlithgow solicitor. She determined to go to the Bar and achieved an impressive list of 'firsts' — as the first woman member of the Scottish Bar (1923), the first woman QC (1948) and the first woman (part-time) sheriff of a county (Dumfries 1960–6, Perth 1966–74). She also served as keeper of the Advocates' Library (1956–69), and was Vice-President of the British Federation of University Women.

She was made DBE in 1975 and LLD twice (Dundee, 1982; Edinburgh, 1984). On her death she was described by a colleague as having 'paved the way for women in the legal profession and in the Scottish Bar in a way no one else could have done'.

Kincaid, Jamaica, *originally* Elaine Potter Richardson

Born 1949
Caribbean-born American novelist, short-story
writer and journalist

Elaine Richardson was born in St John's, Antigua, and educated at state schools there before moving to the USA at the age of 16. Under the assumed name of Jamaica Kincaid, she began her writing career with short stories that were published in the magazine *Ingenue* and in the *New Yorker*. Her first collection was *At the Bottom of the River* (1983).

Her novels include *Annie John* (1985) and *Lucy* (1991). The latter is the sensitive tale of a young West Indian girl who, having fled to New York, grows ever more appreciative of, and eager to return to, her own land. The book is, in part, autobiographical — Kincaid herself has made the same journey, and is currently (since 1976) a staff writer for the *New Yorker*.

She has also written a non-fictional account of her home island, *A Small Place* (1988), and enjoys a certain cachet among a feminist audience.

Kincaid-Smith, Priscilla

Born 1926
South-African born Australian physician who has
specialized in kidney diseases

Priscilla Kincaid-Smith was born in Johannesburg, South Africa. She trained in medicine in South Africa and after junior medical positions there, relocated to London as registrar at the Royal Postgraduate Medical School, and at the Hammersmith Hospital (1953–8).

She moved to the University of Melbourne as a Research Fellow in 1958 and became Professor of Medicine and the Director of Nephrology there in 1967.

King, Billie Jean, *originally* Moffitt

Born 1943
American tennis player whose domination of
women's singles and doubles tennis for over 15
years elevated the status of the game

Billie Jean Moffitt was born in Long Beach, California. Between 1965 (the year of her marriage to Larry King) and 1980 she was one of the dominant players in women's tennis and won a record 20 titles at Wimbledon, consisting of six singles titles, 10 women's doubles and four mixed doubles.

In 1974 she founded the magazine *Women's Sports* and was one of the founders of the Women's Tennis Association — as its first president she played a prominent role in working for the improvement of remuneration and playing conditions for women in professional tennis.

She has commentated on television and written several books, including *Tennis to Win* (1970), *Billie Jean* (1974), *Secrets of Winning Tennis* (1975) and *Billie Jean King* (1982).

King, Carole, *née* Klein

Born 1942
American composer and singer whose memorable
songs express the angst of romance

Carole King was born in Brooklyn, New York. She co-wrote numerous songs with her future husband Gerry Goffin, including 'Will You Still Love Me Tomorrow', which was a number-one single for the Shirelles. Her other songs include 'Natural Woman', 'The Locomotion', 'Up on the Roof' and 'It's Too Late'.

In 1971 King's solo album *Tapestry* won four Grammy awards, including Album of the Year;

it has since sold over 10 million copies world-wide. She was inducted into the Rock & Roll Hall of Fame in 1990, and in 1994 appeared on Broadway in *Blood Brothers*.

King, Coretta Scott, *née* Scott

Born 1927
African-American singer, civil rights campaigner,
writer and wife of Martin Luther King, Jr

Coretta Scott was born in Marion, Alabama, and trained in music at the New England Conservatory. She made her concert début in 1948, and married Martin Luther King, Jr in 1953.

Two years later, the Montgomery (Alabama) bus strike led the couple into the struggle for civil rights for black Americans. After her husband's assassination in 1968, Coretta continued her husband's legacy of non-violent resistance by fighting (successfully) for a national holiday in his honour and by establishing the Martin Luther King, Jr Center for Nonviolent Social Change. She currently serves as its president.

King, Jessie Marion

Born 1875 Died 1949
Scottish designer and internationally renowned
book illustrator

Jessie Marion King was born in New Kilpatrick (now Bearsden), the daughter of a minister. She studied at the Glasgow School of Art (1895–9), and won a travelling scholarship to Italy and Germany. In 1908 she married the designer Ernest Archibald Taylor.

She participated in the decoration of Charles Rennie Mackintosh's Scottish Pavilion at the Exposizione Nazionale in Turin, and won a gold medal for the design of a book cover. She was much sought-after as a book illustrator and also worked with Liberty's, designing fabrics and part of the Cymric silver range.

With her husband, she moved to Paris in 1911 and returned to Scotland at the outbreak of World War I. She lived in Kirkcudbright and exhibited up to the time of her death.

King, Micki (Maxine)

Born 1944
American US Air Force officer who is better
known as a champion diver

Micki King was born in Pontiac, Michigan. Even though she competed in diving in high school and college, she did not have the financial support to train full-time after graduation. She joined the US Air Force as an officer

candidate and received her commission as a second lieutenant.

In 1969 she entered the World Military Games and competed against men, performing dives that no other woman had done in competition. She finished fourth in the platform event and third overall in the springboard event. Between 1969 and 1972 she won 10 national springboard and platform diving championships, and at the 1972 Olympics she won a gold medal in the springboard event.

Having risen to the rank of captain, in 1973 she became the first woman to hold a faculty position at the Air Force Academy when she became the diving coach.

Kingsford, Anna, *née* Bonus

Born 1846 Died 1888
English doctor and religious writer whose concerns
also included women's education

Anna Bonus was born in Stratford, Essex. In 1867 she married a Shropshire clergyman, Algernon Kingsford, and converted to Catholicism (1870). She wrote for the *Penny Post* and in 1872 bought and edited *The Lady's Own Paper*. She was an antivivisectionist, a vegetarian, and MD of Paris (1880) — her thesis was extended and published as *The Perfect Way in Diet* — as well as a Theosophist and a supporter of the cause for higher education for women.

In 1875 she wrote *Keys of the Creeds* with Edward Maitland, and in 1884 collaborated with him to found the Hermetic Society, which attempted to reconcile Christianity and Eastern religions. After her death Maitland published her collection of 'illuminations', *Clothed With the Sun* (1889).

Kingsley, Mary Henrietta

Born 1862 Died 1900
English traveller, writer and ethnologist who
ventured into parts of Africa where no European
had been before

Mary Kingsley was born in Islington, London, the daughter of the traveller George Kingsley, and niece of the writer Charles Kingsley. She was not formally educated, but was a voracious reader in her father's scientific library.

When her parents became invalids Mary took over the running of the household, and after they died she went on the first of two remarkable journeys to West Africa. This took place in 1893, when she lived among and bartered with the natives while retaining European dress. Returning from her second journey in 1895, she wrote *Travels in West*

Africa (1899), which was based on her diaries. *West African Studies* also appeared in 1899. The places she visited included the coastal area between what is now Zaire and the Congo, southeast Nigeria, part of Equatorial Guinea, the French Congo and Gabon, where she travelled through the territory of a reputedly cannibalistic tribe and had several life-threatening adventures.

Latterly she was consulted by colonial administrators, for her expertise was wide and her understanding of African culture broad-based. She died of enteric fever while serving as a nurse in the second Boer War.

Kingsley, Mary St Leger, *pseud*
Lucas Malet

Born 1852   Died 1931
English novelist who earned a literary reputation on her own, and not her father's, merit

Mary Kingsley was daughter of the writer Charles Kingsley (1819–75). In 1876 she married the Rev W Harrison, rector of Clovelly. She adopted the pen-name Lucas Malet to avoid association with her father, and completed his *Tutor's Story* in 1916.

She wrote over 20 works, among them such novels as *Mrs Lorimer* (1882), *Colonel Enderby's Wife* (1885), *The Wages of Sin* (1890), *The Carissima* (1896) and *Sir Richard Calmady* (1901). She became a Roman Catholic in 1899.

Her style is reminiscent of the 19th century in its characterization and is now considered sentimental, but she was awarded a civic pension in 1930 for her contribution to literature.

Kinnaird, Alison

Born 1949
Scottish studio glass artist and engraver whose work is inspired by myths and legends, music, naturalism and personal experiences

Alison Kinnaird was born in Edinburgh. She was educated at George Watson's Ladies College, Edinburgh, and went on to study Celtic history and archaeology at Edinburgh University, graduating in 1970. In her final year at university she took a course in glass engraving at Edinburgh College of Art run by Helen Munro Turner. Since 1971 she has worked as a glass artist on a freelance basis.

Her work exploits the qualities of her medium and she specializes in copper-wheel engraving as a decorative technique. She was awarded the Worshipful Company of Glass Sellers of London prize for artistic achieve-

ment in glass in 1987 and has exhibited widely in Britain and abroad.

Examples of her work can be seen in the National Museum of Scotland, Glasgow Museum and Art Gallery, Kelvingrove, Huntly House Museum in Edinburgh, and in the Corning Museum of Glass in New York.

Kinnaird, Lady Mary Jane, *née* Hoare

Born 1816   Died 1888
English philanthropist who co-founded the Young Women's Christian Association (YWCA)

Mary Hoare was born at Northwick Park, Northamptonshire, the daughter of a London banker. In 1843 she married Arthur Fitzgerald Kinnaird, a fellow philanthropist who supported her endeavours to raise the social standing of women. He became the tenth Baron Kinnaird in 1878.

Among her many activities, Mary founded a training school for domestic servants (1841) and edited a book of 'servants' prayers' (1848). She worked with Lady Canning to send nursing aid to the Crimea, and helped found the British Ladies' Female Emigration Society and the Zenana Bible and Medical Mission. In 1855 she founded hostels and institutes for young working women in London. In 1877 these came together with the Prayer Union founded by Miss Emily Robarts to form the Young Women's Christian Association.

Kirkland, Gelsey

Born 1952
American ballet dancer who formed a celebrated partnership with Mikhail Baryshnikov

Gelsey Kirkland was born in Bethlehem, Pennsylvania. After studying at the School of American Ballet, she joined New York City Ballet as its youngest member in 1968, where she became a principal in 1972. Roles were created for her by choreographers George Balanchine (*The Firebird*, 1970) and Jerome Robbins (*The Goldberg Variations*, 1971, and *An Evening Walze*, 1973), and by Antony Tudor in his last two ballets, *The Leaves Are Fading* (1975) and *The Tillers in the Fields* (1978).

She moved to the American Ballet Theatre in 1975 and partnered the Russian-born Mikhail Baryshnikov (1948–   ); the couple became one of the decade's most celebrated partnerships. A troubled personal life curtailed Kirkland's career in the early 1980s, but she made a dramatic and successful comeback in *Swan Lake* with the Royal Ballet in London, where she was guest dancer in 1980, 1981 and 1986. She returned to the American Ballet Theatre in 1992 to teach.

Her flawed but dazzling career is documented in her controversial autobiography, *Dancing on My Grave* (1986).

Kirkpatrick, Jeane Duane Jordan,
née Jordan

Born 1926
American academic and stateswoman with a reputation for independent thought who was permanent representative to the UN (1981–5)

Jeane Jordan was born in Duncan, Oklahoma. She was educated at Columbia University and Paris University, and became a research analyst for the state department (1951–3). She married Evron M Kirkpatrick in 1955 and concentrated on a career as an academic, at Trinity College and at Georgetown University, Washington DC, where she became Professor of Government in 1978.

Noted for her 'hawkish', anti-communist defence stance and advocacy of a new Latin-American and Pacific-orientated diplomatic strategy, she was appointed permanent representative to the United Nations by President Reagan in 1981, remaining there until 1985. Formerly a Democrat, she joined the Republican Party in 1985.

Her books include *Political Woman* (1974), *The Reagan Phenomenon* (1983) and *The Withering Away of the Totalitarian State* (1990).

Kitt, Eartha Mae

Born 1928
Creole American singer and actress who became a star of cabaret, stage and screen

Eartha Kitt was born in North, South Carolina. She graduated from the New York School of the Performing Arts, and made her New York début as a member of **Katherine Dunham's** dance troupe in *Blue Holiday* (1945). She toured throughout Europe and was subsequently cast by Orson Welles in his production of *Dr Faustus* (1951). Her theatrical credits include *New Faces of 1952*, *Shinbone Alley* (1957) and *The Owl and the Pussycat* (1965–6).

With her sinuous grace, vocal vibrancy, fiery personality and cat-like singing voice, she became a prime cabaret attraction across the world and a top recording artist. Since her début in *Casbah* (1948), her film appearances have included *New Faces* (1954), *St. Louis Blues* (1957), *Anna Lucasta* (1958), the documentary *All By Myself* (1982) and *Boomerang* (1991). She first appeared on television in

Eartha Kitt, 1989

1953, received the Golden Rose of Montreux for *Kaskade* (1962) and was appropriately cast as Catwoman in the series *Batman* (1966).

Later theatre work includes *Timbuktu!* (1978–80), *Blues in the Night* (1985), a showstopping appearance in *Follies* (1988–9), and a one-woman show. Her autobiographies include *Thursday's Child* (1956), *Alone With Me* (1976) and *I'm Still Here* (1989).

Kitzinger, Sheila Helen Elizabeth,
née Webster

Born 1929
British childbirth educationalist who has published widely on her subject

Sheila Webster was educated at Bishop Fox's School, Taunton, and at Ruskin and St Hugh's Colleges, Oxford. She married in 1952 and has five daughters. From 1952 to 1953 she conducted research into social anthropology, and she has worked with the Open University and the National Childbirth Trust.

She has long been a campaigner for more natural childbirth procedures and her 1980 book *Pregnancy and Childbirth* sold over one million copies. Her other books, which cover all aspects of pregnancy and childbirth, include *The Good Birth Guide* (1979), *Birth over Thirty* (1982), *Homebirth* (1991), *Ourselves as Mothers* (1992) and *The Year After Childbirth* (1994).

Kizer, Carolyn Ashley

Born 1925
American poet who won the Pulitzer Prize for
poetry in 1985 for 'Yin' (1984)

Carolyn Kizer was born in Spokane, Washington. She was educated at Columbia University and the University of Seattle, and founded the journal *Poetry Northwest* in Seattle. She worked briefly for the State Department as an adviser on Pakistan, and has taught at a number of universities.

Her first collection, *Poems* (1959), was followed by *The Ungrateful Garden* (1961). Subsequent volumes include *Knock Upon Silence* (1965), *Midnight Was My Cry* (1971), *Mermaids in the Basement: Poems for Women* (1984) and *The Nearness of You: Poems for Men* (1986). Her translations from several languages, including Urdu and Chinese, are collected in *Carrying Over* (1988).

Klein, Anne Hannah, *née* Hannah Golofski

Born c.1921 Died 1974
American fashion designer who pioneered fashions
in sophisticated but practical clothes for women

Hannah Golofski was born in New York. In 1938 she started her career as a sketcher on Seventh Avenue. In 1948, Junior Sophisticates was launched, and Anne Klein & Co was established in 1968.

She was a noted leader in designing sophisticated, practical sportswear for young women. She recognized early a need for blazers, trousers, and separates. Her designs were popular in America, where her company still thrives.

Klein, Melanie

Born 1882 Died 1960
Austrian-born British psychoanalyst who
pioneered the application of psychoanalysis to
children

Melanie Klein was born in Vienna. She studied medicine at first, but when she was in Budapest she was analyzed by Sigmund Freud's follower Sandor Ferenczi, and trained with him in his children's clinic. She studied under Karl Abraham in Berlin, where she was a member of the Berlin Psychoanalytic Institute (1921–6), then moved to London in 1926.

She pioneered the now widely used techniques of 'play therapy' and was the first to apply psychoanalysis to small children, working on such areas as the death instinct and the Oedipus complex. Her belief that neuroses are fixed in the earliest months of life

was always controversial and caused dissent among her colleagues; among those who disagreed with her was **Anna Freud**.

Klein's ideas and methods are expressed in her books, among them *The Psychoanalysis of Children* (1932).

Knight, Dame Laura, *née* Johnson

Born 1877 Died 1970
English artist who was one of the early women
members of the Royal Academy

Laura Johnson was born in Long Eaton. She studied at Nottingham Art School and in 1903 married her fellow-student, the portrait-painter Harold Knight (1874–1961).

Also in that year she began exhibiting at the Royal Academy, of which she became a member in 1936, the first woman to be an Academician since the founder-members **Mary Moser** and **Angelica Kauffman**.

She travelled in many parts of the world and produced a long series of oil paintings of the ballet, and of the circus and gypsy life, in a lively and forceful style, and also executed a number of landscapes in watercolour.

Knight, Gladys

Born 1944
American soul and r'n'b singer, who brought
together The Pips

Gladys Knight was born in Atlanta, Georgia. She began singing in church, joining the Maurice Brown and Wings Over Jordan gospel choirs. At the age of eight, she won a television talent competition, and the same year formed a close-harmony group called the Pips with her brother and two cousins. They began to record in 1958 and in 1966 switched to the Tamla Motown label where a string of hits followed, including 'I Heard it Through the Grapevine'.

Knight's rich, gospelly voice also lent itself to secular music and in 1972 she scored a huge hit with 'Help Me Make It Through the Night'. She left Motown in 1973 and had further success on the Buddah label with 'Midnight Train to Georgia' and 'The Way We Were'. Despite only sporadic activity since then, she remains one of the most successful black entertainers of all time.

Koch, Marita

Born 1957
German athlete who dominated the 200 and 400
metres events for over more than a decade

Marita Koch was born in Wismar and studied paediatric medicine. Competing for East

Germany, she won the Olympic 400 metres title in 1980 and the European title three times, remaining undefeated over 400 metres between 1977 and 1981.

In the 200 metres race, she won three indoor European championship titles and a world Student Games title. She set the world 400 metres record seven times and the 200 metres four times, and has set 16 world records in total.

She retired in 1986 and married her coach Wolfgang Meier. Her 400 metres record still stands a decade after she set it.

Koechlin-Smythe, Pat *see* Smythe, Pat

Koehler, Florence

Born 1861 Died 1944
American artist-craftswoman and jeweller, a
leading figure in the Craft Revival in America

Florence Koehler lived and worked in Chicago, which became one of the two centres for the Arts and Crafts Movement, Boston being the other. The Chicago Arts and Crafts Society, which was founded in 1897, helped to promote Koehler's work.

From around 1900 her jewellery designs became extremely popular in aesthetic and intellectual circles. Her designs for jewellery in the Art Nouveau style owed more to France than England.

Along with the work of L C Tiffany, the craft jewellery produced by Koehler is considered to be the best of the period.

Kolb, Barbara

Born 1939
American composer whose works feature an
emphatic recurrence of themes

Barbaro Kolb was born in Hartford, Connecticut, and educated at the Hartt School of Music there. She worked with the Hartford Symphony as a clarinettist (1960–6), before returning to Hartt as an instructor (1962–4). In 1962 she moved to New York City, but spent much of the early 1970s in Rome.

The early *Soundings* (1971–2) remains her best-known piece. Her later compositions are often influenced by the visual arts, as in the orchestral *Grisaille* (1978–9) and the later *Umbrian Colors* for violin and guitar (1986), and *Millefoglie* (1987), which won her the Kennedy Center Friedheim Award. Stylistically, she unites Debussy with jazz.

Kollontai, Alexandra Mikhaylovna, *née* Domontovich

Born 1872 Died 1952
Russian feminist and revolutionary who became
the world's first female ambassador

Alexandra Domontovich was born in St Petersburg into an upper-class family, but she rejected her privileged upbringing and became interested in socialism. She married an army officer, but nevertheless joined the Russian Social Democratic party, and for her revolutionary behaviour was exiled to Germany in 1908.

In 1915 she travelled widely in the USA, begging the nation not to join World War I, and urging the acceptance of socialism. In 1917, following the Revolution, she returned to Russia, where she became People's Commissar for Public Welfare in 1920. In this post she agitated for domestic and social reforms, including collective childcare and easier divorce proceedings. Although her private liaisons shocked the party, she was appointed minister to Norway (1923–5, 1927–30) as the first woman to hold that rank, and to Mexico (1926–7) and Sweden (1930–45). She rose to the rank of ambassador in 1943 and played a vital part in negotiating the termination of the Soviet–Finnish war (1944).

Her works, such as *The New Morality and the Working Class* (1918), and her collection of short stories, *Love of Worker Bees* (1923), aroused considerable controversy because of their open discussion of subjects like sexuality and women's place in society and the economy. Her autobiography, written in 1926, was not published in Russia.

Kollwitz, Käthe, *née* Schmidt

Born 1867 Died 1945
German graphic artist and sculptor whose
characteristic themes were tragic

Käthe Schmidt was born in East Prussia, the daughter of a Free Congregation pastor. She studied in Königsberg, then Berlin, where she studied drawing and married a medical student, Karl Kollwitz, who went on to work in a poor quarter of the city.

Although she has been called an Expressionist, she was uninterested in the fashions of modern art. Instead she was influenced by the prints of the German etcher, painter and sculptor Max Klinger (1857–1920), and chose serious, tragic subjects, with strong social or political content, as shown in her early etchings the *Weaver's Revolt* (1897–8) and the *Peasants' War* (1902–8).

From c.1910 she preferred lithography, and

after being expelled by the Nazis in 1933 from the Prussian Academy (its first woman member) she made a moving series of eight prints on the theme of *Death* (1934–5).

Komisarjevskaya, Vera Fedorovna,
also spelt Vera Fyodorovna Komissarzhevskaya

Born 1864 Died 1910
Russian actress and manager whose style impressed the Russian symbolists

Vera Komisarjevskaya was born in St Petersburg. Her father was an operatic tenor, and her younger brother Theodore became a noted director and designer. She became the leading Russian actress of her day, and was particularly valued not only by Anton Chekov, but also by the new school of Russian symbolist writers led by Aleksandr Blok and Andrey Bely, who admired her mystical, sensitive style and ethereal presence.

She was already established as an actress when she founded her own experimental theatre in St Petersburg in 1905, and engaged Vsevolod Meyerhold to produce there. The artistic relationship did not succeed, and she closed the theatre in 1908, intending to open a drama school, but died of smallpox on a fund-raising trip to Tashkent.

Königsmark, Marie Aurora, Countess of

Born 1662 Died 1728
German–Swedish noblewoman who became the King of Poland's mistress and a prominent figure in the court of Saxony

The Countess of Königsmark was born in Stade, Bremen, the daughter of a German nobleman in Swedish employment. She was the sister of Count Philipp Christoph of Königsmark, who allegedly had a love affair with Sophia Dorothea, wife of the future George I of Britain (who was then electoral prince of Hanover).

In 1694 Philipp suddenly disappeared (probably murdererd) and the Countess of Königsmark went to Dresden to look for him. There she met and became the mistress of Augustus II 'the Strong', elector of Saxony and future king of Poland. In 1696 she bore him a son, Maurice of Saxony, who was to become marshal of France (Marshal de Saxe).

In 1702 King Augustus sent her on a mission to arrange peace between himself and Charles XII of Sweden, but it was a failure. She fell

from favour and was pensioned off as prioress of Quedlinburg, though she continued to enjoy court life.

Korbut, Olga

Born 1956
Russian gymnast who gave gymnastics a new lease of life as a sport

Olga Korbut was born in Grodno, Belorussia. As a young woman of very slight stature, at the age of 17 she captivated the world at the 1972 Olympics at Munich with her lithe grace. She won a gold medal as a member of the winning Soviet team, as well as individual golds in the beam and floor exercises and silver for the parallel bars.

By 1976 she felt burned out. After retiring, she married a pop star, Leonid Bartkevich, and became a coach. As a mother she steered her son away from what she termed the 'self flagellation' of a childhood dominated by sport.

Kotopoúli, Maríka

Born 1887 Died 1954
Greek actress, regarded as one of the three top actresses of her day

María Kotopoúli was born to parents who were actors. She seemed destined for the theatre, and along with Kyvéli Andrianoú (1887–1978) and Katína Paxinoú (1900–73), became one of the leading Greek actresses of her day.

Her ability to switch from vaudeville and low comedy to classical drama and tragedy with equal conviction led to her being regarded as the most versatile and wide-ranging of that distinguished trio. She ran her own independent theatre company in Athens for over 30 years, and devoted herself to the revival of ancient Greek drama toward the end of her career.

Kovalevskaya, Sofya Vasilyevna

Born 1850 Died 1891
Russian mathematician and novelist who had an unusual gift for both activities

Sofya Kovalevskaya was the daughter of a Moscow artillery officer. She married a brother of the Russian embryologist Alexander Kovalevsky, and made a distinguished name for herself throughout Europe as a mathematician. As a woman she found it impossible to obtain an academic post in Europe until finally she obtained a lectureship at Stockholm, followed by a professorship in 1889.

She worked on Abelian integrals, partial differential equations and the form of Saturn's rings. She also made a name as a novelist, her works including *Vera Brantzova* (1895) and the novella *The Nihilist Girl* (1890), which reveal her lively gift as a storyteller. In 1878 she published her autobiography, *A Russian Childhood*.

Kovalskaya, Elizaveta Nikolayevna, *née* Solntseva

Born 1851 Died 1943
Russian revolutionary worker who later earned
respect as a historian

Elizaveta Solntseva was born in Kharkov and began her revolutionary work there by organizing a study group which was closed by the police in 1869. After 13 years of work in the revolutionary movement she founded the 'Southern Russian Workers' League' in Kiev (1880) which committed terrorist acts against officialdom. However, she was arrested and sentenced to hard labour in Siberia.

On her release in 1903 she went to Switzerland and returned to Russia in 1917 to become a distinguished historian of the Russian Revolution at the Petrograd Archives of Revolutionary History. In 1926 she published *The 1880–81 Southern Russian Workers' League*.

Kovács, Margit

Born 1902
Hungarian potter inspired by Hungarian folk art
in her use of heraldic motifs and painted
decoration

Margit Kovács was born in Györ. She began studying art in 1924, and went to Budapest to study ceramics. She left Hungary in 1926 and worked with H Bucher in Vienna, then studied modelling under the sculptor Karl Miller and ceramics under A Niemeyer in Munich in 1928–9.

She returned to Hungary in 1929 and had a successful exhibition in Budapest. She then worked in Copenhagen and for 18 months at the Sèvres factory, also fulfilling commissions in Paris. She won an honorary diploma at the Paris International Exhibition in 1937, and the major prize at the Brussels Exhibition in 1958.

Her work includes figures and relief panels both modelled, or sculpted, and thrown, or made on a pottery wheel. Among her later works is a series of figures entitled *Mourning Women*, large murals depicting figures in scenes from folklore and country life. A museum has been established at Szentendre, near Budapest in recognition of her work as a ceramic sculptor.

Kowalski, Karla

Born 1941
Austrian architect who collaborates with her
husband to design stimulating and provocative
buildings

Karla Kowalski was born in Oberschleisen, which is now part of Poland. She was trained at the Technical University in Darmstadt, Germany, and at the Architectural Association Planning Department (1968–9) and has run a practice with her husband, Michael Szyszhowitz, in Graz, Austria, since 1973.

Their work is strongly emotional and incorporates imagery and names from folklore. They have won many awards for their work since 1978, including the Geramb medal (1982), the Austrian Architects Association prize (1982) and the Styrian Region Great award (1983) for their renovation of and additions to Grosslobming Castle.

Their other work includes the Institute of Biochemistry, Graz (1985–90), a church interior, Graz-Ragnitz (1984–7) and the German Rheumatism Centre, Berlin (1988).

Kramer, Dame Leonie Judith, *née* Gibson

Born 1924
Australian academic, writer and administrator

Leonie Gibson was born in Melbourne and educated at Melbourne University and at St Hugh's College, Oxford. She married Harold Kramer in 1952. She was appointed Professor of Australian Literature at Sydney University (1968–89), the first ever to hold such a post. As a scholar and critic she has held positions on a number of influential bodies, being a member of the board of the Australian Broadcasting Commission (1977–81) and its Chairman (1981–3), member of the Universities Council (1977–86), council member of the Australian National University, Canberra (1984–7), and Chairman of the board of the National Institute of Dramatic Art from 1987.

Her published works include three critical volumes on the Australian author H H Richardson. She has co-authored two books on language and literature, edited the *Oxford History of Australian Literature* (1981), co-edited the companion *Oxford Anthology of Australian Literature* (1985), and edited other volumes of poetry including *David Campbell: Collected Poems* (1989).

She was created a DBE in 1983.

Kreps, Juanita, *née* Morris

Born 1921
American economist, first woman Director of the
New York Stock Exchange, and first woman
Secretary of Commerce

Juanita Morris was born in Lynch, Kentucky, and educated at Berea College and Duke University. She taught economics at Denison College (1945–50), and returned to Duke University in 1958, becoming Professor there in 1967 and its first woman vice-president in 1973. She became director of the New York Stock Exchange (1972–7), and under President Carter served as Secretary of Commerce (1977–9). She continues to serve on the boards of several major companies.

Her political interests have principally focused on such issues as sexual and racial equality in business, and the economic consequences of women's patterns of work.

Her works include *Lifetime Allocation of Work and Income* (1971), *Sex in the Marketplace: American Women at Work* (1971) and *Women and the American Economy* (1976).

Kristeva, Julia

Born 1941
French theorist and critic, a leading voice among
French intellectuals and in feminist criticism

Julia Kristeva was born in Bulgaria. She became a practising psychoanalist and, influenced by Sigmund Freud and Jacques Lacan, she was led to question Western claims concerning philosophy, literary criticism, linguistics and politics.

Her work focuses on language, literature and cultural history. *Desire in Language* (1977, Eng trans 1980) applies semiotics to literature and art. *Revolution in Poetic Language* (1974, Eng trans 1984) paved the way for a sociology of literature based on language. And *About Chinese Women* (1975, Eng trans 1976) and *Polylogue* (1977, Eng trans 1980) have brought her work to the forefront of feminist criticism.

Kristiansen, Ingrid, *née* Christensen

Born 1956
Norwegian athlete who has held several records
for long-distance running

Ingrid Christensen was born in Trondheim. She attained champion status in cross-country skiing, and then became an outstanding long-distance runner.

In 1986 she became the only person to hold world best times for the 5,000 metres, 10,000 metres, and marathon. She had knocked 45.68 seconds off the world 10,000 metres record,

and easily won the European title, but since then the record for the 10,000 metres has been broken, most recently by Wang Junxia (1993: 29 minutes 31.78 seconds).

Kristiansen has won most of the world's major marathons, including Boston, Chicago, and London, and was the world cross-country champion in 1988.

Kristina *see* Christina

Krone, Julie

Born 1963
American jockey, the most successful woman
jockey to date

Julie Krone was born in Benton Harbor, Michigan. She became the first woman to win a racing title when she won the riding title at Atlantic City in 1982. Until the 1970s few women had made their living as jockeys, and in 1988 Krone became the leading female jockey in history on winning her 1,205th race.

She rode in the annual Breeders' Cup races at Churchill Downs, the first woman ever to race in that event, and in 1991 became the first woman to race in the Belmont Stakes. By that year, with $31 million dollars in purses and 2,000 wins, she had become the most successful female jockey of all time.

Krüdener, Barbara Juliana von, *née* von Vietinghoff

Born 1764 Died 1824
Russian noblewoman who became a mystic, and
saw the Holy Alliance as her own work

Barbara von Vietinghoff was born in Riga, the daughter of Baron von Vietinghoff. In 1782 she married Baron von Krüdener, Russian ambassador at Venice, but they separated in 1785. From 1789 she lived in Riga, St Petersburg and Paris. In 1803 she published a remarkable novel, *Valérie*, supposed to be autobiographical, and presently gave herself up to an exaggerated mysticism.

In 1815 she met the Tsar Alexander I and was instrumental in his conversion, crediting herself with the Holy Alliance of Russia, Austria, and Prussia, which he orchestrated that year. Expelled in 1817–18 from Switzerland and Germany, and repulsed by Alexander (apparently because he disliked the people she mixed with and disagreed with her plans for him to conquer Greece), she retired to her paternal estates near Riga, where she entered into relations with the Moravian Brethren.

Krupskaya, Nadezhda Constantinovna

Born 1869 Died 1939
Russian political figure, a leading Bolshevik and
wife of V I Lenin

Nadezhda Krupskaya was born in St Petersburg to an aristocratic but impoverished family. Typically among young women of her class in late 19th-century Russia, she became a committed socialist, having first trained as a teacher. The Russian socialist women's movement tended to draw its members not from the working classes, but from relatively privileged sections of society, because of the suppression of trade union activity or any organized labour movement among the working classes.

She married V I Lenin in 1896, and was one of a number of women prominent in the leadership of the Marxist Russian Social Democratic Party. In 1900 she published *The Woman Worker*, a pamphlet which applied **Clara Zetkin**'s analysis of the female condition to the position of women in Russia.

Kübler-Ross, Elisabeth

Born 1926
Swedish-born American psychiatrist and
physician, concerned with the care of the
terminally ill

Elisabeth Kübler-Ross was born in Zurich. She decided to train in medicine after being a hospital volunteer during World War II. She graduated MD from the University of Zurich in 1957, and shortly afterwards married E R Ross and moved to the USA.

She specialized in psychiatry and in 1965 became assistant professor at the University of Chicago Medical School. Treatment of terminally ill patients led her to write *On Death and Dying*, identifying an area of concern previously unrecognized.

Kulisciov, Anna

Born 1854 Died 1925
Italian socialist and feminist of Russian birth

Anna Kulisciov was born at Simferopol in the Crimea, and studied at Zurich where she was influenced by the anarchist Mikhail Bakunin. Subsequently, she was exiled from Russia in 1877 for her political activities.

She moved to Florence in 1878, and became active in Italian politics. She became a socialist, moved to Milan (where she spent the rest of her life) and became a doctor.

From 1892 Kulisciov and her partner Filippo Turati were leading figures in the newly-founded Italian Socialist Party, with Kulisciov significantly involved in women's issues.

Being a socialist, she saw women's emancipation as inseparable from the emancipation of the working-classes, unlike **Anna Maria Mozzoni** for example, who prioritized women's causes. However in 1910 Kulisciov opposed the majority of her fellow members of the Socialist Party in demanding a commitment to women's suffrage.

Kumin, Maxine

Born 1925
American poet, novelist and writer for children,
America's Consultant in Poetry in 1981–2

Maxine Kumin was born in Philadelphia and educated at Radcliffe College. Her first novel, *Through Dooms of Love* (1965), describing the clash between a radical, college-educated girl and her pawnbroker father, was directly autobiographical.

As a poet Kumin has been tagged 'Roberta Frost', but she is more than the Earth Mother poet this nickname implies. Although her work is autobiographical it is not confessional in the manner of her friend and collaborator **Anne Sexton**.

She is a prolific writer whose other work includes *Up Country* (1972), which won a Pulitzer Prize in 1973, and *Nurture* (1989), which, like much of her later work, focuses on threatened species and is passionately environmental. During her term as Consultant in Poetry (a post renamed poet laureate in 1987), she set up poetry workshops for women.

Kurys, Diane

Born 1948
French film director who has established a strong
individual voice in her work

Diane Kurys was born in Lyons. Her parents were Jewish immigrants from Russia. She began as an actress in Paris in 1970, working on stage and in films, including *Fellini's Casanova* (1976). Her first film, *Diabolo Menthe* (1978, *Peppermint Soda*), was a surprise success, and launched her as an important European filmmaker.

Much of her work has been autobiographical in its inspiration. *Cocktail Molotov* (1980) looked back on the events of 1968 in Paris, while *Coup de Foudre* (1983, *At First Sight*) dealt with the theme of divorce. It was nominated for an Academy Award as best foreign film.

I

La Barbara, Joan Linda, *née* Lotz

Born 1947
American vocalist and composer who has been an
influential figure in experimental music since the
1970s

Joan La Barbara was born in Philadelphia and was trained in singing (1965–8) and composition (1968–70) in New York City. She sang in the ensembles of composers Steve Reich (1971–4) and Philip Glass (1973–6), before establishing a solo career as a composer-performer specializing in 'extended' techniques such as circular breathing and multiphonics (the simultaneous sounding of two or more pitches). John Cage and Morton Feldman have written pieces for her.

She married the composer of electronic music Morton Subotnick in 1979 and studied acoustic processing with him, from which *October Music: Star Showers and Extra-terrestrials* (1980) was an early outcome. More recently, La Barbara has concentrated on 'sound-paintings' of places; *In the Dreamtime* (1990) is a 'sonic self-portrait'.

Labé, Louise, *originally* Louise Charlieu *or* Charly

Born c.1520 Died 1566
French poet whose love poetry caused a scandal
and challenged conventional views on women

Louise Charlieu was born in Parcieux, Ain, the daughter of a rope maker. She was educated in the Renaissance manner, learnt Latin and music, and was a skilled rider. In 1542 she fought, disguised as a knight, at the siege of Perpignan, and in 1550 she married a wealthy rope manufacturer, Ennemond Perrin, in Lyons, thereafter being called 'la Belle Cordière' (the Lovely Ropemaker).

In 1555 she published her *Oeuvres*
('Works'), which included three elegies and 23 sonnets in the Petrarchan manner. She also wrote a prose work, *Débat de Folie et d'Amour* (1555, 'Debate Between Folly and Love'), and was noted for her love affairs, which are reflected in her work.

Labille-Guiard, Adelaide

Born 1749 Died 1803
French artist, teacher and portraitist who painted
members of the French royal family

Adelaide Labille-Guiard's first formal training was with François Elie Vincent. From 1769 to 1774 she trained with Quentin de la Tour, then studied oil painting with François André Vincent (1746–1816), the son of her first teacher. Their relationship became something of a scandal, but they dismissed the rumours and married in 1800.

In order to be accepted into the Academy, Adelaide was forced to execute a series of pastel portraits of prominent (misogynist) Academicians. This apparently satisfied the Academy that her husband was not responsible for producing her work and she was elected on 31 May 1783.

In the 1790s she painted the portraits of members of the new Revolutionary government. Her greatest disappointment was the destruction during the Revolution of her vast painting entitled *The Chevalier Receiving the Order of St Louis*.

Lacey, Janet

Born 1903 Died 1988
English philanthropist, the first director of
Christian Aid

Janet Lacey was brought up in Sunderland. She worked for the YWCA in Kendal, Dagenham, and at the end of World War II with BAOR (British Army of the Rhine) in Germany. She joined the British Council of Churches as

Youth Secretary in 1947, moving to the Inter-Church Aid department, which she directed from 1952 to 1968. Christian Aid Week was started in 1957, the name Christian Aid being adopted in 1964.

Lacey moved on from Christian Aid to the Family Welfare Association and the Churches' Council for Health and Healing. She was the first woman to preach in St Paul's Cathedral and received an honorary Lambeth DD in 1975. Her views on aid are expressed in *A Cup of Water* (1970).

Lacombe, Claire

Born 1765 Died after 1795
French actress who advanced women's rights in turbulent times and was decorated by French Revolutionaries for helping to storm the Tuileries

Claire Lacombe was born in Pamiers. She became a professional actress in the provincial theatre but, attracted by the real-life drama of revolutionary Paris, she took up residence there in 1792.

She was awarded a civic crown for her part in helping to storm the Tuileries on 10 August that year, and she was later nicknamed 'Red Rosa' for her red cap as she became recognized as a leading member of a left-wing group known as the *Enrages*.

Her demand that women should be allowed to bear arms made her enemies in the new power structures evolving in Paris, and when her group was proscribed in 1794, she was imprisoned for nearly a year. Her later fate is unknown.

Lacoste, Catherine

Born 1945
French golfer, the youngest-ever winner of the American Women's Open

Catherine Lacoste was born in Paris, the daughter of René Lacoste, one of the world's greatest tennis players, and Simone (formerly de la Chaume), who won the British Women's golf championship and was also the first French player to win the British girls' championship.

Catherine shared first place in the individual competition at the Espirito Santo world team championships in 1964 and enjoyed a historic victory at the American Women's Open in 1967, when she became the youngest player ever to win the trophy. She also won her first French Open title the same year. In 1969 she followed in her mother's footsteps to win the British women's championship as well as the US, French and Spanish amateur titles.

La Fayette, Marie Madeleine Pioche de Lavergne, Comtesse de

Born 1634 Died 1693
French novelist and reformer of French romance-writing whose La Princesse de Clèves is considered to be the first modern French novel

Marie de Lavergne was born in Paris, the daughter of the governor of Le Havre. She married the Comte de La Fayette in 1655, but they separated about four years later. During the early 1660s she formed a liaison with La Rochefoucauld which lasted until his death in 1680 and led to the formation of a distinguished literary circle.

Right up to the end of her life she played a leading part at the French court, as was proved by her *Lettres inedites* (1880, 'Unabridged Letters'); prior to their publication it was believed that her last years were given to devotion. Her novels are *Zaïde* (1670, Eng trans *Zayde: A Spanish History*, 1678) and *La Princesse de Clèves* (1678, Eng trans *The Princess of Cleves*, 1679), a study in conflict between love and marriage in the court-life of her day. It is considered to be a landmark in French fiction and led to reaction against the long-winded romances of Gautier Calprenède and **Madeleine de Scudéry**.

Laforet, Carmen

Born 1921
Spanish writer of novels and short stories, the first woman novelist to come to notice after World War II

Carmen Laforet was born in Barcelona. She studied at Barcelona University and then moved to Madrid, achieving instant fame in 1944 with her first novel *Nada* ('Nothing'), which portrays economic and psychological depression in the wake of civil war and is based on her own arrival in Barcelona in 1939.

La isla y los demonios (1952, 'The Island and the Devils'), set in the Canaries, conjures up an equally unsettling picture of family life gently simmering with neurosis and sexual frustration. In 1955 she published an ambitious but less well-received novel based on her conversion to Catholicism in 1951, *La mujer nueva* ('The New Woman').

Her later works include *La insolación* (1963, 'Sunstroke'), which traces 20 years of Nationalist rule in Spain.

Lagerlöf, Selma Ottiliaa Lovisa

Born 1858 Died 1940
Swedish novelist who was the first woman winner of the Nobel Prize for Literature

Selma Lagerlöf was born at the manor house in Mårbacka and had a sheltered childhood largely because she was disabled. She taught at Landskrona (1885–95), and first sprang to fame with her novel *Gösta Berlings saga* (1891, 'The Story of Gösta Berling'), based on the traditions and legends of her native Värmland, as were many of her later books, such as her trilogy on the Löwensköld family (1925–8, Eng trans *The Rings of the Lowenskolds*, 1931). She also wrote the children's classic *Nils Holgerssons underbara resa genom Sverige* (1906–7, 'The Wonderful Adventures of Nils').

Although she was a member of the neoromantic generation of the 1890s, her work is characterized by a social and moral seriousness, as in *Antikrists Mirakler* (1897, 'The Miracles of Anti-Christ') and *Bannlyst* (1918, 'The Outcast'). When she was awarded the Nobel Prize for Literature in 1909 she used the prize money to buy back her childhood home that her father had had to sell in the 1880s. In 1914 she became the first woman to enter the Swedish Academy.

Laine, Cleo, *originally* Clementina Dinah Campbell

Born 1927
English jazz musician and actress whose musical partnership with her husband has been a success for over 30 years

Clementina Campbell was born in Southall, Middlesex. Early in her career she sang with the big band of her husband-to-be John Dankworth (1927–   ), who was a founder-member (on clarinet and alto saxophone) of the legendary Club 11 (1948). She became a highly successful singer, with her wonderfully distinct delivery that has opened up opportunities in musical theatre and in straight acting.

Dankworth later acted as her musical director and assumed a less prominent public role, concentrating on composition and arrangement. Though their musicianship has often been underestimated, and despite a brief artistic 'divorce' when they opted to work apart, they have remained a significant musical partnership for over 30 years, running an annual workshop/festival for young musicians near their home at Wavendon, Buckinghamshire, since 1970.

Lakshmi Bai

Born 1835   Died 1858
Maratha Rani (Queen) of Jhansi, regarded by some as the best and bravest military leader of the Indian forces during the war of 1857

Lakshmi Bai was the daughter of the political adviser to the Peshwa of Bithur. She was brought up in a palace beside the Ganges, and from an early age rode horses and elephants and became adept in the martial arts; she also developed a strong Hindu faith.

She was married to Gangadhar Roa, the Raja of Jhansi in   northern India. The marriage was childless however, so they had adopted an heir, who was entrusted to the regency of Lakshmibai on the Raja's death in 1853. But the British refused to recognize the adopted boy as heir and immediately absorbed the state of Jhansi under the annexation policy made by Lord Dalhousie. According to this policy, all 'dependent' Indian states without direct heirs were to lapse to the British.

In 1857 a brutal rebellion against the British took place in Cawnpore, which led to Jhansi being besieged and taken despite desperate resistance from the Rani. The Rani fled on horseback to the fortress of Kalpi and persuaded the Indian leaders, including Tantia Topee (d.1859), to seize the fortress of Gwalior where she proclaimed the Nana Sahib (c.1820–59) as Peshwa. She died fighting in 1858.

Lamballe, Marie Thérèse Louise de Savoie-Carignan, Princesse de

Born 1749   Died 1792
French aristocrat who was murdered for being a close friend of Marie Antoinette

Marie de Savoie-Carignan was born in Turin, a daughter of the Prince de Carignan. In 1767 she married Louis de Bourbon, Prince de Lamballe, but he died the following year. She was beautiful and charming, and entered the court at Versailles when she was appointed superintendent of the Queen's household (1774) by **Marie Antoinette**, who also made her an intimate companion.

After the start of the French Revolution in 1789 she moved to Paris with the Queen and is thought to have taken part in her counter-revolutionary intrigues. She escaped to England in 1791, but returned to share the Queen's imprisonment in the Temple, and refused to take the oath of detestation of the king, queen, and monarchy. As she left the courtroom she was torn to pieces by the mob.

La Motte, Jeanne de Valois, Comtesse de

Born 1756   Died 1791
French adventuress who was a key player in the Diamond Necklace Affair

The Comtesse de La Motte, in association with the Italian adventurer Count Alessandro di

Cagliostro (properly Giuseppe Balsamo, 1743–95), duped the French prelate Cardinal Rohan-Guéménée (1734–1803), whose mistress she had become, into standing security for the acquisition of a diamond necklace, allegedly at the request of **Marie Antoinette**.

When the plot was revealed she was branded and imprisoned (1786), but escaped from gaol the following year and joined her husband in London, where she died as a result of a drunken fall from a three-storey window.

Lancefield, Rebecca, *née* Craighill

Born 1895 Died 1981
American pathologist whose work on streptococcus bacteria was fundamental in understanding their role in disease

Rebecca Craighill was born in Fort Wadsworth, New York, to an army family. She graduated from Wellesley College and received her masters degree from Columbia University in 1918. Also that year she married Donald Lancefield and accepted a position at the Rockefeller Institute, where she remained until her death.

She was widely honoured, somewhat late in life, and elected to the National Academy of Sciences in 1970.

Landowska, Wanda

Born 1879 Died 1959
Polish pianist, harpsichordist, and musical scholar

Wanda Landowska was born in Warsaw. In 1900 she went to Paris, and in 1912 became professor of the harpsichord at the Berlin Hochschule. After World War I, during which she was detained, she undertook many extensive concert tours, and in 1927 she estabished her École de Musique Ancienne at Saint-Leu-la-Forêt near Paris, where she gave specialized training in the performance of old works.

In 1940 she had to flee first to the south of France, then to Switzerland, and finally in 1941 to the USA. She excelled as a player of J S Bach and Handel, and Manuel de Falla wrote his harpsichord concerto for her. She renewed 20th-century interest in the harpsichord and her techniques now underlie contemporary playing.

She herself composed songs and piano and orchestral pieces. She also made a profound study of old music and on this subject wrote *La Musique ancienne* (1908, translated 1927). Among her other writings are *Bach et ses Interprètes* (1906) and many articles.

Lane, Dame Elizabeth, *née* Coulbourn

Born 1905 Died 1988
English lawyer who became the first woman High Court judge in Britain

Elizabeth Coulbourn was educated privately and at Malvern Girls College. She married a barrister, Henry Lane CBE (d.1975), in 1926 and the death of her only child led her to study for the Bar and become a barrister in 1940. She was the third woman to be appointed QC in 1960, and became a Master of the Bench in 1965.

She was assistant Recorder of Birmingham from 1953 to 1961, and then became Recorder of Derby and Commissioner of the Crown Court at Manchester in 1961–2. She was then the first woman circuit court judge until 1965, when she became the first woman to be appointed a judge of the High Court, working in the Family Division.

In 1971–3 she chaired the committee on the working of the Abortion Act, continuing to serve at the High Court until her retirement in 1979. She was created DBE in 1965.

lang, k d (kathy dawn)

Born 1962
Canadian singer, gay icon with a controversial approach and a leading exponent of New Country

k d lang spent her childhood in Alberta, where she learnt to play the piano and guitar by the age of 10. She attended drama college in Vancouver and had formed a group called the reclines (in memory of **Patsy Cline**) by the age of 21. Her first album, *A Truly Western Experience* (1983), brought her to the attention of a New York recording company.

She made a major breakthrough with non-reclines vocalists with *Shadowland* (1988), which was in the style of traditional US country and western, and returned to perform with the reclines on the successful *Absolute Torch and Twang* (1989). *Ingenue* (1992) confirmed her status as a star, and was followed by the film soundtrack for *Even Cowgirls Get the Blues*, and the impassioned pop album *All You Can Eat* (1995).

Lange, Dorothea, *originally* Nutzhorn

Born 1895 Died 1965
American photographer whose evocative pictures epitomized the Depression

Dorothea Nutzhorn was born in Hoboken, New Jersey. She studied at Columbia and learnt photography under Clarence White (1871–1925) who was prominent in the group

Photo-Secession. After travelling for a time, selling her photographs to pay her way, she established a studio in San Francisco in 1916, but became dissatisfied with the role of a society photographer and turned to recording the misery caused by the Depression.

She is best known for her social records of migrant workers, share-croppers and tenant farmers throughout the south and west of the USA in the Depression years from 1935, especially for her celebrated study, 'Migrant Mother' (1936). Some of her pictures were so powerful that they brought about state aid for the migrant workers.

With her husband, economist Paul Taylor, she collaborated on a book, *An American Exodus: A Record of Human Erosion* (1939). After World War II she worked as a freelance photo-reporter in Asia, South America, and the Middle East (1958–63). Her work has influenced many later photo-journalists.

Lange, Helene

Born 1848 Died 1930
German educationalist who championed women's rights in Germany

Helene Lange was born into a middle-class family in Oldenberg. She devoted herself to women's causes in Germany, first as a teacher, and later as an activist. Although politically conservative, she argued successfully for the higher education of women, founding the German Women Teachers' Association in 1889 and the Berlin Women's Association five years later.

Lange persuaded the Progressive Party to adopt the cause of female emancipation and set a personal example to women by undertaking voluntary service in the World War I. An expert proponent of the written word to spread her message, she published a collection of her writings in 1930, two years before her death in Berlin.

Lange, Jessica

Born 1949
American film actress who often chooses diverse roles that have a connection with her own concerns

Jessica Lange was born in Minnesota. She travelled America and Europe with her first husband Paco Grande, then settled for a time in Paris to study at the Opéra Comique before returning to New York. She made her film début as the screaming blonde beauty in the 1976 remake of *King Kong*, but public indifference to the film damaged her aspirations. Nevertheless, she continued to find work

and won critical acclaim for her roles in *The Postman Always Rings Twice* (1981), *Frances* (1982), and *Tootsie* (1982), for which she won a Best Supporting Actress Oscar. She has been drawn to roles of tortured and anguished women and has lent her star name to work that reflects some of her political and environmental concerns.

Her roles continued to be diverse, from a Southern sister in *Crimes of the Heart* (1986) to an indignant lawyer facing up to her father's Nazi past in *The Music Box* (1990). Box-office success with the remake of *Cape Fear* (1991) led to a reunion with the co-star Robert De Niro on a remake of the 1950s film noir *Night and the City* (1992), and a Best Actress Oscar for her role in *Blue Sky* (1994).

Langer, Susanne K(nauth)

Born 1895 Died 1985
American philosopher who was influential in the field of linguistic analysis and aesthetics

Susanne Langer was born in New York and educated at Radcliffe College, where she taught from 1927 to 1942. She subsequently held positions at the University of Delaware, Columbia University and Connecticut College.

She was greatly influenced by the German–Jewish philosopher Ernst Cassirer (1874–1945) and published important works on linguistic analysis and, more especially, aesthetics, such as *Philosophy in a New Key: A Study in the Symbolism of Reason, Rite and Art* (1942), which proposes a theory of art as the articulation of human emotion, *Feeling and Form* (1953), *Problems of Art* (1957) and *Mind: An Essay on Human Feeling* (3 vols, 1967–82).

Langley, Eve

Born 1908 Died 1974
Australian novelist who won acclaim for her epic novel The Pea Pickers

Eve Langley was born in Forbes, New South Wales. She moved to New Zealand in 1932 and had a short and unhappy marriage despite raising three children. Back in Sydney she threw herself into the literary milieu but later lived, and tragically died, as a recluse.

She wrote a number of novels of which the best are *The Pea Pickers* (1942), about a couple of women who go adventure-seeking in male disguise, and its sequel *The White Topee* (1954), in which the feminine 'hero' Steve plays out her own fantasies of virginal love, which possibly mirror the sexual conflicts of her author.

Langley's interest centres also on her personal quirks, such as wearing trousers before it became usual, always carrying a gun or sheath knife, and changing her name to 'Oscar Wilde'.

Langtry, Lillie (Emilie Charlotte),
née Le Breton

Born 1853 Died 1929
British actress and the alleged mistress of the
Prince of Wales

Lillie Le Breton was born in Jersey, the daughter of the dean of the island. She married Edward Langtry in 1874, and made her first important stage appearance in 1881. She was one of first 'society' women to go on stage and caused a sensation more for this reason and for her beauty than for her acting, though in time the critics began to recognize her ability.

Her nickname, *'The Jersey Lily'*, originated in the title of the portrait of her by John Millais (1829–96). She was widowed in 1897, married Hugo Gerald de Bathe in 1899 and continued to act until 1917. Her best roles included Rosalind in *As You Like It*. Her beauty brought her to the attention of several distinguished admirers, including the Prince of Wales, later Edward VII, whose mistress she allegedly became for a time.

In 1901 she became manager of the Imperial Theatre (originally the Old Aquarium Theatre) but it was not a successful venture, though she did later become a noted racehorse owner. She wrote *All at Sea* (as Lillie de Bathe) in 1909, and her reminiscences, *The Days I Knew* (1925).

Lansbury, Angela Brigid

Born 1925
English-born American actress of film, Broadway
and television

Angela Lansbury was born in London. She was under contract to the Metro-Goldwyn-Meyer film studios from 1943 to 1950, and appeared in such films as *Gaslight* (1944), *National Velvet* (1944), and *Samson and Delilah* (1949). She became a naturalized American citizen in 1951. After she became freelance she made many more films, including *The Reluctant Debutante* (1958), *The Manchurian Candidate* (1963), *Bedknobs and Broomsticks* (1972) and *Death on the Nile* (1978).

She made her Broadway stage début in Georges Feydeau's *Hotel Paradiso* in 1957, and became noted as an actress in such musicals as Stephen Sondheim's *Anyone Can Whistle* (1964) and *Sweeney Todd* (1979). She also played Gertrude in *Hamlet* at the National Theatre, London, in 1975, and has appeared frequently in American television series, such as *Murder, She Wrote* (1984–   ), becoming one of the highest earning British women of the mid-1990s.

Lansing, Sherry

Born 1944
American film executive who became the first
woman to head a major studio in Hollywood

Sherry Lansing was born in Chicago. She taught in high school in Los Angeles before becoming an actress in 1970. Her real ambitions lay behind the camera, and she rose from script reader to Vice President in Charge of Production at Columbia.

She became the first woman ever to head a Hollywood studio when she was appointed President of Twentieth Century-Fox in 1980, and remained there until 1982. She formed her own production company with Stanley R Jaffe. Their highly successful films include *Fatal Attraction* (1987), *The Accused* (1988) and *Indecent Proposal* (1993). Appointed Chairman of Paramount Pictures in 1992, she has consolidated her status with such hits as *Ghost* and *Forrest Gump*.

La Plante, Lynda

Born 1946
English actress and writer of novels and
screenplays who is best known for Prime Suspect

Lynda La Plante was born in Formby, Liverpool, and educated at Streatham House School for Ladies, Corby, and at RADA. She began her acting career in 1972, touring with Brian Rix, and working in both theatre and television, a period which included roles in the popular television series *The Sweeney* (1974–8) and *Minder* (1979–86).

She has written several novels, but her greatest successes have been screenplays for television, including *Widows* (1982), the BAFTA award-winning thrillers *Prime Suspect* (1991) and *Prime Suspect 2* (1992), and the controversial and violent drama about soldiers returning to civilian life, *Civvies* (1992).

However, *The Lifeboat*, her 1994 television series on the experiences of a Pembrokeshire lifeboat crew, was less successful. It was followed by the series *The Governor* (1995).

Lasker, Mary, *née* Elwin

Born c.1910
American civic worker and philanthropist whose
foundation gives awards to medical and health
research

Mary Elwin was born in Watertown, Wisconsin. She was educated at Radcliffe College and graduated with a law degree from the University of Wisconsin. Her second marriage was to Albert Lasker in 1940, the owner of an advertising agency.

In 1942 they established the Albert and Mary Lasker Foundation which gives annual awards for contributions to medical research and public health, several recipients of which have subsequently received Nobel Prizes.

Mary Lasker, too, has received several honours, including the Presidential Medal of Freedom 1968.

Laski, Marghanita

Born 1915 Died 1988
English novelist who was really best known as a
critic and broadcaster

Marghanita Laski was born in Manchester, a niece of the socialist politcal scientist Harold Laski. She was educated in Manchester and at Somerville College, Oxford, and married John E Howard in 1937. She wrote extensively for newspapers and reviews and her first novel, *Love on the Supertax*, appeared in 1944. Her later novels include *Little Boy Lost* (1949) and *The Victorian Chaise-longue* (1953).

She also wrote a play, *The Offshore Island* (1959), as well as editing and writing various studies and critical works; it was as a critic and broadcaster that she was best known. She contributed to the radio programmes *The Brains Trust*, *Any Questions* and *The Critics*, and also contributed extensively to the four-volume supplement to the *Oxford English Dictionary.*

Lathrop, Julia Clifford

Born 1858 Died 1932
American social reformer whose work led to
significant improvements in child welfare

Julia Clifford Lathrop was born in Rockford, Illinois, and educated at Vassar College. After working in her father's law office for about 10 years, in 1890 she joined **Jane Addams**'s Hull House Settlement in Chicago, remaining until 1909, and as the first woman member of the Illinois State Board of Charities from 1893, she worked to help underprivileged children and the mentally ill. She also saw female doctors employed in state hospitals for the first time and helped to establish the first US juvenile court (1899).

She was one of the founders of the Chicago Institute of Social Science (1903–4), was associated with the Chicago School of Philanthropy from 1908 to 1920, and was the first head of the Federal Children's Bureau (1912–21), in which position she commissioned groundbreaking research on such subjects as child labour, infant mortality and delinquency, and proposed the elements relating to maternity and child welfare that would eventually be incorporated into the Social Security Act. She was a member of the Child Welfare Committee of the League of Nations from 1925 to 1931.

Lathrop, Rose Hawthorne, *name in religion* Mother Alphonsa Lathrop, *née* Hawthorne

Born 1851 Died 1926
American nurse, founder and first Mother
Superior of the St Rose of Lima nursing order

Rose Hawthorne was born in Lenox, Missouri. As her father was in the diplomatic service she spent much of her girlhood in Europe, and in 1871 she married a Londoner, George Parsons Lathrop. They had one son, Francis, who died of diphtheria in 1881 at the age of five.

In 1895 Rose left her husband because of his alcoholism and decided to nurse dying cancer patients in the New York slums. Following his death in 1898, she became a Dominican tertiary and her work with fellow volunteer nurses developed into a church-based organization. She founded the St Rose of Lima order (the Servants of Relief for Incurable Cancer) in December 1900, becoming its first Mother Superior, and the following year a mother house, novitiate, and cancer ward were established at Rosary Hill House, Westchester County.

Latynina, Larissa (Semyonovna), *née* Diril

Born 1935
Ukrainian gymnast who won a remarkable
number of Olympic medals

Larissa Latynina was born in Kharsan. In 1956 and 1964 she collected 18 Olympic medals for the USSR, a record for any sport, winning nine golds. During her 13-year career she won 24 Olympic, World, and European titles. She retired in 1966.

Lauder, Estée, *née* Mentzer

Born 1908
American businesswoman and beautician who co-
founded a massive cosmetics and fragrance
company

Estée Mentzer was born in New York City, the daughter of poor Hungarian immigrants. She worked her way up in the cosmetics industry

Estée Lauder, 1966

by selling a face cream made by her uncle who was a cosmetic chemist.

Together with her husband Joe Lauder (d.1982) she founded Estée Lauder Inc in 1946. They spent their small advertising budget on making samples of their products which they gave away to the public, immediately capturing an eager market. They had great success with Youth Dew bath oil in the 1950s, and Clinique anti-allergic products and the Aramis men's range in the 1960s.

Lauder was named one of 100 women of achievement by *Harper's Bazaar* in 1967, and named one of the Top Ten outstanding women in business in 1970. The family have used their fortune to build adventure parks and assist the restoration of the Palace of Versailles. She published her autobiography, *Estée: A Success Story*, in 1985.

Laurence, (Jean) Margaret, *née* Wemyss

Born 1926 Died 1987
Canadian writer of Scots–Irish descent, one of the most respected novelists of her country

Margaret Wemyss was born in the prairie town of Neepawa, Manitoba. Her first stories appeared in the high-school paper. Aged 18, she left home to study at United College (now Winnipeg University), from which she gradu-

ated in 1947, the same year she married John Laurence, a civil engineer. His job took them to England, Somaliland and, in 1952, to Ghana, where they spent five years before moving to Vancouver.

A Tree for Poverty (1954), a collection of translated Somali poetry and folk-tales, and the travel book *The Prophet's Camel Bell* (1963), came from her East African experience. *This Side Jordan* (1960), her first novel, was set in Ghana. In 1962 she separated from her husband and moved to England; a year later a collection of stories, *The Tomorrow-Tamer*, set in West Africa, appeared. In Penn, Buckinghamshire, she wrote her famous Manawaka series based on her home town: *The Stone Angel* (1964), *A Jest of God* (1966), *The Fire-Dwellers* (1969), *A Bird in the House* (1970) and *The Diviners* (1974). She then returned to Canada for the rest of her life and turned to writing stories for children.

She received Governor-General Awards in 1967 and 1975, and in 1972 was made a Companion of the Order of Canada.

Laurencin, Marie

Born 1885 Died 1956
French artist and designer known for her gentle paintings of elegant-looking women

Marie Laurencin was born in Paris and trained at the Académie Humbart. She exhibited in the Salon des Indépendents in 1907. She was mistress to the poet Guillaume Apollinaire from 1908 and among their artistic friends was Picasso, who influenced her art and features in her group portrait *The Guests* (1908). Although she lived among its exponents, she did not join the Cubist movement itself.

She is best known for her portraits of women in misty pastel colours, such as *The Rehearsal* (1936). She also illustrated many books with watercolours and lithographs, and designed costumes for Sergei Diaghilev's Ballets Russes.

La Vallière, Louise Françoise de La Baume le Blanc, Duchesse de

Born 1644 Died 1710
French aristocrat who was the mistress of Louis XIV (reigned 1643–1715)

Louise de La Baume le Blanc was born in Tours and brought to court by her mother to be maid of honour to Louis XIV's sister-in-law Henrietta Anne of England. She became mistress to Louis XIV in 1661 (though he had been married to Maria Theresa for only a year) and bore him four children. However she was not acknowledged as official mistress, due to

Louis's fear of upsetting his mother, **Anne of Austria** (1601–66) and partly to her own timidity.

When the Marquise de **Montespan** superseded her in 1667 she was forced to remain at court as official mistress because the Marquise's husband was planning to humiliate his wife. She was made a duchess in recompense but eventually managed to retire to a Carmelite nunnery in Paris (1674), where she adopted an ascetic regime.

Réflexions sur la miséricorde de Dieu par une dame pénitente (1680) is attributed to her.

Lavenson, Alma Ruth

Born 1897 Died 1989
American photographer who was best known for her dramatic still life, architectural and industrial images

Alma Lavenson was born into a prosperous business family in San Francisco, and moved with them to Oakland in 1906. She graduated in psychology from the University of California, Berkeley, in 1919, and began taking photographs on a seven-month tour of Europe with her family in 1922. Her work was first exhibited in pictorialist salons in the 1920s. In 1932 she was represented in San Francisco in the inaugural exhibition of the influential purist Group f/64, by several of whose members she was strongly influenced, especially **Imogen Cunningham**. In 1933 she married lawyer Matt Wahrhaftig and they had two sons.

She began photographing California Gold Rush ghost towns c.1933, and in 1935 the family moved to Piedmont, California. She was represented in the 1955 'Family of Man' exhibition at the Museum of Modern Art, New York, organized by photographer and curator Edward Steichen (1879–1973), had a retrospective at the California Museum of Photography in 1979, and was exhibited at the Friends of Photography in 1987 and 1990. After the death of her husband in 1957, she travelled and photographed people in their environments throughout the 1960s and 1970s in Europe, Latin America, Asia and elsewhere.

One of Lavenson's most moving images is *Child with Doll*, a close-cropped study of the hands of a child, made for the 1932 exhibition 'Showing of Hands' at the de Young Memorial Museum in San Francisco.

Lavin, Mary

Born 1912 Died 1996
Irish short-story writer and novelist who earned comparison with Chekhov

Mary Lavin was born in East Walpole, Massachusetts. Her parents returned to Ireland when she was nine and she was educated at University College, Dublin, and later settled in County Meath. 'Miss Holland', her first short story, was published in the *Dublin Magazine* where it was admired by the Irish writer Lord Dunsany (1878–1957) who encouraged her and later wrote an introduction to her first collection, *Tales from Bective Bridge* (1942), which was awarded the James Tait Black Memorial prize.

Notwithstanding two early novels — *The House in Clewe Street* (1945) and *Mary O'Grady* (1950) — she concentrated on the short story and published many collections, including *A Memory and Other Stories* (1972), *The Shrine and Other Stories* (1977) and *A Family Likeness* (1985).

Her laurels include the **Katherine Mansfield** prize, two Guggenheim awards and the Gregory Medal, founded by W B Yeats to be 'the supreme award of the Irish nation'.

La Voisin, *real name* Catherine Deshayes Monvoisin

Died 1680
French poisoner who played a key part in the Poison Affair

La Voisin was the assumed name of Catherine Monvoisin, a midwife and fortune-teller who grew wealthy through concocting potions and selling them to the ladies at the court of Louis XIV. When the poison plots were discovered in 1679, in a scandal known as the Poison Affair involving such well-known figures as **Marie Anne** and **Olympe Mancini** and the Marquise de **Montespan**, La Voisin was found to be responsible after an examination by a secret tribunal. She was burned as a poisoner and sorceress in 1680.

Lawrence, Andrea Mead

Born 1932
American Alpine skier, the only US skier to win two Olympic medals in one year

Andrea Mead Lawrence was born in Rutland, Vermont. She is noted for having won two gold medals at the 1952 Olympics — in the grand slalom and slalom events — and for becoming the only American skier to win two gold medals in the same Winter Olympics.

Three years previously she had received the White Stag Trophy for the best Ladies Combined Downhill.

Lawrence received the Beck International Trophy as the outstanding American skier in international competition in 1952, was inducted into the National Ski Hall of Fame in 1958, and was named to the International Women's Sports Hall of Fame in 1983.

Lawrence, Carmen Mary

Born 1948
Australian politician who entered politics after becoming an eminent psychologist

Carmen Lawrence was born in Western Australia and educated in Perth. She trained as a psychologist and worked at the University of Western Australia from 1979 until 1983, when she became a research psychologist in the Research and Evaluation Unit of the Psychiatric Services in Western Australia's Health Department. She entered politics in 1986 on becoming a member of the House of Representatives. She was Minister for Education (1988–90), Minister of Eduation and Aboriginal Affairs and Premier of Western Australia (1990–3) and became Leader of the Opposition, shadow Treasurer and shadow Minister for Employment in 1993.

She became a member of the federal parliament in 1994 on being appointed Minister for Health and Human Services.

Lawrence, Gertrude, *originally* Gertrud Alexandra Dagmar Lawrence Klasen

Born 1898 Died 1952
English actress who was a great star of the musical stage

Gertrude Lawrence was born in London. Although an undistinguished dancer and technically indifferent singer, she became one of the great stars of the Broadway musical stage. She had huge successes with musicals like *Oh, Kay!* (1926) and *Lady in the Dark* (1944).

She was also a much-acclaimed comic actress, and was particularly associated with the work of Noël Coward, beginning with *Private Lives* in 1931. Her last stage appearance came in one of her most famous productions, *The King and I* (1951).

Lawrence, Marjorie Florence

Born 1908 Died 1979
Australian operatic soprano whose period as a leading Wagnerian singer was cut short by poliomyelitis

Marjorie Lawrence was born in Deans Marsh, Victoria. She won a singing competition in nearby Geelong in 1928, and her parents were persuaded by the operatic singer John Brownlee (1900–69) to let her study overseas. She made her operatic début in 1932 with the Monte Carlo Opera, and the following year appeared in Paris. She became a member of the Metropolitan Opera, New York, in 1935 where for four years she was a leading Wagnerian soprano.

In 1941, while touring in Mexico, she contracted poliomyelitis. Returning to the USA she was treated there by Sister **Elizabeth Kenny**, and by the end of the following year was making guest appearances at 'The Met' in a wheelchair. During World War II she travelled extensively to entertain the troops, including visits to the Pacific and to Europe.

Her autobiography was filmed as *Interrupted Melody*. Later she took up teaching at the University of Southern Illinois.

Lawrence, Susan

Born 1871 Died 1947
English Labour politician who became Chairman of the Labour Party

Susan Lawrence was the daughter of a solicitor. She was educated at University College London, and won the Rothschild Exhibition for pure mathematics in 1893.

After educational appointments to the London School Board and in 1904 and 1913 to the London County Council (LCC), she committed her life to fight to improving conditions for working women.

Elected to parliament as member for East North Ham in 1923–4 and 1926–31, she became Parliamentary Private Secretary to the President of the Board of Education, Parliamentary Secretary to the Minister of Health (1929–31) and Chairman of the Labour Party (1929–31).

Lawson, Louisa, *née* Albury

Born 1848 Died 1920
Australian writer, social reformer and suffragist hailed as the originator of female suffrage in Australia

Louisa Albury was born in Guntawang, near Mudgee in New South Wales. In 1866 she married Niels Hertzberg Larsen, a Norwegian immigrant sailor-turned-goldminer, and on the birth of their son Henry (1867–1922, later a well-known writer), the family name was anglicized to Lawson. The family lived in harsh conditions in the Australian bush until Louisa left her husband and went with her five children to Sydney in 1883, where she worked as a seamstress to support them.

Soon involved in radical and feminist politics and social reform, in 1887 she bought the *Republican*, editing it with Henry until in 1888 she founded the journal *Dawn*, which she edited for 17 years, offering household advice, stories and reports on women around the world. In 1889 she founded the Dawn Club, a group that campaigned through *Dawn* mainly for female suffrage but also for 'health, temperance, social purity, education, dress reform and physiological matters'. In 1900 Lawson was thrown from a train and suffered physical and pyschological injuries from which she never fully recovered.

Australian women were given the vote in 1902, and though Lawson had played a major part in this achievement, she lived the rest of her life in poverty and died in a hospital for the insane.

Lazarus, Emma

Born 1849 Died 1887
American poet and essayist who wrote 'The New Colossus' which is inscribed on the base of the Statue of Liberty

Emma Lazarus was born in New York. She published striking volumes of poems and translations, including *Admetus and other poems* (1871), *Songs of a Semite* (1882) and *By the Waters of Babylon* (1887). She also wrote a prose romance, *Alide: An Episode of Goethe's Life* (1874), and a verse tragedy, *The Spagnaletto* (1876).

From about 1881 she championed the cause of oppressed Jews and worked to help Jewish immigrants in the USA. The sonnet, 'The New Colossus' (1883), for which she is best known, is inscribed on the Statue of Liberty in New York harbour and expresses her faith in her country as a place of sanctuary for the tired and homeless.

Leach, Janet, *née* Darnell

Born 1918
American potter who became the first foreign woman to study pottery in Japan

Janet Darnell was born in Texas and left home to study sculpture in New York City in 1937. She worked as a sculptor's assistant on the Federal Arts Project — a project designed by the US government to assist artists who had been hard hit by the Depression — and during World War II was a welder on Navy destroyers. Her interest in ceramics began to grow in 1947, and she studied at the Inwood Pottery and Alfred University.

She became interested in the philosophy and technique of Japanese pottery and, after

meeting Bernard Leach (whom she later married) and Shoji Hamada, she went on to study in Japan, travelling widely.

Her work in reduction fired stoneware (for which the air in the kiln is kept to a minimum for various effects) is influenced by both the 'Leach tradition' and Shoji Hamada; it has a ragged quality and is often decorated in freely coloured slips and drip glazes.

Leakey, Mary Douglas, *née* Nicol

Born 1913
English archaeologist and anthropologist whose excavations and fossil finds in East Africa revolutionized ideas about human origins

Mary Nicol was born in London. Her interest in prehistory was roused during childhood trips to south-west France, where she collected stone tools and visited the painted caves around Les Eyzies. She met her future husband Louis Leakey while preparing drawings for his book *Adam's Ancestors* (1934), and moved shortly afterwards to Kenya where she undertook pioneering archaeological research (1937–42) at sites such as Olorgesailie and Rusinga Island.

In 1948, at Rusinga, in Lake Victoria, she discovered *Proconsul africanus*, a 1.7 million-year-old dryopithecine (primitive ape) that brought the Leakeys international attention and financial sponsorship for the first time. From 1951 she worked at Olduvai Gorge in Tanzania, initially on a modest scale, but more extensively from 1959 when her discovery of the 1.75 million-year-old hominid *Zinjanthropus* (subsequently reclassified as *Australopithecus*), filmed as it happened, captured the public imagination and drew vastly increased funding. *Homo habilis* — a new species contemporary with, but more advanced than *Zinjanthropus* — was found in 1960 and published amidst much controversy in 1964. Perhaps most remarkable of all was her excavation in 1976 at Laetoli, 30 miles south of Olduvai, of three trails of fossilized hominid footprints which demonstrated unequivocally that our ancestors already walked upright 3.6 million years ago.

Her books include *Olduvai Gorge: My Search for Early Man* (1979) and an autobiography, *Disclosing the Past* (1984). Her son Richard Leakey (1944–   ) also became a distinguished palaeoanthropologist.

Lease, Mary Elizabeth, *née* Clyens

Born 1853 Died 1933
American reformer who was renowned for her powerful rhetoric and energetic campaigning

Mary Clyens was born in Ridgway, Pennsylvania, the daughter of an Irish political refugee. She married Charles Lease in 1873 and became an energetic orator for such causes as women's suffrage and prohibition of alcohol. In 1885–7 she gave a series of lectures on Irish matters which gained her recognition.

She worked effectively for the Populist Party in 1890–6, earning the nickname of the 'Kansas Pythoness' for the strength of her populist rhetoric. Her command to 'raise less corn and more hell' became the Party's slogan.

In 1902, the year of her divorce, she became lecturer for the New York City Board of Education, a post she held for 16 years. She also wrote on political matters, publishing *The Problem of Civilization Solved* in 1895.

Leavis, Q(ueenie) D(orothy), *née* Roth

Born 1906 Died 1981
English literary critic whose real influence was on and through the work of her well-known husband

Q D Roth was born in London. She studied at Girton College, Cambridge, under the scholar and critic I A Richards. Though her powerful sociological analysis of 19th-century fiction made a substantial impact on her literary critic husband F R Leavis (1895–1978), whom she married in 1929, she has only rarely (and posthumously) received full credit for it.

Despite writing regularly for Leavis's journal *Scrutiny*, and continuing to publish perceptive essays and papers on literary subjects, she wrote only one book — *Fiction and the Reading Public* (1932). This may be the reason for her contribution usually being overlooked.

Though by no means a doctrinaire feminist, she had a particular interest in women's writing and wrote shrewdly about the **Brontë** sisters, **Jane Austen** and **Edith Wharton**. Some of her best essays were posthumously collected.

Leavitt, Henrietta Swan

Born 1868 Died 1921
American astronomer who discovered that there is a relationship between period and luminosity in certain stars

Henrietta Leavitt was born in Lancaster, Massachusetts, the daughter of a Congregational minister. She was educated at Radcliffe College, where she developed an interest in astronomy. She became a volunteer research assistant at Harvard College Observatory and joined the staff there in 1902, quickly becoming head of the department of photographic photometry. Like **Annie Jump Cannon**, her colleague, she was very deaf, and she too discovered (four) novae and numerous variable stars.

She is best known for her discovery of the period–luminosity relationship of Cepheid variable stars — stars whose brightness varies for periods lasting from a few days to several months. Whilst studying Cepheids she noticed that the brighter they were, the longer their period of light variation. By 1912 she had succeeded in showing that the apparent magnitude decreased linearly with the logarithm of the period.

This simple relationship proved invaluable as the basis for a method of measuring the distance of stars, including their distances from Earth, and the size of the Milky Way.

Lecouvreur, Adrienne

Born 1692 Died 1730
French tragic actress who was extraordinarily popular in her lifetime and lastingly inspirational after her suspicious death

Adrienne Lecouvreur was born near Chalons. She made her début at the Comédie Française in 1717 as the title role in Prosper Jolyot de Crébillon's *Électre*, and soon became famous for her naturalistic style of acting, and for her admirers, amongst whom were Marshal de Saxe (her lover during the 1720s), Voltaire and Lord Peterborough.

She had rivals among other leading actresses, but managed to secure highly successful parts in the plays of Molière and Racine. Some ascribed her death to poisoning by a jealous aquaintance. Since she had not officially renounced her profession as an actress, she was refused a Christian burial — a hypocritcal outrage, in Voltaire's opinion, that prompted him to write a lament.

Her life is the subject of the play *Adrienne Lecouvreur* (1848) by Eugène Scribe and Ernest Legouvé in which **Élisa Rachel** and subsequently **Sarah Bernhardt** starred.

Lee, Ann, *known as* Mother Ann

Born 1736 Died 1784
English-born American mystic who founded the main Shaker settlement

Ann Lee was the illiterate daughter of a Manchester blacksmith. In 1762 she married Abraham Stanley, also a blacksmith. Four years previously she had joined a radical branch of the Quakers called the 'Shaking Quakers' or 'Shakers'.

In 1770 she was imprisoned for street-preaching, and she claimed to have had a vision in prison which convinced her that it was essential for people to remain celibate if they wanted to succeed in doing Christ's work. Responding to another vision, she emigrated with her husband and followers to the USA in 1774, and in 1776 founded the parent Shaker settlement at Niskayuna (now Watervliet), near Albany, in what is now New York state. The Shakers saw in her the second coming of Christ, for she embodied the apparently missing female half of the divine dual nature, and accepted her as their leader.

Mother Ann was imprisoned for her pacifism for a time in 1780 and then on her release toured New England in 1781–3, preaching and allegedly performing miracles of healing as she went.

Lee, Brenda, *née* Brenda Mae Tarpley

Born 1945
American singer who as a rising star became known as 'Little Miss Dynamite'

Brenda Lee was born in Lithonia, Georgia. She began her career in 1956 as a child country star regularly appearing on Red Foley's country-and-western television show *Ozark Jubilee*.

During the 1950s she became a rock 'n' roll star and was nicknamed 'Little Miss Dynamite' because her of her small stature and very powerful voice. She is best known for the song 'I'm Sorry'.

She moved to country music in the 1970s and had virtually retired by the 1980s.

Lee, Gypsy Rose, *stage name of* Rose Louise Hovick

Born 1914   Died 1970
American burlesque star, the first to receive widespread fame and gain entrance into Broadway revues

Gypsy Rose Lee was born in Seattle, Washington. She performed in a vaudeville routine with her sister June as a child from 1922 to 1928, and by the age of 17 had joined the striptease troupe at Minsky's Burlesque in New York.

She developed a sophisticated song style to accompany her suggestive, teasing dancing, and became the first burlesque artist to achieve widespread fame. She was also the first to transfer her act to the legitimate Broadway stage when she played in the *Ziegfeld Follies* (1936), as well as in other prominent venues.

She was the author of plays and stories, and her autobiography, *Gypsy* (1957), was adapted for the stage as a musical comedy.

Gypsy Rose Lee

Lee, (Nelle) Harper

Born 1926
American novelist who is known for her modern classic To Kill a Mockingbird

Harper Lee was born in Alabama and educated at Alabama State University. Her only novel, *To Kill A Mockingbird* (1960), was an immediate success, and has subsequently enhanced its reputation as a modern classic. Narrated by Scout, a six-year-old white tomboy in the American south, it is centred on a trial at which Scout's father is the defence lawyer for a black man accused of raping a white woman. It won a Pulitzer Prize in 1961, and was made into a highly successful film (1962) starring Gregory Peck.

Lee, Vernon, *pseud of* Violet Paget

Born 1856   Died 1935
English aesthetic philosopher, critic, and novelist
whose reputation oscillated between excellence
and condemnation

Violet Paget was born in Boulogne of English parentage. She travelled widely in her youth and lived in Florence for a time. She wrote successful studies of Italian and Renaissance art which were followed by her philosophical study, *The Beautiful* (1913), one of the best expositions of the empathy theory of art.

She also wrote travel books including *Genius Loci* (1899) and *The Sentimental Traveller* (1908), the novels *Miss Brown* (1884) and *Vanitas* (1892), which were not well received, a play *Ariadne in Manuta* (1903), and a dramatic trilogy *Satan the Waster* (1920), which gave full rein to her pacifism. In all she produced some 45 volumes.

Her family in England disapproved of her homosexuality, so she spent some time in Paris attending the famous salon in the Rue Jacob, which was frequented between the wars by such literary figures as **Janet Flanner**, **Djuna Barnes** and **Natalie Barney**.

Lee of Asheridge, Jennie Lee, Baroness

Born 1904   Died 1988
Scottish Labour politician who became Britain's
first Minister of Arts

Jennie Lee was born in Lochgelly, Fife, the daughter of a miner. She graduated from Edinburgh University with degrees in education and law. At the age of 24, as a Labour MP for North Lanark, she became the youngest member of the House of Commons. She was a dedicated socialist, and campaigned with great wit and intelligence.

In 1934 she married the Welsh politician Aneurin Bevan (1897–1960) and, despite her feminist principles, consciously stepped to one side as he rose within the Labour party. After being appointed as Britain's first Arts Minister in 1964, she doubled government funding for the arts and was instrumental in setting up the Open University.

She published two autobiographies, *Tomorrow is a New Day* (1939) and *My Life with Nye* (1980).

Lee-Smith, Diana

Born 1940
British architect who works to aid African poverty
and housing conditions

Diana Lee-Smith trained at the Architectural Association, London, where she received her diploma in 1964. She took up a teaching post in the University of East Africa in Nairobi, Kenya, in 1969, where she realised that her professional skills were not adequate to deal with the problems facing poverty-stricken communities. With her Kenyan-born husband and other professionals, she set up a non-profit research and development organization. The group's aim was to improve local building material production, construction skills and housing standards.

In 1981 Lee-Smith became editor of Settlements Information Network Africa, which links 32 African countries. Since 1987, the International Year of Shelter for the Homeless, she has been a co-ordinator of Habitat International Coalition and she was responsible for setting up the HIC Women and Shelter network.

LeFanu, Nicola Frances

Born 1947
English composer whose best-known work is The
Old Woman of Beare *which draws on medieval*
Irish texts

Nicola LeFanu was born in Wickham Bishops, Essex, the daughter of Dame **Elizabeth Maconchy**. She was educated in Wiltshire, and at Oxford and the Royal College of Music, London (1968–9).

Her first published compositions, which established a pattern of meticulous lyricism, often with a Celtic flavour, were followed by post-graduate composition study at Harvard under Earl Kim (1973–4). *The Old Woman of Beare* appeared in 1981.

In 1979 she married the Australian composer David Lumsdaine. She shared a senior teaching post with him at King's College London from 1977 to 1993, the year she was appointed Professor of Musical Composition.

Lefauchaux, Marie-Helene, *née* Postel-Vinay

Born 1904   Died 1964
French Resistance fighter who became an
international spokeswoman for the rights of
women worldwide

Marie-Helene Postel-Vinay was born in Paris. She was a middle-class intellectual who is best remembered for the part she played, along with her husband Pierre Lefauchaux, in the French Resistance of World War II. A woman of great resourcefulness as well as courage, she succeeded in having her husband released from Buchenwald, and her service in the War brought her a number of decorations, including the Croix de Guerre and Chevalier of the Legion d'Honneur.

She became prominent in the municipal administration of Paris both before and immediately following the War, before she embarked on a career as a professional diplomat for women's rights, particularly those of students for French colonial Africa. A member of France's United Nations delegation of seven years in the period 1946–59, she was awarded the presidency of the International Council of Women from 1957 to 1963. She died in a plane crash in the USA.

Le Fort, Gertrud von

Born 1876 Died 1971
German novelist and poet whose work explores
religious themes within historical backgrounds

Gertrud von Le Fort was born into an aristocratic, originally Huguenot, family in Minden. She wrote her most famous collection of poems, *Hymnen an die Kirche* (1924, Eng trans *Hymns to the Church*, 1937) as a Protestant; then she became a Catholic, and wrote dedicated novels and poems in the interests of her new faith.

Her *Die Letze am Schafort* (1931, Eng trans *The Song of the Scaffold*, 1953) formed the basis for Poulenc's well-known opera *Dialogues de Carmelites* (1956), which in turn inspired the film script by French writer Georges Bernanos on the same theme. Selected novellas are in *The Judgement of the Sea* (1962).

Le Gallienne, Eva

Born 1899 Died 1991
English actress, director and producer who became
an influential figure in American theatre

Eva Le Gallienne was born in London, the daughter of the writer Richard Le Gallienne. She was brought up in Paris, and made her début in London in 1914 in *Mona Vanna*, before studying for a year under Herbert Beerbohm Tree and moving to New York.

After a series of bit parts and big disappointments, she began to come to notice in the early 1920s, beginning with such roles as Elsie Dover in Arthur Richman's *Not So Long Ago*. She was the founder (1926) and director of the Civic Repertory Theater on 14th Street in New York, acting in and directing most of the 37 plays produced there before it closed in 1935. She was then co-founder and director of the American Repertory Theatre (1946–8).

She continued to act until the early 1980s, and was renowned for her Chekhovian roles.

Her honours included the National Medal of the Arts (the highest award for an artist in the USA).

Legge, Diane

Born c.1950
American architect who won an American
Institute of Architects Distinguished Building
Award

Diane Legge was born in Englewood, New Jersey, and trained at Stanford University (1972) and Princeton University (1975). In 1977 she joined the Chicago office of Skidmore, Owings and Merrill and worked on many of Chicago's famous modern buildings, becoming a partner in charge of design in 1982.

In 1984 she won an American Institute of Architects Distinguished Building Award for the Boston Globe Printing Plant, Billerica, Massachusetts. Her design skills made what could have been a vast, featureless shed into a sophisticated and enjoyable place of work. Her other work includes the Arlington International Racecourse in Illinois (1988), and the Bethesda Metro development in Maryland (1989).

Le Guin, Ursula, *née* Kroeber

Born 1929
American science-fiction writer whose creation of
new cultures shows up the deficiencies of modern-
day society

Ursula Kroeber was born in Berkeley, California, the daughter of anthropologist Alfred Louis Kroeber (1876–1960). She was educated at Radcliffe College and Columbia University. She is a prolific writer both for adults and children, and has demonstrated that it is possible to work in genre and be taken seriously as a writer.

Much of her work focuses on subjective views of a universe incorporating numerous habitable worlds, each spawned by beings from the 'Hain'. Hain novels include *Rocannon's World* (1966), *Plant of Exile* (1966), *The Left Hand of Darkness* (1969), and *The Word for World is Forest* (1976).

In a prodigious oeuvre for children, known as the 'Earthsea' trilogy — *A Wizard of Earthsea* (1968), *The Tombs of Atuan* (1971) and *The Farthest Shore* (1972) — she depicts a magical but threatening world where every village has its small-time sorcerer and the forces of evil are uncomfortably close. She continued this trilogy in an overtly feminist vein with *Tehanu* (1990).

Lehmann, Beatrix

Born 1903 Died 1979
English actress, writer, director and producer

Beatrix Lehmann was born in Bourne End, Buckinghamshire, a daughter of the journalist Rudolph Chambers Lehmann and sister of **Rosamond Lehmann** and the poet John Lehmann. She was trained as an actress at RADA.

In 1924 she made her London début in the role of Peggy in *The Way of the World* at the Lyric, Hammersmith, following which she appeared in such successful plays as *Family Reunion*, Peter Ustinov's *No Sign of the Dove*, and *Waltz of the Toreadors*.

In 1946 she became director and producer of the Arts Council Midland Theatre Company. She also acted in films and wrote two novels and several short stories.

Lehmann, Inge

Born 1888 Died 1993
Danish geophysicist who in 1936 made the discovery of the Earth's inner core

Inge Lehmann was born in Copenhagen. She was educated at a school founded by an aunt of the physicist Niels Bohr, where girls were encouraged to study the same subjects as boys, and entered Copenhagen University in 1907 to read mathematics. After a year at Newnham College, Cambridge (1910–11), she pursued a career in insurance until 1918, though she maintained an interest and contacts in science. Her studies were resumed in 1918, and she received her degree in 1920. She was awarded her PhD at the University of Copenhagen in 1928.

From 1928 until her retirement in 1953, she was chief of the seismological department of the newly founded Danish Geodetic Institute, taking responsibility for the seismological stations in Greenland. Lehmann's research involved the interpretation of seismic events detected by European stations; in this work she discovered that the presence of a distinct inner core of the Earth was required to explain the data received from large epicentral distances.

In collaboration with the German-born American geophysicist Beno Gutenberg (1889–1960) she also endeavoured to resolve a velocity structure compatible with the revised traveltime tables of the English physicist Harold Jeffreys (1877–1946), and found a low-velocity layer at 200 kilometres depth. This fitted well with European seismic data and became accepted generally.

Lehmann, Lilli

Born 1848 Died 1929
German operatic soprano who sang in the first performance of the Ring cycle

Lilli Lehmann was born in Würzburg. She was taught singing in Prague by her mother, and made her début there in *Die Zauberflöte* (1865). Developing an enormous repertory of around 170 roles, she sang mainly in Berlin, New York and Bayreuth, where she took part in the first performance of Wagner's *Ring des Nibelungen* (1876). She also sang at the Salzburg festival (1901–10), which she helped to organize, and in Danzig, Leipzig, London, and elsewhere.

She was hailed as a magnificent Isolde in Wagner's opera *Tristan und Isolde* and also became known for her lieder singing. She retired from the operatic stage in 1909, but continued to give recitals until 1920.

Lehmann, Liza (Elizabeth) Nina Mary Frederika

Born 1862 Died 1918
English soprano and composer who is known especially for her song-cycles

Liza Lehmann was born in London. She had a successful career as a concert singer until 1894, then devoted herself to composition.

Her works include ballads, light operas such as *The Vicar of Wakefield* (1906), and song-cycles, particularly *In a Persian Garden* (1896), which has words from Edward Fitz-Gerald's translation of *Rubáiyát of Omar Khayyám*.

Lehmann, Lotte

Born 1888 Died 1976
German-born American soprano famed for singing Schumann's songs and Strauss's operas

Lotte Lehmann was born in Perleberg. She studied in Berlin, made her début in Hamburg in 1910, and sang at the Vienna Staatsoper (1914–38). She also appeared frequently at Covent Garden between 1924 and 1938 and at the New York Metropolitan (1934–45).

She was noted for her performances of Robert Schumann's songs and for her roles in operas by Richard Strauss, including the Marschallin in *Der Rosenkavalier* and for the premières of his *Die Frau ohne Schattin* (1919, 'The Woman without a Shadow') and *Intermezzo* (1924).

She took US nationality, and in 1951 retired to teach in Santa Barbara.

Lehmann, Rosamond Nina

Born 1901 Died 1990
English writer whose novels show insight into
character and a brilliant portrayal of women

Rosamond Lehmann was born in High Wycombe, Buckinghamshire, a daughter of the journalist Rudolph Chambers Lehmann and the sister of **Beatrix Lehmann** and the poet, editor and publisher John Lehmann. She was educated at Girton College, Cambridge, which provided the background for her first novel, *Dusty Answer* (1927), and was co-director of her brother's company John Lehmann Ltd from 1946 to 1953.

Among her other books are *A Note in Music* (1930), *An Invitation to the Waltz* (1932) and its sequel *The Weather in the Streets* (1936), and *The Echoing Grove* (1953). Her last novel was *A Sea-Grape Tree* (1970). She also wrote a play, *No More Music* (1939), and a volume of short stories, *The Gypsy's Baby* (1946). She produced the autobiographical *The Swan in the Evening* in 1967.

She later developed a belief in spiritualism, and became President of the College of Psychic Studies.

Vivien Leigh in *Gone With the Wind*, 1939

Leigh, Vivien, *originally* Vivian Mary Hartley

Born 1913 Died 1967
English actress who won Oscars for her
performances in Gone With the Wind *and* A Streetcar Named Desire

Vivien Leigh was born in Darjeeling, India. After studying at RADA she made her professional début in the film *Things Are Looking Up* (1934). Her stage début followed in *The Green Sash* (1935) and in the same year she was an overnight sensation in the comedy *The Mask of Virtue*.

A charming, vixenish actress of great beauty, she was married to actor Laurence Olivier from 1940 to 1961 and appeared opposite him in numerous classical plays including *Romeo and Juliet* (1940, New York), *Antony and Cleopatra* (1951, New York), and *Macbeth* (1955, Stratford). Persistent ill health and frequent bouts of manic depression curtailed her career, but she did give two electrifying Academy Award-winning performances in *Gone With the Wind* (1939) and *A Streetcar Named Desire* (1951).

After her divorce from Olivier she worked on stage and made a final film appearance in *Ship of Fools* (1965). She died from tuberculosis.

Leighton, Clare Veronica Hope

Born 1901 Died 1989
English-born American artist best known for her
wood engravings

Clare Leighton was born in London to a literary family. She trained at the Brighton School of Art and the Slade School of Art prior to learning engraving under Noel Rooke at the Central School of Arts and Crafts. She wrote several books on engraving, then moved to the USA in 1939, becoming a US citizen in 1945.

Although she continued to paint, she was best known for her wood engravings which have a monumental quality using large areas of dark, defined by finely engraved lines often depicting labourers, farm workers or the fishermen of Cape Cod.

She held many titles, including Vice-President of both the National Institute of Arts and Letters and the Society of American Graphic Art. Boston Public Library lists some 789 engravings by her as well as work in other media such as stained glass and mosaic.

Leighton, Margaret

Born 1922 Died 1976
English actress who was a leading stage actress of
her generation

Margaret Leighton was born near Birmingham. She was the tall, slender, very distinguished leading lady in a large number of stage plays and films, and became one of the best known actresses of her era.

She trained for the stage as a teenager, and joined the Old Vic under Olivier and Richardson in the 1940s, and made her Broadway début in 1946. Her major plays include Terence Rattigan's *Separate Tables* (1956) and Tennessee Williams's *The Night of the Iguana* (1961). She was nominated for an Academy Award for the film *The Go-Between* (1971). She died from multiple sclerosis.

Leitch, Cecil (Charlotte Cecilia Pitcairn)

Born 1891 Died 1977
English golfer whose excellent performance led to the introduction of plus handicapping

Cecil Leitch was born in Silloth, Cumbria, the daughter of a Scottish doctor. The Ladies Golf Union (LGU) re-wrote their eligibilty rules to allow her to play for England.

Used to practising with her local male county team, she fulfilled her early promise in a famous match against Harold Hilton in 1910, where she was given a stroke on the even holes and defeated him convincingly. She was instrumental again in changing golf history when her performances prompted the LGU to introduce plus handicapping.

Despite the fact that her career was dissected by World War I, she won the British championship four times — a record equalled only by her contemporary **Joyce Wethered**, as well as two English and five French titles.

Lenclos, Ninon de, *pseud of* Anne de Lenclos

Born 1620 Died 1705
French feminist and light poet who is more famous for her lifestyle than for her literature

Anne de Lenclos was born and died in Paris. She had many high-society lovers from literary and political milieux, founded a *salon* which favoured Jansenists, was a close friend to Saint Évremond, and could hold her own with La Rochefoucauld and the other thinkers and wits of her time.

Her ungodly behaviour cost her a spell in a convent in 1656 at the behest of **Anne of Austria**, but her popularity ensured a swift release, and afterwards she wrote *La Coquette vengée* (1659) in her own defence. Celebrated nearly as much for her manners as for her beauty, she was sometimes sent the children of respectable families in the hope that they would acquire taste, style, and politeness.

In later life, when she had retired from

being a 'courtesan', her salon acquired great respectability.

Leng, Virginia Helen Antoinette, *married name* Elliot, *née* Holgate

Born 1955
British equestrian event rider who was a frequent winner during the 1980s

Virginia Leng was born in Malta. She was the European junior champion in 1973, and won the team gold at the senior championship in 1985, 1987 and 1989, and individual titles in 1985 (on 'Priceless'), 1987 (on 'Night Cap') and 1989 (on 'Master Craftsman').

In the World Championship she won team silver in 1984 and 1988, and the individual title in 1986 on 'Priceless'. In the Olympic Games she has won the bronze individual medal twice: in 1984 (on 'Priceless') and in 1988 (on 'Master Craftsman'). She has also won three times at Badminton (1985, 1989, 1993), and five times at Burghley (1983–6, 1989). Her first marriage was to Hamish Leng, and in 1993 she married Michel Elliot and adopted his surname.

Lenglen, Suzanne

Born 1899 Died 1938
French tennis player who is regarded as one of the best female players of all time

Suzanne Lenglen was born in Compiègne and was trained by her father. She became famous in 1914 by winning the women's world hardcourt singles championship at Paris at the age of 15 and went on to be the dominant woman player from 1919 to 1926.

She was the ladies champion of France (1919–23, 1925–6), and her Wimbledon championships were the women's singles and doubles (1919–23, 1925) and the mixed doubles (1920, 1922, 1925). She also won the singles and doubles gold medals at the 1920 Olympic Games.

She became a professional in 1926, toured the USA, and retired in 1927 to found the Lenglen School of Tennis in Paris. She published *Lawn Tennis, the Game of Nations* (1925) and a novel, *The Love-Game* (1925), and set a new fashion in female tennis dress.

Lenngren, Anna Maria, *née* Malmstedt

Born 1754 Died 1817
Swedish poet and journalist whose elegant satires invigorated Swedish journalism

Anna Maria Malmstedt was born in Uppsala. She received a good education and became an accomplished translator from French and Latin. In 1780 she married Carl Lenngren, co-founder and later editor of the radical *Stockholms-Posten* and, anonymously, began to contribute to his newspaper.

She published — up to 1797 anonymously — elegant satires as well as sharply observed and humorously realistic poems. These latter are superbly skilful in their handling of metre and rhyme and are characterized by a simple and mercilessly precise language, conveying vivid images of a broad range of contemporary life, and exposing the ruling classes to an intrepid satire.

A number of her poems were set to music and remain popular songs to this day.

Lennox, Annie

Born 1954
Scottish pop singer who is a former member of
The Eurythmics

Annie Lennox was born in Aberdeen. She was waitressing in Hampstead in 1977 when she met musician and composer Dave Stewart. The pair formed The Tourists, a band which recorded three albums before splitting up in 1980.

Lennox and Stewart stayed together as The Eurythmics, and continued the group even after their personal relationship ended the following year. The band's albums have included *Sweet Dreams* (1982), *Touch* (1983), *Be Yourself Tonight* (1985), and *Savage* (1987).

Although she had become one of Scotland's best-known pop singers she took a break from music in 1990, but returned in 1992 to launch a solo career with the album *Diva*.

Lenshina, Alice

Birthdate unavailable
Zambian leader whose millenarian movement
opposed the Zambian President

Alice Lenshina was the leader of a millenarian movement called the Lumpa Church which from 1964 led opposition to the newly independent regime in Zambia. The church and its followers represented the split between urban politics and rural aspirations, between modernizers and traditionalists.

Lenshina's church became a major focus of opposition to the regime of President Kenneth Kaunda, who was premier from 1964 to 1991.

Lenya, Lotte, *originally* Karoline Wilhelmine Blamauer

Born 1900 Died 1981
Austrian actress and cabaret singer who is
considered the supreme interpreter of Kurt Weill's
work

Karoline Blamauer was born in Hitzing, Vienna. She made her public bow in a local circus at the age of six and was tightrope-walking two years later. In 1914 she moved to Switzerland and studied ballet at the Stadt Theatre in Zürich. She became a talented, all-round performer, and moved to Berlin in 1920 where she came to represent the spirit of that decadent era with her husky and emotional voice.

In 1926 she married the German composer Kurt Weill (1900–50) and starred in many of his works, such as *The Little Mahagonny* (1927) and *The Threepenny Opera* (1928). In 1933 the couple fled to Paris and in 1935 settled in the USA. Her New York stage appearances include *The Eternal Road* (1937), *Candle in the Wind* (1941) and *The Firebrand of Florence* (1945). After Weill's death she became the public custodian of his legacy.

Later stage appearances include *The Threepenny Opera* (1954), *Brecht on Brecht* (1962), *Cabaret* (1966) and *Mother Courage* (1972) and among her rare film roles are *The Threepenny Opera* (1931), *From Russia With Love* (1963) and *Semi-Tough* (1977).

Lerner, Gerda

Born 1920
American historian whose wish is to change the
perspective of historical study

Gerda Lerner was born in Vienna, Austria. She has challenged traditional history by exposing its male bias. Her goal is to change the study of history by recovering the role of women in history and correcting the distortions of androcentrism.

Her works include *The Woman in American History* (1971) and *The Female Experience: An American Documentary* (1977).

Leslie, Ann Elizabeth Mary

Birthdate unavailable
British journalist and broadcaster, known mainly
for her work for the Daily Mail

Ann Leslie was born in Pakistan. Educated in convent schools in Derbyshire and Sussex, and at Oxford University, she joined the staff of the *Daily Express* in Manchester in 1962 and after five years went freelance. She married Michael Fletcher in 1969 and now works mainly as foreign news correspondent for the *Daily Mail*. Over the course of her career she has reported from 70 countries, including Zimbabwe, Ethiopia, China, Russia, South Africa, as well as on the Gulf War and the war in the former Yugoslavia.

Leslie is a respected figure in her field and has received several awards for her journalism and broadcasting, including the Variety Club Woman of the Year Award in 1981, and four British Press Awards Commendations.

L'Esperance, Elise, *née* Strang

Born 1878 Died 1959
American physician and founder of women's
cancer clinics

Elise Strang was born in Yorktown, New York. She studied at the Women's Medical College in New York established by **Elizabeth Blackwell**, receiving her MD in 1900. She studied and worked in paediatrics for some years, during which time she married and divorced David L'Esperance.

In 1910 she moved to the department of pathology at Cornell University, where she remained until 1932, becoming the first woman assistant professor there in 1920. Her research on cancer stimulated her to found the Kate Depew Strang clinics in memory of her mother.

Important work carried out at the Strang clinics included the development by Dr George Papanicolacu of the 'Pap' smear to detect cervical cancer. L'Esperance was active in many women's organizations, medical and non-medical, and was widely honoured for her work.

Lespinasse, Julie Jeanne Eléanore de, *also known as Claire Françoise de Lespinasse*

Born 1732 Died 1776
French hostess who presided over one of Paris's
most brilliant salons

Julie de Lespinasse was born in Lyons, an illegitimate daughter of the Countess d'Albon. At first a teacher, in 1754 she became companion to the ailing Marquise du **Deffand**, hostess of a leading Paris salon, where she formed a deep platonic relationship with the philosopher Jean d'Alembert.

In 1764 Mademoiselle de Lespinasse broke with the Marquise and, taking with her some of the elder lady's admirers, created a brilliant salon of her own for the literary figures of her day. Although not strikingly beautiful, she formed liaisons with the Marquis de More and the Comte de Guibert, to whom she wrote beautifully crafted letters of ardent (but unrequited) love that were later published (*Lettres*, 1809).

Lessing, Doris May, *née* Tayler

Born 1919
British writer whose work considers the effects of
political and social changes

Doris Tayler was born in Kermanshah, Persia (called Iran since 1935), the daughter of a British army captain. Her family moved to Southern Rhodesia (Zimbabwe since 1979) and she lived in Salisbury 1937–49, when she became involved in politics and helped to start a non-racialist left-wing party. She was married twice while living in Rhodesia (Lessing is her second husband's name).

Her experiences of life in working-class London after 1949 are described in *In Pursuit of the English* (1960). She joined the Communist Party but left it in 1956, in which year Rhodesia declared her a 'prohibited immigrant'. Her first published novel was *The Grass is Singing* (1950), a study of the sterility of white civilization in Africa. *This was the Old Chief's Country* (1951), a collection of short studies, continued this theme. In 1952 *Martha Quest* appeared, the first novel in her sequence *The Children of Violence* (completed in *A Proper Marriage*, 1954, *A Ripple from the Storm*, 1958, *Landlocked*, 1965, and *The Four-Gated City*, 1969), throughout which runs the theme of the ideal city where there is no violence. The city is, however, unattainable, and political and personal catastrophe is seen as inevitable. Other novels include *The Golden Notebook*

Doris Lessing

(1962) and *Briefing for a Descent into Hell* (1971) and other collections of short stories include *A Man and Two Women* (1963), *African Stories* (1964), and *The Story of a Non-marrying Man* (1972).

Latterly, in *Canopus in Argos: Archives*, a quintet of novels, Lessing has attempted science fiction but her commitment to exploring political and social undercurrents in contemporary society can still be seen to potent effect in *The Good Terrorist* (1985) and *The Fifth Child* (1988). She published the autobiographical volume, *Under My Skin*, in 1994.

Lessore, Thérèse

Born 1884 Died 1945
English painter of landscapes, interiors and theatre subjects, associated with the London Group

Thérèse Lessore was born in Brighton, a daughter of the artist Jules Lessore. She studied at the South Western Polytechnic Art School before attending the Slade (1904–9), where she won the Melville–Nettleship prize in her final year.

She married the artist William Sickert in 1926, becoming his third wife, and was very much influenced by his work, particularly the music-hall paintings which captured fleeting moments of human interest. Both she and **Sylvia Gosse** carried out the preparatory work on his paintings as he became older.

Her first one-person exhibition was held in 1918 and her association with the Leicester Gallery, which had begun in 1924, ended with a memorial exhibition in 1946.

Leverson, Ada, *née* Beddington

Born 1865 Died 1936
English novelist and journalist who wrote witty novels and was a loyal friend to Oscar Wilde

Ada Leverson was born in London. After being educated privately, she married Ernest Leverson at the age of 18 and became a member of the circle which included the writers Max Beerbohm and Oscar Wilde, whom she bravely supported during his trials in 1895. Wilde referred to her as 'The Sphinx'.

Having published literary parodies in *Punch*, she contributed stories for *The Yellow Book* and, as 'Elaine', wrote over 100 columns for *The Referee*, in some of which she satirized other advice columnists.

Her six novels, written between 1907 and 1916, include such titles as *Love's Shadow* (1908), *Tenterhooks* (1912) and *Love at Second Sight* (1916). They are domestic stories of difficult marriages (not unlike her own to the gambler Ernest Leverson), and rely for their readability mainly on the author's wit.

Levertov, Denise

Born 1923
English-born American poet and essayist whose work questions political and cultural issues

Denise Levertov was born in Ilford, Essex, into a literary household. She was the daughter of a Welsh mother and a Russian Jewish father who became an Anglican clergyman. She was educated privately, served as a civilian nurse during World War II, emigrated to the USA in 1948, and was appointed poetry editor of *The Nation* in 1961.

The Double Image (1946) was her first collection of verse and others have appeared steadily. A 'British Romantic with almost Victorian background', she has been outspoken on many issues (Vietnam, feminism, etc) and her poetry is similarly questioning. Her attachment to the 'Black Mountain' poets like Charles Olson and William Carlos Williams is palpable but her voice is distinctive. *With Eyes at the Back of Our Heads* (1959), *Relearning the Alphabet* (1970), *To Stay Alive* (1971) and *Footprints* (1972) particularly stand out.

Levi-Montalcini, Rita

Born 1909
Italian neuroscientist and joint Nobel Prize winner for her discovery of the nerve growth factor

Rita Levi-Montalcini was born and educated in Turin, where she graduated in medicine in 1936. She began studying the mechanisms of how nerves grow, but from 1939 onwards was prevented, as a Jew, from holding an academic position, and worked from a home laboratory. During the latter part of World War II she served as a volunteer physician.

In 1947 she was invited by Viktor Hamburger to Washington University in St Louis, where she remained until 1981 (Research Associate 1947–51; Associate Professor 1951–8; Professor 1958–81), when she moved to Rome. Her work has primarily been on chemical factors that control the growth and development of cells, and she isolated, originally from mouse salivary glands, a substance now called nerve growth factor that promotes the development of sympathetic nerves. Her work continued on locating further sources of the factor, on determining its chemical nature (it comes from diverse sources but is chemically a protein), and examining its biological activity in isolated tissues and whole neonatal and adult animals. This work has provided powerful new insights into processes of some neurological diseases and possible repair therapies, into tissue regeneration, and into cancer mechanisms.

In 1986 she shared the Nobel Prize for Physiology or Medicine with American biochemist Stanley Cohen (1922–   ).

Levison, Mary Irene, *née* Lusk

Born 1923
English Presbyterian reformer and minister who
helped to bring about the Church of Scotland's
decision to ordain women

Mary Lusk was born in Oxford. She studied philosophy at Oxford University and theology at Edinburgh, Heidelberg, and Basel, eventually beginning work as a deaconess of the Church of Scotland in 1954. After a period as assistant chaplain to Edinburgh University, she petitioned the General Assembly in 1963 to be ordained to the Ministry of Word and Sacrament, setting in motion a process of debate that was to culminate in the historic decision of the General Assembly (1968) to permit the ordination of women.

Although Levison was not, in the end, the first woman minister of the Church of Scotland (Catherine McConachie of Aberdeen enjoyed that honour in 1968), she inspired and engendered the momentum that made such a possibility a reality, and the integrity, intelligence and dignity with which she so effectively made her case did much to hasten the process.

Levison was herself ordained to serve as the assistant minister at St Andrew's and St George's Parish Church in Edinburgh in 1978. Later appointed the first female Chaplain to the Queen (1991–3), she was an extra Chaplain to the Queen in Scotland from 1993. She published *Wrestling with the Church* in 1992.

Levitt, Helen

Born 1913
American photographer best known for her
poignant and witty urban documentation,
especially of New York street life

Helen Levitt was born in Brooklyn, New York. She worked for a portrait photographer in the Bronx in 1931, studied at the Art Students League in New York, in 1956–7, and was strongly influenced by photographer Henri Cartier-Bresson (1908–   ) who lived in New York in 1935.

She began small-camera street photography in 1936, and in 1937 started to photograph children at play, while teaching art to East Harlem children under a Federal Art Project. In 1938 she assisted the photographer Walker Evans (1903–75) with his exhibition 'American Photographs' at the Museum of Modern Art, New York. Working as a freelance, her photographs have been widely published in such journals as *Time*, the *New York Post* and *Harper's Bazaar*.

She has also worked in film, as assistant film cutter with director Luis Buñuel (1900–83) and as assistant editor in the Film Division of the Office of War Information in 1944–5. With James Agee and painter and art historian Janice Loeb, she made the film *In the Street* (1945–6) and with Loeb, Agee and Sidney Myers she made *The Quiet One* (1946–7). She returned to still photography in 1959 and taught at the Pratt Institute, Brooklyn, in the mid-1970s.

Lewald, Fanny

Born 1811   Died 1889
German novelist whose works provide an insight
into women's position in society

Fanny Lewald was born in Königsberg (now Kaliningrad). She was Jewish by birth, but became a Lutheran convert in 1828 to marry a young theologian, who died just before the wedding. In 1845 she met Adolf Stahr (1805–76), a Berlin critic, with whom she lived until he was free to marry in 1855.

She was an enthusiastic champion of women's rights, and aired her opinions in her early novels, *Clementine* (1842), *Jenny* (1843) and *Eine Lebensfrage* (1845, 'A Question About Life'). Her later works were family sagas, like *Von Geschlecht zu Geschlecht* (1863–5, 'From Generation to Generation') and *Die Familie Darner* (3 vols, 1887, 'The Darner Family').

She also wrote records of travel in Italy (1847) and Great Britain (1852), and published an autobiography, *Meine Lebensgeschichte* (1861–3, 'The Story of my Life') which social historians in particular find to be of lasting interest.

Lewis, Agnes Smith, *née* Smith

Born 1843   Died 1926
Scottish Oriental scholar who discovered Old
Syriac biblical manuscripts

Agnes Smith was born in Irvine, Ayrshire, and educated at Irvine Academy and privately. She married the Rev Samuel Savage Lewis, fellow of Corpus, Cambridge, in 1887. On his death in 1891 she lived with her twin sister Margaret Dunlop (1843–1920), whose husband James Young Gibson had died in 1886.

In 1892 the sisters made their first visit to St Catherine's monastery, Mount Sinai, where Agnes found the Old Syriac Gospels. These are fourth- or fifth-century palimpsest manuscripts, preserved only because their valuable codices had been used again, which contain texts dating from the second or third century. The Gospels (fully edited in 1910) and other Syriac manuscripts discovered then and later were catalogued in 1894. Margaret, who co-wrote some of the scholarly studies that followed, wrote up Agnes's journals as *How the Codex was Found* (1898).

Agnes received the Royal Asiatic Society gold medal (1915) and honorary degrees from St Andrews, Heidelberg, and Dublin.

Lewis, Edmonia

Born 1845 Died after 1909
American sculptor whose art was influenced by civil rights and neoclassicism

Edmonia Lewis was born in Greenbush, New York, to a black father and half-Chippewa, half-black mother. At the age of 20 she went to Rome where she did much of her work, and where she later retired after converting to Catholicism in the 1880s.

Self-taught, she was strongly influenced by the neoclassic style, and her sculptures reflect her interest in racial equality and women's rights; they include *Hagar in the Wilderness* (1868).

Many of her works were praised as original and striking but not pretty, and her popularity faded generally when interest in the neoclassic style waned.

Lewis, Ida

Born 1842 Died 1911
American lighthouse keeper honoured for 50 years of lifesaving exploits

Ida Lewis was born in Newport, Rhode Island, the daughter of a sea captain who was the lighthouse keeper on Lime Rock in Newport Harbour. Accustomed to rowing her siblings to school, she took over her father's duties when he suffered a stroke.

For 50 years she manned the lighthouse, performing many rescues which began in 1858 when she saved four men whose boat had capsized.

Lewis won public recognition in 1869 and **Susan B Anthony** reported her exploits in her suffrage journal *The Revolution*. She was awarded a gold medal by Congress and a pension by the Carnegie Hero Fund.

Leyster, Judith

Born 1609 Died 1660
Dutch painter who is probably the best-known female painter of the 17th century

Judith Leyster was born in Haarlem, the daughter of a brewer, Jan Willemsz, who took his surname from his Haarlem brewery, the 'Ley-ster(re)'. She was an exceptionally talented child whose artistic abilities were noted by the poet Samuel Ampzingh in his history of Haarlem. She married an artist, Jan Molenaer, in 1636.

Her lively paintings of revellers include *The Jolly Toper*, which was attributed to Franz Hals (c.1580–1666) until her own monogram was revealed during cleaning. Her self portrait (c.1635) hangs in the National Gallery of Art in Washington, and many of her genre scenes of everyday Dutch life hang in the leading museums of Europe.

Li, Florence Tim Oi

Born 1906 Died 1992
Hong Kong Christian and the first Anglican woman priest

Florence Tim Oi Li was ordained priest in 1944 to minister to the Anglican congregation in Macao, where she already served as deacon, during the Japanese occupation of South China. This extraordinary wartime measure by R O Hall, the Anglican Bishop of Hong Kong, was disowned by the Archbishop of Canterbury, Geoffrey Fisher, in 1945. Hall refused to suspend Li, so to save him from having to resign, she voluntarily gave up her priestly ministry.

Li was appointed a teacher at Canton Theological Seminary. Later, since Hong Kong, like other Anglican Provinces outside England, had made its own decision (1971) to ordain women priests, she was able to celebrate the fortieth anniversary of her ordination in Westminster Abbey in 1984 and to take part in the consecration of **Barbara Harris** as the first Anglican bishop in 1989.

Lidman, Sara Adela

Born 1923
Swedish author, one of the most highly acclaimed modern writers in Sweden

Sara Lidman was born into a religious family in Missenträsk in the county of Västerbotten in the far north of the country. She attended Uppsala University, but had her studies interrupted by tuberculosis and turned to writing. The area of her childhood was the setting for her early novels such as *Tjärdalen* (1953, 'The Tar Still') and *Hjortronlandet* (1955, 'Cloudberry Land').

The support for the underdog visible in these novels became more overtly political in the 1960s after her experiences of South Africa, Kenya and Vietnam. In the highly-acclaimed series of novels beginning with *Din tjänare hör* (1977, 'Thy Servant Heareth'), Lidman returns to her roots and takes as her theme the building of the railways of the north, which is underpinned by a desire to examine social conditions.

She has experimented with documentary forms of writing and has also written plays.

Lieberman-Cline, Nancy

Born 1958
American basketball player whose success at college led her into professional play

Nancy Lieberman-Cline was born in Brooklyn, New York. A successful competitor in high school, she was recruited by Old Dominion University where she earned All-American honours three times and led her team to national titles in 1979 and 1980. She herself won the Wade Trophy for the outstanding female college basketball player.

In 1979 she joined the US national team that won the world women's basketball championship. She became a professional player when she signed with the Dallas Diamonds of the Women's Basketball League. After leading the team to a division title, she was named All-Pro and Rookie of the Year before the League folded. In 1988 she played on the Washington Generals team against the Harlem Globetrotters.

Lieberman-Cline was named Jewish Athlete of the Year and was awarded the Broderick Cup as the top female college athlete in 1980, and has been given a place in the Naismith Memorial Basketball Hall of Fame. She has written two autobiographies: *Basketball My Way* (1982) and *Lady Magic: The Autobiography of Nancy Lieberman-Cline* (1991).

Lillie, Bea(trice) Gladys, *married name* Lady Peel

Born 1894 Died 1989
Canadian comic actress and revue singer

Bea Lillie was born in Toronto and educated in Ontario. After an unsuccessful start as a drawing-room ballad singer, she found her true talent in London in 1914 at the Chatham Music Hall. She began as a serious singer but was encouraged as a comedienne by André Charlot and entered into the new vogue of 'intimate revue' which he had brought over from Paris.

Bea Lillie

She entertained the troops on leave during World War I, worked with Noël Coward in London (making famous his 'Mad Dogs and Englishmen'), made her début in the USA in 1932, and entered cabaret in London at the Café Royal (1938). In 1920 she married Robert Peel, who succeeded to his baronetcy in 1925. During World War II she made many tours to entertain the troops and was decorated by General de Gaulle.

During the 1950s she developed her own television series in the USA. She also appeared in films throughout her career, but was at her best with a live audience. Her autobiography, *Every Other Inch a Lady,* appeared in 1973.

Limerick, Sylvia Rosalind Pery Lush, Countess of, *née* Lush

Born 1935
British health visitor and social campaigner

Sylvia Lush was educated at Lady Margaret Hall, Oxford, then became a research assistant at the Foreign Office (1959–62) until after her marriage to Viscount Glentworth (now 6th Earl of Limerick) in 1961.

She joined the headquarters staff of the British Red Cross Society (1962–6), and has since served on several hospital governing boards, area health authorities, community health councils, and numerous other health care organizations, including the Health Visitors Association (Vice-President 1978–84; President 1984–) and the Foundation for the Study of Infant Deaths (Vice-Chairman 1971–).

In 1985 she was appointed Chairman of the British Red Cross and co-wrote *Sudden Infant Death*.

Lincoln, Abbey, *originally* Anna Marie Woolfridge *also known as* Gaby Lee

Born 1930
American jazz singer and actress who was over 60 years old when her singing career revived

Abbey Lincoln was born in Chicago, Illinois. She began her career on the West Coast as a conventional nightclub singer, a background still evident on albums like *Abbey is Blue* (1958).

Following her marriage to drummer Max Roach she changed direction, recording *We Insist! Freedom Now Suite* (1960) with him, an important document of Black nationalism in the USA.

She divorced Roach and sidetracked into acting, but her singing career revived spectacularly in the 1990s with records for the Verve label, including *You Gotta Pay the Band* (1991) and *Devil's Got Your Tongue* (1992).

Lind, Jenny (Johanna Maria), *known as the* Swedish Nightingale

Born 1820 Died 1887
Swedish soprano who sang in opera and oratorio with a remarkably controlled and pure voice

Jenny Lind was born of a humble family in Stockholm. At the age of nine she entered the court theatre school of singing and following many appearances as a child she made her operatic début in Stockholm in 1838 as Agathe in Weber's *Der Freischütz*. After studying under Manuel García in Paris she attained great international popularity, becoming a master of coloratura, with her pure and flexible voice, and singing parts written for her by Giacomo Meyerbeer and Giuseppe Verdi, among others.

Her most celebrated roles were Alice in Meyerbeer's *Robert le diable*, Marie in Gaetano Donizetti's *La fille du régiment* and Amina in Vincenzo Bellini's *La sonnambula*. In 1852 she married her accompanist Otto Goldschmidt; they settled in England in 1858. Her earnings were largely devoted to founding and endowing musical scholarships and charities in Sweden and England, and after retiring from the stage in 1883 she taught at the Royal College of Music, London, for three years.

Lindgren, Astrid

Born 1907
Swedish author of Pippi Longstocking, *a dominant influence in Scandinavian children's literature*

Astrid Lindgren was born in Vimmerby. At 18 she had an illegitimate child who was raised by her parents; she portrayed them in *Samuel August från Seudstorp och Hanna: Hult* (1975). She established her reputation with *Pippi Långstrump* (1945, Eng trans *Pippi Longstocking*, 1954), and while she wrote at least 50 more books, including *Mästerdetektiven Blomkvist* (1946, Eng trans *Bill Bergson Master Detective*, 1951), none has eclipsed its popularity.

Lingard, Joan

Born 1932
Scottish novelist whose main themes concern emotions engendered by relationships or social change

Joan Lingard was born in Edinburgh and educated in Belfast, where she was brought up from the age of two until 18. She trained as a teacher in Edinburgh and published *Liam's Daughter* in 1963, since when she has been a prolific writer of novels for both adults and children, most of which have been set in either Belfast or Edinburgh.

The Prevailing Wind (1964) exposes the veneer of respectability behind which the staunch Edinburgh bourgeoisie shelter from emotional engagement, a theme to which she has returned with some frequency. She began writing for children and teenagers in 1970, and has established a considerable reputation in the field.

Her persistent themes are the complexities of family relationships, and the problems and fluctuations facing characters caught up in the whirlpool of social change.

Linton, Eliza Lynn, *née* Lynn

Born 1822 Died 1898
English novelist and polemicist whose writing style changed and matured as she emerged from a sheltered Lake District upbringing

Eliza Lynn was born in Keswick, the daughter of a Cumberland cleric. After leaving home for London in 1845 to begin a career as a novelist, she soon also gained a professional position in journalism and met many contemporary writers, including Charles Dickens.

While her early fiction is now regarded as whimsical and unrealistic, she matured considerably after meeting William James Linton, a writer and engraver who was also a widower with seven children. They married and published *The Lake Country* together in 1864, although their marriage broke up soon afterwards. Eliza Lynn Linton's later novels, such as *Joshua Davidson*, and her unusual autobiography written from a male point of view, are little remembered nowadays, while her opposition to female enfranchisement appears dated.

Lioba, *also called* Liofe, Leoba *or* Liobgytha

Born c.700   Died 782
Anglo-Saxon abbess and leader of the nuns sent to help St Boniface of Crediton convert Germany to Christianity

Lioba was born in Wessex. In 748 she was appointed leader of the 30 nuns sent from Wimborne, Dorset, to help her kinsman Boniface convert the Germans.

She founded a monastery at Bischofsheim, near Mainz. Her advice was sought from near and far by people in all levels of society, and she was a close friend of Hildegard of Kempton, the wife of Charlemagne.

Her latter years were spent at Schönersheim and she was buried near Boniface, at Fulda monastery. Her life is known through her letters and a biography written 50 years after her death.

Lipman, Maureen Diane

Born 1946
English actress and writer well-known for her expertise in both spoken and written comedy

Maureen Lipman was born in Hull, Yorkshire, and trained at the London Academy of Music and Dramatic Art. She made her theatrical début in 1969 and was first seen in London's West End in Shaw's *Candida* in 1976. Acclaimed for her Maggie in *Outside Edge* in 1978, she won a Laurence Olivier award for her role as Miss Skillen in *See How They Run* in 1984. She has had many other stage successes, including a one-woman show *Re: Joyce* (1988), about **Joyce Grenfell**.

Perhaps better known as a television actress, Lipman has appeared in her husband Jack Rosenthal's play *The Evacuees* and in Alan Bennett's *Rolling Home*. She won the *TV Times* Comedy Actress award for playing the lead in the comedy *All at No 20* in 1989, and starred as Jane Lucas in four series of *Agony*, a sitcom about an agony aunt. She was also the memorable Beattie in the British Telecom commercials, for which she won a BAFTA advertising award. Her films include *Educating Rita* (1983).

Also acclaimed as a humourous writer who can capture the comedy of everyday situations, she has been a columnist for *Options, She* and *Good Housekeeping* magazines, and has published books including *How Was it for You?* (1985), *You Got an 'Ology?* (1989) and *When's It Coming Out?* (1992).

Lisle, Alicia, *née* Beckenshaw

Born c.1614   Died 1685
English parliamentarian executed for her part in the Duke of Monmouth's rebellion against James II and VII

Alicia Beckenshaw married John Lisle, a member of Oliver Cromwell's House of Lords and a regicide, in 1630. She was widowed in 1664. At Charles I's execution in 1649 she said that her 'blood leaped within her to see the tyrant fall'.

She sheltered two of the Duke of Monmouth's rebels after the Battle of Sedgemoor (1685), for which, by order of Judge Jeffreys during the series of trials known as the 'Bloody Assizes', she was beheaded at Winchester.

Lispector, Clarice

Born 1917   Died 1977
Ukrainian-born Brazilian novelist, perhaps the first major women writer from Latin America

Clarice Lispector was trained in law in Rio de Janeiro and spent much of her adult life abroad; her husband was in the Brazilian diplomatic service. Though she is considered to be one of Latin America first major women writers, her reputation has been slow to develop in the English-speaking world and her concerns are neither exclusively nor narrowly feminist.

Her early fiction — *Perto do coracao salvagem* (1944) and *O lustre* (1949) — is still virtually unknown in the anglophone countries and even the more direct narrative of *A maçâ no escuro* (1961, Eng trans *The Apple in the Dark*, 1967) occasionally falls foul of untranslatable elements and rhythms in the original Portuguese. This is particularly true of *A paixao segundo G H* (1964, Eng trans *The Passion According to G H*, 1988).

Her most popular book is *A hora da estréla* (1977, Eng trans *The Hour of the Star*, 1986), a winsome and slightly formulaic novel prepared for the press shortly before her death. Lispector also wrote short fiction, but is more effective in her longer evocations of developing consciousness.

Littlewood, Joan Maud

Born 1914
English stage director who championed the
performance of socially significant experimental
plays

Joan Littlewood was born in London and
trained at RADA. In 1935 she founded Theatre
Union, an experimental company in Manchester, which re-formed in 1945 as Theatre
Workshop, and opened at the Theatre Royal,
Stratford East, London, in 1953 with *Twelfth
Night*. The group quickly won acclaim and
was invited to represent Britain at the Théâtre
des Nations in Paris in 1955 and 1956, and
played at the Moscow Art Theatre.

She also directed the first British production of Bertolt Brecht's *Mother Courage*, in
Barnstaple in 1955, in which she played the
title role. The ideology of the Theatre Workshop company was aggressively left-wing,
aiming to offer the theatre as a place where
the thoughts and feelings of the time could
illuminate its social history. Their artistic
policy revolved around both a fresh, political
approach to established plays and the staging
of new, working-class plays, notably Brendan
Behan's *The Quare Fellow* (1956), **Shelagh
Delaney**'s *A Taste of Honey* (1958) and *Fings
Ain't Wot They Used T'Be* (1959).

In 1963 she directed the musical for which
she is perhaps best known — *Oh, What a
Lovely War!*, and since 1975 she has worked
abroad. Her autobiography, *Joan's Book*, appeared in 1994.

Lively, Penelope Margaret

Born 1933
English novelist and children's author whose work
is characterized by her interest in the effect of time

Penelope Lively was born in Cairo, Egypt, and
educated at Oxford where she read history. A
preoccupation with the relationship between
the present and the past, and a vivid sense of
time and place, form the central thread of
much of her writing.

In her children's book *The Ghost of Thomas
Kempe* (1973), a present-day family is haunted
by a 17th-century sorcerer, while the heroine
of *A Stitch in Time* (1976) finds strange links
between herself and the child who, a hundred
years previously, had embroidered a sampler
hanging in her family's home.

The adult novel *Moon Tiger* (1987), which
won the Booker Prize, chronicles the life of
intellectual, independent historian Claudia
Hampton, while in *Cleopatra's Sister* (1992), a
palaeontologist and a young journalist meet
when the aircraft on which they are travelling

is hijacked and forced to land at Callimba, a
fictitious state on the north African coast.

Lively has also written *The Presence of the
Past: An Introduction to Landscape History*
(1976).

Livermore, Mary Ashton, *née* Rice

Born 1820 Died 1905
American reformer and editor of suffragist
publications

Mary Rice was born in Boston. She trained
as a teacher and married the Rev Daniel P
Livermore in 1845. Together they edited the
New Covenant, a Chicago church periodical
(1857–69).

She became active in the women's suffrage
movement and was founder-editor of *The Agitator* (1869–72) and later the *Woman's Journal*,
into which it was merged.

Livia Drusilla, *later called* Julia Augusta

Born 58BC Died AD29
Roman empress as the powerful, ambitious and
devoted wife of Caesar Augustus (ruled 27BC–
AD14)

Livia Drusilla was the third wife of Octavian
(later the emperor Augustus), whom she
married in 39BC after divorcing her first
husband, Tiberius Claudius Nero. From her
first marriage she had two children — Tiberius the future emperor (who succeeded
Augustus) and Nero Claudius Drusus — but
her marriage with Augustus did not result in
offspring.

She was believed to have had a strong
influence on Augustus, and rumour credited
her with promoting the interests of her sons
at the expense of Augustus' kinsmen, by fair
or foul means. She was adopted into the Julian
family by Augustus at his death in AD14, when
her name was changed in his will to Julia
Augusta. When he was deified shortly after
his death, she became priestess of his cult.

Relations with her son Tiberius after his
accession became strained, as she sought to
exert influence, and when she died he did not
execute her will or allow her to be deified. Her
great-grandson, the future Emperor Caligula,
nicknamed her 'Ulysses in Petticoats'.

Llewellyn Davies, Margaret Caroline, *originally* Margaret Davies

Born 1861 Died 1944
English campaigner for women's rights and
divorce law reform, remembered especially for her
work with the Women's Co-operative Guild

Margaret Davies, niece of **Emily Davies**, was born in Marylebone, London and adopted the family name Llewellyn. She was educated at Queen's College, and Girton, Cambridge. She became involved the Women's Co-operative Guild through voluntary social work in Marylebone. In 1909 she gave evidence on behalf of the Guild to a Royal Commission on Divorce Law, advocating divorce equality for women.

In 1921 she co-founded the International Women's Co-operative Guild, becoming the first woman President of the Co-operative Congress (1922). Her works include *The Women's Co-operative Guild 1883–1904* (1904), *Maternity Letters from Working Women* (1915), and a book of guild members' reminiscences, *Life as We Have Known It* (1931).

Lloyd, Chris Evert , *see* Evert, Chris

Lloyd, Marie, *originally* Matilda Alice Victoria Wood

Born 1870 Died 1922
English music hall entertainer famed for
portraying working-class Londoners

Matilda Wood was born in Hoxton, the daughter of a waiter and eldest of 11 children. She made her first appearance as Bella Delmare at the Royal Eagle Music Hall (later The Grecian) in 1885. After choosing a new stage name, she had her first great success with a song called 'The Boy I Love Sits Up in the Gallery'. She went on to become one of the most popular music hall performers of all time with a wittily improper act that was often criticized for coarseness.

She appeared in music halls throughout the country and in the USA, South Africa, and Australia. She continued on the stage until a few days before her death. Among her most famous songs were 'Oh! Mr Porter', 'My Old Man Said Follow the Van', and 'I'm One of the Ruins that Cromwell Knocked About a Bit'.

Lochhead, Liz

Born 1947
Scottish poet and dramatist acclaimed for her use
of irony and of the Scots language

Liz Lochhead was born in Motherwell, Lanarkshire. After studying at Glasgow School of Art (1965–70), she worked as an art teacher at Bishopbriggs High School, Glasgow, before becoming a full-time writer in 1979. A frank and witty poet, with a nice line in irony, she has published several collections, including *Dreaming Frankenstein and Collected Poems* (1984) and *True Confessions and New Clichés*

(1985), a collection of songs, monologues, and performance pieces.

Her most powerful work has been written for the stage, where she has profitably reworked the staples of Scottish history in *Mary Queen of Scots Got Her Head Chopped Off* (1987), literary biography (**Mary Shelley** in *Blood and Ice*, 1982), popular culture in *The Big Picture* (1988), and horror fiction in a version of Bram Stoker's *Dracula* (1985), which restored the serious intent of the original, all from a thoroughly modern perspective.

She translated Molière's *Tartuffe* (1985) into demotic Glaswegian, and has written for radio and television, her use of Scots reflecting her belief in a renewal of self-confidence in the language. She wrote the text for the epic music theatre production *Jock Tamson's Bairns* in Glasgow in 1990.

Locke, Bessie

Born 1865 Died 1952
American pioneer of kindergarten education

Bessie Locke was born in West Cambridge (now Arlington), Massachusetts. She herself attended a private kindergarten (then a recent importation from Germany), and went on to Brooklyn public schools and Columbia University, but took no degree. She is said to have been deflected from business to education by her observation of a friend's kindergarten in a slum area of New York City.

Convinced that the kindergarten was second only to the Church as an agency for improvement, she founded the National Association for the Promotion of Kindergarten Education (National Kindergarten Association) in 1909, and became chief of the kindergarten division of the US bureau of education (1913–19), working to improve kindergarten teacher training. She has helped to open over 3,000 kindergartens, serving over 1.5 million children.

From 1917 she published home education articles for parents which became very influential.

Lockwood, Belva Ann, *née* Bennett

Born 1830 Died 1917
American lawyer and reformer who became the
first woman to practise before the Supreme Court

Belva Bennett was born in Royalton, Niagara County, New York. She was educated at Genesee College, graduated in 1873 from the National University Law School in Washington and was admitted to the Bar. In 1868 she married Ezekiel Lockwood (d.1877) as her second husband (she had been a widow since 1853).

A skilled and vigorous supporter of women's rights, after much campaigning to lift the 'custom' that forbade a woman to speak, she became the first woman to practise before the Supreme Court, and helped to promote various reforms, such as the Equal Pay Act for female civil servants (1872). In 1884 and 1888, as a member of the National Equal Rights party, she was nominated to run for the US presidency.

She also held strong pacifist views, and was a member of the nominating committee for the Nobel Prize for Peace.

Lockwood, Margaret

Born 1911 Died 1990
English character actress of film, stage and television

Margaret Lockwood was born in Karachi, India. She studied at the Italia Conti School, and made her stage début as a fairy in *A Midsummer Night's Dream* (1928). She then trained at RADA before making her film début in *Lorna Doone* (1934). Signed to a long-term contract with British Lion, she made a fresh and spirited young heroine in films like *Midshipman Easy* (1935) and *The Beloved Vagabond* (1936) before achieving stardom in the classic thriller *The Lady Vanishes* (1938) and *Bank Holiday* (1938).

Briefly in Hollywood before World War II, she returned to Britain and found her greatest renown as scheming doxies in costume melodramas like *The Man in Grey* (1943) and *The Wicked Lady* (1945). By 1946 she was judged to be Britain's favourite female star, but subsequent role choices failed to sustain her stardom and she played her last leading role in *Cast a Dark Shadow* (1955).

She retained her popularity on stage and television over the next two decades, and returned to the cinema for a final appearance as the wicked stepmother in *The Slipper and the Rose* (1976) before spending her last years as a publicity-shy recluse.

Lombard, Carole, *originally* Jane Alice Peters

Born 1908 Died 1942
American actress and one of Hollywood's most popular stars at the time of her death in an air crash

Carole Lombard was born in Fort Wayne, Indiana, and later lived in California. She was spotted by director Allan Dwan and cast as a tomboy in the film *A Perfect Crime* (1921). After completing her studies she returned to filmmaking in 1925 where her blond hair and beauty made her a decorative addition to many comedy shorts for the Canadian filmmaker Mack Sennett (1880–1960). She married the actor Clark Gable in 1939.

After she was signed to a long-term contract with Paramount in 1930, her roles gradually improved and she revealed a delicious comic flair in *Twentieth Century* (1934). A glamorous, sophisticated woman, she was unafraid to play for laughs and her witty, wacky effervescence made her the perfect heroine of screwball comedies like *My Man Godfrey* (1936), *Nothing Sacred* (1937) and *To Be or Not to Be* (1942) whilst her dramatic potential was glimpsed in *They Knew What They Wanted* (1940).

Longman, Evelyn Beatrice

Born 1874 Died 1954
American sculptor considered to be the most successful woman sculptor of her time

Evelyn Longman was born near Winchester, Ohio. She attended evening classes at Chicago Art Institute and Mount Oliver College in Michigan prior to returning to Chicago where she studied under Lorado Toft, graduating with honours in 1900.

She became the only female assistant to Daniel French before opening her own studio, gaining a series of monumental commissions, such as the bronze doors for the chapel of the US Naval Academy, her *Victory* for the St Louis exposition and her most famous sculpture, *Genius of Electricity*, originally installed on top of a building in Manhattan. She also executed many portrait commissions in a decorative classical style.

She collected many awards, including the honour of being the first woman elected to the National Academy of Design.

Longo, Jeanne

Born 1958
French cyclist, widely considered the best female road cyclist of all time

Jeanne Longo was born in Annecy. Her numerous wins include the Women's Tour de France three times, the Colorado equivalent four times and the world title a record eight times. She was French Women's Champion on the road 11 times between 1979 and 1989 and won the Tokyo and Osaka Grand Prix events and set numerous world records indoors and out.

Her career was never highlighted by an Olympic gold medal, although she came out of retirement for the Barcelona Olympics in 1992 and won a silver in the road race that year.

She is married to her coach Patrice Ciprelli, who was himself a former Alpine skiing internationalist, and they now live in Grenoble.

Longueville, Anne-Geneviève de Bourbon-Condé, Duchesse de

Born 1619 Died 1679
French noblewoman whose political activities lead to her being called the 'soul of the Fronde'

Anne-Geneviève de Bourbon-Condé was the only daughter of the Prince de Condé, born in prison in Vincennes where her parents were being held for their opposition to the Marquis d'Ancre, the favourite of **Marie de' Médicis**. She was educated in a Carmelite convent in Paris and in 1639 was married to the Duc de Longueville, who was at least 20 years her senior. She exerted a considerable influence on politics, in which she first began to interest herself as the mistress of the Duc de la Rochefoucauld.

In the first war of the Fronde (1648), the uprising by some nobles and others against Cardinal Mazarin and **Anne of Austria**, she sought in vain to win over her brother, the Great Condé, but he persisted in loyally suppressing it. However in the second (1650) she won him over, but he was ultimately defeated by the royal armies.

After the death of her husband (1663) and her desertion by la Rochefoucauld, she lived in Paris and became increasingly convinced by Jansenism. She became the Jansenists' protectress; during her lifetime the nuns of Port-Royal des Champs were safe. She later retired to the convent that educated her but continued to have influence at court.

Lonsdale, Dame Kathleen, *née* Yardley

Born 1903 Died 1971
Irish crystallographer who made important analyses of certain atoms

Kathleen Yardley was born in Newbridge, County Kildare. She entered Bedford College, London (1919), to study mathematics, but changed to physics at the end of her first year. On graduation in 1922 she was invited by William Bragg to join his crystallography research team, first at University College London (UCL), and then at the Royal Institution. She remained at the latter until 1946, apart from a short period when she worked at Leeds (1929–31).

In 1946 she became Reader in Crystallography in the chemistry department of UCL and in 1949 she was promoted to Professor of Chemistry. In 1945, when the Royal Society agreed to admit women fellows, she was one of the first two women to be elected FRS; she was awarded the society's Davy Medal in 1957.

Of her many contributions to crystallography, the most celebrated was her X-ray analysis in 1929 of hexamethylbenzene and hexachlorobenzene, which showed that the carbon atoms in the benzene ring are coplanar and hexagonally arranged. She also made important contributions to space-group theory and to the study of anisotropy and disorder in crystals.

She became a Quaker in 1935 and later worked tirelessly for various causes including peace, penal reform, and the social responsibility of science. She was appointed DBE in 1956 and retired in 1968.

Loos, Anita

Born 1888 Died 1981
American novelist and scriptwriter, one of Hollywood's most influential screenwriters

Anita Loos was born in California. She started her literary career at the age of 10, when she wrote for her father's paper, and began writing filmscripts and silent-film subtitles for D W Griffith in 1912.

Her comic masterpiece, *Gentlemen Prefer Blondes* (1925), with its naive, gold-digging heroine Lorelei Lee, summed up the mood of the Roaring Twenties. It scored a huge success as novel, musical, and movie, and she became one of Hollywood's most influential screenwriters, working with her second husband, director John Emerson.

She also wrote stage-plays, including *Gigi* (1952), an adaptation of **Colette**'s novel, and two gossipy Hollywood memoirs, *A Girl Like I* (1966) and *Kiss Hollywood Goodbye* (1974). Doubt has been cast on her commonly accepted birthdate by her biographer, Gary Carey, who suggests she was born in 1888.

Lopez, Nancy

Born 1957
American golfer who raised the profile of women's golf

Nancy Lopez was born in Torrance, California. Competing as an amateur in high school and college, she won the national championships of the Association for Intercollegiate Athletics for Women in 1976. Two years later she joined the professional tour and by 1991 had taken 44

LPGA (Ladies Professional Golf Association) victories and won more than \$3.2 million.

Her powerful play, shown in her great strength enabling long drives, her impeccable putting, and impressive poise in pressurized situations, is considered to be one of the reasons that women's professional golf has attracted large purses and corporate sponsorship.

Lopez was inducted into the LPGA Hall of Fame in 1987 and the PGA (Professional Golfers Association) Hall of Fame in 1989. The Associated Press selected her as the Female Athlete of the Year in 1978 and 1985, and she has been the LPGA Player of the year four times — in 1978, 1979, 1985 and 1988.

Lorde, Audre Geraldine

Born 1934 Died 1992
American poet and feminist

Audre Lorde was born in New York of West Indian parents and educated at the National University of Mexico, Hunter College, and Columbia University. She was proud to be black, feminist, lesbian *and* a mother of two children.

From her earliest collection, *The First Cities* (1968), through to the later *Our Dead Behind Us* (1987), she singlemindedly explored themes of race and sex, using memories of her own childhood and the efforts of a light-skinned mother to 'beat me whiter every day'. Her prose work includes *The Cancer Journals* (1980), about her experience of the disease, and *Burst of Light* (1988).

Loren, Sophia, *originally* Sofia Scicolone

Born 1934
Italian actress who became a statuesque leading lady in Italian cinema before making her name worldwide

Sofia Scicolone was born in Rome. She was a teenage beauty queen and model, and entered films in 1950 as an extra in *Cuori sul Mare*. Under contract to Carlo Ponti, later her husband, she blossomed into a stunningly beautiful star with a talent for earthy drama and vivacious comedy.

An international career followed and she won an Academy Award for *Two Women* (*La Ciociara*, 1961). Frequently seen in partnership with Italian actor Marcello Mastroianni, she has attempted a wide range of characterizations with varying degrees of success. Her many films include *The Millionairess* (1961), *Marriage Italian Style* (1964), *Cinderella — Italian Style* (*C'Era Una Volta*,

1967) and *A Special Day* (*Una Giornata Particolare*, 1977).

In 1979 she published *Sophia Loren: Living and Loving* (with A E Hotchner) which was filmed for television as *Sophia Loren: Her Own Story* (1980) with the actress playing both herself and her mother. Her career continues with television films like *Courage* (1986) and *The Fortunate Pilgrim* (1988).

Loriod, Yvonne *and* Jeanne

Yvonne born 1924 Jeanne born 1928
French musicians, specializing in piano and ondes Martenot respectively

Yvonne Loriod was born in Houilles, Seines-et-Oise. In 1962 she became the second wife of the composer Olivier Messiaen (1908–92), and was the first interpreter of all his piano parts from then until his death. She was also the dedicatee of Pierre Boulez's Second Piano Sonata (1950). Jeanne was responsible for the ondes Martenot part in Messiaen's *Turangalîla-Symphonie* (1946–9).

Lorraine, Mary of *see* Mary of Guise

Los Angeles, Victoria de, *originally* Victoria López Cima

Born 1923
Spanish lyric soprano who won fame for her interpretations of Spanish songs

Victoria de Los Angeles was born in Barcelona, where she gave her first public concert (1944) and made her operatic début at the Liceo theatre in 1945. She then performed at the Paris Opéra and La Scala, Milan (1949), Covent Garden (1950), the New York Metropolitan (1951) and subsequently at all the great houses and festivals throughout the world, becoming noted for her 19th-century Italian roles and for her performances of Spanish songs, in particular Carmen, Dido, Puccini's heroines, Mozart roles and Elisabeth in *Tannhäuser* (Bayreuth, 1961).

After retiring from the stage in 1969 she continued to give recitals.

Loudov, Ivana

Born 1941
Czech composer whose individuality has brought her international recognition

Ivana Loudov was born at Chlumec nad Cidlinou. She studied composition at Prague Conservatory (1968–71), at Darmstadt summer courses (1967–9) and under Olivier Messiaen in the ORTF (Office de Radiodiffusion-Télévision Française) experimental studio (1971).

In 1973 she married Milos Haase, and the following year won the Young Czech Composer competition with *Concerto*, a piece that developed the orchestral language of *Spleen* (1971), written during her period in Paris.

Important later works are the choral *Italian Triptych* (1982) and the *Double Concerto* for violin, percussion and strings (1989), which confirmed the individuality that has brought her increasing international recognition.

Loughlin, Dame Anne

Born 1894 Died 1979
English trade unionist who rose to be the first
woman president of the TUC

Anne Loughlin was born in Leeds. When she was 12 her mother died, and as eldest daughter she looked after the family as well as working in a clothing factory. She became involved in union affairs, and was a full-time organizer by the time of the Hebden Bridge strike by 6,000 clothing workers in 1916.

In 1920 she was appointed women's officer of the Tailors and Garment Workers Union, and worked tirelessly to improve the working conditions and to increase union strength. In 1948 she became general secretary of the National Union of Tailors and Garment Workers.

She served on many government committees, as well as the Royal Commission on Equal Pay. In 1943 she became the first trade unionist to be created DBE, and also the first woman president of the Trades Union Congress.

Louisa

Born 1776 Died 1810
Queen of Prussia as the wife of Frederick-William
III (ruled 1797–1840)

Louisa was born in Hanover, where her father, Duke Karl of Mecklenburg-Strelitz, was commandant. Married to the Crown Prince of Prussia, the future King Frederick-William III, in 1793, she was the mother of Frederick-William IV and William I, who afterwards became emperor.

She endeared herself to her people with her spirit and energy during the period of national calamity that followed the battle of Jena, and especially by her patriotic and self-denying efforts to obtain concessions at Tilsit from Napoleon, though he had shamelessly slandered her.

Louisa Maximilienne Caroline *see* Albany, Countess of

Løveid, Cecilie

Born 1951
Norwegian poet, novelist, and playwright who is
internationally recognized

Cecilie Løveid grew up in Bergen, studied at art college, and had her first literary text published in 1969. Her work, which often employs a collage technique and transcends the conventional notions of genre, is heavily dependent on the effects of imagery and sound, the experimental language centring on the female body.

The poetic novel *Most* (1972) focuses, like so many of her subsequent works, on a female–male relationship, while *Alltid skyer over Askoy* (1976, 'Always Clouds over Askoy') traces the changing experiences of several generations of women. The novel *Sug* (1979, Eng trans *Sea Swell*, 1986), with its kaleidoscopic composition and stylistic experimentation, highlights a search for feminine identity which also becomes a search for language. Linguistic boldness is also characteristic of her radio drama *Måkespisere* (Eng trans *Seagull Eaters*, 1989), which was first performed in 1982 and won the Prix Italia the following year.

Lovelace, (Augusta) Ada King, Countess of, *née* Byron

Born 1815 Died 1852
English mathematician and writer who became
the first computer programmer by creating a
program for Charles Babbage's 'analytical engine'

Ada, Lady Byron, was born in Picadilly Terrace, Middlesex (now part of London), the daughter of the poet Lord Byron, whom she never knew because he left Britain when she

Ada, Countess of Lovelace

was a baby. Encouraged by her mother, she taught herself geometry, and was trained in astronomy and mathematics. Her tutors included Augustus de Morgan (1806–71), London University's first Professor of Mathematics. In 1835 she married William King, 8th Baron King, and became Countess of Lovelace when he became an earl in 1838.

She translated and annotated an article on the analytical engine of the computer pioneer Charles Babbage (1792–1871), written by Italian mathematician L F Menabrea, adding many explanatory notes of her own, including how it could be programmed. This *Sketch of the Analytical Engine* (1843) is an important source on Babbage's work. The high-level universal computer programming language ADA was named in her honour, and is said to realize several of her insights into the working of a computer system.

Low, Bet

Born 1924
Scottish artist whose evocative watercolours of the Scottish Islands are the equivalent of visual poetry

Bet Low was born in Gourock and trained at Glasgow School of Art (1942–5) and at Hospitalfield under James Cowie. She married fellow artist Tom MacDonald, and exhibited with him at the Blythswood Gallery, Glasgow, in 1969. In 1963 she had become a co-founder of the new Charing Cross Gallery. Later she was elected to the RSW (Royal Scottish Water Colour Society, 1974), RGI (Royal Glasgow Institute of Artists, 1980) and ARSA (Associate of the Royal Scottish Academy, 1988).

In her watercolours she captures the ambience and spirit of place by subtle use of colour and form, painstakingly built up to create the haunting images which are her unique trademark. She has exhibited widely and has works in many public and private collections.

Low, Juliette (Magille Kinzie) Gordon, *née* Gordon

Born 1860   Died 1927
American founder of the Girl Scouts of America

Juliette Gordon was born into a wealthy family in Savannah, Georgia. While in her early twenties, she began a pattern of travel and extensive visits that continued throughout her unhappy marriage to William M Low (begun in 1886) and throughout her life. Due to the mistreatment of an earache, she became increasingly deaf.

When in England in 1911 she met General Sir Robert Baden-Powell, who had founded the Boy Scouts (now the Scout Association) in Britain in 1908. Captivated by the idea, she returned to the USA to found the Girl Scouts of America in 1915. As their first president, she was the US delegate to the first International Council of Girl Scouts and Girl Guides in 1919, then served as president until the following year and continued to work for the organization until her death.

Lowell, Amy

Born 1874   Died 1925
American imagist poet who helped to popularize imagism and modernist poetry

Amy Lowell was born into an extremely wealthy family in Brookline, Massachusetts, a sister of the political scientist Abbott Lowell and the astronomer Percival Lowell. She travelled extensively with her parents in Europe, and bought the parental home, 'Sevenals', in 1903.

Identifying herself with the work of H D (**Hilda Doolittle**), she wrote volumes of *vers libre* which she named 'unrhymed cadence', starting with the conventional *A Dome of Many-Colored Glass* (1912) and *Sword Blades and Poppy Seeds* (1914). She also wrote polyphonic prose. Her other works include *Six French Poets* (1915), *Tendencies in Modern American Poetry* (1917), *What's O'Clock* (1925), for which she posthumously received a Pulitzer Prize in 1926, and a biography of the English poet John Keats (1925).

Loy, Myrna, *originally* Katerina Myrna Adele Williams

Born 1905   Died 1993
American film actress and comedienne of incisiveness and humanity

Myrna Loy was born in Radersburg, Montana, of Welsh ancestry. She moved with her family to Los Angeles in 1919 and was performing in a movie house chorus when she was spotted by Rudolph Valentino. She made her début in *Pretty Ladies* (1925) and then appeared in scores of silent features.

After her role as the sadistic daughter in *The Mask of Fu Manchu* (1932), she moved to comedy and her appearance opposite William Powell (1892–1984) as the husband-and-wife detectives Nick and Nora Charles in *The Thin Man* (1934) began a long and happy partnership in which their impeccable timing, witty bantering and evident affection contributed to a more sophisticated dramatic view of the married couple. Together they made 13 films.

Loy was successful also in *Test Pilot* (1938), as the feckless socialite in *The Rains Came* (1939) and as the loyal, level-headed homefront wife in *The Best Years of Our Lives* (1946). In later life she became a discriminating character actress. She made a belated Broadway début in 1974 and completed her acting career opposite Henry Fonda in the television film *Summer Solstice* (1981). Her autobiography, *Being and Becoming* (1987), displays the qualities of wit and charm that had been evident throughout her career.

Lü

Died 180BC
Empress of China, a formidable person who was China's first woman ruler

Lü was the wife of Liu Bang (Liu Pang) or Gaozu (Kao tsu), the founder of the Han Dynasty, and when he died in 195BC, she was virtual regent for 15 years, first for her son Hui Ti and then, after his death (188), for two other infants.

By the time of her death, she had firmly established the authority of the ruling Liu family, although Chinese historiography condemns her for her resort to nepotism and employment of eunuchs at court.

Luce, (Anne) Clare Boothe, *née* Boothe

Born 1903 Died 1987
American writer, ambassador, socialite and wit best known for her magazine articles

Clare Boothe was born in New York City. She married for the first time at the age of 20, but divorced in 1929 and married the millionaire publisher Henry Luce (1898–1967) in 1935. She began writing for *Vogue* and *Vanity Fair* in 1930, becoming associate editor of the former and associate editor and managing editor of the latter (1930–4).

She was elected to the House of Representatives as a Republican in 1942 and was selected by President Dwight D Eisenhower to be American ambassador to Italy in 1953, but she resigned due to ill health in 1956. Though chosen as ambassador to Brazil in 1959, she did not take up the post.

She had several Broadway successes as a writer, including *The Women* (1936), a stinging satire on the manners of Manhattan's female élite, to which she belonged, *Kiss the Boys Goodbye* (1938) and *Margin for Error* (1939). Her other works include a collection of her satirical articles for *Vanity Fair* entitled *Stuffed Shirts* (1933), *Europe in the Spring* (1940) and *Slam the Door Softly* (1970).

Lucretia

6th century BC
Roman matron whose tragic tale has been retold in poetry and music

Lucretia is a legendary figure, a virtuous woman who was married to Lucius Tarquinius Collatinus and who was raped by Sextus Tarquinius (son of the tyrannical King of Rome Tarquinius Superbus). She summoned her husband and friends, made them take an oath to drive out the Tarquins, and then plunged a knife into her heart. The Tarquins were later expelled by Lucius Junius Brutus, an event which marked the beginning of the Roman Republic.

The tale has formed the basis of several works, notably Shakespeare's narrative poem *The Rape of Lucrece* and the opera *The Rape of Lucretia* by Benjamin Britten.

Lucy, St

Died AD304
Christian virgin and martyr, one of the earliest Christian saints to attain widespread popularity

Lucy, according to tradition, was born into a wealthy family in Sicily but rejected worldly comforts and marriage in favour of celibacy. A rejected suitor denounced her as a Christian to the Roman authorities and she was condemned to a period in a brothel, but miraculously the order remained unfulfilled as no one could move her. When sentenced to burn she remained unharmed by the flames and so was eventually martyred by the sword under Diocletian at Syracuse in Sicily.

She is the patron saint of the blind, from a legend telling that her eyes were plucked out but miraculously restored, and of Syracuse. Her feast day is 13 December, which in Sweden marks the first day of Christmas festivites.

Ludmilla, St, *also spelt* Ludmila

Born c.860 Died 921
Slavic martyr and patron saint of Bohemia who was instrumental in the spread of Christianity in that country

Ludmilla was born near Mělník, Bohemia. She married Borivoj, who was the first Czech prince to embrace Christianity. Together they built the first Christian church in Bohemia, which was situated near Prague.

Ludmilla was the grandmother of St Wenceslas, whom she raised as a Christian. When her son (his father) Ratislav died she tried to persuade Wenceslas to oppose the anti-Christians who had taken over the government of the country. However, Ludmilla's daughter-in-law Drahomira, who was regent and a pagan, became resentful of Ludmilla's influence and arranged her murder at Tetin Castle, near Podébrady.

Ludwig, Christa

Born 1924
German mezzo-soprano with a rich, expressive voice

Christa Ludwig was born in Berlin. She made her début in Frankfurt in 1946 and joined the Vienna State Opera in 1955, tackling both classical and modern roles. In 1957 she married the Austrian bass-baritone Walter Berry (marriage dissolved 1970), with whom she often performed.

Her repertoire favours Romantic music, and she has made a particular specialism of Brahms and Mahler.

Lulu, *real name* Marie McDonald Mclaughlin Lawrie

Born 1948
Scottish pop singer and entertainer who came to fame with the title song from To Sir With Love

Marie Lawrie was born in Glasgow. With her band The Luvvers she had the first Scottish hit of the Beat era with a cover of the Isley Brothers' 'Shout' in 1964. Opting for a solo career in 1966, she had her greatest success in the USA the following year with the title song from the film *To Sir With Love*, in which she also acted.

During the 1970s she became better known as an entertainer and television personality than as a pop singer, and she had her own BBC series *It's Lulu*. She was married to Maurice Gibb of the Bee Gees from 1969 to 1973.

Her albums have included *New Routes* (1969) and *Lulu* (1981). 'Shout' was re-released and brought fresh chart success in 1986, and in 1993 she entered the charts again with 'Independence'.

Lumley, Joanna

Born 1946
British comic actress who has earned great popularity on UK television

Joanna Lumley was born in Srinagar, Kashmir. She worked as a model for three years in the UK and continental Europe before becoming an actress, mainly of the small screen. She came to notice in such series as *The New Avengers* (1976–8) and won a BAFTA award in 1994 for her performance in the second series of **Jennifer Saunders**'s *Absolutely Fabulous*, in which she played the show-stopping nympho-

maniac and dypsomaniac best friend Patsy to Saunders's Edina.

Though seldom seen on stage, she has appeared in such plays as Noel Coward's *Blithe Spirit* and *Private Lives*, and was acclaimed as the 1920s colonialist accused of murder in Somerset Maugham's *The Letter* in 1995. Her cinema appearances include two of the *Pink Panther* films and *Shirley Valentine*.

Her memoirs, *Stare Back and Smile*, were published in 1989.

Lupescu, Magda

Born c.1902 Died 1977
Romanian adventuress who became the unpopular but influential mistress and second wife of Charles II of Romania (ruled 1930–40)

Magda Lupescu was born in Iaşi. In the 1920s she became the mistress of Prince Charles (or Carol, 1893–1953) who was the heir apparent, but because of the scandal surrounding their affair, he renounced his claim to the throne in 1925. When he returned to Romania in 1930 to reclaim his throne, having become reconciled with his wife, Princess Helen of Greece, it was on condition that Lupescu remained abroad. However she too returned and took up residence in the palace, upon which the Prime Minister, Iuliu Maniu, resigned.

It was her Jewish descent as much as her dissolute behaviour that earned her the disapproval of Romanian society, itself notorious for its profligacy. She became extremely unpopular at court, but continued to exert excessive influence until Charles abdicated (1940) and the couple fled the country. Upon her marriage in 1947 to Charles, she took the name Princess Elena and lived in exile with the former king in Estoril, Portugal, where she remained after his death.

Lupino, Ida

Born 1918 Died 1995
English film actress and director who excelled in delineating the darker side of the female psyche

Ida Lupino was born in London, the daughter of popular comedian Stanley Lupino (1893–1942). She trained at RADA and was still a teenager when she made her leading role début in *Her First Affaire* (1932). She moved to Hollywood the following year and eventually rose to prominence as the adulterous murderess in *They Drive By Night* (1940).

Under contract to Warner Brothers, she appeared in several musicals and comedies, and was highly successful in a series of roles expressing inner torment, repression and malevolence. She was most memorable as the gangster's moll in *High Sierra* (1941), the murderous housekeeper in *Ladies in Retirement* (1941), the compulsively ambitious sister in *The Hard Way* (1943) and the torch singer in *Road House* (1948).

When she left Warner Brothers in 1947 she formed her own company, producing, co-writing and directing *Not Wanted* (1949). She continued to act, but focused increasingly on direction, tackling the issue of rape in *Outrage* (1950) and bigamy in *The Bigamist* (1953). With the formation of Four Star Productions (with Charles Boyer, David Niven and Dick Powell), she worked extensively for television, and also appeared in *Mr Adams and Eve* (1957–8) with her third husband Howard Duff (1917–90).

Lurie, Alison

Born 1926
American writer whose work revolves around an ironic examination of social mores

Alison Lurie was born in Chicago and educated at Radcliffe College, Massachusetts. She has taught at Cornell University since 1968 (as Professor of English since 1976) and academic life forms the backdrop to her first three books, the ironically titled *Love and Friendship* (1962), *The Nowhere City* (1965) and *Foreign Affairs* (1984), which won the 1985 Pulitzer Prize. The second and the third also deal with cultural displacement — Easterners in the Far West and an American in London respectively.

Her skill in using enclosed, even hermetic worlds to reflect the progress and problems of the wider culture can be gauged in *Imaginary Friends* (1967), about a chiliastic cult, and in *The War Between the Tates* (1974), set against the background of the Vietnam War. *The Truth about Lorin Jones* (1988) is a more recent novel, but Lurie has increasingly turned to non-fictional commentary, brilliantly in *The Language of Clothes* (1981), often contentiously in *Don't Tell the Grown-ups: Subversive Children's Literature* (1990).

Lutyens, (Agnes) Elizabeth

Born 1906   Died 1983
English composer, one of the first British composers to adopt the 12-tone technique

Elizabeth Lutyens was born in London, the daughter of architect Edwin Lutyens. She studied in Paris and at the Royal College of Music and had a setting of Keats's poem *To Sleep* performed while still attending the College. Her *Chamber Concerto No. 1* (1939), composed in her own personal interpretation of the 12-tone technique, was a remarkably original work.

Her compositions were, in general, not immediately well-received — the chamber opera *Infidelio* (1954) and cantata *De Amore* (1957) were not performed until 1973 — but later she became accepted as a leading British composer.

Her work includes *O Saisons, O Châteaux* (1946), the chamber opera *The Pit* (1947), *Concertante* (1950), *Quincunx* (1959), *The Country of the Stars* (1963), *Vision of Youth* (1970) and *Echoi* (1979). She published her autobiography, *A Goldfish Bowl*, in 1972.

Lutz, Bertha

Born 1899   Died 1976
Brazilian scientist who successfully campaigned for women's rights at home and in the international arena

Bertha Lutz was a Brazilian biology lecturer who, after studying in Paris, successfully challenged male predominance in the government scientific service in her own country by gaining an appointment in the National Museum at Rio de Janeiro.

After campaigning successfully for female enfranchisement, she was able to establish a government department to examine women's subjects, while taking her crusade into the international arena. At the first United Nations meeting in 1945 she won a major victory by having sexual discrimination given equal weight with discrimination on grounds of race, creed or colour.

She was founding President of the Brazilian Federation for the Advancement of Women from 1922 until she died.

Luxemburg, Rosa, *known as* Bloody Rosa

Born 1871   Died 1919
German left-wing revolutionary and influential political theoretician

Rosa Luxemburg was born into a Jewish family in Zamość in Poland, which was then under Russian rule. She became a communist in 1890, took part in underground activities in Poland and founded the Polish Social Democratic party (later the Polish Communist party). She was educated in Zürich, then moved to Berlin in 1898 and became a leader of the left-wing movement and the author of such tracts as *Sozialreform oder Revolution?* (1889, 'Reform or Revolution?') which defended Marxism and championed revolution. A compelling speaker and gifted politi-

Rosa Luxemburg, 1908

cal writer, she believed that socialism could be attained worldwide through mass action by the proletariat. Her other publications include *Die Akkumulation des Kapitals* (1913).

At the outbreak of World War I, together with Karl Liebknecht (1871–1919) and **Clara Zetkin**, she formed the *Spartakusbund* (Spartacus League), which aimed to end the war through revolution and the establishment of a proletarian government. It later grew into the Communist Party of Germany. Luxemburg spent most of the War in prison; after her release in 1919 she took part in an abortive uprising known as the Spartacus Revolt, and was murdered with Liebknecht in Berlin.

In 1986 a film about her life by **Margarethe Von Trotta** was released.

Lydia

1st century AD
Biblical character who was St Paul's first Christian convert in Europe

Lydia was a prosperous trader in purple dye from Thyatira, in the district of Lydia, western Asia Minor. She was a religious woman, who had become attracted to the Jewish faith even before she heard Paul's message at Philippi.

Either widowed or unmarried, Lydia was head of her own household and was baptized with them. Her offer of hospitality to Paul and his companions may have been the origin of the Philippian Church's reputation for generosity.

Lyman, Mary Redington Ely, *née* Ely

Born 1887 Died 1975
American theologian and educator

Mary Ely was born in St Johnsbury, Vermont. She studied at Mount Holyoke College, Union Theological Seminary, New York (as the only woman in her class), Cambridge and Chicago.

She was Professor of Religion at Vassar College (1921–6) and lectured at Columbia University and at Union Theological Seminary (1928–40), where she married Eugene William Lyman (1872–1948), Professor of the Philosophy of Religion. On his retirement in 1940 she became Dean and Professor of Religions at Sweet Briar College, Virginia, but returned to Union as Dean of Women and Professor of English Bible (1950–5).

Lyman was ordained to the Congregational ministry in 1949, was active in the YWCA and the World Council of Churches, and wrote several books.

Lympany, Dame Moura, *originally* Mary Johnstone

Born 1916
English concert pianist who began her career as a child prodigy and made a remarkable comeback in her seventies

Moura Lympany was born in Saltash, Cornwall. Her mother was a liberated, educated woman and, wanting her children to speak several languages, sent them to school in Europe. Lympany played her first concerto at the age of 12, then was awarded a scholarship to study at the Royal Academy of Music. She also studied in Liège and under Tobias Matthay (1858–1945).

By the late 1930s she had won several prestigious prizes and developed a glamourous international career, becoming the first Western pianist to play in Russia after World War II. She developed a repertoire of 60 concertos, specializing in 20th-century English music. However she disappeared from the concert stage for many years, during which she married twice and suffered the early death of her son. In later life she succeeded in recreating her career and continued to impress all over the world through the 1990s. She was created DBE in 1992.

Lynn, Loretta, *née* Webb

Born 1935
American country singer who shrugged off her deprived background to become a star

Loretta Lynn was born into rural poverty in Butcher's Hollow, Kentucky, and married at the age of 14. Her first single, 'I'm a Honky-Tonk Girl' became a minor hit and earned her an invitation to perform in *The Grand Ole Opry* country music show in Nashville, following which *Cashbox* magazine named her the Most Programmed Female Country Star for 1962.

From that early award, Lynn established herself as a major singles and album artist with albums such as *Blue Kentucky Girl* (1965) and *Woman of the World* (1969). In 1976 her autobiography *Coal Miner's Daughter* became a bestseller; it was made into a major motion picture in 1979.

Lyon, Mary Frances

Born 1925
English biologist whose work has been invaluable in the study of hereditary disease

Mary Lyon was born in Norwich and educated at Cambridge. She joined the UK Medical Research Council's staff in 1950 and began working at their Radiobiology Unit, Harwell/Chilton, in 1955, becoming head of its Genetics Division in 1962, and deputy director from 1986 until 1990, when she officially retired.

Lyon has published on many aspects of mammalian genetics and metagenesis. Her name is particularly associated with the 'Lyon hypothesis' of random inactivation of the mammalian X chromosome, which she propounded in 1961. She suggested that one of the two X chromosomes in female mammals is inactivated in early development (becoming the 'sex chromatin' found in the nucleus of normal female, but not male cells), so that females are in effect mosaics of different genetic cell lines (characterized by which of the X chromosomes is switched off). This idea has been widely confirmed and has proved to be of great value in studies on clinical genetics and imprinting.

She has extended knowledge of the mam-malian X, especially with respect to human–mouse homologies. Her long-term research on the t-complex region of mouse chromosome 17 has elucidated many puzzling features and made it the most thoroughly studied part of the mouse genome, and her studies of the genetic effects of low radiation doses and female germ-cell exposures have strengthened genetic risk assessment.

She is a Foreign Associate of the US National Academy of Sciences and Foreign Honoraria Member of the Genetics Society of Japan. She chaired the Committee on Standardized Genetic Nomenclature for Mice (1975–90), as well as the Mouse Genome Committee of the Human Genome Organization (HUGO). She was elected a Fellow of the Royal Society in 1973, and was awarded its Royal Medal in 1984.

Lytton, Constance Georgina

Born 1869 Died 1923
English suffragette who was among the most ardent campaigners of her time

Constance Lytton was born in Vienna and spent her childhood between Vienna, Paris, Lisbon, India, and the family home at Knebworth, Hertfordshire. She was educated at home by governesses.

Around 1906 she was introduced to the Esperance Guild for Working Girls and became involved with women's suffrage. She visited suffragettes in Holloway jail, joined the Women's Social and Political Union, and became an ardent campaigner.

In 1909 she was arrested herself but released when her identity was discovered. Thereafter she gave a false name, was imprisoned as Jane Warton and force-fed eight times. She gave an account of her experiences at a public meeting which was instrumental in the cessation of force-feeding; all of this is related in her book *Prison and Prisoners* (1914).

m

McAliskey, (Josephine) Bernadette, née Devlin

Born 1947
Northern Irish political activist who was a key figure in Irish politics in the 1970s

Bernadette Devlin was born into a poor Catholic family and brought up in Dungannon, County Tyrone. She was educated at St Patrick's Girls' Academy, Dungannon, and Queen's University, Belfast. While at university she became the youngest MP in the House of Commons since William Pitt the Younger when she was elected as an Independent Unity candidate in 1969, aged 21.

Her aggressive political style led to her arrest while leading Catholic rioters in the Bogside and she was sentenced to nine months' imprisonment, but in 1971 she lost Catholic support when she gave birth to an illegitimate child. She married two years later and did not stand in the 1974 general election.

In 1979 she unsuccessfully sought a seat in the European parliament, and in 1981 actively supported the IRA hunger strikers, making a dramatic appearance in Spain after her recovery from an attempted assassination in which she and her husband were shot. She was a co-founder of the Irish Republican Socialist party in 1975–6 and was appointed Chairman of the Independent Socialist Party. She wrote her autobiography, *The Price of My Soul*, in 1969.

McAllister, Anne Hunter

Born 1892 Died 1983
Scottish pioneer in speech training and therapy

Anne McAllister was born in Biggar, Lanarkshire, and began her career teaching in city schools in Glasgow. In 1919 she joined the staff of the college which later became Jordanhill College of Education, where for 30 years she blazed the trail for speech training in the education of teachers — personally training the teachers, writing their text-books, broadcasting, and conducting research (which won her a DSc from Glasgow University).

Concurrently she studied for the new degree of BEd at Glasgow University and, from 1926, assisted in the educational pioneer William Boyd's clinic. She established the Glasgow School of Speech Therapy in 1935 and was a founder of the College of Speech Therapists, the British headquarters of the profession she had helped to create.

Macarthur, Elizabeth, née Veale

Born 1766 Died 1850
English-born Australian pioneer who help to found the wool industry in Australia

Elizabeth Veale was born in Bridgerule, Devon. She married John Macarthur (1767–1834) in 1788 and sailed with him and their son to New South Wales in 1789 on the second fleet. In 1793 Macarthur received a grant of land near Parramatta, New South Wales, which he named Elizabeth Farm.

During her husband's prolonged absences from the colony, she was left, with their seven surviving children, to manage his involved business ventures. (He led the 'Rum Rebellion' against Governor William Bligh in 1808–10, and was banished to England until 1816). With the support of her husband's nephew, Hannibal Hawkins Macarthur (1788–1861), she introduced merino sheep to Elizabeth Farm and to their new grant of land at Camden, New South Wales, and successfully carried out experiments in the breeding of sheep for fine wool which led to the establishment of the Australian wool industry.

In 1816 Governor Macquarie gave an additional 600 acres to the Macarthurs in special recognition of Elizabeth's work for the betterment of the colony's agriculture. She is generally regarded as the first 'educated' woman in Australia.

MacArthur, Mary Reid

Born 1880 Died 1921
Scottish trade unionist who fought for better working conditions, especially for women

Mary Reid MacArthur was born in Glasgow. She was educated at Glasgow High School before working in her father's draper's shop. She joined the Shop Assistants' Union in 1901, became President of the Scottish National District and, on moving to London, became Secretary of the Women's Trade Union League (1903).

Maintaining an 'exuberant and contagious joy of life', she organized strikes and fought for better conditions and minimum wages. Her most famous campaigns concerned sweated labour (1906), outworkers (1907) and chain-makers (1910). She was delegate to the International Congress of Women in Berlin and the USA (1904, 1908), founded the National Federation of Women Workers (1906), the journal *Woman Worker* (1907), and was on the National Council of the Independent Labour Party (1909–12); also during this time she married W C Anderson.

During World War I she campaigned for women workers in munitions factories, becoming well known throughout Britain and the USA, and an unlikely friend of Queen Mary (**Mary of Teck**). Her last major engagement was as British labour representative in the USA in 1920.

Macaulay, Catherine Graham, *née* Sawbridge

Born 1731 Died 1791
English historian who wrote one of the earliest English history books by a women

Catherine Sawbridge was born in Wye, Kent, and educated at home by her father in Greek and Latin. She married George Macaulay, an obstetrician, in 1760.

Her *History of England* (which ran to eight volumes) was published from 1763 and met with both critical acclaim and condemnation. She visited Paris and met the intellectuals of the day at home and abroad. Most famously she is said to have dined with Dr Johnson and to have invited the footman to dine with them.

Her husband died in 1766 and in 1778 she married William Graham who was almost half her age, thus incurring much censure. In 1785

she visited the USA and was the guest of George Washington for 10 days.

Macaulay, Dame (Emilie) Rose

Born 1881 Died 1958
English novelist, travel writer and essayist whose style was intelligent and satirical

Rose Macaulay was born in Rugby, Warwickshire, the daughter of a Cambridge university lecturer in classical literature, and educated at Somerville College, Oxford, where she read history.

Her first novel was *Abbots Verney* (1906), followed by *Views and Vagabonds* (1912) and *The Lee Shore* (1920), which won a £1,000 publishers' prize. Her later novels included *Potterism* (1920), *Dangerous Ages* (1921, which won the Femina Vie Heureuse prize), *Told by an Idiot* (1923), *Orphan Island* (1924), *Crewe Train* (1926), *Keeping Up Appearances* (1928), *They were Defeated* (1932), *I Would be a Private* (1937) and *And No Man's Wit* (1940).

After World War II she wrote two further novels, *The World My Wilderness* (1950), and *The Towers of Trebizond* (1956), which won the Tait Black Memorial prize. Her travel books included *They Went to Portugal* (1946), *Fabled Shore* (1949) and *The Pleasure of Ruins* (1953). She was created DBE in 1958.

McAuley, Catherine Elizabeth

Born 1787 Died 1841
Irish nun who founded the order of the Religious Sisters of Mercy

Catherine McAuley was born in Dublin, a Roman Catholic. When her Protestant adoptive parents left her some money, she had a large building built in Dublin which she opened in 1827 as the House of Our Blessed Lady of Mercy, a school for orphans and poor children and a residence for working women.

She was persuaded by the Archbishop of Dublin to enter the religious life and in 1831 she and two others took the vows of poverty, chastity and obedience, thus founding the order of the Religious Sisters of Mercy (RSM). McAuley was its superior for the first 10 years.

The RSM opened a house in London in 1839 and was to become one of the largest congregations in the English-speaking world, still active in social work and education to this day.

Macbeth, Ann

Born 1875 Died 1948
English embroideress and a member of the 'Glasgow School'

Ann Macbeth was born in Little Bolton. She studied at Glasgow School of Art (1897–1900) and was a member of its staff from 1901 to 1920, latterly as head of the embroidery department. She was influential in advocating new methods of teaching embroidery through lecturing, teaching, and through several books, including an instruction manual called *Educational Needlecraft* (1911).

She executed a number of ecclesiastical commmissions and her embroidered panels decorate many Glasgow interiors. She was a member of the famous 'Glasgow School', and received the Lauder award in 1930.

MacBride, Maud *see* Gonne, Maud

McCarthy, Mary Thérèse

> Born 1912 Died 1989
> *American novelist and critic noted for her acerbic observations on marriage, sexuality, intellectualism and urban society*

Mary McCarthy was born in Seattle, Washington, of mixed Catholic, Protestant and Jewish descent. She and her three younger brothers were orphaned in 1918 and were raised by grandparents, uncles and aunts. At the age of eight she won a state prize for an article entitled 'The Irish in American History'. She was educated at Forest Ridge Convent, Seattle, and Anne Wright Seminary, Tacoma, and graduated from Vassar College, New York in 1933. She married an actor, Harold Johnsrud, who died in a fire.

She began to write book reviews for the *Nation* and the *New Republic* and in 1936–7 was an editor for *Covici Friede*; from 1937 to 1948 she was an editor and theatre critic for the *Partisan Review*, during which period she wrote articles, stories and eventually novels. In 1938 she married the critic Edmund Wilson, who encouraged her to write fiction, but they divorced soon afterwards. In 1948 she married Bowden Bowater, whom she divorced in 1961 to marry James West, an information officer.

Her voice has often been described as scathing, yet although she brought little emotional warmth to her work, she was a highly intelligent, observant novelist. Her best-known fiction is *The Company She Keeps* (1942), *The Groves of Academe* (1952) and *The Group* (1963), a bestseller about eight Vassar graduates and their sex lives. She also wrote documentary denunciations of US involvement in the Vietnam war, in *Vietnam* (1967) and *Hanoi* (1968). Other works include *A Charmed Life* (1955), *Sights and Spectacles* (1956), the autobiographical *Memories of a*

Catholic Childhood (1957) and *Cannibals and Missionaries* (1979).

McCauley, Mary Ludwig Hays, *known as* Molly Pitcher

> Born 1754 Died 1832
> *American Revolutionary War heroine*

Mary Hays was born near Trenton, New Jersey. She earned her nickname by carrying water to her husband, John Hays (or Heis), and the other men of the 7th Pennsylvania Regiment during the Battle of Monmouth on 28 June 1778. When her husband collapsed from the heat, like (or perhaps confused with) **Margaret Corbin**, she took his place at his cannon for the remainder of the battle. For this act of bravery she was rewarded with a government pension in 1822. After her husband's death she married a man named George McCauley.

McClintock, Barbara

> Born 1902 Died 1992
> *American geneticist whose pioneering work included the discovery of 'controlling elements' in genes*

Barbara McClintock was born in Hartford, Connecticut. She received a PhD in botany in 1927 from Cornell, where she worked from 1927 to 1935. Later she held posts at the University of Missouri (1936–41) and Cold Spring Harbor (1941–92). In 1927, with Harriet Creighton, she showed that changes in the chromosomes of maize resulted in physical changes in the colour of the corn kernels; this ultimate proof of the chromosome theory of heredity was published in 1931.

In the 1940s she showed how genes in maize are activated and deactivated by 'controlling elements' — genes that control other genes, and which can be copied from chromosome to chromosome. She presented her work in 1951 at a Cold Spring Harbor symposium, but its significance was lost on the attendees who mainly worked with bacteria. It was not until the 1970s, after the work of the French biochemists François Jacob (1920–) and Jacques Monod (1910–76), that her work began to be appreciated. At a 1976 symposium, McClintock's research was acknowledged with the introduction of the term 'transposon' to describe her 'controlling elements'.

Finally in 1983, she was awarded the Nobel Prize for Physiology or Medicine. She continued to work on maize genetics at Cold Spring Harbor until her death.

McClung, Nellie (Letitia), *née* Mooney

Born 1873 Died 1951
Canadian suffragist, writer and public speaker
who was influential in Canadian politics

Nellie Mooney was born in Chatsworth, Ontario, and educated in Manitoba. She married in 1896 and had five children. In 1908 she published her first novel, *Sowing Seeds in Danny*, the heroine of which reappears as a suffragist in later novels, such as *The Second Chance* (1910) and *Purple Springs* (1921). She also wrote short stories, many of which reflect her social concerns, including women's suffrage, immigrants and prohibition.

She rose to prominence through the Women's Christian Temperance Union and the suffrage movement, and after moving to Edmonton in 1916 she continued to campaign for prohibition and suffrage there. After being elected as a Liberal to the Alberta Legislative Assembly (1921), she attempted to make Alberta's divorce laws more liberal, among other activities, but was defeated in 1925.

McColgan, Liz (Elizabeth)

Born 1964
Scottish middle- and long-distance runner

Liz McColgan was born in Dundee and committed to athletics from an early age. She studied at the University of Alabama before returning to Scotland, where she won her first major success — the 10,000 metres gold medal in the 1986 Commonwealth Games, held in Edinburgh. She won the silver medal at the Seoul Olympics of 1988, then retained her Commonwealth title in Auckland in 1990, as well as winning a bronze in the 3,000 metres behind her great rival, **Yvonne Murray**.

Already possessed of great mental resolve and physical stamina, she returned to the sport after the birth of her daughter, seemingly stronger than ever, and won the 1991 New York Marathon in two hours, 27 minutes, the fastest female marathon début. Also that year, in a remarkable performance of front-running, she won the 10,000 metres at the World Championship in Tokyo, but failed to take the expected gold in the same distance at the 1992 Barcelona Olympics.

In 1993 she had two knee operations and was advised to give up racing, but continued her career regardless and resumed training in Gainsville, Florida, coached by her husband Peter. She returned to racing in 1995 to come fifth in the London Marathon and, representing Britain for the first time since 1992,

finished fourth in the 10,000 metres in the European Cup and set her sights on the 1996 Olympic marathon in Atlanta. She is also an enthusiastic worker with young athletes, and has been the Athletics Development Officer of Dundee District Council since 1987.

McCormick, Patricia

Born 1930
American diver, twice the winner of two Olympic gold medals

Patricia McCormick was born in Seal Beach, California. In 1951 she became the first woman to win all the American Athletics Union indoor and outdoor diving championships.

At the 1952 Olympics she won gold medals in both the platform and springboard events, a performance she repeated at the 1956 Olympics, becoming the only woman in Olympic history to achieve the 'double double'.

By the time she retired in 1956 she had won five Pan-American Games medals and 27 national championships. She was chosen the Associated Press Female Athlete of the Year in 1956 and became the second woman to receive the James E Sullivan Award as the Amateur Athlete of the Year.

McCracken, Esther Helen, *née* Armstrong

Born 1902 Died 1971
English actress and playwright known for her domestic comedies

Esther Armstrong was born in Newcastle-upon-Tyne. Her first husband, Lt-Col Angus McCracken, died in action in 1943, and she married Mungo Campbell in 1944.

She acted with the Newcastle Repertory Company from 1924 to 1937 and her first play, *The Willing Spirit*, was produced in 1936, but it was with *Quiet Wedding* (1938) that her reputation was made as a writer of domestic comedy. Other successes were *Quiet Weekend* (1941) and *No Medals* (1944).

McCullers, (Lula) Carson, *née* Smith

Born 1917 Died 1967
American novelist whose characters embody everyday inner human problems

Carson Smith was born in Columbus, Georgia. She went to high school there and then attended writing classes at Columbia University, New York, and at New York University. In 1937 she married Reeves McCullers, with whom she moved to Charlotte, North Carolina; in 1941 they moved to Greenwich

Village and divorced, but were re-married in 1945, finally divorcing again in 1948.

The Heart is a Lonely Hunter, her first book, about a deaf mute, appeared in 1940, distinguishing her immediately as a novelist of note. She wrote the best and the bulk of her work in a six-year spell through World War II. Along with William Faulkner, Tennessee Williams and Truman Capote she is credited with fashioning a type of fiction labelled by critics as Southern Gothic. Fusing, in her own words, 'anguish and farce', she peopled her work with grotesque characters who are expressionistic extensions of normal, universal human problems.

Reflections in a Golden Eye appeared in 1941, followed by *The Member of the Wedding* (1946), *The Ballad of the Sad Cafe* (1951) and *Clock Without Hands*, a last ironic look at the South, in 1961.

McCullough, Colleen

Born 1937
Australian novelist who became famous when her bestselling saga The Thorn Birds *was televised*

Colleen McCullough was born in Wellington. She is best known for the Cleary family's saga of sex, religion and disaster, *The Thorn Birds* (1977), later produced as a televison series. Her earlier book *Tim* (1974) was also filmed, as was *An Indecent Obsession* (1981). A delicate novella, *The Ladies of Missalonghi* (1987) showed that she is capable of some fine writing, and her latest books, a series of six novels set in Ancient Rome, starting with *The First Man in Rome* (1990), demonstrate a concern for historical detail.

MacDonald, Elaine Maria

Born 1943
Scottish ballet dancer, the Scottish Ballet's leading ballerina for 20 years

Elaine MacDonald was born in Tadcaster. She trained at the Royal Ballet School, joined Western Theatre Ballet in 1964 and moved with the company to Glasgow when it became Scottish Ballet in the late 1960s. She was their leading ballerina from 1969 to 1989.

Though her career has been limited by a total loyalty to this company, she became a dancer of international standard and created many roles for the choreographer–director Peter Darrell, including *Sun Into Darkness* (1966), *Beauty and the Beast* (1969), *Tales of Hoffman* (1972), *Mary Queen of Scots* (1976) and *Five Ruckert Songs* (1978).

She was artistic controller of the company in 1988–9, and was appointed associate artistic director of the Northern Ballet Theatre in 1990.

Macdonald, Flora

Born 1722 Died 1790
Scottish Jacobite heroine whose role in helping Bonnie Prince Charlie escape has become the subject of many legends and songs

Flora Macdonald was born in South Uist in the Hebrides, the daughter of a tacksman or farmer who died when she was two. At the age of 13 she was adopted by Lady Clanranald, the wife of the chief of the clan.

After the Battle of Culloden (1746) which finally broke the 1745 Jacobite Rising, she conducted the Young Pretender, Prince Charles Edward Stuart, disguised as her maid 'Betty Burke', from Benbecula to Portree. For this perilous feat she was much fêted during her year's captivity on the troopship in Leith Roads and in the Tower of London.

In 1750 she married Allan Macdonald, the son of Macdonald of Kingsburgh in Skye, where in 1773 she entertained Dr Johnson. The following year she emigrated with her husband to North Carolina. In 1776 Allan became a brigadier-general in the War of Independence. He was taken prisoner and Flora returned to Scotland in 1779. After two years she was rejoined by him, and they settled again at Kingsburgh.

MacDonald, Frances

Born 1873 Died 1921
Scottish painter and designer who was a major exponent of Art Nouveau

Frances MacDonald was born in Glasgow. She was one of the internationally influential Glasgow 'Group of Four', the prime exponents of Art Nouveau in Scotland. The other three members were her sister **Margaret Mackintosh**, brother-in-law Charles Rennie Mackintosh, and her husband Herbert MacNair. Frances MacDonald's paintings and decorations are generally strongly poetic, incorporating insubstantial figures in symbolic settings.

MacDonald, Margaret *see* Mackintosh, Margaret

MacDonald, Sharman

Born 1951
Scottish playwright and novelist

Sharman MacDonald was born in Glasgow and educated at Edinburgh University. She became an actress before embarking on a full-time writing career. Her first play, *When I Was a Girl I Used to Scream and Shout*, a bitter and wry study of Scottish childhood and adolescence, produced at the Bush Theatre, London (1984), was an immediate success and won the *Evening Standard* Most Promising Playwright award for that year.

Also for the Bush Theatre she has written *The Brave* (1988), which is set in Morocco where a Scottish woman is visiting her refugee terrorist sister. *When We Were Women* (1989) was written for the National Theatre Studio; set in Scotland, it is a more lyrical and shrewd piece exploring a woman's relationship with her boyfriend and her parents during World War II. *Shades* (1992) develops further MacDonald's recurring theme of the relationship between parents and their children, as does *The Winter Guest* (1995). Her novels *The Beast* (1986) and *Night Night* (1988) however, have had less success.

McEwan, Geraldine, *originally* McKeown

Born 1932
English actress who has been equally successful in classical and contemporary drama

Geraldine McEwan was born in Windsor. She gained her first acting experience there with the local repertory company, and played a number of light comedies in London.

She came to notice in *The Member of the Wedding* in 1958, and confirmed her promise with the Shakespeare Memorial Theatre in Stratford-upon-Avon. She made her New York début in 1963 in Sheridan's *The School For Scandal*, and went on to earn a glowing reputation as an intelligent and versatile actress who is able to rise to the challenge of widely differing roles, and is equally at home in the classics and contemporary drama.

McGinley, Phyllis

Born 1905 Died 1978
American author of skilful light verse

Phyllis McGinley was born in Oregon. Many of her verses appeared in the *New Yorker* and she became known for her humorous verse about various aspects of modern life.

In 1961 she won the Pulitzer Prize for poetry for her *Times Three: Selected Verse from Three Decades* (1960). She was praised by such highly thought of critics as W H Auden, but her work has failed to last, not being quite of the order of that of Harry Graham, Ogden Nash and others of that calibre. McGinley also wrote successful and charming books for children.

MacGregor, Sue (Susan Katriona)

Born 1941
English BBC radio presenter who has achieved success in a highly competitive field

Sue MacGregor was born in Oxford and educated mainly in South Africa. Her first job was as an announcer and producer with the state-run South African Broadcasting Corporation (1962–7).

She moved to London and joined the BBC as a reporter in 1967, working on *World at One*, *World this Weekend* and *PM*, before beginning her 15-year position as presenter of *Woman's Hour* for Radio 4 in 1972. She also worked on *Tuesday Call* (1973–84) and has had her own radio series, *Conversation Piece*, since 1978.

Highly respected in her field, MacGregor has been a presenter of BBC Radio 4's *Today* programme since 1984, and is also known to be very knowledgeable about South African affairs and to enjoy a firm friendship with Helen Suzman.

McIntosh, Genista Mary, *née* Tandy

Born 1946
English arts administrator who is a prominent figure in the world of British theatre

Genista Tandy was born in London and educated at the University of York. She married Neil McIntosh in 1971 (divorced 1990). She began her career working with the York Festival of the Arts before joining the Royal Shakespeare Company, where she was casting director (1972–7), planning controller (1977–84), senior administrator (1984–90) and associate producer in 1990. That year she was appointed executive director of the Royal National Theatre.

Mack, (Marie) Louise Hamilton

Born 1874 Died 1935
Australian children's author, novelist and journalist who was the first woman war correspondent

Louise Mack was born in Hobart, Tasmania. Her sister Amy Mack (1876–1939) was a naturalist and children's writer. Louise's first juvenile novel *The World is Round* appeared in 1896; the trilogy *Teens* (1897), *Girls Together* (1898), and the much later *Teens Triumphant* (1933), drew on her own school experiences.

She moved to London in 1901 and wrote the popular *An Australian Girl in London* (1902); nine other adult novels include *The Red Rose of Summer* (1909) and *The Music Makers* (1914).

She spent some years in Florence during

which she edited the English-language *Italian Gazette* (1904–7). In 1914 she went to Belgium for the London *Daily Mail* and *Evening News* as the first woman war correspondent; her adventures were published in 1915 as *A Woman's Experiences in the Great War*.

McKay, Heather Pamela, *née* Blundell

Born 1941
Australian squash player who was unbeaten between 1962 and 1980

Heather Blundell was born in Queanbeyan, New South Wales, one of 11 children. As a schoolgirl she played hockey for Australia, then at the age of 18 was Queanbeyan tennis champion. Having taken up squash rackets at 17 to keep fit for hockey, she went on to win 14 Australian titles (1960–73), as well as the British Open in 16 successive years (1962–77) and to be World Champion in 1976 and 1979.

She married another top squash player, Brian McKay, in 1965 and 10 years later moved to Canada, where she became Canadian racketball champion.

Heather McKay, 1962

Mackay, Jessie

Born 1864 Died 1938
New Zealand poet who is recognized as the first significant native-born poet

Jessie Mackay was born in Rakaia Gorge, Canterbury, of Scottish descent. Her verse drew heavily on the vocabulary of Celtic and Scan-

dinavian myth, but she was a liberal thinker and ardent feminist.

She fought for the issues of the day, as in her 'Vigil, April 10, 1919' on the eve of a Prohibition referendum. Her first collections were *The Spirit of the Rangatira* (1889), *The Sitter on the Rail* (1891) and *From the Maori Sea* (1908), and her last was *Vigil* (1935).

Mackellar, Dorothea

Born 1885 Died 1968
Australia's most often quoted poet whose fame rests on one single poem

Dorothea Mackellar was born in Sydney. Her fame rests solely on 'My Country', which was first published in the London *Spectator* in 1908. Later revised and included in her first collection *The Closed Door* (1911), its opening lines 'I Love a Sunburnt Country,/A Land of Sweeping Plains —' evoke an emotional response from Australians the world over.

She published three further volumes of verse between 1914 and 1926, all in pastoral and patriotic vein, and three novels, two of them in collaboration with **Ruth Bedford**. Ill health circumscribed her writing, but she lived to 83, still revered as the author of one poem.

McKenna, Siobhán

Born 1923 Died 1986
Northern Irish actress whose loyalty to the work of her fellow Irishmen resulted in a fine reputation

Siobhán McKenna was born in Belfast. She made her stage début in Galway, then joined the Abbey Theatre in Dublin in 1944, playing leading roles in both Gaelic and English.

She made her London début in 1947 and first appeared in New York in 1955, and went on to play with distinction in Shakespeare, Chekov, Shaw, O'Neill and Brecht, among others. However her reputation was firmly founded on her many Irish roles, from the generation of Sean O'Casey and J M Synge through to contemporary playwrights. Her one-woman show *Here Are Ladies* (1975) incorporated work by Yeats, Beckett and Joyce.

McKenzie, Julia Kathleen

Born 1941
English actress, singer and director known for her interpretation of Stephen Sondheim's musicals

Julia McKenzie trained at the Guildhall School of Music and Drama. Her London musical appearances include *Maggie May* (1965),

Mame (1969), Sondheim's *Company* (1972); the anthologies *Cowardy Custard* (1973), *Cole* (1974), and *Side by Side* by Stephen Sondheim (1977); Frank Loesser's *Guys and Dolls* (1982); and Sondheim's *Follies* (1987).

She has interspersed musicals with plays, notably Bertolt Brecht's *Schweyk in the Second World War* (1982), three plays by Alan Ayckbourn — *The Norman Conquests* (1974), *Ten Times Table* (1979) and *Woman in Mind* (1986) — and has also appeared in television films such as *Adam Bede* (1992) and in the feature film *Shirley Valentine* (1989).

Following her directorial début, *Stepping Out*, in 1984, she has directed such plays as *Steel Magnolias* (1989) and *Putting It Together* (1992).

McKillop, St Mary Helen

Born 1842 Died 1909
Australian nun, known as Mother Mary of the
Cross, who became the first Australian saint

Mary McKillop was born in the Fitzroy district of Melbourne, Victoria, the daughter of Scottish parents who had married soon after emigrating. With Father Tenison-Woods she founded the Society of the Sisters of St Joseph of the Sacred Heart in Penola, South Australia, in 1866. Although the Society quickly grew, establishing 170 schools and 160 Josephite convents, diocesan rivalry caused Mother Mary to be excommunicated in 1871 but she was reinstated two years later by Pope Pius IX, who approved the Sisterhood in the same year.

In 1875 Mother Mary was confirmed as superior-general of the order, which is popularly known as the 'Little Joeys'. Its work is highly regarded, and it is devoted to the education of poorer children and care of orphans and unmarried mothers. The case for the beatification of Mother Mary, the first step towards canonization, was made in 1925, and in 1975 her cause was formally introduced by the Vatican. She was beatified by Pope John Paul II in 1995, making her Australia's first saint.

MacKinnon, Catherine

Born 1946
American feminist writer and legal scholar who
has fervently addressed gender-related issues in her
bid for sexual equality

Catherine MacKinnon was born in Minneapolis, Minnesota. She studied at Smith College and Yale Law School (graduating in 1977) before undertaking a post-graduate degree in political science at Yale. Her first publication arose from an extended student essay, *Sexual Harassment of Working Women: A Case of Sex Discrimination* (1979). In 1986 her fight for equality in the workplace bore fruit, when the Supreme Court decreed that sexual harassment was sex discrimination.

MacKinnon then pursued in earnest her crusade against pornography, which she identified as a key issue reinforcing the inequality of women. With feminist writer **Andrea Dworkin**, she formulated an ordinance which classified pornography as a human rights violation; it was, however, rejected in the courts. She has also lectured and written extensively on the related issues of rape and abortion, as well as working with Croatian and Muslim women demanding justice for Serbian sexual atrocities.

Her publications include *Feminism Unmodified: A Discourse on Life and Law* (1987) and *Only Words* (1994).

Mackintosh, Elizabeth see Tey, Josephine

Mackintosh, Margaret, *née* MacDonald

Born 1865 Died 1933
English artist who was a major exponent of Art
Nouveau in Scotland

Margaret MacDonald was born in Staffordshire. She studied at the Glasgow College of Art, and married the Scottish architect Charles Rennie Mackintosh in 1900. She was one of the internationally influential Glasgow 'Group of Four', the prime exponents of Art Nouveau in Scotland. The other three members were her husband, her sister **Frances MacDonald**, and her brother-in-law Herbert MacNair.

Best known for her work in watercolours and stained glass, she exhibited widely on the Continent, winning the Diploma of Honour at the Turin International Exhibition of 1902. She collaborated with her husband in much of his work.

McLachlan, Jessie

Born 1834 Died c.1899
Scottish convicted murderer who was at the centre
of a highly controversial crime

McLachlan had once been a servant in the Glasgow house where a murder took place. The victim was killed while the family was absent, with the exception of the house-owner's father, a Mr Fleming. When the body was discovered Fleming was arrested on suspicion of having committed the murder. He was released after a week and McLachlan, who was friendly with both Fleming and the victim, was then charged, convicted (1862) and sentenced to death.

Fleming denied any involvement in the offence. McLachlan likewise denied all knowledge of the deed and entered a special defence naming the old man as the murderer. He appeared as the chief prosecution witness. After the conviction and sentence a petition was raised which attracted over 50,000 signatures protesting McLachlan's innocence and seeking justice.

In the absence of a court of criminal appeal, parliament set up a private enquiry which resulted in McLachlan being granted a conditional royal pardon, the condition being that she be detained in prison for the rest of her life. She spent 15 years in prison and subsequently emigrated to the USA. Fleming spent the rest of his life under a cloud of suspicion.

MacLaine, Shirley, *originally* Shirley McLean Beaty

Born 1934
American actress whose freshness and frankness has brought her unconventional leading roles

Shirley MacLaine was born in Richmond, Virginia, a sister of the filmmaker Warren Beatty (1937–) who changed the spelling of his surname). She entered showbusiness as a teenager and made her film début in Alfred Hitchcock's black comedy *The Trouble With Harry* (1955).

Adept at light comedy, her impish good-humour and waif-like manner made her an unconventional leading lady and Hollywood struggled at first to showcase her talent. She won the first of five Best Actress Oscar nominations for her role opposite Frank Sinatra in *Some Came Running* (1958), and a second for her heart-rending performance in Billy Wilder's *The Apartment* (1960). She appeared in several lavish 1960s productions, which generally had little success, but was acclaimed in the musical *Sweet Charity* (1968).

Increasingly successful in later years, she has starred in such films as *Being There* (1979), *Terms of Endearment* (1983), for which she finally won her coveted Best Actress Oscar, *Steel Magnolias* (1989), and *Postcards From The Edge* (1990).

McLaren, Agnes

Born 1837 Died 1913
Scottish Catholic doctor and missionary who campaigned for priests and nuns to be given medical training

Agnes McLaren was born in Edinburgh. She studied medicine there and in Dublin but had to go to France to graduate, where she became the first woman graduate in medicine at Montpellier in 1878 before practising in Nice.

She became a Roman Catholic at the age of 60 and in 1910 founded the first Catholic medical mission in India: St Catherine's Hospital, Rawalpindi (now in Pakistan). It was a hospital for women, run by women, as Islam requires.

Lay associates under the leadership of her Austrian successor, Anna Dengel, became the Medical Mission Sisters when in 1936 the Vatican ban against medical training for priests and nuns was lifted — development stemming at least in part from McLaren's own persistent appeals to Rome.

McLaren, Dame Anne Laura

Born 1927
Welsh developmental biologist and geneticist, influential in cancer research

Anne McLaren was brought up in Tal-y-cafn, near Conwy in Wales, a daughter of the 2nd Baron of Aberconway (d.1953). She was educated at the University of Oxford, where she obtained her PhD, and after post-doctoral work in London she joined the Agricultural Research Council's Unit of Animal Genetics in Edinburgh (1959). She was Director of the Medical Research Council's Mammalian Development Unit from 1974 until she retired in 1992 and became a Principal Research Associate at the Wellcome Trust/Cancer Campaign Research Institute in Cambridge.

She has published extensively on reproductive biology and embryology, genetics and immunology, and is best known for her discovery and isolation of the embryonal carcinoma cell line. This cell type is of great value in studying the nature of carcinogenesis, among other things.

McLaren received the Scientific Medal of the Zoological Society of London in 1967, was elected FRS in 1975 (Foreign Secretary 1991 and Vice-President 1992, the first woman to serve as an officer of the Royal Society), and was created DBE in 1993.

McLaughlin, (Mary) Louise

Born 1847 Died 1939
American artist who discovered the secret of Limoges underglaze painting

Louise McLaughlin studied drawing, wood carving and china painting at the McMicken

School of Design in Cincinnati. She began to experiment with slip-painting after having been impressed with the work of the French ceramicist Ernest Chaplet at the Exposition or exhibition of fine pottery by the Haviland firm from Limoges, who were considered to be the finest producers of Limoges porcelain. Her work with the underglazing techniques known as 'Faience' led her style to be known as 'Cincinnati Limoges' or 'Cincinnati Faience' ware. She was forced to abandon this work in 1885 due to a lack of facilities.

She founded the Cincinnati Art Pottery Club in 1879 with Clara Newton and **Laura Ann Fry** to encourage other women, and fired their work at the Coultry Pottery. In 1881 they began to use the facilities at the Rookwood Pottery but the following year were refused them, due to rivalry between the members of the Club and the pottery designers.

In 1895 Louise resumed full-scale ceramic work and patented a new method of decoration called 'American Faience'. Her most successful work, produced around 1901, was named 'Losanti' (the original name for Cincinnati being Losantiville), a high-fired translucent porcelain carved and filled with delicate glazes. McLaughlin abandoned ceramics entirely in 1906.

McLean, Una

Born 1930
Scottish actress and comedienne

Una McLean was born in Strathaven, Lanarkshire, and educated at Larkhall. She trained at the Royal Scottish Academy of Music and Drama, and made her professional début at the Byre Theatre, St Andrews, in 1955. She joined the Citizen's Theatre, Glasgow, in 1959, appearing as Emilia in *Othello*, and has consistently asserted her dramatic prowess in such productions as *The Wild Duck* (1969), *Woman in Mind* (1988), *The Guid Sisters* (1989), *Ines De Castro* (1989) and *Sky Woman Falling* (1991).

A versatile comedienne with a rasping cackle of a laugh, she served as a foil to some of Scotland's top entertainers in the fondly recalled *Five Past Eight Shows* of the 1960s, and has proved herself a stalwart of pantomime since her début in *Mother Goose* (1958). Her musical talents have been displayed in the likes of *The Boyfriend* (1970) and *The Beggar's Opera* (1981) and she is a veteran of countless television shows, including the award-winning *Dreaming* (1990). In 1991 she married her frequent co-star Russell Hunter.

Maclehose, Agnes, *née* Craig

Born 1759   Died 1841
Scottish literary figure remembered for her acquaintance with Robert Burns

Agnes Craig was born in Edinburgh, the daughter of a surgeon. In 1776 she married a Glasgow lawyer, from whom she separated in 1780. She met the poet Robert Burns (1759–96) at a party in Edinburgh in 1787, and subsequently carried on with him the well-known correspondence under the name 'Clarinda'. A number of Burns's poems and songs were dedicated to her.

McLish, Rachael Elizondo

Born 1958
American body-builder whose occupation has prompted discussion of the conflicts of ideals inherent in female body-building

Rachel McLish was born in Harlington, Texas. She was Miss Olympia in 1980 and 1982.

In 1985 McLish was featured in the film documentary *Pumping Iron II*, which examined the conflict between judging women's body-building on female ideals of beauty and body-building's concepts of musculature and strength.

Macmillan, Chrystal

Born 1882   Died 1937
Scottish lawyer who used her position as an early woman graduate to champion women's rights and pacifism

Chrystal Macmillan was born in Edinburgh. She was educated at St Leonard's School, St Andrews, and Edinburgh University where, as one of its first women graduates, she obtained a first-class degree before further study in Berlin. She was called to the Bar in 1924, but never practised, instead immersing herself in feminist causes.

As the first woman to address the House of Lords (1908), she appealed for the right of women graduates to vote and served on a plethora of committees, as well as being a leader of the National Union of Suffrage Societies, Secretary of the International Woman Suffrage Alliance, and founder of the Open Door Council (1929) which opposed legal restraints on women.

As a pacifist, she was an instigator of the International Women's Congress at the Hague (1915) and Secretary of the International Alliance of Women (1913–23). She stood unsuccessfully as a Liberal candidate in the 1935 election.

McMillan, Margaret

Born 1860 Died 1931
American-born British educational reformer

Margaret McMillan was born in New York, brought up near Inverness, and educated in Frankfurt, Geneva and Lausanne. She joined the suffrage movement in London and became an active member, and in 1893 joined the newly-formed Independent Labour Party.

As a member of Bradford School Board, she agitated ceaselessly in the industrial north of England for medical inspection and school clinics. In 1902 she joined her sister Rachel (1859–1917) in London, where they opened the first school clinic (1908) and the first open-air nursery school (1914).

After Rachel's death, the Rachel McMillan Training College for nursery and infant teachers was established as a memorial.

McMillan, Rachel

Born 1859 Died 1971
American-born British educationalist who pioneered schools for young children

Rachel McMillan was, like her sister **Margaret McMillan**, born in America and brought up in Scotland. She became a socialist in her twenties and sold Christian–Socialist tracts during the dockers' strike. After moving to London, she learnt about women's working conditions while running a working girl's hostel. Then she trained as a sanitary inspector and taught on hygiene.

She established the Rachel McMillan Open Air Nursery School in 1913–14, which became a blueprint for future nursery schools.

McMillan, Terry

Born 1951
African-American writer and educator

Terry McMillan's novels explore the lives of African-American women. They include *Mama* (1987), *Disappearing Acts* (1989) and *Waiting to Exhale* (1992). In 1990 she edited *Breaking Ice: An Anthology of African-American Fiction*.

Macnamara, Dame (Annie) Jean

Born 1899 Died 1968
Australian physician whose influence extended from polio to the iron lung and myxomatosis

Jean Macnamara was born in Beechworth, Victoria, and educated at Melbourne University. She began her career in local hospitals where she developed a special interest in 'infantile paralysis'. During the poliomyelitis epidemic of 1925, she tested the use of immune serum and, convinced of its efficacy, she visited England, the USA and Canada with the aid of a Rockefeller scholarship.

With Macfarlane Burnet (1899–1985), she found that there was more than one strain of the polio virus, a discovery which led to the development of the 'Salk vaccine' (named after American virologist Jonas Salk, 1914–). She also supported the experimental treatment developed by **Elizabeth Kenny**, and introduced the first artificial respirator (iron lung) into Australia.

She was created a DBE in 1935, and later became involved in the controversial introduction of the disease myxomatosis as a means of controlling the rabbit population of Australia. In the early 1950s it was estimated that as a result of her efforts the wool industry had saved over £30 million.

McNeill, Florence Marian

Born 1885 Died 1973
Scottish writer who specialized in the folklore and culinary history of Scotland

Florence McNeill was born in Saint Mary's Holm, Orkney, and educated there and at the universities of Glasgow and Edinburgh. She spent two years travelling before returning to take up a position as Secretary to the Association for Moral and Social Hygiene. She was busy in these years as a suffragette and, after the breakdown of her health, as a tutor in Athens and a freelance journalist in London. After settling in Scotland in 1926, she worked for the Scottish National Dictionary.

McNeill is best known for her work as a folklorist, her reputation being based upon *The Scots Kitchen* (1929), which examines Scottish culinary history, its links to France, and includes many traditional recipes. Her comprehensive *The Silver Bough* (1957–68) is a four-volume study of the folklore, festivals and traditions of Scotland. In a similar vein, her work *Hallowe'en* (1970) uses photographs and illustrations to explore the origins of the rites and ceremonies associated with this occasion in Scotland. Her only novel is *The Road Home* (1932), a romance based upon her life in Glasgow and London.

MacNicol, Bessie, *married name* Mrs Alexander Frew

Born 1869 Died 1904
Scottish artist who died in childbirth just as she was gaining a favourable reputation

Bessie MacNicol was born in Glasgow. She studied at the Glasgow School of Art (1887–92) and at the Atelier of Colarossi in Paris. She was a direct contemporary of the 'Glasgow Boys', and was influenced by such artists in that group as George Henry, Edward Arthur Hornel and James Guthrie.

She set up her own studio in 1895 in St Vincent Street, Glasgow, and produced a series of well executed, stylish portraits in a decorative manner. In 1899 she married Dr Alexander Frew and moved to a house previously owned by the artist Sir David Young Cameron with a design by Charles Rennie Mackintosh.

Maconchy, Dame Elizabeth Violet

Born 1907 Died 1994
English composer known especially for her chamber music

Elizabeth Maconchy was born in Broxbourne, Hertfordshire, of Irish parentage. She studied under Ralph Vaughan Williams at the Royal College of Music and in 1929 went to Prague, where her first major work, a piano concerto, was performed the following year. Her suite, *The Land*, was performed at the London Proms in 1930 and her early works were often written for festivals of the International Society for Contemporary Music.

Among her best-known compositions are her *Symphony* (1953) and overture *Proud Thames*, also written in Coronation Year, a carol cantata *A Christmas Morning* (1962), a choral and orchestral work *Samson and the Gates of Gaza* (1963), an opera for children *The King of the Golden River* (1975), *Heloise and Abelard* (1978) and *My Dark Heart* (1981).

She also wrote a group of one-act operas, 12 string quartets and songs. She was made a DBE in 1987. Her daughter is the composer **Nicola LeFanu**.

Macphail, Agnes Campbell, *née* Campbell

Born 1890 Died 1954
Canadian suffragette and politician who was the first woman in Canada's parliament

Agnes Campbell was born in Grey County, Ontario. She became a schoolteacher and was involved with the women's suffrage movement. She became MP for the United Farmers of Ontario in 1921 and, as the first woman to enter Canada's parliament, served until her defeat in 1940.

Afterwards she was a member of the Ontario legislature (1943–5, 1948–51) as well as a leading member of the Co-operative Commonwealth Federation Party of Canada, which had been formed in 1933. She also represented Canada in the Assembly of the League of Nations.

MacPhail, Alexandrina Matilda

Born 1860 Died 1946
Scottish doctor who became the Free Church of Scotland's first female medical missionary

Alexandrina MacPhail was born in Skye. After graduating from the London School of Medicine for Women in 1887, she went to Madras, India.

She set up a dispensary for women and children, and then a hospital in her own bungalow; these were replaced in 1914 by the purpose-built Christina Rainy Hospital. MacPhail also helped found a tuberculosis sanatorium and taught at Vellore women's medical school. During World War I she was chief medical officer of a Scottish hospitals' unit for female Serbian refugees.

She was awarded the Kaiser-i-Hind Medal in 1912 and the OBE in 1930.

Macphail, Katherine Stewart

Born 1888 Died 1974
Scottish paediatrician who used her expertise particularly in the former Yugoslavia

Katherine Stewart Macphail was born in Coatbridge, Lanarkshire. She graduated in medicine at Glasgow in 1911, and during World War I went to Salonika with the Scottish Women's Hospital Unit and later worked at the headquarters of the Serbian Army and its military medical unit. From the autumn of 1917 she worked behind the enemy lines for the civilian population in Macedonia.

In 1918 she returned to Belgrade and the following year founded a hospital for children which later became the Anglo-Yugoslav Children's Hospital. She was superintendent until 1933, and organized the building of a hospital for surgical tuberculosis at Kamenica on the Danube, which she felt was much needed for children. She remained in Yugoslavia until the Germans arrived in 1941, then was interned by the Italians but was later released and worked for two years in Lanarkshire.

In 1944, at the request of Save the Children Fund, she returned to Yugoslavia and headed the Funds's first medical relief unit there. In 1945 she returned to her hospital which she re-organized and remained as its head until 1947, when she retired to Scotland. She received many Yugoslav decorations and in 1932 she was awarded the Russian Red Cross insignia for her work among white Russian refugees and children.

McPherson, Aimee (Elizabeth) Semple, *née* Kennedy

Born 1890   Died 1944
Canadian-born American evangelist famed for her healing ministry and the controversy surrounding her activities

Aimée Kennedy was born near Ingersoll, Ontario, into a Salvation Army family. She became a Pentecostalist and in 1908 married a Pentecostal preacher, Robert Semple. They went to China as missionaries but her husband died in 1910 and she returned to North America with her daughter. In 1912 she married Harold McPherson (divorced 1921), but left him to become an itinerant evangelistic preacher. A third marriage, in 1931, also ended in divorce.

She was flamboyant and imaginative, and hugely successful as an evangelist. In 1918, aided by her mother Minnie Kennedy as business manager, she founded the International Church of the Foursquare Gospel in Los Angeles, and for nearly two decades she conducted a preaching and healing ministry in the Angelus Temple, Los Angeles, which had cost her followers $1.5 million to construct. She had her own radio station, Bible school, magazine, and social service work.

Aimee Semple McPherson, 1928

Considerable controversy surrounded her in the form of continuous embroilment in legal suits against her, as well as a bizarre and unexplained five-week disappearance in 1926 (she claimed to have been kidnapped). Even her death raised questions; authorities differ on whether it was due to a heart attack or from an overdose of barbiturates. Her books include *This is That* (1923), *In the Service of the King* (1927) and *Give Me My Own God* (1936).

Macpherson, Annie

Born c.1824   Died 1904
Scottish teacher and missionary who worked with underprivileged teenagers

Annie Macpherson was born in Campsie, Stirlingshire. She trained as a teacher under the educationalist Dr Friedrich Froebel, founder of the kindergarten system, and established her first orphanage in Spitalfields, London, in 1864.

This was followed by a Farm Home that provided agricultural training for disadvantaged youngsters before she arranged for them to be re-settled in Canada. With the help of her sisters, over 14,000 child emigrants settled with families in the backwoods of Ontario and Quebec.

Macrina the Younger

Born c.330AD   Died AD379 or 380
Eastern Christian ascetic who established an early community of women ascetics

Macrina was born in Neocaesarea, Cappadocia, the granddaughter of Macrina the Elder. She was the elder sister of the Cappadocian theologian Basil of Caesarea — whom she turned from a secular career to the priesthood, along with another brother, Peter of Sebaste, and Gregory of Nyssa.

She established an early community of women ascetics at Pontus. Her life, written by Gregory, includes an account of their meeting on her deathbed. Her cult was strong in the Eastern Churches.

Macy, Anne Mansfield Sullivan, *née* Sullivan

Born 1866   Died 1936
*American educator who was the successful teacher and faithful companion of **Helen Keller***

Anne Sullivan was born in Feeding Hills, Massachusetts. She lost most of her sight in childhood due to an infection and attended the Perkins Institute for the Blind in Boston. She regained some of her sight through operations, but nevertheless learnt the manual alphabet in order to communicate with other disabled people. In 1887 she was chosen to teach the blind, deaf and mute child **Helen Keller**. Using the manual alphabet and a method of touch teaching in which she allowed the child to hold objects rather than have their properties explained, she was dramatically successful in instructing her.

She later accompanied Keller to Radcliffe College and on worldwide lecture tours. In 1905 she married John Macy, a writer and critic, but continued in her work for the blind, particulary during the 1920s when she championed the cause of the new American Foundation for the Blind.

Madison, Dolley Payne Todd, née Payne

Born 1768 Died 1849
American society hostess and First Lady as the
wife of James Madison, fourth US President

Dolley Payne was born in Guilford County, North Carolina. She was already a widow when she married Madison in 1794 (Todd is her first husband's name). She became famous as a vivacious Washington hostess, especially after Madison had become Secretary of State (1801–9).

As First Lady (1809–17), she restored formality to the White House and was considered a premier hostess and society figure. In 1814 when the British captured Washington and burned government buildings including the White House, she salvaged many important state documents and artistic artefacts.

Madonna, originally Madonna Louise Veronica Ciccone

Born 1958
American pop singer who has been influential in
young society and fashion

Madonna Ciccone was born in Rochester, Michigan. She trained as a dancer at Michigan University before moving to New York, where she began her professional career as a backing singer and then played with a number of New York groups.

She hired pop singer Michael Jackson's manager prior to releasing *Madonna* (1983), an album which included five US hit singles. Subsequent albums have included *Like A Virgin* (1984), *True Blue*, *You Can Dance* (1987), *Erotica* (1992) and *Bedtime Stories* (1994). She has sold over 55 million records worldwide and has also acted in films, including *Desperately Seeking Susan* (1985), *Shanghai Sur-*

prise (1986), *Body of Evidence* (1992) and *Dangerous Game* (1993).

She was an influential role model for teenagers in the 1980s, and her success has been greatly enhanced by clever promotion and image-making, though following the publication of her book *Sex* (1993) some thought she had perhaps overreached herself. With the help of couturiers Jean Paul Gaultier and (Stefano) Dolce and (Domenico) Gabbana, she has also infuenced fashion by popularizing the craze for wearing underwear as outerwear.

Magnani, Anna

Born 1908 Died 1973
Italian actress who was acclaimed as the greatest
Italian star of her time

Anna Magnani was born in Alexandria, Egypt, the illegitimate daughter of an Italian mother and Egyptian father, and raised in poverty in Rome. She first made her living as a night-club singer. Her screen début was in *Scampolo* (1927) but she did not concentrate on film acting until around 1934. She married the director Goffredo Alessandrini in 1935 (separated 1940, marriage annulled 1950), who gave her a supporting role in his film *Cavalleria* (1936).

She played mainly minor roles for several years until achieving recognition in Roberto Rossellini's *Roma città aperta* (1945, 'Rome, Open City'). She won an Oscar for her first Hollywood film *Rose Tattoo* (1955), but much of her later work was for the Italian stage and television, although she appeared in a cameo role in Federico Fellini's *Roma* (1972).

Mahony, Marion

Born 1871 Died 1961
American architect to whom some of Frank Lloyd
Wright's work may be attributed

Marion Mahony was the first woman to receive a degree in architecture from the Massachusetts Institute of Technology. After graduating she worked in Frank Lloyd Wright's Oak Park Studios and became his chief draftsman, designing several of her own commissions.

In 1910 Wright's work was published by Wasmuth: of 27 attributable drawings, 17 were Mahony's and the other 10 were the joint work of Mahony and others. In 1916 Wright included two Decatur Houses in an exhibition of his work which were entirely Mahony's work, but she was shunned by Wright in later years.

In 1911 Mahony had married Walter Burley Griffin, a colleague in Wright's office, and they inherited some of Wright's commissions when he left for Europe.

Mahy, Margaret May

Born 1936
New Zealand writer of prize-winning children's fiction

Margaret Mahy was born in Whakatane and had her first work published as a schoolgirl. She was educated at Auckland University and then worked in the School Library Service in Christchurch. Her early tales show her characteristic use of fantasy, and include *The Dragon of an Ordinary Family* and *Miss Discombobulous* (both 1969).

She did not take up writing full-time until 1980, but her books soon became internationally recognized: *The Haunting* (1982) won the Carnegie Medal, as did *The Change-over: A Supernatural Romance* (1984). Her work ranges from texts for picture books, through short stories, to novels for younger readers and teenagers and, in *Aliens in the Family* (1986), to science fiction. Her younger tales are also full of fantasy but in *The Tricksters* (1986) and the award-winning *Memory* (1987) she adopts contemporary settings and raises current concerns and is considered the most distinguished New Zealand children's author of her generation.

Maillart, Ella Kini

Born 1903
Swiss sportswoman and travel writer

Ella Maillart was born in Geneva. She represented Switzerland in the 1924 Olympic Games in Paris in the single-handed sailing competition, captained the Swiss Ladies Hockey Team in 1931 and skied for her country from 1931 to 1934. She taught in Wales, and worked on an archaeological dig in Crete, before travelling to Moscow to study film production.

In 1932 she crossed Russian Turkestan and wrote of her tribulations in both French and English. In 1934, working as a journalist for *Petit Parisien*, she went to Mongolia to report on the Japanese invasion and returned via Peking across Tibet and into Kashmir with the writer Peter Fleming, described in *Oasis interdites* (1937, Eng trans *Forbidden Journey,* 1937).

She worked and journeyed in Iran and Afghanistan, and then spent the war years living in an ashram in southern India under the tutelage of Sri Ramama. She was one of the first travellers into Nepal when it opened in 1949, and wrote *The Land of the Sherpas*

(1955). In later life she settled in Switzerland and worked as a travel guide.

Maintenon, Françoise d'Aubigné, Marquise de

Born 1635 Died 1719
French mistress and influential second wife of Louis XIV (ruled 1643–1715)

Françoise d'Aubigné was born near the concièrgerie of Niort, where her father was a prisoner, and her childhood was spent in penury. She was the granddaughter of the Huguenot Théodore Agrippa d'Aubigné (1552–1630). In her teens she was converted to Roman Catholicism and in 1652 she married the poet Paul Scarron, whose death in 1660 left her penniless again.

In 1669 she was appointed governess of the two illegitimate sons of her friend the Marquise de **Montespan** and Louis XIV, and became the king's mistress. In 1674, with the king's help, she bought the estate and marquisate of Maintenon, after which she became known as 'Madame de Maintenon'. Following the death of Queen Maria Theresa in 1683, Louis married her in secret. She was accused of wielding enormous influence over him, particularly concerning the bloody persecution

Madame de Maintenon, 1692

of Protestants after the Revocation of the Edict of Nantes (1685).

She founded a home for impoverished noblewomen, the Maison Royale de Saint-Louis at Saint Cyr, to which she retired when the king died in 1715.

Mairet, Ethel

Born 1872 Died 1952
English weaver whose workshop 'Gospels' became a creative centre for many international weavers

Ethel Mairet was born in Barnstaple. After visiting Ceylon (now Sri Lanka) between 1903 and 1906, she worked with the designer and architect Charles Robert Ashbee and the Guild of Handicrafts. She started weaving in Devon in 1911.

After marrying Philip Mairet (as her second husband), she established her workshop, 'Gospels', at Ditchling in Sussex, which was visited by weavers from many different countries.

Mairet also wrote a great deal, revealing a desire for rethinking the educational approach to handweaving and a reassessment of its relationship to power loom production.

Maiz, Marta

Born 1959
Spanish architect whose bold designs incorporate strong geometric shapes and dramatic use of space

Marta Maiz trained at the Polytechnic University of Madrid, where she graduated in 1985, having in 1984 been awarded a grant for postgraduate studies by the Spanish government.

Now a principal of her own practice, which she runs with Enrique Romero in Madrid, she has designed 12 individual houses and several interiors for fashion shops throughout Spain. She has also designed furniture, clocks and a telephone booth.

Her work has been exhibited in Paris and Salamanca (1985) and she has held teaching posts at the School of Architecture, Madrid (1983–4), and at the School of Design and Fashion (1986–9).

Makarova, Natalia Romanovna

Born 1940
Russian ballet dancer who defected and became one of the most celebrated dancers of the 1970s

Natalia Makarova was born in Leningrad (now St Petersburg). After studying there she joined the Kirov Ballet in 1959 and became one of their star dancers. Stopping in London on tour in 1970, she defected to the West, and went on to earn widespread acclaim, particularly in the title role of *Giselle*.

Associating herself with the American Ballet Theatre in New York from 1970 until she retired from dancing in 1992, she often appeared with the Royal Ballet, Covent Garden and other companies. While specializing in the classics, she also created roles for contemporary choreographers like Antony Tudor, George Balanchine and Glen Tetley. Her work as a producer includes *La Bayadère* (1980) for American Ballet Theatre, *The Kingdom of the Shades* (1985) and *Swan Lake* (1988), both for London Festival Ballet.

In 1988 in London she became the first dancer in exile to appear with her home company, the Kirov, and in 1991 she acted in the play *Tovarich* in St Petersburg.

Makeba, Miriam

Born 1932
South African-born American singer, the first African singer to gain an international following

Miriam Makeba was born in Johannesburg but was exiled from South Africa because of her political views. She settled in the USA and became widely known in the 1960s as 'the empress of African song', making concert tours and recording several albums. She gained an international following and played a vital role in introducing the sounds and rhythms of traditional African song to the West.

Her marriage in the late 1960s to the militant black leader, Stokely Carmichael, effectively ended her career in the USA, as she was declared persona non grata; she moved to Guinea, and virtually disappeared from the international concert arena, emerging only occasionally to take part in special, politically-orientated events.

Makin, Bathsua Pell, *née* Pell

Born 1608 Died 1675
English writer described as the most highly educated woman in England in her time

Bathsua Pell was born in Southwick, Sussex, the daughter of a local cleric. She grew up in an erudite family — her brother John was a mathematician who served both royalty and the Roundheads — and she became probably the best-educated Englishwoman of her time.

She was appointed as tutor to the children of Charles I, a post for which she later claimed she was insufficiently remunerated, and went on to establish a school at Tottenham High Cross. Noted for her radical views, she published *Essay to Revive the Antient Education of*

Gentlewomen, her best-remembered publication, in 1673.

Malakhovskaya, Natalya

Born 1947
Russian feminist whose writings were suppressed by the authorities

Natalya Malakhovskaya graduated from the faculty of letters in Leningrad (now St Petersburg) with a degree in philosophy in 1973. Initially a teacher, she became involved with the feminist movement, organizing and contributing to a feminist review, and founding the proscribed Club Maria.

She was co-author of *Women and Russia*, a *samizdat* or underground self-printed work, first circulated in St Petersburg in 1979 and smuggled to London for publication in 1980. Her contribution, 'The Matriarchal Family', deplores the traditional patriarchy of Russia and ends with the words, '—so women survive the living death devised by man and nature'.

The group's second issue, entitled *Rossianka* (*Russian Women*) was published in Paris, but according to some accounts, four of the feminist organizers were sent into exile.

Malibran, Maria Felicita

Born 1808 Died 1836
Spanish mezzo-soprano who was the most famous female singer of her time

Maria Malibran was born in Paris, the daughter of the Spanish singer Manuel Garcia, who was her most important teacher.

She was a spirited singer and made her operatic début in London in 1825, following which she became very popular.

In 1836 she divorced her first husband and remarried, but was killed the same year following a fall from a horse.

Mallet-Joris, Françoise, *pseud of* Françoise Lilar

Born 1930
Belgian-born French novelist, an important figure in modern French literature

Françoise Lilar was born in Antwerp and educated in the USA and at the Sorbonne. Her first novel, the bestselling *Le Rempart des Béguines* (1950), appeared in the USA as *The Illusionist* (1952) and in the UK as *Into the Labyrinth* (1957). Until the 1980s she was routinely translated, often miscasting her vivaciously individual feminism as a sober intellectual stance rather than as a more instinctive reaction to social conditioning.

Affected by existentialism, she is deeply concerned with personal authenticity, a theme that emerges strongly in the brilliant *Les Mensonges* (1956, Eng trans *House of Lies*, 1957) and *L'Empire Céleste* (1958, Eng trans *Café Céleste*, 1959), for which she was awarded the prestigious Prix Femina. The autobiographical *Lettre à moi-même* (1963, Eng trans *A Letter to Myself*, 1964) traces her conversion to Roman Catholicism.

For many years she worked in publishing and as a songwriter, she is on the jury for the Prix Femina, and in 1973 she was elected President of the Académie Goncourt.

Mancini, Hortense, Duchesse de Mazarin

Born 1646 Died 1699
Italian beauty and memoir-writer, and allegedly a mistress of Charles II

Hortense Mancini was born in Italy, and like her four sisters, **Laura**, **Marie Anne**, **Marie** and **Olympe**, followed her uncle Cardinal Mazarin (1602–61) to France. He married her off to Armand Charles de la Porte, who assumed the Mazarin title.

After separating from her husband she became famous for her beauty in London at the court of Charles II, whose mistress she allegedly became. She established a literary circle there. Her memoirs appeared in 1675, but have also been attributed to the historical novelist Saint-Réal.

Mancini, Laura, Duchesse de Mercoeur

Born 1636 Died 1657
Italian noblewoman renowned for her beauty

Laura Mancini was the sister of **Hortense**, **Marie Anne**, **Marie** and **Olympe Mancini**. She came to the French court with her uncle Cardinal Mazarin and was married to Louis de Vendôme. The famous Duc de Vendôme was their son.

Mancini, Marie Anne, Duchesse de Bouillon

Born 1649 Died 1714
Italian noblewoman and alleged poisoner

Marie Anne Mancini was the sister of **Hortense**, **Laura**, **Marie** and **Olympe Mancini**. She moved with them and their uncle Cardinal Mazarin to France and became renowned for her beauty, her literary salon and for her patronage of the French poet Jean de La Fontaine.

She was banished in 1680, having been involved in the *cause célèbre* of the notorious sorceress **La Voisin** known as the 'Affair of the Poisons'.

Mancini, Marie, Princess de Colonna

Born 1640 Died 1715
Italian noblewoman and memoir-writer, and
allegedly a mistress of Louis XIV

Marie Mancini was the sister of **Hortense, Marie Anne, Olympe** and **Laura Mancini**. She moved with them to France and became a mistress of Louis XIV, who was prevented from marrying her only by the machinations of her uncle, Cardinal Mazarin. She lived in Spain for most of her life. Her memoirs appeared in 1678, but like those of her sister Hortense, these are attributed by some to the historical novelist Saint-Réal.

Mancini, Olympe, Comtesse de Soissons

Born 1639 Died 1708
Italian beauty, mistress of Louis XIV and alleged
poisoner

Olympe Mancini was the sister of **Hortense, Marie Anne, Laura** and **Marie Mancini**. She went with her sisters and her uncle Cardinal Mazarin to France and, like Marie is thought to have done, became a mistress of Louis XIV.

She was involved with her sister Marie Anne in the **La Voisin** intrigues and, accused of poisoning her husband and the Queen of Spain, fled to the Netherlands.

Her son was Prince Eugene of Savoy, who renounced his country and entered the service of the Austrian Emperor Leopold I, later becoming a celebrated general in the Austrian army.

Mandela, (Nomzano) Winnie (Winifred), *Xhosa surname* Madikizela

Born 1934
South African civil rights activist, former wife of
South African President Nelson Mandela

Winnie Mandela was born in Bizana, the daughter of a provincial missionary school-teacher and descendant of a tribal chief. She trained in social work, becoming South Africa's first black social worker, began working with Nelson Mandela, future President of South Africa, in 1956, and married him in 1958. She became active in his work for the African National Congress (ANC), which was banned in 1960.

When he was put in prison by the South

Winnie Mandela, 1990

African government (1964–90), she too was banned, imprisoned (1969–70), and forced into internal exile, being kept in Brandfort from 1977 to 1985, out of the public eye. In 1985 she returned to Soweto and became involved in the militant politics of the township. Throughout Nelson Mandela's 26 years' incarceration, she campaigned ceaselessly for black rights on his behalf, as well as for his release.

Her popularity declined in 1988–9 when her bodyguards were implicated in the kidnapping, beating and murder of a black youth. She was convicted of the kidnapping alone and sentenced to six years in prison, but this was commuted to a £9,000 fine. She and Mandela separated in 1992, but in the new government of South Africa two years later she was appointed deputy Minister of Arts, Culture, Science and Technology. However in March 1995 she was removed from this post, although she did retain her seat in parliament, her membership of the ANC and her position as President of the ANC Women's League.

Mandrell, Barbara

Born 1948
American country singer and musician

Barbara Mandrell was born in Houston, Texas. An accomplished steel guitarist and saxophone player by the age of 10, she began playing Las Vegas with country headliners such as Tex Ritter and Cowboy Copas.

She became a singer and toured with country stars such as Johnny Cash and **Patsy Cline**. Her first number-one hit was 'Sleeping Single in a Double Bed' in 1978.

She was declared the Country Music Association (CMA) Female Vocalist of the Year in 1979 and 1981 and the CMA Entertainer of the Year in 1980–1.

Mangeshkar, Lata

Born 1928
Indian singer credited with being 'the most recorded voice in the world'

Lata Mangeshkar became a singer to support her family following the early death of her father, and travelled widely to studios all over in India, gaining a deep love of her country's music.

In 1948 she was employed by the Indian film industry, and went on to provide the singing voice of actresses in over 2,000 musical films, making about 30,000 recordings over 36 years. She also performed to sell-out audiences in London in the 1980s and retired in 1984.

Manley, Mary de la Rivière, *also spelt* Delarivier

Born 1663 Died 1724
British writer, the first woman to write a bestseller, the first to be arrested for her writing and the first professional woman journalist

Mary de la Rivière Manley was born in Jersey, the daughter of a future governor of Jersey. After her father's death in 1688, her cousin John Manley of Truro, MP, quickly lured her into a bigamous marriage, but soon deserted her. She went to England, where she had a success with the publication of her letters.

In 1696 she wrote two plays, *The Lost Lover* and *The Royal Mischief*, which were not successful. She did have success however with her gossipy political chronicles disguised as romantic fiction, especially the scandalous anti-Whig *The New Atalantis* (1709); this led to her arrest for libel.

In 1711 she succeeded Jonathan Swift as editor of *The Examiner*, becoming the first professional woman journalist. She wrote a fictional account of her own early struggles in *The Adventures of Rivella* (1714), and her last work was *The Power of Love, in Seven Novels* (1720).

Mannin, Ethel

Born 1900 Died 1984
English novelist, travel writer and short-story writer

Ethel Mannin was born in London, of Irish ancestry. In the 1930s she was involved in the struggle for women's rights and was a member of the Independent Labour Party. Her early works include *Venetian Blinds* (1933), a novel set in working-class south London around World War I.

She wrote over 40 novels, of which *Red Rose* (1941), based on the life of the anarchist **Emma Goldman**, most closely reflects her own concerns. Her commitment to the far left is evident in such works of non-fiction as *Women and the Revolution* (1938) and *Rebels' Ride* (1964). She travelled widely, and wrote several books on the Middle East (such as *A Lance For The Arabs*, 1963) as well as volumes on Germany, Burma and Japan.

Manning, Dame (Elizabeth) Leah, *née* Perrett

Born 1886 Died 1977
English politician, one of the most colourful personalities in British left-wing politics in the 1930s

Leah Perrett was born in Rockford, Illinois. Her early years were strongly influenced by the legend of her great-grandmother (by marriage), the Methodist philanthropist Susan Tappin, who did good works among the poor of London's East End. She trained as a teacher at Homerton College, Cambridge, where she also began her involvement with the Fabian Society, and in 1914 married William Manning.

Manning was twice a member of parliament, in the Labour Government of 1929–31 and again from 1945 to 1950. Throughout her educational career she was an ardent trades unionist within the National Union of Teachers, and as a politician she tirelessly championed the Republican cause during the Spanish Civil War.

Her publications include *What I Saw in Spain* (1933), in which she strongly advocates a policy of non-intervention and her autobiography, *A Life for Education* (1970). She was created DBE in 1966.

Manning, Olivia

Born 1908 Died 1980
English novelist applauded for her fictional account of life in the war years, Fortunes of War

Olivia Manning was born in Portsmouth, the daughter of a naval officer. Much of her youth was spent in Ireland and she had 'the usual Anglo-Irish sense of belonging to nowhere'. She trained at art school, and then went to

London, and published her first novel, *The Wind Changes*, in 1937.

She married in 1939 and went abroad with her husband, Reggie Smith, a British Council lecturer in Bucharest. Her experiences there formed the basis of her Balkan trilogy, comprising *The Great Fortune* (1960), *The Spoilt City* (1962) and *Friends and Heroes* (1965). As the Germans approached Athens, she and her husband evacuated to Egypt and ended up in Jerusalem. She returned to London in 1946, where she resided until her death.

She was a prolific author whose publications include *Artist Among the Missing* (1949), *School for Love* (1951), *A Different Face* (1953), and her Levant Trilogy, comprising *The Danger Tree* (1977), *The Battle Lost and Won* (1978) and *The Sum of Things* (1980). The Balkan Trilogy and the Levant Trilogy form a single narrative entitled *Fortunes of War* which critic Anthony Burgess described as 'the finest fictional record of the war produced by a British writer'.

Mansfield, Katherine, *pseud of* Kathleen Mansfield Beauchamp

Born 1888 Died 1923
New Zealand short-story writer who had a lasting influence on her genre and became New Zealand's most famous writer

Katherine Mansfield was born in Wellington, the daughter of a successful businessman and cousin of **Mary von Arnim**. She was educated at Queen's College, London, returned to New Zealand for two years to study music, and left again for London in 1908, determined to pursue a literary career. She lived on the breadline and like a bohemian and met, married, and left her first husband, George Bowden, in the space of three weeks.

Finding herself pregnant (not by her husband) she was installed by her mother in a hotel in Bavaria, but she miscarried. The experience bore fruit in the stories collected in *In A German Pension* in 1911, most of which had previously appeared in *The New Age*. That same year she met the British writer and critic John Middleton Murry (1889–1957), and thereafter her work began to surface in Murry's *Rhythm*. From 1912 the couple lived together (they did not marry until 1918), mingling with the literati, particularly the novelist D H Lawrence (1885–1930), who portrayed them as Gudrun and Gerald in *Women in Love*. In 1916 she and Murry founded the short-lived magazine *Signature*, but she began to suffer from tuberculosis which precipitated her premature death.

Her first major work was *Prelude* (1917), a recreation of the New Zealand of her childhood. *Bliss, and other stories* (1920), containing the classic stories 'Je ne parle pas francais' and 'Prelude', confirmed her standing as an original and innovative writer, named in company with Anton Chekhov despite the backstabbing of her near-contemporary, **Virginia Woolf**. The only other collection published before her death at Fontainebleau was *The Garden Party, and other stories* (1922). Her other collections are *The Dove's Nest and Other Stories* (1923) and *Something Childish and Other Stories* (1924, published in the USA as *The Little Girl and Other Stories*, 1924). *The Letters of Katherine Mansfield*, edited by Murry, appeared in 1928 and *Katherine Mansfield's Letters to John Middleton Murry 1913–1922*, detailing the couple's stormy but tender relationship punctuated by lengthy separations, in 1951. Vincent O'Sullivan edited a selection, *Poems of Katherine Mansfield* (1988), and her work for the theatre was collected in *Katherine Mansfield: Dramatic Sketches* (1988).

Manton, Irene

Born 1904 Died 1988
English botanist and cytologist who worked on plankton structure, one of the first two sisters to be elected FRS

Irene Manton was born in London, the younger sister of **Sidnie Manton**. She read botany at Cambridge and spent a year studying cytology in Sweden before accepting an assistant lectureship in Manchester in 1929.

She remained there until 1946 when she became Professor of Botany at the University of Leeds and collaborated, amongst others, with **Mary Parke** on the structure of plankton.

She retired in 1969, having been elected a Fellow of the Royal Society in 1961, an event which created a unique situation as two sisters had never before been awarded such distinction. She received several awards and honorary degrees from around the world.

Manton, Sidnie Milana

Born 1902 Died 1979
English zoologist whose work greatly improved knowledge of invertebrates

Sidnie Manton was born in London and educated at Girton College, Cambridge, where from 1935 to 1942 she was Director of Studies in Natural Science. In 1943 she moved to King's College in London as a lecturer (1943–9) and reader in zoology (1949–60).

In studies of arthropods she investigated

feeding and locomotive mechanisms, and related the different evolutionary forms, introducing the new phylum Uniramia to encompass the Onychophora, Tardigrada, Hexapoda and Myriapoda.

Elected FRS in 1948, and awarded the Linnaean Gold Medal in 1963, she retired as Research Fellow of Queen Mary College, London, in 1967.

Manus, Rosa

Born 1880 Died 1942
Dutch campaigner for women's rights who met her
death at Auschwitz

Rosa Manus was born into a middle-class family in Amsterdam. She devoted her life to the struggle for female enfranchisement, firstly in her native Netherlands, and when this was achieved, in the rest of Europe and South America, where she worked with **Carrie Chapman Catt**.

She organized peace conferences in various European cities, and an International Women's Congress in Istanbul in 1935, but when the Netherlands were invaded in 1940, her activities were anathema to the Nazis, and she perished in Auschwitz concentration camp two years later.

Manzolini Anna Morandi, *née* Morandi

Born 1716 Died 1774
Italian anatomist whose wax anatomical models
were used all over Europe

Anna Morandi was born in Bologna. At the age of 20 she married Giovanni Manzolini, a professor of anatomy at the University of Bologna with whom she had six children.

He taught her to construct wax anatomical models, and when he became ill she lectured in his place, and was elected professor after his death in 1760. She was invited to lecture at several foreign academies and her models were used all over Europe.

Margaret, *known as the* Maid of Norway

Born 1283 Died 1290
Infant Queen of Scotland from 1286 until her
untimely death at sea

Margaret was the granddaughter of Alexander III of Scotland, being the only child of Alexander's daughter Margaret (who died in childbirth), and King Erik II of Norway. When Alexander III died in 1286, Margaret was the only direct survivor of the Scottish royal line and was proclaimed queen.

In 1289 she was betrothed to the infant Prince Edward (the future Edward II of England), son of Edward I, but she died at sea the following year on her way from Norway to the Orkneys.

In 1301 a woman claiming to be Margaret was burned to death in Bergen. Many believed her to be the real Margaret, and thereafter revered her as a saint.

Margaret (Rose), Princess, Countess of Snowdon

Born 1930
British princess who is Queen **Elizabeth II**'s only
sister

Princess Margaret was born at Glamis Castle in Scotland, the younger daughter of George VI and the only sister of Elizabeth II. She was the first scion of the Royal House in the direct line of succession to be born in Scotland for more than three centuries. An outstandingly beautiful young woman, in 1955 she rejected a possible marriage to Group-Captain Peter Townsend, whose previous marriage had been dissolved. This she did allegedly out of strong loyalty to her sister the Queen, which has continued ever since.

In 1960 she married Antony Armstrong-Jones (1930–), a photographer, who was later created Earl of Snowdon. The marriage was dissolved in 1978. Their children are David, Viscount Linley (1961–), who married the Hon Serena Stanhope in 1993, and Lady Sarah Armstrong-Jones (1964–), who married Daniel Chatto in 1994.

Princess Margaret is patron or president of numerous charities and organizations, including the NSPCC, the Guide Association, London Lighthouse, and the Royal Ballet.

Margaret, St

Born c.1046 Died 1093
English princess who became Queen of Scotland
as the wife of Malcolm Canmore (ruled 1057–93)

Margaret was born during the exile in Hungary of her father Edward the Ætheling. After the Norman Conquest, she fled from Northumberland to Scotland with her mother, sister, and young brother, Edgar the Ætheling. Young, lovely, learned, and pious, she won the heart of the Scottish king, Malcolm Canmore, who married her at Dunfermline in 1069.

Much of her reputation derives from her confessor and biographer, Turgot. She brought Benedictine monks to Dunfermline and stimulated a certain amount of change in usages in the Celtic Church, but institutional change and the real influx of new orders belong to the reigns of her stepson Duncan and sons Edgar, Alexander and David.

She was canonized by Innocent IV in 1251, and remains the only Scottish royal saint.

Margaret of Angoulême, *also known as* Margaret of Navarre

Born 1492 Died 1549
Queen of Navarre and one of the most brilliant women of her age

Margaret was born in Angoulême in France, the sister of Francis I of France. She married first the Duke of Alençon (d.1525) and then, in 1527, Henry d'Albret (titular King of Navarre), to whom she bore **Jeanne d'Albret**, mother of Henri IV of France (known as Henry of Navarre).

Margaret had from her youth a strong interest in Renaissance learning, and was much influenced by the Dutch humanist scholar Erasmus and the religious reformers of the Meaux circle, who looked to her for patronage and protection. Although she remained a Roman Catholic, she was also influenced by Martin Luther's writings, with which she had a certain sympathy. She encouraged agriculture, learning, and the arts, and her court was the most intellectual in Europe. She became the patron of men of letters, including the heretical poet Clément Marot, and was herself a prolific writer.

Her works included long devotional poems published as *Le Miroir de l'âme Pécheresse* (1531, 'The Mirror of a Sinner's Soul') and *Les Marguerites de la Marguerite des princesses* (1547, 'The Daisies of Princess Marguerite'), the shorter *Chansons religieuses* ('Religious Songs'), dramas, and the secular poem *La Coche* ('The Coach'); her last works, written at the end of her life in some mental anguish, were found and published in 1895 as *Les Dernières poésies* ('The Last Poems'). Her most celebrated work was *Heptaméron*, a collection of stories on the theme of love, modelled on the *Decameron* of Boccaccio.

Margaret of Anjou

Born 1430 Died 1482
Queen of England as the wife of Henry VI (ruled 1445–82)

Margaret was born probably in Pont-à-Mousson, Lorraine, the daughter of René of Anjou. She was married to Henry VI in 1445 and, owing to his weak intellect, or madness, she was the virtual sovereign and became deeply involved in political life. The war of

1449, in which Normandy was lost, was laid by the English to her charge.

In the Wars of the Roses (1455–85), Margaret was a leading Lancastrian and, after a brave struggle of nearly 20 years to obtain the Crown for her son Edward (1453–1471), she was finally defeated at Tewkesbury (1471), where Edward was slain. She lay in the Tower for four years, until she was ransomed by Louis XI. She then retired to France, where she died in poverty.

Margaret of Antioch, St, *also called* Marina

3rd or 4th century
Virgin martyr and saint who was very popular in the Middle Ages despite being almost certainly a fictitious character

Margaret is traditionally held to have been born in Antioch, Syria, the daughter of a pagan priest who rejected her when she became a Christian, forcing her to find work as a shepherdess.

She attracted and spurned the attention of Olybrius, the prefect of Antioch, who consequently reported her to the authorities and had her subjected to horrific and fantastic tortures. These included being swallowed by Satan in the form of a dragon, but the cross which she carried so irritated his throat that she was spewed out unharmed (perhaps the reason for her being invoked in childbirth). Attempts to execute her by fire and drowning also failed; the crowds watching these miracles were converted and executed in their turn.

Finally, Margaret was beheaded with most of her converts in the persecutions of Diocletian. Her feast day is 20 July.

Margaret of Austria

Born 1480 Died 1530
Duchess of Savoy and regent of the Netherlands

Margaret of Austria was born in Brussels, the daughter of the future Holy Roman Emperor Maximilian I and **Mary of Burgundy**. In 1497 she married the Infante Juan of Spain, who died within a few months. Then, in 1501, she married Philibert II, Duke of Savoy, but he died in 1504.

From 1507 to 1515, appointed by her father, she was Regent of the Netherlands and guardian of her nephew, the future Emperor Charles V, who had succeeded her brother Philip I, the Handsome (1478–1506). In 1519 she was appointed regent again, this time by Charles V, who was busy securing the German throne for himself.

Her policies abroad were rigidly pro-English, and at home involved the imposition of heavy taxes to support military efforts to increase Habsburg possessions. By 1528 Habsburg dominion had extended to Friesland (1524) and included the Bishop of Utrecht's lands. In 1529 Margaret represented her nephew at the Treaty of Cambrai, negotiating the 'Paix des dames' with Louise of Savoy, who was representing her son, Francis I.

Margaret of Parma

Born 1522 Died 1586
Regent of the Netherlands who was a masterful and able administrator

Margaret of Parma was the illegitimate daughter of the emperor Charles V. She married first Alessandro de' Medicis (1536) and second Ottavio Farnese, Duke of Parma (1538), to whom she bore Alessandro Farnese (later Duke of Parma) in 1546.

Margaret of Parma

She was Regent of the Netherlands from 1559 to 1567, when she proved herself to be masterful and able. A staunch Catholic, in 1567 she suppressed a Calvinist revolt, but was replaced by the Duke of Alva.

When her son Alessandro became governor of the Netherlands (1578–86), ruling as regent for Philip II of Spain, Margaret returned with him as head of the civil administration for a time.

Margaret of Valois

Born 1553 Died 1615
Queen of Navarre and Queen of France as the wife of Henri IV (known as Henry of Navarre, ruled 1589–1610)

Margaret of Valois was the daughter of Henri II of France and **Catherine de' Medicis**, and sister of Francis II, Charles IX and Henri III.

In 1572 she married Henri of Navarre, who became King Henri IV of France in 1589. The marriage was childless, and was dissolved by the pope in 1599 in order to allow Henri to marry **Marie de' Médicis**.

Margaret was noted for her beauty and learning and became famous for her *Memoires*, published in 1628.

Margaret Tudor

Born 1489 Died 1541
Queen of Scotland as the wife of James IV (ruled 1488–1513)

Margaret Tudor was born in London, the elder daughter of Henry VII. In 1503 she married James IV of Scotland, but the marriage did not improve relations between the Scots and the English, and her husband died fighting the latter in 1513. During the minority of their son James V, Margaret was a significant, but shifting, enigma in the Scottish political arena, alternating her support between the pro-English and pro-French factions.

Her marriage in 1514 to Archibald Douglas, Earl of Angus, showed pro-English tendencies, so she was replaced as regent by the pro-French Duke of Albany, John Stewart, and exiled to England for a time. Having divorced Douglas in 1527, she married Henry Stewart, later Lord Methven, and found acceptance again at the Scottish court.

She and her husband became James V's advisers when he took governmental control in 1528, but six years later it was found that she had betrayed state secrets to her brother, Henry VIII, and she was forced to retire from her influential position.

Margareta I, *also called* Margaret *or* Margrethe

Born 1353 Died 1412
Queen of Denmark, Norway and Sweden, one of the greatest of the Scandinavian monarchs

Margareta was born in Søborg, Denmark, the daughter of King Valdemar IV 'Atterdag' of Denmark. She was married to King Haakon VI of Norway in 1363 at the age of 10. On the death of her father without male heirs in 1375 the Danish nobles offered her the Crown of Denmark in trust for her five-year-old son Olav, for whom she acted as regent. By Haakon's death in 1380, Margareta became Regent of Norway too, thus attaining the unification of the two countries that was to last until 1814.

Olav died suddenly in 1387 at the age of 17, leaving her sole ruler of Denmark–Norway. In 1388 the Swedish nobles, affronted by their German king, Albrekt (Albert) of Mecklenburg, offered her his Crown, whereupon she invaded Sweden, took Albrekt prisoner, and took over the rule of Sweden. In 1389 she had her seven-year-old great-nephew, Erik of Pomerania, adopted as her successor to the three Scandinavian kingdoms.

In 1397 she effected the Union of Kalmar, whereby the three kingdoms should remain for ever under one ruler, each retaining its separate laws, and presenting a united front against the threat of dominance by the German Hanseatic League. Erik was thereupon crowned king of the triple monarchy (as Erik VIII), but Margareta retained all real power in her own hands until her death at Flensburg.

Margrethe II, *full name* Margrethe Alexandrine Thorhildur Ingrid

Born 1940
Queen of Denmark who acceded to the throne in 1972

Margrethe II is the daughter of King Frederik IX, whom she succeeded in 1972, and Queen Ingrid. She was educated at the universities of Copenhagen, Aarhus and Cambridge, the Sorbonne in Paris, and the London School of Economics, and became an archaeologist.

In 1967 she married a French diplomat, Count Henri de Laborde de Monpezat, now Prince Henrik of Denmark. Their children are the heir-apparent, Prince Frederik André Henrik Christian (1968–   ) and Prince Joachim Holger Waldemar Christian (1969–   ).

Her publications include *The Valley* (1988) and *The Fields* (1989).

Maria II, *known as* Maria Da Glória

Born 1819 Died 1853
Queen of Portugal (1834–53), responsible for several crises during her reign

Maria was born in Rio de Janeiro, the daughter of Peter I of Brazil and IV of Portugal. She was proclaimed queen in 1826 under a regency following the renunciation by her father of his rights on the death of her grandfather, John IV. After being overthrown in 1828 by her uncle, Michael, she fled to England and Brazil. A civil war between Liberals and Absolutists ensued, which returned Maria to the throne in 1834.

In November 1836 she tried to engineer a coup d'etat against a leftist government. Similarly, the civil war of 1846–7 was caused by Maria's imposition of the conservative Sal-

danha as Prime Minister. Although Maria was forced to abdicate, the English and Spanish enforced the Peace of Gramido (June 1847), which restored her to power until her death in childbirth.

Through both her interference and her favouritism, she undoubtedly exacerbated the political instability of the years 1836–51.

Maria Carolina

Born 1752 Died 1814
Queen of Naples as the wife of Ferdinand IV of Naples and (later) of the Two Sicilies

Maria Carolina was the daughter of the Emperor Francis I and **Maria Theresa** of Austria. In 1768 she married Ferdinand IV of Naples (1759–1806, Ferdinand I of the Two Sicilies, 1816–25), who fell completely under her influence.

She appointed as Prime Minister her lover, the English naval officer Sir John Acton, and joined an Austrian–British coalition against France. She was forced to flee during the uprising that led to the brief Parthenopean republic (1798–9), and again in 1806 when the French invaded Naples. She died in exile in Austria.

Maria Christina

Born 1806 Died 1878
Queen of Spain as the fourth wife of Ferdinand VII (ruled 1808–33)

Maria Christina was the daughter of Francis I, King of the Two Sicilies. She persuaded her husband Ferdinand to change the law of succession so that their daughter Isabella could become queen, and on his death in 1833 she became regent for the three-year-old **Isabella II**.

A Carlist war broke out because Ferdinand's brother Don Carlos had been deprived of the throne, and in 1836 Maria Christina was forced to grant a constitution; in 1840 she was driven to France, but she returned in 1843.

Her share in the schemes of Louis-Philippe over the marriage of her daughters in 1846, and her reactionary policy, made her unpopular. A revolution in 1854 again drove her into exile in France where, except for a time in Spain (1864–8), she spent the rest of her life.

Maria Theresa

Born 1717 Died 1780
Holy Roman Empress, Archduchess of Austria, and Queen of Hungary and Bohemia

Maria Theresa was born in Vienna, the daughter of the emperor Charles VI. By the 'Pragmatic Sanction', for which the principal

European powers became sureties, her father appointed her heir to his hereditary thrones. In 1736 she married Francis of Lorraine, afterwards Grand Duke of Tuscany and Holy Roman Emperor as Francis I; and at her father's death in 1740 she became Queen of Hungary and of Bohemia, and Archduchess of Austria.

At her accession the chief European powers put forward claims to her dominions. The young Queen was saved by the chivalrous fidelity of the Hungarians, supported by Britain. The War of the Austrian Succession (1741–8) was terminated by the Peace of Aix-la-Chapelle. She lost Silesia to Prussia, and some lands in Italy, but her rights were admitted and her husband was recognized as Emperor Francis I.

Maria Theresa instituted financial reforms, fostered agriculture, manufacturing and commerce, and nearly doubled the national revenues, while decreasing taxation. Marshal Daun reorganized her armies; Prince Wenzel von Kaunitz-Rietberg took charge of foreign affairs. But the loss of Silesia rankled in her mind and, with France as an ally, she renewed the contest with the Prussian king, Frederick II, the Great. The issue of the Seven Years' War (1756–63), however was to confirm Frederick in the possession of Silesia. After the peace she carried out a series of reforms; after the death of her husband in 1765, her son Joseph (Emperor Joseph II) was associated with her in the government. She joined with Russia and Prussia in the first partition of Poland (1772), securing Galicia and Lodomeria; while from the Porte she obtained Bukovina (1777), and from Bavaria several districts.

A woman of majestic figure and an undaunted spirit, she combined tact with energy and won not merely the affection and even enthusiastic admiration of her subjects, but raised Austria from a wretched condition to a position of assured power. Although a zealous Roman Catholic, she sought to correct some of the worst abuses in the Church. Of her 10 surviving children, the eldest son, Joseph II, succeeded her; Leopold, Grand Duke of Tuscany, succeeded him as Leopold II; Ferdinand became Duke of Modena; and **Marie Antoinette** was married to Louis XVI of France.

Marie de France

Floreat c.1160–90
French poet, the first to write in a European vernacular, whose Lais *were a landmark in French literature*

Marie de France was born in Normandy. She spent much of her life in England, where she wrote her *Lais* sometime before 1167 and her *Fables* sometime after 1170. She was the first to write in a European vernacular, and there is a certain amount of conjecture as to her identity.

She translated into French the *Tractatus de Purgatorio Sancti Patricii* (c.1190, 'St Patricius's Treatise on Purgatory') and her works contain many classical allusions. The *Lais*, her most important work and dedicated to 'a noble king', probably Henry II of England, comprises 14 romantic narratives in octosyllabic verse based on Celtic material.

Marie de' Médicis, *Italian* Maria de' Medici

Born 1573 Died 1642
Queen of France as the second wife of Henri IV (known as Henry of Navarre, ruled 1589–1610), and Regent of France as the mother of Louis XIII

Marie de' Médicis was born in Florence, the daughter of Francesco de' Medici, Grand Duke of Tuscany (also known as Francis I). She married Henri in 1600 (following his childless marriage to **Margaret of Valois**) and became regent (1610–17) for her nine-year-old son in 1610 when her husband was assassinated.

She was unwise in her choice of counsellors, dismissing her husband's able minister the Duke of Sully, and relying instead on a coterie of unscrupulous favourites, especially her Italian lover Concino Concini (Marquis d'Ancre). The disaffected nobles obliged her to convoke the Estates General in 1614, where the Queen received support from the young Richelieu, Bishop of Luçon and future Cardinal de Richelieu, who was given charge of foreign affairs in 1616. In 1615 she had arranged a marriage for her son Louis with the Infanta **Anne of Austria** (daughter of Philip III of Spain), and for her eldest daughter Elizabeth to the heir to the Spanish throne (the future Philip IV), thus bringing an end to the war with the Habsburgs.

In 1617 young Louis assumed royal power; he arranged for the assassination of Concini, and exiled his mother and her supporters to the provinces. Thanks to the mediation of Richelieu she was reconciled to her son in 1620 and was readmitted to the council in 1622. When Richelieu was again given office in 1624 her influence as figurehead of the strongly Catholic *dévot* party remained important. When the king was absent on campaign in Italy in 1629 she acted as regent once again. She plotted tirelessly against her former protégé, Richelieu, but Richelieu broke her power and she went into exile in Brussels. Her lasting achievement was the building of the Luxembourg Palace in Paris, whose galleries were decorated by the Flemish painter Peter Paul Rubens.

Marie d'Oignies

Born 1176 Died 1213
French laywoman who was the inspiration behind
the Béguine movement

Marie d'Oignies was born in Nivelles, Brabant. She married at 14, and persuaded her husband to join her in nursing lepers in their home. Later, shunning publicity, she went to live in a cell attached to the Augustinian priory at Oignies for 31 years, aiming to imitate the poverty of Christ.

Her life, as told by her spiritual director Jacques de Vitry (d.1240), became the start of the Béguine movement — austere semi-religious sisterhoods, mainly committed to manual work and philanthropy. Their mysticism of devotion to Christ's Passion and to the Eucharist was suspected of heresy because of their association with the Spiritual Franciscans, an extreme group within the Franciscans.

Marie Amélie

Born 1782 Died 1866
Queen of France as the wife of Louis-Philippe
(ruled 1830–48)

Marie Amélie was born in Caserta, the daughter of Ferdinand IV of Naples (who was Ferdinand I of the Two Sicilies from 1816). She married Louis-Philippe in 1809.

She took little interest in politics and after the revolution of 1848, she was exiled and lived with her husband in Claremont, England.

Marie Antoinette, Josephe Jeanne

Born 1755 Died 1793
Queen of France as the wife of Louis XVI (ruled
1774–93)

Marie Antoinette was the fourth daughter of the empress **Maria Theresa** and Emperor Francis I. In 1770 she was married to the dauphin, who became King Louis XVI in 1774. Young and inexperienced, she aroused criticism by her extravagance and disregard for conventions, and on becoming queen she soon deepened the dislike of her subjects by her devotion to the interests of Austria, as well as by her opposition to all the measures devised by the economists Turgot and Necker for

Marie Antoinette with Louis-Joseph (1781–9) and Marie-Thérèse

relieving the financial distress of the country.

The miseries of France became identified with her extravagance, and in the affair of the Diamond Necklace (1784–6, *see* Jeanne de Valois, **Comtesse de La Motte**) her guilt was taken for granted. She made herself a centre of opposition to all new ideas, and prompted the poor vacillating king into a retrograde policy to his own undoing. She was capable of strength rising to the heroic, and she possessed the power of inspiring enthusiasm. Amid the horrors of the march of women on Versailles (1789), she alone maintained her courage. But to the last she failed to understand the troubled times; and the indecision of Louis and his dread of civil war hampered her plans.

She had an instinctive abhorrence of the liberal nobles like Lafayette and Mirabeau, but was at length prevailed on to make terms with Mirabeau (July 1790). But she was too independent to follow his advice, and his death in April 1791 removed the last hope of saving the monarchy. Less than three months later occurred the fatal flight to the frontier, intercepted at Varennes. The storming of the Tuileries and slaughter of the brave Swiss guards, and the trial and execution of the king (21 January 1793) quickly followed, and soon she herself was sent to the Conciergerie like a common criminal (2 August 1793). Her second son, Louis-Charles (1785–95), then became titular king as Louis XVII. After eight weeks more of insult and brutality, the 'Widow Capet' was herself arraigned before the Revolutionary Tribunal. She bore herself with dignity and resignation. Her answers were short with the simplicity of truth. After two days and nights of questioning came the inevitable sentence, and on the same day, 16 October 1793, she died by the guillotine.

Marie Louise

Born 1791 Died 1847
Austrian princess who became Empress of France as Napoleon's second wife

Marie Louise was born in Vienna, the daughter of Francis I of Austria. She became Empress of France on her marriage to Napoleon in 1810 (after the divorce of **Joséphine**), and in 1811 bore him a son, who was created king of Rome, Duke von Reichstadt, and later Napoleon II. On Napoleon's abdication she returned to Austria, was awarded the duchies of Parma, Piacenza, and Guastalla, and refused to join him in exile.

Following Napoleon's death in 1821 she contracted a morganatic marriage with the father of two of her children, Count von Neipperg, and governed the duchies with him, allegedly with little wisdom or strength of character. After his death (1829) the more stringent policies of the new secretary of state in Parma led to a rebellion. Marie Louise fled but was restored by the Austrians, whose policies she had to adopt thereafter. Her third marriage, again morganatic, was with Charles René, Count de Bombelles (1784–1856).

Marillac, St Louise de

Born 1591 Died 1660
French Catholic co-founder of the Sisters of Charity

Louise de Marillac was born in Ferrières-en-Brie, near Meaux, and lost both parents by the age of 15. She married Antony Le Gras in 1613 but was widowed in 1925. She took Vincent de Paul as her spiritual director, who saw her as the right person to train girls and widows to help the sick and the poor.

In 1633 four girls started work in her Paris home. From this modest beginning sprang the Sisters of Charity, who ministered in hospitals, orphanages and schools in Paris and beyond. They did not take vows until 1642, and then only for a year at a time, a practice that continues today.

Lousie de Marillac was canonized in 1934 and named the patron of Christian social work in 1960.

Marin, Maguy

Born 1951
French dancer and choreographer who is a central figure in the European world of dance

Maguy Marin was born in Toulouse. She studied dance as a child, and secured her first job with the Strasbourg Opera Ballet before continuing to train at the Mudra school in Brussels. This led to her joining Maurice Béjart's Ballet of the 20th Century in the mid-1970s.

In 1978 she won first prize at the Bagnolet international choreographic competition outside Paris. That same year she founded her own troupe, which in 1981 became the resident company of Creteil, a Paris suburb.

She has choreographed for major European companies including Paris Opéra Ballet, Dutch National Ballet, and, most notably, a 1985 version of *Cinderella* for Lyon Opéra Ballet, in a style that is as much theatre as dance.

Marion, Frances, *originally* Frances Marion Owens

Born 1887 Died 1973
American screenwriter, novelist and one of the first female war correspondents

Frances Marion Owens was born in San Francisco. She worked as a commercial artist, model and reporter with the *San Francisco Examiner* before arriving in Hollywood in 1913 as the protégé of director Lois Weber. During the silent era, she was often associated with actress **Mary Pickford** on such films as *Rebecca Of Sunnybrook Farm* (1918) and *Pollyanna* (1920).

During the latter stages of World War I she served as one of the first female war correspondents, and afterwards she tried her hand at directing with such films as *Just Around The Corner* (1921) and *The Love Light* (1921). As a screenwriter she became adept at heart-tugging melodrama, hard-bitten adventure yarns, and epic romances, and was also much praised for her skilled adaptations of *Stella Dallas* (1925), *The Scarlet Letter* (1926) and *The Wind* (1928).

Surviving the transition to sound, she wrote star vehicles for the likes of **Greta Garbo** and **Jean Harlow** and received Academy Awards for *The Big House* (1930) and *The Champ* (1931). She retired from screenwriting in 1940 and subsequently wrote novels including *Westward The Dream* (1948) and *The Powder Keg* (1954).

Markham, Beryl

Born 1902 Died 1986
English-African aviator who completed the first east–west trans-Atlantic solo flight

Beryl Markham was born in England. In 1906 she moved with her father to East Africa and she grew up playing with native Murani children, learning Masai and Swahili. She apprenticed with her father as a horse trainer and breeder, until he left Africa for Peru in 1919. She decided to remain in her adopted homeland and later turned to aviation.

From 1931 to 1936 she carried mail, passengers and supplies in her small plane to remote corners of Africa, including the Sudan, Tanganyika, Kenya and Rhodesia. In 1936, she became the first person to fly solo across the Atlantic from east to west, taking off in England and crash-landing in Nova Scotia 21 hours and 25 minutes later.

Her autobiography *West With the Night* (1942) contains reflections on Africa and flying.

Markievicz, Constance Georgine, Countess, *née* Gore-Booth

> Born 1868 Died 1927
> *Irish nationalist who was the first British woman MP but refused to take her seat at Westminster*

Constance Gore-Booth was born in London, the daughter of Sir Henry Gore-Booth of County Sligo. A society beauty, she studied art at the Slade School in London and in Paris, where she met Count Casimir Markievicz and married him in 1900. They settled in Dublin in 1903, and in 1908 she joined Sinn Féin and became a friend of **Maud Gonne**. Her husband left in 1913 for the Ukraine and never returned.

Countess Markievicz fought in the Easter Rising in Dublin (1916) and was sentenced to death, but reprieved in the general amnesty of 1917. In 1918 she was elected Sinn Féin MP for the St Patrick's division of Dublin — the first British woman MP — but refused to take her seat. She was elected to the first Dáil Eireann in 1919 and became Minister for Labour, but was imprisoned twice. After the Civil War she was a member of the Dáil from 1923.

Markova, Dame Alicia, *stage-name* of Lilian Alicia Marks

> Born 1910
> *English ballet dancer who helped to establish some top UK ballet companies*

Lilian Alicia Marks was born in London. She joined Sergei Diaghilev's Ballets Russes in 1924, and on her return to Britain appeared for the Camargo Society and the Vic–Wells Ballet (now the Royal Ballet). She then formed a partnership with dancer and choreographer Anton Dolin (1904–83), which led to the establishment of the Markova–Dolin Ballet Company in 1935.

In addition to performing Dolin's choreography in the joint company, they made guest appearances together around the world and were famed for their interpretation of *Giselle*. Their touring group, assembled in 1950, developed into the London Festival Ballet, which became the English National Ballet in 1988.

She was created DBE in 1963, was a director of the Metropolitan Opera Ballet (1963–9), and a governor of the Royal Ballet from 1973.

Marlborough, Duchess of *see* Churchill, Sarah

Marozia

> Died 938
> *Roman noblewoman of infamous reputation who helped her son become pope*

Marozia was the daughter of Theodora and Theophylactus. She was thrice married: first to Alberic, second to Guido of Tuscany, and third to Hugh, king of Italy. She was also the mistress of Pope Sergius III, and mother of Pope John XI and grandmother of Pope John XII.

She had influence enough at court to secure the deposition of Pope John X, her mother's lover, and the election of her own son as Pope John XI. She died in prison in Rome, put there in 932 by her son Alberic II.

Mars, Mademoiselle, *originally* Anne Françoise Hippolyte Boutet

> Born 1779 Died 1847
> *French actress who excelled performing Molière and Marivaux*

Anne Boutet was the daughter of the actor and playwright Monvel. She began her acting career as a child in Versailles and then followed Mademoiselle **Montansier** to Paris and starred at the Comédie Française from 1795.

She excelled in the plays of Molière and Marivaux, insisting their work was brought back into the company's repertoire, and by 1839 she had created 109 roles there. For three decades she was a fashion leader, and she developed a following of thousands of fans, including Napoleon I.

She retired in 1841 and wrote *Mémoires* (2 vols, 1849) and *Confidences* (3 vols, 1855).

Marsden, Kate

Born 1859 Died 1931
English humanitarian and traveller who devoted
much of her life to the leper colonies of Siberia

Kate Marsden was born in North London, the daughter of a solicitor. She trained as a nurse, and went to Bulgaria to treat casualties of the Russo-Turkish war of 1878, before going to New Zealand to tend to her dying sister.

She had witnessed the plight of lepers in the war and, inspired to help them, she planned an expedition to Yakusk, 2,000 miles across Siberia, for which she enlisted the patronage of Empress Marya of Russia, wife of Tsar Alexander III, as well as that of the Princess of Wales (later Queen **Alexandra**) and via her, Queen **Victoria**. Marsden's account of the gruelling journey, *On Sledge and Horseback to Outcast Siberian Lepers* (1893), was greeted with both admiration and scepticism, the latter because it seemed so implausible and it was feared that her patrons would be discredited when it became known that she was a lesbian.

In 1892 she became one of the first women elected to Fellowship of the Royal Geographical Society.

Marsh, Dame (Edith) Ngaio

Born 1899 Died 1982
New Zealand detective novelist and theatre
director

Ngaio Marsh was born in Christchurch. After a brief career on stage and as an interior decorator, she introduced her detective-hero Roderick Alleyn in *A Man Lay Dead* (1934), which was followed by 30 more stories ending with *Light Thickens* (1982).

In theatre, she toured with the Wilkie company in Shakespeare during the early 1920s, and devoted much time to theatrical production in New Zealand in the 1940s and 1950s. She also founded the Little Theatre in Christchurch.

She wrote on art, theatre, and crime fiction, as well as the libretto for a fantasy-opera *A Unicorn for Christmas* (1962) to music by New Zealand composer David Farquhar. Her autobiography is *Black Beech and Honeydew* (1966, revised edition 1981). She was appointed DBE in 1948.

Marshall, (Sarah) Catherine, *née* Wood

Born 1914 Died 1983
American religious and inspirational writer and
publisher

Catherine Wood was born in Johnson City, Tennessee. While at Agnes Scott College, Georgia, she met her husband-to-be, the Scottish pastor Peter Marshall (1902–49). Their move to a church in Washington DC, his ministry as chaplain to the US Senate, his sudden death and Catherine's bereavement are related in the best-selling *Mr Jones, Meet the Master* (1950), *A Man Called Peter* (1951), which was made into a film in 1955, and *To Live Again* (1957).

In 1959 she married Leonard LeSourd, executive editor of *Guideposts,* and worked with him on the magazine and later in their own publishing company. Her writing continued apace with a dozen titles, ranging from the novel *Christy* (1967) to books on prayer, and the autobiography *Meeting God at Every Turn* (1980).

Marshall, Margaret Anne

Born 1949
Scottish soprano who has performed in the world's
major opera houses since the mid-1970s

Margaret Marshall was born in Stirling. She studied at the Royal Scottish Academy of Music and Drama, and with Hans Hotter. She won first prize in the Munich International Competition (1974) and has since performed in opera and concerts at most of the principal European festivals and music capitals.

She made her London début in 1975; her operatic début at Florence, as Euridice in Christoph Gluck's *Orfeo ed Euridice* in 1978; her American concert début in 1980, and she was first heard at Covent Garden that year (as the Countess in *Figaro*). In 1982 she made débuts at La Scala, Milan, and in Salzburg (Fiordiligi).

For Scottish Opera her roles have included Pamina and the Countess.

Marshall, Paule

Born 1929
American author whose Brown Girl,
Brownstones *has become a classic of black*
American literarure

Paule Marshall was born in Brooklyn, New York, to parents who had emigrated from Barbados during World War I, and she grew up in Brooklyn during the Depression. In 1948 she studied at Hunter College, New York City, but left prematurely because of illness. Later she graduated from Brooklyn College and worked for *Our World Magazine*.

Her first novel, *Brown Girl, Brownstones* (1959), is regarded as a classic of black American literature. It tells the story of the coming of age of Seling Boyce, the daughter of Barbadian immigrants living through the Depression and World War I. Later novels are *The Chosen Place* (1969), *The Timeless People* (1969) and *Praisesong for the Widow* (1983), and she also writes short stories.

Marshall, Penny, *originally* Penny Marscharelli

Born 1942
American film director, and comedienne

Penny Marshall was born in Brooklyn, New York. She established her initial reputation as a comedy actress in television shows like *The Odd Couple* (1971–5) and *Laverne and Shirley* (1976–83).

She made her début as a film director with *Jumpin' Jack Flash* (1986), starring **Whoopi Goldberg**, and scored a box office success with *Big* (1988), in which Tom Hanks played a young boy magically transplanted into an adult body. Her other films include *Awakenings* (1990) and *A League of Their Own* (1992).

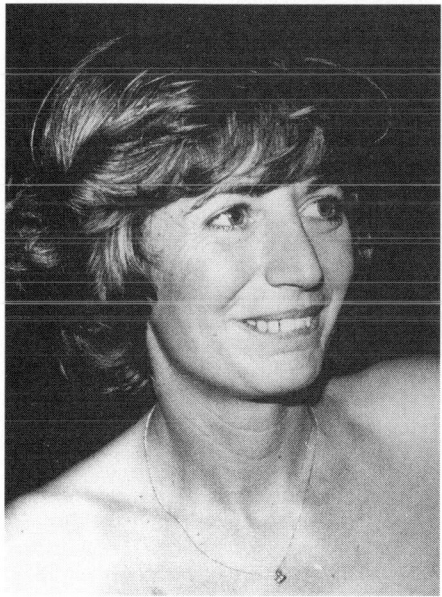

Penny Marshall, 1980

Marshall, Sheina Macalister

Born 1896   Died 1977
Scottish zoologist who was influential in identifying and utilising British sources of agar jelly

Sheina Marshall was born in Rothesay and educated locally and at the University of Glasgow. She graduated in 1919 and held a Carnegie Fellowship from 1920 to 1922, and was awarded a DSc in 1934. In 1923 she moved to the Millport Marine Laboratory, an independent laboratory later taken over by the Scottish Marine Biological Association, where she remained for her entire career, becoming its first Honorary Fellow on her retirement.

Her work, often published jointly with Dr A P Orr, was mainly on the classification, distribution and metabolism of plankton and provided important information about marine biology and productivity. In particular, her discoveries of British sources of agar jelly, formerly obtained from Japanese algae, were put to practical application in World War II. Agar jelly is an important component of medical, scientific and other commercial processes.

In 1949 she was elected a Fellow of the Royal Society of Edinburgh, in 1963 a Fellow of the Royal Society and was created OBE in 1966.

Marson, Una

Born 1905   Died 1965
Jamaican poet and playwright and a campaigner for black and feminist issues

Una Marson was educated at Hampton School, Malvern. She trained as a social worker but was equally interested in journalism, founding and editing the *Cosmopolitan* magazine. She worked in England (1932–6) as secretary to the League of Coloured Peoples, then private secretary to Emperor Haile Selassie. She also became involved in the movement supporting colonial dependence.

She wrote the first play performed by black colonials in London (*At What a Price*, 1932). In Jamaica she was a dynamic figure in many fields: she founded the Save the Children Fund, the Readers' and Writers' Club, and a progressive paper, *Public Opinion*. Subsequent plays produced in Jamaica include *London Calling* (1937) and *Pocamania* (1938).

Between 1930 and 1945 she published four books of verse, and during World War II she presented the BBC's influential 'Caribbean Voices' programme in London. By her use of jazz rhythms and Jamaican dialect in verse and her focus on issues of gender, race and identity, she pioneered a new movement in Jamaican writing in the 1940s.

Martha

1st century AD
Biblical character who is usually remembered for attending to domestic duties while she could have been sitting at Christ's feet

Martha lived in Bethany, near Jerusalem, and was possibly the wife or widow of Simon the Leper. She was devoted to Jesus Christ, like her sister — allegedly the **Mary** who anointed him — and brother, the Lazarus whom he raised from the dead (John 11). Perhaps unfairly, she is chiefly remembered for the incident in which Jesus rebuked her for fussing over domestic arrangements and being irked that Mary just sat listening to him (Luke 10.39–42).

In later Christian tradition Mary and Martha have been taken as symbols for the two paths of contemplative and active spirituality and used in arguments about the superiority of one over the other.

Martin, Agnes

Born 1912
Canadian painter whose work is characterized by abstract grids of vertical and horizontal lines

Agnes Martin was born in Maklin, Saskatchewan. After studying at Columbia University in the 1940s she began painting in a style called Biomorphic Abstraction. She lived in New Mexico from 1956 to 1957.

In 1959 she began painting the repetitive abstract grids of vertical and horizontal lines which have preoccupied her ever since. She has held various retrospective exhibitions throughout the USA, as well as in London and Amsterdam.

Martin, Violet Florence *see* Somerville, Edith

Martin-Spencer, Lilly (Angelique Marie), *née* Martin

Born 1822   Died 1902
American painter who acquired a reputation for her genre paintings

Lilly Martin was born in Exeter, Devon, to French parents. In 1830 they emigrated to the USA and settled in Marietta, Ohio, where her parents worked to establish a utopian co-operative society and were deeply involved in reform movements. She refused a patron's offer of help to study in Boston or Europe and settled in Cincinnati.

In 1844 she married Benjamin Rush Spencer, an English tailor and painter of stereoptican slides, with whom she had 13 children. They moved to New York, where she exhibited successfully for many years. A series of engravings and etchings were produced from her paintings.

She was widowed in 1890, but kept painting tirelessly and died after spending a morning at her easel.

Martineau, Harriet

Born 1802   Died 1876
English writer and important 19th century literary figure

Harriet Martineau was born in Norwich, the sixth of eight children of a textile manufacturer of Huguenot descent. Her brother was the Unitarian theologian James Martineau (1805–1900). In 1821 she wrote her first article for the (Unitarian) *Monthly Repository,* and then produced *Devotional Exercises for the Use of Young Persons* (1826), and short stories about machinery and wages. Her next book was *Addresses for the Use of Families* (1826).

In 1829 the failure of the house in which she, her mother and sisters had placed their money obliged her to earn her living. In 1832 she became a successful author through writing tales based on economic or legal ideas, in *Illustrations of Political Economy,* followed by *Poor Laws and Paupers Illustrated* (1833–4), and settled in London. She was often consulted on economic and social matters by her politician friends. After a visit to the USA (1834–6) she published *Society in America* and a novel, *Deerbrook,* in 1839, followed by a second novel, *The Hour and the Man,* about the Haitian revolutionary leader Toussaint l'Ouverture.

From 1839 to 1844 she was an invalid at Tynemouth but recovered through mesmerism (her subsequent belief in which alienated many friends), and made her home at Ambleside in 1845, the year of *Forest and Game-law Tales.* After visiting Egypt and Palestine she issued *Eastern Life* (1848). In 1851, in conjunction with H G Atkinson, she published *Letters on the Laws of Man's Social Nature* which was so agnostic that it gave much offence, and in 1853 she translated and condensed Comte's *Philosophie positive.* She also wrote much for the daily and weekly press and the larger reviews. *An Autobiographical Memoir* was published posthumously in 1877.

Martín Gaite, Carmen

Born 1925
Spanish novelist, one of Spain's most important women writers

Carmen Martín Gaite was born in Salamanca. She became one of the three most important female novelists in Spain in the latter half of the 20th century (the others are **Carmen Laforet** and **Ana María Matute**). Since receiving her doctorate from the University of

Madrid, she has written scholarly works on the 18th century and literary criticism.

She gained her reputation as a social realist writer and member of the Postwar Generation, but more recently has worked in psychological novels and the fantastic. Her main themes are the lives of women in society, communication, the isolation of the individual and the deeper side of reality.

She has won many literary honours, including the Premio Nadal (1959) and the Premio Nacional de Literatura (1979).

Marx, Eleanor

Born 1855   Died 1898
British daughter of Karl Marx who adopted her father's ideals

Eleanor Marx was the youngest of Karl Marx's three daughters and was more committed to her father's cause than her siblings. She grew up in Soho, London, in a milieu of politics and international socialism and earned herself financial independence through typing, teaching and translating.

However it was through her own writings and public speaking that she became well respected in the socialist movement. Her identification with the struggles of the poor led her to support 'Bloody Sunday' in 1887 and the strikes of 1889.

After Marx's death she edited the fourth volume of *Das Kapital*. She lived with a socialist named Edward Aveling for 24 years but it was an unhappy relationship and she committed suicide aged 43.

Mary I, *also called* Mary Tudor *and* Bloody Mary

Born 1516   Died 1558
Queen of England from 1553, the first to rule in her own right

Mary Tudor was born in Greenwich, the daughter of Henry VIII by his first wife, **Catherine of Aragon**. She was well educated, a good linguist, fond of music, devoted to her mother, and devoted to the Roman Catholic Church. Her troubles began with her mother's divorce, when Henry forced Mary to sign a declaration that her mother's marriage had been unlawful. During the reign of her half-brother Edward VI she lived in retirement, and no threats could induce her to conform to the new religion of Protestantism.

On his death (1553) she became entitled to the Crown by her father's testament and the parliamentary settlement. The Duke of Northumberland had, however, induced Edward

Queen Mary I

and his council to set Henry's will aside in favour of his daughter-in-law Lady **Jane Grey**, but the whole country favoured Mary, who entered London on 3 August in triumph. Northumberland and two others were executed, but Lady Jane and her husband were, for the present, spared. The Queen proceeded very cautiously to bring back the old religion. She reinstated the Catholic bishops and imprisoned some of the leading reformers, but dared not restore the pope's supremacy.

The question upon which all turned was the Queen's marriage. She obstinately set her heart on Philip II, King of Spain, and ignored national protests. The unpopularity of the proposal brought about Thomas Wyatt's rebellion, quelled mainly through the Queen's courage and coolness. Lady Jane was then executed, with her husband and father. Princess **Elizabeth**, her youger half-sister, was suspected of complicity and committed to the Tower. Injunctions were sent to the bishops to restore ecclesiastical laws to their state under Henry VIII.

In 1554 Philip was married to Mary, remaining in England for over a year. Later that year the English prelate Reginald Pole entered England as papal legate, parliament petitioned for reconciliation to the Holy See, and the realm was solemnly absolved from the papal censures. Soon after, the persecution which gave 'Bloody Mary' her name began. In 1555 the Protestant reformers Nicholas Ridley and Hugh Latimer were brought to the stake;

Thomas Cranmer followed in March 1556; Pole, now archbishop of Canterbury, was left supreme in the councils of the Queen. How far Mary herself was responsible for the cruelties practised is not exactly known, but during the last three years of her reign 300 victims were burned. Mary died, broken down with sickness, with grief at her husband's heartlessness, and with disappointment at her childlessness.

Mary II

Born 1662 Died 1694
Queen of Great Britain and Ireland from 1689
who ruled jointly with her husband William

Mary was born in St James's Palace, London, the daughter of the Stuart Duke of York (later James VII and II) and his first wife, Anne Hyde (1638–71). Mary was married in 1677 to her first cousin, William, Stadtholder of the United Netherlands, who in November 1688 landed in Torbay with an Anglo-Dutch army in response to an invitation from seven Whig peers hostile to the arbitrary rule of James II.

When James fled to France, Mary came to London from Holland and was proclaimed queen on 13 February 1689. She shared the throne with her husband, who became King William III. Both sovereigns accepted the constitutional revolution implicit in the Declaration of Rights. Mary was content to leave executive authority with William (except when he was abroad or campaigning in Ireland) but she was largely responsible for raising the moral standard of court life and enjoyed a popularity in the kingdom which her husband never attained.

Mary suffered several miscarriages, and the marriage was childless. She died of smallpox in Kensington Palace.

Mary, Queen of Scots

Born 1542 Died 1587
Queen of Scotland described variously as Catholic
martyr or papist plotter

Mary was born in Linlithgow, the daughter of James V of Scotland by his second wife **Mary of Guise**. Her father died soon afterwards and she became queen from the age of just one week. Her betrothal to Prince Edward of England was annulled by the Scottish parliament, precipitating a war with England in which the Scots were defeated at Pinkie (1547).

Mary was then offered in marriage to the Dauphin of France (Francis II from 1559), the eldest son of Henri II of France and **Catherine de' Médicis**, and sent to be brought up at the glittering French court. She married in 1558 but was widowed in 1560 and the following year returned to Scotland, where Protestant riots threatened the celebration of mass in her private chapel at Holyrood. A Catholic with a clear dynastic aim, she was ambitious for the English throne, and in 1565 married her cousin, Henry Stewart, Lord Darnley, a grandson of **Margaret Tudor**, but was disgusted by his debauchery and soon alienated from him. The vicious murder of David Rizzio, her Italian secretary, by Darnley and a group of Protestant nobles in her presence in 1566 confirmed her insecurity. She gave birth to a son, the future James VI and I (June 1566), but the event failed to bring a lasting reconciliation.

When on 10 February 1567 Darnley was found strangled after an explosion at Kirk o' Field, the chief suspect was the Earl of Bothwell, who underwent a mock trial and was acquitted. The queen's involvement is unclear but after only three months she succumbed to her apparent infatuation and married the recently divorced Bothwell, a fatal step that united her nobles in arms against her. Let down by her own army, she surrendered at Carberry Hill (15 June), and was imprisoned on an island in Loch Leven and compelled to abdicate.

The following year she escaped and raised an army but was defeated on 13 May 1568 at Langside near Glasgow. Placing herself under the protection of Queen **Elizabeth I**, she found herself a prisoner for life. Her presence in England stimulated numerous Catholic plots to depose Elizabeth and finally, after the Babington conspiracy (1586), she was brought to trial for treason. She was executed in Fotheringary Castle, Northamptonshire.

Mary's beauty and personal accomplishments have never been disputed, though often undervalued. She spoke or read in six languages, including Greek; she sang well, played various musical instruments, and had by 1567 a library of over 300 books, which included the largest collection of Italian and French poetry in Scotland. Her own poetry is less important than the revival of vernacular poetry which has now been traced to the court during her personal reign, including the important collection, *The Bannatyne Manuscript*.

Mary, *known as* the Blessed Virgin Mary, *Hebrew* Miriam, *Greek* Mariam

Born 1st century BC Died 1st century AD
New Testament character who was selected by
God to be the mother of Jesus Christ

Mary is assumed to be of the same family as Joseph, a carpenter who was a descendant of King David and through whom the genealogy of Jesus in the Gospel of Matthew is traced. She lived in Nazareth as a child and became engaged to Joseph.

As related in the Gospel of Luke, an angel of God appeared to tell Mary that she would conceive a child by the Holy Spirit and give birth to God's son, even though she was not yet married, a momentous event called the Annunciation. Mary's deep humility and unswerving obedience to God have made her an exemplary subject of veneration for generations of Christians, particularly of the Roman Catholic faith.

John reports that she was present at the Crucifixion. The last mention of her in the New Testament is in the Acts of the Apostles (1.14), where Luke includes her in a group of women who devoted themselves to prayer following the ascension of Christ. The date of her death is often given as AD63; the tradition of her having been assumed into heaven was defined as doctrine in 1950, and is celebrated in the festival of the Assumption.

Mary of Agreda *see* Agreda, María de

Mary of Burgundy

Born 1457 Died 1482
Duchess of Burgundy whose marriage contributed to the Netherlands coming under Habsburg control

Mary was born in Brussels, the daughter of Charles the Bold, Duke of Burgundy (1433–77), and Isabella of Bourbon. She inherited all the Burgundian possessions in France and the Netherlands, as Duchess, in 1477.

The King of France, Louis XI, who wanted Mary to marry his son Charles, repossessed Burgundy and Picardy while the Netherlands rose up against her, but Mary married instead the future Holy Roman Emperor Maximilian I, son of Ferdinand III and archduke of Austria, who helped to restore order in Mary's dominions, and, most importantly, gained the vast Burgundian possessions for the Habsburgs. His actions nevertheless led to war with France, in which Louis XI was defeated.

Mary's son Philip I, 'the Handsome', succeeded her in 1482 when she fell from her horse while hunting and died. His marriage to **Joanna the Mad**, daughter of Ferdinand of Aragon and **Isabella I**, continued the extension of Habsburg rule. Their son became the Emperor Charles V and their daughter **Mary of Hungary**.

Mary of Egypt

Born c.344AD Died 421
Desert mother who became a popular subject of many legends

Mary of Egypt led an evil life in Alexandria between the ages of 12 and 29, but when she went on pilgrimage to Palestine, she was converted to Christianity in Jerusalem. As penance for her wasted years, she settled in the desert, beyond the river Jordan.

After 47 years she met the priest and monk Zosimus and asked him to give her communion on Holy Thursday. According to legend she died the same day, as he discovered when he returned exactly a year later, by arrangement, and found her corpse, preserved by the sand and dry air, awaiting burial.

Mary of Guise, *also known as* Mary of Lorraine

Born 1515 Died 1560
*French noblewoman whose daughter **Mary** became Queen of Scots*

Mary of Guise was the daughter of Claude of Lorraine, 1st Duke of Guise from 1527. In 1534 she married Louis of Orléans, Duke of Longueville, and in 1538 James V of Scotland, at whose death in 1542 she was left with one child, **Mary, Queen of Scots**.

During the troubled years that followed, she acted with wisdom and moderation as Queen Mother, but after her accession to the regency in 1554 she allowed the Guises so much influence that the Protestant nobles raised a rebellion (1559), which continued to her death in Edinburgh Castle.

Mary of Hungary

Born 1505 Died 1558
Queen of Hungary and Bohemia as the wife of Louis II (ruled 1516–26)

Mary was the daughter of Philip I of Castile and **Joanna the Mad**. She married Louis II of Hungary and Bohemia in January 1522, a month after he was declared of age. Their life of debauchery soon disqualified the king from affairs of state, and he is said to have drowned whilst fleeing from a battle in which his forces were routed by marauding Ottoman Turks.

Hungary was thereafter divided between the Turks and the Austrian Habsburgs. In 1531 Mary's brother, Emperor Charles V, confident of her administrative capabilities, asked her to act as regent in his Low Countries possessions, which she did from 1531 to 1555.

Despite her patronage of the arts and her efficient government, Mary's rule subjugated the interests of the Netherlands provinces to those of Spain and the empire, which, along with the persecution of Protestant heretics, helped lay the ground for the Eighty Years War, a series of uprisings (1568–1648) by the Low Countries against the Spanish Habsburg rule.

Mary of Modena, *née* Marie Beatrice d'Este

Born 1658 Died 1718
Queen of Great Britain and Ireland as the second wife of James VII and II (ruled 1685–8)

Marie Beatrice d'Este was born in Modena, the only daughter of Alfonso IV, Duke of Modena. She grew up a devout Roman Catholic and married James in 1673 when he was Duke of York. They lost five daughters and a son in infancy, but in 1688 she gave birth to James Francis Edward Stewart (the future 'Old Pretender').

On the pretext that the child had been adopted to ensure a Catholic heir, William of Orange (the future William III) landed in England later that year at the start of the 'Glorious Revolution'. Mary escaped to France with the infant, and was joined there later by her deposed husband. She spent the rest of her life at St Germain.

Mary of Teck, *originally* Princess Victoria Mary Augusta Louise Olga Pauline Claudine Agnes

Born 1867 Died 1953
Queen of the United Kingdom as the wife of George V (ruled 1910–36)

Princess May (as she was known) was born in Kensington Palace, London, the only daughter of Francis, Duke of Teck, and Princess Mary Adelaide of Cambridge, a granddaughter of George III. In December 1891 she accepted a marriage proposal from the eldest son of the Prince of Wales, the Duke of Clarence, who within six weeks died from pneumonia. The Princess then became engaged to his brother, the Duke of York, and married him in 1893. After his accession (as George V) in 1910, Queen Mary accompanied him to Delhi as Empress of India for the historically unique Coronation Durbar of December 1911.

Although by nature stiff and reserved, Queen Mary was more sympathetic to changing habits than her husband, whom she helped to mould into a 'people's king'. She organized women's war work (1914–18), devoted her time to the interests of women and children, and continued with many public and philanthropic activities even after the death of her husband. She was known and loved as a regal and in many ways a highly individual figure with a keen sense of duty. She was also a discerning collector of antiques and objets d'art.

After the abdication of her eldest son, Edward VIII, in 1936 she applied her wide experience to strengthening once again the popular appeal of the monarchy throughout the reign of her second son, George VI, whom she survived by 13 months. She died at Marlborough House, London, less than three months before the coronation of her granddaughter, **Elizabeth II**.

Mary Magdalene, St, *also called* Mary of Magdala

Born 1st century BC Died 1st century AD
Early follower of Jesus Christ who represents the archetypal repentant sinner

Mary Magdalene was born probably in Magdala on the west coast of the sea of Galilee, hence her name. Luke 8.2 reports that Jesus exorcized seven evil spirits from her, and throughout the Church's history she has epitomized the archetypal repentant sinner. She features also in the narratives of Jesus's passion and resurrection as, seemingly with other women, she was present at the Cross and later at the empty tomb.

Most memorably, as related in John 20 and Mark 16, she was the first to encounter the risen Lord, who appeared to her in the garden of his burial; blinded by her tears, she at first supposed him to be the gardener. Her cult was influenced greatly by her identification with Mary the sister of **Martha** (John 11–12) and also with the woman in Luke 7 who anointed Jesus's feet and dried them with her hair. However, nowadays these are thought to be three separate people. One tradition holds that she accompanied St John the Evangelist to Ephesus where she later died and was buried. Her feast day is 22 July.

Masham, Abigail, *née* Hill

Died 1734
*English courtier who secured herself the position of confidante to Queen **Anne***

Abigail Hill was a cousin of **Sarah Churchill**, Duchess of Marlborough, through whose influence she entered the household of Queen Anne. In 1707 she married Samuel (later Baron) Masham.

She was a subtle intriguer and a strong Tory, and gradually turned the Queen against the Marlboroughs to the extent that by about 1707 she managed to supersede her cousin as the Queen's confidante and the power behind the throne.

Masham, Damaris, *née* Cudworth

Born 1658 Died 1708
English educationalist who overcame poor eyesight to become a noted theological author

Damaris Cudworth was born in Cambridge, the daughter of a local cleric, and became Lady Masham on her marriage to Sir Thomas Masham in 1685. She was a friend of the philosopher John Locke (1632–1704), who lived with the Mashams for 13 years and formed a high opinion of her intellect.

While she dedicated herself to the education of her only child and her step-children, she advocated the greater education of women, even if only to prepare them for the role of becoming teachers in their own turn.

Despite poor eyesight, Lady Masham wrote a number of theological tracts, including *Discourse concerning the love of God* (1696).

Masina, Giulietta, *originally* Giulia Anna Masina

Born 1920 Died 1994
Italian actress who is best known as Fellini's leading woman

Giulietta Masina was born near Bologna. She met Federico Fellini while both were students in Rome, and they married in 1943. She made her film début in Rossellini's *Paisà* (1946, *Paisan*), then worked briefly on the stage, but her reputation rests on her work with Fellini.

As Italy's leading director, he regarded her as an inspiration as well as his leading actress, and they created a number of memorable roles in films like *La Strada* (1954, *The Road*), *Giulietta degli Spiriti* (1965, *Juliet of the Spirits*), and *Ginger e Fred* (1986, *Fred and Ginger*).

Masiotene, Ona, *née* Brazauskaité

Born 1883 Died 1949
Lithuanian feminist active in promoting women's rights in both Lithuania and Russia

Ona Brazauskaité was born in Slavenae, but received advanced education in Moscow. Inspired by the cause of female rights being fought for in Western nations, she returned to her homeland in her early twenties and founded the Alliance of Lithuanian Women.

An educationalist by profession, she taught in both Vilnius and Moscow, working for the nationalist cause during the Russian Revolution from 1917. She later headed the women's movement back in Lithuania and published a major work on women's role in society.

Mata Hari, *stage-name of* Margaretha Gertruida MacLeod, *née* Zelle

Born 1876 Died 1917
Dutch dancer and convicted spy who took lovers from opposing sides in World War I

Mata Hari was born in Leeuwarden. She married a Scottish army officer in the Dutch colonial army in 1895 and travelled with him for some years until they separated in 1905 and she became a dancer in France.

She was a beautiful women with allegedly few qualms about near-nudity on stage, and soon saw success. She also had many lovers, several in high military and governmental positions (on both sides).

Though the facts of her duplicity remained uncertain, she was found guilty of espionage for the Germans, and shot in Paris.

Mata Hari

Mather, Margrethe

Born 1855 Died 1952
American photographer and antique dealer

Margrethe Mather was born in or near Salt Lake City, Utah. To escape an unhappy situation in the home of her adoptive parents (whose surname she took), she ran away to San Francisco around 1910 and supported herself as a prostitute, later turning to photography.

In 1912 or 1913 she met photographer Edward Weston (1886–1958). After about a year they became partners in a studio in Glendale; Mather had a strong influence on Weston's work. She is best known for her portraits, and for elegant formalist nudes and still lifes. She continued to practise commercial photography until 1930. After Weston's departure for Mexico in 1922, she lived platonically with artist and designer William Justema from 1923 to 1927. Much of her work was made with a 10" × 8" view camera and usually contact-printed in silver or platinum

In 1934 Mather turned to dealing in antiques, but occasionally photographed friends.

Matilda, *also known as* Maud

Born c.895   Died 968
German queen as the philanthropic wife of Henry I the Fowler (ruled 919–36)

Matilda was born at Engern, Westphalia, the daughter of Count Dietrich of Westphalia and Reinhold of Denmark. She was married to Henry I the Fowler (c.876–936), King of Germany, and their sons included Emperor Otto I 'the Great' (912–73) and St Bruno (925–65), Archbishop of Cologne.

During her 32 years as a widow, she bore ill-treatment and criticism from two of her sons, Otto and Henry 'the Quarrelsome', for giving much of her wealth to the poor and to the Church.

Matilda of Tuscany, *also called* Matilda of Canossa, *known as the* Great Countess of Tuscany

Born c.1046   Died 1115
Countess of Tuscany and supporter of the papacy

Matilda was the daughter of the Margrave Boniface II of Canossa, and as an infant she inherited vast tracts of land in northern Italy. She grew up to be intelligent, well-educated and determined, and married first Godfrey the Hunchback, Duke of Lorraine (d.1076), and later, at the age of 43, the 17-year-old Guelf of Bavaria, a member of the Este family, but they separated in 1095.

She was a devoted supporter of the papacy and, in particular, Pope Gregory VII (Hilde-brand), even taking the field at the head of her troops to aid him in his struggle against the Holy Roman Empire. In 1077 it was at her stronghold of Canossa that the Emperor Henry IV did barefoot penance to the pope.

After Gregory's death in 1085 her lands were ravaged by Henry's allies, but she refused to make peace or recognize the anti-pope Clement III; instead she steadfastly supported Pope Urban II until his death in 1099. She died at the Benedictine monastery of Polirone, near Mantua.

Matilda, *known as* Empress Maud

Born 1102   Died 1167
English princess, wife of Holy Roman Emperor Henry V and claimant to the English throne

Matilda was the only daughter of Henry I. In 1114 she married the Emperor Henry V (ruled 1111–25), but returned to England as 'Empress Maud' after his death in 1125 and was acknowledged as the heir to the English throne.

In 1128 she married Geoffrey Plantagenet of Anjou, by whom she had a son, 'Henry FitzEmpress', the future Henry II of England. When Henry I died in 1135, his nephew Stephen of Blois seized the throne in a swift *coup d'état*. In 1139 Matilda invaded England from Anjou with her half-brother, Robert, Earl of Gloucester and after capturing Stephen, she declared herself 'Lady of the English', but was never crowned.

Stephen and his queen gradually regained control, and in 1148 Matilda left England and returned to her son in Normandy.

Matthews, Jessie

Born 1907   Died 1981
English actress who was a leading star of the musical stage

Jessie Matthews was born in London, one of 11 children of a poor family. She made her stage début at 10, and danced in chorus lines as a teenager. She became a hugely popular star in musical revues in the 1920s, and translated that success into film roles in the 1930s.

These films were largely undistinguished, but her appeal transcended their limitations. She chose to remain in Britain rather than go to Hollywood to enhance her career, and worked only sporadically after World War II. She directed the short film *Victory Wedding* in 1944.

Matto de Turner, Clorinda

Born 1854   Died 1909
Peruvian novelist, poet, and playwright

Clorinda Matto de Turner occasionally wrote under the pseudonym of 'Carlota Dumont' and is claimed by some critics as an early feminist. She is most famous however for her *Aves sin nido* (1889, 'Birds Without a Nest'), the only Indianist novel of the 19th century and the first novel about contemporary South American Indian life to emerge from South America. It has a Romantic plot, realist detail, a strong anti-clerical message, and displays elements of *criollismo* (narratives on popular customs and language).

Her other major work was *Tradiciones cuzqueñas* (1884–6, 'Traditions of Cuzco'), a development of the uniquely Peruvian genre invented by the writer Ricardo Palma (1883–1919). She is regarded as one of the most important Latin-American women writers of the 19th century.

Matute, Ana María

Born 1926
Spanish novelist, one of Spain's major 20th-century female writers

Ana María Matute was born in Barcelona. She decided to remain in Spain after the Civil War and to denounce injustice under the eyes of the censors.

She came into prominence in the 1950s and 1960s as one of a generation who had experienced the war as children: her best-known novel, the long *Los hijos muertos* (1958, Eng trans *The Lost Children*, 1965), examines just this problem in the objectivist manner then almost statutory in a Spain where little that was directly critical of the regime could appear.

She has continued to explore the themes of war and children in a series of novels and stories upon which critical opinion is divided: one school holds that her work is, though worthy, poorly written and excessively rhetorical, the other that she is a major novelist. Among them are *Los soldados lloran de noche* (1964, 'Soldiers Cry at Night') and *La torre vigía* (1971, 'The Watchtower').

Maude, Clementina, Lady Hawarden

Born 1822 Died 1865
Scottish amateur photographer whose work possessed a lightness rare at the time

Clementina Maude was born at Cumbernauld House, the daughter of the Hon Charles Elphinstone-Fleming (MP for Stirlingshire). She married Cornwallis Maude, 4th Viscount Hawarden, in 1845 and spent the rest of her life in England, much of it in London. In 1864

she met and became a close friend of Charles Dodgson (Lewis Carroll).

Her photographs, apparently made over relatively few years, in the late 1850s and early 1860s, are mainly of women in country-house interiors. They are romantic and sensuous, often conspiratorial in feeling, and are unusually light in comparison with the ponderous seriousness of much contemporary work.

Maura, Carmen

Born 1945
Spanish actress who became an international star in the films of Pedro Almodovar

Carmen Maura was born in Madrid. Her family were very conservative, and her decision to give up teaching in favour of acting caused a serious rift. She made slow progress at first, but became nationally known as the host of the television show *Esta Noche* (*Tonight*) in the 1970s.

Her career took off internationally in the 1980s through her collaboration with the controversial Spanish director Pedro Almodovar. She has appeared in a number of his films, and won the Best Actress award at the European Film Awards in 1988 for her performance in his *Woman on the Verge of a Nervous Breakdown*.

Maximilla

Died c.179 AD
Ecstatic prophetess and co-leader of the Montanist sect

Maximilla was a prophetess who, with Montanus and fellow prophetess Priscilla, co-led the Montanists, a heretical Christian sect that believed that the Holy Spirit had told them that Christ's return was imminent. Their belief was that he would establish the New Jerusalem near the village of Pepuza, in Phrygia, Asia Minor.

Maximilla resisted attempts by local bishops to exorcize her, and seems to have outlived her companions. Though she had prophesied that war and revolution would follow her death, these prophecies were not fulfilled, a fact that was taken by the orthodox to invalidate all her teaching.

May, Elaine, *originally* Elaine Berlin

Born 1932
American screenwriter and film director who specializes in satirical comedy

Elaine May was born in Philadelphia, the daughter of Jack Berlin, a well-known Yiddish actor. She was a child actress, then met Mike Nicols while studying at the University of Chicago. They developed a successful writing partnership for the stage until their break-up in 1961.

She went on to write for both stage and screen, and shared an Academy Award for best screenplay with Warren Beatty for *Heaven Can Wait* (1978). Her directing career stumbled disastrously with the failure of the big-budget comedy *Ishtar* in 1987, and she returned to acting.

May, Julian

Born 1931
American writer and publisher of science books for children and fantasy novels for adults

Julian May was born in Chicago, Illinois. She has had an extremely prolific writing and publishing career in juvenile works in science, technology and mythology.

Her fantasy novels for adults have intricate plots and study the complex interplay of people. They include *The Many Colored Land* (1982), *The Golden Torc* (1981) and *Jack the Bodiless* (1992).

Mayer, Hélène

Born 1910 Died 1953
German-born American fencer, regarded as the finest stylist in the world

Hélène Mayer was born in Offenberg. She won her first national foil title at the age of 13 and the Olympic title at 17. She went on to win the 1929 and 1931 world foil championships but was expelled from her local fencing club in Germany while studying in America because her father was Jewish.

Blonde, statuesque and often described as typically Aryan in appearance, she was invited back to represent Germany at the Berlin Olympics to dispel criticism of the Nazi anti-semitic régime. She finished second behind Ilona Elek, who was also Jewish, but defeated her in 1937 to take the world title again.

Mayer later became an American citizen and won the US championship eight times.

Mayo, Katherine

Born 1868 Died 1940
American journalist who criticized society's wrongdoings

Katherine Mayo was born in Ridgeway, Pennsylvania. She is remembered for her books exposing social evils, especially *Isles of Fear* (1925), condemning American admin-

istration of the Philippines, and *Mother India* (1927), a forthright indictment of child marriage and other Indian customs.

Mayreder, Rosa

Born 1858 Died 1938
Austrian writer regarded as a leading feminist of her time

Rosa Mayreder is now principally remembered for her writings on feminist theory, although her early years in Vienna involved her in direct campaigning. She was appalled by the Austrian authorities' attitude to prostitution, and agitated sucessfully for the reform of laws affecting prostitutes. From the time of World War I, in which she was a convinced pacifist, she used the pen to disseminate her beliefs.

Mayreder's principal feminist essay is *A survey of the women problem* (1913), but she also distinguished herself as an artist, exhibiting in Vienna and at an international exhibition in the USA. She also wrote an opera libretto for Hugo Wolf. Her final years were made difficult for her by her husband's mental illness.

Mbande, Jinga

Born c.1582 Died 1663
Angolan queen who struggled against the Portuguese and fought to quell the slave trade

Jinga Mbande was born in the West African kingdom of Kongo and Ndongo, the daughter of the King of Ndongo. Her life was committed to the struggle against the Portuguese who in 1576 had founded Luanda, beginning a lucrative trade exporting slaves to Brazil. Jinga first made herself known in 1622 when she entered into negotiations for Ndongo's independence from the Portuguese on behalf of her brother Ngola. In order to add strength to her cause she apparently converted to Christianity and changed her name to Anna de Sousa.

On Ngola's death (by murder or suicide), Jinga renounced her Christianity, seized power, and declared war on the Portuguese. Ousted from Ndongo almost immediately, she travelled east and conquered the kingdom of Matamba; here she presided over the Jaga tribe, making alliances both with neighbouring tribes to control the slave routes, and with the Dutch, who had captured Luanda in 1641. She continued to organize debilitating raids on the Portuguese until 1643, when they imprisoned her sister and recaptured Luanda.

Jinga went into hiding in the Matamba hills until in 1656 she negotiated a peaceful settlement with the Portuguese, receiving her sister in exchange for 130 slaves as well as military protection whenever she needed it. She returned to ruling the Jaga, weaning them from practising infanticide and cannibalism and converting them to Christianity.

Mead, Margaret

Born 1901 Died 1978
American anthropologist whose writing
popularized interest in her field of study

Margaret Mead was born in Philadelphia. She was appointed assistant curator of ethnology at the American Museum of Natural History in 1926, associate curator from 1942, and curator from 1964. After expeditions to Samoa and New Guinea she wrote *Coming of Age in Samoa* (1928) and *Growing up in New Guinea* (1930). Later publications included *Male and Female* (1949) and *Growth and Culture* (1951).

In these works she argued that personality characteristics, especially as they differ between men and women, are shaped by cultural conditioning rather than heredity. Her writings have proved very popular, and made anthropology accessible to a wide public, though more recently her early findings have been called into question and strongly criticised.

Mechtild of Magdeburg

Born c.1210 Died 1282
German mystic who had visions from the age of
12, one of the key mystics of her time

Mechtild of Magdeburg is not to be confused with her contemporary, Mechtild of Helfta or Hackeborn. At the age of about 21 she became a Béguine at Magdeburg.

She suffered considerable opposition to her mystical experiences, as well as to her criticism of the clergy, and for the last 12 years of her life she was obliged to find shelter in the Cistercian convent at Helfta.

Her poetic and individualistic visions and revelations, *The Flowing Light of the Godhead*, were recorded in six parts, with a seventh added later. The lost Low German original survives in High German and Latin versions.

Mee, Margaret Ursula

Born 1909 Died 1988
English botanical artist who campaigned for the
protection of the Amazon

Margaret Mee was trained at the Camberwell School of Art. She first visited the Amazon forests when she was 47 and 10 years later, having settled in Brazil, she began her outstanding career as a botanical artist. Travelling

extensively in the Brazilian Amazonia, she collected new species and painted many others, some of which have since become extinct.

She was well known for her outspoken anger at the destruction of the Amazonia, which she called 'a valley of death', and the Margaret Mee Amazon trust was set up in 1988 to draw attention to the area's ecological crisis.

Meinhof, Ulrike Marie

Born 1934 Died 1976
German terrorist who acted on her belief that
brutality would result in social change

Ulrike Meinhof was born in Oldenburg, the daughter of a museum director. While studying at Marburg University, she campaigned for the creation of a neutral, nuclear-free 'Greater Germany'. Subsequently she became a respected left-wing journalist.

In 1961 she married the communist activist, Klaus Rainer Röhl (divorced 1968), by whom she had twin daughters. After an interview with the imprisoned arsonist Andreas Baader (1943–77), she became committed to the use of violence to secure radical social change. In May 1970, she helped free Baader and they both then headed an underground urban guerrilla organization, the Red Army Faction, which conducted brutal terrorist attacks against the post-war West German 'materialist order'.

As the Faction's chief ideologist, she was arrested in 1972, and in 1974 was sentenced to eight years' imprisonment. She committed suicide in Stammheim high-security prison.

Meir, Golda, *married name* Goldie Myerson, *née* Mabovich

Born 1898 Died 1978
Israeli Labour politician, a founder of the state of
Israel who became its fourth Prime Minister

Golda Mabovich was born in Kiev. Her family emigrated to Milwaukee, USA, when she was eight years old. She married in 1917 and settled in Palestine in 1921, where she took up social work and became a leading figure in the Labour movement supporting the Zionist cause. During World War II Meir was acting head of the Political Department of the Jewish Agency, working for the release of Jewish activists imprisoned by the British.

In 1948 she was a signatory to Israel's declaration of independence and became Israeli ambassador to the Soviet Union (1948–9). Her later appointments included Minister of Labour (1949–56), during which she improved housing and roads and promoted the unre-

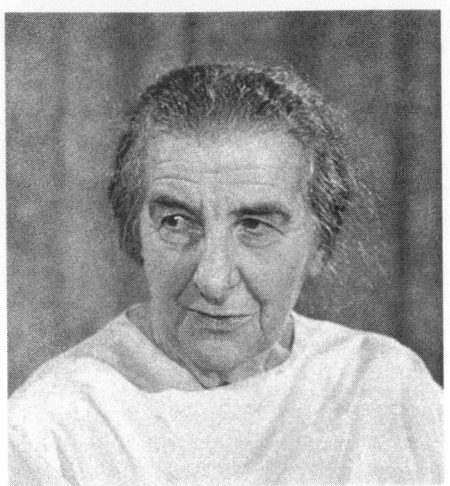

Golda Meir, 1969

stricted immigration of Jews into Israel, and Foreign Minister (1956–66), during which she strove to improve Arab–Israeli relations, which she continued to do after her election as Prime Minister in 1969. Despite her extensive travels and efforts to make peace, the fourth Arab–Israeli war broke out in 1973. She resigned in 1974 but remained a respected figure in international politics until her death from leukaemia.

Meireles, Cecília

Born 1901 Died 1964
Brazilian Catholic poet, critic, and dramatist who
is considered her country's greatest poet

Cecília Meireles was born in Rio de Janeiro. She was an orphan, and unhappily married, and her convincing rejection of the consolations of 'ordinary' experience is in itself replete with experience. Though she was well established as a poet from 1919, when she published her first collection, she later rejected everything she had written before *Viagem* (1939, 'Voyages').

Her poetry, which crosses the metaphysical and the lyrical in a fluid, dream-like manner, has been described as second only, in her century, to that of **Laura Riding**. Two representative poems are translated in the *Penguin Book of Latin American Verse* (1971, ed E Curacciolo-Trejo).

Meitner, Lise

Born 1878 Died 1968
Austrian physicist who with Otto Frisch
discovered and elucidated fission of the
uranium nucleus

Lise Meitner was born in Vienna and educated at the university there. She became professor at Berlin (1926–38) and member of the Kaiser Wilhelm Institute for Chemistry (1907–38), where together with the German radiochemist Otto Hahn (1879–1968) she set up a laboratory for studying nuclear physics. In 1917 she shared with Hahn the discovery of the radioactive element protactinium.

In 1938 she fled to Sweden to escape persecution by the Nazis. Shortly afterwards, Hahn observed radioactive barium in the products of uranium bombarded by neutrons. He wrote to Meitner telling her of the discovery, and with her nephew Otto Frisch (1904–79), she proposed that the production of barium was the result of the uranium nucleus being split in two by nuclear fission. Frisch was able to verify the hypothesis within a few days.

Meitner worked in Sweden until retiring to England in 1960. Recently nuclear physicists named the element of atomic number 108 after her.

Melania the Younger

Born c.383AD Died AD438
Romano-Spanish heiress who founded
monasteries in Africa with her husband

Melania was the granddaughter of Melania the Elder (345–410). She was married at 14 to her cousin, the senator Pinianus, and after the death of two infants they decided to live together in chastity and give away their wealth.

On the Gothic invasion of 410 they fled to Thagaste, North Africa, where they founded two monasteries. Around 417 they moved to Jerusalem and met Jerome, and entered the male and female monasteries founded by **Paula** at Bethlehem.

After Pinianus's death Melania became abbess at a new monastery on the Mount of Olives. She influenced the spiritual writer Evagrius of Ponticus. Returning from a journey to Constantinople, she died in Jerusalem.

Melanie, *professional name of* Melanie Safka

Born 1947
American singer-songwriter

Melanie Safka was born in Queens, New York. She married Peter Schekeryk, who managed her later career, rescuing her from the false start of 'Beautiful People' (1966), recorded while still in her teens.

She made a successful comeback with *Melanie* (1969) and became hugely popular, appearing at the Woodstock Festival. Her recording of *Candles in the Rain* (1970), inspired fans to wave lighters at her concerts, a practice that has spread to other rock bands.

'Brand New Key' from the album *Gather Me* (1971) was a hit, but Melanie's career was in decline and *Garden in the City* (1972) was memorable only for having a perfumed sleeve.

Melba, Dame Nellie, *stage-name of* Helen Armstrong, *née* Mitchell

Born 1861   Died 1931
Australian operatic soprano of international fame

Helen Mitchell was born in Richmond, near Melbourne, from which she took her professional name. Her musical skills were obvious from childhood, but she trained as a pianist and did not study singing until 1882.

She sang in Sydney and London, and made her operatic début, using her stage-name, in Brussels in 1887, singing Gilda in Verdi's *Rigoletto*. She appeared at Covent Garden in 1888, and the wonderful purity of her soprano voice won her worldwide fame. Her most popular roles included Violetta in Verdi's *La Traviata*, Marguerite in Gounod's *Faust*, and Mimì in Puccini's and Leoncavallo's *La Bohème*.

She published her autobiographical *Melodies and Memories* in 1925 and was created DBE in 1927. Her name has been given to peach Melba and Melba toast — the former was concocted for her by the French chef Auguste Escoffier (as *pêche melba*), and the latter, legend has it, arose from the occasion she was served overcooked toast in the Savoy, London. Rather than sending it back, she enjoyed eating it, which resulted in it being added to the menu.

Mellanby, Lady May, *née* Tweedy

Born 1882   Died 1978
British nutritional scientist who connected diet with the development of strong teeth

May Tweedy spent her early years in Imperial Russia, where her father worked in the oil industry. In 1902 she entered Girton College, Cambridge, and was permitted to attend several lectures not normally open to women. She was awarded the equivalent of a second class honours degree in 1906 (women not being allowed to graduate from Cambridge at this time) and became a research fellow, then lecturer in physiology at Bedford College for women in London.

In 1914 she married Edward Mellanby

whom she had met at Cambridge, and collaborated with him on several nutritional researches. She also developed an important independent, but complementary, research line on dental development, arising from a chance observation in 1917 that her husband's dogs, suffering from experimentally induced rickets, had structural abnormalities in their teeth. From animal experiments she showed that vitamins A and D were essential for the proper postnatal development of teeth, and she was the first woman to present a paper to the British Orthodontics Society in 1919.

She travelled widely, examining the teeth of adults and children, and carrying out controlled experiments in children's homes and hospitals, and authored important special reports for the Medical Research Council on the relationship between diet, and dental structure and disease.

Mellis, Margaret

Born 1914
Scottish painter and constructivist artist

Margaret Mellis was born in China of Scottish parents. She studied at Edinburgh College of Art under Samuel John Peploe and won several awards, including a travelling scholarship that enabled her to visit Spain, France, where she worked with Andre Lhote, and Italy.

Before World War II she studied in London with the Euston Road School. She then married the artist Adrian Stokes and lived in Cornwall from 1939 to 1947. She was friendly with the artists Ben Nicholson, Naum Gabo, **Barbara Hepworth** and Peter Lanyon. After separating from Stokes, she married the artist Francis Davison in 1947.

She was originally a painter, but has worked in collage as a constructivist (that is, an artist who pieces the work together rather than moulding, casting or carving it), with relief carving, and she also executed a series of colour structures between 1963 and 1973. Retrospectives have been held in the Redfern Gallery and in Nottingham Art Gallery, both in 1987.

Menchik-Stevenson, Vera (Francevna), *née* Menchik

Born 1906   Died 1944
Russian-born British chess player, the best woman player of her time

Vera Menchik was born in Moscow. She became a British citizen on her marriage in 1937.

She earned recognition as the finest of all

female chess players, and held the world title from 1927 onwards (the first champion). She was killed during a London air-raid.

Menchu, Rigoberta Tum

Born 1959
Guatemalan activist for the rights of indigenous
people and Nobel Prize laureate

Rigoberta Menchu was born near San Marcos, in western Guatemala. She has worked as a domestic servant and as a labourer in the cotton fields of Guatemala. Her campaign for human rights began when she was a teenager and later she had to flee to Mexico when her brother and parents were killed by security forces in 1980.

In 1983 her book *I Rigoberta Menchu* was published and her cause was taken up by Madame Danielle Miterrand, wife of President Mitterand of France (1916–96). In 1986 Menchu narrated the film *When the Mountains Tremble*, which portrays the difficulties experienced by the native Quiche people. In 1992 she was involved in organizing opposition to the 500th anniversary of the arrival of Columbus in America and that same year was awarded the Nobel Peace Prize.

Menken, Adah Isaacs, *née* Adèle Bertha Theodore

Born 1835 Died 1868
American actress who earned a place in theatrical
history for riding near-naked on horseback

Adèle Theodore was born near New Orleans. She had many husbands, including Charles Dickens, and many literary friends. She appeared on stage in New York in 1859, and later appeared in *Mazeppa* with immense success in London (1864) and elsewhere.

No reports of her acting ability are extant and her reputation appears to rest on her audacity, which reached its apotheosis when she appeared on stage in a state of virtual nudity after she was bound to the back of a horse, a role she performed throughout America in the early 1860s.

Menten, Maude

Born 1879 Died 1960
Canadian histochemist and pathologist

Maude Menten was educated at the University of Toronto and graduated MD from there in 1911. She worked in Toronto, the Rockefeller Institute, Western Reserve University and

Berlin, before earning a PhD in biochemistry at the University of Chicago.

She became Professor at the University of Pittsburgh School of Medicine and served as chief pathologist at the city's Children's Hospital. The histochemical and biochemical assay techniques that she developed became essential tools in others' work determining cellular and molecular mechanisms of disease.

Mercouri, Melina (Anna Amalia)

Born 1923 Died 1994
Greek film actress who became a prominent
politican

Melina Mercouri was born in Athens. She began her career in films in 1955, playing successfully in *Stella*, which also established her as a notable interpreter of contemporary Greek music. In 1960 she found international fame with *Never on Sunday.* She married the director Jules Dassin as her second husband in 1966 and subsequently collaborated in several features with him.

She was always politically involved, and during her exile from Greece (1967–74) she played in several British and US productions, such as *Topkapi* (1964) and *Gaily, Gaily* (1969).

She returned to be elected to parliament in 1977, and became Minister of Culture and Sciences (1981–5, 1993–4) and Minister of Culture, Youth, and Sports (1985–90). Among her many concerns was her tireless campaign to have the Elgin marbles returned to Greece.

Méricourt, Théroigne de, *also known as* La belle Liègeoise, *originally* Anne-Joseph Théroigne

Born 1762 Died 1817
Belgian-born public figure active in Paris during
the French Revolution

Anne-Joseph Théroigne was born in Marcourt near Liège, Belgium, later adopting the name of her village in the form 'de Méricourt'. After a brief education at a convent school in Liège, she worked variously as a farmworker, as a dressmaker, and as a governess. After training as a singer in London she moved to Paris in 1785 where she co-founded the *Club des Amies de la Loi.*

She was a frequent visitor to the National Assembly and her public pronouncements were ridiculed in the royalist press. When the mob stormed the Tuileries she was in the thick of the battle but was attacked, stripped and publicly flogged for her support of Brissot. By the end of 1794 she was insane and was committed to the Salpétrière Institute.

Merman, Ethel, *née* Ethel Agnes Zimmerman

Born 1909 Died 1984
American singer and star of Broadway and film musicals

Ethel Merman was born in Astoria, New York. Her first break was in 1930, when she got a supporting role in the Broadway production of George Gershwin's *Girl Crazy*. She sang just one song — 'I Got Rhythm' — but it was enough to highlight her powerful voice and bring her enduring fame.

Her later performances on Broadway include *Annie Get Your Gun* (1946) and *Call Me Madam* (1950). Her many appearances in movie musicals include *Stage Door Canteen* (1943) and *Call Me Madam* (1953).

Messalina, Valeria, *also spelt* Messallina

Born c.25AD Died c.48AD
Roman empress as the wife of Emperor Claudius (ruled 41–54) who abused her powerful position

Valeria Messalina was the third wife and second cousin of the emperor Claudius, whom she married at the age of 14. She bore him two children: Octavia, who married Nero (whose mother **Agrippina, the Younger** married Claudius in AD49 and persuaded him to adopt her son as his successor); and Britannicus, who was named in honour of his father's triumph in Britain and who was supplanted as Claudius's heir and later poisoned by his stepbrother Nero.

Messalina's name has become a byword for avarice, lust and cruelty, for she stage-managed many murderous intrigues and had senators executed when they refused her amorous propositions. In the emperor's absence she publicly married one of her favourites, the consul-designate Silius, and the emperor was at last persuaded she was plotting against him and had her executed.

Mészáros, Marta

Born 1931
Hungarian film director whose films focus on the daily realities of women's lives

Marta Mészáros was born in Budapest but was forced to leave Hungary for Russia in 1936. Both her parents died early, an experience that was to affect Mészáros's subject matter in later life, but she managed to obtain a scholarship to Moscow's VGIK Film School. She made her directorial début with the short *Ujra Mosoly-gonak* ('Smiling Again') in 1954 and over the next 14 years made over 30 documentaries

designed to popularize science in Romania and Hungary.

Her first feature-length film was *Eltávozott Nap* (1968, 'The Girl'), a plaintive portrait of an orphan's disillusioning search for the parents who had abandoned her. This was followed by *A 'Holdudvar* (1968, 'Binding Sentiments') and the semi-musical romance *Széplányok, Ne Sirjatok* (1970, 'Don't Cry Pretty Girls').

Other significant films are *Ök Killan* (1977, 'Two Women'), a tale of women finding more emotional support in their female friendships than in their inadequate male partners, and an insightful trilogy on the history of postwar Hungary: *Naplo Gyermekeimnek* (1982, 'Diary for My Children'), *Naplo Szerelmeimnek* (1987, 'Diary for My Loves') and *Naplo Apamnak Anya'Mnak* (1990, 'Diary for My Father and My Mother').

Mew, Charlotte Mary

Born 1869 Died 1928
English poet and short-story writer whose works were revived in feminist literature in the 1970s

Charlotte Mew was born in London and essentially self-educated. Her work largely concerned the problems of women in a society that provided few reliable terms of reference or role models for female individuality. The critical support of those such as Walter de la Mare and Thomas Hardy, who predeceased her only briefly, sustained her reputation and led to her being awarded a civil pension.

The circumstances of Mew's suicide, following the death of her sister, has fostered a certain romantic cult around her. In the late 1970s, Mew was rediscovered by the feminist movement; her collected verse and prose, reissued by Virago Press, made a significant impact on a revisionist awareness of post-Victorian social and cultural attitudes.

Her most famous poem is 'The Farmer's Bride' (1915), a vigorous narrative about an emotionally restricted life.

Meyers, Ann

Born 1955
American basketball player who played in the first women's Olympic team

Ann Meyers was born San Diego, California. She was one of the first women to go to UCLA (University of California at Los Angeles) on a full athletic scholarship, and was named All-American in each of her four years of college play.

At the 1976 Olympics she played in the first Olympic women's basketball tournament, where the US team won a silver medal.

In 1978 she was named UCLA Athlete of the year and was chosen Collegiate Woman Athlete of the Year by the National Association for Girls and Women In Sports; she also became the first woman inducted into the Naismith Memorial Hall of Fame. Also that year she left amateur sports for a successful commercial and media career.

Meynell, Alice Christiana Gertrude, *née* Thompson

Born 1847 Died 1922
English essayist and a lyrical and mystical poet

Alice Thompson was born in Barnes, London, the daughter of a scholar and a concert pianist, and sister of the painter **Elizabeth Butler**. She spent her childhood on the Continent, and became a convert to Catholicism.

Her volumes of essays include *The Rhythm of Life* (1893), *The Colour of Life* (1896) and *Hearts of Controversy* (1917). She published several collections of her own poems, starting in 1875 with *Preludes*, and anthologies of the poet Coventry Patmore (1823–96), of lyric poetry, and of poems for children.

In 1877 she married Wilfrid Meynell (1852–1948), author and journalist, with whom she edited several periodicals. Her poetry was highly praised, especially by other writers such as **George Eliot**.

Mhac An tSaoi, Máire, *née* MacEntee

Born 1922
Irish Gaelic poet, short-story writer and essayist, known for her Irish-language poetry

Máire Mhac An tSaoi was born in Dublin and educated at University College there and at the Sorbonne in Paris. She was called to the Bar in 1944. She married the writer and politician Conor Cruise O'Brien (1917–   ) in 1962.

She has written and translated a remarkable and singular oeuvre of 'feminist-orientated' poems and verses in Gaelic. She has always emphasized, as in *Cré na Mna Tí* (1958, 'The Housewife's Credo') for example, that it is essential to realize and utilize creativity despite the dictates of domesticity: 'like Scheherazade, you will *need* to write poetry also'. Her sense of the present being interdependent on a richly cultivated past is most in evidence in the invaluable English translations *A Heart Full of Thought* (1959).

In collaboration with her husband she published *A Concise History of Ireland* in 1972.

Michaëlis, Karin

Born 1872 Died 1950
Danish novelist, short-story writer, and journalist known for her explorations of female sexuality

Karin Michaëlis was born in Randers. She left home at the age of 20, married the poet Sophus Michaëlis and started writing. Her novel *Barnet* (1902, 'The Child'), the first to be noticed outside Denmark, focuses on the theme of childhood. *Den farlige Alder* (1910, Eng trans *The Dangerous Age*, 1912), which resulted in international fame, is an epistolary and diary novel about a menopausal woman, pinpointing the lies and dissimulation which are part of the social construction of the feminine role.

Her extensive output includes the seven-volume series for children about Bibi (1929–39) and two autobiographical series, *Træt på godt og ondt* (1924–30, 'The Tree of Good and Evil') and *Vidunderlige Verden* (1948–50, 'Marvellous World').

Also involved in politics, Michaëlis became a well-known figure in Denmark, and always championed the causes of women and the underprivileged.

Michel, (Clémence) Louise

Born 1830 Died 1905
French anarchist who spent many years of her life preaching revolution

Louise Michel was born in Vroncourt and trained as a teacher in Paris. She devoted much of her life to preaching revolution through violence and class war rather than political reform, and periodically suffered imprisonment as a result.

In 1871 she fought with the National Guard to defend the Paris Commune against the government troops; she escaped massacre but was sentenced to long-term imprisonment. Free after the amnesty of 1880, she returned to her anarchist activities and undertook lecture tours throughout France, which caused a riot and landed her in prison for three years from 1883.

She lived for 10 years in London (1886–96), remaining aware of revolutionary interest on the Continent, and returned to Paris to spread anarchist propaganda and instill in people a sense of social consciousness. She wrote *Mémoires* (1886) and various other works.

Midler, Bette

Born 1945
American comedienne, actress and singer

Bette Midler was born in Honolulu, Hawaii. She studied drama at the University of Hawaii and then was hired as an extra in the film *Hawaii* (1966) before moving to New York, where she made her stage début in *Miss Nefertiti Regrets* (1966). She then developed a popular nightclub act as a chanteuse and purveyor of outrageously bawdy comic routines.

Her album *The Divine Miss M* (1974) won her a Grammy award as Best New Artist, and the same year she received a Tony award for her record-breaking Broadway show. Her dramatic performance in the film *The Rose* (1979) earned her an Academy Award nomination and she has continued to excel in all media, writing a modest memoir *A View from A Broad* (1980) and enjoying considerable commercial success in a string of film farces including *Outrageous Fortune* (1987) and *Big Business* (1988). She sang the soundtrack for *Beaches* (1988) and appeared in the children's comedy *Hocus Pocus* (1993).

Mildmay, Lady Grace, *née* Sherrington

Born 1552 Died 1620
English journal keeper and writer on medicine
who left provision for scholars at Emmanuel
College

Grace Sherrington was the second daughter of Sir Henry Sherrington, a Wiltshire landowner, who trained her in religion and the arts of medicine. She married Anthony Mildmay in 1570.

Her journal, kept until her husband's death in 1617, shows how she ran the home while he was constantly away at court, taking responsibility for the household's religious observance, medical and other needs.

In her will she made provision for the poor, for tradesmen, and for scholars at Emmanuel College, Cambridge, which had been founded by her father-in-law, Sir Walter Mildmay.

Mill, Harriet Taylor, *née* Hardy

Born 1807 Died 1858
English feminist philosopher, essayist and political
theorist, one of the first to champion women's
suffrage

Harriet Hardy was born in London, and little is known of her early life. Her first husband was John Taylor, upon whose death she married her philosopher friend John Stuart Mill (1806–73) in 1851. One of the first writers in England to press for women's rights and suffrage, she wrote essays in the 1850s that confidently and authoritatively rejected the legal and political traditions subordinating women with a firmness uncharacteristic of the age. Her suggested remedies for the improvement of the position of women lay in education, law and politics. A strong and pioneering advocate of women's suffrage as early as 1851, she claimed full legal and political citizenship for women, and promoted equality in higher education.

She was not able to remain politically active because of bad health, but continued to pursue her cause through the activities of her husband, who acknowledged her indispensable contribution to his thought and work. She collaborated with him in particular on his classic expression of feminist thought, *The Subjection of Women* (1869). Among her works are the important *Essays on Sex Equality.*

Millar, Margaret

Born 1915 Died 1994
American novelist and short-story writer known
mainly for her detective fiction

Margaret Millar was born in Kitchener, Canada, and educated at the University of Toronto. She worked as a screenwriter for Warner Brothers and was the President of Mystery Writers of America in 1957–8. The *Los Angeles Times* voted her Woman of the Year in 1965.

She wrote over 20 novels and several short stories, mostly in the detective fiction genre — though she probed more deeply into the psychology of her characters than most crime writers.

She wrote her first novel, *The Invisible Worm*, in 1941. *Beast in View* (1955) won her the Mystery Writers of America Edgar Allan Poe award, as did *Banshee* nearly 30 years later, in 1983.

Millay, Edna St Vincent

Born 1892 Died 1950
American poet and Pulitzer Prize-winner

Edna St Vincent Millay was born in Rockland, Maine. Her first poem was published when she was a student at Vassar College. Moving into Greenwich Village, then at its height as a meeting place for artists and writers, she published *A Few Figs from Thistles* (1920). In 1923 came *The Harp Weaver and Other Poems*, for which she was awarded a Pulitzer Prize.

During her lifetime she was a feminist and though she was latterly dismissed as arrogant, egotistic and whimsical, the admiration of writers like **Maya Angelou** has caused her to be re-evaluated and there has been renewed interest in her sonorous verse.

Miller, Cheryl

Born 1964
African-American basketball player, the first woman to 'dunk' the ball

Cheryl Miller was born in Riverside, California. She is noted as the first woman to dunk a basketball in regulation play (ie to score by thrusting the ball downward through the basket).

In high school competitive girls' basketball, Miller holds the California Interscholastic Federation records for the most career points and the most points scored in one season. As a collegiate athlete at USC (the University of Southern California), she won nearly every major basketball award, including the Naismith Trophy (1984, 1985, 1986); the Broderick Award as college player of the year (1984, 1985); and the Women's Basketball Coaches' Association Player of the Year (1985, 1986). USC retired her number in 1986, marking the first time a basketball player had been so honoured. (This means that the number she was assigned as a team athlete will never be reassigned, but always associated with her.) She now works as the women's basketball coach at USC.

Miller was inducted into the International Women's Sports Hall of Fame in 1991.

Miller, Lee

Born 1907   Died 1977
American photographer known for powerful documentary work and fashion photography

Lee Miller was born in Poughkeepsie, New York, and was taught photography by her father. She studied in Paris (1925) and at the Art Students League, New York (1927–9), during which time she also modelled, notably for photographer and curator Edward Steichen (1879–1973). She returned to Paris in 1929 to study with photographer and painter Man Ray (1890–1976) until 1932, when she returned to the USA to run her own photography studio in New York until 1933.

The following year she married Egyptian businessman Aziz Eloui Bey (separated 1939, divorced 1947) and lived in Egypt and Europe until 1939. She left Bey to live in England with painter and future author Roland Penrose, whom she married in 1947 and with whom she had a son, Anthony (b.1947), who was later to write her biography, *The Lives of Lee*

Miller (1985). From 1940 she became a photographer in London for *Vogue*, and in 1942 she became official war correspondent for the US forces, photographing the liberation of Paris and of Dachau and Buchenwald concentration camps in 1945. She then returned to *Vogue* as a freelance journalist and photographer (1946–54).

Retrospective exhibitions of her work were held at the Statey-Wise Gallery in New York (1985), the Photographers' Gallery, London (1986), and the San Francisco Museum of Modern Art (1987). Her publications include *Grim Glory: Pictures of Britain under Fire* (1941, with E Carter).

Millett, Kate (Katherine) Murray

Born 1934
American feminist, writer and sculptor

Kate Millett was born in St Paul and educated at the University of Minnesota, St Hilda's College, Oxford, and at Columbia University, New York, where she graduated PhD in 1970. Her thesis became the bestseller and feminist classic, *Sexual Politics* (1970).

Early in her career as a sculptor she spent some time in Tokyo (1961–3), and has exhibited in Tokyo, New York, Los Angeles and Berlin. She also founded the Women's Art Colony at Poughkeepsie, New York.

Her other publications include *The Prostitution Papers* (1973), the autobiographical *Flying* (1974), *Going to Iran* (1982) and *The Loony Bin Trip* (1990).

Mills, Barbara Jean Lyon

Born 1940
English lawyer who has risen to the top of her profession

Barbara Mills was born in Chorley Wood, Hertfordshire, and educated at St Helen's School, Northwood, and Lady Margaret Hall, Oxford. She was called to the Bar in 1963, made a Recorder of the Crown Court in 1982, and a QC in 1986. She was a Junior Treasury Counsel to the Central Criminal Court in the 1980s, during which time she became known for prosecuting Michael Fagin for breaking into the bedroom of **Elizabeth II**.

In 1990 she was made director of the Serious Fraud Office, and then in 1992 became the first woman to head the Department of Public Prosecutions, at a time when its activities were under scrutiny following damaging revelations of miscarriages of justice.

Barbara Mills, 1992

Milner, Brenda Atkinson, née Langford

Born 1918
English-born Canadian psychologist, significant
in the growth of neuropsychology

Brenda Langford studied at Cambridge and at McGill University, Montreal. She worked at the Ministry of Supply (1941–4), before emigrating to Canada where she taught at the Université de Montreal (1944–52), leaving to join McGill University and then becoming head of the Neuropsychology Research Unit at the Montreal Neurological Institute (1953).

Her contributions to the field of neuropsychology have been mainly empirical, the best-known being a series of investigations of a man rendered profoundly amnesic following a radical brain operation for the relief of epilepsy. This work has formed the basis for a large body of subsequent research, in which the brain structures implicated in laying down a new memory, and their mode of function, are now becoming better understood. Other important research has concerned the asymmetrical activities of the two sides of the brain, particularly in relation to the temporal lobes (at the side of the brain), but also in relation to the frontal lobes. As well as contributing to our knowledge of how the brain works, much of her research has also had application to the clinic, particularly in relation to the surgical treatment of temporal-lobe epilepsy.

She won the Distinguished Scientific Con-

tribution award of the American Psychological Association (1973) and the Ralph W Gerard Prize of the Society for Neuroscience (1987).

Min

Born 1851 Died 1895
Queen of Korea as the wife of King Kojong (ruled 1864–1907)

Min was the leader of a powerful faction at court, mainly comprising members of her own family, which was strongly opposed to increased Japanese influence in Korea. Though her husband Kojong (or I T'aewang) was king, she was the real holder of the ruling power, but for this she struggled with her father-in-law Hungson (or Tai Wen Kun) who was official regent from 1864 to 1873 but remained a dominant political figure until his death in 1898.

Min was assassinated in a palace coup instigated by the Japanese Minister to Korea, Miura Goro, in an attempt to secure Japanese control over the Korean king. The plot misfired, however; Miura was cashiered by his own government while King Kojong increasingly looked to China for protection.

Mink, Paule, née Mekarska

Born 1839 Died 1900
French socialist feminist who had to flee the country because of her beliefs

Paule Mekarska was born into a family of Polish descent who had settled at Clermont-Ferrand in France. She moved to Paris and undertook a variety of jobs, while becoming involved in political and feminist groups. When the Franco-Prussian war broke out, she organized the defence of the town of Auxerre and supported the Paris Commune, actions for which she had to flee the country.

After returning to France in 1880 under amnesty, she campaigned for women's rights through journalism, but stood for the National Assembly in 1893, and led the Socialist Women's Movement in France from 1896 until her death. Such was her popularity that the crowds attending her funeral had to be policed by more than 1,000 troops.

Minnelli, Liza May

Born 1946
American singer and actress who has followed in her mother's star-studded footsteps

Liza Minnelli was born in Los Angeles, daughter of director Vincente Minnelli (1910–86) and **Judy Garland**. She first appeared on screen in her mother's film *In The Good Old*

Summertime (1949) and acted in a school production of *The Diary of Anne Frank* (1960). She made her off-Broadway début in *Best Foot Forward* (1963) and became the youngest actress to win a Tony award for *Flora, the Red Menace* (1965).

Seen on television and in cabaret, her vibrant vocal talents and emotional rendition of plaintive songs earned comparisons with her mother. Dramatic roles in films like *Charlie Bubbles* (1967), *The Sterile Cuckoo* (1969) and *Tell Me That You Love Me, Junie Moon* (1970) revealed her as a skilled portrayer of social outcasts: the fragile, insecure and gauche. She won an Academy Award for *Cabaret* (1972), and a television special, *Liza with a Z* (1972), confirmed her many talents. Subsequent dramatic appearances include *New York, New York* (1977), the television film *A Time to Live* (1985) and *Stepping Out* (1991).

Her private life has often appeared to emulate the volatility of her mother's but she remains a potent attraction as a recording artist and concert performer, her activities including a well-received tour in Russia in 1994.

Minton, Yvonne Fay

Born 1938
Australian operatic and concert mezzo-soprano
whose voice is well suited to Wagnerian roles

Yvonne Minton was born in Earlwood, Sydney. She attended the New South Wales Conservatorium of Music, and after winning a scholarship and the Shell aria contest, studied in London where in 1961 she won the **Kathleen Ferrier** prize. She made her operatic début in 1964 at the Royal Opera House, Covent Garden, where she was principal mezzo-soprano from 1965 to 1971.

Minton has also been a guest member of the Cologne Opera since 1969, and guest artist with the New York Metropolitan, the Chicago, Paris, and Australian opera companies. She created the role of Thea in Michael Tippett's *The Knot Garden* (1970) and is noted for her Octavian in Strauss's *Rosenkavalier*.

Miranda, Carmen, *professional name of* Maria do Carmo Miranda Da Cunha

Born 1909 Died 1955
Brazilian singer and actress, the 'Brazilian Bombshell'

Carmen Miranda was born near Lisbon and raised in Rio de Janeiro, where she became a film and radio personality before being brought to the USA by Lee Shubert in 1939.

She became known as the 'Brazilian Bombshell', compensating for (and making fun of) her diminutive stature by wearing platform shoes and towering hats of fruits and flowers. Her American début was in the Broadway show *The Streets of Paris* (1939) with George Abbott and Tom Costello. She went on to star in *Down Argentine Way* (1941) and *The Gang's All Here* (1943), which included the song 'The Lady in the Tutti Frutti Hat'.

After World War II, she topped the bill at the London Palladium for the 1948 season. She died suddenly while preparing a television special with Jimmy Durante.

Miriam

Floreat c.1526 BC
Biblical character, the sister of Aaron and Moses

Miriam was the daughter of Amram and Jochebed, and sister of the Israelite leaders Aaron and Moses. She watched over the baby Moses hidden in the bulrushes and suggested that her mother be employed as the nurse to bring him up in the Egyptian court.

During the Israelites' escape from Egypt by crossing the Red (or Reed) Sea, she led the women in music, dancing and singing. When she took Aaron's side against Moses in a leadership dispute, she was struck by leprosy for a short time. Later tradition has her as the wife of Caleb and mother of Hur.

Mirren, Helen, *originally* Ilyena Mironoff

Born 1945
English actress who has become a leading star in film, theatre and television

Helen Mirren was born in Southend. Her father was a Russian who came to England as a child. She was a member of the National Youth Theatre, and worked briefly with the Manchester Repertory Theatre before joining the Royal Shakespeare Company in 1967, where she spent much of the next 15 years.

A fiery young performer, unafraid to express a strong sexuality in her roles, her memorable stage performances include Ophelia in *Hamlet* (1970), *Miss Julie* (1971), and Lady Macbeth in *Macbeth* (1974). She made her film début in *Herostratus* (1967) and won acclaim for her roles in *The Long Good Friday* (1980) and *Cal* (1984), for which she received the Best Actress prize at the Cannes Film Festival. Her subsequent film roles include *The Mosquito Coast* (1986), *The Cook, The Thief, His Wife and Her Lover* (1989) and *Where Angels Fear to Tread* (1991).

Attempting to maintain a transatlantic career (she lives in the USA with her partner, director Taylor Hackford, whom she met when he directed her in *White Nights,* 1984), she has appeared on stage in such plays as *Extremities* (1984), *Two-Way Mirror* (1989), *Sex Please, We're Italian* (1991) and Turgenev's *A Month in the Country* (1994). She received the BAFTA Best Actress award three times for her performance as a middle-aged police inspector fighting her male colleague's prejudice in **Lynda La Plante**'s television drama *Prime Suspect* (1991) and its sequels, *Prime Suspect 2* (1992), and *Prime Suspect 3* (1993).

Mistinguett, *stage-name of* Jeanne Marie Bourgeois

Born c.1875 Died 1956
French dancer, singer, and actress who was a
symbol of Parisian gaiety

Jeanne Marie Bourgeois was born in a suburb of Paris, the daughter of parents who had a furniture shop in Montmorency. She was given her stage name by the friends with whom she travelled on the train to Paris, who thought that 'Miss' characterized her 'English' looks. She made her début in 1895 and reached the height of success with Maurice Chevalier at the Folies Bergère. Although not a classic beauty due to having protruding front teeth, her legs (allegedly insured for one million francs) were renowned for their shapeliness.

She was noted for her vivacity as a stage personality, and made up for her weak voice with a remarkable versatility and originality in comedy. She also distinguished herself as a straight actress in *Madame Sans-Gène* and *Les Misérables.* Among her best-remembered songs are 'Mon Homme' and 'J'en ai marre'.

She published her memoirs *Toute ma vie* (*Mistinguett, Queen of the Paris Night*) in 1954.

Mistral, Gabriela, *pseud of* Lucila Godoy de Alcayaga

Born 1889 Died 1957
Chilean poet, diplomat and teacher and winner of
the Nobel Prize

Gabriela Mistral was born in Vicuña. As a teacher she won a poetry prize with her *Sonetos de la muerte* ('Sonnets of Death') at Santiago in 1915. She taught at Columbia University, Vassar, and in Puerto Rico, and was formerly consul at Madrid and elsewhere. The cost of publication of her first book, *Desolación* (1922, 'Desolation'), was defrayed by the teachers of New York.

Her work is inspired by religious sentiments and a romantic preoccupation with sorrow and death, infused with an intense lyricism. Her career as a teacher led her to write a great deal of work for children, notably the songs in *Ternura* (1924); much of her children's writing is translated in *Crickets and Frogs* (1972). She was awarded the Nobel Prize for Literature in 1945.

Mitchell, Hannah, *née* Webster

Born 1871 Died 1956
English working-class feminist who overcame
class prejudice to be a magistrate

Hannah Webster was born in Derbyshire, the daughter of a farmer. She had no formal schooling and grew up resenting the limitations placed on working-class women. She married Gibbon Mitchell, a socialist, and had one son.

After joining the Independent Labour Party, she took part in the suffrage movement, working with the **Pankhursts** in 1904–5. She later worked for the Women's Social and Political Union and in 1907 for the Women's Freedom League.

She was a pacifist during World War I and afterwards was elected to the Manchester City Council, becoming a magistrate in 1926.

Mitchell, Joni (Roberta Joan), *née* Anderson

Born 1943
Canadian singer and songwriter who progressed
from folk to rock

Joni Anderson was born in McLeod, Alberta, and studied commercial art for a time. Her compositions, which are highly original and personal in their lyrical imagery, first attracted attention among folk music audiences in Toronto while she was still in her teens. She married folk singer Chuck Mitchell in 1965, but the marriage was over within two years.

She moved to the USA in the mid-1960s and in 1968 recorded her first album, *Song to a Seagull.* Other highly successful albums that followed include *Clouds, Ladies of the Canyon, Blue* and *The Hissing of Summer Lawns. Turbulent Indigo* appeared in 1994. Many of her songs, notably 'Both Sides Now', have been recorded by other singers.

Mitchell, Juliet

Born 1934
New Zealand-born British feminist and writer on
the subject of psychoanalysis

Juliet Mitchell was born in New Zealand. She moved to Britain with her family in 1944 and was educated at King Alfred School, Hampstead, London and at St Anne's College,

Oxford. She undertook postgraduate study at Oxford and subsequently lectured at the University of Leeds (1962–3) and at the University of Reading (1965–70). Since 1971 she has been a freelance writer and broadcaster and has lectured on her subject, psychoanalysis, throughout the world.

Her publications include *Women's Estate* (1972), *Psychoanalysis and Feminism* (1974) and *Women: The Longest Revolution* (1966). She has also co-authored *The Rights and Wrongs of Women* (1976) and edited *What is Feminism* (1986), both with **Ann Oakley**.

Mitchell, Margaret

Born 1900 Died 1949
American novelist famed for her single work,
Gone with the Wind

Margaret Mitchell was born in Atlanta, Georgia. She studied for a medical career, but turned to journalism. After her marriage to J R Marsh in 1925, she began the 10-year task of writing her only novel, *Gone with the Wind* (1936), which won the 1937 Pulitzer Prize, sold over 25 million copies, was translated into 30 languages and was the subject of a celebrated film in 1939.

Mitchell, Maria

Born 1818 Died 1889
American astronomer, one of the first women to
make discoveries and teach in this field

Maria Mitchell was born in Nantucket into a serious-minded Quaker family. Her father's activities included regulating chronometers for whaling ships in which his daughter took part from an early age. In 1836 the US Coast Survey equipped an observatory at their home as a local station with her father in charge, where Maria, a librarian in the local Athenaeum, had an opportunity to practise astronomy.

Her discovery of a comet in 1847 brought her to public notice and earned for her the King of Denmark's Gold Medal (1848) for first discoverers of telescopic comets, and election to the American Academy of Arts and Sciences, its first woman member. Her first professional commission was the computing of tables of the planet Venus for the American Ephemerides and Nautical Almanac, a duty she performed for 20 years (1849–68).

In 1865 she was appointed Professor of Astronomy at the newly founded Vassar College for women at Poughkeepsie, where she was an inspiring teacher and a doughty campaigner in the women's rights and anti-slavery

movements. In failing health she retired to her native Nantucket in 1888. She was inducted into the National Women's Hall of Fame in 1994.

Mitchison, Naomi Margaret, *née* Haldane

Born 1897
Scottish novelist, poet and travel writer

Naomi Haldane was born in Edinburgh, the daughter of the Scottish physiologist J S Haldane, and educated at the Dragon School, Oxford. She married Gilbert Richard Mitchison (1890–1970, created life peer in 1964) in 1916. He was a Labour MP (1945–64), and joint Parliamentary Secretary, Ministry of Land (1964–6), and she too became involved with the Labour Party and advocated women's rights and pacifism.

She won instant attention with her brilliant and personal evocations of Greece and Sparta in a series of novels such as *The Conquered* (1923), *When the Bough Breaks* (1924), *Cloud Cuckoo Land* (1925) and *Black Sparta* (1928). In 1931 came the erudite *Corn King and Spring Queen*, which brought to life the civilizations of ancient Egypt, Scythia and the Middle East.

She has travelled widely, and in 1963 was made Tribal Adviser and Mother to the Bakgatla of Botswana. She has written more than 70 books, including her memoirs in *Small Talk* (1973), *All Change Here* (1975) and *You May Well Ask* (1979), among many other writings. Since 1937 she has lived in Carradale in the Mull of Kintyre, Scotland.

Mitchison, Rosalind Mary, *née* Wrong

Born 1919
English historian, leading feminist historian who
wrote A History of Scotland

Rosalind Mitchison was born in Manchester, the granddaughter of George Mackinnon Wrong, a leading Canadian historian. She was educated at Channing School, Highgate, London, and Lady Margaret Hall, Oxford, and became assistant lecturer in history first at Manchester University (1943–6), and then at Edinburgh (1954–7). She moved to Glasgow as assistant lecturer (1962–3), then lecturer (1966–7), then returned to Edinburgh as lecturer in social and economic history (1967–76).

In 1970 she published *A History of Scotland*, which was conspicuous for its forthright language and integration of economic and social history with political history, and became a standard text for the next 20 years. She was Professor of Social History at Edinburgh from 1981 to 1986, and her many works include *British Population Change since 1869* (1977), *Lordship and Patronage: Scotland 1603–1745* (1983) and *People and Society in Scotland, 1760–1830* (1988).

A vigorous and inspirational lecturer and teacher, she was the foremost authority on the Scottish poor law. A trenchant analyst of class and property interests in the Scottish past, she has in recent years become the judicious but firm leader of Scottish feminist historians. She has been married since 1947 to the cell biologist Professor John Mitchison (1922–).

Mitford, Jessica Lucy

Born 1917
English-born American writer whose work is inspired by her observations of American society

Jessica Mitford was born in Gloucestershire, the fifth of the six daughters of the 2nd Baron Redesdale, and sister of **Nancy Mitford**. She went to the USA in 1939 and joined the US Communist Party, her experiences of which were the subject for *A Fine Old Conflict* (1977).

Her observation of various aspects of American society provided material for her works, such as her bestselling *The American Way of Death* (1963), an exposé of the funeral industry's unethical practices. *The Trial of Dr Spock* (1970), based on the trials of anti-Vietnam War activists, was inspired by her interest in civil-rights cases.

Her other works include *Hons and Rebels* (1960), which is her autobiography and the story of the unconventional Mitford childhood, and *The Making of a Muckraker* (1979).

Mitford, Mary Russell

Born 1787 Died 1855
English playwright and poet who is best known for her sketches of village life in England

Mary Mitford was born in Alresford, Hampshire, the daughter of George Midford (as he spelled the name), a doctor who gambled compulsively, bringing the family into considerable hardship. She was given a lottery ticket for her tenth birthday and won £20,000, with which she attended Mrs St Quintin's School in Hans Place, London, and had a family house built in Reading. In an attempt to offset her father's continuing profligacy and maintain the family on an even financial keel, Mitford began to write poetry and sketches. However in 1820, in virtual poverty, the family was forced to move from Reading to a small, damp cottage in the nearby village of Three Mile Cross, in Berkshire.

Mitford's first play, *Julian*, a tragedy, was produced at Covent Garden in 1823, with the bombastic actor William Charles Macready in the title role. It was followed by *Foscari* (1826) and *Rienzi*, produced in 1828 at Drury Lane. Mitford's other two tragedies, *Mary, Queen of Scots* (1831) and *Charles I* (1834), were staged at the Victoria Theatre. She also wrote the libretto for *Salak and Kalasrade, or The Waters of Oblivion* (1835), an opera composed by Charles Packer (1810–83).

She remains best known for her amiable sketches of rural characters and manners, based on events in Three Mile Cross, and which appeared in several magazines before being collected in *Our Village* (5 vols, 1824–32). Similar works followed, including *Country Stories* (1837). She was awarded a civil list pension in 1837, which was increased on her father's death in 1842 from subscriptions raised to pay his funeral expenses. In 1852 she published *Recollections of a Literary Life*. Her plays were published in two volumes, with an autobiographical introduction, in 1854.

Mitford, Nancy Freeman

Born 1904 Died 1973
English novelist, biographer and journalist responsible for classifying 'non-U' behaviour

Nancy Mitford, 1931

Nancy Mitford was one of the six daughters of the 2nd Baron Redesdale and sister of **Jessica Mitford**. She established a reputation with her witty novels such as *Pursuit of Love* (1945) and *Love in a Cold Climate* (1949), followed by *The Blessing* (1951) and *Don't Tell Alfred* (1960).

After World War II she settled in France and wrote her major biographies *Madame de Pompadour* (1953), *Voltaire in Love* (1957), *The Sun King* (1966) and *Frederick the Great* (1970). As one of the essayists in *Noblesse Oblige*, edited by herself (1956), she seemed to enjoy the comedy of upper-class manners and helped to originate the famous 'U', or upper-class, and 'non-U' classification of linguistic usage and behaviour.

Mnouchkine, Ariane

Born 1938
French stage director and dramatist who founded the Théâtre du Soleil

Ariane Mnouchkine was born in Boulogne-sur-Seine. In 1959 she founded the Association Théâtrale des Étudiants de Paris with fellow students of the Sorbonne, putting on plays and organizing workshops and lectures. In 1962 she travelled to Cambodia and Japan and on her return in 1963 founded the Théâtre du Soleil as a theatre co-operative.

The early productions were influenced by the teachings of Stanislavsky, and their first major success came with a production of Arnold Wesker's *The Kitchen* in 1967. After the student uprising of May 1968, the company performed a series of collective improvizations based on techniques of collage, circus, and continuous and discontinuous narrative.

One of the company's best-known works is *1789*, first produced in 1970.

Model, Lisette, *née* Elise Amelie Felicie Stern

Born 1901 Died 1983
Austrian-born American photographer, best known for perceptive photographs of people

Lisette Stern was born in Vienna to an Austrian-Italian physician and musician father and a French mother, who changed their surname to Seybert in 1903. She studied music with composer Arnold Schoenberg in 1918–20 and in Paris in 1922.

She began to paint in 1932 and to photograph in 1937, both for her own pleasure and hoping for employment as a darkroom technician. In 1936 she married the Russian painter Evsa Model, with whom she moved

to New York in 1938 because of the political situation in Europe. In New York she worked as a freelance photographer, for *Harper's Bazaar* and other publications (1941–57). She also taught photography at the New School for Social Research, New York (1951–82), where **Diane Arbus** was among her students.

Her work was first exhibited in 1940 in the exhibition 'Sixty Photographs: A Survey of Camera Esthetics' at the Museum of Modern Art, New York. Retrospectives were held at the New Orleans Museum of Art, 1981 and the National Gallery of Canada, Ottawa, 1990. She continued to photograph and lecture until almost the end of her life. Her street photographs, some of them of 'deviant' people, are characterized by the way that their human subjects often almost fill the frame, and her fashion images are made in small- and medium-format black-and-white.

Modersohn-Becker, Paula, *née* Becker

Born 1876 Died 1907
German painter at the beginning of the German Expressionist movement

Paula Becker was born in Dresden. After art school in London and academic training in Berlin (1896–8), she joined an artists' colony at the village of Worpswede, and married a fellow-artist, Otto Modersohn.

She made several trips to Paris between 1900 and 1906 where she came under the influence of *avant-garde* painters such as Paul Gauguin and Paul Cézanne. Her subsequent paintings, in which personal response in the form of simple forms and strong colour takes precedence over realistic portrayal, place her at the beginning of the German Expressionist movement.

Modjeska, Helena, *née* Opid

Born 1844 Died 1909
Polish-born American actress

Helena Opid was born in Cracow. She began to act in 1861, and made a great name in Cracow in 1865. She married first an actor, Gustav Modrzejewsji (also spelt Modjeska), and second a politician, Count Bozenta Chalpowski, and from 1868 to 1876 she was the first actress of Warsaw.

After learning English she achieved her greatest triumphs in the USA and in the UK, in such roles as Juliet, Rosalind, and Beatrice, and in *La Dame aux camélias*. Her repertory totalled 260 roles, some of which she could perform in Polish and in English. She wrote *Memories and Impressions* (1910).

Modotti Mondini, Tina (Assunta Adelaide Luigia)

Born 1896 Died 1942
Italian-born Mexican photographer, model and revolutionary

Tina Modotti (sometimes referred to as Tina Modotti Mondini, using her mother's name too) was born in Udine, Italy. After working in a textile factory in Udine, she emigrated in 1913 to San Francisco, USA, to join her machinist father Giuseppe Modotti, who had gone there in 1906. She worked as a seamstress and dressmaker until 1917, when she married the American poet and painter Roubaix de l'Abrie Richey ('Robo') and began working as an actress, entering Hollywood in 1918. She met photographer Edward Weston (1886–1958) around 1920. After the death of her husband, she lived with Weston in Mexico (1923–6), where she modelled for him and also for muralists Diego Rivera and José Orozco.

She learned photography there and became a partner with Weston in a photographic studio, working on illustrations for books, newspapers and magazines. After joining the Communist Party in Mexico in 1927 she became increasingly involved with revolutionary politics, giving up photography c.1931 and forming liaisons with the Cuban revolutionary Julio Antonio Mella in 1928 and then with the communist Vittorio Vidali from about 1933 until her death. She was deported from Mexico in 1929 and lived briefly in Berlin before moving to Moscow (1931–4) and Spain (1935–8), where she worked for the relief organization Red Aid. She returned with Vidali to Mexico in 1939, where she died.

She is best known in photography for strong portraits, mainly of artist friends and Mexican peasants, formalist still lifes and plant studies, and documentary work. She is also celebrated for her courage and dedication to her revolutionary political ideals.

Moiseiwitsch, Tanya

Born 1914
English stage designer whose sets are notable for their simplicity

Tanya Moiseiwitsch was born in London. Her father was the pianist Benno Moiseiwitsch, and her mother the violinist Daisy Kennedy, but she turned to theatre rather than music. Her career as a designer was launched at the Abbey Theatre in Dublin (1935–9), and carried on in Oxford (1941), the Old Vic (1944), and Stratford-upon-Avon (1949), where she began with a celebrated set for *Henry VIII*.

Her most permanent achievements are the theatre auditoriums she designed for the Stratford (Ontario) Festival in 1957, and the Guthrie Theatre in Minneapolis in 1963. Her sets have made a virtue of simplicity, directness and a strong sense of visual aptness to the production.

Molesworth, Mary Louisa, *née* Stewart

Born 1839 Died 1921
Scottish novelist and writer of children's stories featuring strong female characters

Mary Stewart was born in Rotterdam. She spent her childhood in Manchester, Scotland and Switzerland, and married Major Richard Molesworth in 1861, but separated in 1878.

She began writing as a novelist under the pseudonym 'Ennis Graham', her main theme being the problems women encounter in marriage, but she is best known as a writer of stories for children blending magic and realism, such as *Carrots: Just a Little Boy* (1876), *The Cuckoo Clock* (1877), *The Tapestry Room* (1879), and the more realistic *Two Little Waifs* (1883).

Molony, Helena

Born 1884 Died 1967
Irish trade unionist and actress who took up the gun in her support of her nation's freedom

Helen Molony became an Irish nationalist during her teens, and not only agitated for Irish freedom by editing a monthly political magazine and founding the Irish Women Workers Union, but also took up arms. Her active participation in the attack on Dublin Castle in 1916 earned a period of imprisonment in Aylesbury gaol.

Molony had also found time to be a member of the famous Abbey Theatre Company in Dublin over an 11-year period from 1909. Returning to trade union activity in later life, she was honoured with the presidency of the Irish Trades Union Congress before ill-health forced her to retire prematurely in 1945.

Monica, St, *also spelt* Monnica

Born AD322 Died AD387
Devout Christian whose son, Augustine of Hippo, was a great Latin Church father

Monica was born in Thagaste, Numidia (now Souk-Ahras, Algeria). She was a Christian woman married to the dissolute and violent pagan Patricius, whom she brought to faith in 370, shortly before his death.

Widowed at the age of 50, she worked and prayed for Augustine's conversion (386), and followed him to Carthage, Rome, and Milan, as related in his *Confessions*. His brother Navigius was also converted, and one of his sisters became head of a convent in Hippo.

Monica died at Ostia after a brief illness just before a return journey to Africa. Some of her relics were moved to to Arras, France, in 1162; others to Rome in 1430. Her feast day is 4 May.

Monk, Maria

Born 1816 Died 1849
Canadian impostor and author who made her
fortune from fabricated stories of a nunnery

Maria Monk was born in Saint-Jean-sur-Richelieu, Quebec. Slightly brain-damaged from childhood from having stuck a slate pencil in her ear, she was a difficult girl and turned to prostitution at an early age. She was institutionalized in 1834, but escaped to New York the following year and pretended to have witnessed various horrific activities in the Hôtel Dieu nunnery in Montreal, including the murder of a nun who had refused to satisfy the monks' lascivious desires. She also claimed to have become pregnant by one of the monks and, knowing the fate of babies in that place to be strangulation, she ran away.

Her first set of fabrications, *Awful Disclosures by Maria Monk* (1836), fuelled anti-Catholic prejudice and led to various inquiries. A journalist inspected the Hôtel Dieu and declared her story false, but apparently not before she had reaped the benefit of her bestselling *Further Disclosures*. Though she married in 1838 her husband soon tired of her debauchery and deserted her. She was finally arrested in a brothel, accused of stealing from a client.

Monk, Meredith

Born 1942
American dancer, choreographer, and musician
who formed her own company

Meredith Monk was born in Lima, Peru, the daughter of a professional singer. She took dance classes as a child and began composing music as a teenager. She was briefly associated with the experimental Judson Dance Theatre in the mid-1960s, but broke away to develop multimedia music/theatre/dance events of her own. These are either solos or inventive group performances featuring her own company, The House (formed in 1968). They frequently occur in unconventional venues (churches, museums, car parks) and utilize film, props, sound, gestures and other movement, public history, and personal myth.

Monnot, Marguerite

Born 1903 Died 1961
French songwriter who wrote Irma la douce *and songs for* **Edith Piaf**

Marguerite Monnot was born in Decize, Nièvre département, the daughter of the composer Marius Monnot, under whom she studied. As well as being a brilliant pianist, she began writing early, scoring a hit with 'L'étranger' for Annete Lajon. She is really best known for her songs for Yves Montand and (especially) Edith Piaf, for whom she wrote 'Milord', 'Hymne à l'amour' and 'Un coin tout bleu'. Her most substantial success was the musical *Irma la douce* (1956), which became an international success rivalling British and American productions.

Monroe, Harriet

Born 1860 Died 1936
American poet and critic who strengthened the early career of some famous poets

Harriet Monroe was born in Chicago. In 1912 she founded the magazine *Poetry*, which was influential in publicizing the work of Vachel Lindsay, T S Eliot, Ezra Pound and Robert Frost, among others.

She wrote the 'Columbian Ode' for the Chicago World's Columbian Exposition in 1892, celebrating the 400th anniversary of the West's 'discovery' of America.

In 1917 she edited the influential free verse anthology, *The New Poetry*. Her own work was collected in *Chosen Poems* (1935).

Monroe, Marilyn, *originally* Norma Jean Mortenson, *later* Baker

Born 1926 Died 1962
American film star, symbol of Hollywood's ruthless exploitation of beauty and youth

Marilyn Monroe was born in Los Angeles. After a disturbed childhood spent largely in foster homes because of her mother's mental illness, she became a photographer's model in 1946. Following several small film parts and a high-powered studio publicity campaign, she became the star of many successful films as a beautiful, sexy 'dumb blonde' in, for instance, *How to Marry a Millionaire* and *Gentlemen Prefer Blondes* (both 1953).

She developed her flair for light comedy in *The Seven Year Itch* (1955) and *Some Like It Hot* (1959). Wanting more serious roles (she had studied at Lee Strasberg's Actors' Studio), she went on to win acclaim in *Bus Stop* (1956) and *The Misfits* (1961), written for her by her third husband, Arthur Miller. She came to London to make *The Prince and the Showgirl* (1957) with Sir Laurence Olivier, returning after two years to Hollywood.

She and Arthur Miller divorced in 1961, and she died the following year of an overdose of sleeping pills. She is described by **Gloria Steinem** as an 'icon of enduring power'.

Montagu, Elizabeth, *née* Robinson

Born 1720 Died 1800
English writer and society leader around whom grew the famous 'bluestocking' circle

Elizabeth Robinson was born in York, the sister of **Sarah Scott**. In 1742 she married Edward Montagu, grandson of the 1st Earl of Sandwich and cousin of Edward Wortley Montagu (husband of Lady **Mary Wortley Montagu**). Known as the 'Queen of the Blues', she had £10,000 a year and was one of the first 'bluestockings'.

She established a salon in Mayfair which became the heart of London's social and literary life and welcomed people like George Lyttelton (to whose *Dialogues of the Dead* she contributed in 1760), David Garrick, Joshua Reynolds (who painted her portrait) and Samuel Johnson. Her coterie also included **Elizabeth Carter**, **Hannah More**, **Mary Delany** and **Fanny Burney**. Among her writings was an essay on Shakespeare (1768).

She received a fortune on the death of her husband, and with it extended his Priory at

Elizabeth Montagu

Sandleford and built Montagu House (1781, now 22 Portman Square), London.

Montagu, Lady Mary Wortley, *née* Pierrepont

Born 1689 Died 1762
English writer, traveller and society hostess who introduced vaccination against smallpox into Britain

Mary Pierrepont was born in London, the daughter of the Earl (later Duke) of Kingston. Mostly self-educated, she taught herself Latin and wrote poetry from childhood. In 1712 she eloped with Edward Wortley Montagu and lived in London, where she gained a reputation for wit and was on close terms with Joesph Addison, Alexander Pope and others. From 1716 to 1718 she lived in Constantinople while her husband was on embassy; the sparkling letters she wrote from Turkey were published posthumously (1763).

On her return she was prominent in intellectual and court circles for 20 years, became a friend of the feminist **Mary Astell**, was involved in a bitter literary feud with Pope, wrote satirical verse, published political essays (1737–8) in support of Sir Robert Walpole, and campaigned successfully for the introduction into Britain of the smallpox inoculation. In 1739 she travelled to Italy in vain pursuit of a young writer Francesco Algarotti with whom she had fallen in love, then stayed on the Continent until shortly before her death.

As a poet and essayist she was versatile, witty and accomplished, but her letters, whether written for publication or as personal correspondence, are in a class apart for candour, intelligence, keen observation and vivid expression.

Montansier, Mademoiselle, *stage name of* Marguerite Brunet

Born 1730 Died 1820
French actress, theatre manager and salon hostess, a prominent figure during the ancien régime *and at the start of the Revolution*

Marguerite Brunet was born in Bayonne. She fell in love with an actor, Honoré Bourdon de Neuville (1736–1812) and followed him onto the stage but, perhaps due to her accent, did not have great success as an actress. She and Neuville then entered a successful career in theatre management.

Under the patronage of **Marie Antoinette**, she became manager of the theatre at Versailles in 1768, was invited to present productions at court, and in 1777 built a new theatre at Versailles bearing her name. She opened a number of provincial theatres and by 1778 had the monopoly on all theatrical productions in the northern half of France, which she could subcontract as she wished.

On the outbreak of the Revolution she went to Paris and presided over a salon situated in the foyer of her theatre in the Palais-Royal; this was visited by Napoleon, among other prominent figures. Montansier also built the large Théâtre National. She was accused of being a Royalist in 1793 but was saved from the guillotine during the Thermidor coup, married Neuville and returned to managing the Palais-Royal theatre until 1806.

Montesi, Wilma

Born 1932 Died 1953
Italian model whose mysterious death prompted a close scrutiny of corrupt governmental practices

Wilma Montesi was born in Rome, the daughter of a middle-class carpenter. The finding of her body on the beach near Ostia in April 1953 led to prolonged investigations involving sensational allegations of drug and sex orgies in Roman society.

After four years of debate, scandal, arrests, re-arrests and libel suits, the son of a former Italian foreign minister, a self-styled marquis and a former Rome police chief, were tried in Venice for complicity in her death, but there were many conflicts of evidence and the trial ended in their acquittal.

The trial left the mystery unsolved, but exposed corruption in high public places and helped to bring about the downfall of the Scelba government in 1955.

Montespan, Françoise Athénais de Rochechouart, Marquise de

Born 1641 Died 1707
French courtier who was the mistress of Louis XIV for over 13 years

Françoise Athénais de Rochechoart was the daughter of the Duc de Mortemart. In 1663 she married the Marquis de Montespan, and became attached to the household of Queen Maria Theresa. Her beauty and wit captivated Louis XIV, and about 1668 she became his mistress.

The marquis was flung into the Bastille, and in 1676 his marriage was annulled. The Marquise de Montespan reigned supreme till 1682, and bore the king seven children, who were legitimized. She lasted through the Affair of the Poisons (1679) when she was alleged to have bought poison from the witch **La Voisin**.

She was supplanted by Madame de **Maintenon**, the governess of her children. In 1691 she left the court, and retired to a convent.

Montessori, Maria

Born 1870 Died 1952
Italian physician and educationalist who founded the Montessori system of education

Maria Montessori was born in Rome and was the first woman in Italy to receive a medical degree (1894). She became interested in the education of children with learning disabilites and was director of a school for them (1899–1901), where her innovative methods proved successful. Her philosophy focused on a child's potential for self-education and creativity when given suitable materials and non-intrusive supervision, and highlighted the unsuitablility of classrooms. The children were provided with such objects such as wooden cylinders for small-muscle development, beads arranged in special ways to encourage counting, and small blocks constructed to make the eye follow left-to-right reading movements.

Gradually she developed a system of education for normal children of three to six, based on spontaneity of expression and freedom from restraint. She opened the first Montessori school for children in the slums of Rome in 1907 and then travelled to many countries, establishing teacher-training programmes, lecturing, and writing. The system was later worked out for older children, and applied in Montessori schools throughout the world.

After leaving Italy in 1934 she eventually retired to The Netherlands. Her works range from *Il metodo della pedagogia scientifica* (1909, Eng trans *The Montessori Method*, 1912) to *La mente assorbente* (1949, Eng trans *The Absorbent Mind*, 1949).

Montez, Lola, *originally* Maria Délores Eliza Rosanna Gilbert

Born 1818 Died 1861
Irish-born American dancer who took advantage of the King of Bavaria's infatuation with her

Maria Gilbert was born in Limerick. After an unsuccessful marriage she turned dancer at Her Majesty's Theatre in London (1843), and while touring Europe, went to Munich (1846), where she soon won over the eccentric artist-king, Ludwig I of Bavaria.

She had a scandalous affair with him (1847–8), which gave a great boost to her career as a dancer. She was created Countess of Landsfeld and used her not insubstantial influence to persuade him to oppose the Jesuits and make liberal policies. However her control aroused much hostility; not only was she forced to flee, but Ludwig had to abdicate (1848).

Following dancing tours of the USA and Australia, she decided to turn to lecturing on fashion and beauty and settled in California.

Montgomery, L(ucy) M(aud)

Born 1874 Died 1942
Canadian novelist who wrote Anne of Green Gables

Lucy Maud Montgomery was born in Clifton, Prince Edward Island. She qualified as a schoolteacher from Prince of Wales College, Charlottetown, and after studying at Dalhousie College, Halifax, Nova Scotia, she returned to Cavendish to care for her grandmother for 13 years.

She published as her first book the phenomenally successful *Anne of Green Gables* (1908), the story of an orphan girl adopted in error for a boy by an elderly brother and sister. She followed it with several sequels, of which *Rilla of Ingleside* (1921) is an invaluable description of the impact of World War I on the island community.

She married Ewan MacDonald, a Presbyterian minister, in 1911, and moved to his manse at Leaskdale, Ontario. Her works are sometimes highly satirical; at her best she captures memorably the mysteries and terrors of early childhood, as in *Magic for Marigold* (1929), while her later works show qualities which recall the French novelist Guy de Maupassant (1850–93).

Montpensier, Anne Marie Louise d'Orléans, Duchesse de

Born 1627 Died 1693
French noblewoman prominent in the French court during the minority (1643–51) of Louis XIV

Anne d'Orléans was the daughter of Gaston de France, Duc d'Orléans. She became known as 'La Grande Mademoiselle' because he was called 'Monsieur', and as a niece of Louis XIII, she held high aspirations for her marriage. However she was prevented by the government from marrying the future Louis XIV and, for lack of a peace agreement with the Habsburgs, she could not marry the future Holy Roman Emperor Ferdinand III either.

She was an enemy of Cardinal Mazarin, who was effectively running the country with **Anne of Austria**, and supported her father and the Prince de Condé (having persuaded them to collaborate) in the revolt of the Fronde (1651–2), where she commanded an army that occupied Orléans and later the Bastille, saving Condé's army from total destruction by the royal army.

After a couple of periods in disgrace she returned to the court and wished to marry the Comte de Lauzun, but the King, probably due to the lovers' difference in rank, refused his consent for many years. When at last he did agree in 1670 his advisers were so horrified that Lauzun was imprisoned until Montpensier managed to have him freed, 10 years later. Her marriage in the end was not successful and her last years were spent in religious duties. She wrote her *Mémoires* about her life up to 1688.

Moodie, Susanna, *née* Strickland

Born 1803 Died 1885
English-born Canadian writer whose best works evoke her harsh life in the wilderness of Ontario

Susanna Strickland was born in Bungay, Suffolk, and emigrated to Canada in the early 1830s, shortly after her marriage to Dunbar Moodie in 1831. She began contributing her stories to annuals and in 1830 published a volume of poetry, *Patriotic Songs*, with her sister Agnes. Her own *Enthusiasms; and Other Poems* followed in 1831. In Canada her husband took up farming, and she continued writing to supplement their income.

Considered more romantic and sentimental than those of her sister, **Catherine Parr Traill**, her works for children and her poetry show a strong interest in religion, particularly the Quaker faith. Her *Roughing It In The Bush; or, Life in Canada* (1852) and *Life in the Clearings versus the Bush* (1853) have many fictional elements but reflect her life as a frontier woman and a diversity of interests.

In 1972, **Margaret Atwood**'s book of poems, *The Journals of Susanna Moodie* brought Moodie increased literary prominence.

Moody, Helen Wills *see* Wills, Helen

Moon, Lorna, *pseud of* (Helen) Nora Wilson Low

Born 1886 Died 1930
Scottish writer who became a success in America with tales based on her Scottish upbringing

Lorna Moon was born in Strichen, Aberdeenshire, the daughter of a plasterer who worked mostly abroad. After an itinerant life he acquired the Temperance Hotel in Strichen, a haunt of commercial travellers. One, an American called Hebditch, who dealt in jewellery, married Lorna, and they left for America, where they had one child. Eventually she reached Hollywood, where she wrote scripts for MGM, who employed her on the screenplay for *Mr Wu*, starring Lon Chaney, which was a huge success.

She became a friend of **Frances Marion** and **Anita Loos**, and wrote for magazines in her spare time, contributing stories about Strichen, barely disguised as 'Pitouie'. Her first book, *Doorways in Drumorty* (1926), was a collection of stories; when it was published in Britain it was banned from the local library in Strichen, as was her novel *Dark Star* (1929). Wickedly and deftly puncturing her parents' social pretensions and the foibles of village life, she combined Gothic tragedy with black humour, sharpened no doubt by distance from her targets.

Mooney, Ria

Born 1903   Died 1973
Irish actress and teacher who became the Abbey Theatre's first woman director

Ria Mooney was born in Dublin. She began acting at the age of six, and first appeared at the Abbey Theatre in Dublin in 1924. She attracted significant attention in Sean O'Casey's *The Plough and The Stars* (1926), and made her American début in 1927.

After a short spell at the Gate Theatre in Dublin, she returned to the Abbey in 1935, and was placed in charge of their experimental Peacock Theatre in 1937, where she directed her first play.

In 1948 she became the first woman director of the Abbey Theatre, and served with distinction until her retirement in 1963.

Moore Sitterly, Charlotte

Born 1898 Died 1990
American astronomer and spectroscopist who documented thousands of wavelengths

Charlotte Moore Sitterly was born in Enciltoun, Pennsylvania, and educated at Swarthmore College. She was an assistant to the astronomer Henry Russell (1877–1957) at Princeton from 1920 to 1925 before moving to Mount Wilson Observatory to work on the revision and extension of the table of wavelengths in the solar spectrum, originally the work of Henry Rowland (1848–1901) from 1895 to 1897.

In the revised table, which she published jointly with Charles Edward St John and others (1928), over 58,000 wavelengths were tabulated in which 57 chemical elements were reported as present in the Sun. A second revision, with 10,000 more lines (1966) was later produced under her direction. She returned to Princeton (1931–45) where she produced her famous *Multiplet Tables of Astrophysical Interest* (1945), and in 1945 joined the Bureau of Standards, Washington (1945–68), where she published *Ultraviolet Multiplet Tables* (1946) and *Atomic Energy Levels* (1949–58).

After her formal retirement, she was attached to the Naval Research Laboratory, Washington, and remained active in spectroscopy until past her ninetieth birthday.

Moore, C(atherine) L

Born 1911
American science-fiction writer who created Northwest Smith and Jirel of Jory

C L Moore was born in Indianapolis, Indiana. She began writing in the 'golden age' of science fiction in the 1930s and 1940s, when her short stories appeared in periodicals such as *Amazing Stories* and *Weird Tales*.

She became known for the two characters Northwest Smith and Jirel of Jory. The latter was a 15th-century warrior queen who had heroic adventures, one of the first female characters in science fiction to move beyond the victim stereotype. Moore's main themes include the pursuit of otherness and an understanding of female psyche.

Her works include *Northwest of Earth* (1954), *Doomsday Morning* (1960) and *Earth's Last Citadel* (1964, with Henry Kuttner).

Moore, Marianne Craig

Born 1887 Died 1972
American poet acclaimed as America's most popular 20th-century female poet

Marianne Moore was born in Kirkwood, Missouri, and educated at Bryn Mawr College. She taught commercial studies at Carlisle Commercial College, tutored privately, and was a branch librarian in New York (1921–5).

She contributed to the Imagist magazine, *The Egoist*, from 1915, and edited *The Dial* from 1926 until its demise in 1929. Though she was acquainted with seminal modernists like Ezra Pound and T S Eliot, New York was her milieu, not Paris, and she associated with the Greenwich Village group that included William Carlos Williams and Wallace Stevens. She was much liked and admired by contemporaries, even those — like Eliot — who were at odds with her artistic beliefs.

Idiosyncratic, a consummate stylist and unmistakably modern, she has supplied a much-quoted definition of the creative ideal as 'imaginary gardens with real toads in them'. Her first publication was *Poems* (1921); among her later titles are *Selected Poems* (1935), *The Collected Poems* (1951), which won a Pulitzer Prize in 1952, and *The Complete Poems* (1968), which brought her the National Medal for Literature. She published *Predilections*, a collection of essays, in 1955.

Moore, Mary Tyler

Born 1936
American actress who has become immensely popular in television comedy

Mary Tyler Moore was born in Brooklyn, New York. She trained as a dancer, and her first professional job was as the Happy Hotpoint Pixie in a series of television commercials in 1955. Small acting roles followed and she was seen in the series *Richard Diamond, Private Eye* (1957–9) and made her film début in *X-15* (1961).

The series *The Dick Van Dyke Show* (1961–6) highlighted her talent for domestic comedy and won her Emmys in 1964 and 1965. Her small-screen popularity was used to launch a multi-media career on Broadway with *Breakfast at Tiffanys* (1966) and in the cinema, but she returned to television with *The Mary Tyler Moore Show* (1970–7) where her charm and self-reliance were seen to embody the average single working girl. Among numerous awards, the series won her Emmys in 1973, 1974 and 1976. She subsequently won an Emmy for *First, You Cry* (1978), a Tony for *Whose Life Is It Anyway?* (1980), and an Oscar nomination for *Ordinary People* (1980).

Unable to repeat the success of earlier series she has appeared in television films like *Finnegan, Begin Again* (1984), *Heartsounds* (1984), *Lincoln* (1988) and *The Last Best Year* (1990). MTM Enterprises, formed with her second husband Grant Tinker in 1970, has been responsible for such television series as *Lou Grant* and *Hill Street Blues*.

Moorehead, Agnes Robertson

Born 1906   Died 1974
American character actress of stage, film and television

Agnes Moorehead was born in Clinton, Massachusetts, the daughter of a Presbyterian minister. She made her first appearance on stage at the age of three and her professional début aged 11 with the St Louis Municipal Opera Company. A graduate of the University of Wisconsin, she taught English before committing herself to an acting career and studying at the American Academy of Dramatic Arts. Her early stage appearances include *Marco's Millions* (1928) and *Scarlett Pages* (1929). She was a noted radio actress in the 1930s, but joined Orson Welles's Mercury Theater Group in 1940 and followed him to Hollywood to make her film début in *Citizen Kane* (1941).

Her richly textured perfomance as the lonely spinster aunt in *The Magnificent Ambersons* (1942) earned her the New York Critics Best Actress Award and sealed her career in film. Her most vivid characterizations include a chic Frenchwoman in *Mrs Parkington* (1944), a sympathetic prison warden in *Caged* (1950) and a slatternly maid in *Hush...Hush, Sweet Charlotte* (1964).

Later stage work includes tours of *Don Juan In Hell* (1950–4), her one-woman show *The Fabulous Redhead* (1954) and the Broadway musical *Gigi* (1973). On television, she appeared as the witch Endora in the long-running comedy series *Bewitched* (1964–71).

Mary Tyler Moore, 1969

Morante, Elsa

Born 1912   Died 1985
Italian novelist, poet and short-story writer, one of Italy's most prominent 20th-century writers

Elsa Morante was born and educated in Rome. Her first publication, a collection of short stories called *Il gioco segreto* (1941, 'Secret Jest'), coincided with her marriage to the writer Alberto Moravia (1907–90), but the marriage did not last. In her writing she depicts a partly mythical or imaginary world evoking through it the difficulties of coming to terms with reality. Her second book, *Menzogna e sortilegio* (1948, 'Lies and Riddles'), won the Viareggio Prize and was later published in the USA as *House of Liars* (1951). Its successor, *L'isola di Arturo* (1957, Eng trans *Arturo's Island*, 1959), was a lyrical-elegiac account of childhood and the violation of innocence. It won Morante the prestigious Strega Prize.

Morante's greatest single achievement, however, was *La storia* (1974, Eng trans *History*, 1977), a large-scale, almost Faulknerian narrative about the degeneracy of the Italian family under fascism. Though politically engaged and consistently espousing Morante's Christian-Marxist principles, the novel never deteriorates into a tract.

Her verse includes *Il mondo salvato dai ragazzini e altri poemi* (1968), and she also translated **Katherine Mansfield** into Italian.

Morata, Olympia Fulvia

Born 1526 Died 1555
Italian humanist scholar and poet whose genius remained largely unfulfilled

Olympia Morata was born in Ferrara, the daughter of the poet and scholar Pellegrino Morato who was tutor to the young sons of Alphonsus I. Her father recognized her genius and she entered court life to study with the princess of Ferrara. Her swift mastery of Latin and Greek and her ability to give public lectures at the age of 15 astonished everyone, but when her father died her mother fell ill and she was obliged to return to household affairs.

Having in 1548 married the German physician Andreas Grundler, she became a Protestant and followed him to Schweinfurt in Franconia. She narrowly escaped the siege of that city but died penniless, leaving numerous Latin and Greek poems, a treatise on the Roman statesman Cicero, dialogues and letters.

More, Hannah

Born 1745 Died 1833
English playwright and religious writer who was a member of the 'bluestocking' circle

Hannah More was born in either Stapleton or Fishponds, near Bristol, the daughter of a schoolteacher who taught her Latin while she was educated and learnt French, Italian and Spanish at the nearby boarding school run by her elder sisters, where she wrote verses at an early age. She was engaged in 1767 to a Mr Turner, who failed to marry her for six years and eventually settled £200 a year on her and left her. In 1773 she published *The Search after Happiness*, a morally improving pastoral drama for young ladies, and then went to London in 1774, where she joined the 'bluestocking' coterie of **Elizabeth Montagu** and her friends.

Her plays included a very successful tragedy, *Percy* (1777), which was produced by her friend, the actor and theatre manager David Garrick; it was followed by *The Fatal Falsehood* (1779). Led by her religious views to withdraw from society, she retired to Cowslip Green near Bristol, where she did much to improve the condition of the poor. She published *Sacred Dramas* (1782), a collection of religious poems in *Bas Bleu* (1786), and an essay *Estimate on the Religion of the Fashionable World* (1790). Her moral tracts for the poor, *Village Politics by Will Chip* (1793) and *Cheap Repository Tracts* (1795–8), which took only four years to sell two million copies, led to the founding of the Religious Tracts Society. She also wrote on female education in *Strictures on the Modern Systen of Female Education* (1799) and a didactic novel, *Coelebs in Search of a Wife* (1809).

Although well-meaning, she was proprietorial; **Ann Yearsley**, whose poetry she promoted assiduously, interpreted More's management of her affairs as intrusive and meddling.

Moreau, Jeanne

Born 1928
French actress and director who rose to fame with the Nouvelle Vague

Jeanne Moreau was born in Paris. She trained at the Conservatoire National D'Art Dramatique, made her stage début with the Comédie Française in *A Month in the Country* (1948) and her film début in *Dernier Amour* (1948). An association with the directors of the French *Nouvelle Vague*, or New Wave, brought her recognition as an intense, hypnotic film actress, capable of immersing her own personality in a succession of generally worldweary, sensual characterizations.

Her most famous films include *Les Amants* (1958), *La Notte* (1961), *Jules et Jim* (1961), *Diary of a Chambermaid* (1964) and *Viva Maria* (1965). Occasional English-language ventures met with little acclaim but she proved herself a formidable director with *La Lumière* (1976) and *L'Adolescente* (1978), and later appeared on television in *Clothes in the Wardrobe* (1992) and *A Foreign Field* (1993).

Morgan, Agnes, *née* Fay

Born 1884 Died 1968
American biochemist and nutritionist who researched the dietary role of vitamins

Agnes Fay was born in Peoria, Illinois. She graduated in chemistry from the University of Chicago in 1905 and taught chemistry in various colleges, until her husband Arthur Morgan, whom she married in 1908, encouraged her to return to Chicago to obtain her PhD, which she received in 1914.

She spent most of her subsequent career in the College of Agriculture at Berkeley. She particularly addressed issues associated with food chemistry and nutrition, and organized national and international meetings on nutritional standards and healthy eating. She acted as a governmental adviser on nutritional matters at both state and national level, and was awarded several academic honours.

Morgan, Ann Haven

Born 1882 Died 1966
American zoologist and ecologist active in research, education and conservation

Ann Haven Morgan was born in Waterford, Connecticut. She graduated in biology from Cornell University in 1906 and received her PhD in 1912 for a dissertation on mayflies. She moved to Mount Holyoke College as an instructor in zoology (1912), becoming associate professor in 1914 and full professor in 1918 (until 1947).

Her research covered many biological problems, including the zoology of aquatic insects, the comparative physiology of hibernation, conservation and ecology.

She was keen to communicate her subject, and her *Field Book of Ponds and Streams* (1930) encouraged many amateur naturalists.

Morgan, Barbara Brooks, *née* Johnson

Born 1900 Died 1992
American photographer and writer whose best-known work includes portraits and montages

Barbara Johnson was born in Buffalo, Kansas. She grew up in southern California and studied art at the University of California, Los Angeles (UCLA), where she became interested in ideas concerned with rhythm and harmony derived from Eastern philosophies. She then painted and taught art in San Fernando (1923–4) and at UCLA (1925–30). In 1925 she married

photographer and writer Willard D Morgan, with whom she moved to New York City in 1930 and had two sons.

From 1935 she worked mainly in photography, setting up a studio in Scarsdale, New York, in 1941. She was co-owner of the publishing company Morgan and Morgan.

She is best known for vibrant black-and-white photographs of dancers, especially **Martha Graham** and Merce Cunningham (1935–40), for dramatic experimental photomontages and light abstractions (late 1930s), and for portraits and photographs of children. Her publications include *Summer's Children: A Photographic Cycle of Life at Camp* (1951), *Martha Graham: Sixteen Dances in Photographs* (1941) and *Barbara Morgan: Photomontage* (1980).

Morgan, Julia

Born 1872 Died 1957
American architect who in 1904 became the first female architect to register in California

Julia Morgan first trained in engineering at the University of California. There she met Bernard Maybeck, who encouraged her to go to the École des Beaux-Arts in Paris. She tussled with the French government for two years to get a place on the course, but succeeded and at the age of 30 became the first woman to graduate in architecture from the École.

She opened her own office in California in 1906 and was a very reclusive architect, although it is believed that in her career she completed 800 buildings.

Her most famous works include the residences at San Simeon for Mr Hearst, the movie empire magnate. A commission lasting from 1919 to 1937, it is a vast exotic complex, showing Morgan's mastery of light, space and scale. She also completed a large number of works for women's organizations, including the Berkeley Women's City Club (1930), which is still in use today.

Morgan, Robin

Born 1941
American feminist writer and editor who documents the feminist movement

Robin Morgan was born in Lake Worth, Florida. Her main work has been to chronicle the American women's liberation movement from its early history, and in 1970 she became the editor of the first published anthology to collect feminist essays, *Sisterhood is Powerful*.

Her works include poetry, reporting, and reflection on an evolving movement, such as the collection *The Anatomy of Freedom* (1982). Her second anthology, *Sisterhood is Global* (1984), collects essays from the international feminist movement.

Morgan, Sally, *née* Milroy

Born 1951
Australian writer and artist inspired by her
Aboriginal ancestry

Sally Milroy was born in Perth, Western Australia. She majored in psychology at the University of Western Australia, graduating in 1974, and also holds a post-graduate diploma in counselling psychology from the Western Australian Institute of Technology. She married Paul Morgan in 1972.

Although she is of Aboriginal ancestry, this fact was concealed from her by her mother and grandmother; her autobiographical book *My Place* (1987) is an important link between cultures. Her paintings form part of several collections and some may be seen in the Australian National Gallery.

Morgan, Lady Sydney, *née* Owenson

Born 1776   Died 1859
*Irish writer who, like **Maria Edgeworth**, was*
one of the first Irish novelists

Sydney Owenson was born either in Dublin or on board ship, the daughter of a theatrical manager and actor who got into financial difficulties. She supported the family, first as governess, next as author of sentimental poems and novels. In 1812 she married a surgeon, Thomas Charles Morgan (1783–1843), who was later knighted.

Her works — lively novels, verse and travels — include *St Clair* (1804), *The Wild Irish Girl* (1806), *O'Donnel* (1814), *The O'Briens and the O'Flahertys* (1827) and *Memoirs* (1862). In 1837 she became the first woman to be awarded a civil pension (£300) for her contribution to literature. In later life she lived in London and became a well-known society figure.

Morgner, Irmtaud

Born 1933   Born 1990
German novelist whose work broke free from the
conventions imposed by authoritarian
government

Irmtaud Morgner was born into a working-class family in Chemnitz. She began a writing career at the age of 25 after studying in Leipzig. Her early works conform to the strictures of communist realism dictated by the authoritarian government of what was then East Germany, but during the 1960s her work matured into a more daring personal style, particularly after the publication of her novel *Hochzeit in Konstantinopel* (1968).

She was fascinated by the conflict between fantasy and reality, often expressed through the gender of her characters, and for this she is regarded as a leading feminist writer of her time. Literary critics regard her work as being in the forefront of a revival in the German romantic tradition.

Morison, Harriet Russell

Born 1862   Died 1925
New Zealand feminist and labour leader who
triumphed over the tyranny of the sweatshop

Harriet Russell Morison was born in Ireland, the daughter of a tailor, and was brought to Dunedin, New Zealand, as a child. She found work in the garment business there but, incensed at the sweatshop conditions, organized the first women's union, the Tailoresses' Union, in 1889, and succeeded in improving working conditions.

A deeply religious woman who never married, she later worked with the mentally ill before being appointed as a factory inspector, and then as Head of Women's Employment Bureau in Auckland from 1908 to 1913.

Morisot, Berthe Marie Pauline

Born 1841   Died 1895
French painter who was the leading female
exponent of Impressionism

Berthe Morisot was the granddaughter of the Rococo painter Jean Honoré Fragonard. Her Impressionist paintings were often of women and children, and she exhibited regularly at the Salon and in most of the Impressionist exhibitions.

Her early work shows the influence of her friend and mentor Jean Baptiste Camille Corot, but her later style owes more to Auguste Renoir. She herself influenced Édouard Manet (whose brother Eugène she married), such as in encouraging him to practise *plein-air* painting and to use the rainbow palette.

Morpurgo, Rahel

Born 1790   Died 1871
Hebrew poet whose achievement as a modern
Hebrew poet is considered to be outstanding

Rahel Morpurgo was born in Trieste. Her work was a part of the great flowering of Jewish literature which took place in the 18th and early 19th centuries, and with her boldly magnificent ode dedicated to the revolutions of

1848, she well deserves her title of first modern Hebrew poet.

It has been said that no woman who hopes to make a mark in poetry can afford to neglect study of Morpurgo's achievement. English translations of her work can be found in *Collected Poems and Letters* (1890).

Morris, Jan, *formerly* James Morris

Born 1926
English journalist, historian, essayist and prolific travel writer

James Morris was born in Somerset of Anglo-Welsh parentage and was educated at Lancing College and Oxford University. He began his career as a young journalist on the editorial staff of *The Times* (1951–6). In 1953 he was assigned to cover the expedition to climb Mount Everest, and reported the successful ascent on the day of Queen **Elizabeth's** Coronation. He underwent a gender change in 1972 and continued to write, publishing under the name of Jan Morris from 1973.

As a freelance travel writer, Jan has visited almost every major city in the world and produced a prolific number of books, earning **Rebecca West**'s description: 'perhaps the best descriptive writer of our time'.

Among her best-known books, imbued with a political flavour and a strong sense of place, are *Venice* (1960), *The Oxford Book of Oxford* (1978), the *Pax Britannica* trilogy, and her autobiography *Conundrum*, (1974).

Morris, Margaret

Born 1891 Died 1980
English dancer, choreographer, designer, director, author and teacher

Margaret Morris was born in London. As a child she appeared in pantomime and plays and in 1907 joined the Frank Benson Shakespearian Company as principal dancer. In 1910 she designed the decor and costumes for Marie Brema's production of Gluck's *Orfeo ed Euridice* and in the same year founded the MMM School of Dancing in London, basing classes around her own dance technique, Margaret Morris Movement.

In the interwar period she founded a summer school in Devon (which was to run throughout her life), lectured to doctors on the remedial possibilities of her dance and, after 1931, opened training schools in Paris, Cannes, Edinburgh, Glasgow, Aberdeen and Manchester. In 1939 she and her husband, painter J D Fergusson (1874–1961), settled in Glasgow, where she formed the Celtic Ballet Club, touring to the USA in 1954 and to Russia,

Austria and Czechoslovakia in 1958, the same year that she founded a studio theatre in the centre of Glasgow.

The school closed in 1961, but her teaching, writing and courses continued until her death.

Morris, May (Mary)

Born 1862 Died 1938
British designer and embroiderer who designed jewellery, wallpaper and fabrics

May Morris studied with her father, the designer and writer William Morris (1834–96), and in 1885 she took over the running of the embroidery department of the firm Morris & Co. Along with many leading members of the Arts and Crafts Movement, she was very active in the Socialist League.

She also lectured on embroidery and jewellery in the USA and taught embroidery at the Central School of Arts and Crafts, London.

Morrison, Toni, *née* Chloe Anthony Wofford

Born 1931
American novelist whose powerful works portray the African-American experience

Chloe Anthony Wofford was born in Lorain, Ohio. She was educated at Howard University and Cornell University, and taught at Howard

Toni Morrison, 1993

before moving to New York in 1965. She worked in publishing as senior editor at Random House before turning to fiction, and was appointed to the chair in humanities at Princeton University in 1989.

Labelled as a black James Joyce or William Faulkner, she explores in rich vocabulary and cold-blooded detail the story of black Americans. *The Bluest Eye* (1970) focuses on the incestuous rape of an 11-year-old girl; *Sula* (1974) again confronts a generation gap, but between a grandmother and the eponymous scapegoat; *Song of Solomon* (1977) is a merciless study of genteel blacks.

Her most recent novels, *Tar Baby* (1981), *Beloved* (1987), which won a Pulitzer Prize in 1988, and *Jazz* (1992), are formidable in their mastery of technique and courageous in their subject-matter. Morrison won the Nobel Prize for Literature in 1993, the first African-American to do so.

Mortimer, Penelope Ruth, *née* Fletcher

Born 1918
Welsh novelist who examines the comedy in domestic relationships

Penelope Fletcher was born in Rhyl, Flint, and educated at a variety of schools, and at University College, London. Her first novel, *Johanna* (1947), appeared under the name of Penelope Dimont (her first husband's surname). Her other novels, many of which look at the female experience of life among the English professional classes, include *Daddy's Gone A-Hunting* (1958), *My Friend Says It's Bullet-Proof* (1967) and *The Handyman* (1983).

Her most famous novel, *The Pumpkin Eater* (1962), describes a woman who imagines that pregnancy will give a direction to her life, but who is persuaded by her husband to have an abortion. She was married from 1949 to 1972 to dramatist John Mortimer (1923–) and published her autobiography, *About Time Too*, in 1993.

Moser, Mary

Born c.1744 Died 1819
English flower painter who helped to found the Royal Academy

Mary Moser was the daughter of the Swiss goldsmith and enameller George Michael Moser. She painted in the Dutch manner, earning admiration for her work and exhibiting at the Society of Artists from 1760 to 1768.

With her father, she was one of the founder members of the Royal Academy. Also an inti-

mate friend of the royal family, she was employed for a time by Queen **Charlotte**, consort of George III.

Moser-Pröll, Annemarie, *née* Pröll

Born 1953
Austrian alpine skier whose remarkable career culminated in an Olympic gold medal

Annemarie Pröll was born at Kleinarl. She won a women's record 62 World Cup races (1970–9), and was overall champion (1979), downhill champion (1978, 1979), Olympic downhill champion (1980), world combined champion (1972, 1978) and world downhill champion (1974, 1978, 1980).

She temporarily retired in 1975–6, after her marriage, and finally retired after winning the gold medal for downhill in the 1980 Olympics.

Moses, Anna Mary, *known as* Grandma Moses, *née* Robertson

Born 1860 Died 1961
American primitive artist whose naïve depictions of rural American life became widely popular

Anna Mary Robertson was born in Washington County, New York. As a child she used to colour her drawings with natural juices, but this creativity was put to one side when she married a farmer, Thomas Moses, in 1887. They lived in Staunton, Virginia, and then in New York State, where she continued to farm for about nine years after he died in 1927.

She did a number of embroidered worsted pictures but with the onset of arthritis in her mid seventies she turned to painting, choosing as her subject mainly country scenes remembered from her childhood — 'old, timey things . . . all from memory' — such as *Catching the Turkey for Thanksgiving*.

These naïve, colourful and romantic depictions of late 19th- and early 20th-century rural life were sold at first in a drugstore, but it was not long before she was 'discovered' by a dealer and they had become popular throughout the USA, being exhibited nationwide and reproduced on Christmas cards. Grandma Moses also had 15 one-woman exhibitions in Europe.

Mosley, Lady Cynthia, *née* Curzon

Born 1899 Died 1933
English Labour politician whose loyalty to her husband superseded loyalty to her party

Cynthia Curzon was the daughter of Lord Curzon of Kedleston. She married Sir Oswald Mosely and, as the mother of two young children, developed a particular interest in education and child welfare.

Elected to parliament as MP for Stoke in the so-called Flapper Election of 1929, she resigned from the Labour Party in 1931 and joined her husband in the formation of his New Party — the forerunner of the British Union of Fascists. This was a move her friends suspected to be made out of loyalty to her husband rather than from political conviction. Shortly thereafter she died from peritonitis.

Moss, Kate

Born 1974
English model who began her career as a teenage
waif

Kate Moss was born in Croydon. In 1988, aged 14, she was 'discovered' at JFK airport in New York by the owner of Storm model agency.

She became fully established in 1992 when her controversial waif-like presence took to the fashion catwalks of top designers in Paris, Milan, New York and London, her short, skinny physique establishing her as the antithesis of 1980s style. She was the icon of the grunge and deconstructivist period of fashion, before gaining a few pounds and re-inventing herself as a supermodel of the mid-1990s.

She has advertising contracts with St Laurent for Opium perfume and with Calvin Klein (she is his muse) for his fashion collection and Obsession perfume. 'Kate', a retrospective photographic essay of her work, was published in 1995.

Moss-Carlsson, Pat (Patricia), *née* Moss

Born 1934
English rally driver, the first woman to win a
major international race

Pat Moss began a career in international showjumping but was taught to drive by her famous brother Stirling Moss and quickly followed in the family tradition of excellence. Her mother Eileen had been an expert trials driver in the 1930s and her father Alfred had raced internationally in the 1920s.

Pat Moss won countless Coupes des Dames and won the European ladies championship in 1958 with Ann Wisdom. They went on to be outright winners of the tough Liège-Rome-Liège race in 1960, and so became the first female team to win a major international race. In 1962 Moss finished third in the East African Safari. She married top rally driver Erik Carlsson in 1963.

Mosseen, Annalena

Born 1952
Swedish architect whose housing project in
Gothland was a massive success

Annalena Mosseen trained at the Royal Academy of Technology, Stockholm, where she graduated in 1976. She initially worked with Ralph Erskine but turned down a partnership with him to start her own practice with three other architects in native Gothland. Their practice, Visby Arkitektgrupp, is now the largest in Visby.

In 1982 the Gothland housing association approached Mosseen to address the problem of unpopular housing estates. In discussion with tenants at Grabo housing estate, she drew up a four-year plan for improvements, which were to provide a better social mix of housing as well as many individual physical improvements.

In a different area of work Mosseen's practice sought funding to renovate a medieval block of Visby town, known as the Triangle. Their work on this project, which reflected the need for historical accuracy and modern requirements, won the prestigious Europa Nostra award in 1990.

Mota, Rosa

Born 1958
Portuguese athlete with an unparalleled record for
the marathon

Rosa Mota was born in Foz do Douro. Her first marathon race was in Athens in 1982, when she won the European title. She went on to improve her time on the next seven occasions she competed.

Weighing in at slightly over seven stones (44kg), she possesses surprising reserves of stamina which helped her to win 10 of her first 13 marathons. She has had victories in Tokyo, Boston, Chicago, Rotterdam, London and Osaka, as well as a further two European titles, the world championship title in 1987 and the Olympic gold medal in 1988.

Her Olympic win also made her the first Portuguese woman to win an Olympic medal.

Mott, Lucretia, *née* Coffin

Born 1793 Died 1880
American feminist and reformer who pioneered
the US women's rights movement

Lucretia Coffin was born in Nantucket, Massachusetts. She married James Mott (d.1868) in 1811, and bore him six children. Beginning in 1817, she rose to prominence as a speaker at Quaker meetings and became an active cam-

Lucretia Mott

paigner for temperance, peace, women's rights and anti-slavery. She attended the Anti-Slavery Convention of 1833 and was organizer and president of the Philadelphia women's branch but was denied membership in the World Anti-Slavery Convention in London, for which the Irish political leader Daniel O'Connell savagely denounced it.

She was strongly supported by her husband in this, and under her influence he left his commission business because of its connection with slave-produced cotton, in which he had dealt throughout the 1820s. In 1841 James Mott published *Three Months in Great Britain*, describing their ill-fated mission of the previous year. Lucretia Mott and **Elizabeth Cady Stanton** organized the first Woman's Rights Convention in 1848. She remained prominent and active in the feminist movement until her death.

Mountbatten of Burma, Edwina Cynthia Annette, Countess, *née* Ashley

Born 1901 Died 1960
English leader in the St John Ambulance Brigade and the last vicereine of India

Edwina Ashley was the elder daughter of the 1st Lord Mount Temple. She married Louis, Lord Mountbatten (1900–79, later Earl Mountbatten of Burma and Admiral of the Fleet) in 1922, and together they became central figures in the fashionable young society of the time.

During the London 'blitz' (1940–2) she rendered distinguished service to the Red Cross and St John Ambulance Brigade, of which she became superintendent-in-chief in 1942. When her husband was appointed the last Viceroy of India (1947), she became Vicereine and her compassionate work in social welfare throughout the country brought her the friendship of Mahatma Gandhi and Pandit Nehru.

She died suddenly in her sleep during an official tour of Borneo for the St John Ambulance Brigade.

Mourning Dove, *also called* Hum-Ishu-Ma, *English name* Christine Quintasket

Born 1888 Died 1936
American writer and the first Native American woman to publish a novel

Mourning Dove was born in a canoe on the Kootenai River in Idaho while her parents were making a ferry crossing. She received little formal education and worked for most of her life as a migrant farm labourer, travelling always with her typewriter on which she produced the stories she heard from the Okanogans with whom she lived and worked, and which formed the basis of her published collection, *Coyote Stories* (1933).

She was a member of the Colville Confederated Tribes of Eastern Washington. Passionately concerned with recording the threatened traditions and oral literature of her people, and encouraged by her friend and literary collaborator, Lucillus McWhorter, she also travelled and lectured to audiences in the east about Okanogan traditions. Her first novel, *Cogewea, the Half-Blood* (1927), describes the trials of a young mixed-blood woman ranch-hand, combining the plot of a frontier romance with descriptions of Okanogan culture and lively colloquial dialogue.

Her autobiographical writings have been collected and published as *Mourning Dove: a Salishan Autobiography* (1990, ed Jay Miller).

Mowlam, Marjorie

Born 1949
English Labour politician, known for her strong opinions and desire to implement change

Marjorie Mowlam was educated in Coventry, and at Durham University and Iowa University, gaining a PhD from the latter. After lecturing at Florida State University (1977–8) she moved to Newcastle-upon-Tyne (1979–83), before turning to administration.

In 1987 she was elected as MP for Redcar. Within a year she was an assistant front bench spokesperson on Northern Ireland (1988–9) and then was deputy co-ordinator for Labour's successful European parliament campaign in 1989. Continuing her rise through the Labour Party ranks, she was spokesperson for city and corporate affairs (1989–92), for the Citizen's Charter and women (1992–3), for national heritage (1993–4) and for Northern Ireland (1994–), seeing her role to voice Labour's support for the peace process and ensure its continuation during a change to a Labour government in the UK.

Mozzoni, Anna Maria

Born 1837 Died 1920
Spanish women's rights campaigner from an upper-class background who adopted socialist ideals

Anna Maria Mozzoni was born into an upper-class family in Milan. She became involved in the fight for Italian women's rights, arguing that employment was essential for women's development, opposing all forms of discrimination and advocating equal political and educational rights for women.

Despite her comfortable background, Mozzoni embraced socialist ideals, believing that Italian women were less emancipated than they had been in 1789. She employed her pen to advance her cause, her best-known work being *La Liberazione delle donne*.

M'Rabet, Fadéla

Born 1935
Algerian feminist and writer and broadcaster on issues concerning Algerian women

Fadéla M'Rabet was born in Constantine, Algeria, where she graduated from the University of Algiers. She is an ardent proponent of feminism, and has worked in broadcasting, organizing women's programmes for Algerian radio.

In addition she has written about women's experience in Algeria in a number of publications including *La femme algérienne* (1962) and *L'Algérie des illusions* (1973).

Muir, Jean Elizabeth

Born 1928 Died 1995
Scottish dressmaker who captured the essence of modernity in her designs

Jean Muir was born in London of Scottish parentage and educated at Dame Harper School, Bedford. She started as a salesgirl with Liberty's in London in 1950, then moved to Jaeger in 1956 and specialized in knitwear design. In 1961 she started on her own as Jane & Jane. In 1966 she established her own company, Jean Muir, of which she was co-owner and designer-director until 1975.

Dubbed the Miss Jean Brodie of design, throughout her career she shunned the fads of fashion and crafted clothes noted for their classic shapes and their softness and fluidity. Her purpose was to enhance the body and movement of any modern woman, not just those with model-like figures, and her fastidiousness about colour was reflected in the range of sombre colours — especially deep, navy blues — with which her designs became associated.

Muir, Willa, *pseud* Agnes Neill Scott, *née* Anderson

Born 1890 Died 1970
Scottish novelist and translator who collaborated with her famous literary husband Edwin Muir and wrote about the role of women in Scotland

Willa Anderson was born in Montrose, Angus. She showed an early aptitude for languages as a child, speaking both her parents' Shetland dialect and English, and was educated at St Andrews University. She taught classics and educational psychology in London until forced to resign on marrying the 'atheist' poet Edwin Muir in 1919.

Despite her ill health, brought on by poor medical treatment after the birth of their son Gavin in 1927, the Muirs punctuated their lives in Scotland with much travelling, and lived for short periods in Prague, Rome and the USA. They translated jointly (although often only Edwin was credited), and were influential in spreading the work of the Austrian novelist Franz Kafka in the 1930s.

Her essay *Women: An Enquiry* (1925) dealt with the demoralizing effects of Scottish small-town life, a subject she returned to in her novel *Imagined Corners* (1931). *Mrs Grundy in Scotland* (1936) examined the role of women in Scottish culture. She wrote a moving account of her long and creative partnership with Edwin Muir, *Belonging* (1968), and finished his project *Living With Ballads* (1965) after his death.

Muller, Mary

Born 1820 Died 1902
New Zealand feminist who helped to establish equality in property law and voting rights for her country's women

Mary Muller was born in Britain, but little is now known of her early life. Following the death of her first husband, a man named Griffiths, she went to New Zealand at the age of 30. She soon married S L Muller, whose disapproval of her feminist views led to her secretly publishing these anonymously through a local newspaper.

Her feminist tract *An Appeal to the Men of New Zealand* won her international acclaim, and she was instrumental in having a women's property act passed in 1884, and in achieving female suffrage in her adopted homeland 10 years later.

Munro, Alice, *née* Laidlaw

Born 1931
Canadian writer known for her short stories set in rural Ontario

Alice Laidlaw was born in Wingham, Ontario, and attended the University of Western Ontario before marrying and moving to British Columbia. She wrote short stories from an early age, waiting until she was 'ready' to write the 'great novel'.

Her only novel to date, *Lives of Girls and Women* (1971), accomplished though it is, cannot claim to be great, though her stories, published for many years without being collected, are recognized as among the finest of the day. They are invariably set in rural and semi-rural Ontario, the landscape of her childhood.

She has published several collections, from *Dance of the Happy Shades* (1968) — winner of the Governor-General's award for Fiction — and *The Progress of Love* (1987) to *Friend of My Mouth* (1990) and *Something I've Been Meaning to Tell You* (1992).

Münter, Gabriele

Born 1877 Died 1962
German Expressionist painter of landscapes and interiors

Gabriele Münter was born in Berlin in 1877. She enrolled at the Women's Academy in Düsseldorf in 1897, but tired of her studies and left to travel across America for the next three years. Her parents had previously emigrated to America but they had returned to Germany at the outbreak of the Civil War. Being a woman, Münter was unable to study at the Academy in Munich, so she attended classes under the painter and art critic Wassaly Kandinsky (1866–1944) at his Phalanx School there.

She and Kandinsky then travelled throughout Europe (1903–8) and while in France she was influenced by Fauvism and the work of Paul Gauguin (1848–1903). They settled in Murnau where she evolved her own style, working closely with two other Russian artists, Von Werefkin and Jawlensky. Kandinsky moved towards abstract art while Münter and the two Russians retained their interest in more figurative painting.

Her relationship with Kandinsky deteriorated, coming to an end in 1916, but with the encouragement of her partner Johannes Eicher, she returned to painting in the late 1920s, and from 1945 until her death she promoted the work of the *Blaue Reiter* (Blue Rider) group.

Murasaki, Shikibu

Born c.970 Died c.1015
Japanese author who wrote the first great work in Japanese, if not the first great novel in the world

Shikibu Murasaki was a member of the Fujiwara family, one of the most powerful aristocratic dynasties in Japan, but her real name is unknown: 'Shikibu Murasaki' is a later fictive construction.

Her *Genji Monogatari* (Eng trans *The Tale of Genji*, 1925–35) was the first great work in Japanese; indeed, there are many who think it still the greatest piece of literature Japan has ever produced. Complex, delicate, and often sublimely beautiful, it far outclasses anything produced elsewhere in its day.

Like many other aristocratic ladies in late Heian Japan, Murasaki also wrote a *Nikki* ('Diary') which, apart from being beautifully constructed, contains valuable insights into court life of the period, for after being widowed at the age of 21 she became lady-in-waiting to the empress Akiko, for whose entertainment *Genji* may have been written.

Murdoch, Dame (Jean) Iris

Born 1919
Irish novelist, playwright and philosopher

Iris Murdoch was born in Dublin of Anglo-Irish parents. She was educated at Badminton School, Bristol, and Oxford University, where she was Fellow and tutor in philosophy at St Anne's College from 1948 to 1963. She published a study of Jean-Paul Sartre (like her, both a novelist and a philosopher) in 1953 and two important but unfashionable philosophical works, much influenced by Plato, *The Fire and the Sun* (1977) and *The Sovereignty of the Good* (1970). These deal with the relationships between art and philosophy, and between love, freedom, knowledge, and morality. A later philosophical work is *Meta-*

physics as a Guide to Morals (1992).

She began writing novels as a hobby. *Under the Net* appeared in 1954, to be followed by more than 20 titles in the next 25 years, including such works as *The Sandcastle* (1957), *The Bell* (1958), *A Severed Head* (1961), *An Unofficial Rose* (1962), *The Red and the Green* (1965), *The Nice and the Good* (1968), *The Black Prince* (1972), *The Sea, The Sea* (1978), which won the Booker Prize, *Nuns and Soldiers* (1980), *The Good Apprentice* (1985), *The Book and the Brotherhood* (1987), *The Message to the Planet* (1989) and *The Green Knight* (1993). The popularity of the fiction derives largely from her narrative skill in controlling tangled and shifting patterns of relationships, the ironic or even startling circumstances in which the characters find themselves, and the pervasive blend of realism and symbolism.

She has also written several plays, including *A Severed Head* (adapted with J B Priestley in 1963), *Servants and the Snow* (1970), *The Two Arrows* (1972) and *Art and Eros* (1980).

Murphy, Dervla

Born 1931
Irish travel writer who is prolific and amusing

Dervla Murphy was born in Cappoquin, County Waterford. She attended the Ursuline Convent, Waterford, but left school early to look after her invalid mother. She read avidly and went cycling in Europe, and after her mother's death in 1962 she cycled to India to work with Tibetan refugees. Her first two books, *Full Tilt* (1965) and *Tibetan Foothold* (1966), financed further journeys to Nepal and Ethiopia.

Murphy's daughter Rachel was born in December 1968 and they subsequently made several long journeys together in southern India, trekking through the Karakoram Mountains and 1,300 miles along the Andes.

Murphy has won several literary awards and has also written books on subjects closer to home, including Northern Ireland, racial conflict and the nuclear controversy.

Murphy, Emily Gowan, *pseud* Janey Canuck *née* Ferguson

Born 1868 Died 1933
Canadian journalist and feminist, a major campaigner for divorce law reform

Emily Murphy was born in Cookstown, Ontario, and educated at Bishop Strachan School, Toronto. She married Arthur Murphy in 1887.

On moving to Edmonton, Alberta, in 1907, she became involved in the women's movement and campaigned with **Nellie McClung** for legal reform which would entitle a wife to one third of her husband's property (The Dower Act, 1911). In 1916 she was the first woman in the British Empire to be appointed magistrate but this was opposed on the grounds that as a woman she was a non-person.

She was the President of the Canadian Women's Press Club (1913–20) and was literary editor of the *Winnipeg Telegram* and *Edmonton Journal*. She published many books, including *The Impressions of Janey Canuck Abroad* (1902), *Janey Canuck in the West* (1910), *Open Trails* (1912) and *Black Candle* (1922).

Murray, Anne

Born 1945
Canadian singer and winner of several awards for her country music

Anne Murray was born in Springhill, Nova Scotia. Her first American album, *About Me*, contained the song 'Snowbird' which earned a gold record (ie, sold over one million copies) in 1970. Her songs, such as 'Danny's Song' in 1973, have been consistent hits.

In 1980 she won a Grammy for Best Country Vocal Performance. She has also won four Junos, the Canadian equivalent of the Grammy award.

Murray, Judith Sargent, *née* Sargent

Born 1751 Died 1820
American writer of essays, poems and plays

Judith Sargent was born into a wealthy Massachusetts family. She studied with her brother and in her twenties, against a background of social change brought on by the revolutionary atmosphere, she began writing.

In 1790, now married to the Rev John Murray, she published a paper in favour of education for women. Convinced of the need to encourage women to be self-supporting as an alternative to marriage, she was one of two women whose writing appeared in the earliest known American anthology, published in 1794.

Her best-known literary work is the collection of essays, poems and plays entitled *The Gleaner*, published in 1798.

Murray, Margaret Alice

Born 1863 Died 1963
British scholar and Egyptologist who became a university professor

Margaret Murray was born in Calcutta, India, and educated privately both in England and Germany. Although she had commenced a career as a nurse in Calcutta, when she returned to England permanently in 1886 she abandoned nursing.

In 1894 she studied Egyptology at University College, London, and in 1899, despite the fact that she had never been to school and had never taken an examination, she became a junior lecturer at University College; 1925 she was assistant professor.

Her publications include *Elementary Coptic Grammar* (1911), *The Witch-Cult in Western Europe* (1921) and *My First Hundred Years* (1963).

Murray, Yvonne

Born 1964
Scottish middle-distance runner who has had most wins over 3,000 metres

Yvonne Murray was born in Musselburgh, near Edinburgh. She first came to prominence in 1982, breaking the UK junior record for the 3,000 metres when she won the Scottish championships. Although also a 1,500-metre runner, her main successes have all come at 3,000 metres. In 1986 she was a bronze medallist at the Commonwealth Games, and a silver medallist at the European championships. She won bronze at the 1988 Olympics, and Commonwealth silver again in 1990 before, also in 1990, winning the European championships in Split, Yugoslavia.

Though she was not placed at the 1991 World championships or the 1992 Barcelona Olympics, in 1993 she won gold at the World Indoor Athletics championships and also beat **Liz McColgan** to win the 5,000 metres at the BUPA Festival of Road Running in Aberdeen, which enforced her aim to compete in the 6,000 metres at the 1996 Olympics. In 1994 she won the 10,000 metres at the Commonwealth Games and the 3,000 metres at the World championships.

An ebullient but modest figure, perceived as becoming a tougher competitor by the year, she was awarded the MBE in 1990 for services to sport.

Musgrave, Thea

Born 1928
Scottish composer whose work ranges from concertos, operas and orchestral pieces to vocal works and electronic music

Thea Musgrave was born in Edinburgh. She studied at Edinburgh University, the Paris Conservatoire, and with **Nadia Boulanger**. Her early work was largely Scottish in inspiration: her *Suite o'Bairnsangs* (1953) and the ballet *A Tale for Thieves* (1953) were followed

by *Cantata for a Summer's Day* (1954), a chamber opera *The Abbot of Drimock* (1955) and her *Scottish Dance Suite* (1959).

In the late 1950s her work became more abstract, and she has used serial and aleatory devices. Her music includes two works for chorus and orchestra, *The Phoenix and the Turtle* (1962) and *The Five Ages of Man* (1963); an opera *The Decision* (1964–5); a full-length ballet *Beauty and the Beast* (1968); works for instruments and prerecorded tapes; the chamber opera *The Voice of Ariadne* (commissioned for the Aldeburgh Festival of 1974); the operas *Mary, Queen of Scots* (1977) and *A Christmas Carol* (1979); a radio opera, *An Occurrence at Owl Creek Bridge* (1981); and the orchestral works *The Seasons* (1988) and *Rainbow* (1990).

Myles, Lynda

Born 1947
Scottish film and television producer who raised the profile of the Edinburgh Film Festival and scored a success with The Commitments

Lynda Myles was born in Arbroath, Angus. Whilst studying philosophy at Edinburgh University, she became involved in the running of the Edinburgh International Film Festival. Serving as its director from 1973 to 1980, she raised the event's international reputation through her informed championing of the New German Cinema, underappreciated Hollywood veterans, and the new generation of American directors, an enthusiasm that led her to co-author the book *The Movie Brats* (1979).

She worked as curator of the Pacific Film Archive in California between 1980 and 1982, then returned to Britain and worked for Channel 4 and Enigma Films, where she produced the political thriller *Defence of the Realm* (1985). After being senior Vice-President of European Production for Columbia Pictures during David Puttnam's brief reign as studio head, she subsequently worked for the BBC before returning to independent film production with the highly successful *The Commitments* (1991). Later films include *The Snapper* (1993) and Stephen Frears's *The Van* (1996).

In 1981 she received a BFI Special Award for sevices to the film industry.

Myrdal, Alva Reimer, *née* Reimer

Born 1902 Died 1986
Swedish sociologist, politician and peace reformer, joint recipient of the Nobel Prize for Peace

Alva Reimar was born in Uppsala. She was

educated at the universities of Uppsala, Stockholm and Geneva, and in 1924 married the economist and politician Gunnar Myrdal (1898–1987).

A proponent of child welfare and equal rights for women, she was director of the United Nations department of social sciences (1950–6). Appointed Swedish ambassador to India, Burma and Ceylon from 1955 to 1961, she was elected to the Swedish parliament in 1962, acting as Swedish representative on the UN Disarmament Committee from 1962 to 1973. As Minister for Disarmament and Church Affairs (1966–73), she played a prominent part in the international peace movement; her works include *The Game of Disarmament: How the United States and Russia Run the Arms Race* (1977).

She was awarded the 1980 Albert Einstein Peace Prize, and in 1982 received the Nobel Prize for Peace, jointly with the Mexican diplomat Alfonso García Robles.

n

Naidu, Sarojini, *née* Chattopadhyay

Born 1879   Died 1949
Indian feminist, poet and political activist who
was the first Indian woman to lead the National
Congress

Sarojini Chattopadhyay was born in Hyderabad and educated at Madras, London and Cambridge. She organized flood-relief in Hyderabad (1908), and lectured and campaigned on feminism, particularly the abolition of purdah. She was associated with Mahatma Gandhi, and became in 1925 the first Indian woman to be President of the Indian National Congress, a position that **Annie Besant** had held from 1917 to 1923.

She was imprisoned several times for civil disobedience incidents, and took part in the negotiations leading to independence. In 1947 she was appointed govenor of United Provinces (now Uttar Pradesh), again the first Indian woman to hold such a position.

For her literary output she became known as the 'nightingale of India', and she published three volumes of lyric verse: *The Golden Threshold* (1905), *The Bird of Time* (1912) and *The Broken Wing* (1915).

Nairne, Carolina Nairne, Baroness, *née* Oliphant

Born 1766   Died 1845
Scottish song writer whose music expressed
Jacobite sentiments

Carolina Oliphant was born in Gask, Perthshire, the daughter of a Jacobite laird. In 1806 she married her second cousin, Major Nairne (1757–1830), who became 5th Baron Nairne of Nairne in 1824. She lived in Edinburgh, but travelled widely in Ireland and Europe after her husband's death.

Collecting traditional airs, she wrote songs to them under the pseudonym 'Mrs Bogan of Bogan', which were published in *The Scottish Minstrel* (1821–4), and posthumously as *Lays from Strathearn*. They include the lament for Prince Charles Edward Stuart, 'Will ye no' come back again', 'The Land o' the Leal', 'Caller Herrin', 'The Laird o' Cockpen', 'The Rowan Tree' and 'The Auld Hoose', as well as the martial setting for 'The Hundred Pipers'.

Nalkowska

Born 1884   Died 1954
Polish novelist and dramatist best known for
psychological and sketches based on Nazi crimes

Nalkowska was born in Warsaw, the daughter of a famous geographer and his wife, who gave her a sound education. She was initially associated with the so-called Positivist movement, which preceded that of the neo-romantic 'Young Poland' (Mloda Polska). Her first novel, *Kobiety* (1906, Eng trans *Women*, 1920), published when she was only 22, was well intentioned, but too closely reflected what she thought she ought, as a Positivist, to believe; however, its characterization bore sure signs that she was a woman of unusual genius, who did not pander to male notions of women.

Eighteen years later she had matured beyond recognition: *Romans Teresy Hennert* (1924, 'Teresa Hennert's Affair') is a scathing account of the bourgeois attitude to 'illicit' love in Poland after World War II. She wrote at least three more excellent psychological novels, of which *Granica* (1935, 'The Boundary') is perhaps the finest. She is most famous, however, for *Medaliony* (1946, Eng trans of part of it in *Introduction to Modern Polish Literature*, 1964, H Gillon and L Krzyzanowski eds); as a member of the International Commission to Investigate Nazi Crimes, she had, early, to investigate torture and concentration camps in Poland, and in these sketches, amongst the most harrowing and ironic ever written on this subject, she reported her findings. 'Professor Spanner', about making soap from prisoners, is peculiarly memorable for its bland summaries of the good reasons advanced for this process.

Naomi

*Biblical character in the Old Testament, mother-in-law of **Ruth***

Naomi's name means 'my delight' in Hebrew. She is described in the stories of the Book of Ruth as the mother-in-law of Ruth and Orpah. After Naomi was widowed, and her two sons had also died, she persuaded Orpah to return to her own people.

Ruth however made an oath to remain with Naomi and returned with her from Moab to Bethlehem, where Naomi helped to arrange the marriage of Ruth with Boaz, one of the secondary kinsmen of Naomi's deceased husband. Ruth and Boaz had a son called Obed, who was to be the father of Jesse, who in turn was the father of David.

Nation, Carry Amelia, *née* Moore

Born 1846   Died 1911
American temperance agitator who undertook violent missions at home and abroad

Carry Moore was born in Garrard County, Kentucky. She had little formal education but was influenced by evangelical crusaders and by the beliefs of the negro slaves whom she knew as a child. In 1867 she married Charles Gloyd, but he was an alcoholic and she soon left him; he died within the year. She turned to teaching to provide for her young daughter and in 1877 married David Nation, who divorced her in 1901 for desertion.

From 1899 Nation lived in Kansas, a state with prohibition laws, and became convinced of her divine appointment to ensure the closure of illicit saloons. At nearly six feet tall, she was a large, powerful woman of volcanic emotions, and she went on saloon-smashing expeditions brandishing a hatchet, often accompanied by hymn-singing women. She took her campaign to other American cities and to the UK, was frequently imprisoned for breach of the peace and also encountered and survived physical attacks.

She financed her mission and her fines by the sale of souvenir hatchets and of her publications, including her autobiography *The Use and Need of the Life of Carry Nation* (1904). Although her eccentric techniques prevented her being supported by official temperance movements, her activities are thought to have swung public opinion in favour of the ratification in 1919 of the Prohibition Amendment to the US Constitution. She was also a firm advocate of women's suffrage, but did not

Carry Nation

receive much support from suffrage organizations either. In later life she became mentally unbalanced and retreated to a remote mountain farm in Arkansas.

Navratilova, Martina

Born 1956
Czechoslovakian-born American tennis player
who won Wimbledon a record nine times

Martina Navratilova was born in Prague. For three years she played for Czechoslovakia in the Federation Cup, but in 1975 she defected to the USA and immediately turned professional, taking US nationality in 1981.

Her rivalry with **Chris Evert** was one of the great features of the game from 1975 (Evert won Wimbledon in 1974, 1976 and 1981). Navratilova won Wimbledon a record nine times (1978–9, 1982–7, 1990) and the US Open four times (1983–4, 1986–7) and recorded more than 100 tournament successes. She is also the only woman to have won the Grand Slam twice. Her impressive number of wins in both singles and doubles matches makes her second only to **Margaret Smith Court**.

After reaching the final at Wimbledon in 1994, Navratilova announced her retirement from competitive singles tennis. Her books include *Martina* (1985) and *Feet of Clay* (1996).

Naylor, Gloria

Born 1950
African-American writer whose works focus on
the lives of black American women

Gloria Naylor was born in New York City and educated at Brooklyn College and Yale. Her novels reflect the experiences of urban African-American women in the 20th century.

Her best-known novel is *The Women of Brewster Place* (1981), which comprises seven stories, each focusing on the experiences of a different African-American woman. Her other works include *Linden Hills* (1985) and *Mama Day* (1988).

Nazimova, Alla, *originally* Leventon

Born 1879 Died 1945
Russian-born American actress who specialized
in the plays of Ibsen, Turgenev, Chekhov and
O'Neill

Alla Leventon was born in the Crimea. She studied in Moscow under Stanislavsky and made her début in St Petersburg in 1904. Soon established as a leading lady, she toured Europe and America and in 1906, having learnt English in less than a year, appeared in New York as Hedda Gabler.

Her success over the next few years led the theatre-owning Shubert brothers to build the Nazimova Theatre (later the 39th Street Theatre) for her, which she opened in 1910 with a performance of Ibsen's *Little Eyolf*. She became a highly popular emotional actress, and in 1915 began a successful period in films, which included *The Brat, Camille, A Doll's House, The Red Lantern* and her own *Salomé*, based on Aubrey Beardsley's illustrations to Oscar Wilde's play.

She became a US citizen in 1927, returned to the stage and continued to act on both stage and screen into her sixties.

Neagle, Dame Anna, *originally* Marjorie Robertson

Born 1904 Died 1986
English actress who was acclaimed in historical
roles, musicals and films

Marjorie Robertson was born in London. She studied dance as a child and was an instructor before becoming a chorus girl in *Charlot's Revue of 1925*. She graduated to leading roles in *Stand Up and Sing* (1931), making her film début in *Should A Doctor Tell?* (1930).

Under the tutelage of director Herbert Wilcox, who became her husband in 1943, she emerged as a major star of historical film dramas, offering genteel portraits of inspiring heroines in *Victoria, the Great* (1937), *Nurse Edith Cavell* (1939), *Odette* (1950) and *The Lady With the Lamp* (1951). A series of escapist musicals opposite Michael Wilding made her Britain's number one box-office attraction but later attempts to tackle contemporary subjects were ill-judged and she retired from the screen after *The Lady is a Square* (1958). She retained the affection of British audiences with appearances in such productions as *Charlie Girl* (1965–71), *No, No, Nanette* (1973) and *My Fair Lady* (1978–9).

She was created DBE in 1969, and wrote two autobiographies: *It's Been Fun* (1949) and *There's Always Tomorrow* (1974).

Neal, Patricia (Patsy Louise)

Born 1926
American actress and leading lady whose ill-
health forced her into semi-retirement

Patricia Neal was born in Packard, Virginia. She studied drama at Northwestern University and worked as a model before making her Broadway début in *The Voice Of The Turtle* (1946). She joined the New York Actors Studio, won a Tony award for *Another Part Of*

The Forest (1946) and made her film début in *John Loves Mary* (1949). She is a deep-voiced woman of obvious intelligence and sophistication, but Hollywood squandered her talents on a succession of conventional roles, though she later proved her worth in films like *A Face In The Crowd* (1957), *Breakfast At Tiffany's* (1961) and *Hud* (1963), in which her performance as the world-weary housekeeper earned her a Best Actress Oscar.

Felled by a series of massive strokes, she fought to regain her health, receiving the Heart of the Year award from President Johnson for her bravery and a further Oscar nomination for *The Subject Was Roses* (1968). Her subsequent career has provided few first-rate roles, but she has given notable performances in such television productions as *The Homecoming* (1971) and *Things In Their Season* (1974). She was married to the writer Roald Dahl from 1953 to 1983 and has written an autobiography *As I Am* (1988).

Nedreaas, Torborg

Born 1906   Died 1987
Norwegian novelist and critic of Jewish extraction whose books highlight social life and class struggle

Torborg Nedreaas was born in Bergen. She was a left-wing feminist and turned to writing late in life, after World War II.

Her especially powerful works include *Musikk fra en blå brønn* (1960, Eng trans *Music from a Blue Well*) and *Ved neste nymåne* (1971, Eng trans *At the Next New Moon*), about a girl called Herdis growing up in Bergen between the wars. Nedreaas's stories were collected in *Stoppested* (1953, 'Stopping Place').

Needham, Dorothy Mary Moyle, *née* Moyle

Born 1896   Died 1987
English biochemist who carried out important research on the muscle

Dorothy Needham was born in London and educated at Girton College, Cambridge. She began research into the physiology and biochemistry of muscle in the Biochemical Laboratory there in 1920, where she remained until 1963. She published extensively on the metabolism of muscle tissue and also on the history of biochemistry, especially in relation to studies of muscle. She married a fellow biochemist, Joseph Needham (1900–   ), in 1924, and in 1948 joined her husband as a Fellow of the Royal Society.

Nefertiti

14th century BC
Egyptian queen as the wife of King Akhenaten (reigned 1379–1362BC)

Nefertiti is believed to have been born an Asian princess in Mitanni. She and her husband, King Akhenaten, had six children, and she was closely associated with him, as is evident from the painted reliefs in the Aten temple at Karnak, where she figures prominently, and at El Amarna in tomb scenes.

In his sixth year as king, he had instigated a religious revolution and forced the adoption of the cult of the sun-disc Aten, changing his name from Amenhotpe IV to Akhenaten, and moving the capital from Thebes to El Amarna. Nefertiti was an ardent follower of the new cult of the Aten but it continued to appeal only to the king and his family, rather than to the population as a whole.

After Akhenaten's death two of their daughters became consorts of his successors: one married Smenkhkare (who may have reigned jointly with him for a time) and the other married Tutankhamun, who, with Nefertiti's approval, reinstated the former religion of the sun-god Amun. She is immortalized in the beautiful sculptured head found at Amarna in 1912, now in the Ägyptisches Museum, Berlin.

Negri, Ada

Born 1870   Died 1945
Italian poet whose work examines social and political issues

Ada Negri was born in Lodi. She became a teacher in a small primary school, and made her literary debut with *Fatalità* (1892, 'Destiny'), a derivative and idealistic collection of humanitarian poems.

Her subsequent works, nine more volumes of verse and a number of prose works, refined the political, feminist, and mystical basis of her work. She won several literary prizes and was a member of the Accademia d'Italia.

Neilson, Julia Emilie

Born 1868   Died 1957
English actress who celebrated her stage jubilee in 1938

Julia Neilson was born in London. After a brilliant career at the Royal Academy of Music, she made her début at the Lyceum in 1888; her greatest success was as Rosalind in the record-breaking run of *As You like It* (1896–8).

She met and married **Ellen Terry's** brother

Fred (1863–1933), while they were co-starring in *The Dancing Girl* (1891). From 1900 until his retirement in 1929 he often appeared with her as his leading lady, and he also partnered her in management.

Their children Dennis (1895–1932) and Phyllis (1892–1977) Neilson-Terry also became famous for their acting, the latter especially in the title role of *Trilby*, and for their productions.

Nemcová, Bozena, *née* Panklová

Born 1820   Died 1862
Czech novelist who became the first truly eminient Czech woman writer

Bozena Panklová was born in Vienna of an Austrian father, a coachman on an estate in Bohemia, and a Czech mother. She garnered her considerable wisdom from her old grandmother, whom she lovingly and memorably portrayed in *Babicka* (1855, Eng trans *Granny*, 1962), one of the great books of the 19th century. At 17 she married unhappily — her husband, an excise man much older than her, could not reconcile his duties to his Austrian masters with her habits of thinking for herself and writing, and they parted in 1850.

Nemcová was beautiful, sensitive, intense, and became (almost like **George Eliot** in England) the subject of much vulgar gossip, since she chose to have many love affairs (which were as unhappy as her marriage had been). However, she also became a highly respected writer — *Granny* has gone through over 300 Czech editions since it first appeared, and through many more in other Slavonic languages. She wrote many more novels and stories, some of them folk- and fairy-tales.

She died prematurely, while trying to collect an edition of her works, as a result of exhaustion and disappointment. Some of her fairy-tales are translated in *The Shepherd and the Dragon* (1930).

Nesbit, E(dith)

Born 1858   Died 1924
English writer of stories and novels for children

Edith Nesbit was born in London, the daughter of an agricultural chemist who died when she was three. She was educated at a French convent, and began her literary career by writing poetry, having met **Christina Rossetti** and her circle. In 1880 she married the Fabian journalist Hubert Bland.

To help with the family finances she turned to popular fiction and children's stories about the Bastaple family, including *The Story of the*

Treasure Seekers (1899), *The Would-be-Goods* (1901), *Five Children and It* (1902), *The New Treasure Seekers* (1904), *The Railway Children* (1906) and *The Enchanted Castle* (1907). She also wrote other novels, and ghost stories. She was emulated by many later children's writers.

After her husband's death in 1914 she married an engineer, Terry Tucker, in 1917. Her last novel was *The Lark* (1922).

Neuberger, Julia Babette Sarah, *née* Schwab

Born 1950
British rabbi, writer and broadcaster, the first female rabbi in Britain

Julia Schwab was born in London and educated at Cambridge. She took a Rabbinic Diploma at Leo Baeck College, where she later returned as lecturer in 1979. She married Anthony Neuberger in 1973. From 1977 to 1989 she was rabbi of the South London Liberal Synagogue, and she was picked to front *Choices* on BBC1 in 1986 and 1987.

Noted for her liberal and reasonable approach, she is often asked to comment in the media on aspects of daily British life and has been involved in religious and secular advisory committees on such topics as health and human rights. In 1993 she became Chancellor of the University of Ulster, the second non-Royal female chancellor of a UK university (Dame **Margot Fonteyn** was the first, when she became Chancellor of the University of Durham in 1982); also that year she was appointed to the chair of the Camden and Islington Community Health Services NHS Trust.

Neumann, Theresa

Born 1898   Died 1962
German mystic and stigmatic

Theresa Neumann was born in Konnersreuth, Bavaria. Sickness and accident from 1918 onwards were followed by a string of illnesses up to 1925 that were cured without medical intervention.

During Lent in 1926 she had visions of the Passion of Christ accompanied by stigmata on her hands, feet and left side. She is said to have had no food from 1927 onwards, apart from daily Holy Communion.

Her life attracted much interest, but claims that miraculous healing and survival proved her a saint have not been accepted as reaching the standards required by Church authority.

Nevelson, Louise, *née* Berliawsky

Born 1899
Russian-born American printmaker and sculptor,
known for her abstract and 'environmental'
sculptures

Louise Berliawsky was born in Kiev. Her family settled in Portland, Maine, in 1905. After marrying Charles Nevelson in 1920, she studied at the Art Students' League in New York (1929–33) and (after separating from her husband) with the influential theorist Hans Hofmann in Munich. In 1932 she worked as an assistant to the Mexican mural-painter Diego Rivera.

She is best known for her 'environmental' sculptures — abstract, wooden box-like shapes stacked up to form walls and painted white or gold — and in 1966 she began to use lucite, plexiglass and aluminium, adding reflected light to her work.

Her works include *Transparet Sculpture VI* (1967–8) in lucite, *Transparent Horizon* (1975) in steel, and the white-painted wooden interior *Bicentennial Dawn* (1976).

Neville-Jones, Dame (Lilian) Pauline

Born 1939
English diplomat who reached a higher rank than
any other woman in the Foreign Office

Pauline Neville-Jones, the daughter of two doctors, was educated in Leeds and won a scholarship to study history at Oxford University. She entered the Foreign Office in 1963. Apparently sacrificing marriage for a single life of success (for until 1972 women in the Foreign Office had to resign if they married), she worked her way through the diplomatic ranks, her early foreign postings including Rhodesia (now Zimbabwe) in 1964–5, Singapore (1965–8) and Washington DC (1971–5).

She worked in the Foreign and Commonwealth Office (FCO) in 1968–71 and 1975–7, as Chef de Cabinet for the European Commissioner for Budget in 1977–82 and at the Royal Institute for International Affairs (1982–3) before becoming the FCO Head of Planning Staff in 1987. Since then her positions have included being deputy in Bonn (1988–91) and Chairman of the Joint Intelligence Committee in the Cabinet Office (1993–4).

In 1994, on Prime Minister John Major's recommendation, she became the second highest official in the FCO as Political Director and Deputy Under-Secretary of State. She played a key role as head of the British del-egation during the Bosnian peace talks in Dayton, Ohio, in 1995, and was an obvious candidate for the Grade One posting of ambassador to Paris in 1996. Passed over for this however, she left the FCO to join the investment banking department of NatWest as European specialist. She had been created DBE earlier that year.

Newbery, Jessie, *née* Rowat

Born 1864 Died 1948
Scottish art embroideress who pioneered the
approach to embroidery as an art form

Jessie Rowat was born in Paisley, the daughter of a shawl manufacturer. She was educated in Paisley, Edinburgh, and at the Glasgow School of Art, and married the Director of the school, Francis Newbery, in 1889. In 1894 she was appointed to the staff of the Art School and introduced embroidery into the curriculum, but also taught enamelling and mosaic work.

It is for her needlework and embroidery and her approach to the teaching of these subjects that she is best known. Her work was exhibited in Britain, Germany, France and America, and was often illustrated in journals such as *The Studio*, *Das Elgenkleid der Frau* and *Modern Stickerian*. In collaboration with **Frances MacDonald**, **Margaret Mackinstosh** and **Ann Macbeth**, she played an important role in the development of the Glasgow Style of Art Nouveau. In terms of design and technique her work was original, underpinned by a belief that embroidery should be conceived as an art form, a philosophy which had a major influence on her students.

She retired from the Art School in 1908 and moved to Corfe Castle in Dorset with her husband in 1918.

Newby-Fraser, Paula

Born 1962
South African athlete, the most outstanding
female triathlete of the present day

Paula Newby-Fraser was born in Zimbabwe and brought up in South Africa. She has won the women's event at the gruelling Hawaii Ironman Triathlon a record five times and is also the only woman to have won it more than once. She has won the Nice Triathlon four years in a row and the US Triathlon series in 1990 and 1991.

A regular challenger of the best male athletes, her time for the triathlon is the fastest women's time ever and is also among the top 10 times of all time for the event, male or female. She was voted athlete of the year by the Women's Sport Foundation in 1990.

Newcastle, Duchess of *see*
Cavendish, Margaret

Newton-John, Olivia

Born 1948
British singer of rock and country music, noted for her role in the film Grease!

Olivia Newton-John was brought up in Australia. She won a talent contest and after several false starts, had a hit with Bob Dylan's 'If Not for You', and a further success with soft rock/country songs 'Banks of the Ohio' and 'Take Me Home Country Roads'.

Her association with Cliff Richard and romance with Shadows member Bruce Welch did much to underline her squeaky-clean image. In 1974, with 'Long Live Love', she was the UK's Eurovision Song Contest entrant, but failed to win.

A move to the USA and a role in the movie version of *Grease!* (1978) started realignment of her career and persona. The albums *Xanadu* and *Physical* were altogether more adult in orientation, but later, raunchier records failed to catch. During the early 1990s, Newton-John successfully fought cancer.

Ngoyi, Lilian Masediba

Born 1911 Died 1980
Black South African campaigner who suffered frequent and lengthy imprisonment for her opposition to apartheid

Lilian Ngoyi was born near Pretoria. Her education was cut short because of family poverty, and she worked in a variety of menial jobs, before marrying, bearing three children, and being widowed by the age of 40.

Her experience of work conditions in clothing factories fired her determination to campaign for a fair society in South Africa, and she agitated against the infamous Pass Laws with such persistence that she was arrested and imprisoned for her beliefs. Later activity, in 1956, led to her being charged with treason; although she was acquitted, she was imprisoned again while awaiting trial, and endured no fewer than 71 days in solitary confinement.

A brilliant orator, Lilian Ngoyi did not live to see the dismantling of apartheid, for she died under house arrest in 1980.

Nice, Margaret, *née* Morse

Born 1883 Died 1974
American biologist and ornithologist

Margaret Morse was born in Amherst, Massachusetts. She graduated in natural science from Mount Holyoke College in 1906 and moved to Clark University to study biology. In 1909 she married Leonard Nice and whilst bringing up five daughters, she undertook ornithological research relying on close observation, a technique she later applied to studying child psychology.

She also became particularly involved in conservation issues and campaigned against the indiscriminate use of pesticides.

Nicholson, (Rose) Winifred, *also known as* Winifred Dacre, *née* Roberts

Born 1893 Died 1981
English painter of botanical and abstract art

Winifred Roberts was born in Oxford into an aristocratic family who encouraged her to practice art. She attended the Byam Shaw School of art and married the artist Ben Nicholson in 1920. Throughout her career she worked in Paris, Lugano, India and the Hebrides. She lived in Cumbria and became a member of the Seven and Five Society (1925–35).

After 1931, the year Ben Nicholson left to live in London with **Barbara Hepworth**, she moved away from her highly respected figurative works, painted from nature, to experiment with abstraction. From 1935 to 1945 she exhibited under her mother's surname of Dacre.

Despite the demands of her three children, she continued to paint, also researching colour theory with the use of prisms, for the rest of her life.

Nidetch, Jean

Born 1923
American entrepreneur who founded the revolutionary dieting organization 'Weight Watchers'

Jean Nidetch was born in Brooklyn, New York. She embarked on a diet to lose five stone in 1961 and found it to be much easier when she had the support of a group of overweight friends with a similar goal. From this simple idea grew an organization, launched in 1963, and an international empire that foreshadowed a major boom in the diet and fitness industries. Since then 37 million people have joined, seeking the answer to their weight problem.

The technique of Weight Watchers International combines teaching on nutrition and diet with the opportunity to share the experience with other dieters in local 'clubs'. Since 1978 the company has been owned by Heinz, who market calorie-counted products under the Weight Watchers® name.

Nightingale, Florence, *known as the* Lady of the Lamp

Born 1820 Died 1910
English nurse and hospital reformer, credited with founding the modern nursing profession

Florence Nightingale was born in Florence, the daughter of William Edward Nightingale of Embly Park, Hampshire. She trained as a nurse at Kaiserswerth in Germany (1851) and in Paris and in 1853 became superintendent of a hospital for invalid women in London.

In the Crimean War she volunteered for duty and took 38 nurses to Scutari in 1854. She organized the barracks hospital after the Battle of Inkerman (5 November) and through discipline and sanitation brought about a drastic reduction in the hospital mortality rate. She returned to England in 1856 and a fund of £50,000 was subscribed to enable her to form an institution for the training of nurses at St Thomas's and at King's College Hospital.

She devoted many years to the question of army sanitary reform, to the improvement of nursing, and to public health in India. Her main work, *Notes on Nursing* (1859), went through many editions.

Nijinska, Bronislava

Born 1891 Died 1972
Russian ballet dancer who became principal choreographer for Serei Diaghilev

Bronislava Nijinska was born in Minsk, the sister of the dancer Vaslav Nijinsky (1890–1950). Her parents were professional dancers and she, like her brother, studied at the Imperial Ballet School in St Petersburg; she graduated in 1908 and became a soloist with the Maryinsky company.

She danced with Sergei Diaghilev's Ballets Russes in Paris and London before returning to Russia during World War I, when she started a school in Kiev, but went back to Diaghilev in 1921, following Léonide Massine as principal choreographer. Among the ballets she created for the company were her masterpieces *Les Noces* (1923) and *Les Biches* (1924).

After working in Buenos Aires and for Ida Rubinstein's company in Paris she briefly formed her own company in 1932. From 1935 she choreographed for many companies in Europe and the USA, but lived mainly in the USA and started a ballet school in Los Angeles (1938). She was persuaded to stage a notable revival of *Les Noces* and *Les Biches* at Covent Garden in 1964.

Nikolaevna, Klavdiya Ivanovna

Born 1893 Died 1944
Russian activist who campaigned for Russian and Soviet women's rights

Klavdiya Nikolaevna was born in St Petersburg and worked as a bookbinder. From an early age she was involved in revolutionary activities, being frequently arrested from 1908 onwards.

After 1917 she organized women's groups in Petrograd (the name for St Petersburg in 1914–24) and in 1924 she was appointed head of *zhenotdel*, the women's section of the Communist Party of the Soviet Union.

In 1926 she was dismissed for supporting the rebellious politician Grigoriy Zinoviev but survived to hold various lower rank appointments until her death.

Nilsson, (Märta) Birgit

Born 1922
Swedish operatic soprano, the leading Wagnerian singer of her time

Birgit Nilsson was born near Karup, Kristianstadslaen. She was educated at the Stockholm Royal Academy of Music, where her teachers included the Scottish tenor Joseph Hislop (1884–1977).

Following her début in 1946, she sang with the Stockholm Royal Opera (1947–51), at the New York Metropolitan from 1959, and at the Bayreuth Festival almost annually from 1953 to 1970. With her voice of exceptional power, stamina and intense personality, she became the leading Wagnerian soprano of that period.

She sang at most of the great houses and festivals of the world, and her repertoire included Verdi, Puccini and Strauss. She retired from the stage in 1982.

Nilsson, Christine

Born 1843 Died 1921
Swedish operatic singer who became a leading performer of the 19th century

Christine Nilsson was born in Sjöabol, near Vexiö, and trained in Stockholm and Paris. She made her début as Violetta in Paris in

1864, and became a leading prima donna in Europe and the USA.

Her acclaimed roles included the title role in the French composer Ambroise Thomas's *Mignon* (1866) and Ophelia in his *Hamlet* (1868). In 1883 she played Marguerite in Charles Gounod's *Faust*, at the opening performance of the Metropolitan Opera House in New York.

She made regular appearances in London from 1864 to 1881, and retired in 1888, though she gave a farewell performance in 1891.

Nin, Anaïs

Born 1903 Died 1977
French-born American writer, a seminal figure in the new feminism of the 1970s

Anaïs Nin was born in Paris to parents of mixed Spanish–Cuban descent. She spent her childhood in Europe until the age of 11, when she left France to live in the USA. Ten years later, after her marriage to Hugh Guiler, a banker, she returned to Paris, where she studied psychoanalysis under Otto Rank, became acquainted with many well-known writers and artists and began to write herself.

Her first novel, *House of Incest*, was published in 1936 and was followed by volumes of criticism, among them *The Novel of the Future* (1968), and a series of novels including *Winter of Artifice* (1939), *A Spy in the House of Love* (1954) and *Collages* (1964). She also published an early collection of short stories, *Under a Glass Bell* (1944). Ultimately, however, her reputation as an artist and feminist rests on her seven *Journals* (1966–83). Spanning the years 1931–74, they are an engrossing record of an era and some of its most intriguing and avant garde players, as well as a passionate, explicit and candid account of one woman's voyage of self-discovery.

Nino, *also called* Nina

Died c.340AD
Former slave whose prayers brought Christianity to Georgia

Nino was a slave-girl from Cappadocia — unnamed in the earliest account — whose prayers cured the Queen of Georgia and turned her to Christianity in 333. Shortly afterwards the king, Mirian, had a prayer answered and was also converted.

Mirian asked Constantine for a political alliance and for priests to instruct his people in the faith. The country became officially Christian in 337, a policy supported by his son and successor.

Nino, who is known as Christiana in Roman martyrology, spent the latter part of her life as a recluse in Bodbe, Kakhetia.

Noailles, Anna Élisabeth de Bibesco-Brancoven, Comtesse de

Born 1876 Died 1933
French poet and novelist who was acclaimed in the pre-war period as 'Princesse des lettres'

Anna de Bibesco-Brancoven was born in Paris of Romanian and Greek descent. She married Comte Mathieu de Noailles, a French count. With her first book, a collection of sensual and musical poems, *Le Coeur innombrable* (1901, 'The Innumerable Heart'), written under the influence of the writer Francis Jammes, she won the hearts of the French poetry-reading public. This verse has now dated, but the best of it is still worthy of attention. However, her last poems show her at her most original.

She presided over a literary salon in Paris and was a friend to novelist and politician Maurice Barrès, but was greatly disliked by some French critics, and has hardly had her posthumous due.

Noddack, Ida Eva, *née* Tacke

Born 1896
German chemist whose identification of nuclear fission is seldom acknowledged

Ida Tacke was educated in Berlin, where she met her husband Walter Karl Friedrich Noddack (1893–1960) whilst working in a testing laboratory. Together they discovered the elements masurium and rhenium (named after the Rhine) in 1925.

Ida Noddack was one of the first scientists to identify the occurrence of nuclear fission (1934), though the theory was apparently disregarded until **Lise Meitner** and Otto Frisch suggested it five years later.

Noether, (Amalie) Emmy

Born 1882 Died 1935
German mathematician, a leader in the development of abstract algebra

Emmy Noether was born in Erlangen, the daughter of the mathematician Max Noether, and educated at Erlangen and Göttingen. Though invited to Göttingen in 1915 by the mathematics professor there, David Hilbert, as a woman she could not hold a full academic post at that time, but worked there in a semi-honorary capacity until, expelled by the Nazis as a Jew, she emigrated to the USA in 1933 to Bryn Mawr College and the Institute for Advanced Study, Princeton.

A leader in the development of abstract algebra, she made fundamental discoveries in ring theory and the theory of ideals; the theory of Noetherian rings has been an important subject of later research. She developed it to provide a neutral setting for problems in algebraic geometry and number theory, with a view to enabling their essential features to stand out from the technicalities.

Nogarola, Isotta

Born 1418 Born 1466
Italian intellectual and writer whose brilliant career of scholarship was not tarnished by sexual smears

Isotta Nogarola was born into an aristocratic family in Verona. Famed by the time she was 18 for her command of the Latin language and her knowledge of the classics, she suffered the collapse of the world around her when, at the age of 20, she was accused of incestuous and promiscuous behaviour.

Forcing her to move to Venice, the accusations made her reclusive by nature and she turned her attention to religious studies. However her scholarship was unimpaired and continued to attract praise at home and abroad. Her written work emphasised gender roles, even to the extent of defending **Eve's** participation in Adam's banishment from Eden.

Noonuccal, Oodgeroo Moongalba,
originally Kath(leen Jean) Walker

Born 1920 Died 1993
Australian Aboriginal artist and writer who became the first to be published

Kath Walker was born in Brisbane, Queensland, and brought up with the Noonuccal tribe on Stradbroke Island, Queensland. From the age of 13 she worked in domestic service in Brisbane, gaining her education mainly from the libraries of her employers. She joined the Australian Women's Army Service during World War II, and afterwards became involved in Aboriginal activism.

In 1964 she became the first Aboriginal writer to be published, with her collection of poems *We are Going*, followed by *The Dawn is at Hand* (1966). With other works these were republished in 1970 as *My People, a Kath Walker Collection*. In 1972 she published a book of Aboriginal stories, *Stradbroke Dreamtime*. She won a number of awards, including the **Mary Gilmore** Medal. She visited the USA on a Fulbright Scholarship from 1978 to

1979, lecturing on Aboriginal rights, and was active on many Aboriginal interest committees including the Aboriginal Arts Board. In 1985 she published *Quandamooka, the Art of Kath Walker*. She also ran a Centre for Aboriginal Culture, for children of all races, on Stradbroke Island.

Australian composer Malcolm Williamson has set some of her poems for choir and orchestra; *The Dawn is at Hand* was premiered in 1989. In 1988 she adopted the Aboriginal name Oodgeroo of the tribe Noonuccal.

Nordenflycht, Hedvig Charlotta

Born 1718 Died 1763
Swedish writer of poetry and prose, one of the first female Swedish authors to make a living from her work

Hedvig Nordenflycht was born in Stockholm and received a good education. Her first book of poetry, *Den sörgande Turtur-Dufwan* ('The Mourning Turtle-dove'), was published in 1742, introducing a new subjectivity and a strongly feminine self-assertion. Between 1744 and 1750 she published four volumes of poetry, all under the title of *Qvinligt Tankespel* ('A Woman's Thoughts').

In 1753 she became one of the leading members of a new literary society in Stockholm (*Tankebyggarorden*, 'The Society of Thought Builders') and subsequently published works in conjunction with other members. Famous for the love poetry she wrote late in her life, she is also renowned as the author of a challenge to Jean-Jacques Rousseau's misogynism, *Fruentimrets försvar* (1761, 'The Defence of Woman').

Norman, Jessye

Born 1945
American dramatic soprano noted for her expressive voice and masterful technique

Jessye Norman was born in Augusta, Georgia. She won a scholarship to Howard University, Washington DC, and continued her training at Michigan University.

She made her operatic début as Elisabeth in Wagner's *Tannhäuser* at the Deutsche Oper, Berlin (1969), and began performing at both La Scala and Covent Garden in 1972. Her US début was at the Hollywood Bowl (1972) and she first sang at the New York Metropolitan Opera in 1983.

She is widely admired in opera and concert music for her beauty of tone, breadth of register and mastery of dynamic range.
(*See photograph on next page.*)

Jessye Norman, 1980

Norman, Marsha

Born 1947
American dramatist and novelist whose themes
include the nature of responsibility

Marsha Norman was born in Louisville, Kentucky. She graduated from the University of Georgia and for two years worked with emotionally disturbed children. The heroine of *Getting Out* (1977), her first play to be produced, is a murderer represented as both Arlie and Arlene, a double character from whose dialogue the audience learns of her complex emotional background.

Norman's best-known play is the Pulitzer Prize-winning *'night Mother* (1982), a much more naturalistic piece dealing with the relationship between a woman who is about to commit suicide and her mother. The mother and daughter theme is continued in *The Fortune Teller* (1987), a novel examining the ethics of abortion.

Noronha, Joana Paula Manso de

Born c.1850 Deathdate not known
South American journalist who fearlessly
proclaimed a feminist message to a hostile
community

Joana de Noronha was born in Argentina. She moved to Brazil after an unsuccessful marriage and took up journalism and literary criticism in Rio de Janeiro. Through her establishment of radical journals she publicised improvements in women's conditions internationally, despite the fact it made her unpopular in conventional Brazilian society.

Norris, Kathleen, *née* Thompson

Born 1880 Died 1966
American novelist and short-story writer whose
first book was a bestseller

Kathleen Thompson was born in San Francisco and educated at home. She wrote stories to entertain her younger siblings and later sold these to women's magazines in New York, where she moved after marrying the novelist Charles Norris in 1909.

In 1911 her first novel, *Mother*, about Californian family life, became a bestseller. After that she wrote many more short stories and more than 70 popular novels, including *Certain People of Importance* (1922) and *Over at the Crowleys* (1946).

North, Marianne

Born 1830 Died 1890
English botanical painter who travelled to many
countries in search of unknown plants

Marianne North was born into a wealthy family in Hastings. At the age of 40, after the death of her father, who had introduced her to travelling, she set off to paint colourful and exotic flowers in many countries.

Her first major trip in the early 1870s took her to Canada, the USA, Jamaica and Brazil. In later years she visited Japan, Java, Ceylon and India. In 1880, at Charles Darwin's suggestion, she went to Australia to improve her botanic collections. Occasionally, she discovered unclassified plants, such as the *Northia seychellana* capucin tree in the Seychelles.

Encouraged by the botanist Sir Joseph Dalton Hooker, director of the Royal Botanic Gardens at Kew, she gave her valuable collection to Kew Gardens where they can be seen in a gallery, opened in 1882, which bears her name (the North Gallery).

Norton, Caroline Elizabeth Sarah, *née* Sheridan

Born 1808 Died 1877
Irish writer and reformer who campaigned for
improvements in the laws of marriage and divorce

Caroline Sheridan was born in London, a granddaughter of the Irish dramatist Richard Brinsley Sheridan. She married a dissolute barrister, the Hon George Chapple Norton (1800–75), in 1827 and bore him three sons.

She took up writing to support the family, and published a successful book of verse, *The Sorrows of Rosalie* (1829).

In 1836 she separated from her husband, who brought an action of 'criminal conversation' (adultery) against her friend the Prime Minister Lord Melbourne, obtained custody of the children and tried to obtain the profit from her books. Her spirited pamphlets led to improvements in the legal status of women in relation to infant custody (1839) and marriage and divorce (1857). She married Sir William Stirling-Maxwell in 1877, but died soon afterwards.

Her other books of verse included an attack on child labour in *Voice from the Factories* (1836), *The Dream* (1840) and *The Lady of Garaye* (1862), and she also published three novels. She was the model for George Meredith's central character in his novel *Diana of the Crossways* (1885).

Norton, Mary, *née* Pearson

Born 1903 Died 1992
English children's novelist known for her stories about the Borrowers

Mary Norton was born in Leighton Buzzard, Bedfordshire, and the splendid Georgian house where she spent her childhood became the setting for several of her stories. She wanted to become an actress and joined **Lilian Baylis's** Old Vic Theatre Company in the 1920s, but marriage in 1927 to Robert Norton took her to Portugal, where she first began to write, and later to America during World War II.

She published *The Magic Bed-knob* in America in 1943, the year of her return to Britain. Its British edition appeared two years later, followed in 1947 by her second book, *Bonfires and Broomsticks*; the two were later combined as *Bed-knob and Broomstick* (1957).

But it was *The Borrowers* (1952), an enchanting story about tiny people living beneath the floorboards of a big house, which established her reputation. It won the Carnegie Medal and had four sequels, the last being *The Borrowers Avenged* (1982).

Norton, Mary Teresa Hopkins, *née* Hopkins

Born 1875 Died 1959
American politician who championed the rights of working women and combatted racial discrimination

Mary Hopkins Norton was born in Jersey City, New Jersey. In 1912 she formed a non-sec-tarian day-care centre for children of working women. She was its secretary for three years and president for 12 years. She became the first woman to serve on the New Jersey State Democratic Committee, serving as either vice-chair or chair from 1921 to 1944.

In 1925 she was elected to US Congress, where she served until 1951, the first woman to be in that position on her own political strength. As the first woman to head a congressional committee, she chaired the District of Columbia Committee. She became chair of the Labor Committee in 1937, and fought successfully for the Fair Labor Standards Act.

Novak, Helga, *pseud of* Helga Maria Karlsdottir

Born 1935
German writer who examines the interface between political issues and personal experience

Helga Karlsdottir was born in Berlin. She lived first in East Germany, then (from 1961 to 1970) in Iceland, and since then in her native city. She could not publish until 1965, when her first collection of satirical poems, *Ballada von der reisenden Anna* ('Ballad of Wandering Anna'), an early criticism of the socialist government's repressive policies, appeared. She was forced out of East Germany in 1966 and settled in West Germany.

Her most characteristic work is the overtly feminist and, once more, satirical *Eines Tages hat sich die Sprechpuppe nicht mehr ausziehen lassen* (1972, 'One Day the Talking Doll Refused to be Undressed'). Translations of her work are available in *German Women Writers of the Twentieth Century* (1978). Her two-volume autobiography — *Die Eisheiligen* (1979, 'Saints of Ice') and *Vogel Federlos* (1982, 'Featherless Bird') — provides important comment on Germany before, during and after World War II.

Nur Jahan, *originally* Mih-run-Nisa

Born 1571 Died 1645
Powerful wife of the Mughal Emperor Jahangir (ruled 1605–27)

Mih-run-Nisa was the daughter of Itimadud-daula, who was made joint Diwan by her future husband Jahangir, who was the eldest son of Emperor Akbar the Great. After the death of her first husband, Sher Afghan Kan, she became lady-in-waiting to Jahangir's step-mother. In 1611 she married Jahangir, who honoured her as his favourite wife with the name Nur Jahan, 'Light of the World'.

Along with her father and brother, whom

Jahangir had already honoured, and in alliance with Jahangir's third son Prince Khurram (Shah Jahan), Nur Jahan formed a group or *junta* which 'managed' Jahangir (who may have had a tendency to drink) and his political activities. This led to the division of the court into two factions. Although her precise political role in this period is not clear, Nur Jahan was a dominant figure in the royal household and set new fashions based on Persian traditions.

Nyro, Laura

Born 1947
American singer-songwriter whose work has been influential

Laura Nyro was born in the Bronx, New York. As a child she was enrolled at the High School of Music and Art. Her first recording was *More Than a New Discovery* (1966). The following year she sang at the Monterey Rock Festival, but, as on record, her music and her delivery proved to be too subtle and understated for the majority of rock fans.

Many of her best songs were made hits by other artists, such as **Barbra Streisand** and the Fifth Dimension; they include 'Blowin' Away', 'Stoned Soul Picnic' and 'Time and Love'. Her albums *Eli and the Second Coming* (1968) and *New York Tendaberry* (1969) were critical if not commercial successes and influenced a later generation of songwriters.

Nzinga

Died 1663
Queen of Matamba who fought to establish a kingdom independent of the Portuguese

Nzinga was a royal princess of the Ndongo (a small kingdom adjoining the Portuguese colony of Angola). In 1623 she went personally to Angola to negotiate with the governor and was baptized a Christian as Dona Aña de Souza.

The following year she was driven out of Ndongo by Portuguese troops. She created the new kingdom of Matamba, where she trained up military élites to resist the Portuguese. She also allied herself with the Dutch following their capture of Luanda, the Angolan capital, in 1641.

Although she had abandoned Christianity, she re-converted towards the end of her life, by which time Matamba had become a thriving commercial kingdom (largely through acting as a broker in the Portuguese slave-trade).

O

Oakley, Ann, *née* Titmuss

Born 1944
British sociologist, writer, and feminist

Ann Titmuss was educated at Chiswick Poly-technic and Somerville College, Oxford. She married Robin Oakley in 1964 but they later divorced.

Since 1991 she has been Professor of Sociology and head of the Thomas Coram Research Unit at the Institute of Education, University of London. She is a prolific writer and her work focuses largely on gender roles.

Her best-known work in recent years is *The Men's Room* (1988) which was made into a BBC television serial. Other works include *Sex, Gender and Society* (1972), *The Sociology of Housework* (1974), *Scenes Originating in the Garden of Eden* (1993) and *Essays on Women, Medicine and Health* (1994), as well as two books on which she collaborated with **Juliet Mitchell**, *The Rights and Wrongs of Women* (1976) and *What is Feminism* (1986).

Annie Oakley

Oakley, Annie, *stage-name of* Phoebe Anne Oakley Moses

Born 1860 Died 1926
American rodeo star and sharp-shooter whose remarkable skill became legendary

Phoebe Anne Oakley Moses was born into an Ohio Quaker family. She learned to shoot at an early age, helping to provide food for her family after her father's death, and married Frank E Butler in 1880 after defeating him in a shooting match. They formed a trick-shooting act, and from 1885 toured widely with the Buffalo Bill Wild West Show.

A tiny woman just under five feet tall, she shot cigarettes from her husband's lips, and could shoot through the pips of a playing card tossed in the air (hence an 'Annie Oakley' for a punched free ticket).

She retired in 1922 and her story was fictionalized in the Irving Berlin musical comedy *Annie Get Your Gun* (1946), starring **Ethel Merman**.

Oates, Joyce Carol

Born 1938
American writer whose award-winning work examines the meaning of violence in US culture

Joyce Carol Oates was born in Millersport, New York, and educated at Syracuse University and the University of Wisconsin. She married Raymond Smith in 1961, taught English at the University of Detroit (1961–7), then was appointed Professor of English at the University of Windsor in Ontario. Her first published novel was *With Shuddering Fall* (1964)

She became a prolific novelist, story writer and essayist. Her fiction, which is splintered with violence and impressive in its social scope, challenges received ideas about the nature of human experience. *Them* (1969), her fourth novel, won a National Book award. Later novels include *Marya: A Life* (1986) and *You Must Remember This* (1989). Her interest in pugilism emerged in *On Boxing* (1987), first published in the *Ontario Review*, with which she has long had a connection.

O'Brien, Edna

Born 1932
Irish novelist, short-story writer and playwright

Edna O'Brien was born in Tuamgraney, County Clare, and educated at the Convent of Mercy, Loughrea, and at the Pharmaceutical College of Dublin, following which she practised pharmacy briefly before becoming a writer. 'My aim', she has written, 'is to write books that in some way celebrate life and do justice to my emotions'.

Among her celebrated books are *The Country Girls* (1960), which was an early and shockingly frank expression of female sexuality, *The Lonely Girl* (1962), *Girls in Their Married Bliss* (1964), *August is a Wicked Month* (1965) and *A Pagan Place* (1970). *The Collected Edna O'Brien*, containing nine novels, was published in 1978, and she has also published several collections of short stories. Recent novels include a collection of *The Country Girls Trilogy* with an epilogue (1986), and *The High Road* (1988).

She has also written a number of plays and screenplays, a book of verse, *On the Bone* (1989), and some non-fiction.

O'Brien, Kate

Born 1897 Died 1974
Irish playwright and novelist whose writing broke new ground in Irish literature

Kate O'Brien was born in Limerick and educated at Laurel Hill Convent, Limerick, and University College, Dublin. At 30 she began a career in London as playwright and in 1931 she published *Without My Cloak*, which won the Hawthornden Prize, followed by *Mary Lavelle* (1936), *Pray for the Wanderer* (1938), *The Land of Spices* (1941), *The Last of Summer* (1943), *That Lady* (1946) and *As Music and Splendour* (1958).

A remarkable observer of life, she was injured by a deeply unhappy marriage to the Dutch historian Gustaaf Johannes Renier, and

her novels are best understood through appreciation of her consciousness of a lesbian sexual identity.

Her work reflected deep knowledge of Ireland and Spain as may be seen from her *Farewell Spain* (1937) and *My Ireland* (1962).

Ocampo, Silvina

Born 1903 Died 1993
*Argentinian writer who with her sister **Victoria Ocampo** was one of the most important women writers in Latin America*

Silvina Ocampo was born into a wealthy family in Buenos Aires. She and her husband Adolfo Bioy Casares held an influential literary *tertulia* (conversation group) which included writers and poets like Jorge Luis Borges, **María Luisa Bombal** and Ezequiel Martinez Estrada.

Ocampo wrote dramatic and amorous poetry, as well as collections of short stories and juvenile fiction. Her titles include *Sonetos del jardin* (1948, 'Garden Sonnets') and the short-story collection *Informe del cielo y del infierno* ('Report on Heaven and Earth'). She was also an accomplished painter.

Ocampo, Victoria

Born 1891 Died 1979
Argentinian writer who made her reputation as the driving force behind the literary journal Sur

Victoria Ocampo was born into a wealthy family in Buenos Aires. She lived in Paris and London as a child, and learned French, English and Italian. She and her sister **Silvina Ocampo** earned a reputation as Latin America's most important early 20th-century women writers.

Victoria Ocampo is most highly regarded as the editor and motivational force behind one of Latin America's major literary journals, *Sur*, which combined the mission of publishing new Latin-American writers (like Jorge Luis Borges) and translations of major North American and European writers.

Her literary creations are extensive, including biography (*338171 T.E.*, 1942, a biography of T S Eliot), essays and criticism (*Testimonios* is a 10-volume collection of these), novels and translations.

O'Cathain, Detta O'Cathain, Baroness

Born 1938
Irish businesswoman who was MD of London's Barbican Centre for nearly five years

Detta O'Cathain was educated in Limerick and at University College, Dublin. In 1968 she married Bill Bishop, an organ scholar. She became an expert in economics and marketing and worked her way up through the ranks of private-sector industry, from Aer Lingus through Tarmac, Rootes, Vyella, British Leyland and Unigate to the Milk Marketing Board, which she headed in 1985–8, proving herself extremely capable.

In 1990 she was appointed managing director of the Barbican Centre in the City of London, reputedly the biggest arts centre in Europe. She won increased funding from the City of London, which owns the Barbican Centre, procured enhanced funding for the London Symphony Orchestra, and won a £9.7 million refurbishment of the Centre.

Despite these and other successes, O'Cathain's management style was not that of the professional arts-loving impresario that the great arts centre appeared to need and she left in November 1994. She was awarded a life peerage in 1991.

Sandra Day O'Connor with President George Bush, 1991

O'Connor, (Mary) Flannery

Born 1925   Died 1964
American novelist who is also regarded as one of the finest short-story writers of her generation

Flannery O'Connor was born in Savannah, Georgia, whose environs she rarely left during her short life. She was educated at Peabody High School, Midgeville, Georgia, graduating in 1942. Thereafter she attended Georgia State College for Women and the University of Iowa. Brought up a Catholic and in the 'Christ-haunted' Bible-belt of the Deep South, she homed in on the Protestant fundamentalists who dominated the region.

The characters in her work seem superficially similar to those photographed by **Diane Arbus**: grotesque, deformed, freakish. This to her, however, was reality, and her heightened depicton of it is unforgettable. *Wise Blood* (1952), the first of her two novels, is a bizarre tragi-comedy, and its theme of vocation is taken up again in her second, *The Violent Bear It Away* (1960).

Her brilliant work in the short-story form can be found in *A Good Man Is Hard To Find and other stories* (1955) ('nine stories about original sin') and *Everything That Rises Must Converge* (1965), affected by the pain she was suffering in the closing stages of chronic disseminated lupus. *The Habit of Being: Letters of Flannery O'Connor* was published in 1979.

O'Connor, Sandra Day, *née* Day

Born 1930
American judge and first woman to become associate justice of the US Supreme Court

Sandra Day was born in El Paso, Texas. She studied law and was admitted to the Bar in California but then took up practice in Arizona, where she became assistant attorney-general (1965–9) and then a state senator.

She was then a superior court judge of Maricopa County (1974–9) and a judge of the Arizona Court of Appeals (1979–81) before being named an associate justice of the Supreme Court of the US, the first woman to attain that office.

Octavia, *known as* Octavia Minor

Born c.69BC   Died 11BC
Roman wife of Mark Antony who abandoned her for **Cleopatra**

Octavia was the daughter of Gaius Octavius and his second wife Atia, and sister of Octavian (later the emperor Augustus). Distinguished for her beauty and 'womanly' virtues, she married Gaius Marcellus and had two daughters and a son.

On the death of her husband she consented in 40BC to marry Marcus Antonius (Mark Antony), a marriage that was intended to reconcile him and her brother. When there was a dispute between them in 37BC, Octavia's influence resulted successfully in the Treaty of Tarentum. In 36BC Antony travelled east to fight and once in Egypt he continued his affair with **Cleopatra**, for whom he forsook and divorced Octavia in 32BC.

After his death in 30BC Octavia faithfully looked after her children together with Antony's by both first wife Fulvia (d.40BC) and by Cleopatra (d.30BC).

O'Day, Anita, *professional name of* Anita Belle Colton

Born 1919
American jazz vocalist

Anita Colton was born in Kansas City, Missouri. She started out as a marathon dancer (during which time she adopted her new name), but was spotted singing by drummer and bandleader Gene Krupa and joined him in 1941. Apart from a brief stint with Stan Kenton's 'modernist' band, she remained with Krupa for five years, during which time she recorded the hit 'Let Me Off Uptown'.

Her subsequent career was interrupted by the narcotics problems frankly discussed in her autobiography *High Times, Hard Times* (1981), but she made a brilliant return at the Newport Festival in 1958, a performance documented in the film *Jazz on a Summer's Day.*

She is a practical feminist like **Betty Carter**, and has founded her own label, Emily Records. Renewed health has sustained an active career into the 1990s.

Odetta, *originally* Odetta Holmer Gordon Shead Minter

Born 1930
African-American singer who was drawn to the reforming aspect of folk

Odetta was born in Birmingham, Alabama. Deeply affected by the social reform associated with folk-singers, she taught herself to play the guitar and started singing in Los Angeles and New York's Greenwich Village.

Her eclectic repertoire contains gospel, blues, spirituals and folk-songs, such as 'Old Cotton Fields at Home', 'Sometimes I Feel Like A Motherless Child' and 'Blowin' in the Wind'.

Ogilvie, Bridget Margaret

Born 1938
Australian parasitologist and director of the Wellcome Trust, the major British medical research charity

Bridget Ogilvie was born in Glen Innes, New South Wales. She studied agricultural science before undertaking postgraduate research at the University of Cambridge. After obtaining her PhD she became a member of the scientific staff of the Medical Research Council's National Institute for Medical Research in London, working in the Parasitology Division.

Her work focused on the biology of intestinal parasites, especially the worm *Nippostrongylus*, and the immune responses of their infected hosts. After secondment to the Wellcome Trust in 1979, the direction of her career changed towards scientific administration and she joined the Trust full time, becoming its director in 1991. In 1993 she was the only woman appointed to the Council of Science and Technology.

O'Hara, Maureen, *originally* Maureen Fitzsimons

Born 1929
Irish actress and flame-haired beauty who frequently played opposite John Wayne

Maureen O'Hara was born near Dublin and joined the Abbey Players at the age of 14. She made her film début in *Kicking The Moon* (1938) and her Hollywood début as the gypsy Esmerelda in *The Hunchback of Notre Dame* (1939). Over the next three decades she proved the equal of any man as a swashbuckling spitfire in such adventure yarns as *The Black Swan* (1942) and *At Sword's Point* (1952).

Often cast as fiery shrews tamed by chauvinistic males, she was a favourite co-star of John Wayne (1907–79), with whom she appeared in such films as *The Quiet Man* (1952), *McLintock* (1963) and *Big Jake* (1971).

She returned to the screen, little changed after a 20-year absence, in *Only The Lonely* (1991).

O'Keeffe, Georgia

Born 1887 Died 1986
American painter known for her abstract depictions of desert landscapes

Georgia O'Keeffe was born in Sun Prairie, Wisconsin. She studied at several prominent art schools, including the Art Institute of Chicago, and later headed the art department of the West Texas Normal School, now West Texas State University.

She devoted herself full-time to art from 1918, and in 1924 married the photographer and art dealer Alfred Stieglitz (1864–1946), who was responsible for bringing many European *avant-garde* works to the USA.

Now regarded as a pioneer of modernism in the USA, she became known for her abstract paintings, not of geometrical shapes, but of the detail of plants (eg *Black Iris*, 1949). She settled in New Mexico, and the southwest desert strongly influenced her paintings. Works such as 'Summer Days' depict the colours, flowers, and animal bones found in the desert landscape.

Oldfield, Anne

Born 1683 Died 1730
English actress, one of the most popular actresses of her time

Anne Oldfield was born in London. She was allegedly 'discovered' by the Irish playwright George Farquhar, by whom she was loved, though she never married. She was encouraged by John Vanbrugh and made her début in 1700. It was not until 1704 however, when Colley Cibber recognized her talent and cast her as Lady Betty Modish in *The Careless Husband*, that her reputation was secure.

By 1705 she had become one of the most popular actresses of her time. Around 1706 she began to take over from **Anne Bracegirdle** and played such roles as Mrs Millamant in *The Way of the World*. Other roles in which she excelled were Lady Townley in the *Provoked Husband* and Calista in Nicholas Rowe's *Fair Penitent*.

Equally successful in comedy and tragedy, she continued to act until the last year of her life. She was the first actress to be buried in Westminster Abbey, but was given no monument due to having had two illegitimate children.

Olga, St, *also called* Helga

Born c.890 Died c.969
Russian saint, princess and Russia's first female ruler, sought to spread Christianity in Russia

Olga was married to Prince Igor of Kiev, who was murdered in 945 when he tried to impose crippling taxes. She seems to have been the first female ruler in Russia, and ruled Kiev during the minority of her son Syvatoslav (945–64), a period that she commenced with ruthless revenge on Igor's murderers.

She was also the first member of the ruling family to embrace Christianity, being baptized at Constantinople (c.657). On her return to Russia, she became a champion of the new creed. Although Svyatoslav remained a pagan, her grandson, later St Vladimir I, continued the christianization of Russia.

Olga is the first saint of the Russian Orthodox Church, and her feast day (observed by Russian and Ukrainian Churches) is 11 July.

Oliphant, Margaret, *née* Wilson

Born 1828 Died 1897
Scottish novelist who wrote prolifically, often using the background of small-town life

Margaret Wilson was born in Wallyford, Midlothian. When she was 10 years old her family moved to England. At that time she took her name from her mother; little is known about her father, Francis Wilson, except that he once 'took affadavits' in a Liverpool customs house. She was a precocious teenager, and wrote a novel when she was 16, but her first published work was *Passages in the Life of Mrs Margaret Maitland* (1849). Two years later she began her lifelong connection with the Edinburgh publishers Blackwood and *Blackwood's Magazine*, which culminated in a history of the firm that was published posthumously (1897). In 1852 she married her cousin, Frances Oliphant, an artist, but she was widowed in 1859 and found herself £1,000 in debt with an extended family to support and educate.

Her output was astonishing and uneven, hardly surprising in an author who wrote almost 100 novels, the best known of which are in the group known as *The Chronicles of Carlingford*, consisting of *The Rector and the Doctor's Family* (1863), *Salem Chapel* (1863), *The Perpetual Curate*, (1864), *Miss Majoribanks* (1866) and *Phoebe Junior* (1876), which have earned her the sobriquet, a 'feminist Trollope'. She wrote novels of Scottish life, including *The Minister's Wife* (1869), *Effie Ogilvie* (1886) and *Kirsteen* (1890). Other notable works include *Hester* (1883), *Lady Car* (1889), *The Railway Man and His Children* (1891) and *Sir Robert's Fortune* (1895).

She was awarded a Civil List pension in 1868, but her industry was unabated and she produced a spate of biographies, literary histories, translations, travel books, tales of the supernatural, and an autobiography (1899).

Olive, 'Princess', *assumed title of* Mrs Olivia Serres, *née* Wilmot

Born 1772 Died 1834
English impostor who claimed to be due a legacy as the niece of George III

Olivia Wilmot was born in Warwick, the daughter of a house painter. She became an artist, exhibiting at the Royal Academy (1794–1808), and in 1806 was appointed landscape painter to George, Prince of Wales (later George IV).

In 1817 she claimed to be an illegitimate daughter of the Duke of Cumberland, brother of George III, then in 1821 had herself rechristened as Princess Olive, legitimate daughter of the Duke and his first wife, Olive. Also in 1821 she was arrested for debt, but managed to produce an alleged will of George III, leaving £15,000 to her as his brother's daughter. However in 1823 her claims were found to be baseless, and she died in the King's Bench Prison.

Her elder daughter, Mrs Lavinia Ryves (1797–1871), took up her mother's claim of legitimacy, which a jury finally repudiated in 1866.

Oliver, Mary Jane

Born 1935
American poet whose work has earned comparison
with that of Robert Frost

Mary Jane Oliver is not to be confused with the Spanish writer Maria Oliver. She was born in Ohio and educated at the state university, but has spent most of her adult life in Provincetown, Massachusetts.

She was awarded a Pulitzer Prize in 1984 for *American Primitive* (1983) which, like all her work, contained modest reflections on the pastoral life. She has, especially since her move to New England, been compared with Robert Frost.

Any malevolence to be found in her poetry is seen as ultimately friendly and controllable.

Oliveros, Pauline

Born 1932
American accordionist and composer mainly of
electronic music who teaches the usefulness of
mediation as a guide to improvisation

Pauline Oliveros was born in Houston, Texas, and educated at the university there. She joined the improvising group Sonics in 1961, the year she became co-director of the San Francisco Tape Music Center. Since 1967, she has taught at the University of California, San Diego.

Oliveros has written a substantial body of music for her own instrument, including *The Roots of the Moment* (1987), as well as for other forces; *To Valerie Solanas and Marilyn Monroe in Recognition of their Desperation* (1970) is one of her few orchestral pieces. In the 1980s, Oliveros founded and led a movement called 'Deep Listening', the philosophy of which is anticipated in her texts *Pauline's Proverbs* (1976) and *Software for People* (1981).

Olsen, Tillie, *née* Lerner

Born 1913
American novelist, critic, short-story writer and
lecturer on her working-class feminist analysis

Tillie Lerner was born in Omaha, Nebraska, to Russian–Jewish parents. She did not publish her first volume of stories, *Tell Me A Riddle*, until 1962, when she was almost 50. A novel, *Yonnondio: From the Thirties*, followed in 1974 and *Silences*, a collection of essays, four years later.

Her writing draws upon her own working-class experiences and identifies poverty as being the root of individual despair and political oppression. In the title story of *Tell Me A Riddle*, an elderly working-class woman looks back over her life and blames the failure of her hopes upon the pressures of being a wife and mother, while in the novel, a young woman recounts her family's journey from country to city in a disastrous attempt to find economic salvation.

Olympias

Born c.375BC Died 316BC
Queen of Macedon as the wife of Philip II (ruled
359–336BC), and mother of Alexander the Great

Olympias was the daughter of King Neoptolemus of Epirus. She married Philip II of Macedon in 359BC, but he divorced her and in 337BC married Cleopatra, niece of Attalus. He was assassinated the following year and succeeded by Alexander 'the Great'.

On her divorce Olympias returned to Epirus, which she ruled by herself, meanwhile gaining great influence during her son's rule (336–232BC). She is said to have brought about the murder of Cleopatra. After Alexander's death in 323BC she returned to Macedon, where she secured the death of his half-brother and successor, and made Alexander's posthumous son, Alexander IV, king.

Eventually Cassander (the regent Antipater's son who had failed to succeed on his father's death in 319BC and now waged war against Polyperchon who had succeeded as regent) besieged her in Pydna, and on its surrender put her to death.

Onassis, Jackie (Jacqueline) Kennedy, *née* Lee Bouvier

Born 1929 Died 1994
American First Lady as the glamorous wife of
President John F Kennedy, and an influential
fashion leader

Jackie Lee Bouvier was born in Southampton, New York, and was a photographer with the Washington *Times–Herald* in 1952. She married John F Kennedy in 1953 and during his presidency (1961–3), she supervised the restoration of the White House and wielded a powerful and widespread influence on fashion.

Her simple outfits of shift dresses worn knee-length under overblouses started a craze, as did her gilt-chained bags, white gloves and low-heeled shoes. Young women all over the world copied her hatless ensembles, wearing hairbands, bows and pillboxes on combed-back hair as she did.

After her husband's assassination she returned to private life, and in 1968 she married Aristotle Onassis, the Greek shipping magnate. She later worked with Viking Publications (1975–7), and Doubleday and Co as editor (1978–82).

Ono No Komachi

Born c.810   Died c.880
Japanese poet who is known in Japan as one of the Six Poetic Geniuses

Ono No Komachi was born probably in Kyoto in the classical period of Japanese literature. Like many of the other great figures of classical literature in Japan, she was a court poet, writing in a rarefied form of the vernacular — it was more common for men to write in a form of Chinese, which is why so much surviving classical Japanese literature is by women (see **Shikibu Murasaki**). She was a supreme writer of the verse form *tanka*.

Ono, Yoko

Born 1933
Japanese artist, writer, singer and campaigner who married John Lennon

Yoko Ono was born in Tokyo. She moved to the USA after World War II, married the composer Toshi Ichiyanagi (later divorced) and established a reputation as an avant-garde filmmaker, occasionally branching out into experimental music. She married John Lennon (1940–80) in 1969, and was criticised for her role in the Beatles' break-up in 1970.

She subsequently became Lennon's collaborator in the Plastic Ono Band and in various well-publicized peace protests. Her book *Grapefruit* (1970) and album *Approximately Infinite Universe* (1972) suggest she was more talented than detractors still claim.

Since Lennon's murder, she has protected his unpublished work and continued to campaign for peace.

Opie, Iona

Born 1923
English folklorist and specialist in children's literature

Iona married Peter Mason Opie (1918–82) in 1943 and the birth of their first child prompted them to study the folklore of childhood. This culminated in *The Oxford Book of Nursery Rhymes* (1951), acknowleged widely for its scholarship as well as its sense of humour.

Through their work on this they amassed the peerless Opie Collection of children's books which is now housed in the Bodleian Library. In 1993 Iona published *The People in the Playground*, based on the research she had done with her husband for their earlier books. Iona also collects publications by contemporary illustrators.

Orbach, Susie

Born 1946
British-American psychotherapist and feminist author who confronts the fears raised by differences between the sexes

Susie Orbach was born in London, and studied in both London and New York. She became a psychotherapist in 1972, co-founding the Women's Therapy Centre in London in 1976, and the Women's Therapy Centre Institute in New York in 1981.

Her book *Fat is a Feminist Issue* (1976) addresses women's mixed feelings about food, fat and femininity, and argues that dieting and the obsession with food that it induces, actually makes women fat. Her later works include *Understanding Women* (1982, co-authored) and *Hungerstrike* (1985).

In 1991 she presented the BBC television programme *Behind the Headlines*, as well as becoming a columnist for *The Guardian* newspaper. The latter post gave her a platform for tackling topical issues and their relation to psychoanalysis, and for re-defining the role of the psychotherapist in contemporary society.

Orczy, Emmuska, Baroness

Born 1865   Died 1947
Hungarian-born British novelist and playwright remembered for The Scarlet Pimpernel

Emmuska Orczy was born in Tarnaörs, the daughter of a musician. *The Scarlet Pimpernel* (1905) was the first success in the Baroness's long writing career. It was followed by many popular adventure romances, including *The Elusive Pimpernel* (1908) and *Mam'zelle Guillotine* (1940), which never quite attained the success of her early work.

Orzeskowa, Eliza

Born 1841   Died 1910
Polish realistic novelist who was one of the most educated women of her time

Eliza Orzeskowa was born in Grodno, and her notable work is mostly associated with the surrounding area. Her extensive education was largely owing to her enlightened father's library. She was associated with the 'Positivist' movement — a reaction to the 'romanticism' which had led to the unsuccessful uprisings of 1863–4 — and her huge fictional output deals with 'ordinary people', though she gradually became more idealistic.

As a whole, her work, which has been undervalued until recently, may be compared to that of the French novelist Honoré de Balzac (1799–1850). She dealt with women, Jews, and — adeptly — with political censors. Her books remain eminently readable.

Novels available in English include *Meir Ezofowicz* (1878, Eng trans *An Obscure Apostle*, 1898), *Argonauci* (1899, Eng trans *The Modern Argonauts*, 1901), and *Piesn Przerwana* (1896, Eng trans *The Interrupted Melody*, 1912).

La Belle Otero, 1904

O'Shane, Pat(ricia)

Born 1941
Australian lawyer, the first person of Aboriginal descent to become a barrister

Pat O'Shane was born in Mossman, Queensland, the daughter of an Irish father and Aboriginal mother. She trained at the University of New South Wales, the first Aborigine to graduate in law there, and was called to the Bar in 1976.

She was head of the Ministry of Aboriginal Affairs of the state of New South Wales from 1981 to 1986, when she became a magistrate in the local courts. She is known for her progressive attitude, as shown especially in decisions concerning women and Aboriginal people.

Oslin, K(ay) T(oinette)

Born 1941
American country singer and songwriter

K T Oslin was born in Crossett, Arkansas. Her album *80's Ladies* garnered her a Grammy award in 1987 for Country-Best Vocal Performance-Female. The 1988 album, *Hold Me*, won two Grammys — for Country-Best Song and Country-Best Female Vocal Performance.

In 1988 Oslin was declared Top Female Vocalist of the Year by the Academy of Country Music.

Otero, La Belle, *originally* Caroline Puentovalga

Born 1868 Died 1965
Spanish dancer and courtesan whose list of lovers reads like an International Who's Who

Caroline Puentovalga was born in Cádiz, the daughter of a gypsy woman whose lover killed Caroline's father in a duel. She took her first lover when she was 12 or 13 and ran away with him to Lisbon where she began her career on the stage. About the age of 16 she married an Italian baritone and moved to Paris, but he soon gambled their money away and she turned again to singing and dancing, quickly gaining a reputation for her beauty and sensuality and receiving offers of work from all over Europe.

By the time she had spent a period in the USA, she had acquired a stream of lovers and immense wealth in jewels and money, which she gambled away in the subsequent years. Among her lovers were tsar Nicholas II (shortly before his engagement to **Alexandra (Alix) Feodorovna**), Edward Prince of Wales (later Edward VII of England), Kaiser Wilhelm I of Germany, the US financier Cornelius Vanderbilt, multi-millionaire Joseph Kennedy, the Italian poet Gabriele d'Annunzio, and King Alfonso of Spain.

Otto, Kristin

Born 1966
German swimmer who won six gold medals for East Germany in the 1988 Olympics

Kristin Otto was born in Leipzig. Between 1982 and 1986 she won a total of seven world championship medals — three individual and four relay — and between 1983 and 1989 she won nine gold medals at the European Cup — four individual and five relay.

By winning six gold medals in the 1988 Olympics, she broke the record for the most medals won by any woman in one sport at the same Olympic Games. They were for the 50 metres freestyle, 100 metres freestyle, 100 metres butterfly, 100 metres backstroke, and two relay races.

Otto was also the first woman to break the minute barrier for the 100 metres backstroke in a short course (25m) pool. She is now a coach and commentator.

Otto-Peters, Luise, *née* Otto

Born 1819 Died 1895
German novelist who became a revolutionary before taking up the pen again as a propaganda weapon

Luise Otto was orphaned at the age of 16, but she completed her education and began to write, achieving considerable success as a novelist. Using the pseudonym Otto Stern of Konigsberg, she highlighted women's causes in her fiction. In 1848, a year of revolution, she played a more active role, but her demands for female equality and emancipation were in vain.

Following this setback, she propagated her views through journalism. In 1858 she married the revolutionary August Peters, and after his death in 1864 she modified her campaign, later concentrating on the campaign for divorce law reform.

Ouida, *pseud of* Marie Louise de la Ramée

Born 1839 Died 1908
English writer of best-selling popular romantic novels

Marie Louise de la Ramée was born in Bury St Edmunds. Her mother was English, her father a French teacher. 'Ouida' was a childish mispronunciation of 'Louise'. She was educated in Paris, and settled in London in 1857. Starting her career by contributing stories to magazines, in particular to *Bentley's Miscellany* (1859–60), her first success was *Held in Bondage* (1863). This was followed by *Strathmore* (1865), another three-decker aimed at the circulating libraries.

She was soon established as a writer of hothouse romances, often ridiculed for her opulent settings, preposterous heroes, and improbable plots, as well as for her ignorance of male sports and occupations. But her narratives were powerful, readers responded to her emotional energy and until her popularity waned in the 1890s, she was a bestseller. From 1860 she spent much time in Italy and in 1874 settled in Florence where she lived lavishly in a style recognizable from her novels.

She wrote almost 50 books, mainly novels, such as *Under Two Flags* (1867), *Folle-Farine* (1871), which was praised by the writer Edward Bulwer-Lytton, *Two Little Wooden Shoes* (1874), *A Village Commune* (1881) and *In Maremma* (1882) — but also animal stories, essays, and tales for children. Latterly her royalties dried up; she fell into debt, moved to Lucca in 1894, and spent her last years in destitution in Viareggio.

Ozick, Cynthia

Born 1928
American novelist, critic and short-story writer who expresses the Jewish ethos

Cynthia Ozick was born in New York City and educated at New York University and Ohio State University. She has said she began her first novel, *Trust* (1966), as an American writer and ended it six and a half years later a Jewish one.

Her slight but significant oeuvre, characterized by its evocation of central European Jewish culture, includes *The Pagan Rabbit and Other Stories* (1971), *Bloodshed* (1976), *Levitation: Five Fictions* (1982), *The Cannibal Galaxy* (1983) and *The Messiah of Stockholm* (1987).

p

Page, Geraldine

Born 1924   Died 1987
American actress who starred on both stage and screen

Geraldine Page was born in Missouri and trained at the Goodman Theatre Dramatic in School in Chicago. She made her New York début in 1945, but it was not until her success in Tennessee Williams's *Summer and Smoke* in 1952 that she became established there.

Credited with great versatility and sensitivity, her notable roles included Alexandra del Lago in Williams's *Sweet Bird of Youth* (1959) and Mother Miriam Ruth in *Agnes of God* (1982). She acted in many films, and won an Academy Award in 1985 for *The Trip To Bountiful*.

Paglia, Camille

Born 1947
American academic, essay writer, media personality, and internationally recognized public thinker

Camille Paglia was born in Endicott, New York, of Italian parentage. She was educated at Yale University before securing a job teaching at Bennington College (1972–80). She then lectured at Wesleyan University and Yale and became an assistant professor at the Philadelphia College of Performing Arts (now called the University of the Arts) in 1987. Remaining there, she was appointed first associate professor (in 1987) and then Professor of Humanities in 1991.

Described as an anti-feminist feminist with one of the biggest egos in US art and entertainment, Paglia has become renowned both for her powerful intellect, and for being contentious and belligerent in her attempt not only to pour scorn on modern feminism, but also to promote her theory of women as the innately powerful sex whose destiny is neither to serve nor to demean men, but to rule them.

Her publications include *Sexual Personae: Art and Decadence from Nefertiti to Emily Dickinson* (1990), *Sex, Art, and American Culture: Essays* (1992) and *Vamps and Tramps* (1995).

Paige, Elaine, *originally* Elaine Bickerstaff

Born 1952
English actress and singer who rose to fame in stage musicals

Elaine Bickerstaff was born in Barnet. After attending drama school, where she changed her name, she joined the West End cast of *Hair* in 1969, but it was her performances in *Jesus Christ Superstar* (1972) and *Billy* (1974) that established her as a musicals actress.

She appeared at Chichester Festival Theatre and at Stratford East before she became a star as *Evita* in 1978. In 1981 she played in *Cats*, followed by *Chess* (1986) and *Anything Goes* (1989-).

She released her eleventh solo album, *Time and Romance*, in 1993, and the same year starred as **Edith Piaf** in **Pam Gems**'s biographical play *Piaf*.

Paley, Grace, *née* Goodside

Born 1922
American short-story writer and poet who is also an active feminist and pacifist

Grace Paley was born in New York City and educated at Hunter College, New York. She has taught in several US colleges. Her fiction has all been in the short-story form, usually set in New York, and often with Jewish settings and themes.

Her sharp ear for convincingly realistic dialogue is evident in all her stories. Those in *Little Disturbances of Man* (1959) have a wider range of social settings than *Enormous Changes at the Last Minute* (1974), which are all set in the run-down world of inner-city slums, but they share a common wit, compassion, and characteristic tone of voice.

She helped to found the Greenwich Village Peace Center in 1961 and her support of the peace movement is evident in *Later the Same Day* (1985), as well as in the non-fiction *365 Reasons Not to Have Another War* (1989). Other writings include *Begin Again: New and Collected Poems* (1992), and an essay collection, *Long Walks and Intimate Talks* (1991).

Palm, Etta Aelders

Born 1743 Died after 1793
Dutch woman who proclaimed women's rights during the French Revolution

Little is known of the early life of Etta Palm, except that she was born in the Netherlands and already married by the time she settled in Paris some 15 years before the Revolution in 1789.

The highlight of her career as a feminist occurred in 1791, when she led a women's deputation to the newly-established Assembly, arguing for female equality in all aspects of society. She was active in women's revolutionary clubs at grass-roots level, and by 1793 had returned to the Netherlands.

Palmer, Nettie (Janet Gertrude), *née* Higgins

Born 1885 Died 1964
Australian writer who was an influential advocate of new writers

Nettie Higgins was born in Bendigo, Victoria, and educated at Melbourne University. She travelled and studied in Europe, and married the writer Vance Palmer (1885–1959) in London in 1914, creating a partnership that for nearly 40 years dominated the literary left.

She was a prolific writer for contemporary journals but little of her criticism has been collected, except for the ground-breaking *Modern Australian Literature 1900–1923* (1924).

Her major contribution to Australian literature was in the advocacy of other, especially women, writers. She was among the first to recognize the worth of **H H Richardson** and to promote such diverse authors as **Barbara Baynton**, Shaw Nielson and **Katharine Susannah Prichard**.

Pandit, Vijaya Lakshmi, *née* Swarup Kumari Nehru

Born 1900 Died 1990
Indian politician and diplomat, the first woman President of the UN General Assembly

Swarup Kumari Nehru was born in Allahabad in Uttar Pradesh, the sister of Jawaharlal Nehru (Prime Minister 1947–64). She was given her name Vijaya Lakshmi ('victory and prosperity') on the occasion of her marriage in 1921 to advocate Ranjit Pandit (d.1944).

She entered politics in 1935 and was Local Government and Health Minister (1937–9). As a member of the Opposition she was imprisoned in 1940 and 1941 for her nationalist campaigns. On the Congress Party's return to power, she led the Indian delegation to the United Nations (1946–8 and 1952–3), and also held several ambassadorial posts (1947–51). In 1953 she became the first woman President of the UN General Assembly, quickly dispelling any doubts about a woman's ability to hold such high office, and from 1954 to 1961 she was Indian High Commissioner in London.

Outspoken against the policies of her niece **Indira Gandhi**, and subsequently Indira's son and successor Rajiv Gandhi, she took part in the successful campaign against the Congress Party in the 1977 general elections, but declined to take any office afterwards. She later retired to the town of Dehra Dun in the Himalayan foothills to concentrate on her writing. Among her works are *The Evolution of India* (1958) and her memoirs, *The Scope of Happiness* (1979).

Pankhurst, Adela Constantia

Born 1885 Died 1961
English campaigner for the causes of woman suffrage, pacifism and Australia's international policies

Adela Pankhurst was born in Manchester, the youngest daughter of Richard Marsden and **Emmeline Pankhurst**. Like her sisters before her she quickly became involved in the movement for woman suffrage, but disagreements with her mother prompted her to sail for Australia. There she helped direct the socialist-feminist movement with **Vida Goldstein** of the Women's Political Association.

With the outbreak of World War I Adela threw herself into the anti-conscription campaign, holding talks and writing such polemics as *Put up the Sword!* (1915). In 1916 she travelled to New Zealand where she met Tom Walsh, a militant socialist; a year later she had joined the Victorian Socialist Party as an organizer, married Walsh and taken up editing

Dawn, a monthly socialist newsletter for children. Married life saw her pursuing a succession of causes, as a member of both the Australian Women's Guild of Empire (which sought to build Australia as part of the British Empire) and the Australia First Movement (which supported an alliance with Japan). She resigned from the latter following the attack on Pearl Harbour, althought this did not prevent her internment.

Following the death of her husband in 1943, financial need forced her to take work as a nurse for retarded children.

Pankhurst, Christabel Harriette

Born 1880 Died 1958
English militant suffragette and joint founder of
the Women's Social and Political Union (WSPU)

Christabel Pankhurst was born in Manchester, the eldest daughter of Richard Marsden and **Emmeline Pankhurst**. In 1903 she founded the WSPU with her mother in an attempt to further the cause of female suffrage. Although initially a peaceful movement, the militant campaigning that Christabel undertook with **Annie Kenney** in 1905 resulted in their arrest, and stimulated a wave of militant action throughout the country with large-scale imprisonment and forcible feeding of suffragettes. She encouraged such tactics until 1914, when her efforts were channelled into meetings and tours in support of World War I. With the end of the War in 1918 and the granting of the vote to women over the age of 30, Christabel turned to preaching on Christ's Second Coming.

She edited *The Suffragette* from 1912 to 1920, and wrote her political memoirs, *Unshackled: The Story of How We Won the Vote* (1959), at the very end of her life.

Pankhurst, Emmeline, *née* Goulden

Born 1857 Died 1928
English suffragette who is possibly the most
famous name in the fight for women's rights

Emmeline Goulden was born in Manchester. In 1879 she married Richard Marsden Pankhurst (d.1898), a radical Manchester barrister who had been the author of the first women's suffrage bill in Britain and of the Married Women's Property Acts of 1870 and 1882.

In 1889 she founded the Women's Franchise League, and in 1903, with her daughter **Christabel Pankhurst**, the Women's Social and Political Union, which fought for women's suffrage with extreme militancy. The former achieved in 1894 the right for married women to vote in local elections, though not for

Westminster offices. Pankhurst was frequently imprisoned and underwent hunger strikes and force-feeding. She later joined the Conservative party.

Her 40-year campaign reached a peak of success shortly before her death, when the Representation of the People Act of 1928 was finally passed, establishing voting equality for men and women. She wrote her autobiography in *My Own Story* (1914). Her daughter **Sylvia Pankhurst** was also a suffragette.

Pankhurst, (Estelle) Sylvia

Born 1882 Died 1960
English campaigner for woman suffrage, Labour
politics, pacificism and internationalism

Sylvia Pankhurst was born in Manchester, the second of Richard Marsden and **Emmeline Pankhurst**'s three daughters. Scholarships enabled her to study at both the Manchester Municipal School of Art and the Royal College of Art in London; alongside her education she worked in London's East End for the Women's Social and Political Union (WSPU), a suffrage organization founded jointly by her mother and her elder sister, **Christabel Pankhurst**. However her relations with the WSPU deteriorated; in 1913 she left the East End branch and a year later her objections to World War I stood in sharp contrast to the support of Emmeline and Christabel.

An irrepressible campaigner, she wrote extensively advocating not only woman suffrage but also Ethiopian independence, socialism and international and domestic issues. Her works include *The Suffragette Movement* (1931) and *Ethiopia: A Cultural History* (1955).

Paraskeva

Died c.304AD
Early Christian martyr, the patron saint of
working women

Paraskeva came from Iconia, Asia Minor. An eighth-century Life tells of her martyrdom in the Diocletian persecution. When asked to state her name she is said to have ignored the question and explained her faith, arguing that giving the name of eternal life must come before giving the name of temporal existence.

Paraskeva's name in Greek and Russian (Piatnitza) means Friday; the association with market day led her to be regarded, especially by Slavs, as the patron saint of working women and trade.

Pardo Bazán, Emilia, Condesa de

Born 1851 Died 1921
Spanish writer and the first Spanish woman of
note to sustain a feminist campaign

Emilia Pardo Bazán was born into an aristo-cratic Galician family. Her literary vocation was formed early, then developed when the family moved to Madrid. This gave her access to the literary circles of the capital and cultivated her interest in contemporary European thought and affairs; her interests ranged over Darwinism, feminism and science, into Russian and French literature.

Besides her novels, she produced over 500 short stories, articles, criticism, poems and travel literature, as well as giving lectures. She was strongly influenced by the French naturalist writers, and this can be seen in her first novel, *Pascual Lopez* (1879). Her best-known books in this genre are *Los Pazos de Ulloa* (1886, 'The Manors of Ulloa') and *La Madre Naturaleza* (1887, 'Mother Nature'), both set in the rural decadence of her native Galicia. Later novels such as *La Quimera* (1905, 'The Chimera') and *La Sirena Negra* (1908, 'The Black Mermaid') are unmistakably modernist in atmosphere and psychology.

Latterly she came under the influence of *fin-de-siècle* spiritualism and adopted more idealistic values. She also published works on the French novelist Émile Zola (1840–1902) and naturalism, the revolution in Russia, and modern French literature. Amongst many other feminist activities, she ran a library for women.

Pardoe, Julia

Born 1806 Died 1862
English author of historical and descriptive works who travelled widely to gather material

Julia Pardoe was born in Yorkshire, the daughter of an army officer who served at Waterloo. She published her first volume of poems at the age of 13, followed by a historical novel set in the time of William the Conqueror.

In 1835 she travelled with her father to Constantinople (now Istanbul) where she acquired an in-depth knowledge of the East, rivalled only by that of Lady **Mary Wortley Montagu**. On her return she wrote *The City of the Sultan and Domestic Manners of the Turks* (1837).

A later tour of the Austrian Empire produced a set of well-researched historical novels, and in 1847 she began writing historical works on French history including *The Court and Reign of Francis the First* (1849).

Paretsky, Sara N

Born 1947
American crime writer whose feminist concerns find voice through the character of her female detective

Sara N Paretsky was born in Ames, Iowa, and educated at the University of Kansas and the University of Chicago, where she received an MBA and a PhD in history. She worked for a research firm and as a marketing manager for an insurance company, before becoming a full-time writer in 1986. That same year she co-founded Sisters in Crime, an organization devoted to promoting women crime writers.

Her novels feature the feisty female detective V I Warshawski (played on screen by **Kathleen Turner** in 1992), who faces such diverse problems as toxic waste and anti-abortionists. From these situations Paretsky looks at the nature of relationships between women, and at the line between the personal and professional as experienced by her outwardly tough but essentially warm-hearted heroine.

Her later works include *Burn Marks* (1990) and *Guardian Angel* (1992).

Pargeter, Edith, *pseud* Ellis Peters

Born 1913 Died 1995
English novelist and crime writer who popularized 'Mystorical' detective fiction

Edith Pargeter was born in the tiny hamlet of Horsehay in Shropshire. Largely self-educated, she did not attend university, working instead as a chemist's assistant during the 1930s and writing in her spare time. She was a prolific writer for many years, including in her work a string of quietly successful detective novels, many featuring Inspector Felse (*Fallen into the Pit*, 1951, was the first of these).

Real success, however, came when she was in her sixties. On reading about a historical incident in which the relics of St Winifred were moved to Shrewsbury Abbey, she hit upon the idea of Brother Cadfael, a medieval detective. *A Morbid Taste for Bones: A Mediaeval Whodunnit* (1977, as Ellis Peters) was an instant hit, and a series was born. By no means as literary as Umberto Eco's comparable *The Name of the Rose*, the Cadfael books are, nevertheless, prime examples of the sort of quintessentially English detective fiction where there is no gore and anything too unpleasant is described from a discreet distance. The period setting, though a strong selling point, is incidental.

Pargeter was awarded the Crime Writers' Association's highest award, the Diamond Dagger, in 1993.

Park, Maud May, *née* Wood

Born 1871 Died 1955
American suffrage leader and first President of the League of Women Voters

Maud Wood was born in Boston, Massachusetts. She was educated at Radcliffe College, where she had a glittering career, and with Inez Haynes Gillmore (Irwin) she joined the Massachusetts Woman Suffrage Association. In 1897, while still at college, she married an architect, Charles Edward Park, but he died in 1904.

Becoming more deeply involved in woman suffrage issues, she became co-founder and leader of Boston Equal Suffrage Association for Good Government and with Inez Gillmore founded the College Equal Suffrage League in 1901, aiming to involve young women in the fight for equality. In 1908 she was secretly married to a theatrical agent, Robert Hunter (d.1928).

Following the success of the 19th Amendment, which secured the vote for women, she became first President of the League of Women Voters (1920–4), and shortly afterwards head of the Women's Joint Congressional Committee. Following her retirement from the LWV she continued to lecture and advise.

Park, Ruth

Born c.1923
New Zealand-born Australian writer

Ruth Park was born near Hamilton and educated at the University of Auckland. She went to Australia in 1942 and married the author D'Arcy Niland. Her first success was in 1947 with the novel *The Harp in the South*, which won a newspaper competition. This story of slum life in the Surry Hills district of Sydney has been translated into 10 languages and forms a trilogy with *Poor Man's Orange* (1949) and the retrospective *Missus* (1986). *Swords and Crowns and Rings* (1977) won the **Miles Franklin** award for its sensitive tale of an outcast of society.

Park created the popular books based on an ABC children's series about *The Muddle-Headed Wombat* between 1962 and 1981, and has also written novels for adolescent readers including two set in Victorian Sydney, *Come Danger, Come Darkness* (1978) and the haunting *Playing Beatie Bow* (1980, filmed 1987). The autobiographical *A Fence Round the Cuckoo* (1992) was awarded the Foundation for Australian Literature Studies award. A second volume of autobiography was published in 1993 as *Fishing in the Styx*.

Parke, Mary Winifred

Born 1908 Died 1989
English botanist and specialist in phycology, the study of algae

Mary Parke was born and educated in Liverpool, gaining a PhD in 1932 before moving to the university's marine station at Port Erin on the Isle of Man, where she compiled detailed accounts of the life histories and ecology of many species of algae.

During World War II she was transferred to the Marine Biological Association's Laboratory at Plymouth, where she remained until retirement in 1973. There she continued and extended her previous research on the growth of seaweeds, and on the classification of marine plankton, setting high standards for phycology in Britain. Her research has been of international significance for oceanographers and fish farmers.

She was elected to Fellowship of the Royal Society in 1972.

Parker, Agnes Miller

Born 1895 Died 1980
Scottish artist and printmaker particularly skilled in her depiction of light

Agnes Miller Parker was born in Irvine, Ayrshire. She studied at Glasgow School of Art where she also taught for two years. She married the artist William McCance and together they worked at Greggnog press alongside **Gertrude Hermes** and Blair Hughes-Stanton.

Her work was unusual in that she produced brilliant images that could convey any effect of light using a series of bold shapes enhanced by subtle lines from a palette of silvery greys.

The list of her works is long and distinguished and in addition to her work at Greggnog, she illustrated many works for the Limited Edition Club, New York. She moved back to Glasgow in 1962 and later retired to the Island of Arran.

Parker, Bonnie

Born 1911 Died 1934
American thief who with Clyde Barrow formed the notorious partnership 'Bonnie and Clyde'

Bonnie Parker and Clyde Barrow met in 1932 when Parker was working as a waitress. Shortly after, when Barrow was convicted of theft and sentenced to two years in jail, Parker smuggled a gun to him and he escaped. Parker herself spent a short time in jail on suspicion of car theft.

With their gang, which included Barrow's brother and wife, Parker and Barrow continued to rob and murder until they were shot dead in their car by police at a road-block in Louisiana on 23 May 1934. Despite the popular romantic image of the duo as glamorous robbers, they and their gang were also responsible for a number of murders.

Their demise was predicted by Parker in a poem, variously called *The Story of Bonnie and Clyde* and *The Story of Suicide Sal*.

Parker, Dorothy, *née* Rothschild

Born 1893 Died 1967
American wit, writer and co-founder of the
Algonquin Hotel Round Table luncheon group

Dorothy Rothschild was born in West End, New Jersey, the daughter of a clothes salesman. Her mother died when she was five and her father re-married, but Dorothy could barely contain her antipathy to her stepmother and refused to address her. Her formal education ended in 1908 at the age of 14, but she was a voracious reader and, having read Thackeray when she was 11, decided to make literature her life. In 1916 she sold some of her poetry to the editor of *Vogue*, and was given the job of writing captions for fashion photographs and drawings. She then became drama critic of *Vanity Fair* (1917–20), where she met Robert Benchley (1889–1945) and Robert Sherwood (1896–1955) and formed with them the nucleus of the legendary Algonquin Hotel Round Table luncheon group.

Famed for her spontaneous wit and acerbic criticism, she was at her most trenchant in book reviews and stories in the early issues (1927–33) of the *New Yorker*, a magazine whose character she did much to form. Her work continued to appear in the magazine at irregular intervals until 1955. Her reviews were collected in *A Month of Saturdays* (1971). She also wrote for *Esquire* and published poems and sketches. Her poems are included in *Not So Deep as a Well* (1930) and *Enough Rope* (1926), which became a bestseller. Her short stories were collected in *Here Lies* (1936). She also collaborated on several film scripts, including *The Little Foxes* and *A Star Is Born*.

Twice married (1917 and 1933), she took her surname from her first husband. Both marriages foundered, there was a string of lacerating love affairs, abortive suicide attempts, abortions, debts and drinking bouts, and she died alone in a Manhattan apartment with Troy, her poodle, at her side.

Parkes, Bessie Rayner

Born 1829 Died 1925
English feminist and editor of the
Englishwoman's Journal

Bessie Rayner Parkes was born into a Unitarian family, the great-granddaughter of the clergyman and chemist Joseph Priestley (1733–1804). She formed a lifelong friendship with **Barbara Bodichon**, with whom she was a founding member of the women's movement; this included supporting the unsuccessful Married Woman's Property Bill.

In 1858 Parkes bought the *Englishwoman's Journal*, which she edited with the help of Bodichon, **Emily Faithfull** and Jessie Boucherett (owner of *The Englishwoman's Review*). The journal became the voice of the woman's movement.

Parkes married Louis Belloc, a French barrister, in 1867, and became the mother of the future writers Marie Adelaide Belloc (1868–1947, later Mrs Lowndes) and Hilaire Belloc (1870–1953).

Parkin, Sara Lamb

Born 1946
English environmentalist who played an active
role in the Green Party in its early days

Sara Lamb Parkin was educated in Coventry and at Edinburgh Royal Infirmary, and began her working life as a nurse (1973–9). Her environmental career began when she became International Liaison Secretary for the newly-formed Green Party in 1983. She held the post of co-secretary of European Green Coordination (1985–90) and was Speaker for the UK Green Party from 1990 for two years, during which time she frequently appeared on radio and television as a spokesperson for the environmental movement.

Following her resignation she lived in Lyons, France. In 1994 she published *The Life and Death of Petra Kelly* about the co-founder of the German Green Party, her friend and fellow-campaigner **Petra Kelly**, who was discovered shot dead at her Bonn home in October 1992.

Parks, Rosa Lee

Born 1913
American civil rights protester and symbol of the
non-violent protest

Rosa Lee Parks was born in Tuskegee, Alabama. While she was employed as a seamstress, her action as a black woman refusing to give up her seat to a white man on a bus in Montgomery, Alabama, led not only to her imprisonment but also in 1955 to the 381-day Montgomery bus boycott by the black community, which was organized by the young Martin Luther King, Jr. Hers was a test case to challenge segregation, and, together with the boycott, it led to the Supreme Court decision in 1956 that declared bus segregation unconstitutional.

Although both Parks and King belonged to the National Association for the Advancement of Colored People, the movement also resulted in the formation of the Southern Christian Leadership Conference, which was led by clergy and had King as its president. Parks moved to Detroit in 1957 and continued her work in civil rights.

Parr, Catherine

Born 1512 Died 1548
Queen of England as the sixth and last wife of
Henry VIII (ruled 1509–47)

Catherine Parr was the daughter of Sir Thomas Parr of Kendal. She married first Edward Borough, and next Lord Latimer, and in 1543 married King Henry VIII. She was distinguished for her learning and knowledge of religious subjects, her discussion of which with the king almost brought her to the block.

She persuaded Henry to restore the succession to his daughters Mary (**Mary I**) and **Elizabeth**. Very soon after Henry's death (1547) she married a former lover, Lord Thomas Seymour of Sudeley, but died in childbirth the following year at Sudeley Castle near Cheltenham.

Parra, Violeta

Born 1917 Died 1967
Chilean folklorist, songwriter and singer

Violeta Parra was born in San Carlos. She had a varied career, which included a period in Paris (1961–5), and became internationally celebrated. Her whose work inspired the New Chilean Song movement of the later 1960s.

Parren, Kalliroe

Born 1861 Died 1940
Greek teacher who pioneered the campaign for
female equality in Greece

Kalliroe Parren trained as a teacher and spent 10 years as headmistress of a girls' school before deciding to give up her promising career to become a journalist advocating women's rights in her native Greece. She had already started a woman's newspaper, directly addressing her fellow Greeks about the discrimination against them, as well as providing practical information on matters important to them.

Parren represented her country at international women's conferences, as well as founding three national bodies to advance the cause of women in Greece. While her objective of female emanciaption was not achieved until after her death, she is regarded as the pioneer of women's rights in her own country.

Parsons, Emily Elizabeth

Born 1824 Died 1880
American woman who overcame deafness and
partial blindness to tend the wounded during the
Civil War

Emily Parsons was born into comfortable surroundings in Cambridge, Massachusetts. She overcame a number of physical disabilities, including complete deafness and partial sight, to forge a career for herself as a nurse at the age of 37. She insisted on working in army hospitals as the Civil War raged, and soon became Supervisor of Nurses at the 2,500-bed Benton Barracks Hospital.

When malaria forced her to return to the family home in Cambridge, for she had never married, she organized a local hospital; this was the forerunner of the present Cambridge Hospital, founded six years after her death.

Parsons, Louella Oettinger

Born 1881 Died 1972
American gossip columnist who held sway during
the heyday of the Hollywood studio system

Louella Parsons was born in Freeport, Illinois. Few reliable details of her early years remain, a fact as much attributable to her embroidered accounts of the past as to the vagaries of history. She became a reporter for the *Chicago Tribune* in 1910 and also wrote screenplays for silent films, publishing the book *How to Write for the Movies* in 1915. In New York from 1919 and Hollywood from 1926, she rose to prominence writing a daily, syndicated gossip column on the lives and loves of Hollywood movie stars.

Feared within the film community for her influence, in time she could make or break a career and was said to have 'ruled as a queen'. She also hosted a number of radio shows, including *Hollywood Hotel* (1934–8), and wrote the books *The Gay Illiterate* (1944) and *Tell It To Louella* (1961).

She retired in 1964, but remains a symbol of an era when the Hollywood dream factory dominated the world's cinema screens, when movie stars were treated as gods and when all of them 'told it' to Louella.

Dolly Parton, 1983

Parton, Dolly

Born 1946
American country singer, songwriter and actress
known for her elaborate blonde wigs, flamboyant
clothes and curvaceous figure

Dolly Parton was born in Sevier County, Tennessee. She was a child television star, and, writing songs with her uncle Bill Owens, had recorded several times by the age of 15. Her marriage to builder Carl Dean has lasted since 1966 and remains intensely private.

She joined the Porter Wagoner television show in 1967 and partnered him until the international success of her single 'Jolene' (1974), which he produced. 'Jolene' gave her a much wider pop following than earlier work and the album *New Harvest. . .First Gathering* (1977) was a chart hit. In 1980 she made her acting début in *9 to 5*. She went on to star in such films as *The Best Little Whorehouse in Texas* (1982), for which she wrote new songs, and *Steel Magnolias* (1989).

Health problems, allegedly involving repercussions from cosmetic surgery, hampered her career in the later 1980s, but she continued to perform and to write, including 'I Will Always Love You', a huge hit for **Whitney Houston**. In 1995 she published her autobiography *Dolly: My Life and Other Unfinished Business.*

Pasionaria, La, *see* Ibarruri, Dolores

Paterson, Emma, *née* Smith

Born 1848 Died 1886
English trade unionist, the first woman delegate
at the Trades Union Congress

Emma Smith was born in London and educated by her father who was a headmaster. She became an apprentice book-binder but on his death she assisted her mother as a teacher.

In 1872 she became secretary of the Women's Suffrage Association and, following her marriage to Thomas Paterson and their honeymoon in America, she founded the Women's Protective and Provident League to aid the establishment of trade unions on the model of the Umbrella Makers' Union in New York.

She was the first woman to be admitted as a delegate to the Trades Union Congress (1875) and she co-founded and edited the *Women's Union Journal* (1876).

Patkau, Patricia

Born 1950
Canadian architect whose work tends to be in very
isolated sites

Patricia Patkau was born in Winnipeg, Manitoba, and trained in interior design at the University of Manitoba (1973) and in architecture at Yale University, where she graduated in 1978, having accumulated six academic awards. With her husband John Patkau, she has run Patkau Architects in Edmonton and Vancouver since 1979.

They have won several prizes for their innovative designs, including the Governor-General's Medal for Architecture (1986) and the British Columbia Honour Award (1988) for the Pyrch Residence in Victoria, British Columbia and The Canadian Clay and Glass

Gallery in Waterloo, Ontario (1989), for which they also won first prize in a design competition in 1986. The Seabird Island Indian School in Aggasiz, British Columbia (1989), is another of their major projects.

Patkau has taught at the University of British Columbia (1984–7) and the University of Pennsylvania (1987), and now teaches at the University of California.

Paton Walsh, Jill (Gillian Honoinne Mary)

Born 1937
English author known as a children's writer but whose adult novel Knowledge of Angels *achieved a place on the Booker Prize short list*

Jill Paton Walsh was born in London and educated at Oxford. She began writing when she left teaching to raise a family. Her first book was *Hengest's Tale* (1966), a rather dour historical novel set in the Dark Ages. This was followed by *The Dolphin Crossing* (1967), about two boys helping at Dunkirk, but both were significantly surpassed by *Fireweed* (1970), a novel set in the London Blitz.

Goldengrove (1972) and its sequel *Unleaving* (1976), taking their titles from a Gerard Manley Hopkins poem, are considered to be some of her finest work. She won the Whitbread award for *The Emperor's Winding-Sheet* (1974), and the Smarties Prize for *Gaffer Samson's Luck* (1984). Recent works have consolidated her focus on adolescence rather than childhood.

She has also written books for adults, including *Knowledge of Angels* (1994), which was short-listed for the Booker Prize. In 1996 she was appointed a CBE for services to children's literature.

Patti, Adelina

Born 1843 Died 1919
Spanish-born British operatic soprano

Adelina Patti was born in Madrid, the daughter of the Sicilian tenor Salvatore Patti. At seven she sang in New York, and made her début there as Lucia in Gaetano Donizetti's *Lucia di Lammermoor* in 1859. She appeared in London in 1861 and thereafter performed in the major venues of Europe and America, becoming one of the greatest prima donnas in operatic history.

In 1866 she married the Marquis de Caux, and, on her divorce in 1886, the Breton tenor Ernesto Nicolini (1834–98), followed in 1899 by the Swedish Baron Cederström. Her home was Craig-y-nos Castle near Swansea, and in 1898 she became a British citizen.

Her sister Carlotta (1840–89) was also a fine soprano.

Pattison, Dorothy Wyndlow, *known as* Sister Dora

Born 1832 Died 1878
English philanthropist and nurse

Dorothy Pattison was born in Hauxwell, a sister of the scholar and critic Mark Pattison. In 1861 she became schoolmistress at Little Woolston near Bletchley, and in 1864 joined the Sisterhood of the Good Samaritan at Coatham near Redcar.

As 'Sister Dora' she became a nurse at Walsall, and in 1877 became head of the municipal epidemic hospital at Walsall (mainly for smallpox).

Pauker, Ana, *née* Rabinsohn

Born 1893 Died 1960
Romanian politician who helped to establish the communist regime in Romania

Ana Rabinsohn was the daughter of a Moldavian rabbi. She joined the Social Democrat Party in 1915 and took part in revolutionary movements in Romania (1917–18). She married Marcel Pauker (1920) and with him joined the Communist Party, becoming a member of the Central Committee in 1922.

She was arrested in 1925, but escaped to the USSR where she worked for Comintern. She returned to Romania in 1934 and was again arrested. A 'Moscow communist' who spent World War II in the USSR, she returned home after the overthrow of the Fascist dictator Ion Antonescu (September 1944).

Summoned to Moscow with the Romanian communist politician Gheorghiu-Dej (January 1945), she was instructed by Stalin to establish a government under the control of the National Democratic Front, the communist front in Romania. She entered the Foreign Ministry in 1947 and took part in organizing the collectivization of all land. With Stalin's consent, she was relieved of her offices in 1952.

Paul, Alice

Born 1885 Died 1977
American feminist and social reformer who wrote the first draft of the Equal Rights Amendment

Alice Paul was born into a Quaker family in Moorestown, New Jersey, and educated at Swarthmore College and the University of Pennsylvania. She spent some years in England, where she became involved in the militant branch of the suffrage movement, and was several times arrested and imprisoned.

On her return to the USA in 1912, she joined the National American Woman Suffrage Association (NAWSA) and became head of its congressional committee. She organized a march of 5,000 women in Washington to coincide with the first inauguration of President Woodrow Wilson in 1912, but the crowds attacked the women and they had to be rescued. In 1913 Paul broke away from NAWSA and formed the Congressional Union for Woman Suffrage (later the National Woman's Party), to which her magnetic, forceful personality attracted wide support and equally wide mistrust.

After seeing women's suffrage become law in 1920, she pioneered the campaign for the equal rights amendment (ERA). In Geneva in the late 1930s she represented the World Women's party, on whose executive committee she served, and lobbied for an Equal Rights Treaty that would guarantee women equality under the law in all signatory nations. She returned to the USA in 1941 and achieved both the inclusion of a statement recognizing the equal rights of men and women in the UN charter and, in 1946, the adoption of a woman-suffrage resolution.

New legislation concerning working conditions during the New Deal revived interest in the ERA and Paul, who was now head of the National Women's party, resumed her campaign for a constitutional amendment; though it was passed, a rider had been added that made legislatory changes unnecessary. The indefatigable Paul also took part in the renewed campaign for equal rights in the 1970s.

Paula

Born AD347 Died AD404
Roman matron and friend and patron of Jerome

Paula was a rich widow and mother of five who dedicated herself to asceticism, sleeping on the ground and taking a bath only when dangerously ill. She took instruction in Hebrew and Bible study from Jerome, and with her third daughter **Eustochium** followed him in AD385 by way of Egypt and Palestine to Bethlehem.

There was a year of exploration and pilgrimage to holy places before they settled down and she founded a monastery and a convent. Their upkeep used up all her wealth and she died in debt. Her feast day is 26 January.

Pavlova, Anna Pavlovna

Born 1885 Died 1931
Russian ballet dancer and legendary figure in ballet history

Anna Pavlova was born in St Petersburg. She trained there at the Imperial Ballet School at the Mariinsky Theatre (later the Kirov State Theatre), graduating to the Imperial Ballet in 1899 and becoming a prima ballerina in 1906. She soon became world famous, creating roles in work by Michel Fokine, in particular *The Dying Swan* (1907).

After a period with Sergei Diaghilev's Ballet Russe in 1909, she toured in partnership with Mikhail Mordkin and began touring Europe with her own company. Among the 23 ballets in her repertoire was her famous interpretation of *Giselle*. She is also remembered for choreographing *Autumn Leaves* (1919).

With her captivating grace and poetic movement Pavlova did much to create the somewhat magical, if now stereotyped, image of the ballerina which persists today.

Payne-Gaposchkin, Cecilia Helena, *née* Payne

Born 1900 Died 1979
British-born American astronomer who became a professor at Harvard

Cecilia Payne was born in Wendover, Buckinghamshire, the daughter of a barrister. She attended St Paul's Girls' School in London and entered Newnham College, Cambridge, as a scholar in 1919 to study natural sciences. Having listened to a lecture by English astronomer Sir Arthur Eddington (1882–1944), she determined to become an astronomer, and on graduating from Cambridge in 1922 was able to fulfil her wish by going to the USA to work under Harlow Shapley (1885–1972) at Harvard College Observatory.

The topic of her doctoral thesis (1925), *Stellar Atmospheres*, continued to be the special field of research which led to her pioneering work on the determination of the relative abundances of chemical elements in stars of various types and in the universe at large. She remained at Harvard for the rest of her life and became a professor there in 1956.

With her husband and colleague Sergei I Gaposchkin, she masterminded an immense programme of identifying and measuring variable stars on photographic plates, involving more than a million observations, which resulted in a catalogue of variable stars published in 1938. A similar project on variable stars in the Magellanic Clouds was later carried out by the Gaposchkins in 1971.

Peabody, Elizabeth Palmer

Born 1804 Died 1894
American reformer, abolitionist and educator
through whose efforts the kindergarten was
accepted into American public education

Elizabeth Palmer Peabody was born in Billerica, Massachusetts. She established a school in
Massachusetts, but though a gifted teacher,
was not a good businesswoman, and the
venture collapsed. In 1840 she opened a bookshop in Boston which flourished for several
years as a literary centre frequented by such
people as **Margaret Fuller**, who edited *The
Dial*, the transcendentalist journal that
Peabody published.

In 1860 she founded in Boston the first
English-speaking kindergarten; this became a
showcase for Fredrich Froebel's ideas concerning child nurture and education, concepts
that she went to Europe to study further in
1867–8. Upon her return, she travelled and
lectured extensively to establish kindergartens and kindergarten training schools
throughout the USA. She also convinced publishers Ernst Steiger and Milton Bradley to
produce materials for children.

Peale, Anna Claypoole

Born 1791 Died 1878
American artist known for her portrait miniatures
and one of the first two women elected to the
Pennsylvania Academy

Anna Peale was born into one of the most
famous families of American painters and was
trained by her father James Peale and her
uncle Charles Willson Peale, both notable
painters of the late 18th century.

When her father's eyesight began to fail,
Anna assisted him with his miniatures and
became well known in her own right for her
portrait miniatures. Anna and her younger
sister **Sarah Peale** often shared commissions,
Anna executing the miniatures and Sarah the
full-scale portrait oils. The sisters were elected
the first women Academicians by the Pennsylvania Academy in 1824.

Anna married twice, stopping her work
periodically, but outlived both her husbands
and continued to work until late in life.

Peale, Sarah Miriam

Born 1800 Died 1885
American artist who is recognized by many as the
first professional woman painter in the USA

Sarah Peale was born in Philadelphia, the
younger sister of **Anna Peale**. She too was
taught to paint by her artist father James

Peale. She became a famous portrait painter to
prominent US families and painted the Secretary of State Daniel Webster, Senator
Thomas Hart Benton and the Marquis de
Lafayette, among many others. Sarah often
shared commissions with her sister as it was
common for patrons to request both a minia-
ture, executed by Anna, and a full portrait
which Sarah undertook.

She visited her cousin Rembrandt Peale in
Baltimore for tuition in oil painting and
glazing techniques and in 1825 moved to Baltimore, remaining there for 20 years. In 1846
she moved to St Louis where she undertook a
series of still life paintings whilst remaining
the foremost portrait painter. She returned to
Philadelphia in 1877.

Pearce, (Ann) Philippa

Born 1920
English children's novelist and short-story writer

Philippa Pearce was born in Great Shelford,
Cambridgeshire. From 1945 she spent 13 years
as a scriptwriter in the BBC's schools broadcasting department, then became an editor,
first with Oxford University Press and later
with André Deutsch.

Her first novel, *Minnow On the Say* (1955),
combines the excitement of a treasure-hunt
with the relaxed, at times poetic, depiction of
her home territory. Her second, *Tom's Midnight Garden* (1958), won the Carnegie Medal;
a magical but credible story of time travel and
nascent sexuality, it is among the most endur-
ingly popular of post-war novels for children.

Her other books include *A Dog So Small*
(1962), set, again, just south of Cambridge, *The
Strange Sunflower* (1966), about a boy's dream
trip to Sunflower Land, and *The Battle of
Bubble and Squeak* (1978), which won the
Whitbread award.

Pearl, Minnie, *real name* Sarah Ophelia Colley Cannon, *née* Colley

Born 1912 Died 1996
American country entertainer whose
characteristic attire was a gaudy flowered straw
hat with the price tag attached

Minnie Pearl was born in Centerville, Tennessee. Her aim was to entertain by combining
comedy and country music. She first appeared
at the *Grand Old Opry* in Nashville in 1940 and
became one of the show's most beloved stars.

Her albums include *The Story of Country
Music* and *Answer to Giddyup and Go*. She has
received numerous awards, including the
Pioneer Award from the Academy of Country

Music (1987). She was named to the Country Music Hall of Fame in 1975.

Peck, Annie Smith

Born 1850 Died 1935
American mountaineer, feminist and Greek
scholar

Annie Smith Peck was born in Providence, Rhode Island, and educated at the University of Michigan before becoming the first woman to attend the American School of Classical Studies in Athens. She later taught Greek at the prestigious Purdue University and at Smith College.

She began climbing in the Alps at the age of 45 with an ascent of the Matterhorn, and was a founder-member of the American Alpine Club in 1902. She held the record for the highest peak ever climbed by a woman when she climbed Orizaba (5,699m) in 1897, and again when she climbed the North peak of Huascaran (6,650m) at the age of 58.

A lifelong feminist, in 1910 she unfurled a banner on the summit of the volcano Coropuna, proclaiming 'Votes for Women'. She continued climbing and travelling well into her seventies.

Peeters, Clara

Born 1594 Died after 1657
Flemish artist who was one of the leading pioneers
of still life painting

Clara Peeters was born in Antwerp, but little is known of her early life, except that in 1639 she was married in the same church where she was baptized.

Between the years of 1608 and 1657 she completed over 32 signed works in several still-life categories, including flower paintings and elaborate 'food' and vessel paintings.

She is perhaps best known for her highly detailed 'meal' still lifes, often depicting fish and many reflective surfaces. Four of these paintings are in the Prado, Madrid, and others are in Vienna and the USA.

Pelletier, Madeleine

Born 1874 Died 1939
French militant feminist who campaigned for
women's rights and was arrested and
incarcerated for her beliefs

Madeleine Pelletier was born into a middle-class Parisian family, but had an unhappy childhood. She left school at 12, but nevertheless went on to qualify in medicine and receive an official medical appointment by the age of 25. She adopted male attire and, like

Emmeline Pankhurst in Britain, was prepared to employ illegal methods to publicise her belief in female enfranchisement.

Assuming the presidency of *Le Groupe de la Solidarité des Femmes* in 1906, she embraced both communism and anarchism, and undertook a journey alone through the turbulent Soviet Union in 1922. In later years she campaigned on such issues as birth control and women's right to abortion, performing operations herself, even after suffering a stroke in 1937. Arrested in 1939 for performing an abortion, she was confined to a mental hospital where she died shortly afterwards.

Pembroke, Countess of *see* St Pol, Marie de *or* Herbert, Mary

Pentreath, Dolly

Born 1685 Died 1777
English fishwife who is thought to have been the
last native Cornish speaker

Dolly Pentreath was born in Mousehole on Mounts Bay, Cornwall. She is reputed, due to the inscription on her gravestone, to have been the last person to speak native Cornish. It is said also that she did not learn English until the age of 20. She was an itinerant fishwife and fortune-teller, married to a man named Jeffery, and would charge money to say anything in Cornish to a stranger.

Peratrovich, Elizabeth

Born 1911 Died 1958
American Indian activist whose efforts were
responsible for the Alaskan Anti-Discrimination
Bill of 1945

Elizabeth Peratrovich was born to the Raven clan of the Tlingit Indians in south-east Alaska. She was the Grand President of the Alaska Native Sisterhood (ANS).

During her tenure she fought against unfair treatment of natives by businesses of Alaska, but because it was during World War II, her efforts branded her as disloyal. She nevertheless continued to work for native rights in Alaska and the Anti-Discrimination Bill was her crowning achievement.

Perey, Marguerite Catherine

Born 1909 Died 1975
French physicist credited with the discovery of the
element francium

Marguerite Perey was born in Villemomble. She was educated in Paris and from 1929 worked at the Radium Institute under **Marie Curie**. She later moved to the University of

Strasbourg, becoming Professor of Nuclear Chemistry in 1949 and Director of the Centre for Nuclear Research in 1958.

During studies of the radioactive decay of actinium-227, Perey discovered the element francium (originally known as actinium K) in 1939. In 1962 she was appointed the first female member of the French Academy of Sciences.

Her death was thought to be due to prolonged exposure to radiation.

Peri Rossi, Cristina

Born 1941
Uruguayan militant, iconoclastic, feminist
novelist, short-story writer, poet and journalist

Cristina Peri Rossi was born in Montevideo of Italian immigrant parents. Her work is among the best experimental fiction written by a Latin-American writer, and tests the limits of genre, language and form. Her main interests lie in shifting literature, society and gender roles, and both her poetry and her prose employ humour and irony to illustrate the disintegration of out-dated modes of social interaction.

Among her awards are the Benito Pérez Galdós Prize for *La rebelión de los niños* (1976, 'The Children's Rebellion') and the Ciudad de Palma Prize for *Linguistica General* (1979). She was persecuted for her stance against oppression and has lived in exile in Barcelona since 1972.

Perkins, Frances

Born 1882 Died 1965
American social reformer and politician, the first
woman to hold Cabinet rank in the USA

Francis Perkins was born in Boston, Massachusetts, into a well-off middle-class family. She was educated at Mount Holyoke College, Massachusetts, where a speech by **Florence Kelley** first sparked her interest in feminism. Later, while a teacher, she visited various Chicago settlement houses, in particular Hull House, and grew convinced that the workers' conditions would be improved by practical deeds not political doctrines.

She moved to New York and became secretary of the New York Consumers' League (1910–12), during which time she campaigned with enormous energy on many fronts. She achieved several legislative successes as secretary of the Committee on Safety of the City of New York. In 1918 she became the first woman member of the New York State Industrial Commission (Chairman 1926, Commissioner 1929). She joined the Democratic

Frances Perkins

party and for 30 years played a significant role in introducing women's issues into party policy.

She was appointed US Secretary of Labor (1933–45) in President Franklin D Roosevelt's Cabinet, and in this post made perhaps her greatest contribution to women's rights, child labour and factory legislation in her supervision of the New Deal labour regulations, which included the Social Security Act (1935) and the Wages and Hours Act (1938). A controversial figure, she resigned from President Harry S Truman's cabinet in 1945, but served on the Civil Service Commission until 1952. Her memoir, *The Roosevelt I Knew* (1946), was the first, and in many ways remains one of the best recollections of the New Deal.

Perón, Evita, *popular name of* María Eva Duarte de Perón, *née* Duarte

Born 1919 Died 1952
Argentine political figure who used her position as
President's wife to improve social welfare and
agitate for women's suffrage

Eva Duarte was born into a poor family in Los Toldos, Buenos Aires. She became a radio and stage actress before her marriage as the second wife of Juan Perón in 1945. After helping in his successful presidential campaign the following year, she became a powerful political influence and mainstay of the Perón government, meanwhile agitating for women's suffrage (she founded the Peronista Feminist Party in 1949) and acquiring control of newspapers and business companies.

As *de facto* Minister of Health and Labour, she gained politcal support for her husband from among the working classes. Idolized by the populace herself, she founded the Eva Perón Foundation for the promotion of social welfare. After her death, support for her husband waned. When he was overthrown in 1955 her body was stolen and kept hidden until the early 1970s; it was repatriated by **Isabelita Perón** after Juan Perón's death in 1974.

Evita Perón's life story was the theme of the Andrew Lloyd-Webber and Tim Rice musical *Evita* (1978).

Perón, Isabelita, *popular name of* María Estela Martínez de Perón, *née* Cartas

Born 1931
Argentine political figure who was unsuccessful as
President of Argentina in 1974–6

Maria Cartas was born in La Rioja Province and adopted the name Isabel when she began her career as a dancer. She became the third wife of the deposed President Juan Perón ('El Líder') in 1961, living with him in Spain until his triumphal return to Argentina as President in 1973, when she was made Vice-President.

She took over the presidency at his death in 1974, but her inadequacy in office led to a military coup in 1976. She was imprisoned for five years on a charge of abuse of public property and on her release in 1981 settled in Madrid.

Perovskaya, Sophie

Born 1854   Died 1881
Russian feminist socialist who was executed for
assassinating Tsar Alexander II

Sophia Perovskaya was born in rural Russia to a moderately prosperous family and, typically for the period, was one of hundreds of relatively financially privileged young women in the 1860s and 1870s who left home in order to study and become politically active.

She became a member of the Russian 'Amazons', a network of study groups promoted and supported by **Elizaveta Kovalskaya**, which evolved into conspiratorial revolutionary organizations. She was publicly hanged, with four men, for assassinating Tsar Alexander II in 1881.

The entry of women into Russian universities, which had been permitted since 1876, was subsequently forbidden on the basis that a woman had been responsible for

the death of the Tsar. This was not re-instated until the 1905 revolution.

Perpetua

Died AD203
Early Christian martyr who perished during the
persecutions led by Septimus Severus

Perpetua was the daughter of Vibia Perpetua of Carthage, North Africa. She was thrown into prison for her faith during the persecutions of Septimus Severus, along with her slave Felicitas, two fellow catechumens and their catechist Saturus.

The Passion of Perpetua, possibly edited by Tertullian, includes accounts of visions received in prison by Perpetua while she awaited death in the amphitheatre.

Since Perpetua and Felicitas were both Christians, they were jointly honoured by a church built on the site of their burial, which was identified in 1907. Other inscriptions dating from the sixth century have been discovered.

Perry, (Mary) Antoinette

Born 1888   Died 1946
American actress and director who gave her name
to the Tony award

Antoinette Perry was born in Denver, Colorado. She had a long career on the stage from 1905 and as a director from 1928. Among the successful plays that she co-produced were *Strictly Dishonourable, Personal Appearance* and *Kiss the Boys Goodbye*.

She became known for encouraging young entrants to the world of the theatre and in 1941 founded the American Theatre Wing. The annual Antoinette Perry or 'Tony' awards of the New York theatre are named after her.

Pert, Candace, *née* Beebe

Born 1946
American pharmacologist who has researched the
relationships of chemicals to neural functioning

Candace Beebe was born in Manhattan, New York, and educated at Bryn Mawr College and Johns Hopkins University Hospital Medical School. She received her PhD in pharmacology in 1974 and stayed at Johns Hopkins as Research Fellow (1974–8) and Research Pharmacologist (1978–82) until her appointment as chief of the section of brain chemistry of the National Institute of Mental Health.

Her doctoral research, under the supervision of Solomon Snyder, was stimulated by the realization that the highly specific effects of synthetic opiates at very small doses indicated that they must bind to highly selective target receptor sites. She began a search for these sites, using radioactively labelled compounds. In 1973 she first reported the presence of such receptors in specialized areas of the mammalian brain. From this arose the suggestion that there might be natural opiate-like substances in the brain that used these sites, as later discovered by the British pharmacologists Hans Kosterlitz and John Hughes.

Peterkin, Julia

Born 1880 Died 1961
American novelist who won the Pulitzer Prize for fiction in 1929

Julia Peterkin was born in South Carolina. She married a plantation manager, and became known as the leading depictor of (and spokeswoman for) the region's Gullah Blacks.

Her Pulitzer Prize-winning *Scarlet Sister Mary* (1928) was dramatized, with white actors (such as **Ethel Barrymore**) in blackface. *Black April* (1927) was also a major novel. It is likely that criticism has not yet caught up with her achievement.

Peters, Mary Elizabeth

Born 1939
Northern Irish athlete who won an Olympic gold in 1972

Mary Peters was born in Halewood, Lancashire. She started competing in the pentathlon, a gruelling discipline covering five events over two days, at the age of 17. She won the gold medal at her third Olympics in 1972, at the age of 33, setting a new world record (4801 points). She was also the Commonwealth champion twice, winning the shot as well in the 1970 Games.

Perennially cheerful and good-natured, she campaigned for more sports facilities in Northern Ireland, and an athletics stadium in Belfast, where she now lives, is named after her. Since 1977 she has been managing director of her own sports company and in 1990 she was appointed CBE.

Pethick-Lawrence, Emmeline, *née* Pethick

Born 1867 Died 1954
English suffragette and social worker

Emmeline Pethick was born in Clifton, Bristol, and went to boarding school at Devizes. She founded the Esperance Working Girls' Club with Mary Neal in 1895 and Maison Esperance, a dressmaking co-operative, in 1897.

In 1901 she married the Liberal-Unionist MP Frederick Lawrence (later Baron Pethick-Lawrence). When Emmeline became treasurer of the Women's Social and Political Union, they edited the newspaper *Votes for Women* and financed the campaign to extend the franchise. As the suffrage campaign became increasingly militant, she formed the non-violent Votes for Women Fellowship.

She was one of the organizers of the International Peace Conference in The Hague (1915) and describes her life in *My Part in a Changing World* (1938).

Petry, Ann

Born 1911
American novelist and short-story writer, the first black woman writer to sell over a million copies of a book

Ann Petry was born in Old Saybrook, Connecticut, and educated at the University of Connecticut. She moved to New York in 1938 and worked as a reporter for *Amsterdam News* and *People's Voice*. She published her first short story, 'On Saturday the Siren Sounds at Noon', in 1943, after studying creative writing at Columbia University.

Social realism characterizes her work: her first novel, *The Street* (1947), is an account of slum life and domestic unrest which ends in a tragic death, while *The Narrows* (1951) focuses on an inter-racial marriage, and again has a tragic outcome.

Pfeiffer, Ida, *née* Reyer

Born 1797 Died 1858
Austrian traveller who enlarged the British museum natural history collection

Ida Reyer was born in Vienna. After making two journeys around the world (1846–8, 1851–4), mainly making botanical and mineralogical collections for the British Museum, among others, in 1856 she went on an expedition to Madagascar, endured terrible hardships, and came home to die. She wrote accounts of all her journeys.

Pfeiffer, Michelle

Born 1958
American film actress, currently one of the most respected in Hollywood

Michelle Pfeiffer was born in Santa Ana, California. She was spotted by a theatrical agent at a beauty contest, and began her career in television commercials before making her feature-film début in *Falling in Love Again* (1980).

Despite her beauty, hers was a vapid set of

credits before she stunned the critics with the conviction of her performance as the coke-sniffing wife of a drugs baron in *Scarface* (1983). Her first major commercial success was in *The Witches of Eastwick* (1987), and the purity and delicacy of her playing in *Dangerous Liaisons* (1988) brought her a Best Supporting Actress Oscar nomination.

Her new-found star status was endorsed by her performance in *The Fabulous Baker Boys* (1989). Becoming one of the most highly-respected female stars in Hollywood, she later featured in *The Russia House* (1990) and *Frankie and Johnny* (1991), and gave a scene-stealing performance of physical agility and emotional complexity in *Batman Returns* (1992).

Philippa of Hainault

Born c.1314   Died 1369
Queen of England as the wife of Edward III (ruled 1327–77)

Philippa was the daughter of William the Good, Count of Hainault and Holland. Following her marriage to Edward III, her second cousin, in York in 1327, she brought Flemish weavers to England, encouraged coal-mining and made the French poet and historian Jean Froissart her secretary.

Contrary to the tenedencies of many foreign queens, she was known for her compassionate nature and did not alienate the upper classes by finding positions at the English court for her family. She accompanied her husband on his successful Scottish campaign in 1333 and is said to have roused the English troops before the defeat of the Scots at the Battle of Neville's Cross in 1346. She also allegedly interceded with Edward for mercy for the burgesses of Calais after the long siege in 1347.

She bore him five daughters and seven sons, one of which was Edward, the Black Prince. The Queen's College, Oxford, founded by Philippa's chaplain in 1341, was named after her.

Philips, Katherine Fowler, *pseud*
'Orinda', *née* Fowler

Born 1631   Died 1664
English poet who was the first woman poet in England to have her work published

Katherine Fowler was born in London, the daughter of a merchant, and became known as 'the matchless Orinda'. At 16 she married James Philips of Cardigan Priory, and there have been attempts to claim that 'Ephelia' was her daughter.

In 1659 she received a dedication from the English theologian Jeremy Taylor (*Discourse on the Nature, Offices and Measures of Friendship*). She is the first English woman poet to have her work published (it included an address to the Welsh poet Henry Vaughan). She also translated Corneille's *Pompée*, which was performed in Dublin in 1663, and the greater part of his *Horace*. Her poems, surreptitiously printed in 1663, were issued in 1667. The literary salon that she ran is described in the *Letter of Orinda to Poliarchus* (1705).

She died of smallpox on a visit to London.

Phillips, Jayne Anne

Born 1952
American novelist and short-story writer of stories of working-class lives

Jayne Phillips was born in Buckhannon, West Virginia, and educated at the universities of West Virginia and Iowa. She first became known in the UK as part of the 'dirty realism' school of American writers, but this is an inappropriate label as her work, while based in a recognizable real world, is also —as shown by her short-story collection *Black Tickets* (1979) — impressionistic, fanciful, and at times a touch precious.

Machine Dreams (1984), her only novel to date, is easily her most accomplished and engaging work. The story of two generations of an American middle-class family who grow up to lose their illusions and see their dreams die, it is acted out against a background of social dislocation and the Vietnam War. Her other publications include the short-story collection *Fast Lanes* (1984).

Phillips, Marion

Born 1818   Died 1932
Australian-born British socialist

Marion Phillips was born in Melbourne, Australia, of an Australian father and a New Zealand mother. She was educated at Melbourne Presbyterian Ladies' College, Ormond College and Melbourne University. She came to England in 1904 to study at the London School of Economics.

Following a period of social research for the Webbs and for a Royal Commission on the Poor Laws, she became Labour councillor for Kensington (1912) and campaigned for improved social conditions. From 1913 to 1918 she was secretary of the Women's Labour League and in 1918 she became the chief woman officer of the Labour Party and editor of *Labour Woman*.

In 1929 Phillips was elected Labour MP for Sunderland.

Phillpotts, Dame Bertha Surtees

Born 1877   Died 1932
English Scandinavian scholar and educationalist

Bertha Phillpotts was born in Bedford. She studied medieval and modern languages at Girton College, Cambridge (1898–1902), and was a research student in Iceland and Denmark (1903–6). In 1913 she was appointed the first Lady Carlisle Fellow at Somerville College, Oxford, and in 1920 became Principal of Westfield College, London.

She was mistress of Girton (1922–5), and director of Scandinavian Studies at Cambridge from 1926 to 1932. She wrote *The Elder Edda and Ancient Scandinavian Drama* (1920) and *Edda and Saga* (1931). In 1931 she married the astronomer Hugh Frank Newall (1857–1944).

Phipson, Joan

Born 1912
Australian writer of fiction for children whose first novel won an award

Joan Phipson was born in Warrawee, New South Wales. Her first novel, *Good Luck to the Rider* (1953), won the Children's Book of the Year award, as did the later *The Family Conspiracy* (1962).

Her books range over a variety of themes, from fantasy to adventure, and from a historical re-creation *Bass and Billy Martin* (1972) to contemporary themes of the environment and urban life.

Phryne, *popular name of* Muesarete

4th century BC
Greek courtesan who became so wealthy that she offered to rebuild the walls of Thebes

Muesarete was born in Thespiae, Boeotia, and nicknamed Phryne ('toad') because of her wan complexion. She became enormously rich through her many lovers and is said to have offered to finance the rebuilding of the walls of Thebes, which had been destroyed by Alexander the Great (c.335BC).

She was reportedly the inspiration and the model for Apelles' painting of Aphrodite rising from the sea (*Aphrodite Anadyomene*) and for the statue *Aphrodite of Cnidus* by her lover Praxiteles. When she was accused of the capital offence of blasphemy through profaning the Eleusinian mysteries, she was defended by the orator Hyperides, who, legend relates, threw off her robe in court,

Phryne

showing her loveliness, and so gained the verdict.

Piaf, Edith, *originally* Edith Giovanna Gassion

Born 1915   Died 1963
French singer who became internationally famous for her sad and nostalgic songs

Edith Gassion was born in Paris, the daughter of the acrobat Jean Gassion. She led a life that was marred by trauma and tragedy, beginning with desertion by her mother and the loss of her own sight through meningitis from the ages of three to seven. She started her career by singing in the streets, and she soon graduated to music hall and cabaret, becoming known as Piaf, from the Parisian argot for 'little sparrow', which perfectly suited her waif-like appearance and the 'life at street-level' subject-matter of her songs.

She appeared in stage-plays — Jean Cocteau wrote *Le Bel Indifferent* for her — and in films, including Renoir's *French-Cancan*. However it was for her songs with their undercurrent of sadness and nostalgia, written by herself and songwriters such as Jacques Prévert, that she became legendary, travelling widely in Europe and America.

After a severe illness she made a greatly successful but brief return to the stage in 1961, before recurring ill health resulted in her death two years later. Among her best-remembered songs are 'Le Voyage du pauvre nègre', 'Mon Légionnaire', 'Un Monsieur m'a suivi dans la rue', 'La vie en rose' and 'Non, je ne regrette rien'.

Picasso, Paloma

Born 1949
French designer who uses bold, geometric patterns

Paloma Picasso was born in Paris, the daughter of Pablo Picasso and Françoise Gilet. After training in jewellery design, she designed sets and costumes for her husband's Paris theatre productions before producing her first costume jewellery collection, which Yves Saint Laurent showed in 1969.

She was commissioned by the Greek jewellery company Zolotas in 1971 and 1973, and launched her first semi-precious jewellery collection for Tiffany in 1980. Her eye for bold, geometric designs in vibrant colours is also reflected in her own perfume bottles—Paloma Picasso (1984) and Minotaure (1992) — and cosmetics for L'Oréal.

She has boutiques in Paris, Japan and Hong Kong, and designs bone china, crystal, silverwear and tiles for Villeroy & Bosch, as well as hosiery, eyewear, home linens, wallcoverings and fabrics for other top companies. She is a devotee of haute couture and lives in New York and Paris.

Pickford, (Gladys) Mary, *née* Smith

Born 1893 Died 1979
Canadian-born American actress who epitomized sweetness and innocence on the silent screen

Mary Smith was born in Toronto. She first appeared on the stage at the age of five, and in 1909 made her first film, *The Violin Maker of Cremona*, directed by D W Griffith (1875–1948).

Her beauty and ingenuous charm soon won her the title of 'The World's Sweetheart' and her many successful films include *Rebecca of Sunnybrook Farm* (1917), *Poor Little Rich Girl* (1917), and *The Taming of the Shrew* (1929). In 1929 she made her first talkie, *Coquette*, earning herself the second Best Actress Oscar to be awarded, and retired from the screen in 1933.

Also a keen businesswoman, she cofounded the United Artists Film Corporation in 1919 with Charlie Chaplin (1889–1977) and Douglas Fairbanks, Senior (1833–1939), who

from 1920 to 1935 was the second of her three husbands.

Pickford, (Lillian) Mary

Born 1902
Scottish physiologist who researched kidney function and blood pressure regulation

Mary Pickford was born in Jabbalpore, India. She was educated at Wycombe Abbey School and after taking a BSc at Bedford College, London (1925), she graduated in medicine from University College Hospital Medical School, London, in 1934. After holding a Beit Memorial Research Fellowship at Cambridge (1936–9) she became a lecturer in physiology at the University of Edinburgh Medical School (1939) where she remained throughout her career, apart from visiting professorships in Nottingham and Brisbane.

She was awarded the DSc of London in 1957 and was elected FRS in 1966 as well as being appointed to a personal chair in physiology in Edinburgh. In 1991 she received an honorary DSc from Heriot-Watt University. She was an outstanding teacher, greatly respected by her colleagues and students.

Her contribution was to the knowledge of the regulation of the kidney function and the regulation of blood pressure through the interaction of drugs, and of hormones, with the nervous system. Her book *The Central Role of Hormones* (1968) was an important contribution to the field.

Piercy, Marge

Born 1936
American novelist and poet whose writing stems from strongly held political and feminist views

Marge Piercy was born in Detroit, Michigan. She was educated at the University of Michigan and has taught in a number of colleges.

Her poetry employs vernacular language and speech rhythms to good effect, and her novels *Going Down Fast* (1969), *Small Changes* (1973) and *Vida* (1980) are revealing documents of the emerging feminist consciousness of the 1960s and 1970s. *Woman On the Edge of Time* (1976) was a science-fiction narrative which contrasted a future utopia with the economic, environmental, and gender abuses of contemporary America.

Later novels include *Gone to Soldiers* (1987), set during World War II, and *Mars and Her Children* (1992).

Pieterse, Zola, *née* Budd

Born 1966
South African athlete whose achievement as a champion has been clouded by politics

Zola Budd was born in Bloemfontein. Dogged by controversy, she set a world-record time of 15 minutes 1.83 seconds for the 5,000 metres while still a South African citizen, competing under her maiden name. In April 1984 she was accorded British citizenship on the strength of her parental background, and became eligible to participate in the 1984 Olympic Games. But her presence was not universally welcomed, and her disappointing performance was best remembered for her accidental clash with US athlete Mary Decker (now **Mary Decker Slaney**), which put Decker out of the race.

She set further world records for the 5,000 metres in 1984 and 1985, reducing the time to 14 minutes 48.7 seconds, but her refusal to condemn apartheid outright and her apparent lack of commitment to her British residency brought her career in the UK to a premature end. She returned to South Africa in 1988 and later resumed competitive running under her married name, Pieterse. Competing for South Africa, she was unsuccessful in the 3,000 metres at the 1992 Olympics, the first time the country had taken part in the event for 32 years.

Pilcher, Rosamunde

Born 1924
English novelist who has been widely known since the publication of The Shell Seekers

Rosamunde Pilcher was born in Lelant, Cornwall. She worked in the Women's Royal Naval Service but, from the age of 18 when her first story was published in *Woman and Home* magazine, pursued another career as a writer, at first publishing under the pseudonym Jane Fraser.

The romance *A Secret To Tell* (1955) was the first book to appear under her own name, but three decades passed before that name became more widely known with the publication of the bestselling *The Shell Seekers* (1987). A romance of a bittersweet nature, it is the story of an artist's daughter who, finding that a painting of her father's is worth a small fortune, suddenly has the financial power to become independent — to the possible detriment of her family.

The success of *The Shell Seekers* was followed in 1989 by *September*. Later novels include *Coming Home* (1995).

Pilkington, Laetitia, *née* Van Lewen

Born 1712 Died 1750
Irish writer whose memoirs provide a lively account of her wild living and her famous literary acquaintances

Laetitia Van Lewen was born in Dublin, the daughter of an obstetrician of Dutch origin. She was an intimate friend of Jonathan Swift (1667–1745) and wrote verse from an early age.

When she was 17 she married a clergyman and minor writer, Matthew Pilkington, who deserted her. She followed him to London but he divorced her in 1738 on grounds of adultery. She tried to provide for herself and her children by writing, such as *The Statues: Or, the Trial of Constancy* (1739), but led a profligate lifestyle and was jailed for debt in 1742. She later supported herself by bookselling.

Her vivacious *Memoirs* (1748–54) give a candid, racy account of her life and adventures, with revealing anecdotes of Swift, Alexander Pope, Samuel Richardson and other authors. They include her poems: usually light-hearted or satirical, she could also write with dignity and feeling about personal misfortune.

Pinckney, Eliza, *née* Lucas

Born 1723 Died 1793
American pioneer and letter writer

Eliza Lucas was born in Antigua in the West Indies and educated in England. She first went to Carolina where her family owned plantations in 1739, later taking over the running of family affairs to develop indigo as a crop which became vital to regional economies.

In 1744 she married Charles Pinckney and their sons became distinguished politicians. In later life she was financially ruined as a result of British raids on her property during the American War of Independence.

Her journal detailing her life and her feminist viewpoint has been published as *The Journal and Letters of Eliza Lucas* (1850).

Pinkham, Lydia E(stes)

Born 1819 Died 1883
American housewife and manufacturer of a highly successful 'cure-all' herbal remedy

Lydia Pinkham was born in Lynn, Massachusetts, and trained as a teacher. She espoused various causes such as temperance and abolition, and married Isaac Pinkham in 1843. When he went bankrupt in 1875, she began selling a home remedy made from herbs and roots (and alcohol as preservative) specifically aimed at 'female complaints'.

Its phenomenal success resulted in a successful family business and national fame for Pinkham, who corresponded personally with her customers. For many years after her death her 'Vegetable Compound' remained the best-known patent medicine in the USA.

Pintasilgo, Maria de Lourdes

Born 1930
Portuguese politician who has raised the profile of
women's rights in Portugal

Maria Pintasilgo was born in Abrantes. She
trained in chemical engineering and while still
a student was President of Pax Romana, a
Catholic student organization. She honed her
oratorical skills and developed left-wing and
feminist views, and from 1970 to 1974 she
chaired the National Committee on the status
of women.

After the 1974 revolution she was made
Minister for Social Affairs, legislating above
all on women's rights. In 1976–9 she was
Ambassador to UNESCO, and from 1979 to
1980 acted as caretaker Prime Minister, then
was adviser to the President from 1981 to
1985.

She has also been a member of the World
Policy Institute since 1982 and has written
widely on international affairs and women's
issues.

Pitcher, Molly *see* McCauley, Mary

Jenny Pitman with Royal Athlete, 1995

Pitman, Jenny (Jennifer Susan), *née* Harvey

Born 1946
English National Hunt racehorse trainer, the first
woman to train a Grand National and Gold Cup
winner

Jenny Pitman was born in Hoby, Leicestershire. She married Richard Pitman in 1965
(separated 1978) and set up her first training
stables with him. Among the races that her
horses have won are the Midland National,
the Massey Fergusson Gold Cup, the Welsh
National, the Cheltenham Gold Cup, the
Henessey Gold Cup and the Whitbread
Trophy.

Corbiere won the Grand National in 1983,
while Esha Ness won the abandoned Grand
National in 1993 (the race was void because of
problems at the start), and Royal Athlete won
it in 1995. Burrough Hill Lad won the King
George VI Cup, the Hennessey Gold Cup and
the Cheltenham Gold Cup in 1984.

Pitman has been declared the Piper Heid-
sieck Trainer of the Year several times (1983–4,
1989–90) and the Golden Spurs Best National
Hunt Trainer (1984). She published her autobiography *Glorious Uncertainty* in 1984. Her
son Mark is a National Hunt jockey and assistant trainer at her stables.

Pitter, Ruth

Born 1897 Died 1992
English poet whose award-winning work is
characterized by formal metrical language

Ruth Pitter was born in Ilford, Essex, the
daughter of a schoolmaster. She wrote verse
from a very early age and later was encouraged
by the poet Hilaire Belloc (1870–1953). Her
writing belongs to no particular school and
for inspiration she drew drawn mainly upon
the beauty of natural things and upon her
Christian faith.

In 1955 she became the first woman to be
awarded the Queen's Gold Medal for Poetry,
having already won the Hawthornden Prize
in 1936 with *A Trophy of Arms*. Other volumes
include *First and Second Poems* (1927), *A Mad
Lady's Garland* (1934), *Urania* (1951), *The
Ermine* (1953), *Still by Choice* (1966), and *End
of Drought* (1975). A *Collected Poems* appeared
in 1990.

Pitt-Rivers, Rosalind Venetia, *née* Henley

Born 1907 Died 1990
English biochemist and medical researcher

Rosalind Henley was born in London and educated at Bedford College, London. She gradu-

ated in 1931, the year she married George Pitt-Rivers (d.1966), and gained her PhD in 1939. She then joined Charles Harington at University College Hospital and moved with him in 1942 to the Medical Research Council's National Institute for Medical Research and became head of the Chemistry Division there (1969–72). She worked on the biochemistry of the thyroid gland and discovered the thyroid hormone triiodothyronine.

She published many papers and co-wrote several influential books on the subject, and was elected a Fellow of the Royal Society in 1954.

Pizarnik, Alejandra

Born 1936 Died 1972
Argentinian poet regarded as one of the foremost female Latin-American poets of the 20th century

Alejandra Pizarnik lived in Argentina and France, where she contributed to a number of literary magazines. Her work is characterized by mystery, surrealism and a dreamy quality, which attempt to make reality greater than it is in normal life. Important themes are death, the loss of innocence, nostalgia and longing.

She committed suicide at the age of 36. Her works include *El deseo de la palabra* (1975, 'Desire of the Word') and *El Infierno musical* (1971, 'The Musical Hell').

Pizzey, Erin (Patricia Margaret), *née* Carney

Born 1939
British women's rights campaigner and writer especially concerned about battered women

Erin Carney was born in China and endured an unhappy childhood, leaving home at the age of 17 on her mother's death.

Her marriage in 1961 to broadcaster Jack Pizzey was subsequently dissolved. In 1971 she founded the first refuge in Britain for battered women. Her book *Scream Quietly or the Neighbours Will Hear* (1974) was followed by the controversial book *Prone to Violence* (1982) which she wrote with her second husband, the psychologist Jeff Shapiro, from whom she later divorced.

She has written numerous books, including novels, and now lives in Italy where she was the recipient of the San Valentino d'Oro prize for literature in 1994.

Placidia, (Aelia) Galla

Born c.390AD Died AD450
Roman empress, who was the daughter, sister, wife and mother of emperors

Galla Placidia was the daughter of the Roman emperor Theodosius I. After the fall of Rome in 410 she was imprisoned by the Goths under Alaric and married to his heir, Ataulphus, in 414. When her husband was assassinated the following year she was restored to her people in Ravenna.

She was forced in 417 to marry Constantius III (ruled 421), with whom she was declared co-ruler and Augusta. On his death she went to Constantinople, where her nephew Theodosius II was eastern emperor. She later went to Rome where her son was hailed as the new emperor Valentinian III (b.419; ruled 425–455), and for whom she acted as regent during the early part of his reign (425–437).

She died at Ravenna, where a small chapel allegedly still houses her tomb.

Plaidy, Jean *see* Holt, Victoria

Plamnikova, Franciska

Born 1875 Died 1942
Czech campaigner for women's rights who died for her beliefs

Franciska Plamnikova worked as a teacher and school inspector in Czecholslovakia when it was still part of the Austrian Empire, and devoted her life to improving the welfare of women. After founding two women's associations by 1905, she stood successfully for election to the Prague city council in 1918, and five years later became the head of the Czech Council of Women and Vice-Chairman of the International Council of Women.

Her political career continued to thrive, with Plamnikova being elected a Senator in 1929. She never ceased to campaign for female equality, and this undoubtedly caused her death. She visited Britain in 1939 to seek help against Nazi invaders, but was arrested on her return to the now-occupied Czechoslovakia and perished in a concentration camp.

Plath, Sylvia

Born 1932 Died 1963
American poet whose work challenges its readers to think afresh on the nature of writing, female identity, suffering and madness

Sylvia Plath was born in Boston, Massachusetts, the daughter of a German-born Professor of Biology and a schoolteacher. Educated at Bradford High School and Smith College, where she suffered from deep depression and attempted suicide, she won a Fulbright Fellowship to Newnham College, Cambridge, in 1956, where she studied English and met and married English poet Ted Hughes (1930–   ). After a spell of teaching in the USA they settled in England, first in London and then in Devon, but separated in 1962; a year later Sylvia committed suicide.

She wrote poetry from early childhood; her first volume, *A Winter Ship* (1960), was published anonymously, but she put her name to her second volume, *The Colossus* (1960). After the birth of her second child she wrote a radio play, *Three Women* (1962), set in a maternity home. She is often termed a 'confessional' poet because of the inclusion in her work of personal details about her own life and the influence of poets such as Robert Lowell (1917–77); her earlier, highly controlled poetry gave way to an almost visionary expression and intensity, reaching its culmination in the last few days before her death.

This late poetry was published posthumously in *Ariel* (1965), *Crossing the Water* (1971) and *Winter Trees* (1972). *Collected Poems*, edited by Ted Hughes, was published in 1981 and won the Pulitzer Prize for poetry the following year. Plath's only novel, *The Bell Jar* (1963), about her student collapse, was published just before her death, under the pseudonym Victoria Lucas.

Plato, Ann

Floreat c.1841
African-American author of essays and poems published in 1841 which encouraged other black American women authors to achieve self-expression

Ann Plato was born free and appears to have been a protegee of the former slave Dr James Pennington, of whose church she was a devout member.

She lived in Hartford, Connecticut, where she published a volume of essays and poems in 1841. Her essays are mainly religious in nature, and not particularly remarkable, but her poems include a paean of praise to the British Empire for freeing slaves in the British West Indies in 1838, some time before the USA followed suit.

It was the fact that her work was published at all which served as an encouragement to later black women writers. Nothing is known of Plato's later life, marital status, or her death.

Pleasant, Mary Ellen, *known as* Mammy Pleasant

Born 1814 Died 1904
American entrepreneur and former slave who influenced San Francisco's economic and political life for over 50 years

Mary Pleasant was born into slavery in the American South. She came to California in 1850, a widow with a legacy of several thousand dollars from her deceased husband. She invested in a boarding house, and set about attracting influential financiers and politicians into her sphere. Having discovered the city's financial mysteries she was soon able to invest in further property, to lend money at exorbitant interest, and to offer her services as a financial adviser.

It is said that she contributed $30,000 to fund John Brown's raid on Harper's Ferry in 1859. Her most significant exploit was her successful suing in 1864 of San Francisco streetcar companies for refusing her right to board, on grounds of colour.

So successful, intelligent and sophisticated was Mammy Pleasant, that the only explanation San Francisco society could offer for her success as a black woman was that she used black magic. This reputation plagued her during her long life in the city, and caused her to be implicated in numerous rumours of poisonings and other deaths and double dealings.

Pleydell-Bouverie, Katherine

Born 1895 Died 1985
English potter who specialized in stoneware with wood ash glazes

Katherine Pleydell-Bouverie studied at the Central School of Arts and Crafts in London and with potter Bernard Leach (1887–1979) at St Ives, Cornwall, in 1924.

She established a pottery in Coleshill, Wiltshire, where she produced domestic wares in stoneware and experimented with wood and vegetable ash glazes, carrying out the first systematic study of their use. Norah Braden (1901–   ) worked with her there from 1928 to 1936.

In 1946 Pleydell-Bouverie established an oil-fired kiln in Kilmington Manor near Warminster where her output consisted of a series of unique small works often decorated with vertical ribbing.

Plisetskya, Maiya Mikhailovna

Born 1925
Russian ballet dancer who became a prima ballerina of the Bolshoi

Maiya Plisetskya was born in Moscow into a family with dance in its blood (she was the niece of Asaf and Sulamith Messerer) and trained at the Bolshoi school. Success came early and she was made a principal immediately on joining the company in 1943.

Celebrated for her dazzling, fast technique, she shone in classical roles like Odile/Odette in *Swan Lake* and came to represent the epitome of the Bolshoi style. A performer of great charisma both on and off stage, she was able to travel at a time when this was difficult for most Soviet artists.

Perhaps best known for the role created for her in *Carmen Suite* (1967) by Alberto Alonso, she also danced in Roland Petit's company in *La Rose malade* (1973) and in Maurice Béjart's company in 1979. Film roles, both dancing (*Vernal Floods*, 1975) and acting (*Anna Karenina*, 1972), punctuated her illustrious career.

Plowden, Lady Bridget Hortia, *née* Richmond

Born 1907
English educationalist whose Plowden Report marks a watershed in the development of English primary education

Bridget Richmond went to school at Downe House and married Baron Plowden in 1933. As well as serving on numerous councils and advisory boards, she was the first woman to chair the Central Advisory Council for Education (1963–6), and subsequently chaired the Independent Broadcasting Authority (1975–80).

Her report, *Children and their Primary Schools* (1967), concentrated public attention on the relationship between the primary school and the home and social background of children. It argued that education must be concerned with the whole family and that increased resources were needed for nursery education and for areas starved of new investment — 'educational priority areas'.

It took child-centred approaches to their logical limits, insisting on the principle of complete individualization of the teaching/learning process and holding it impossible 'to describe a standard of attainment that should be reached by all or most children'. Much of her report was implemented during **Margaret Thatcher**'s administration. She was appointed DBE in 1972.

Plowright, Joan Ann, Lady Olivier

Born 1929
English actress and stage director acclaimed for her remarkable range and versatility

Joan Plowright was born in Brigg, Lincolnshire, and trained at the Laban Art of Movement Studio in Manchester and Old Vic

Joan Plowright, 1993

Theatre School. She first appeared on stage in 1951 and became a member of the English Stage Company at the Royal Court Theatre, London, in 1956, where she played opposite Laurence Olivier (1907–89), whom she married in 1961. In 1957 she played Jean Rice in John Osborne's *The Entertainer*, and Beattie in Arnold Wesker's *Roots* in 1959. In 1963 she joined the National Theatre in its first season, remaining their leading actress until 1974. She also appeared in New York from 1958.

A formidably talented classical actress, she is also an accomplished stage director, and in more recent years has worked in television, winning two Golden Globe awards for Best Supporting Actress in 1993 for the film *Enchanted April* and the mini-series *Stalin*.

Pocahontas, *Native American name* Matoaka

Born 1595 Died 1617
Native American princess who negotiated peace between her tribe and the colonists and earned herself a place in American folk history

Pocahontas was reputedly the favourite daughter of the Algonquin chief Powhatan. According to the English adventurer John Smith (1580–1631), she saved his life on two occasions when he was at the mercy of her tribe. She is also said to have helped the survival of the infant colony of Jamestown by informing the colonists, who were at war with

Powhatan, of her father's belligerent plans.

In 1612 however, she entered a long period as a captive of the English; Powhatan reluctantly agreed to a truce which lasted until 1622. Pocahontas embraced Christianity, was baptized Rebecca, and in 1614 married an Englishman, John Rolfe (1585–1622), and came to England with him in 1616, where she was received by royalty.

Having embarked for Virginia the following year, she died of smallpox off Gravesend. She left one son, and several Virginia families claim descent from her.

Pollard, Eve

Birthdate unavailable
British publisher who became editor of the
Sunday Express *newspaper*

Eve Pollard began her impressive career in 1967 as fashion editor first for *Honey* and then for the *Daily Mirror* magazine. She became women's editor for the *Observer* magazine in 1970, and moved the following year to the Mirror Group as women's editor for the *Sunday Mirror* (1971–81) and then assistant editor of the *Sunday People*.

In 1983 she joined TV-am as features editor and presenter, remaining for two years before moving to New York where she set up *Elle USA* magazine, working as editor-in-chief there (1985–6) and freelancing for the *Sunday Times*. After a short time with the *News of the World's Sunday* magazine in 1986, she took up the editorship of *You* magazine (1986–8), and then that of the *Sunday Mirror*, for which she launched a magazine section in 1988. From 1991 to 1994 she was with the Express group as editor of the *Sunday Express* and its magazine, the first woman to edit a Sunday newspaper of that level. She has been married to Sir Nicholas Lloyd, editor of the *Daily Express*, since 1979.

Pompadour, Jeanne Antoinette Poisson, Marquise de

Born 1721 Died 1764
French nobewoman who wielded great influence
as mistress and confidante of Louis XV

Jeanne Poisson was born in Paris, the child of a financier who had to flee the country when she was very young. She was raised by a wealthy financier friend, Le Normant de Tournehem, and in 1741 married his nephew, Le Normant d'Étoiles. She became a queen of fashion (later giving her name to a particular hair-style and to a square-cut, low bodice) and attracted the eye of the King at a ball.

Obtaining a legal separation from her husband, she was installed at Versailles and ennobled as Marquise de Pompadour. She was the King's mistress from 1745 for about five years.

Though modern scholarship credits Louis XV with more decision-making ability than was previously thought, Madame de Pompadour, as she is known, is thought to have assumed control of public affairs and to have swayed the policy of the state for 20 years. She reversed the traditional policy of France because Frederick II, the Great, lampooned her. She filled all public offices with her nominees and made her own favourites ministers of France but her policy was disastrous, and her wars (she is blamed for leading France into the Seven Years War) unfortunate — the ministry of Choiseul was the only fairly creditable portion of the reign.

A lavish patron of the arts, she heaped her bounty upon architects and painters, though had less success in literature than the decorative arts because she could not arouse the King's interest in it. She founded the École Militaire and the royal factory at Sèvres. She held her difficult position to the end, and retained the king's favour by managing all his business, by diverting him with private theatricals, and at last by countenancing his debaucheries. The *Mémoires* (1766) are not genuine.

Poniatowska, Elena

Born 1933
French-born Mexican writer, one of the most
important in Latin America

Elena Pontiatowska was born in Paris. Her father was Polish and her mother was Mexican, and the family emigrated to Mexico when she was 10 years old. She is a fiercely original writer whose works include journalism (she contributes to several of the best newspapers in Mexico), testimonial literature, short stories, novels (notably *Hasta no verte, Jesus mío*, 1969, 'Until I See You, dear Jesus') and literary criticism. She is also one of the most respected interviewers in Mexico.

Her most famous work is the collage *La noceh de Tlatelolco* (1971, Eng trans *Massacre in Mexico*, 1975). One of her main areas of interest is re-creating the modes of speech of the Mexican popular classes.

Pons, Lily (Alice Joséphine)

Born 1898 Died 1976
French-born American soprano who sang with the
New York Metropolitan Opera for over 30 years

Lily Pons was born in Draguignan, near Cannes. She studied in Paris and made her début in 1928 in Delibes's *Lakmé*, in which she could reach the high F that no singer had sung for 50 years.

She became a fine dramatic coloratura, with a high-pitched voice and vivacious manner, and excelled in her small opera repertory, achieving immense success in Paris, London, South America, and especially at the New York Metropolitan.

She also sang in films, and during World War II toured North Africa and the Far East.

Ponselle, (Ponzillo) Rosa

Born 1897 Died 1981
American soprano whose voice was described as 'vocal gold'

Rosa Ponselle was born in Meridan, Connecticut. Her career began in vaudeville. At the Italian tenor Enrico Caruso's suggestion she appeared as Leonora opposite him in *La forza del destino* at the New York Metropolitan (1918).

She sang in leading French and Italian grand opera roles there until 1937, her powerful, opulent voice and dramatic presence making her immensely successful in operas by Verdi, Meyerbeer, Mozart, and Bellini.

She also appeared at Covent Garden in 1929–31. She later taught and directed opera in Baltimore. Her sister Carmela (1888–1977) was an operatic mezzo-soprano.

Ponsonby, Sarah *see entry on* Butler, Lady Eleanor

Popova, Liubov Sergeevna, *née* Eding

Born 1889 Died 1924
Russian painter and stage designer who contributed greatly to the Constructivist school

Liubov Eding was born near Moscow. After studying in Paris (1912–13) she returned to Russia where she met Vladimir Tatlin, the founder of Soviet Constructivism. She became a member of the Russian avant-garde and contributed a great deal to the Constructivist school, developing her interest in colour and space within the painting and in what she termed the 'architectonic value' of the picture.

Her work was especially important for its exploration of abstract colour values, for she used subtly graduated colours, making them appear to rotate within the painting, and also tried to emphasize the flat, two-dimensional nature of the painted surface, avoiding any suggestion of space or volume.

In the year before her death she designed textiles for the First State Textile Print Factory, Moscow, where there was a memorial exhibition in her honour in 1924.

Popp, Adelheid, *née* Dworak

Born 1869 Died 1939
Austrian trade unionist who led the earliest women's strikes

Adelheid Dworak was born in Inzersdorf, near Vienna, and attended the local *Volksschule* for three years. From the age of eight she earned money to supplement the family income and educated herself by reading socialist works during periods of illness.

In the 1880s she became a militant trade unionist and led the first women's strike in four clothing factories (1893). From 1892 she edited *Arbeiterinnen Zeitung,* the paper of the Austrian Socialist Women's Movement. She also co-founded the reading and discussion club Libertas (1893) which promoted education and debating skills for women.

She married in 1894 and her reminiscences have been published in English as the *Autobiography of a Working Woman* (1912).

Popp, Lucia

Born 1939 Died 1994
Austrian soprano who had a bright voice and charming stage presence

Lucia Popp was born in Uhoršk Veš, Czechoslovakia. She was married twice, to her accompanist György Fischer, and to the tenor Peter Seiffert. She made her début in Bratislava in 1963 as the Queen of the Night in Mozart's *Die Zauberflöte* and joined the Vienna State Opera later that year. Her first British appearance was as Oscar in Verdi's *Un ballo in maschera* at Covent Garden in 1966.

Her clear, bell-like voice and boyish physique made her a certain choice for the so-called 'trouser roles', but she matured to bring a sophisticated presence to the Marschallin in Richard Strauss's *Der Rosenkavalier* and other demanding parts.

Poppaea Sabina

Died AD65
Roman society beauty who married the Emperor Nero

Poppaea Sabina divorced her first husband in favour of her lover, Nero's playboy friend, the future Emperor Otho. Then she became Nero's mistress, and divorced Otho to marry him in AD62.

Her influence over Nero allegedly extended to his having his mother **Agrippina, the Younger** and his former wife Octavia put to death, and ordering the philosopher Seneca to commit suicide.

Poppaea Sabina shared the then fashionable interest in Judaism, and has been thought by many to have encouraged Nero in his vicious attack on the Christians in the aftermath of the Fire of Rome (AD64). Tradition relates that she was kicked to death by Nero.

Porète, Marguerite de

Born c.1265   Died 1310
French Béguine writer and martyr, recognized as
a prominent mystic of the 13th century

Marguerite de Porète originally came from Valenciennes. She became a Béguine, a member of the movement begun by **Marie d'Oignies**. Her work on mystical love, *The Mirror of Simple Souls*, proved unacceptable to the church authorities, and they had her burnt at the stake as a heretic in the Place de Grève, Paris.

The Council of Vienne condemned Béguine teachings generally in 1311–12, although some of the sisterhoods' concerns, including writing in the vernacular instead of Latin, survived with the German Dominican mystic Meister Eckhart (c.1260–1327), who visited Paris the year after Porète's death.

Porter, Eleanor, *née* Hodgman

Born 1868   Died 1920
American novelist whose Pollyanna *became a*
lasting success

Eleanor Hodgman was born in Littleton, New Hampshire. She studied music at the New England Conservatory, and married in 1892. Her early novels include *Cross Currents* (1907) and *Miss Billy* (1911).

In 1913 *Pollyanna* appeared; it was an immediate success and has retained its popularity ever since. A sequel, *Pollyanna Grows Up*, was published in 1915, and two volumes of short stories, *The Tangled Threads* and *Across the Years*, appeared posthumously in 1924.

Porter, Gene(va) *see* Stratton-Porter, Gene

Porter, Helen Kemp, *née* Archbold

Born 1899   Died 1987
English biochemist, elected a Fellow of the Royal
Society in 1956 for innovative work on plant
metabolism

Helen Archbold was born in Farnham, Surrey, and entered Bedford College, London, in 1917 to study sciences. In 1922 she was appointed to work on a project based at Imperial College, London, to study the biochemistry of apples, in which she was later joined by **Elsie Widdowson**. This was of concern because of deterioration during cold storage and transport.

Despite short breaks during World War II, she remained at Imperial College until retirement in 1964, becoming the College's first woman professor in 1959. She married the physician William Porter in 1937 but was widowed after only a few years, and married the physiologist Arthur St George Huggett in 1962, but had no children from either marriage.

Porter, Jane

Born 1776   Died 1850
English writer who made her name with the
romance Thaddeus of Warsaw

Jane Porter was born in Durham, the daughter of an army surgeon and sister of the battle-painter Robert Ker Porter (1775–1842) and Anna Maria Porter (1780–1832), who became the author of such novels as the highly successful *The Hungarian Brothers* (1807), about the French Revolution. Jane made a great reputation in 1803 with her high-flown romance, *Thaddeus of Warsaw*, and had even more success in 1810 with *The Scottish Chiefs*, although her stage tragedy *Switzerland* (1819) was a failure.

Other books were *The Pastors' Fireside* (1815), *Duke Christian of Lüneburg* (1824), *Tales Round a Winter's Hearth* (with her sister Anna Maria, 1824) and *The Field of Forty Footsteps* (1828). *Sir Edward Seaward's Shipwreck* (1831), a clever fiction, edited by her, was almost certainly written by her eldest brother, Dr William Ogilvie Porter (1774–1850).

Porter, Katherine Anne Maria Veronica Callista Russell

Born 1890   Died 1980
American writer who won acclaim for her lengthy
short stories, unusual in their depth and richness
of character depiction

Katherine Anne Porter was born in Indian Creek, Texas, and brought up by a grandmother near Kyle, Texas. She ran away and got married at 16, but divorced at 19. She worked as a reporter and actress, moved to Greenwich Village, then went to Mexico (1920–2) and took up Mexican causes.

She had started writing at a very early age,

but allowed nothing to be published until 1928, when her first collection of stories, *Flowering Judas*, appeared. Later, in Paris, she married a consular official (divorced 1938), and wrote her first novel, *Hacienda* (1934). Back in the USA she was married for a third time, to a professor of English, but divorced four years later. Three short novels, published as *Pale Horse, Pale Rider* (1939), were a success.

Ship of Fools (1962), an immense allegorical novel analysing the German state of mind in the 1930s, aroused great controversy. A volume of essays, *The Days Before*, appeared in 1952, and *The Collected Stories* (1965) won the 1966 Pulitzer Prize for fiction.

Portsmouth, Louise de Kéroualle, Duchess of

Born 1649 Died 1734
French courtesan who became the mistress of
Charles II of Britain

Louise de Kéroualle was born in Brittany. She went to England in 1670 ostensibly as a lady-in-waiting to Charles II's cherished sister, **Henrietta Anne**, Duchess of Orléans, but had secretly been charged to influence the King in favour of the French alliance, the secret Treaty of Dover.

On the sudden death of Henrietta Anne, Louise joined the ladies in waiting of Charles's queen, **Catherine of Braganza**. Charles soon made her his mistress and ennobled her (1673) and her son, who became Duke of Richmond. An able poltician herself, she could influence the King in favour of the politicians whom she befriended, who in turn protected her position, and continued to receive honours from the French King, Louis XIV.

'Madame Carwell', as she was known, was rapacious and haughty however, and universally detested.

Post, Emily, *née* Price

Born 1873 Died 1960
American writer and socialite whose name
became synonymous with proper etiquette

Emily Price was born into a wealthy family in Baltimore, Maryland, and educated in New York. She married in 1892 but divorced after having two children and began her career writing novels and society journalism, gradually allowing her interest in correct social behaviour to develop.

Intending to shape the nation's manners, she found lasting fame with *Etiquette in Society, in Business, in Politics and at Home* (1922), which became better known as *Etiquette: The Blue*

Book of Social Usage. By the time of her death it had sold more than a million copies and had brought Post many newspaper column inches and radio broadcasts.

She also wrote *How to Behave Though a Debutante* (1928) and a book about interior decorating, *The Personality of a House* (1930). In 1946 she founded the Emily Post Institute for the Study of Gracious Living.

Postan, Eileen Edna Le Poer, *née* Power

Born 1889 Died 1940
English expert on women's historical studies who
achieved eminence in academia as well as the
world of literature

Eileen Power was born in Altringham, Cheshire, into a London stockbroker's family. She excelled in her scholastic career at Cambridge, in Paris, and at the London School of Economics. She became fascinated by women's role in economic history, and had been appointed Professor of Economic History at LSE, before she married her colleague Michael Postan.

Now recognized as an expert in British women's historical studies, Eileen Postan produced an outstanding series of publications, from *Medieval English Nunneries* in 1922 through the *Economic History Review*, which she founded in 1927, to *Medieval Women*, published 35 years after her death.

Potter, (Helen) Beatrix

Born 1866 Died 1943
English author and illustrator of books for
children

Beatrix Potter was born in Kensington, London, into a wealthy family. The atmosphere at home was oppressively quiet and Beatrix, supervised by nurses and educated by governesses, grew up a lonely town child longing for the country. She taught herself to draw and paint, and while still quite young did serious natural history studies of fungi with the intention of making a book of watercolours.

She turned to sketching pet animals dressed as human beings to amuse younger children. The original version of *The Tale of Peter Rabbit* was enclosed with a letter to her ex-governess's child in 1893 and later published at her own expense, with fuller illustrations, in 1900, as was *The Tailor of Gloucester* (1902). When Frederick Warne took over publication in 1903, Potter had her first popular success with *The Tale of Squirrel Nutkin* (1903). In an

Beatrix Potter, 1889

appreciative, if gently satirical, review, Graham Greene considered *The Roly-Poly Pudding* (1908, later changed to *The Tale of Samuel Whiskers*) to be her masterpiece. Miss Potter was not amused.

In 1913, eight years after she had moved to a farm at Sawrey, near Lake Windermere (where six of her books are set), she married William Heelis, a Lake District solicitor. Thereafter she devoted herself almost entirely to farming and the new National Trust. *Johnny Town-Mouse* (1918) was her last book in the familiar style. She devised an elaborate cryptic diary whose code was broken by Leslie Linder and published as *The Journal of Beatrix Potter 1881–1897* (1966). She was the outstanding writer and artist of picture-story books of her time, and Peter Rabbit, Jemima Puddle-Duck, Mrs Tiggy-Winkle, Benjamin Bunny, and the rest have become classic characters in children's literature.

Powell, (Ada) Louise, *née* Lessone

Born 1882 Died 1956
English designer and decorator responsible for the revival of hand painting in the Wedgwood factory

Louise Lessone was born into a distinguished French family of artists. She studied at the Central School of Art in London and was closely associated with the Arts and Crafts Exhibition Society. She and her husband Alfred Powell painted pottery for the Wedgwood factory from c.1904, training artists in freehand work and establishing a separate department in the 1920s.

On the whole Powell's images concentrated on armorial designs, flowing patterns, flowers and foliage, drawing loosely on Islamic and Renaissance traditions. After leaving Wedgwood she worked mainly to commission, also selling her work through a number of London galleries.

Powell, (Elizabeth) Dilys

Born 1901 Died 1995
British film critic and writer who was with the Sunday Times *for 40 years*

Dilys Powell was educated first at Bournemouth High School and then at Somerville College, Oxford, where she met her first husband, Humfry Payne. In 1926 she married Payne, now living full-time in Greece, and two years later started work at the *Sunday Times*. She travelled enthusiastically in Greece before Payne's sudden death in 1936, which prompted Powell to write, amongst other works, *The Traveller's Journey is Done* (1943) and *The Villa Ariadne* (1973).

She worked as a film critic for the *Sunday Times* between the years 1939 and 1979, marrying its literary editor, Leonard Russell, in 1943. She sat on the Board of Governors at the British Film Institute (1948–52) and from 1976 wrote about films on television. In 1979 she took up writing film reviews for *Punch*, which she continued to do until that magazine's demise in 1992.

Her reviews have been published as *The Golden Screen* (1989) and *The Dilys Powell Film Reader* (1991).

Praed, Rosa

Born 1851 Died 1935
Australian novelist, best known as a writer of romantic fiction under the name of Mrs Campbell Praed

Rosa Praed was born in Bromelton, Logan River, Queensland. The privations of her early married life on outback Queensland stations resulted in *An Australian Heroine* (1880) and *The Romance of a Station* (1889). In 1875 she left with her husband for London where she became a popular novelist and the 'Queen' of circulating libraries, mixing in literary circles which included Oscar Wilde.

During the next 40 years she produced almost as many novels, many with an Australian setting. *Policy and Passion* (1881) dealt, as did many of the others, with the disillusion which marriage brings. She questioned the permanency of marriage in *The Bond of Wedlock* (1887), which created controversy as a play.

The failure of her marriage, and the death of her four children in tragic circumstances, turned her to aspects of spiritualism and she set up house with a 'medium', Nancy Harward (1899–1927), producing a number of occult books.

Press, Irina Natanovna

Born 1939
Soviet athlete, an excellent all-rounder and multiple record-breaker

Irina Press was born in Kharkov, the younger sister of **Tamara Press**, and graduated from the Leningrad Institute of Railway Engineers in 1962. Between 1959 and 1966 she proved her versatility on the athletics field, becoming USSR national champion in a variety of fields, including pentathlon.

At the 1960 Olympics she was 80 metres hurdles champion and also ran in the USSR Olympic sprint relay team; in 1964 she picked up a bronze in the 80 metres hurdles and became pentathlon champion.

Over the course of her career Irina Press set six world records at 80 metres hurdles and eight at pentathlon, and became an Honoured Master of Sport.

Press, Tamara Natanovna

Born 1937
Soviet athlete whose domination of the shot and the discus lasted the length of her career

Tamara Press was born in Kharkov and graduated in building engineering. She is the elder sister of **Irina Press**. She came to prominence when she won the shot and finished third in the discus at the 1958 European championships. Two years later at the Olympic Games she won the gold medal in the shot and the silver in the discus. At the next European championships in 1962 she took the double, winning both the shot and the discus, a victory she repeated at the 1964 Olympics.

Over the course of her career, Tamara Press set six world shot records and six world discus records, winning 16 national titles for shot and discus. She retired in 1966.

Preston, Margaret Rose

Born 1875   Died 1963
Australian artist and teacher whose work shows the influence of Aboriginal painting

Margaret Preston was born in Adelaide, South Australia, and educated in Sydney and Melbourne. In 1904 she went to Germany where she attended the Government Art School for Women in Munich. She travelled widely in Europe before returning to Sydney in 1919.

An enthusiastic traveller, she visited various south Pacific islands, south-east Asia, and China in the 1920s, and Africa and India in the late 1950s. She was an active champion of Aboriginal painting, and its influence is clearly seen in her still lifes of Australian flowers and her wood and linocut engravings with their strong design and use of colour.

Previn, Dory, *née* Langdon

Born c.1936
American singer, lyricist and playwright whose work ranges from film songs to autobiographical verse

Dory Langdon was born in Woodbridge, New Jersey. She sang and danced as a child, then studied acting. Her song lyrics interested film and television companies and she collaborated with André Previn (1929–), to whom she was married from 1959 to 1970. She received Oscar nominations for some of her film songs, including 'The Faraway Part of Town' (1960), sung by **Judy Garland**.

Her own singing emerged on three semi-autobiographical and semi-fictional albums recorded in 1971 and 1972: *Mythical Kings and Iguanas*, *Reflections in a Mud Puddle*, and *Mary C Brown and the Hollywood Sign*. Her verse was collected in *On My Way to Where* (1973), and she has written memoirs concerning her struggle with schizophrenia and various kinds of abuse.

Price, (Mary Violet) Leontyne

Born 1927
American lyric soprano who worked to combat racial discrimination in her profession

Leontyne Price was born in Laurel, Mississippi, where she sang in the church choir as a child. After studying at the Juilliard Music School in New York City, she was successful early in her career as a notable Bess (1952–4) in George Gershwin's *Porgy and Bess*. In 1955 she became the first black opera singer to perform on television, when she took the title role in a production of *Tosca*.

She performed at many of the major European opera houses during the 1950s, then based herself at the New York Metropolitan Opera House from 1961 to 1985, when she retired.

As well as being remembered as an outstanding Verdi singer, she was much associated with Samuel Barber's music, especially in the role of Cleopatra, which he created for her.

Price, Dame Margaret Berenice

Born 1941
Welsh operatic and concert soprano

Margaret Price was born in Blackwood, near Tredegar. She trained at Trinity College of Music in London and made her début in 1962 with Welsh National Opera as Cherubino in the *Marriage of Figaro*, repeating the role for her first appearance at Covent Garden the following year. From 1968 she appeared at Glyndebourne, performing some of her most impressive Mozart roles there, such as Fiordiligi in *Così fan tutte*. Her many Verdi roles are notable too, and she has made a recording of Wagner's *Tristan and Isolde*.

She has performed in the major opera houses of Europe and the USA, receiving rapturous praise for her performance of Desdemona during her tour of the USA with Paris Opéra in 1976, and making her début at the New York Metropolitan (again as Desdemona) in 1985. She continues to impress internationally on both the concert and operatic stage.

Prichard, Katharine Susannah

Born 1883 Died 1969
Australian writer and prominent figure in literary circles whose work reflects her socialist ideals

Katharine Susannah Prichard was born in Levuka, on Ovalau, where her father was editor of the *Fiji Times*. She started work on a Melbourne newspaper, for which she made a trip to London in 1908. Four years later she returned to journalism in London. In 1915 her first novel, *The Pioneers*, won the 'colonial' section of a publisher's competition; it was filmed in Australia the following year. In 1916 she returned to Australia, married Captain Hugo Throssell VC and over the next 50 years produced 12 novels, many poems, plays, and short stories, and an autobiography, *Child of the Hurricane* (1963).

In 1920 she had become a founding member of the Australian Communist Party, and her socialist convictions coloured much of her subsequent work, especially her powerful trilogy set in the West Australian goldfields, *The Roaring Nineties* (1946), *Golden Miles* (1948) and *Winged Seeds* (1950). Her last novel, *Subtle Flame* (1967), was a study in the conflicts facing a newspaper editor.

Her son, Ric Prichard Throssell, wrote a play *For Valour* (1960, published 1976), the study of the economic and personal decline of a returned war hero, closely modelled on his father, and a biography of his mother, *Wild Weeds and Wind Flowers* (1975).

Priest, Ivy Maud Baker, *née* Baker

Born 1905 Died 1975
American politician who helped to pioneer a place for women in high governmental office

Ivy Baker Priest was born in Kimberly, Utah. Her dynamic speaking ability and her organizational skills brought her a succession of offices in the Republican party, including President of Utah Young Republicans (1934–6), co-chair of the Young Republicans for 11 western states (1936–40) and President of the Utah Legislative League (1937–9). Also during the 1930s she was a leader in the effort to enact a minimum wage law for working women in Utah.

She ran unsuccessfully for the Utah State Legislature in 1934 and for Congress in 1950, but in 1952 President Dwight D Eisenhower appointed her treasurer of the USA. She was the second woman to hold that post and served eight years. In 1966 she was elected to the post of treasurer for the state of California, where she also served for eight years. In 1968 she placed Ronald Reagan in nomination for the Republican party's candidate for US President, the first woman to perform that act.

Her autobiography *Green Grows Ivy* (1958) discusses the conflicts of work and family.

Primus, Pearl

Born 1919 Died 1994
American dancer, choreographer, anthropologist and teacher whose dances reflected her black heritage

Pearl Primus was born in Trinidad. She was a star athlete in school, and studied medicine and anthropology at Columbia University before making an accidental dance début in 1941 as a last-minute replacement. Her first solo recital followed two years later, and the first appearance of her own group in 1944. *African Ceremonial* that year was her first important choreographic work.

She continued to present concerts and choreographed on Broadway, but her real direction lay in dance and anthropological research in Africa. She made the first of several extended study trips there in 1948. On subsequent trips she was assisted in the preservation of primitive dance forms by her husband, dancer Percival Borde. She took a PhD in educational anthropology at New York University in 1978.

Pringle, Mia Lilly Kellmer

Born 1920 Died 1983
Austrian educational psychologist whose publications have influenced parent–child relationships

Mia Pringle was born in Vienna and educated at Vienna Grammar School, and at King's College and Birkbeck College, London. After teaching in primary schools from 1942 to 1945, she was appointed psychologist in the Hertfordshire School Psychology and Child Guidance Service (1945–50), deputy head of the Child Study Centre (1954–63) and lecturer (senior lecturer from 1960) in educational psychology at Birmingham University (1950–63).

She was director of the National Children's Bureau from 1963 to 1981. Her many publicatons include *Early Child Care and Education* (1974) and *Psychological Approaches to Child Abuse* (1980).

Printemps, Yvonne, *stage-name of* Yvonne Wigniolle-Dupré

Born 1894 Died 1977
French actress who became a leading performer in musical theatre

Yvonne Wigniolle-Dupré was born in Ermont, Seine-et-Oise. She made her first appearance at the Théâtre Cigale, Paris, in 1908, and appeared regularly in revue and musical comedy at both the Folies Bergère and the Palais-Royal. In 1916 she began to work with the French actor and dramatist Sacha Guitry (1885–1957), appearing in many of his plays. She subsequently (in 1919) became the second of his five wives.

She appeared in London, for example in Guitry's *Nono* in 1920 and his *Mozart* in 1926, and in New York, but did not undertake English parts until 1934, when she played in Noël Coward's *Conversation Piece*. She divorced Guitry and took for her second husband in 1932 the actor Pierre Fresnay, with whom she had great success in *Trois Valses* (1937).

In 1937 she returned to Paris as manager of the Théâtre de la Michodière where she also appeared in musicals and comedies until the late 1950s.

Priscilla, *also called* Prisca

1st century AD
Biblical character, an early Jewish Christian

Priscilla was married to a leather worker or tent maker called Aquila, and was apparently more important (or perhaps more forceful) in Church or society than her husband for, except for the first mention of the couple in Acts and a reference made by Paul in 1 Corinthians, she is always named first.

Priscilla and Aquila were close friends and co-workers with Paul (also a leather worker or tent maker) in Corinth, and in Ephesus where a church met in their house and they helped the Alexandrian Jew Apollos to Christian faith. They had come to Corinth after the expulsion of Jews from Rome by Claudius, and seem to have returned there after his death.

Procter, Adelaide Ann, *pseud* Mary Berwick

Born 1825 Died 1864
English poet and feminist who numbered Charles Dickens among her admirers

Adelaide Procter was born in London, the daughter of the poet Bryan Waller Procter (pseud Barry Cornwall). In 1851 she became a Roman Catholic. Among her admirers was Charles Dickens, who wrote the foreword to her *Complete Works* (1905). Her *Legends and Lyrics* (1858–60), some of which were previously written for Dickens's magazine *Household Words*, won poetical renown.

Her poems, many of which were sentimental, included *The Lost Chord*, which was set to music by Sir Arthur Sullivan. Procter was also editor of an anthology of verse, *Victoria Regia*, which was published in 1861 by **Emily Faithfull**'s Victoria Press.

Her activity as a feminist included helping to found the Society for Promoting the Employment of Women and donating the profits from her *Chaplet of Verses* (1862) to a refuge for homeless women.

Procter, Dod, *née* Doris M Shaw

Born 1892 Died 1972
English artist and traveller best known for her painting Morning

Doris Shaw was born London. In 1907 she and her brother studied at Elizabeth and Stanhope Forbes's painting school at Newlyn. She then went on to study at the Atelier of Colarossi in Paris in 1910.

In 1912 she married the artist Ernest Procter and with him designed the decoration for the Kokine Palace in Rangoon in 1920. This commission awakened her interest in travel which she continued after the death of her husband in 1935.

She first exhibited at the Royal Academy in 1913 and was elected an RA in 1942. Her work has a rounded, sculptural quality which has been attributed to the early influence of Cubism. Her most famous painting, *Morning*, was acclaimed picture of the year in 1927 and

Dod Procter, 1938

was purchased by the *Daily Mail* for the Tate Gallery.

Prout, Margaret Millicent, *née* Fisher

Born 1875 Died 1963
English artist who painted mostly landscape and flower studies in an impressionist manner

Margaret Fisher was born in Chelsea, London, the only daughter of the English impressionist Mark Fisher. Her childhood was spent in England and France where she painted with her father prior to studying at the Slade School of Art (1894–7). She taught life classes at Hammersmith School of Art and married John Prout in 1908.

As she painted, she developed interesting techniques, such as washing out pigment and adding body colour and charcoal to great effect. She exhibited at the RWS (Royal Society of Painters in Water Colours) and the NEAC (New English Art Club), was elected associate member of the Royal Academy in 1948 and awarded a medal from the Paris Salon. She was still showing in the RA 42 years after the appearance of her first exhibit.

Pulcheria

Born AD399 Died AD453
Byzantine empress who became a schism healer and church founder

Pulcheria was the daughter of Emperor Arcadius, and was made regent at the age of 15 for her younger brother Theodosius II. She arranged his marriage, but his wife Athenais (who became a Christian and took the name **Eudocia**) became her rival and they disagreed on contemporary theological controversies, with Pulcheria supporting orthodoxy.

Pulcheria restored John Chrysostom's relics to Constantinople in 438, which brought about the healing of a church schism. She was forced from court in 440 but returned in 450, when the elderly soldier-statesman Marcian was nominal Emperor. She convened the Council of Chalcedon in 451, founded three churches and left her goods to the poor.

Pye, Edith Mary

Born 1876 Died 1965
English Quaker midwife and international relief organizer

Edith Mary Pye was born in London. She trained as a nurse and midwife, becoming Superintendent of District Nurses in 1907.

After becoming a Quaker in 1908, she did World War I relief work in France, later working in Vienna, Germany and Spain. During and after World War II she worked for famine relief in France and Greece. In the 1920s and 1930s she served on the executive of the Women's International League for Peace, and in 1934 she was President of the British Institute of Midwives.

Pym, Barbara Mary Crampton

Born 1913 Died 1980
English novelist who gently satirizes the frustrated lives of middle-class spinsters

Barbara Pym was born in Shropshire. She was educated at St Hilda's College, Oxford, and later worked at the International African Institute in London. Her fiction is deliberately confined within narrow bounds, characteristically exploring the tragi-comic lives of frustrated middle-class spinsters in a delicate, understated fashion.

She published three novels in the 1950s, the best of which is *A Glass of Blessings* (1958), then lapsed into obscurity until, partly through the support of Philip Larkin, her *Quartet in Autumn* appeared in 1977.

The Sweet Dove Died (1979) was the last book published in her lifetime, but four more novels, *A Few Green Leaves* (1980), *An Unsuitable Attachment* (1982), *Crampton Hodnet* (1985) and *An Academic Question* (1986), appeared posthumously.

q

Qiu Jin (Ch'iu Chin)

Born 1875   Died 1907
Chinese feminist and revolutionary who was
executed for her alleged activities

In 1904 Qiu Jin abandoned her family to study
in Japan, where she became actively involved
in radical Chinese student associations calling
for the overthrow of the Manchu Qing (Ch'ing)
Dynasty.

On her return to China in 1906, she founded
a women's journal in which she argued that
the liberation of women was an essential pre-
requisite for a strong China.

In 1907 Qiu Jin was implicated in an abortive anti-Manchu uprising and was executed
by the Qing authorities.

Quant, Mary

Born 1934
English fashion designer who helped make London
a fashion centre

Mary Quant was born in London. She studied
at Goldsmith's College of Art and began
fashion design when she opened a small boutique in Chelsea in 1955. Two years later she
married one of her partners, Alexander Plun-
kett Greene.

Her clothes became extremely fashionable
in the 1960s when the geometric simplicity of
her designs, especially the mini-skirt, and the
originality of her colours, became an essential
feature of the 'swinging Britain' era. As well
as the 'mod' or 'Chelsea' look, she introduced
the 'wet' look for her young clientele, characterized by close-fitting vinyl clothing.

In the 1970s she extended into cosmetics
and textile design.

Quimby, Harriet

Born 1882   Died 1912
American aviator and journalist, the first licensed
woman pilot

Harriet Quimby was born in Arroyo Grande,
California. In 1911, eight years after the first
flight of the Wright Brothers, she became the
first woman to earn her pilot's licence. She was
also the first woman to fly across the English
Channel on 12 April, 1912, which Louis Blériot
had done for the first time in 1909.

r

Rachel

*Biblical character for whose hand in marriage
Jacob had to work for 14 years*

Rachel was the daughter of Laban and wife of
Jacob. Jacob worked seven years to earn Rachel as his wife, but was tricked into taking
her elder sister Leah (because traditionally the
younger sister could not be given in marriage
before the elder), and had to work another
seven for Rachel (Genesis 29).

At first Rachel was barren, but God gave
her a child, Joseph (Genesis 30.24); she died
when giving birth to her second son Benjamin
during the long journey to Ephrathath (Bethlehem) in Canaan.

Rachel, originally Élisa Félix

Born 1821 Died 1858
*French tragedienne who was unrivalled in
classical roles, and scored her greatest triumph
as Phèdre*

Rachel was born in Mumpf in Switzerland,
the daughter of Jewish-Alsatian pedlars.
Brought to Paris about 1830, she received
singing and elocution lessons, and made her
début in *La Vendéenne* in 1837 with moderate
success.

In June 1838 she appeared as Camille in
Horace at the Théâtre Français, and was
unrivalled in classical roles for the rest of her
career. Though barely five feet tall, she had an
imposing stage presence and came to dominate
the affairs of the Comédie-Française during
her 17 years there. She also had immense
success in *Adrienne Lecouvreur*, written for her
by Ernest Legouvé and Eugène Scribe.

She visited London (and was witnessed by
Charlotte Brontë), Brussels, Berlin and St Petersburg, everywhere meeting with enthusiastic applause. In 1855, in America, her health
gave way. She died of consumption.

Rachilde, *pseud of* Marguerite Eymery

Born 1860 Died 1935
*French writer who wrote novels characterized by
the abnormal sexuality of their protagonists*

Marguerite Eymery was born at Le Cros in the
Perigord. Her father was a cavalry officer who
would have preferred a son, and her mother
an intellectual, and she spent much of her
lonely childhood in her grandfather's library.
With the prospect of marriage at 14 to a
middle-aged soldier she attempted suicide, so
the engagement was cancelled and she took to
writing, publishing stories under the pseudonym 'Rachilde'.

Following an encouraging response from
Victor Hugo to one of her stories, she moved
to Paris and entered its literary circles, often
dressing as a man. She married Alfred Vallette,
editor of the *Mercure de France*. Her first major
success, *Monsieur Venus*, was published in
Belgium in 1884. Both shocking and impressive, its story of a woman removing parts of her
deceased lover to create a male version of the
anatomical female model 'Venus' caused such
a scandal that Rachilde was threatened with
imprisonment if she ever went to Belgium.

It also launched her long literary career,
which continued with *The Marquise de Sade*
(1887), the story of a girl's warped development in a society characterized by misogyny;
Les Hors Nature (1897, 'Nature's Outcasts'),
about two incestuous brothers; and *La Souris
japonaise* (1912, 'The Japanese Mouse'), which
centres on the theme of paedophilia. She
herself became increasingly misogynisitc, and
expressed her views in an autobiographical
pamphlet *Pourquois je ne suis pas feministe*
(1928, 'Why I Am Not a Feminist').

Rackham, Clara, née Tabor

Born 1875 Died 1965
English feminist and factory inspector

Clara Tabor was the daughter of a farmer. She was educated at Cambridge, where she developed and interest in politics. After her marriage in 1901 to Harris Rackham, a Fellow of Christ's College, she served on local boards, becoming aware of the need for women to be involved in local government.

In 1915 she was appointed one of the first women factory inspectors, working in Lancashire to start with, then in London. Elected to the Cambridge Borough Council in 1919, she was later elected to the City Council, and she stood twice as Labour parliamentary candidate, for Chelmsford in 1922 and for Saffron Walden in 1935. She published a book on *Factory Law* in 1938.

Radcliffe, Ann, née Ward

Born 1764 Died 1823
English novelist who became known for Gothic romances such as The Mysteries of Udolpho

Ann Ward was born in London. At the age of 23 she married William Radcliffe, a graduate of Oxford and student of law, who became proprietor and editor of the weekly *English Chronicle*. In 1789 she published the first of her Gothic romances, *The Castles of Athlin and Dunbayne*, followed by *A Sicilian Romance* (1790), *The Romance of the Forest* (1791), *The Mysteries of Udolpho* (1794) and *The Italian* (1797).

She travelled much, and her journal shows how keen an eye she had for natural scenery and ruins. A sixth romance, *Gaston de Blondeville*, with a metrical tale, 'St Alban's Abbey', and a short biography, was published in 1826. Her reputation among her contemporaries was considerable. She was praised by Sir Walter Scott, and influenced writers such as Byron, Shelley and **Charlotte Brontë**.

Her particular brand of writing found many imitators, most of them unfortunately inferior to herself, and prompted **Jane Austen**'s satire *Northanger Abbey.*

Radclyffe-Hall, Marguerite *see* Hall, (Marguerite) Radclyffe

Radegund, *also spelt* Radegunda

Born 518 Died 587
Early Christian who escaped her arranged marriage to do good works

Radegund was the daughter of King Berthar of Thuringia. She was taken as a hostage to France in 531 and forced at the age of 16 to marry Clotaire, the son of Clovis and St **Clotilda**. She escaped to a convent, became a deaconess, and founded a double monastery at Poitiers which attracted many high-born converts.

Her good works included promoting reconciliation among warring kings. Her secretary, the Latin poet Venantius Fortunatus, later Bishop of Poitiers, wrote her first biography. One of his hymns was inspired by the fragment of the True Cross that she obtained for her convent from Emperor Justin II.

Rae, Barbara

Born 1943
Scottish artist who uses bold blocks of colour, sensitive line and differing surface textures

Barbara Rae was born in Edinburgh. She studied at Edinburgh College of Art from 1961 to 1965, and used a travelling scholarship to paint in France and Spain in 1966. She was elected RSW (Royal Scottish Water Colour Society) in 1975 and ARSA (Associate of the Royal Scottish Academy) in 1980, and has received many awards, including the Guthrie medal and the William Gillies award, both from the RSA. In 1985 she was awarded an Arts Council grant and spent three months working in Spain and in Santa Fe, New Mexico, USA.

Rae's work shows a preoccupation with her response to the man-made marks of urban and rural landscape, both in her native Scotland and in the Spanish uplands. She has exhibited in Britain and the USA and has works in private and public collections there and in Europe.

Raeburn, Agnes Middleton

Born 1872 Died 1955
Scottish artist associated with Charles Rennie Mackintosh and his circle

Agnes Middleton Raeburn was born in Glasgow and trained at Glasgow School of Art. She contributed to the *Magazine* as early as 1893.

Her early work was influenced by Glasgow symbolism and her later landscapes from France and Holland, as well as her flower studies, are fluid in style and freely painted.

She was elected RSW (Royal Scottish Water Colour Society) in 1901 and exhibited many works in the RSA (Royal Scottish Academy).

Rahab

Floreat c.1400 BC
Biblical character, a prostitute who was saved when Jericho fell because of her obedience to God

Rahab was a prostitute who protected Joshua's spies while they surveyed the defences of Jericho. In return for helping them, she and her family were saved when the city fell to the Israelites.

She is probably the Rahab named as the mother of Boaz, and so an ancestor of King David and of Jesus Christ. The New Testament also cites her as an example of faith (Hebrews 11.31). Her reputation is enhanced in Jewish traditions that stress either her former way of life as a first-rate source of information or her latter life as the wife of Joshua.

Raicho Hiratsuka *see* Hiratsuka, Raicho

Rainer, Yvonne

Born 1934
American experimental dancer, choreographer and filmmaker who has been one of the greatest influences on post-modern dance

Yvonne Rainer was born in San Francisco, California. She moved to New York in 1956, took classes at the **Martha Graham** School, and returned in 1969 to California where she joined Anna Halprin's experimental summer course, which had a profound effect on her future work.

Back in New York she studied with Merce Cunningham, and enrolled in Robert Dunn's pioneering composition class along with **Trisha Brown**, Steve Paxton, David Gordon and **Lucinda Childs**. The radical Judson Dance Theatre, for which she was the most prolific choreographer, was born out of these alternative sessions.

Trio A (part of the larger work *The Mind is a Muscle*), her signature piece, was made to be performed by anyone of any age whether trained or not. *Continuous Project — Altered Daily* was started in 1970 and *Grand Union Dreams* was made in 1971. In 1973, she gave up her involvement in dance and took up filmmaking. Her films include *Film About a Woman Who. . .* (1974) and *Kristina Talking Pictures* (1976).

Rainey, Gertrude Pridgett, *known as* Ma Rainey, *née* Pridgett

Born 1886   Died 1939
American singer who is considered to be the first of the great black blues singers

Gertrude Pridgett was born in Columbus, Georgia. She began her career as a singer in the Negro minstrel shows in the South, but did not become well known until Paramount hired her to record songs with an urban flavour.

Her style of singing preserves the continuity from early Negro music to jazz, and her contribution to jazz, which only became widely acknowledged after her death, includes the songs 'See See Rider' and 'Slow Driving Moan'.

Raitt, Bonnie

Born 1949
American country blues singer and guitarist

Bonnie Raitt was born in Burbank, California, the daughter of John Raitt, a stage singer. She worked with Freebo and with Bluesbusters between 1969 and 1971, when her eponymous début album was released.

Raitt is perhaps too musicianly for mass appeal, and her records *Give It Up* (1972) and *Streetlights* (1974) had an unmarketable jazz tinge. However, she continued to develop and became a minor cult with blues fans, particularly after her collaboration with John Lee Hooker on his *The Healer* (1989). In the 1990s however, she had a huge breakthrough in popularity and became a major star in the USA, winning Grammy awards and gaining access to perform in large concerts.

Ramabai, Sarasvati, *also known as* Pandita Ramabai

Born 1858   Died 1922
Indian Christian educator who was a champion of female emancipation

Ramabai Sarasvati was born near Mangalore in southern India, the daughter of a Brahmin. She was orphaned in 1874, but survived by reciting Hindu Scriptures, and her skill in Sanskrit earned her the name Pandita ('teacher' or 'mistress of learning').

After only two years of marriage, she was widowed. She went to England (where she and her daughter were baptized) for education (1883–6) and to the USA for study and fund-raising (1886–9), returning to Bombay to open a boarding school for high-caste child widows. Following the 1896–7 famines, she established the Mukti Sadan (House of Salvation) orphanage and training institute for women and children at Kedgaon, near Poona.

She wrote *The High Caste Hindu Woman* (1887) and *Testimony* (1917), translated the Bible into Marathi, and was awarded the Kaiser-i-Hind gold medal in 1919.

Rambert, Dame Marie, *stage-name of* Cyvia Rambam

Born 1888 Died 1982
Polish-born British ballet dancer, teacher and founder of the Ballet Rambert

Cyvia Rambam was born in Warsaw. She was sent to Paris to study medicine, but became involved in artistic circles and began to study eurhythmics. In 1913 she worked on Stravinsky's *Rite of Spring* with Sergei Diaghilev's Ballet Russe. She moved to London and began to dance and teach, and married playwright Ashley Dukes in 1918.

In 1931, 11 years after opening her own dance studio, she formed the Ballet Club, a permanent producing and performing organization which featured the dancer **Alicia Markova** and the choreographer Frederick Ashton. She was particularly interested in promoting new ballets, always encouraging her pupils to produce works, and this inevitably led to periodical financial shortages. Her company (which had become Ballet Rambert in 1935) had been expanding since the 1940s, but by 1966 was reduced to a small group which concentrated on new works and began to embrace modern dance techniques.

In the mid-1970s the company performed work by Glen Tetley, John Chesworth and Christopher Bruce, and has grown to become one of Britain's major contemporary touring dance companies. She was created DBE in 1962.

Rambouillet, Catherine de Vivonne, Marquise de

Born 1588 Died 1665
French noblewoman whose salon had an influence on the classical literature of 17th-century France

Catherine de Vivonne was born in Rome, the daughter of Jean de Vivonne, Marquis of Pisani. At the age of 12 she was married to the son of the Marquis de Rambouillet, who succeeded to the title in 1611. Virtuous and spiritual, she disliked both the morals and manners of the French court and sought to make her townhouse, the famous Hôtel Rambouillet, a place where cultured conversation could take place between nobles and men of letters without the insidious intrigues of court life.

For 50 years she led a salon frequented by the talent and wit of France culled from both the nobility and the literary world. With its hallmarks of refinement and elegant language, and its members' penchant for psychological exploration, the salon had a very significant and positive influence on the classical literature of 17th-century France, despite providing material for satire in Molière's comedy *Les Précieuses Ridicules* (1659).

Rame, Franca

Born 1929
Italian actress and playwright whose career is directed towards campaigning against authoritarian regimes at home or abroad

Franca Rame was born into a family of professional comedians near Milan and made her stage début at the age of eight days as a babe-in-arms. Growing up as an actress skilled in improvisatory techniques, Rame married playwright Dario Fo (1926–), and in 1956 co-founded a theatre company with him, which was soon hailed as a leading exponent of political avant-garde theatre in Europe.

By the 1970s, Rame had begun campaigning for the rights of political prisoners and against gender discrimination through her own writing and presentations. Along with her husband, from whom she was separated for some years, she remains among Europe's most important politically active actors and writers.

Rankin, Dame Annabelle Jane Mary

Born 1908 Died 1986
Australian politician, the first Australian woman to enter various ranks of politics and diplomacy

Annabelle Rankin was born in Brisbane, Queensland, the daughter of a former Minister of the Queensland parliament. Appointed senator for the state in 1946, she became the first Queensland woman to enter federal politics.

She became the first woman whip in the British Commonwealth, serving as opposition whip (1947–9) and government whip (1951–66), and then was also the first Australian woman of ministerial rank, holding the housing portfolio (1966–71).

In 1971 she was Australia's first woman head of a diplomatic mission on being appointed high commissioner to New Zealand, from which position she retired in 1974. She was appointed DBE in 1957.

Rankin, Jeannette

Born 1880 Died 1973
American feminist and pacifist who became the first female member of the US Congress

Jeanette Rankin was born near Missoula, Montana, and educated at Montana University and the New York School of Philanthropy. She went on to work as a social worker in Seattle (1909), where she became involved in the fight for women's rights.

In 1914 she was appointed legislative secretary of the National American Woman Suffrage Association, and in 1916 entered the House of Representatives as a Republican, the first woman to do so. During her two terms there (1917–19 and 1941–3) she consistently voted against American participation in both world wars, promoted women's welfare and rights, and was instrumental in the adoption of the first bill granting married women independent citizenship.

Continuing to campaign for women's issues throughout her career, she worked for the National Council for the Prevention of War from 1928 to 1939, and led the Jeannette Rankin March (1968) in which 5,000 women gathered on Capitol Hill, Washington DC, to protest against the Vietnam War.

Ransome-Kuti, Olufunmilayo, *née* Thomas

Born 1900 Died 1978
Nigerian teacher and politician who campaigned
successfully for women's enfranchisement and
against gender discrimination

Olufunmilayo Thomas was born in Abokuta, and was fortunate in receiving a good education, both in Nigeria and in the UK. She married the Rev Israel Ransome-Kuti and had four children before throwing herself into the struggle for women's rights in Nigeria.

During World War II she agitated against a local ruler's discriminative market practices and succeeded in having him deported by the British authorities. She then campaigned successfully for the enfranchisement of Nigerian women, later travelling widely as a highly-respected ambassador for African women in general, and Nigerian women in particular.

Rantzen, Esther Louise

Born 1940
English television presenter and producer, a
well-known personality in the UK

Esther Rantzen was born in Berkhamsted and educated at Somerville College, Oxford. She joined the BBC in 1963, making sound effects for radio drama. Shifting into research for *Man Alive* (1965–7), she joined *Braden's Week* (1968–72) as a reporter.

Since 1973 she has produced, written and presented *That's Life*, a populist consumer programme combining investigative journalism with a potpourri of comical items. She also produced the talent show *The Big Time*

(1976) and *Esther Interviews. . .* (1988), and has used her position of influence to campaign on issues of child abuse and drug problems in a variety of documentaries such as *Childwatch* (1987).

In 1977 she married broadcaster Desmond Wilcox (1931–); their joint publications include *Kill the Chocolate Biscuit* (1981) and *Baby Love* (1985). In 1988 she received the Richard Dimbleby award for her contributions to factual television and in 1991 she was created OBE.

Rathbone, Eleanor Florence

Born 1872 Died 1946
English feminist, pacifist and social reformer

Eleanor Rathbone was born in Liverpool into a philanthropic merchant family of Quaker ancestry. After reading classics at Somerville College, Oxford, she made an extensive study of the position of widows under the poor law, and became the leading British advocate for family allowances in *The Disinherited Family* (1924) and *The Case for Family Allowances* (1940).

She was a leader in the constitutional movement for female suffrage, and as independent member of Liverpool city council from 1909 she worked vigorously in the housing campaign between the wars. Elected as independent MP for the Combined English Universities, she fought to gain the franchise for Indian women, denounced child marriage in India (*Child Marriage: The Indian Minotaur*, 1934), and attacked appeasement of Hitler in *War Can Be Averted* (1937), non-intervention in the Spanish Civil War, and Italian aggression in Ethiopia.

She was a vigorous worker in the service of refugees, as a result of which she became an enthusiastic proponent of Zionism.

Rattenbury, Alma

Died 1935
Alleged murderer of unknown extraction who may
have helped her lover to murder her husband

Alma Rattenbury was married to a successful British architect, Francis Rattenbury (1867–1935), who was reputedly 30 years her senior, and whom she had met and married in Canada in 1928. Upon her husband's retirement, the couple settled in Britain.

In 1934, Alma advertised for a chauffeur/handyman. The employee, 18-year-old George Stoner, soon became her lover. On 24 March 1935 Alma found her husband with blood streaming from his head at their home, Villa Madeira, in Bournemouth. He later died.

The murder weapon was found to be a mallet. Alma and Stoner confessed independently. At the trial Stoner was found guilty and sentenced to death, but Alma was acquitted. She then committed suicide.

Following a petition with over 300,000 signatures, Stoner was reprieved shortly afterwards.

Ratushinskaya, Irina

Born 1954
Russian poet, human rights activist and literary cause célèbre who was imprisoned by the Soviet authorities but found favour in the West

Irina Ratushinskaya was brought up in Odessa and educated as a physicist. She was gaining a reputation as a skilled poet with a concern for social issues in Moscow when, in the 1970s, she began to get into trouble with the Soviet authorities who found her work distasteful. Eventually in 1983 she was sentenced to seven years' internal exile for anti-Soviet activities.

Her cause was, however, taken up in the West, where she found fame and a market for her verse. *No I'm Not Afraid* (1986) was, for a poetry book, very successful, and was followed by further volumes, notably *Dance with a Shadow* (1992). On her release from prison camp she and her husband went to live in the West.

She has since published two volumes of autobiography: *Grey is the Colour of Hope* (1989) and *In the Beginning* (1991).

Irina Ratushinskaya, 1986

Rau, Dhanvanthi Rama

Born 1893 Died 1987
Indian feminist who campaigned for improved family planning

Dhanvanthi was born into an aristocratic Indian family, and was one of the first Indian women to attend university. She became a lecturer in English at Queen Mary's College in Madras.

After marrying Sir Bengal Rama Rau, she devoted herself to campaigning for women's rights in general, and birth control in particular. She was a supporter of the Indian Family Planning Association for 14 years, and she presided over the International Planned Parenthood Association for 18 years.

Ravera, Camilla

Born 1889
Italian communist thinker who was imprisoned for 13 years for her beliefs

Camilla Ravera was born into a middle-class family in Acqui and came under the influence of her father's atheistic views. After moving to Turin, where she took up a teaching career, she became politically active. She joined the Communist Party in 1917, quickly becoming one of its most prominent members in Italy, and began a new career in journalism to disseminate her beliefs.

After meeting Lenin and spending some time in Moscow, Ravera returned to Italy, now a Fascist state, in 1930. There she was imprisoned and held under house arrest for 13 years. Following World War II however, she was free to broadcast her views once again through a series of publications. She was also elected to the Chamber of Deputies, and took up the cause of women's rights.

Raverat, Gwendolen Mary, *née* Darwin

Born 1885 Died 1957
English artist and critic who is best known for her landscape work

Gwendolen Darwin was born in Cambridge. She studied at the Slade School of Art under Frederick Brown and Henry Tonks, and whilst studying at the Sorbonne in Paris, she met and married Jacques Pierre Raverat. They moved to Venice in 1920 with their two young daughters. After the death of her husband in 1925, Gwendolen returned to live in Cambridge.

From 1928 to 1939 she worked as critic for *Time and Tide*, and she also worked with Robert Gibbings on the Penguin Illustrated Classic series. Many of her earlier works were taken from the stories of Hans Christian Andersen and although small in scale, contain some of the finest images of the period. Her career was cut short by a stroke in 1951.

Rawlings, Marjorie

Born 1896 Died 1953
American novelist and regionalist writer who won the 1939 Pulitzer Prize for fiction

Marjorie Rawlings was born in Washington DC and educated at the University of Wisconsin, Madison. She worked as a journalist, an editor, and a syndicated verse writer before devoting herself to full-time creative writing in 1928. She was awarded the O Henry award in 1933 for her short story 'Gal Young Un'.

She published her first novel, *South Moon Under*, in the same year but is best remembered for her Pulitzer Prize-winning novel *The Yearling* (1938), later filmed, which centres on a young boy's attachment to his pet fawn. Her autobiographical work, *Cross Creek* (1942), heightened her reputation as a 'regionalist' writer.

Rayner, Claire Berenice, *pseuds* Ruth Martin, Sheila Brandon, Ann Lynton

Born 1931
English writer, broadcaster, journalist and agony aunt

Claire Rayner was raised and educated in London. She trained and worked there as a nurse and midwife before becoming the medical correspondent for *Women's Own* magazine (as Ruth Martin 1966–75, and as Claire Rayner 1975–87). She also wrote advice columns as the 'agony aunt' for several national newspapers and entered television and radio broadcasting, again as public problem-solver.

Drawing on her medical knowledge and experience of common family concerns, since *Mothers and Midwives* (1962) she has published over 75 books, many on such subjects as pregnancy and parenthood, gardening, marriage, sex and family health. She also writes fiction, both under her own name and as Sheila Brandon, and contributes to medical journals under the name Ann Lynton. The 12-book saga *The Performers* is perhaps her best-known.

Raziya

Floreat 1236–40
First woman ruler of the Delhi Sultanate of the Mamluk ('Slave') Dynasty

Raziya was named by her father Iltutmish as his successor, since none of her brothers were considered worthy of the throne. The nomination of a woman in preference to a man was a novel step and, in order to assert her claim, Raziya had to contend with the hostility of her brothers as well as that of powerful Turkish nobles.

In the event, she retained the throne for only four years. Though brief, however, her rule had a number of interesting features. It marked the beginning of a power-struggle between the monarchy and the Turkish chiefs, sometimes called 'the forty' or the *chahalgani*. She put up a brave defence against these hostile forces, discarding female apparel and holding court with her face unveiled, as well as hunting and leading the army.

This behaviour, coupled with her attempt to create her own party and to raise non-Turks to high positions was, however, found unacceptable; a powerful group of provincial nobles banded against her and, despite a spirited defence, she was defeated and killed.

Read, Mary

Born 1690 Died 1720
Englishwoman who adopted male attire, gaining fame and notoriety as both soldier and sailor

Mary Read's earliest years are undocumented, but her adoption of male attire may have resulted from a fraudulent attempt by her mother to claim an inheritance through male primogeniture. After leaving home, Read retained her masculine appearance, and served on board a warship before enlisting in the British army in Flanders. Here she fell in love with an officer, revealed her true gender, and, much to the astonishment of the regiment, married him.

After her husband's early death, Read sailed to the West Indies, but was captured by pirates led by Anne Bonney. The two women appear to have had an intimate relationship, although Read also enjoyed heterosexual affairs. When captured off Jamaica, it was only the fact that she was pregnant that prevented her execution, and she died of fever in captivity there at the age of 30.

Reagan, Nancy Davis, *originally* Anne Francis Robbins

Born 1923
Former First Lady of the USA as the wife of President Ronald Reagan

Nancy Robbins was born in New York City and educated at Smith College, Massachusetts. She was an MGM contract player from 1949 to

1956, during which time she married Ronald Reagan (1911–   ) in 1952.

Her husband was US President from 1981 to 1989 and as First Lady, she campaigned against substance abuse, winning numerous honours and awards. She was honourary chair of the Just Say No Foundation and the National Federation of Parents for Drug Free Youth.

She was thought to have a considerable behind-the-scenes influence on her husband. Her book of memoirs, *My Turn*, was published in 1989.

Rebekah, *also spelt* Rebecca

Floreat c.1860BC
Biblical character in Genesis who favoured her son
Jacob while Isaac favoured Esau

Rebekah was the daughter of Abraham's nephew Bethuel. She married Isaac and after 20 childless years of marriage, Isaac's prayers were answered with the birth of the twins Esau and Jacob. An oracle foretelling their future rivalry was born out by Rebekah coming to favour Jacob while Isaac favoured Esau.

As Isaac's death approached, Rebekah planned Jacob's impersonation of Esau in order to obtain the blessing that belonged by right to the firstborn son. When the deception was discovered she protected Jacob from revenge by sending him away to her brother Laban.

Rebuck, Gail

Born 1952
English businesswoman who has become one of
the most successful women in publishing

Gail Rebuck was born in London and went to school at the Lycée Français there before attending the University of Sussex. She entered publishing as production assistant at Grisewood & Dempsey (1975–6) and progressed through the editorial ranks at Robert Nicholson Publications to become publisher (1976–8). She joined the Hamlyn Group in 1979 and helped to establish its mass-market paperbacks, before becoming a founding director at Century Publishing (1982–5), where she played a major part in the company's growth.

When the merger with Century Hutchinson took place in 1985, Rebuck was appointed publisher, and in 1989 when the company was taken over by Random House Inc, she became Chairman of the Random House Division. In 1991 she was appointed Chairman and Chief Executive of Random House UK Ltd, taking on the responsibility for the group and its subsidiaries in South Africa, New Zealand and Australia.

Récamier, (Jeanne Françoise) Julie (Adélaïde), *née* Bernard

Born 1777 Died 1849
French salon hostess of wit and beauty whose
salon attracted prominent literary and political
figures

Julie Bernard was born in Lyons, the daughter of a banker with whom she moved to Paris. In 1792 she married a rich banker, Jacques Récamier, whose age was three times her own. Her salon was soon filled with the brightest wits of the day, but her temperament prevented any hint of scandal.

When her husband was financially ruined by Napoleon's policies and she was exiled from Paris, she stayed with Madame de **Staël** at Coppet (1806), who featured her in her novel *Corinne* (1807). Here she met Prince August of Prussia. A marriage was arranged, provided M Récamier would consent to a divorce. He did, but Madame Récamier could not desert him in adversity.

After Napoleon's defeat at Waterloo in 1815 she returned to Paris but additional financial loss left her in straitened circumstances. She moved to a suite in the Abbaye-aux-Bois and continued to entertain there. The most distinguished friend of her later years was the writer and statesman Vicomte François de Chateaubriand.

Redgrave, Vanessa

Born 1937
English actress who is active in all media and has
proved herself one of the most distinguished
performers of her generation

Vanessa Redgrave was born in London, the eldest daughter of the actor Michael Redgrave and actress Rachel Kempson. She trained at the Central School of Speech and Drama (1954–7), made her professional début at the Frinton Summer Theatre (1957), her London stage début opposite her father in *A Touch of the Sun* (1958), and became a classical actress with the Royal Shakespeare Company. She made her film début in *Behind the Mask* (1958) and achieved stardom with her performances in *Morgan!* (1965) and *Blow-Up* (1966). Other film roles include Miss Amelie in *The Ballad of the Sad Café* (1991), an ailing Ruth Wilcox in *Howard's End* (1992), and Clara's mother in *The House of the Spirits* (1994).

Her luminous grace, conviction and integrity have served a vast emotional spread of characterizations. On stage her work includes *The Prime of Miss Jean Brodie* (1966), *The Lady from the Sea* (1976–7), *Orpheus Descending* (1988–9) and *When She Danced* (1991). She has received Academy Award nominations for *Morgan!*, *Isadora* (1968), *Mary, Queen of Scots* (1971) and *The Bostonians* (1984), winning an Oscar for *Julia* (1977). On television she won an Emmy for *Playing for Time* (1980).

She is noted for her espousal of various left-wing and humanitarian causes, and with her brother Corin she has set up a company called Moving Theatre, for which she performed in *Brecht in Hollywood* (1994) with Bertolt Brecht's son-in-law Ekkehard Schall.

Redpath, Anne

Born 1895 Died 1965
Scottish painter considered to be one of the most important modern Scottish artists

Anne Redpath was born in Galashiels, Selkirkshire, the daughter of a tweed designer. She studied at Edinburgh College of Art (1913–18), and lived in France from 1920 to 1934 with her architect husband, during which time she did little work.

Returning to Scotland, she began to paint, revealing the influence of her travels abroad. She is one of the most important modern artists in Scotland, and her paintings in oil and watercolour show great richness of colour and vigorous technique.

She was elected a member of the RSA in 1952.

Redpath, Jean

Born 1937
Scottish singer who has made a reputation as an interpreter of Scots ballads

Jean Redpath was born in Edinburgh and educated at Edinburgh University, where she became involved in folk music. In 1961 she emigrated to the USA, where her outstanding ability, particularly as an interpreter of traditional Scots ballads and the songs of Robert Burns, was quickly recognized.

She made her mark at academic level, too, and for several years lectured in music at Wesleyan University. In the mid-1970s she returned to live and perform in Scotland, but she continued to pay frequent visits to the USA, where she had already embarked on a project to record all of the songs of Robert Burns — numbering more than 300 — to musical arrangements written by the US composer, Serge Hovey.

Reeve, Clara

Born 1729 Died 1807
English novelist of the 'Gothic' school

Clara Reeve was born in Ipswich, the daughter of the rector of Freston. She translated the Scottish satirical writer John Barclay's allegorical romance *Argenis* from Latin as *The Phoenix* (1772), and wrote *The Champion of Virtue, a Gothic Story* (1777), renamed *The Old English Baron*, which was an imitation of Horace Walpole's *The Castle of Otranto*.

Her other novels were *The Two Mentors* (1783), *The Exiles* (1788), *The School for Widows* (1791), *Memoirs of Sir Roger de Clarendon* (1793) and *Destination* (1799). She also wrote *The Progress of Romance* (1785).

Reger, Janet

Born c.1935
English lingerie designer who began her career designing beachwear

Janet Reger was born in London. She attended Leicester College of Art and Technology and was a freelance beachwear designer in Zurich before returning to London in the late 1960s. There the large Fenwick store placed her first significant order of lingerie designs.

Reger's name was made during the 1970s as a designer of glamorous, sexy underwear in silky satin and lace. In 1983 her company was bought out by Berlei, though Reger continues to design under her own name.

Janet Reger, 1993

Rego, Paula

Born 1935
Portuguese artist best known for her narrative
psychological paintings

Paula Rego was born in Lisbon. She studied at the Slade School of Art (1952–6), then returned to Portugal where she established her reputation as a narrative artist. Her childhood playroom, an interest in folk and fairy tales, illustrative art and strip cartoons have all played a part in influencing her subject matter.

Her early work used animals to express human behaviour, but more recently these animals have been replaced by human figures collectively exploring issues such as power, gender stereotypes, sexuality and undercover human emotions. All these factors combine to give a slightly eerie, menacing feel to her work that draws from the surrealist movement. She has lived and worked in Britain since 1976.

Reibey, Molly (Mary), *née* Haydock

Born 1777 Died 1855
Australian businesswoman and philanthropist

Mary Haydock was born in Bury, Lancashire. Orphaned, she ran away at 13 dressed as a boy and was sentenced to death for horse-stealing, but on her sex being discovered she was transported instead. On arrival in Sydney in 1792 she became a nursemaid. She married Thomas Reibey, an Irish East India Company employee, in 1794, and helped him and a partner set up business as ship-owners and merchants. When the two men died in 1811, she took over and expanded the business. By 1816 her property was valued at £20,000 and she was a benefactor of charities and education. The first office of the Bank of New South Wales opened in her home in 1817.

Reid, Beryl

Born 1920
English comedienne and actress who has
progressed from revue to character acting

Beryl Reid was born in Hereford. She first appeared on stage in 1936 at the Floral Hall, Bridlington. In the ensuing years she built a reputation as a variety entertainer and soubrette-cum-impressionist, particularly in revues and pantomimes. Her comic character of schoolgirl Monica was established in the radio series *Educating Archie* (1952–6); her other creations include Midlands Teddy girl Marlene.

She made her film début in *Spare a Copper* (1940), and her many television roles include the series *The Most Likely Girl* (1957), *Man o' Brass* (1964), and *The Secret Diary of Adrian*

Mole (1985). *The Killing of Sister George* (1965) established her as a serious actress and she won a Tony award for its Broadway production (1966).

Finding herself in demand for eccentric character roles and malaprops, she appeared in other films such as *Star!* (1968) and *Entertaining Mr Sloane* (1969). Her stage work encompasses *Blithe Spirit* (1970), *Spring Awakening* (1974), *Born in the Gardens* (1979–80) and *Gigi* (1985). On television she received a BAFTA award for *Smiley's People* (1982). Her books include *The Kingfisher Jump* (1991) and her autobiography, *So Much Love* (1984).

Reiniger, Lotte

Born 1899 Died 1981
German film animator, an important pioneer

Lotte Reiniger was born in Berlin. She studied design at Max Reinhardt's theatre school in 1916, and developed a special technique of silhouette animation. She became a leading innovator in that art, and utilised her techniques in many films.

She made the first ever full-length animated feature film, *Die Abenteuer des Prinzen Achmed* (*The Adventures of Prince Achmed*) in 1926. She moved to England in 1935 until the war ended, and returned there permanently in 1950. She worked for the celebrated animation section of the National Film Board of Canada in the 1970s, and wrote books on animation.

Reitz, Dana

Born 1948
American dancer and choreographer whose work
is noted for its quiet energy and gestural detail

Dana Reitz was born in New York and spent some of her teenage years in Japan, before studying dance theatre at the University of Michigan, Ann Arbor. She graduated in 1970 and moved to New York to study classical ballet and t'ai chi chuan, and to study with Merce Cunningham.

She was briefly a member of **Twyla Tharp** and **Laura Dean**'s companies, and began choreographing in 1973. Although she is best known as a soloist, she has collaborated with other dancers, musicians and lighting designers. She made a significant contribution to the Robert Wilson and Philip Glass opera *Einstein on the Beach* (1976).

Réjane, *originally* Gabrielle Charlotte Réju

Born 1856 Died 1920
French actress who was acclaimed in comic roles
and founded a theatre bearing her name

Gabrielle Charlotte Réju was born in Paris, the daughter of a refreshment vendor. She began her career at the Théâtre du Vaudeville in 1875 and was noted for her playing of such parts as Zaza and the title role of Victorien Sardou's *Madame Sans-Gêne*, as well as the first French Nora in Henrik Ibsen's *The Doll's House*.

She married the Vaudeville's director Porel in 1893 (divorced 1905). In 1906 she founded the Réjane Theatre, where Maeterlinck's *L'oiseau bleu* (1909) was first staged in France.

Equally gifted in both tragic and comic roles, she was regarded in France almost as highly as **Sarah Bernhardt**, and was also popular in England and the USA.

Renault, Mary, *pseud of* (Eileen) Mary Challans

Born 1905 Died 1983
English historical novelist who wrote stories of
life in ancient Greece, such as The King Must Die

Mary Challans was born in London and educated at Oxford. She worked in medicine before turning to writing serious novels about war and hospitals, the best of which is *The Charioteer* (1953).

After emigrating to South Africa in 1948, she began writing her eminently readable adventure novels set in ancient Greece, with which she found her greatest success. These include a trilogy about Alexander and several retellings of the Greek myths. The best known include the first two, *The Last of the Wine* (1956) and *The King Must Die* (1958), a retelling, with modern psychological insights, of the story of Theseus, and the spy-thriller *The Mask of Apollo* (1966).

Rendell, Ruth Barbara, *also writes as* Barbara Vine

Born 1930
English detective novelist and one of the country's
highest earning women

Ruth Rendell was born in London. Her 'Wexford' books have become her most popular. These began with her first novel, *From Doon With Death* (1964), which introduces Chief-Inspector Reginald Wexford, a compassionate, humane man serving with the Kingsmarkham CID in southern England. Wexford's cases take place within a domestic, often middle-class and apparently comfortable world.

In the twelfth Wexford novel, *Kissing the Gunner's Daughter* (1992), the discovery of three bodies leads him into a mire of greed, fear and obsession. These preoccupations find a darker home in the much more psychologically macabre novels Rendell writes under

the name of Barbara Vine, of which *King Solomon's Carpet* (1991) is representative.

Renée, *Maori name* Ngati Kahungunu, *in full* Renée Gertrude Taylor, *née* Jones

Born 1929
New Zealand playwright and novelist, one of the
few prominent lesbian writers in New Zealand

Renée Jones was born in Napier, the daughter of farm-workers. Her father committed suicide when she was four and she was raised by her Maori mother. She went to work from a young age, and worked in a woollen mill and as a journalist before attending Massey University. After her marriage foundered in 1981 she 'acknowledged her lesbian identity' and abandoned her married name Taylor, calling herself solely by her Christian name.

A radical feminist, she has been involved in drama workshops as writer and director since the mid-1960s. Her stage plays feature all-women casts, except for a male policeman who appears in her first play, *Setting the Table*, which was broadcast, then produced on stage in 1981. Her first success on the professional stage was *Wednesday to Come* (1984), the story of four generations of working-class women. This became the central play of a trilogy, a female perspective on the relationship between the economy and social class, with *Jeannie Once* appearing in 1990 and *Pass It On* in 1986. The feminist theme is carried on in *What Did You Do in the War, Mummy?* (1982) and *Asking for It* (1983).

Renée has also written the novels *Finding Ruth* (1987) and *Willy Nilly* (1990).

Renée of Ferrara, *also called* Renée de France

Born 1510 Died 1575
French-Italian aristocrat who was a supporter of
Calvin and other Protestants

Renée was the daughter of Louis XII of France, and sister-in-law of Francis I. She married Duke Ercole of Ferrara and welcomed to her court Protestant religious refugees from France, including the poet Clément Marot and the reformer John Calvin in 1535–6. A decade later she supported Italians Protestants like Fanino Fanini of Faenza and the reformer Bernardino Ochino, but her husband Ercole asked the king of France to send inquisitors to make her change her views, which she did in 1554, to Calvin's dismay.

On Ercole's death she returned to France, and before long was embroiled in the wars of religion that involved all her relatives. She was of liberal outlook, both caring for Huguenot victims in her principality of Montargis, near Orleans, in the face of family opposition, and rejecting Calvin's views on Hell as the destination of all Catholics — which would have included all her relatives and descendants.

Reno, Janet

Born 1938
American politician and lawyer, the first female Attorney-General in US history

Janet Reno was born in Miami, Florida. She was educated at Cornell and Harvard universities and was admitted to the Florida Bar in 1963.

After practising for 10 years she became administrative assistant state attorney for the 11th Judiciary Circuit Florida, Miami (1973–6). She was state attorney in Florida from 1978 to 1993, the year she was nominated and confirmed as the US Attorney-General.

Janet Reno, 1993

Reszke, Joséphine de

Born 1855 Died 1891
Polish operatic soprano who often performed with her two highly acclaimed brothers

Joséphine de Reszke was born in Warsaw. She made her début in Venice in 1874 and sang at the Paris Opéra (1874–84), during which time Massenet created the role of Sita for her in *Le Roi de Lahore* (1877).

She was a sister of the de Reske brothers

Edouard (bass) and Jean (tenor), with whom she sang in Jules Massenet's *Hérodiade* in 1884 and in other performances.

She withdrew from the stage when she married Baron von Kronenburg, but continued to sing in charity concerts in Warsaw.

Retton, Mary Lou

Born 1968
American gymnast, the youngest Olympic athlete to win five medals

Mary Lou Retton was born in Fairmont, West Virginia. In the 1984 Olympics she became the youngest and most decorated Olympic athlete when she won five medals.

She shared the 1984 Women's Sports Foundation Sportswoman of the Year Award with **Joan Samuelson**, was selected by the Associated Press as Female Athlete of the Year and became the youngest athlete inducted into the US Olympic Hall of Fame (1985). She maintains her amateur status and has a successful career as a motivational speaker, drawing on her experience of success, training and hard work.

Reverdy, Michèle

Born 1943
French composer and musicologist who composes mainly for ensembles and solo instruments

Michèle Reverdy was born in Alexandria, Egypt, and educated at the Conservatoire National Supérieur de Musique in Paris under Olivier Messiaen and Claude Ballif.

After a period as bursar at the Casa de Velazquez in Madrid, in 1983 she was appointed Professor of Analysis at the Conservatoire National. That same year, she wrote perhaps her most important work to date: *Scenic Railway* for 13 instruments.

She has also written two important books about Messiaen: *L'oeuvre pour piano* (1978) and *L'oeuvre pour orchestre* (1990). Her style synthesizes serialist technique with Messiaen's concepts of rhythm.

Rhead, Charlotte

Born 1885 Died 1947
English pottery designer whose speciality was for designs in tube lining

Charlotte Rhead was born in Burslem into a talented family who were heavily involved in the potteries (such as Minton and Wedgwood). She first worked for the firm of T & R Boote and then designed for a number of firms, including the Crown pottery and Burgess & Leigh.

Her subject matter ranged from fruit and

flowers through 'Jazz age' patterns influenced by Persian motifs to Eastern and Chinese designs. Her most noted work uses tube lining, where the decoration is applied in outline with a raised seam of coloured slip. Her last position was as art director for Wood & Sons who continued to produce work from her designs after her death.

Rhodes, Zandra Lindsey

Born 1940
English fashion designer noted for her distinctive,
exotic designs in floating chiffons and silks

Zandra Rhodes was born in Chatham, Kent. She studied textile printing and lithography at Medway College of Art, then won a scholarship to the Royal College of Art (1961–4).

She designed and printed textiles, and, with others, opened The Fulham Road Clothes Shop, afterwards setting up on her own. She showed her first dress collection in 1969, and by the 1970s had gained a reputation as a designer of punk fashions.

She was British Designer of the Year in 1972. In 1984 she won an Emmy for her costumes for the televised *Romeo and Juliet on Ice* and 10 years later launched a cosmetics range in the UK and USA.

Rhondda, Margaret Haig Thomas, Viscountess

Born 1883 Died 1958
Welsh feminist and owner-editor of Time and
Tide *which often published radical work*

Margaret Thomas was born in London, the daughter of David Alfred Thomas (1st Viscount Rhondda). She studied, briefly, at Somerville College, Oxford (before women were permitted to take degrees at Oxford), became a suffragette, and was arrested for attempting to destroy the contents of a postbox using a chemical bomb, but was released after hunger-striking. She worked in her father's business during his wartime goverment service as food controller; she had previously been lucky to escape from the *Lusitania*, which was sunk off the Irish coast by a German submarine in 1915.

On her father's death in 1918 she attempted to take her seat in the House of Lords as Viscountess Rhondda, but was kept out after extensive legal proceedings. In 1920 she founded *Time and Tide*, a weekly journal of politics and literature, and personally ran it from 1926. It was largely liberal right-wing, with a warm welcome for refugees and outcasts whose work was boycotted elsewhere. George Orwell published his exposé of Sta-

linist repression in Republican Spain in it after it was rejected by the *New Statesman,* and he later became its film critic with visible effects in *1984.*

It probably tapped a more fruitful and more independent cross-section of British intellectual life than most journals, but it was in deep financial trouble when Viscountess Rhondda died.

Rhys, Jean, *pseud of* Gwen Williams

Born 1894 Died 1979
British novelist whose best-known work is Wide Sargasso Sea

Gwen Williams was born in the West Indies. Her father was a Welsh doctor, her mother a Creole. She was educated at a convent in Roseau, Dominica, and moved to England in 1910 to train at the Royal Academy of Dramatic Art, but her father's death after only one term obliged her to join a touring theatre company. At the end of World War I she married a Dutch poet, Max Hamer, and went to live on the Continent, spending many years in Paris where she met writers and artists, including Ernest Hemingway, James Joyce and Ford Madox Ford (the last-named in particular encouraged her writing).

In 1927 she published *The Left Bank and Other Stories,* set mostly in Paris or in the West Indies of her childhood. Four novels followed: *Quartet* (originally published as *Postures,* 1928), *After Leaving Mr Mackenzie* (1930), *Voyage in the Dark* (1934) and *Good Morning Midnight* (1939); her heroines were women attempting to live without regular financial support, adrift in European cities between the worlds of wealth and poverty.

After nearly 30 years she published in 1966 what was to become her best-known novel, *Wide Sargasso Sea,* based on the character of Rochester's mad wife in **Charlotte Brontë's** *Jane Eyre.* Further short stories followed in *Tigers are Better Looking* (1968) and *Sleep It Off, Lady* (1976); an autobiography, *Smile Please,* was published posthumously in 1979.

Ricard, Marthe, *née* Betenfeld

Born 1889 Died 1982
French pilot and spy who served her country in
two world wars and later agitated against the
sexual exploitation of women

Marthe Betenfeld was born in Alsace-Lorraine. She qualified as a pilot in 1911, and after losing her husband in World War I, undertook secret intelligence work for France. Her seduction of a German baron in Spain enabled her to elicit important naval information, and she was later decorated with the Légion d'Honneur.

In World War II, she worked with the Resistance against the invader, and after her third marriage, as Marthe Ricard, she was elected to the municipal council in Paris. Campaigning successfully to rid the city of its prostitutes, she pioneered national legislation to eradicate what she viewed as female exploitation.

In later years she appears to have modified her views, believing that a controlled sex industry was less exploitative.

Ricci, Nina

Born 1883 Died 1970
Italian couturier who founded one of Paris's longest-running couture houses

Nina Ricci was born in Turin, Italy. She became a dressmaker's apprentice at the age of 13, was in charge of an atelier by 18 and head designer at 20. In 1932 she opened her own Paris couture house with her jeweller husband Louis. Her son, Robert, has managed the business since 1945.

She created clothes in superb detail, becoming known for a high standard of workmanship that appealed to an elegant and wealthy clientele. She also made trousseaux for young brides-to-be.

Her perfume, L'air du Temps, launched in 1948 in a Lalique flaçon with a frosted glass stopper, is still one of the top sellers worldwide.

Rice-Davies, Mandy (Marilyn)

Born 1944
Welsh model and show girl whose friendship with **Christine Keeler** *involved her in the scandalous Profumo Affair of 1963*

Mandy Rice-Davies was born in Wales, the daughter of a police officer. She grew up in the West Midlands where she worked in a department store after leaving school. Her striking looks and figure won her a contract as a model in the promotion of the new Mini motor car and, with her appetite for show business whetted, she moved at an early age to London, where she became a show girl at Murray's Cabaret Club.

There she met and became close friends with Christine Keeler and, through the osteopath Stephen Ward, was introduced to influential London society, receiving several marriage offers. As a witness at Ward's trial on the charge of living off immoral earnings, in reply to a suggestion that Lord Astor denied

knowing her, she gave the celebrated retort: 'He would, wouldn't he?'

After the trial she moved to Israel, where she established two night clubs called Mandy. She married twice and published her autobiography, eventually returning to live in London.

Rich, Adrienne Cecile

Born 1929
American feminist poet, one of the most influential feminists writing today

Adrienne Rich was born into a Jewish family in Baltimore, Maryland, and educated at Radcliffe College, Cambridge, Massachusetts. Her first volume of verse, *A Change of World* (1951), was published while she was still an undergraduate, but it foreshadowed her emergence as the most forceful American woman poet since **Elizabeth Bishop** and **Sylvia Plath**.

Later collections include *Snapshots of a Daughter-in-Law* (1963) and *The Will to Change* (1971). The latter took her up to the point of her husband's suicide. Thereafter, Rich began to align herself more directly with the women's movement, often dating poems as if they documented stopovers on a campaign trail. Her prose became almost as influential as her verse. *Of Woman Born* (1976) is a ruggedly unsentimental account of maternity. *On Lies, Secrets, and Silence* (1979) collected the best of her occasional prose. In *Blood, Bread, and Poetry* (1986) she aligned herself with radical lesbianism, defined in a broad non-sexual way that embraces the entire cathexis that binds woman to woman.

Later verse appeared as *The Dream of a Common Language* (1978), *A Wild Patience Has Taken Me This Far* (1981), which established her lineage from **Emily Dickinson**, and *An Atlas of the Difficult World: Poems 1988–1991* (1991), which examined her connection with Jewish heritage. *The Fact of a Doorframe* (1984) collected her poetry from 1950. She received the Commonwealth Poetry Prize in 1991.

Richards, Ann Willis, *née* Willis

Born 1933
American politician who has served as state governor of Texas

Ann Willis was born in Lakeview, Texas, and educated at Baylor University and the University of Texas. She worked as a teacher for a time before taking up local offices in Texas such as Treasurer of State (1983–91), and serving as governor of Texas (1991–5).

She was chair of the Democratic National Convention in 1992 and has written a book, *Straight From the Heart* (with Peter Knobler), published in 1989.

Richards, Audrey

Born 1899 Died 1984
English social anthropologist who combined fieldwork among primitive tribes with a career of academic excellence

Audrey Richards was born in London, the daughter of a lawyer in the British colonial service in India, where she spent most of her childhood. After returning to Britain in 1911, she went on to study at Newnham College, Cambridge, where she graduated in 1921.

Never lacking in confidence, she published her first study of primitive tribal life in 1932 without carrying out any fieldwork, but later undertook first-hand field studies among primitive societies in Rhodesia.

Her academic career culminated in her appointment as director of the East African Institute of Social Research in Uganda in 1950. She retired 16 years later and died unmarried.

Richards, Ellen Henrietta Swallow, *née* Swallow

Born 1842 Died 1911
American chemist who devoted considerable energy to furthering scientific education for women

Ellen Richards was born in Westford, Massachusetts. Financial difficulties meant that she had to work and save before she could enter Vassar College in 1868. She graduated two years later and joined the Massachusetts Institute of Technology in 1870 as a non fee-paying student. She later discovered this was a deliberate device so that the Institute could deny her presence on the student roll, should anyone complain, for she was the first woman to study there. She remained at MIT, gaining a Masters degree in chemistry and marrying Robert Richards, an engineering professor, in 1875.

To further the cause for women's education, she helped establish the Woman's Laboratory at MIT, and to co-found what later became the American Association of University Women. She became particularly concerned about the impact of industrialization on the environment and on the family, and was involved in developing influential home economics programmes across the country, with an aim to simplifying housekeeping to free women for other activities.

Richards, Renée, *originally* Richard Raskind

Born 1934
American doctor, tennis player and transsexual

Renée Richards was born in New York City. Born a male, he began a life of academic and athletic accomplishment, being scouted for baseball by the Yankees and captain of Yale's tennis team. He later became a leading ophthalmologist.

As a teenager, he became aware of his feeling that he was really a woman. After asserting his female identity through dress and hormone treatments, he underwent transsexual surgery in 1975 and was renamed Renée Richards. Her 1983 book, *Second Serve*, details her life, her surgery and her struggles to be accepted in women's tennis.

Richardson, Dorothy M(iller)

Born 1873 Died 1957
English novelist and first exponent of the 'stream of consciousness' style later made famous by **Virginia Woolf**

Dorothy Richardson was born in Abingdon, Berkshire. After her mother's suicide in 1895 she moved to London and worked as a teacher, a clerk, and a dentist's assistant. She became a Fabian, and had an affair with the writer H G Wells which led to a miscarriage and a near-collapse in 1907. In 1917 she married a painter, Alan Odle.

She started her writing career with works on the Quakers and George Fox (1914). Her first novel, *Painted Roofs* (1915), was the first of a 12-volume sequence entitled *Pilgrimage*, culminating with *Clear Horizon* (1935) and *Dimple Hill* (1938).

Richardson, H(enry) H(andel), *pseud of* Ethel Florence Lindesay Richardson

Born 1870 Died 1946
Australian novelist and short-story writer

Ethel Richardson was born in Fitzroy, Melbourne, the daughter of an Irish immigrant doctor, who claimed descent, through her grandfather, from the ancient Irish Earls of Lindesay. After an unhappy childhood in which her father died insane, she travelled widely with her mother and younger sister and studied music with distinction at Leipzig Conservatorium, graduating with honours in 1892. She married a fellow-student, John George Robertson, and they moved to London.

Her first novel, *Maurice Guest*, was published there in 1908, under her masculine-sounding pseudonym, followed by *The Getting of Wisdom* in 1910. Her major work was the trilogy *The Fortunes of Richard Mahoney*; the first book, *Australia Felix* (1917), was followed in 1925 by *The Way Home*. This sold so poorly that the final book, *Ultima Thule*, was initially privately published at her husband's expense, but the three were re-published together in 1930. In *Maurice Guest* and in her later novel *The Young Cosima* (1939), a study of the interwoven lives of Liszt, Wagner, and Wagner's second wife Cosima von Bülow, her deep musical sympathies are evident.

One of the first Australian novelists to receive international acclaim, and arguably the greatest of her time, she also wrote some short stories, and a rather imaginative 'autobiography', *Myself when Young* (posthumous, 1948).

Ride, Sally Kristen

Born 1951
American astronaut and astrophysicist who became the first American woman in space

Sally Ride was born in Los Angeles and educated at Westlake High School, Los Angeles, and Stanford University. While a student she achieved national ranking as a tennis player, but chose not to pursue this as a career.

She gained a PhD in physics in 1978. That same year she was selected as an astronaut candidate by NASA, and became a mission

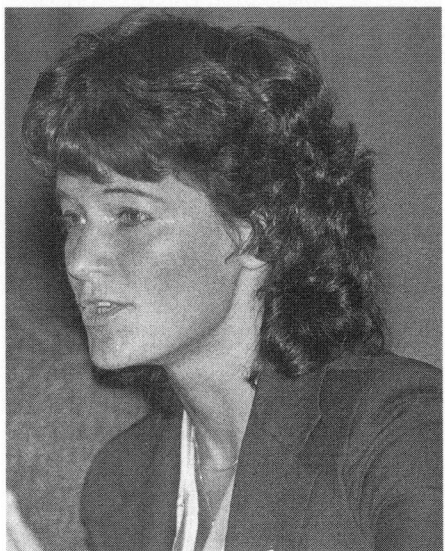

Sally Ride, 1983

specialist on future Space Shuttle flight crews until 1989. She was selected to serve on a planned six-day flight of the orbiter *Challenger* in June 1983 and she also helped to design the Space Shuttle's robot arm.

In August 1987 she published a report to the Administrator of Nasa on 'Leadership — and America's Future in Space'. In 1989 she was appointed director of the California Space Institute and Professor of Physics at the University of California, San Diego.

Riding, Laura, *originally* Reichenfeld, *married names* Laura Riding Gottschalk, *and, after 1941* Laura (Riding) Jackson

Born 1901 Died 1991
American poet, critic, story writer, novelist and polemicist who examines the reasons for human existence

Laura Reichenfeld was born in New York City, the daughter of an Austrian immigrant. She took some courses at Cornell University, and married Louis Gottschalk, a history instructor there. Her first collection of poetry, *The Close Chaplet*, appeared in England, under the imprint of the Hogarth Press, run by Leonard and **Virginia Woolf**. She was the lover (1926–9) and then the literary associate (1929–39) of Robert Graves, with whom she lived in Mallorca, London, and Rennes.

In 1941 she married Schuyler Jackson, a minor poet and farmer, with whom she wrote a long (unpublished) study of language. It is generally agreed that her poetry is superior to her prose, which became increasingly convoluted and denunciatory of those whom she regarded as her enemies (chiefly, and notoriously, Graves himself).

Her poetry is quite unlike any other poetry of this century: based, rhythmically, on a very surely-handled four-accent line, it seeks unabashedly to examine the reasons for human existence, and to establish human obligations. It has attracted the attention of many, including Graves, W H Auden, Philip Larkin, Robert Fitzgerald, and her friend Robert Nye, but has never received satisfactory critical exegesis. *First Awakenings* (1992), edited by Nye and assistants, adds considerably to the canon.

Rie, Dame Lucie, *née* Gomperz

Born 1902 Died 1995
Austrian-born British studio potter who was a 20th-century leader in her craft

Lucie Gomperz was born in Vienna and trained at the Kunstgewerbeschule. She was married to Hans Rie from 1926 to 1940, and in 1938 fled with him to England where Bernard Leach (1887–1979), who became a lifelong friend despite his very different, more rustic approach, was the dominant force in studio ceramics.

After World War II Rie shared a workshop with a young German, Hans Coper (1920–81), producing ceramic jewellery and buttons while continuing her individual work. They were a source of inspiration to each other and worked together until 1960, during which time Rie pioneered the production of stoneware in an electric kiln and, rejecting the fashionable Oriental influence of the time, created an individual style rooted in Modernism.

She produced stoneware, tin glazed earthenware, and porcelain pots throughout her working life with a precision and technical control that has influenced many of today's leading contemporary potters and, it is said, bridged the gap between the craft of pottery and the art of sculpture. Although commercial galleries have been showing works by Rie and Coper for several years, in 1994 the New York Metropolitan Museum of Art became the first national institution to devote an entire exhibition to her work. She was appointed DBE in 1991.

Riefenstahl, Leni (Helene Berte Amalie)

Born 1902
German film director and photographer noted for
her propagandist Nazi film Triumph Des
Willens

Leni Riefenstahl was born in Berlin. A student of fine art and ballet, she was a professional dancer before making her film début in *Der Helige Berg* (1926). She appeared in some of the mountaineering films made by Arnold Fanck (1889–1974), who has been credited with training her. In 1931 she formed Riefenstahl Films and made her directorial début with *Das Blaue Licht* (1932, 'The Blue Light') and was appointed film expert to the Nationalist Socialist Party by Hitler.

Her *Triumph Des Willens* (1934, 'Triumph of the Will') was a compelling record of a Nazi rally at Nuremberg. With expert editing and photography it used over 40 cameramen to create a record of the event, glorifying Hitler's magnetism and the future he offered Germany. *Olympische Spiele 1936* (1938, 'Olympiad') was another propagandisitic documentary of impressive technique. Whilst it is impossible to deny the beauty and filmmaking artistry of her work, it is as difficult to view Riefenstahl

as merely a documentarist creating an objective record of events as it is to divorce judgement of her work from the cause it served.

At the end of World War II she was interned by the Allies and held on charges of pro-Nazi activity that were subsequently dropped. She never fully resumed her filmmaking, but enjoyed a further career as a photojournalist under the name of Helen Jacobs, covering the 1972 Olympic Games for the *Sunday Times* and building a portfolio of work on the East African tribe of Mesakin Nuba. She published her autobiography, *The Sieve of Time*, in 1992.

Rigby, Cathy

Born 1952
American gymnast whose success increased the
status of gymnastics in the USA

Cathy Rigby was born in Los Alamitos, California. Before her participation in international gymnastic competition, gymnastics had been a minor sport in the USA.

She won a silver medal in the 1970 world championships, the first US woman to win an individual medal in world competition. The following year she gained a gold medal in the all-around competition (ie participating in all four events — horse-vault, uneven bars, balance beam and floor) in the World Cup gymnastics championships, and in 1972 she won the American Athletics Union women's gymnastics all-around title. In the 1972 Olympics she led the women's team to a fourth-place finish and achieved high placings in the individual competitions.

On her retirement from amateur competition in 1973, she began a successful business and acting career.

Rigg, Dame Diana

Born 1938
English actress in many media, best remembered
as kinky-boot clad Emma Peel in The Avengers

Diana Rigg was born in Doncaster. After studying at RADA, she joined the Royal Shakespeare Company in 1959 and made her London début with them in 1961. She has subseqently appeared in several roles with the RSC, and many with the National Theatre, including, in 1972, creating the part of Dorothy in *Jumpers* and playing a much-acclaimed Lady Macbeth.

Other distinguished appearances include Célimène in *The Misanthrope* (1972), Eliza Doolittle in *Pygmalion* (1974), and in 1992 she played a much-admired title role in *Medea*. Her film appearances include *On Her Majesty's Secret Service* (1969) and *Evil Under The Sun*

(1981), and she has also had success on television, such as in *The Avengers* (1965–7) and
Mother Love (1990), for which she won a
BAFTA award. Equally recognized in comedy
and serious work, she extended her range
further in the 1987 musical *Follies*.

In recent years she has used her fame to
do 'positive work within the arts', working
closely with such organizations as the British
Museum Development Fund and the Association for Business Sponsorship of the Arts,
chiefly to raise funding. She was appointed
DBE in 1994.

Riley, Bridget Louise

Born 1931
English op artist, the first English painter to win
the major painting prize at the Venice Biennale
(1968)

Bridget Riley was born in London and educated at Cheltenham Ladies' College. She
trained at Goldsmith's College of Art (1949–
52) and at the Royal College of Art (1952–5),
and held her first one-woman show in London
at Gallery One in 1962; this was followed by
others worldwide.

She is a leading op artist, manipulating
overall flat patterns, originally in black and
white but later in colour, using repeated
shapes or undulating lines which dazzle the
beholder, often creating an illusion of movement, for example in *Fall*, 1963.

Rimington, Dame Stella

Born 1935
English former director-general of the Secret
Service

Stella Rimington was born in London. She
read English at Edinburgh University, then
joined MI5. She is thought to have made a big
impact as head of the F2 branch, which deals
with domestic 'subversion'. F2 played an
important role in government action against
the miners' strike of 1984–5.

Towards the end of the 1980s she became
director of counter-terrorist activities, then
director-general of MI5 in 1992. The appointment's being made public symbolized a new
chapter of relative openness for the security
service. She was appointed DCB (Dame Commander of the Order of the Bath) in 1996, the
year in which she retired from MI5.

Ristori, Adelaide

Born 1822   Died 1906
Italian tragedienne, the leading Italian actress of
her day before earning international acclaim

Adelaide Ristori was born in Cividale in Friuli,
the daughter of travelling players. She began
acting at the age of 14 but her marriage with
the Marquis del Grillo in 1847 temporarily
interrupted her dramatic career.

She won a complete triumph before a
French audience in 1855, when **Élisa Rachel**
was at the height of her fame, and earned
international renown as she gained fresh
laurels in nearly every country of Europe, in
the USA (1866, 1875, 1884–5), and in South
America.

She retired from the stage in 1885 and three
years later published *Memoirs and Artistic
Studies* (trans 1907).

Rita of Cascia, St

Born 1377   Died 1457
Italian Augustinian nun and mystic

Rita was born in Roccaporena, near Spoleto.
Following her parents' wishes, she led an
exemplary life as the wife of a difficult
husband for 18 years before being widowed
when he was murdered. She then, around
1407, obtained permission to become an
Augustinian nun at Cascia, Umbria, where she
cared for sick nuns and counselled sinners
before dying from tuberculosis.

Biographies, written nearly 150 years after
her death, credit her with supernatural experiences, including a mystical wound on her
forehead like that caused by a crown of thorns
which persisted for 15 years. She was beatified
in 1626, canonized in 1900 and is highly
popular in present-day Italy as the patron of
desperate cases (such as failing marriages). Her
feast day is 22 May.

Ritchie, Anne Isabella Thackeray, Lady

Born 1837   Died 1919
English writer who had an influence on her niece
Virginia Woolf

Anne Thackeray was born in London, the
daughter of novelist William Makepeace
Thackeray (1811–63), of whom she was a close
companion. She became well acquainted with
his friends of literary and artistic note, contributed valuable personal reminiscences to an
1898–9 edition of his works, and also wrote
memoirs of their contemporaries, such as
Alfred, Lord Tennyson and John Ruskin. She
also knew Robert and **Elizabeth (Barrett)
Browning**, **Charlotte Brontë** and **George
Eliot**.

Her novels include *The Village on the Cliff*

(1867), *Old Kensington* (1873) and *Mrs Dymond* (1885). She was the aunt of **Virginia Woolf**, who based the character of Mrs Hilbery in *Night and Day* (1919) on her.

Ritchie, Jean Atkinson Smail

Born 1913
Scottish nutritionist whose teaching has improved the health of women and children in Africa and South-East Asia

Jean Ritchie was born in Edinburgh and educated at Edinburgh College of Domestic Science. In 1939 she received the MSc in Nutrition from the University of Chicago. Following war service as an ambulance driver she joined the Rowett Institute in Aberdeen and worked with the biologist Lord Boyd Orr (1880–1971).

After a period with the Ministry of Food and the United Nations Relief and Rehabilitation Administration (1944–6), she joined the Food and Agriculture Organization (FAO) (1946–78) as Regional Nutrition Officer for Africa and Regional Adviser to the Economic Commission for Africa. She taught at the London School of Hygiene and Tropical Medicine and University of Ibadan (1963–9).

She has published *Teaching Better Nutrition* (1950), *Learning Better Nutrition* (1967) and *Nutrition and Families* (1983). Active in improving nutritional standards through education in Africa and South-East Asia, through workshops and seminars she has improved the situation of women, including their health and nutrition. In 1977 she received the Sen award (FAO) for field work.

Ritter, Erika

Born 1948
Canadian playwright and stand-up comic with a shrewd observation of life

Erika Ritter was born in Regina, Saskatchewan. She writes comedies which set independent and intelligent women at loggerheads with the urban world.

She is not a 'soap-boxing' playwright and this, coupled with her authentic feel for comedy, has helped bring success at the box-office, as with *Automatic Pilot* (1980), which concerned the autobiographical routine of a female comic.

Her collection of essays *Ritter In Residence* (1987), like *Urban Scrawl* (1984), shows that she can communicate her shrewd angle on life in essay form as well as on the stage.

Rivers, Joan, *originally* Joan Alexandra Molinsky

Born 1933
American comedienne and writer whose caustic wit has earned her renown

Joan Rivers was born in Larchmont, New York. A starstruck child, keen on amateur dramatics, she was an extra in the film *Mr Universe* (1951). After graduating from college, she became a fashion co-ordinator for Bond stores whilst still harbouring notions of a showbusiness career. Concentrating on these aspirations from 1958, she appeared in *Seawood* (1959) and other minor plays before working with the Chicago improvisational troupe Second City (1961–2) and developing her prowess as an acid-tongued, stand-up comedienne dealing in personal intimacies and vituperative assaults on public figures.

Success came with an appearance on *The Tonight Show* in 1965. She made her Las Vegas début in 1969, wrote a regular column in *The Chicago Tribune* (1973–6), directed the film *Rabbit Test* (1978), recorded an album *What Becomes A Semi-Legend Most* (1983), and was the regular guest host of *The Tonight Show* (1983–6). She has also hosted *The Late Show* (1986–7), *Hollywood Squares* (1987–), and the morning talk show *Joan Rivers* (1989–), which won a Daytime Emmy award in 1990.

Her books include *Having A Baby Can Be A Scream* (1974) and the autobiographies *Enter Talking* (1986) and *Still Talking* (1991).

Roberts, Elizabeth Madox

Born 1881   Died 1941
American novelist and poet whose novels centre around Kentucky pioneers

Elizabeth Madox Roberts was born in Perrysville, Kentucky. Opinions are still divided as to her merits, but she was regarded in her day as a major novelist. Some have seen her as over-poetic and over-diffuse — as 'indeterminate'; others as transcending regionalism.

Her works include *The Time of Man* (1926), about Kentucky hill-dwellers, *My Heart and my Flesh* (1927), a study of a family in decline, and *The Great Meadow* (1930), a historical novel about the settlement of Kentucky by emigrants from Virginia. Criticism has yet to assess her.

Roberts, Julia

Born 1967
American film actress, a 'pretty woman' who attracts audiences by her presence alone

Julia Roberts was born in Smyrna, Georgia. Though her earliest ambition was to be a veterinarian, she decided to study acting, at the same time attaching herself to a modelling agency. Her film début was in *Blood Red* (1987), which did little to advance her career, but she caught the eye as the town beauty in *Mystic Pizza* (1988), and was nominated for a Best Supporting Actress Oscar as the diabetic daughter of **Sally Field** in *Steel Magnolias* (1989).

The phenomenal success of *Pretty Woman* (1990) hailed her as a box-office name, able to attract audiences on her presence alone, which was the case with *Flatliners* (1990) and *Sleeping With The Enemy* (1991). Also in 1991 she appeared as a tomboyish but startlingly amorous Tinkerbell in the critically-reviled but popular *Hook*.

Roberts, Kate

Born 1891 Died 1985
Welsh novelist and short-story writer, the most respected Welsh prose writer of the 20th century

Kate Roberts was born in Rhosgadfan, near Caernarfon, Gwynedd, and educated at the University College of North Wales, Bangor. Sometimes described as 'the Welsh Chekhov', she is generally regarded as the most distinguished prose writer in Welsh this century.

She was a teacher of Welsh at Ystalyfera (1915–17) and Aberdare (1917–28), and later (with her husband Morris T Williams) bought Gwasg Gee, the publishers of the newspaper *Baner ac Amserau Cymru* (later *Y Faner*), and settled in Denbigh.

Robertson, Anne Strachan

Born 1910
Scottish archaeologist who has become a leading authority on Roman artefacts, especially coins

Anne Robertson was born in Glasgow and educated at Glasgow and London universities. She became Reader and later Keeper of the Roman Collections and Hunter Coin Cabinet in Glasgow University, where in 1974 she was made Professor of Roman Archaeology.

Her excavations and research on the Antonine Wall elucidated many aspects of its history, and in 1960 she published a classic handbook, *The Antonine Wall*. She is a leading authority on Roman coins, and has published many papers as well as catalogues of the Anglo-Saxon and Roman Imperial coins in the Hunter Coin Cabinet. Her work on Roman artefacts found on native settlements helped to clarify the relationship between the Roman army and the native population.

Robertson, Belinda

Born 1959
Scottish fashion designer who is recognized as one of the world's leading cashmere designers

Belinda Robertson was born in Glasgow. She had a varied career in modelling, teaching and marketing before settling for fashion design. Self-taught, she designs Scottish cashmere, fine merino wool, and merino silk from yarn supplied mostly by Todd and Duncan in Kinross.

She operates from her workshop and showroom in Edinburgh, with her main factory in Hawick, Roxburghshire, creating what she describes as 'classics with an innovative twist'. Special commissions include 'own-label' collections for several international couture houses.

She trades mostly with the Far East, the USA, France and Germany, but is developing outlets in Italy and Scandinavia.

Robertson, Grace

Born 1930
British photographer and photojournalist, known for her empathetic and witty coverage of a wide range of human subjects

Grace Robertson was born in Manchester, the daughter of the Scottish journalist Fyfe Robertson. She decided to become a photographer in 1948, having left school to care for other members of her family due to her mother's illness, and became a regular photographer for *Picture Post* from 1950. She was asked to join the staff in 1954 but declined; she also turned down an associate staff position at *Life* magazine in 1956. In 1954 she married photographer and journalist Godfrey Thurston Hopkins, and with him had two children, Joanna (b.1960) and Robert (b.1961).

After the birth of her children she worked for 12 years as a primary school teacher. She has continued to carry out freelance work for magazines including *Picture Post* (until its closure in 1957) and *Life*, and for the BBC. A retrospective of her work was held at the Royal National Theatre, London, 1993.

Her publications include *Grace Robertson: Photojournalist of the Fifties* (1989).

Robertson, Jeannie

Born 1908 Died 1975
Scottish folk-singer described by the US folklorist Alan Lomax as 'a monumental figure of world folk-song'

Jeannie Robertson was born in Aberdeen. She was virtually unknown beyond the north-east of Scotland, until her talent was recognized in 1953 by the Scottish folklorist, composer and poet Hamish Henderson (1919–   ).

Although she spent most of her life in Aberdeen, she belonged to the 'travelling folk', whose music was passed down orally from generation to generation, and she represented an important link with this ancient culture.

Her huge repertoire of classic traditional ballads and other songs, together with her powerful and magnetic singing style, exerted a profound influence on the folk music revival.

Robertson, Muriel

Born 1883 Died 1973
Scottish-born microbiologist who carried out extensive research on parasites

Muriel Robertson was born in Glasgow. She was educated privately at home and then at Glasgow University, from which she graduated MA (1905) and achieved a DSc (1922).

After extensive travelling, in 1909 she moved to the Lister Institute in London to continue the work she had begun on blood parasites, especially trypanosomes. She remained at the Institute, with intermittent breaks to work abroad, until her retirement in 1961, studying the life cycles of parasites and aspects of their immunology.

She was elected a Fellow of the Royal Society in 1947.

Robineau, Adelaide Alsop, *née* Alsop

Born 1865 Died 1929
American ceramic designer and decorator

Adelaide Alsop Robineau was born in Connecticut. She taught herself china painting from books and in her early twenties taught the subject in Minnesota. She then moved to New York to study painting under William Chase, while still earning her living from china painting. In 1899 she married Samuel Robineau and began editing a highly successful magazine called *Keramic Studio*. In it she urged women to continue using their talents while raising children and running a home.

The Robineaus moved to Syracuse, New York, where they built a workshop and kiln and, later, a house next door. Adelaide began working in porcelain in 1903, throwing her own shapes and experimenting with different glazes to achieve her distinctive cystalline effects. Her work was exhibited in many international exhibitions and sold in Tiffany & Co, New York.

She met Edward Gardner Lewis in 1909, and moved to University City, St Louis, to work in the pottery he had founded along with Taxile Doat whom he had persuaded from Sèvres. During the next two years Adelaide produced some of her finest work including the Scarab Vase which took 1,000 hours to make and won the Grand Prize at the Turin International Exhibition.

Robins, Elizabeth

Born 1865 Died 1952
American playwright, actress, novelist and campaigner for women's equality

Elizabeth Robins was born in Kentucky. She made her acting début in 1880, joining a touring company. In 1885 she married an actor, but he committed suicide two years later. In 1888 Robins went to London, where she had an affair with the critic William Archer (1856–1924) and established herself as one of the leading actresses of her generation. She appeared in the British premières of several of Henrik Ibsen's plays, including title role in *Hedda Gabler* (1891), Hilde Wangel in *The Master Builder* (1893) and Ella Rentheim in *John Gabriel Borkman* (1897), and retired from the stage in 1902, her last role being that of Alice Manisty in **Mrs Humphry Ward's** *Eleanor*, in order to devote herself to writing, and to campaigning for the rights of women.

She wrote novels under the pseudonym of C E Raimond, but wrote her most important play, *Votes for Women!* (1906), under her own name. Her other plays include *Alan's Wife* (1893), written in association with Florence Bell (1851–1930) and produced anonymously, since the subject of merciful infanticide was considered too shocking for the authors to identify themselves.

Robins also co-founded the Actresses Franchise League in 1908. The same year she became the first President of the Women Writers' Suffrage League (1908–12). She was also a committee member of the Women's Social and Political Union (1907–12).

Robins, Margaret Drier

Born 1868 Died 1945
American reformer and labour activist

Margaret Drier Robins was born in Brooklyn, New York, into a prosperous German immigrant family. She was educated privately. In 1905 she married Raymond Robins and the couple moved to Chicago.

In 1907 she became president of both the Chicago and National Women's Trades Union League, working with **Rose Schneiderman** to organize the garment workers' strikes in New York, Philadelphia and Chicago. She was closely linked with the pacifist groups of the 1920s and affiliated to the suffrage movement.

On her resignation from the Trades Union League in 1922, she became President of the International Federation of Working Women.

Robinson, Joan Violet, *née* Maurice

Born 1903 Died 1983
English economist, one of the most influential
economic theorists of her time

Joan Maurice was born in Camberley, Surrey, and educated at Girton College, Cambridge. She married an economist, Austin Robinson, in 1926, and after a brief period in India taught economics at Cambridge from 1931 to 1971 (in 1965 she succeeded her husband as professor).

As one of the most influential economic theorists of her time, she was a leader of the Cambridge school, which developed macroeconomic theories of growth and distribution, based on the work of J M Keynes (1883–1946).

Her books include *The Economics of Imperfect Competition* (1933), *Introduction of the Theory of Employment* (1937), *Essay of Marxian Economics* (1942), *The Accumulation of Capital* (1956), *Essays in the Theory of Economic Growth* (1962) and *Economic Heresies* (1971).

Robinson, Marilynne

Born 1943
American novelist and essayist who wrote the
feminist classic Housekeeping

Marilynne Robinson was born in Sandpoint, Idaho, and educated at Brown University and the University of Washington. Her first novel, *Housekeeping* (1980), was later filmed and has been hailed as a feminist classic; this lyrical novel focuses on the different life choices of two previously inseparable sisters.

Robinson's work has been strongly influenced by the American Transcendentalists. In 1989 she published her first non-fiction book, *Mother Country: Britain, The Nuclear State, and Nuclear Pollution*.

In 1982 she received both the Hemingway Foundation award and the American Academy Rosenthal Foundation award.

Robinson, Mary ('Perdita'), *née* Darby

Born 1758 Died 1800
English poet and novelist whose adventures
included a period as mistress to the future
King George IV

Mary Darby was born in Bristol, the daughter of a merchant, and educated at schools in Bristol and London. Her adventures and tribulations started with marriage at the age of 16; at 17 she was imprisoned for debt with her husband and infant daughter, and she also published her first poems. She became an actress in 1776, and was the mistress of the Prince of Wales, later George IV, but he deserted her in 1780.

Saved from destitution by an annuity secured by the Liberal statesman Charles James Fox (1749–1806), she travelled to France with her lover, Col Banastre Tarleton (1754–1833), but from 1783 was lamed by partial paralysis. Tarleton left her in 1792 and thereafter she struggled to support her family by writing. She associated with radical intellectuals, and her poems were highly admired by the influential poet Samuel Taylor Coleridge.

Her prolific output included satirical verse, love-sonnets (*Sappho and Phaon*, 1796), a long poem on the French Revolution, *Lyrical Tales* (1800), showing affinities with the nascent Romantic movement, two plays, and several novels of sentiment and Gothic romance, including the bestselling *Vancenza* (1792).

Robinson, Mary, *née* Bourke

Born 1944
Irish politician who became President of Ireland
in 1990

Mary Bourke was trained as a lawyer and was Professor of Law at Trinity College, Dublin, from 1969. She was a member of the Irish Senate (1969–89) and participated in numerous legal associations in the European Community. She became an activist on many social issues, including women's and single-parents' rights and the decriminalization of homosexuality.

Although she had resigned from the Labour Party in 1985 over the Anglo-Irish Agreement, she was nominated as presidential candidate and unexpectedly defeated the Fine Fáil candidate Brian Lenihan in the presidential elections of November 1990. She soon became an internationally respected head of state.

Robscheit-Robbins, Freda

Born 1893 Died 1973
American pathologist whose work on iron
metabolism furthered the study of pernicious
anaemia

Freda Robscheit-Robbins was born in Germany and was educated at the universities of Chicago and California. She received her PhD from the University of Rochester, where she began working with George Whipple in 1917. She remained his research partner for 36 years.

Their joint work on iron metabolism led to the discovery of the factors that caused pernicious anaemia, and the usefulness of liver therapy in its treatment, for which Whipple was awarded a share of the Nobel Prize in 1934. Robscheit-Robbins retired in 1955, still holding the junior position of associate professor.

Robson, Dame Flora

Born 1902 Died 1984
English actress who gained an excellent reputation on stage and screen

Flora Robson was born in South Shields and trained at the Royal Academy of Dramatic Art. She made her first appearance on stage in 1921 at the Shaftesbury Theatre, London, in **Clemence Dane**'s *Will Shakespeare*. Dissatisfied with professional acting, she left in 1924 and worked in a factory, but returned to the stage five years later and rose to fame mainly in historical roles in plays and films, such as Queen **Elizabeth** in *Fire over England* (1931) and Thérèse Raquin in *Guilty* (1944).

Her first major success on stage was in 1931 as Abbie Putnam in *Desire Under the Elms*, followed by Mary Paterson in James Bridie's *The Anatomist* and Gwendolen Fairfax (later Miss Prism) in *The Importance of Being Earnest*. Though she never dominated the major female roles, her typically 'supporting' performances were always intelligent and sensitive, and often witty.

She consolidated her reputation with memorable stage performances in George Bernard Shaw's *Captain Brassbound's Conversion* (1948) and Henrik Ibsen's *Ghosts* (1958). She was made DBE in 1960 and had almost completely retired by 1969.

Rochefort, Christiane

Born 1917
French novelist who writes about people struggling against conventional society

Christiane Rochefort was born in Paris. None of her novels has made the same impact as her first, *Le Repos du guerrier* (1958, Eng trans *Warrior's Rest*, 1959). This well-written and ironically told story of a girl's submission to a sadistic alcoholic contained much scabrous detail, and won the Prix de la Nouvelle Vague.

Her novels typically involve a social outcast struggling against the oppressiveness of conventional society, as in her second, *Les Petits*

Enfants du siècle (1961, Eng trans *Children of Heaven*, 1962, and *Josyane and the Welfare*, 1963), which is also well known through being studied in schools.

Roddick, Anita Lucia, *née* Perella

Born 1942
English retail entrepreneur who founded the immensely successful Body Shop chain

Anita Perella was born in Brighton. She was a teacher for 14 years and then in 1976, with her husband Thomas Gordon Roddick, she founded Body Shop International to sell cosmetics 'stripped of the hype' and made from natural materials. The company now has over 1,200 stores worldwide (many of them franchised) in 45 countries. Anita Roddick was managing director until 1994, when she became chief executive.

A proponent of 'caring capitalism', she put her vision of a new type of British management into practice by pioneering childcare

Anita Roddick, 1988

in her company; she also lectures on green issues and conducts campaigns with Friends of the Earth.

In 1989 she won the UN environmental award and two years later published her book, *Body and Soul*.

Rodnina, Irina Konstantinova

Born 1949
Soviet figure skater, one of the greatest pairs skaters of all time

Irina Rodnina was born in Moscow. Her initial partner on the skating rink was Aleksey Ulanov, with whom she won four world championships. In 1972 she paired up with the younger and stronger Aleksandr Zaitsev, who became her husband in 1976, and with him achieved a perfect six mark from all judges at the European championships in 1973 and went on to win the world championships six times.

As well as her record 10 world championship wins, she also won the Olympic pairs three times and the European championship 11 times, another record.

She retired after the 1980 Olympics, having had a baby in 1979.

Rodoreda, Mercè

Born 1909 Died 1983
Catalan writer regarded by many as the best female novelist of 20th-century Spain

Mercè Rodoreda was born in Barcelona. She began her career as a writer soon after the proclamation of the Spanish Republic, and published prolifically between 1932 and 1937. Five novels, plus numerous short stories in literary magazines, established her as a rising star of Catalan literature, but with the end of the Spanish Civil War and the suppression of the Catalan language, her books were banned and she fled to France to live in exile.

Unable to write during this time, she published her first book for 20 years in 1957 (*Vint-i-dos Contes*, 'Twenty-two Stories'), followed in 1962 by her masterpiece, *La Plaça del Diamant* ('Diamond Plaza'), a stream-of-consciousness novel depicting the psychic and material horrors of the Civil War through the experiences of an ordinary Catalan woman. *Carrer de les Camèlies* ('Camellia Street'), a novel set in war-torn Barcelona in the 1940s and 1950s, was published in 1966 and *La Meva Cristina i Altres Contes* ('My Christina and Other Stories') in 1967.

Rodoreda returned to Spain in 1979, after Franco's death. Her books have been translated into many languages.

Rogers, Ginger, *originally* Virginia Katherine McMath

Born 1911 Died 1995
American actress and dancer who with Fred Astaire formed the most famous dance team of all time

Ginger Rogers was born in Independence, Missouri. Encouraged by her mother, she took singing and dancing lessons and had already turned down one film contract before making her professional début in vaudeville at the age of 14. She pursued a career in the theatre, progressing to leading roles in the Broadway musicals *Top Speed* (1929) and *Girl Crazy* (1930–1).

She moved to Hollywood in 1931 and had appeared as wise-cracking chorusgirls and cheerful golddiggers before being cast opposite Fred Astaire (1899–1987) in *Flying Down To Rio* (1933). It was the beginning of a lengthy partnership that produced some of the most graceful, romantic musicals in cinema history. Their finest work together includes *Top Hat* (1935) and *Swing Time* (1936). As a solo performer, she enjoyed success in films such as *Stage Door* (1937) and *Bachelor Mother* (1939) and won a Best Actress Oscar for *Kitty Foyle* (1940). She made her last film appearance in *Harlow* (1965).

Her many stage appearances include *Hello Dolly!* (1965) on Broadway, and *Mame* (1969) in London. She was a fashion consultant in the 1970s, and was wheelchair bound in her later years, but published a lively kiss-and-tell autobiography, *Ginger: My Story*, in 1991.

Rogers, Mary Josephine

Born 1882 Died 1955
American founder of the Maryknoll Missionaries

Mary Josephine Rogers was born in Boston, Massachusetts. She worked as a science teacher for a time, then returned to Smith College on a fellowship. In organizing a mission study group for Catholic students, she was inspired by the author and translator James A Walsh.

She joined the foundation at Maryknoll in 1912, and when what was then an auxiliary to the Catholic Foreign Mission Society of America (the Maryknoll Missionaries) became autonomous in 1920, she was chosen to be its superior. Five years later she became Mother General, remaining until her retirement in 1947.

The Foreign Mission Sisters of St Dominic were known from 1954 as the Maryknoll Sisters of St Dominic, and had by then trained and placed over 1,000 missionary sisters in some 70 countries.

Rohde, Ruth, *née* Bryan

Born 1885 Died 1954
American diplomat and feminist, the first US woman to hold a diplomatic post

Ruth Bryan was born in Jacksonville, Illinois. Her father was the politician and lawyer William Jennings Bryan (1860–1925), and she gained political insight from a young age. She was educated at Monticello Female Academy and Nebraska University, but left soon after entering to get married (1903). After divorcing in 1909 with two children, in 1910 she married Reginald Owen, an English army major, by whom she also had two children. Her husband was badly injured in service, and was left a chronic invalid. He died in 1927.

In order to support her family, Ruth took to public speaking and in 1926 entered politics as a Democrat in Florida. In 1928 she successfully ran for Congress, becoming the first Congresswoman from the deep South. Defending herself against accusations of ineligibility for Congress because of dubious citizenship (the result of marrying an alien), she won a brilliant victory on feminist grounds which resulted in an amendment to the Cable Act. As a member of Congress she continued to campaign for women's rights and in 1933 she was appointed US minister to Denmark, the first American diplomatic post ever held by a woman.

In 1936 she married Börge Rohde, a Danish soldier, and was obliged to resign her ministerial post. Returning to the USA, she continued to lecture and write, helped to draft the United States Charter, and received the OM from King Frederik IX of Denmark.

Romanov, Anastasia *see* Anastasia, Romanov

Rook, Jean

Born 1931 Died 1991
English journalist who was nicknamed the 'First Lady of Fleet Street'

Jean Rook was born in Hull. She graduated from London University with a degree in English before starting her career on local Yorkshire newspapers.

She moved to Fleet Street, first to the *Daily Sketch*, then the *Daily Mail*, and finally the *Daily Express*, where her outspoken and individual viewpoint and her 'common touch' made her the highest-paid of female journalists and earned her the title 'First Lady of Fleet Street'.

Roosevelt, (Anna) Eleanor

Born 1884 Died 1962
American humanitarian, an invaluable support to the 32nd President of the USA and an active UN worker after his death

Eleanor Roosevelt was born in New York City, the niece of Theodore Roosevelt. She married Franklin D Roosevelt in 1905. She took up extensive political work during her husband's illness with polio and proved herself an invaluable social adviser to him when he became president in 1933.

In 1941 she became assistant director of the office of civilian defence. After her husband's death in 1945 she extended the scope of her activities, and was a delegate to the UN Assembly in 1946, Chairman of the UN Human Rights Commission (1947–51) and US representative at the General Assembly (1946–52). She was also Chairman of the American UN Association.

Her publications include *This Is My Story* (1937), *The Lady of the White House* (1938), *The Moral Basis of Democracy* (1940), *India and the Awakening East* (1953), *On My Own* (1958) and her autobiography (1962).

Roper, Margaret, *née* More

Born 1505 Died 1544
English scholar and humanist remembered for her erudite writings

Margaret More was the eldest of Sir Thomas More's three daughters. He valued education for women and she learned philosophy, Latin and Greek. She married William Roper, who later became her father's biographer, when she was 16, and gave birth to five children, one of whom, Mary Roper Basset, continued the family literary tradition.

Margaret Roper corresponded with her father's friend, the Dutch humanist Desiderius Erasmus, and translated his work *A Devout Treatise Upon the Pater Noster* (1524). She is also remembered for her essays on the Four Last Things and for the letters to her father as he awaited execution (1534–5).

Rose of Lima, St, *originally* Isabel de Santa Maria de Flores

Born 1586 Died 1617
Peruvian visionary who is the patron saint of all South America

Isabel de Santa Maria de Flores was born into a wealthy family in Lima and known as Rosa from an early age. From girlhood she lived a life of self-imposed austerity, refusing the attentions of young men attracted by her beauty (which she tried to destroy by defacing her smooth skin) and working hard to alleviate her parents' financial hardship.

Although they longed for her to marry, Rosa made a vow of lifelong virginity, taking **Catherine of Siena** as her role model. She joined the Dominican tertiaries in 1606 and retired to a hut in the family garden, where it is said she experienced many visions and increased the austerity of her lifestyle by wearing a crown of thorns. News of her mystical experiences spread, and when earthquakes hit the city Rosa was often credited with the survival of its inhabitants.

Despite her reclusive life, she devoted time to the concerns of others and is regarded as the founder of Peru's social service. Her feast day is 23 August.

Rosenblatt, Wibrandis

Born 1504   Died 1564
Swiss Protestant who endured the deaths of four husbands and four children

Wibrandis Rosenblatt was born in Basel. She married in turn the humanist Cellarius (Ludwig Keller) in 1524, and the Protestant reformers Oecolampadius (1482–1531) in 1528, Capito (1478–1541) in 1532, and Bucer (or Butzer, 1491–1551) in 1542, but outlived them all.

Her life illustrates the close-knit nature of the emerging Protestant community (the reformers married her after taking advice from each other) and the transience and uncertainty of life at the time. Wibrandis had one child by Cellarius and three by Oecolompadius (of which two survived); she was the second wife of Capito, by whom she had five children (three survived), and the second wife of Bucer, by whom she had two children (one survived).

Her feats of household organization included taking the whole family to England to be with Bucer and bringing it back after his death. Killed by the plague of 1564, she was buried at Basel cathedral, beside Oecolampadius.

Rosewoman, Michele

Born 1953
American jazz pianist whose style is influenced by African and Cuban percussion

Michele Rosewoman was born in Oakland, California, to an eclectically musical family. She began playing piano as a child, but also studied African and Cuban percussion, which has strongly influenced her style.

Moving to New York City in 1978, she made a striking début with saxophonist Oliver Lake,

worked with violinist Billy Bang and formed her own groups, the ambitious big band New Yor-Uba and, later, Quintessence, in which she combined avant-garde piano technique with rhythms drawn from so-called 'World Music'.

Records such as *Contrast High* (1989) and *Occasion to Rise* (1991) have confirmed her growing stature.

Ross, Diana, *professional name of* Diane Earle

Born 1944
American pop singer and film actress who was a founder-member of the Supremes, the most successful black female group of all time

Diana Ross was born in Detroit, where she grew up in a poor housing project. Together with Florence Ballard and Mary Wilson, she formed the Primettes, later to become the Supremes. Their classic hits 'Baby Love' (1964) and 'Stop! In the Name of Love' (1965) were characteristic of their style. Ross assumed leadership and the group was renamed as if her backing band: Diana Ross and the Supremes.

The group split in 1970 and Ross began her solo career with 'Reach Out and Touch'. She was (mis)cast in the role of **Billie Holiday** in *Lady Sings the Blues* (1972) and later acted in *Mahogany* (1975) and *The Wiz* (1978). *Diana* (1980) is her most accomplished solo album to date, rivalled by *Swept Away* (1984).

In recent years, Ross has returned to her sanitized version of Holiday's style, having relaunched herself in 1990 as a jazz diva.

Ross, Mother *see* Davis, Christian

Rossetti, Christina Georgina

Born 1830   Died 1894
English poet whose work of technical virtuosity and wide-ranging imagination ranks her among the best female Victorian poets

Christina Rossetti was born in London, the daughter of the writer Gabriele Rossetti and sister of the poet and painter Dante Gabriel Rossetti. She was educated at home and was to have been a governess, but she retired through ill health which may originally have been feigned or psychosomatic. She was poetically precocious, and had a pamphlet printed by her grandfather before she was in her teens. She was engaged to James Collinson, the painter, but this was broken off when he returned to the Catholic faith, Christina being a devout High Anglican.

Her first lyrics, including 'An End' and

Christina Rossetti

'Dream Lane', were published in the first issue of *The Germ* (1850) under the pseudonym Ellen Alleyne. *Goblin Market*, her first and best-known collection, was published in 1862, and in 1866 came *The Prince's Progress. Sing Song: A Nursery Rhyme Book*, illustrated by Arthur Hughes, appeared in 1872. By the 1880s recurrent bouts of illness had made her an invalid, but she still continued to write, later works including *A Pageant and Other Poems* (1881), *Time Flies: A Reading Diary* (1895) and *The Face of the Deep: A Devotional Commentary on the Apocalypse* (1892).

Roudy, Yvette, *née* Saldou

Born 1929
French politican, writer and feminist activist

Yvette Saldou was born in Bordeaux and educated at the Collège de Jeune Filles. She married Pierre Roudy in 1951.

In 1964 she became secretary of the Mouvement Démocratique Féminin and was the founder and editor-in-chief of *La Femme du 20ème siecle*. In 1969 she wrote *La réussite de la femme*, followed by *La femme en marge*. She led the women's division of the French Socialist Party and in 1979 was elected as deputy to the European parliament in Strasbourg. From 1981 to 1986 she was the Minister in charge of Women's Rights, and in 1986 she was elected Socialist Deputy for Calvados.

Rowbotham, Sheila

Born 1943
English social historian and feminist whose books have provoked controversy

Sheila Rowbotham was born in Leeds and educated at Oxford. She became involved in the women's movement in the late 1960s. She also became an active socialist and wrote for several socialist papers, provoking controversy with her book *Beyond the Fragments: Feminism and the Making of Socialism* (1979, with Segal and Wainwright).

Among her most important historical works are *Women, Resistance and Revolution* (1972), *Hidden from History* (1973) and *Woman's Consciousness, Man's World* (1973).

Rowson, Susannah Haswell

Born c.1762 Died 1824
American writer and actress who may be America's first professional novelist

Susannah Rowson was born in Portsmouth, England. She moved to the USA as a child, returned to England in 1777, and went back to America in 1793.

Possibly the first woman to earn a living by writing, she published seven sometimes sensational novels, including *Charlotte Temple, A Tale of Truth* (1791 in the UK, 1794 in the USA), a seduction tale modelled on English novelist Samuel Richardson's *Clarissa*. It sold badly in Britain but became a huge bestseller in America. For the stage she wrote a series of social comedies, including *The Female Patriot* (1794) and *Americans in England* (1796).

Keenly interested in education for women, she wrote several tracts and essays on the subject, and in 1797 left the Boston theatre where she had been acting in order to found a boarding school for girls.

Roy, Gabrielle

Born 1907 Died 1983
Francophone Canadian novelist whose prize-winning depiction of the life of a poor family was the first to bring her acclaim

Gabrielle Roy was born in St Boniface, Manitoba, and was later resident in Quebec. Her first novel, *Bonheur d'occasion* (1945), translated as *The Tin Flute* (1947), was the first French–Canadian work to be awarded the Prix Femina. It was a realistic and compassionate novel about a slum family and a young woman's role in a society dominated by religion and the Church.

Subsequent novels drew on Roy's prairie childhood and were marked by a strong and straightforward narrative style. Her autobiography, *La Détresse et l'enchantment* (1984, Eng trans *Enchantment and Sorrow: The Auto-*

biography of Gabrielle Roy, 1987), was published posthumously.

Royden, (Agnes) Maude

Born 1876   Died 1956
English social worker and preacher who took a
religious and moral approach to women's suffrage

Maude Royden was born in Liverpool and educated at Cheltenham Ladies' College and Lady Margaret Hall, Oxford. She was a prominent campaigner in the women's suffrage movement, though less interested in its political goals than its religious and moral aims.

After working in Liverpool at the Victoria Women's Settlement she moved to Rutland where she began a long association with the Rev Hudson Shaw, whom she was to marry more than 40 years later. From 1917 to 1920 she was assistant preacher at the City Temple in London, and then until 1936 was a founder-leader of the Fellowship Guild. During this time she travelled worldwide, preaching and expressing her radical views on social issues.

She wrote *A Threefold Chord* (1947) about her long friendhsip with Hudson Shaw and his first wife, and also published works including *Woman and the Sovereign State, The Church and Woman* and *Modern Sex Ideals.*

Royds, Mabel Alington

Born 1874   Died 1941
English artist printmaker whose use of the
medium of woodcuts combined her interest in
colour and line to great effect

Mabel Royds was born in Little Barford, Bedfordshire, the fifth of 11 children. She won a scholarship to the Royal Academy Schools but turned it down in favour of the Slade, where she studied under the artist Henry Tonks. She was also influenced by the German-born painter Walter Richard Sickert, whom she met in Paris at the turn of the century.

From 1911 she taught at Edinburgh College of Art and in 1914 married the printmaker Ernest Stephen Lumsden. She travelled extensively, particularly in India and Tibet. She was an accomplished printmaker and her works are in many public collections including the Victoria and Albert and British Museums.

Royer, Clémence Augustine

Born 1830   Died 1902
French naturalist and writer

Clémence Royer was born in Nantes, Brittany. She is noted especially for providing the first French translation of Charles Darwin's *On the Origin of Species* in 1862. She revised and expanded this, and published *The Origins of Man and Society* in 1870. Her books were read extensively and caused much controversy, especially in religious and scientific circles.

Rozeanu, Angelica, *née* Adelstien

Born 1921
Romanian table tennis player who won a record
six successive world titles

Angelica Rozeanu was born in Bucharest. She first won Hungarian national championships in 1936, and went on to win them every year until her retirement in 1961. She often struggled with political pressures in her country, being denied a passport to take part in the 1938 world championships in London by her strongly anti-semitic government.

The first of her record six successive world championship wins was in 1950, and the high point of her career came in 1953 when she won the singles, ladies doubles and mixed doubles at the world championships and helped win the Corbillon Cup.

For several years she was ranked number one in the world.

Rubens, Bernice Ruth

Born 1928
Welsh novelist and playwright who writes on
Jewish, social and psychological themes

Bernice Rubens was born and educated in Wales. She trained as a teacher and was an English mistress at a boys' school in Birmingham before working for the United Nations as a documentary filmmaker.

Her first novel was *Set on Edge* (1960), followed by *Madame Sousatzka* (1962, subsequently adapted for film by **Ruth Prawer Jhabvala**), *Mate in Three* (1965) and *The Elected Member* (1969, published in the USA as *Chosen People*), for which she was awarded the 1970 Booker Prize. These were more overtly Jewish in subject-matter than subsequent books, but they clearly marked out Rubens's interest in familial guilt and the psychic damage caused by withdrawn or compromised love. In later books Rubens showed an interest in marginal social and sexual types, the 'cold and chosen ones'.

Later novels include *A Five Year Sentence* (1978) and *Mr Wakefield's Crusade* (1985); there is some sense that in the later 1980s and early 1990s she, like Graham Greene and, arguably, **Iris Murdoch**, interspersed more serious novels with lighter 'entertainments'.

However, *A Solitary Grief* (1991) found her at the top of her powers, being a work of genuine profundity.

Rubinstein, Helena

Born 1870 Died 1965
Polish-born American businesswoman who founded a cosmetics empire that bears her name

Helena Rubinstein was born in Kraków, Poland, into a Jewish family with seven other daughters who later became involved in Helena's business. She studied medicine and went to Australia in 1902, taking with her a facial cream made by her mother, and found that she could sell it to Australian women whose skin had been coarsened by the climate. She quickly opened a shop in Melbourne, where she offered advice to customers interested in her product, and then decided to study dermatology in depth and launch her business in Europe.

Her Maison de Beauté opened in London in 1908 and in Paris in 1912, and when World War I broke out she went to the USA and opened salons there, starting in New York City. In 1917 she began what was to become the major element of her business — wholesale distribution of the products — and after World War II she built cosmetics factories all over the world. She created a personal fortune of around $100 million and remained active in the running of Helena Rubinstein Inc into her nineties.

As well as a business executive, Rubinstein was a philanthropist, and in 1953 she established the Helena Rubinstein Foundation, through which she patronised the arts and education and endowed institutions for the poor. Her autobiography, *My Life for Beauty*, was published in 1965.

Ruddock, Joan Mary

Born 1943
British anti-nuclear campaigner and Labour politician who concerns have also included homelessness and racism

Joan Ruddock was born in Pontypool, Wales, and educated in Wales and at Imperial College, London. She worked for Shelter, the national campaign for the homeless, from 1968 to 1973, and was then director of an Oxford housing aid centre.

In 1977 she joined the Manpower Services Commission with special responsibilities for the young unemployed, and chaired the Campaign for Nuclear Disarmament (CND) from 1981 to 1987. That year she entered parliament

Joan Ruddock, 1993

as Labour MP for Lewisham, Deptford, almost immediately becoming a member of the Opposition Front Bench.

Her published work includes *The CND Story* (1983), *CND Scrapbook* (1987) and *Voices for One World* (1988).

Rudolph, Wilma

Born 1940 Died 1994
American athlete who has been described as one of the greatest sprinters of all time

Wilma Rudolph was born in Clarksville, Tennessee, the twentieth of 22 children. She weighed less than five pounds at birth but overcame childhood scarlet fever and polio and doctors' predictions that she would never walk properly to come to prominence as a teenager as part of an athletics team known as the 'Tennessee Belles'. At six feet tall, she was also an excellent basketball player.

As a 16-year-old she won a sprint relay bronze medal at Melbourne in the 1956 Olympic Games, and she became the first American woman to be decorated with three Olympic gold medals, all won at Rome in 1960 — in the 100 metres, 200 metres, and sprint relay events. She won the Sullivan award in 1961 and retired in 1964. She was an inspiration to black female athletes, particularly **Jackie Joyner-Kersee**, and was inducted into the National Women's Hall of Fame in 1994.

Ruether, Rosemary Radford, née Radford

Born 1936
American theologian whose writing examines
religion from a feminine viewpoint

Rosemary Radford was born in Minneapolis, Minnesota. As Professor of Applied Theology at Garrett-Evangelical theological seminary, Evanston, since 1976 she has written extensively on women and theological issues.

Her books, which analyze the effects of male bias in official Church theology and seek to affirm the feminine dimension of religion and the importance of women's experience, include *New Woman/New Earth* (1975), *Mary: The Feminine Face of the Church* (1979), *Sexism and God-Talk* (1983), *Women-Church* (1985) and *Gaia and God: Ecofeminism and Earth-Healing* (1992).

Rukeyser, Muriel

Born 1913 Died 1980
American poet, biographer, translator and
activist who believed in the motivational
power of poetry

Muriel Rukeyser was born in New York. She was educated at Vassar College (at the same time as **Mary McCarthy** and **Elizabeth Bishop**) and Columbia University. From the end of World War II until 1960 she was Vice-President of the House of Photography; technical and scientific ideas and processes play an important role in her verse. Her first collection, *Theory of Flight* (1935), reflects this most directly.

In later volumes she develops a terse, imagistic style, stripped of rhetorical artifice and false emotion; collections include *Beast in View* (1944) and *Body of Waking* (1958). An important selection appeared as *Waterlily Fire* in 1962, and a full-scale *Collected Poems* two years before her death.

Rukeyser wrote biographies of Willard Gibbs (1942), Wendell Wilkie (1957) and Thomas Hariot (1971), reflecting her political interests. Her experiences as a social activist included imprisonment during the protests against the Vietnam War. She also translated the Mexican poet Octavio Paz and the Swedish poet Gunnar Ekelöf .

Rule, Jane Vincent

Born 1931
Canadian novelist and short-story writer whose
lesbian writing has increased awareness of
feminist and homosexual issues and literature

Jane Rule was born in Plainfield, New Jersey, and educated in California and London. Her first novel was *Desert of the Heart* (1964), a bold study of two women tentatively approaching a lesbian relationship. Later books, such as *This is Not for You* (1970) and *Against the Season* (1971), explore similar territory, though in the latter book the range of characters is widened considerably. In *The Young in One Another's Arms* (1977) and *Contact with the World* (1980) homosexuality is used more broadly and metaphorically as an index of the estrangement felt by artists in an essentially philistine world.

Typically, Rule uses a multiple narrative perspective. In 1975, she published the important study *Lesbian Images*, followed a decade later by *A Hot-Eyed Moderate* (1985), which includes essays on earlier lesbian writers such as **Radclyffe Hall** and **Vita Sackville-West**. Her short stories are collected in *Themes for Diverse Instruments* (1975), *Outlander* (1981), a volume that also includes non-fiction, and *Inland Passage* (1985).

Rushforth, (Margaret) Winifred, née Bartholomew

Born 1885 Died 1983
Scottish pioneer of psychotherapy in Scotland

Winifred Bartholomew was born in Winchburgh, West Lothian, and educated at Edinburgh Medical School and University. In 1909 she sailed to India, where she spent 20 years as a medical missionary. Influenced by the works of William McDougall and Sigmund Freud, she decided to become a psychoanalyst. After a period of personal analysis at the Tavistock Institute in London, she moved to Edinburgh and set up practice as a private analyst.

In 1939 she founded the Davidson Clinic in Edinburgh, with the aim of bringing analysis within the reach of anyone, regardless of income. In time the clinic expanded to include children's play therapy and family therapy. After the clinic's closure in 1973 she practised from home, concentrating particularly on dream therapy, which she conducted until the day before her death.

Her publications include *Something is Happening* (1981), her autobiography *Ten Decades of Happenings* (1984) and *Life's Currency: Time, Money and Energy* (1985). Maintaining always a remarkable breadth and openness of mind, she exemplified in her life one of her favourite sayings: 'They will know we are old not by the frailty of the body but by the strength and creativity of the psyche'.

Russ, Joanna

Born 1937
American science-fiction writer whose powerful
female characters succeed without men's help

Joanna Russ was born in New York City. She
published her first story in 1959. Her early
work was more conventional in genre terms,
but the novel *Picnic on Paradise* (1968), later
incorporated in *Alyx* (1976), introduced the
female adventurer to centre stage, and revised
genre expectations in the process.

Her most important novel is *The Female
Man* (1975), a complex feminist study which
postulates four alternate lives for its female
protagonist, before bringing them together on
the utopian female planet Whileaway.

Her stories are collected in several volumes,
and she has also written fantasy and juvenile
novels, and criticism such as *Why Men Sup-
press Women's Writing*, now a classic in feminist literary criticism. She was appointed
Professor of English at the University of Washington in 1977.

Russell, Anna, *stage-name of* Claudia Anna Russell-Brown

Born 1911
English singer internationally successful concert
comedienne

Anna Russell was born in London. She studied
singing, and began an orthodox operatic
career before realizing the possibilities of
satire offered by opera and concert singing.

She worked on television and radio before
she first appeared in 1948 as a concert comedienne in New York, debunking musical fads,
since when she has achieved universal fame in
this medium.

She starred in *Anna Russell and her Little
Show* on Broadway (1953) and travelled
throughout Britain, North America, Australia,
the Orient and South Africa, before settling in
Canada. Her autobiography is *I'm Not Making
This Up, You Know*.

Russell, Dora, *née* Black

Born 1894 Died 1986
British feminist and former wife of philosopher
Bertrand Russell

Dora Black was educated at Sutton High
School, and graduated with a first class
honours degree in modern languages from
Girton College, Cambridge (1915). She continued her studies with research at University
College London and became a Junior Fellow
at Girton.

She visited Russia and China in the early
1920s and married Bertrand Russell (1872–
1970) in 1921. They established a progressive
school near Petersfield in 1927, which she continued to run after their divorce in 1935. She
later married Pat Grace.

She was a founder member of the National
Council for Civil Liberties and took part in a
CND rally when she was 90. Her publications
include *The Prospects of Industrial Civilization*
(1923) which was written with Russell, and
her autobiography *The Tamarisk Tree* (1975–
85).

Russell, Jane Anne

Born 1911 Died 1967
American endocrinologist who did pioneer work
on the role of growth hormone

Jane Russell was born in California and graduated from the University of California at Berkeley in 1932. She gained her PhD in 1937 on
carbohydrate metabolism and the role of pituitary hormones. She co-operated in research
projects with Carl and **Gerty Cori**, and moved
to Yale University in 1938.

In 1940 she married her collaborator Alfred
Wilhelmi and, despite lack of formal recognition from her university, won international acclaim for her work. In 1950 she and
her husband moved to Emory University in
Atlanta, where she did pioneer work on the
role of growth hormone, and achieved public
recognition for her service on many national
science policy committees. Despite this she
was not promoted to full professorship until
1965 when she was already terminally ill.

Russell, (Ernestine) Jane (Geraldine)

Born 1921
American actress whose ample bosom led her to
stardom

Jane Russell was born in Bemidji, Minnesota,
the daughter of a former actress. She worked
as a chiropodist's receptionist and photographer's model before studying acting with
Maria Oupenskaya (1876–1949). However, it
was her voluptuous figure that brought her
fame as the star of *The Outlaw* (1943), an
innocuous western that won notoriety for the
censor's concern over the amount of Russell's
cleavage exposed on screen. One Baltimore
judge commented that her bosom 'hung over
the picture like a thunderstorm over a landscape'.

She subsequently displayed some talent as
a comedienne, actress and singer in such films
as *The Paleface* (1948) and *Gentlemen Prefer
Blondes* (1953). As her film career faded, she

appeared in cabaret, endorsed Playtex bras on television, starred on Broadway in *Company* (1971) and on television in the series *Yellow Rose* (1983).

An autobiography, *My Path and Detours* (1985), revealed her alcohol-related problems and staunch religious beliefs.

Ruth

12th century BC
Biblical character who was widowed young but with God's help found a new husband

Ruth was a Moabite woman who had married one of the two sons of Elimelech and **Naomi**. When Naomi's husband and, later, both sons had died, she decided to return to her home town of Bethlehem. Ruth insisted on accompanying Naomi, believing that the God of Israel would look after her, and she later married a distant relative, the wealthy landowner Boaz.

The story, in the Book of Ruth, can be interpreted as a parable of divine providence and devotion to duty, or a reaction against teaching banning mixed marriages. Perhaps all three themes are combined in the New Testament mention of Boaz as an ancestor of King David and so of Jesus Christ.

Rutherford, Dame Margaret

Born 1892 Died 1972
English stage and film actress whose repertory included several notably eccentric roles

Margaret Rutherford was born in London. She made her first stage appearance in 1925 at the Old Vic theatre, and her film début in 1936.

She gradually gained fame as a character actress and comedienne, her gallery of eccentrics including such notable roles as Miss Prism in *The Importance of Being Earnest* (stage 1939, film 1952), Madame Arcati in *Blithe Spirit* (stage 1941, film 1945) and Miss Whitchurch in *The Happiest Days of Your Life* (stage 1948, film 1950). She also scored a success as **Agatha Christie**'s Miss Marple in a series of films from 1962, appearing with her husband, the actor Stringer Davis (1896–1973), whom she married in 1945.

She won an Oscar as Best Supporting Actress for her part in *The VIP's* (1963), and was created DBE in 1967.

Ruysch, Rachel

Born 1664 Died 1750
Dutch artist, the most celebrated Dutch flower painter of the 18th century

Rachel Ruysch was born in Haarlem, Holland. She studied with the flower painter Willem von Aelst and in 1693 married the portrait painter Juriaen Poole. The couple were both admitted into the Hague Corporation of Painters in 1701.

In 1708 they were appointed court painters to the Elector Palatine, and so lived in Dusseldörf, painting exclusively for the Prince, until his death in 1716, when they returned to Amsterdam. During this period Rachel also managed to have 10 children.

Ruysch was interested in producing a faithful depiction of nature and worked slowly, probably from her studies of flowers rather than from the blooms themselves.

Ryan, Elizabeth

Born 1892 Died 1979
American lawn tennis player whose record number of wins held for 45 years

Elizabeth Ryan was born in Anaheim, California. She won 19 Wimbledon titles (12 doubles and 7 mixed doubles), a record which stood from 1934 until 1979, when it was surpassed by **Billie Jean King**. Six of her women's doubles titles were with **Suzanne Lenglen**.

Ryder of Warsaw, Sue Ryder, Baroness

Born 1923
English philanthropist who promotes residential care for the sick and disabled

Sue Ryder was born in Leeds and educated at Benenden School in Kent. She joined the First Aid Nursing Yeomanry in World War II and worked with the Polish section of the Special Operations Executive in occupied Europe.

As a result of her experiences she determined to establish a 'living memorial' to the dead and those, like refugees, who continued to suffer. The Sue Ryder Foundation, begun at Cavendish, near Sudbury, Suffolk, in 1953, now links 80 centres worldwide. In some countries projects function under the auspices of the Ryder–Cheshire Foundation, which links her work with that of the English philanthropist Leonard Cheshire (1917–92), whom she married in 1959.

She has written *And the Morrow Is Theirs* (1975) and her autobiography, *Child of My Love* (1986).

Rye, Maria Susan

Born 1829 Died 1903
English feminist and social reformer

Maria Susan Rye was born in London, the daughter of a solicitor, and was educated at home. She joined the campaign for women's rights as secretary of the committee to promote the Married Women's Property Bill and became a member of the Society for Promoting Employment of Women.

In 1859 she opened a law stationer's business and was involved in the founding of the Telegraph School. She procured sponsorship for an emigration plan and in 1861 founded the Female Middle Class Emigration Society. Her ambitions extended to the training of pauper children, for whom she found employment in Canada. She retired to Hemel Hempstead in 1886.

S

Saariaho, Kaija Anneli

Born 1952
Finnish composer whose impressionistic music
often makes use of electronics

Kaija Saariaho was born in Helsinki and educated at the Rudolf Steiner school and the university there. She studied composition at the Sibelius Academy under Paavo Heininen, graduating in 1981. She is married to Jean-Baptiste Barrière, and now lives in France.

She makes considerable use of electronics in her work, both in tape pieces and in electroacoustic works, like the three *Jardins secrets* (1984–7). These followed her first orchestral essay *Verblendungen* (1982–4) and anticipated techniques in her remarkable ensemble piece *Lichtbogen* (1985–6), inspired by the Aurora Borealis.

Sabin, Florence Rena

Born 1871   Died 1953
American medical researcher who studied the
embryology of blood cells and lymph vessels

Florence Sabin was born in Central City, Colorado. She graduated in science from Smith College in 1893 and in medicine from Johns Hopkins in 1900, where in 1902 she became the first woman member of staff as an assistant in the Department of Anatomy. In 1917 she became the first woman professor there.

At the time when she was the first woman elected to the National Academy of Sciences in 1925, she was also serving as the first woman President of the American Anatomical Society, concurrently with her appointment as the first woman member of staff at the Rockefeller Institute for Medical Research in New York, which was where she began studying the aetiology of tuberculosis.

Following her retirement in 1938 she became deeply involved in public health legislation in her native Colorado.

Sacajawea, *also called* Bird Woman

Born c.1786   Died 1812
Native American woman famous for the part she
played on an expedition across America

Sacajawea was a member of the Shoshone. She was captured at the age of 12 and eventually sold into slavery to a French–Canadian trader, Toussaint Charbonneau. He married her and took her with him in 1804–6 when, as interpreter, he joined the US transcontinental expedition led by Meriwether Lewis and William Clark.

She was the only woman on the expedition and proved an invaluable guide, especially when they reached the upper Missouri River and the mountains where she had grown up. When they encountered other Native American tribes, Sacajawea, who was carrying her infant son on her back, allayed their hostility, and helped to negotiate for horses and guides. Her participation was vital to the success of the expedition, which established an American presence in the Pacific Northwest, and her fortitude in the face of much hardship has raised her to folkloric status.

Some historians claim that she did not die in 1812, but that a missionary met her in 1875 and she actually died in 1884.

Sacco, Nicola

Born 1891   Died 1927
American political radical and chief figure in a
possible miscarriage of justice

Nicola Sacco was born in Italy. She was one of the chief figures (the other was Bartolomeo Vanzetti, 1888–1927) in an American *cause célèbre* (known as the Sacco–Vanzetti case,

1920–1) which had worldwide reverberations.

Sacco and Vanzetti were accused and found guilty of murder and the theft of $16,000 payroll and were committed in 1920. Seven years later they were electrocuted in spite of conflicting and circumstantial evidence, and the confession of another man to the crime.

Both had been anarchists, and the suspicion that this had provoked deliberate injustice aroused an outcry all over the world, and led to the declaration 50 years later that the verdict had indeed been unjust and a result of prejudice.

Sachs, Nelly Leonie

Born 1891   Died 1970
German-born Swedish poet and playwright whose writing expresses the anguish of the Jews

Nelly Sachs was born in Berlin into a wealthy Jewish family. Between the wars she published a book of stories, *Tales and Legends* (1921), and several volumes of lyrical poetry.

With the rise of Nazi power she studied Jewish religious and mystical literature, and in 1940 escaped to Sweden through the intercession of the Swedish royal family and **Selma Lagerlöf**. After World War II she wrote plays and poetry about the anguish of the Jewish people.

She was awarded the 1966 Nobel Prize for Literature, jointly with the Israeli novelist Shmuel Yosef Agnon.

Sackville-West, Vita (Victoria Mary)

Born 1892   Died 1962
English poet and novelist who was the model for
Virginia Woolf's *Orlando*

Vita Sackville-West was born in Knole House, Kent, a daughter of the 3rd Baron Sackville. She received a private education and started writing novels and plays as a child. In 1913 she married the diplomat Harold Nicolson (1886–1968), and their marriage survived despite Nicolson's homosexuality and her own lesbian affair with Violet Trefusis.

Her first published works were a collection of poems, *Poems of West and East* (1917), and a novel, *Heritage* (1919). In her *Orchard and Vineyard* (1921) and her long poem *The Land*, which won the 1927 Hawthornden prize, her close sympathy with the life of the soil of her native county is expressed. Her prose works include the novels *The Edwardians* (1930), *All Passion Spent* (1931) and *No Signposts in the Sea* (1961), an account of her family in *Knole and the Sackvilles* (1947), and studies of Andrew Marvell and **Joan of Arc**. *Passenger*

to Teheran (1926) records her years in Persia (now Iran) with her husband.

She was a passionate gardener at Sissinghurst in Kent, her married home, and wrote a weekly gardening column for the *Observer* for many years.

Sadler, Flora Munro, *née* McBain

Born 1912
Scottish astronomer and first female employee of the Royal Greenwich Observatory

Flora McBain was born in Aberdeen and educated at Aberdeen University, where she graduated in mathematics and natural philosophy. She was a member of the British Expedition which successfully observed the total eclipse of the Sun in Omsk, Siberia, in June 1936. The following year she was appointed to the scientific staff of the Royal Observatory, Greenwich, the first woman scientist ever to be employed there.

Her work in the Observatory's Nautical Almanac Office, where she was Principal Scientific Officer until 1973, involved the production of astronomical and navigational tables and almanacs for the use of astronomers. She represented Great Britain on the International Astronomical Union's Commissions on the Moon and Astronomical Ephemerides from 1948 to 1970, and played an active part in the affairs of the Royal Astronomical Society, becoming its first woman secretary from 1949 to 1954.

Sagan, Françoise, *pseud of* Françoise Quoirez

Born 1935
French novelist, playwright and short-story writer

Françoise Quoirez was born in Cajarc in the Lot region, and educated at a convent in Paris and private schools. At the age of 18 she wrote, in only four weeks, the bestselling *Bonjour tristesse* (1954, Eng trans 1955; filmed 1958), followed by *Un Certain Sourire* (1956, Eng trans *A Certain Smile*, 1956; filmed 1958), both remarkably direct testaments of wealthy adolescence, written with the economy of a notable literary style. Her use of polite everday language to describe emotion lends a superficial simplicity to her work.

Irony creeps into her third, *Dans un mois, dans un an* (1957, Eng trans *Those Without Shadows*, 1957), but moral consciousness takes over in her later novels, such as *Aimez-vous Brahms...* (1959, Eng trans 1960; filmed 1961 as *Goodbye Again*) and *La Chamade* (1966, Eng trans 1966). A ballet to which she gave the central idea, *Le Rendez-vous manqué* ('The Missed Rendezvous'), enjoyed a temporary *succès de scandale* in Paris and London in 1958.

Her later works, including several plays, such as *Château en Suède* (1960, 'Castle in Sweden'), *Les Violons, parfois. . .* (1961, 'Sometimes, Violins. . .') and *Un Piano dans l'herbe* (1970, 'A Piano on the Grass'), and novels such as *L'Echarde* (1966, 'The Splinter'), *Le lit défait* (1977, Eng trans *The Unmade Bed*, 1978), *La Femme Fardée* (1981, Eng trans *The Painted Lady,* 1983) and *Un orage immobile* (1983, Eng trans *The Still Storm*, 1984) have had a mixed critical reception.

Sager, Ruth

Born 1918
American geneticist who postulated that DNA exists in cell cytoplasm as well as in the nucleus

Ruth Sager received her PhD in genetics from Columbia University in 1948 and worked as a research fellow in several institutions before becoming Professor of Biology at Hunter College (1966–75) and then Professor of Cellular Genetics at Harvard (1975–   ).

Most of her experimental work used the single-celled algae *Chlamydmonas* which she observed through numerous mutations, and in 1963 provided the clinching evidence that DNA existed in the cytoplasm. She postulated cytoplasmic inheritance — the inheritance of genes contained in the cell body or cytoplasm — in addition to the well-established inheritance of genes in the cell nucleus.

Sager was elected to the National Academy of Sciences in 1977.

Saint Denis, Ruth, *originally* Ruth Dennis

Born 1879 Died 1968
American dancer, director, choreographer and teacher of modern dance

Ruth Dennis was born in Newark, New Jersey, the daughter of a farmer and inventor. She began performing in vaudeville at an early age and became known, first in Europe, for the exotic, colourful eastern dances which were to characterize her work (*Cobras, The Incense* and *Radha* were all made in 1906).

She constituted the other half of the Denishawn partnership with Ted Shawn (1891–1972), whom she married in 1914 on her return to the USA, and founded a school and company with him in Los Angeles in 1915 (later in New York), which was frequented by many Hollywood stars. In 1916 she choreographed the Babylonian dances for D W Griffith's film *Intolerance*.

Fusing all manner of dance forms together, from ballet to Indian style, the company toured the USA until it folded in 1931, when the couple separated. She continued to dance into her eighties. Her autobiography, *An Unfinished Life*, was published in 1939.

St Pol, Marie de, Countess of Pembroke

Born c.1304 Died c.1377
French philanthropist who founded Pembroke College, Cambridge

Marie de St Pol was the daughter of Guy V of Châtillon-sur-Marne and Mary of Brittany. Her brief marriage (1321–4) to Aymer de Valance, Earl of Pembroke, left her a wealthy widow.

She acquired rights over the manor of Denney in 1327, and refounded and re-endowed the abbey (1339–42), chiefly by moving all but the most recalcitrant nuns from a foundation at Waterbeach. She began buying land in Cambridge for a college in 1346, and founded Pembroke Hall in 1347. She took a close interest in its management and endowments, and acquired more land in 1351.

Sainte-Marie, Buffy (Beverly)

Born 1941/42
Native American singer and songwriter whose work reflects her concern for Indian rights

Buffy Sainte-Marie was born of Cree descent in Saskatchewan, Canada. She was orphaned before she was a year old and raised in Massachusetts by her adoptive parents Albert C and Winifred Kendrick Sainte-Marie, a part-Micmac couple. In the 1960s she graduated from the University of Massachusetts and went to New York City to sing folk music.

An early hit was her classic antiwar protest song 'Universal Soldier', which was included in her first album *It's My Way* (1964). 'My Country 'Tis Of Thy People You're Dying' and 'Now That The Buffalo's Gone' vocalized her support of the Indian rights movement. 'Until It's Time for You to Go' was a love song which became a hit when sung by Elvis Presley in 1972, and her song 'Up Where We Belong', the theme tune for the film *An Officer and a Gentleman* (1982), won an Academy Award in 1983. Although her music has not sold in large quantities in the USA, perhaps because of her continuing involvement with protest movements, it is nevertheless considered to be of very high calibre.

She founded Native Creative to help increase cultural awareness in American children, and writes on North American Indian life for periodicals such as *Thunderbird* and *American Indian Horizons*.

Sallé, Marie

Born 1707 Died 1756
French dancer who inspired such personalities as Handel and Voltaire

Marie Sallé was born in Paris, the daughter of an acrobat, and became a child performer. She appeared in London in pantomime, and made her Paris début in 1718. She studied with François Prévost there and first performed with the Paris Opéra in 1727.

She was a rival of **Maria Camargo**, the other illustrious dancer of the time, and knew a large number of great talents, including Handel and Voltaire, who were inspired by her. She is known to have excelled in Jean Philippe Rameau's *Les indes gallantes* (1735) and *Castor et Pollux* (1737) and in the comedy ballets of Molière and Jean Baptiste Lully. She created some roles of her own, most notably a sensational *Pygmalion* (1733), and Terpsichore, in the prologue to *Pastor fido* (1734) by Handel.

Having worked all her career between London and Paris, she resigned in 1739. She rejected displays of technical virtuosity, masks and restrictive costumes in favour of dramatic, expressive gestures and loose flowing hair, and is known today as one of the pioneers of the ballet d'actions.

Salome

1st century AD
Judaean princess in the New Testament who requested the head of John the Baptist as a prize for her dancing

Salome was the granddaughter of Herod the Great and daughter of Herod Antipas's wife Herodias by her first husband Herod Philip. The historian Josephus identified her as the unnamed daughter in Mark 6.17–28 and Matthew 14.1–12, which relate how she was asked to choose a reward for dancing before Herod Antipas. At her mother's instigation, she requested the head of John the Baptist, for he had inveighed against Herodias's marriage to Herod Antipas, the brother of Herod Philip.

Josephus states in *Antiquities* that Salome later married Herod the Great's son, her uncle Philip the Tetrarch. Other sources claim she had a second husband, Aristobulus, King of lesser Armenia. Salome's dance is a favourite theme in art and literature, and her story is the subject of a play by Oscar Wilde (1894), on which is based an opera by Richard Strauss (1905).

Salote Tupou III

Born 1900 Died 1965
*Queen of Tonga remembered in Britain for her colourful and engaging presence during her visit in 1953 for the coronation of Queen **Elizabeth II***

Salote was educated in New Zealand and she succeeded her father, King George Tupou II, in 1918. Her prosperous and happy reign saw the reunion, for which she was mainly responsible, of the Tongan Free Church majority with the Wesleyan Church (1924).

Salt, Dame Barbara

Born 1904 Died 1975
English diplomat, the first British woman to be given an ambassadorial posting

Barbara Salt was educated at Seaford in Sussex and at universities in Munich and Cologne. During World War II she acted as vice-consul in Tangier before joining the Foreign Office as a first secretary to the United Nations.

Promoted to counsellor in 1955 and to ambassador to Israel in 1962, she was unable to take up the latter posting due to an illness which resulted in the loss of both her legs. Nevertheless she remained in the Foreign Office and became head of the Special Operations Executive, a post she held from 1967 until her retirement in 1972.

Samoilova, Konkordiya Nikolaevna

Born 1876 Died 1921
Russian socialist, political activist, writer and journalist, one of the great woman leaders of the Bolshevik period

Konkordiya Samoilova was born in Siberia, the daughter of a priest, and was educated in Leningrad. In 1905 she married a lawyer who died 13 years later.

She was a political activist and supporter of Lenin who played a variety of roles in the revolutionary movement; these included being an editor of *Pravda* from its foundation in 1912 and a co-editor of the journal *Rabotnitsa*, the women's newspaper.

In 1921 Samoilova contracted cholera while on a mission for the Soviet government in the Volga Region and died from the illness.

Sampson, Agnes

Died 1592
Scottish witch who claimed to have prompted the appearance of Satan himself

Agnes Sampson was born in Haddington, East Lothian. She was a lay-healer, and appears to have been an active witch rather than a victim of suspicion. She was put on trial after being named by a fellow and accused as the 'eldest witch of them all'.

Following severe torture, she confessed to celebrating black Mass, where the devil himself appeared and gave instructions to plot the death of the King and Queen. She also said she had organized meetings in North Berwick at Hallowe'en, when 200 people had danced in a circle by the sea.

Sampson was finally interrogated by James VI himself, and was subsequently executed.

Samuelson, Joan Benoit, née Benoit

Born 1957
American long-distance runner and women's
marathon world record holder

Joan Benoit was born in Cape Elizabeth, Maine. Competing under her maiden name, she won the Boston marathon on her second attempt, and set a new American record. On winning her second marathon in 1983, she set both a Boston Marathon record and a women's world record.

At the 1984 Olympics, she won a gold medal in the first women's Olympic marathon, setting the record at 2 hours 24 minutes and 52 seconds. Also that year she received the Sullivan Memorial Trophy as the nation's best amateur athlete, and shared the Women's Sports Foundation Sportswoman of the Year Award with **Mary Lou Retton**.

Sand, George, *pseud of* Amandine Aurore Lucie Dupin, Baronne Dudevant

Born 1804 Died 1876
French novelist who scandalized bourgeois society
with her unconventional ways and her love affairs

Amandine Dupin was born in Paris, the illegitimate daughter of Marshal de Saxe. She grew up principally at Nohant in Berri with her grandmother, Madame Dupin, on whose death she inherited the property. At the age of 18 she married Casimir, Baron Dudevant, and had two children, but after nine years left him and went to Paris with her children to make her living through writing in the Bohemian society of the period (1831).

For nearly 20 years her life was spent in the company of various distinguished men. Her first lover was Jules Sandeau, from whose surname she took her pseudonym, and with whom she wrote a novel, *Rose et Blanche* (1831, 'Pink and White'). She was always interested in poets and artists, including Prosper

George Sand

Mérimée, Alfred de Musset, with whom she travelled in Italy, and Chopin, who was her lover for 10 years. In the second decade her attention shifted to philosophers and politicians, such as Lamennais, the socialist Pierre Leroux, and the republican Michel de Bourges. After 1848 she settled down as the quiet 'châtelaine of Nohant', where she spent the rest of her life in outstanding literary activity, varied by travel.

Her work can be divided into four periods: candidly erotic novels such as *Indiana* (1832, Eng trans 1850), which shared in the Romantic extravagance of the time; socialistic rhapsodies such as *Spiridion* (1838, Eng trans 1842); studies of rustic life such as *La Mare au diable* (1846, Eng trans *The Haunted Marsh*, 1848), which are, by modern standards, her best works; and the miscellaneous works of her last 20 years. Her complete works (over 100 vols), besides novels and plays, include the autobiographical *Histoire de ma vie* (1855, 'The Story of My Life'), *Elle et lui* (on her relations with de Musset, 1859, Eng trans *He and She*, 1900), and delightful letters, published after her death.

Sandel, Cora, *pseud of* Sara Fabricius

Born 1880 Died 1974
Norwegian author and painter, one of the finest
writers of the inter-war period in Scandinavia

Sara Fabricius was born in Oslo and brought up in Tromsø in northern Norway. She lived as a painter in Paris from 1906 until 1921 and published her first novel, *Rosina*, in 1922. In many of her novels she condemns small-town and middle-class mores; another important theme in her work is the difficulty experienced by women in achieving artistic self-realization. Her poignant and subtly ironic manner of narration conveys great psychological insight and a profound knowledge of human nature.

Following *Rosina*, her writing career began in earnest with the 'Alberte' trilogy (*Alberte* (1926), *Alberte og Friheten* (1936, 'Alberte and Freedom') and *Bare Alberte* (1939, 'Just Alberte'), in which she describes a woman's experiences of power and powerlessness. In the short novel collection *Vårt vanskelige liv* (1960, 'Our Difficult Life'), Sandel addresses women's longing for acknowledgement and self-determination, while a further collection, *Barnet som elsket veier* (1973, 'The Child who Loved Roads'), reflects her empathy with a child's view of the world.

Although her protagonists belong to the perpetually powerless, they revolt unremittingly against their oppressive environment by means of obstinacy and fantasy, and sublime optimism pervades all her writing.

Sanderson, Tessa (Theresa Ione)

Born 1956
English sportswoman who entered television after retiring from javelin throwing

Tessa Sanderson was born in Wolverhampton. She first threw the javelin for Great Britain in 1974 and, along with her great rival **Fatima Whitbread**, kept the country at the top of the event for the ensuing decade.

In a career latterly dogged by injury she won three Commonwealth gold medals (1978, 1986, 1990) as well as one Olympic gold — at the Los Angeles games of 1984.

An ebullient, cheery figure, she made regular guest appearances on the ITV quiz show *Sporting Triangles*, and in 1989 became a sports newsreader for Sky TV.

Sanford, Agnes Mary, *née* White

Born 1897 Died 1982
American spiritual healer and author and champion of the work of the Holy Spirit

Agnes White was born in China, the daughter of Presbyterian missionaries. In 1923 she married Edgar Lewis Sanford, and shortly afterwards returned to the USA, to Moorestown, New Jersey, where he became an Episcopalian rector.

The discovery that she had a gift of healing started her on a career as a spiritual healer, especially as a healer of memories, a story told in *The Healing Light* (1947). Pentecostal experiences of the Holy Spirit around 1953–4 led her to promote charismatic renewal within the mainstream churches and, with her

husband, a school of pastoral care. Her autobiography, *Sealed Orders*, appeared in 1972.

Sanford, Katherine

Born 1915
American medical researcher, the first person to clone a mammalian cell

Katherine Sanford was born and educated in Wellesley, Massachusetts. She received her PhD from Brown University and then moved to the National Cancer Institute where she spent her entire research career. She worked initially with Dr Virginia Evans and colleagues, developing tissue-culture techniques and examining ways of promoting cancerous transformations in cultured cells.

Her cloning of a mammalian cell —the isolation of a single cell in order that it could propagate itself, producing a colony of identical cells — has become a vital tool for the detailed pathological study of cancer-causing mechanisms.

Sanger, Margaret Louise, *née* Higgins

Born 1883 Died 1966
American social reformer who founded the birth control movement

Margaret Higgins was born in Corning, New York, and educated at Claverack College. She trained as a nurse, and married her first husband William Sanger in 1902. (They divorced in 1920, and she married J Noah H Slee in 1922). Appalled by the tragedies she encountered as a nurse, she published a radical feminist magazine, *The Woman Rebel*, with advice on contraception, in 1914.

In 1916 she founded the first American birth-control clinic, in Brooklyn, New York, for which she was imprisoned. After a world tour, she founded the American Birth Control League in 1921, serving as its president until 1928. The first World Population Conference in Geneva in 1927 was the result of Sanger's organization.

Her many books include *What Every Mother Should Know* (1917), *Motherhood in Bondage* (1928) and *My Fight for Birth Control* (1931).

Sanger, Ruth Ann

Born 1918
Australian-British haematologist who discovered a sex-linked antigen carried on the X-chromosome

Ruth Sanger was born in Southport, Queensland, and moved to Armidale, New South Wales, at the age of two. After graduating in science from the University of Sydney in 1939, she joined the Sydney Red Cross Blood Transfusion Service, remaining until 1946. She then became assistant to Robert Russell Race (1907–84), the director of the Medical Research Council's Blood Group Reference Laboratory in London, and they collaborated extensively on investigating blood group systems.

On the death of Race's first wife in 1956, they married, and in 1973, on her husband's retirement, Sanger succeeded him as director of the MRC Blood Group Unit. She was elected a Fellow of the Royal Society in 1972.

Santamaria, Haydée

Born 1932
Cuban revolutionary who helped establish the new regime in 1959

Haydée Santamaria took part in the infamous attack on the Moncada Barracks in 1952 and was later imprisoned. Although the attack itself was relatively bloodless, around 70 students were subsequently killed as troops carried out arrests.

On her release from prison she continued to work in the underground movement with her close friend, the revolutionary leader Che Guevara and fought in the Sierra Maestra. Following Castor's coup in 1959 she helped establish the new regime.

Sappho

Born c.612BC
Greek lyric poet, regarded as the greatest woman poet of antiquity

Sappho was born on the island of Lesbos. She went into exile about 596BC from Mytilene to Sicily, but after some years returned to Mytilene. She married Cercylas, and had a daughter, Cleis.

She seems to have been the centre of a circle of women and girls, probably her pupils, perhaps as the priestess of a love cult. Tradition represents her as homosexual because of the love and admiration she expresses in some of her poems addressed to girls. Her lyrics were virtually unsurpassable in their depth of feeling, passion and grace. Only two of her odes are extant in full, but many fragments have survived.

It is from her that the 'lesbian' has acquired its modern meaning and the four-line sapphic stanza (used in Latin by Catullus and Horace) its name.

Sarah, *also spelt* Sarai

19th century BC
Biblical character in the Old Testament, whose name means 'princess' in Hebrew

Sarah was the wife of Abraham and mother of Isaac. She accompanied Abraham from Ur to Canaan (Genesis 12–23) and on account of her beauty she posed as Abraham's sister before Pharaoh in Egypt and Abimelech in Gerar, since their desire for her may have endangered her husband's life. Pharaoh took her as his wife, and Abraham prospered, but when the truth was revealed, Pharaoh banished them both. Long barren, she eventually gave birth to Isaac in her old age, fulfilling God's promise that she would be the ancestor of nations (Genesis 17.16). She died at the age of 127 in Kiriath-arba.

In the New Testament Paul uses the miracle of the birth of Isaac through God's promise to the free-born Sarah (rather than the slave-woman **Hagar**, who bore Abraham's first son) to explain to the Galatian Christians that they were freed by the covenant of Christ and therefore inheritors of the heavenly Jerusalem (Galatians 4.22–31). Peter cites her as an exemplary wife who afforded her husband due obedience and respect (1 Peter 3.6).

Sarandon, Susan Abigail, *née* Tomalin

Born 1946
American film actress perhaps best known as Thelma's friend Louise Sawyer in the road movie

Susan Tomalin was born in New York City, the eldest of nine children. She studied drama at the Catholic University in Washington DC, where she met her future husband, actor Chris Sarandon. She made her film début in *Joe* (1970) and worked extensively in television soap operas and in theatre before graduating to more interesting supporting roles in cinema, such as the naïve newly-wed Janet in *The Rocky Horror Picture Show* (1975).

Despite being a Best Actress Oscar nominee for her role in *Atlantic City* (1980), she did not receive much good work until cast in *The Witches of Eastwick* (1987) and *Bull Durham* (1988). Increasingly in demand as mature women displaying a strong sexuality, she subsequently triumphed in *White Palace* (1990), *Thelma and Louise* (1991), *Lorenzo's Oil* (1992) and won a Best Actress Oscar for her role in *Dead Man Walking* (1996).

Sarin, Madhu

Born 1945
Indian architect who uses her architectural skills to aid the poorest sector of India's population

Madhu Sarin trained in architecture at the Punjab University, Chandigarh (1962–7), and completed a postgraduate course in Tropical

Studies at the Architectural Association, London (1969–70). After graduating she worked in London for seven years as consultant to the UN Economic and Social Commission for Asia and the Pacific, responsible for co-ordinating policies concerning slums. In 1977 she returned to Chandigarh, India, and became consultant to the Indian government, speaking at conferences all over the world.

In response to a fuel shortage, she designed an energy-efficient stove that has benefited thousands of people worldwide. She has also developed ferro-cement roofing components to use in areas where traditional timber roofs are unavailable due to deforestation.

In 1988 Sarin was appointed to the Indian Ministry of Education National Resource Group to work on Education for Women's Equality.

Sarraute, Nathalie, *née* Tcherniak

Born 1902
Russian-born French writer, a leading exponent of the nouveau roman school

Nathalie Tcherniak was born in Ivanova. She and her mother settled in France when she was a child. She was educated at the Lycée Fénelon and the Sorbonne, graduating in arts and law. She spent a year at Oxford (1922–3) doing graduate studies, and then studied sociology in Berlin, before becoming a member of the French Bar and practising law in Paris, which she continued until she turned to writing full time. Her first book was a collection of sketches on bourgeois life, *Tropismes* (1939, Eng trans *Tropisms*, 1934), in which she rejected traditional plot development and characterization to describe a world between the real and the imaginary.

As a leading exponent of the *nouveau roman* school, she developed her theories further in her later novels: *Portrait d'un Inconnu* (1948, Eng trans *Portrait of a Man Unknown*, 1958), *Martereau* (1953, Eng trans 1959), *Le Planétarium* (1959, Eng trans 1960), *Les Fruits d'or* (1963, Eng trans *The Golden Fruits*, 1964), *Entre la vie et la mort* (1968, Eng trans *Between Life and Death*, 1969) and *Vous les entendez?* (1972, Eng trans *Do You Hear Them?*, 1973).

She has also written plays, *Le Silence, suivi de Le Mensonge* (1967, Eng trans *Silence, and The Lie*, 1969), *Isma* (1970, Eng trans *Izzuma*, 1980), *Elle est là* (1978, Eng trans *It Is There*, 1980) and collections of essays.

Sarton, (Eleanor) May

Born 1912 Died 1995
Belgian-born American poet and novelist whose key theme was solitude, its nature and its benefits

May Sarton was born in Wondelgem, Belgium. She emigrated with her family to the USA at the age of four, and became a naturalized citizen in 1924. She founded and directed the Associated Actors Theatre in 1933 but in 1936 decided to become a full-time writer.

Her first book, the poetry volume *Encounter in April* (1937), was followed by six more, including *Collected Poems* (1974). *The Silence Now*, a volume of new and uncollected early poems, appeared in 1989. Interspersed with these are novels such as *The Single Hound* (1938), dealing with a young English poet; *The Birth of a Grandfather* (1957), sympathetically examining the issue of growing older; and *Mrs. Stevens Hears the Mermaids Singing* (1965), looking at lesbian experience.

Saunders, Dame Cicely Mary Strode

Born 1918
English founder of the modern hospice movement

Cicely Saunders was born in Barnet, Greater London. She was educated at Roedean School and St Anne's College, Oxford, and trained at St Thomas's Hospital Medical School and the Nightingale School of Nursing. She founded St Christopher's Hospice, Sydenham, in 1967 and was its medical director until 1985, when she became chairman (1985–   ).

She promotes the principles of dying with

Cicely Saunders, 1984

dignity, maintaining that death is not a medical failure but a natural part of life and that its quality can be enhanced by sensitive nursing and effective pain-control. She was appointed DBE in 1980, and has received many other awards for her pioneering work, including the Templeton prize (1981) and the BMA gold medal (1987), and was appointed to the Order of Merit in 1989.

She has written and edited a number of books, including *Care of the Dying* (1960), *The Management of Terminal Disease* (1978), *Hospice: The Living Idea* (1981), *Living With Dying* (1983), *St Christopher's in Celebration* (1988) and *Beyond the Horizon* (1990).

Saunders, Jennifer

Born 1958
English comedienne and actress who wrote the TV comedy sensation of 1994: Absolutely Fabulous

Jennifer Saunders was born in Sleaford, Lincolnshire, and trained at the Central School of Speech and Drama in London. There she met **Dawn French**, with whom she created a highly successful comedy double-act, starting at the Comedy Store in London. In 1980 they joined the new Comic Strip club, from which the careers of several contemporary comedians were launched. It was not long before they appeared on television together, such as in *Girls on Top*, which they co-wrote, and were given their own television series, exploiting the hilarious idiosyncrasies of human, particularly female, relationships.

Saunders went on to write the *Absolutely Fabulous* series for BBC2 in 1992, starring in it as the fashion public relations executive Edina, and winning an Emmy award for the script and a BAFTA for her perfomance. On the strength of its popularity (it had eight million viewers) it transferred to BBC1 for the second series, which also starred **Joanna Lumley**.

Sauvé, Jeanne, *née* Benoit

Born 1922
Canadian politician, journalist and broadcaster

Jeanne Benoit was born in Saskatchewan and educated at the universities of Ottowa and Paris. From 1942 to 1947 she was National President of the Jeunesse Étudiante Catholique in Montreal. She married Maurice Sauvé in 1948.

She worked for UNESCO in Paris, and on returning to Canada made her career as a journalist and broadcaster for CBC. In 1972 she became a member of parliament representing Montreal-Ahuntsic and was Secretary of State for Science and Technology.

Her successful political career led to her appointment as the first woman Speaker of the House of Commons, and in 1983 she became Governor-General of Canada.

Sayers, Dorothy L(eigh)

Born 1893 Died 1957
English detective-story writer, dramatist, poet and essayist

Dorothy L Sayers was born in Oxford and educated at the Godolphin School, Salisbury, and Somerville College, Oxford (she took a first in modern languages). She taught for a year and then worked in an advertising agency until 1931. In 1924 she had an illegitimate son, and in 1926 married Captain Oswald Fleming.

In her novels, beginning with *Whose Body?* (1923) and *Clouds of Witness* (1926), she tells the adventures of her hero Lord Peter Wimsey in various accurately observed milieux — such as advertising in *Murder Must Advertise* (1933) or campanology in *The Nine Tailors* (1934). Her other stories include *Strong Poison* (1930), *Gaudy Night* (1935), *Busman's Honeymoon* (1937) and *In the Teeth of the Evidence* (1939).

She also earned a reputation as a leading Christian apologist with two successful plays, *The Zeal of Thy House* (1937) and *The Devil to Pay* (1939), a series for broadcasting (*The Man Born to be King*, 1943) and a closely reasoned essay (*The Mind of the Maker*, 1941). A translation of Dante's *Inferno* appeared in 1949 and of *Purgatorio* in 1955. The *Paradiso* was left unfinished at her death.

Sayers, Peig

Born 1873 Died 1958
Irish Gaelic storyteller who retained her hold on a disappearing language

Peig Sayers was born in Dunquin, County Kerry, among purely Irish-speaking neighbours. She lived most of her life on the Great Blasket Island. The disappearance of the Irish language from most of Ireland made her powers of recollection and her hold on traditional narratives deeply respected by scholars, and she is one of few women to have held such an authoritative position.

Her prose, as recorded in *Peig* (edited by Máire Ní Chinnéide, 1936) and *Machtnamh Sean-Mná* (1939, translated as *An Old Woman's Reflections*, 1962), is straightforward and clear, with decided authority and a touch of complacency.

Scharrer, Berta, née Vogel

Born 1906 Died 1995
American endocrinologist known for her work on neurosecretion

Berta Vogel was born and educated in Munich. She married her fellow student Ernst Scharrer in 1934, and began a personal and professional collaboration that ended with his death in 1965. Their employment prospects in Germany in the mid-1930s were poor, so Ernst qualified in medicine and Berta became a school teacher. In 1940 Ernst was able to move to the Western Reserve University in the USA and Berta followed him, the first of several moves in which she was included.

In 1965 after Ernst's death she was no longer subject to the prohibition of husbands and wives holding appointments at the same university and was appointed Professor of Anatomy at the Albert Einstein School of Medicine in New York. Their extensive work on the comparative anatomy and physiology of neurosecretion, the ability of some specialized nerve cells to behave like gland cells of the endocrine system, was fundamental in establishing it as an important biological concept. Berta's work in the 1970s was important in extending and re-fashioning the concept.

Honoured by many academies and societies, she was elected a member of the National Academy of Sciences in 1978.

Schiaparelli, Elsa

Born 1890 Died 1973
Italian-born French fashion designer who made inventive use of bright colours and traditional fabrics

Elsa Shiaparelli was born in Rome, the daughter of a professor of oriental languages. She studied philosophy and lived in the USA for a time, working as a film script writer. Her husband left her and in 1920 she took her daughter and moved to Paris.

The first garment that she designed and wore was a black sweater knitted with a white bow that gave a *trompe l'œil* effect. It resulted in her receiving orders from an American store, which started her in business in 1929.

Her designs were inventive and sensational, and she was noted for her use of colour, including 'shocking pink', and her original use of traditional fabrics. She featured zippers and buttons, and made outrageous hats. She

opened a salon in New York in 1949, and retired in 1954.

Schiffer, Claudia

Born 1970
German supermodel, the muse for Chanel and an occasional television presenter

Claudia Schiffer was born in Krefeld. She is the daughter of a lawyer and had ambitions in the law herself before she was discovered by a model agent at a Düsseldorf disco in 1988. Her début with the publicity campaign for Guess Jeans in the USA led to her catwalk career at Chanel in 1990. Karl Lagerfeld has made her his muse there, and she also models for his other collections, as well as for Versace and Valentino.

As well as producing fashion calendars, she has an exclusive publicity contract with Revlon and is a partner with supermodels **Naomi Campbell** and Elle Macpherson in the expanding Fashion Café empire. Her books *Claudia Schiffer: Memories*, a photographic essay, and *Claudia Schiffer by Karl Lagerfeld*, a collection of photographs, appeared in 1995. She is engaged to the American magician and illusionist David Copperfield.

Schlafly, Phyllis, née Stewart

Born 1924
American writer and anti-feminist, a well-known media figure

Phyllis Stewart was born in St Louis and studied at Washington University, St Louis (BA, 1944), Harvard University (MA, 1945) and Niagara University (LLD, 1976). She married Fred Schlafly in 1949.

She became well known as a syndicated columnist and as a broadcaster with CBS and the Cable TV News Network. She served on the Commission on the Status of Women (1975–85) and on President Ronald Reagan's Defence Policy Advisory Group.

Her publications *include A Choice Not an Echo* (1964), *The Power of the Positive Woman* (1977), *Equal Pay for Unequal Work* (1984) and *Who Will Rock the Cradle* (1989).

Schmidt, Birgit, née Fischer

Born 1962
German canoeist who has the most successful record of any female throughout canoeing history

Birgit Fischer was born in Brandenberg. Her husband is Jorg Schmidt, who is also a world champion canoeist. A physical education teacher, she has won four Olympic gold medals — three for East Germany and one for Germany — one in 1980 for K1, two in 1988 at K2 and K4 and a record-breaking fourth in 1992 for K1.

Her final Olympic gold was part of a stunning comeback to competition following a three-year break from the sport while she had her second child. She also has five world championship K1 titles, seven K2 titles and seven K3 titles.

Schneiderman, Rose, *known as* Rachel

Born 1884 Died 1972
American trade unionist, labour leader and
social reformer

Rose Schneiderman was born in Poland. She emigrated to the USA when she was eight, and after the sudden death of her father, a tailor, she spent much time in institutions as her mother was unable to support her. She worked from the age of 13.

In 1904 she was elected to a union executive board, the highest position yet held by a woman in any American labour organization. After 1908 she worked mainly with the Women's Trade Union League. During Roosevelt's presidency, she was the only woman in the National Recovery Administration, and from 1937 to 1943 she was Secretary of the New York State Department of Labour.

A dynamic orator, she lectured widely, and by the end of her long life she had become one of the most respected spokespersons and activists for improving the conditions of working people.

Scholastica, St

Born c.480AD Died c.543AD
Italian nun who was an early Christian founder
and the first Benedictine nun

Scholastica was born in Nursia, traditionally the twin sister of St Benedict of Nursia, who founded Western monasticism. Her life is known from the *Dialogues* of Gregory the Great.

She established a convent at Plombariola, not far from her brother's headquarters at Monte Cassino. They met once a year to discuss spiritual matters. She is said to have prolonged their last meeting by invoking a storm through prayer to prevent him leaving. She was buried at Monte Cassino a few years before her brother. Her feast day is 10 February.

Schoonmaker, Thelma

Born 1945
American film editor who is best known for her
work with Martin Scorsese

Thelma Schoonmaker grew up in Africa. She is one of the leading editors in contemporary American cinema. She met Martin Scorsese at New York University, and has been closely associated with his films since his début, *Who's That Knocking At My Door?* (1968).

She has been influential in helping create his distinctive visual style. She received an Academy Award for her stunning work on *Raging Bull* (1980), and was also nominated for *Goodfellas* in 1990, and for the rock documentary *Woodstock* in 1970. She was married to the English film director Michael Powell from 1984 until his death in 1990.

Schreiber, Adele

Died 1957
Austrian feminist, journalist and politician

Adele Schreiber was born in Vienna, the daughter of a doctor. She married and became a correspondent for the *Frankfurter Zeitung* in Berlin.

She was a founder of the International Woman Suffrage Alliance and of the German Association for Rights of Mothers and Children (1910). After World War I she became a member of the first Reichstag of the Wiemar Republic, the author of several books and President of the Red Cross.

After Hitler gained control of Germany, she lived in exile first in the UK and then Switzerland, where she becameVice-President of the International Alliance of Women.

Schreiber, Lady Charlotte Elizabeth, *née* Bertie

Born 1812 Died 1895
Welsh scholar diarist and creator of some now
famous collections of artefacts

Lady Charlotte Bertie was born in Uffington, Lincolnshire, a daughter of the Earl of Lindsey. She became interested in the literature and traditions of Wales after her marriage in 1833 to the Welsh industrialist Sir Josiah John Guest, whose ironworks at Dowlais, Merthyr Tydfil, she managed after his death in 1852. In 1855 she married Charles Schreiber, former MP for Cheltenham and Poole.

She is best known for her part in translating and editing *The Mabinogion* (1838–1849), with helped from Thomas Price, John Jones and others. She was also a lifelong collector, and became an authority on fans and playing cards, her collections of which she bequeathed to the British Museum. Her famous collection of china was presented to the Victoria and Albert Museum.

Schreiner, Olive

Born 1855 Died 1920
South African author and feminist who wrote the
first significant novel to come from Africa

Olive Schreiner was born in Wittebergen Mission Station, Cape of Good Hope, the daughter of a German Methodist missionary and an English mother. She grew up largely self-educated and at the age of 15 became a governess to a Boer family near the Karoo desert. She lived in England (1881–9), where her novel, *The Story of an African Farm* (1883) — the first sustained, imaginative work to come from Africa — was published under the pseudonym Ralph Iron.

She had a fiery, rebellious temperament and a lifelong hatred of her mother; in her later works the creative artist gave way to the passionate propagandist for women's rights, pro-Boer loyalty, and pacifism. These include the allegorical *Dreams* (1891) and *Dream Life and Real Life* (1893), the polemical *Trooper Peter Halket* (1897), a sociological study, *Woman and Labour* (1911), and her last novel *From Man to Man* (1926).

In 1894 she married S P Cronwright, who took her name, wrote a biography of her (1924) and edited her letters (1926).

Schulenburg, Ehrengard Melusina, Gräfin (Countess) von der

Born 1667 Died 1743
German noblewoman who became the mistress of
George I of Britain

Gräfin von der Schulenburg was born in Emden, Saxony. Nicknamed 'the Maypole' because of her lean figure, she joined the household of George's mother **Sophia** and became his mistress about 1690, going after him to England when he became its first Hanoverian king in 1714.

She exerted a queen-like influence on the King and became a great friend of Robert Walpole (*de facto* Prime Minister 1721–42), though her lucrative dealings in South Sea stock and selling of titles, not to mention her avarice and physical plainness, earned her little respect from the populace. She herself received many titles, among them Duchess of Kendal in 1719.

After George's death in 1727 she retired to Kendal House, Middlesex.

Schumann, Clara Josephine, *née* Wieck

Born 1819 Died 1896
German pianist and composer who often went
on tour with her Romantic composer husband
Robert Schumann

Clara Wieck was born in Leipzig, the daughter of Friedrich Wieck, a Leipzig pianoforte teacher who trained her to be one of the most brilliant concert pianists of her day. She gave her first *Gewandhaus* concert when only 11 and the following year four of her Polonaises were published.

In 1840 she married the composer Robert Schumann (1810–56), who wrote many of his best known piano pieces for her, and went on concert tours with him to Hamburg. She bore him eight children, which partly curtailed her career, but she did undertake solo tours to Copenhagen (1842) and to Russia. From 1856 she very often played for the Philharmonic Society in London, fostering her husband's work wherever she went.

Her own compositions include piano music and songs. From 1878 she was principal pianoforte teacher in the Frankfurt-am-Main Conservatory.

Schumann, Elisabeth

Born 1889 Died 1952
German-born American operatic soprano who
was noted also for her interpretation of lieder

Elisabeth Schumann was born in Merseburg. In 1919 she was engaged by Richard Strauss for the Vienna State Opera and sang in his and Mozart's operas all over the world, making her London début in 1924.

Latterly she concentrated more on lieder by such composers as Schubert, Hugo Wolf and Richard Strauss. She left Austria in 1936 and in 1938 became a US citizen.

Schumann-Heink, Ernestine, *née* Rössler

Born 1861 Died 1936
Czech-American contralto (and later mezzo-
soprano) with great dramatic presence

Ernestine Schumann-Heink was born in Lieben, near Prague. She was married three times, and her professional name hyphenated the surnames of her first and second husbands. She studied singing in Graz and made her début in Dresden, aged 17.

She moved to Hamburg Opera in 1882 and remained there until 1897, singing Wagner roles under Gustav Mahler. She also performed in Bayreuth *Rings* between 1896 and

World War I. Her American début was in 1899 and she became a regular performer at the Metropolitan Opera, with a pure, flexible voice which become higher pitched as her career advanced. She continued to work on the opera stage in Europe until 1932, when she retired, aged 70.

Schurman, Anna Maria van

Born 1607 Died 1678
Dutch polymath, feminist, artist and poet

Anna Maria van Schurman was born in Holland and educated in the reformed Protestant religion by her father. Intent on following the advice given by him on his deathbed, she avoided marriage. Instead she became joint leader with Jean de Labadie of a religious community which had many similarities to the Quaker religion.

Her influential book, *De Ingenii Muliebris*, was published in 1641 and was translated and published, with some of her letters, as *The Learned Maid*. She wrote her autobiography at the age of 70.

Schwarzkopf, Dame Elisabeth (Olga Maria Elisabeth Frederike)

Born 1915
German-born Austrian-British soprano who made a speciality of Mozartian roles

Elisabeth Schwarzkopf was born in Berlin, where she studied (1938–42) before joining the Vienna Opera. In 1953 she married the record executive Walter Legge (d.1979).

Her British début was in 1947, and four years later she sang in the première of Stravinsky's *The Rake's Progress*, creating the role of Anne Trulove. Generally, though, she favoured classical repertoire, with Mozart a particular speciality.

In 1974 she was awarded the Grosses Verdienstkreuz for her services to music in Germany and in 1992 she was appointed DBE.

Schwimmer, Rosika

Born 1877 Died 1948
Hungarian feminist and pacifist who spent her life campaigning for peace and against Fascism

Rosika Schwimmer was born in Budapest. As a journalist she was active in the Hungarian women's movement, and was a co-founder of a feminist-pacifist group. She became Vice-President of the Women's International League for Peace and Freedom, and from 1918 to 1919 was Hungarian Minister to Switzerland.

In 1920, fleeing from the country's anti-semitic leadership, she emigrated to the USA, but was refused citizenship since, as a pacifist, she could not promise to fight should war break out.

For the rest of her life she continued to campaign for pacifism and before the outbreak of World War II was outspoken in her criticism of growing European Fascism.

Scott, Rose

Born 1847 Died 1925
Australian feminist and social reformer, a key figure in the early suffrage movement

Rose Scott was born in Glendon, near Singleton in New South Wales, and educated by governesses. After her father's death in 1879 she moved to Sydney, where she was a founder of the Women's Literary Society in 1889. This developed into the Women's Suffrage League, of which she became secretary in 1891. She lobbied tirelessly for women's suffrage until 1902, when the Women's Suffrage Act was passed in New South Wales. She was active in other reforms too, especially protective legislation, and campaigned for juvenile offenders to be tried in special children's courts and for the 'age of consent' for girls to be raised to 16.

Refusing to marry, saying 'life is too short to waste on the admiration of one man', she worked for the International League of Women and was President of the Peace Society from 1907. She remained true to her pacifist views throughout World War I and earned a reputation as a patron of Australian art and literature.

Scott, Sarah, *née* Robinson

Born 1723 Died 1795
English novelist who wrote the first depiction of an ideal existence by a woman

Sarah Robinson was born into a well-connected family in Kent, a sister of the 'bluestocking' **Elizabeth Montagu**. She was educated at home, travelled widely in England, was married briefly and unhappily (1751–3) to the Prince of Wales's tutor, then lived with her friend Lady Barbara Montagu in a female community near Bath, teaching poor children (1754–65).

Most of her six novels are conventional tales of moral sentiment, but *A Description of Millennium Hall* (1762), her most popular work, is interesting as one of the first female Utopias; narrated through a series of personal stories, it portrays life in a caring community of women as an appealing alternative to marriage.

Scott, Sheila, *originally* Sheila Christine Hopkins

Born 1927 Died 1988
English pilot who made several record-breaking long-distance solo flights

Sheila Hopkins was born in Worcester. She left school at 16, joined the Royal Naval Section of the Voluntary Aid Detachment, and after World War II spent a year acting with a repertory company under the stage-name of Sheila Scott. Following an unhappy marriage (1945–50), she worked as a model and actress until 1959, when she took her pilot's licence and came fifth in the first race she competed in — from London to Cardiff.

Supported financially by several sponsors, she took part in many races and gained wide flying experience and a commercial pilot's licence. In 1966, in 33 days and 189 flying hours, she flew 31,000 miles (49,888km), the longest solo flight in a single-engined aircraft. She followed this with further light-aircraft records, including in 1971 a solo flight from equator to equator, over the North Pole.

She wrote three books describing her career: *I Must Fly* (1968), *On Top of the World* (1973) and *Bare Feet in the Sky* (1974).

Scott Brown, Denise

Born 1931
American architect and urban planner with an international outlook who has developed a wide range of disciplines

Denise Scott Brown was born in Nkana, Zambia. She trained at the Architectural Association, London, and at the University of Pennsylvania, where she was assistant professor for five years. She also served on the Massachusetts Institute of Technology board of advisers for 10 years. Since 1967 she has worked in the world-renowned Philadelphia practice of Venturi, Scott Brown and Associates, where she is a principal and where she introduced a planning division strongly based on the ideas of urban design.

She has also designed fabrics, china, glassware, wallpaper, jewellery and furniture for international companies such as Knoll International. Her best-known work includes the extension to the National Gallery in London (completed in 1989) and her contributions to 25 urban planning schemes, including the master plan for part of Austin, Texas. Her numerous awards include the National Medal of Arts (1992) and the RSA Benjamin Franklin Award (1993).

With her architect husband and business partner Robert Venturi, she published *A View from the Campidiglio: Selected Essays 1953–84* (1984) and she also wrote *Urban Concepts* (1990).

Scudder, Ida Sophia

Born 1870 Died 1960
American missionary pioneer of female nursing and medical education in India

Ida Scudder was born in Ranipet, Madras. At first she was unwilling to follow the family missionary tradition, but her mind was changed by an incident on a brief visit to India. Three times in the same night there were calls to help Hindu and Muslim women in childbirth. In each case the husband refused to let a male doctor see his wife and the woman died.

Back in India as a qualified doctor in 1900, Scudder began work from a dispensary in her house in Vellore, moving to her first hospital in 1902. Training courses for nurses (1907) and women doctors (1918) followed. From these small beginnings evolved Vellore Christian medical college (1942, co-educational from 1947), the largest teaching hospital in Asia.

Scudéry, Madeleine de

Born 1608 Died 1701
French novelist whose works were very popular in their time and raised the status of women writers

Madeleine de Scudéry was born in Le Havre, a sister of the writer Georges de Scudéry. Left an orphan at the age of six, she went to Paris in 1639 and with her brother was accepted into the literary society of Madame de **Rambouillet**'s salon. It was not long before she had established her own salon which met on Saturdays (*Samedis*). She lived with her brother in Paris and Marseilles until his marriage in 1654.

She had begun her literary career with the romance *Ibrahim ou l'illustre Bassa* (1641, Eng trans *Ibrahim; or, The Illustrious Bassa*, 1652), but her most famous work was the 10-volume *Artamène, ou le Grand Cyrus* (1649–59, Eng trans *Artamenes, or the Grand Cyrus*, 1653–5), written with her brother, followed by *Clélie* (10 vols, 1654–60, Eng trans *Clelia*, 1656–61). These highly artificial, ill-constructed pieces, full of pointless dialogue, were popular at the court because of their sketches of and skits on public personages. Her last novel was *Mathilde d'Anguilon* (1667).

She was a notable *Précieuse*, one of a group of 17th-century salon-going literary women who prided themselves with their ever-increasing knowledge and social graces, as well as their independence from men, and was satirized by Molière in *Les précieuses ridicules* (1659, 'The Conceited Young Ladies').

Seacole, Mary Jane, *née* Grant

Born 1805 Died 1881
Jamaican nurse, Crimean War heroine,
adventurer and writer

Mary Grant was born in Kingston, Jamaica. Her father was a Scottish soldier and her mother, from the mulatto community, ran a boarding house for the military which Mary took over on her death. She was well educated and in 1836 she married Edward Seacole, who died soon afterwards.

A a skilled nurse with experience in treating the prevalent diseases of the day, such as cholera and yellow fever, she offered to tend to the sick at Crimea. Although she was rejected she did what she could to help unofficially. Following the war she was penniless and wrote her memoirs, *The Wonderful Adventures of Mrs. Seacole in Many Lands* (1857), to earn an income. The book was a great success and she became a popular public figure.

Seaman, Elizabeth Cochrane, *pseud* Nellie Bly

Born 1867 Died 1922
American journalist who made her name writing
about her journey around the world

Elizabeth Cochrane Seaman was born in Cochran's Mills, Pennsylvania. As a journalist for the *Pittsburgh Dispatch*, she adopted her pen name from a popular song, and reported on issues of reform and taboo subjects such as divorce.

Moving to New York, she worked for Joseph Pulitzer's *World*, writing dramatic exposés of working conditions, women prisoners and other issues. She was given an assignment to travel around the world in less than 80 days, which she achieved in 1889.

Her stories of her trip by commercial transportation became front-page news and were widely read, and she also wrote about the experience in *Nelly Bly's Book: Around the World in Seventy-Two Days*.

Sears, Eleanora

Born 1881 Died 1968
American athlete and early advocate of women in
sport

Eleanora Sears was born in Boston, Massachusetts. As a member of Boston's social élite, Sears had the opportunity not only to play sports, but also to challenge the conventions regarding 'proper' feminine behaviour in sport.

In 1912 she became the first woman to play the game of polo, and in 1928 she played a major part in founding the US Women's Squash Racquets Association. From winning its first singles championship that year, she maintained a lifelong devotion to sports, and competed in the women's veteran division of the national squash championships at the age of 72.

Sedgwick, Catharine Maria

Born 1789 Died 1867
American novelist and poet, an early writer of
fiction for a female readership

Catharine Sedgwick was born in Stockbridge, Massachusetts. She was the author of *A New England Tale* (1822), considered to be an early example of fiction addressed primarily to a female audience, and went on to become a bestselling novelist noted for her depiction of the simple domestic virtues.

Her novels are valuable historical records of American social customs, and are deceptively satirical. *A New England Tale* was intended as an attack on Calvinism and *Hope Leslie* (1927), by common consent her best book, was based upon careful research into Puritan documents.

She was active in the Unitarian church and, despite the domestic settings for so much of her fiction, a staunch defender of women's right to lead a single life — a position which she argued at length in *Married or Single* (1857).

Seefried, Irmgard

Born 1919 Died 1988
Austrian soprano who rose to fame with the
Vienna State Opera in the 1940s

Irmgard Seefried was born in Köngetried, Germany. She studied in Augsburg and made her début in 1940 in Aachen as the Priestess in Verdi's *Aïda*. She was famous for her performances with Vienna State Opera from 1943, especially in the operas of Richard Strauss and Mozart, such as Fiordiligi in *Così fan tutte* and Susanna in *Le nozze di Figaro*, which she sang at Covent Garden in 1947. She also became a noted Lieder singer, often appearing in concert with her husband, the violinist Wolfgang Schneiderhan.

Seghers, Anna, *pseud of* Netty Radványi, *née* Anna Reiling

Born 1900 Died 1983
German novelist whose work was dominated by
her communist sympathies

Anna Reiling was born in Mainz, the daughter of a Jewish antique-dealer. Her faith in communism dominated her work, and led her ultimately to become a willing purveyor of socialist realism. Her first novel, *Aufstand der Fischer von St Barbara* (1928, Eng trans *The Revolt of the Fishermen*, 1930), essentially expressed the view that revolution lends meaning and solidarity to hopeless and helpless individual lives.

Seghers fled from Hitler in 1933 to France and Mexico, where she wrote the vastly successful (in part through the movie made by Fred Zinnermann) *Das siebte Kreuz* (1942, Eng trans *The Seventh Cross*, 1942), which was her best novel and a powerful indictment of the cruelties of the Nazi regime.

Her novels of the 1930s resembled her first one, and her later novels, written in East Germany, are documents more or less completely convinced of the rightness of the new rulers.

Ségur, Sophie Rostopchin, Comtesse de

Born 1799 Died 1874
Russian-born French author whose fairytales were
popular with several generations of children

Sophie Rostopchin was born in Russia, the daughter of a soldier and statesman. She moved to Paris in 1815, married Comte Eugène de Ségur, and gave birth to eight children. Virtually invalided for several years afterwards, when she recovered (c.1856) she published the first of her children's books, *Nouveaux Contes de fées* (*New Fairytales*). She is better remembered for her stories based on a central character called 'Sophie', such as *Les malheurs de Sophie* (1859, *The Misfortunes of Sophie*) and *Mémoires d'un Âne*.

She began by focusing on aristocratic children, but later depicted with sensitivity the lives of the Parisian working classes, providing for the modern adult reader an interesting historical document of life during the Second Empire (1852–70).

Seidelman, Susan

Born 1952
American film director who in the 1980s became
the most consistently employed woman director
in contemporary American cinema

Susan Seidelman was born in Abington, Pennsylvania. After studying at Drexel University she worked for her local television channel and then enrolled at New York University Graduate School of Film and TV in 1974. Her satirical short film *And You Act Like One, Too* (1976) won a student Oscar, whilst *Yours, Truly, Andrea G Stern* (c.1978) won prizes at several international festivals.

Her first feature, the self-financed *Smithereens* (1982), told of a rootless young girl from the suburbs and her false dreams of finding success in the punk rock scene of New York. It became the first independent US feature to be accepted in the main competition at the Cannes Film Festival. Moving into the mainstream, she directed *Desperately Seeking Susan* (1985), a contemporary screwball comedy that made excellent use of its New York locale and the popular image of emerging music sensation **Madonna**.

Seidelman's best work shows a strong visual sensibility, appreciation of pop culture and a flair for creating appealing feminist heroines from the unlikeliest of characters.

Seles, Monica

Born 1973
Yugoslav tennis player ranked joint world No. 1
with **Steffi Graf**

Monica Seles was born in Novi Sad and moved to the USA in 1986. Since turning professional at the age of 15 in 1989, she has won the French Open three times (1990–2), the US Open twice (1991–2) and the Australian Open three times (1991–3). In 1992 she was defeated by Steffi Graf in the Wimbledon singles final.

During a tournament in Hamburg in April 1993, she was injured in a knife attack by a member of the crowd and was unable to compete for 27 months. After her comeback she won every match she played until in September 1995 she was narrowly beaten by Graf in the US Open final.

Semiramis, *also called* Sammu-Ramat

9th century BC
Semi-legendary Queen of Assyria who made
Babylon a magnificent place and set about the
conquest of distant lands

Semiramis, according to one legend, was the daughter of a goddess. Traditionally she was the wife of Menones, the governor of Nineveh (ruled 811–808BC), whom she assisted during the siege of Bactria. Attracted by her beauty, King Ninus of Assyria requested her hand in marriage, and when Menones committed suicide, Ninus made her his wife but fell under her influence. She persuaded Ninus to give her his regency for one day, during which she ordered his execution so that she could be sole ruler.

She is said to have built Babylon into a magnificent city, channelled water into arid plains, and begun the conquest of remote countries, which included the defeat of the King of India at the River Indus. On her return she found her son Ninyas conspiring against her, so she handed the government of the kingdom to him. He is said to have killed his mother in the 25th year of her reign, when she was 62 years old.

The historical germ of the story seems to be the three years' regency (811–808BC) of Sammu-ramat (Greek for 'Semiramis'), widow of Shamshi-Adad V (823–811BC), but the details are legendary, derived from Ctesias and other Greek historians, with elements of the Astarte myth.

Senesh, Hannah

Born 1921   Died 1944
Hungarian and Israeli World War II heroine

Hannah Senesh was born in Budapest and educated there at a private school. In 1939 she emigrated to Palestine and trained at Nahalal Agricultural School before going to work on the Sdot-Yam kibbutz in Caesarea.

When news of the extermination of European Jews reached Palestine she volunteered to be parachuted into Yugoslavia as a member of the British Armed Forces to warn Jews of the danger they were in and to help rescue as many as possible. She was trained as a radio officer and following the drop, made her way to the Hungarian border.

She was captured, tortured, tried and executed. In 1950 her body was re-buried with military honours in Israel. Her diary and poems were published posthumously.

Serao, Matilde

Born 1856   Died 1927
Italian novelist and journalist who wrote in a number of styles, often focusing on the experiences and position of women

Matilde Serao was born in Patras in Greece, the daughter of a Greek father and a Neapolitan political refugee. She graduated as a teacher in Naples, where she spent most of her life, worked in a telegraph office, and started writing articles for newspapers (1876–8).

Her first novel of Neapolitan life was *Cuore Infermo* (1881), after which she joined the Rome newspaper *Capitan Fracassa*. She had a huge success with her next romantic novel,

Fantasia (1882), followed by *Conquista di Roma* (1886, 'Conquest of Rome'), *Riccardo Joanna* (1887), *All' Erta Sentinella* (1889) and *Il Paese di Cuccagna* (1891). She was one of the most translated writers of her time.

Seton, St Elizabeth Ann, *née* Bayley

Born 1774   Died 1821
American nun who established parochial education and became the first native-born saint of the USA

Elizabeth Bayley was born into New York upper-class society. She married at 19 into a wealthy trading family, and in 1797 founded the Society for the Relief of Poor Widows with Small Children. When her husband lost his fortune they travelled to Italy, where she was attracted by the Roman Catholic faith. In 1803 she herself was left a destitute widowed mother of five.

Following her return to America, she converted to Catholicism from Episcopalianism, but was unable to find work until invited by a priest to found a Catholic elementary school in Baltimore. In 1809 she founded the USA's first religious order, the American Sisters of Charity, where, though still the guardian of her children, Seton became superior. The order, which was based on the rule of St Vincent de Paul, concentrated on poor relief and parish school education, hence the credit that is given Mother Seton for paving the way for the American parochial school system.

She was beatified by Pope John XXIII in

Mother Seton

1963, and canonized in 1975. Her feast day is 4 January.

Sévèrine, *pseud of* Caroline Rémy, *née* Guebhardt

Born 1855 Died 1929
French journalist who used her work as a platform for social change

Caroline Rémy was born in Paris. She was married at 16 and later divorced. In 1881 she met and had an affair with Jules Vallès, a socialist writer. At this time she began to write for his paper, *Le Cri du peuple*, taking it over on his death in 1885.

She also contributed to a number of other publications including *Le Reveil, Gil Blas, La France, Le Matin*, and later the feminist paper, *La Fronde*. In 1920 she joined the Communist Party for a short time.

Her other works include *Pages Rouges* (1893), *Notes d'une Frondeuse* (1894), *En Marche* (1896) *and Vers la lumière — impressions vécues* (1900).

Sévigné, Madame de, *née* Marie de Rabutin-Chantal

Born 1626 Died 1696
French author who is arguably Europe's most famous letter-writer

Marie Rabutin-Chantal was born in Paris. She was orphaned at an early age and was carefully brought up by an uncle, the Abbé de Coulanges, at the Abbaye de Livry in Brittany. She married the dissolute Marquis Henri de Sévigné in 1644, but he was killed in a duel in 1651. From then on, in the most brilliant court in the world, her thoughts were centred on her children, Françoise Marguerite (b.1646) and Charles (b.1648).

On the marriage of the former to the Comte de Grignan in 1669, Madame de Sévigné began the series of letters to her daughter which grew sadder as friend after friend passed away. She died of smallpox, after nursing her daughter through a long illness. Her 25 years of letters reveal the inner history of the time of Louis XIV in wonderful detail, but the most interesting thing in the whole 1,600 (one-third letters to her from others) remains herself.

Seward, Anna

Born 1747 Died 1809
English poet who became known as the 'Swan of Lichfield'

Anna Seward was born in the rectory of the village of Eyam, Derbyshire. She lived from the age of 10 at Lichfield, where her father,

himself a poet, was canon. He died in 1790, but she continued to live on in the bishop's palace, and wrote romantic poetry.

Her 'Elegy on Captain Cook' (1780) was commended by Dr Johnson and brought her to public notice, as did her elegy on David Garrick. She bequeathed all her poems to Sir Walter Scott, who published them in 1810 (*Poetical Works*).

Sewell, Anna

Born 1820 Died 1878
English novelist whose Black Beauty *has become a classic of children's literature*

Anna Sewell was born in Yarmouth. She was an invalid for most of her life and depended on horses to move around. Her single work, *Black Beauty, The Autobiography of a Horse* (1877), written as a plea for the more humane treatment of animals, is perhaps the most famous fictional work about horses.

Sexton, Anne, *née* Harvey

Born 1928 Died 1974
American writer of 'confessional' poetry whose frankness provoked controversy

Anne Harvey was born in Newton, Massachusetts. In 1948 she married Alfred Sexton and had two daughters. She began writing to assist her recovery after a suicide attempt in 1956 and became a confessional poet in the mould of her teacher, Robert Lowell, and her friend **Sylvia Plath**, with whom she is often bracketed. She wrote frankly about her personal experiences, including a nervous breakdown, and examined the relationship between the psyche, the body and art.

Her poetry was published in journals such as the *New Yorker*, and her first collection was *To Bedlam and Part Way Back* (1962); others are *All My Pretty Ones* (1962), *Live or Die* (1966), which won the 1967 Pulitzer Prize, *Love Poems* (1969), *Transformations* (1971), *The Book of Folly* (1972), *The Death Notebooks* (1974), *The Awful Rowing Towards God* (1975), and the posthumously published *45 Mercy Street* (1976).

Sexton taught at Boston University (1969–71) and Colgate (1971–2) and her *Complete Poems* were published in 1981, seven years after she committed suicide.

Seymour, Jane

Born c.1509 Died 1537
Queen of England as the third wife of Henry VIII (ruled 1509–47)

Jane Seymour was the daughter of the soldier

Sir John Seymour. She was lady in waiting to both of Henry's former wives, **Catherine of Aragon** and **Anne Boleyn**. She married Henry 11 days after Anne Boleyn's execution in 1536, and gave birth to Henry's only legitimate son, Edward (the future Edward VI), but died 12 days later.

Seymour, Lynn

Born 1939
Canadian dancer best known for her passionate
interpretations of the choreography of Kenneth
MacMillan and Frederick Ashton

Lynn Seymour was born in Wainwright, Alberta. She trained in Vancouver and spent two years at the Royal Ballet School in London, making her début in 1956 with the Sadler's Wells branch of the company. After being cast by Kenneth MacMillan in *The Burrow* (1958), she was frequently teamed up with Christopher Gable.

Her dancing career was a volatile one and disappointments such as being shifted out of MacMillan's première of *Romeo and Juliet* in favour of **Margot Fonteyn** took their toll, though the roles in Ashton's *Five Brahms Waltzes in the Manner of Isadora Duncan* and *A Month in the Country* (both 1976) were outstandingly performed. In 1979 she spent an unsuccessful season as director of the Bavarian Opera in Munich, but in later years she returned as a mature ballerina as Tatiana in *Onegin* and the mother in Gable's *A Simple Man* (both 1988).

While best known as a dancer, she has choreographed several pieces, including *Rashomon* (1976) and *Wolfi* (1987). Her book *Lynn: leaps and boundaries* (1984) describes the trials and triumphs of her life as a ballerina.

Shange, Ntozake, *pseud of* Paulette Williams

Born 1948
American playwright, poet, and novelist who
draws on her African-American heritage and
fuses her writing with dance and music

Paulette Williams was born in Trenton, New Jersey. On moving to St Louis she suffered racial segregation and survived several suicide attempts before attending Barnard College and the University of Southern California. She adopted her Zulu name in 1971, after leaving the latter.

In 1975 her remarkable 'choreopoem' *for colored girls who have considered suicide/when the rainbow is enuf* was produced on Broadway, a benchmark in the articulation of black feminist consciousness in America. The piece uses female personae, identified by colour, to articulate aspects of black American history.

Later works have been less startling in impact. Other plays include *A Photograph: A Study of Cruelty* (1977) and *Spell # 7: A Geechee Quick Magic Trance Manual* (1979).

Shange has also written novels — *Sassafrass, Cypress & Indigo* (1976, rev edn 1982), *Betsey Brown* (1985) — and poetry, most notably *A Daughter's Geography* (1983).

Sharaff, Irene

Born 1910 Died 1993
American costume designer who rose to become a
leader in her field

Irene Sharaff was born in Boston. She studied art in New York and Paris, and began her career as a costume designer with the Civic Repertory Theatre Company in 1929. She went on to be a successful designer in Hollywood.

Her costumes graced such famous musicals as *An American In Paris* (1951), *Brigadoon* (1954), *Guys and Dolls* (1955), *West Side Story* (1961) and *Hello Dolly!* (1969). She was nominated for 16 Academy Awards, and won five, including *The King and I* (1956) and *Who's Afraid of Virginia Woolf?* (1966).

Sharman, Helen

Born 1963
English chemist who became the country's first
cosmonaut in 1991

Helen Sharman was born in Sheffield, where she trained as a chemist at Sheffield University. Her first job was as a research technologist with Mars Confectionery.

As the winner of a contest, she joined the Anglo-Soviet Juno mission in May 1991 and flew on the *Soyuz TM-12* spacecraft 250 miles above the Earth to the Soviet *Mir* space station. There she worked for one week, carrying out scientific and medical tests. She was the first Briton ever to enter space.

Shaw, Anna Howard

Born 1847 Died 1919
English-born American suffragist and minister,
one of the most influential leaders of the suffrage
movement

Anna Howard Shaw was born in Newcastle-upon-Tyne and emigrated with her family to the USA as a young child (1851). She chose her vocation at the age of about 18 on listening to a female Universalist preacher. After high school she acquired a preacher's license (1871), attended Albion College for two years, then Boston University (1876–8, during which time the Women's Foreign Missionary Society saved her from starvation), and then applied for a permanent position in the Methodist Episcopal Church. Rejected on account of her gender, she turned to the Methodist Protestant Church and in 1880 became their first ordained woman preacher.

In 1886 she graduated as a doctor from Boston University, but decided to devote herself entirely to the cause of women's suffrage. She was an eloquent, powerful lecturer, and campaigned widely. She joined the National American Woman Suffrage Association in 1892, when **Susan B Anthony** was president, and in 1904 she took over the presidency from **Carrie Chapman Catt**; when she resigned in 1915, Catt resumed her post.

Shaw was head of the Women's Committee of the Council of National Defense during World War I. The 19th Amendment providing for women's suffrage was declared on 28 August 1920, little more than a year after her death. She published her autobiography, *The Story of a Pioneer*, in 1915.

Shaw, Fiona, *originally* Bolton

Born 1958
Irish actress hailed as one of the most brilliant in British theatre today

Fiona Shaw was born and brought up in Cork, the daughter of an eye-surgeon. Her family encouraged her to perform, and she learnt to play the piano and the cello, and to recite poetry. She took a degree in philosophy and trained at RADA, making her début in 1982. Her genius was recognized early by director Peter Wood, and she appeared as Julia in his production of *The Rivals* at the National Theatre in 1983.

She went on to perform for the Royal Shakespeare Company — such as Madame de Volanges in *Les Liasons Dangereuses* (1985) and Katharina in *The Taming of the Shrew* (1987) — and came to be associated with highly emotional and heart-rending parts, including the title roles in *Electra* and *Hedda Gabler*.

A frequent collaborator with **Deborah Warner**, she played King Richard in *Richard II* in 1995 and, though her performance was criticised by those who regarded her natural femininity overbearing, most thought she rose admirably to the challenge to her intellect and skill.

Sheba, Queen of, *Arabic name* Bilqīs, *Ethiopian name* Makeda

10th century BC
Biblical monarch famous particularly for her visit to test the wisdom of King Solomon

The Queen of Sheba was the ruler of the Sabeans, a people who seem to have occupied a part of SW Arabia (modern Yemen), though they are placed by some in N Arabia.

She journeyed to Jerusalem to test the wisdom of Solomon, King of Israel, and exchange extravagant gifts, such as spices, gold and jewels, although this may imply a trade pact. The story as depicted in 1 Kings 10 and 2 Chronicles 9, describes the splendour of Solomon's court and extols his great wisdom, thus emphasizing the growing importance of Jerusalem and depicting the sagacious and diplomatic nature of international relations in the ancient Near East.

The story of the Queen of Sheba and Solomon can also be read in the Qur'an. According to later, Ethiopian tradition, the couple married and their son founded the royal dynasty of Ethiopia.

Sheehy-Skeffington, Hannah, *née* Sheehy

Born 1877 Died 1946
Irish patriot and feminist, a militant campaigner for Home Rule and equality

Hannah Sheehy was born in Kenturk, County Cork, and graduated from the National University of Ireland. She became a teacher and was a founder-member of the Irish Women Graduates' Association (1901).

With **Margaret Cousins** she established the Irish Women's Franchise League (1908) which was in her own words 'an avowedly militant association'. In 1912 she was imprisoned in Mountjoy Jail for three months for rioting at Dublin Castle in protest at the exclusion of women from the Home Rule Bill.

Her husband Francis Skeffington, a pacifist, was shot during the course of the Easter Rising in 1916 when he witnessed the shooting of an unarmed boy.

Shelley, Mary Wollstonecraft, *née* Godwin

Born 1797 Died 1851
English writer whose only well-known work is the novel Frankenstein

Mary Godwin was the daughter of the writers William Godwin and **Mary Wollstonecraft**.

In 1814 she eloped with the poet Percy Bysshe Shelley, and married him as his second wife in 1816. They lived abroad throughout their married life. Her first and most impressive novel was *Frankenstein* (1818), her second *Valperga* (1823). After her husband's death in 1822 she returned from Italy to England with their son in 1823.

Her husband's father, in granting her an allowance, insisted on the suppression of the volume of Shelley's *Posthumous Poems* edited by her. *The Last Man* (1826), a romance of the ruin of human society by pestilence, fails to attain sublimity. In *Lodore* (1835) the story is told of Shelley's alienation from his first wife. Her last novel, *Falkner,* appeared in 1837.

Of her occasional pieces of verse the most remarkable is 'The Choice'. Her *Journal of a Six Weeks' Tour* (partly by Shelley) tells of the excursion to Switzerland in 1814; *Rambles in Germany and Italy* (1844) describes tours of 1840–3; her *Tales* were published in 1890. Two unpublished mythological dramas, *Proserpine* and *Midas*, were edited and published in 1922.

Shephard, Gillian, *née* Watts

Born 1940
English Conservative politician and a prominent Cabinet member during the 1990s

Gillian Watts was born in Norfolk, the daughter of a cattle dealer. She was educated at Oxford University, and worked as an education officer and schools inspector in Norfolk from 1963 to 1975. That year she married Thomas Shephard, who became the headmaster of a comprehensive school. Between 1965 and 1987 she lectured for the Cambridge University extra-mural department; she also became a magistrate, deputy leader of Norfolk County Council, where she was councillor from 1977 to 1989, and health authority chairman, first of west Norfolk and Wisbech (1981–5) and then of Norwich (1985–7).

She entered parliament as MP for South West Norfolk in 1987 and was swiftly promoted, rising through several junior posts to enter the Cabinet in 1992 as Secretary of State for Employment. In 1993 she became Minister of Agriculture, Fisheries and Food and in 1994 she was appointed Secretary of State for Education, in which position she used her experience of the state education system to attempt to procure pay rises for teachers and calm the turmoil in the teachers' unions. The next year she was given the joint Education and Employment portfolio.

Sheppard, Kate (Catherine Wilson), *née* Malcolm

Born 1848 Died 1943
British-born New Zealand women's rights campaigner

Kate Malcolm, who was of Scottish descent, was born in Liverpool and emigrated to New Zealand in the late 1860s. She is thought to have been educated in Nairn in Scotland. In 1871 she married a Christchurch councillor, Walter Sheppard.

A member of the Women's Christian Temperance Union, she saw female enfranchisement as the way in which to improve conditions for women and children, and mounted a vigorous suffrage campaign. After the vote was won (1893) she became the first President of the National Council of Women and campaigned further to obtain the right for women to stand for parliament.

She published many pamplets including *An Address on the Subject of Woman Suffrage* (1889), *Sixteen Reasons for Supporting Women's Franchise* (1891) and *Women's Suffrage in New Zealand* (1907).

Sherlock, Dame Sheila Patricia Violet

Born 1918
British physician and liver specialist

Sheila Sherlock trained in medicine at Edinburgh University and was a Beit Research Fellow from 1942 to 1947. After a period at Yale University in 1948, she was appointed physician and lecturer in medicine at the Royal Postgraduate Medical School in London (1948–59), and then Professor of Medicine at the Royal Free Hospital Medical School in London.

She has published extensively on liver function, structure and disease and received honorary degrees and fellowships from several universities and medical colleges. Among the many medical organizations that she has served is the Royal College of Physicians (Councillor 1964–8, Censor 1970–2, Senior Censor and Vice-President 1976–7). She was created DBE in 1978.

Sherwood, Mary Martha, *née* Butt

Born 1775 Died 1851
English writer of books for children characterized by religous fervour and keen observation of child behaviour

Mary Butt was born in Stanford, Worcestershire, the daughter of a chaplain to George II. In 1803 she married her cousin, Capt Henry

Sherwood, and went to India with him (1805–16), where she taught in an army school and cared for orphans. She had already written a story about a pious servant girl for the Sunday school in which she taught before her marriage, and now began to write in earnest, beginning c.1810 with an adaptation of *The Pilgrim's Progress*.

After their return to England the Sherwoods settled in Worcestershire and she continued to produce tracts, essays and pamphlets as well as the moralistic children's tales for which she is best known. She produced over 350 works in all, including *Little Henry and his Bearer* (1815) and the long-popular *History of the Fairchild Family* (1818, 1842, 1847).

Shipton, Mother

Born 1488   Died c.1560
English witch who has given her name to a small
British moth with wing-markings resembling a
witch's face

Mother Shipton was born near Knaresborough and baptized as Ursula Southiel. According to S Baker, who edited her 'prophecies' (1797), she had married a builder called Tony Shipton at the age of 24 and had died at over 70 years of age. A book (1684) by Richard Head tells how she was allegedly carried off by the devil and bore him an imp.

Shirreff, Emily Anne Eliza

Born 1814   Died 1897
English writer and pioneer of education for women
and pre-school children

Emily Shirreff was largely self-educated beyond her teenage years. With her sister **Maria Grey** she wrote *Thoughts on Self-Culture, Addressed to Women* (1850) to encourage women to educate themselves, and in 1858 she alone wrote *Intellectual Education and Its Influence on the Character and Happiness of Women*.

In 1871 she founded the National Union for Promoting the Higher Education of Women, for which she co-edited the *Journal of the Women's Education Union*. Other works published with her sister are the novels *Passion and Principle* (1853) and *Love Sacrifice* (1868).

Shirreff was mistress of Girton College, Cambridge (1870–97), and also published works on kindergartens and the Froebel system. From 1875 until her death she was President of the Froebel Society, which founded a training college for kindergarten teachers.

Shore, Jane

Died c.1527
English courtesan, the mistress first of Edward IV
and then several other political figures

Jane Shore was born in London. She was married from an early age to William Shore, a goldsmith. In 1470 she captivated Edward IV with her wit and beauty and became his mistress. Her husband abandoned her, but she lived in luxury and increasing influence till Edward's death in 1483.

Thereafter she became the mistress of Thomas, Lord Hastings, and on his death, it is said, of the Marquis of Dorset. Edward IV's brother, now Richard III, accused her of sorcery, imprisoned her, and caused the Bishop of London to make her walk in open penance, taper in hand, dressed only in her kirtle (outer petticoat). She died in poverty.

Jane Shore's life is the subject of a play by Nicholas Rowe, *The Tragedy of Jane Shore* (1714).

Short, Clare

Born 1946
English Labour politician who is an increasingly
prominent figure in that party

Clare Short was educated at the universities of Keele and Leeds before joining the Home Office (1970–5). She married a former Labour MP, Alexander Ward Lyon (d.1993), in 1981 and was elected to parliament as MP for Birmingham Ladywood in 1983.

Gradually gaining recognition, she has been an influential member of the National Executive Committee since 1988 and has held the positions of Opposition front bench spokesperson on employment (1985–8), social security (1989–91), environmental protection (1992–3), women's issues (1993–5), and transport (1995–   ).

Sibley, Dame Antoinette

Born 1939
English ballet dancer who became the prima
ballerina of the Royal Ballet

Antoinette Sibley was born in Bromley, Kent. She trained with the Royal Ballet, and appeared as a soloist for the first time in 1956 when, due to the principal dancer's illness, she was given the main role in *Swan Lake*. It was an unprecedented casting move which hit the headlines and made her famous overnight.

She is a dancer of great sensuality and beauty, and her roles in Frederick Ashton's *The Dream* and Kenneth MacMillan's *Manon* are among her most celebrated. Her partnership with Anthony Dowell was one of enchanting compatibility, leading them to be dubbed 'The Golden Pair'. A knee injury forced an early retirement in 1976, but she was persuaded by Ashton to dance again five years later to great acclaim.

She was appointed President of the Royal Academy of Dancing in 1991, having served as Vice-President since 1989. She was appointed DBE in 1996.

Siddons, Sarah, née Kemble

Born 1755 Died 1831
English tragic actress whose perfection led her
portrait painters to call her the 'tragic muse' and
'tragedy personified'

Sarah Kemble was born in Brecon, Wales, the eldest child of Roger Kemble, manager of a small travelling theatrical company, of which Sarah was a member from her earliest childhood. In 1773 she married her fellow actor, William Siddons.

Her first appearance at Drury Lane in December 1775 as Portia was unremarkable, but her reputation grew so fast in the provinces that in 1782 she returned to Drury Lane, and made her appearance in October as Isabella in David Garrick's adaptation of Thomas Southerne's *Fatal Marriage*. Her success was immediate, and from then on she was the unquestioned queen of the stage. In 1803 she followed her brother, John Philip Kemble, to Covent Garden, where she continued until her formal farewell to the stage as Lady Macbeth, on 29 June 1812.

Thereafter she appeared occasionally, and sometimes gave public readings. Endowed with a gloriously expressive and beautiful face, a queenly figure, and a voice of richest power and flexibility, she worked assiduously to cultivate her gifts until as a tragic actress she reached a height of perfection. In comedy, however, she was less successful.

Sidgwick, Nora (Eleanor Mildred), née Balfour

Born 1845 Died 1936
Scottish suffragette, a moderate campaigner who
fought for women's rights in education

Nora Balfour was born into a political family in East Lothian, the sister of the future Prime Minister Arthur Balfour. In 1870 she married Henry Sidgwick, her brother's tutor at Cambridge, and through him was drawn into the development of Newnham College, Cambridge.

Appointed principal of Newnham College in 1892, remaining until 1910, Sidgwick de-

plored the tactics of the militant suffragettes but campaigned to have women admitted to Cambridge on the same basis as men.

Signoret, Simone, *originally* Simon-Henriette Charlotte Kaminker

Born 1921 Died 1985
French film actress who became one of France's
best character actresses

Simon-Henriette Kaminker was born in Wiesbaden, Germany. She left her job as a typist to become a film extra in *Le Prince Charmant* (1942) and soon graduated to leading roles. She was frequently cast as a prostitute or courtesan, and her warmth and sensuality found international favour in such films as *La Ronde* (1950), *Casque d'Or* (1952) and *Les Diaboliques* (1954).

Though a rare participant in English-language productions, she won an Academy Award for *Room at the Top* (1959) and gained further distinction for *Ship of Fools* (1965). Unafraid to show her age, she matured into one of France's most distinguished character actresses, in films including *Le Chat* (1971) and *Madame Rosa* (1977).

She was married to actor Yves Montand (1921–91) from 1951, and later turned to writing, completing an autobiography, *Nostalgia Isn't What It Used To Be* (1976), and a novel, *Adieu Volodia* (1985).

Sigourney, Lydia Howard Huntley

Born 1791 Died 1865
American poet and essayist who was acclaimed
as a 'female Milton'

Lydia Sigourney was born in Norwich, Connecticut. She began publishing her work anonymously because her husband, a wealthy businessman, feared his reputation would be damaged if it was known that his wife was a writer, especially one supporting such causes as that of the Native Americans. *Traits of the Aborigines of America* (1822) records Native American legend in blank verse. Native American themes recur in *Pocahontas and Other Poems* (1841).

From the early 1830s, as a result of her husband's business collapsing, Sigourney was publishing under her own name. She was also successful — the appearance of *Poems* in 1834 resulted in her being acclaimed as a 'female Milton'. Later books include *Pleasant Memories of Pleasant Lands* (1842), an entertaining record of her travels.

Sigurðardóttir, Frída Á

Born 1940
Icelandic short-story writer and novelist who
examines the female experience

Frída Sigurðardóttir was born in Hesteyri, in
the west of Iceland. She worked as a librarian
before concentrating on writing. The short
stories in her first book, *Þetta er ekkert alvar-
legt* (1980, 'This Isn't Serious'), focus on
marital relationships, while her novel *Sólin og
skugginn* (1981, 'The Sun and the Shadow')
explores feminine powerlessness. *Við gluggann*
(1984, 'By the Window') is a book of short
stories in which her earlier realism becomes
marginalized by a style dependent on metaphor and stream of consciousness. Her novel
Meðon nóttin líður (1990, 'While the Night is
Passing') confronts a modern career woman
with memories of six generations of women,
all of them less independent than she is but
enjoying an affinity with their families and
their world that she lacks. The novel won the
1992 Nordic Council Literature Prize.

Silko, Leslie Marmon

Born 1948
American novelist and short-story writer regarded
as one of the most important Native American
writers of her time

Leslie Marmon Silko was born in Albu-
querque, New Mexico. Of mixed Laguna, Mexican and White descent, Silko was brought
up on the Laguna Pueblo reservation in New
Mexico, and the Laguna cultural traditions
and Southwestern desert landscape are central
to her work.

The poems in *Laguna Woman* (1974), her
first publication, display the richly sensuous
imagery combined with humour and naturalistic dialogue that characterize her work.
Her novel *Ceremony* (1977) describes the spiritual and cultural reconstruction of a young
Pueblo war veteran, fighting the destructive
power of witchery over his people, while in
the autobiographical *Storyteller* (1981), Silko
blends personal family history and photography with stories and poems drawing on
Laguna oral tradition and contemporary life.

Through the publication of *Ceremony,* Silko
began a correspondence with the poet James
Wright, and their letters were published in
1985 as *The Delicacy and Strength of Lace.* The
novel *Almanac of the Dead* (1992), published
with poetic irony in the year of the Columbus
quincentennial, is a dark, millennium-end
account of the Native American people's re-
taking of their ancestral lands in the face of an
Anglo-American society in moral, psychological and ecological collapse.

Beverley Sills, 1977

Sills, Beverley, *originally* Belle Miriam Silverman

Born 1929
American coloratura soprano who became
managing director of the Metropolitan Opera

Belle Silverman was born in Brooklyn, New
York, of Russian Jewish descent. After a
varied and remarkable career as a child star,
she made her operatic début in 1947, subsequently appearing with various American
companies, and in Vienna and Buenos Aires
(1967), La Scala in Milan (1969), and at Covent
Garden and the Deutsche Oper Berlin (1970).

A highly musical, intelligent and dramatically gifted coloratura, she was with New
York City Opera from 1955 until she retired
from the stage aged 50. She was general director of New York City Opera (1979–88) and
became managing director of the Metropolitan
Opera, New York, in 1991.

Silver, Joan Micklin

Born 1935
American filmmaker known for her closely
observed social comedies

Joan Micklin Silver was born in Omaha, Nebraska. She studied music at Sarah Lawrence

College in New York, then taught in Cleveland. She directed community theatre productions and educational films, then made her feature début as a screenwriter with *Limbo* (1972).

Disappointed with the results, she opted to direct her subsequent work herself. She was the daughter of Russian–Jewish immigrants, and her most successful films have explored the social and historical milieu of the Jewish community in New York's Lower East Side, notably in *Hester Street* (1985) and *Crossing Delancey* (1988).

Silvia

Born 1943
Queen of Sweden as the wife of Carl XVI Gustaf
(ruler since 1973)

Silvia Renate Sommerlath was born in Heidelberg, the daughter of a German businessman, Walther Sommerlath, and his Brazilian wife, Alice (née Soares de Toledo). She lived for many years in São Paulo in Brazil, where her father represented a Swedish company.

Back in the Federal Republic of Germany, she attended the Interpreters' School in Munich and graduated in 1969 as an interpreter in Spanish. In 1971 she was appointed Chief Hostess in the Organization Committee for the Olympic Games in Munich in 1972, where she met Carl Gustaf, then heir to the Swedish throne.

He acceded in 1973 and they were married in Stockholm Cathedral in 1976. They have three children, Crown Princess Victoria (1977–), Prince Carl Philip (1979–), and Princess Madeleine (1982–).

Simmons, Jean Merilyn

Born 1929
English film actress who moved to Hollywood in the 1950s but was rarely seen in films to match her talent

Jean Simmons was born in London and trained at the Aida Foster School of Dancing. She made her film début in *Give Us the Moon* (1944) and quickly rose to the forefront of young English actresses with accomplished performances as Estella in *Great Expectations* (1946) and Ophelia in Laurence Olivier's *Hamlet* (1948).

Maturing into a talent of beauty and great skill, she was under contract to Howard Hughes in Hollywood from 1951 but found few roles worthy of her abilities. Her best film work includes *The Actress* (1953), *Elmer Gantry* (1960) and *The Happy Ending* (1969), for which she received an Oscar nomination.

She continues to bring distinction to a range of television work and won an Emmy in 1983 for *The Thorn Birds* (1982). Her rare stage appearances include *Big Fish, Little Fish* (1964) and *A Little Night Music* (1976).

Simon, Carly

Born 1945
American composer and singer who was married to James Taylor

Carly Simon was born in New York City. She began her career in 1964, recording with her sister Lucy as the Simon Sisters, and received a Grammy for Best New Artist in 1971, the year she had hits with 'That's The Way I Always Heard It Should Be' and 'Anticipation'. The following year she married singer/songwriter James Taylor (1948–).

Her single 'Let the River Run' for the 1988 film *Working Girl* won an Academy Award for Best Original Song in 1989. Among her other singles are 'You're So Vain' and the James Bond movie theme, 'Nobody Does It Better'. Her albums include *Carly Simon* (1971), *Anticipation* (1972) and *Letters Never Sent* (1994).

Simone, Nina, *professional name of* Eunice Kathleen Waymon

Born 1933
American singer, pianist and composer who incorporates political statement into her music

Nina Simone was born in Tryon, North Carolina. She was a gifted child pianist and her home town raised cash for her musical education at the Juilliard School in New York City. She became a nightclub singer in Atlantic City and began writing her own highly charged, often overtly political, material in the early 1960s.

Her first hit was Gershwin's 'I Loves You, Porgy' (1959), but later songs like 'Mississippi Goddam', a response to the race murder of children, were more typical. Simone left the USA in the later 1960s, living in Africa and then France.

Though her subsequent career has been dogged by personal problems, she has enjoyed continued success, often through use of her material on television commercials.

Simpson, Myrtle Lillias, *née* Emslie

Born 1931
Scottish Arctic explorer, travel writer, mountaineer and long-distance skier

Myrtle Emslie was born in Aldershot to Scottish parents and educated in many different places, including India, as her father was an army officer. She spent her early twenties climbing in New Zealand and Peru. In 1957 she married the medical researcher and explorer Dr Hugh Simpson, with whom she travelled Surinam and the Arctic.

In 1965, as a member of the Scottish Trans-Greenland Expedition, she became the first woman to ski across the Greenland ice cap. In 1969 she attempted unsuccessfully to ski to the North Pole unsupported, hauling a sledge for 45 days and covering a distance of 90 miles from Ward Hunt Island. She nevertheless reached the most northerly point a woman had ever attained unsupported.

She is the author of several books and chaired the Scottish National Ski Council for a time.

Simpson, Wallis *see* Windsor, Duchess of

Sinclair, May

Born 1863   Died 1946
English novelist, and early exponent of the 'stream of consciousness' style later made famous by **Virginia Woolf**

May Sinclair was born in Rock Ferry, Cheshire, and educated at Cheltenham College. She was an advocate of women's suffrage, and took an interest in psychoanalysis, which is revealed in some of her 24 novels. They include *The Divine Fire* (1904), *The Creators* (1910), *The Three Sisters* (1914) and *The Dark Night* (1924).

Her novels *Mary Olivier* (1919) and *The Life and Death of Harriett Frean* (1922) reveal her adoption of the 'stream-of-consciousness' method; *Mary Olivier* contains clear autobiographical echoes. She also wrote books on philosophical idealism.

Siouxsie Sioux, *professional name of* Susan Janet Dallion

Born 1957
English punk/new wave singer who has had lasting fame with The Banshees

Susan Dallion was born in Bromley, London. She formed Siouxsie and the Banshees (1976) in imitation of the Sex Pistols, but did much to suggest both musical and style alternatives; Siouxsie virtually patented the 'panda' look.

Her first album was *The Scream* (1978), which was criticised for anti-Semitism; a later single, 'Israel' (1980), attempted to redress the balance. Other hits include 'Hong Kong Garden' (1979) and the later 'Miss the Girl'.

Siouxsie briefly split to form The Creatures, a duo with percussionist Budgie, but she has continued to perform with The Banshees, updating their act steadily.

Sirani, Elisabetta

Born 1638   Died 1665
Italian artist of exceptional talent who had the avant-garde idea of opening a studio for women artists

Elisabetta Sirani was born in Bologna. She learned to paint in the workshop of her father Gian Andrea, a local artist, and by the age of 19 was recognized to have exceptional talent. She duly earned enough to keep her entire family.

In 1664 Cosimo, Crown Prince of Tuscany, visited Bologna and after watching her paint a portrait of his uncle, Prince Leopold, he commissioned a Madonna for himself. She also painted the *Baptism of Christ* for the Church of the Certosini at Bologna and executed many highly regarded etchings of biblical subjects before her sudden death at the age of 27.

The somewhat mysterious circumstances of her death — poisoning or stomach ulcers both being suggested but neither proved — have added to her reputation in her native city and beyond.

Sitwell, Dame Edith Louisa

Born 1887   Died 1964
English poet whose fame was the product of both her literary skill and her aristocratic eccentricity

Edith Sitwell was born in Scarborough, Yorkshire, a daughter of the eccentric Sir George Sitwell, and sister of the writers Osbert and Sacheverell Sitwell. She had a lonely and frustrated childhood until her governess introduced her to music and literature, especially the poetry of Algernon Charles Swinburne and the Symbolists.

She first attracted notice by her editorship of an anthology of new poetry entitled *Wheels* (1916–21). This was a new type of poetry which repudiated the flaccid quietism of Georgian verse, but her shock tactics were not fully displayed till *Façade* appeared in 1923, with William Walton's music, and was given a stormy public reading in London. Following her *Elegy for Dead Fashion* (1926), the short poems of her romantic period, 'Colonel Fantock', 'Daphne', 'The Strawberry' and above all 'The Little Ghost who died for Love' are probably the most beautiful things she ever wrote, and at its close she suddenly flamed into indignation over the evil in society to express the horror underlying civilization in *Gold Coast Customs* (1929).

In the 1930s she turned to prose work.

During World War II she denounced with great vehemence the cruelty of man in the prophetic utterance of *Street Songs* (1942), *Green Song* (1944) and *The Song of the Cold* (1945). She set out to refresh the exhausted rhythms of traditional poetry by introducing the rhythms of jazz and other dance music and there is a certain lack of control in her poems on the age of the atom bomb — *The Shadow of Cain* (1947) and *The Canticle of the Rose* (1949). Other works include *The English Eccentrics* (1933), *Victoria of England* (1936), *Fanfare of Elizabeth* (1946), *The Outcasts* (verse; 1962) and *The Queens and the Hive* (1962). Her autobiography, *Taken Care Of*, was published posthumously in 1965.

Skoblikova, Lidiya Pavlovna

Born 1939
Soviet ice skater who won six Olympic speed-skating gold medals

Lidiya Skoblikova was born in Zlatoust, Chelyabinsk. The most decorated female Olympian of all time, in 1960 she won the 3,000 metres and 1,500 metres titles at the Olympics, setting a world record for the latter which she improved upon in 1964, the year she accomplished a clean sweep of titles over every distance (500m, 1000m, 1500m, 3000m) and claimed four further golds.

This performance made her the first woman ever to achieve the Olympic 'Grand Slam' and she set three Olympic records in the process — at 500 metres, 1,000 metres and at 1,500 metres. She also won two world championship titles in 1963 and 1964.

Skobtsova, Maria

Born 1891 Died 1945
Russian Orthodox nun who worked among society's cast-offs until she was executed by the Nazis

Maria Skobtsova was born in Riga. She early identified herself with the Social Revolutionaries as a student in St Petersburg, where she was the first woman to enrol at the Ecclesiastical Academy. Bolshevik excesses having disillusioned her, she was among those who escaped to France.

She began work with the Russian Orthodox Student Christian Movement which also administered to refugees. She was unconventional and radical by nature, and in 1932, despite having had two divorces, became a nun and worked to feed and house the underprivileged in society.

Nazi measures against the Jews in wartime Paris provided a new challenge. She was arrested and sent to Ravensbrück concentration camp in 1943, to which she brought Christian light and hope despite appalling conditions. She was gassed on the eve of Easter, 1945, reportedly going voluntarily 'in order to help her companions to die'.

Skram, (Bertha) Amalie, *née* Alver

Born 1847 Died 1905
Norwegian feminist novelist regarded as the first naturalistic writer in Norway

Amalie Alver was born in Bergen, the commercial life of which provided the main setting for her work. After divorcing her first husband in 1878, she worked as a critic and short-story writer. In 1884 she married Erik Skram, a Danish writer, and following this wrote a collection of novels in which she explored women's issues, and sex in particular.

Her best-known works include *Constance Ring* (1885, Eng trans 1988), the tetralogy *Hellemyrsfolket* (1887–98, 'The People at Hellemyr'), which is considered a classic of Norwegian naturalism, and *Foraadt* (1892, Eng trans *Betrayed*, 1987). She was divorced from Skram in 1900, and thereafter never recovered her mental health, ironically reflecting the plight she had fictionalized in *Professor Hieronimus* (1895, Eng trans 1899) and *På St Jørgen* (1895, 'At St Jorgen's').

Sky, Alison

Born 1946
American architect and founding member of SITE, a multi-disciplinary group of architects and environmental artists

Alison Sky trained at Adelphi and Columbia universities in New York before founding SITE, a group renowned for radical ideas, preferring their work to be called 'De-Architecture'. They produce their architecture by transforming the conventions of society into a form of public art, strengthening the relationship between architecture and art.

One of the group's biggest clients is the discount sales company BEST, which has commissioned several retail outlets, giving SITE massive publicity. The showrooms have brick façades that peel away at the edges, have holes punched through them, and appear to defy gravity. Some of the BEST projects are Indeterminate Façades (1974–5), Notch project (1976–7), Tilt Showroom (1976–8) and Hialeah Water Showrooms (1978–9).

Slaney, Mary Tereza Decker, *née* Decker

Born 1958
American athlete, pushed forward as a child and
pushed out as a champion

Mary Decker was born in New Jersey. Acclaimed as the 'Golden girl' of American athletics, she was pushed so hard as a youngster that she suffered from injury problems throughout her career.

She made her international début against Russia at the age of 14 but had to undergo operations and spend periods in plaster before she set world records for the mile and the 5,000 metres in 1982, which she followed up a year later with an incredible double at the world championships in Helsinki, taking gold in the 3,000 metres and 1,500 metres.

Married first to marathon runner Ron Tabb and later to English discus thrower Richard Slaney, she was frequently in the news and publicly voiced opposition to America's boycott of the 1980 Moscow Olympics. She is often rememberd however for her collision with Zola Budd (now **Zola Pieterse**) in the 3,000 metres at the Los Angeles Olympics in 1984, which put her out of the race.

Slessor, Mary Mitchell

Born 1848   Died 1915
Scottish missionary who devoted her life to
working among the native Nigerians

Mary Slessor was born in Aberdeen. She worked as a mill girl in Dundee from childhood but, conceiving a burning ambition to become a missionary, got herself accepted by the United Presbyterian Church for teaching in Calabar, Nigeria (1876). She spent many years of devoted work among the natives there, concentrating less on converting them to Christianity than on eradicating cruel tribal customs such as human sacrifice. Known among them as 'Great Mother', she was given legal authority in their territories by the British government.

Slick, Grace, *née* Wing

Born 1939
American rock vocalist who is a powerful
performer and an underrated lyricist

Grace Wing was born in Chicago, Illinois. Along with her husband Jerry Slick and his brother, she formed The Great Society (1965). She then joined Jefferson Airplane (1966), with whom she recorded two classic albums: *Surrealistic Pillow*, which includes the songs

'White Rabbit' and 'Somebody to Love', and *After Bathing at Baxters*. The later *Crown of Creation* (1968) was weaker.

Slick co-founded the Grunt label (1970), on which later records appeared, including her own solo *Manhole* (1974). Also in 1974, she became lead vocalist with Jefferson Starship. She left in 1978 but later returned to record with the renamed Starship until 1988.

Small, Annie Hunter

Born 1857   Died 1945
Scottish missionary, author and educationalist

Annie Hunter Small was born in Redding, Falkirk. She followed in her father's footsteps as a missionary to India, serving in Chindwara and a girls' school in Pune from 1876 to 1892.

Having returned home as an invalid, she became the first principal (1894–1913) of the Free Church (later the United Free Church) women's missionary training institute in Edinburgh that was to become St Colm's College. Here community life and worship underpinned theoretical and practical training.

Her publications include *Light and Shade in Zenana Missionary Life* (1890), *Buddhism and Islam* (1905) and *The Psalter and the Life of Prayer* (1914).

Smedley, Agnes

Born 1890   Died 1950
American writer and feminist whose strongly held
early beliefs cost her her job and her freedom

Agnes Smedley was born in Missouri and brought up in extreme poverty. Her education was sporadic and she became a teacher in Arizona in 1911. In 1912 she married Ernest Brundin and taught and studied at San Diego Normal School until 1916, when she lost her job because of her socialist beliefs.

In 1918 she moved to New York and later was arrested for her support of Indian nationalism. She started to write when she was in jail and on her release settled first in Germany (1920) and then in China, where she became well known as a journalist observing the revolution at first hand and working for the *Manchester Guardian*.

Her works include the autobiographical novel *Daughter of Earth* (1929), *Battle Hymn of China* (1943) and *Portraits of Chinese Women in Revolution* (1976).

Smetanina, Raisa Petrovna

Born 1952
Soviet cross-country skier who amassed 23 World
and Olympic medals

Raisa Smetanina was born in Mokhcha, Komi ASSR. Her 23 medals won between 1974 and 1992 included a record 10 Olympic skiing medals — four gold, five silver and one bronze. In the world championships she won her first medal, a silver, in 1979, but rose to take gold in 1981, before winning another silver in 1984.

Her incredibly long-lasting excellence enabled her to compete in the Olympics within two weeks of her fortieth birthday in 1992, 20 years after she made her début. As part of her national relay team (called the United Team) which won the gold medal that year, Smetanina became the oldest-ever Olympic skiing medalist.

Smiley, Jane

Born 1949
American novelist who won a Pulitzer Prize for
A Thousand Acres

Jane Smiley was born in Los Angeles and brought up in Saint Louis. She graduated from the University of Iowa with a PhD in creative writing and went on to hold teaching positions both there and at Iowa State University, where she is Distinguished Professor.

Her first novel, *At Paradise Gate* (1981), was followed by the short stories and novellas gathered in *The Age of Grief* (1988) and *Ordinary Love and Good Will* (1989). Her most ambitious work to date is the novel *A Thousand Acres* (1991), a remarkable re-working of the *King Lear* story, set in a contemporary farming community in Iowa. It was awarded a Pulitzer Prize in 1992.

Smith, Bessie (Elizabeth)

Born 1894   Died 1937
American blues singer whose talent was
recognized in her nickname: 'The Empress
of the Blues'

Bessie Smith was born in Chattanooga, Tennessee. She began her career in the modest circuit of vaudeville tents and small theatres, but her magnificent voice, blues-based repertoire, and vivacious stage presence soon gained her recognition as one of the outstanding black artistes of her day.

She made a series of recordings throughout the 1920s, accompanied by leading jazz musicians such as Louis Armstrong, and these are regarded as classic blues statements. In 1929 she had the leading role in a film, *St Louis Blues*, the title of one of her favourite songs. She died following a car crash.

Smith, Delia

Born 1941
English cookery writer and broadcaster, arguably
the UK's most influential and popular cookery
personality

Delia Smith was born in Woking, Surrey. She left school at 16 and worked in a hairdressing salon, a travel agency and as a dishwasher before she was allowed to help with the cooking in the establishment where she was employed as a waitress. Meanwhile she attempted to discover why English food had such a bad reputation by reading about it in the British Library.

In 1969 she wrote for the *Daily Mirror* magazine, where her future husband, Michael Wynn Jones, was deputy editor, and she began her 12-year association with the *Evening Standard* in 1972. The following year she published her first cookery book, *How to Cheat at Cooking*. She built up a large popular following which was swelled by the viewers of her many television series. By the time she presented *Delia Smith's Christmas* (television programme and book, 1990), she had sold five million copies of her cookery books, and raised aspirations to produce delicious food, elegantly presented, in millions of cooks. This success was followed by her bestselling *Summer Collection* (1993) and by the *Winter Collection* (1995).

Her style is less intimidating than that of some other famous television chefs, which may explain her very wide influence. She is a committed Christian (Roman Catholic) and also writes religious books, including *A Feast for Lent* (1983) and *A Journey into God* (1980). In 1995 she was made an OBE.

Smith, Dodie (Dorothy Gladys),
pseud (until 1935) C L Anthony

Born 1896   Died 1990
English playwright, novelist and children's writer

Dodie Smith grew up in Manchester and trained as an actress at the Royal Academy of Dramatic Art. After some time spent in the theatre, she worked in Heal's furniture store and had an affair with the designer Sir Ambrose Heal (1872–1959). She moved in with a colleague, Alec Beesley, married him after 10 years, and moved to the USA at the start of World War II. There she became a Hollywood scriptwriter and made friends with the homosexual writer Christopher Isherwood (1904–86), who influenced her writing.

Her first play, *Autumn Crocus* (1930), was

an instant success and enabled her to devote all her time to writing. Other plays include *Dear Octopus* (1938), *Letter from Paris* (adapted from *The Reverberator* by Henry James, 1952) and *I Capture the Castle* (adapted from her own novel, 1952). Other works include the highly popular children's book *The Hundred and One Dalmations* (1956), the film rights to which were sold to Walt Disney for $25,000. Her four volumes of autobiography are *Look Back with Love* (1974), *Look Back with Mixed Feelings* (1977), *Look Back with Astonishment* (1979) and *Look Back with Gratitude* (1985), and her biography by Valerie Grove, *Dear Dodie*, appeared in 1996.

Smith, Hannah Whitall, *née* Whitall

Born 1832   Died 1911
American Quaker, author of The Christian's Secret of a Happy Life *(1875)*

Hannah Whitall was born in Philadelphia. She married Robert Pearsall Smith in 1851, who like her was from a Quaker background. She was converted in 1858, but came to a new experience of faith as a spiritual victory in 1867. Influenced by the Methodist holiness movement, Hannah and Robert promoted the 'Higher Christian Life' at meetings in the USA and UK. At one point they left the Quakers, or Society of Friends, for other denominations, but rejoined the Friends later.

They moved to England in 1872, where their interdenominational meetings led to the foundation in 1874 of the Keswick Convention in the Lake District. This was an annual summer conference for spiritual renewal through prayer, preaching and bible study, which continues to meet to this day.

Hannah Whitall Smith was also a founder of the Woman's Christian Temperance Union in 1874 and a speaker on women's education and suffrage in the 1880s.

Smith, Madeleine Hamilton

Born 1835   Died 1928
Scottish gentlewoman who is notorious as the accused in a sensational murder trial

Madeleine Smith was born in Glasgow, the daughter of an architect. In 1857 she stood trial at the High Court in Edinburgh for the alleged murder by arsenic poisoning of her former lover Pierre Émile L'Angelier, a clerk and native of Jersey (Channel Islands) whom she had met in Glasgow in 1855. Her uninhibited love letters to him, published during the trial, stirred up considerable resentment against her. But although she had sufficient

motive for ridding herself of L'Angelier, after her engagement to a more wealthy suitor, William Minnoch, and although she had purchased arsenic on three occasions, evidence was lacking of any meeting between them on the last days or nights prior to his last violent illness. She was brilliantly defended by John Inglis, Dean of the Faculty of Advocates, and the verdict was 'not proven'.

Spurned by her family, she moved to London, where she became a popular social figure. In 1861 she married an artist-publisher George Wardle, an associate of William Morris, and after a normal family life in Bloomsbury, separated from her husband and eventually emigrated to the USA, where she married again, refusing all Hollywood offers to play herself in a silent film of her life.

Smith, Dame Maggie (Margaret Natalie)

Born 1934
English actress regarded as one of the greatest in Britain today

Maggie Smith was born in Ilford, Essex, and trained at the Oxford Playhouse School. She made her stage début with the Oxford University Dramatic Society in a production of *Twelfth Night* (1952) and, after revue experience, appeared in New York as one of the *New Faces of '56*. In 1967 she married the actor Robert Stephens (1931–   ), but the marriage did not last. Their two sons have become actors. In 1975 she married the playwright Beverly Cross (1931–   ). Her inimitable vocal range, mastery of stagecraft, and precise timing have enabled her to portray vulnerability to both dramatic and comic effect. Gaining increasing critical esteem for her performances in *The Rehearsal* (1961) and *Mary, Mary* (1963), she joined the National Theatre to act in *Othello* (1963), *Hay Fever* (1966) and *The Three Sisters* (1970), among others.

Her film début in *Nowhere to Go* (1958) was followed by scene-stealing turns in such films as *The VIPs* (1963) and *The Pumpkin Eater* (1964) but her *tour de force* was in *The Prime of Miss Jean Brodie* (1969), gaining her an Academy Award. Later stage work includes *Virginia* (1980) and Peter Shaffer's *Lettice and Lovage* (1987, written as a birthday present), while her selection of film roles shows a penchant for eccentric comedy and acid spinsters, and includes award-winning performances in *California Suite* (1978), *A Private Function* (1984, BAFTA award for Best Actress), *A Room With a View* (1985) and *The Lonely Passion of Judith Hearn* (1987).

Created DBE in 1990, in 1992 she was the Mother Superior in *Sister Act*, a wizened Wendy in *Hook*, and made a welcome return to the stage as Lady Bracknell in *The Importance of Being Earnest*. The following year she appeared on television in *Suddenly Last Summer* (1993).

Smith, Margaret Chase, *née* Chase

Born 1897 Died 1995
American Republican politician, the first woman to be elected to both houses of the US Congress

Margaret Chase was born in Skowhegan, Maine, the daughter of a barber. After being a teacher for a time she worked on a newspaper and married its publisher, Clyde Smith, in 1930. He became US Representative in Washington and when he died in 1940 she took over his position, becoming the first American woman politician to wield power through having both political influence and political office.

Eight years later she became Maine's first congresswoman, and the first woman elected a US Senator in her own right, and in 1949 she became the first woman to read the address to the Senate. She was re-elected three times, serving until 1973. During this time she became one of the first Republican senators to speak out against Senator Joseph McCarthy,

Margaret Chase Smith, 1949

and in 1964 she campaigned for the office of US President, the first woman to do so since **Victoria Woodhull**.

She wrote the books *Gallant Women* (1968) and *Declaration of Conscience* (1972).

Smith, Margaret *see* Court, Margaret Smith

Smith, Maria Ann

Born c.1801 Died 1870
Australian orchardist who gave her name to the popular Granny Smith apple

Maria Smith was growing various seedlings on her orchard in Eastwood, near Sydney, in the 1860s and experimented with a hardy French crab-apple from the cooler climate of Tasmania. From this was developed the late-ripening 'Granny Smith' apple which, because of its excellent keeping qualities, formed for many years the bulk of Australia's apple exports.

Smith, Robyn, *married name* Mrs Fred Astaire

Born 1943
American jockey who for six years led the field in the USA

Robyn Smith began her thoroughbred riding career in 1969. In 1972 she was seventh in international jockey standing — and the only American in international standing — with 98 mounts and 20 per cent of the winnings.

She maintained her top US rank from 1972 to 1978. In 1973 she was the first woman jockey to win a stakes race when she rode North Sea to victory in the Paumonok Handicap.

She married film star and dancer Fred Astaire (1899–1987) in 1980.

Smith, Sophia

Born 1796 Died 1870
American philanthropist whose fortune enabled the foundation of Smith College, Massachusetts

Sophia Smith was born in Hatfield, Massachusetts. Shy and retiring by nature, she depended on her sister Harriet (d.1859) for guidance and support for most of her life. On inheriting her brother Austin's fortune in 1861, she felt burdened by the responsibility it incurred and sought the advice of a young pastor, John Morton Greene. He wisely suggested she kept a journal, to allow her introspective nature to speak, and found hers to be a mind longing for forgiveness and self improvement rather than fulfilled ambition and material prosperity.

Due to her own deafness, she first planned to bequeath the money for an institution for the deaf, but on the foundation of the Clarke School for the Deaf, she changed her will to enable the foundation of a women's college, a vision credited to Greene's wisdom, foresight and planning. Five years after her death, Smith College in Northampton, Massachusetts, was opened.

Smith, Stevie, *pseud of* Florence Margaret Smith

Born 1902 Died 1971
English poet and novelist who drew on suburban life and religion in much of her work

Florence Smith was born in Hull. At the age of three she moved with her family to the house in the London suburb of Palmer's Green where she was to live with her aunt for most of her life. She attended the local High School and the North London Collegiate School for Girls before working for the Newnes publishing company. In 1935 she took a collection of her poems to a publisher, who rejected them and advised her to try a novel. This she did, and the result was *Novel on Yellow Paper*, published in 1936, a largely autobiographical monologue in an amusing conversational style, which proved a success and was followed in 1938 by *Over the Frontier*, in similar style. *The Holiday* (1949) was again to a great extent autobiographical but had a more conventional structure and told the story of a doomed love affair.

Meanwhile her reputation as a poet was becoming established. *A Good Time Was Had By All* was published in 1937, the poetry light and childlike in tone, with chatty amusing language and short verses. She developed a more serious tone, with stronger themes, moving towards the concepts and language of Christianity. Loneliness is often her theme, as in *Not Waving but Drowning* (1957), and she is considered to be a comic writer, but one who talks of serious matters in an amusing tone. Her work also includes *Mother, What is Man?* (1942), *Harold's Leap* (1950), *Selected Poems* (1962), *The Frog Prince* (1966) and *Scorpion* (1972). She wrote many reviews and critical articles, and produced a volume of the line-drawings that often accompanied her poems, entitled *Some Are More Human Than Others* (1958). Her *Collected Poems* appeared in 1975.

Smithson, Alison Margaret, *née* Gill

Born 1928 Died 1993
English architect who worked with Team X, a theoretical group that challenged pre-war ideas

Alison Gill was born in Sheffield. From 1950 she was in private practice with her husband Peter Smithson (1923–) and the couple became an internationally renowned team. They are best known for their involvement with the Team X group of the Congress Internationaux d'Architecture Moderne which attempted to break down the barriers between the arts and the sciences.

The Smithsons' work includes the Secondary Modern School in Hunstanton (1950–2) and the 'House of the Future' at the Ideal Homes Exhibition (1956), both of which are inspired by their modern thinking and attention to all aspects of the construction process. Their more recent work includes the Economist complex in Westminster, London.

Smithson, Harriet (Henrietta) Constance

Born 1800 Died 1854
English actress who was acclaimed in Paris after being ignored in London

Harriet Smithson was born in Ireland. She made her London début at Drury Lane in 1818, but did not make much of an impression either there, or in subsequent roles in the city.

In Paris, on the other hand, she created a huge sensation when she played as part of Charles Kemble's company in 1827. Particularly acclaimed for her interpretations of Shakespearian heroines, she became the darling of the young Romantics intent on remoulding French theatre.

Her fame was transient, however, and she retired from the stage in 1836 to suffer the consequences of an ill-judged and unhappy marriage with the composer Hector Berlioz.

Smyth, Dame Ethel Mary

Born 1858 Died 1944
English composer and suffragette who wrote 'The March of the Women'

Ethel Smyth was born in London. After studying at Leipzig she composed a Mass in D Minor, symphonies, choral works, and operas like *Der Wald* (1901), *The Wreckers* (1906) and *The Boatswain's Mate* (1916).

As a crusader for women's suffrage she composed the battle-song of the Women's Social and Political Union ('The March of the Women', 1911), and was imprisoned for three months.

Created DBE in 1922, she later wrote the autobiographical *Female Pipings for Eden* (1933) and *What Happened Next* (1940).

Smythe, Pat(ricia Rosemary),
married name Koechlin-Smythe

> Born 1928 Died 1996
> British show jumper and writer who was the first female Olympic rider

Pat Smythe was born in Barnes, London. She was a member of the British show jumping team from 1947 to 1964, and won the European ladies championship a record four times on 'Flanagan' (1957, 1961–3). In 1956 she was the first woman to ride in the Olympic Games, winning a bronze medal in the team event. Among her numerous victories — she won more grand prix events on her own horses in more countries than anyone else — is her winning of the Queen Elizabeth II Cup on 'Mr Pollard' in 1958.

She did very little competitive riding after her marriage in 1963 to the Swiss lawyer and businessman Sam Koechlin (d.1985), but continued to write. After *Jump for Joy: Pat Smythe's Story* was published in 1954 she wrote over 20 books, including several for children and her autobiography *Jumping Life's Fences* (1992). In her later years she suffered illnesses related to falls during her riding career, but served charities and her local Cotswolds community and was President of the British Show Jumping Association (1986–9)

Snell, Hannah, *also known as* James Gray

> Born 1723 Died 1792
> English soldier who succeeded in disguising herself as a man

Hannah Snell was born in Worcester and orphaned in 1740 when she went to live with her sister in Wapping. Around 1743 she married James Summs, a Dutch seaman who left her expecting a child.

In 1745 she disguised herself as a man and went to find him, first enlisting as a foot soldier and then as a sailor in a sloop bound for the East Indies. She was involved in action near Pondicherry and, despite serious injuries, managed to conceal her true identity. On obtaining a return passage to Europe she learned that her husband was no longer alive.

She returned to Britain in 1750 and profited from the publication of her story, *The Female Soldier; Or, The Surprising Life and Adventures of Hannah Snell* (1750). She is also reputed to have received an annuity as a Chelsea pensioner.

Snow, Sophia *see* Baddeley, Sophia

Södergran, Edith

> Born 1892 Died 1923
> Finno-Swedish Expressionist poet whose brief career remains influential

Edith Södergran was born in Petrograd, the daughter of a peasant who worked in the factory of Alfred Nobel, the Swedish chemist and manufacturer who invented dynamite. Her family moved to the Karelia peninsula, where the landscape and contact with the people had a profound effect.

Following an unhappy love affair, she published *Dikter* (1916, 'Poems'). This was followed by *Septemberlyran* (1918, 'September Lyre'), *Rosenaltaret* (1919, 'The Rose Altar') and the ironically titled *Fremtidens skugga* (1920, 'The Shadow of the Future'), each of which attested to a growing sense of the poet as a prophetic, almost magical figure.

Though she died when barely past 30, having suffered from tuberculosis since the age of 16, Södergran now exerts considerable influence on younger Swedish poets, who value her passionate, almost visionary imagery, and a robust metre that occasionally suggests the works of **Emily Dickinson**.

Söderström, Elisabeth Anna

> Born 1927
> Swedish operatic soprano who is particularly well suited to Janáček's operas

Elisabeth Söderström was born in Stockholm and trained at the Stockholm Opera School. Engaged by the Royal Opera, Stockholm, in 1950, she made her débuts at Glyndebourne in 1957, the Metropolitan Opera Company in 1959, and Covent Garden in 1960, and has sung in all the leading international opera houses and toured extensively in Europe, the USA and the USSR.

Her roles range from Nero in Monteverdi's *Poppea*, through Mozart, Tchaikovsky's Tatyana, Strauss, Débussy's Mélisande to Janáček's Jenúfa and Elena Makropoulos and Daisy Doody in Blomdahl's *Aniara*. In the 1959 season she sang all three leading female roles in *Der Rosenkavalier.*

She has published two autobiographical works, *I min tonart* (1978) and *Sjung ut, Elisabeth* (1986), and became artistic director of Drottingholm Court Theatre in 1993.

Sokolow, Anna

Born 1912
American dancer, choreographer and teacher who founded the first modern dance company in Mexico

Anna Sokolow was born in Hartford, Connecticut. She studied at the School of American Ballet and Metropolitan Opera Ballet School, leaving home as a teenager to become one of **Martha Graham**'s original dancers (1930–9).

She started choreographing in 1934, began her own troupe and, in 1939, founded the first modern dance company in Mexico, called La Paloma Azul. She retired from the stage in 1954, but continued to teach and make dances for her own and other companies, stage, television and film.

As a choreographer, she is an uncompromising social critic. She has also conducted pioneering collaborations with experimental jazz composers.

Somerville, Edith (Anna Oenone)
and **Violet Florence Martin**, *née* Ross, *pseud* Martin Ross

Edith born 1858; died 1949
Violet born 1862; died 1915
Irish novelists who formed a successful literary partnership called 'Somerville and Ross'

Edith Somerville was born in Corfu, the daughter of an army officer. As a baby she returned to the family home of Drishane in Skibbereen, County Cork. She was educated at Alexandra College, Dublin, studied painting in London, Düsseldorf and Paris, and became a magazine illustrator. In 1886 she met her cousin Violet Martin, (pseud 'Martin Ross'), who was born in County Galway, and began a lasting literary partnership as 'Somerville and Ross'.

They are known chiefly for a series of novels making fun of the Irish. Starting with *An Irish Cousin* (1889), they completed 14 works together, including *The Real Charlotte* (1894) and *Some Experiences of an Irish RM* (1899), the success of which led to two sequels, *Further Expenses...* (1908) and *In Mr Knox's Country* (1915). Violet also wrote travel books about the Irish countryside, and two autobiographical works, *Some Irish Yesterdays* (1906) and *Strayaways* (1920).

After Violet's death in 1915, Edith continued to write as 'Somerville and Ross', producing *Irish Memoirs* (1917) and *The Big House at Inver* (1925). A forceful character, she became the first woman Master of Foxhounds in 1903, and was Master of the West Carberry

pack from 1912 to 1919. She was also a founder-member of the Irish Academy of Letters (1933).

Somerville, Mary Greig, *née* Fairfax

Born 1780 Died 1872
Scottish mathematician and astronomer who supported the emancipation and education of women

Mary Fairfax was born in Jedburgh, the daughter of a naval officer. She was inspired by the works of Euclid, and studied algebra and classics, despite intense disapproval from her family. From 1816 she lived in London, where she moved in intellectual and scientific circles, and corresponded with foreign scientists.

In 1826 she presented a paper on *The Magnetic Properties of the Violet Rays in the Solar Spectrum* to the Royal Society, and in 1831 she published *The Mechanism of the Heavens*, her account for the general reader of Pierre Simon Laplace's *Mécanique Céleste*. This had great success and she wrote several further expository works on physics, physical geography and microscopic science.

She was summed up as follows by the *Dictionary of National Biography*: 'the fair hair, delicate complexion, and small proportions which had obtained for her in her girlhood the sobriquet of "the rose of Jedburgh", formed a piquant contrast to her masculine breadth of intellect'. Oxford University's Somerville College (1879) is named after her.

Somerville, Mary

Born 1897 Died 1963
Scottish educationalist and broadcasting executive who became the BBC's first female Controller

Mary Somerville was born in New Zealand. She was brought up as a daughter of the manse in Gullane, East Lothian, and educated at Somerville College, Oxford, where she met John (later Lord) Reith. Seeing radio as a powerful educational tool, she asked Reith to employ her on a trial basis at the British Broadcasting Company (later Corporation) in 1925.

She was a formidable lady, and by 1929 had secured responsibility for all broadcasting to schools. In 1947 she was made Assistant Controller, Talks, with a wider remit, and rose to Controller, Talks, in 1950, the first woman to hold the post of Controller in the BBC.

On her retirement the BBC acknowledged that 'the service of broadcasting to schools is Miss Somerville's great monument'.

Song Qingling (Soong Ch'ing-ling)

Born 1892 Died 1981
Chinese wife of revolutionary leader Sun Yat-sen
(Sun Yixian) who continued to be active in politics
after his death

Song Qingling received a Christian education in the USA. She became Sun Yat-sen's English-language secretary in 1913 and married him the following year. After his death in 1925 she played an increasingly active political role and became associated with the left wing of the Guomindang (Kuomintang), being elected to their Central Executive Committee in 1926. In 1927 she became a member of the left-wing Guomindang government established at Wuhan that year in opposition to Chiang Kai-shek. (Ironically her younger sister, Meiling, married Chiang Kai-shek (Jiang Jieshi) in 1927.)

After the collapse of the Wuhan government, Song Qingling spent two years in the USSR (1927–9). During the 1930s she was a prominent member of the China League for Civil Rights, which was constantly harrassed by Chiang Kai-shek's government. She stayed on in China following the victory of the Chinese communists (1949), becoming one of three non-communist vice-chairpersons of the People's Republic.

As the widow of Sun Yat-sen, of whom the communists claimed to be the legitimate heirs, she was accorded much respect by the Chinese Communist Party, although her presence in the new government remained an honorary one.

Sontag, Susan

Born 1933
American critic, intellectual and director of film
and theatre best known for her erudite essays on
modern life

Susan Sontag was born in New York City. Though she emerged first as an experimental fiction writer, author of *The Benefactor* (1963) and *Death Kit* (1967), her main impact has been as a critic. She was formerly married to the Freudian intellectual Philip Rieff and absorbed significant concerns from him.

Her influential books include *Against Interpretation* (1966), *Styles of Radical Will* (1969), *On Photography* (1976) and *Illness as Metaphor* (1978), a study of the mythology of cancer (Sontag was later a sufferer herself), which she revised in 1989 to take account of AIDS, another disease whose social and imaginative construction presents an intellectual challenge.

She has made four films, of which the first two were published as screenplays: *Duet for*

Susan Sontag, 1964

Cannibals (1969), *Brother Carl* (1971), *Promised Lands* (1974), and *Unguided Tour* (1983). Returning to fiction, she wrote the novel *The Volcano Lover* (1992) and the play *Alice in Bed* (1993). Hugely well-read and polymathic, she is a major commentator, not just on the American scene.

Sophia, *also called* Sophia of the Palatinate

Born 1630 Died 1714
Electress of Hanover and George I's mother who
presided over a glittering, cultural court

Sophia was the youngest daughter of Frederick V, Elector Palatinate of the Rhine, and **Elizabeth of Bohemia**, who was a daughter of James I of England. In 1658 Sophia married Ernest Augustus, Duke of Brunswick-Lüneburg, who became Elector of Hanover in 1692.

The British Act of Settlement (1701) stated that Sophia would inherit the throne after Queen **Anne** (in order to avoid many Roman Catholics in the line of succession and secure a Protestant as monarch); however she predeceased Anne by a couple of months, leaving her son to inherit the British throne as George I, the first of five kings ruling both Hanover and England.

The court that had developed around Sophia was a place of culture, frequented by such prominent figures as the composer George Frideric Handel and the philosopher Gottfried Wilhelm Leibniz. George is said to have thought little of England and frequently returned to the delights of Hanover.

Sophia Alekseyevna

Born 1657 Died 1704
Regent of Russia from 1682 to 1689 for her brother Ivan V and half-brother Peter I, 'the Great'

Sophia was the daughter of Tsar Alexei I Mikhailovich and his first wife Maria Mioslavskaya. On the death of her brother, Tsar Fyodor III in 1682, Sophia opposed the accession of her half-brother Peter and took advantage of a popular uprising in Moscow to press the candidature of her mentally deficient brother Ivan. A compromise was reached whereby both Ivan and Peter were proclaimed joint Tsars, with Sophia as regent.

Supported by her adviser and lover Prince Vasily V Gallitzin (or Golitsyn), she became the *de facto* ruler of Russia. During her regency a treaty of 'permanent peace' was signed with Poland and treaties were also signed with Sweden and Denmark (1684) and with China (1689). However, unsuccessful campaigns against the Turks in the Crimea (1687, 1689) did much to discredit the regent and in 1689 a faction of the nobility succeeded in removing her from power.

She spent the rest of her life in a convent in Moscow and was obliged to take the veil under the name of Susanna.

Sophia Charlotte

Born 1668 Died 1705
Queen of Prussia as the wife of Frederick I (ruled 1701–13), and sister of George I of Britain

Sophia Charlotte was the daughter of Ernest Augustus, the first Elector of Hanover, and **Sophia**, youngest daughter of **Elizabeth of Bohemia**. In 1684 she became the second wife of Prince Frederick, who became Elector of Brandenberg as Frederick III in 1688, and the first King of Prussia in 1701.

She greatly encouraged his patronage of learning and the arts and became a friend of the eminent philosopher Gottfried Wilhelm Leibniz.

The district of Charlottenburg in West Berlin was named after her.

Sophie Frederica Mathilda

Born 1818 Died 1877
Queen of the Netherlands as the wife of William III (ruled 1849–90)

Sophie Frederica Mathilda was the daughter of King William of Württemberg and Catherine Pavlovna of Russia. She married her cousin William in 1839, who succeeded to the Dutch throne in 1849.

Sophie bore her husband three sons, none of whom outlived their father. Their marriage was not a success, and she lived estranged from her husband until her death in The Hague.

Sophonisba

Died c.204BC
Carthaginian noblewoman whose life inspired tragedies by Corneille, Voltaire and Alfieri

Sophonisba was the daughter of a Carthaginian general. She was betrothed to the Numidian prince Masinissa but, for reasons of state during the 2nd Punic War (218–202BC), married his rival Syphax.

In 203 Syphax was defeated by a Roman army led by Masinissa, who took Sophonisba captive and married her. The Romans objected to this marriage and Masinissa gave her up, but sent her poison to prevent her being taken as a captive to Rome.

Sorabji, Cornelia

Born 1866 Died 1954
Indian lawyer, the first woman to practise law in India

Cornelia Sorabji was educated as the first female student at Decca College, Poona. Being top of her year, she was due a British university scholarship, but this was refused due to her sex. Eventually some friends arranged for her to attend Somerville College, Oxford, in 1888.

Sorabji continued her studies in law at Lincoln's Inn and became the first woman to sit the Bachelor of Civil Law examination in 1893, though women were not admitted to the English Bar for 30 more years. She returned to India and took up the cause of women in purdah who were wards of court, being appointed legal adviser for such people in Assam, Orissa and Bihar in 1904. In 1923 she moved to Calcutta and practised as a barrister. Her publications include *India Calling* (1934) and *India Recalled* (1936) and many studies of Indian life.

Soraya, *properly* Princess Soraya Esfandiari Bakhtiari

Born 1932
Queen of Persia during her marriage to Muhammad Reza Shah Pahlavi (ruled 1941–80)

Soraya Bakhtiari was born in Isfahan of Persian and German parents. She was educated at Isfahan, and later in England and Switzerland, and became Queen of Persia in 1951 when she married his majesty Muhammad Reza Shah Pahlavi (1919–80) as his second wife. On her failure to produce a male heir, the marriage was dissolved in 1958 and he married Farah Diba (1938–) the following year.

Sorel, Agnès, known as Dame de Beauté

Born c.1422   Died 1450
French mistress of Charles VII of France (ruled 1422–61) and the first mistress to be officially acknowledged

Agnès Sorel was born in Fromenteau, Touraine. She was in the employment of Isabel of Lorraine, the wife of Charles's brother-in-law René of Anjou (Charles was married to Marie of Anjou) and was the king's mistress from 1444 until her death. Sorel was the first to be publicly acknowledged as the 'official' mistress of the king, a position that at first was considered scandalous but nevertheless was to have immense importance during the *ancien régime*.

A beautiful woman beloved by Charles, she exerted considerable influence over him, and, among other gifts, was given an estate at Beauté-sur-Marne, hence her nickname. Soon after the birth of her fourth child, she died of dysentery, but the atmosphere of intrigue that had developed at the court resulted in her death being attributed to poison. The dauphin (later Louis XI) was suspected, probably by scandal-mongers trying to discredit him before the king.

Southcott, Joanna

Born c.1750   Died 1814
English religious fanatic who attracted a large following with her prediction of the second coming of Christ

Joanna Southcott was the daughter of a Devon farmer. She was employed as a servant until about 1792 when she pronounced herself to be the woman of Revelation XII, declaring the imminent arrival of Christ.

She came to London on the invitation of William Sharp the engraver (1749–1824), and published *A Warning* (1803) and *The Book of Wonders* (1813–14). At length she announced that she was to give birth on 19 October 1814, to a second Prince of Peace. She allegedly had about 100,000 followers (called Southcottians) who received this announcement with devout reverence. But she fell into a coma and died of a brain tumour in December 1814.

The Southcottians, believing that she would rise again, still numbered over 200 in 1851, and were not yet extinct at the beginning of the 20th century.

Souza, Madame de, née Adelaïde Marie Emilie Filleul

Born 1761   Died 1836
French novelist who emphasizes the importance of emotional needs in her depictions of aristocratic life

Adelaïde Filleul was born in the Norman château of Longpré. She married the Comte de Flahaut (1727–93), who perished in the Revolution, and in 1802 married the Marquis de Souza-Botelho (1758–1825), Portuguese minister in Paris. Her books provide a fine account of the life of the French aristocracy in the early 19th century.

At the outbreak of the French Revolution (1789) she found refuge with her only son in Germany and England, and there learned of her husband's execution at Arras. She turned to writing, and her first book was the delightful *Adèle de Sénange* (1794). Later novels include *Émilie et Alphonse* (1799), *Charles et Marie* (1801) and *Eugène de Rothelin* (1808).

Spark, Dame Muriel Sarah, née Camberg

Born 1918
Scottish novelist, short-story writer, biographer and poet who wrote The Prime of Miss Jean Brodie

Muriel Camberg was born in Edinburgh, the daughter of a Jewish engineer. She was educated in Edinburgh at James Gillespie's School for Girls (the model for Marcia Blaine School in *The Prime of Miss Jean Brodie*) where she was 'the school's Poet and Dreamer', and at Heriot-Watt College (now University). After her marriage in 1938 she spent a few years in Central Africa. She came back to England in 1944 when her marriage broke down, and worked in the Political Intelligence Department of the Foreign Office, and stayed on in London after the war to become General Secretary of the Poetry Society and Editor of *Poetry Review* (1947–9). Since then she has devoted herself to writing, from the early 1960s living mainly in New York and Italy. She became a Catholic in 1954, an event of central importance to her life and work.

Her early books include poetry and a biographical study of **Emily Brontë** (1953), but she is pre-eminently a novelist and short-story writer. *The Comforters* (1957) was hailed by

Evelyn Waugh as 'brilliantly original and fascinating', so she continued with *Memento Mori* (1959), *The Ballad of Peckham Rye* (1960) and *The Bachelors* (1961), but it was only with the publication of her sixth novel, *The Prime of Miss Jean Brodie* (1961), an eerie portrait of a schoolteacher with advanced ideas and her influence over her 'crème de la crème' pupils, that she achieved popular success.

Her many novels include *The Girls of Slender Means* (1963). *The Abbess of Crewe* (1974), an allegorical fantasy set in an abbey and *A Far Cry from Kensington* (1988). Her stories were collected in 1967 and 1985, and the first volume of her autobiography, *Curriculum Vitae*, was published in 1992. She was created DBE in 1993.

Spears, Laurinda

Born 1951
American architect who co-founded one of the most prolific practices in the USA

Laurinda Spears trained at Brown University, Rhode Island, and Columbia University, New York. She is a principal and co-founder of the Arquitectonica International Corporation, which employs over 80 architects, planners, designers and other related professions. In its first 12 years the firm designed over 60 buildings with a combined value of over $500 million.

Initially it became known for its bold, modernist style of architecture, mainly in Miami, and their hallmark was the incorporation of a giant rectangular void into their buildings. More recently they have expanded into New York, Chicago and San Francisco, with the practice growing in strength and picking up several architectural awards along the way, such as the South Florida Chapter Honor Award for the Palace Apartment block in Miami (1982), the Banco de Credito Corporate headquarters in Peru (1989) and the North Blade Justice Centre. The firm also received the Virginia Chapter Award for the Centre of Innovative Technology in Fairfax, Virginia, in 1989.

Spears has also taught at the University of Miami and lectured internationally on the work of Arquitectonica.

Spence, Catherine Helen

Born 1825 Died 1910
Scottish-born Australian writer, feminist and social reformer remembered as the 'Grand Old Woman of Australia'

Catherine Spence was born near Melrose. She arrived in Adelaide, South Australia, in 1839

with her parents, with the ambition to be 'a teacher first and a great writer afterwards'. While working as a governess she wrote the first novel of Australian life by a woman, published anonymously in London in 1854 as *Clara Morison: a Tale of South Australia during the Gold Fever*. Her second novel, also anonymous, was *Tender and True: a Colonial Tale* (1856). Under her own name she wrote *Mr Hogarth's Will* (1865) and *The Author's Daughter* (1868). Both of these had previously been serialized in Adelaide newspapers, as was *Gathered In* in 1881, though not published in book form until 1977; her last novel, *Handfasted*, was not published until 1984.

A concern with social problems led her into the public arena in the 1870s. She worked for orphaned children and destitute families and wrote Australia's first social studies textbook, *The Laws We Live Under* (1880). She also made lecture tours of Britain and the USA. In the political arena, she had pressed for proportional representation in *A Plea for Pure Democracy* (1861). She later formed the Effective Voting League of South Australia, and stood for the Federal Convention in 1897, thereby becoming Australia's first woman candidate. *Catherine Helen Spence: an Autobiography* was unfinished at her death; it was completed by her companion Jeanne Young in 1910.

Spender, Dale

Born 1943
Australian feminist writer, editor and teacher

Dale Spender was born in Newcastle, New South Wales, and studied first at the University of Sydney and later at London University. She worked as a series editor for Penguin Australia's Women's Library, and was co-originator of the international database on women, *Women's International Knowledge: Encyclopedia and Data*.

Spender worked as a lecturer and taught Women's Studies courses on the politics of knowledge and the intellectual aspects of sexism, as well as being the Australian representative for a number of international academic journals. She became a member of various advisory boards, and sat on the management committee of the Australian Society of Authors.

She has edited several anthologies of literature, as well as the journal *Women's Studies International Forum*. Her feminist books include *Man Made Language* (1981), *Invisible Women* (1982) and *There's Always Been A Women's Movement this Century* (1983).

Speyer, Leonora

Born 1872 Died 1956
American poet and violinist who won the Pulitzer Prize for poetry in 1927

Leonora Speyer was born in Washington, DC. Her early collection, *A Canopic Jar* (1921), showed much promise, which was fulfilled by her Pulitzer Prize-winning *Fiddler's Farewell* (1926).

At their best Speyer's poems speak with wit and perception about the female condition, but *Naked Heel* (1931) marked a withdrawal into a constrained formalism and halted her growing reputation. Her work has not, as yet, benefited from reappraisal.

Spheeris, Penelope

Born 1945
American film director who overcame a difficult childhood to succeed in Hollywood

Penelope Spheeris was born in New Orleans. Her parents worked for a travelling carnival, but her father was killed in a knife fight, leaving her alcoholic mother to bring up four children in California. She worked as a waitress to fund her film studies at UCLA, and began directing short films for *Saturday Night Live* on television.

She attracted wider attention with *The Decline of Western Civilisation* (1981), a documentary on the nihilistic punk rock scene, and its subsequent follow-up, *The Metal Years* (1989). Her major commercial success arrived with the adolescent comedy *Wayne's World* in 1992.

Spiridonova, Mariya Aleksandrova

Born 1884 Died 1941
Russian revolutionary who was not thwarted by many years' hard labour

Mariya Spiridonova was born in Tambov to a wealthy family. She became a member of the Socialist Revolutionary Party and in 1906 shot Tsarist General Luzhenovski, Vice-Governor of Tambov, who was in charge of suppressing peasant uprisings.

She was arrested and sentenced to death, but this was later commuted to hard labour for life in Siberia. She was exiled to Nerchinsk and released after the 1917 Revolution when she became a socialist leader and was involved in further revolutionary activities in Moscow.

On her subsequent arrest she was imprisoned, never to be released again. It is thought that she was executed in 1941 by the Russian Secret Service during a 'purge' of prisons.

Spottiswood, Alicia Ann, Lady John Scott

Born 1810 Died 1900
Scottish poet who wrote such well-known songs as 'Annie Laurie' and 'Durrisdeer'

Alicia Spottiswood was born in Westruther, Berwickshire. She became a friend of the Scottish antiquary Charles Kirkpatrick Sharpe, and was a busy collector of traditional songs. She wrote 69 of her own, often reworking original material, as with her most famous compositions, 'Annie Laurie' and 'Durrisdeer'. In 1836 she married Lord John Scott, a brother of the 5th Duke of Buccleuch.

Springfield, Dusty, *professional name of* Mary O'Brien

Born 1939
English pop singer whose first solo hit was 'I Only Want To Be With You'

Dusty Springfield was born in Hampstead, London. She left the Lana Sisters to form The Springfields (1961), together with her brother Tom and Mike Hurst.

Her first solo single was 'I Only Want To Be With You' (1964), which was followed by 'You Don't Have To Say You Love Me' (1966) and 'Son of a Preacher Man' (1968), all of which capitalized on her dramatic presence and strong voice evoking gospel music. The album *Dusty in Memphis* (1969) took her back to the music's roots.

She largely vanished in the 1970s, but made a cultish comeback with the theme song to the movie *Scandal* (1989, based on the events connected with **Christine Keeler** in the 1960s) and subsequent collaborations with The Pet Shop Boys, who boosted her standing as a gay icon.

Spry, Constance

Born 1886 Died 1960
English flower arranger and cookery-book writer

Constance Spry was born in Derby. She spent her childhood in Ireland, where she was educated, returning to England during World War I, when she did welfare work in London's East End. She began to work with flowers in the 1920s, opening flower shops and becoming Chairman of the Constance Spry Flower School. She excelled in organization, and was adviser to the Ministry of Works on flower decoration for the coronation of **Elizabeth II**.

She became joint Principal, with Rosemary Hume, of the Cordon Bleu Cookery School in London and of the 'finishing school' at Winkfield in Berkshire which aimed to train young women in the arts of cooking and entertaining. Her philosophy of cooking is expressed in the very influential book she co-authored with Rosemary Hume, *The Constance Spry Cookbook* (1956); she wrote many books on flower arranging, including *How to do the Flowers*, *Simple Flowers* and *Favourite Flowers*.

Staal, Marguerite-Jeanne, Baronne de, *formerly* Delaunay, *née* Cordier

Born 1684 Died 1750
French writer of memoirs who describes life during the minority of Louis XV

Marguerite-Jeanne Cordier was born in Paris, the daughter of a poor Parisian painter, whose name she dropped for that of her mother, Delaunay. She became ladies' maid and then secretary to the Duchess of Maine, and began writing entertainments for the court. Her involvement with her employer's plot against the Crown (the proposed kidnap of the regent Philippe, duc d'Orléans, and installation of Philip V of Spain instead as regent for Louis XV) brought her two years in the Bastille, where she had a love affair with the Chevalier de Menil. In 1735 she married the Baron Staal.

Her *Mémoires* (1755, Eng trans 1892) describe the world of the regency with intellect, observation and a subtle irony, and are written in a clear, firm and individual style. Her *Ouvres complètes* appeared in 1821.

Staël, Germaine de, *in full* Anne-Louise-Germaine Necker, Baronne de Staël-Holstein

Born 1766 Died 1817
French woman of letters and salon hostess who wrote a theory of Romanticism

Anne-Louise-Germaine Necker was born in Paris, the only child of the financier and statesman Jacques Necker. In her girlhood she attended her mother's salon and was soon the author of romantic comedies, tragedies, novels, essays and *Lettres sur Rousseau* (1789). In 1786 she married Baron Eric Magnus of Staël-Holstein (1742–1802), the bankrupt Swedish ambassador in Paris. She bore him three children, but the marriage was unhappy and she had many affairs.

Her brilliant Parisian *salon* became the centre of political discussion, but with the Revolution she had to leave for Coppet, by Lake Geneva, in 1792. By 1795 she had returned to Paris, where her husband had re-established himself as ambassador. She pre-

pared for a political role by her *Réflexions sur la paix intérieure* (1795, 'Reflections on Civil Peace'), but was advised to return to Coppet. Her *Influence des passions* appeared in 1796.

She published her famous *Littérature et ses rapports avec les institutions sociales* (Eng trans *The Influence of Literature upon Society*, 1812) in 1800, followed by the novel *Delphine* (Eng trans 1903) in 1802. She had returned to Paris but Napoloen made her unwelcome and in December 1803, now a widow, she set out with her children for Germany, where she dazzled the Weimar court, met the German writers Schiller, Goethe and August von Schlegel, pioneer of the German Romantic movement. In 1805 she returned to Coppet and wrote *Corinne* (1807, Eng trans 1807), a romance which brought her European fame.

She visited Germany at the end of 1807, and her famous work *De l'Allemagne* (Eng trans *Germany*, 1813) was finished in 1810 and partly printed, when the whole impression was seized and destroyed, and she herself was exiled; she escaped secretly to Berne, and from there made her way to St Petersburg, Stockholm and (1813) London, where admiration reached its climax on the publication of *De l'Allemagne*. It revealed Germany to the French and made Romanticism — she was the first to use the word — acceptable to the Latin peoples.

Louis XVIII welcomed her to Paris in 1814 but the return of Napoleon drove her away, and she spent the winter in Italy with Albert de Rocca, an Italian officer in the French service, whom she had married secretly in 1816. She returned to Paris, where she died. Her surviving son and daughter published her unfinished *Considérations sur la Révolution française* (1818, Eng trans *Considerations on the Principal Events of the French Revolution*, 1818), considered her masterpiece by the great French literary critic Charles Sainte-Beuve, the *Dix Années d'exil* (1821, Eng trans *Ten Years' Exile*, 1821), and her complete works (1820–1).

Stafford, Jean

Born 1915 Died 1979
American novelist who is also one of America's most admired short-story writers

Jean Stafford was born in Covina, California. Her father had an unsuccessful career as a writer of westerns under the pseudonyms Jack Wonder and Ben Delight. She was educated at Colorado University, and won a travelling scholarship to Heidelberg, Germany, in 1936. Returning to the USA she met literary establishment figures Randall Jarrell and

Robert Lowell, and she married the latter against his family's wishes in 1940.

She worked on the *Southern Review* and taught at Flushing College. *Boston Adventure*, her first novel, was published in 1944 to great praise; *The Mountain Lion*, her second, appeared in 1947. However, her stormy marriage to Lowell collapsed and she was admitted to psycho-alcoholic clinics. Divorced from Lowell in 1948, she married Oliver Jensen, an editor on *Life*, in 1950. In 1952 *The Catherine Wheel* was published. She was divorced for a second time in 1955 and later married the writer A J Liebling.

She taught throughout the 1960s and published diverse books: short stories, children's books, and interviews with the mother of President John F. Kennedy's alleged assassin, Lee Harvey Oswald, entitled *A Mother in History* (1966). Her *Collected Stories* appeared in 1969 and was awarded a Pulitzer Prize the following year.

Stampa, Gaspara

Born c.1523 Died 1554
Italian poet considered the finest Italian woman poet of the Renaissance

Gaspara Stampa was born in Padua. Her substantial *Rime d'amore* (1554, 'Love Poems'), published after her death by her sister, tell the story of her love (in Venice) for the Count Collitano do Collato, who betrayed her.

Her poems, Petrarchan in style, but often subtly mocking male pretensions, are opulent, passionate and challenging to the prevailing ideas of the time. Since their rediscovery in the last century, by romantic critics, they have been much reinterpreted — and she has justly been compared, although she did not share all her predilections, with **Sappho**.

Stanhope, Lady Hester Lucy

Born 1776 Died 1839
English traveller and eccentric who spent the last 25 years of her life presiding over mountain people in western Syria (now Lebanon)

Lady Hester Stanhope was the eldest daughter of Charles, 3rd Earl Stanhope. She went in 1803 to reside with her uncle, William Pitt, and as mistress of his establishment and his most trusted confidante, had full scope for her queenly instincts. On Pitt's death (1806) the king gave her a pension of £1,200, but the change from the excitements of public life was irksome to her.

In 1809 she was grieved by the death at La Coruña of her brother Major Stanhope, and of Sir John Moore, whom she had loved, so the following year she left England, wandered in the Levant, went to Jerusalem, camped with Bedouins in Palmyra, and in 1814 settled on Mount Lebanon.

She adopted Eastern manners, interfered in Eastern politics, and obtained a wonderful ascendancy over the tribes around her, who regarded her as a sort of prophetess. Her last years were poverty-striken on account of her reckless liberality.

Stanton, Elizabeth Cady, *née* Cady

Born 1815 Died 1902
American social reformer who launched the suffrage movement in the USA

Elizabeth Cady was born in Johnstown, New York. While studying law under her Congressman father, she determined to readdress the inequality that she discovered in women's legal, political, and industrial rights, and in divorce law. In 1840 she married the lawyer and abolitionist Henry Brewster Stanton, insisting on dropping the word 'obey' from the marriage vows. She accompanied him to the international slavery convention in London, where she encountered, with much indignation, a ruling that women delegates were excluded from the floor.

In 1848, with **Lucretia Mott**, she organized the first women's rights convention at Seneca Falls, New York, which launched the women's suffrage movement and accepted the set of resolutions for the improvement of the status of women which Stanton had drawn up. Woman suffrage was included, although Mott allegedly did not agree. Stanton teamed up with **Susan B Anthony** in 1850, producing the feminist magazine *Revolution* (1868–70), and founding the National Woman Suffrage

Elizabeth Cady Stanton

Movement in 1869. Stanton was President of the National Woman Suffrage Association (called from 1890 the National American Woman Suffrage Association) from 1869 to 1892.

With Mott and **Matilda Joslyn Gage** she compiled three out of the six volumes of the *History of Woman Suffrage* (1881–6). She also wrote her autobiography *Eighty Years and More 1815–1897* (1898). Stanton's daughter was the suffragette **Harriot Stanton Blatch**.

Stanwyck, Barbara, *originally* Ruby Stevens

Born 1907 Died 1990
American film and television actress who became a major star in the 1930s

Ruby Stevens was born in Brooklyn, New York. A working girl from the age of 13, she became a dancer, appearing in the *Ziegfeld Follies of 1923*, and made her dramatic stage début in *The Noose* (1926), when she adopted her name. Her first film was *Broadway Nights* (1927).

She is best remembered as gutsy, pioneering women in westerns like *Annie Oakley* (1935) and *Union Pacific* (1939), or as sultry femmes fatales in such films noirs as *Double Indemnity* (1944). A durable leading lady, she was frequently seen as strong-willed women, often struggling to escape from the wrong side of the tracks, although her range also extended to melodramas like *Stella Dallas* (1937) and deft comic performances as in *Lady Eve* (1941) and *Ball of Fire* (1941).

She was also active in radio and television, and enjoyed a long-running series *The Big Valley* (1965–9). She received a special Academy Award in 1982.

Stapleton, Maureen

Born 1925
American actress who became known as a major interpreter of the plays of Tennessee Williams

Maureen Stapleton was born in Troy, New York. She made her New York début in J M Synge's *The Playboy of the Western World* in 1946. Her first Williams role, Serafina in *The Rose Tattoo* (1951), brought her great acclaim. She followed it with Flora in *Twenty-Seven Wagons Full of Cotton* (1955), Lady Torrance in *Orpheus Descending* (1957), and the turbulent Amanda Wingfield in a revival of *The Glass Menagerie* in 1965.

She has been acclaimed as one of the great American stage actresses, and has also appeared in a number of films, including *A View from the Bridge* (1962), *Cocoon* (1985) and *Nuts* (1988).

Stapleton, Ruth, *née* Carter

Born 1929 Died 1983
American evangelist and faith healer, and sister of former US President Carter

Ruth Carter was born in Plains, Georgia, the younger sister of President Jimmy Carter. She is said to have been influential in his conversion to Christianity. Unlike many of her fellow Southern Baptists, she co-operated with other Christians, including Roman Catholics, and used her graduate training in psychology in a remarkable ministry which stressed the necessity for inner healing ('communicating love to the negative, repressed aspects in a human being').

In the 1976 presidential campaign she addressed the National Press Club, Washington, DC largely on her brother's behalf — reportedly the first time that it had listened to a woman preacher.

Starhawk, *originally* Miriam Simos

Born 1951
American peace activist, writer and witch

Starhawk learned of the earth-centered religion of Wicca in college and became dedicated to helping people discover their power and spirituality.

She founded Reclaiming, a feminist collective through which she leads demonstrations against nuclear power and military bases and also teaches spirituality.

Her books include *The Spiral Dance: A Rebirth of the Ancient Religion of the Great Goddess* (1979), *Truth or Dare* (1987) and *Dreaming the Dark* (1982).

Stark, Dame Freya Madeline

Born 1893 Died 1993
English writer and traveller who became an expert in Arab affairs

Freya Stark was born in Paris. She spent her childhood in England and Italy, and attended Bedford College, London University, under the tutelage of W P Ker, Professor of Literature. She was a nurse on the Italian front during World War I, and afterwards studied Arabic at the School of Oriental and African Studies, London University, and was invited to Baghdad by the Prime Minister.

There she worked on the *Baghdad Times*, followed the crusader routes and mapped the Valley of the Assassins in Luristan, described in *Valley of the Assassins* (1934). During World

War II she worked for the Ministry of Information in Aden and Cairo, and was personal assistant to Lady Wavell, describing her experiences in *West is East* (1945). She travelled extensively, financed by her writings, in Europe, the Middle East and Asia.

She produced more than 30 titles, including *The Southern Gates of Arabia* (1938), *Traveller's Prelude* (1950), *Beyond Euphrates* (1951), *The Coast of Incense* (1953), *Dust in the Lion's Paw* (1961) and *The Journey's Echo* (1963).

Starkie, Enid Mary

Born 1897 Died 1970
Irish critic of French literature who wrote on
Baudelaire, Gide and Rimbaud, among others

Enid Starkie was born in Killiney, County Dublin, a daughter of the classicist W J M Starkie and sister of the Hispanicist Walter Starkie (the author of *Raggle-Taggle*, *Spanish Raggle-Taggle* and *Scholars and Gypsies*). She was educated at Alexandra College, Dublin, Somerville College, Oxford, and the Sorbonne, where she wrote a doctoral thesis on the Belgian poet Émile Verhaeren.

She taught modern languages at Exeter and Oxford, wrote perceptively on Baudelaire (1933) and Gide (1954), played a major part in establishing the poetic reputation of Arthur Rimbaud (1938), and crowned her work by two outstanding volumes on Flaubert (1967, 1971).

In 1951 she campaigned successfully to have the quinquennially-elected Professor of Poetry at Oxford be a poet rather than a critic, whereby C S Lewis was defeated by C Day Lewis. She portrayed her early life in *A Lady's Child* (1941).

Starr, (Myra) Belle, *née* Shirley

Born 1848 Died 1889
American outlaw who eventually commanded a
notorious gang

Belle Shirley was born in the area of Carthage, Missouri. Having reputedly born a child by Thomas Coleman Younger around 1869, she eloped with Jim Reed, a notorious outlaw, and became involved in holding up a stagecoach.

She settled in Dallas where she ran a livery stable and dealt in stolen horses. In 1880 she married a Cherokee, Sam Starr and they settled near Fort Smith, Arkansas, in a cabin which became a hide-out for outlaws who preyed upon the Chisholm Trail.

She gained the reputation of being the mastermind of an outlaw gang herself, and died of gunshot wounds.

Stasova, Elena Dmitrievna

Born 1873 Died 1966
Russian revolutionary and feminist, a prominent
figure in early 20th-century politics

Elena Stasova was born in St Petersburg and educated at St Petersburg High School. In 1898 she helped run Sunday workers' schools.

After several years of subversive activities, she became the secretary of the Northern Bureau of the Central Committee of the St Petersburg Marxists, and then worked in Geneva from 1905 to 1906. Later she worked as a propagandist in Tbilisi (1907–12) before being arrested and exiled to Siberia in 1913.

Following the 1917 Revolution she became secretary of the Central Committee of the Bolshevik Party until 1920. From 1921 she worked at the Comintern and in 1938 she was appointed staff editor of the *Inostrannaia Literatura*. She is buried in the Kremlin wall.

Stead, Christina Ellen

Born 1902 Died 1983
Australian novelist, teacher and short-story
writer

Christina Stead was born in Rockdale, Sydney, the daughter of David George Stead, a leading English naturalist and writer. She trained as a teacher, but in 1928 left Australia for Europe, where she lived in London and Paris, working as a secretary in a Paris bank (1930–5). She went to live in Spain but left at the outbreak of war and, with her banker husband, settled in the USA. From 1943 to 1944 she was an instructor at the Workshop in the Novel at New York University, and in 1943 became a senior writer for MGM in Hollywood.

The Salzburg Tales, her first collection of stories, was published in 1934, but it was *Seven Poor Men of Sydney* (1934) which attracted attention, with its interweaving of dissimilar but casually connected lives. Her own experience was used to good effect in *House of All Nations* (1938), a critical look at the world of big finance, and her autobiographical novel, *The Man Who Loved Children* (1940), describes suffocating family life under an egoistical father. Her later novels of suburban American and European life were less successful. In all she published 11 novels, including *A Little Tea, A Little Chat* (1948), *The People with the Dogs* (1952), *Cotter's England* (1956) and *Miss Herbert (The Suburban Wife)* (1976).

The author of several novellas and the contributor of many short stories to the *New Yorker*, she left the USA in 1947 and settled in England, but finally returned to her homeland in 1974, in which year she was the first winner of the Patrick White Literary award. *I'm Dying Laughing*, a novel begun in the 1940s and ridiculing American Hollywood radicals, was published posthumously in 1986.

Stebbins, Emma

Born 1815 Died 1882
American painter and sculptor whose works are displayed in some prominent public places

Emma Stebbins was born in New York City. Her amateur portraits of family and friends won her election as an associate of the National Academy of Design in New York City.

Her sculptures include a bronze of US educationalist and politician Horace Mann in front of the state house in Boston and *The Angel of the Waters* for the Bethesda Fountain in Central Park in New York City.

Steel, Dawn

Born 1946
American film executive and producer whose ambition and drive earned her a reputation as the 'Queen of Mean'

Dawn Steel was born in New York City. She was an ambitious graduate of the NYU School of Commerce, and worked as a sports reporter and merchandise editor for *Penthouse* magazine, as well as enjoying success marketing novelty items like monogrammed toilet paper, before moving to Los Angeles in 1978 and securing a position as director of merchandising for Paramount Pictures.

Subsequently vice-president, senior vice-president and president of production, she was instrumental in the making of such commercially successful films as *Flashdance* (1983), *Top Gun* (1986) and *Fatal Attraction* (1987). In 1987 she was appointed President of Columbia Pictures, a position she held for two and a half years. Her films as an independent producer have included *Cool Runnings* (1993).

She has chronicled her rise through the corporate ranks and struggle against male prejudice in her autobiography *They Can Kill You But They Can't Eat You* (1993).

Steel, Flora Annie, *née* Webster

Born 1847 Died 1929
Scottish social reformer, novelist and chronicler of life in Northern India

Flora Webster was born in Harrow-on-the-Hill, London, the daughter of the Sheriff-Clerk of Forfarshire, and moved to Forfar at the age of nine. In 1867 she married Henry William Steel of the Indian Civil Service, with whom she travelled to the Punjab.

She became an active member of the local Punjabi community as a health worker and campaigner for the education of women. She was the first female Inspector of Schools in India (1884) and served on the Provincial Education Board (1885–8). In 1887 she published (with her friend Grace Gardiner) *The Complete Indian Housekeeper and Cook*, written in both English and Urdu.

Her husband retired to England in 1889, but she returned to India in 1894 to research her most celebrated novel, *On the Face of the Waters* (1896), an account of the Indian Mutiny.

Stein, Charlotte von, *née* von Schardt

Born 1742 Died 1827
German writer who was a friend of Goethe and a significant influence on his work

Charlotte von Schardt was born in Eisenach, a daughter of the master of ceremonies at the Weimar court, where she was employed as a lady-in-waiting to **Anna Amalia** in 1758. In 1764 she married Friedrich von Stein, the master of the horse to the Duke of Saxe-Weimar.

In 1775 she met Goethe, who fell in love with her and saw in her the ideal of femininity. Their friendship was broken suddenly in 1788 due to Goethe's relationship with Christiane Vulpius, but renewed before Von Stein's death.

She was the inspiration for many of his love poems and plays, including the character of Iphigenie in the verse drama *Iphigenie auf Tauris* (1787), and she herself wrote dramas such as the humorous *Rino* (1776) and the tragedy *Dido* (1792).

Stein, Edith, *known as* Sister Teresa Benedicta of the Cross

Born 1891 Died 1942
German Carmelite philosopher who was martyred at Auschwitz

Edith Stein was born in Breslau to a Jewish family. She converted to Catholicism in 1922, and began interpreting the phenomenology she had learned under Edmund Husserl from a Thomistic point of view — a project completed when she entered the Carmelite convent in Cologne in 1934. For safety, in 1938 she transferred to the house in Echt, Holland, where she wrote a phenomenological study of St John of the Cross.

She was executed in Auschwitz concentration camp, among priests and nuns with

Jewish connections who had been rounded up following Church criticism of Nazi anti-semitism. She was beatified in 1987.

Stein, Gertrude

Born 1874 Died 1946
American writer, modernist and lesbian, whose home in Paris was a centre for Cubist artists and avant-garde writers

Gertrude Stein was born in Allegheny, Pennsylvania. She spent her early years in Vienna, Paris and San Francisco, and then studied psychology at Radcliffe College under William James, and medicine at Johns Hopkins University, but settled in Paris, where she was absorbed into the world of experimental art and letters. She sometimes attempted to apply the theories of abstract painting to her own writing, which led to a magnified reputation for obscurity and meaningless repetition. From 1907 she shared an apartment with her lifelong companion from San Francisco, Alice B Toklas. Her influence on contemporary artists — particularly Picasso — is probably less than she imagined, though her personal collection of pictures was representative of the best of its era.

Her first book, *Three Lives* (1908), reveals a sensitive ear for speech rhythms, and by far the larger part of her work is immediately comprehensible. The prose of *Tender Buttons* (1914) is repetitive, canonic and extremely musical. *The Making of Americans* (1925) is a vast, virtually unreadable family saga. She took a more ironic stance in the playfully titled *The Autobiography of Alice B. Toklas* (1933) and *Everybody's Autobiography* (1937). *Four Saints in Three Acts* (1934) and *The Mother Of Us All* (1947) were operas with music by Virgil Thomson. She stayed in Germany in the village of Chloz during World War II, and afterwards wrote *Wars I Have Seen* (1945) and the novel *Brewsie and Willie* (1946) about the liberation by American soldiers.

Steinem, Gloria

Born 1934
American feminist and writer who became an articulate spokesperson for the women's rights movement

Gloria Steinem was born in Toledo, Ohio. In the 1960s her emergence as a leader in the women's rights movement was accompanied by voluble protests against the Vietnam War and racism and many appearances in lecture halls and on television.

She co-founded Women's Action Alliance in 1970 and the National Women's Political

Gloria Steinem, 1970

Caucus in 1971, and was the founding editor of the militant *Ms Magazine* (1971–87) which treated contemporary issues from a feminist viewpoint.

Among her works are a collection of her essays *Outrageous Acts and Everyday Rebellions* (1983) and *Revolution from Within: A Book of Self-Esteem* (1992).

Stepanova, Warwana

Born 1894 Died 1958
Russian painter and avant-garde textile designer, a leading proponent of Russian Constructivism

Warwana Stepanova was born in Lithuania and trained at the Kazan Art School (1910–11). She moved to Moscow in 1912 and studied at the Stroganov School. She taught at the Fine Art Studio of the Academy of Social Education from 1921 and in the Textile Department of the Vkhutemas from 1924 to 1925.

With two other leading proponents of Russian Constructivism, Alexei Gan and her husband Aleksandr Rodchenko, she founded the First Working Group of Constructivists in 1921. She was involved in the journals *LEF* (1923–5) and *Novyi* (1927–8), and produced her own futurist books, working with the poet Vladimir Mayakovskii in the 1930s and 1940s.

Stephenson, Elsie

Born 1916 Died 1967
English nurse and champion of strong links
between hospitals and homes

Elsie Stephenson was born in County Durham and trained as a nurse at the West Suffolk General Hospital. She qualified in midwifery at Queen Charlotte's Hospital, London, in 1938. After war service in the Red Cross in Egypt, Italy, Yugoslavia, and later in Germany among refugees, in 1946 she was awarded a fellowship to study advanced public health administration at Toronto University. She then undertook missions to Germany, Singapore, North Borneo, Brunei and Sarawak on behalf of the British Red Cross Society.

In 1948 she became the County Nursing Officer for East Suffolk where she developed the public health, district nursing and home-help services as well as infant welfare. In 1950 she became Nursing Officer for Newcastle-upon-Tyne, where she created links between the hospital and the community and was one of the working party producing the influential Jameson Report 'An Inquiry into Health Visiting' (1956). She was a member of the World Health Organization (WHO) Advisory Panel of the Expert Committee on Nursing.

In 1956 she took up the post of Director of Nursing Studies Unit at Edinburgh University. This was the culmination of efforts by the Scottish Home and Health Department, the Scottish Board of the Royal College of Nursing, the Rockefeller Foundation and Edinburgh University to create the first academic nursing studies unit in Europe. In 1964 WHO established an International School of Nursing within the Nursing Studies Unit. With her broad background, drive and charismatic manner Stephenson was able to create a unit which had great influence on nursing throughout the world.

Stephenson, Marjorie

Born 1885 Died 1948
English microbiologist and biochemist known for
her work on microbial metabolism

Marjorie Stephenson was born near Cambridge. She studied Natural Sciences at Newnham College, Cambridge, and then, because of financial difficulties, became a teacher in domestic science.

In 1913 she was awarded a Beit Fellowship, which she relinquished to work with the Red Cross during World War I, and resumed research in 1919 in the Biochemical Laboratory, Cambridge, where she remained until her death.

In 1936 she was awarded a DSc by Cambridge University and in 1945 was one of the first two women to be elected to Fellowship of the Royal Society (the other being the crystallographer **Kathleen Lonsdale**).

Stevens, Nettie Maria

Born 1861 Died 1912
American biologist, one of the first to show that
sex is determined by a particular chromosome

Nettie Stevens was born in Cavendish, Vermont. She began her career as a librarian, but later entered Stanford University to study physiology. She received a PhD from Bryn Mawr College, Pennsylvania (1903), and was subsequently appointed to research posts there. The college eventually created a research professorship for her, but she died before she could take up the position.

Stevens was one of the first to show that sex is determined by a particular chromosome: fertilization of an egg by a sperm carrying the X chromosome will result in female offspring and that Y-carrying sperm will produce a male embryo (a discovery made independently by Edmund Wilson).

She extended this work to studies of sex determination in various plants and insects, demonstrating unusually large numbers of chromosomes in certain insects and the paired nature of chromosomes in mosquitoes and flies. She was inducted into the National Women's Hall of Fame in 1994.

Stevenson, (Ella) Savourna

Born 1961
Scottish composer, pianist, and noted player of the
Celtic harp or clarsach

Savourna Stevenson was born in West Linton, Peebles-shire. She has successfully embraced a varied repertoire of clarsach music, ranging through classical, jazz and international folk styles.

Her most acclaimed work for her own instrument is the seven-movement suite, *Tweed Journey* (1989). She has also composed incidental music for theatre, radio and television.

Stewart, Belle

Born 1906
Scottish traditional singer and songwriter who is
considered an important folklore source

Belle Stewart was born in a 'wee bow tent' by the River Tay near Caputh, Perthshire. The best known of the singing 'Stewarts of Blair' family, she came from travelling stock and married a traveller, Alec, in 1925. They had nine children, five of whom died in infancy.

Her songs are rooted in the 'tinker' tradition, with emphasis on the ancient, classic ballads, but not to the exclusion of lighter material. She is much in demand at folk festivals in Scotland and overseas, and her best-known composition is 'The Berryfields of Blair', which can be heard on her recording *Queen Amang the Heather* (1977).

Stewart, Frances Teresa, Duchess of Richmond and Lennox

Born 1647 Died 1702
Scottish noblewoman who allegedly became a
favourite mistress of Charles II

Frances Stewart was the daughter of the 6th Duke of Lennox. Known as 'la belle Stewart' for her remarkable beauty, she was appointed maid of honour to Charles II's queen, **Catherine of Braganza**.

She is thought to have become one of Charles's mistresses, and posed as the effigy of Britannia on the coinage. In 1667 she married the 3rd Duke of Richmond, and fled the court. In later years she was restored to the King's favour.

Stirling, Fanny (Mary Ann), *née* Kehl

Born 1816 Died 1895
English actress whose career lasted over 50 years

Mary Ann Kehl was born in Mayfair, London, and educated in France. Her first husband was the Drury Lane stage manager, Edward Stirling, and in 1894 she married Sir Charles Hutton Gregory.

She made her début in 1832 under the name of Fanny Clifton and continued to perform mainly under her married name until 1886. Her finest roles were playing the part of **Peg Woffington** in *Masks and Faces* and the Nurse in *Romeo and Juliet*.

Stirling, Ruth

Born 1957
Scottish photographer who explores the
relationship between outer appearance and
inner structure

Ruth Stirling trained at Edinburgh College of Art, where she took a post-graduate diploma in 1987. She came to photography through painting and established herself in residencies at the Marine Biological Station, Isle of Cumbrae, the Gatty Marine Laboratory at St Andrews University, and the Eastern Arctic Research Laboratories at Igloolik in Canada (resulting in the exhibition, *Igloolik; Towards the Night, the Light*).

In 1989 she set up an independent studio on the Isle of Cumbrae, and in 1991 she began the first stage of a long-term project to establish a resource centre for cultural, artistic and scientific exchange, based in the Western Isles. Her work eludes traditional categories of art, science and technology to explore the relationship between outer appearance and inner structure, from the biological to the spiritual. She has used electron and light microscopes to extend her research into a dimension of the visual world hitherto reserved for scientists.

Stobart, Kathy (Florence Kathleen)

Born 1925
English saxophonist and educator, widely
acknowledged as an influence on younger players,
particularly women

Kathy Stobart was born in South Shields, County Durham. She made her professional début aged 14 and moved to London at the end of World War II. There she worked with the Vic Lewis band and with trumpeter Bert Courtney, whom she married.

A gifted player on tenor, soprano and baritone saxophones in a wide-ranging mainstream style, she formed a long association with Humphrey Lyttleton, working with him into the mid-1990s. She has also played with Johnny Griffin, Earl Hines and Zoot Sims. Unfortunately, her recorded output scarcely reflects her talent or experience.

Stöcker, Helene

Born 1869 Died 1943
German feminist and essayist

Helene Stöcker was born of a southern German family and was a prolific writer from an early age. After studying German literature, she settled in Berlin (1892) and became an enthusiastic supporter of the women's movement.

In 1905 she established the Association for Sexual Reform and the Protection of Mothers and campaigned for women's rights. She is best remembered for her essays which have been published in *Die Liebe und die Frauen* (1905) and for her novel, *Liebe* (1922).

Stocks, Mary Danvers Stocks, Baroness

Born 1891 Died 1975
English educationalist and broadcaster

Mary Stocks was born in Kensington, London, and educated at St Paul's School and the London School of Economics. After working as an assistant lecturer at the LSE (1916), she became lecturer in economics at King's College for Women (1918).

She had married the academic J L Stocks in 1913 and when he moved from Oxford to Manchester University, she continued her academic career on a part-time basis. She was also appointed magistrate in Manchester. Following her husband's sudden death in 1937 she became Principal of Westfield College in London in 1939.

She was widely known as a participant in BBC radio programmes and her publications include *The Workers' Educational Association, The First Fifty Years* (1953) and *My Commonplace Book* (1970). She was raised to the peerage in 1966.

Stone, Lucy

Born 1818 Died 1893
American feminist, a pioneer of the Women's Rights movement in the USA

Lucy Stone was born in West Brookfield, Massachusetts. She studied at Oberlin College and soon started giving lectures on abolitionism and women's suffrage. She called the first national Women's Rights Convention at Worcester, Massachusetts, in 1850.

In 1855 she married a fellow-radical, Henry Brown Blackwell, but with his agreement retained her maiden name as a symbol of equality and in protest against the inequality of laws applicable to married women ('doing a Lucy Stone' became a standard phrase).

During the 1880s she became a close associate of **Susan B Anthony** and **Anna Shaw** and campaigned throughout the USA. She helped to form the American *Women's Journal*, which she co-edited with her husband. It was later edited by their daughter, Alice Stone Blackwell (1857–1950).

Stopes, Marie Charlotte Carmichael

Born 1880 Died 1958
Scottish birth-control pioneer and palaeobotanist who wrote the first sex manual and founded the first British birth-control clinic

Marie Stopes was born in Edinburgh. She studied at University College, London, and took a PhD at Munich, and in 1904 became the first female science lecturer at Manchester, specializing in fossil plants and coalmining. In 1907 she lectured at Tokyo, and with Professor Sakurai wrote a book on the *Plays of Old Japan, The Nö* (1913).

In 1916 the annulment of her first marriage (to R R Gates) turned her attention to the marital unhappiness caused by ignorance

Marie Stopes, 1953

about sex and contraception and she began a crusade to disseminate information about these subjects. In 1916 her book *Married Love* caused a storm and was banned in the USA. In 1918 she married the aircraft manufacturer Humphrey Verdon Roe (brother of aircraft manufacturer Alliot Verdon Roe), with whom she opened the first British birth control clinic, in North London.

Her 70 books include *Wise Parenthood* (1918), *Contraception: Its Theory, History and Practice* (1923), *Sex and the Young* (1926), *Sex and Religion* (1929) and a play, *Our Ostriches* (1923).

Stoppard, Miriam, *née* Moore-Robinson

Born 1937
English physician, writer and broadcaster who specializes in taking the fear out of common medical concerns

Miriam Moore-Robinson was born in Newcastle-upon-Tyne. She trained as a doctor at the Royal Free Hospital School of Medicine in London and at King's College Medical School in Durham, specializing in dermatology, and after working in various hospitals, worked for a pharmaceutical company as a research director before entering television. From 1972 to

1992 she was married to the playwright Tom Stoppard (1937–).

After making her television début in *Don't Ask Me* (1973–7), she appeared in such programmes as *So You Want to Stop Smoking?* (1981–2), *Where There's Life* (1981–9), *Baby & Co* (1984–7) and *Miriam Stoppard's Health and Beauty Show* (1988–). She has also written books on similar topics, including her own *Book of Babycare* (1977) and *Health and Beauty Book* (1988), *Conception, Pregnancy and Birth* (1993), *The Menopause* (1994) and *The Breast Book* (1996), and contributes to medical journals and women's magazines.

Storace, Nancy (Anna Selina)

Born 1765 Died 1817
English soprano and actress of Italian descent who created the role of Susanna in The Marriage of Figaro

Nancy Storace was born in London, a sister of the composer Stephen Storace. She began singing as a child, and sang in Florence at the age of 15 and at La Scala, Milan, and in London.

Her gift for comedy earned her great popularity, particulary in Vienna, where she married the English composer John Abraham Fisher and met Mozart, for whom she was the original Susanna in *Le Nozze di Figaro* (1786).

She later sang in her brother's operas in London, and after his death in 1796 she toured the Continent with the tenor John Braham, with whom she lived until 1816 and had a child (1802).

Storkey, Elaine, *née* Lively

Born 1944
English Chrisitian writer and broadcaster on contemporary and feminist issues

Elaine Lively was born in Wakefield, Yorkshire. She studied at the University of Wales, McMaster University, Ontario, and the University of York before becoming a lecturer in philosophy, ethics and sociology in the UK and USA. She married Alan Storkey, now a writer and teacher at Oak Hill Theological College, in 1968.

She has been a member of the General Synod of the Church of England since 1987 and became Executive Director of the Institute of Contemporary Christianity ('Christian Impact') in London in 1992. A regular broadcaster and international speaker, Storkey is a skilled and perceptive communicator who conveys, in a style at once intellectual and down-to-earth, not only the relevance of Christian faith in today's society but also the intrinsic value of being human.

Her publications include many essays on religious, sociological, sexual and feminist issues and the books *What's Right With Feminism* (1985), *Mary's Story, Mary's Song* (1994), *Contributions to Christian Feminism* (1995), *The Search for Intimacy* (1995) and *God and Sexuality* (1996).

Storni, Alfonsina

Born 1892 Died 1938
Argentinian feminist, poet and dramatist whose early poetry is largely concerned with love, sexual passion and the sea

Alfonsina Storni was born in Switzerland. Her father died when she was young and she had to work in a factory in Rosario. She then became a teacher and wrote pieces for magazines, which was not a common thing to do in 1910. She also acted with a travelling theatrical company. She had a child and in 1911 moved to Buenos Aires, where she taught drama and languages and worked as a journalist.

Her first book was *La inquietud del rosal* (1916, 'The Solicitude of the Rosebush'). Others include *El dulce daño* (1918, 'Sweet Injury'), *Languidez* (1921, 'Languor'), for which she won prizes, *Ocre* (1925, 'Ochre'), which focuses on the sea, and *Mascarillo y trébol* (1938). Her most famous poem, *Hombre pequeñito* ('Little Man'), is an expression of hatred for men.

She committed suicide on discovering that she was suffering from cancer. An edition of her verse appeared in 1961.

Stowe, Emily Howard, *née* Jennings

Born 1831 Died 1903
Canadian doctor who could not practise when she qualified because of her sex

Emily Jennings was born in Norwich, Ontario. She was educated at home by her mother and at the age of 15 became a schoolteacher in nearby Summerville. In 1853 she entered Normal School in Toronto, graduating in 1854.

When she married John Stowe in 1856 she left her position as principal of Brantford public school, and subsequently decided to train as a doctor. She was refused permission to train in Canada on grounds of gender, but she graduated from New York College for Women (1867). However, she was not granted a licence to practise in Canada until 1880.

She established the Toronto Women's Literary Club (1877) to campaign for women's rights and became the first President of the Dominion Women's Enfranchisement Association in 1889, a post which she held until her death.

Stowe, Harriet (Elizabeth) Beecher, *née* Beecher

Born 1811   Died 1896
American novelist who came to notice with her anti-slavery novel Uncle Tom's Cabin

Harriet Beecher was born in Litchfield, Connecticut, the daughter of Lyman Beecher. She was brought up with puritanical strictness and joined her sister **Catherine Beecher** at her Connecticut Female Seminary at Hartford in 1824. In 1836 she married the Rev Calvin Ellis Stowe, a theological professor at Lane Seminary, with whom she settled in Brunswick, Maine, in 1850.

She contributed sketches of southern life to *Western Monthly Magazine*, and won a short-story competition with *A New England Sketch* (1834). She became famous for her *Uncle Tom's Cabin* (1852), prompted by the passing of the Fugitive Slave Law, which immediately focused anti-slavery sentiment in the North. Her second anti-slavery novel, *Dred* (1856), had a record sale in Britain, largely thanks to a review by **George Eliot**, but she lost her popularity with *Lady Byron Vindicated* (1870), although the charges made against Lord Byron in the book were later proven.

She wrote a host of other books, fiction, biography and children's books. Her best works are about New England life, such as *The Minister's Wooing* (1859) and *Old Town Folks* (1869).

Strachey, Philippa

Born 1871   Died 1968
English pioneer in the equal rights struggle for women

Philippa Strachey was the elder sister of the biographer Lytton Strachey (1880–1932). She grew up in Gordon Square in the heart of the Bloomsbury Set, in an atmosphere that could not fail to make her aware of the social injustices of the day.

She became involved in the struggle for women's suffrage from an early age and was secretary to the London Women's Suffrage (later the Fawcett) Society. An excellent administrator, she organized the society's 'Mud March', an open-air rally of women who marched from Hyde Park to the Strand, upon which basis many future marches were based.

Strachey, Ray (Rachel) Conn, *née* Costelloe

Born 1887   Died 1940
English feminist involved in organizing work for women during and after World War II

Ray Costelloe was born in London and educated at Kensington High School, Newnham College, Cambridge, and Bryn Mawr College, Pennsylvania. In 1911 she married her cousin Oliver Strachey.

She became Parliamentary Secretary for the London Society for Women's Suffrage in 1915 and during World War I was Chairwoman of the Women's Service Bureau, organizing war work for women. From 1930 to 1939 she was the first Chairman of Cambridge University Women's Employment Board.

For many years she played an active part in politics, both as an unsuccessful Independent parliamentary candidate and as secretary to Viscountess **Nancy Astor**. Ray Strachey's best-known work is a history of the women's movement, *The Cause* (1928); her other works include *The World at Eighteen* (1907), *Marching On* (1923) and *Shaken By the Wind* (1927).

Stratton-Porter, Gene(va), *née* Stratton

Born 1868   Died 1924
American novelist whose illustrated works were very popular in the early 20th century

Gene Stratton was born on a farm in Wabash County, Indiana. She married Charles D Porter in 1886, and as Gene Stratton-Porter attained great popularity with *Freckles* (1904), about an apparently orphaned boy who is reunited with his father. She continued her popularity with *A Girl of the Limberlost* (1909), the story of Freckles's companion Eleanora who sells moths to finance her education, *The Harvester* (1911), and other stories full of sentiment and nature study, usually illustrated with her own drawings. She was an advocate for the Limberlost, a primeval forest in Indiana.

Streatfeild, (Mary) Noel

Born 1895   Died 1986
English children's author made famous by Ballet Shoes, *the first 'career novel' for children*

Noel Streatfeild was born in Amberley, Sussex, the daughter of a clergyman who brought up his five children in a strict Victorian manner. Resentful of her restrictive upbringing she became a rebellious child whose bitter sentiments are often reflected in the fictitious characters in her stories. She showed a talent for the stage, attended the

Dramatic Art in London and became an actress, but gave this up after a few years to write.

Though she began with adult books, the massive success of her first children's book, *Ballet Shoes* (1936), established her as the long-standing doyenne of children's writers. She followed this delightful backstage story of strong-willed child performers with further 'career' novels such as *Tennis Shoes* (1937), *The Painted Garden* (1949) and *White Boots* (1951). *The Circus is Coming* (1938), perhaps her finest book, won the Carnegie Medal.

Although the later work never surpassed her first successes, she continued to write popular and accomplished novels with sparky, believable characters.

Streep, Meryl (Mary Louise)

Born 1949
American character actress who has become
firmly established as a first-rank star

Meryl Streep was born in Summit, New Jersey, and educated at Vassar College. After training at Yale Drama School, she made her New York stage début in *The Playboy of Seville* (1969). She appeared in summer stock, off-Broadway and in *Trelawney of the Wells* (1975) before making her film début in *Julia* (1977). This was followed by *The Deerhunter* (1978) and *Kramer vs. Kramer* (1979), for which she won her first Academy Award (Best Supporting Actress). In 1978 she married Don Gummer, a sculptor; they live with their three children on a farm in Connecticut.

Streep has consistently underlined her range, showing sensitivity and a facility with accents, in a series of acclaimed characterizations in films like *The French Lieutenant's Woman* (1981), *Sophie's Choice* (1982), for which she won a second Academy Award (Best Actress), *Silkwood* (1983), *Out of Africa* (1985), *Ironweed* (1987), *A Cry in the Dark* (1988), *Postcards from the Edge* (1991), *Death Becomes Her* (1992), *The House of the Spirits* (1994) and *The Bridges of Madison County* (1995).

Street, Lady Jessie Mary Grey

Born 1889 Died 1970
Australian feminist and writer, an early activist
for women's rights in Australia

Jessie Street was born in Ranchi province of Chota Nagpur, north-east India, where her father was in the Indian civil service. She was educated at private schools in England and at Sydney University and soon developed a concern for social reform, becoming an early activist for the League of Nations.

In 1920 she became secretary to the National Council of Women, and later was President of the Feminist Club. In 1929 she became founding President of the United Associations of Women, an umbrella group for the New South Wales feminist movement. She stood as Labor candidate in the federal election of 1943 and again in 1946. Meanwhile, in 1945, she was the only woman delegate to the formative San Francisco conference, from which evolved the United Nations organization.

Her husband, Sir Kenneth Whistler Street (1890–1972), was lieutenant-governor and chief justice of New South Wales, as was their son, Sir Laurence Whistler Street (1926–   ), who was chief justice (1974–88) and lieutenant-governor (1974–89); he was knighted in 1976.

Street-Porter, Janet

Born 1944
English television programme producer and
presenter

Janet Street-Porter was born in London. After studying architecture for a year (1965–6), she worked as a journalist for various newspapers, including the *Evening Standard* and the *Daily Mirror*. She started presenting evening television shows in the mid-1970s, such as *Saturday Night People* with Auberon Waugh, developing an image as an outrageous symbol of youth culture.

When she moved into production for ITV and Channel 4, her 1980s current affairs programme *Network 7*, which was aimed at the under-25s, won her a BAFTA award for originality and a job at the BBC; in 1988 she became the BBC's first commissioning editor for youth programmes. Following the success of her *Def II* programmes, among others, both youth-oriented and mainstream, she was promoted to head of youth and entertainment in 1991, since when her programmes have included the documentary fashion series *The Look* (1992) and the five-part opera adaptation, *The Vampyr* (1992).

Passed over for the controllership of BBC1 and BBC2, she was appointed head of independent production for BBC TV's entertainment group early in 1994, but later that year left the Corporation to become managing director of the Mirror Group's new national cable television channel, Live TV. However she resigned suddenly in 1995. Three times divorced, she retains the surname of her first husband, photographer Tim Street-Porter.

Alison Streeter, 1985

Streeter, Alison

Born 1964
English swimmer, known as the 'Queen of the Channel'

Alison Streeter was born in Surrey. She first took up swimming to help her asthma but has since clocked up more English Channel crossings than any other female in the world, with the tally still rising, and is the only woman to cross the Channel three times without stopping.

In 1988 she broke the world record, previously held by a man, for the fastest crossing from Scotland to Ireland, and she also set world records for the fastest swims around the Isle of Wight and around Jersey. She is the only person ever to succeed in the 'impossible' task of swimming up the Thames and has raised over £80,000 for charity through sponsorship of her swims.

In 1995 she swam the Channel five times, making her the overall record-holder for cross-Channel swims, and marking the first time a woman has ever held that honour. Streeter was awarded the MBE in 1991 for her achievement in swimming.

Streisand, Barbra Joan, *originally* Rosen

Born 1942
American actress, director and best-selling female singer of all time

Barbra Streisand was born in Brooklyn, New York. Her career began after she was spotted in an amateur talent contest as a teenager, and her New York début in *Another Evening with Harry Stones* (1961) was followed by Broadway successes in *I Can Get It For You Wholesale* (1963) and *Funny Girl* (1964), the success of

which she repeated in the film version (1968), in which she made her film début and earned herself an Academy Award. She followed this with *Hello Dolly* (1969), *The Way We Were* (1973) and *A Star Is Born* (1976), which she produced.

A multi-talented entertainer, with an air of vulnerability in her personal life that seems to add to her appeal (she was married to actor Elliott Gould 1961–71), she won five Emmy awards for her 1965 television special, *My Name is Barbra*, and has been the recipient of numerous Grammy awards, including three as best female vocalist (1964, 1965, 1978).

She has maintained parallel careers as a top-selling recording artist and film actress, and diversified further in 1983 as the producer, director and co-writer of *Yentl*, in which she also acted and sang. She later acted in and directed *Prince of Tides* (1990). In 1994, ending a 27-year break from the mainstream concert stage, she made a comeback in Las Vegas and in London, which was the first time she had been heard live in the UK since in *Funny Girl* in 1966.

Stritt, Marie

Born 1856 Died 1928
German feminist, an important early 20th-century campaigner

Marie Stritt was the prime activist for women's suffrage in Germany for a number of years around the turn of the century. In 1891 she became a member of Hedwig Kessler's women's group, Reform, which promoted educational equality regardless of gender, and by 1895 had become its leader. As a radical campaigner for women's rights, she later joined the Federation of German Women's Associations and was elected President in 1899.

She also became President of the German Imperial Suffrage Union and played a leading role in the Association for Sexual Reform and the Protection of Mothers, the group established in 1905 by **Helene Stöcker**, which promoted a woman's right to control her own fertility.

Struther, Jan, *pseud of* Mrs Joyce Anstruther Placzek

Born 1901 Died 1953
English writer whose most successful creation was Mrs Miniver

Jan Struther was born in London. Her Mrs Miniver, the English middle-class housewife character whose activities were first narrated in articles to *The Times* became the subject of a book, *Mrs Miniver* (1939), and of William Wyler's famous 1942 film of World War II, which has even been credited with helping the Allies to win the war. Its sequel, *The Miniver Story* (1950), tells of Mrs Miniver's suffering from cancer.

Stuart, Arabella

Born 1575 Died 1615
English heiress whose claim to the throne led to conspiracy and her death in the Tower

Arabella Stuart was the daughter of Charles Stuart, Earl of Lennox, younger brother of Lord Darnley, and thus the great-grand-daughter of **Margaret Tudor**. Although she was in the line of royal succession immediately after James VI and I, her supporters argued that she had a superior claim, having been born and brought up in England. Since **Elizabeth I** was jealous of any marriage that might transmit a claim to the throne, Arabella was arrested shortly before the Queen's death, on suspicion of planning to marry William Seymour, heir of the Suffolk line.

James, on his accession, restored her to favour and invited her to live at court, but she was rumoured to have been involved in Lord Cobham's Main plot (in which Sir Walter Raleigh was implicated) to dethrone James and crown her in his place. She constantly complained of poverty and in 1609 was again arrested on a charge of planning an illicit marriage. James relented, released her and awarded her an annual pension of £1,600.

In 1610 she became engaged to Seymour, but he retracted the engagement before the Privy Council and Arabella received further financial support. In July, however, the couple secretly married, but were discovered and arrested. She was put in the custody of the Bishop of Durham in March 1611, but broke her journey north at Barnet, on the plea of ill health. In June she fled on board a French ship, but was captured at sea and brought to the Tower of London, where she died.

Sturrock, Mary Arbuckle Newbery,
née Newbery

Born 1890 Died 1985
Scottish decorative artist of watercolours, embroidery and ceramic decoration in a distinctive linear style

Mary Newbery was the daughter of Fra and **Jessie Newbery**. She studied at the Glasgow School of Art where she met her lifelong friend **Cecile Walton**. She married the artist Aleck Riddell Sturrock in 1918.

Her distinctive linear style of ceramic decoration was influenced by her friend Charles Rennie Mackintosh, and she was a regular exhibitor at the RSA and the RGI (Royal Glasgow Institute of Artists).

Suggia, Guilhermina

Born 1888 Died 1950
Portuguese cellist who first played in public at the age of seven

Guilhermina Suggia was born in Oporto. A child prodigy, she became a member of the Oporto City Orchestra at the age of 12 and, aided by a royal grant, she subsequently studied at Leipzig and under the Spanish cellist, conductor, and composer Pablo Casals, with whom she lived from 1906 to 1912.

She appeared at concerts with him under the name Madame Casals-Suggia, though it is said that they were never legally married. After extensive concert tours she settled in England in 1914, last appearing in public at the 1949 Edinburgh Festival. There is a famous portrait of her by Augustus John, painted in 1923.

Sullavan, Margaret

Born 1911 Died 1960
American actress known particularly for her roles in contemporary drama

Margaret Sullavan was born in Norfolk, Virginia. She worked in amateur and stock productions for several years prior to her Broadway début in *A Modern Virgin* in 1931.

Her striking blonde looks and throaty voice appealed to audiences and critics alike, and she went on to become one of the USA's best-known theatre actresses, especially in contemporary drama. She committed suicide in 1960.

The actress Brooke Heyward, Sullavan's daughter by producer Leland Heyward, wrote about her parents' stormy relationship in *Haywire* (1977).

Sullerot, Evelyne Annie Henriette,
née Hammel

Born 1924
French sociologist and writer particularly interested in the working woman

Evelyne Hammel was born at Montrouge, Hauts de Seine. She was educated at the colleges of Compiègne, Royan and Uzès, and at university in Paris and Aix-en-Provence, followed by a distinguished academic career. She has been a member of the French Economic and Social Council since 1974. Her particular area of interest is the way in which women's work outside the home impacts on family life, and she has carried out research for a number of bodies including UNESCO, the EEC, and the International Labour Organization.

She is co-founder of the French Family Planning Association and her many publications include *La Presse féminine* (1963), *La femme dans le monde moderne* (1970), *Histoire et mythologie de l'amour* (1976) and *Pour meilleur et sans le pire* (1984).

Sumac, Yma, *professional name of* Imperatriz Charrari Sumac del Castillo

Born c.1928
Peruvian singer of astonishing vocal range who maintained an aura of mystery

Yma Sumac claimed to be descended from Inca royalty, though cynics said her name was a reversal of Amy Camus, and her Peruvian background a fictitious stunt.

With her arranger husband Moises Vivianco, she performed the strange songs on *Voice of the Xtabay* (1950) and other discs, achieving considerable success, which was enhanced by her statuesque figure (she is over six feet tall) and elaborate costumes.

Sumac retired in 1962, but gave comeback concerts in New York City 25 years later.

Summer, Donna, *professional name of* LaDonna Adrian Gaines

Born 1948
American popular singer and actress whose early songs were banned from radio broadcast

Donna Summer was born in Boston, Massachusetts, where she made her professional début in local rock bands. She won a part in the German production of *Hair!*, and lived in Europe for a time. Her first hit was the controversial 'Love to Love You, Baby' (1975), a graphically sexual disco anthem which became a hit despite (or because of) being banned by some radio stations. 'I Feel Love' (1977) was a self-conscious follow-up. Albums like *Waitress in a Donut Shop* (1979) presented Summer as a sassy feminist, while the single 'State of Independence' (written by Vangelis and Jon Anderson) was a late excursion into soul for a black female singer.

Summer's substantial gay audience was dismayed by her comments on homosexuality and AIDS, and she was obliged to recant.

Summerskill, Edith Clara Summerskill, Baroness

Born 1901   Died 1980
English doctor and politician who campaigned tenaciously for women's welfare

Edith Summerskill was born in London and educated at King's College there before practising medicine in a London practice shared with her husband. She worked with the Socialist Medical Association, and became a member of Middlesex County Council (1934).

From 1938 to 1955 she was Labour MP for Fulham West, continuing an unremitting fight for women's welfare on all issues, and often provoking great hostility. She became Under-Secretary to the Ministry of Food (1949), and was Chairman of the Labour Party (1954–5). She was created a life peeress in 1961.

Sumner, Mary Elizabeth, *née* Heywood

Born 1828   Died 1921
English founder of the Church of England Mothers' Union

Mary Heywood was born in Swinton, Manchester, the youngest child of a Liverpool banker. She was educated privately and in 1848 married George Henry Sumner, the son of the Bishop of Winchester and nephew of the Archbishop of Canterbury. After parish livings in Crawley and Farnham Castle, they moved to Old Alresford, Hampshire where they stayed for 34 years. George was appointed Bishop of Guildford in 1888.

In 1876 Mary — who held that 'If everyone would sweep before their own door, the streets of the new Jerusalem would be clean' — started the meetings that became the country-wide Mothers' Union; these gathered momentum particularly after she expounded her ideals at a Church Congress at Portsmouth in 1885. Her 51 years of marriage were a potent witness to the validity of her beliefs.

Susann, Jacqueline

Born c.1926   Died 1974
American popular novelist who wrote about ambitious, sexually active 1960s women

Jacqueline Susann was born in Philadelphia, Pennsylvania. After a moderately successful career as a Broadway actress she turned to writing. Her first novel, *Valley of the Dolls* (1966), became an immediate bestseller and *The Love Machine* (1969) enjoyed the same success.

One of the first to examine female sexuality in an explicit and titillating language, she made no literary claims for her work but admitted to writing to provide her readers with an escape from their daily lives into the more sensational world of show business, where ruthless ambition leads to frustration and unhappiness.

Susanti, Susi

Born 1971
Indonesian badminton player, widely considered the greatest female badminton player of all time

Susi Susanti was born in Malaysia. She plays for the club Jaya Raya. In 1992 she won the women's singles at the Olympics, and in 1994 she won her record-breaking fourth consecutive world Grand Prix title, as well as the Indonesian, Malaysian, Thailand, Japanese and Chinese Taipei Opens, the World Cup, the Uber Cup final, and the All-England championship.

She has competed in the last-mentioned competition five times, and has won it four times. In 1994 (her fourth victory) she took just 28 minutes to defeat number-two seed Ye Zhaoying. Unsurprisingly, Susanti is ranked best in the world.

Sutcliff, Rosemary

Born 1920 Died 1992
English writer of sophisticated historical fiction, mostly for younger readers

Rosemary Sutcliff was born at West Clanden, Surrey, and trained at Bideford School of Art. Her skill as a miniaturist is also evident in her prose, which is sharply detailed and coloured.

Her first novel was *The Armourer's House* (1951), but she received greatest praise for *The Eagle of the Ninth* (1954), a story of the Romans in Britain, and for *The Lantern Bearers* (1959).

Their vividness was enhanced by line drawings from C Walter Hodges (later illustrators included Charles Keeping and Shirley Felts). Though seriously affected by osteoarthritis, Sutcliff continued to write into the 1980s.

Sutherland, Dame Joan

Born 1926
Australian soprano of international acclaim

Joan Sutherland was born and educated in Sydney. She made her début there as Dido in Henry Purcell's *Dido and Aeneas* in 1947 and came to London in 1951 to continue her training, joining the Royal Opera in 1952 and remaining resident soprano for seven years. Her first appearance at Covent Garden was as the First Lady in *The Magic Flute*.

In 1954 she married her accompanist and coach Richard Bonynge (1930–   ), who became her principal conductor and encouraged her in the coloratura roles for which she became so highly acclaimed. He later became musical director of the Australian Opera Company (1976–85).

She gained international fame in 1959 with her roles in Donizetti's *Lucia de Lammermoor* and Handel's *Samson* and has sung regularly in opera houses and concert halls all over the world, returning to Australia in 1965 for a triumphant tour with her own company. She was created DBE in 1979 and admitted to the Order of Merit in 1991, the year she retired from the stage.

Sutherland, Dame Lucy Stuart

Born 1903 Died 1980
Australian-born British historian, and principal of Lady Margaret Hall

Lucy Sutherland was born in Australia and educated in South Africa and at Oxford, where she became a tutor and in 1928 a Fellow in history; she was also the first woman to speak at the Oxford Union. During World War II she took a post at the Board of Trade, to which she was to return as chairman after the War.

Also in 1945 Sutherland was appointed principal of Lady Margaret Hall, and her contribution to 18th-century studies was recognized when she was elected to a fellowship of the British Academy. Under her leadership the college doubled in size, and she became the first woman pro-Vice-Chancellor of Oxford University (1961–9). She was created DBE in 1969.

Sutherland, Margaret Ada

Born 1897 Died 1984
Australian composer who has written in a variety of forms

Margaret Sutherland was born in Adelaide, South Australia. She studied at the Melbourne Conservatorium of Music and at the age of 19 appeared as piano soloist with the New South Wales State Orchestra under Henri Verbrugghen. She went in 1923 to study in Vienna and London, returning to Australia in 1925, where for many years she was active in music administration and promotional work.

Recognition came late, but her violin concerto (1954) was warmly received and her opera, *The Young Kabbarli*, based on the life of **Daisy Bates**, was performed in 1965. She has written much chamber music, and has set a number of song cycles including one by Australian poet **Judith Wright**.

Suttner, Bertha Félicie Sophie, Freifrau (Baroness) von, née Kinsky

Born 1843 Died 1914
Czech (Austro-Hungarian) novelist and one of the
first women to be a prominent pacifist

Bertha Kinsky was born of Bohemian descent in Prague, the daughter of an imperial general, Count Kinsky. She married Baron Arthur von Suttner (1850–1902), a novelist and engineer, in 1876 and in 1891 founded an Austrian pacifist organization called the Austrian Society of Friends of Peace.

She edited a pacifist journal, *Die Waffen nieder*, which was later published in book form (1889, Eng trans *Lay Down Your Arms, the Autobiography of Martha von Tilling*, 1892). It shocked her readers by its pacifism and was translated into many European languages.

She wrote many other books on pacifism and from 1876 to 1896 corresponded with Alfred Nobel on the subject, which persuaded him to add provision for a peace award to the endowment in his will. Baroness Bertha von Suttner herself was awarded the Nobel Prize for Peace in 1905.

Helen Suzman, 1989

Suzman, Helen, née Gavronsky

Born 1917
South African liberal politician who spoke out for
human rights and against apartheid during her 36
years in parliament

Helen Gavronsky was born in Germiston, in the Transvaal, the daughter of a Lithuanian immigrant. After graduating in economics and statistics from Witwatersrand University, she married Dr Moses Suzman (d.1994) at the age of 20 and then lectured part time at Witwatersrand (1944–52).

Deeply concerned about the apartheid system erected by the National party under Daniel Malan, she joined the opposition United party and was elected to parliament in 1953. She remained with the United party until 1961, when she became MP for the Progressive party (later the Progressive Reform party and Progressive Federal party); for 13 years — until 1974 — she was its sole representative. She gradually gained the respect of the black community, including the ANC leader Nelson Mandela, and, as a member of the South African Institute of Race Relations, was a fierce opponent of apartheid. In 1978 she received the UN Human Rights award.

After 36 uninterrupted years, she retired from parliament in 1989, the year she was created an honorary DBE. She has twice been nominated for the Nobel Peace Prize. Her auto-

biography, *In No Uncertain Terms*, appeared in 1993.

Suzman, Janet

Born 1939
British actress who played many roles for the
RSC and in modern drama

Janet Suzman was born in Johannesburg, South Africa, the niece of the anti-apartheid campaigner **Helen Suzman**. She came to England to complete her studies, and made her acting début in *Billy Liar* in Ipswich in 1962.

That year she joined the newly-formed Royal Shakespeare Company, and became one of its most distinguished players in the course of a lengthy association. She proved at least equally gifted in modern drama, and won great acclaim in plays by Chekov, Ibsen, Fugard and Pinter, among many others.

She has also worked widely in television and film, her roles including Peter Greenaway's celebrated *The Draughtsman's Contract* (1981). From 1969 to 1986 she was married to the director Trevor Nunn, and from 1983 she began to devote more time to teaching her craft.

Swain, Clara A

Born 1834 Died 1910
American physician who became the first female
western missionary doctor in India

Clara Swain was born in Elmira, New York. After some time as a teacher, she entered medicine, graduating from the Women's Medical College of Pennsylvania in 1869.

In 1870 she went to Bareilly, north India, as a missionary of the Methodist Episcopal Church. There she worked among women and children, founding a dispensary and the first women's hospital in India (1874).

In 1885 she started again in another area, becoming medical adviser to the women of the palace of the Rajah of Khetri in Rajpunta, and continuing medical and educational work among local people. She wrote *A Glimpse of India* (1909).

Swanborough, Stella Isaacs, Baroness, *née* Charnaud

Born 1894 Died 1971
English pioneer of social services and founder of the WRVS

Stella Charnaud was born in Constantinople (now Istanbul), and returned to England with her family before World War I. In 1931 she married Rufus Isaacs, 1st Marquess of Reading (d.1935), becoming Marchioness of Reading, and the following year began her volunteer work.

She was invited by the Home Secretary in 1938 to form a women's organization to help with air-raid precautions and by the outbreak of World War II in 1939 the Women's Voluntary Service for Civil Defence (as it was then called) was able to assist with the evacuation of women and children, and with setting up canteens and services for the troops. The organization continued after the war, when 'for Civil Defence' was dropped from the title. (When 'Royal' was added in 1966, it became widely known as the WRVS.) The WVS pioneered community service in the form of 'meals on wheels' and 'home helps'.

Lady Reading was made a life peer in 1958, and was one of the first women to take her seat in the House of Lords.

Swanson, Gloria, *originally* Gloria May Josephine Svensson

Born 1897 Died 1983
American actress who came to fame as a glamorous star during the silent era

Gloria Svensson was born in Chicago. After studying as a singer she entered the nascent film industry as an extra and bit part player in 1915. She became one of Mack Sennett's bathing beauties before an association with director Cecil B de Mille brought her leading roles as chic sophisticates in the front line of the battle of the sexes.

Her many silent features include *Male and Female* (1919), *The Affairs of Anatol* (1921) and *Manhandled* (1924). She formed her own production company and despite the extravagances of the unfinished *Queen Kelly* (1928), she survived the arrival of sound, receiving Academy Award nominations for both *Sadie Thompson* (1928) and *The Trespasser* (1929). However, her film career gradually dwindled away despite a sensational comeback in *Sunset Boulevard* (1950).

Never relinquishing her glamorous star status, she continued to appear on stage and television. She was married six times, and published her autobiography, *Swanson on Swanson*, in 1980.

Swanwick, Helena, *née* Sickert

Born 1864 Died 1939
British suffragette who used journalism to propound her views

Helena Sickert was born in Munich, Bavaria, and educated at a boarding school in France and Notting Hill High School in London. She graduated from Girton College, Cambridge, in 1885.

After a period working as a lecturer in psychology at Westfield College, London, she married Frederick Swanwick (1888), and later became a reviewer for the *Manchester Guardian*, contributing articles on feminist and domestic topics. At the same time she became a member of the North of England Suffrage Society, and edited the suffragist newspaper *The Common Cause* (1909–14).

In 1915 she became the Chairman of the Women's International League for Peace. Her publications include *The Small Town Garden* (1907), her autobiography *I Have Been Young* (1935) and the controversial *Collective Insecurity* (1937) and *Roots of Peace* (1938).

Switzer, Katherine Virginia

Born 1947
American distance runner, the first woman to run the Boston Marathon

Katherine Switzer was born in Amberg, Germany. In 1967 she was unable to gain official entry to the Boston Marathon because of her gender, so she registered as K Switzer. Race officials and other runners attempted to hinder her from finishing by pushing her and tearing her entry number.

As a consequence, the AAU (American Athletic Union) pressured the Boston Marathon to admit women by barring women from all competitions with men (a boycott that had economic impact and resulted in negative publicity).

In 1972 Katherine Switzer ran the Boston Marathon again, this time officially.

Syers, Madge (Florence Madeline), *née* Cave

Born 1882   Died 1917
English ice-skater, a pioneer of women's figure skating

Madge Syers was born in Surrey. As a pioneer in her sport, she tried to break down the old-fashioned attitudes shown towards women competitors. In 1902 she took the bold step of entering the world championships, as there was no real rule preventing women from doing so, and she finished second, much to the horror of the establishment.

Women were afterwards barred from that event, but Syers went on to win two British championships from her male competitors in 1903 and 1904. A women's world championship event was introduced in 1906, which she won in its inaugural year and in 1907. She went on to win a gold medal at the 1908 Olympics as well as a bronze medal in the pairs, skating with her husband Edgar.

Szewinska, Irena

Born 1946
Polish athlete who became the greatest female athlete of her generation

Irena Szewinska was born in Leningrad (now St Petersburg), Russia. Her career spanned five Olympiads from 1964 to 1980. In the first of these she won a gold medal in the sprint relay.

Four years later, at Mexico, she won the 200 metres gold medal. Her greatest triumph came at the Montreal Games of 1976, when she won the 400 metres in a world record time of 49.28 seconds.

Szold, Henrietta

Born 1860   Died 1945
American Zionist leader, founder of Hadassah and a leader in international social service

Henrietta Szold was born in Baltimore, Maryland. She became a teacher, established some of the earliest evening classes for Jewish immigrants, and co-founded the Jewish Publication Society of America, for which she edited the Jewish Yearbook (1892–1916). Following a visit to Palestine in 1909, she became an ardent champion of Zionism (a movement aimed at securing national priveleges and territory in Palestine for the Jews), working to establish peace between Arabs and Jews and a binationalist state.

In 1912 she founded the women's organization Hadassah, serving as its president until 1926. It began to help Jewish refugees and to upgrade medical and child welfare in Palestine. Four years later Szold went to live in Palestine, and in 1927 she became the first woman to be elected to the World Zionist Organization.

With the Nazi rise to power in 1933 she founded Youth Aliyah, through which Jewish children could escape the Holocaust, and in 1940 she founded Lemaan ha-Yeled (later the Szold Foundation), also to promote child welfare. She also found time to translate works from German, French and Hebrew.

t

Tabei, Junko, *née* Ishibashi

Born 1939
Japanese mountaineer, the first woman to climb
Mount Everest

Junko Tabui was born in Miharu Machi. She founded the Japanese Ladies Climbing Club in 1969, and made the second ascent of Annapurna III by a new route the following year. In 1975, International Women's year, she became the first woman to climb Mount Everest as part of an all-female expedition organized by herself and Eiko Hisano. Though injured in an avalanche midway through the climb on May 4th, her strength and stamina prevailed and she refused to call off the expedition. She reached the summit, by the South Col route, on May 16th, a feat described at the time as '99 percent impossible'.

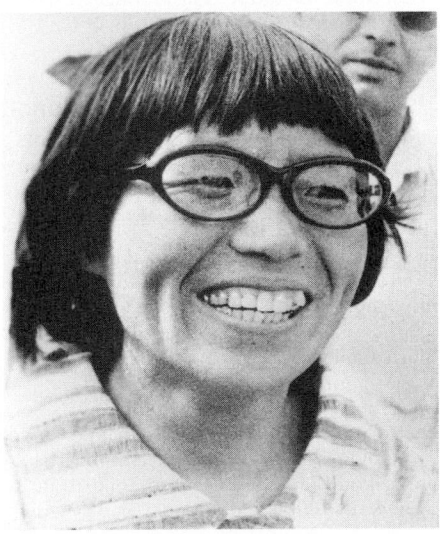

Junko Tabei, 1975

Her expedition was organized on so tight a budget that it cost less than half that of Japan's previous expedition and less than seven times the cost of the Italian expedition of 1973. It was followed by ascents of Shisha Pangma (1981), Peak Communism (1985) and Aconcagua (1987). Junko Tabei has now climbed the highest summits on five continents. A major force in Japanese mountaineering, she is a trustee of the Himalayan Adventure Trust and encourages the conservation of mountain environments.

Taft, Jessie

Born 1882 Died 1961
American social scientist and psychiatric
counsellor who identified the crucial social issue
of her day to be the resolution of social conflict

Jessie Taft was born in Wisconsin. She lived her personal life apart from men, preferring the company of women. She was not a political activist, but she believed that she and other social scientists like herself had a special role to play in the women's movement. Her work is of particular importance because of its emphasis on the social construction of masculine and feminine gender identity, in contrast to the prevailing views on the innateness of differences between women and men.

Implicit in her work were the concepts of 'marginality' of women and 'role strain' — sociological concepts which were developed more fully between 1920 and 1940 in the work of the US sociologists Robert Park (1864–1944) and Talcott Parsons (1902–79), among others.

She considered the primary issue in women's subordination to be psychological rather than political, and was an early exponent of social work and reform work, emphasizing clients' inner psychological problems. Also active in prison reform, she published several essays and research reports, including *Problems in Delinquency — Where do they Belong?* (1922).

Taglioni, Maria

Born 1804   Died 1884
Italian ballet dancer who epitomized the early
19th-century Romantic style

Maria Taglioni was born in Stockholm, the daughter of a Swedish mother and the Italian ballet master Filippo Taglioni, by whom she was trained. She made her début in Vienna in 1822.

Though badly formed and plain, she danced with astonishing grace and individuality, and after some initial setbacks triumphed with her creation of *La Sylphide* in 1832 which marked the great romantic era in ballet. She was one of the first to dance on pointe and is credited with creating a new style of dance incorporating such moves as the arabesque.

She married Count de Voisins in 1832, and ended her career teaching deportment to the British royal children. Her brother Paul (1808–84) and his daughter Marie Paul (1833–91) were also famous dancers.

Tailleferre, Germaine, *originally*
Taillefesse

Born 1892   Died 1983
French composer and longest surviving member of
'Les Six' whose individual achievement is widely
recognized

Germaine Taillefesse was born at Parc-St-Maur, near Paris. She studied at the Paris Conservatory and took lessons from Maurice Ravel. In 1926 she was briefly married to the American writer Ralph Barton; her second husband was the lawyer Jean Lageat.

She became the only female member (and the longest surviving representative) of *Les Six*, an informal grouping of young, like-minded French composers who performed together for a few years from 1917 (the others were Auric, Durey, Honegger, Milhaud and Poulenc). Critical prejudice downgraded her achievement, suggesting that works like the *Concertino* for harp and orchestra (1926) and the *Chansons françaises* (1930) were pale imitations of her male counterparts' works; such views are now unfashionable.

In 1974 Tailleferre (who changed her surname to escape the unfortunate pun it invited) published an autobiography, *Mémoires à l'emporte pièce*.

Takei, Kei

Born 1939
Japanese post-modern dancer and choreographer
whose company is called Moving Earth

Kei Takei was born in Tokyo. She studied there and then travelled on a scholarship to the Juilliard School of Music, where **Anna Sokolow** taught dance. In 1969 she formed her own company, Moving Earth, and began her major work, *Light*, a many-part epic which has over 25 parts lasting at least an hour each. Fifteen sections of this harsh depiction of survival, which starts with the Vietnam War and includes both primitive and contemporary images, were shown in a single performance in 1981.

Talbot, Mary Anne, *known as the*
British Amazon

Born 1778   Died 1808
English woman soldier who served in the army
and the navy disguised as a man

Mary Anne Talbot was an orphan from an early age. After eloping with a Capt Bowen, she accompanied him to St Domingo in disguise as 'John Taylor', a footboy. She later served as a drummer boy in Flanders (1792–3), when she took part in the capture of Valenciennes. Following a destitute period incurred by her own desertion, she found work as a cabin boy and powder monkey in the navy (1793–6). This period included a four-month period in hospital because she was wounded in battle in 1794, a return to sea, and then capture by the French and 18 months' imprisonment. Her sex was finally disclosed when she was seized by a press gang.

In receipt of a small pension because of her war wounds, she was irresponsible with her money and from 1804 to 1807 worked as a domestic servant to Robert S Kirkby, a London publisher, who published her story in the second volume of his *Wonderful Museum* (1804) and in *The Life and Surprising Adventures of Mary Anne Talbot* (1809). Her story is similar to that of **Christian Davies** and **Hannah Snell**.

Tallchief, Maria

Born 1925
American ballet dancer credited with helping
place American ballet on an aesthetic level with
European ballet

Maria Tallchief was born of a Scots-Irish mother and Native American (Osage chief) father in Fairfax, Oklahoma. She studied dance with **Bronislava Nijinska**, and with

George Ballanchine (to whom she was later married, 1946–52) at the School of American Ballet, New York.

She danced with the Ballet Russe de Monte Carlo from 1942 to 1947, when she joined the New York City Ballet and became the principal dancer, appearing in *Swan Lake, Firebird* and others. She danced for the American Ballet Theater (1960–3) and returned to the New York City Ballet in 1963 until her retirement in 1965. She founded the Chicago City Ballet in 1979.

Tamara, Queen, *also called* Thamar

Born before 1160 Died 1212
Queen of Georgia, in Asia, whose empire was greatly expanded during her intelligent and courageous rule

Tamara became co-ruler with her father King George III in 1178 and succeeded to his throne when he died six years later. In need of an heir, she married George Bogolyubski, a debauched warrior prince from Kiev, but after two years she showered him with gifts and sent him into exile. She then had a more fruitful marriage with David Sosland, a prince from the royal house of Bragrationi, and gave birth to a son and a daughter.

Unlike her father, who eliminated potential rivals and castrated his heir and nephew Demna, Tamara kept an eye on her nobles, including Demna's supporters, by insisting on compulsory attendance at court and by accompanying them on their hunting trips. Occasionally she instigated military campaigns and, with her soldiers shouting 'King Tamara', would ride at the head of the army. One such battle involved the defeat in 1205 of a vast Turkish army under the Sultan of Rum at Basiani.

By the time of her death her empire was at the peak of its power and included parts of Russia, Persia, Armenia and Turkey, but her children proved too weak to rule and it was ultimately destroyed by the Mongols. Georgia's national poet, Shota Rustaveli, was reputedly in love with Tamara. His *The Knight in Panther's Skin* is an epic poem about a mythological heroine in a world where men and women are equal.

Tan, Amy

Born 1952
Asian-American writer who focuses on the Chinese immigrant experience

Amy Tan was born in Oakland, California, to Chinese immigrant parents. She became a freelance writer in 1981.

Her novel *The Joy Luck Club* (1989), which looks at the relationship between first-generation American daughters and their Chinese mothers, became a bestseller and was made into a film. Her other novels include *The Kitchen God's Wife* (1991), which continues the themes of mother-daughter relationships and male domination, and *Moon Lady* (1992).

Tandy, Jessica

Born 1907 Died 1994
English-born actress who became a leading stage and screen actress in America

Jessica Tandy was born in London and became a naturalized American citizen in 1954. She made her London début in 1929, and on Broadway the following year. She established herself as a major stage star, with roles opposite Gielgud in *Hamlet* (1934) and as Blanche Du Bois in *A Streetcar Named Desire* (1947) among her many credits.

She appeared in a number of plays on Broadway with her second husband, Hume Cronyn (1911–), including *A Delicate Balance* (1966), *The Gin Game* (1977) and *Foxfire* (1982). She acted in many films, and won an Academy Award for her title role in *Driving Miss Daisy* (1989).

Tarbell, Ida Minerva

Born 1857 Died 1944
American journalist and writer, one of the first women to be labelled a 'muckraker' for her investigative journalism

Ida M Tarbell was born in Erie County, Pennsylvania, and educated at Allegheny College. She was associate editor of *The Chautauquan* (1883–91) and then studied in Paris at the Sorbonne (1891–4) and joined *McClure's Magazine* on the editorial staff (1894–1906). Her explosive denunciation of John D Rockefeller's fortune-building methods, *History of the Standard Oil Company* (published in book form in 1904), established the place of women in the new 'muckraking' journalism.

Her previous books had been conventional lives of Napoleon, Madame Roland and Abraham Lincoln. She joined Lincoln Steffens (1866–1936) and other *McClure's* writers in running the *American* magazine (1906–15), campaigning against corruption and big business interests. Her feminist writing included *The Business of Being a Woman* (1912) and *The Ways of Women* (1915). Her history, *The Nationalizing of Business* (1936), was a standard work on American post-Civil War economic growth for 20 years. Her last book was an autobiography, *All in the Day's Work* (1939).

Taussig, Helen Brooke

Born 1898 Died 1986
American paediatrician who pioneered cardiac
surgery for children

Helen Brooke Taussig was born in Cambridge, Massachusetts. She received her MD from Johns Hopkins University in 1927 and later became the first woman to become a full professor there.

Her work on the pathophysiology of congenital heart disease was done partly in association with the cardiac surgeon Alfred Blalock (1899–1954), and between them they pioneered the 'blue baby' operations which heralded the beginnings of modern cardiac surgery. The babies were blue because of a variety of congenital anomalies which meant that much blood was passing directly from the right chamber of the heart to the left without being oxygenated in the lungs.

Taussig was actively involved in the diagnosis and after-care of the young patients on whom Blalock operated, and their joint efforts helped create a new specialty of paediatric cardiac surgery. She also drew attention in 1962–3 to the danger associated with the use of the tranquillizer thalidomide which had caused many babies in Europe to be born deformed.

Taylor, (Winifred) Ann, *née* Walker

Born 1947
British Labour politician and a significant
presence on the Opposition front bench

Ann Walker was born in Motherwell, Scotland, and educated at Bradford and Sheffield universities. She trained as a teacher, became an Open University tutor, and married David Taylor in 1966. In 1974 she entered parliament as MP for Bolton West (1974–83) and then returned in 1987, representing Dewsbury, West Yorkshire.

She was appointed deputy education spokesperson to Neil Kinnock in 1979, and in 1981–3 was shadow housing minister. In 1990 she was given the first Cabinet-level portfolio dealing with the environment — shadow minister for environmental protection — until in 1992 she became shadow Secretary of State for Education. In 1994 she was appointed shadow Leader of the House of Commons and shadow Chancellor of the Duchy of Lancaster, retaining the former position but relinquishing the latter in the shadow Cabinet reshuffle of 1995.

Taylor's publications include *Choosing Our Future — Practical Politics for the Environment* (1992).

Taylor, Annie Royle

Born 1855 Died c.1918 or 1920
English Christian missionary and traveller, the
first European woman to enter Tibet

Annie Taylor was born in Cheshire. She was a sickly child and her schooling was irregular but she felt a strong calling to God's service. In 1884 she joined the China Inland Mission and worked amongst Tibetans in China and India for seven years, before attempting to travel into Tibet to continue her work. In September 1892, disguised as a pilgrim, with her servant Pontso as companion, she set out on her 1,300-mile journey. After seven months of incredible hardship, during which she was spurred on by her faith, she was betrayed by her guide and arrested just three days from Lhasa.

She was the first European woman to enter Tibet and got closer to Lhasa than anyone else had for nearly 40 years. She later established the Tibetan Pioneer Mission at Yatung, and retired to England around 1908.

Taylor, Elizabeth

Born 1932
American film actress as famous for her private
life as for her acclaimed appearances on the silver
screen

Elizabeth Taylor was born in London of American parents. In 1939 she moved with her family to Los Angeles, where her beauty took the eye of the Hollywood film world, and she made her screen début in 1942 at the age of 10, in *There's One Born Every Minute*. As a child star she made a number of films including two 'Lassie' stories (1943 and 1946), *National Velvet* (1944) and *Little Women* (1949). She was first seen as an adult in *The Father of the Bride* (1950) at the time of her first marriage, to Nick Hilton of the hotelier family. Her career continued through the 1950s with films including *Raintree County* (1957), *Cat on a Hot Tin Roof* (1958), and *Suddenly Last Summer* (1959), for all of which she received Oscar nominations. In 1960 she won her first Academy Award for *Butterfield 8*.

She married first Nick Hilton, 1950, then the actor Michael Wilding in 1952, then the producer Mike Todd in 1957, who was killed in an air-crash the following year. In 1959 she married Eddie Fisher, divorcing him in 1964. The making of the spectacular *Cleopatra* (1962) provided the background to her well-publicized romance with her co-star Richard Burton whom she married for the first time in 1964. She made several films with Burton, including *Who's Afraid of Virginia Woolf?* in

1966, for which she won her second Academy award. Divorced from and remarried to Richard Burton, she was divorced from him again in 1976, and married the US Senator John Warner in 1978, from whom she separated in 1981. She married Larry Fortensky in 1991 but separated from him in 1995.

Taylor's other films include *Reflections in a Golden Eye* (1967), *A Little Night Music* (1976) and *The Mirror Crack'd* (1981). She made her stage début in New York in 1981 with *The Little Foxes*. After treatment for alcohol addiction, she resumed acting, mostly in television with *Malice in Wonderland* (1985), *Poker Alice* (1986) and other films.

Taylor, Elizabeth, *née* Coles

Born 1912 Died 1975
English novelist whose hallmark is observation of middle-class life in the south-east of England

Elizabeth Coles was born in Reading, Berkshire, the daughter of an insurance inspector. She was educated locally at the Abbey School and worked as a governess and librarian. She married John Taylor, the director of a sweet factory, when she was 24, and wrote her first novel, *At Mrs Lippincote's* (1945), while her husband was in the Royal Air Force.

This was followed by such novels as *Palladian* (1946), *A Wreath of Roses* (1949), *A Game of Hide-and-Seek* (1951), *Angel* (1957), *The Wedding Group* (1968), *Mrs Palfrey at the Claremont* (1971) and *Blaming*, published posthumously in 1976.

Her shrewdly observant writing about middle-class English life is reminiscent of **Jane Austen**, with whom she is quite often compared. Like Austen, her life was more domestic than literary. Her stories, collected in four volumes (1954–72), are no less admired than her novels.

Taylor, Helen

Born 1831 Died 1907
English women's rights activist and school reformer

Helen Taylor was the stepdaughter of philosopher and social reformer John Stuart Mill (1806–73). After his death in 1873 she entered politics in London.

She was a radical member of the London School Board (1876–84), and agitated for wide-ranging reforms of the capital's industrial schools. An advocate of land nationalization and taxation of land values, she founded the Democratic Federation in 1881 and campaigned for female suffrage, but after failing

to be nominated to enter parliament in 1885, she retired to Avignon.

On returning to England in 1904, her ability as a public speaker was used to great advantage by the emerging suffragette movement.

Tchalenko, Janice

Born 1942
English ceramicist who specializes in high-fired stoneware and coloured glazes

Janice Tchalenko was born in Rugby, Warwickshire. After six years in the Foreign Office, she studied at Putney School of Art (1965–7) and at Harrow School of Art (1969–71). In 1971 she set up her own studio in East Dulwich, London, and taught part-time at Camberwell and Croydon schools of art.

Her work has a strong sense of form, and in 1979 she started experimenting with the use of brighter colours for decoration of her pots. Her works continue to be basically functional in form, but are increasingly sculptural with an exuberance and boldness of colour and decoration.

Since 1984 Tchalenko has worked with the Dart Pottery, designing new ranges of shapes and colours for their domestic pottery. She also lectures at the Royal College of Art. In 1988 she won the Radio 4 Enterprise Award, and her work can be seen in the collections of the Victoria & Albert Museum, London, Los Angeles Museum of Art, USA and many others worldwide.

Teasdale, Sara

Born 1884 Died 1933
American poet, the first recipient of the Pulitzer Prize for poetry

Sara Teasdale was born in St Louis, Missouri, and educated at the Mary Institute and Hosmer Hall.

She received her Pulitzer Prize in 1918 for her collection *Love Songs* (1917), and initially earned a reputation as a writer of 'feminine' love poetry. However, much of her poetry is in fact based on her own sheltered early life and unhappy marriage, and expresses the conflicting needs for independence and freedom, love and security.

She wrote nine collections of poetry, two of which were published after her death, a suspected suicide.

Tebaldi, Renata

Born 1922
Italian operatic soprano whose most impressive roles included Violetta in Verdi's La Traviata *and the title role in Puccini's* Tosca

Renata Tebaldi was born in Pesaro and trained at Parma Conservatory. She made her début as Elena in Boito's *Mefistofele* at Rovigo in 1944, and was invited by Toscanini to appear at the post-war re-opening of La Scala, Milan, in 1946, remaining there until 1954.

She first performed in the USA in San Francisco in 1950, and at the Metropolitan, New York, in 1955, and has appeared in England, France, Spain, and South America.

Te Kanawa, Dame Kiri Janette

Born 1944
New Zealand operatic soprano whose
performances and recordings have brought her
worldwide fame

Kiri Te Kanawa was born in Gisborne, Auckland, of Maori and British parentage. She began her career as a pop singer and after winning many prizes and awards in New Zealand and Australia she came to the London Opera Centre, and made her début with the Royal Opera Company in 1970.

Her first major role was the Countess in Mozart's *Marriage of Figaro*, which has been followed by a brilliant international career of soprano roles, including those of Donna Elvira, Desdemona, Mimi and Micaela.

She was made a DBE in 1982 and published *Land of the Long White Cloud: Maori myths and legends* in 1989.

Tekawitha, Kateri

Born c.1656   Died 1680
Native American Catholic convert whose
exemplary life earned her the title 'Lady of the
Mohawk'

Kateri Tekawitha was born in the Native American village of Ossernenon, New York. Her mother was a Christian Algonquin who had been brought up among the French but had been captured by the Iroquois and married to a Mohawk chief. Smallpox at the age of four left Kateri orphaned and nearly blind.

On conversion to Christianity in 1676, she was rejected by her people and fled nearly 200 miles to the Indian Christian village of Sault St Louis, near Montreal. She received her first communion at Christmas 1677 and took a private vow of chastity in 1679.

She was credited with many miracles, and beatified in 1980.

Telakowska, Wanda

Born 1905   Died 1986
Polish designer and printmaker who was active in
the Modernist Movement

Wanda Telakowska was born in Poland and she began her designing and printmaking career as a member of the Polish design group LAD. After World War II she organized and ran the production department of the Ministry of Culture in Poland. From 1950 she was a director of the Institute of Industrial Design, a research body in Warsaw, and throughout the difficult Stalinist period, until 1956, she protected and sponsored many Modernist designers.

Telakowska was an advocate of modern design derived from Polish roots and she continued the Cracow School tradition into the communist period in Poland. During the mid-1950s she organized collaborative projects, bringing together professional designers, folk artists and children. These projects resulted in both ceramics and textiles being produced from the 1950s onwards.

Tempest, Dame Marie, *stage name of* Mary Susan Etherington

Born 1864   Died 1942
English actress who gave her name to a special
type of hinge

Marie Tempest was born in London. She trained as a singer, and appeared in light opera and musical comedy in the early part of her career. After a success as Nell Gwynn in the comedy *English Nell* in 1900, she abandoned the musical stage, and concentrated on theatrical comedies.

She toured extensively in the international arena, and was especially admired for her interpretation of the elegant, charming women who populated the work of writers like Noël Coward, St John Ervine, or two of her three husbands, Cosmo Gordon-Lennox and W Graham Browne.

She was appointed DBE in 1937, and retired in 1938. A type of hinge used to secure doors on raked stages is named after her, due to her insistence on their use.

Temple, Shirley

Born 1928
American child entertainer during the Depression
and later a diplomat and ambassador

Shirley Temple was born in Santa Monica, California. She was precociously talented and appeared in a series of short films from the age of three and a half, graduating to full stardom with a leading role in *Little Miss Marker* (1934). An unspoilt personality who sang, danced, and did impressions, she captivated Depression-era audiences and becoming the world's favourite golden-haired moppet in films like *Curly Top* (1935) and *Dimples* (1936).

Her appeal faded, however, and when attempts at an adult comeback floundered, she retired from the screen and became involved with Republican party politics as Mrs Shirley Temple Black. She was appointed America's representative to the United Nations General Assembly in 1969 and served as Ambassador to Ghana (1974–6), White House chief of protocol (1976–7) and Ambassador to Czechoslovakia (1989–92).

ten Boom, Corrie

Born 1892 Died 1983
Dutch evangelist and author who helped Jews
escape from Germany and survived imprisonment
at Ravensbruck

Corrie ten Boom was born in the Netherlands. She worked as a watchmaker in her father's shop in Haarlem, and started clubs for teenage girls.

The family's wartime role in helping some 700 Jews escape the Germans led to their imprisonment in 1944. On unexpected release from Ravensbruck concentration camp in 1945, Corrie carried out plans made with her sister Betsie (who did not survive) to establish a home for rehabilitating concentration camp victims in Holland and a home for refugees in Darmstadt, Germany.

The royalties on her many books, such as *The Hiding Place* (1971, filmed 1973), *Tramp for the Lord* (1974) and *In My Father's House* (1976), were used to support Christian missionaries.

Tencin, Claudine Alexandrine Guérin de

Born 1681 Died 1749
French writer and courtesan, one of 18th-century
society's most prominent figures

Claudine Guérin de Tencin was born in Grenoble. She entered a convent at 16 but managed to be absolved from her vows and in 1714 moved to Paris, where her wit and beauty attracted a crowd of lovers, among them the regent Philippe d'Orléans and Cardinal Dubois. She had much political influence, enriched herself, and facilitated the rise to power of her brother, Cardinal Pierre Guérin de Tencin (1680–1758).

With the death of the regent and the cardinal in 1723, her importance waned and in 1726 she was imprisoned for a short time in the Bastille, after one of her lovers had shot himself in her house. Her later life was more decorous, and her salon one of the most popular in Paris. The writer Bernard le Fon-

Madame de Tencin

tenelle (1657–1757) was one of her oldest lovers, and the mathematician and philosopher Jean d'Alembert (1717–83) one of her children.

Her romances include *Mémoires du Comte de Comminges* (1735, 'Memoirs of the Count of Comminges'), *Le Siège de Calais* (1739, 'The Siege of Calais') and *Les Malheurs de l'amour* (1747, 'Misfortunes of Love').

Tennant, Emma Christina

Born 1937
English novelist who uses features of established
genres in an unconventional way

Emma Tennant was born in London and brought up in Scotland. Her first novel was published under the name 'Catherine Aydy' in 1964. Her fiction has shown a willingness to deal in imaginative and unconventional fashion with themes drawn from genre models, including fantasy, the supernatural, science fiction and detection, as in the apocalyptic *The Time of the Crack* (1973), in which a strange faultline threatens London, or *Hotel de Dream* (1976), in which dream and reality merge.

Gothic strains are evident in *The Bad Sister* (1978), arguably her best book, and *Wild Nights* (1980). She draws directly on literary predecessors in *Two Women in London: The Strange Case of Ms Jeykll and Mrs Hyde* (1989) and *Faustine* (1992), while *Sisters and Strangers: A Moral Tale* (1990) is a fable in which Adam and Eve have survived until the present.

She writes from a feminist perspective, and founded and edited the radical literary magazine *Bananas* (1975–9) which published the early work of **Angela Carter**, **Elaine Feinstein** and Sara Maitland, among others.

Tennant, Kylie

Born 1912 Died 1988
Australian novelist, historian and children's author

Kylie Tennant was born in Manly, New South Wales, and educated at the University of Sydney. Her earliest books, from *Tiburon* (1935) to the award-winning *The Battlers* (1941), describe the 1930s Depression as experienced in city and outback. Her portrayal of the Australian character is achieved with affection, sympathy and humour.

Tennant spent a week in gaol in search of authenticity for *Tell Morning This* (1978), which pictures the seamy underside of Sydney in wartime; it was originally published in a censored version in 1953 as *The Joyful Condemned*. Her children's non-fiction work *All the Proud Tribesmen* (1959) won the Children's Book Award in 1960; she also wrote three plays for children.

Her last book, *Tantavallon* (1983), is a surreal story which effectively combines the tragic and comic strands pre-eminent in her writing.

Teresa of Ávila, St, *also called* Santa Teresa de Jésus

Born 1515 Died 1582
Spanish Carmelite mystic and writer whose writings have become spiritual classics

Teresa was born into a noble family in Ávila, Old Castile, where in 1533 she entered a Carmelite convent. About 1555 her religious exercises reached an extraordinary pitch of asceticism; she experienced ecstasies, and the fame of her sanctity spread. In 1562, with papal permission, she founded the Convent of St Joseph to re-establish the ancient Carmelite rule, with additional observances, later extending her reforms, which were adopted by many convents within her lifetime.

Although she wrote some poetry, she is remembered mainly for her prose works, primarily her autobiography, *Libro de la vida* (1562) and *Las moradas* (1577, 'The Interior Castle'), in which she discusses her spiritual experiences by comparing the soul to a castle which contains many secret chambers, *Camino de perfección* ('Way of Perfection', 1583), and her *Libro de las fundaciones* (1610, 'The Book of Foundations'), in which she describes her struggle to found various convents, but which is also a detailed and revealing chronicle of her tempestuous times.

She stresses the physical aspects of her experiences and uses erotic imagery to convey a sense of spiritual rapture. Her distinctive prose style effectively captures the rhythm and intimacy of the spoken language. She was canonized in 1622.

Teresa of Calcutta, Mother, *originally* Agnes Gonxha Bojaxhiu

Born 1910
Albanian Roman Catholic nun and missionary to India who worked with slum-dwellers and lepers

Agnes Bojaxhiu was born in Yugoslavia of Albanian parents. She lived in Skopje as a child. She went to India in 1928, where she joined the Sisters of Loretto (an Irish order in India) and taught at a convent school in Calcutta, taking her final vows in 1937. She became principal of the school but in 1946 she received a definite call from God to serve him by helping the poor, and left the convent two years later to work alone in the slums.

She went to Paris for some medical training before opening her first school for destitute children in Calcutta. She was gradually joined by other nuns and her House for the Dying was opened in 1952. Her sisterhood, the Order of the Missionaries of Charity (started in 1950), became a pontifical congregation (subject only to the pope) in 1956. The congregation now has 2,000 sisters in 200 branch houses in several countries. In 1957 she started work with lepers and established a leper colony called Shanti Nagar ('Town of Peace') near Asanol.

She was awarded the Pope John XXIII peace prize in 1971 and the Nobel Prize for Peace in 1979.

Tereshkova, Valentina Vladimirovna

Born 1937
Russian astronaut and politician, the first woman in space and the tenth human being in orbit

Valentina Tereshkova was born in Maslennikovo, Yaroslavl, the daughter of a farmer. She was a cotton mill worker and amateur parachutist with 126 jumps to her credit before she joined the cosmonaut corps in 1962. As a 2nd Lieutenant in the Soviet air force she was the solo pilot in the space capsule Vostock 6 which was launched from the Tyuratam Space Station in the USSR on 16 June 1963. She remained in orbit for three days, returning after 48 orbits and travelling a distance of 1,242,800 miles.

She then took up a career in politics, becoming deputy to the USSR Supreme Soviet (1966–

89), chair of the Soviet Women's Committee (1968–87) and a member of the Supreme Soviet Praesidium (1974–89). Subsequently she became USSR People's Deputy (1989–91), head of the USSR International Cultural and Friendship Union (1987–91), and chaired the Russian Association of International Cooperation from 1992.

She was twice the recipient of the Order of Lenin, among other honours, was proclaimed 'Hero of the Soviet Union', and published *Valentina, First Woman in Space* in 1993.

Terry, Dame Ellen Alice

Born 1848 Died 1928
English actress who from 1878 to 1902 dominated
the English and American theatre

Ellen Terry was born in Coventry, the daughter of a provincial actor and sister of the actor Fred Terry. She was apprenticed to the stage from infancy, and at eight appeared as Mammilius in *The Winter's Tale* at the Prince's Theatre, London. From 1862 she played in Bristol and after a brief marriage to the painter George Frederick Watts in 1864, and a second retirement from the stage (1868–74) — during which time her two children, Edith and Edward Gordon Craig (later an actor and stage designer), were born to her lover, architect Edward William Godwin — she established herself as the leading Shakespearian actress in London.

Her natural gentleness and vivacity made her excel, particularly as Portia and Ophelia, and she would have made an ideal Rosalind, but Henry Irving's professional jealousy withheld such an opportunity at the Lyceum. In 1903 Terry went into theatre management without Irving and engaged her son to produce Ibsen's *Vikings*. James Barrie and George Bernard Shaw wrote parts especially for her, such as Lady Cicely Waynflete in the latter's *Captain Brassbound's Conversion* (1905).

She married Charles Kelly (Wardell) in 1876 and in 1907 the American actor, James Carew. She was created DBE in 1925.

Tetrazzini, Luisa

Born 1871 Died 1940
Italian coloratura soprano who dazzled with her
voice rather than her appearance

Luisa Tetrazzini was born in Florence, a sister of the soprano Eva Tetrazzini. She made her début in 1890 in Florence as Inez in Giacomo Meyerbeer's *L'Africaine*. Following successes in Spain, Portugal, Russia and South America, she made her début in the USA in 1904 and in London in 1907.

She appeared mostly in Italian opera of the older school, achieving some of her most notable successes in *Lucia di Lammermoor, La Traviata* and *Rigoletto*. She sang in London and in America — with the Manhattan (1908–10), Metropolitan (1911–12), and the Chicago Opera companies (1913–14).

In 1921 she published *My Life of Song* and 10 years later retired from the concert stage. It is said that her third husband was responsible for squandering her vast fortune before she died.

Tewkesbury, Joan

Born 1936
American screenwriter and director best known
for her work with Robert Altman

Joan Tewkesbury was born in Redbanks, California. She trained as a dancer as a child, and later choreographed and directed productions at the Little Theatre in Los Angeles. She was encouraged by the film director Robert Altman, who made her script supervisor on *McCabe and Mrs Miller* (1971).

Her best-known works are her screenplays for Altman's films *Thieves Like Us* (1974) and the acclaimed *Nashville* (1976). She made her début as a film director with *Old Boyfriends* in 1979, but to a muted critical reception. She has also directed for stage and television.

Tey, Josephine, *pseud of* Elizabeth Mackintosh

Born 1897 Died 1952
Scottish crime writer and playwright who often
wrote under the pseudonym 'Gordon Daviot'

Elizabeth Mackintosh grew up in Inverness and trained as a PE teacher. Her main invention, police inspector Alan Grant, tended to prefer cerebral rather than physical exercise. He was introduced in Tey's first novel, *The Man in the Queue* (1929, published in the USA as *Killer in the Crowd*, 1954).

Her most famous novel, and most extreme example of Grant's aversion to exercise, is *The Daughter of Time* (1952), in which Grant conducts a masterpiece of retrospective investigation from his hospital bed and solves the mystery of Richard III's alleged murder of the little princes in the Tower of London.

Miss Pym Disposes (1946) and *The Franchise Affair* (1948) were non-Grant mysteries, as was the popular *Brat Farrar* (1949, published in the USA as *Come and Kill Me*, 1951); it dealt with double and demonic 'twins' and unconsciously revealed Tey's essential Scottishness. This also emerged in her plays *Queen of Scots* (1934) and *Leith Sands* (1946), and in an impressive biography of Claverhouse (1937).

Thais

4th century BC
Athenian courtesan famous for her wit and beauty

Thais was, according to a doubtful legend, the mistress of Alexander the Great, whom she accompanied on his campaign to Asia and whom she induced during a fit of drunkenness to burn down the royal palace at Persepolis (330BC).

After Alexander's death (323BC), she had several children by Ptolemy Lagos, King of Egypt.

Tharp, Twyla

Born 1941
American dancer and choreographer who creates modern dance with a popular appeal

Twyla Tharp was born in Portland, Indiana. An accomplished musician and dancer as a child, she danced with the Paul Taylor Dance Company (1963–5), and founded her own small troupe in 1965. Her work was at first structural and sombre but from *Eight Jelly Rolls* (1971, set to the jazz piano of Jelly Roll Morton), she struck a note which delighted audiences.

Coupe, a piece made to music by the Beach Boys for the Joffrey Ballet in 1973, was a sensation, as was *Push Comes to Shove* (1976), the first dance made by an American choreographer for the Russian star Mikhail Baryshnikov, then at the American Ballet Theatre.

Her work includes *The Bix Pieces* (1971), *Sue's Leg* (1976), *Nine Sinatra Songs* (1982), *Bach Partita*, for American Ballet Theatre (1984), two Broadway works (*When We Were Very Young*, 1980, and *The Catherine Wheel*, with music by David Byrne, 1983), and dance for the films *Hair* (1979), *White Nights* (1985) and *I'll Do Anything* (1992). In 1995 she created a new ballet for the Royal Ballet using music by Rossini — *Mr Wordly-Wise*. Her autobiography, *Push Comes to Shove*, appeared in 1992.

Tharpe, Sister Rosetta, *née* Rubin

Born 1915 Died 1973
American gospel and blues singer, especially famous as a gospel performer

Sister Rosetta Tharpe was born in Cotton Plant, Arkansas. She sang and accompanied herself on electric guitar, switching without discomfort between sacred songs and very earthy blues material. With the important exception of **Mahalia Jackson**, she has been the most successful female gospel performer ever, with wartime hits like 'Didn't It Rain' (1944). Her appearance at the Newport Jazz Festival in 1968, like Jackson's 10 years earlier, was sensational and revived her career.

She recorded doggedly through her last years, despite losing a leg due to a thrombosis which also impaired her speech. She died in Philadelphia on the eve of a recording session.

Thatcher, Margaret Hilda Thatcher, Baroness, *née* Roberts

Born 1925
English Conservative stateswoman who became Britain's first woman Prime Minister

Margaret Roberts was born in Grantham, the daughter of Alderman Alfred Roberts, a grocer with a small, but expanding, business. She lived over the premises with her parents and sister and assisted in the shop. She was educated at Grantham High School and at Somerville College, Oxford, where she read chemistry. She stood unsuccessfully as a Conservative candidate for Dartford in 1950 and 1951, in which year she married Denis Thatcher. She studied law, specializing in tax law, and was called to the Bar in 1953.

In 1959 she was elected MP for Finchley, and from 1961 to 1964 was joint Parliamentary Secretary to the Ministry of Pensions and National Insurance. She joined the shadow Cabinet in 1967. She was Secretary of State for Education and Science (1970–4) and joint shadow Chancellor (1974–5). In 1975 she was elected leader of the Conservative party, the first woman party leader in British politics.

The Conservative party was elected to government in May 1979 and re-elected with a large majority in June 1983, despite the worst unemployment figures for 50 years. She was greatly assisted by the tide of popular feeling generated by the Falklands War and by the disarray in the opposition parties. Under her leadership, the Conservative party moved towards a more right-wing position, placing considerable emphasis on the market economy and the shedding of public sector commitments through an extensive privatization programme. She also embarked on trade union reform, aided by Norman Tebbit. The coal dispute of 1984–5 ended in victory for the government. Despite the persistence of high unemployment she maintained her parliamentary majority in the 1987 general election, again greatly helped by a fragmented opposition.

Margaret Thatcher, 1991

Two years later her resistance to the growing influence of other EC member states over the British economy and to their plans for economic union triggered the resignation of Chancellor Nigel Lawson and of Foreign Secretary Geoffrey Howe in 1990. Her leadership was challenged, and in November 1990 she was succeeded by John Major. In 1992 she did not stand for parliament in the general election and launched the Thatcher Foundation to promote free enterprise and democracy thoughout the world, particularly in Eastern Europe.

During her 11 years in office she established a personal political philosophy, popularly spoken of as 'Thatcherism', based on a mixture of values gained during her formative years and the resolution to persevere with policies despite objections from her critics and doubts among her supporters. She was made a life peer in 1992. In 1993 she published her autobiography *The Downing Street Years 1979–1990*, and made a BBC documentary on the same subject.

Theodora

Born c.500 Died 548
Byzantine empress as the wife of Justinian I (ruled 527–65)

Theodora was the daughter of a circus beartamer. An actress and noted beauty, she became mistress to Justinian, who raised her rank, and married her in 525. As his most trusted counsellor, she wielded enormous

influence in the work of government, leading many to believe that it was she rather than Justinian who was the real ruler of Byzantium.

She promoted the religious and social policies that she considered important, and saved the throne by her courage at the crisis of the Nika riots (532). During this incident she persuaded her husband not to flee Constantinople, but to face the political factions (the Blues and Greens) who were organizing a massive protest against the acts of the government. The rebels were finally forced into the Hippodrome by the general Belisarius and executed.

Theodora was also known for lavishing her bounty on the poor, especially the unfortunate of her own sex.

Theophano

Born c.955 Died 991
Byzantine princess and Holy Roman Empress as the wife of King Otto II (ruled 973–83)

Theophano was the daughter of the Byzantine Emperor Romanus II. In 972 she married King Otto II in Rome as a symbol of the union of the Eastern and Western Empires. He ruled as Holy Roman Emperor, with Theophano as Empress, from 973 until his death in 983.

Theophano had six children, including the future Emperor Otto III. She took an active role in politics and with her mother-in-law **Adelaide** secured the throne for Otto on his father's death and ruled as co-regent from 983 to 991. She dealt successfully with enemies at home and abroad during his minority, including Henry the Wrangler and Boleslav II of Bohemia, and secured Lotharingia for the empire. Her influence is visible in many of his later policies, especially his ambitions for the empire.

Thérèse of Lisieux, St, *also called* Theresa, *originally* Marie Françoise Thérèse Martin

Born 1873 Died 1897
French nun and virgin saint whose brief, holy life inspired many

Marie Martin was born in Alençon, France, the youngest daughter of a watchmaker. An intensely religious child, she entered the Carmelite convent of Lisieux in Normandy at the age of 15, where she remained until her death from tuberculosis nine years later.

She lived commendably under the Carmelite regime, embracing simple obedience to the Gospels and rejecting the easier path of external mortification. During her last years she was asked to write a spiritual account of her childhood and later life which was edited and published posthumously as the *Histoire d'une âme*. Showing how the most ordinary and insignificant person can attain sainthood by following her 'little way' of simple, childlike, trusting and obedient Christianity, the book immediately gained great popularity and the young nun was credited with interceding in innumerable miracles, attracting near-universal veneration.

She was canonized in 1925, and in 1947 associated with **Joan of Arc** as patron saint of France. Her feast day is 3 October.

Thirkell, Angela Margaret, *née* Mackail

> Born 1891 Died 1961
> *English novelist who created lives for the descendants of characters created by Trollope*

Angela Mackail was born in London, the daughter of the Scottish classical scholar and Oxford Poetry Professor John William Mackail, granddaughter of the painter Sir Edward Burne-Jones, and cousin of Rudyard Kipling. After a five-year marriage that ended in divorce in 1917, she married the Australian George Thirkell and spent the years 1920–9 in Australia before returning to England when the marriage came to an end. She lived in her parents' home in Kensington, where she enjoyed a lively social life and began to write.

Her first novel was *Ankle Deep* (1933), which was followed by *Trooper to the Southern Cross* (1934), and more than 30 novels set in 'Barsetshire', dealing with the descendants of characters from Anthony Trollope's Barsetshire novels, including *Coronation Summer* (1937) and *Growing Up* (1943).

Her son was the novelist Colin MacInnes (1914–79).

Thomas, (Martha) Carey

> Born 1857 Died 1935
> *American feminist and educationalist who helped to create high standards in women's education*

Carey Thomas was born into a Quaker family in Baltimore, Maryland, the daughter of an eminent physician. Educated privately and at Cornell University, she wanted to take a PhD at the newly founded Johns Hopkins University, of which her father was a trustee, but was allowed to attend only if she concealed herself behind a screen. Eventually the Swiss allowed her to undertake a postgraduate degree at Zürich (1882) and on her return she helped with the establishment of Bryn Mawr

College for girls in Philadelphia, being appointed its first Dean.

Quickly realising the need for a high-quality preparatory school to feed into the college, she set about founding the Bryn Mawr School for girls in Baltimore with Mary Garrett, who became its president, and three others. It opened in 1885, with Thomas as treasurer.

An ardent suffragist, she was the first President of the National College Women's Equal Suffrage League in 1908, and later an active member of the National American Woman Suffrage Association. She also established summer schools for women working in industry (1921) and wrote *The Higher Education of Women* (1900).

Thomas, Margaret Haig see

Rhondda, Margaret Haig Thomas, Viscountess

Thompson, Dorothy

> Born 1894 Died 1961
> *American writer and feminist, one of the 20th century's most famous journalists*

Dorothy Thompson was born in Lancaster, New York, the daughter of a Methodist minister, and educated at the Lewis Institute of Chicago and Syracuse University. She began her career in the 1920s as a foreign correspondent in Europe, and came to notice in 1921 when she interviewed Empress Zita of Austria after Zita's husband Charles, the last of the Habsburg emperors, had been unsuccessful in his attempt to regain the throne of Hungary.

While working for the *New York Evening News* in Berlin, Thompson met the novelist Sinclair Lewis (1885–1951). They married in London in 1928 and returned to the USA for a time (divorced 1942). Back in Europe in the 1930s, she began reporting on the rise of Nazism, only to become in 1934 the first foreign correspondent to be expelled by Adolf Hitler. In 1936 she began the highly popular newspaper column 'On the Record' for the *New York Herald Tribune*, and she also continued her aggressive antifascist writings, speeches and broadcasts, for which she is perhaps best remembered. She also wrote for the *Ladies Home Journal* for 20 years.

Voted in 1935 second only to **Eleanor Roosevelt** in female importance in the USA, Thompson was also an ardent suffragist and influential writer. Her books include *New Russia* (1928), *I Saw Hitler!* (1932) and *The Courage to Be Happy* (1957).

Thompson, Edith

Died 1923
English murderer whose trial at the Old Bailey
was sensational at the time

Edith Thompson and her accomplice Frederick Bywaters were tried in 1922 for stabbing her husband on the way home from a London theatre. The trial took place at the Old Bailey, the couple were found guilty, and in spite of many petitions for reprieve were executed.

Thompson, Emma

Born 1959
English actress whose many awards include an
Oscar for her screenplay of Sense and Sensibility

Emma Thompson was born in London and eduated at Newnham College, Cambridge. She began performing as a member of the Cambridge Footlights and worked extensively as a comedienne and in the long-running West End musical *Me and My Girl* (1985–6) before asserting her dramatic capabilities with diverse, award-winning roles in John Byrne's television series *Tutti Frutti* (1987) as spiky Glaswegian art student Suzi Kettles, and *Fortunes of War* (1988) as the witty, vulnerable **Olivia Manning**.

A one-woman series *Thompson* (1988), in which she wrote and performed comedy sketches, has been the one major disappointment in a career of almost unbroken success. She married Kenneth Branagh in 1989 (separated 1995), and appeared opposite him on stage in the likes of *Look Back in Anger* (1989) and in such films as *Henry V* (1989), *Dead Again* (1991), *Peter's Friends* (1992) and *Much Ado About Nothing* (1993). Her other films include *The Tall Guy* (1988), *Howards End* (1992), for which she received both the BAFTA Best Actress award and the Academy Award for Best Actress as well as several international prizes, *In the Name of the Father* (1993) and *Carrington* (1995), based on the life of the artist Dora Carrington (d.1932), a fringe member of the Bloomsbury group who fell in love with the homosexual biographer Lytton Strachey.

Thompson was again nominated for the Academy Award for her performance in *The Remains of the Day* (1993), but it was won by **Holly Hunter** for her performance in *The Piano*. However in 1996 she won two prestigious Golden Globe awards — for screenwriting and best dramatic picture — and an Oscar for her adaptation of **Jane Austen's** *Sense and Sensibility*. She starred in the film

Emma Thompson, 1993

as Elinor Dashwood and won another BAFTA Best Actress award.

Thompson, Flora Jane, *née* Timms

Born 1876 Died 1947
English social historian who, from memory,
documented the erosion of rural society

Flora Thompson was born in Juniper Hill, Oxfordshire. She left school at 14 to work in the local post office. She married young and with her postmaster husband settled in Bournemouth, writing mass-market fiction to help support her increasing family.

In her sixties she published the semi-autobiographical trilogy combined as *Lark Rise to Candleford* (1945), its three parts — *Lark Rise* (1939), *Over to Candleford* (1941) and *Candleford Green* (1943) — having appeared separately.

It is an outstanding feat of observation and memory, showing the erosion of rural society before modern industrialism. Though she was accused of snobbery as an author, Thompson depicted the upper classes who were on the verge of extinction and satisfied many hundreds of readers.

Thompson, Helen Bradford (Woolley), *née* Bradford

Born 1880 Died 1954
American psychologist, social scientist and social
reformer who specialized in the study of mental
differences between men and women

Helen Bradford Thompson surveyed the literature of the previous 25 years and found that the prevailing scientific opinion was that physiological differences between men and women correlated with psychological differences and mental capacity, and in turn with the different social roles ascribed to men and women. She was thus one of the first social scientists to identify, elaborate, and proceed to refute the 'biological theory' of the psychological and social differences between the sexes and had a significant influence on later research into the relationship between human physiology and psychology.

In 1900, when experimental study of mental traits was still a novelty and IQ tests had not been developed, she set out to obtain a complete and systematic statement of the psychological similarities and differences of the sexes by the experimental method. She was innovative in her field for her time, in seeking similarity when presented with raw data, and environmental causes when presented with variance of data.

Influential in her insistence that science should both guide, and be informed by, social reform, she went on to work in the fields of child development, social reform and women's suffrage. Among her publications is an account of her research into sex differences, *Mental Traits of Sex* (1900).

Thompson, Mary Harris

Born 1829 Died 1895
American doctor and medical pioneer

Mary Thompson was born in New York State and worked as a teacher to pay for her college education. In 1863 she graduated from the New England Female Medical College in Boston. She moved to Chicago where she opened a hospital for women and children in 1865, and founded the Women's Medical College (1870), both of which were burned down in the Chicago fire (1871), but re-opened in 1871 and 1873 respectively.

In later life she became Professor of Clinical Obstetrics and was elected to the American Medical Association in 1886 where she was the first woman to present a paper.

Thorndike, Dame (Agnes) Sybil

Born 1882 Died 1976
English actress who helped to make the Old Vic a famous centre of Shakespearian production

Sybil Thorndike was born in Gainsborough. She trained as a pianist but turned, despite considerable discouragement, to the stage. She made her first stage appearance with Ben Greet's Pastoral Players in *The Merry Wives of Windsor* in 1904. After four years spent touring the USA in Shakespearian repertory, she became a prominent member of **Miss Horniman's** Repertory Company in Manchester.

She worked at the Old Vic from 1914 to 1919, and subsequently collaborated with her husband, actor-manager Sir Lewis Casson, whom she married in 1908, on a biography of **Lilian Baylis**. In 1924 she played the title role in the first English performance of George Bernard Shaw's *Saint Joan*, and during World War II she was a notable member of the Old Vic Company, playing at the New Theatre, London.

To mark their golden wedding, Thorndike and Casson appeared together in *Eighty in the Shade* (1958), which **Clemence Dane** had written for them. Thorndike continued to act well into her eighties, creating a gallery of notable elderly lady characters. She was created DBE in 1931.

Tilley, Vesta, *professional name of* Lady de Frece, *née* Matilda Alice Powles

Born 1864 Died 1952
English comedienne who delighted music-hall audiences with her impersonations of men

Matilda Powles was born in Worcester. She first appeared as The Great Little Tilley, aged four, in Nottingham, and did her first male impersonation the following year. She adopted the name of Vesta Tilley and became, through her charm, vivacity and attention to sartorial detail, the most celebrated of all male impersonators.

Of the many popular songs sung by her, 'Burlington Bertie', 'Following in Father's Footsteps', 'Sweetheart May', and 'Jolly Good Luck to the Girl who Loves a Soldier' are the best known. She wrote *Recollections of Vesta Tilley* (1934).

Ting Ling *see* Ding Ling

Tinsley, Pauline

Born 1928
English dramatic soprano with a wide-ranging repertory which takes her all over the world

Pauline Tinsley was born in Wigan. She studied singing in Manchester, at the Opera School, London, and with Eva Turner. She made her début in London in 1951 as Desdemona in Rossini's opera *Otello*.

She excels as a singing actress in roles as diverse as Elektra, Turandot, the Dyer's Wife (in Strauss's *Die Frau ohne Schatten*), Lady

Macbeth, Kostelnička (*Jenufa*), Brünnhilde (*Die Walküre*), Santuzza (*Cavalleria rusticana*) and Lady Billows (*Albert Herring*).

In additon to the UK, she has sung at houses throughout the USA, at La Scala Milan, Hamburg, Amsterdam, and elsewhere in Europe.

Tituba

Born c1648   Died 1692
Caribbean Indian woman who nearly perished in the Salem Witch Hunt

Tituba was born in a Spanish settlement in the West Indies and brought as a slave to Salem Village, Massachusetts, by the Rev Samuel Parris.

Local girls and women would consult her to tell them their fortunes and stories, but they accused her of witchcraft during the Salem witchcraft trials in 1692.

Though tried and found guilty, she was eventually acquitted because of her penitence and the intervention of the governor's wife.

Tivy, Joy

Born 1924
Irish geographer who has done important work in the field of organic resources

Joy Tivy was educated at the universities of Dublin and Edinburgh. After periods in teaching and planning she started her lecturing career at Edinburgh University and was later appointed to Glasgow University, where she became Professor of Georgraphy and head of the geography department.

She has held various posts, being editor of the *Scottish Geographical Magazine* (1955–65), chairing the Scottish Field Studies Association (1984–7, 1990), and serving on the Scottish Advisory Committee to the Nature Conservancy Council (Scotland) (1974–80) and the Geography Board of the Committee for National Academic Awards (1976–84).

She has published widely; *Biogeography: The Role of Plants in the Ecosphere* (1982) is regarded as a pioneering text in the geography of organic resources.

Tizard, Dame Catherine Anne

Born 1931
New Zealand politician who served as the Queen's representative from 1990 to 1996

Catherine Tizard was born in Auckland. After teaching at the university there for 20 years (1963–83), during which time she served as city councillor from 1971, she became Mayor

of Auckland in 1983. Outspoken and popular, she achieved the completion of the Aotea Centre for the performing arts and continued her wide-ranging involvement in the life of the city.

She was appointed DBE in 1984 and the first woman Governor-General of New Zealand in 1990. Her term ended in 1996.

Tomlin, Lily (Mary Jean)

Born 1939
American comedy actress of stage and screen noted for her versatility and finely honed characterizations

Lily Tomlin was born in Detroit, Michigan. A pre-med student at Detroit's Wayne State University, she dropped out to pursue a career performing in local cabaret and later moved to New York. Modestly active in all areas of showbusiness, her big break came as part of the ensemble in television's *Laugh-In* (1960–72) where her most popular characters included malicious telephone operator Ernestine and willful toddler Edith Ann.

She received an Oscar nomination for a dramatic role in her film début *Nashville* (1975) and her subsequent, often infrequent film appearances include *The Late Show* (1977), *Nine To Five* (1980), *Short Cuts* (1983) and *All Of Me* (1984).

She is also a television performer and recording artist, and her comic skills and acute sense of observation were seen to their best advantage in the one-woman stage shows *Appearing Nitely* (1977) and *The Search For Signs Of Intelligent Life In The Universe* (1985–6).

Torvill, Jayne

Born 1957
English ice-skater best known for her award-winning pairs skating with Christopher Dean

Jayne Torvill was born in Nottingham. She started skating at the age of 10, and met her skating partner Christopher Dean in 1975. The pair were six times British champions, and won the 'Grand Slam' of World, Olympic, and European ice-dance titles in 1984. With her partner she received a record 136 perfect '6s' (the highest award a judge can give in ice-skating).

After retiring from amateur competition in 1985, she performed professionally with Dean in their own ice-show and also worked as a choreographer. At the height of their success, Torvill and Dean's personal relationship had become the fascination of tabloid newspapers, but Torvill married Phil Christiansen, a rock and roll sound engineer, in 1990.

In 1994 she and Dean returned to competitive skating and won the European Championship in January. Apparently disappointed with their bronze medal won at the Winter Olympics at Lillehammer, they decided to pull out of the World Championships and return to professional skating. That year they published their story, *Fire on Ice*.

Tourtel, Mary

Born 1874 Died 1948
English writer and illustrator who created the
character of Rupert the Bear

Mary Tourtel was born in Canterbury and educated at Canterbury Art School. She began her career in the 1890s but found lasting fame with her 'Rupert the Bear' cartoon strip in the *Daily Express* between 1920 and 1935, after which time Rupert was carried on by others.

About 50 Rupert books were published. Her hero is usually accompanied in his adventures by such characters as Bill Badger, Algy Pug and Podgy Pig; sometimes a pair of magic flying boots appears or there is an encounter with smugglers; other occasions involve simply a pleasant trip to the seaside.

Unlike the work of A A Milne or **Beatrix Potter**, Tourtel's Rupert has insufficient wit or irony to please many older readers.

Tower, Joan Peabody

Born 1938
American composer whose rejection of serial
music has resulted in a more relaxed style

Joan Tower was born in La Rochelle, New York, and raised in South America. On her return to the USA, she studied at Bennington College, Vermont, and at Columbia University, New York City. After graduating in 1967, she was co-founder and pianist of the Da Capo Chamber Players (1969–84).

Since 1972 she has taught at Bard College, Annandale-on-Hudson. *Breakfast Rhythms I/II* (1974–5) dramatized Tower's growing disillusionment with serial music; mid-composition, she revised her style in favour of a less strict, more tuneful approach evident in her three great concerti — for clarinet (1988), flute (1989) and orchestra (1991).

Townsend, Sue (Susan)

Born 1946
English humorist, novelist and playwright who
made her name with the Adrian Mole diaries

Sue Townsend was born in Leicester. She is best known for *The Secret Diary of Adrian Mole Aged 13¾* (1982) and *The Growing Pains of Adrian Mole* (1984). Witty and perceptive works, they are written in the form of a diary from the point of view of an intellectually ambitious adolescent boy living in the Midlands, who copes with a precarious family life and emotional problems and fantasies (mostly involving the beautiful teenager Pandora Braithwaite). His adventures continue in three further books, including *Adrian Mole: The Wilderness Years* (1993), in which Mole, aged 23¾, battles on in a perplexing world.

Her plays include *Womberang* (1979), a comedy set in the waiting room of a hospital gynaecology department, *Bazaar and Rummage* (1983), which explores the problems faced by women suffering from agoraphobia, and *The Great Celestial Cow* (1984), which looks at the cultural problems of Asian women in Leicester. Her novel, *The Queen and I* (1992), which imagines the demise of the British Royal family, became a bestseller and, in 1994, Townsend's most successful stage play.

Traba, Marta

Born 1930 Died 1984
Argentinian novelist, short-story writer, literary
critic and art historian in the forefront of new
Latin American feminist writing

Marta Traba was born in Argentina, the daughter of Spanish immigrants. She graduated from the Universidad Nacional in Argentina with a doctorate in literature in 1950, but spent most of her life in other countries, most notably Colombia, where she took nationality the year she died.

She founded the magazine *Prisma* in 1954 and Bogotá's Museum of Modern Art in 1965, and the following year won the Casa de las Americas Prize for her novel *Las ceremonias del verano* ('Ceremonies of Summer'). She was an outspoken advocate of human rights and democracy and was expelled from Colombia in 1967 for protesting against the presence of the military at the university.

Her most widely acclaimed novels are *Homérica Latina* (1979, 'Homeric Latin'), *Conversación al sur* (1981, 'Conversation of the South') and *En cualquier lugar* (1984, 'Anywhere'). One of her main themes is the difference between the utterable and the unutterable, the said and the understood. She was killed in a plane crash on the way to the first Spanish American Culture Conference in Bogotá.

Traill, Catherine Parr, *née* Strickland

Born 1802   Died 1899
English-born Canadian writer whose work focused
on the social conditions and experiences of
frontierswomen

Catherine Parr Strickland was born in Kent, England. She distrusted fiction, believing that it seduced judgement. Instead she devoted herself to narratives on flora and fauna and, later, to depicting life in the Canadian wilderness. By the age of 30 she had written several books for children and on natural history. In 1832 she emigrated to Upper Canada with her new husband Thomas Traill.

She is best known for *The Backwoods of Canada: Being Letters from the Wife of an Emigrant Officer; Illustrative of the Domestic Economy of British America* (1836), which focuses on the problems of pioneer women on the Canadian frontier.

She and her sister **Susanna Moodie** left behind a body of work on the Canadian frontier. Traill's reflected the social conditions, culture and natural beauty of Ontario, Canada. One of her last publications was *Pearls and Pebbles; or, Notes of an Old Natulalist* (1895).

Traquair, Phoebe Anna

Born 1852   Died 1936
Irish embroiderer, illustrator and enameller, one
of the most renowned enamellers of her period

Phoebe Anna Traquair was born in Dublin and educated at Dublin School of Art. In 1873 she married Ramsay Traquair, the head of the Natural History Museum in Edinburgh. Her work featured regularly in *Studio* magazine and she came to be regarded as one of the best enamellers of her time.

Much of her later work was of a religious nature and throughout her career she carried out various commissions, mainly enamelled, bright, figurative triptychs, including work for the Scottish architect Sir Robert Lorimer, St Mary's Cathedral, Edinburgh, and many other churches and public buildings in Scotland.

She was awarded medals at the International Exhibitions in Paris, St Louis, and London. In 1887 she remarried, her full name becoming Phoebe Anna Traquair Reid.

Trask, Betty (Margaret Elizabeth)

Born 1895   Died 1983
English writer of light romantic novels whose
recurring theme is the triumph of true love

Betty Trask lived reclusively in Frome, Somerset. She published the first of more than 50 novels, *Cotton Glove Country*, in 1928, and continued writing until the late 1950s. Her books tend towards the heart-throb genre, with decent, middle-class characters and such florid titles as *Desire Me Not* (1935) and *Thunder Rose* (1952).

Trask is best known today for her bequest, in 1983, of about £400,000 in order to create an annual award for novels of a non-experimental nature (the first winner of which was Ronald Frame).

After her death, it was noted in *The Times* that although her novels dwelt upon love, there had never been any reported romance in her own life.

Trason, Ann Bethune

Born 1960
American ultra-runner who is generally
acknowledged to be the best, regardless of gender

Ann Trason was born in San Francisco, California. Ultra-running is an endurance sport consisting of races on road and/or trails longer than the 26.2-mile/41.3km marathon, typically 50 or 100 miles (80.5 or 160.5km).

Trason has won the sport's premier event, the Western States 100 Mile Endurance Run, four times and with each of these victories set a new women's course record. The sporting goods manufacturer Nike sponsors her as the alpha athlete of ultra-running; she is the only ultra-runner to be sponsored.

In 1994 she was first in the world in the races covering 100 miles, 50 miles, 100 kilometres and 50 kilometres.

Traubel, Helen

Born 1899   Died 1972
American opera singer who became the leading
Wagnerian soprano at The Met

Helen Traubel was born in St Louis, where she made her début in 1923. She first sang at the New York Metropolitan in 1937, then again two years later as Sieglinde.

She became the leading Wagnerian soprano there after **Kirstin Flagstad**'s departure in 1941, but resigned in 1953 after a dispute over her nightclub appearances.

She later worked in film and television, and wrote detective novels.

Travers, Mary

Born 1937
American folk-singer and activist who sang with
Peter, Paul and Mary

Mary Travers was born in Louisville, Kentucky. In 1961 she formed a folk-singing trio, Peter, Paul and Mary, with Paul Stookey and Peter Yarrow. Their music combined folk music with a social idealism, popularizing the songs of such writers as Woody Guthrie, Pete Seeger and Bob Dylan.

Their signature songs include 'Puff the Magic Dragon', John Denver's 'Leaving on a Jet Plane', Seeger's 'If I Had A Hammer' and Dylan's anti-war 'Blowin' in the Wind'.

When the group disbanded in 1971, Travers pursued a solo singing and lecture career combined with social activism. In 1980 the trio reunited with the *Reunion* album.

Tremain, Rose

Born 1943
English novelist, dramatist, historian, and
short-story writer

Rose Tremain was born in London and educated at the Sorbonne and East Anglia University, where she began lecturing in Creative Writing in 1984. Her first two books appeared only in the USA: *The Fight for Freedom for Women* (1973) surveys the suffragette movement in Britain and the US, while her life of Stalin (1975) makes a special study of his upbringing in order to analyse his adult actions.

Her first novel, *Sadler's Birthday*, was published in 1976. Others include *The Swimming Pool Season* (1985), *Restoration* (1989), which looks at the reign of Charles II in order to study contemporary Britain and is her best-known novel, and *Sacred Country* (1992), which won the James Tait Black Memorial Prize.

She has also written for the stage and radio, and her *Temporary Shelter* was published in *Best Radio Plays of 1984*.

Triduana, St

4th century
Christian religious and virgin saint who gouged
out her own eyes because of their beauty

Triduana is said to have come to Scotland with St Regulus (also called St Rule), the traditional bearer of St Andrew's relics to Scotland, and lived at Rescobie in Angus. Legend relates that, troubled by the attentions of the local king and learning of his admiration for her eyes, she plucked them out and sent them to him.

She retired to Restalrig, near Edinburgh, where there is a well once famous as a cure for eye diseases, for which Triduana is invoked.

Until the 16th century the church at Restalrig was an important centre of pilgrimage, but it was razed by Scottish reformers. Triduana's feast day is 8 October.

Trier Mørch, Dea

Born 1941
Danish novelist and artist who writes on family
life and the predicament of the working woman

Dea Trier Mørch grew up in Copenhagen with her unmarried architect mother and several siblings. She trained in graphics in Denmark and continued her education at art colleges in Eastern Europe before working in the socialist artist's collective '*Røde Mor*' ('Red Mother'). Her first published books record her impressions of the Soviet Union and Poland.

She made her breakthrough with *Vinterbørn* (1976, Eng trans *Winter's Child*, 1986), a collective novel set in a maternity ward at a Copenhagen hospital, and lovingly illustrated by the author. With the women's perspective predominating, the text depicts pregnancy and childbirth as radicalizing experiences, carrying with them the potential of an alternative community. The novel achieved considerable success in Denmark and abroad, and has also been made into a film.

Kastaniealleen (1978, 'Chestnut Avenue') is a sensitive exploration of the relationships between an elderly couple and their grandchildren, while *Den indre by* (1980, 'The Inner City') highlights the problems of combining family life with an active political commitment, especially for women.

Trimmer, Sarah, *née* Kirby

Born 1741   Died 1810
English author and promoter of Sunday schools
whose success attracted the Queen's interest

Sarah Kirby was born in Ipswich, the only daughter of the artist John Joshua Kirby. The family moved to London around 1755, and later to Kew, where her father was Palace clerk of works. She married James Trimmer of Brentford in 1762, and outlived him and all her children.

From the experience of educating her six sons and six daughters, she became interested in establishing Sunday Schools for children and adults. Her success at Brentford in 1786 led to Queen **Charlotte** seeking her advice for the town of Windsor. A textbook on education followed.

Trimmer compiled religious and other textbooks for charity schools, and produced picture-books and classroom charts for pre-school children.

Tristan (y Moscosa), Flora Céleste Thérèse Henriette

Born 1803   Died 1844
French socialist who wrote an important
manifesto for women's emancipation

Flora Tristan y Moscosa was born in Paris, the illegitimate daughter of a Peruvian nobleman and a Frenchwoman. Her father died very suddenly when she was very young, and she had only a sporadic education.

In 1821 she married her employer, Chazal, a lithographer, but was unable to divorce under French law. In 1833 she travelled to Peru in an attempt to reclaim her inheritance and on her return to Paris she became part of the literary group which published *Gazette des Femmes*.

She subsequently travelled to London to see working-class conditions there for herself and published her findings in *Promenade dans Londres* (1840). She is best remembered for her work *L'Union ouvrière* (1843), a manifesto for women's emancipation

Trollope, Frances, *née* Milton

Born 1780   Died 1863
English novelist who wrote 115 volumes in all,
now mostly forgotten, unlike those of her
famous son

Frances Milton was born in Stapleton, near Bristol. In 1809 she married Thomas Anthony Trollope (1774–1835), a failed barrister and fellow of New College, Oxford. They had six children, of which one, Anthony Trollope (1815–82), became a famous novelist.

In 1827 her husband fell into dire financial difficulties, which were not relieved by moving to Cincinnati, Ohio, in 1827. During her three years in the USA, Mrs Trollope amassed the material for her *Domestic Manners of the Americans* (1832), a critical and witty book much resented in America. Left a widow in 1835, she travelled widely on the Continent, writing articles and fiction for her livelihood, and eventually settled in Florence (1843), where she lived until her death.

Of her novels, the most successful were *The Vicar of Wrexhill* (1837), and *The Widow Barnaby* (1839), with its sequel, *The Widow Married* (1840).

Trotula

11th century
Italian obstetrician and early medical practitioner

Trotula is thought to have lectured on child-birth at the University of Salerno in the 11th century, and she is generally regarded as one of the earliest medical practitioners. Some historians attribute to her a treatise on gynaecology in a 15th-century manuscript which was originally written in Salerno, an important medical teaching centre at the time, during the 11th or 12th century.

Trubnikova, Mariya Vasilevna, *née* Vasilevna

Born 1835   Died 1897
Russian feminist and educator who found ways of
helping disadvantaged women

Mariya Vasilevna was born in Chita in Siberia and educated by her grandmother. When she was 18 she married Constantin Trubnikov and they lived in Moscow, socializing with the leading intellectuals of the day.

In the 1860s she established a feminist group which became known as 'The Triumvirate' with two friends, Nadezhda Stasova and Anna Filosova. Together they set up societies which provided income, education and accommodation for poor women.

She is best remembered for her campaigning work for a university education specifically designed for women which resulted in the foundation of the *Alarchinskii* and *Vladimir* programmes.

Truth, Sojourner, *originally* Isabella Van Wagener

Born 1797   Died 1883
American black evangelist, a leading orator who
fought for women's suffrage and the abolition of
slavery

Isabella Van Wagener was born a slave in Ulster County, New York. After working for several years for a variety of owners, she eventually gained her freedom and settled in New York, taking her surname from her previous master, and becoming an ardent evangelist.

Having had visions since childhood, in 1843 she felt called by God to change her name to Sojourner Truth, and to fight against slavery and for women's suffrage. As she preached across the USA, her infectious style of speaking drew large crowds. In 1850 she produced a biography to support herself entitled *The Narrative of Sojourner Truth*, which she had dictated to Olive Gilbert.

Influenced by the women's suffrage movement from the early 1850s, she worked for that cause for the rest of her life, much encouraged by **Lucretia Mott**. In 1864 she was appointed counsellor to the freedmen of Washington by Abraham Lincoln, and continued to promote Negro rights, including educational opportunities, until her retirement in 1875.

Tsushima Yuko

Born 1947
Japanese writer and novelist, one of the first to become popular writing about women's issues

Tsushima Yuko was born in Tokyo, the daughter of writer Osamu Dazai (1909–48). She became a prolific and popular writer of short stories, one of the first of a generation of Japanese women writers to achieve a degree of popular success whilst writing about what might broadly be termed 'women's issues'. 'Silent Traders' and 'The Light of Night Runs After Me' have both won prizes.

Tsushima has also written novels: *Choji* (1978, Eng trans *Child of Fortune*, 1983) is the tale of a divorcee who finds herself pregnant in a society where there is considerable stigma attached to unmarried motherhood.

Tsvetayeva, Marina

Born 1892   Died 1941
*Major Russian poet, dramatist and memoirist who holds a high position similar to that of **Anna Akhmatova** among Russian 20th-century poets*

Marina Tsvetayeva was brought up mainly in Moscow, the daughter of a university professor father and pianist mother. She travelled widely with her parents and studied at the Sorbonne, publishing her first collection, *Vecherny albom* ('Evening Album') in 1910. Her pallid, romantic early poetry was technically well accomplished and gained her a high reputation, but now receives little attention.

Her husband Sergei Efron fought against the Bolsheviks (for her, Satan), and much of the poetry of her middle period — in particular *Lebediny stan* (1917–22, 'The Swans' Encampment') — is anti-Bolshevik in spirit. She also wrote a number of historical verse plays. Boris Pasternak, in writing of her *Versty* (1922, 'Versts'), spoke of the 'intense lyrical power of her poetic form'.

She emigrated in 1922, and became, in Paris, a symbol of Russia-in-exile. Her memoirs of such writers as the Russian poets Alexander Blok, Maximilian Voloshin, and Mikhail Kuzmin are illuminating, although somewhat nervously self-centred. She proved too individualistic to be able to remain in Paris, returned to Russia in 1939, but was evacuated to a remote town in 1941 and hanged herself. Her poetry has been outstandingly well translated by **Elaine Feinstein**.

Tubman, Harriet

Born c.1820   Died 1913
American abolitionist who was known as 'the Moses of her people'

Harriet Tubman escaped from slavery in Maryland in 1849, and from then until the American Civil War (1861) she was active on the slave escape route (the Underground Railroad), making a number of dangerous trips into the South and leading over 300 people to freedom.

A committted Christian who acknowledged that her strength and guidance came from God, she acquired fame among abolitionists, and counselled John Brown before his attempt to launch a slave insurrection in 1859.

During the Civil War she was a Northern spy and scout, but despite her work for the Federal Army was denied a federal pension until 1897.

Tucker, Sophie, *professional name of* Sonia Kalish

Born 1884   Died 1966
Russian-born American singer and vaudeville entertainer

Sophie Tucker made her début in New York as a blackface comedienne and retained strong blues and jazz elements in her singing style. Together with her larger-than-life persona, it won her the title 'the last of the red hot mommas'. Like **Ethel Waters**, she made a significant contribution to perceptions of women in entertainment.

She remained close to African-American composers like Eubie Blake and Shelton Brooks, who wrote her theme song 'Some of These Days', the title of which she appropriated for her 1945 autobiography.

Tucker, Tanya

Born 1958
American country singer who sang 'Delta Dawn' as a teenager

Tanya Tucker was born in Seminole, Texas. In 1972, at the age of 14, she recorded 'Delta Dawn', which reached the Top Ten in three recording industry charts. Her albums include *Delta Dawn* (1973), *Here's Some Love* (1976), *Tanya Tucker's Greatest Hits* (1978), *TNT* (1979), *Changes* (1982) and *Tennessee Woman* (1990).

In 1991 Tucker received the Country Music Association Female Vocalist of the Year award.

Tuckwell, Gertrude Mary

Born 1861 Died 1951
English trade unionist who worked to improve women's working conditions

Gertrude Tuckwell was born in Oxford and educated at home by her father, a master at New College School. In 1885 she became a teacher in London.

From 1893 she worked as secretary for her aunt **Emily Dilke**, the wife of MP Sir Charles Dilke, and became interested in politics. She later became President of the Women's Trade Union League and campaigned for better working conditions for women.

She was one of the first female Justices of the Peace and in 1926 served on the Royal Commission on National Health Insurance. A life-long philanthropist, she published *The State and its Children* in 1894.

Turischeva, Lyudmila Ivanovna

Born 1952
Soviet gymnast, one the great classical gymnasts of all time

Lyudmila Turischeva was born in Grozny, Checheno-Ingushkaya ASSR. She began gymnastics in 1965, was a member of the Soviet team by the following year, and went on to win all four of the world's major titles: world championship, Olympic, World Cup and European.

She won the world title in 1970 and the European title in Minsk in 1971. She won the combined gold at the Munich Olympics in 1972, although she did not claim gold at any individual piece of apparatus, but in 1973 at the European championships she took gold in every discipline, going on to take the world championship title again the following year and the World Cup in 1975. She later became coach to the Soviet team.

Turlington, Christy

Born 1969/70
American model who was the first to achieve supermodel status

Christy Turlington was born and raised in San Francisco, the daughter of an American father and Salvadoran mother. While she was competing in a gymkhana in Miami, a photographer took her picture and sent it to a model agency.

She began modelling at the age of 15 and after three years moved to New York to work regularly for *Vogue*. In 1988 she signed an exclusive multi-million-dollar contract with Calvin Klein to promote fashion and Eternity perfume, and moved to Los Angeles. However she tired of this and after the contract was terminated by mutual consent in 1989, she returned to full-time modelling.

Since then Turlington has given up catwalk modelling, but has an advertising contract with Maybelline cosmetics and continues to work for magazines. Though at the top of her profession, she began with no ambitions to be a model and plans to write when she retires.

Turner, Ethel Mary

Born 1870 Died 1958
English-born Australian novelist and children's author whose first book became a classic of Australian literature

Ethel Turner was born in Balby, Yorkshire. Her father, Bennett George Burwell, died before she was two, and for her writing she took her stepfather's surname. She moved to Australia at the age of nine. With her sister Lilian she started *Iris*, a magazine for schoolgirls, for which Ethel wrote the children's page, later doing the same for the *Illustrated Sydney News* and the *Bulletin*.

Her first book, *Seven Little Australians* (1894), is now a classic of Australian literature. It has been in print ever since publication, was filmed as early as 1939, and has been adapted for British and Australian television and as a stage musical. A sequel, *The Family at Misrule*, came out in 1895 and there followed a steady stream of juvenile books, short stories and verse.

Her daughter Jean Curlewis (1899–1930) edited the children's column in the Sydney *Daily Telegraph*, wrote a number of books for older children including *The Ship that Never Set Sail* (1921), and collaborated with her mother on such books as *The Sunshine Family: a Book of Nonsense for Girls and Boys* (1923).

Turner, Kathleen

Born 1954
American film actress whose clinched her successful career in the early 1980s playing Joan Wilder opposite Michael Douglas

Kathleen Turner was born in Springfield, Missouri. She studied at the Central School of Speech and Drama in London, then returned to New York and was eventually cast in a television soap opera (1978–80). Her first feature film appearance was as the conniving wife in the contemporary film noir *Body Heat* (1981).

Though she was an exceptional femme fatale, with her honey-blonde hair, sensuous lips and an ebullient, no-nonsense manner, she managed to avoid stereotyping and appear in a varity of roles. Her stardom was consolidated with the popular cliffhanger *Romancing The Stone* (1984), following by its sequel, *Jewel Of The Nile* (1985).

Later accomplishments have included *Crimes Of Passion* (1984), *Prizzi's Honor* (1985), and *Peggy Sue Got Married* (1986), for which she was nominated for a Best Actress Oscar. She later provided Jessica Rabbit's husky tones in *Who Framed Roger Rabbit* (1988) and appeared in *House of Cards* (1992) and *Serial Mom* (1993).

Turner, Lana (Julia Jean Mildred Frances)

Born 1920 Died 1995
American film actress whose beautiful figure earned her the nickname 'Sweater Girl'

Lana Turner was born in Wallace, Idaho. Legend has it that as a teenager she was spotted sipping a soda at Schwab's Drugstore on Sunset Boulevard and asked if she would like to be in the movies. She duly appeared as an extra in *A Star Is Born* (1937) and came under contract to MGM, cast in a string of undemanding but decorative roles.

Groomed for stardom, she appeared opposite Clark Gable (1901–60) in *Honky Tonk* (1941), and though her glamour meant she was rarely called upon to act, she did have some more persuasive appearances as the femme fatale in *The Postman Always Rings Twice* (1946) and the alcoholic movie star in *The Bad And The Beautiful* (1952). Later, she suffered in style through a succession of glossy, racy melodramas including the popular *Peyton Place* (1957) and *Imitation Of Life* (1959).

She has also appeared on stage and in such television series as *The Survivors* (1969) and the soap opera *Falcon Crest* (1982–3). Married seven times, she often won more attention through her stormy private life than her professional activities. In 1982 she published an autobiography *Lana: The Lady, The Legend, The Truth*.

Turner, Tina, *professional name of* Annie Mae Bullock

Born 1938
American pop singer who recorded hits with her former husband Ike and became a superstar in middle age

Annie Mae Bullock was born in Nutbush, Tennessee. She met Ike Turner in a nightclub in St Louis, Missouri, joined his Revue and then married him (1958). Together they made hits like 'Poor Fool' (1961), 'River Deep, Mountain High' (1966), allegedly one of the greatest pop records ever made, and 'Nutbush City Limits' (1973), and developed a sexy stage routine before divorcing in 1976.

Tina turned to acting in Pete Townshend's *Tommy* (1974) and he produced her *Acid Queen* album (1975). Her career was in decline in the later 1970s, but the success of 'Let's Stay Together' and the album *Private Dancer* (1984) propelled her to huge stardom and endless media hype of the 'sexiest granny' sort.

Turner-Warwick, Dame Margaret Elizabeth Harvey, *née* Moore

Born 1924
English physician, first woman President of the Royal College of Physicians of London (1989–92)

Margaret Moore was born in London. After medical education at Lady Margaret Hall, Oxford, and University College Hospital, London, she undertook post-graduate training at University College Hospital and at the Brompton Hospital in London. In 1950 she married the urologist and surgeon Richard Turner-Warwick (1925–).

She became a Consultant Physician at the **Elizabeth Garrett Anderson** Hospital (1962–7) and at the Brompton and London Chest Hospitals (1967–72), concurrently serving as senior lecturer at the Institute of Diseases of the Chest. Appointed Professor of Thoracic Medicine at the Cardiothoracic Institute, University of London, in 1972, she became Emeritus Professor on her retirement in 1987; she was also Dean of the Institute (1984–7).

She was created DBE in 1991.

Tussaud, Marie, *née* Grosholtz

Born 1761 Died 1850
Swiss modeller in wax who gave her name to the famous musem known as 'Madame Tussaud's'

Marie Grosholtz was born in Strasbourg. She was apprenticed to her uncle Dr Philippe Curtius in Paris at an early age and inherited his wax museums after his death in 1794. After the Revolution, she attended the guillotine to take death masks from the severed heads. Following a short imprisonment, she married a French soldier, François Tussaud, but separated from him in 1800 and went to England with her younger son, Francis.

She toured Britain with her life-size portrait waxworks, a gallery of heroes and rogues, and in 1835 set up a permanent exhibition in Baker Street, London, which moved to Marylebone Road in 1884. These premises were destroyed by fire in 1925, but were rebuilt on the same site. The exhibition still contains her own handiwork, notably of **Marie Antoinette**, Napoleon, Sir Walter Scott, and Burke and Hare in the Chamber of Horrors, the last two having been joined by a succession of notable murderers, including John Christie with his kitchen sink.

Tutin, Dorothy

Born 1930
English actress who made her name in classical, contemporary and cinematic drama

Dorothy Tutin was born in Surrey. She made her stage début in 1949, and was a member of both the Bristol Old Vic and the Old Vic in London, where she began to build her reputation with distinguished performances in plays by Graham Greene, Anouilh and Ibsen, among others.

She joined the Shakespeare Memorial Company in Stratford-upon-Avon in 1958, where she was widely admired in both Shakespeare and contemporary roles, scoring a particular success in John Whiting's *The Devils* (1961), and later in works by Harold Pinter.

She went on to build a very distinguished career in both classical and modern drama, and in film, and was appointed CBE in 1967.

Twiggy, 1966

Twiggy, *originally* Leslie Hornby, married name Twiggy Lawson

Born 1949
English model whose figure and fashions became a symbol of the 1960s

Leslie Hornby was born in London. She was launched into the heady fashion scene of 1966 by entrepreneur Justin de Villeneuve, and quickly shot to fame as a fashion model in newspapers and magazines worldwide, including *Elle* in France and the UK and American *Vogue*.

Her adolescent gaucheness was emphasized by the girlish 1960s mini dresses, pale tights and loon pants she modelled. With short hair styled by Vidal Sassoon she epitomized the boyish look in vogue at the time. She became known as the 'Face of 1966' and her waif-like figure and huge eyes became the symbol of the decade.

She later proved she could sing, dance and act, and appeared in the films *The Boyfriend* (1971) and *The Blues Brothers* (1980).

Twining, Louisa

Born 1820 Died 1912
English poor law reformer who achieved better medical facilities in the workhouses

Louisa Twining was born in London and was educated at home. She became involved in social work when she visited her old nurse in a workhouse, and instituted a series of visits. In 1855 she published a report entitled *A Few Words about the Inmates of our Union Workhouse* and travelled widely visiting workhouses and promoting improvements.

She also campaigned for trained medical staff and better conditions for workhouse infirmaries and in 1879 established the Workhouse Infirmary Nursing Association. In 1867 she assisted with the relief of cholera victims in the East End of London by setting up a convalescent home.

As well as writing many articles on Poor Law and workhouses she presented a paper at the first conference of the National Association for the Promotion of Social Science

(1857). Her publications include *Recollections of Life and Work* (1893) and *Workhouses and Pauperism* (1898).

Tyler, Anne

Born 1941
American novelist, short story writer and Pulitzer Prize-winner who writes against a background of Southern life

Anne Tyler was born in Minneapolis, Minnesota, and raised in Raleigh, North Carolina. She graduated from Duke University at 19, where she twice won the Anne Flexner award for creative writing, and has been a Russian bibliographer and assistant to the librarian at McGill University Law Library.

Writing mainly of life in Baltimore or in small Southern towns, and concerned with the themes of loneliness, isolation and human interactions, she has had a productive career since her début in 1964 with *If Morning Ever Comes*.

Significant subsequent titles include *Morgan's Passing* (1980), *Dinner at the Homesick Restaurant* (1982), *The Accidental Tourist* (1985), and *Breathing Lessons* (1989), for which she won the Pulitzer Prize for fiction.

Tynan, Katharine

Born 1861   Died 1931
Irish poet and novelist who was a leading author of the Celtic literary revival

Katharine Tynan was born in Clondalkin, County Dublin. She was a friend of Charles Stewart Parnell, Wilfred and **Alice Meynell**, and Dante Gabriel and **Christina Rossetti**, and in 1893 she married H A Hinkson, who was a resident magistrate in County Mayo from 1914 to 1919.

Her journalism established her reputation, but she also wrote some 18 volumes of tender, gentle verse, over 100 novels, including *Oh! What a Plague is Love* (1896), *She Walks in Beauty* (1899) and *The House in the Forest* (1928), and around 40 other books, including five autobiographical works, the last of which was *Memoires* (1924). Her *Collected Poems* appeared in 1930.

Tyus, Wyomia

Born 1945
African-American track and field athlete, winner of two consecutive Olympic gold medals

Wyomia Tyus was born in Griffin, Georgia. Competing as a sprinter in high school and college, she won the 1962 Girls' AAU (American Athletic Union) championships in the 100 yard dash, 50 yard dash and the 75 yard dash. Two years later she won the AAU 100 metre title.

At the 1964 Olympics, she won a gold medal in the 100 metres and a silver in the 4 × 100 metre relay. In the 1968 Olympics she won a second gold in the 100 metres to become the first athlete to win two consecutive gold medals in that event. She won another gold medal in the 4 × 100 metre relay.

Tyus is a founding member of the Women's Sports Foundation, which serves to promote women in all sports. She was elected to the National Track and Field Hall of Fame in 1980 and became a member of the International Women's Sports Hall of Fame in 1981.

Tz'u Hsi *see* Cixi

U

Ulanova, Galina

Born 1910
Russian ballet dancer who became the leading
ballerina of the USSR

Galina Ulanova studied at the Petrograd State
Ballet and made her début in *Les Sylphides* at
the Kirov Ballet in Leningrad (now St
Petersburg) in 1928. She joined the Bolshoi
Ballet in 1944, became the country's leading
ballerina, and was four times a Stalin prize-
winner.

She visited London in 1956 with the Bolshoi
ballet, when she gave a memorable perfomance
in *Giselle*, perhaps her most famous role. She
has appeared in several films made by the
Moscow State Ballet Company and in 1957 was
awarded the Lenin prize. She retired in 1962,
but continued to teach at the Bolshoi.

Ullman, Tracey

Born 1959
English singer, comedienne and actress who has
achieved success as a television star in the USA

Tracey Ullman was born in Buckinghamshire.
She went to stage school in London and had
parts in musicals *Elvis* and *Grease!* before
breaking through as a comic in *Three of a Kind*
(1981).

Her singing career consisted largely of
cover versions — 'Breakaway', **Doris Day's**
'Move Over Darling', and 'They Don't Know'
(Labour Party leader Neil Kinnock appeared
in the video) — and a return to acting seemed
inevitable.

After mixed critical fortunes in Britain, she
moved to the USA, where the *Tracey Ullman
Show* (1987–   ) has achieved a startling five
Grammy awards.

Ullmann, Liv Johanne

Born 1938
Norwegian actress whose brilliant work with
Ingmar Bergman is especially acclaimed

Liv Ullmann was born in Tokyo, Japan. She
studied acting at the Webber-Douglas School
in London before beginning her career with a
repertory company in Stavanger. She made her
film début in *Fjols til Fjells* (1957) but her
screen image was largely defined through a
long professional and personal association
with the Swedish director Ingmar Bergman in
which she laid bare the inner turmoil of
women experiencing various emotional and
sexual crises.

Their films together include *Persona* (1966),
Viskningar och Rop (1972, 'Cries and
Whispers'), *Ansikte mot Ansikte* (1975, 'Face
to Face') and *Herbstsonate* (1978, 'Autumn
Sonata'). Her work for other filmmakers has
been less challenging, particularly in English-
language productions like *Lost Horizon* (1973).
She made her Broadway début in *A Doll's
House* (1975) — her regular theatre appear-
ances include *I Remember Mama* (1979) and
Old Times (1985, London) — and her direc-
torial début with the film *Sophie* in 1993.

The first female recipient of Norway's Peer
Gynt award, she has worked extensively for
the charity UNICEF and written two autobiographical works, *Changing* (1977) and
Choices (1984).

Ulmann, Doris

Born 1884 Died 1934
American photographer, best known for
straightforward and respectful portraits, often
taken in rural communities, and for still lifes

Doris Ulmann was born to a wealthy family in
New York. She studied with the photographer,
teacher and social reformer Lewis Hine (1874–

1940) at the Ethical Culture School, New York (1900–3), then took psychology and law at Columbia in 1907 and photography with Clarence White at Columbia in 1907 and at his own school in 1914, when she became seriously interested in photography. She married Charles H Jaeger c.1917 (divorced 1925).

She began her photographic career as a portraitist in 1918 and published several books in the early 1920s. From 1925 to 1933 she photographed life in rural communities in the eastern states of the USA, sometimes in the company of folk-singer John Jacob Niles. Her publications include *Roll, Jordan, Roll* (1933, text by J M Peterkin).

Ulrika Eleonora

Born 1688 Died 1741
Queen of Sweden whose brief reign coincided with the start of the decline of royal power

Ulrika Eleonora was born in Stockholm, the younger sister of the unmarried Karl XII. Her elder sister Hedvig Sophia died in 1708, leaving her heir to the Swedish throne.

In 1715 she was married to Prince Frederick of Hesse-Kassel, and she was elected queen in 1718 after her brother's death. A new constitution, however, inaugurated the so-called 'Era of Liberty' (1718–71), and saw the abolition of royal absolutism, giving the majority of power to the Riksdag (parliament).

Ulrika was so displeased that she abdicated in 1720 in favour of her husband, who ascended the throne as Fredrik I.

Under, Marie

Born 1883 Died 1977
Estonian poet considered by many to be the greatest in her language

Marie Under has been compared to the Austrian poet Rilke and even to the German poet Goethe. She was the leading poet in the expressionistic and Futurist 'Siuru' Group (named after a fabulous bird in Estonian mythology), which in 1917 ushered in the most colourful and exciting period in this Finno-Ugric literature.

Her work developed from a delicately impressionistic love poetry to one of magnificent visionary power; she is one of the great woman poets of the century in international terms, and her work only awaits adequate translation for it to be so recognized.

Translations of some of her poetry are in W K Matthews (ed), *Anthology of Modern Estonian Poetry* (1953).

Underhill, Evelyn

Born 1875 Died 1941
English poet and mystic whose writing helped mystical theology to be recognized

Evelyn Underhill was born in Wolverhampton and educated at King's College, London. In 1907 she married Herbert Stuart Moore, a barrister, and in 1921 became lecturer on the philosophy of religion at Manchester College, Oxford.

A friend and disciple of the theologian Baron Friedrich von Hügel, she found her way intellectually from agnosticism to Christianity, and wrote numerous books on mysticism, including *The Life of the Spirit* (1922), volumes of verse, and four novels. Her *Mysticism* (1911) became a standard work.

From 1924 she led retreats and became a respected religious counsellor.

Undset, Sigrid

Born 1882 Died 1949
Norwegian novelist of worldwide fame and winner of the Nobel Prize for Literature

Sigrid Undset was born in Kalundborg, in Denmark, the daughter of a noted Norwegian archaeologist from whom she inherited an interest in medieval Norway. From 1899 she worked in an office, and the problems facing young contemporary women formed the basis of her early novels, including *Jenny* (1911).

Her masterpiece, *Kristin Lavransdatter* (3 vols, 1920–2), which tells a graphic story of love and religion in 14th-century Norway, was followed by *Olav Audunsson* (4 vols, 1925–7), *Gymnadenia* (1929, Eng trans *The Wild Orchid*, 1931) and *Den trofaste hustru* (1936, Eng trans *The Faithful Spouse*, 1937). She became a Roman Catholic in 1924, after which her work deepened in religious intensity, and received the Nobel Prize for Literature in 1928.

During World War II she was exiled in the USA where she continued to write and lecture, an outspoken opponent of Nazism.

Ursula, St

Possibly 4th century
Legendary saint and martyr who was murdered with 11,000 other virgins

Ursula, according to one legend, was the daughter of a Christian king in Britain. On being betrothed against her will to a pagan prince, she secured a delay of three years in which to enjoy her virginity and set sail on a pilgrimage with 10 companions, each one accompanied by a ship of 1,000 virgins.

They sailed up the Rhine to Switzerland

and then on to Rome, but on their return to Cologne, where St Ursula is especially honoured, she and the 11,000 virgins were slain by a horde of pagan Huns, enraged because Ursula refused to marry their chief.

She became the patron saint of many educational institutions, particularly the teaching order of the Ursulines. Her feast day (which was removed from the universal calendar in 1969) is 21 October.

Ustvolskaya, Galina Ivanovna

Born 1919
Russian composer whose spiritual symphonies show an unusual approach to instrumentation

Galina Ustvolskaya was born in Petrograd (Petersburg) and educated at Leningrad Arts School (1937–9) and at the Leningrad Conservatory under Dmitri Shostakovitch, who later asked her to comment on his work-in-progress. She married Konstantin Makukhin in 1966.

Though she taught composition classes at the Leningrad Conservatory from 1948 to 1977, Ustvolskaya has remained profoundly reclusive and her deeply spiritual work was unknown in the West until the 1980s.

Her most substantial achievement is the symphonic cycle begun in 1955 and continued with Symphonies Two, *True and Eternal Bliss* (1979), Three, *Jesus Messiah, Save Us!* (1983), Four, *Prayer* (1985–7), and Five, *Amen* (1989–90), all of which demonstrate her unusual approach to instrumentation.

Uttley, Alison

Born 1884   Died 1976
English author of children's stories

Alison Uttley was born on a farm in Derbyshire. She was widowed in 1930 and turned to writing to support herself and her young son. *The Country Child* (1931) was followed by a flood of books, mainly for children, which revealed her great love for and knowledge of the countryside and country lore. Many of her books were in the **Beatrix Potter** tradition, featuring much-loved characters such as Grey Rabbit and Sam Pig.

V

Vadasz, Christine

Born 1946
Hungarian-born Australian architect with a great
respect for art and craftsmanship

Christine Vadasz trained at the University of
Adelaide, South Australia. As a student she
worked for I M Pei's office in New York, and
after graduating she worked with Bill Lucas
in Sydney. This period gave her a sensitive
and creative approach to the environment
which was to be one of the hallmarks of all
her subsequent work.

She is the director of Christine Vadasz
Architects, Byron Bay, New South Wales,
which she founded in 1974. Her practice
embodies her attitudes and tends to shy away
from overt commerciality. Her subtle and
innovative approach to designs for the Australian Tourist Board have won her repeat
commissions and spread her reputation far
afield.

In 1984 she won the President of the Royal
Australian Institute of Architects award for
her development of a Regional Approach to
architecture, and in 1987 she won the Duncan's Award for Design Excellence in Timber
for Bedarra Bay Resort, North Queensland.
Since 1985 she has taught at Sydney University.

Vala, Katri, *pseud of* Karin Alice Heikel, *née* Wadenström

Born 1901 Died 1944
Finnish poet credited with the introduction of free
verse into Finnish literature

Karin Alice Wadenström was born in Muonio,
Lapland, the daughter of a forester. Following
his early death she was brought up in poverty,
but she became a teacher and on the publication of her first two volumes of poetry, she

was established as an important poet of her
generation. She became the leading woman
poet of the semi-modernist Tulenkantajat
('Torchbearers') Group, who fearlessly expressed their optimistic views about change.

Vala's early poems, characterized by her use
of free verse, celebrated life and light. Later,
once the Torchbearers has dispersed in the
late 1920s, her work changed in style from
being Expressionist and stylized to being political and formal, advocating social reform and
political justice. Rather than becoming revolutionary however, they had a tragic and
strongly personal voice.

She was, like **Edith Södergran**, another
Finnish victim of the scourge of tuberculosis,
and died in exile in Sweden.

Valadon, Suzanne, *originally* Marie-Clémentine Valadon

Born 1865 Died 1938
French painter who earned international acclaim
in the 1920s and 1930s

Suzanne Valadon was born near Limoges. At
the age of 18 she became the mother of
Maurice Utrillo (1883–1955), who also became
a famous painter. She became an artist's model
after an accident ended her career as an
acrobat, modelling for Auguste Renoir and
others.

With the encouragement of Henri Toulouse-Lautrec, Edgar Degas and Paul Cézanne,
she took up painting in about 1892 and
excelled in her realistic treatment of nudes,
portraits, figure studies and landscapes, her
work having some affinity with that of Degas.
She employed well-built models as subjects
and made bold use of colour and linework, for
example in *The Blue Room* (1923).

Valenzuela, Luisa

Born 1938
Argentinian writer and journalist regarded as one
of the most important women writers of Latin
America

Luisa Valenzuela was born in Buenos Aires.
She moved to the USA in 1979, as a result of
the political situation in Argentina, but since
the re-establishment of democracy, has returned to Argentina.

She has written seven novels and three collections of stories. Most of her work is highly
experimental, including such techniques as
linguistic distortion, shifting points of view,
and use of metaphor to communicate an ironic
view of gender relations. Titles include the
short-story collection *Cabio de armas* (1975,
'Other Weapons'), the narrative collection *El
gato eficaz* (1972, 'Cat-o-Nine-Deaths') and
Cola de lagartija (1983, 'The Lizard's Tail').

She has won several awards, including a
Fulbright scholarship and a Guggenheim fellowship.

Valois, Dame Ninette de, *stage-name* of Edris Stannus

Born 1898
Irish ballet dancer whose contribution to dance
has been outstanding

Dame Ninette de Valois, 1951

Ninette de Valois was born in Baltiboys, Blessington, County Wicklow. She studied under
the Italian Enrico Cecchetti and made her first
appearance in 1914 in the pantomime at the
Lyceum Theatre. She subsequently appeared
with the Beecham Opera Company and at
Covent Garden. After a European tour with
Sergei Diaghilev (1923–5), she partnered
Anton Dolin in England and became director
of ballet at the Abbey Theatre, Dublin.

She was a founding member of the Camargo
Society and the Vic–Wells Ballet (which
became Sadler's Wells Ballet and the Royal
Ballet). She was artistic director of the Royal
Ballet until 1963. In 1935 she married Dr A
B Connell. She organized the National Ballet
School of Turkey (1947) and was created DBE
in 1951.

She wrote *Invitation to the Ballet* (1937) and
her autobiography, *Come Dance with Me*
(1957). Her rarely performed choreographic
works include *The Rake's Progress, Checkmate*
and *Don Quixote.*

Vanbrugh, Dame Irene, *originally* Barnes

Born 1872   Died 1949
English actress who became a leading exponent of
Pinero and Barrie heroines

Irene Barnes was born in Exeter, the fifth of
six children of a clergyman, and a younger
sister of **Violet Vanbrugh**. She was educated
at Exeter High School, travelled to the Continent with her father, and went to school in
London when the family moved there. She
followed the example and early career of her
sister, changing her name, being trained by
Sarah Thorne and entering J L Toole's
company. Her first appearance was at Margate
as Phoebe in *As You Like It* (1888).

She married Dion Boucicault the younger in
1901, and acted with Beerbohm Tree, George
Alexander, Robertson Hare and Charles
Frohman, winning a reputation as an
interpreter of James Barrie and Arthur Pinero
heroines, including Sophie Fullgarney in
Pinero's *The Gay Lord Quex*, the title role in
Letty, Nina Jesson in *His House in Order* and
Zoe Blundell in *Mid-Channel*. In 1895 she was
the first Gwendolen Fairfax in Oscar Wilde's
The Importance of Being Earnest.

She was created DBE in 1941. Her brother
Sir Kenneth Barnes, principal of the Royal
Academy of Dramatic Art from 1909 to 1955,
named its Vanbrugh Theatre in honour of his
sisters.

Vanbrugh, Violet Augusta Mary, originally Barnes

Born 1867 Died 1942
English actress who had great success in both
Shakespearian and modern roles, and when
performing with her husband Arthur Bourchier

Violet Barnes was born in Exeter, the elder sister of **Irene Vanbrugh**. Her decision to go on stage was very unusual for a person of her standing. She managed to gain the interest and friendship of **Ellen Terry**, who suggested she change her name and recommended to J L Toole (1832–1906) that he take her into his company.

Vanbrugh first appeared in burlesque in 1886 and two years later played Ophelia at Margate, where she had been trained by Sarah Thorne. She joined **Madge Kendal** and her husband for their US tour and on her return played **Ann Boleyn** in Henry Irving's production of *Henry VIII*.

She married Arthur Bourchier in 1894 and enhanced many of his successes with her elegance and ability. Her brother Sir Kenneth Barnes, principal of the Royal Academy of Dramatic Art from 1909 to 1955, named its Vanbrugh Theatre in honour of his sisters.

Van Damm, Sheila

Born 1922 Died 1987
English motor racing driver and theatre owner

Sheila Van Damm first drove in a rally in 1950, as a publicity stunt to advertise the Windmill Theatre, which belonged to her father. She achieved a run of success in the ladies' sections, and won the Ladies' European Touring Championships in 1954.

She was also occupied with her father's theatre, which she inherited from him in 1960; she turned to full-time management but was forced to close it down in 1964, and retired to Sussex.

In 1957 she published her autobiography, *No Excuses*.

Vanderbilt-Cooper, Gloria

Born 1924
American artist, actress, model, socialite and
fashion designer who created the first-ever
'designer' jeans

Gloria Vanderbilt-Cooper was born in New York. In November 1934, aged 10, she was the subject of a sensational custody trial between her mother (Gloria Morgan Vanderbilt, widowed at 19 after being married for two years to sportsman Reginal Vanderbilt) and her millionaire aunt Harry (Gertrude) Payne Whitney. Her aunt gained custody until Gloria was 14 — at which age Gloria's estate was valued at some $4 million.

In 1955 she made her professional acting début on Broadway (in *The Time of Your Life*) and also that year published the first of her six books, *Love Poems*.

The winner of several design awards, she designs stationery, fabrics, clothing, household accessories and gave her name to the Vanderbilt perfume and jeans. She was married to her fourth husband, Wyatt Cooper, from 1963 until his death in 1978.

Van de Vate, Nancy Jean, pseudonyms Helen Huntley *and* William Huntley, *née* Smith

Born 1930
American composer who in 1975 founded the
International League of Women Composers

Nancy Van de Vate was born in Plainfield, New Jersey, and has been resident in Vienna since 1985. She studied piano at the Eastman School in New York City (1948–50), and theory at Wellesley College, Massachusetts (1949–52). She married Dwight Van de Vate Jr in 1952 (marriage dissolved 1976) and Clyde Arnold Smith in 1979.

She has worked as a concert pianist and has held a number of academic posts, living in Hawaii (1976–80) and in Indonesia (1982–5) before settling in Europe.

Her orchestral pieces *Dark Nebulae* (1981), *Distant Worlds* (1985) and *Chernobyl* (1987) are typical of her sonorous style, influenced by the Polish modernists.

Van Duyn, Mona Jane

Born 1921
American poet who won a Pulitzer Prize in 1991
and became the first female US poet laureate

Mona Van Duyn was born in Waterloo, Iowa. She was educated at the University of North Iowa and the University of Iowa, and taught English at a number of universities, including the University of Louisville, Kentucky, and Washington University, St Louis.

Her first collection, *Valentines in the Wide World* (1959), was followed by a small but admirable body of skilfully crafted and insightful poems in *A Time of Bees* (1964), *To See, To Take* (1970), *Bedtime Stories* (1972), *Merciful Disguises* (1973) and *Letters from a Father* (1982).

A gap of eight years passed before her next volume, *Near Changes* (1990), which won her the Pulitzer Prize for poetry in 1991. She was appointed US poet laureate in 1992.

Van Praagh, Dame Peggy (Margaret)

Born 1910   Died 1990
English ballet dancer, teacher and producer who
made a remarkable contribution to ballet

Peggy Van Praagh was born in London. Having acquired exceptional technical skills as a child (she could perform 100 fouettés on point), she trained with Margaret Craske, joined the Ballet Rambert in 1933 and created many roles with that company, chiefly in works by Antony Tudor, *Jardin aux Lilas* (1936) and *Dark Elegies* (1937). She moved to Tudor's newly-formed London Ballet in 1938, introducing the revolutionary idea of lunchtime performances during the Blitz.

In 1941 she joined the Sadler's Wells Ballet as dancer and teacher, and worked as producer and assistant director with **Ninette de Valois** at the Sadler's Wells Theatre Ballet until 1956. She produced many ballets for BBC television and for international companies, and in 1960 became artistic director for the Borovansky Ballet in Australia.

She was founding artistic director for the Australian Ballet between 1962 and 1979, and a member of the council and guest teacher until 1982. She was created DBE in 1970.

Varda, Agnès

Born 1928
French film writer and director who views
personal issues in a social context

Agnès Varda was born in Brussels, Belgium, and educated at the Sorbonne in Paris. She was studying art history at the École du Louvre when she began evening classes in photography and decided to make a career of it. She made her directorial début with *La Pointe Courte* (1954), the story of a couple trying to salvage their marriage and of fishermen struggling to survive against severe competition; it is often cited as an early influence on the *nouvelle vague*.

Though she has maintained a commitment to the documentary throughout her career, exploring political situations in such films as *Salut les Cubains* (1963, 'Salute to Cuba'), she co-wrote the feature *Ultimo Tanga A Parigi* (1972, 'Last Tango in Paris') and has also made such films as *Lion's Love* (1969), the award-winning *Sans Toit Ni Loi* (1985, 'Vagabonde'), the autobiographical *Jacquot de Nantes* (1990), about a young boy's desire to become a filmmaker, and *Les 100 et 1 Nuits* (1994).

She was married to the director Jacques Demy from 1962 until his death in 1990, and published her autobiography *Varda par Agnès* in 1994.

Vare, Glenna Collette

Born 1903   Died 1989
American golfer, six times US women's champion

Glenna Vare was born in Providence, Rhode Island. At the age of 19 she won the amateur championships of the North, the South and the East. She went on to win six US Women's championships in the 1920s and the Canadian Women's Amateur in 1922.

She was inducted into the World Golf Hall of Fame in 1975 and the International Women's Sport's Hall of Fame in 1981. In 1952 the Ladies Professional Golf Association began presenting the Vare Trophy for the player with the lowest scoring average.

Varnhagen von Ense, Rahel Friederike Antonie, *née* Levin

Born 1771   Died 1833
Jewish salon hostess whose home in Berlin was a
leading centre for Romanticist intellectuals

Rahel Levin was born in Berlin, the daughter of a Jewish merchant called Levin Markus. From c.1790 to 1806 (when Napoleon invaded Berlin) her salon attracted all the leading intellectuals of Berlin society.

She became engaged to Count Karl von Finckenstein, but their relationship (1795–1800) was broken off, probably because she was Jewish. In 1814 she converted and married Karl August Varnhagen von Ense (1785–1858). They went to Vienna (1814–15) where he was a member of the diplomatic corps at the Congress of Vienna, then lived in Karlsruhe, where he was Prussian *chargé d'affaires*, before returning to Berlin in 1819.

Rahel is known to us through her husband's memoirs and papers, and through her letters to Jewish novelist Regina Frohberg. **Hannah Arendt**'s study, *Rahel Varnhagen: The Life of a Jewess* (1957) has reawakened interest in her.

Vasconcelos, Carolina Wilhelma Michaëlis de, *née* Michaëlis

Born 1851   Died 1925
German-born Portuguese scholar and writer who
specialized in romance philology and literature

Carolina Michaëlis was born in Berlin. Following her marriage in 1876 to historian and art critic Joaquim de Vasconcelos (b.1849), she lived in Oporto, Portugal, where she did much scholarly research on the Portuguese language, its literature, and especially its folk literature. Her extensive scholarship earned her the first university chair to be awarded to a woman in Portugal (1911).

Most noteworthy amongst her writing is her edition of the late 13th- or early 14th-century *Cancioneiro da Ajuda* (1904, 'Book of Songs of Help'). Other works include *Notas Vicentinas* (1912, 'Vincentian Notes'), an edition of the poetry of Francisco Sá de Miranda (1481–1558), and essays, studies, and correspondence with other Portuguese scholars.

She was also a firm advocate of education for women and declared that a feminist movement would only be possible in Portugal if more women were educated and financially independent.

Vaughan, Dame Janet

Born 1899 Died 1993
English haematologist and radiobiologist who researched the treatment of pernicious anaemia by liver therapy

Janet Vaughan was the daughter of the headmaster of Rugby School, who met his future wife through his first cousin, **Virginia Woolf**. After education at home the 15-year-old Janet was allowed to attend a day school, where her headmistress considered her 'too stupid' for further education. She failed the Oxford entrance examinations twice before being admitted to Somerville College, where she gained first-class honours in physiology.

She went on to pursue clinical studies at University College Hospital in London, qualifying in 1924, and became assistant pathologist there, developing an interest in the new treatment of a then fatal disease, pernicious anaemia, with a diet including raw liver extract. After studies in the USA with George Minot, who was to be joint winner of the Nobel Prize in 1934 for the discovery, Vaughan returned to London to work on blood and bone, and published *The Anaemias* in 1934.

The Spanish Civil War stimulated her interest in storing blood and she played an important role in establishing transfusion depots in London during World War II, for which she was awarded an OBE. In 1945 she went to Belsen with Dr Charles Dent and Dr **Rosalind Pitt-Rivers** to assess the value of concentrated protein solutions in treating starvation. She returned to Oxford that year as Principal of her old College, remaining in that position until 1967. She also led a successful research group working on the effect of radioactive isotopes on bone formation and metabolism. She was the author of several scientific papers and books and contributed to many university and Government committees.

She was created a DBE in 1957 and elected a Fellow of the Royal Society in 1979.

Vaughan, Sassy (Sarah Lois)

Born 1924 Died 1990
American jazz singer and pianist

Sassy Vaughan was born in Newark, New Jersey. As a child she sang gospels in church and spent 10 years studying the organ. Winning a talent competition in 1942 at the Apollo Theatre, Harlem, she came to the attention of singer Billy Eckstine, and through him of Earl Hines, who promptly hired her as a singer and pianist.

In 1944 she made her first recording with 'I'll Wait and Pray', the following year launching out on a solo career. By the early 1950s she was internationally acclaimed, and a leader of the new jazz known as bebop. A master of vibrato, range, and expression, her abilities could inspire envy in opera singers, and her singing was once described as 'instrumental stunt flying'.

Her most notable hits include 'It's Magic', 'Send in the Clowns' and 'I cried for you'.

Veil, Simone, *née* Jacob

Born 1927
French politician and former lawyer devoted to reconciliation in Europe

Simone Jacob was born in Nice. In 1944 she and her Jewish family were imprisoned in the Nazi concentration camps Auschwitz and Bergen–Belsen, but she survived to marry Antoine Veil in 1946, have three children, and to study law at the Institute d'Études Politiques in Paris.

She joined the Ministry of Justice in 1957 and progressed through its ranks, an expert on the law particularly concerning prisoners, women and children. As Minister of Health (1974–6), then of Health and Social Security (1976–9) in the Giscard d'Estaing administration, she won the controversial legalization of abortion in 1974, made contraception more easily available, upgraded medical services for the poor and promoted the reform of medical schools.

In 1979 Veil became a member of the European parliament, where she was the first president (1979–82), chaired the legal affairs committee (1982–4) and the liberal and democratic group (1984–9), and initiated the 42-nation summit in Paris in 1994 to mark World AIDS day. An MEP until 1993, she has received numerous honorary degrees, prizes, medals and foreign decorations for her work.

Verdy, Violette, *originally* Nelly Guillerm

Born 1933
French ballet dancer and director who has won a
following on both sides of the Atlantic

Nelly Guillerm was born in Pont-L'Abbé-Lambour. She made her début with Ballets des Champs-Élysées in 1945, and subsequently appeared in films and theatre as an actress and dancer.

She joined Roland Petit's Ballets de Paris in 1950, later freelancing with a string of companies including London Festival Ballet (1954), American Ballet Theatre (1957) and New York City Ballet (1958–77).

She was artistic director of Paris Opéra Ballet (1977–80) and an associate of Boston Ballet.

Veronica, St

1st century
Early Christian woman who received her cloth
back from Jesus permanently marked with his
features

According to legend, when Veronica devotedly offered a cloth for Christ to wipe his anguished brow as he stumbled beneath his Cross on the way to Calvary, it was returned miraculously imprinted with the divine features.

'St Veronica's Veil' is said to have been preserved in St Peter's, Rome, from about 700, and was exhibited as recently as 1933. Some believe the name *Veronica* to be derived from *vera icon* ('true image') and that the legend of the saint developed in order to explain the existence of the veil. Her feast day is 12 July.

Vestris, Lucia Elizabeth, *née* Bartolozzi

Born 1797   Died 1856
English actress, opera singer and theatre manager

Lucia Bartolozzi was born in London, a granddaughter of the Italian engraver Francesco Bartolozzi. At 16 she married the dancer Armand Vestris (1787–1825), member of an originally Florentine family that gave to France a series of distinguished chefs, actors and ballet dancers.

In 1815 they separated and Madame Vestris, as she was known, went on the stage in Paris. She appeared at Drury Lane in 1820, became famous in *The Haunted Tower*, was even more popular as Phoebe in *Paul Pry*, and in light comedy and burlesque was equally successful.

She had been seven years lessee of the Olympic when in 1838 she married the comedian Charles James Mathews (1803–78). She afterwards undertook the management of Covent Garden and the Lyceum. She introduced the box set to the London stage and was one of the first to use historically accurate costumes.

Viardot-García, (Michelle Ferdinande) Pauline, *née* García

Born 1821   Died 1910
Spanish mezzo-soprano who exerted a wide
influence during her successful career

Pauline García was the daughter of the tenor and composer Manuel García, in whose opera company she sang with her brother Manuel and sister **Maria Malibran**. She travelled with them to sing in New York City and Mexico. She first sang in London in 1839 and the following year she married Louis Viardot.

Her immensely successful career was spent singing mainly in London and Paris, though she was very well received in St Petersburg in 1843–6. She created the character of Fidès in Giacomo Meyerbeer's *Le prophète*, which was written for her, and provided the inspiration for Charles Gounod's *Sapho* and Camille Saint-Saëns's Dalila in his *Samson et Dalila*, among others.

Her wide influence, for example on the Russian writer Ivan Turgenev, who collaborated in her operettas *Trop de femmes* (1867), *Le dernier sorcier* (1867) and *L'ogre* (1868), included the promotion of Russian music in the west. In addition to operettas she also composed songs. Her daughter Louise Viardot, later Héritte-Viardot (1841–1918), was a contralto singer and composer of such works as the comic opera *Lindoro* (1879), and her son Paul Viardot (1857–1941) was a violinist and composer.

Victoria, *in full* Alexandrina Victoria

Born 1819   Died 1901
Queen of the United Kingdom of Great Britain and
Ireland, and (in 1876) Empress of India

Victoria was born in Kensington Palace, London, the only child of George III's fourth son, Edward, Duke of Kent, and Victoria Maria Louisa of Saxe-Coburg, sister of Leopold I of Belgium. Companioned in girlhood almost exclusively by older folk, her precocious maturity and surprising firmness of will were noticeable as soon as she was called to the British throne, which occurred on the death of her uncle, William IV, in 1837. However the provisions of Salic Law excluded her from

Queen Victoria, 1864

married Frederick III of Germany; Albert Edward, afterwards Edward VII; Alice, who married the Duke of Hesse; Alfred, Duke of Edinburgh and of Saxe-Coburg-Gotha; Helena, who married Prince Kristian of Schleswig-Holstein; Louise, who married the Marquis of Lorne; Arthur, Duke of Connaught; Leopold, Duke of Albany; and Beatrice, who married Prince Henry of Battenberg. Strongly influenced by her husband, with whom she worked in closest harmony, after his death in 1861 the grief-stricken Queen went into lengthy seclusion, which brought her temporary unpopularity. But with the adventurous Disraeli administration vindicated by the Queen's recognition as Empress of India, Victoria rose high in her subjects' favour.

Her experience, shrewdness, and innate political flair brought powerful influence to bear on the conduct of foreign affairs, as did the response to the country's policy made by her innumerable relatives amongst the European royal houses. Unswerving in her preference for ministers of conservative principles, such as Melbourne and Benjamin Disraeli, rather than for counsellors of more radical persuasion, such as Lord Palmerston and William Gladstone, in the long run the queen's judgement of men and events was rarely to be faulted, although her partiality for all things German had the effect of throwing her heir almost too eagerly into the arms of France.

Her *Letters*, although prolix and pedestrian in style, bear witness to her unwearying industry, her remarkable practicality, and her high sense of mission. She published *Leaves from the Journal of our Life in the Highlands* (1869) and *More Leaves* (1884).

dominion over Hanover, which passed to another uncle, Ernest Augustus, Duke of Cumberland.

Following her coronation at Westminster on 28 June 1838, she speedily demonstrated her clear grasp of constitutional principles and knowledge of the scope of her own prerogative, for she had been paintstakingly instructed by letter in these things by her uncle, Leopold I of Belgium, who remained her constant correspondent. With the fall of Lord Melbourne's government in 1839 she resolutely exercised her prerogative by setting aside the precedent which decreed dismissal of the current ladies of the bedchamber. Robert Peel thereupon resigned, and the Melbourne administration, which she personally preferred, was prolonged till 1841. Throughout the early formative years of her reign, Melbourne was both her prime minister and her trusted friend and mentor. His experience and thoroughly English outlook served as a useful counter-balance to that more 'Continental' line of policy of which 'Uncle Leopold' was the untiring and far from unprejudiced advocate.

On reaching marriageable age, the Queen became deeply enamoured of Prince Albert of Saxe-Coburg-Gotha, to whom she was married in 1840. Four sons and five daughters were born: Victoria, the Princess Royal, who

Viebig, Clara, *pseud of* Clara Viebig Cohn

Born 1860 Died 1952
German writer who wrote Zolaesque novels and short stories and was very widely read in her day

Clara Viebig was born in Trier. Now neglected, Viebig began as a follower of Émile Zola (1840–1902). The background of her fiction is the menacing landscape of her native Eifel, and she often examines the lives of women trapped by fate.

Das schlafende Heer (1904, Eng trans *The Sleeping Army*, 1929) depicts Polish peasants under the Germans. Her most famous novel, telling the story of the life of a servant girl, was *Das tägliche Brot* (1900, Eng trans *Our Daily Bread*, 1908).

Vigée Lebrun, (Marie) Élisabeth Louise, née Vigée

Born 1755 Died 1842
French painter who is listed among the most
successful women painters of all time

Élisabeth Vigée was born in Paris, the daughter of a painter. In 1776 she married J B P Lebrun, a picture dealer and grandnephew of the historical painter Charles le Brun.

Her great beauty and the charm of her painting speedily made her work fashionable. Her portrait of **Marie Antoinette** (1779) led to a lasting friendship with the Queen and she painted numerous portraits of the royal family.

She left Paris for Italy at the outbreak of the Revolution and undertook a triumphal progress through Europe, finding success as a portraitist, especially of women and children, wherever she went. She arrived in London in 1802 and painted portraits of the Prince of Wales, Lord Byron, and many others, before returning to Paris in 1805.

Vik, Bjørg

Born 1935
Norwegian short-story writer, playwright,
novelist and leading figure in Norwegian
literary life

Bjørg Vik grew up in Oslo and began her career as a journalist, publishing her first volume of short stories in 1963. Elegant and complex, her short stories focus the situation of the middle-class housewife trapped by family duties and the demands of materialism.

The texts in *Kvinneakvariet* (1972, Eng trans *An Aquarium of Women*, 1987), depicting women of different ages at times of crisis, reflect her involvement with 'second-wave' feminism, as does her successful play *To akter for fem kvinner* (1974, 'Two Acts for Five Women'). She has also published a semi-autobiographical novel, *Små nøkler store rom* (1988, 'Small Keys Large Rooms').

Villiers, Barbara, Duchess of Cleveland, *married name* Countess of Castlemaine

Born 1640 Died 1709
English noblewoman who was a favourite mistress
of Charles II

Barbara Villiers was the daughter of William Villiers, 2nd Viscount Grandison, and grew up to be a noted society hostess. In 1659 she married Roger Palmer, who was created Earl of Castlemaine as a consolation when she became the king's mistress.

She became a Roman Catholic in 1663 but was nonetheless notorious for her amours, as well as for trafficking in the sale of offices. In 1670 she was created Duchess of Cleveland. Supplanted in the king's favours by the Duchess of Portland in 1673, she moved to Paris, where in 1705 she bigamously married Robert 'Beau' Fielding (the marriage was annulled in 1707).

She had seven children, five of whom were acknowledged by Charles as his: Anne, Countess of Suffolk (b.1661); Charles Fitzroy, Duke of Southampton (b.1662); Henry Fitzroy, Duke of Grafton (b.1663); Charlotte, Countess of Lochfield (b.1664); and George Fitzroy, Duke of Northumberland (b.1665).

Vionnet, Madeleine

Born 1876 Died 1975
French couturier innovative in her use of material
and in her techniques

Madeleine Vionnet was born in Aubervilliers. She opened her own Paris house in 1912 and became one of the most innovative designers of her time. She is credited with inventing the bias cut for her body-skimming evening and day dresses, and with dispensing with the corset before her contemporaries **Coco Chanel** and Poiret.

She was also the first to use crepe de chine as a fabric and not a lining, also favouring pliant materials such as silk, organdy, chiffon and lamé. She used lingerie techniques such as faggotting, pintucking and rolled hems to sew her exquisitely fluid dresses that often had no fastenings. She also popularized the cowl and halter neck. Vionnet retired in 1939.

Vivonne, Catherine de *see* Rambouillet, Marquise de

Vogt, Marthe Louise

Born 1903
German-born British neuroscientist who studied
the chemistry and pharmacology of the brain

Marthe Vogt was born in Berlin, the daughter of two distinguished neuro-anatomists, and reared in the heady atmosphere of intellectual Berlin. She qualified in medicine and gained a PhD in chemistry. By 1935 she had become Head of the Institute for Brain Science in Berlin, but the political upheavals in Germany under Hitler encouraged her to go abroad, and she moved to the Medical Research Council's National Institute of Medical Research in London to work with Sir Henry Dale on the pharmacology of nerve transmission.

After a brief period in Cambridge she

returned to London to the School of Pharmacy (1941–6), moved to the Department of Pharmacology, Edinburgh (1947–60), and then returned to Cambridge as the Head of Pharmacology in the Agricultural Research Council's Unit of Animal Physiology at Babraham.

Her work on the brain, in which she elaborated the functional roles of naturally occurring chemicals such as acetylcholine, was of importance in understanding both normal healthy brain tissue, and also the clinical problems when such systems were disturbed. She was elected a Fellow of the Royal Society in 1952.

Voigt, Cynthia

Born 1942
American author who writes primarily for
children and from 1981 has published at least
one book a year

Cynthia Voigt was born in Boston, Massachusetts, and educated at Smith College. She has worked as a high school teacher since 1965 and has received the Newbery Medal (1983) and the Mystery Writers of America Edgar Allan Poe award (1984).

Her novels tend to focus on independent adolescents, 'outsiders', who gradually come to create bonds with family and friends; several of them, including her first, *Homecoming* (1981), centre on one family, the Tillermans.

Von Krusenstjerna, Agnes

Born 1894 Died 1940
Swedish novelist whose sexually explicit works
aroused controversy

Agnes Von Krusenstjerna was born in Växjö into an upper-class family. Her schooling was limited, and the psychiatric problems which were to recur throughout her life surfaced while she was still a child.

Her first major work was the trilogy centring on Tony Hastfehr (1922–6), an *entwicklungsroman* in which the young girl's discovery of sexual desire becomes a significant element. The seven-volume *Fröknarna von Pahlen* (1930–5, 'The Misses von Pahlen') is a radical exploration of the feminine psyche and women's lives, culminating in the ideal of the maternal family. The sexual explicitness of this work resulted in a wide-ranging public controversy. The four-volume *Fattigadel* (1935–8, 'Petty Nobility') traces the development of an upper-class woman in a perceptively depicted social setting on the verge of change.

Von Trotta, Margarethe

Born 1942
German film director and actress who explores
female characters and their position in the
social order

Margarethe Von Trotta was born in Berlin. She studied acting in Munich before making a number of critically applauded stage and television appearancese such as *Baal* (1969), her first collaboration with future husband Volker Schlöndorff (1939–   ). She also appeared in such films as *Der Plötzliche Reichtum der Armen Leute von Kombach* (1971, 'The Sudden Fortune of the Poor People of Kombach'), which she also co-wrote.

Working as a scriptwriter on most of Schlöndorff's projects, she wrote and co-directed *Die Verlorene Ehre der Katharina Blum* (1975, 'The Lost Honour of Katharina Blum'), a potent critique of police practices and the excesses of the gutter press as a young woman faces public disgrace after unwittingly spending a night with a terrorist suspect. Von Trotta was sole director for the first time with *Das Zweite Erwachen der Christa Klages* (1977, The Second Awakening of Christa Klages), which signalled her interest in the social position of women.

Later films include *Schwestern Oder Die Balance des Glücks* (1981, 'Sisters, or the Balance of Happiness'), a biographical film about **Rosa Luxemburg** (1986), *L'Africana* (1990, 'The Return') and *I lungo silencio* (1992).

Vorse, Mary Heaton

Born 1874 Died 1966
American journalist concerned with workers'
rights

Mary Vorse was born in New York City. She enjoyed a comfortable existence until the death of her husband in 1912, when she turned to journalism to support herself and her two children.

Shocked that year by the conditions she witnessed when covering the textile mill strike in Lawrence, Massachusetts, she committed the next 30 years of her life to reporting on working conditions worldwide, helping the middle classes understand the needs of the workers. During World War II she reported on the welfare of the women and children.

Vreeland, Diana, *née* Dalziel

Born c.1903 Died 1989
French-born American fashion editor who
maintained the dialogue between American and
European fashion

Diana Vreeland was born in Paris and moved to New York when she was eight. Her first column for *Harper's Bazaar*, 'Why Don't You...?' drew attention with such idiosyncratic advice as '...put all your dogs in yellow collars and leads like all the dogs in Paris?'. She worked as fashion editor there from 1939 to 1962, during which time her startling memos to staff became legendary and she was parodied as the flamboyant fashion editor who tells staff to 'Think pink!' in the 1956 film *Funny Face*.

Nevertheless, Vreeland was a committed promoter of fashion, especially during the 1960s. She had an admirable visual eye and furthered the careers of many models, photographers and designers.

After being managing editor of American *Vogue* (1962–71) she became special consultant to the Costume Institute of the Metropolitan Museum of New York where she used fashion history to create spectacular annual exhibitions. She was awarded the French Order of Merit in 1970 and the French Legion of Honour in 1976.

W

Waddell, Helen Jane

Born 1889 Died 1965
English medievalist who wrote a major work
about the travelling scholar monks of the
Middle Ages

Helen Waddell was born in Tokyo and educated at Queen's University, Belfast. Her best known work is *The Wandering Scholars* (1927), a study of the scholar monks, whom she called 'Vagantes', who travelled Europe in the Middle Ages.

She also published translations of *Lyrics from the Chinese* (1913) and *Mediaeval Latin Lyrics* (1929), a novel *Peter Abelard* (1933), based on the life of the French scholar and philosopher of that name who lived from 1079 to 1142, and *The Desert Fathers* (1936), amongst others.

Waddington, Miriam, *née* Dworkin

Born 1917
Canadian poet acclaimed as one of the finest lyric
poets of her time

Miriam Dworkin was born in Winnipeg to Yiddish-speaking Russian-Jewish parents. She was educated at the University of Toronto and married a journalist, Patrick Waddington. She was a social worker for many years and lived in Montreal before separating from her husband (1960) and returning to Toronto to teach literature at York University.

Her work is personal and confessional, but highly intelligent. She published her first collection, *Green World*, in 1945, to much acclaim; in the collections *Dream Telescope* (1972) and *The Visitants* (1981) she began to use short lines and a truncated syntax reminiscent of **Gertrude Stein**. Later she introduced a celebratory approach to the process of ageing. She has also published a short-story collection, *Canadian Jewish Short Stories* (1990).

Virginia Wade, 1992

Wade, (Sarah) Virginia

Born 1945
English tennis player who had a remarkably long
competitive career

Viriginia Wade was born in Bournemouth and brought up in South Africa. She competed at Wimbledon for 20 years, and won the singles there in 1977 when she was ranked number two. In 1968 she took the US Open title, and she also won the Italian Championship in 1971 and the French Championship in 1972.

She was a Wightman Cup player for 16 years, and towards the end of her career captained the side. She served on the All England Lawn Tennis Club Committee (1983–91) and in 1980 became a tennis commentator for BBC Television.

Wägner, Elin Matilda Elisabeth

Born 1882 Died 1949
Swedish novelist and journalist, feminist, and
pacifist

Elin Wägner was born in Lund and eduated at a girls' high school. She embarked on a career as a journalist and retained a journalistic style in her books, the first of which was *Från jordiska muséet* (1907, 'From our Earthly Museum'). She was an ardent advocate of women's rights and better care of the environment, and her experiences of the Swedish women's suffrage movement are reflected in *Pennskaftet* (1910, 'Pen Woman'), which combines wit and irreverence with poignancy and earnestness.

Åsa-Hanna (1918), perhaps her best novel, is a many-faceted investigation of the plight of a peasant woman facing the misogyny of society, including the Church. Notions of a matriarchal past, translated into subtle mythical patterns, result in increasingly critical perspectives on the present, as in *Dialogen fortsätter* (1932, 'The Dialogue is Continuing'). The remarkable eco-feminist essay *Väckarklocka* (1941, 'Alarm Clock') highlights the need for respect and restraint between human beings and towards Mother Earth.

Waitz, Grete

Born 1953
Norwegian athlete, one of the world's best female
distance runners

Greta Waitz was born in Oslo. She rose to prominence in 1975, when she set a world record at 3,000 metres (9 minutes 34.2 seconds, and later, in 1977, 8 minutes 46.6 seconds), and for more than a decade rivalled **Ingrid Kristiansen** as the world's greatest female distance runner.

Waitz has set a unique four world best times for the marathon. In 1979, in the New York marathon — a race she won eight times — she became the first woman to run it in under two and a half hours. By 1983 she had brought her time down to 2 hours 25 minutes and 29 seconds. As winner of the marathon at the inaugural world championships in 1983, she became the first official world champion ever.

Walburga, St, *also called* Walpurgis *or* Walpurga

Born c.710 Died 779
English abbess who presided over the only double
monastery in Germany at the time

Walburga was born in Wessex, sister of St Willibald and St Winebald. She joined St Boniface on his mission to Germany and helped him organize the Frankish Church.

Appointed by her brother Winebald as abbess over the nuns at his double monastery at Heidenheim, the only one of its kind in 8th-century Germany, when he died in 761 she extended her rule over the whole monastery. On her death she was buried there, but her relics were transferred (c.870) to Eichstätt and placed on a rock which is said to exude a mysterious fluid containing healing properties.

Walpurgis night (April 30) arose from the confusion between the day of the transfer of her remains (the night of 1 May), and the popular superstitions regarding the flight of witches on that night. Her feast day is 25 February.

Wald, Lilian

Born 1867 Died 1940
American nurse and social worker, organizer of
nursing schemes

Lilian Wald was born in Cincinnati, Ohio, and educated at private schools. She attended the New York Hospital Training School for Nurses (1889–91). In 1893 she founded the Nurses Settlement (later called the Henry Street Settlement) and established an insurance company nursing scheme and the first public school nursing scheme in the world.

In 1912 the district nursing branch of the American Red Cross was set up at her suggestion and she was also instrumental in the foundation of the Federal Children's Bureau (1912). She published two books on her experiences in the settlement, *The House on Henry Street* (1915) and *Windows on Henry Street* (1934).

Walewska, Marie, Countess

Born 1789 Died 1817
Polish countess and mistress of Napoleon

Countess Walewska was a patriot who had hopes that Napoleon would revive her country. He fell in love with her during a visit to Warsaw. Their illegitimate son was the French statesman Count Walewski (1810–68).

Walker, Alice Malsenior

Born 1944
American novelist and poet instrumental in the
development of black feminist literature

Alice Walker was born in Eatonville, Georgia, into a poor black family. Educated at Spelman College, Atlanta, and Sarah Lawrence College, she has been employed registering voters, as a social worker, and as a teacher and a lecturer.

Her collection of essays *In Search of Our Mothers' Gardens* is an important rediscovery of a black female literary and cultural tradition and includes criticism of such authors as **Zora Neale Hurston**.

Though an accomplished poet, as seen in *Horses Make a Landscape Look More Beautiful* (1984), Walker is better known for her novels, of which *The Color Purple* (1982) is her third and most popular. The winner of the 1983 Pulitzer Prize for fiction and later made into a successful film, it tells in letters the story of two sisters in the cruel, segregated world of the Deep South between the wars. It was preceded by *The Third Life of Grange Copeland* (1970) and *Meridian* (1976).

Her other works include the novel *The Temple of My Familiar* (1988), the collection *Living By the Word: Selected Writings 1973– 1987* and *Possessing the Secret of Joy* (1992), a polemical novel about an African-American girl who returns to her tribe in Africa to undergo 'female genital mutilation' in an attempt to establish her identity.

Walker, Dame Ethel

Born 1861 Died 1951
Scottish painter and sculptor who was a prominent member of the New English Art Club after 1900

Ethel Walker was born in Edinburgh. From 1870 she lived in London, where she was educated privately. She attended Putney Art School, the School of Art at Westminster, and then the Slade School of Art (1892–4). Thereafter she divided her time between London, where she was a familiar figure in Chelsea, and Yorkshire, where she painted notable seascapes from her cottage in Robin Hood's Bay.

Her early work is mannered in the style of the New English Art Club (a group of non-Academicians whose original aim was to revive naturalistic painting) and Walter R Sickert, but she gradually developed a more individual style which owed something to her study of Impressionism, particularly in her work after World War I.

She is best known for her portraits (often of young girls), flower paintings and seascapes, and for more visionary canvases like *Nausicaa* (1920) or *The Zone of Love* (1931– 3), which reflected her idealized vision of a golden age. She was created DBE in 1943.

Walker, Kath *see* Noonuccal, Oodgeroo Moongalba

Walker, Mary Broadfoot

Born c.1895 Died 1974
British pharmacologist who suggested the drug physostigmine as a treatment for myasthenia gravis

Mary Walker graduated in medicine from the University of Edinburgh in 1913, from which she received a gold medal for her MD thesis in 1935.

She suggested the use of the drug physostigmine whilst working in a junior position at St Alfege's Hospital, Greenwich, but although her discovery became the standard treatment for a distressing and chronic disease, which is marked by abnormal fatigue and muscle weakness, she never received due acknowledgement for it.

Walker, Mary Edwards

Born 1832 Died 1919
American physician and the first woman surgeon in the US Army

Mary Edwards Walker was educated at Syracuse Medical College and then joined her husband Albert Miller in a practice in New York State. She campaigned for rational dress for women, revised marriage and divorce laws and women's rights and often wore male evening dress for her lectures.

During the American civil war she volunteered for army service, becoming the US Army's first female surgeon, and was the only woman to receive the Congressional Medal of Honour.

Wallace, Sippie, *originally* Beulah Thomas

Born 1898 Died 1986
African-American blues singer whose music emphasized rural vocal phrases and risqué lyrics

Sippie Wallace was born in Houston, Texas. The majority of her work was done between 1923 and 1927, when she was accompanied by Louis Armstrong and others, singing songs like 'Bedroom Blues' and 'Special Delivery Blues'.

After the death of her husband and her brothers, she did not record anything until her comeback in 1966 when she recorded an album of blues standards with Victoria Spivey entitled *Sippie Wallace and Victoria Spivey*.

In 1970, after a stroke, she recorded *Sippie*

which won a W C Handy Award for Best Blues Album.

Walter, Lucy, *also known as* Mrs Barlow

Born 1630 Died 1658
English courtesan and mistress of the future
Charles II of Scotland and England

Lucy Walter was born probably in Dyfed, Wales, the daughter of a Welsh royalist. She and Charles (who later ruled 1660–85) met in the Channel Islands when he was fleeing England in 1644 during the Civil War, and she became his mistress (1648–50) during his exile in Holland and France.

She bore him a son, James, Duke of Monmouth (1649–85), who on Charles's death, supported by the Whigs, made an unsuccessful Protestant claim to the throne in opposition to the Catholic James, Duke of York (later James II). She also gave birth to a daughter, Mary, in 1651, after their affair had ended.

Walter returned to being a courtesan but was accused of being a spy in 1656 and was banished to France, where she died.

Walters, Julie

Born 1950
English actress who has triumphed in all spheres
of the British entertainment media

Julie Walters was born in Birmingham. She worked as a nurse before studying at the Manchester Polytechnic School of Theatre, and subsequently worked at the Liverpool Everyman Theatre. The role of the indomitable, working-class hairdresser in *Educating Rita* (1980) established her reputation and she received an Academy Award nomination for her reprise of the character in the 1983 screen version.

Rejecting offers of employment in the USA, she has continued to triumph in Britain, revealing a talent that is as likely to provoke howls of laughter as tears of compassion. A skilled mimic, comedienne, and versatile character actress, her stage work includes *Macbeth* (1985), *Frankie and Johnny in the Clair de Lune* (1989) and *The Rose Tattoo* (1991). A frequent television performer, her work ranges from numerous comedy skits in partnership with **Victoria Wood**, to the role of a septuagenarian Irish matriarch in the drama series *GBH* (1991).

Her films include *Personal Services* (1987), *Buster* (1988), *Stepping Out* (1991) and *Wide Eyed and Legless* (1993). She is also the author of *Babytalk* (1990), a frank and funny account of motherhood.

Walton, Cecile

Born 1891 Died 1956
Scottish artist and illustrator, the first woman
painter to receive the Royal Scottish Academy's
prestigious Guthrie Award

Cecile Walton was born in Glasgow, the elder daughter of the Scottish painter Edward Arthur Walton. She studied in Paris, Florence and Edinburgh and displayed a prodigious talent as a painter and illustrator. Although she illustrated a number of books, it was as a painter in oils that she attained her major achievements.

She married the artist Eric H M Robertson in 1914 and with him became a leading figure in the Edinburgh Group of artists that flourished from 1912 to 1921. In the late 1920s she turned to theatre decor and a few years later joined the BBC as organizer of the Scottish Children's Hour. She retired in 1948 to Kirkcudbright where she took up painting again.

Wang Guangmei (Wang Kuang-mei)

Born 1921
Chinese politician who has held several important
positions

Wang Guangmei was born in Beijing and educated at Furen and Yanjing Universities. She is the widow of the Chinese politician Liu Shaoqi (Liu Shao-ch'i), Mao's one-time deputy, who was denounced during the Cultural Revolution, and who is reported to have died in detention c.1970.

She has held a number of important political posts including that of director of the Foreign Affairs Bureau (1979), and has served as a member of successive standing committees of the Chinese People's Political Consultative Conference from 1979.

During the Cultural Revolution she is reported as having been persecuted and maltreated by **Jiang Qing**.

Ward, Elizabeth Stuart Phelps, *originally* Mary Gray Phelps

Born 1844 Died 1911
American feminist and author of a string of
emotionally religious novels

Mary Phelps was born in Boston. In 1852 her mother Elizabeth Stuart Phelps died and she adopted her name. She began to write fiction the following year. The early inspiration for her religious novels about Heaven, *The Gates Ajar* (1868), *Beyond The Gates* (1883), *The Gates Between* (1889) and *Within The Gates* (1901), was drawn from the bitter experience of the death of her own beloved husband in the Civil War. *The Gates Ajar* was an immediate bestseller, selling over 180,000 copies in the USA and England.

She vowed never to marry another and threw her energies into writing, but in her mid-forties relented and married the 27-year-old Herbert Dickinson Ward. Feminists have applauded her insistence on women's right to self-fulfilment and her *Doctor Zay* (1882) broke new ground in representing women in the medical profession.

Ward, Dame (Lucy) Geneviève Teresa

Born 1838 Died 1922
American-born British singer and actress, the first to be created DBE

Geneviève Ward was born in New York. In her youth she was a great opera singer (as Ginevra Guerrabella) and when her voice failed she became a great tragedienne, primarily on the English stage, beginning her career as Lady Macbeth in Manchester in 1873.

She did gain an international reputation however, particularly after her enormous success in 1879 at the Lyceum, of which she was manager for a time, with a little-known play by Herman Merivale and F C Grove called *Forget-Me-Not*. Among her famous roles were Portia, **Eleanor of Aquitaine** in *Becket*, which Lord Tennyson requested her to play, and Queen Margaret (**Margaret of Anjou**) in *Richard III*. She was still acting at 83.

She wrote *Both Sides of the Curtain* (1918) with Richard Whiteing and was created DBE in 1921, the first actress to be so honoured.

Ward, Henrietta Mary Ada, *née* Ward

Born 1832 Died 1924
English painter who received many portrait commissions from Queen Victoria and Prince Albert and taught several of the royal children

Henrietta Ward was the only child of two artistic parents. Her talents were encouraged from an early age, when she was instructed initially by her father and grandfather, before she undertook further training. At the age of 11 she had met the artist Edward Ward (no relation) who was then 27; they became engaged in 1847 but had to marry secretly in 1848 because of parental hostility to their union, which continued until their death.

Henrietta had eight children, but nevertheless continued to paint and was regarded as exceptional, painting both domestic and historical subjects and undertaking several

royal commissions. On the death of her husband in 1879, Henrietta decided to open an Art School for 'young ladies' in London.

She continued to exhibit, albeit more rarely, and some of her work was shown at the Chicago Exposition of 1893 and in the Royal Academy in 1924, when she was 91.

Ward, Mrs Humphry, *née* Mary Augusta Arnold

Born 1851 Died 1920
English scholar, anti-suffragette and novelist

Mary Augusta Arnold was born in Hobart, Tasmania, a granddaughter of the scholar Dr Thomas Arnold of Rugby, and niece of poet and critic Matthew Arnold. The family returned to Britain in 1856 and, after attending private boarding schools, she joined them in Oxford in 1867. In 1872 she married Thomas Humphry Ward (1845–1926), a Fellow and tutor of Brasenose College, Oxford, member of the staff of *The Times*, and editor of *The English Poets* (5 vols, 1880–1918).

Mrs Ward contributed to *Macmillan's* and, as a student of Spanish literature, wrote Lives of early Spanish ecclesiastics for the *Dictionary of Christian Biography* edited by Sir William Smith (1813–93). In 1879 she became secretary to Somerville College, Oxford, before moving to London in 1881, where she wrote for various periodicals. A children's story, *Milly and Olly* (1881), *Miss Bretherton* (1884), a slight novel, and a translation (1885) of Henri Frédéric Amiel's *Journal intime* preceded her greatest success, the bestselling spiritual romance *Robert Elsmere* (1888) which controversially suggested that social commitment rather than theology could form the basis of faith and inspired the philanthropist Passmore Edwards to found a settlement for the London poor in 1897 in Tavistock Square.

Her later novels, all on social or religious issues, include *Marcella* (1894), *Sir George Tressady* (1896), and *The Case of Richard Meynell* (1911). She was an enthusiastic social worker and anti-suffragette, believing that women would lose their moral influence if they gained the vote, and became first President of the Anti-Suffrage League in 1908. She published *A Writer's Recollections* in 1918.

Ward, Mary, *originally* Joan Ward

Born 1585 Died 1645
English religious reformer and educator

Mary Ward was born in Yorkshire. She founded various schools in France and Germany, then returned to England to found in 1609 a Catholic society for women, modelled on the Society of Jesus. She and her devotees founded schools and taught in them, giving up the cloistered existence and the habit of nuns to work in the community.

Although their work was not questioned, these innovations were, for pastoral work was thought by the English Catholic leaders to be unsuitable for women, whilst door-to-door visiting was considered potentially scandalous. During the time they appealed to Rome, Ward contined to found schools in Italy, Germany, Austria and Hungary. Pope Urban VIII at last called her to Rome and suppressed her society in 1630.

When she did not stop her work, she was arrested as a heretic, but managed to continue in Rome until she was allowed to return to England in 1639. Her institute was fully restored, with papal permission, in 1877 and became the model for modern Catholic women's institutes.

Deborah Warner being congratulated by Franco Zeffirelli, 1992

Wardle, Elizabeth, *née* Wardle

Born 1834 Died 1902
English embroiderer who founded the Leek School
of Art Embroidery

Elizabeth Wardle was born in Leek, Staffordshire. In 1857 she married her cousin Thomas Wardle, whose silk firm provided most of the technical knowledge behind William Morris's specially dyed fabrics and silks for embroidery. Elizabeth founded the Leek Embroidery Society in 1879 to promote the works of the middle-class lady embroiderers, while employing professional embroideresses and reminding the ladies that they could not hope to 'make a living from it'. Around 1881 she founded the Leek School of Art Embroidery.

Thomas Wardle was knighted for his services to the silk industry in 1897, an honour that was certainly helped by his wife's involvement in the Society and School of Art Embroidery, both of which he used to promote his own business interests.

Warner, Deborah

Born 1959
English theatre director who has already won two
Olivier awards for her work

Deborah Warner was born in Oxford. She was educated at Sidcot School, Avon, and St Clare's College, Oxford, then at the Central School of Speech and Drama. She founded the Kick Theatre Company in 1980, and was its artistic director from 1980 to 1986, during which time its success at the Edinburgh Festival Fringe regularly overshadowed that of the better-

known theatre companies. Warner then became resident director at the Royal Shakespeare Company (1987–9) and associate director of the Royal National Theatre in 1989.

She repeated the success of the Kick Theatre's productions of Brecht's *The Good Woman of Szechwan* (1980) and Shakespeare's *King Lear* (1985) at the National Theatre in 1989 and 1990, and won the *Evening Standard* and Laurence Olivier awards for direction in 1988 for her acclaimed *Electra*, which was revived in 1992. She also won an Olivier for her production of Ibsen's *Hedda Gabler* at the Abbey Theatre in Dublin in 1991. She is renowned for her collaborations with actress **Fiona Shaw**, which have included a contoversial *Richard II* (1995).

She began directing opera in 1992 and went on to work at the Salzburg Festival (1993) and at the Glyndebourne Festival (1994).

Warner, Marina Sarah

Born 1946
English literary critic and writer at the forefront
of modern feminist writing

Marina Warner was born in London and educated at St Mary's Convent, Ascot, and at Lady Margaret Hall, Oxford. She was the Paul Getty Scholar at the Getty Centre for the History of Art and the Humanities (1987–8) and the Tinbergen Professor at Erasmus University, Rotterdam (1990–1).

In 1969 she was Young Writer of the Year, and she was also awarded the Fawcett Prize in 1986 and the Commonwealth Writers' Prize

(Eurasia) in 1989. In 1994 she delivered the Reith Lectures — a series entitled 'Six Myths of Our Time', which has since been published as *Managing Monsters* (1994). Other publications include *Alone of all her Sex: The Myth and Culture of the Virgin Mary* (1976), *Monuments and Maidens* (1985) and *Mermaids in the Basement* (1993).

Warner, Susan Bogert, *pseud of* Elizabeth Wetherell

Born 1819 Died 1885
American novelist who wrote one of the first bestsellers in the USA

Susan Bogert Warner was born in New York. She wrote to support her family and had a huge success with *The Wide, Wide World* (1851), followed by *Queechy* (1852) and other sentimental and emotional tales.

She collaborated in many books with her sister Anna Bartlett (1827–1915) who, sometimes under the name Amy Lothrop, wrote popular stories such as *My Brother's Keeper* (1855) and *Stories of Vinegar Hill* (6 vols, 1892) and was the author of popular children's hymns like 'Jesus Loves Me, This I Know' and 'Jesus bids us Shine'.

Warner, Sylvia Townsend

Born 1893 Died 1978
English musicologist, communist and writer in many forms

Sylvia Townsend Warner was born in Harrow. A student of music, she researched music in the 15th and 16th centuries and was one of the four editors of the 10-volume *Tudor Church Music* (1923–9).

She was a communist and a lesbian, and lived most of her life with the extraordinary Valentine Ackland, an alcoholic amazon. Together they strongly resisted the rise of Fascism in Europe, a commitment which Warner expresses through her writing. She published seven novels, four volumes of poetry, essays, and eight volumes of short stories, many of which had previously appeared in the *New Yorker*.

Ranging widely in theme, locale, and period, significant titles are *Lolly Willowes* (1926), *Mr Fortune's Maggot* (1927), *Summer Will Show* (1936), *After the Death of Don Juan* (1938) and *The Corner That Held Them* (1948).

Warwick, Dionne, *also spelt* Warwicke

Born 1940
American soul and pop singer popular during the 1960s and 1970s

Dionne Warwick was born in East Orange, New Jersey, to a musical family (which includes Cissy and **Whitney Houston**). She was discovered by songwriters Burt Bacharach and Hal David, who wrote 'Anyone Who Had a Heart', 'Walk on By' (1964), 'I Say A Little Prayer' (1967) and 'Do You Know the Way to San Jose' (1968) for her, among other songs; in the UK, her thunder was stolen by **Cilla Black**'s cover versions.

Warwick was less successful after splitting from Bacharach/David, but had a number-one hit with The Spinners on 'Then Came You' (1974). She had added the final 'e' to her name for extra class, but dropped it again in the mid-1970s.

Washington, Dinah, *stage name of* Ruth Jones

Born 1924 Died 1963
American jazz and rhythm-and-blues singer

Dinah Washington was born in Tuscaloosa, Alabama. After an apprenticeship in gospel with the Sara Martin Singers, she made a gradual (though never complete) switch to jazz, joining the Lionel Hampton band in 1943 and shortly thereafter making her first recordings as leader.

Commercial success afforded her considerable freedom and she was able to divide her activities between lucrative r'n'b sessions and more taxing encounters with improvisers like trumpeter Clifford Brown.

She attempted to assuage personal problems with alcohol and serial monogamy, but her lifestyle took its toll and she died aged just 38, too soon to see her crossover approach become the dominant style in Black popular music in the USA.

Wasserstein, Wendy

Born 1950
American playwright who won the 1989 Pulitzer Prize for Drama for The Heidi Chronicles

Wendy Wasserstein was born in Brooklyn, New York City, and educated at Mount Holyoke College and Yale Drama School. She has written adaptations and screenplays for television, notably John Cheever's *The Sorrows of Gin*.

Her early stage plays include *Any Woman Can't* (1974), which deals with the obstacles confronting an aspiring career woman who eventually settles for marriage, and the punningly titled *When Dinah Shore Ruled the Earth*

(1975), a parody of beauty contests, written with Christopher Durang. *Uncommon Women and Others* (1977) and *Isn't It Romantic* (1981) are accounts of the lives of contemporary young women in New York.

She won a Pulitzer Prize in 1989 for *The Heidi Chronicles* (1988), a play about an unfulfilled feminist lecturer reflecting on the achievements and failures of the women's movement. Wasserstein's most recent work includes the comedy *The Sisters Rosensweig* (1990).

Waters, Ethel, *née* Howard

Born 1896 Died 1977
American jazz singer and actress who was still performing at the age of 80

Ethel Waters was born in Chester, Pennsylvania. She made her first recordings in 1921, when she was backed by the Fletcher Henderson orchestra, and later worked with Duke Ellington, Benny Goodman and others.

From the late 1930s she branched out into acting roles, notably in *Cabin in the Sky* (1943). Growing up in the North gave her a less secure blues feel than either **Bessie Smith** or **Ma Rainey** and she was much influenced by white vaudevilleans. However, her vocal improvisations made a considerable impact on **Ella Fitzgerald**.

Waters's autobiography, *His Eye is on the Sparrow* (1951), is a powerfully moving narrative, documenting how religious faith sustained her through years of prejudice and neglect.

Waterston, Jane Elizabeth

Born 1843 Died 1933
Free Church of Scotland missionary who became a pioneer educationalist and physician in South Africa

Jane Waterston was born in Inverness. As a missionary commissioned by the Free Church of Scotland, she went out to South Africa. She was head of Lovedale girls' school (1866–73) in Lovedale, South Africa, before returning to Europe to train as a doctor.

Though appointed as an assistant to Robert Laws at Livingstonia, a personality clash forced *Noqataka* — the unconventional and forceful 'mother of activity' as she was known — to return to Lovedale. Failing to get mission support to carry out medical work there, she set up a private medical practice in Cape Town in 1883, where she also became famous for philanthropic and political work.

Watkins, Margaret, *originally* Meta Gladys Watkins

Born 1884 Died 1969
Canadian photographer transitional between pictorialism and the modernist 'new objectivity'

Meta Watkins was born in Hamilton, Ontario, to emigré Scottish parents. She studied at the Clarence White School of Photography in New York City, where she taught from 1917 and became an influential colleague and teacher of photographers such as **Laura Gilpin**, Paul Outerbridge and **Doris Ulmann**. In about 1916 she opened her own photographic studio in New York, specializing in highly professional advertising work for major companies.

Her still-lifes celebratory of mundane objects, notably *Kitchen Sink* and *Domestic Symphony* (both 1919), were forerunners of the formalist images of the *Neue Sachlichkeit* ('new objectivity'). Her work, which also included sensitive portraits and nude studies, was widely exhibited in the USA (with a solo show at the Art Center, New York, in 1923) and internationally. In 1926 she was resident Vice-President of the Pictorial Photographers of America.

After the early death of Clarence White (1925), Watkins went to Europe in 1928 and visited her mother's three elderly sisters in the family home in Glasgow. There she remained, caring for them and making trips to other parts of Europe, including the USSR, but finding it difficult to make a living from her work. When the last of the aunts died in 1939, she found herself still stranded in Glasgow by the outbreak of World War II. She lived a reclusive life until her death, and her work was rediscovered by her executor, Joseph Mulholland; it has since been re-exhibited and its importance recognized.

Watson, Janet Vida

Born 1923 Died 1985
Scottish geologist who was the first and, to date, the only female President of the Geological Society of London (1982–4)

Janet Watson was born in London, the daughter of David Watson, the vertebrate palaeontologist. Inspired first by Herbert Leader Hawkins at Reading University and then by Herbert Harold Read at Imperial College, London, she embarked on her life's work, the study of crystalline basement rocks. This she did with her fellow student John Sutton, whom she married in 1949, thus forming one of the most remarkable partnerships in the history of geology.

Their classic work, first published in 1951, on the Lewisian basement of north-west Scotland, led to the recognition of the older Scourian events, separated by some 1,000 million years from the younger Laxfordian. Watson's gentle and unassuming manner belied great intellect and many honours were bestowed upon her, including a personal chair at Imperial College and fellowship of the Royal Society of London.

Watt, Elizabeth Mary

Born 1886 Died 1954
Scottish artist known for her painted wooden
boxes and decorated ceramics

Elizabeth Mary Watt was born in Dundee and studied at Glasgow School of Art from 1906 to 1917.

She painted portraits (mainly children) and flower and landscape studies in watercolour. Her well-known painted wooden boxes and decorated ceramics are striking in their linear design, ranging from abstract patterns to fairyland subjects.

In 1939 she lamented to Nan Muirhead Moffat: 'now, alas, I paint butter dishes for the proletariat!'

Weaver, Sigourney (Susan Alexandra)

Born 1949
American film and stage actress first known as
Ripley in the Alien *trilogy*

Sigourney Weaver was born in New York City, the daughter of an actress and the former President of NBC. She read English at Stanford University and studied drama at Yale before entering the acting profession in off-Broadway plays and as an understudy to **Ingrid Bergman** in *The Constant Wife* (1974). She made her film début with a tiny role in *Annie Hall* (1977) and achieved her first major success in *Alien* (1979).

A tall, patrician woman, able to project cool intelligence and steely determination, she brought a gutsy physical presence to the astronaut Ripley in the entire *Alien* trilogy and was equally powerful in such dramatic roles as the obsessive naturalist **Dian Fossey** in *Gorillas In The Mist* (1988) and the vengeance-seeking torture victim in *Death And The Maiden* (1994).

Her flare for comedy was also revealed in *Ghostbusters* (1984) and as the bitchy boss in *Working Girl* (1988). Her frequent stage appearances include *Old Times* (1981), *Hurlyburly* (1984) and *The Merchant Of Venice* (1986).

Webb, (Martha) Beatrice, *née* Potter

Born 1858 Died 1943
English social reformer, social historian and
economist

Beatrice Potter was born in Gloucester, the eighth daughter of a businessman. Much of her education was gleaned through talking to her father's friends and reading. Following the failure of a relationship with the Liberal statesman Joseph Chamberlain to result in marriage, she undertook social work in London, learning about the life of the working class and their own organizations — the labour unions — and wrote the book *The Cooperative Movement in Great Britain* (1891), which drew on her earlier experiences of visiting relatives in Lancashire.

Her social work made her realize that the root causes of poverty could only be addressed through proper knowledge of the affected section of society, and it was while researching labour unions and working-class economic conditions that she was introduced in 1890 to Sidney James Webb, later Baron Passfield (1859–1947), an early member of the Fabian Society. They married in 1892 and formed a remarkably complementary partnership that was dedicated to Fabian Socialist values and to a radical, pioneering approach to social reform.

Together they established the London School of Economics and Political Science (1895) and became highly influential in many areas of society. Most of the social and political reforms of the time came about as a result of the Webb's research and political insight. From 1914 they actively supported the Labour Party, providing intellectual leadership. Sidney became an MP in 1922 and they continued with their joint publications, which include *Decay of Capitalist Civilisation* (1923). By 1932 however, the Webbs had become disillusioned with the Labour Party; they paid a visit to the Soviet Union and were so impressed that they wrote *Soviet Communism: A New Civilization?* (1935). Beatrice Webb alone also wrote *Factory Acts* (1901).

Webb, Mary Gladys, *née* Meredith

Born 1881 Died 1927
English writer best known for Precious Bane *and*
other novels based in Shropshire

Mary Meredith was born in Leighton, near the Wrekin in Shropshire. In 1912 she married Henry B L Webb and lived mostly in Shropshire, market gardening and novel-writing. *Precious Bane* (1924) won her belated fame as a writer of English and a novelist of the soil, the dialect, and superstition of Shropshire, expressing 'the continuity of country life'. The emotional intensity of her work has sometimes brought comparison with that of Thomas Hardy.

Her other works include the novels *The Golden Arrow* (1916), *Gone to Earth* (1917), *The House in Dormer Forest* (1920), *Seven for a Secret* (1922) and the unfinished *Armour Wherein He Trusted* (1929); nature essays, *The Spring of Joy* (1917); and poems.

Her novels were later parodied by **Stella Gibbons** in *Cold Comfort Farm*.

Webb, Phyllis, née Bane

Born 1927
Canadian poet and teacher of literature and creative writing recognized as one of Canada's leading poets

Phyllis Bane was born in Victoria, British Columbia, and educated at the University of British Columbia. Whilst doing graduate work at McGill University, Montreal, she published *Trio* (1954) with two other poets, and after some other volumes she received a Governor General's award for *The Vision Tree* (1982), a collection of poetry spanning 30 years.

Her poetry has been described as 'honed down to an extraordinary intellectual spareness', but this judgement excludes the conversational tone that Webb uses to convey her complex ideas and surreal imagery.

Weber, Helene

Born 1881 Died 1962
German politician honoured with the Grosse Bundeverdiendstyren *for her work*

Helene Weber was born at Elberfeld in North Rhine–Westphalia. After teaching for five years in a state primary school she studied history, French and philosophy at Bonn and Grenoble.

In 1917 she took over the *Soziale Frauenschule* in Cologne, a welfare school for women which operated under the auspices of the German Catholic Women's Federation. Three years later she joined the Prussian Ministry of Social Welfare and from 1919 to 1933 was a member of the National Assembly, representing the Zentrum Party, until the rise of the Nazis.

During World War II she carried out private welfare work and after the War she joined the Christian Democratic Party and was elected to the NRW assembly. In 1957 she was awarded the *Grosse Bundeverdiendstyren*, the highest civilian award.

Webster, Margaret

Born 1905 Died 1972
English actress and director, the first woman to direct an opera at the Met

Margaret Webster was born in New York, where her actor parents were performing. She was a child actress from 1917, and made her adult début in the chorus of a classical Greek drama in 1924. Having established her acting career in London, she went back to New York in 1936, where she began to concentrate more (although not exclusively) on directing.

She had a major success directing Paul Robeson in *Othello* on Broadway in 1943, and three years later co-founded the influential American Repertory Company with **Cheryl Crawford** and **Eva Le Gallienne**. She toured Shakespeare in the USA, and later became the first woman to direct an opera at the Metropolitan Opera House in New York.

Weddington, Sarah Ragle

Born 1946
American lawyer renowned for her success in the case of Roe v Wade

Sarah Weddington was born in Abilene, Texas. After entering the Bar in Texas, Washington DC and in District Court, she practised law in Austin, Texas.

In 1973 she made her name by successfully arguing the abortion/privacy case Roe v. Wade before the US Supreme Court, a landmark case that resulted in the legalization of abortion.

In 1992 she wrote *A Question of Choice*.

Wedgwood, Dame (Cicely) Veronica

Born 1910
English historian who is a specialist in 17th-century history

Veronica Wedgwood was born in Stocksfield, Northumberland, and educated at Lady Margaret Hall, Oxford.

As a specialist in 17th-century history, she has published such books as biographies of *Strafford* (1935), *Oliver Cromwell* (1939), *William the Silent* (James Tait Black Memorial prize, 1944) and *Montrose* (1955) as well as *The Thirty Years' War* (1938), *The King's Peace* (1955), *The King's War* (1958) and *The Trial of Charles I* (1964).

She was created DBE in 1968.

Weigel, Helene

Born 1900 Died 1972
Austrian-born actress and manager who performed working-class roles in the plays of her husband Bertolt Brecht

Helene Weigel began her acting career in Frankfurt but went to Berlin in 1923 and met Bertolt Brecht (1898–1956), whom she married in 1929. She appeared in the title role of his adaptation of Maxim Gorky's *The Mother* in 1932.

In 1933 she accompanied him in his exile from Germany. On their return to East Berlin in 1948, she and Brecht co-founded and ran the Berliner Ensemble, regarded as one of the great world theatre companies. She found her greatest role as Mother Courage in *Mother Courage and her Children* (1949) and perfectly exemplified his 'alienation' theory of acting.

After Brecht's death in 1956 she managed the Ensemble on her own.

Weil, Simone

Born 1909 Died 1943
French social philosopher and mystic who was influential in France and England

Simone Weil was born in Paris. After a brilliant career as a student she worked for an anarchist trade union and in a factory (to experience the psychological effects of such labour), shared her wages with the unemployed, and lived in poverty. She trained to fight against Franco in the Spanish Civil War in 1936, but became a camp cook because of her pacifism. During World War II she moved to Marseille and wrote for publications supporting the Resistance. She then moved to England, where she died, in Ashford, Kent, of 'self-imposed privation and anorexia'.

Although she was not a creative writer *per se*, Weil's essays reach a singular beauty of creative utterance, and she has influenced countless writers with her quest for purity and justice. In her profound theological thinking she concluded that God, who certainly existed and exists, withdrew himself from the universe after creating it; man is obliged to withdraw himself likewise, from material considerations, and thus return to God. Her prose style is important because in it she increasingly and successfully strove to make herself clear to her reader, eschewing all pretension. She has been accused of over-paradoxicality, but, whether that is just or not, she commands wide respect for her ruthless sincerity and lucidity.

She is at her best in her notebooks, *Cahiers* (1951–6, Eng trans *Notebooks*, 1956), and in *Seventy Letters* (1965). Other influential books include *L'Attente de Dieu* (1949, Eng trans *Waiting for God*, 1959) and *L'Enracinement* (1949–50, Eng trans *The Need for Roots*, 1955).

Weill, Claudia

Born 1947
American film director best known for her television work

Claudia Weill was born in New York City. She is a distant cousin of composer Kurt Weill. She began making films while still at Radcliffe College, and studied painting with Oskar Kokoschka in Salzburg, and photography with Walker Evans (1903–75) at Yale. She combined making experimental short films with directing for television.

She was nominated for an Academy Award with **Shirley MacLaine** for *The Other Half of the Sky* in 1975. Her feature début, *Girlfriends* (1978), was a commercial success. Much of her subsequent work has been for television, where she directed the cult series *thirtysomething*.

Weir, Judith

Born 1954
Scottish lecturer and composer of her operas, vocal and instrumental works

Judith Weir was born in Cambridge of an Aberdeenshire family. Her composition teachers were John Tavener, Robin Holloway and Olivier Messiaen. She was educated at King's College, Cambridge, and was Cramb Fellow, Glasgow University (1979–82) and Composer-in-Residence at the Royal Scottish Academy of Music (1988–91).

She had notable success with her operas *The Black Spider* (1984), *A Night at the Chinese*

Judith Weir, 1974

Opera (Kent Opera, 1987) and *The Vanishing Bridegroom* (Scottish Opera, 1990). Other vocal works include *The Consolations of Scholarship* (1985), *Lovers, Learners and Libations* (1987), *Missa del Cid* (1988) and *HEAVEN ABLAZE* (1989, with two pianos and eight dancers). Her instrumental works include keyboard music, a string quartet (1990), *Sederunt Principes* (1987, for chamber orchestra), and many other works.

Weir, Molly (Mary)

Born 1920
Scottish actress and writer who has been
successful on stage, screen, radio, television and
the printed page

Molly Weir was born in Glasgow, a sister of the hillwalker and broadcaster Tom Weir. Though she was determined to enter showbusiness, she nevertheless studied at commercial college, achieving a shorthand speed of 300 words a minute. Her boundless energy soon took her into the acting profession.

After making her film début in *2000 Women* (1944), she appeared in *Flesh and Blood* (1951) and *The Prime of Miss Jean Brodie* (1969), among others, but achieved her greatest renown as the creator of such well-loved radio characters as Tattie Mackintosh in *ITMA* (1939–49) and the housekeeper Aggie in *Life With the Lyons*, which ran throughout the 1950s and also spawned the films *Life with the Lyons* (1954) and *The Lyons in Paris* (1955).

She has appeared in numerous television series, acted on stage, served as a radio panellist and culinary expert, and also earned a place in the Guinness Book of Records for the longest piece of female autobiographical writing, which began with *Shoes Were for Sunday* (1970), and has continued with such volumes as *Best Foot Forward* (1972) and *Spinning Like a Peerie* (1983).

Welch, Raquel, *originally* Raquel Tejada

Born 1940
American actress who came to fame as a sixties
sex symbol

Racquel Tejada was born in Chicago, Illinois. As a child she studied ballet and began entering beauty contests as a teenager. She was a model, waitress and television weatherforecaster before making her film début in *A House is Not a Home* (1964). She was launched as a curvaceous sex symbol after her scantilyclad appearance in *One Million Years B.C.* (1966).

Rarely challenged by later roles, she did evince some comic ability in *The Three Musketeers* (1973), for which she received a Best Actress Golden Globe award. Absent from the cinema since 1979, she continues to be regarded as one of the world's great beauties and her professional career has included nightclub entertaining, the Broadway musical *Woman of the Year* (1982), and the publication of *The Raquel Welch Total Beauty and Fitness Programme* (1984) and related videos.

Weldon, Fay

Born 1931
English novelist and author of television
screenplays who takes an ironic look at sexual
politics and at the role of women in modern society

Fay Weldon was born in Alvechurch, Worcestershire, and educated at St Andrews University. She became a successful advertising copywriter and is credited with creating the slogan: 'Go to work on an Egg'. Her early writing for television was marked by the award-winning first episode of *Upstairs, Downstairs*.

Her first novel, *The Fat Woman's Joke*, appeared in 1967. It has been followed by many more, in which her recurring themes include the nature of women's sexuality and experience in a patriarchal world. Although her women are usually morally and culturally more sophisticated than the men around them, they can also exert uncompromising revenge upon the world, as in *The Life and Loves of a She-Devil* (1983), in which an ugly and rejected heroine seeks retribution. Weldon later adapted this for television.

Other novels include *Puffball* (1980), which looks at pregnancy and womanhood, and *The Cloning of Joanna May* (1989), which considers genetic engineering.

Wells, Kitty, *née* Muriel Deason Wright

Born 1919
American country-and-western singer, the first
woman to have a number-one country hit

Kitty Wells was born in Nashville, Tennessee, where she sang in gospel choirs as a child. She performed on radio in the early 1930s and in the 1950s became a regular on *The Grand Ole Opry* country music show in Nashville.

She became the first woman to have number-one country hit with her signature song, 'It Wasn't God Who Made Honky Tonk

Angels' in 1952, and was named to the Country Music Hall of Fame in 1976.

Wells-Barnett, Ida, *née* Wells

Born 1862 Died 1931
African-American journalist and activist who led
an anti-lynching crusade in the 1890s

Ida Wells was born in Holly Springs, Mississippi, to parents who were slaves. She became a teacher then turned to journalism, writing under the pseudonym Iola for newspapers owned by blacks. In 1895 she married Ferdinand Lee Barnett, the editor of the *Chicago Conservator*. She was an active campaigner against lynching and chronicled the crimes in a pamphlet entitled *Southern Horrors* (1892).

She was also one of two women who signed a call for the formation of the NAACP (National Association for the Advancement of Colored People) and, on her own, founded the first black woman suffrage organization, the Alpha Suffrage Club of Chicago.

Welty, Eudora

Born 1909
American novelist and short-story writer

Eudora Welty was born in Jackson, Mississippi. She was educated at the Mississippi State College for Women, the University of Wisconsin, and the Columbia University School of Advertizing in New York. After leaving college she was a publicity agent with the Works Progress Administration in Mississippi which involved extensive travel through the state. She took numerous photographs which were published as *One Time, One Place: Mississippi in the Depression: A Snapshot Album*, in 1971.

During World War II she was on the staff of the *New York Review of Books*. She started writing short stories with 'Death of a Travelling Salesman', and published several collections from 1941 to 1954. She has also written five novels, mostly drawn from Mississippi life: *The Robber Bridegroom* (1942), *Delta Wedding* (1946), *The Ponder Heart* (1954), *Losing Battles* (1970) and *The Optimist's Daughter* (1972), which won the 1973 Pulitzer Prize. *The Collected Stories of Eudora Welty* was published in 1980, and *Eudora Welty Photographs* in 1989. Her autobiography, *One Writer's Beginnings*, was published in 1984.

Among her many accolades, she has received two Guggenheim Fellowships, three O Henry awards and the National Medal for Literature.

Wenzel, Hanni

Born 1956
Liechtenstein alpine skier who has won a record
number of Olympic golds for skiing

Hannie Wenzel was born in Staubirnen, Germany. At the 1980 Olympics she won the gold medal in the slalom and giant slalom, and the silver in the downhill. Her total of four Olympic gold medals (including a bronze in 1976) is a record for any skier. She was combined world champion and overall World Cup winner in 1980.

Wertmuller, Lina, *originally* Arcangela Felice Assunta Wertmuller von Elgg

Born 1928
Italian film director who has courted controversy
in her work

Lina Wertmuller was born in Rome. Although a rebellious child, she became a teacher, but soon turned her attention to the theatre. She spent 10 years as an actress, writer and director, but eventually moved into film through her friendship with Marcello Mastroianni, who introduced her to Federico Fellini.

Her best-known film as a director is *Pasqualino Sette Bellezze (1976, Seven Beauties)*, set in a Nazi concentration camp, which brought her the distinction of being the first woman director to be nominated for an Academy Award.

Wesley, Mary, *pseud of* Mary Aline Mynors Siepmann, *née* Farmar

Born 1912
English novelist who came to notice with The
Camomile Lawn *at the age of 70*

Mary Farmar was born in Englefield Green, Berkshire, the daughter of a distinguished soldier, and educated at home until she was allowed to attend lectures at the London School of Economics. She became Baroness Swinfen on marrying Charles, 2nd Baron Swinfen, but the marriage did not last. She met Eric Siepmann (d.1970), a journalist, during World War II, changed her name by deed poll, and remained with him until he died, leaving her virtually destitute. She wrote two children's books, *Speaking Terms* and *The Sixth Seal* (both 1969), before publishing her first adult novel, *Jumping the Queue*, in 1983, at the age of 70.

She has since produced a succession of books dealing with middle-class mores, each written with ironic, detached amusement and taking an unblinkered though compassionate look at sexual values.

The Camomile Lawn (1984) considers sexual and emotional relationships in the turmoil of war, while *Second Fiddle* (1988) deals with the relationship between a middle-aged woman and a young, hopeful male novelist. Others include *A Sensible Life* (1990), *A Dubious Legacy* (1993) and *An Imaginative Experience* (1994).

Wesley, Susanna, *née* Annesley

Born 1669 Died 1742
English mother of Charles and John Wesley, the founders of Methodism

Susanna Annesley was one of three survivors of the 24 children of Samuel Annesley, a dissenting London minister. In 1688 she married Samuel Wesley, rector of Epworth, Lincolnshire, 1697–1735. She had become an Anglican at 13 but never lost her Puritan heritage of serious devotion to spiritual and practical responsibilities.

She kept a spiritual journal, read widely in theology, ran a disciplined and obedient household, and gave her children six hours' instruction in reading and writing a day from age five. John (1703–91), her fifteenth child (out of 19) and second surviving son, was prepared for Confirmation when he was eight. She was always concerned for his spiritual welfare, and he, in his turn, felt able in his early ministry to consult her on theological questions. Charles (1707–88) is best remembered as the author of over 5,500 hymns.

When Susanna's husband was away, she supplemented what she considered the curate's meagre spiritual offerings by holding informal kitchen meetings on Sunday evenings. They were intended for family and servants but attracted audiences of over 200.

West, Dottie

Born 1932 Died 1991
American country music singer and songwriter, and originator of 'Here Comes My Baby'

Dottie West was born in McMinnville, Tennessee. She began her career in 1961 with a duet with Jim Reeves entitled 'Is this Me?'. With her husband Bill West she co-wrote the song 'Here Comes My Baby', which has been recorded by more than 100 artists.

Her awards include Best Female Artist Grammys in 1965 for 'Here Comes My Baby' and in 1972 for 'Coca Cola Girl', and the Country Music Association award for Best Vocal Duo (with Kenny Rogers) in 1978 and 1979.

West, Mae

Born 1893 Died 1980
American actress and sex symbol who apparently never did say: 'Why don't you come up and see me sometime?'

Mae West was born in Brooklyn, New York. She made her début on Broadway in 1911, specializing in roles of sultry sexual innuendo, and became known as an archetypal sex symbol whose vulgarity and mockery was ultimately endearing.

She wrote many of the plays she starred in, like *Sex* (1926) and *Diamond Lil* (1928, later filmed as *She Done Him Wrong* with Cary Grant, 1933), which are riddled with double meanings. Her other films included *I'm No Angel* (1933), *Klondyke Annie* (1934) and *My Little Chickadee* (1940). She returned to the screen in 1970 in *Myra Breckenridge*.

The 'Mae West', an inflatable life-jacket, is affectionately named after her.

West, Dame Rebecca, *adopted name of* Cecily Isabel Fairfield

Born 1892 Died 1983
Irish novelist, biographer, journalist, and critic who was witty, incisive and combative

Cecily Fairfield was born in County Kerry. Her father, a journalist, left her mother and the family moved to Edinburgh where they lived in straitened circumstances. She was educated at George Watson's Ladies College, and trained for the stage in London, where in 1912 she adopted the *nom de plume* Rebecca West, the heroine of Ibsen's *Rosmersholm* which she had once played, and who is characterized by a passionate will.

From a formative age she was involved with the suffragettes and in 1911 joined the staff of the *Freewoman*, the following year becoming a political writer on the *Clarion*, a socialist newspaper. Her love affair with H G Wells (1866–1946) began in 1913 and lasted for 10 turbulent years during which time she bore him a son and laid the foundations for her career as a writer. Her first published book (1916) was a critical study of Henry James (1843–1916); her second, a novel, *The Return of the Soldier* (1918), describes the homecoming of a shell-shocked soldier. After the final break with Wells she went to the USA where she lectured and formed a long association with the *New York Herald-Tribune*.

In 1930 she married Henry Maxwell Andrews, a banker, and they lived in Buckinghamshire until his death in 1968. She published eight novels including *The Judge* (1922), *Harriet Hume* (1929), *The Thinking Reed*

(1936), and the largely autobiographical *The Fountain Overflows* (1957); her last (unfinished) novel was *Cousin Rosamund* (1988). She was described by George Bernard Shaw as handling a pen 'as brilliantly as ever I could and much more savagely'. In the mid-1930s she made several trips to the Balkans to gather material for a travel book, but her interest deepened and resulted in her masterful analysis of the origins of World War II, *Black Lamb and Grey Falcon*, published in two volumes in 1941. It is generally considered her magnum opus.

During World War II she superintended BBC broadcasts to Yugoslavia and in its aftermath she attended the Nuremberg War Crimes Trials. From this and other cases came *The Meaning of Treason* (1949) and *A Train of Powder* (1955).

West, Rosemary

Born 1953
English murderer whose Gloucester home was dubbed the 'house of horror'

Rosemary West married a divorced builder named Frederick (1941–95) in 1972. She had seven children. The couple came to public notice when the remains of their daughter Heather, who had not been seen since the age of 16 in 1987, were found underneath the floor of their home at 25 Cromwell Street, Gloucester. The remains of eight more bodies of young women and girls were discovered there, in addition to three at other sites, some of which had been buried in the 1970s.

The couple were arrested, but before reaching trial Fred was found hanged in his prison cell on 1 January 1995 and the 12 murder charges against him were dropped. In November 1995 Rosemary West was found guilty of murdering 10 young women, including one of her daughters, and sentenced to life imprisonment.

Westbrook, Kate (Katherine Jane), *née* Barnard

Born 1936/37
English jazz vocalist and composer who has collaborated with her husband and established her own group

Kate Barnard was born in Guildford, Surrey, supposedly around 1936 or 1937. She initially studied art and worked as a painter in the USA and Britain.

While teaching at Leeds College of Art, she joined the Mike Westbrook Brass Band as singer and tenor horn player. She and Westbrook subsequently married and have since collaborated on a range of jazz and jazz-influenced compositions, most notably *The Cortege* (1982) and *London Bridge is Broken Down* (1987), together with settings of Rimbaud, Lorca and Blake.

Her own compositions and Grand Guignol vocal style are featured on *Peter Lorre is Dead* (1991) and with her own group, The Skirmishers.

Weston, Dame Agnes Elizabeth

Born 1840 Died 1918
English philanthropist who founded Sailors' Rests in England

Agnes Weston was brought up in Bath, where her father was a barrister. Here she helped in the reading and coffee rooms laid on annually for the assembling of the Somerset Militia. After being persuaded to address a sailors' wives meeting at Devonport, she joined with Sophia Wintz in the fight against intemperance in the navy.

From 1873 she spoke for the National Temperance League. The first Sailors' Rests, Christian social club alternatives to pubs which offered food and accommodation, were set up in Devonport (1879) and Portsmouth (1881). Weston also had an enduring concern for the welfare of naval widows and orphans. Her work was recognized by an honorary degree from Glasgow (1901), and a naval burial.

Westwood, Vivienne

Born 1941
English fashion designer of worldwide renown who began with punk designs in the King's Road

Vivienne Westwood was born in London. She was a primary-school teacher in early adulthood, but turned her attention to clothes design on meeting Malcolm McLaren. If not, as they would claim, the inventors of punk, the pair were certainly its leading costumiers. Based from 1971 in a shop — known variously as 'Sex' and 'Seditionaries' — on the King's Road, London, they created designs using rubber, leather, and bondage gear, which were influenced by the paraphernalia of pornography.

Since her split from McLaren in 1983, Westwood has become accepted by the mainstream, and recognized as a highly original designer; she was Designer of the Year in 1990 and 1991. Hers is a peculiarly English genius, a contradictory combination of reverence and iconoclasm (padded bottoms were a feature of her 1994 collection), nonetheless greatly esteemed in international fashion.

Wethered, Joyce, *married name* Lady Heathcoat Amory

Born 1901
English golfer, a great ambassador for the sport who always enjoyed golf for the sake of the game

Joyce Wethered was born in Surrey and was taught to play golf by her brother Roger, who was a British champion and Walker Cup player. She entered the English women's championship in 1920 just for fun and ended up defeating **Cecil Leitch**, the best player of the day, winning the title on what was to be the first of five occasions.

She also won the British championship a record four times, three times before she retired in 1925 and then again when she returned to the sport to play at St Andrews in 1929. In the same year her family lost their fortune in the Wall Street crash and she gave up her amateur status.

In 1935 she took part in a four-and-a-half month professional tour of America where she played with Bobby Jones, among others, who claimed she was the best golfer he had ever seen. A couple of years later she married Sir John Heathcoat Amory (d.1972) and together they created the famous gardens at their home in Knightshayes Court, which now belong to the National Trust.

Wharton, Edith Newbold, *née* Jones

Born c.1861 Died 1937
American novelist and short-story writer, a novelist of manners and a witty and satirical observer of society

Edith Jones was born in New York into a wealthy and aristocratic family. She was educated at home and in Europe. In 1885 she married Edward Wharton, a friend of the family, and they travelled widely before settling in Paris in 1907. Her husband, however, was mentally unbalanced and they were divorced in 1913. Socially gregarious, she formed a durable friendship with the novelist Henry James (1843–1916) who did much to encourage and influence her work, and corresponded with, among others, the art critic Bernhard Berenson (1865–1959).

The Greater Inclination (1899), her first collection of short stories, was followed by a novella, *The Touchstone* (1900), but it was *The House of Mirth* (1905), a tragedy about a beautiful and sensitive girl destroyed by the very society her upbringing has designed her to meet, that established her as a major novelist. Almost 50 other works followed, including travel books and volumes of verse, but she is known principally as a novelist of manners. Her most uncharacteristic novel is *Ethan Frome* (1911), which deals partly with her unhappy marriage, and partly with primitive people in rural America.

Important later works are *The Age of Innocence* (1920), which won the 1921 Pulitzer Prize, *The Mother's Recompense* (1925), *The Children* (1928) and *Hudson River Bracketed* (1929). Her approach to her work is discussed in *The Writing of Fiction* (1925). *A Backwards Glance* (1934) is her revealing autobiography.

Wheatley, Phillis

Born c.1753 Died 1784
American poet who in 1770 became the first black woman to have work published

Phillis Wheatley was born in Africa, possibly Senegal. As a child she was shipped to the slave-market in Boston, Massachusetts (1761), and sold as a maidservant to the family of a Boston tailor, John Wheatley, who educated her with the rest of his family. She studied Latin and Greek, and started writing poetry in English at the age of 13.

She published *Poems on Various Subjects, Religious and Moral* (1783) and visited England in that year, to huge popular interest, although some cast doubt on her poems' authenticity. In 1778 she married John Peters, a free Negro of Boston.

Her poetry is given classic status in North American literature, and a *Collected Works* appeared in 1988.

Wheeler, Anna, *née* Doyle

Born 1785 Died 1848
Irish feminist and advocate of women's emancipation

Anna Doyle was the daughter of an enlightened Irish landlord. At 15 she married an alcoholic from whom she escaped with her two children in 1812. She was widely read, and she travelled between London and the Continent where her friendships in different political circles enabled her to influence political thinking. Settling in London in 1824, she devoted herself the cause of woman's emancipation. The socialist William Thompson acknowledged that many of the ideas in his *Appeal of One Half the Human Race* (1825) which advocated the right to vote for women, originated with Wheeler.

Whitbread, Fatima, *originally* Fatima Vedad

Born 1961
English javelin thrower whose excellence disproved preconceptions concerning her height

Fatima Vedad was abandoned by her parents as a baby and brought up in a children's home in east London. Her physical education teacher, former British international javelin thrower Margaret Whitbread, recognized her talent, trained her and later adopted her.

Fatima Whitbread, 1987

Traditionally considered too short at 1.36 metres to excell at the javelin, Whitbread secured an Olympic bronze in 1984 and in 1985 became the first women to throw a javelin over 76 metres. She set a world record of over 77 metres the following year (the record is now held by Petra Felke at nearly 80 metres). She took the world championship title in Rome in 1987 and the Olympic silver medal in 1988.

White, Ellen Gould, *née* Harmon

Born 1827 Died 1915
American Seventh-day Adventist leader

Ellen Gould Harmon was born in Gorham, Maine. She was converted to Adventism in 1842 through the preaching of William Miller (1782–1849). In 1846 she married an Adventist minister, James White.

She was said to have experienced during her lifetime 'two thousand visions and prophetic dreams'. She became leader on the official establishment of the Seventh-Day Adventist Church in 1863, and her pronouncements were regarded as the 'spirit of prophecy'.

She wrote more than 60 works, one of which, *Steps to Christ*, has sold more than 20 million copies.

White, Pearl Fay

Born 1889 Died 1938
American cinema actress who found fame in long-running serialized melodramas

Pearl Fay White was born in Green Ridge, Missouri, the daughter of a farmer. She went on stage as a child and later joined a circus as an equestrienne but incurred a spinal injury after a fall and had to leave to join a travelling theatre troupe. She found a secretarial job with the Powers film company and was soon noticed by film director Joseph A Golden.

She began her film career in 1910, making her name at first in silent slapstick comedies and then as the heroine of *The Perils of Pauline* (1914), *The Exploits of Elaine* (1914–15), *The Black Secret* (1919–20), and others, gaining an enormous reputation as the exponent *par excellence* of the type of melodramatic serialized film or chapter play popularly called 'cliff-hanger', carrying out nearly all her own stunts.

The genre declined in popularity with the advent of the feature film and, having made over 100 comedies, serials and westerns, in 1924 White retired and went to live in France. She was married twice, both times to actors — Victor C Sutherland (1907–14) and Wallace McCutcheon (1919–20).

Whitelaw, Billie

Born 1932
English actress who is noted as an interpreter of the plays of Samuel Beckett

Billie Whitelaw was born in Coventry. She made her London début in Feydeau's *Hotel Paradiso* in 1956, and joined the National Theatre in 1964, appearing in Beckett's one-act *Play*. Having risen in the 1960s to become a leading lady of the stage and small screen (also with Gwen Walford, 1927–94), she joined the Royal Shakespeare Company in 1971 and returned to Beckett in 1973 to play Mouth in *Not I*.

She played in Beckett's *Footfalls* at the Royal Court in 1976, and in a revival of Beckett's *Happy Days* at the Royal Court in 1979. She has played many other modern roles on stage, and appeared in several films, including *Charlie Bubbles* (1968), for which she won a British Film Academy award.

Whitney, Anne

Born 1821 Died 1915
American sculptor not permitted to win a major competition because she was a woman

Anne Whitney was born in Watertown, Massachusetts. Her early works, created in Boston, reflect her interest in social justice. Following the American Civil War, she travelled and studied extensively in Europe, and continued sculpting well into her eighties.

In 1893, at the age of 72, she anonymously entered a competition to create a memorial to US statesman Charles Sumner. Her sculpture won but the honour was withdrawn when it was discovered that she was a woman.

At least 100 of her works have been catalogued and are owned by such institutions as the Smithsonian and the National Collection of Fine Arts.

Whitney, Gertrude Vanderbilt, *née* Vanderbilt

Born 1875 Died 1942
American sculptor who was a prominent patron of the arts

Gertrude Vanderbilt was born into a wealthy family in New York City and married Harry Payne Whitney (1872–1930), a financier, in 1896. She then trained at the Art Students League of New York and in Paris, where she was inspired by the work of August Rodin.

During World War I she established a hospital and worked as a nurse, later transforming the horror she felt at the suffering into such works as two panels for the *Victory Arch* (1918–20) and *The Washington Heights War Memorial* (1921), both in New York City. Other works include the *Aztec Fountain* (1912) for the Pan American building in Washington DC and the monumental *Titanic Memorial* (1914–31), which symbolizes the words in Revelation 20.13: 'The sea gave up its dead'.

In 1930 Whitney donated her collection of 500 works of 20th-century art, and bought 100 more, to found the Whitney Museum of Modern Art in Greenwich Village, where she had opened a studio in 1907. The museum, which opened in 1931, is now located in West 75th Street in Madison Avenue.

Whitworth, Kathy (Kathrynne Ann)

Born 1939
American golfer, the most successful woman golfer to date

Kathy Whitworth was born in Monahans, Texas. She has won 88 tournaments on the US Women's circuit, including all the women's 'Majors', except the US Open.

She turned professional in 1958, and won the US Ladies Professional Golf Association Championship four times (1967, 1971, 1975, 1982). Between 1965 and 1973 she was the leading money-winner eight times.

Whyte, Kathleen

Born 1909
Scottish embroiderer and teacher best known for her ecclesiastical work

Kathleen Whyte was born in Arbroath, and travelled with her family in India in 1911–13 and 1920–3. The move to Jamshedpur made an impact on her, the rich colours and textiles being so very different from those of Scotland. She studied at Gray's School of Art, Aberdeen (1927–32), under Dorothy Angus and James Hamilton, winning the Founder's Prize, the Alexander Barker Prize and the Former Students' Association Prize. In 1948 she joined the staff of the Glasgow School of Art to teach embroidery, and in 1950 introduced machine embroidery and tapestry weaving there.

Her commissions include pulpit falls for St Martin's Church, Port Glasgow, St Brendan's Church on Bute, Cathcart South Church, Glasgow, and Westerton Church, Bearsden. She also designed a stole for **Elizabeth**, the Queen Mother to commemorate the opening of the Tay Bridge in 1966.

In 1969 she developed eyesight problems, but despite the alteration to her visual perception, she continued to work effectively. She retired from the Glasgow School of Art in 1974, and a large retrospective exhibition of her work was shown in Edinburgh in 1987. She was created MBE for her services to the Decorative Arts in Scotland.

Widdecombe, Ann Noreen

Born 1947
English Conservative politician described as treating politics as a crusade as well as a career

Ann Widdecombe was born in Bath. She spent her early years in Singapore where her naval father was based before returning to attend a Catholic convent in Bath, followed by Birmingham and Oxford universities. From 1975 to 1987 she was a senior administrator at the University of London, and she had an early involvement in politics when she was elected councillor for Runnymede District Council in 1976.

In 1987 she entered parliament as MP for Maidstone, immediately taking part in the anti-abortion motion and supporting the Bill to reduce the number of weeks during which abortion was legal. Promoted to Under-Secretary of State for Social Security in 1990, she then moved in 1993 to the Department of Employment, becoming its Minister of State the following year and earning respect for her tough talking. In 1995 that department was abolished and she became Minister of State at the Home Office. Dubbed the 'Minister for Trouble', she was soon required to defend the government on such controversial issues as police use of CS gas spray and the shackling of pregnant prisoners.

In 1993 when the Church of England approved the ordination of women as priests, apparently the last of a number of attitudes with which she disagreed, Widdecombe made a public move to join the Roman Catholic Church.

Widdemer, Margaret

Born 1884 Died 1978
American poet and novelist who won the 1919
Pulitzer Prize for poetry

Margaret Widdemer was born in Pennsylvania. She first came to notice with a poem denouncing the employment of children. It was reprinted as the title poem in her first collection, *The Factories and Other Poems* (1915). In the same year her novel, *The Rose-Garden Husband*, which told the story of a young librarian (Widdemer was herself a trained librarian), became a bestseller.

Her later poetry lost the hard edge of *The Factories* and in 1919 she won a prize from the Poetry Society (which became the Pulitzer Prize) for *Old Road to Paradise*. Her best verse is to be found in *Collected Poems* (1957).

In addition to her romantic and historical novels for adults she also wrote the 'Winona' series for girls.

Widdowson, Elsie May

Born 1906
English nutritionist who developed an extensive
programme on the effects of nutrition on growth
and development

Elsie Widdowson grew up in London and studied chemistry at Imperial College there, one of three women amongst 100 men. She did PhD research with **Helen Porter** on the chemistry of apples, and was awarded the degree in 1933.

Employment difficulties led her to becoming a dietician, in which capacity she met the physiologist R A McCance, with whom she began a career-long collaboration, first at King's College London, and then in Cambridge from 1938 onwards. Their research focused on the chemical composition and nutritional value of foodstuffs.

Elected a Fellow of the Royal Society in 1976, she has received academic honours from around the world. She was created CBE in 1979 and a Companion of Honour in 1993.

Wiggin, Kate Douglas, *née* Smith

Born 1856 Died 1953
American novelist whose greatest success was
Rebecca of Sunnybrook Farm

Kate Smith was born in Philadelphia. She trained as a kindergarten teacher and after moving to California with her mother and stepfather, established a kindergarten in the San Francisco slums, the first one west of the Rocky mountains. In 1881 she married and moved to New York. It was to help the kindergarten that she began writing, publishing *The Story of Paisy* in 1883.

She went on to write novels for both adults and children, but was more successful with the latter. *Rebecca of Sunnybrook Farm* (1903) is probably her best-known book, although the *Penelope* exploits, *The Birds' Christmas Carol* (1888) and *Mother Carey's Chickens* (1911), were all firm favourites.

Wightman, Hazel Hotchkiss

Born 1886 Died 1974
American tennis player who made radical changes
in women's tennis

Hazel Hotchkiss Wightman was born in Healdsburg, California. Later known as the 'Queen Mother of Tennis', she began tournament play in 1902 and introduced more active play for women, employing volley and net play for the first time. She also challenged the restrictive women's dress of the day.

The winner of the national triple — the singles, the doubles and the mixed doubles — in 1909, 1910 and 1911, in 1919 she promoted international competitions for women, and in the 1920s began teaching. She published *Better Tennis* in 1933.

A donated vase to the United States Lawn

Tennis Association became known as the 'Hazel Hotchkiss Wightman Trophy'.

Wigman, Mary, *originally* Marie Wiegmann

> Born 1886 Died 1973
> German dancer, choreographer, and teacher, the most influential German dancer of her era

Mary Wigman was born in Hanover. After studying eurhythmics with Émile Jaques-Dalcroze, she assisted Rudolf von Laban during World War I. She subsequently made her name as a soloist, but her ensemble dances were landmarks in the German Expressionist style and she exerted a great influence on European modern dance. She opened a school in Dresden in 1920, branches of which grew throughout Germany and, through her star pupil **Hanya Holm**, in the USA; the Nazis later closed the German schools. She retired from the stage in 1942, but continued to choreograph and opened another school in West Berlin in 1949.

Wilcox, Ella Wheeler, *née* Wheeler

> Born 1850 Died 1919
> American journalist and poet who wrote 'Laugh and the world laughs with you, Weep and you weep alone' ('Solitude')

Ella Wheeler was born in Johnstown Center, Wisconsin. She had completed a novel before she was 10, and later wrote at least two poems a day. In 1884 she married Robert M Wilcox (d.1916).

The first of her many volumes of verse was *Drops of Water* (1872). *Poems of Passion* (1883) was instantly successful, partly because it was seen to rebel against the conventional code of literary propriety. Though much of her prolific verse is now considered sentimental, she was very popular in her day. She also wrote a great deal of fiction, and contributed essays to many periodicals. Her *Story of a Literary Career* (1905) and *The World and I* (1918) were autobiographical.

Wilde, Lady Jane Francesca, *known as* 'Speranza'

> Born 1826 Died 1896
> Irish poet, folklorist and hostess, and mother of Oscar Wilde

Lady Jane Wilde was born in Dublin. An ardent nationalist, she contributed poetry and prose to the *Nation* from 1845 under the pen-name of 'Speranza'. She was married to Sir William Wilde from 1851; their son was Oscar Wilde.

After her husband's death she moved to London, and published several works on folklore and Celtic myth, on which she was an authority, including *Ancient Legends of Ireland* (1887) and *Ancient Cures* (1891).

Wilder, Laura Ingalls

> Born 1867 Died 1957
> American author of the 'Little House' series of children's books drawn from her own childhood in the Midwest

Laura Ingalls Wilder was born in Pepin, Wisconsin. She lived on a farm all her life, and it was not until she was in her sixties, when her daughter suggested that she write down her childhood memories, that her evocative 'Little House' series began to appear.

Little House in the Big Woods (1932) gained instant popularity in the USA and was followed by several sequels: *Little House on the Prairie* (1935), *By the Shores of Lake Silver* (1939), *Little Town on the Prairie* (1941), *Farmer Boy* (1933) and *Those Happy Golden Years* (1943). A television series in the 1970s assured their success in Britain.

Wilhelm, Kate

> Born 1928
> American science-fiction writer considered one of the most subtle and intelligent voices in the genre

Kate Wilhelm was born in Toledo, Ohio. A slowly maturing author, she won a Nebula award in 1969 for her short story 'The Planners', but did not begin to produce her best work as a novelist until around a decade later.

Where Late The Sweet Birds Sang (1976), set in a post-holocaust America, won a Hugo award. *Juniper Time* (1979), which takes place in a drought-stricken US, is one of the most effective of the genre's many works with an ecological theme. She has also written several mainstream novels.

She was married to the science-fiction author and editor Damon Knight (1922–).

Wilhelmina, Queen, *in full* Wilhelmina Helena Pauline Maria of Orange-Nassau

> Born 1880 Died 1962
> Queen of the Netherlands (1890–1948)

Wilhelmina was the daughter of William III, whom she succeeded at a very early age in 1890. Her mother, Queen **Emma**, acted as regent until 1898. During her reign Wilhelmina fully upheld the principles of constitutional monarchy. She won the admiration of her people especially during World War II, when, though compelled to seek refuge in Britain, she steadfastly encouraged Dutch resistance to the German occupation by broadcasting to her people from London.

In 1948, in view of the length of her reign, she abdicated in favour of her daughter **Juliana** and assumed the title of Princess of the Netherlands. Her memoirs, *Eenzaam maar niet alleen* (1959, *Lonely but not Alone*, 1960), give an insight to the religious faith that underpinned her life.

Wilkinson, Ellen Cicely

Born 1891 Died 1947
English feminist, trade unionist, and Labour politician, the first female education Minister

Ellen Wilkinson was born in Manchester. She became an active campaigner for women's suffrage and was an early member of the Independent Labour party (1912). From 1915 she helped to organize the Union of Shop, Distributive and Allied Workers and in 1920 she joined the Communist party, but had left it by 1924, when she became Labour MP for Middlesbrough East.

From 1929 to 1931 she was Parliamentary Private Secretary to the Chairman of the Labour Party, **Susan Lawrence**. She lost her seat in 1931, but re-entered parliament in 1935 as member for Jarrow. The following year, when most areas of southern England were beginning to recover from the Depression, she led the Jarrow March. This consisted of unemployed workers walking to London to present the cause of the people in the Durham area who were continuing to suffer severe hardship.

In 1940 she became Parliamentary Secretary to the Ministry of Home Security, and in 1945 Minister of Education, the first woman to hold such an appointment.

Wilkinson, Jemima

Born 1752 Died 1819
American religious leader who convinced followers of her own resurrection

Jemima Wilkinson was born into an affluent Quaker family in Cumberland, Rhode Island. Influenced by the preaching of the Methodist George Whitefield, and later by **Ann Lee**, founder of the Shakers, she called herself 'Public Universal Friend'.

After a fever in 1774 in which she claimed to have died and had her body taken over by the 'Spirit of Life', she held open-air meetings and established churches. On being forced to leave New England when her disciples' claims that she was Christ prompted opposition, she established a colony called 'Jerusalem' in Yates County in 1794.

The movement, which depended on her personal magnetism, fell apart after her death.

Willard, Emma, *née* Hart

Born 1787 Died 1870
American educationalist whose pioneering campaign for equal educational opportunities for women paved the way for co-education

Emma Hart was born in Berlin, Connecticut, and educated at Berlin Academy. In 1809 she married Dr John Willard (d.1825). From her husband's nephew, who was studying at Middlebury College, she learned about the subjects studied there, such as geometry and philosophy, which were never taught to women.

In 1814 she opened Middlebury Female Seminary, offering an unprecedented range of subjects, in order to prepare women for college. Unsuccessful in gaining funding for her school, she moved to Troy, New York, where she received financial help. The school developed fast, and she wrote several highly-regarded history text-books.

Emma Willard

Willard, Frances Elizabeth Caroline

Born 1839 Died 1898
American educator who was a prominent figure in the temperance campaign

Frances Willard was born in Churchville, New York. She studied at the Northwestern Female College, Evanston, Illinois, and became Professor of Aesthetics there. She was appointed president when the college became the Evanston College for Ladies, and Dean of Women when it merged with the Northwestern University (1873–4).

In 1874 she became secretary of the newly founded National Women's Christian Temperance Union (WCTU) and was its president from 1879, also serving as president of the first worldwide WCTU from 1891. She also edited the Chicago *Daily Post* and, as first President of the National Council of Women (1888–90), helped to found the International Council of Women.

She also campaigned for women's suffrage and for safety regulations for female industrial workers.

Willenbrandt, Mabel Walker, *née* Walker

Born 1896 Died 1963
American lawyer and government official, the second woman US Assistant Attorney General

Mabel Walker was born in Woodsdale, Kansas. She received her law degree from the University of Southern California and was appointed as a non-salaried public defender with special responsibility for women's cases, meanwhile developing a private practice.

During World War I she was appointed the head of the Legal Advisory Board, the largest draft board in Los Angeles, and after the war she was recommended for the post of Assistant Attorney General of the United States (1921). She was the second woman to hold that post, and the first to hold it for an extended term, during which she became involved in tax, prison and prohibition activities.

She resigned in 1928 to return to private practice.

Williams, Betty

Born 1943
Northern Irish peace activist who co-founded the peace movement in Northern Ireland

Betty Williams was born in Belfast. As a Roman Catholic housewife in Belfast, she founded with **Mairéad Corrigan-Maguire** the Northern Ireland Peace Movement in 1976

(the 'Peace People Community') after witnessing the accidental deaths of three children by a car whose terrorist driver had been shot.

She broke away from the movement in 1980 after four years of campaigning for the end of sectarian violence in the province. She and Corrigan-Maguire were jointly awarded the Nobel Prize for Peace in 1976.

Williams, Cicely Delphine

Born 1893 Died 1992
British specialist and pioneer in maternal and child health

Cicely Williams was born in Kew Park, Jamaica, into a plantation-owning family. She read history at Somerville College, Oxford, before switching to medicine; she qualified from King's College Hospital in 1923. After a year in Greece working in rural areas, she joined the Colonial Medical Service in the Gold Coast in 1929, where nutrition and mother and child care became her primary concern, leading to her vivid clinical description in the *Lancet* (1935) of the condition kwashiorkor (a disease in newly weaned children caused by protein deficiency).

She was in Singapore in 1942 when the Japanese invaded; imprisoned in Changi, she was held in cages with the dead and the dying. She survived this experience and was the first head of Mother and Child Health (1948–52) in the World Health Organization, Geneva. She lectured in more than 70 countries promoting breast-feeding and combined preventative and curative medicine.

Williams, Esther Jane

Born 1923
American swimmer and film actress whose supreme acquatic abilities made her a star

Esther Williams was born in Inglewood, near Los Angeles in California. She became a record-breaking swimmer, was selected for the cancelled 1940 Olympics, and entered the fringes of showbusiness as part of a San Francisco Aquacade in 1940. Seen by a Hollywood talent scout, she signed with MGM and made her film début in *Andy Hardy's Double Life* (1942).

She became a star in *Bathing Beauty* (1944) and spent the next decade in a lavish series of colourful musicals and escapist romances all designed to showcase her athletic acquatic abilities. She was a top box-office attraction whose many films include *Neptune's Daughter* (1949), *Dangerous When Wet* (1953) and *Jupiter's Darling* (1955). Serious dramatic roles in films like *The Unguarded Moment* (1956) and

The Big Show (1961) revealed her limitations and comedienne **Fanny Brice** once remarked: 'Wet she is a star. Dry she ain't'.

She later designed a range of swimwear, promoted swimming pools, worked as a sports commentator and saw synchronized swimming become a competitive sport at the summer Olympics. Her success in business led *Life Magazine* to give her the title of 'The Mermaid Tycoon'. She was a recent on-screen host of *That's Entertainment 111* (1994), a nostalgic celebration of MGM's past.

Williams, Ivy

Born 1877 Died 1966
English barrister who never practised, preferring
academia to law

Ivy Williams was educated at the universities of London and Oxford, where she lived most of her life. In January 1920 she became one of the first English women to be called to the Bar, on being admitted to the Inns of Court and joining the Inner Temple.

She never practised law however, choosing instead an academic career, as tutor and lecturer in law to the Society of Oxford Home Students, in which capacity she inspired many young women. She was elected Honorary Fellow of St Anne's College in 1956. In her retirement she published a Braille primer.

Williams, Mary Lou

Born 1910 Died 1981
American jazz pianist, arranger, and composer

Mary Lou Williams was born in Atlanta, Georgia, and brought up in Pittsburgh. She interrupted her high school studies to become a touring show pianist; her first important period as a performer and arranger was during the 1930s with the Kansas City-based Andy Kirk and his Clouds of Joy.

Her outstanding qualities as an arranger brought her work from the jazz giants Duke Ellington (for whom she arranged the well-known *Trumpets No End*), Earl Hines and Benny Goodman, among others. Her *Waltz Boogie* (1946) was one of the first jazz pieces in 3/4 time, and she later embraced the bebop style as well as writing several sacred works, such as 'Mary Lou's Mass' (1970).

Williams of Crosby, Shirley Vivien Teresa Brittain Williams, Baroness

Born 1930
English politician and co-founder of the SDP

Shirley Williams is the daughter of **Vera Brittain**. She worked as a journalist before becoming a Labour MP in 1964. After holding ministerial posts in Education and Science (1967–9) and the Home Office (1969–70), she was appointed Secretary of State for Prices and Consumer Protection (1974–6), then for Education and Science (1976–9), the only woman in the Cabinet.

She was a co-founder of the Social Democratic Party (SDP) in 1981 and became its first elected MP later that year. She became President of the SDP the following year, but lost her seat in the 1983 general election. In 1988 she joined the new, merged SLDP (Social and Liberal Democratic party). In the same year she married, for the second time. Her first husband (1955–74) was Bernard Williams, Professor of Moral Philosophy at Oxford University and her second husband, Richard Neustadt, Professor of Politics at Harvard.

After her second marriage she moved to the USA and in 1988 became Professor of Elective Politics at Harvard's John F Kennedy School of Government, but remains involved in British politics. She was awarded a life peerage in 1993.

Wills, Helen Newington, *married name* Moody

Born 1905
American tennis player who dominated women's
tennis for over a decade

Helen Wills was born in Centreville, California. From the retirement of **Suzanne Lenglen** in 1926 until the outbreak of World War II she dominated women's tennis, winning eight singles finals at Wimbledon (1927–30, 1932–3, 1935, 1938) and seven US championships (1923–5, 1927–9, 1931).

While she was married (1929–37) she added her husband's name to her own, becoming Helen Wills Moody. Her great rivalry with Helen Jacobs (US Open winner 1932–5, Wimbledon winner 1936) drove her to continue to play during the 1938 Wimbledon final, despite being severely handicapped by injury. She retired in 1939.

Wilson, Harriet

Born c.1807 Died 1870
American writer, author of the first novel by an
African-American woman

Harriet Wilson was born in Fredericksburg, Virginia. Her book *Our Nig: or, Sketches from the Life of a Free Black, in a Two-Story White House, North, Showing that Slavery's Shadows Fall Even There. By 'Our Nig'* (1859) was written in the style of the sentimental 19th-century novel, telling the story of a mixed marriage.

When the book's authorship was first discovered, oversimplistic parallels were drawn between Wilson's own life and the story she told. Since the book's reprinting in 1983 Wilson has been given the credit due for her stylistic intelligence and the cool way in which she handles the power struggles at play in a nominally Christian family.

Wilson, Harriette, *née* Dubochet

Born 1786 Died 1855
English courtesan whose popularity evaporated when she published her memoirs

Harriette Dubochet was born in Mayfair, London, of French descent. Her long career as a genteel courtesan began at the age of 15 with the Earl of Craven; subsequent paramours included the Duke of Argyll, the Duke of Wellington, the Marquis of Worcester and a host of others.

All these men figured in her lively but libellous *Memoirs*, brought out in parts from 1825 to the accompaniment of a barrage of suggestive advance publicity aimed at blackmail of the victims, most of whom echoed the celebrated outburst of Wellington on the occasion — 'Publish and be damned!'

Wilson, Nancy

Born 1937
African-American singer who has produced more than 40 albums and had her own TV show

Nancy Wilson was born in Chillicothe, Ohio. In 1956 she dropped out of college to tour with the Rusty Bryant Band. Three years later she moved to New York City to embark on a solo career.

She got a recording contract with Capitol Records almost immediately and released her first album, *Guess Who I Saw Today*, in 1960. In 1964 she won a Grammy award for 'How Glad I Am'. Her later albums include *Lady With a Song*, *Nancy Now* and *With My Lover Beside Me*.
In 1980 her US career peaked but she still remains popular in Japan. She has appeared frequently on television and had her own show in 1967–8. Among her honours are a 1975 Emmy award for the *Nancy Wilson Show* and the Urban Network Achievement Award (1990).

Winchilsea, Anne Finch, Countess of, *née* Kingsmill

Born 1661 Died 1720
English poet whose verse has been quoted in admiration by later prominent writers

Anne Kingsmill was born in Sidmonton, near Southampton, the daughter of Sir William Kingsmill. She was a maid of honour to **Mary of Modena** and in 1684 she married Heneage Finch, Earl of Winchilsea (from 1712).

Her longest poem, a Pindaric ode called *The Spleen*, was printed in 1701, and her *Miscellany Poems* in 1713. She was a friend of Pope, Swift and Gay, and her nature poems were admired by Wordsworth in his *Lyrical Ballads*.

Windsor, (Bessie) Wallis Warfield, Duchess of

Born 1896 Died 1986
American socialite whose marriage to Edward VIII resulted in his abdication

Wallis Warfield was born in Blue Ridge Summit, Pennsylvania. She was an extrovert character, and in 1916 married Lieutenant Earl Winfield Spencer of the US navy, but in 1927 the marriage was dissolved. The following year, in London, she married Ernest Simpson, an American-born Briton. She became well known in London society, and met Edward, the Prince of Wales, at a country house party in 1931.

In 1936, the year of his accession, she obtained a divorce in England, and the king subsequently made clear to Prime Minister Stanley Baldwin and his government his determination to marry her, even if it meant giving up the throne. He abdicated, and they married in 1937 in France, but she was not accepted by the British royal family until the late 1960s.

She and Edward lived in France and the Bahamas; after Edward's death she lived virtually as a recluse in Paris. In 1956 she published her memoirs, *The Heart has its Reasons*.

Winfrey, Oprah Gail

Born 1954
American actress and talk-show host

Oprah Winfrey was born on a farm in Kosciusko, Mississippi. A bright child with a talent for public oratory, she was a contestant in the Miss Black America Pageant in 1971 and later secured a job co-hosting the evening news on WTVF–TV in Nashville.

Committed to a career in television, she became the co-host of *Baltimore is Talking* (1977–84) before moving to host *A.M. Chicago* in January 1984. By September of the following year the programme had been re-titled *The Oprah Winfrey Show* (1985–   ). Dedicated to changing the lightweight image of daytime television, she proved a fearless instigator of debate on a wide range of controversial topics

Oprah Winfrey, 1994

Party '57 (1977). Her first really successful appearance was in *Urban Cowboy* (1980).

She came into her own as the factory girl swept off her feet by Richard Gere in *An Officer And A Gentleman* (1982), and as the turbulent, terminally ill daughter of **Shirley MacLaine** in *Terms Of Endearment* (1983). Both films earned her Best Actress Oscar nominations. She had one of her best roles in *Black Widow* (1987), and, despite choosing to work with the world's most renowned directors rather than in obviously commercial projects, she starred in the thriller *Betrayed* (1988). Included in her burst of 1990s activity are *Wilder Napalm* (1992), *Shadowlands* (1993) and *Forget Paris* (1995), and among her more eclectic credits is *E.T.* (1982), for which she supplied the homesick extra-terrestrial's voice. She has a reputation for outspokenness and total dedication to her craft.

After living in Los Angeles for a time, she moved with her son Noah to live on a remote farm, which she manages herself, in the foothills of the Catskill mountains in New York State.

Winifred, St

7th century
Legendary Welsh virgin saint who survived
decapitation and founded Holywell

Winifred's legend relates that after she refused a marriage proposal from Prince Caradog, he chased and decapitated her. Her head rolled down a hill, and where it stopped a spring gushed forth, creating a still-famous place of pilgrimage, Holywell in Clwyd.

St Beuno restored her head and, according to one tradition, she went on to become abbess of a nunnery at Holywell; another has her spending most of the rest of her life as a nun in a remote valley in the mountains.

Winkworth, Catherine

Born 1827   Died 1878
English hymn translator and pioneer of women's
higher education

Catherine Winkworth was born in London, the fourth daughter of a silk merchant. Her mother died when she was 14, and her father remarried four years later. The family lived in or near Manchester from 1829, moving in 1862 to Clifton, Bristol.

Catherine devoted herself to the emerging cause of women's higher education, working towards what became Bristol University. She helped found Clifton High School and was a governor of other girls' schools.

She translated over 300 hymns from

and became a Mother Earth figure to the American viewer, renowned for her quick wit, spontaneity, genuine compassion and a publicly waged battle with the bulge. In 1996 she published a diet book, *In the Kitchen with Rosie*.

As an actress, she received an Academy Award nomination for her film début in *The Colour Purple* (1985) and has appeared in such television dramas as *The Women of Brewster Place* (1990) which she also produced through her company Harpo Productions. Among her many honours are Emmy Awards for Best Daytime Talk Show Host in 1987, 1991 and 1992. She is also the first woman to own and produce her own talk show and the first black person to own a large television studio. She was inducted into the National Women's Hall of Fame in 1994.

Winger, Debra

Born 1955
American film actress who combines a raw
sensuality with a vibrant independence

Debra Winger was born in Cleveland, Ohio, the daughter of orthodox Hungarian–Jewish parents. Determined to become an actress after a fall that threatened permanent injury, she gained a wide variety of television exposure and made her feature film début in *Slumber*

German to English, writing books that were constantly reprinted. Several of her hymns, like 'Praise to the Lord the Almighty' and 'Now thank we all our God' remain popular today. Catherine also translated German studies on charity work and a biography of Theodor Fliedner (1800–64), who founded both the first Protestant hospital and the female diaconate, an order of nurses, in the Lutheran Kaiserwerth community.

Winnemucca, Sarah

Born 1844 Died 1991
Native American activist and educator whose knowledge of English helped her adversaries but not her people

Sarah Winnemucca was born of Northern Paiute descent near the Humboldt River in western Nevada. Because she knew English, she was used as an interpreter during the Snake War in 1866. In 1872 the Paiutes were relocated to the Malheur reservation in Oregon, where she assisted reservation agent Samuel Parrish with his agricultural programmes and was an interpreter and teacher. His replacement refused to pay the Paiute for their agricultural labour and this led to the Bannock War.

Winnemucca was again used as an interpreter and peacemaker, but the Paiute were forced to another reservation. She began a lecture tour in 1879, travelling in California and the East, but she never managed to raise the money needed to return the Paiute to Malheur. She wrote *Life Among the Paiutes: Their Wrongs and Claims*. She returned to Nevada and established a school for Native American children. In 1994 she was inducted into the National Women's Hall of Fame.

Winterson, Jeanette

Born 1959
English novelist, a confident, often provocative writer, whose work is deliberately challenging

Jeanette Winterson was born in Manchester. After graduating from Oxford, she worked in London fringe theatre and in publishing. Her first novel, the autobiographical *Oranges Are Not the Only Fruit* (1985), recounts an upbringing as the daughter of fundamentalist Christian parents and the emergence of her lesbian sensibilities.

It was critically acclaimed, as was *Sexing the Cherry* (1989), a far more experimental novel set in a fantastical 17th century. *Written On*

the Body (1992) was followed in 1994 by *Art and Lies*.

Withers, Googie (Georgette Lizette)

Born 1917
English actress who found fame in London, New York and Australia

Googie Withers was born in India and made her stage début as a child actress in 1929. She earned her initial reputation on the English stage in contemporary English plays by J B Priestley and Noël Coward, and was particularly admired for her role as Georgie Elgin in Clifford Odets's *Winter Journey* in 1952.

She married the Australian-born actor and director John McCallum in 1948, and they moved to Australia in 1958, shortly after she made her début in Shakespeare at Stratford-upon-Avon. She performed for the first time in New York in 1961, and was seen occasionally in London, but much of her subsequent career was in Australia, where she added to her already considerable reputation.

Witt, Katerina

Born 1965
German ice-skater who dominated the sport during the 1980s

Katerina Witt was born in Karl-Marx-Stadt. She was the figure-skating champion of East Germany in 1982, and won the first of six successive European titles in 1983. She was world champion in 1984–5 and 1987–8, and Olympic champion in 1984 and 1988.

After six years on the professional circuit a change in the regulations concerning participation by professionals allowed her to qualify for the 1994 Olympics, but in the event she achieved only seventh place, Oksana Baiul and Nancy Kerrigan winning gold and silver respectively.

Wittig, Monique

Born 1935
French novelist and critic who expresses her lesbian and feminist ideals through innovative language

Monique Wittig is a radical lesbian and the founder of the group Féministes Révolutionnaires. She gained notoriety in 1978 by claiming that 'Lesbians are not women', by which she meant that the conventional man–woman opposition is inadequate for the gender analysis feminism should be undertaking.

In *The Straight Mind and Other Essays* (1992) she describes her own position as 'Materialist Lesbianism' (despite the idealism), believing that 'it is oppression that creates sex'. Her avant-garde utopian novel *Les guérillères* (1969) intersperses scenes of an all-woman community fighting against men with blank pages containing series of women's names in capitals.

Wockel, Barbel, *née* Eckert

Born 1955
German athlete who won two gold medals for East
Germany at both the 1976 and 1980 Olympics, a
record for a female track and field athlete

Barbel Wockel was born in Leipzig and studied education. She began to make a mark in her athletics career by winning European Junior gold medals and setting records for 200 metres and 100 metres hurdles in 1973.

In 1974 she gained a European senior gold relay medal and finished seventh in the 100 metres. Her Olympic wins in 1976 and 1980 were in the 200 metres and sprint relay, and she then won a silver medal for 100 metres and a gold at 200 metres at the 1982 European championships. She also shared in a total of four East German world relay records.

Woffington, Peg (Margaret)

Born 1720 Died 1760
Irish actress famous for her beauty and vivacity
and for her 'breeches' roles

Peg Woffington was born in Dublin, the daughter of a bricklayer and a laundress. She played on the Dublin stage from the age of 17 to 20 and made her London début at Covent Garden as Sylvia in *The Recruiting Officer* in 1740. The prominent theatre manager and actor David Garrick was one of her many lovers.

Among the 'breeches' parts for which she was particularly famous was the role of Sir Harry Wildair in *The Constant Couple*. She played at Drury Lane until 1746, then Covent Garden, with a triumphant return to Dublin (1750–4). Despite her lack of vanity she was notorious for her tempestuous relationships with other successful actresses and in 1756 she stabbed **George Anne Bellamy**. The following year Woffington was taken ill on stage, never to return.

Her last days were given to charity and good works, endowing alms houses in Teddington. She was a character in the play *Masks and Faces* (1852) by Tom Taylor and Charles Reade, and the subject of the latter's first novel, *Peg Woffington* (1853) .

Wolcott, Marion Post, *née* Post

Born 1910 Died 1990
American photographer, best known for sensitive
but trenchant social documentary work

Marion Post Wolcott was born in Montclair, New Jersey. She enrolled at the New York School for Social Research and at New York University and in 1933 went on to study child psychology at the University of Vienna; her sister Helen had been studying photography in Vienna, and it was there that Marion made her first photographs. She trained in photography under Ralph Steiner in New York City in 1935.

She became a freelance photographer and from 1938 to 1941 worked on the staff of the US Farm Security Administration (FSA), documenting mainly rural situations, migrants and small-town life at the time of the 'New Deal'. In 1941 she married widowed government official Lee Wolcott, whose children Gail and John she brought up with their own daughter Linda (b.1942) and son Michael (b.1945).

Lee became Professor of Government at the University of New Mexico (1954–9) and then worked abroad for the Agency for Internal Development (1959–68), accompanied by Marion, who took teaching jobs in American schools in Iran and Pakistan. In the late 1960s they returned to California. Her photographic work was shown in the important FSA group exhibition at the Witkin Gallery, New York, in 1976.

Wolf, Christa

Born 1929
German novelist, East Germany's most prominent
woman writer

Christa Wolf was born in Landsberg, Warthe (now in Poland), and educated at Leipzig and Jena universities. She spent her early career in the Eastern bloc, a fact which has significantly restricted her publishing career.

She rose to be East Germany's most highly regarded woman writer on the publication of *Der geteilte Himmel* (1963, Eng trans *The Divided Heaven*, 1965), but many of her books received only limited circulation in that country. The most important of them, *Nachdenken über Christa T* (1968), was published in English translation as *The Quest for Christa T* (1982). Her novel/essay *Kassandra: Erzahlung* (1983) appeared in English two years later, but the *Moskauer Novelle* (1961, 'Moscow Novella') have not so far been translated.

Wolf examines the fate of personality in totalitarian situations, by which she means something larger and more universal than the specific political situation in her homeland.

Wolf, Kate

Born 1942 Died 1986
American singer and guitarist who left a lasting impression in folk history

Kate Wolf was born in San Francisco, California. Her first albums, *Black Roads and Lines on Paper*, were released on her own label. She worked from her home area and organized the Santa Rosa folk festivals.

She is highly regarded in American folk music circles for her clear, beautiful voice, her original compositions and her interpretations of other folk songwriters' works.

Her other albums include *Give Yourself to Love* (1983) and the posthumous *The Wind Blows Wild* (1988).

Wolfe, Elsie (Ella Anderson) de, married name Lady Mendl

Born 1865 Died 1950
American interior designer, hostess and champion of 'good taste'

Elsie de Wolfe was born in New York City. She went to school in Edinburgh before launching herself into New York society. She became a professional actress in about 1890, but left the stage in 1905 to learn interior design. During World War I she nursed soldiers in France, for which she received the Croix de Guerre. She married Sir Charles Mendl in 1926 and enjoyed her well-dressed position in high society.

With her hallmark focus on visual unity and use of pale colours and mirrors to emphasize space, she introduced a new, anti-Victorian fashion of interior design to America. Her commissions included the Trellis Room of the Colony Club in New York (1906) and a Manhattan version of London's Wallace Collection for the industrialist and art patron Henry Clay Frick. She published *The House in Good Taste* in 1913, confirming the popularity of her chosen profession.

Wolff-Bekker, Elizabeth, originally Betje Wolff

Born 1739 Died 1804
Dutch novelist, poet, critic and translator whose
Willem Leevend *is considered one of the great novels written by a woman*

Betje Wolff was born in Flushing. In 1759 she married a parson 30 years older than herself, and until his death in 1777 studied literature (of which she had an extensive and profound knowledge), wrote amusing verse, and in-

dulged her admiration for Rousseau. Then she set up house with **Aagje Deken**, with whom she wrote epistolary novels in the style of **H H Richardson**.

Willem Leevend (1784–5), her masterpiece (for it was she who did most of the real work), has been described as superior even to Richardson, on account of her refusal to resort to melodrama. It has been pronounced to be too long; but this is to fail to see the significance of its lengthy and often satirical theological passages. A translation is overdue: acute psychologically, sardonic, tolerant, humane, it is one of the great novels written by women, and remains to be discovered by English-speaking feminists.

In 1788 Wolff-Bekker, who sometimes used the pseudonym 'Sylvania', had to go into exile in France with her friend Deken; when 10 years later they could return, they were forced to do hack translations. They died within a few weeks of each other.

Wollstonecraft, Mary, married name Mary Godwin

Born 1759 Died 1797
Anglo-Irish feminist and writer, a strong advocate of equality for women in society and education

Mary Wollstonecraft was born in London. After a number of jobs she obtained work with a publisher (1788) as a translator and became acquainted with a group of political writers and reformers known as the English Jacobins, including her future husband William Godwin (1756–1836).

In 1790 she wrote *Vindication of the Rights of Man* (a response to Edmund Burke's *Reflections on the French Revolution*, 1790), and in 1792 produced her controversial *Vindication of the Rights of Woman*, which advocated equality of the sexes and equal opportunities in education. That year she went to Paris to witness the Terror and collect material for her *View of the French Revolution* (vol 1, 1794). She met an American timber-merchant, Captain Gilbert Imlay, by whom she had a daughter, Fanny Imlay (1794, committed suicide 1816); on being deserted by him, she tried to commit suicide.

In 1797 she married William Godwin, and gave birth to a daughter, Mary (the future **Mary Shelley**), but died soon afterwards.

Wood, Mrs Henry, née Ellen Price

Born 1814 Died 1887
English novelist who had a huge success with her moralizing novel East Lynne

Ellen Price was born in Worcester, the daughter of a manufacturer. A spinal disease confined her to bed or a sofa for most of her life. She married Henry Wood, a ship agent living in France, but returned to England with him in 1860. After his death in 1866 she settled in London, and wrote for magazines.

Her second published novel, *East Lynne* (1861), had an immense success. She never rose above the commonplace in her many novels, but showed some power in the analysis of character in her anonymous *Johnny Ludlow* stories (1874–80).

In 1867 she bought the monthly *Argosy,* which she edited, and her novels went on appearing in it long after her death.

Wood, Natalie, *originally* Natasha Gurdin

Born 1938   Died 1981
American film actress whose career blossomed during the 1960s

Natalie Wood was born in San Francisco. She was spotted as a teenager by director Irving Pichel (1891–1954) and cast in his wartime melodrama *Happy Land* (1943). Subsequent films usually featured her as the daughter, sister or younger relation of the more prominent star, enabling her to study first-hand their talents, though she never became a front-rank child star like **Elizabeth Taylor** or **Shirley Temple**. In 1955 she was cast in the highly influential *Rebel Without a Cause* (1955), earning a Best Supporting Actress nomination for her role as the young woman drawn moth-like to the dangerous charms of malcontented teenager James Dean.

She followed this with a role in another key 1950s film, the western *The Searchers* (1956), as the girl who is captured and raised by Native Americans. Two years later she graduated to stardom with the lead in *Marjorie Morningstar* (1958). Though her performances lacked the emotional intensity, commitment, or even eccentricity that marked out the great actresses that she had hoped to emulate, she enjoyed starring roles in *Splendor In The Grass* (1961), *West Side Story* (1961) and *Love With The Proper Stranger* (1963).

During the 1970s the momentum of her career slowed, and in 1981 she was found drowned with a high blood-alcohol level after having been reported missing from her yacht — a tragic and mysterious death.

Wood, Victoria

Born 1953
English comedienne and writer who has become a stalwart of British television and stand-up comedy

Victoria Wood was born in Prestwich, Lancashire. She studied drama at Birmingham University and began singing her own comic songs on local radio and television while still a student. In 1976 she secured a regular slot on national television in *That's Life.* Her first play, *Talent* (1978), was adapted for television and won her the Pye award for Most Promising New Writer.

The creator of all her own sketches, songs, and stand-up routines, she is a bubbly, outsize personality who offers witty observations on everyday life, sexual relations, and inexpert soap-operas. Her television series include *Wood and Walters* (with **Julie Walters**, 1981–2), *Victoria Wood As Seen on Television* (1984–7) and *An Audience With Victoria Wood* (1988, British Academy award). Her frequent stage tours include *Funny Turns* (1982), *Lucky Bag* (1984) and *Victoria Wood* (1987).

She has also published several books, including *Up To You, Porky* (1985), *Barmy* (1987) and *Mens Sana in Thingummy Doodah* (1990).

Woodard, Lynette

Born 1959
African-American basketball player, the first of the Harlem Globetrotters' women players

Lynette Woodard was born in Wichita, Kansas. She was a four-time collegiate All-American (1978–81), who set several records. In 1981 she won the Wade Trophy and the Broderick Award as the nation's outstanding women's collegiate basketball player. At the 1979 World University Games, she played on the gold medal-winning US women's basketball team, and in 1983 the US team on which she played won the gold medal at the Pan-American Games and the silver medal at the World University Games.

In the 1984 Olympics, she was on the women's basketball team which won a gold medal, and the following year she became the first woman basketball player for the Harlem Globetrotters. In 1986 the Women's Sports Foundation selected her as Professional Sportswoman of the Year.

Woodhull, Victoria, *née* Claflin

Born 1838   Died 1927
American reformer who advocated women's suffrage and free love and was the first woman to run for the US presidency

Victoria Claflin was born in Homer, Ohio. One of a large family which earned a living by giving fortune-telling and medicine shows, she performed a spiritualist act with her sister,

Tennessee Claflin. From 1853 to 1864 she was married to Dr Canning Woodhull, but on her divorce returned to the family business.

In 1868 she went with Tennessee to New York where they persuaded the rich Cornelius Vanderbilt to set them up as stockbrokers. At this time they became involved with a socialist group called Pantarchy, and began to advocate its principles of free love, equal rights and legal prostitution. In 1870 they established the magazine *Woodhull and Claflin's Weekly* (1870–6), outlining these views. A vigorous speaker, Victoria won support from the leaders of the woman suffrage movement, and became the first woman nominated for the presidency.

In 1877 she moved to London, with Tennessee, where she continued to lecture and write. Her publications include *Stirpiculture, or the Scientific Propagation of the Human Race* (1888) and *The Human Body the Temple of God* (1890, with Tennessee).

Woodville, Elizabeth

Born c.1437   Died 1492
Queen of England as the wife of Edward IV (ruled 1461–83)

Elizabeth Woodville was the eldest daughter of Sir Richard Woodville, 1st Earl Rivers. In 1461 she married Sir John Grey, who was killed at St Albans that same year, and in 1464 she was married privately to Edward IV, being crowned in 1465.

When Edward fled to Flanders in 1470, she sought sanctuary in Westminster. In 1483 her sons, Edward V and Richard, Duke of York, (the 'Princes in the Tower') were murdered.

After the accession of Henry VII in 1485 her rights as dowager queen were restored, but soon she was forced to retire to the abbey of Bermondsey, where she died. Her eldest daughter, **Elizabeth of York**, married Henry in 1486.

Woodward, Joanne

Born 1930
American film and television actress who is married to Paul Newman

Joanne Woodward was born in Thomasville, Georgia. She appeared on Broadway and in numerous television dramas before Twentieth Century-Fox noticed her and cast her in a minor western, *Count Three And Pray* (1955). Two years later she won a Best Actress Oscar for her performance as a woman suffering multiple personalities in *The Three Faces of Eve*, and followed this with notable performances as a suburban housewife in *No Down Payment* (1957), the Southern belle in *The Long Hot*

Summer (1958), and the title character in *The Stripper* (1963).

Her career floundered in the 1960s, but she was acclaimed again in *Rachel, Rachel* (1968), directed by her husband Paul Newman. She was successful as the discontented matriarch in *Mr and Mrs Bridge* (1990) and as the mother of AIDS sufferer Andy (Tom Hanks) in *Philadelphia* (1993) but has increasingly worked on stage and in TV-movie drama.

Woolf, Virginia, *née* Stephen

Born 1882   Died 1941
English novelist, critic and essayist, the archetypal modernist who had an immense influence on the form of the novel in English

Virginia Stephen was born in London, a daughter of the scholar and critic Sir Leslie Stephen and sister of **Vanessa Bell**. She was taught at home, by her parents and governesses, and received an uneven education.

In 1891 she started the *Hyde Park Gate News* which was read by adults and appeared weekly until 1895. In it appeared her first efforts at fiction. Her father died in 1904 and the family moved to Bloomsbury where they formed the nucleus of the Bloomsbury Group, comprising — among others — Keynes, E M Forster, Roger Fry, Duncan Grant, and Lytton Strachey: philosophers, writers, and artists. A year later she began her long association with the *Times Literary Supplement*. She married Leonard Woolf in 1912 and her first novel, *The Voyage Out*, was published in 1915. It was greeted cordially and though realistic, there were hints of the lyricism which would later become her hallmark.

In 1917 she and Leonard formed the Hogarth Press, partly for therapeutic reasons, for she suffered poor health and depression. Its first publication was *Two Stories*, one by each of the founders. Her second novel, *Night and Day,* appeared in 1919. Again its mode is realistic; some critics still think it her best work. *Jacob's Room* (1922) marked a turning point in her fiction and made her a celebrity.

In 1924 she went to Cambridge to speak on 'Character in Modern Fiction'; the result was *Mr Bennett and Mrs Brown*, an attack on the 'Georgian novelists' Arnold Bennett, John Galsworthy, and H G Wells, and can be read as her own aesthetic manifesto. Regarded now as an archetypal Modernist, she published in six years the three novels that have made her one of the century's great writers: *Mrs Dalloway* (1925), *To the Lighthouse* (1927) and *The Waves* (1931). But her work took its toll on her health and though she wrote prolifically

Virginia Woolf

---

she was beset by deep depressions and debilitating headaches. Throughout the 1930s she worked on *The Years*, which was published in 1937. A year later appeared *Three Guineas*, provisionally titled 'Professions for Women', intended as a sequel to *A Room of One's Own* (1929), regarded as epochal by feminists. In this she stated that 'A woman must have money and a room of her own if she is to write fiction'.

In 1941 she forced a large stone into her pocket and drowned herself in the River Ouse, near her home at Rodmell in Sussex. She is, with James Joyce (whose novel, *Ulysses*, the Hogarth Press declined to publish), regarded as one of the great modern innovators of the novel in English.

Woolley, Hannah

Born c.1623 Died after 1677
English teacher and writer of books on cookery

Hannah Woolley may have been orphaned as a child, for little of her early life is known, but at the age of 15 she was running her own school. She later became a governess to the nobility. In 1647 she married a Mr Woolley, a master of the Free School in Newport, Essex, where she continued teaching and also published a cookery book, *The Ladies' Directory,* followed by *The Cook's Guide* (1664).

Widowed with four sons, she began to resent the lack of educational and employment opportunities available to women, and trained gentlewomen to enter service whilst encouraging them to study. She married her second husband, Francis Challinor, in 1666.

Her most successful publications *include The Queen Like Closet* (1670) and *The Gentlewoman's Companion* (1673), a guide to social behaviour.

Wootton of Abinger, Barbara Frances Wootton, Baroness

Born 1897 Died 1988
English social scientist and prominent public figure interested in assimilating social and natural sciences

Barbara Wootton was born in Cambridge, the daughter of a don. She studied and lectured (1920–2) in economics at Girton College, Cambridge before becoming a research worker of the Labour party (1922–5), principal of Morley College, London (1926–7), director of studies (1927–44) and Professor in Social Studies (1948–52) at London.

She was frequently appointed as a royal commissioner and London magistrate, and remains best known for her work, *Testament for Social Science* (1950), in which she attempted to assimilate social to the natural sciences. Another work was *Social Science and Pathology* (1959). She was awarded a life peerage in 1958.

Wordsworth, Dorothy

Born 1771 Died 1855
English writer who lived most of her life alongside her famous brother William

Dorothy Wordsworth was born in Cockermouth, Cumberland, the only sister of the poet William Wordsworth (1770–1850). She was his constant companion through life, both before and after his marriage, and on tours to Scotland, the Isle of Man and abroad, the records of which are to be found in her *Journals.*

These *Journals* show that Dorothy's keen observation and sensibility provided a good deal of poetic imagery for both her brother and his friend Samuel Taylor Coleridge — more than that, they regarded her as the embodiment of that joy in Nature which it was their object to depict.

In 1829 she suffered a breakdown from which she never fully recovered. Her *Recollections of a Tour made in Scotland* AD1803 (1874) is a classic.

Wordsworth, Dame Elizabeth

Born 1840 Died 1932
English educationalist and first principal of
Lady Margaret Hall

Elizabeth Wordsworth was the daughter of the headmaster of Harrow School, later Bishop of Lincoln, and was mostly educated at home by her father and by governesses.

She became a devoted churchwoman, and in 1878 was appointed principal of Lady Margaret Hall, Oxford, where she supported higher education for women whilst placating those who opposed it. In 1886 she founded St Hugh's Hall, later St Hugh's College, followed a year later by the Lady Margaret Hall Settlement for social services in Lambeth.

Wordsworth was also a novelist, but her best-known work is her biography of her father, written with J H Overton in 1888.

Worth, Irene

Born 1916
American actress, equally at home on both sides
of the Atlantic

Irene Worth was born in Nebraska. After working as a teacher, she made her professional début with a US touring company in 1942, and appeared on Broadway a year later. In 1944 she moved to London, where she spent many of the next 30 years.

She created the role of Celia Copplestone in T S Eliot's *The Cocktail Party* at the 1949 Edinburgh Festival. In 1951 she joined the Old Vic and in 1953 appeared in the inaugural season at Stratford, Ontario. She played the title role in the German dramatist Johann von Schiller's *Mary Stuart* (1800, translated by Stephen Spender) in New York in 1957.

After joining the Royal Shakespeare Company at Stratford-upon-Avon in 1960, she continued to act on stage and screen — from *Orders to Kill* (1958) to *Eyewitness* (1981) — until the 1980s.

Wray, Fay

Born 1907
American actress remembered as the object of
desire who caused King Kong's downfall

Fay Wray was born in Canada, near Cardston, Alberta, and raised in Los Angeles. She made an early film début in *Blind Husbands* (1919) and had appeared in many small roles before securing the lead in *The Wedding March* (1928). After *King Kong* (1933), she proved an asset to several influential horror films of the period as distressed damsels screaming for help.

Her stage work includes *Nikki* (1931) and *Golden Wings* (1941). She first retired from the screen in 1942 but returned for a handful of matronly character parts before her final appearance in *Dragstrip Riot* (1958).

She later wrote plays and acted on television in *Gideon's Trumpet* (1980). Her autobiography, *On The Other Hand*, was published in 1989.

Wright, Fanny (Frances), *married name* Madame Darusmont

Born 1795 Died 1852
Scottish-born American reformer and abolitionist

Frances Wright was born in Dundee, the heiress to a large fortune. She emigrated to the USA in 1818 and the following year produced her play *Altorf*, which deals with the Swiss struggle for independence. She toured widely, publishing *Views of Society and Manners in America* in 1821, and a historical novel, *A Few Days in Athens*, in 1822.

In the company of the reformer Marie Joseph Lafayette, in 1825 she founded the short-lived community called Nashoba for freed slaves in western Tenessee. Settling in New York in 1829, she published with Robert Dale Owen a socialist journal, *Free Enquirer*. She was also one of the early suffragettes, and campaigned vigorously against religion and for the emancipation of women.

In 1831 she began an unhappy marriage with a Frenchman, William P Darusmont (or Guillaume Philquepal d'Arusmont). They had one daughter and after many separations and legal battles, divorced in 1850. After her marriage, the issues she championed grew increasingly controversial, such as birth control and the equal division of wealth. She was inducted into the National Women's Hall of Fame in 1994.

Wright, Judith

Born 1915
Australian poet, the first Australian to receive the
Queen's Medal for Poetry

Judith Wright was born in Armidale, New South Wales, and brought up on the family sheep farm, Wallamumbi, in pastoral New South Wales. She was educated at Sydney University and travelled in Britain and Europe before returning to Sydney (1938–9) to concentrate on her writing. The war disrupted her plans and lack of work led her back to her rural roots in the Queensland mountains, the source of her inspiration.

The Moving Image (1946) was her first collection, since when she has been an industrious poet, critic, anthologist, editor and short-story writer. Her main volumes of poetry are *Woman to Man* (1949), *The Gateway* (1953), *The Two Fires* (1955), *Birds* (1962), *City Sunrise* (1964), *The Other Half* (1966), *Alive* (1973) and *Fourth Quarter and Other Poems* (1976). Her *Collected Poems 1942–1970* and *The Double Tree: Selected Poems: 1942–1976* were published in 1971 and 1978 respectively. Her literary criticism was published in *Preoccupations in Australian Poetry* (1965). *The Cry for the Dead* (1981) is an account of the impact of European immigration on the Aborigines. A collection of essays on Aboriginal culture, *Born of the Conquerors*, was published in 1991.

She edited the Oxford anthology *A Book of Australian Verse* in 1956, and has written on the Australian poets Charles Harpur (1813–68) and Henry Lawson (1867–1922). In *The Generations of Men* (1959) and *The Cry for the Dead* (1981) she recreates from family documents the life of her pioneering pastoralist forebears, and in doing so demonstrates her own abiding affection for the Australian landscape.

In 1993 she received the Queen's Medal for Poetry, awarded on the recommendation of the Poet Laureate.

Wright, Mickey

Born 1935
American golfer, a consistent high-achiever

Mickey Wright was born in San Diego, California. After beginning professional competition in 1955, she consistently won more valuable prizes than any woman golfer, winning at least one LPGA (Ladies Professional Golf Association) tournament each year for 14 consecutive years (1956–69).

Her victories include four LPGA championships and four US Women's Open titles. In 1961 she won the Grand Slam of women's golf — the Titleholders (Masters), the US Women's Open and the LPGA championship.

She was inducted into the LPGA Hall of Fame in 1964, the World Golf Hall of Fame in 1976, and the International Women's Sports Hall of Fame in 1981.

Wright, Patience Lovell, *née* Lovell

Born 1725 Died 1786
American sculptor considered to be America's first professional sculptor

Patience Lovell was born in Bordentown, New Jersey, one of nine children of a fanatical Quaker farmer. She and her siblings were dressed in white, wore wooden shoes and could only go out veiled, as a protection from sin. At 20 she ran away to Philadelphia, and in 1748 married Joseph Wright and raised three children. She continued throughout this period to model figures in clay.

Her husband died when she was 44, leaving her to support four children (one born just after his death). Her sister suggested that she should make portrait busts and her gift for uncanny likenesses made her work an immediate success. She travelled to England in 1772 and settled in the West End of London near to George III's palace.

She became known as 'The Promethean Modeler' and was eventually asked by the king himself to model his portrait. In her highly opinionated manner, she berated the king for his policies towards the New World, remarks that resulted in her departure for Paris after the start of the Revolution. In Paris she modelled a portrait of Benjamin Franklin. She hoped to return to America and had arranged with George Washington to model his portrait but died, after a fall, in England.

Wrightson, Patricia

Born 1921
Australian writer of award-winning children's fiction

Patricia Wrightson was born in Lismore, New South Wales. Her first book, *The Crooked Snake* (1955), marked the arrival of a writer sensitive to the concerns of youth and was followed by *The Bunyip Hole* (1957) with its introduction of Aboriginal lore.

She came to notice with *The Rocks of Honey* (1960), which blended the supernatural with realism and native legend and became highly popular with *I Own the Racecourse!* (1968), an engaging study of a subnormal boy, which won the Hans Christian Andersen International Medal. Her trilogy of adventure stories featuring an Aboriginal boy, *The Ice is Coming*, *The Dark Bright Water* and *Behind the Wind*, was published as *The Book of Wirrun* in 1983.

Wrinch, Dorothy

Born 1894 Died 1970
American theoretical biologist and the first woman to receive a DSc from Oxford

Dorothy Wrinch was born in Rosario, Argentina, to English parents. She was educated in England, read mathematics at Girton College, Cambridge, and was appointed lecturer in mathematics at University College London in 1918. She married the physicist John Nicholson in 1922, but the marriage was dissolved in 1937.

In 1929 she became the first woman to be awarded a DSc by the University of Oxford. She was also a member of the Theoretical Biology Club at Cambridge which pioneered what is now known as molecular biology. In the late 1930s she took sabbatical leave in America and remained there, accepting a joint professorship with the biologist Otto Glaser, whom she also married. The theory of protein structure that she proposed in the 1930s was the focus of much fruitful debate until it was finally disproved in the 1950s.

Wu, Chien-Shiung

Born 1912
Chinese-born American physicist who proved the
principle of parity conservation in weak decays

Chien-Shiung Wu was born in Shanghai. She studied at the National Centre University in China, and from 1936 in the USA, at the University of California at Berkeley. From 1946 she was on the staff of Columbia University, New York, where she was appointed professor in 1957.

In 1957 Wu and her colleagues carried out an experiment to test Tsung-Dao Lee and Chen Ning Yang's hypothesis that parity is not conserved in weak decays; this would result in the decay not being mirror symmetric, ie having a preferred direction. The experiment was performed by cooling cobalt-60 nuclei in a magnetic field so that their spins were aligned.

They observed that the electrons resulting from the beta decay of the nuclei were emitted preferentially in one direction, proving that the principle of parity conservation was indeed violated in weak interactions. This was later explained by the V-A theory of weak interactions proposed by Richard Feynman and Murray Gell-Mann.

Wu Zhao (Wu Chao)

Born 625 Died 705
Chinese concubine and empress credited with
unifying the empire

Wu Zhao was concubine to the emperors Tai Zong (T'ai Tsung) and Gao Zong (Kao Tsung) and rose to become the only female sovereign in the history of China, appointing herself empress after Gao Zong's death.

She is said to be responsible for the conquest of Korea (655–675). Subsequently she manipulated power by passing control of the empire between her sons Zhong Zong (Chung Tsung) and Rui Zong (Jui Tsung), although she eventually claimed the throne again in 690.

Wurdemann, Audrey Mary

Born 1911 Died 1960
American poet and youngest recipient of the
Pulitzer Prize for poetry

Audrey Wurdemann was born in Seattle, Washington. She graduated from the University of Washington and lived in New York, where she married the writer Joseph Auslander (1897–1965); they collaborated on two books, including *The Islanders* (1951).

She published her first collection of poems, *The House of Silk* (1936), when still in her mid-teens, and became the youngest recipient of the Pulitzer Prize for poetry in 1935 for her collection *Bright Ambush* (1934).

Her other collections are *The Seven Sins* (1935), *Splendour in the Grass* (1936) and the sonnet sequence *Testament of Love* (1938).

Wylie, Elinor Hoyt

Born 1885 Died 1928
American author reputedly as famous for her
beauty as for her poetry

Elinor Wylie was born in Somerville, New Jersey. Her first marriage was unhappy and in 1910 she ran away to England with Horace Wylie, whom she married when her first husband died. Though they later divorced and she married the poet and editor William Rose Benét in 1923, she continued to write under the name Wylie.

Her first volume of poetry, *Nets to Catch the Wind*, which won the Julia Elsworth Ford Prize in 1921, was followed by several more collections and by four highly individual novels, *Jennifer Lorn* (1923), *The Venetian Glass Nephew* (1925), *The Orphan Angel* (1927) and *Mr Hodge and Mr Hazard* (1928). The fiction is as fantastic and artificial as the poetry is terse, direct and positive.

Wyman, Jane, *originally* Sarah Jane Fulks

Born 1914
American actress, equally at home in drama and
comedy

Jane Wyman was born in St Joseph, Missouri. She was a child actress, and made her first breakthrough as a radio singer. It was not until her performance in the film *The Lost Weekend* (1945) that she was recognized as a serious actress of real talent.

She was nominated for an Academy Award for *The Yearling* (1946), and won one for *Johnny Belinda* (1948), in which she played a deaf mute. She acted in many films, and starred in the television soap opera *Falcon Crest* in the

1980s. She was married to Ronald Reagan from 1940 to 1948.

Wynette, Tammy, *professional name of* Virginia Wynette Pugh

Born 1942
American country singer who remains the epitome of success in her field

Tammy Wynette was born in Tupelo, Mississippi, and raised in Alabama. She married her second husband, country singer George Jones, in 1969 (marriage dissolved 1975), and recorded songs like 'D-I-V-O-R-C-E' (1970) and 'Stand By Your Man' (1971), which were taken to be comments on the marriage.

Wynette has not changed her singing style in nearly 30 years, and she remains, through personal upheavals and remarriage in the 1970s and 1980s, the archetypal tear-jerking country singer.

Wyon, Olive

Born 1881   Died 1966
English theological translator and writer on prayer

Olive Wyon was born in Hampstead, London, and trained at St Colm's Missionary College, Edinburgh. She served with the London Missionary Society; her Free Church background and Anglican sympathies prepared her for ecumenical contacts and work with the World Council of Churches. Her final appointment (1951–3) was as Principal of St Colm's, 40 years after she had been a student there.

She translated the Swiss theologian Emil Brunner's *The Mediator* (1934) and *The Divine Imperative* (1937). Her belief in the value of Christian community living and interest in new British and Continental developments is reflected in *Living Springs* (1963). Her other enduring books include *The School of Prayer* (1943) and *The Altar Fire* (1954).

y

Yalow, Rosalyn, *née* Sussman

Born 1921
American biophysicist whose influential work on
RIA earned her a Nobel Prize

Rosalyn Sussman was born in New York City. She was the first woman to graduate in physics from Hunter College, New York (1941), and obtained a PhD from the College of Engineering of the University of Illinois in 1945, having married Aaron Yalow in 1943. She taught physics at Hunter College until 1950, and in 1947 became consultant to the Radioisotope Unit at the Bronx Veterans Administration (VA) Hospital.

From 1950, Yalow collaborated with

Rosalyn Yalow, 1977

Solomon Berson, and during the course of research on diabetes they developed 'radioimmunoassay' (RIA). This is an ultrasensitive method of measuring concentrations of substances in the body which relies upon 'labelling' molecules with radioactive isotopes. Yalow and Berson found that in adult diabetics, the rate of clearance of injected labelled insulin from the blood is surprisingly low, and suggested that antibodies inactivating the insulin are formed.

In 1977, for her work on RIA, Yalow shared the Nobel Prize for Physiology or Medicine with the French–American physiologist Roger Guillemin and the American biochemist Andrew Schally. Besides diabetes, Yalow has used RIA in work on dwarfism, leucaemia, peptic ulcers, and neurotransmitters in the brain.

Since 1969 she has been Chief of the Radioimmunoassay Reference Laboratory and from 1973 to 1992 she was Director of the Solomon A Berson Research Laboratory of the VA Medical Centre.

Yamada, Koma Takashi

Born 1948
Japanese dance-theatre artist who choreographs
and performs as an avant-garde team with
Eiko Otake

Koma Takashi Yamada was born in Niigata, Japan, but is now resident in New York City. She and Eiko Otake (1952–) met in 1971 as political science and law students who joined butoh master Tatsumi Hijikata's company in Toyko. What began as an experiment developed into an exclusive partnership in which they perform and choreograph only their own work.

They made their début in 1972, and began studying with Kazuo Uhno, the other central figure of Japan's mid-20th-century avant-garde. That same year their interest in the roots of German modern dance took them to Hanover, where they studied with a disciple of **Mary Wigman**. They made their American début in 1976 and since then have regularly toured North America and Europe with both short and full-length pieces.

Their choreographed works include *White Dance* (1976), *Fluttering Black* (1979) and *Fission* (1979).

Yarmouth, Sophia von Walmoden, Countess of

Died 1765
German noblewoman and mistress of George II (ruled 1717–60)

Sophie von Walmoden made the aquaintance of George II in Hanover. On the death of his wife, **Caroline of Anspach**, in 1737 she was brought to England as his mistress, and created a countess.

Yearsley, Ann, *née* Cromartie

Born 1753 Died 1806
English author in whose poetry (rather than her plays) her radical ideas are best expressed

Ann Cromartie was born in Bristol to humble parents and taught to read by her brother. She married a labourer in 1774 and brought up a large family in poverty, working as a milk-woman and reading and writing at night. She was taken up by **Hannah More** who organized publication of her *Poems on Several Occasions* (1785) and tried to govern her life.

Yearsley fiercely rejected More's patronage and made her way thereafter largely by her own efforts. In 1793 she opened a circulating library, but in her last years she retired to Melksham and became a recluse. She published four more books of verse, a historical play *Earl Goodwin*, performed at Bristol in 1791, and a novel *The Royal Captives* (1795) about the Man in the Iron Mask.

Yevonde, Madame, *also known as* Philonie Yevonde *and* Edith Plummer, *née* Yevonde Cumbers

Born 1893 Died 1975
English photographer best known for her dramatic portrait studies

Yevonde Cumbers was born in London. She was educated privately and then at boarding schools, followed by studies at the Sorbonne in 1910. She decided upon photography as a career on her return to London and became

an apprentice (1911–14) to Lallie Charles, the best-known female portraitist of the time. She is sometimes incorrectly referred to as Edith Plummer, an appellation which arose due to a researcher's error.

She set up her own photographic studio and after 1918 she became a successful and innovative society and advertising photographer. She is noted for her early and effective use of colour, and her costumed 'Goddesses' series of debutantes (1935) is her most famous set of portraits.

She was married to playwright Edgar Middleton from 1921. A major retrospective of her work was shown at the Royal Photographic Society of Great Britain in 1973.

Yonge, Charlotte M(ary)

Born 1823 Died 1901
English novelist who wrote successfully for the sake of the Church

Charlotte Yonge was born in Otterbourne, Hampshire. She achieved great popular success with *The Heir of Redclyffe* (1853) and its successors, publishing some 120 volumes of fiction. Her work was high church in tone, but she was a skilled enough author that their religiosity did not prevent their enduring popularity.

Part of the profits of her *Heir of Redclyffe* were devoted to fitting out the missionary schooner *Southern Cross* for Bishop George Selwyn, and she gave the profits of the *Daisy Chain* (£2,000) to the building of a missionary college in New Zealand.

She also published historical works, a book on *Christian Names* (1863), a *Life of Bishop Patterson* (1873) and a sketch of *Hannah More* (1888). She edited the girls' magazine, *Monthly Packet*, from 1851 to 1890.

York, Susannah, *originally* Susannah Yolande Fletcher

Born 1941
English actress of the 1960s who is more recently famous as Superman's mother

Susannah York was born in London, and brought up in Scotland. She graduated from RADA, and worked in repertory theatre and pantomime, but is best known as a film actress. She has also written screenplays and children's stories.

She became one of the quintessential faces of the 1960s, and built on her artistic reputation with films like *Tom Jones* (1963), *The Killing of Sister George* (1968), in which she played a controversial lesbian love scene, and

They Shoot Horses, Don't They? (1969). She played the eponymous hero's mother in the *Superman* films of the 1980s.

Yosano Akiko

Born 1878 Died 1941
Japanese poet who successfully revived the verse form tanka

Yosano Akiko was born in Sakai. She chose to specialize in the verse form called *tanka*, which had been the standard form since medieval times but which, in the 19th century, had been replaced by *haiku* and *waka*, which were thought more capable of conveying emotional power.

Her versions of the form, however, were like none that had gone before and her collection *Midaregami*, on its publication in 1901, caused great controversy because of its attempts to reform the tanka.

Exquisitely crafted, her poems combine great emotional depth with an instant appeal which is not common in Japanese poetry. There is an English translation — *Tangled Hair: Selected Tanka from Midaregami* (1971).

Young, Elizabeth

Floreat 1558
English Protestant exile during the reign of Bloody Mary

Elizabeth Young was a member of the group of Protestant refugees who fled to the Continent in an attempt to avoid persecution during the Catholic restoration of **Mary I**. She was also one of the messengers who smuggled propaganda across the English Channel.

Married and the mother of three children, she was captured and imprisoned in London whilst distributing copies of John Olde's tract *Antichrist*. During 13 different interrogations she refused to betray her accomplices or her faith. She was finally released after agreeing to an ambiguous wording on a declaration concerning the nature of the sacrament.

Young, Sheila

Born 1950
American ice-skater and cyclist, triple Winter Olympic gold winner

Sheila Young was born in Birmingham, Michigan. She won her first two speed-skating titles, the US national outdoor competition and the North American Outdoor championship, in 1970. The following year, she defended both titles and won the Amateur Bicycle League of America women's national sprint title.

At the 1976 Olympics she became the first American in the history of the Winter Olympics to earn three medals — gold in the 500 metres, silver in the 1,500 metres and bronze in the 1,000-metre speed-skating events.

Young was a founding member of the Women's Sports Foundation and has served on numerous boards, including the US Cycling Federation and the Special Olympics International. She was named the US Olympic Committee's Sportswoman of the Year in 1981 and is in the International Women's Sports Hall of Fame, the US Cycling Federation Hall of Fame and the Speed Skating Hall of Fame.

Younghusband, Dame Eileen Louise

Born 1902 Died 1981
English social work pioneer who set up one of the first CABs

Eileen Younghusband was born in London, but brought up in Kashmir, where her father was senior British diplomat. On returning to England she did university settlement work in Bermondsey and Stepney, and studied at the London School of Economics, where she taught from 1929 to 1957.

During World War II she worked for the National Association of Girls' Clubs, directed courses for the British Council for Social Welfare, and set up one of the first Citizens Advice Bureaux. Later she compiled reports on social work training and social work (1947, 1951) and was principal adviser to the National Institute for Social Work Training (1961–7). From this unrivalled perspective she wrote a history of *Social Work in Britain, 1950–75* (1978).

Yourcenar, Marguerite, *pseud of* Marguerite de Crayencour

Born 1903 Died 1987
Belgian-born French novelist and poet, the first woman writer to be elected to the exclusive Académie Française

Marguerite de Crayencour was born in Brussels and educated at home in a wealthy and cultured household. She read Greek authors at the age of eight, and her first poems were privately printed in her teens. She travelled widely, and wrote a series of distinguished novels, plays, poems and essays. She settled in the USA in 1939, taking citizenship in 1947, but was later given French citizenship by presidential decree so that she could be admitted to the 40-member Académie in 1980.

Her novels, many of them historical reconstructions, include *La Nouvelle Eurydice* (1931,

'The New Eurydice'), *Le Coup de grâce* (1939, rev edn 1953, Eng trans 1957), *Les Mémoires d'Hadrien* (1941, Eng trans *Memoirs of Hadrian*, 1954) and *L'oeuvre au noir* (1968, Eng trans *The Abyss*, 1976). She also wrote on her religious experiences in *Préface à Gita-Gavinda* (1958), an anthology of American spirituals (*Fleuve profond, sombre rivière*, 1964, 'The Deep Dark River'), a long prose poem (*Feux*, 1939, Eng trans *Fires*, 1981), and an autobiography, *Souvenirs pieux* (1977, 'Pious Memories').

Z

Zaharias, Babe (Mildred Ella), *née* Didrikson

Born 1914 Died 1956
American golfer and one of the greatest all-round athletes ever

Babe Didrikson was born in Port Arthur, Texas. She was in the All-American basketball team (1930–2), then turned to athletics and won two gold medals (javelin and 80 metres sprint) at the 1932 Olympics in Los Angeles; she also broke the world record in the high jump, but was disqualified for using the new Western Roll technique.

Excelling also in swimming, tennis, rifle-shooting, diving, billiards and lacrosse, in 1934 she turned to golf, and after being briefly banned as an amateur for an unauthorized endorsement, she won the US National Women's Amateur Championship in 1946 and the British Ladies' Amateur Championship in 1947. In 1948 she turned professional and won the US Women's Open three times (1948, 1950, 1954). She was married to George Zaharias from 1938.

Babe Zaharias

Zaimis, Eleanor, *née* Christides

Born 1915 Died 1982
Greek-born British pharmacologist who focused on the interaction of drugs and the body

Eleanor Christides grew up and was educated in Bucharest, Romania. She graduated in medicine from Athens University in 1938, and became an assistant to the Professor of Pharmacology, which she remained until 1947. She was also a member of the Greek national pistol shooting team.

She married her second husband John Zaimis, a diplomat, in 1943, and accompanied him to London. She worked at the University of Bristol, at the National Institute for Medical Research in London and at the School of Pharmacy, London, where she became Reader in 1954. That same year she was appointed Head of the Department of Pharmacology at the Royal Free Hospital School of Medicine, where she remained until retirement in 1980.

She is credited with making important contributions to the understanding and development of local anaesthetics, drugs to lower blood pressure, and neuro-muscular relaxants.

Zakharina, Natalya

Birthdate unavailable
Russian architect who is almost unknown outside her own country

Natalya Zakharina works in and around Leningrad and has won a number of architectural prizes for her work, which includes a Shopping and Community Centre in Zelengorsk (1979–81) and a large-scale housing development in Pushkin (1970–80).

In 1984 she designed another housing scheme which is much smaller in scale and marked a step forward in the development of her style, demonstrating more variety and incorporating lower buildings in brick rather than concrete.

Other buildings include a crematorium designed in 1965 which inexplicably took 18 years to complete, the Communist Party headquarters in Pushkin (1979–86) and student housing in Pushkin (1980–2).

Zakrzewska, Maria

Born 1829 Died 1902
German-born American physician who devoted over 35 years of her life to educating women physicians and treating patients

Maria Zakrzewska was born in Berlin where she trained, as had her mother, to be a midwife. She emigrated in 1853 to study medicine and, through the efforts of **Elizabeth Blackwell**, was admitted to the Cleveland Medical College from which she graduated in 1856.

She worked with Elizabeth and Emily Blackwell in their New York Infirmary for Women and Children. After a brief period as Professor of Obstetrics and Diseases of Women and Children in the Boston Female Medical College, she established the New England Hospital for Women and Children in Boston in 1862.

Zaslavskaya, Tatiana Ivanovna

Born 1927
Russian economist and sociologist, highly influential in the break-up of the Soviet Union and formation of the new Russian government

Tatiana Zaslavskaya was born in Kiev and educated at Moscow University. A member of the Communist Party from 1954 to 1990, she has been a full member of the Russian (formerly Soviet) Academy of Sciences since 1981. She wrote the 'Novosibirsk Memorandum' (1983), a criticism of the Soviet economic system which was one of the factors behind the change of policies in Russia in the late 1980s.

She was President of the Sociological Association of the USSR (now Russia) in 1989–91, USSR People's Deputy (1989–91), personal adviser to President Gorbachev on economic and social matters, and, as an academic, is developing the new discipline, economic sociology.

Her publications range from *The Principle of Material Interest and Wage-Earning on Soviet Kolkhozes* (1958) to *The Second Socialist Revolution* (1991).

Zaturenska, Marya

Born 1902 Died 1982
Russian-born American poet, historian and biographer who won the 1938 Pulitzer Prize for poetry

Marya Zaturenska was born in Kiev. She moved to America at the age of eight, and was educated at the University of Wisconsin, where she met and married the poet and critic Horace Gregory (1898–1982).

Her second collection was the Pulitzer Prize-winning *Cold Morning Sky* (1938). Her poetry was mystical, lyrical, and often meditative, but has failed to last owing to its lack of true originality.

With her husband she wrote the influential *A History of American Poetry, 1900–1940* (1946), and she also wrote one of the best critical biographies of **Christina Rossetti** (1949).

Zayas y Sotomayor, Mariá de

Born 1590 Died c.1660
Spanish poet, novelist and playwright, one of the most dynamic and imaginative women writers of her time

Mariá de Zayas y Sotomayor was born in Madrid but brought up in Naples. She became one of the strongest defenders of women's rights of the century, and has been cited in modern times as one of the most effective premodern feminists.

Though she was greatly praised in her day as a poet by such writers as Lope Félix de Vega Carpio and Castillo Solórzano, she is most famous for her short stories, which draw on the traditions of the Spanish picaresque novel, the pastoral novel and the work of Boccaccio. Her two most important books are *Novelas amorosas y ejemplares* (1637, 'Exemplary and Amorous Novels', published in Zaragoza, where she lived for a large part of her life), and *Desengaños amorosos, parte segunda del sarao y entretenimientos honestos* (1647, 'Disenchantments of Love, the Second Part of the Party and Entertainment').

It is not clear when she died, and she may have spent the last years of her life in a convent.

Zell, Katherina Schütz, *née* Schütz

Born 1497/98   Died 1562
French Protestant reformer, writer, and religious
activist

Katherina Schütz was born in Strasbourg, the daughter of a cabinetmaker. In 1523 she married the Strasbourg reformer Matthew Zell, who became the third priest in Strasbourg to take a wife and be excommunicated from the Catholic Church.

They had two children who died in infancy, so Katherina was free to throw herself into the role of Protestant pastor's wife, welcoming visitors with controversial religious views, and spearheading the city's refugee relief programme for survivors of the Peasants' War of 1524–5.

She also wrote in defence of clerical marriage and in support of clergy wives, and published hymns and meditations. In 1548 she preached at her husband's funeral.

Zenobia, Septimia

3rd century AD
Queen of Palmyra, a strikingly beautiful and high
spirited woman who governed with prudence,
justice and liberality

Septimia Zenobia was born in Palmyra and was probably of Arab descent. She became the wife of the Bedouin Odenathus, lord of the city, who in AD264 was recognized by Gallienus as governor of the East. On her husband's murder (c.267) she embarked on a war of expansion, conquered Egypt in 269 and in 270 overran nearly the whole of the eastern provinces in Asia Minor, declaring independence from Rome and her son Vaballathus the eastern emperor (271).

When Aurelian became emperor in 270 he marched against her, defeated her in several battles, besieged her in Palmyra, and ultimately captured her as she was attempting flight (272). She saved her life by imputing the blame of the war to her secretary, Longinus; he was beheaded and Palmyra destroyed.

Zenobia, adorned with jewels, was led in triumphal procession at Rome, and presented by her conqueror with large possessions near Tivoli, where, with her two sons, she passed the rest of her life in comfort and even splendour, the wife of a Roman senator.

Zetkin, Clara, *née* Eissner

Born 1857   Died 1933
German socialist, feminist and communist leader
who helped to form Germany's Communist Party

Clara Eissner was born in Wiederau, Saxony. While studying at Leipzig Teacher's College for women she became a socialist and staunch feminist, and from 1881 to 1917 was a member of the Social Democratic party. She associated with Russian revolutionaries and in the 1880s was married to an exile, Ossip Zetkin (1848–89), during which time she lived in France and Switzerland, writing and distributing illegal literature, meeting with other socialists, and taking part in the founding congress of the Second Socialist International (1889).

She returned to Germany and from 1892 to 1917 edited *Die Gleichheit* ('Equality'), a socialist magazine for women. A friend of **Rosa Luxemburg**, she was a founder-member of the radical Independent Social Democratic party (called the *Spartakusbund* or Spartacus League) in 1917, and a founder of the German Communist Party (1919).

A strong supporter of the Russian Revolution (1917), she was a personal friend of Lenin and was elected in 1921 to the praesidium of the Comintern (Third International founded in Moscow in 1919). She spent most of her remaining years in the USSR although her influence decreased after Lenin died in 1924.

Zetterling, Mai

Born 1925   Died 1994
Swedish actress and director who became an
important figure in European cinema

Mai Zetterling was born in Vasteras, Sweden. She made both her stage and screen débuts at 16, and went on to become a highly successful actress. Her first major role came in the influential Swedish film *Hets* (USA *Torment*, UK *Frenzy*) (1944).

She played in many British and American films, then turned her attention to directing with her début film, the award-winning documentary *The War Game* (1963), which she co-wrote with her husband David Hughes. She directed a number of feature films in Sweden, often concerned with the role of women in contemporary society, and has also written novels.

Zhang Jie (Chang Chieh)

Born 1937
Chinese short-story writer and novelist, one of the
most important writers to emerge from China
after the death of Mao

Zhang Jie is a graduate of the People's University of Beijing (Peking). She came to writing in middle age but achieved a measure of success (and official disapprobation) almost immediately, winning literary prizes with her very first published stories.

Her writing, which is often satirical in its attitudes to officialdom, marriage, and the small-mindedness of ordinary people, is a potent blend of the domestic and the bizarre, which has no real equivalent in the West. She has yet to gain a significant reputation outside China.

Some of her work has been translated (*Leaden Wings* and *As Long as Nothing Happens, Nothing Will* are both published in English), but the translations to date are not entirely satisfactory.

Zia, Begum Khaleda

Born 1945
Bangladeshi politician and the first woman prime minister of Bangladesh

Begum Zia was the widow of General Ziaur Rahman, President of Bangladesh from 1977 until his assassination in 1981. She became Vice-Chairman of the Bangladesh Nationalist Party (BNP) in 1982, and its leader in 1984, and helped to form the seven-party alliance which forced President Hussain Muhammad Ershad to resign in 1990. Elections were called in which the BNP's main contestant was the Awami League led by Sheikh Hasina Wajed; in the event, the latter only gained 30 per cent of the seats and in 1991 Begum Zia became the first woman prime minister of Bangladesh.

Zita, St

Born c.1218   Died 1272
Italian servant whose life was so exemplary that she became the patroness of domestic servants

Zita was born in Monsagrati, near Lucca. From the age of 12 until her death she served the Fatinelli family. Her diligence did not endear her to fellow servants, nor did her generous donation of provisions to the poor impress her employer, but in due time she became a respected and trusted friend to all.

During the Middle Ages Zita was unofficially venerated, her popularity spreading to England, where she was known as St Sitha. Her remains were inspected in 1446, 1581 and 1652 and were found not to have decomposed. She was canonized in 1696 and declared patroness of domestic workers in 1953.

Zoë

Born 980   Died 1050
Empress of the eastern Roman empire

Zoë was born in Constantinople (now Istanbul). She was the daughter of the Byzantine emperor Constantine VIII, whom she succeeded in 1028, the year she married Romanus III and made him co-emperor.

In 1034 however, she had Romanus murdered and made her paramour emperor as Michael IV Paphiagonian. He died in 1041, and when in 1042 his successor Michael V (who was responsible for shutting Zoë up in a cloister for a time) was deposed, Zoë became joint empress with her sister Theodora. That year Zoë married her third husband, Constantine IX, who ruled jointly with them.

Though riddled with scandal and intrigue, their court was the focus of intellectual brilliance in the empire. The chief event marking their reign was the schism between the Eastern and Western Church, the culmination of much dispute between the papacy and the patriarchate.

Zwilich, Ellen Taaffe, *née* Taaffe

Born 1939
American violinist, lecturer and composer, the first woman to receive the Pulitzer Prize for music

Ellen T Zwilich was born in Miami, Florida. She received her doctorate from the Juilliard School of Music in 1975, the first woman to do so, and has since gone from strength to strength, seeing many of her compositions performed internationally.

She won the Pulitzer Prize in 1983 for her Symphony No.1, originally entitled *Three Movements for Orchestra*; her other honours include a gold medal in the International Composition Competition (1975) and the Marion Freschel Prize (1971, 1972, 1975).

A Women's Chronology
key events and achievements

According to Genesis, Eve is created by God as a partner for Adam in the Garden of Eden

14th century BC EGYPT: Nefertiti becomes Queen of Egypt as the wife of King Akhenaten

10th century BC ARABIA: *politics*: Queen of Sheba makes a diplomatic journey from Arabia to visit King Solomon of Israel in Jerusalem

7th century BC GREECE: *literature*: Sappho is born on Lesbos and becomes a great lyric poet

3rd century BC PERSIA: *religion*: Esther helps to save the Jews from slaughter — the origin of the festival of Purim

4BC ISRAEL: *religion*: Virgin Mary gives birth to Jesus Christ

1st century AD ENGLAND: *warfare*: Boudicca leads an army of British warriors in rebellion against the Romans

AD421 ROMAN EMPIRE: Eudocia marries Theodosius II and becomes an influential figure in the Eastern Roman Empire

c.650 CHINA: Wu Zhao becomes the first and only woman ruler of China

797 ROMAN EMPIRE: Irene becomes ruler in her own right of the Eastern Roman Empire

962 ROMAN EMPIRE: Adelaide is crowned Holy Roman Empress

c.980 GERMANY: *literature*: Hrostwitha is the first known writer of both poetry and plays

1139 ENGLAND: Matilda, wife of Holy Roman Emperor Henry V and mother of Henry II, lands in England to challenge the rule of Stephen

1147–52 GERMANY: *religion*: Hildegard of Bingen's visions are documented in the *Scivias*

1160–70 ALSACE: *literature*: Herrad of Hohenbourg becomes the first woman to organize the compilation of an encyclopedia

1184 ASIA: Tamara becomes Queen of Georgia and proves to be a wise and successful ruler

1346 ENGLAND: *education*: Elizabeth de Burgh founds Clare College, Cambridge

c.1382 ENGLAND: *politics*: Anne of Bohemia persuades her husband, Richard II, to pardon the peasants

1388 SCANDINAVIA: Margareta I becomes Queen of Denmark, Norway and Sweden

1399 FRANCE: *literature*: Christine de Pisan becomes possibly the first professional woman writer

1505 ENGLAND: *education*: Lady Margaret Beaufort, mother of Henry VII, founds Christ's College, Cambridge

1553 ENGLAND: Mary I becomes Queen of England

1558–1603 ENGLAND: Elizabeth I rules as Queen of England

1670 ENGLAND: *literature*: Aphra Behn becomes England's earliest professional woman writer

1740 HUNGARY: Maria Theresa succeeds to the Austrian dominions of Charles VI

1754 UK: *law*: Hardwicke Marriage Act makes parental consent obligatory for minors to marry

1763 UK: *literature*: Catherine Macaulay publishes the first volume of her *History of England*, one of the earliest historical works by a woman

1770 AMERICA: *literature*: Phyllis Wheatley becomes the second American woman and first black woman writer to be published

c.1770 FRANCE: *art*: Marguerite Gerard is one of the earliest women painters to achieve professional success

1775 UK: *law*: George III declares an order that releases women and young children from employment in coal and salt mines, where work is frequently as much as 12 hours a day

1776   USA: *suffrage*: in New Jersey a clause is introduced that gives the vote to women with more than $250 to their name

1786–97   UK: *science*: Caroline Herschel is credited with discovering eight comets

1792   UK: *reform*: Mary Wollstonecraft advocates equality between the sexes, radical social change, and economic independence for women in her *Vindication of the Rights of Women*

1793–1815   UK: during the war with France women assume patriotic roles raising money, providing clothing and making speeches

1812   UK: *medicine*: the first woman doctor is probably 'James Barry', a medicine graduate who practises as a man, and whose true sex is only discovered at her death in 1865

1813   UK: *reform*: Elizabeth Fry visits Newgate prison, where 300 women with their children live in appalling conditions, and is driven to devote herself to prison and asylum reform

1824   USA: *industrial action*: women weavers ally with men at Pawtucket, Rhode Island, in the first joint strike

1829   USA: *women's rights*: Fanny Wright and Robert Dale Owen publish the *Free Enquirer* newspaper in New York, using it as a vehicle to further the cause of women's emancipation

1838   USA: *women's rights*: feminist and social reformer Sarah Moore Grimké lectures on women's emancipation and the abolition of slavery and proposes that women become ministers of religion

1839   USA: *law*: the first married woman's property law is passed in Mississippi, allowing wives to hold property and income in their own names

1839   UK: *law*: Caroline Norton's spirited pamphlets and influential contacts result in the Infant Custody Bill, which improves the legal status of women in relation to infant custody

1840   UK: *women's rights*: the World's Anti-Slavery Convention in London sees women members of the US delegation refused a place on the convention floor

1842   UK: *law*: Mines Act prohibits the employment of women and children in mines

1843   UK: *photography*: the first ever photographically illustrated book, *British Algae: Cyanotype Impressions*, is published by a woman, Anna Atkins

1844   USA: *reform*: Sarah Bagley founds the Lowell Female Labor Reform Association in Massachusetts to promote the 10-hour day; a year later has more than 600 members

1845   USA: *reform*: the first ever investigation into working conditions is made by the Lowell Female Labor Reform Association examining the unhealthy 14-hour working days in Massachusetts textile mills

1847   UK: *law*: the working hours of women and children (aged 13–18) are limited to 10 per day

USA: *science*: Maria Mitchell discovers a comet and goes on to become the first woman member of the American Academy of Arts and Sciences

1848   USA: *law*: in New York a Married Women's Property Act is passed enabling divorced women to keep some of their possessions

USA: *women's rights*: in Seneca Falls, New York, the first women's rights convention determines to fight for female equality in marriage, work and education

UK: *education*: the first women's institution of higher learning, Queen's College, London, is opened

1850   USA: *women's rights*: in Worcester, Massachusetts, Lucy Stone calls the first National Convention for Women's Rights

UK: *education*: the North London Collegiate School for Ladies is founded by Frances Buss, the first woman to call herself a headmistress

1851   USA: *medicine*: Elizabeth Blackwell becomes the first woman physician in the USA

1852   USA: *education*: Antioch College in Yellow Springs, Ohio, the first college claiming to offer equal opportunities to men and women, is founded

1853   USA: *women's rights*: the Constitutional Convention in Massachusetts is subject to a petition for women's suffrage signed by 74 women

1854 USA: *law*: in Massachusetts a Married Women's Property Act is passed, granting every woman married after this date control of her property, and limited rights over that of her husband

1855 USA: *law*: in Massachusetts divorce law is reformed, making it fairer to women

UK: *reform*: the Young Women's Christian Association (YWCA) is founded in London to supply food and a bed to women not living at home

1855 USA: *education*: Elmira Female College, New York, becomes the first US institution to grant academic degrees to women

1856 USA: *theatre*: Laura Keene becomes the first woman theatre manager in the USA

1857 UK: *law*: helped by the efforts of Caroline Norton, the passage of Britain's Matrimonial Causes Act enables women to divorce their husbands more easily and ensures they are better provided for after divorce

1862 FRANCE: *education*: Julie-Victoire Daubié becomes the first woman to obtain the *baccalauréat*

1863 USA: *religion*: Olympia Brown becomes the first woman to be ordained in the USA

1864 UK: *law*: the Contagious Diseases Acts (also 1866 and 1869) stipulate that women in seaports and military towns are liable for compulsory examination for venereal disease, whilst making no reference to men

UK: *labour*: the Society for Promoting Employment of Women is established

1865 USA: *education*: Vassar Female college, Poughkeepsie, New York, is founded, essentially the first US women's college

UK: *medicine*: Elizabeth Garrett Anderson qualifies as a physician, the first woman in England to do so undisguised

1867 UK: *law*: a Reform Bill augmenting female suffrage is passed, supported by John Stuart Mill and MP Henry Fawcett

UK: *suffrage*: the Scottish Women's Suffrage Society meets for the first time

UK: *education*: the North of England Council for Promoting Higher Education of Women is founded by reformers keen to achieve women's examinations at university level

1868 UK: *suffrage*: Britain's National Society for Woman Suffrage meets for the first time

USA: *labour*: the Working Women's Association is founded by Elizabeth Cady Stanton

USA: *labour*: the National Labor Union admits four women to its Congress

1869 UK: *women's rights*: John Stuart Mill, influenced by his wife Harriet, advocates the emancipation and equality of women in *The Subjection of Women*

UK: *education*: Cambridge University allows women to take an examination at university level

1869 USA: *suffrage*: the American Woman Suffrage Association (AWSA) is founded in Boston by Lucy Stone and her husband, Henry Brown Blackwell

USA: *suffrage*: the National Woman Suffrage Association (NWSA) is founded by Susan Brownell Anthony and Elizabeth Cady Stanton

USA: *suffrage*: Mary Ashton Livermore establishes *The Agitator*, a journal aimed at promoting voting rights for women

USA: *suffrage*: in Cheyenne, Wyoming Territory, a new constitution grants women the rights to vote and to hold office

USA: *labour*: the first national women's labour organization, the Daughters of St Crispin (DOSC), is created in Lynn, Massachusetts

1870 USA: *suffrage*: in the Territory of Utah full suffrage is granted to women

USA: women's rights: Victoria Woodhull and her sister Tennessee Claflin establish *Woodhull and Claflin's Weekly*, a magazine advocating free love, equal rights and legal prostitution

1870 UK: *law*: women are now able to retain money they have earned, and are not obliged to hand it over to their husbands

UK: *law*: the Education Act broadens elementary education for girls and boys

UK: *education*: the National Union for Improving the Education of Women is founded

1872   USA: *law*: in Chicago discrimination for reasons of gender becomes illegal, enabling female lawyers to practise

USA: *law*: in Portland, Oregon, married women are allowed to enter business for themselves and their property is legally protected should their husbands desert them

USA: *labour*: Congress passes a law stipulating equal pay for equal work in US federal employment

1873   UK: *law*: divorced women acquire the right to claim custody of their children

USA: *reform*: in Indianapolis, Indiana, the first US prison operated and occupied solely by women is opened

1874   UK: *suffrage*: the Dublin Women's Suffrage Society is founded

USA: *labour*: the first successful law stipulating a 10-hour working day for women is passed in Massachusetts

UK: *education*: the London School Board issues degrees to women for the first time

1875   UK: *labour*: the Trade Union Congress admits women delegates for the first time

1876   USA: *women's rights*: Elizabeth Cady Stanton and Matilda Joslyn Gage compile a charter called the 'Declaration of Rights of the Women of the United States' and present it to the acting US vice president on 4 July at Philadelphia

1877   USA: *politics*: Victoria Woodhull becomes the first woman nominated to run for the US presidency

UK: *education*: the Association for the Higher Education of Women is established in Glasgow

1878   USA: *labour*: the Women's Typographical Union Local closes; women are reluctantly accepted into the printer's union on an equal footing with men

UK: *labour*: the Factory and Workshop Act allows women better protection

1879   USA: *law*: women are allowed to plead a case in the Supreme Court, and the first woman to exercise this right is Belva Lockwood

UK: *education*: Somerville College, an all-women college (until 1994), is founded at Oxford University

1880   USA: *religion*: Anna Howard Shaw becomes the first ordained woman preacher of the Methodist Church

UK: *education*: the first high schools for girls are established

1881   UK: *suffrage*: the Householders in Scotland Act awards some Scottish women the right to vote in local elections

UK: *education*: at the University of Cambridge women are permitted to enroll for honours examinations, but receive certificates in place of degrees

1882   UK: *law*: the Second Married Women's Property Act allows married women to hold property in their own right

1884   UK: *education*: the first women college graduates in Ireland receive their degrees

1885   UK: *education*: St Hilda's College, Cheltenham, the first women's teacher training college, is founded

1886   UK: *law*: following the crusading efforts of Josephine Butler, the Contagious Diseases Acts (*see* 1864) are repealed

UK: *law*: the Guardianship of Infants bill recognizes the mother's role in child care

USA: *labour*: the Noble Order of the Knights of Labor establishes a Woman's Department to research women's work throughout the country

1887   USA: *suffrage*: a 'Protest' petitioning complete women's suffrage is presented to President Cleveland

UK: *sport*: Wimbledon Ladies' Championship is won by Lottie Dod

1888   UK: *sport*: Wimbledon Ladies' Championship is won by Lottie Dod

1890   USA: *education*: the founding charter of the University of Chicago announces its intention to admit women on the same basis as men

1891   UK: *sport*: Wimbledon Ladies' Championship is won by Lottie Dod

1892   UK: *sport*: Wimbledon Ladies' Championship is won by Lottie Dod

1893   INDIA: *law*: Cornelia Sorabji passes the Bachelor of Civil Law examination in London and returns to India to become the first practising woman lawyer there

USA: *suffrage*: in Colorado the male electorate votes for female suffrage

UK: *travel*: Annie Royle Taylor becomes the first European woman to enter Tibet

UK: *sport*: Wimbledon Ladies' Championship is won by Lottie Dod

1894 UK: *suffrage*: the Local Government Act broadens the extent of women's voting rights but does not include national elections

ITALY: *medicine*: Maria Montessori becomes the first woman in Italy to gain a medical degree

1895 USA: *suffrage*: in Utah the constitution is amended to include woman suffrage

1896 USA: *suffrage*: in Idaho the constitution is amended to include woman suffrage

USA: *music*: Mrs H H A Beach becomes the first US woman to write a symphony

1898 UK: *law*: Irish women are granted the right to sit on district councils in Ireland

NEW ZEALAND: *suffrage*: women gain equal voting rights

1899 UK: *women's rights*: the first meeting of the International Women's Congress is held

1902 UK: *suffrage*: women textile workers present a suffrage petition to parliament

1903 UK: *suffrage*: Emmeline Pankhurst and her daughter Christabel found the Women's Social and Political Union to further the cause of female suffrage

USA: *labour*: in Oregon a law prohibits the employment of women for more than 10 hours a day in any factory or laundry

USA: *labour*: the National Women's Trade Union League (WTUL) is founded to encourage women to form trade unions and organize research

Nobel Prize for Physics is won by Marie Curie (with Pierre Curie and Antoine Henri Becquerel)

1904 UK: *suffrage*: a meeting of the International Council of Women is held in Berlin and the International Woman Suffrage Alliance is formed

1905 UK: *suffrage*: following the failure of the Women's Vote Bill, Emmeline and Christabel Pankhurst resort to increasingly militant tactics, for which the latter is imprisoned

Nobel Prize for Peace is won by Baroness Bertha von Suttner

1906 FINLAND: *suffrage*: women gain equal voting rights

UK: *suffrage*: the Labour Party in opposition calls for women's suffrage

1908 UK: *politics*: Elizabeth Garrett Anderson becomes the first woman mayor as Mayor of Aldeburgh

UK: *politics*: Chrystal Macmillan becomes the first woman to address the House of Lords; her subject is the right of women graduates to vote

UK: *suffrage*: 10,000 suffragists storm parliament, resulting in 24 arrests and the barring of women from the building

1908 USA: *arts*: Julia Ward Howe becomes the first woman member of the American Academy of Arts and Letters

1909 USA: *suffrage*: the Men's League for Woman Suffrage is founded

USA: *education*: National training School for Women and Girls, which offers a variety of vocational courses, is founded in Washington DC

1909 Nobel Prize for Literature is won by Selma Lagerlöf

1910 USA: *suffrage*: women gain the right to vote in Washington

1911 USA: *suffrage*: women gain the right to vote in California

USA: *aviation*: Harriet Quimby becomes the first licensed woman pilot

Nobel Prize for Chemistry is won by Marie Curie

1912 USA: *suffrage*: male voters in the states of Michigan, Kansas, Oregon and Arizona vote to amend the constitution to grant women suffrage, but the suggestion is rejected by the Wisconsin electorate

USA: *labour*: in Massachusetts a minimum wage law relating to women and children is passed

USA: *sport*: Eleanora Sears becomes the first woman to play polo

1913 FINLAND: *suffrage*: women gain equal voting rights

USA: *suffrage*: Alice Paul founds the Congressional Union for Woman Suffrage (called the National Woman's Party from 1916)

FRANCE: *music*: the Prix de Rome is won by Lili Boulanger for *Faust et Hélène*

1914   USA: *law*: Florence Allen is admitted to the Ohio Bar

USA: the first meeting of the Women's Peace Party is convened in New York

1914–18   UK: *labour*: during World War I the shortage of manpower enables women to enter the industrial and agricultural workplace, particularly in munitions factories and in transport

1914–18   UK: *science*: during World War I the Ayrton fan, invented by Hertha Ayrton, is used for dispersing poisonous gases

1916   USA: *politics*: Jeannette Rankin becomes the first female member of Congress when she enters the House of Representatives as a Republican

USA: *medicine*: Margaret Sanger, founder of the birth control movement, is imprisoned for opening a birth control clinic

1917   RUSSIA: *suffrage*: women gain equal voting rights

USA: *suffrage*: President Wilson speaks in support of equal suffrage to the New York State Woman Suffrage Party in the White House

1917–18   USA: *labour*: during World War I women are employed in war plants and auxiliary units, or alternatively, as pacifists, decline to support the war

1918   UK: *politics*: an act passed in November enables women to become MPs

UK: *politics*: Constance Markievicz becomes the first British woman MP but does not take her seat in the House of Commons

USA: *suffrage*: the US Woman Suffrage Amendment resolution is rejected by the Senate despite being passed in the House of Representatives

UK: *suffrage*: with the end of World War I, the vote is granted to women of 30 years age and over (and also to men of age 21 and over)

CANADA (most states): *suffrage*: women gain equal voting rights

GERMANY: *suffrage*: women gain equal voting rights

AUSTRIA: *suffrage*: women gain equal voting rights

USA: *literature*: Pulitzer Prize for poetry is won by Sara Teasdale for *Love Songs*

1919   UK: *politics*: Nancy Astor becomes the first woman MP to take her seat in the House of Commons

NETHERLANDS: *suffrage*: women gain equal voting rights

USA: *women's rights*: the Feminist Congress meets for the first time in New York

UK: *labour*: the Sex Disqualification Act allows women to enter the professions

USA: *labour*: International Congress of Working Women is established in Washington DC

USA: *education*: Alice Hamilton becomes the first woman professor at Harvard University

USA: *literature*: Pulitzer Prize for poetry is won by Margaret Widdemer for *Old Road to Paradise* (with Carl Sandburg for *Corn Huskers*)

UK: *sport*: Wimbledon Ladies' Championship is won by Suzanne Lenglen

1920   UK: *law*: Elizabeth Haldane is appointed the first woman Justice of the Peace in Scotland

USA (all states): *suffrage*: women gain equal voting rights, proclaimed on 26 August

USA: *suffrage*: the League of Women Voters is founded by Carrie Chapman Catt to provide support for newly enfranchised women

CZECHOSLOVAKIA (now the Czech and Slovak republics): *suffrage*: women gain equal voting rights

USA: *labour*: Congress passes an act creating the Women's Bureau of the Department of Labor to promote women's working conditions and improve their wages

UK: *education*: Oxford University admits 100 women to study for full degrees and male and female professor status is levelled

UK: *sport*: Wimbledon Ladies' Championship is won by Suzanne Lenglen

1921   CANADA: *politics*: Agnes Macphail becomes the first woman to enter Canada's parliament

SWEDEN: *suffrage*: women gain equal voting rights

USA: *literature*: Pulitzer Prize for fiction is won by Edith Wharton for *The Age of Innocence*

USA: *literature*: Pulitzer Prize for drama is won by Zona Gale for *Miss Lulu Bett*

UK: *sport*: Wimbledon Ladies' Championship is won by Suzanne Lenglen

1922 USA: *law*: the Cable Act grants married women independent citizenship

UK: *sport*: Wimbledon Ladies' Championship is won by Suzanne Lenglen

1923 UK: *politics*: Katharine Atholl becomes the first woman Minister

UK: *law*: the Matrimonial Causes Bill is passed in the House of Commons

UK: *law*: Dame Margaret Kidd becomes the first woman member of the Scottish Bar

USA: *labour*: in Columbia the Supreme Court rules that a minimum wage law in the state of Columbia (passed 1918) is unconstitutional

USA: *literature*: Pulitzer Prize for fiction is won by Willa Cather for *One of Ours*

USA: *literature*: Pulitzer Prize for poetry is won by Edna St Vincent Millay for *The Harp Weaver and Other Poems*

UK: *sport*: Wimbledon Ladies' Championship is won by Suzanne Lenglen

1924 USA: *literature*: Pulitzer Prize for fiction is won by Margaret Wilson for *The Able McLaughlins*

UK: *sport*: Wimbledon Ladies' Championship is won by Kitty McKane (later Kitty Godfree)

1925 USA: *literature*: Pulitzer Prize for fiction is won by Edna Ferber for *So Big*

UK: *sport*: Wimbledon Ladies' Championship is won by Suzanne Lenglen

1926 AUSTRALIA: *art*: Grace Cossington-Smith helps to introduce post-Impressionism by founding the Contemporary Group

Nobel Prize for Literature is won by Grazia Deledda

USA: *literature*: Pulitzer Prize for poetry is won by Amy Lowell for *What's O'Clock?*

USA: *sport*: Gertrude Ederle becomes the first woman to swim the English Channel

UK: *sport*: Wimbledon Ladies' Championship is won by Kitty Godfree

1927 USA: *literature*: Pulitzer Prize for poetry is won by Leonora Speyer for *Fiddler's Farewell*

UK: *sport*: Wimbledon Ladies' Championship is won by Helen Wills

1928 UK: *suffrage*: women gain equal voting rights

ECUADOR: *suffrage*: women gain equal voting rights

GUYANA: *suffrage*: women gain equal voting rights

UK: *suffrage*: the Representatives of the People Act lowers the minimum age of women voters from 30 to 21 years

USA: *aviation*: Amelia Earhart becomes the first woman to fly the Atlantic

Nobel Prize for Literature is won by Sigrid Undset

USA: *film*: Best Actress Oscar is won by Janet Gaynor for her role in *Seventh Heaven*

UK: *sport*: Wimbledon Ladies' Championship is won by Helen Wills

1929 UK: *politics*: Margaret Bondfield becomes the first woman Cabinet Minister

UK: *science*: Amy Johnson becomes the first woman to gain her certificate as a ground engineer

1929 USA: *literature*: Pulitzer Prize for fiction is won by Julia Peterkin for *Scarlet Sister Mary*

USA: *film*: Best Actress Oscar is won by Mary Pickford for her role in *Coquette*

UK: *sport*: Wimbledon Ladies' Championship is won by Helen Wills

1930 UK: *aviation*: Amy Johnson flies solo from England to Australia

UK: *literature*: Virginia Woolf undertakes the cause of independence for women in *A Room of One's Own*

USA: *film*: Best Actress Oscar is won by Norma Shearer for her role in *The Divorcee*

UK: *sport*: Wimbledon Ladies' Championship is won by Helen Wills Moody (formerly Helen Wills)

1931 SPAIN: *suffrage*: women gain equal voting rights

Nobel Prize for Peace is won by Jane Addams (with Nicholas Butler)

USA: *literature*: Pulitzer Prize for fiction is won by Margaret Ayer Barnes for *Years of Grace*

USA: *literature*: Pulitzer Prize for drama is won by Susan Glaspell for *Alison's House*

USA: *film*: Best Actress Oscar is won by Marie Dressler for her role in *Min and Bill*

1932   USA: *politics*: Hattie Caraway becomes the first woman elected to the US Senate

BRAZIL: *suffrage*: women gain equal voting rights

URUGUAY: *suffrage*: women gain equal voting rights

THAILAND: *suffrage*: women gain equal voting rights

MALDIVES: *suffrage*: women gain equal voting rights

USA: *literature*: Pulitzer Prize for fiction is won by Pearl S Buck for *The Good Earth*

USA: *film*: Best Actress Oscar is won by Helen Hayes for her role in *The Sin of Madelon Claudet*

UK: *sport*: Wimbledon Ladies' Championship is won by Helen Wills Moody (formerly Helen Wills)

1933   USA: *politics*: Frances Perkins becomes the first US woman to hold Cabinet rank

USA: *politics*: Ruth Rohde becomes the first US woman diplomat

TURKEY: *suffrage*: women gain equal voting rights

USA: *film*: Best Actress Oscar is won by Katharine Hepburn for her role in *Morning Glory*

UK: *sport*: Wimbledon Ladies' Championship is won by Helen Wills Moody (formerly Helen Wills)

1934   CUBA: *suffrage*: women gain equal voting rights

NEW ZEALAND: *aviation*: Jean Batten flies the England–Australia return journey solo

USA: *literature*: Pulitzer Prize for fiction is won by Caroline Miller for *Lamb in His Bosom*

USA: *film*: Best Actress Oscar is won by Claudette Colbert for her role in *It Happened One Night*

1935   Nobel Prize for Chemistry is won by Irène Joliot-Curie (with Frédéric Joliot-Curie)

USA: *literature*: Pulitzer Prize for fiction is won by Josephine Winslow Johnson for *Now in November*

USA: *literature*: Pulitzer Prize for drama is won by Zoë Akins for *The Old Maid*

USA: *literature*: Pulitzer Prize for poetry is won by Audrey Wurdemann for *Bright Ambush*

USA: *film*: Best Actress Oscar is won by Bette Davis for her role in *Dangerous*

UK: *sport*: Wimbledon Ladies' Championship is won by Helen Wills Moody (formerly Helen Wills)

1936   USA: *labour*: the New York: Supreme Court rules that a minimum wage law (passed 1933) is unconstitutional

USA: *film*: Best Actress Oscar is won by Luise Rainer for her role in *The Great Ziegfeld*

1937   UK: *law*: the new Irish Constitution bans divorce and condemns working mothers

PHILIPPINES: *suffrage*: women gain equal voting rights

USA: *labour*: the Supreme Court upholds a minimum wage for women

UK: *science*: Flora Sadler is admitted to the scientific staff of The Royal Observatory, Greenwich

USA: *literature*: Pulitzer Prize for fiction is won by Margaret Mitchell for *Gone With the Wind*

USA: *film*: Best Actress Oscar is won by Luise Rainer for her role in *The Good Earth*

1938   Nobel Prize for Literature is won by Pearl Buck

1938   USA: *literature*: Pulitzer Prize for poetry is won by Marya Zaturenska for *Cold Morning Sky*

USA: *film*: Best Actress Oscar is won by Bette Davis for the second time for her role in *Jezebel*

UK: *sport*: Wimbledon Ladies' Championship is won by Helen Wills Moody (formerly Helen Wills)

1939   AUSTRIA: *science*: the term 'nuclear fission' is first used by Lise Meitner and her nephew Otto Frisch

UK: *education*: Dorothy Garrod becomes the first woman professor of Cambridge University

USA: *literature*: Pulitzer Prize for fiction is won by Marjorie Rawlings for *The Yearling*

USA: *film*: Best Actress Oscar is won by Vivien Leigh for her role in *Gone With the Wind*

1939–45   UK: *labour*: during World War II the Women's Royal Naval Service, the Auxiliary Territorial Service, the Women's Auxiliary Air Force, the Women's Voluntary Service for Civil Defence, the nursing services, the industrial sector and the Women's Land Army all take on numerous women recruits as part of the war effort

1939–45   UK: *aviation*: during World War II Jacqueline Cochran becomes the first woman to pilot a bomber across the Atlantic

1940   USA: *film*: Best Actress Oscar is won by Ginger Rogers for her role in *Kitty Foyle*

1941   PANAMA: *suffrage*: women gain equal voting rights

USA: *film*: Best Actress Oscar is won by Joan Fontaine for her role in *Suspicion*

1942   USA: *literature*: Pulitzer Prize for fiction is won by Ellen Glasgow for *In This Our Life*

USA: *film*: Best Actress Oscar is won by Greer Garson for her role in *Mrs Miniver*

1942–5   USA: *labour*: during World War II the Women's Army Auxiliary Corps, the Women Accepted for Voluntary Emergency Service and the Women's Auxiliary Ferrying Squadron are all founded to encourage female employment, provide support to the armed forces, and free men for combat; it is estimated that nearly half of all US women hold a position in the uniformed services or in the factories, shipyards and shops

1943   USSR: *politics*: Alexandra Kollontai becomes the the world's first woman foreign ambassador

UK: *labour*: Dame Anne Loughlin becomes the first woman president of the TUC

USA: *film*: Best Actress Oscar is won by Jennifer Jones for her role in *The Song of Bernadette*

1944   FRANCE: *suffrage*: women gain equal voting rights

HONG KONG: *religion*: Florence Tim Oi Li is ordained the first woman priest of the Anglican Church

USA: *film*: Best Actress Oscar is won by Ingrid Bergman for her role in *Gaslight*

1945   ITALY: *suffrage*: women gain equal voting rights

HUNGARY: *suffrage*: women gain equal voting rights

YUGOSLAVIA: *suffrage*: women gain equal voting rights

GUATEMALA: *suffrage*: women gain equal voting rights

SENEGAL: *suffrage*: women gain equal voting rights

IRELAND: *suffrage*: women gain equal voting rights

Nobel Prize for Literature is won by Gabriela Mistral

USA: *literature*: Pulitzer Prize for drama is won by Mary Chase for *Harvey*

USA: *film*: Best Actress Oscar is won by Joan Crawford for her role in *Mildred Pierce*

1946   PALESTINE: *suffrage*: women gain equal voting rights

KENYA: *suffrage*: women gain equal voting rights

LIBERIA: *suffrage*: women gain equal voting rights

VIETNAM: *suffrage*: women gain equal voting rights

UK: *science*: Agnes Arber becomes the first woman botanist elected to the Royal Society

Nobel Prize for Peace is won by Emily Balch (with John R Mott)

USA: *film*: Best Actress Oscar is won by Olivia de Havilland for her role in *To Each His Own*

1947 BULGARIA: *suffrage*: women gain equal voting rights

CHINA: *suffrage*: women gain equal voting rights

NEPAL: *suffrage*: women gain equal voting rights

PAKISTAN: *suffrage*: women gain equal voting rights

VENEZUELA: *suffrage*: women gain equal voting rights

ARGENTINA: *suffrage*: women gain equal voting rights

Nobel Prize for Physiology or Medicine is won by Gerty Cori (with Carl Cori and Bernardo Houssay)

USA: *film*: Best Actress Oscar is won by Loretta Young for her role in *The Farmer's Daughter*

1948 UK: *law*: Dame Margaret Kidd becomes the first woman QC

ISRAEL: *suffrage*: women gain equal voting rights

IRAQ: *suffrage*: women gain equal voting rights

KOREA: *suffrage*: women gain equal voting rights

SURINAM: *suffrage*: women gain equal voting rights

USA: *film*: Best Actress Oscar is won by Jane Wyman for her role in *Johnny Belinda*

1949 CHILE: *suffrage*: women gain the right to vote, but must vote separately from men

INDONESIA: *suffrage*: women gain equal voting rights

COSTA RICA: *suffrage*: women gain equal voting rights

USA: *education*: Harvard Law School admits women

USA: *film*: Best Actress Oscar is won for the second time by Olivia de Havilland for her role in *The Heiress*

1950 INDIA: *suffrage*: women gain equal voting rights

USA: *literature*: Pulitzer Prize for poetry is won by Gwendolyn Brooks for *Annie Allen*; she is the first black laureate

USA: *film*: Best Actress Oscar is won by Judy Holliday for her role in *Born Yesterday*

1951 MONGOLIA: *suffrage*: women gain equal voting rights

USA: *medicine*: Elizabeth Blackwell begins to practise as the first woman doctor in the USA

USA: *film*: Best Actress Oscar is won by Vivien Leigh for the second time for her role in *A Streetcar Named Desire*

1952 GREECE: *suffrage*: women gain equal voting rights

1952 USA: *literature*: Pulitzer Prize for poetry is won by Marianne Moore for *Collected Poems*

USA: *film*: Best Actress Oscar is won by Shirley Booth for her role in *Come Back, Little Sheba*

UK: *sport*: Wimbledon Ladies' Championship is won by Maureen Connolly

1953 INDIA: *politics*: Vijaya Pandit becomes the first woman president of the UN General Assembly

MEXICO: *suffrage*: women gain equal voting rights

SUDAN: *suffrage*: women gain equal voting rights

USA: *film*: Best Actress Oscar is won by Audrey Hepburn for her role in *Roman Holiday*

UK: *sport*: Wimbledon Ladies' Championship is won by Maureen Connolly, who goes on to win the women's tennis Grand Slam

1954 USA: *film*: Best Actress Oscar is won by Grace Kelly for her role in *The Country Girl*

UK: *sport*: Wimbledon Ladies' Championship is won by Maureen Connolly

1955 INDONESIA: *suffrage*: women gain equal voting rights

NICARAGUA: *suffrage*: women gain equal voting rights

USA: *film*: Best Actress Oscar is won by Anna Magnani for her role in *The Rose Tattoo*

1956　EGYPT: *suffrage*: women gain equal voting rights

TUNISIA: *suffrage*: women gain equal voting rights

COMOROS: *suffrage*: women gain equal voting rights

MAURITIUS: *suffrage*: women gain equal voting rights

USA: *literature*: Pulitzer Prize for drama is won by Frances Goodrich (and Albert Hackett) for *The Diary of Anne Frank*

USA: *literature*: Pulitzer Prize for poetry is won by Elizabeth Bishop for *Poems — North and South*

USA: *film*: Best Actress Oscar is won by Ingrid Bergman for her role in *Anastasia*

UK: *sport*: Pat Smythe becomes the first woman to ride in the Olympic Games

1957　HONDURAS: *suffrage*: women gain equal voting rights

MALAYSIA: *suffrage*: women gain equal voting rights

USSR: *politics*: Yekaterina Fursteva becomes the first woman member of the Politburo

USA: *film*: Best Actress Oscar is won by Joanne Woodward for her role in *The Three Faces of Eve*

UK: *sport*: Wimbledon Ladies' Championship is won by Althea Gibson

1958　USA: *literature*: Pulitzer Prize for drama is won by Ketti Frings for *Look Homeward, Angel*

USA: *film*: Best Actress Oscar is won by Susan Hayward for her role in *I Want to Live!*

UK: *sport*: Wimbledon Ladies' Championship is won by Althea Gibson

1959　MADAGASCAR: *suffrage*: women gain equal voting rights

TANZANIA: *suffrage*: women gain equal voting rights

USA: *theatre*: Lorraine Hansberry becomes the first black author of a Broadway play

USA: *film*: Best Actress Oscar is won by Simone Signoret for her role in *The Room at the Top*

UK: *sport*: Wimbledon Ladies' Championship is won by Maria Bueno

1960　SRI LANKA: *politics*: Sirimavo Bandaranaike becomes the world's first woman prime minister

ZAIRE: *suffrage*: women gain equal voting rights

GABON: *suffrage*: women gain equal voting rights

USA: *film*: Best Actress Oscar is won by Elizabeth Taylor for her role in *Butterfield 8*

USA: *sport*: Wilma Rudolph becomes the first US woman to win three Olympic gold medals

UK: *sport*: Wimbledon Ladies' Championship is won by Maria Bueno

1961　RWANDA: *suffrage*: women gain equal voting rights

USA: *literature*: Pulitzer Prize for fiction is won by Harper Lee for *To Kill a Mockingbird*

USA: *literature*: Pulitzer Prize for poetry is won by Phyllis McGinley for *Times Three: Selected Verse from Three Decades*

USA: *film*: Best Actress Oscar is won by Sophia Loren for her role in *Two Women*

1962　ALGERIA: *suffrage*: women gain equal voting rights

USA: *film*: Best Actress Oscar is won by Anne Bancroft for her role in *The Miracle Worker*

1963　MOROCCO: *suffrage*: women gain equal voting rights

CONGO: *suffrage*: women gain equal voting rights

USA: *labour*: the Equal Pay Act claims to guarantee women the same pay as men for the same work

USSR: *science*: Valentine Tereshkova becomes the first woman in space

Nobel Prize for Physics is won by Maria Goeppert-Mayer (with Eugene Wigner and Hans Jensen)

USA: *literature*: Betty Friedan publishes *The Feminine Mystique,* the bestseller which analyses the role of women in American society and articulates their frustrations

USA: *film*: Best Actress Oscar is won by Patricia Neal for her role in *Hud*

UK: *sport*: Wimbledon Ladies' Championship is won by Margaret Smith (later Margaret Smith Court)

1964   USA: *politics*: Margaret Chase Smith runs for the US presidency

Nobel Prize for Chemistry is won by Dorothy Hodgkin

UK: *exploration*: Myrtle Simpson becomes the first woman to ski across the Greenland ice cap

USA: *film*: Best Actress Oscar is won by Julie Andrews for her role in *Mary Poppins*

UK: *sport*: Wimbledon Ladies' Championship is won by Maria Bueno

AUSTRALIA: *sport*: Dawn Fraser becomes the first woman to win gold medals at three consecutive Olympic Games

USSR: *sport*: Lidiya Skoblikova wins the Olympic Grand Slam in ice skating

1965   UK: *law*: Elizabeth Lane becomes the first woman judge

USA: *literature*: Pulitzer Prize for fiction is won by Shirley Ann Grau for *The Keepers of the House*

USA: *film*: Best Actress Oscar is won by Julie Christie for her role in *Darling*

UK: *exploration*: Myrtle Simpson becomes the first woman to ski across the Greenland ice cap

UK: *sport*: Wimbledon Ladies' Championship is won by Margaret Smith (later Margaret Smith Court)

1966   AUSTRALIA: *politics*: Dame Annabelle Rankin becomes the first woman Minister in the Australian parliament

1966   USA: *women's rights*: the National Organization for Women (NOW) is founded by Betty Frieden and other feminists to continue the campaign for equal rights

1966   Nobel Prize for Literature is won by Nelly Sachs (with Shmuel Yosef Agnon)

1966   USA: *literature*: Pulitzer Prize for fiction is won by Katherine Anne Porter for *The Collected Stories*

1966   USA: *film*: Best Actress Oscar is won by Elizabeth Taylor for the second time for her role in *Who's Afraid of Virginia Woolf?*

UK: *sport*: Wimbledon Ladies' Championship is won by Billie Jean King

1967   AUSTRALIA: *suffrage*: women gain equal voting rights

USA: *women's rights*: National Organization for Women (NOW) holds its first national conference, raising such issues as demands for equal opportunities in employment, equal education, equal poverty allowances and maternity leave

UK: *science*: the first pulsar is jointly discovered by Jocelyn Bell Burnell and Antony Hewish

USA: *literature*: Pulitzer Prize for poetry is won by Anne Sexton for *Live or Die*

USA: *film*: Best Actress Oscar is won by Katharine Hepburn for the second time for her role in *Guess Who's Coming to Dinner,* shared with Barbra Streisand for her role in *Funny Girl*

UK: *sport*: Wimbledon Ladies' Championship is won by Billie Jean King

1968   UK: *religion*: Catherine McConachie becomes the first woman minister of the Church of Scotland

USA: *film*: Best Actress Oscar is won by Katharine Hepburn for the third time for her role in *The Lion in Winter*

UK: *art*: Bridget Riley wins the major painting prize at the Venice Biennale

UK: *sport*: Wimbledon Ladies' Championship is won by Billie Jean King

1969   USA: *women's rights*: International Women's Day is revived

USA: *film*: Best Actress Oscar is won by Maggie Smith for her role in *The Prime of Miss Jean Brodie*

UK: *sport*: Wimbledon Ladies' Championship is won by Ann Jones

1970   USA: *law*: New York becomes the first major US city to pass a law against sexual discrimination in public places

USA: *labour*: the 50th anniversary of women's suffrage is celebrated by the Women's Strike for Equality, a 10,000-strong march down New York's Fifth Avenue

USA: *labour*: Margery Hurst becomes the first woman to be elected a member of the New York Chamber of Commerce

UK: *literature*: Booker Prize is won by Bernice Rubens for *The Elected Member*

USA: *literature*: Pulitzer Prize for fiction is won by Jean Stafford for *Collected Stories*

USA: *film*: Best Actress Oscar is won by Glenda Jackson for her role in *Women in Love*

UK: *sport*: Wimbledon Ladies' Championship is won by Margaret Smith Court

1971 SWITZERLAND: *suffrage*: women gain equal voting rights

USA: *suffrage*: the Twenty-sixth Amendment lowers the voting age for men and women from 21 to 18

USA: *politics*: the National Women's Political Caucus is founded to enhance women's political power

USA: *film*: Best Actress Oscar is won by Jane Fonda for her role in *Klute*

UK: *sport*: Wimbledon Ladies' Championship is won by Evonne Goolagong (later Evonne Cawley)

1972 USA: *women's rights*: the Senate votes to submit the Equal Rights Amendment to the states for ratification, proposing equality of rights in law (the deadline is extended in 1978)

UK: *education*: five formerly all-male colleges at Oxford University open their doors to women

USA: *film*: Best Actress Oscar is won by Liza Minnelli for her role in *Cabaret*

UK: *sport*: Wimbledon Ladies' Championship is won by Billie Jean King

1973 USA: *politics*: Barbara Jordan becomes the first African-American to be elected to either house of the US Congress since the Civil War

JORDAN: *suffrage*: women gain equal voting rights

USA: *literature*: Pulitzer Prize for fiction is won by Eudora Welty for *The Optimist's Daughter*

USA: *literature*: Pulitzer Prize for poetry is won by Maxine Kumin for *Up Country*

USA: *film*: Best Actress Oscar is won by Glenda Jackson for the second time for her role in *A Touch of Class*

UK: *sport*: Wimbledon Ladies' Championship is won by Billie Jean King

1974 ANGOLA: *suffrage*: women gain equal voting rights

UK: *literature*: Booker Prize is won by Nadine Gordimer for *The Conservationist* (with Stanley Middleton for *Holiday*)

USA: *film*: Best Actress Oscar is won by Ellen Burstyn for her role in *Alice Doesn't Live Her Anymore*

UK: *sport*: Wimbledon Ladies' Championship is won by Chris Evert (later Chris Evert Lloyd)

1975 UK: *politics*: Margaret Thatcher becomes the first woman leader of a political party

UK: *law*: the Equal Pay Act and Sex Discrimination Act stipulates that women are to receive the same wages as men for the same work

NEW ZEALAND: *civil rights*: Maori leader Whina Cooper leads a march of 5,000 people in support of Maori claims to land taken by Europeans

UK: *literature*: Booker Prize is won by Ruth Prawer Jhabvala for *Heat and Dust*

USA: *film*: Best Actress Oscar is won by Louise Fletcher for her role in *One Flew Over the Cuckoo's Nest*

UK: *sport*: Wimbledon Ladies' Championship is won by Billie Jean King

JAPAN: *sport*: Junko Tabei becomes the first woman to climb Mount Everest

1976 PORTUGAL: *suffrage*: women gain equal voting rights

USA: *women's rights*: the first female cadets are admitted to the Military Academy, West Point, Naval Academy, Annapolis, and Air Force Academy, Colorado Springs

FRANCE: *education*: Hélène Ahrweiler becomes the first woman President of the Sorbonne

Nobel Prize for Peace is won by Mairéad Corrigan and Betty Williams

USA: *film*: Best Actress Oscar is won by Faye Dunaway for her role in *Network*

UK: *sport*: Wimbledon Ladies' Championship is won by Chris Evert

USSR: *sport*: Tatyana Kazankina wins an Olympic double at 800m and 1,500m

1977   USA: *women's rights*: 20,000 supporters of gender-related issues gather for discussion at the National Women's Conference, Houston

Nobel Prize for Physiology or Medicine is won by Rosalyn Yalow (with Roger Guillemin and Andrew Schally)

USA: *film*: Bette Davis becomes the first woman recipient of the American Film Institute's Life Achievement Award

USA: *film*: Best Actress Oscar is won by Diane Keaton for her role in *Annie Hall*

UK: *sport*: Wimbledon Ladies' Championship is won by Virginia Wade

1978   USA: *women's rights*: in recognition of her contribution to sexual equality in all races, Susan B Anthony becomes the first woman to adorn American currency

USA: *education*: Hanna Gray becomes the first woman head of a major US university

USA: *sport*: Janet Guthrie becomes the first woman to complete the Indianapolis 500 motor race

UK: *sport*: Wimbledon Ladies' Championship is won by Martina Navratilova

UK: *literature*: Booker Prize is won by Iris Murdoch for *The Sea, The Sea*

USA: *film*: Best Actress Oscar is won by Jane Fonda for her role in *Coming Home*

1979   UK: *politics*: Margaret Thatcher becomes the first woman Prime Minister of Britain

UK: *medicine*: Dame Josephine Barnes becomes the first woman president of the British Medical Association

Nobel Prize for Peace is won by Mother Teresa of Calcutta

UK: *literature*: Booker Prize is won by Penelope Fitzgerald for *Offshore*

USA: *film*: Best Actress Oscar is won by Sally Field for her role in *Norma Rae*

1980   DOMINICA: *politics*: as Prime Minister of Dominica, Eugenia Charles becomes the first woman Prime Minister in the Caribbean

ICELAND: *politics*: Vigdís Finnbogadóttir is elected President of Iceland, the first elected woman head of state in the world

IRAN: *suffrage*: women gain equal voting rights

USA: *film*: Sherry Lansing becomes the first woman head of a major Hollywood studio

USA: *film*: Best Actress Oscar is won by Sissy Spacek for her role in *Coal Miner's Daughter*

UK: *sport*: Wimbledon Ladies' Championship is won by Evonne Cawley (formerly Evonne Goolagong)

1981   NORWAY: *politics*: Gro Harlem Brundtland becomes the first woman Prime Minister of Norway

USA: *law*: Sandra Day O'Connor becomes the first woman associate justice of the US Supreme Court

AUSTRALIA: *publishing*: Ita Buttrose becomes the first woman editor of a daily or Sunday paper in Australia

USA: *literature*: Pulitzer Prize for drama is won by Beth Henley for *Crimes of the Heart* (with Lanford Wilson for *Talley's Folly*)

USA: *film*: Best Actress Oscar is won by Katharine Hepburn for the fourth time for her role in *On Golden Pond*

UK: *sport*: Wimbledon Ladies' Championship is won by Chris Evert Lloyd (formerly Chris Evert)

1982   USA: *law*: the deadline passes with the Equal Rights Amendment only three states short of ratification, and a year later a bill to revive the amendment is defeated in Congress

USA: *education*: Mississippi University for Women accepts the first male nursing student after a ruling by the Supreme Court

Nobel Prize for Peace is won by Alva Myrdal (with Alfonso García Robles)

USA: *literature*: Pulitzer Prize for poetry is won by Sylvia Plath for *Collected Poems*

USA: *film*: Best Actress Oscar is won by Meryl Streep for her role in *Sophie's Choice*

UK: *sport*: Wimbledon Ladies' Championship is won by Martina Navratilova

1983 USA: *science*: Sally Ride becomes the first US woman in space, serving on the flight of the orbiter *Challenger*

Nobel Prize for Physiology or Medicine is won by Barbara McClintock

USA: *literature*: Pulitzer Prize for fiction is won by Alice Walker for *The Color Purple*

USA: *literature*: Pulitzer Prize for drama is won by Marsha Norman for *'Night Mother*

USA: *music*: Pulitzer Prize for music is won by Ellen Zwilich, the first woman laureate, for her Symphony No.1

USA: *film*: Best Actress Oscar is won by Shirley MacLaine for her role in *Terms of Endearment*

UK: *sport*: Wimbledon Ladies' Championship is won by Martina Navratilova

1984 USA: *politics*: Geraldine Ferraro is the first woman to run as vice-presidential candidate for a major party

UK: *literature*: Booker Prize is won by Anita Brookner for *Hotel du Lac*

USA: *literature*: Pulitzer Prize for poetry is won by Mary Oliver for *American Primitive*

USA: *film*: Best Actress Oscar is won by Sally Field for the second time for her role in *Places in the Heart*

USA: *sport*: Evelyn Ashford becomes the first woman to run the 100m in under 11 seconds in the Olympic Games (Marlies Gohr achieved this outside the Olympics)

UK: *sport*: Wimbledon Ladies' Championship is won by Martina Navratilova

1985 UK: *literature*: Booker Prize is won by Keri Hulme for *The Bone People*

USA: *literature*: Pulitzer Prize for fiction is won by Alison Lurie for *Foreign Affairs*

USA: *literature*: Pulitzer Prize for poetry is won by Carolyn Kizer for *Yin*

USA: *film*: Best Actress Oscar is won by Geraldine Page for her role in *The Trip to Bountiful*

UK: *sport*: Wimbledon Ladies' Championship is won by Martina Navratilova

1986 Nobel Prize for Physiology or Medicine is won by Rita Levi-Montalcini (with Stanley Cohen)

USA: *film*: Best Actress Oscar is won by Marlene Matlin for her role in *Children of a Lesser God*

UK: *sport*: Wimbledon Ladies' Championship is won by Martina Navratilova

1987 UK: *politics*: Diane Abbott becomes the first black woman member of the British parliament

AUSTRALIA: *law*: Mary Gaudron becomes the first woman judge in the High Court of Australia

UK: *literature*: Booker Prize is won by Penelope Lively for *Moon Tiger*

USA: *literature*: Pulitzer Prize for poetry is won by Rita Dove for *Thomas and Beulah*

USA: *film*: Best Actress Oscar is won by Cher for her role in *Moonstruck*

UK: *sport*: Wimbledon Ladies' Championship is won by Martina Navratilova

1988 PAKISTAN: *politics*: as Prime Minister of Pakistan, Benazir Bhutto becomes the first woman leader of a modern muslim nation

UK: *law*: Dame Elizabeth Butler-Sloss becomes the first woman Lord Justice of Appeal

Nobel Prize for Physiology or Medicine is won by Gertrude Elion (with George Hitchings and James Black)

USA: *literature*: Pulitzer Prize for fiction is won by Toni Morrison for *Beloved*

USA: *film*: Best Actress Oscar is won by Jodie Foster for her role in *The Accused*

UK: *sport*: Wimbledon Ladies' Championship is won by Steffi Graf

GERMANY: *sport*: Kristin Otto wins six gold medals for swimming in the Olympic Games

1989 USA: *religion*: Barbara Harris is ordained the first woman bishop in the Anglican Church

USA: *literature*: Pulitzer Prize for fiction is won by Anne Tyler for *Breathing Lessons*

USA: *literature*: Pulitzer Prize for drama is won by Wendy Wasserstein for *The Heidi Chronicles*

USA: *film*: Best Actress Oscar is won by Jessica Tandy for her role in *Driving Miss Daisy*

UK: *sport*: Wimbledon Ladies' Championship is won by Steffi Graf

1990 UK: *literature*: Booker Prize is won by A S Byatt for *Possession*

USA: *film*: Best Actress Oscar is won by Kathy Bates for her role in *Misery*

UK: *sport*: Wimbledon Ladies' Championship is won by Martina Navratilova

1991 UK: *politics*: Stella Rimington is appointed as the head of MI5

FRANCE: *politics*: Edith Cresson becomes the first woman Prime Minister of France

BANGLADESH: *politics*: Begum Zia becomes the first woman Prime Minister of Bangladesh

UK: *science*: Dame Anne McLaren becomes the first woman officer of the Royal Society

UK: *religion*: Mary Levison is appointed the first female chaplain to the Queen

UK: *publishing*: Eve Pollard becomes the first woman editor of the *Sunday Express* newspaper

Nobel Prize for Literature is won by Nadine Gordimer

Nobel Prize for Peace is won by Aung San Suu Kyi

USA: *literature*: Pulitzer Prize for poetry is won by Mona Jane Van Duyn for *Near Changes*

USA: *film*: Best Actress Oscar is won by Jodie Foster for her role in *The Silence of the Lambs*

UK: *sport*: Wimbledon Ladies' Championship is won by Steffi Graf

1992 UK: *law*: Barbara Mills becomes the first woman Director of Public Prosecutions

USA: *education*: college research indicates that women comprise more than half of college students, but less than a third of faculty members

Nobel Prize for Peace is won by Rigoberta Menchu

USA: *literature*: Pulitzer Prize for fiction is won by Jane Smiley for *A Thousand Acres*

USA: *film*: Best Actress Oscar is won by Emma Thompson for her role in *Howards End*

UK: *sport*: Wimbledon Ladies' Championship is won by Steffi Graf

1993 CANADA: *politics*: Kim Campbell becomes the first woman Prime Minister of Canada

TURKEY: *politics*: Tansu Çiller becomes the first woman Prime Minister of Turkey

UK: *labour*: the Women's Royal Naval Service becomes integrated into the Royal Navy

UK: *labour*: Frances Heaton is appointed the first female director of the Bank of England

Nobel Prize for Literature is won by Toni Morrison

USA: *literature*: Pulitzer Prize for poetry is won by Louise Glück for *The Wild Iris*

USA: *film*: Best Actress Oscar is won by Holly Hunter for her role in *The Piano*

UK: *sport*: Wimbledon Ladies' Championship is won by Steffi Graf

1994 SOUTH AFRICA: *suffrage*: women gain equal voting rights

UK: *labour*: the Women's Royal Air Force is integrated into the Royal Air Force

UK: *religion*: the Church of England ordains the first women priests, but the same resolution is defeated in Wales

USA: *literature*: Pulitzer Prize for fiction is won by E Annie Proulx for *The Shipping News*

USA: *film*: Best Actress Oscar is won by Jessica Lange for her role in *Blue Sky*

1995 CHINA: *politics*: the UN Fourth World Conference on Women is hailed as a watershed in women's equality

   UK: *law*: Britain's first woman chief constable is appointed to the Lancashire police force

   USA: *literature*: Pulitzer Prize for fiction is won by Carol Shields for *The Stone Diaries*

   UK: *exploration*: Alison Hargreaves becomes the first woman to climb Mount Everest solo without supplementary oxygen, but dies on K2 in August

   UK: *sport*: Wimbledon Ladies' Championship is won by Steffi Graf

1996 UK: *literature*: the Orange Prize for Fiction is launched, offering £30,000 for the best English-language novel written by a woman

   USA: *film*: Best Screenplay Oscar is won by Emma Thompson for her adaptation of Jane Austen's *Sense and Sensibility*

NB: Although all the Best Actress Oscars and women winners of Pulitzer Prizes for literature and music have been included for consistency, a few have not been selected for inclusion in the dictionary.

Women on Women

Louisa May Alcott

She had a womanly instinct that clothes possess an influence more powerful over many than the worth of character or the magic of manners.
Little Women, 1868

Susan B Anthony

There will never be complete equality until women themselves help to make laws and to elect lawmakers.
Quoted in *The Arena*

Mary von Arnim

. . . far from being half a woman, a widow is the only complete example of her sex. In fact, the finished article.
All the Dogs of My Life, 1936

Mary Astell

If Absolute Sovereignty be not necessary in a State, how comes it to be so in a family?
Some Reflections upon Marriage Occasion'd by the Duke and Duchess of Mazarine's Case which is also consider'd, 1706

If all Men are born free, how is it that all Women are born Slaves? as they must be if the being subjected to the *inconsistent, uncertain, unknown, arbitrary Will* of Men, be the *perfect Condition of slavery*? and if the Essence of Freedom consists, as our Masters say it does, in having a *standing Rule to live by*? And why is Slavery so Much condemn'd and strove against in one Case, and so highly applauded, and held so necessary and so sacred in another?
Ibid.

A Woman indeed can't properly be said to Choose, all that is allow'd her, is to Refuse or Accept what is offer'd.
Ibid.

Nancy Astor

I married beneath me. All women do.
Speech, Oldham, 1951

Jane Austen

But history, real solemn history, I cannot be interested in . . . it tells me nothing that does not vex or weary me . . . the men all so good for nothing, and hardly any women at all.
Northanger Abbey, 1818

A woman especially, if she have the misfortune of knowing any thing, should conceal it as well as she can . . . imbecility in females is a great enhancement of their personal charms.
Ibid.

Mary Austin

When a woman ceases to alter the fashion of her hair, you guess that she has passed the crisis of her experience.
The Land of Little Rain, 1903

Simone de Beauvoir

La femme . . . sait que quand on la regarde on ne la distingue pas de son apparence: elle est jugée, respectée, desirée a travers sa toilette.

Woman . . . knows that when she is looked at she is not considered apart from her appearance: she is judged, respected, desired, by and through her toilette.
Le Deuxième Sexe, 1949 (Eng trans *The Second Sex*, 1952)

A S Byatt

There is something both gratifying and humiliating in watching a man who has taken you for a routinely silly woman begin to take you seriously . . .
Still Life, 1985

Jane Welsh Carlyle

When I think of what I is
And what I used to was,
I gin to think I've sold myself
For very little cas.
Journal entry, 1855

I scorched my intellect into a cinder of stolidity.
Quoted in *New Letters and Memorials of Jane Welsh Carlyle*, 1903

Mrs Patrick Campbell

Do you know why God withheld the sense of humour from women? That we may love you instead of laughing at you.

Angela Carter

Clothes are our weapons, our challenges, our visible insults.
'Notes for a Theory of Sixties Style', 1967

Coco Chanel

Nature gives you the face you have when you are twenty. Life shapes the face you have at thirty. But it is up to you to earn the face you have at fifty.

Caroline Chisholm

If Her Majesty's Government be really desirous of seeing a well-conducted community spring up in these Colonies, the social wants of the people must be considered . . . For all the clergy you can despatch, all the schoolmasters you can appoint, all the churches you can build, and all the books you can export, will never do much good without what a gentleman in that Colony very appropriately called 'God's police' — wives and little children — good and virtuous women.
Emigration and Transportation Relatively Considered; in a Letter, Dedicated, by Permission, to Earl Grey, 1847

Hélène Cixous

Je voudrais tant être une femme sans y penser.
I would like so much to be a woman without thinking about it.
Le Livre de Promethea, 1983

Mary Daly

. . . If God is male, then the male is God. The divine patriarch castrates women as long as he is allowed to live on in the human imagination. The process of cutting away the Supreme Phallus can hardly be a merely 'rational' affair.
Beyond God the Father, 1973

Emily Davies

If neither governesses or mothers know, how can they teach? So long as education is not provided for them, how can it be provided by them?
1868. Paper read at the Annual Meeting of the National Association for the Promotion of Social Sciences, published in *Thoughts on some Questions Relating to Women 1860–1908.*

Emily Wilding Davison

As I am a woman and women do not count in the State, I refuse to be counted. Rebellion against tyrants is obedience to God.

Elizabeth Hanford Dole

There is a ceiling — a 'glass ceiling' ... women ... are blocked ... by invisible and impenetrable barriers.
Quoted in the *New York Times*, 31 July 1990

Andrea Dworkin

The power of money is a distinctly male power. Money speaks, but it speaks with a male voice. In the hands of women, money stays literal, count it out, it buys what it is worth or less. In the hands of men, money buys women, sex, status, dignity, esteem, recognition, loyalty, all manner of possibility.
Pornography: Men Possessing Women, 1981

Edna Ferber

Being an old maid is like death by drowning, a really delightful sensation after you cease to struggle.
Quoted in R E Drennan, *Wit's End*

Marilyn French

All men are rapists and that's all they are. They rape us with their eyes, their laws and their codes.
The Women's Room, 1977

Betty Friedan

In 1960, the problem that has no name burst like a boil through the image of the happy American housewife ... the actual unhappiness of the American housewife was suddenly being reported ... although almost everybody who talked about it found some superficial reason to dismiss it.
The Feminine Mystique, 1963

Women, even though they are almost too visible as sex objects in this country, are invisible people.
Speech, Conference for Repeal of Abortion Laws, 1969

Margaret Fuller, Marchioness Ossoli

It is well known that of every strong woman they say she has a masculine mind.
'The Great Lawsuit,' in *Dial*, July 1843

Charlotte Gilman

The labor of women in the house, certainly, enables men to produce more wealth than they otherwise could; and in this way are economic factors in society. But so are horses.
Women and Economics, 1898

... whatever the economic value of the domestic industry of women is, they do not get it. The women who do the most work get the least money, and the women who have the most money do the least work.
Ibid.

From the day laborer to the millionaire, the wife's worn dress or flashing jewels, her low roof or her lordly one, her weary feet or her rich equipage — these speak of the economic ability of the husband.
Ibid.

Germaine Greer

Freud is the father of psychoanalysis. It had no mother.
The Female Eunuch, 1970

If women understand by emancipation the adoption of the masculine role then we are lost indeed.
Ibid.

Bathsua Pell Makin

A Learned Woman is thought to be a Comet, that bodes Mischief, when ever it appears.
An Essay to Revive the Antient Education of Gentlewomen in Religion, Manners, Art and Tongues, with An Answer to the Objections Against this Way of Education, 1673

Willa Muir

Apparently the average man sees woman alternately as an inferior being and as an angel.
Women: An Enquiry, 1925

Florence Nightingale

Why have women Passion, intellect, moral activity — these three — and a place in society where no one of the three can be exercised?
'Cassandra' I, 1852, part of *Suggestions for Thought to Searchers after Religious Truth*

Look at the poor lives we lead. It is a wonder that we are so good as we are, not that we are so bad.
'Cassandra' II, 1852

The next Christ will perhaps be a female Christ.
'Cassandra' IV, 1852

Margaret Oliphant

A woman who cannot be a governess or a novel-writer must fall back on that poor little needle, the primitive and original handicraft of femininity.
The Condition of Women, 1858

Emmeline Pankhurst

Women never took a single step forward without being pushed back first of all by their opponents.
Speech, Canadian tour, 1912

Women had always fought for men, and for their children. Now they were ready to fight for their own human rights.
My Own Story, 1914

Dorothy Parker

You know, that woman speaks eighteen languages? And she can't say 'no' in any of them.

Brevity is the soul of lingerie

Sylvia Plath

I am afraid of getting married. Spare me from cooking three meals a day — spare me from the relentless cage of routine and rote.
Letters Home by Sylvia Plath, 1949

Adrienne Rich

Male honour also having something to do with killing ... Women's honour, something altogether else: virginity, chastity, fidelity to a husband.
On Lies, Secrets and Silence, Selected Prose, 1966–78, 1979

Sheila Rowbotham

There is no 'beginning' of feminism in the sense that there is no beginning to defiance in women.
Women, Resistance and Revolution, 1972

Olive Schreiner

This pretty ring ... I will give it to the first man who tells me he would like to be a woman. It is delightful to be a woman; but every man thanks the Lord devoutly that he isn't one.
The Story of an African Farm, 1883

Men are like the earth and we are the moon; we turn always one side to them, and they think there is no other, because they don't see it — but there is.
Ibid.

Anne Sexton

I was tired of being a woman,
tired of the spoons and the pots,
tired of my mouth and my breasts tired of the cosmetics and the silks
... I was tired of the gender of things.
Live or Die, 1966

Muriel Spark

... a nice girl should only fall in love once in her life.
The Girls of Slender Means, 1963

Beware of men bearing flowers.
Personal motto

Elizabeth Cady Stanton

Quite as many false ideas prevail as to woman's true position in the home as to her status elsewhere. Womanhood is the great fact in her life; wifehood and motherhood are but incidental relations.
The History of Woman Suffrage 1848–61, 1881–6

Although woman has performed much of the labor of the world, her industry and economy have been the very means of increasing her degradation.
Ibid.

As to woman's subjection, ... it is important to note that equal dominion is given to woman over every living thing, but not one word is said giving man dominion over woman.
Ibid.

'Self-development is a higher duty than self-sacrifice', should be a woman's motto henceforward.
The Woman's Bible, 1898

Dame Freya Stark

The great and almost only comfort about being a woman is that one can always pretend to be more stupid than one is and no one is surprised.
The Valley of the Assassins, 1934

Gloria Steinem

A woman needs a man like a fish needs a bicycle.
Attributed graffiti

Margaret Thatcher

I owe nothing to Women's Lib.
Attrib. in the *Observer*, 1 December 1974

In politics, if you want anything said, ask a man. If you want anything done, ask a woman.
Quoted in *People*, 1975

Diana Vreeland

A little bad taste is like a splash of paprika. We all need a splash of bad taste — it's hearty, it's healthy, it's physical.
D. V., 1984

Mae West

You can say what you like about long dresses, but they cover a multitude of shins.

Dame Rebecca West

Women know the damnation of charity because the habit of civilisation has always been to throw them cheap alms rather than give them good wages.
Clarion, 1912

Mary Wollstonecraft

... I now speak of the sex in general. Many individuals have more sense than their male relatives; and ... some women govern their husbands without degrading themselves, because intellect will always govern.
A Vindication of the Rights of Woman, 1792

Liberty is the mother of virtue, and if women be, by their very constitution, slaves, and not allowed to breathe the sharp invigorating air of freedom, they must ever languish like exotics, and be reckoned beautiful flaws in nature.
Ibid.

Let woman share the rights and she will emulate the virtues of man, for she must grow more perfect when emancipated.
Ibid.

Virginia Woolf

Women have served all these centuries as looking-glasses possessing the magic and delicious power of reflecting the figure of man at twice its natural size.
A Room of One's Own, 1929

I would venture to guess that Anon, who wrote so many poems without signing them, was often a woman.
Ibid.

... it is obvious that the values of women differ very often from the values which have been made by the other sex ... Yet it is the masculine values that prevail.
Ibid.

Women have served all these centuries as looking-glasses possessing the magic and delicious power of reflecting the figure of a man at twice its natural size.
Ibid.

More women on women

Educate a man and you educate an individual — educate a woman and you educate a family.
Agnes Cripps

Until a woman is free to be as incompetent as the average male then she will never be completely equal.
Speech, 1995 Scottish lawyer and politician Roseanna Cunningham (1951–   )

Whatever women do they must do twice as well as men to be thought half so good . . . luckily, it's not difficult.
Canada Month, 1963 Canadian, politician and Mayor of Ottowa Charlotte Whitton (1896–1975)

The more legal and material hindrances women have broken through, the more strictly and heavily and cruelly images of female beauty have come to weigh upon them.
The Beauty Myth, 1990 US writer Naomi Wolf (1962–   )

When women breached the power structure in the 1980s, . . . two economies finally merged. Beauty was no longer just a symbolic form of currency: it literally *became* money.
Ibid.

Listening is one of the lesser-known skills that mistresses offer.
All in the Family: A Survival Guide for Living and Loving in a Changing World, 1988
Canadian dramatist and writer Betty Jane Wylie (1930–   )

Men on Women

Women were brought up to believe that men were the answer. They weren't. They weren't even one of the questions.
Staring at the Sun, 1986 English novelist Julian Barnes (1946–   )

But there's wisdom in women, of more than they have known,
And thoughts go blowing through them, are wiser than their own.
'There's Wisdom in Women', 1913 English poet Rupert Chawner Brooke (1887–1915)

Heav'n has no rage, like love to hatred turn'd,
Nor Hell a fury, like a woman scorn'd.
The Mourning Bride, 1697 English dramatist and poet William Congreve (1670–1729)

a pretty girl who naked is
is worth a million statues
'mr youse needn't be so spry' in *is* 5, 1926 US writer and painter e e cummings (1894–1962)

The chief distinction in the intellectual powers of the two sexes is shewn by man's attaining to a higher eminence in whatever he takes up, than can woman — whether requiring deep thought, reason, or imagination, or merely the use of the senses and hands. We may also infer . . . that if men are capable of a decided pre-eminence over women in many subjects, the average in mental power in man must be above that of woman.
English naturalist Charles Darwin (1809–82)

Female beauty is an important minor sacrament . . . I am not at all sure that neglect of it does not constitute a sin of some kind.
Canadian novelist, playwright and critic Robertson Davies (1913–95)

When a man sits with a pretty girl for an hour, it seems like a minute. But let him sit on a hot stove for a minute — and it's longer than an hour. That's relativity.
Attrib. German-born US scientist Albert Einstein (1879–1955)

The artist has won — through his fantasy — what before her could only win *in* his fantasy: honour, power, and the love of women.
Introductory lectures on Psycho-Analysis, No.23 (1916) Austrian psychiatrist Sigmund Freud (1856–1939)

During my seven years in office, I was in love with seventeen million French women . . . I know this declaration will inspire irony and that English language readers will find it very French.
La Pouvoir et la Vie, 1988 French President Valery Giscard D'Estaing (1926–   )

Why have such scores of lovely, gifted girls
Married impossible men?
'A Slice of Wedding Cake', 1958 English writer Robert Graves (1895–1985)

What a terrifying relection it is, by the way, that nearly all our deep love for women who are not our kindred depends — at any rate, in the first instance — upon their personal appearances. If we lost them, and found them again dreadful to look on, though otherwise they were very same, should we still love them?
She, 1887 English novelist Sir Rider Haggard (1856–1925)

If I had to give a definition of capitalism, I would say: the process whereby American girls turn into American women.
Savages, 1974 English playwright Christopher Hampton (1946–)

Why it was that upon this beautiful feminine tissue, sensitive as gossamer, and practically blank as snow as yet, there should have been traced such a coarse pattern as it was doomed to receive; why so often the coarse appropriates the finer thus, the wrong man the woman, the wrong woman the man, many thousand years of analytical philosophy have failed to explain to our sense of order.
Tess of the D'Urbervilles, 1891 English novelist and poet Thomas Hardy (1840–1928)

Back of every achievement is a proud wife and a surprised mother-in-law.
Brooks Hays

Nature has given women so much power that the law has very wisely given them little.
Letter to John Taylor, 18 August 1763 English writer Samuel Johnson (1709–84)

Women should be obscene and not heard.
Attrib. British songwriter and former Beatles member John Lennon (1940–80)

Thank heaven for little girls,
For little girls get bigger every day.
'Thank Heaven for Little Girls' in the musical *Gigi*, 1958 US lyricist and playwright Alan Jay Lerner (1918–86)

The female sex has no bigger fan than I, and I have the bills to prove it.
The Street Where I Live, 1978 US lyricist and playwright Alan Jay Lerner (1918–86)

There was a little girl
Who had a little curl
Right in the middle of her forehead;
And when she was good
She was very, very good,
But when she was bad, she was horrid.
Attributed to Henry Wadsworth Longfellow by Blanch Roosevelt Tucker Macchetta in *The Home Life of Henry W. Longfellow* (1882)

Who loves not women, wine and song
Remains a fool his whole life long.
Attrib. German religious reformer Martin Luther (1483–1546)

. . . It does make me bitterly angry that my generation, which prided itself so complacently on its soul, on its powers of intelligence and analysis, should have fallen so cloddishly for totalitarian simplicities which declared a war of eternal opposition between men and women.
No More Sex War: The Failures of Feminism, 1992 British journalist and writer Neil Lyndon (1946–)

We in this industry know that behind every successful screenwriter stands a woman. And behind her stands his wife
Attrib. US entertainer Groucho Marx (1895–1977)

With equality of experience and of general faculties, a woman usually sees much more than a man of what is immediately before her.
The Subjection of Women, 1869 English philosopher and social reformer John Stuart Mill (1806–73)

Marriage is the only actual bondage known to our law. There remain no legal slaves, except the mistress of every house.
Ibid.

In so far as the family as an institution turns women into darling little slaves and men into their chief providers and unweaned dependents, the problem of a satisfactory marriage remains incapable of purely private solution.
The Sociological Imagination, 1959 US sociologist C Wright Mills (1916–62)

Dancing is a wonderful training for girls, it's the first way you learn to guess what a man is going to do before he does it.
Kitty Foyle, 1939 US writer and poet, Christopher Darlington Morley (1890–1957)

By the end of the decade, quite a few women will be marrying robots.
Ogdenisms: The Frank Ogden Quote Book, 1994 Canadian Frank Ogden (1920–)

A divorce is the end of a wifetime.
Ibid.

Il y a ainsi un petit nombre d'hommes et de femmes qui pensent pour tous les autres, et pour lesquels tous les autres parlent et agissent.
There is a small number of men and women who think for everyone else and for whom everyone else speaks and acts.
Julie ou la nouvelle Héloise, 1761 French political philosopher and author Jean Jacques Rousseau (1712–78)

She's beautiful and therefore to be woo'd;
She is a woman, therefore to be won.
Henry VI, Part 1, 1592 English playwright William Shakespeare (1564–1616)

'Tis beauty that doth oft make women proud.
Henry VI, Part 3, 1592 English playwright William Shakespeare (1564–1616)

Frailty, thy name is woman.
Hamlet, 1601 English playwright William Shakespeare (1564–1616)

For women are as roses, whose fair flower
Being once displayed, doth fall that very hour
Twelfth Night, 1601 English playwright William Shakespeare (1564–1616)

The recruiting field for the militant suffragists is the million of our excess female population — that million which had better long ago have gone out to mate with its complement of men beyond the sea.
Letter to The Times, 1912 English bacteriologist and one of the most vocal opponents of the suffragettes, Sir Almroth Edward Wright (1861–1947)

Wit is more necessary than beauty; and I think no young woman ugly that has it, and no handsome woman agreeable without it.
The Country Wife, 1675 English dramatist William Wycherley (c.1640–1716)